LSAT®
PrepTests 72–81
Unlocked

Exclusive Data, Analysis, & Explanations for
10 Actual, Official LSAT PrepTests Volume VI

KAPLAN

PUBLISHING

New York

LSAT® is a registered mark of the Law School Admission Council, Inc.

© 2018 by Kaplan, Inc.

Published by Kaplan Publishing, a division of Kaplan, Inc.
750 Third Avenue
New York, NY 10017

ISBN: 978-1-5062-2344-5
10 9 8 7 6 5 4 3 2 1

Kaplan Publishing print books are available at special quantity discounts to use for sales promotions, employee premiums, or educational purposes. For more information or to purchase books, please call the Simon & Schuster special sales department at 866-506-1949.

Introduction

About This Book

This book contains complete explanations to every question from officially released LSAT PrepTests 72 through 81, along with exclusive data and analysis of test taker performance and question difficulty on each one of these LSAT exams. It is the perfect companion to these tests individually, or to the LSAC's bundle of these tests released under the title *10 Actual, Official LSAT PrepTests Volume VI*.

Whether you are taking a prep course or studying on your own, taking officially released LSATs is an essential component of successful preparation. LSAT students are fortunate that LSAC (the organization that develops and administers the test) typically releases three LSATs—the test forms given in June, in the Fall, and in December—each year. It probably goes without saying that practice with recent LSATs is especially valuable, and the tests covered by this book range from the test administration in June 2014 through the one in June 2017. At the time of this book's release, *10 Actual, Official LSAT PrepTests Volume VI* is the most recent bundle of 10 tests released by LSAC.

While practice tests are necessary, LSAT experts will tell you that simply taking and scoring tests isn't sufficient to maximize your score improvement. You need to know why you missed questions, and how to get to the right answers even more efficiently. That's where this companion comes in. For each of the 10 tests explained and analyzed here, Kaplan provides exclusive data about how test takers perceived the tests' difficulty. We then compare that to actual student performance on the test, and we identify each test's 10 most difficult questions and categorize the difficulty of all of the test's questions. You'll also see how representative each test is of the LSAT's most recent trends and learn about anything that makes a particular test administration unique or unusual. Finally, you get complete explanations for every question, game, and passage in the test, including explanations for every wrong answer.

Start by reading the section called "Introduction: How to Use Kaplan LSAT Explanations," so that you get familiar with Kaplan's methods, strategies, and terminology. Then, after taking any of the practice tests covered by this volume, put your practice experience in context by reading the test's "Inside Story" page. Finally, review your performance on any question, game, or passage from the test. Kaplan's LSAT experts encourage you to review every question—even those you got right—to learn how top LSAT scorers use patterns to approach the exam effectively and efficiently.

No matter how you choose to use the information and explanations included in this book, Kaplan is here to encourage and support your study and practice. For over 70 years, our commitment has been to raising scores for every test taker. So, here's to good luck, and, more importantly, good preparation.

How to Review a PrepTest

Taking full-length practice LSAT tests is an essential part of comprehensive preparation for this important exam. Not only do practice tests contain examples of all the questions, games, and passages used by the testmaker, but by taking practice LSATs, you also get a feel for the timing restrictions that make each section of the LSAT so challenging. Moreover, when you take full-length exams, you approximate the endurance and stamina demands of Test Day.

The LSAT is unique among the major post-graduate admissions exams in that the LSAC (the organization that creates and administers the LSAT) releases three previously administered, official LSAT tests each year. To help our students get the most out of these valuable practice resources, Kaplan has a team of LSAT experts who evaluate each test, and write comprehensive explanations for every question (indeed, for every answer choice) immediately after the exam's release. Now, for the first time, we are making these explanations available to everyone who is serious about his or her LSAT preparation.

Here are a few tips for the best way to use the explanations.

1. Learn the Kaplan Methods for Each Section

Every official LSAT contains two sections of Logical Reasoning, and one section each of Logic Games (or Analytical Reasoning, as the LSAC calls it) and Reading Comprehension. Test takers who train with Kaplan learn simple but highly effective methods for the questions, games, and passages in these sections. Thus, our explanations are written so that they follow the steps of those methods consistently. As you review the questions in the test, the explanations here will not only explain why a particular answer is correct, it will show you how an LSAT expert efficiently untangles the question, and how she can demonstrate that all four other answers are incorrect.

The Kaplan Methods for each type of scored section are outlined for each section later in this chapter. The methods are somewhat intuitive, so you'll get the gist of each one pretty quickly. In addition, you'll learn about some of the specific strategies Kaplan students learn in class. Keep an eye out for those strategies again as you review the questions in your test.

Terminology and Definitions

In our comprehensive LSAT prep courses, Kaplan students learn a sweeping vocabulary of terms, categories, and distinctions for the question types, patterns of reasoning, flaws, conclusions, and rhetorical devices employed by the testmaker. If you are not currently in a Kaplan LSAT prep course, you may come across terms with which you're unfamiliar, or unsure how to understand in the context of the test. For such terms, we've created a glossary that you can find at the back of this book.

2. Evaluate Timed Practice Differently than Untimed Practice

We'll stipulate that you have already completed the test. Why else would you be looking at the explanations? Now, a couple of questions: First, did you take the LSAT under strict, timed conditions? If you did, review questions in context. Were you running out of time near the end of the section? Did you have to guess? Did you spend far too long to get one or two questions correct, thus costing yourself the opportunity to try other questions? Many of the explanations in this book will give you

KAPLAN

strategies for answering questions more efficiently and effectively, as well as always explaining how to answer them correctly. Speed and confidence can be important to your score on Test Day—in some cases, as important as expertise.

If you did not time yourself, or if you gave yourself extra time to complete the LSAT, review the questions to assess your mastery of LSAT skills. There is nothing wrong with untimed practice. Indeed, Kaplan's expert LSAT instructors encourage their students to engage in untimed, mastery practice whenever the students learn a new question type. When you are reviewing a test on which you took extra time, your focus should be on assessing how you did on each step of each question, and especially on how well you executed the skills rewarded by the LSAT.

3. Note the Question Difficulty

At the beginning of each section of explanations, you will see a list of the questions in that section of the test. For each question, we provide the question type and a difficulty rating of between 1 star (easiest) and 4 stars (hardest). Pay attention to the difficulty level of the questions you got right and those you missed.

Because our students take official, released LSAT tests for practice during their courses, we at Kaplan have hundreds of thousands of data points on the questions in these released tests. We can accurately determine the difficulty of every question on each exam, and even determine which incorrect answers gave students the most trouble, and which ones they dismissed easily.

Here's how the star ratings work. Four-star questions are the 10 most difficult questions on the test. Typically these are answered correctly by one-third of students or less. The next 20 questions in difficulty are assigned a 3-star rating. The next 30 get a 2-star rating. And, the rest (the easiest 40 or 41 questions on the exam) are given a 1-star rating. On most LSATs, the 1-star questions are answered correctly by 70 percent of students or more.

The difficulty ratings help you assess your performance in two important ways. First, when you miss a 4-star or 3-star question, you're in good company. These questions are difficult for most students. Study the explanation to a 4- or 3-star question carefully, and note the strategic approaches that allows LSAT experts to solve these tough verbal and reasoning puzzles. On the other hand, when you miss a 1- or 2-star question, focus on where you may have misinterpreted the instructions or some key piece of information. While these questions are not too hard for most students, even top scorers occasionally miss 1- and 2-star questions, usually because of same kinds of oversights you'll see cleared up in the explanations in this book.

The second way difficulty ratings can help you is by providing insight into your score. Here is a chart showing how raw score (the number of correct answers a test taker generates) translates into scaled score (the 120 to 180 score law schools see on your score report) and into percentile (the percentage of test takers who scored below you on a given exam).

Raw Score (#correct)	Scaled Score	Percentile
92	172	99th
85	167	95th
81	164	90th
74	160	80th
67	156	70th
63	154	60th
58	151	50th
55	149	40th
50	146	30th
45	143	10th
39	139	10th

How raw score (number of questions correct) translates into
scaled score and percentile ranking

PrepTest 77 (December 2015)

Because the LSAC score report is comparing you to all those who took your test, and to the cohort of applicants likely to apply to law school at the same time you do, the translation from raw score to scaled score and percentile change slightly from test to test. The previous chart, however, provides a good estimate of scoring on most recent LSATs. As you can see, on most tests, you could miss nine of the ten 4-star questions and still score a 172, placing you in the 99th percentile, and giving you a score competitive at any law school in the country. Were you to miss all of the 4- and 3-star questions, you would still get 71 correct answers, producing a scaled score around 158, better than 75 percent of test takers. To place above the 50th percentile (or, to score over 151, if you like), you'll need to get about 58 correct answers, that's all of the 1-star and not quite a majority of the 2-star questions. Now, most test takers get a mixture of easier and harder questions right, and even top scorers occasionally mess up and miss a 1-star question. But, take note of what happens once you are scoring over the 50th percentile: adding between five and ten correct answers to your performance can move your percentile score up ten points or more, making your application stronger than those of thousands of other test takers.

4. Recognize Patterns in the LSAT and in Your Performance

As a standardized test, the LSAT is nothing if not predictable. You won't know the content of the questions or passages you'll see on your official exam, of course, but repeated practice can reveal patterns that will help you improve your performance. As you review multiple tests, you will begin to see that certain question types recur with greater or lesser frequency. Moreover, each question type is amenable to a handful of expert strategies, which are often outlined in the explanations in this book. Beyond the patterns associated with question strategies and correct answers, you'll see that even the incorrect answers regularly fall into a handful of definite types as well. Whenever this is the case, the Kaplan explanations will highlight and articulate the incorrect answer pattern.

Use these patterns and categories to help assess your own performance. Ask yourself the following questions, and answer honestly. Do you regularly struggle with a particular Logic Reasoning question type? Is a certain pattern in Logic Games easier for you? Does another game type trip you up? Do some topics or question types in Reading Comprehension give you more trouble than others? Throughout the test, are there incorrect answer types to which you are routinely susceptible?

In our comprehensive Kaplan LSAT prep courses, we provide tools that help all of our students identify their individual strengths and weaknesses, and then we provide personalized instruction to help them maximize their potential on the test. If you are preparing on your own, identifying the patterns that impact your performance (for better or worse) will require more time and attention, but don't skip this important part of review. Determine your areas of greatest opportunities for improvement, and focus on them as you continue your practice. That leads directly to the next tip.

5. Apply What You Learn

This is the most significant tip of all. Taking a practice LSAT is important. If you complete your practice test under timed, test-like conditions, it will give you a great snapshot of your performance as it stands now. But, to get a genuine understanding of your strengths and opportunities—and, more importantly, to improve your performance—you need to take and review multiple tests.

The greatest value of these explanations is that you can use each practice test to evaluate your performance. That will point you in the right direction the next time you practice. Don't be content with getting a question right. Review the explanation until you are satisfied that you can get a similar question right the next time you see one, and that you can get it right as quickly and efficiently as you'll need to under the time constraints of the test. When you get a question wrong, don't simply read the correct answer and think, "Oh, I get it now." Make sure you know how you misread or misunderstood the question, and why the particular incorrect answer you chose was tempting.

Practice and review the LSAT consistently with the help of expert explanations, and you will improve.

Logic Games Method and Strategies

Every Logic Games section contains four games, each with five to seven questions. To finish the section within the allotted 35 minutes, you need to average around 8 and 1/2 minutes per game. That's a tall order, one most test takers are not able to fill. The Kaplan Method for Logic Games is designed to attain the maximum combination of speed and accuracy within this section.

LOGIC GAMES METHOD
1. Overview
2. Sketch
3. Rules
4. Deductions
5. Questions

You may find it striking that the LSAT expert completes four steps in this Method before turning her attention to the questions. That seems counter-intuitive. Don't we want to get to the questions as quickly as possible? As you study the logic games explanations in this book, however, you'll see that the expert's approach, which involves organizing the game's information first, allows her to answer the questions much more efficiently, sometimes in a matter of seconds. These explanations will demonstrate the enormous power of patience in logic games, and will convince you of the value of consistently applying the Method to every game you encounter.

To understand what each step involves, let's first define the parts of a logic game as they appear in the test booklet. To conduct your overview of the game, you'll examine the game's **setup**, the short description of the game's situation, entities (the people or things you're asked to arrange in the game), and action (the game's task). Beneath the setup, the testmaker always includes some **rules**, which are listed in indented text. These rules provide restrictions on how the entities may behave within the game's action and framework. After that, you'll see the game's **questions**. In most games, one or more of the questions will begin with a hypothetical "If" condition. Such a condition acts like an additional rule, but it applies *only* to that individual question. Keep your Master Sketch with the rules that apply throughout the game separate from your scratchwork on individual questions containing new "If"s that are unique to that question.

Step 1: Overview

The goal here is to have a clear mental picture of your task. Ideally, you could describe your job within the game in a single sentence, e.g., "I will be dividing eight students into two teams of four with no overlap," or "From among seven books, I will select four and reject three." Be as precise as you can without overstating the limitations imposed by the setup. Make sure, for example, that the game asks you to choose "exactly four books" and not "at least four books." In logic games, every word is important.

LOGIC GAMES STRATEGY

Ask the SEAL Questions to Conduct Your Overview

To make sure that they have a strong grasp of the game's layout and task, LSAT experts ask four questions, known to Kaplan students by the acronym SEAL, from the first letter of each word.

What is/are the ...

Situation—What is the real-world scenario being described? What is the deliverable information—an ordered list, a calendar, a chart showing what's matched up?

Entities—Who or what are the "moving parts," the people or things I'm distributing, selecting, sequencing, or matching?

Action—What is the specific action—distribution, selection, sequencing, matching, or a combination of those—that I'm performing on the entities?

Limitations—Does the game state parameters (e.g., select exactly four of the seven, sequence the entities one per day) that determine or restrict how I'll set up and sketch the game?

Throughout Kaplan Logic Games explanations, the LSAT experts will often break down their Overviews just like this. Be sure you see what they see before you move into the complicated rules and deductions.

Step 2: Sketch

Based on your Overview, create a simple framework in which you record and organize the game's information, rules, and limitations. The testmaker uses just a handful of game types, so as you review your work and study the expert's sketches in the explanations, learn to identify the most common actions and the sketches typically associated with them. Here are two good rules of thumb: 1) Always list out the entities in abbreviation (e.g., M O P T W Y) above your sketch framework, and 2) make your framework as simple and easy to copy as possible (since you will want to repeat it when a question offers you a new "If" condition).

LOGIC GAMES STRATEGY

Learn the Standard Sketch for Each Game Type

Every game needs a Master Sketch. It provides a framework into which you can build the rules and restrictions that will allow you to answer the questions. Fortunately, the LSAT uses the same game types test after test, and you can learn some standard patterns that will save you time and frustration on Test Day. Here's how LSAT experts typically set up the most common game actions.

Strict Sequencing—These games ask you to arrange or schedule entities in numbered positions, or on specific days or times. A series of numbered slots (either horizontal or vertical) usually suits this task.

A B C D E F

— — — — — —
1   2   3   4   5   6

Loose Sequencing—These games are similar to Strict Sequencing, but here, the setup does not provide numbered slots or days of the week. Instead, all of the rules describe the relative position of two or more entities. The rules can be combined to show all of the known relationships among the entities.

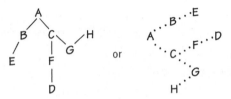

Selection—These games ask you to choose or select a smaller group of entities out of a longer list. All you really need here is a roster of all the entities. Then, you can circle those selected and cross out those rejected.

A̶ B̶ Ⓒ D E̶ F Ⓖ

Matching—These games ask you to match up members of one group with those of another, or to assign certain attributes to some members and different attributes to others. A list or grid fits the bill here.

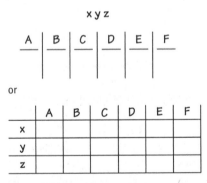

Distribution—These games give you a group of entities and ask you to break it up into smaller groups (two or three smaller groups is most common, but you will see four on occasion).

L M N O P R S

1	2	3
—	—	—
—	—	—

For every game, the Kaplan explanations will show the LSAT expert's initial sketch framework and explain how she chose it. Then, you'll see how the expert develops the sketch to accommodate the rules and deductions provided by the game. Study the sketches carefully and make sure you see why the expert chose the one she did.

Now, some games may have twists or special requirements that require you to vary or add to these standard sketches, and Hybrid games combine two or three of the standard actions together. Don't let these exceptions deter you from learning the standard sketches. Once you know the common patterns, it will be easier to see how LSAT experts can account for the unique features of any game within them.

Step 3: Rules

Once you have created a sketch framework, you will then analyze and sketch each rule. Make sure to consider what each rule does and does not determine. Again, every word in Logic Games is important. A rule stating that "A gives his presentation on a day earlier than the day on which B gives his presentation" is different than one stating that "A gives his presentation on the day immediately before the day on which B gives his presentation," and both are distinct from the rule "A gives his presentation on the day immediately before or the day immediately after the day on which B give his presentation." As you review the explanations, pay careful attention to how the LSAT expert sketched out each rule to make sure you didn't over- or under-determine the rule's scope.

LOGIC GAMES STRATEGY

Build Rules Directly into the Sketch Framework

Always seek to depict rules in the most concrete, helpful way possible. If you can, build them right into the sketch, so that you can see their impact on the setup and the entities.

When you encounter a rule that establishes exactly where an entity should go, your instinct will rightly be to place that entity right into your sketch framework. Consider, for example, a game that asks you to sequence six entities—A, B, C, D, E, and F—into six numbered positions—1 through 6. If you get a rule that says "D will be placed in Position 4," you'll just jot down "D" on top of that slot in your framework. Perfect! The entity can't move, and you'll always see where it is.

With other types of rules, however, many test takers do not add them to the sketch in the most helpful way. When analyzing Logic Games rules, LSAT experts always consider what the rules does and does not restrict. Sometimes, the negative implications of a rule are stronger than its affirmative ones. For example, consider a game that asks you to sequence six entities—A, B, C, D, E, and F—into six numbered positions—1 through 6. A typical rule for that game might say: C must be placed before A. You could jot down something like "C ... A," but that doesn't tell you anything concrete. You cannot easily place that into your sketch framework. The negative implications of that rule, however, are very strict: C absolutely cannot go in position 6, and A absolutely cannot go in position 1. If you write something like "~C" directly underneath slot 6 and "~A" underneath slot 1 in your sketch, you will have a very clear visual depiction of this rule.

Throughout the Kaplan explanations, take time to study how LSAT experts draw and depict the rules. It's okay if your drawings don't look identical to those in the explanations, but you're sure to encounter a few instances in which the expert's sketch makes a lot of sense, and teaches you a few new tactics for handling games and their rules.

Step 4: Deductions

This is the step that most untrained test takers miss, but it is also the step that can transform your performance on a game. Deductions arise when you are able to combine rules and restrictions to determine additional information. Logic games reward test takers for being able to quickly and accurately determine what must, can, and cannot be true about the entities in the game, and deductions can increase your brain's processing power enormously. Take the simplest kind of deduction, accounting for "Duplications," in other words, entities mentioned in more than one rule. Here's the scenario:

In a game that asks you to arrange six entities (call them A, B, C, D, E, and F) into six hour long spots from 1 PM through 6 PM, you have two rules:

B gets an earlier spot than C.
D gets a later spot than C.

Combining those two rules (B ... C and C ... D) produces a three-entity list (B ... C ... D). That's pretty routine, but consider the implications. You now know that D will never take 1 PM or 2 PM, that C will never take 1 PM or 6 PM, and that B will never take 5 PM or 6 PM.

Most deductions are more elusive than that, and some are even more powerful in their effects on the entities within the game. As you review your work and study the explanations, pay attention to the deductions made by the LSAT experts. Especially in games where you feel that you really struggled, discovering that there was an available deduction that you missed can make the entire game clearer and more comprehensible.

LOGIC GAMES STRATEGY

Use the BLEND Checklist to Make All Available Deductions

One of the hardest things to learn to do in logic games is to make all of the deductions quickly, and then to be confident enough that there are no more deductions that you can move on to tackle the question set. To help with this difficult task, Kaplan's LSAT experts have created a mnemonic of the five most common deduction-producing patterns seen in the rules and restrictions. We call it BLEND, for the first letter of each item in the list. Check for these patterns, and you'll be sure you don't overlook an available deduction, and you'll know when there are no more deductions to be found.

Blocks of Entities: When a rule forces two or more entities to occupy adjacent spaces in a list, or to be placed together in a group, check to see where space is available for them, and where they may prevent other entities from appearing.

Limited Options: When a rule (or combination of rules) restricts the entire game to just two or three patterns, LSAT experts will often create dual sketches to depict the game. Pay careful attention to Limited Options in the explanations. They aren't always easy to spot, but when they occur, they make the questions much, much easier to answer.

Established Entities: When a rule (or combination of rules) restricts an entity to just one space in a list, or forces the entity to be placed into a particular group, note it. This is powerful not only because you have firmly placed one entity, but also because that entity's placement may prevent others from being assigned to the same position or group.

Number Restrictions: When rules and limitations within a game restrict the number of entities that may be placed into a particular group, it makes the game much easier to solve. Being asked to split up seven students into two teams doesn't tell you much, but deducing that Team A must have three students and Team B must have four tells you a lot.

Duplications: When an entity appears in two rules, it allows the rules to be combined. We just described the simple B ... C + C ... D = B ... C ... D type of duplication, but duplications can be far more sophisticated, and may appear in any type of logic game.

In the explanations to every game, the expert will note when one or more of these patterns appears, and the term will appear in the glossary in case you've forgotten how it's defined.

Step 5: Questions

We alluded to the fact that logic games reward you for being able to determine what must, can, and cannot be true about the placement of the entities within the game. Scan the questions from any logic games section, and you'll see multiple variations asking "Which one of the following is an acceptable arrangement/could be true/must be false/etc.?" Throughout the explanations, you'll see how an LSAT expert uses the Master Sketch (including the additional deductions he's made) to make short work of these questions.

Quite often, the question stem opens with a New-"If" condition, but then asks one of these same questions given the new constraint or limitation. In most cases, LSAT experts tackle these with new "mini-sketches" so that they can make the new condition concrete. This strategy is discussed briefly below.

LOGIC GAMES STRATEGY

Use "Mini-sketches" to Take Control of New-"If" Questions

One "rookie mistake" that untrained test takers will make in Logic Games is to create a Master Sketch for a game and then try to use it for all of the game's New-"If" questions. Let's say a game has five questions, and when our untrained test taker comes to Question 2, he sees that it begins with a new "If" condition. He then adds the new restrictions into his overall Master Sketch and works out the implications. That's great for that one question, but here are a few reasons why it's a bad strategy for the rest of the game:

Subsequent questions will either have different New-"If" conditions, or they will have no new conditions at all. That means that to use his Master Sketch again, the untrained test taker will have to erase all of the work he did on Question 2. At a minimum, that will be messy and will take up some time. The bigger risk is that the test taker will forget exactly which of the deductions he made at the beginning of the game, and which he made specifically for Question 2. He could wind up inadvertently leaving some of Question 2's work in the sketch, or erasing some of the initial deductions he'd made. Either way, he's now in danger of missing all the subsequent questions associated with the game.

Additionally, if our untrained test taker effectively erases the work in the sketch that was unique to Question 2, he will no longer have that work to refer to. In the next strategy note, you'll learn how LSAT experts sometimes consult their work on earlier questions to help answer later ones. If you are building-erasing-rebuilding your sketch as you go, you won't have a record of the work you've done throughout the question set.

LSAT experts avoid these pitfalls by creating a Master Sketch containing the setup, rules, and deductions for the overall game. And, then, they leave it alone. They can consult the Master Sketch for questions without New-"If" conditions. For each New-"If" question, however, they quickly copy the Master Sketch and label it with the question number of the New-"If" question. They add the question's new "If" condition to this copy, and work out the question's implications there. When they move on, they leave that question's work as a reference, just in case it helps them on a subsequent question.

As you review, study the new "mini-sketches" that experts make for New-"If" questions. You'll learn not only how they got a particular question right, but also how they effectively manage an entire game.

There are a handful of relatively rare Logic Games question types, but well-trained test takers can use the same sketches and techniques to answer them, as well. At times, test takers who have truly mastered the Logic Games Method will even use their work on one or two questions to help them quickly answer another. That's why it is valuable to review an entire game, from Step 1 all the way through the last question, even when you only missed one or two of the questions along the way. Your review will not only reveal where you went off track on the questions you missed, it also will likely show you how you could have handled the entire game more quickly and confidently.

LOGIC GAMES STRATEGY

Use Previous Work to Determine what Could be True

The LSAT always provides enough information to answer every question. That's comforting to know, but open-ended questions that ask you what could be true or must be false in a game without giving you any new conditions or constraints can be very time consuming. For most students, their instincts tell them to try out every answer choice one by one.

LSAT experts know to keep track of the work they do on every question, and when they can use it to help them solve these open-ended questions. If they see that an open-ended question will be very time consuming, or will require them to test every answer choice, they often skip that question temporarily. After working through the other questions in the set, they'll come back to the open-ended question.

Here's how it works. Let's say a question asks "Which one of the following must be false?" You check your Master Sketch, but you don't see anything there that definitively rules out one of the answer choices. Work through the rest of the questions for the game. Along the way, you'll likely encounter one question that asks for an "acceptable arrangement" of entities. You'll probably also have two or three questions with New-"If" conditions, and you'll solve those by creating "mini-sketches" that reveal some additional "acceptable arrangements." Now, the expert test taker uses critical thinking: "Since the correct answer to the open-ended question must be false, all four of its wrong answers could be true." Then, he can check any acceptable arrangement he has discovered or created along the way. Any answer choice for the "must be false" question that appears in an acceptable arrangement is an incorrect answer, and he can cross it out. Sometimes, you may be able to eliminate all four wrong answers in this way.

Students in Kaplan's comprehensive LSAT prep courses drill with the Logic Games Method in class and throughout their homework. They are assigned chapters in Kaplan's LSAT treatise "The LSAT Unlocked" that go over the strategies, tactics, and techniques associated with each step of the Method. They practice it on dozens of real LSAC-released logic games in Kaplan's exclusive Qbank, a library of over 2,000 official LSAT questions. As you review your work in these explanations, follow along with the LSAT experts who make the Logic Games Method their template for accuracy and speed in this section.

Reading Comprehension Method and Strategies

For many students, Reading Comprehension is the section of the LSAT in which they find it most difficult to improve their scores. This is due, in part, to how familiar Reading Comprehension feels. In one way or another, you have been tested from grade school through college on how well you understood or remembered something that you had read. Learning to read actively and strategically, in the way rewarded by the LSAT, takes some getting used to. Kaplan's Reading Comprehension Method is designed to make your performance on this section of the test just as efficient and effective as our Logic Games Method can on that section.

READING COMPREHENSION METHOD

1. Read the Passage Strategically
2. Analyze the Question Stem
3. Research the Relevant Text
4. Predict the Correct Answer
5. Evaluate the Answer Choices

Given that you have four passages (and their accompanying questions) to complete in 35 minutes, time is precious in Reading Comprehension. LSAT experts will usually complete Step 1 for a passage in around 3 to 4 minutes. That leaves between 4 to 5 minutes to tackle the questions, using Steps 2 through 5 for each one. Here's what each step accomplishes.

Step 1: Read the Passage Strategically

LSAT Reading Comprehension passages are excerpts of around 450 to 500 words, typically from academic writing in fields covered by social science, natural science, humanities, and law. The writing is dense, and the topics are rarely, if ever, familiar to the casual reader. This content is pretty intimidating, and students often compound the problem by trying to read and remember the details and facts in these arcane passages.

But, here's what LSAT experts know: The LSAT is far more interested in *how* and *why* the author wrote the passage than it is in *what* the author said about the details. Here's why. Imagine if you saw this question on the LSAT.

> In which of the following years did George Washington lead Continental Army troops across the Delaware River?

This is a question that rewards knowledge, not reading comprehension. If you happen to know the answer, you could get this question right even without the passage. Law schools need to evaluate your skill level in comprehension and analysis. So, the LSAT asks questions more like these.

> The author of the passage would most likely agree with which one of the following statements about Washington's military leadership?

> The author includes a reference to Washington's crossing of the Delaware in order to

The primary purpose of the fourth paragraph of the passage is

To answer LSAT questions, you need to read for the passage's structure, and the author's opinions, and not just for names or dates or facts. Anticipating the kinds of questions that the test asks, LSAT experts read actively, interrogating the author as they proceed. When the author offers an opinion, the expert looks for where and how the author supports it. If the author describes two theories, the expert looks for the author's evaluation of them, or for language in which the author prefers one theory over the other. An LSAT expert's reading is never passive or wayward.

READING COMPREHENSION STRATEGY

Use Keywords to Read Effectively

Given the LSAT's emphasis on opinion and purpose, Kaplan has compiled a list of Keywords that indicate text that is likely to be relevant in answering LSAT questions. These include terms that indicate an author's point of view, her reason for including a detail or illustration, and words that show contrast or correspondence between two things or ideas. LSAT experts circle or underline these Keywords when they encounter them in the passage, and they use Keywords to effectively paraphrase or summarize chunks of text.

To see why Keywords are so helpful, try to answer the following question:

Type X coffee beans grow at very high altitudes. Type X coffee beans produce a dark, mellow coffee when brewed.

With which one of the following statements would the author most likely agree?

1. Coffee beans that grow at high altitudes typically produce dark, mellow coffee when brewed.
2. Coffee beans that grow at high altitudes typically produce light, acidic coffee when brewed.

You cannot answer that question from the text alone. It contains only facts. To understand the author's point of view, and thus to answer the LSAT question about it, you need for the author to supply Keywords that logically connect the facts in a specific way. Observe:

> Type X coffee beans grow at very high altitudes, *but* produce a *surprisingly* dark, mellow coffee when brewed.

Now, choice (2) is the correct answer on the LSAT. Choice (1) is clearly incorrect. But, what if the author had written the following?

> Type X coffee beans grow at very high altitudes, *and so* produce a dark, mellow coffee when brewed.

Now, it's choice (1) that is supported by the passage. Notice that the facts did not change at all, but when the author changes the Keyword, the correct answer on the LSAT changes. Keywords indicating a passage's structure or an author's point of view are not the kinds of words you typically pay attention to when you are reading for school, so you need to train yourself to spot them, and use them, on the LSAT.

Throughout the Kaplan LSAT explanations for Reading Comprehension, LSAT experts will show you the Keywords and phrases that they circled or underlined in the passage text.

Then, as they explain individual questions associated with a passage, they will demonstrate how they refer back to those Keywords to research the passage, predict correct answers, and evaluate the answer choices. The categories of Keywords are defined in the glossary.

By circling or underlining Keywords, and then jotting down succinct notes in the margin next to the passage, an LSAT expert creates a "Roadmap" of the passage. This helps the expert quickly research the text when one of the questions refers to a detail, illustration, or argument in the passage.

While a Roadmap of Keywords and margin notes is helpful on most questions, there are typically a few questions accompanying each passage that call for broader answers, such as the author's "primary purpose" or the passage's "main idea." To prepare for these questions, an LSAT expert also summarizes the "big picture" of the passage as she reads. Keeping in mind the kinds of questions that the LSAT asks, these summaries must go beyond mere subject matter to encompass how and why the author wrote the passage. Big picture summaries are described in the following strategy note.

READING COMPREHENSION STRATEGY

Summarize the Passage's Big Picture

In addition to circling Keywords and jotting down notes in the margins next to the passage, LSAT experts also mentally summarize passages as they strategically read LSAT Reading Comprehension passages. To do this efficiently, experts will usually break down the passage's big picture into Topic, Scope, Purpose, and Main Idea. You'll see these "big picture" terms referenced throughout Kaplan's LSAT explanations, and for most passages, the discussion following the Sample Roadmap will paraphrase the expert's summaries for you.

The Topic means the overall subject matter. It almost always appears in the first paragraph. At this high level, the subject matter is likely to be familiar to you, even if you don't know much about it.

The Scope refers to the aspect of the Topic that interests this author. For example, if the Topic is George Washington, the Scope could be Washington's economic policies, Washington's education, or Washington's service as a general in the Continental Army. Usually, you will have some idea of the Scope from the passage's first paragraph, although occasionally, it may not be entirely clear until the second (or even third) paragraph. The Scope must be narrower than the Topic, and it is important that you recognize *the author's* Scope and avoid imposing your thoughts about a Topic onto the passage.

Identifying the author's purpose is central to your LSAT success. To put your finger on why the author is writing the passage, look to the passage's structure. Does the author begin by describing someone else's idea or theory about the subject? If so, the author's purpose may be to *rebut* the other thinker's idea. On the other hand, the author might go on to *explain* how this other person's theory influenced subsequent ideas on the subject. In another passage structure common on the LSAT, the author opens with a description of an event or phenomenon. She might go on to *evaluate* the importance of the phenomenon, or she might *advocate* for a particular kind of response to it. Notice that all of the italicized words here are verbs, and learn to paraphrase the author's Purpose as a verb in your own summaries.

Remember, you want to capture *why* and *how* the author examines a subject, and not only *what* she says about it.

If you have summarized the Topic, Scope, and Purpose accurately, you can usually combine them into a fairly clear statement of the passage's Main Idea. For example, if the Topic is George Washington, the Scope is Washington's time as commander of the Continental Army, and the author's Purpose is to *illustrate* how his military career influenced his political career, then the Main Idea might be something like: "Washington's generalship trained him to be consultative and decisive in political battles with Congress." In the most academic passages on the LSAT, you may encounter a one-sentence thesis statement or summary that makes the Main Idea explicit, but more often, you will need to paraphrase the Main Idea by combining the Topic, Scope, and Purpose you have identified from the passage structure and the author's point of view.

As you review Reading Comprehension sections using these explanations, you'll see how LSAT experts handle "main idea" and "primary purpose" questions using the kinds of big picture strategies we've just discussed.

In Reading Comprehension, Step 1 should take you around 3–4 minutes. Think of your passage Roadmap much as you would your Master Sketch in a logic game. It highlights and organizes the most important information in the passage, and it gets you ready to answer the questions.

Step 2: Analyze the Question Stem

Reading Comprehension passages are usually accompanied by 5–8 questions. Start your analysis of each question by identifying two things: the question type and any clues that will help you research the passage text. Kaplan always identifies the question type at the start of every question's explanation. The question types are defined in the glossary, as well.

As we've already alluded to, some Reading Comprehension questions ask about the "big picture." Kaplan calls these Global questions, and if you've summarized the Topic, Scope, Purpose, and Main Idea of the passage, you won't need do any further research. Just use your summaries to predict the correct answer.

Other question types focus on the specifics of what the author said. Occasionally, you'll encounter a Detail question. These usually begin with a phrase such as "According to the passage ..." making it clear that the correct answer is something stated in the passage. The LSAT also often tests details through Logic Function questions. These question stems cite the detail from the passage and then ask *why* the author included the detail or *how* he used it. A common phrasing for this question type is: "The author refers to *xxx* (lines 24–26) in order to." Use the detail, and any line or paragraph reference to research the text. Keywords before or after the detail ("*but* xxx is different" or "xxx is *especially important because*") will often demonstrate the author's reason for including it, and will help you predict the correct answer.

By far, the most common question type in Reading Comprehension is the Inference question. These ask you for something that the passage implies, but does not state explicitly. Inference question stems can be open-ended ("With which one of the following statements would the author of the passage most likely agree?") or they may include references to a detail in the passage ("Based on the information presented in the passage, which one of the following economic policies would Washington have been most likely to endorse?"). Whenever a research clue is present, use it to pinpoint the relevant text in the passage. For example, the "economic policies" mentioned in the second Inference question stem would likely take you to a particular paragraph, and maybe even to a particular line in the passage about Washington.

A handful of questions in the Reading Comprehension section will mimic the skills tested in the Logical Reasoning section. A Reading Comprehension question could, for example, ask you to strengthen an argument made by the author, or to identify a method of argument parallel to one in the passage. To manage these questions, LSAT experts employ the skills they've learned for the comparable question types in the Logical Reasoning section. This is a good reminder that you should review complete tests, even when you're primarily concerned with just one or two sections.

Step 3: Research the Relevant Text

Don't answer LSAT Reading Comprehension questions on a whim. Whenever you are able to research the passage, do so. But, be careful. Don't passively re-read the passage, or go on a "fishing expedition" for details you don't remember.

An LSAT expert uses the research clues that he finds in question stems in conjunction with his strategic reading Roadmap to put his finger right on the relevant text in the passage. Moreover, the expert always seeks out Keywords that indicate *why* the author included a detail, or *how* the author used it in the passage. In some questions, the LSAT testmaker will include wrong answers that use words or phrases directly from the passage, but that distort what the author had to say about those words or phrases. The following strategy examines how LSAT experts use research effectively and efficiently.

READING COMPREHENSION STRATEGY

Use Research Clues to Answer Questions Efficiently

Most LSAT test takers are pretty good readers. Given unlimited time, a lot of test takers could probably get all of the Reading Comprehension questions correct. Of course, the LSAT does not give you unlimited time. Indeed, the 35-minute time limit may be your biggest obstacle to Reading Comprehension success.

LSAT experts combat the test's time constraints by very effectively avoiding pointless re-reading. There are five kinds of research clues they recognize in question stems that help them zero in on the relevant text and predict the correct answer.

> **Line References**—Experts research around the referenced detail, looking for Keywords that indicate why the referenced text has been included and how it is used.
> **Paragraph References**—Experts consult their Roadmaps to check the paragraph's scope, and its function in the passage.
> **Quoted Text** (sometimes accompanied by a line reference)—Experts check the context of the quoted term or phrase, and they consider what the author meant by it.
> **Proper Nouns**—Experts check for the context of the person, place, or thing in the passage; they check for whether the author made a positive, negative, or neutral evaluation of it; and they consider why the author included it.
> **Content Clues**—Experts take note when question stems mention terms, concepts, or ideas highlighted in the passage, knowing that these almost always refer to something that the author emphasized, or about which the author expressed an opinion.

If you struggle to maintain your accuracy while trying to complete the Reading Comprehension in time, pay attention to how Kaplan's LSAT experts explain their work in Step 3. It could really change the way you take the test.

Step 4: Predict the Correct Answer

Once you have researched the passage (or, for Global questions, once you have paused to consider your big picture summaries of the passage), take a moment to paraphrase (or "pre-phrase," if you like that term) what the correct answer must contain. Taking a few seconds to predict the correct answer can save you a lot of time as you move through the answer choices. Just as they do in Logical Reasoning explanations, the Kaplan experts who write the Reading Comprehension explanations will always share their predictions with you in their analysis of Step 4. Pay careful attention to this step if you want to improve your speed and accuracy in Reading Comprehension.

Step 5: Evaluate the Answer Choices

Every question on the LSAT has one correct answer and four demonstrably incorrect ones. This is especially important to remember in Reading Comprehension because comparing answer choices back to the text can lead to endless re-reading and wasted time. Armed with a solid prediction (or, at a minimum, with a clear idea of the author's purpose and point of view), evaluate the choices boldly. If (A) does not contain what the correct answer must say, cross it out and move on. Those who master the Reading Comprehension Method often become so confident that once they spot the correct answer, they do not even need to read the rest of the answer choices. In the Kaplan explanations, we always explain why every wrong answer is wrong, even when the correct answer is (A). On Test Day, however, you will be well served by the ability to predict and evaluate consistently.

READING COMPREHENSION STRATEGY

Spot Common Wrong Answer Patterns

LSAT experts use the standardized nature of the LSAT to their advantage in Reading Comprehension (just as they do in Logical Reasoning) by anticipating certain types of wrong answers that occur over and over again.

Many of the wrong answer types in this section are the same ones associated with Logical Reasoning questions. You will see a fair share of Outside the Scope wrong answers, and in Reading Comprehension Global questions particularly, you will see incorrect answers that go beyond the scope, encompassing more than what the author included in her Purpose or Main Idea. You will also see Extreme and 180 incorrect answers similar to those in Logical Reasoning.

Two incorrect answers types that are more common in Reading Comprehension than they are in Logical Reasoning are the Distortion and Half-Right/Half-Wrong answer choices. Distortion incorrect answers are those that stay within the scope of the passage, but then twist what the author has said in a way that misstates the author's position or point of view. Half-Right/Half-Wrong answer choices are those that start off well, matching the passage up to a point, but then incorrectly characterize or contradict the passage in their second half.

Whenever an answer choice fits into one of the common wrong answer categories, the Reading Comprehension explanations will point it out. If there is an incorrect answer type that doesn't make sense to you, check out its description in the glossary.

Students in Kaplan's comprehensive LSAT prep courses make Reading Comprehension a regular part of their practice. They understand that they have to. After all, improvement in Reading Comprehension requires diligent practice. Kaplan instructors encourage both un-timed and timed practice so that students can learn the skills and strategies rewarded by the Reading Comprehension section, and then evaluate them under test-like conditions. In addition to having access to hundreds of released LSAT Reading Comprehension passages, Kaplan students also hone their skill set with *LSAT Channel* lessons covering the full range of ability levels, from Fundamentals to Advanced. Even if Reading Comprehension is your strongest section initially, practice and review it throughout your LSAT prep. Steady improvement in this tough section will lead to a higher score on the exam.

A Note About Formal Logic on the LSAT

In college and university Philosophy departments, Formal Logic is an enormous topic that may cover several semesters and hours and hours of difficult reading. Its reputation as a formidable and intimidating subject is well deserved. The LSAT, however, tests only a small sliver of Formal Logic, a sliver that can be mastered with a few hours of expert instruction and diligent practice.

The aspect of Formal Logic tested on the LSAT is restricted to **conditional statements** (also called "If-then" statements). You'll see them from time to time in Logic Games, and multiple times in Logical Reasoning on every test. Here's a brief introduction to how you will see Formal Logic described and discussed in these explanations.

Conditional Statements: Sufficiency and Necessity

A conditional statement is defined by having a **sufficient** clause and a **necessary** clause. That's a hifalutin' way of saying it has an "If" clause and a "then" clause. Here's a simple example:

> If this car is running, then it has gasoline in its gas tank.

That means that gasoline in the gas tank is necessary for this car to run. So, the necessary clause follows "then." That's always the case. Now, notice that the clause "this car is running" is sufficient to establish that the car has gasoline in its gas tank. The "If" clause is always sufficient (that is, it is enough by itself) to establish the truth of the necessary (or "then") clause.

In the explanations, the LSAT expert will often abbreviate Formal Logic by using an arrow for the "then" clause, like this:

$$\textit{If} \quad \textit{car running} \quad \rightarrow \quad \textit{has gas}$$

Translating Conditional Statements

There are many ways to express conditional logic in the English language, and the LSAT uses them all. For example, on the test, the previous conditional statement might be expressed in any of the following ways:

> This car will run only if it has gasoline in its gas tank.
> This car will not run unless it has gasoline in its gas tank.
> Only if this car has gasoline in its gas tank will this car run.
> If this car does not have gasoline in its gas tank, then this car will not run.

From the perspective of Formal Logic these are all equivalent statements. They all present exactly the same relationship of a sufficient term to a necessary term. LSAT experts learn to recognize conditional statements and to quickly and accurately translate them into the "If-then" format. You'll see this skill demonstrated several times in the explanations to any LSAT test.

The final version of our statement about the car ("If this car does not have gasoline in its gas tank, then this car will not run") is also known as the contrapositive of the original statement. Being able to formulate the contrapositive of any conditional statement is a crucial skill for LSAT success.

Contrapositives

The logic underlying contrapositives is simple. Since the term that follows "then" is necessary for the term that follows "If," when you negate the necessary term, you must also negate the sufficient term. In other words, when you remove something that is necessary, you can't have the thing it's necessary for. So, to abbreviate our previous example:

If   *NO gas*   →   *car NOT running*

If our original statement is true, then this one must be true as well. And, that's it. To form the contrapositive of a conditional statement, reverse *and* negate its sufficient and necessary terms.

Be careful, though, because if you reverse without negating, or if you negate without reversing, you will create illogical statements (and the LSAT will punish illogical statements with wrong answers). For example, here's what we would get by negating our original statement's terms without reversing them too:

If   *car NOT running*   →   *NO gas*

But that could be wrong, couldn't it? If the car is not running, it might have a dead battery, or a broken transmission, or it might even be turned off. In any of those cases, it might have gasoline in its gas tank.

Similarly, here's what we'd get by reversing without negating:

If   *has gas*   →   *car running*

Again, the mistake is obvious in our simple example. Having gasoline is necessary for the car to run, not sufficient for it to run. It could have a full tank of gas, but if its battery is dead, it would not be running.

To see why contrapositives are important on the LSAT, consider a Logic Games rule: "If Katherine is selected, then Malik will be selected." It's easy to translate and jot down:

If   *K*   →   *M*

That will be helpful any time you know that Katherine is selected in the game. But, here's what the test is likely to ask: "If Malik is not selected, then which one of the following must be true?" An LSAT expert may even anticipate a question like this one because as soon as he sees the original conditional statement among the rules, he will also note its contrapositive by reversing and negating the original terms:

$$\textbf{\textit{If}} \quad \textbf{\textit{NOT M}} \quad \rightarrow \quad \textbf{\textit{NOT K}}$$

There's no doubt that if Malik is not selected, then it must be true that Katherine is not selected either.

Conditional Statements with Multiple Terms

From time to time, the LSAT will include conditional statements that have more than one term in the sufficient clause, in the necessary clause, or in both. For the most part, these work just the same as the previous example, but there is one important additional note we need to make about contrapositives in conditional statements with multiple terms. To see this, let's add a term to the necessary clause of our original statement:

$$\textbf{\textit{If}} \quad \textbf{\textit{car running}} \quad \rightarrow \quad \begin{array}{l} \textbf{\textit{has gas AND}} \\ \textbf{\textit{has charged}} \\ \textbf{\textit{battery}} \end{array}$$

This statement now has two terms in the necessary clause, and *both* are necessary: If this car is running, then it has gasoline in its gas tank AND it has a charged battery. Because both conditions are necessary, the negation of either one will cause the car not to run. Thus, the contrapostive would read:

$$\textbf{\textit{If}} \quad \begin{array}{l} \textbf{\textit{NO gas OR}} \\ \textbf{\textit{NO charged}} \\ \textbf{\textit{battery}} \end{array} \quad \rightarrow \quad \begin{array}{l} \textbf{\textit{car NOT}} \\ \textbf{\textit{running}} \end{array}$$

When we reverse and negate to form the contrapositive, we must also change the "and" linking the two necessary terms to "or." This will always work, regardless of whether the "and" or the "or" are found initially in the sufficient clause or in the necessary clause. We can illustrate this with another Logic Games rule. Imagine that the test tells you the following: "If Juliana and Nestor attend the dance, then Patricia will not attend the dance." That is, if J and N are *both* there, P will not be. Here's that rule in Formal Logic shorthand:

$$\textbf{\textit{If}} \quad \textbf{\textit{J AND N}} \quad \rightarrow \quad \textbf{\textit{NOT P}}$$

Now, to form the contrapositive, reverse and negate the terms, and change the "and" to an "or":

$$\textbf{\textit{If}} \quad \textbf{\textit{P}} \quad \rightarrow \quad \begin{array}{l} \textbf{\textit{NOT J OR}} \\ \textbf{\textit{NOT N}} \end{array}$$

That might look funny initially, but it is absolutely true based on the original statement. Patricia will not go to the dance if both Juliana and Nestor go. So, knowing that Patricia *is* at the dance is sufficient to establish that at least one of the other two is absent.

Any time you see a conditional statement, you can form its contrapositive correctly by reversing and negating the terms, and changing "and" to "or" or vice versa.

Combining Conditional Statements

The LSAT often rewards your ability to combine conditional statements to reach valid deductions that may not be apparent at first. The most obvious example is when they give you two statements like these:

$$\text{If} \quad A \quad \rightarrow \quad B$$

$$\text{If} \quad B \quad \rightarrow \quad C$$

From this, we can pretty easily deduce the following:

$$\text{If} \quad A \quad \rightarrow \quad B \quad \rightarrow \quad C$$

And, thus:

$$\text{If} \quad A \quad \rightarrow \quad C$$

When the example is that straightforward, the deduction is pretty easy to see. However, on the LSAT, the testmaker will sometimes add a step or two. Imagine that you see these rules in a logic game:

Danny will audition for any play that Carla directs.

Danny will not audition for a play unless Rebekkah also auditions for that play.

First, you will need to translate those sentences into Formal Logic abbreviations:

$$\text{If} \quad C_{dir} \quad \rightarrow \quad D_{aud}$$

$$\text{If} \quad \sim R_{aud} \quad \rightarrow \quad \sim D_{aud}$$

Now, the result of the first statement (its necessary clause) is that Danny auditions. The trigger (or sufficient clause) of the second sentence is that Rebekkah does *not* audition. Right now, you can't combine those statements. But look what happens when you formulate the contrapositive of the second sentence:

$$\text{If} \quad D_{aud} \quad \rightarrow \quad R_{aud}$$

Now, the trigger (the sufficient clause) of the second statement is that Danny auditions. Thus:

$$\text{If} \quad C_{dir} \quad \rightarrow \quad D_{aud} \quad \rightarrow \quad R_{aud}$$

So, when combined, those statements allow you to deduce that Rebekkah also auditions for any play that Carla directs.

The skill of combining conditional statements doesn't only appear in Logic Games. In fact, it's far more common in Logical Reasoning questions. Wherever they encounter Formal Logic on the test, LSAT experts are adept at spotting conditional statements, translating them into the "If-then" format, formulating their contrapositives, and combining them to reach deductions.

For students in a comprehensive LSAT prep program, they regularly practice Formal Logic in and out of class, in their books, and their homework assignments, and they hone their skills watching Formal Logic *LSAT Channel* sessions. Whenever you encounter Formal Logic in these explanations, the LSAT expert will explain the analysis thoroughly, using abbreviations like those you've seen here. Always give Formal Logic an extra careful review.

PrepTest 72

The Inside Story

PrepTest 72 was administered in June 2014. It challenged 21,803 test takers. What made this test so hard? Here's a breakdown of what Kaplan students who were surveyed after taking the official exam considered PrepTest 72's most difficult section.

Hardest PrepTest 72 Section as Reported by Test Takers

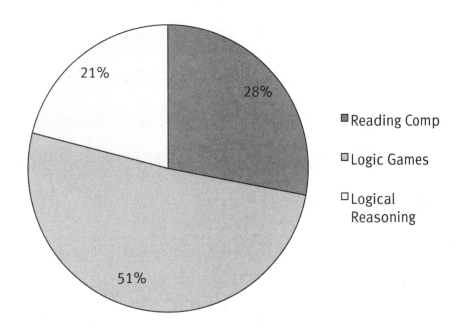

Based on these results, you might think that studying Logic Games is the key to LSAT success. Well, Logic Games is important, but test takers' perceptions don't tell the whole story. For that, you need to consider students' actual performance. The following chart shows the average number of students to miss each question in each of PrepTest 72's different sections.

Percentage Incorrect by PrepTest 72 Section Type

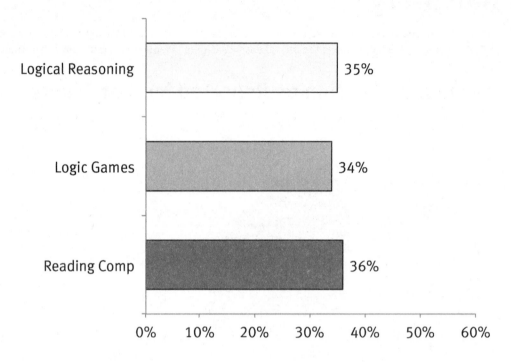

Actual student performance tells quite a different story. On average, students were almost equally likely to miss questions in all three of the different section types, and on PrepTest 72, Reading Comprehension and Logical Reasoning were somewhat higher than Logic Games in actual difficulty.

Maybe students overestimate the difficulty of the Logic Games section because it's so unusual, or maybe it's because a really hard Logic Game is so easy to remember after the test. But the truth is that the testmaker places hard questions throughout the test. Here were the locations of the 10 hardest (most missed) questions in the exam.

Location of 10 Most Difficult Questions in PrepTest 72

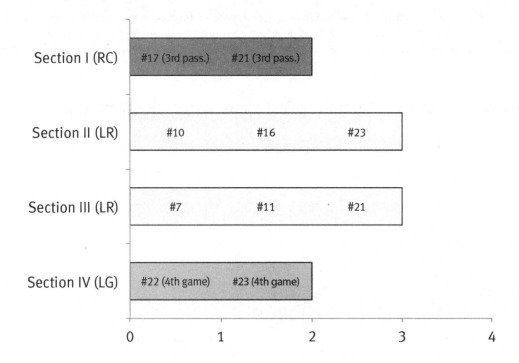

The takeaway from this data is that, to maximize your potential on the LSAT, you need to take a comprehensive approach. Test yourself rigorously, and review your performance on every section of the test. Kaplan's LSAT explanations provide the expertise and insight you need to fully understand your results. The explanations are written and edited by a team of LSAT experts, who have helped thousands of students improve their scores. Kaplan always provides data-driven analysis of the test, ranking the difficulty of every question based on actual student performance. The 10 hardest questions on every test are highlighted with a 4-star difficulty rating, the highest we give. The analysis breaks down the remaining questions into 1-, 2-, and 3-star ratings so that you can compare your performance to thousands of other test takers on all LSAC material.

Don't settle for wondering whether a question was really as hard as it seemed to you. Analyze the test with real data, and learn the secrets and strategies that help top scorers master the LSAT.

7 Can't–Miss Features of PrepTest 72

- PT 72 features the famous "Summit Company Workpieces" game. Although it is classified as a Strict Sequencing game, it involves a very rare quadruple sequence. Check out the explanations for this game, because making a few key deductions makes the questions significantly easier.
- PT 72's Logic Games section starts off with a Hybrid game. It's the first test to do so since October '08 (PT 55).
- This was the first PrepTest since December '06 (PT 51) with no Method of Argument questions.
- Don't expect to easily identify one Humanities, one Law, one Social Science, and one Natural Science passage in the Reading Comprehension section. The four passages straddle topics and no true Humanities passage appears.
- Only three Detail Questions appear in the Reading Comprehension section, that's the lowest since October '10 (PT 61).
- Answer choices (D) and (E) show up the same number of times overall in the LG and RC sections. However, in each individual section one is four times as likely to occur as the other one!
- The 2014 FIFA World Cup would kick off just three days after PrepTest 72 was administered. However, not a single question mentions soccer, host Brazil, or champion Germany!

PrepTest 72 in Context

As much fun as it is to find out what makes a PrepTest unique or noteworthy, it's even more important to know just how representative it is of other LSAT administrations (and, thus, how likely it is to be representative of the exam you will face on Test Day). The following charts compare the numbers of each kind of question and game on PrepTest 72 to the average numbers seen on all officially released LSATs administered over the past five years (from 2012 through 2016).

Number of LR Questions by Type: PrepTest 72 vs. 2012–2016 Average

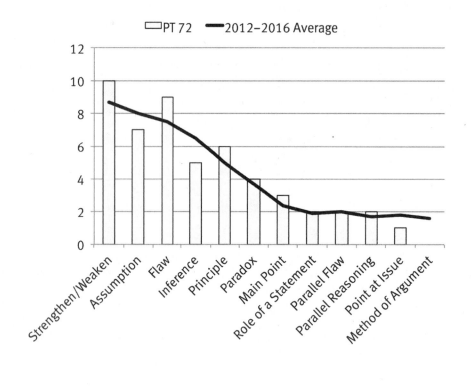

KAPLAN

Number of LG Games by Type: PrepTest 72 vs. 2012–2016 Average

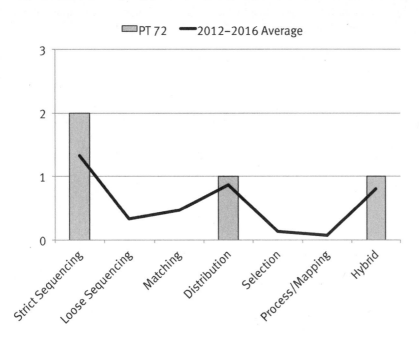

Number of RC Questions by Type: PrepTest 72 vs. 2012–2016 Average

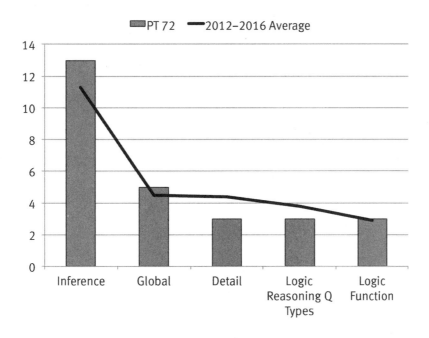

There isn't usually a huge difference in the distribution of questions from LSAT to LSAT, but if this test seems harder (or easier) to you than another you've taken, compare the number of questions of the types on which you, personally, are strongest and weakest. And then, explore within each section to see if your best or worst question types came earlier or later.

Students in Kaplan's comprehensive LSAT courses have access to every released LSAT, and to an online Qbank with thousands of officially released questions, games, and passages. If you are studying on your own, you have to do a bit more work to identify your strengths and your areas of opportunity. Quantitative analysis (like that in the previous charts) is an important tool for understanding how the test is constructed, and how you are performing on it.

Section I: Reading Comprehension
Passage 1: Wildfire Management

Q#	Question Type	Correct	Difficulty
1	Global	D	★
2	Inference	E	★
3	Inference	C	★★★
4	Logic Function	A	★
5	Inference	B	★★
6	Inference	D	★★★

Passage 2: Protecting the Cultural Antiquities of Mali

Q#	Question Type	Correct	Difficulty
7	Global	B	★★
8	Detail	B	★
9	Logic Function	C	★★
10	Inference	A	★★
11	Inference	C	★★
12	Inference	D	★★
13	Inference	B	★★★

Passage 3: The Case for Clinical Equipoise

Q#	Question Type	Correct	Difficulty
14	Global	B	★
15	Logic Function	D	★
16	Detail	C	★★
17	Inference	D	★★★★
18	Global	D	★★
19	Inference	A	★
20	Detail	C	★★
21	Logic Reasoning (Weaken)	A	★★★★

Passage 4: The Fairness of Flat Taxes

Q#	Question Type	Correct	Difficulty
22	Global	C	★
23	Logic Reasoning (Method of Argument)	E	★
24	Logic Reasoning (Strengthen)	D	★
25	Inference	D	★★★
26	Inference	B	★★★
27	Inference	B	★★★

Passage 1: Wildfire Management

Step 1: Read the Passage Strategically
Sample Roadmap

line #	Keyword/phrase	¶ Margin notes
2	powerful	
3	But	
5–6	too much; can be worse than none at all	N Am firefighters do job too well
7	dependent	Some fires necessary
9–10	for example	Ex: ponderosa
20	however	No fire → too much fuel
22–23	so large; total devastation	Fires more intense
27	Because	
30	vulnerable	Forests vulnerable
31	devastating	
31–32	therefore increasingly necessary	Auth: manage, don't eliminate
33	rather than	
34	should; essential	
36	depends on	Factors affect fire behavior
37	three factors	
38	since	
39	only	
40	should therefore focus	Focus on fuel
44	most promising	2-prong approach
48	thereby	(1)
50	both	(2)
56	needed	Maint burns needed
57	more easily; much less	Positive effects

Discussion

An interesting paradox opens this passage. Firefighters have gotten a lot better at battling wildfires over the past 50 years—a little too good. Forest ecosystems depend on periodic fires to keep fuel from building to levels that would make any given fire catastrophic. Lines 9–19 are devoted to the extended example of ancient ponderosa forests, which survived thanks in part to periodic low-intensity fires.

The Keyword *however* at the beginning of paragraph 2 signals a shift. The author lays out the consequences of eliminating fires from forests altogether. Whenever a fire does manage to spring up, it wipes out the entire forest and the wildlife that live within. Firefighters have been so successful in preventing fires that many forests are now vulnerable to these catastrophic fires. The Keyword *therefore* in line 31 signals the author's stance (and hints at the **Main Idea**): Firefighters in North America should manage rather than eradicate wildfires because they have proven useful in forest ecosystems.

The third paragraph gives more detail on the author's proposed policy change. Three factors (topography, weather, and fuel) affect fire behavior, and land managers should focus on fuel because it's the one factor they can influence. Land managers can influence the amount of fuel in a forest through selective harvesting (described in lines 45–49) and prescribed fires (described in lines 50–54). Supplementing this policy with regular "maintenance burns" will keep forests stable and prevent those cataclysmic fires from occurring.

The **Topic**, from the first sentence, is wildfires in North America, and the **Scope** is strategies for managing them. Based on the bulk of paragraphs 2 and 3, the author's **Purpose** is to suggest a new approach to wildfires. That new approach (and the **Main Idea**) is that managing rather than eliminating wildfires is the best policy for preserving forest ecosystems and preventing major fires.

1. (D) Global

Step 2: Identify the Question Type
This is a Global question because it asks for the passage's "primary purpose."

Step 3: Research the Relevant Text
Instead of researching a specific part of the passage to predict your answer, base your prediction on the Purpose you determined during Step 1.

Step 4: Make a Prediction
The Purpose of the passage is to advocate for a new approach to managing wildfires—the Keywords *therefore* in line 31 and *should* in line 34 signal the author's main intent here.

Step 5: Evaluate the Answer Choices
(D) is therefore correct.

(A) is Outside the Scope. The author never offers any explanation for why the policy change advocated in the passage hasn't been enacted.

(B) is also Outside the Scope. The author's proposed policy hasn't been implemented yet, so its effects aren't discussed in the passage.

(C) introduces funding for the author's proposed policy, another concept beyond the scope of the passage.

(E) is a Distortion. The author doesn't attempt to reconcile any contradictory goals of his policy; the author argues for a new kind of policy that will better meet the goals of the current fire management policy.

2. (E) Inference

Step 2: Identify the Question Type
This is an Inference question because it asks you to define a term as it is used in context.

Step 3: Research the Relevant Text
Line 55 is clearly relevant, but you need to read around that line to see how the author uses the term "maintenance burns."

Step 4: Make a Prediction
The sentence prior to the one that mentions maintenance burns says that an effective fire management policy should include "both the intentional lighting of controlled burns and the policy of allowing fires … to burn." So a maintenance burn must be a fire that helps reduce fuel but that is either set intentionally or allowed to burn.

Step 5: Evaluate the Answer Choices
(E) is therefore a match.

(A) is a Distortion. Maintenance burns are part of the author's present-day policy recommendation; the passage never says they occurred in ancient times.

(B) is a 180. The author is hoping to avoid the destruction of mature trees (lines 25–31), so the passage wouldn't recommend maintenance burns to reduce the population of these trees.

(C) is nearly a 180. The author advocates maintenance burns as an alternative strategy to the one currently being employed by firefighters in North America today. That means maintenance burns aren't already happening in today's forests.

(D) twists a detail from paragraph 2, a detail not relevant to the concept of maintenance burns.

3. (C) Inference

Step 2: Identify the Question Type
Any question asking for the sentence that would logically complete a paragraph or passage is an Inference question.

Step 3: Research the Relevant Text

Revisit the last few sentences of the passage to get a sense of the author's argument there.

Step 4: Make a Prediction

At the end of the passage, the author is advocating for a new fire management policy that focuses on fuel: selectively harvesting it and periodically burning it off. The last sentence of the passage gives the author's prediction of the results of implementing the new policy. The next sentence of the passage would continue those predictions.

Step 5: Evaluate the Answer Choices

(C) does just that. **(C)** is quite reasonable given the time frames discussed in the passage, particularly the 15- to 20-year intervals for regular maintenance burns.

(A) introduces a new idea—the threat to private property. The entire passage was all about damage to forest ecosystems.

(B) is unjustified as the last sentence of the passage. The author never hints at the response of the forest community to this recommended new policy.

(D) could possibly be tacked onto the sentence ending in line 49, but by the end of the passage, the author has stopped discussing harvesting smaller trees.

(E) strikes a pessimistic tone about financing that is unwarranted given the author's view of the new policy (consider the phrase "most promising" in line 44).

4. (A) Logic Function

Step 2: Identify the Question Type

This is a Logic Function question because it asks why the author mentioned something in the passage.

Step 3: Research the Relevant Text

The factors of topography, weather, and fuel are discussed at the beginning of paragraph 3.

Step 4: Make a Prediction

Paragraph 3 is an extension of the argument the author makes at the end of paragraph 2, where he recommends a new policy of fire management. The mention of the three factors affecting fire behavior is intended to support the idea that fuel is the only one land managers can control, and thus the one they should focus on (the Keyword *therefore* in line 40 indicates that this is the key point here).

Step 5: Evaluate the Answer Choices

(A) is therefore correct.

(B) is an argument the author doesn't make. In fact, the passage ends on a hopeful note—if land managers follow the author's proposed policy, catastrophic fires will be much less likely to occur.

(C) is in a different part of the passage. The reason why forest fires have become devastating is given at the beginning of paragraph 2.

(D) draws a relationship among the three factors that the author never implies. Fire behavior depends on the three factors of topography, weather, and fuel, but the passage doesn't argue that these three factors depend on each other.

(E) takes something from later in the paragraph (fires set by lightning) and makes it the point of lines 36–40. But the author's main argument in paragraph 3 has little to do with fires set by lightning and more to do with strategies for managing fuel levels.

5. (B) Inference

Step 2: Identify the Question Type

"The passage provides the most support for inferring" is a sure sign of an Inference question.

Step 3: Research the Relevant Text

Ancient ponderosa forests are discussed primarily in lines 9–19. The author briefly mentions ponderosa forests in line 29 also.

Step 4: Make a Prediction

You know the gist of the author's points about ancient ponderosa forests: They were more stable than their modern counterparts thanks to low-intensity fires that cleared away excess fuel (lines 9–14); these low-intensity fires occurred periodically enough to maintain the forests (lines 15–19); and today's version of these ancient forests is more vulnerable to fire damage (lines 27–31). The correct answer *must* be true based on these statements.

Step 5: Evaluate the Answer Choices

(B) is a valid Inference. Lines 12–14 say that low-intensity fires in ancient ponderosa forests "clear[ed] the understory of brush and young trees." Today, because those low-intensity fires have been suppressed, the forests have gotten too crowded and full of fuel, encouraging more devastating fires (lines 20–23, 27–31).

(A) is Outside the Scope. The genetic makeup of ancient ponderosa forests relative to today's forests is never discussed.

(C) is unsupported. The author mentions weather only as one of the three factors that affect fire behavior. No part of the passage hints at changes in weather patterns over time.

(D) is Outside the Scope. You know from the passage that today's fires wipe out more plant life, but you don't know that they wipe out more *types* of plant life.

(E) is unsupported because wildlife populations are only mentioned in the context of the devastating fires more likely to occur today.

6. (D) Inference

Step 2: Identify the Question Type
Any question asking what "can be inferred" from the passage is an Inference question.

Step 3: Research the Relevant Text
The author discusses the recommended fire management policy throughout paragraph 3.

Step 4: Make a Prediction
In lines 50–54, the author's proposed fire management strategy includes "allowing fires set by lightning to burn when the weather is damp enough to reduce the risk of extensive damage." The policy in the question stem talks about letting all fires set by lightning burn themselves out (regardless of weather conditions), which is more extreme than the author's policy.

Step 5: Evaluate the Answer Choices
(D) is therefore correct.

(A) is a Distortion. The author doesn't think that allowing lightning-triggered fires to burn until they died out naturally would lower the vulnerability of forests. In fact, doing so could wipe out entire forests if the weather conditions were unfavorable.

(B) is a Distortion. While the author does consider selective harvesting part of the recommended policy change, the other component of prescribed fire management doesn't allow for letting *all* fires set by lightning to burn uncontrolled.

(C) makes an Irrelevant Comparison between older and younger forests, when nothing in the passage indicates that a lightning-triggered fire would affect these forests differently.

(E) introduces the public perception of wildfires, which is Outside the Scope.

Passage 2: Protecting the Cultural Antiquities of Mali

Step 1: Read the Passage Strategically
Sample Roadmap

line #	Keyword/phrase	¶ Margin notes
3	but	Mali: no excav or export of sculpture
4	certainly	Couldn't enforce it
6	result was	
7	illicitly	Sculptures sold illegally
9	Because	
12	never	Lost knowledge
13	condemn	
14	And	Response: UNESCO doctrine
16	evolved	
18	Essentially	
19	should	
22	Further	Extension of doctrine
23	strengthened; declaring	
25	cannot	
26	Accordingly; reasonable	Mali should decide
30	Regrettably	
30–31	painful irony	Irony: strict regs work against Mali
32	discourage	
33–34	key reasons	
34	For example	Example
41	Suppose	Auth: what Mali could have done
45	greater	
47	Suppose	
52	may; less; less	
53	than	
55	still; avoided; But	Not ideal, but still better outcome
56	better than; ?	

Discussion

The passage starts by describing a quandary faced by the Malian government. Mali prohibited the excavation and export of Djenne-jeno's terra-cotta sculptures, but couldn't enforce that prohibition. So many of the sculptures were illegally excavated and sold, depriving us of valuable knowledge about the culture that produced them. The author uses words like *wonderful* (line 2) and *fine* (line 6) to describe the sculptures, so the tone is clearly one of appreciation for the artifacts. And because the author presents a dilemma faced by the Malian government, you can expect to learn either how the government resolved it or how they *could have* resolved it. The **Topic** of the passage is therefore the cultural antiquities of Mali, and the **Scope** is the policies enacted to preserve their heritage.

Paragraph 2 describes how UNESCO tried to resolve the pillaging problem. The UNESCO doctrine, according to the author, states that cultural artifacts are the property of the culture that produced them. The author then mentions that some countries have gone even further than this doctrine by declaring that their antiquities are "state property that cannot be freely exported" (line 25).

Paragraph 3 applies this idea to Mali. If we follow the doctrine, Mali should be able to decide what happens to the statues of Djenne-jeno. But if Mali goes so far as to prohibit the export of such statues and reacquire them from abroad, Mali will ironically be squelching the preservation of cultural knowledge about these artifacts, which is the goal in the first place.

The author ends the passage with a counterfactual argument. If Mali had worked with UNESCO to license excavations and boost education efforts, or taxed exports of sculptures to fund a museum, or registered excavated objects before they left their dig sites, the sculptures may have suffered a better fate. This last argument confirms that the **Purpose** is to suggest an alternate approach to the draconian laws that Mali instituted. The **Main Idea** is that a more flexible set of laws is better suited to preserve the cultural heritage of artifacts at places like Djenne-jeno.

7. (B) Global

Step 2: Identify the Question Type
Any question asking for the "main point of the passage" is a Global question.

Step 3: Research the Relevant Text
Instead of rereading specific parts of the text, use the work you did in Step 1 to predict your answer.

Step 4: Make a Prediction
The main point is that governments like Mali's have to take a more nuanced approach than simply prohibiting excavation

and export of artifacts if they want to preserve cultural heritage.

Step 5: Evaluate the Answer Choices
(B) is therefore correct.

(A) may be mentioned in the passage, but it leaves out the author's discussion of problems that can arise from a country's prohibition of archaeological excavation, to say nothing of paragraph 4, which is the heart of the author's policy recommendation.

(C) is a 180. The author says explicitly that things would have gone better for Mali's artifacts had Mali worked with UNESCO, which is an international body (lines 41–43).

(D) overemphasizes and distorts a detail from paragraph 4. The author gives recommendations for what Mali should have done, but says that these policies could have worked well even if items were excavated by laypeople.

(E) is a Distortion. The harm to countries like Mali comes not from the idea in **(E)**, which is itself a bastardization of the UNESCO doctrine, but from unenforceable policies prohibiting the excavation and export of artifacts.

8. (B) Detail

Step 2: Identify the Question Type
Direct, categorical language such as "the passage indicates" is a sign of a Detail question.

Step 3: Research the Relevant Text
The author discusses the ways in which countries have made use of the UNESCO doctrine in paragraph 2.

Step 4: Make a Prediction
In paragraph 2, the author says that some countries have adopted and even strengthened the UNESCO doctrine by declaring their cultural artifacts state property that can't be removed from within their borders (lines 22–25).

Step 5: Evaluate the Answer Choices
(B) is therefore correct.

(A) is part of a policy the author recommends toward the end of the passage, but paragraph 2 doesn't say that this is something already being done under the UNESCO doctrine.

(C) is a detail lifted from paragraph 4. **(C)** is an example of something Mali could have done, not something that countries are already doing with the UNESCO doctrine.

(D) is a complicated idea that's never mentioned in the passage. The boundaries of an ancient culture's territory never come into play in the UNESCO doctrine—only the boundaries of the modern country are involved.

(E) is Outside the Scope. The UNESCO doctrine doesn't dictate countries' behavior once antiquities are taken illegally out of a country.

9. (C) Logic Function

Step 2: Identify the Question Type
The phrase "in order to" at the end of the question stem signals a Logic Function question. Determine *why* the author made a certain reference, not *what* the author said in that reference.

Step 3: Research the Relevant Text
The question stem points you to lines 49–51. But understanding the purpose of the entire fourth paragraph will be critical as you predict the answer.

Step 4: Make a Prediction
The entire fourth paragraph is where the author asks the reader to make certain suppositions. All these suppositions are things Mali could have done differently. A tax on exported objects is therefore presented as one of several actions that Mali and countries like it can take to preserve their cultural legacy.

Step 5: Evaluate the Answer Choices
(C) is therefore correct.

(A) lifts the term "cultural patrimony" (line 22) from the UNESCO discussion in paragraph 2 and mashes it up with the national museum from paragraph 4. But no such connection exists in the passage.

(B) is a 180. The tax on exported objects is something the author says Mali *should have done*, not something it already did.

(D) is a Distortion. The tax on exported objects is not intended to encourage careful recordkeeping. It's intended to "fund acquisitions of important pieces for the national museum" (lines 50–51).

(E) is a 180. The author never sets out to expose a flaw in the UNESCO doctrine. The author actually points out that Mali should have worked with UNESCO (lines 41–47).

10. (A) Inference

Step 2: Identify the Question Type
"The author ... would be most likely to agree with" is a phrase signaling an Inference question.

Step 3: Research the Relevant Text
UNESCO is discussed mainly in paragraph 2, but also briefly in the overall arguments made in paragraphs 3 and 4.

Step 4: Make a Prediction
The author makes a couple of important points about UNESCO: that it stepped in to create a doctrine that helps curtail cultural pillaging in countries like Mali and that Mali should have worked with them to further their goal of preserving and recording cultural knowledge.

Step 5: Evaluate the Answer Choices
(A) is directly in line with the author's discussion of UNESCO in paragraph 2. In addition, in paragraph 4, the author's wish that Mali had worked with UNESCO clearly supports **(A)**.

(B) is a Distortion. The author doesn't actually name the impetus for UNESCO to devise its doctrine, so you can't say it came specifically from the situation in Mali.

(C) is an Irrelevant Comparison. UNESCO's effectiveness doesn't depend on the number of states its initiatives involve.

(D), if anything, is a 180. The UNESCO doctrine specifically condemns the pillaging of cultural artifacts in countries like Mali.

(E) is Outside the Scope. The author says that the UNESCO doctrine has been less effective in helping certain countries because those countries passed laws that were too inflexible, not because funding dried up.

11. (C) Inference

Step 2: Identify the Question Type
This is an Inference question because it asks for what "the author ... would be most likely to agree with."

Step 3: Research the Relevant Text
Regulations governing cultural antiquities are discussed primarily in paragraphs 3 and 4.

Step 4: Make a Prediction
From paragraphs 3 and 4, you can gather that the author believes regulations prohibiting exports in countries like Mali to be rigid and counterproductive. Instead, the author advocates for more flexible regulations governing trade. The correct answer will be consistent with the author's ideas on regulations "governing the trade in cultural antiquities." These ideas will have direct textual support.

Step 5: Evaluate the Answer Choices
(C) is supported by lines 51–56, where the author admits that "some people would still have avoided" complying with the rules the passage recommends. Nevertheless, the rhetorical question that ends the passage suggests that the author would still push for these rules.

(A) is unsupported. Nowhere does the author make archaeologists' approval necessary to enact the passage's recommendations.

(B) is also unsupported. The author seems perfectly content with antiquities leaving their home countries under the right circumstances (lines 47–51). No mention is made about what quantity of antiquities should remain in a country.

(D) is Outside the Scope. The author doesn't delve into possible punishments for violators of the recommended regulations.

(E) is also Outside the Scope. The author never ties the effectiveness of regulations to the ease with which people can understand them.

12. (D) Inference

Step 2: Identify the Question Type
Any question asking for what "the author … would be most likely to agree with" is an Inference question.

Step 3: Research the Relevant Text
Cultural antiquities essentially constitute the Topic of the passage, so there's no specific place to do your research.

Step 4: Make a Prediction
Predicting the correct answer to an Inference question is tough without specific lines to reference. Therefore, go straight to the answer choices, selecting only the answer choice that *must* be true based on the information provided.

Step 5: Evaluate the Answer Choices
(D) must be true. Lines 51–54 say that even if Mali had adopted the system recommended by the author, the excavations conducted would be "less well conducted and less informative than proper, professionally administered excavations by accredited archaeologists." So the author believes excavations are ideally conducted by professional archaeologists.

(A) is Extreme. The author's recommendations in paragraph 4 mention funding for a national museum in Mali, but that doesn't mean that all cultural antiquities have to be housed in that museum.

(B) is similarly Extreme. The author's recommendations in paragraph 4 allow for the well-regulated removal of cultural artifacts from their home countries.

(C) is Outside the Scope. The value of the artifacts isn't discussed, and the author never suggests that some of the artifacts must end up in the possession of private entities.

(E) is a 180. The author agrees with the UNESCO doctrine that the artifacts "should be regarded as the property of the culture." So, he doesn't believe the artifacts should belong to whoever finds them.

13. (B) Inference

Step 2: Identify the Question Type
This is an Inference question because it asks about the author's attitude toward something mentioned in the passage.

Step 3: Research the Relevant Text
"Foreign collectors of terra-cotta sculptures from Djenne-jeno" is a Content Clue leading you to lines 6–8.

Step 4: Make a Prediction
In lines 6–8, the author says that due to Mali's inability to enforce its laws, many sculptures were illegally excavated and "sold to foreign collectors who rightly admired them." Thus, the author's attitude toward these collectors is that they have good taste in sculptures.

Step 5: Evaluate the Answer Choices
(B) is a paraphrase of that idea.

(A) is a Distortion. It's not the foreign collectors who want to preserve cultural artifacts; it's the government of Mali.

(C) is Outside the Scope. The author never passes judgment on the collectors or, for that matter, even says the collectors were aware that the sculptures were obtained illegally.

(D) is another negative sentiment never expressed in lines 6–8.

(E) is Outside the Scope. The motives of the collectors (other than to collect fine art) are not discussed.

Passage 3: The Case for Clinical Equipoise

Step 1: Read the Passage Strategically
Sample Roadmap

line #	Keyword/phrase	¶ Margin notes
1	required	Ethical req: best treatment
2	best; ordinary	
4	unproblematic; but	
6	special issues arise	Issue: clinical trial
8	Traditionally; most	
9	agreed	
12	should have no opinion	Trad'l view: no opinion on superior treatment = Equipoise
13	superior	
15	Unfortunately	Auth: theoretical equipoise (T.E.) too strict
16	typically	
17	may be too strict	
18	only	
20	exactly	
20–21	ideal hardly attainable	T.E. unattainable
25	Even if	
27	extremely fragile	
29	Consequently	
30	few	If adhere to T.E. few trials happen
31	even fewer	
33	difficulties	
34	suggest; different notion	Auth: different version better—clinical equipoise (C.E.)
35	should	
36	rigorous	
37–38	without unreasonably constricting	C.E. less strict
38	One reason	
43	but	Conflict in med community is acceptable
48	The very absence of	
49	is what makes	
50	possible	C.E. thrives on no consensus
52	But	
54	must simply	Preference OK

Discussion

The passage begins by describing what is usually the case—a medical practitioner's ethical obligation to prescribe the best available treatment doesn't pose any problems. Then, in typical LSAT fashion, a problem is introduced. When physicians conduct clinical trials, they withhold one or more treatments from a group of patients to do the research properly. And when they are testing a new treatment against an existing one, researchers shouldn't have an opinion on which treatment is superior. The author terms this idea "equipoise." If you caught the Keyword *traditionally* in line 8, then you can guess the next paragraph will raise an objection.

The Keyword *unfortunately* in line 15 highlights that objection. The common, *theoretical* version of equipoise is too strict for the author's tastes. The notion that researchers would find the evidence between two alternative treatments exactly balanced is unrealistic and, even if achieved, wouldn't last long. If clinicians adhered to theoretical equipoise, they'd ultimately find it impossible to do their jobs.

Predictably, the author tears down theoretical equipoise in order to offer an alternative—clinical equipoise. Paragraph 3 gives the author's argument for this new standard. Clinical equipoise allows for different groups of physicians to have honest differences of opinion as to which of two competing treatments is superior.

In the last paragraph, the author turns a perceived weakness of clinical equipoise—the very real preferences researchers have of one treatment or the other—into an asset. As long as the researchers recognize that their less-favored choice is the more-favored choice of other researchers, ethical standards are upheld.

The **Topic** of the passage is clinical trials, and its **Scope** is the ethical standards by which researchers should conduct those trials. Because paragraphs 3 and 4 argue strongly for the author's point of view, the **Purpose** is to advocate for a less-restrictive ethical principle than the one traditionally espoused. Therefore, the **Main Idea** is that clinical equipoise is a preferable version because it is more realistic and doesn't constrict clinicians' ability to conduct trials.

14. (B) Global

Step 2: Identify the Question Type

Any question asking for the passage's "primary purpose" is a Global question.

Step 3: Research the Relevant Text

The entire text is relevant to a Global question. Use your work from Step 1 to predict the answer here.

Step 4: Make a Prediction

The Purpose, as determined during Step 1, is to advocate for a more-realistic, less-restrictive version of equipoise than the traditional one.

Step 5: Evaluate the Answer Choices

(B) is a perfect match.

(A) is too neutral. The author doesn't just explain the differences between clinical and theoretical equipoise; a clear preference is indicated.

(C) is a 180 and Extreme. The author wants a change to a certain ethical standard for clinical trials precisely because it will free up researchers to do their work better. The author does not agree it would *endanger* their ability to gain information.

(D) is Outside the Scope. The author never accuses researchers of insufficiently examining the underpinnings of their ethical standards.

(E) is a Distortion. It's not the scientific methods the author takes issue with; it's the ethical principles behind the research that bother the author.

15. (D) Logic Function

Step 2: Identify the Question Type

This is a Logic Function question because instead of asking for the purpose of the entire passage, it asks for the purpose of one specific part.

Step 3: Research the Relevant Text

Whenever you see a question asking for the purpose of a paragraph, revisit your Roadmap to see how it fits into the passage as a whole.

Step 4: Make a Prediction

The second paragraph is all about theoretical equipoise. The author gives its defining characteristic and then explains its shortcomings.

Step 5: Evaluate the Answer Choices

(D) is therefore correct.

(A) is a Distortion. Paragraph 2 doesn't provide a view that contrasts with one in favor of clinical equipoise. The whole point of the paragraph is to lay the groundwork in support of the author's endorsement of clinical equipoise.

(B) is a Faulty Use of Detail. It is something that paragraph 2 only does in passing, in lines 21–25. This is not the purpose of the entire paragraph.

(C) is another Distortion. The author doesn't criticize theoretical equipoise because it's on shaky moral ground. The author accuses theoretical equipoise of being too strict and unattainable in the world of research.

(E) is too broad. The author doesn't take issue with the general notion of equipoise; in fact, the passage is set up to argue for a specific kind of equipoise.

16. (C) Detail

Step 2: Identify the Question Type
This is a Detail question because it categorically asks for what is true "according to the passage."

Step 3: Research the Relevant Text
The question stem provides no Content Clues, so the correct answer can come from any point in the passage.

Step 4: Make a Prediction
Instead of listing every single statement made by the author, go directly to the answer choices, prepared to research carefully. Don't select an answer until you find where it's stated in the passage.

Step 5: Evaluate the Answer Choices
(C) is the gist of the last paragraph. Lines 50–53 say that a clinician's "decided treatment preference" is "no ethical bar to participation in the trial."

(A) is Extreme. The author never says that trials that meet the standard of theoretical equipoise face *no* additional ethical standards unrelated to equipoise.

(B) is Outside the Scope. The author never mentions conditions under which researchers must suspend clinical trials.

(D) is a 180. The author proposes clinical equipoise because it is less strict than theoretical equipoise.

(E) might be something the author hopes will one day happen, but the passage makes clear that theoretical, not clinical, equipoise is the "conception ... that is typically employed" (lines 15–16).

17. (D) Inference

Step 2: Identify the Question Type
This question stem asks you to determine what would "more likely" happen based on a supposition, so it's an Inference question.

Step 3: Research the Relevant Text
Paragraphs 2, 3, and 4 are relevant here. Use your Roadmap to identify when the author gives requirements for each type of equipoise.

Step 4: Make a Prediction
Theoretical equipoise requires that the evidence in favor of each of two treatments be always in balance. When that balance is disrupted, theoretical equipoise holds than an unethical bias would form that would compromise the trial. Clinical equipoise allows for researchers to have an initial treatment preference, as long as they keep in mind that that

preference doesn't constitute a consensus in the research community. The correct answer will, therefore, disrupt the balance of evidence (jeopardizing theoretical equipoise) but maintain a lack of consensus (protecting clinical equipoise).

Step 5: Evaluate the Answer Choices
(D) would certainly jeopardize theoretical equipoise more than clinical equipoise. Under theoretical equipoise, the trial would be ethically compromised once the balance tipped in favor of one treatment over the other, because the researchers would then become unreasonably biased. Nevertheless, (D) comports with clinical equipoise because the researchers still recognize the lack of consensus even though a treatment preference may be emerging.

(A) would severely jeopardize both theoretical and clinical equipoise. Clinical equipoise is certainly not so lax that it allows researchers to definitively prefer one treatment over another before the trial has even concluded.

(B) is Outside the Scope. The expert clinical community doesn't need to be aware of preliminary results for either type of equipoise to be jeopardized.

(C) threatens not only theoretical equipoise, but also clinical equipoise because it does away with the "absence of consensus" (line 48) that the author sees as central to clinical equipoise.

(E) makes an Irrelevant Comparison between physicians participating in the trial and those in the expert medical community. No such comparison affects one type of equipoise more than the other.

18. (D) Global

Step 2: Identify the Question Type
This is a Global question because it asks for the "main point of the passage."

Step 3: Research the Relevant Text
You already determined the Main Idea during Step 1—no need to reread parts of the passage.

Step 4: Make a Prediction
The Main Idea of the passage is that clinical equipoise is better suited than theoretical equipoise to encourage researchers' work in clinical trials because it is more reasonable and less strict.

Step 5: Evaluate the Answer Choices
(D) is therefore correct.

(A) would be the Main Idea if the passage stopped at paragraph 2. However, the whole reason the author labels theoretical equipoise as overly strict is so that an alternative view can be proposed.

(B) is too general. The author isn't simply saying that the general ethical requirements for medical research are too restrictive. The point of the passage is that the commonly held notion of one specific ethical idea—equipoise—is too restrictive, and a better notion is possible.

(C) is a Faulty Use of Detail. This is a point the author makes in support of the overall argument for clinical equipoise, but it is too narrow to be the main point of the passage.

(E) is also too narrow. The author would agree with this point, but any answer that doesn't discuss the author's preference for the standard of clinical equipoise is incorrect.

19. (A) Inference

Step 2: Identify the Question Type
This is an Inference question because it asks you to define a term as the author uses it in context.

Step 3: Research the Relevant Text
Line 41 is relevant, but as in any question depending on context, you must read around that line as well.

Step 4: Make a Prediction
The term *community* is part of the phrase "expert clinical community" (lines 40–41). This larger term refers to the group of researchers who all work in the same field and have debates about how best to treat a certain illness that shows up in their work.

Step 5: Evaluate the Answer Choices
(A) is therefore correct.

(B) is a blanket dictionary definition of *community*, but nothing in the passage indicates that these researchers all live and work in or near the same physical location.

(C) is a 180. Members of the expert clinical community have real differences of opinion, which comparative clinical trials are often designed to resolve.

(D) is a Distortion. The passage never says that members of the expert clinical community are bound or defined by their shared ethical values. They may share these values incidentally, but that's not what makes them a community in the author's eyes.

(E) is Outside the Scope. The research methods of the expert clinical community are not discussed, nor are those methods compared to those of unrelated disciplines.

20. (C) Detail

Step 2: Identify the Question Type
This is a Detail question because it asks for what is true "according to the passage."

Step 3: Research the Relevant Text
You don't have any Content Clues to point out specific text in the passage, so save your research for Step 5.

Step 4: Make a Prediction
It's all but impossible to predict the answer to a Detail question that is this vaguely worded. Go straight to the

answer choices and select the one that you can find stated or paraphrased directly in the passage.

Step 5: Evaluate the Answer Choices
(C) is taken directly from paragraph 2. The author says that theoretical equipoise is "an ideal hardly attainable in practice" (lines 20–21), and the last sentence of paragraph 2 indicates that if the standard of theoretical equipoise were met, "few … trials would commence and even fewer would proceed to completion" (lines 29–32).

(A) is too broad. The author never makes blanket statements about ethical standards in general, let alone what proportion of trials meets these standards.

(B) is a Distortion. The author says that fewer clinical trials would be conducted if everyone adhered to the standard of theoretical equipoise—but the standard is rarely, if ever, adhered to. Therefore, changing the standard wouldn't automatically affect the number of clinical trials conducted.

(D) is too broad, dealing with general ethical requirements, and also imputes an opinion to *most* physicians and ethicists, which the passage never does.

(E) is Extreme. Lines 38–42 say that one reason comparative clinical trials are conducted is to resolve a conflict of opinion. That doesn't mean that *most* trials are conducted with this goal in mind.

21. (A) Logic Reasoning (Weaken)

Step 2: Identify the Question Type
This question stem closely resembles a Weaken question from the Logical Reasoning section. Use the same techniques to answer this Reading Comp variant.

Step 3: Research the Relevant Text
Review your Roadmap for the third and fourth paragraphs to understand the author's argument.

Step 4: Make a Prediction
Paragraphs 3 and 4 are all about arguing for clinical equipoise. Clinical equipoise, according to the author, is better suited to meet the goals of a comparative clinical trial. One of those goals is to settle a conflict over the preferred treatment for a given illness, each side of the conflict recognizing the validity of the other side. The correct answer will undermine this idea.

Step 5: Evaluate the Answer Choices
(A) is therefore correct. If most trials have proving the consensus treatment superior to the alternative as their goal, then the notion of even-handedness underlying the argument for clinical equipoise is contradicted.

(B) is Outside the Scope. The frequency with which physicians leave comparative trials due to early findings doesn't affect the argument for clinical equipoise.

(C) doesn't affect the author's argument because a decrease in the level of ethical oversight of trials is not a hindrance to clinical equipoise. In fact, it may suggest that a new ethical standard (such as the one the author proposes) is needed.

(D) is an Irrelevant Comparison. The author's argument doesn't depend on having stronger support of medical ethicists relative to clinical researchers.

(E) doesn't weaken the author's argument because clinical equipoise doesn't require that researchers have or develop a strong early treatment preference; it just doesn't disqualify those researchers for having a preference.

Passage 4: The Fairness of Flat Taxes

Step 1: Read the Passage Strategically
Sample Roadmap

line #	Keyword/phrase	¶ Margin notes
Passage A		
3	:	Estonia: flat tax for all
7	seems	Flat tax actually proven practical
8	as well; as it does	
10	further; objection	
11	unfair	Another objection to flat tax: unfair
12	Enlightened; argued	
15	seems	
17	Not so	Auth: flat tax not unfair
19	extent	
21	just	
24	enormous	Other tax sys allows for tax dodging
26	commensurately large; So; unsurprising	
27	usually; as much	High-income earners pay about same amount w/ flat tax
28	as	
Passage B		
30	don't understand	
31	think	People think graduated tax unfair
33	seems unfair; Actually	Auth: graduated tax is fair
36	don't	
37	entire; only	
38	not	
40	but	People equal, not $
42	almost entirely	
44	critical; even; tremendous	Lower-income $ goes to survival
46	but; much greater	Middle-income $ more flexible
48	Even	
49	want	
50	So; since	
51	why	Auth critical of flat tax
53	?; Since	
57	naturally; fall	Middle class pays more b/c of high- and low-tax decreases

Discussion

Passage A begins by saying that Estonia became the first country to institute a flat tax in 1994, showing the naysayers that a flat tax could work "as well in practice as it does on the blackboard" (line 8). With that phrase, it seems that the author is supportive of flat taxes. The second paragraph introduces another objection those naysayers have against flat taxes—they're unfair. Flat taxes go against the principle that higher-income earners should pay a bigger share of their incomes than low-income earners, a principle at work in the tax systems of most developed countries.

You can expect paragraph 3 to counter this objection, and right away the author shuts it down with "[n]ot so" (line 17). A flat tax can be progressive, the author says, if a country makes adjustments to the threshold and/or the tax rate on income above that threshold. Moreover, in most developed countries, the tax systems are so complicated that high-income earners can easily find ways to avoid paying their complete share of taxes. So, the author concludes, high-income earners end up paying as much under flat tax systems as they do under other ones already in place.

The **Topic** of this passage is flat taxes, and the **Scope** is whether or not they are fair. The **Purpose** is to argue that a flat tax is a fair and viable system. Therefore, the **Main Idea** is that contrary to what some believe, flat taxes can be fair to taxpayers of all income levels and can generate as much revenue as graduated systems.

Passage B's author, like the author of passage A, introduces a misconception about taxation. This time, though, it's a misconception about graduated taxes. The author argues that graduated taxes are fair because each taxpayer pays the same rate on equivalent levels of income. The next paragraph explains that while people are equal, their dollars aren't. Lower-income earners spend nearly all their money on essentials and don't have the discretionary money that higher-income earners have.

The last paragraph explains how a flat tax system tries (and, in the author's view, fails) to deal with the difference between survival dollars and discretionary dollars. A certain level of income isn't taxed at all and then the flat rate is applied to money above that. The problem with this, according to the author, is that while it eases the burden on the working poor and high-income earners, it transfers that burden to middle-income earners.

The **Topic** of this passage is also flat taxes. In this passage, the **Scope** is whether or not they are fairer than graduated taxes. The **Purpose** is to argue that graduated taxes are fairer to taxpayers than are flat taxes, and the **Main Idea** is that a flat tax system doesn't account for differences in income levels and creates an unequal tax burden for the middle class.

Passage A posits that a flat tax is fair to everyone and removes incentives for high-income earners to avoid paying taxes, while passage B clearly prefers a graduated tax system and doesn't believe that flat taxes are fair to everyone. Expect that key point at issue to show up in the questions.

22. (C) Global

Step 2: Identify the Question Type
This is a Global question because it asks for a question both passages are concerned with answering. Don't worry if the absence of a word like *primarily* in the question stem led you to classify this as a Detail question. You'll still use the same essential process to answer the question.

Step 3: Research the Relevant Text
Any question answered by both passages would involve the Scope of those passages, which is nearly identical—the relative fairness of flat taxes versus other systems of taxation.

Step 4: Make a Prediction
In Step 1, you determined that the passages reach different conclusions on the same central issue, which is whether or not a flat tax treats taxpayers equally. Passage A says that it does, and passage B says that it doesn't.

Step 5: Evaluate the Answer Choices
(C) is within the scope of both passages. The entirety of paragraph 3 of passage A is devoted to demonstrating that a flat tax can be fair to all taxpayers. Passage B argues that flat taxes leave middle-income taxpayers with a disproportionate share of the tax burden (lines 53–58).

(A) is answered in passage A, which discusses Estonia's successful implementation of a flat tax, but passage B only discusses flat taxes in the abstract.

(B) is explicitly answered in passage B (line 34), but the fairness of graduated progressive taxes isn't discussed in passage A.

(D) isn't addressed in passage A, which only gives objections to flat taxes.

(E) is only addressed in passage A (lines 21–26).

23. (E) Logic Reasoning (Method of Argument)

Step 2: Identify the Question Type
This is a Method of Argument question because it asks how the passages "advance their arguments."

Step 3: Research the Relevant Text
Use your Roadmap and relevant Keywords from the passages to see how the authors structure their arguments.

Step 4: Make a Prediction
Phrases such as "[n]ot so" (line 17) and "a lot of people don't understand" (line 30) indicate that each author introduces a

misconception about flat versus graduated taxes and then corrects it.

Step 5: Evaluate the Answer Choices

(E) is therefore correct.

(A) is a Distortion. Any ostensible *opponents* to the passages' authors aren't accused of shifting their ground; they're accused of misunderstanding how taxes work.

(B) is not a strategy used by both authors. Even if passage A's example of Estonia's 1994 imposition of a flat tax is considered an "historical development," there is no similar evidence in passage B.

(C) is wrong because neither passage uses an analogy, which would be a comparison between taxes and something else.

(D) is incorrect because only passage B employs a rhetorical question, in lines 50–53.

24. (D) Logic Reasoning (Strengthen)

Step 2: Identify the Question Type

This is a Strengthen question because it asks for the answer that "would most support" one author's position over another's.

Step 3: Research the Relevant Text

Go back to your Roadmap for passage B to get the gist of its argument.

Step 4: Make a Prediction

In the third paragraph of passage B, the author argues against a flat tax by pointing to the potential consequences for middle-income taxpayers. In passage B's view, the burden of maintaining revenue levels for the government would "fall on the middle class" (line 57) because high- and low-income taxpayers would pay less under a flat tax.

Step 5: Evaluate the Answer Choices

(D) would, therefore, strengthen passage B's argument by showing that its predictions would come true.

(A) is Outside the Scope. The argument isn't over which tax system generates more revenue; the argument is over which tax system distributes the burden of revenue generation more evenly among taxpayers.

(B) is also Outside the Scope. The argument in passage B is that a flat tax will lead to unfair outcomes for certain groups of taxpayers. The simplicity or complexity of various tax systems doesn't affect that argument.

(C) isn't a valid Strengthener because passage B doesn't point to the beliefs of high-income taxpayers to support its argument.

(E) doesn't support passage B's position. Just because legislators favor a graduated tax doesn't make it automatically superior to a flat tax.

25. (D) Inference

Step 2: Identify the Question Type

This is an Inference question because you have to determine a conclusion drawn in passage A that isn't addressed in passage B. Inference questions often ask you to deal with what's *unsaid* in the passages.

Step 3: Research the Relevant Text

The entire text is relevant, since you need to find something discussed in passage A but not in passage B. Start by going through your Roadmap for passage A.

Step 4: Make a Prediction

The author of passage A makes two main points about flat taxes: that they are not unfair and can be progressive; and that they maintain the amount of tax revenue collected by making it harder for high-income earners to dodge their tax payments. That second point is not addressed in passage B.

Step 5: Evaluate the Answer Choices

(D) is therefore correct.

(A) is addressed by passage B in lines 48–50.

(B) is a 180. Passage A doesn't argue that flat tax proposals aren't practical. That's the argument that the author attempts to debunk, in part by citing the example of Estonia's flat tax.

(C) is Outside the Scope. Passage A doesn't argue anything about the economic effects of raising taxes on high-income earners.

(E) is a conclusion that passage A never draws. Passage A says that a flat tax can be progressive *and* fair.

26. (B) Inference

Step 2: Identify the Question Type

This is an Inference question because it asks what the two authors "would be most likely to disagree over."

Step 3: Research the Relevant Text

Without a clear line reference, the correct answer could come from any part of the passages. Use your Global understanding from Step 1 to form your prediction.

Step 4: Make a Prediction

The authors of these passages are very clear on their positions when it comes to a flat tax. Passage A says that a flat tax can be fair and doesn't let high-income earners off the hook. Passage B argues that a flat tax ends up unfairly shifting the tax burden to middle-income earners. The correct answer will be consistent with this difference.

Step 5: Evaluate the Answer Choices

(B) would certainly be a point of disagreement. The last sentence of passage A says that high-income taxpayers would not pay less under a flat tax, and passage B asserts that they would (line 56).

(A) is incorrect because only passage A says that a flat tax can be progressive (lines 19–21). Passage B doesn't explicitly express an opinion on this. Even if lines 48–50 indicate that passage B acknowledges a flat tax can still be done over two layers, thereby making it progressive, then **(A)** would still be something the authors agree on, rather than disagree on.

(C), if anything, is something the authors might actually agree on. However, passage B doesn't definitively weigh in on whether a flat tax can actually be implemented.

(D) is an apparent misperception that passage B corrects, but passage A doesn't touch on this idea.

(E) is Outside the Scope. The passages don't make any arguments as to exactly how much of a person's income should be subject to taxation. Both passages do though mention a threshold in the event of a flat tax (lines 17–19 and lines 48–50), and the author of passage B indicates that for low-income earners "every dollar is critical; even a small difference causes tremendous changes in quality of life" (lines 43–45). So, if anything, both authors may seem to disagree with **(E)**.

27. (B) Inference

Step 2: Identify the Question Type
This is an Inference question because you have to determine the best way to complete the argument in passage B so that it now responds to the final argument made in passage A.

Step 3: Research the Relevant Text
The final argument of passage A is in its last paragraph. The Keyword *so* in line 26 indicates the conclusion.

Step 4: Make a Prediction
The author of passage A argues that high-income taxpayers pay as much under flat tax systems as they do under other taxation systems. The evidence for this is the complexity of the graduated systems, which provide high-income taxpayers with opportunities to avoid paying taxes. The correct answer will directly challenge this idea in a way that is consistent with the overall argument of passage B.

Step 5: Evaluate the Answer Choices
(B) would be an effective counter to passage A's final argument. It undermines the notion that high-income earners pay less under graduated systems by virtue of them being graduated. In so doing, the author of passage B would be removing one of passage A's criticisms of graduated taxes.

(A) comes close, but isn't an effective counter to passage A's final argument because passage A isn't saying that flat tax systems eliminate *all* opportunities for high-income earners to avoid taxes.

(C) is incorrect because passage A isn't singling out high-income earners as tax avoiders. The author of passage A is merely saying that high-income earners have extra

incentive and opportunity to avoid taxes under a graduated tax system.

(D) isn't a good counter to passage A's final argument because taxpayer preference isn't within the scope of that argument.

(E) is Outside the Scope. Passage B argues that graduated taxes are fairer to taxpayers; it doesn't call for eliminating income taxes altogether.

Section II: Logical Reasoning

Q#	Question Type	Correct	Difficulty
1	Principle (Identify/Strengthen)	D	★
2	Weaken	C	★
3	Strengthen	B	★
4	Main Point	A	★
5	Flaw	E	★★
6	Principle (Identify/Strengthen)	C	★
7	Strengthen	E	★
8	Assumption (Sufficient)	D	★
9	Paradox	D	★
10	Weaken	C	★★★★
11	Paradox	C	★★
12	Assumption (Necessary)	E	★★★
13	Role of a Statement	C	★★
14	Flaw	C	★★
15	Assumption (Necessary)	D	★
16	Flaw	D	★★★★
17	Inference	B	★★
18	Flaw	E	★★
19	Point at Issue	C	★★
20	Flaw	B	★★★
21	Assumption (Necessary)	B	★★
22	Parallel Flaw	C	★★★
23	Strengthen	A	★★★★
24	Inference	A	★★
25	Strengthen	B	★★★
26	Parallel Reasoning	D	★★★

1. (D) Principle (Identify/Strengthen)

Step 1: Identify the Question Type

A question stem that directs you to "justify the reasoning above" using a *principle* indicates an Identify the Principle question that will mimic a Strengthen question. Approach it as you would a Strengthen question, while remaining open to more generally phrased answer choices. The correct answer will typically express the assumption in more general—and potentially more forceful—terms, often just re-stating the evidence and conclusion in broader terms.

Step 2: Untangle the Stimulus

The first sentence defines "treat training" while the next two sentences contrast each other, providing a pro and a con: dogs learn quickly, but most won't obey unless they see food. The conclusion, at the end of the stimulus, alternatively recommends using "praise and verbal correction" for dog training. The evidence Keyword *[s]ince* highlights the essential reason that the author prefers praise and verbal correction to treat training: one cannot always have treats on hand.

Step 3: Make a Prediction

The author's recommendation is based solely on the fact that praise and verbal correction is always available whereas treats are not. The assumption, therefore, is that availability is a key factor in effective training. The correct answer, likely stated as a rule, will assert this.

Step 4: Evaluate the Answer Choices

(D) matches the prediction. If **(D)** is true, then the author is correct in arguing that when training a dog, praise and verbal correction are preferable to treats.

(A) is a 180. The only reference in the stimulus to *quickness* favors the use of treat training, against which the author argues. Rather than justify why the use of praise and verbal correction is optimal, this answer choice explains why many dog trainers might choose treat training.

(B) is tempting, but is a Distortion of the argument. This choice focuses on the overall *frequency* of the use of a stimulus (such as a treat or praise) rather than the consistency of the *availability* of that stimulus. This answer depends on building in an additional assumption, i.e., constant availability is equivalent to more frequent use.

(C) is too weak to affect the argument. First, because treat training teaches most dogs to quickly obey, this choice could very well describe the treat-training method. This would make this a 180. Even if most treat-trained dogs will not obey commands unless they see a treat, it still may be true that this method leads to a high obedience rate in "at least some" circumstances. Second, because the author does not mention whether or not praise and verbal correction results in a high obedience rate in some circumstances, it's unclear if this

choice even presents a rule that supports the author's recommendation.

(E) is Extreme. The stimulus never indicates that the rejected method—treat training—has not been proven effective for *any* dogs. The evidence's claim that *most* treat-trained dogs ignore commands unless they see a treat leaves open the possibility that treat training *has* been proven effective for up to 49 percent of dogs.

2. (C) Weaken

Step 1: Identify the Question Type

The question stem explicitly asks you to Weaken the argument. Identify the assumption and attack it.

Step 2: Untangle the Stimulus

The archaeologist predicts that modern civilizations that rely heavily on irrigation for farming will likely collapse, as did the Sumerian civilization. The reason is that in the ancient Sumerian civilization, irrigation caused a buildup of salt and other impurities in the soil, which in turn, caused the soil to become infertile and ultimately led to the society's destruction.

Step 3: Make a Prediction

The argument displays two argument patterns common on the LSAT: a prediction and an analogy. The archaeologist makes a prediction about the future of modern civilizations based on the assumption that past trends will repeat themselves. Additionally, the archaeologist assumes that the situation in ancient Sumer(ia) is sufficiently similar to modern agriculture in other areas of the world. A valid weakener will point out either a change in circumstances or a difference between the situations. Such a general prediction is not only sufficient but preferable, because specific predictions could be innumerable. However, note that the argument's scope is limited to modern civilizations that continue to rely heavily on irrigation. An Out of Scope answer indicating that at least some civilizations do not rely heavily on irrigation is irrelevant to the archaeologist's prediction, yet likely to appear in the answer choices.

Step 4: Evaluate the Answer Choices

(C) is correct. It attacks the analogy, pointing out an important difference between ancient and modern irrigation methods, and making it less likely that modern farming civilizations will face the same problem the Sumerian civilization did.

(A) broadens the scope of the conclusion. The conclusion specifies only "modern civilizations that continue to rely heavily on irrigation for agriculture"; what percentage of modern civilizations this entails is unclear. However, this answer choice extends the scope to include "*most* modern civilizations." Nevertheless, regardless of how far-reaching the archeologist's conclusion is, this choice doesn't affect the archaeologist's *reasoning* because even if some civilizations need irrigation that doesn't undermine that it may ultimately result in their decline.

(B) is Out of Scope. The archaeologist's prediction is based on what actually *did* cause the collapse of the Sumerian civilization. Even if there *were* other threats to the Sumerian civilization, the archaeologist's conclusion that irrigation is a danger to modern civilizations could still logically follow.

(D) as predicted in Step 3, is a classic wrong answer for an argument that explicitly conditions or limits its conclusion. The archaeologist's conclusion is limited to those modern civilizations that are heavily dependent on irrigation for agriculture and, thus, this answer choice simply doesn't apply.

(E) is ambiguous as to whether it strengthens or weakens the argument because it is unclear whether this is a similarity or difference between the soil in ancient Sumer(ia) and the soil supporting the agriculture of modern civilizations. To qualify as a weakener, this answer choice would need to be comparative, indicating that Sumerian soil initially contained significantly *more* toxic salts and impurities than does the soil in areas that currently rely heavily on irrigation.

3. (B) Strengthen

Step 1: Identify the Question Type
The question stem asks you to Strengthen the argument. Identify the assumption and firm up the bridge between the evidence and the conclusion.

Step 2: Untangle the Stimulus
The contrast Keyword *[h]owever* signals the shift from the background to the researcher's observation of an intriguing phenomenon: Rarely will mineralized dinosaur bones be found near dinosaur tracks in dried mud flats. The conclusion is that the researcher doesn't find this phenomenon to be surprising. His explanation is that scavengers would go to mud flats looking for dinosaur carcasses.

Step 3: Make a Prediction
Here the researcher presents an interesting observed phenomenon, which he remarks is not surprising and then provides a reason why it is not. That is not an uncommon argument pattern on the LSAT. The inherent assumption is that no other explanation is possible. Most commonly, this pattern shows up in Weaken questions, which typically require the identification of an alternative explanation. In this argument, the researcher's explanation actually raises more questions than it answers; the correct answer will actually explain the explanation, almost like the correct answer to a Paradox question. The correct answer will provide a reason why scavengers could find dinosaur carcasses at mud flats yet mineralized bones and preserved dinosaur tracks in mud flats are rarely found together, when the opposite seems like it should be true. However, it is important to remember that

this is *not* a Paradox question, and you are *not* tasked with a blank slate to explain the mystery described in the evidence. Your task is to support the *researcher's* explanation of the mystery: *scavengers*.

Step 4: Evaluate the Answer Choices
(B) meets the predicted need. If scavengers would drag carcasses away from the mud flats, then that would explain why bones and tracks are found in different places, thus strengthening the researcher's argument that scavengers are the reason for the lack of overlap.

(A) is Out of Scope. The researcher is concerned with tracks at mud flats and bones. Dinosaur tracks at places other than mud flats are irrelevant. Additionally, this choice fails to explain how scavengers would be responsible.

(C) is an Irrelevant Comparison. The disparate number of fossils doesn't explain why the two types aren't found in the same places. Additionally, this doesn't strengthen the researcher's assertion that scavengers are the key.

(D) is Out of Scope. Fossils other than mineralized bone or tracks in dried mud flats are irrelevant to the researcher's argument while, just as importantly, scavengers aren't mentioned.

(E) may be tempting at first, but it has a couple problems. First, surely there has been enough time for the dinosaur bones to have mineralized by now, so the length of time is inconsequential. Additionally, as in the other three wrong answer choices, this choice doesn't address scavengers and their relevance to the separation of bones and tracks.

4. (A) Main Point

Step 1: Identify the Question Type
The question stem asks you to identify the *conclusion* of the argument, which makes this a Main Point question. Select the answer that matches the meaning of the part of the argument that you bracket as the conclusion.

Step 2: Untangle the Stimulus
This stimulus does not contain conclusion or evidence Keywords to guide you, which is often the case in Main Point questions. You'll have to use other methods for finding the conclusion. Here, look for which sentence supports the other. The first sentence is a prediction while the second sentence provides facts that support the prediction.

Step 3: Make a Prediction
The correct answer should match in meaning, if not verbatim wording, the prediction that "electric stovetop burners would cause fewer fires if their highest temperature were limited to 350° C."

Step 4: Evaluate the Answer Choices
(A) is a verbatim match of the argument's conclusion.

(B) matches the second clause of the first sentence. By asserting that cooking will be unhindered, this clause removes a possible reason why electric burners *shouldn't* be limited, but it is not the conclusion. The stimulus does not contain any evidence to support this clause because the second sentence is pertinent to fires, not effective cooking.

(C) restates a piece of the evidence. Beyond the fact that this information supports the conclusion about causing fewer fires, straightforward information like this will rarely function as a conclusion.

(D) is another piece of the evidence.

(E) is an assumption that is deducible by combining the evidence and conclusion of the argument, but is never explicitly stated. The conclusion of an argument must be explicitly stated, not just implied.

5. (E) Flaw

Step 1: Identify the Question Type
The question stem asks you to describe the flaw in the argument. Notice any disconnect between the evidence and conclusion; keep in mind that common LSAT flaws will help you both pinpoint the correct answer and reject wrong ones.

Step 2: Untangle the Stimulus
The author's conclusion follows the contrast Keyword *[y]et*, asserting that "Jenkin's conclusion must be rejected." It is imperative to paraphrase the meaning of such a vaguely phrased conclusion. In other words, the author concludes that *Firepower* was actually intended to provoke antisocial behavior. The author's reason is that the movie produced antisocial behavior.

Step 3: Make a Prediction
There is a blatant scope shift from intention to result. The movie ended up producing antisocial behavior, but that does not necessarily mean it *planned* to do so. The author, however, assumes that such is the case.

Step 4: Evaluate the Answer Choices
(E) matches the prediction. Often, the correct answer to a Flaw question will merely describe the evidence and conclusion of the argument, highlighting the mismatched concepts contained therein.

(A) describes an *ad hominem* attack, which focuses on the arguer rather than the argument. However, that flaw type is not in play here. Jenkins, whose argument the author rejects, is not the director of the movie, who is the only person with an identifiable bias. Additionally, the author never mentions bias.

(B) describes a causal flaw, which isn't relevant. In the argument, the *evidence* is a claim of causation, while the conclusion is an accusation of intent.

(C) incorrectly describes a parts-versus-whole flaw. The stimulus concerns a single movie and does not extrapolate information about that movie to be representative of the film industry or another *whole* at all.

(D) is a Distortion. *Jenkins* presents the evidence that preventing antisocial behavior is in the director's best interest (although it's unknown if the director actually *expressed* this interest), and thus it is in fact Jenkins who overlooks this possibility. Other than simply presenting Jenkins's evidence, the author does not touch on the idea of acting for or against one's expressed interest.

6. (C) Principle (Identify/Strengthen)

Step 1: Identify the Question Type
A question stem that directs you to "justify the reasoning in the argument" using a principle in the answer choices indicates an Identify the Principle question that mimics a Strengthen question. Look for the broad idea that would make the author's conclusion more likely to be true.

Step 2: Untangle the Stimulus
The author's conclusion, which follows the Keyword *[s]o*, says reporters should restrict use of the term *loophole* to news stories that include evidence of wrongdoing. The evidence is that the word *loophole* is charged, implying wrongdoing and scandal.

Step 3: Make a Prediction
The mismatched concepts in this stimulus are "implies wrongdoing" and "provide evidence of wrongdoing." The author assumes that, in a news story, the mere implication of wrongdoing requires evidence. The correct answer will state this assumption.

Step 4: Evaluate the Answer Choices
(C) matches the prediction. The breadth and forcefulness of this answer (news stories need to back up *any* suggestions of misconduct) is not a problem for a Principle question that mimics a Strengthen question. This broad rule encompasses use of the word *loophole* and thus supports the author's conclusion.

(A) is a 180 that undermines the author's direction to provide evidence of wrongdoing when asserting that someone used a loophole: there can never be evidence of wrongdoing if the use of loopholes *never* constitutes wrongdoing or scandal. Moreover, this answer choice is also a Distortion, because the author is concerned with the *implication* of the word *loophole*, not whether using a loophole does in fact equal wrongdoing.

(B) is Out of Scope. The author is concerned with the standards of news stories, not the standards of editorials. Therefore, this choice doesn't affect the argument at all.

(D) is also Out of Scope, for the same reason as **(B)**. The author doesn't weigh in on what editorial writers should or should not do. Rather, the conclusion is restricted to news reporters, and so this choice has no effect on its strength.

(E) goes Out of Scope, as the author does not suggest any limitations on the reporting of actual wrongdoing (besides perhaps providing evidence). Public interest is definitely not listed as a limitation.

7. (E) Strengthen

Step 1: Identify the Question Type
The question stem asks you to strengthen the argument. Identify the assumption and firm up the bridge between the evidence and the conclusion.

Step 2: Untangle the Stimulus
The author concludes that "widespread food shortages are inevitable." The reason cited is that there is a ceiling on how much food production can be increased.

Step 3: Make a Prediction
The expert makes a prediction for the future. Prediction conclusions usually mean the author assumes that current or past trends will continue. Here, the expert mentions that both food production and the population have been increasing, but that food production has an upper limit. To conclude that food shortages are *inevitable*, the author must be assuming that the population will continue to grow and will eventually outpace food production. The correct answer will indicate this is the case.

Step 4: Evaluate the Answer Choices
(E) is correct. If the population continues to grow after food production is maxed out, then it's more likely food shortages will occur. Notice that this choice does not *guarantee* that the expert's prediction will come true, but it does increase the probability.

(A) does nothing to strengthen the argument because the evidence already indicates that there is an upper limit on food production. The fact that food resources are *renewable*, if anything, keeps the claim of inevitable shortages in doubt.

(B) is not sufficient to strengthen the argument. Full utilization of a *single* food resource does not affect the author's absolute claim of the *inevitability* of *widespread* food shortages. The oceans, even if fully utilized, might still be limited, and thus the population might still overtake the overall amount of available food.

(C) is a 180. Because the planet's resources have not yet been maxed out, a stabilized population undermines the prediction of future widespread food shortages.

(D) is Out of Scope. While the past can occasionally provide insight on the future, this answer is too weak. "Periodic regional food shortages" are not on the same level as inevitable *widespread* food shortages due to a global limit on food production.

8. (D) Assumption (Sufficient)

Step 1: Identify the Question Type
The phrasing "the conclusion can be properly drawn if ... assumed" indicates a Sufficient Assumption question. These questions require you to identify the additional evidence that proves the conclusion true.

Step 2: Untangle the Stimulus
The author concludes that the technical sophistication of newer video games makes them less compelling to players. The main evidence is a subsidiary conclusion: Players have a hard time identifying with the human figures. These detailed figures are made possible by the games' technical sophistication.

Step 3: Make a Prediction
A common pattern to correct Sufficient Assumption answers is merely a rephrasing of the argument: If evidence, then conclusion. Here, that would mean that if it is difficult for players to identify with the characters they control, then the game becomes less compelling. If this Formal Logic statement is true, then the author's conclusion would be valid.

Step 4: Evaluate the Answer Choices
(D) correctly puts the assumption in the form of: If Evidence (hard to identify with game figures), then Conclusion (find game less compelling). Thus, it matches the prediction and is correct.

(A) is Extreme. While the correct answer to a Sufficient Assumption question can be extreme or absolute, this one misses the mark. This answer forcefully suggests that the trend away from simple icons is universal, but it does not connect the evidence to the conclusion that sophisticated games are less compelling to players.

(B) can be categorized as either Out of Scope or a 180. This choice attacks the draw of early video games, which, at best, doesn't lead to the conclusion that newer games are less compelling and, at worst, weakens it.

(C) is incorrect for several reasons. First, the author's evidence is about those who cannot identify with the figures, whereas this choice focuses on those who can. Second, the author is concerned with whether games are less compelling than they could be, not whether they are "fully compelling" to players. Finally, the author merely suggests that technical sophistication can detract from players' enjoyment; whether it can or can't *by itself* make games compelling is Out of Scope. So ultimately, nothing about **(C)** would guarantee the argument that those who have a hard time identifying with figures find the games less compelling.

(E) is a 180. It flips the pieces of the argument, indicating that if the conclusion is true, then the evidence is—essentially putting the argument in: If Conclusion, then Evidence form. The author's argument is that detailed human figures are sufficient to make a game—at least in some cases—less compelling for players. This answer indicates that such figures are a necessary condition for less-compelling games.

9. (D) Paradox

Step 1: Identify the Question Type
The phrase "resolve the apparent discrepancy" indicates a Paradox question. Identify the two apparently contradictory facts and find the choice that provides an explanation or alternative factor that allows both to be true.

Step 2: Untangle the Stimulus
The stimulus indicates that there are many agricultural regions in North American with a growing season long enough to grow pumpkins without risk of frost. Still, pumpkin production is concentrated in regions where crops are exposed to that risk.

Step 3: Make a Prediction
Your task is to identify a reason why farmers aren't growing pumpkins in places where the weather cooperates. Specific predictions might be that more lucrative crops are grown in temperate regions or that pumpkins benefit in some way from colder climates; however, because such possibilities are innumerable, general predictions are better—the general prediction would be that there is some reason pumpkins are grown in cold rather than temperate regions.

Step 4: Evaluate the Answer Choices
(D) provides a benefit that pumpkins derive from colder climates, i.e., disease control.

(A) is a 180 because it presents a reason why pumpkin farmers would want to avoid early frosts.

(B) is a 180 because it suggests yet another benefit to producing pumpkins in warmer climates.

(C) is a 180 because it deepens the mystery. If the majority of pumpkins are sold in regions with long growing seasons, then it would make even more sense to grow them there, and thereby minimize transportation costs.

(E) is a 180 because it provides another reason to grow pumpkins in areas with long growing seasons, as that is where the seeds are produced. You may have been tempted by the mention of greenhouses, which could possibly protect pumpkins in colder areas; however, notice that they are mentioned here only in relation to seed production, not pumpkin production, and thus cannot help resolve the paradox.

10. (C) Weaken

Step 1: Identify the Question Type
A question stem that asks you to *undermine* the author's conclusion indicates a Weaken question. Identify the assumption and attack it.

Step 2: Untangle the Stimulus
The council chair forcefully recommends that an alternate code, which has been successful elsewhere, replace the traditional code of parliamentary procedure. While the council chair concedes that the traditional code is entrenched and widely accepted, the chair also claims that the traditional code contains a number of obscure, unnecessary rules that lead to quibbling, which, in turn, undermines public confidence, a condition necessary for the council's success.

Step 3: Make a Prediction
Any recommendation conclusion assumes that the balancing of pros and cons comes down in favor of the author's suggested direction. Additional pros or cons that could tip the scales one way or the other will strengthen or weaken the argument. In this instance, the council chair proposes scrapping the traditional code primarily due to a concern with eroding public confidence. The council chair traces this potential erosion of public confidence to the existence of unnecessary rules in the traditional code. This suggests there might be a less-extreme solution than scrapping the entire traditional code, such as removing the unnecessary rules.

Step 4: Evaluate the Answer Choices
(C) undermines the need for entirely scrapping the traditional code. It indicates less-extreme measures are already underway that will rid the code of the rules that the council chair has identified as the cause of the problem.

(A) attempts to undermine the evidence rather than the conclusion. Whether the council's use of the problematic rules is intermittent or not, the council chair's evidence indicates that such use is causing the council to appear unworthy of public confidence. That evidence must be accepted as true; the argument cannot be weakened by implicitly contradicting it.

(B) is incorrect for a couple reasons. First, the council chair's evidence that the alternate code has been successful in the other jurisdictions should be accepted as true. Additionally, a limited counterexample is not typically sufficient to weaken an argument, especially because the negative described (confused opponents) is not necessarily linked to the key problem the council chair identifies (an erosion of public confidence).

(D) is Extreme. The council chair's argument does not depend on it *always* being reasonable to adopt a different code to maintain the public's confidence, only that it be reasonable in this instance. Even if this choice was true, the council chair's specific recommendation could be perfectly valid, if this was one of the instances where it *was* reasonable.

(E) is a 180. It indicates that, contrary to the traditional code, which has a large number of problematic rules, the alternate code has few such provisions. Thus, this choice supports the council chair's recommendation to switch to the alternate code.

11. (C) Paradox

Step 1: Identify the Question Type
A question stem that asks you to *explain* a situation indicates a Paradox question. This question stem points out the paradox for you, leaving you to find the answer choice that allows both financial results to be true.

Step 2: Untangle the Stimulus
The stimulus discusses the findings of a study. Among a group of businesses that sold similar products, a majority of those that used customer surveys saw a decline in profits, while a majority of those that did not use customer surveys did *not* see a decline in profits. The mystery arises from the fact that frequently customer surveys are used by businesses in an attempt to improve sales and profits.

Step 3: Make a Prediction
As with many Paradox questions, myriad potential explanations might leap to mind. Maybe the surveys were counterproductive for some reason, or maybe something else differed between the businesses that used surveys and those that did not. It is important to notice qualifying language in LSAT stimuli. Here, it is indicated that these surveys are *frequently* used in an attempt to improve sales and increase profits. That leaves open the possibility that these surveys are used for other purposes as well, potentially those that could be a factor in declining profits.

Regardless, all that is needed is a general prediction paraphrasing the type of information required to explain the mystery: some reason why those businesses using the surveys were more likely to see a decline in profits.

Step 4: Evaluate the Answer Choices
(C) provides a possible reason why the study found that businesses using the surveys experienced a decline in profits. If, for this particular type of business, the use of the surveys results from customer complaints, then it is probably those complaints (and not the surveys themselves) that explain the declining profits.

(A) is a Distortion. The stimulus says one group did not see a *decline* in profits, but never mentions an *increase* in profits. Moreover, at most this answer could help explain only why some businesses saw a decline in profits while others did not. It doesn't, however, provide any explanation as to why those businesses using the surveys were the ones that typically saw a loss.

(B) is too weak. While *some* businesses may routinely use surveys, it's unclear how many or whether those particular businesses overlap with those in the stimulus. Additionally, this choice doesn't provide any information about what effect routine survey use might have on profits.

(D) is irrelevant. While this choice indicates that businesses might not get accurate feedback from surveys, nothing in this choice indicates that profit is affected by the completeness or accuracy of survey data. Assuming that businesses use that bad information to their detriment is too much of leap.

(E) might explain why the use of surveys did not result in an *increase* in profits, but it doesn't explain why the use of surveys would be correlated with a *decline* in profits. Additionally, *some* might mean only one business, which typically isn't enough to resolve a paradox.

12. (E) Assumption (Necessary)

Step 1: Identify the Question Type
An assumption on which an argument *depends* is a necessary assumption. Build the core basic bridge between the evidence and conclusion. You can use the Denial Test to check your answer.

Step 2: Untangle the Stimulus
The author concludes that modern humans are generally unable to make better choices than could humans in centuries past. The evidence is that humans' emotional tendencies have remained consistent.

Step 3: Make a Prediction
The mismatched concepts in this argument are "emotional tendencies" in the evidence and "choosing wisely" in the conclusion. The author assumes that without a change in emotional tendencies, humans are unable to choose more wisely. Put another way, the author assumes that the ability to make better choices requires a change in emotional tendencies.

Step 4: Evaluate the Answer Choices
(E) matches the prediction. Rephrased, it says that if humans could make wiser choices now, then there must have been a change in humans' emotional dispositions. In other words, a change is required. If the stimulus was considered in the format of "If Evidence (no change in emotion tendencies), then Conclusion (can't make wiser choices)," then **(E)** is just the contrapositive of that statement.

(A) is Extreme. The author does not need it to be true that humans have not changed *at all*. Additionally, this answer doesn't create a link between emotional tendencies and the ability to make good choices.

(B) is a Distortion in several respects. First, there is a difference between "emotional tendencies" and "control of their emotions." Second, the LSAT routinely distinguishes between relative levels (i.e., wiser) and absolute levels (i.e., wise). Third, information about a specific group (humans who make wise choices) is not necessary to a conclusion about humans in general.

(C) is Out of Scope. While the stimulus covers the whole of human history, the argument is not concerned with learning the lessons of the past.

(D) is tempting, especially because it also ties in the author's side observation regarding the wider range of choice available today. However, this choice neglects the most vital component of the argument: the author's judgment that humans today do not choose more *wisely*. Also, the stimulus doesn't discuss *how* humans make choices. Using the Denial Test might help here. Even if humans *don't* choose on the basis of emotions alone, the author's conclusion could still stand.

13. (C) Role of a Statement

Step 1: Identify the Question Type
A question stem that asks you for the *role* of a claim as it is used in an argument indicates a Role of a Statement question. Underline the claim in the stimulus before reading the argument to determine the role the statement plays. Also, notice that the stem asks about how the claim functions in the *ornithologists'* argument, which may be different than the *author's* argument.

Step 2: Untangle the Stimulus
The claim regarding "recent reforestation" is found in the second sentence, right before the ornithologists' conclusion, which is that the threat to songbirds continues to increase. The reason given by the ornithologists is that forest fragmentation, not forest size, endangers songbirds.

Step 3: Make a Prediction
The contrast Keyword *despite* signals the belief of ornithologists that while reforestation is ostensibly a positive step, recent reforestation has not been enough to keep the situation from worsening. So the purpose of mentioning the recent reforestation is basically to point out an apparent paradox: A factor that seems like it ought to counteract the threat to songbirds is, in fact, occurring in conjunction with an overall worsening of forest conditions.

Step 4: Evaluate the Answer Choices
(C) is correct. The Keyword *despite* indicates that ornithologists accept that recent reforestation is occurring in conjunction with the continuing decline of forest conditions. Indeed, the overlap of recent reforestation and the continuing decline of forest health is presented as a paradox, which the ornithologists resolve by explaining that forest fragmentation is the critical factor.

(A) is a subtle Distortion. The fact that reforestation has recently occurred is not itself used to prove that songbirds

will continue to be at risk. Rather, it's an expected solution that is dismissed as not actually having an effect on the problem.

(B) is a 180. The ornithologists accept that there has recently been reforestation; they merely argue that it is not removing the threat. Additionally, the ornithologists never actually mention declining songbird populations, let alone use that to prove deforestation has occurred.

(D) is a Distortion. While predators are mentioned as a threat, there is no conclusion that reforestation is providing a habitat for those predators. According to the stimulus, reforestation isn't *enough* to solve the problem, but it certainly isn't *worsening* it.

(E) is Out of Scope. A threat to songbirds' predators is never even mentioned, and therefore it is impossible for the statement in question to function as evidence for such a claim.

14. (C) Flaw

Step 1: Identify the Question Type
The phrase "vulnerable to criticism" indicates a Flaw question. Notice any disconnect between the evidence and conclusion, and keep in mind the common LSAT flaws.

Step 2: Untangle the Stimulus
The author concludes that reducing excessive chocolate consumption can likely cause an improvement in mood. The evidence is a study that showed a correlation between chocolate consumption and depression. Those in the study who ate the most chocolate were also those who were the most likely to feel depressed.

Step 3: Make a Prediction
This argument contains one of the most important LSAT argument patterns: evidence of a correlation used to support a claim of causation. The correct answer should describe this classic scope shift.

Step 4: Evaluate the Answer Choices
(C) is correct as it describes the classic scope shift of an author using evidence of a correlation (those who ate the most chocolate were most likely to feel depressed) to reach a conclusion of suggesting causation (recommending that people lay off the chocolate to improve their mood indicates that the author assumes a causal connection).

(A) is a Distortion, because it incorrectly describes the evidence. According to this choice, the evidence consists of "the *fact* that a substance causally contributes to a condition." To the contrary, the evidence describes a correlation while the *conclusion* implies a causal connection. However, this answer is tempting because it uses the right words, albeit incorrectly.

(B) describes a representativeness flaw, which often appears in stimuli containing studies. However, the stimulus explicitly indicates that the sample is large and, more importantly, *diverse*, while both the evidence and conclusion center on adults. There is no indication that such a sample would be nonrepresentative.

(D) describes a classic LSAT flaw, but not one that is implicated by this argument. A confusion of necessary and sufficient conditions will usually occur in stimuli with Formal Logic. Though the author suggests that eating less chocolate is almost certainly sufficient to improve one's mood, the evidence never indicates that eating less chocolate is the *only* way (i.e., necessary) to improve one's mood.

(E) is incorrect as the conclusion is sufficiently clear. While more specifically defining what constitutes "excessive chocolate consumption" would be helpful in guiding people who wish to follow this prescription, it is not necessary to assess the logic.

15. (D) Assumption (Necessary)

Step 1: Identify the Question Type
An assumption *required* by the argument is a necessary assumption. Build the core basic bridge between the evidence and conclusion. You can use the Denial Test to check your answer.

Step 2: Untangle the Stimulus
The author concludes that scientific fraud is widespread among authors submitting to a particular journal. The reason is that dozens of authors submitted digital images manipulated in ways that violated the journal's guidelines.

Step 3: Make a Prediction
The argument makes two different jumps. First, there is a difference between manipulated images and scientific fraud. The author assumes that the manipulation of images constitutes fraud, while in actuality it may not. Second, the argument assumes that the fact that "dozens of authors" violated the guidelines indicates a *widespread* problem. However, since dozens of incidents would typically be considered a widespread problem even for a journal with hundreds of submissions, the correct answer is more likely to address the first assumption.

Step 4: Evaluate the Answer Choices
(D) is correct because it links the mismatched concepts of image manipulation with intentional deception.

(A) is Out of Scope. The argument requires that the scientists were aware of the impropriety of manipulating the images, not that they were specifically aware of what technique the journal would use to uncover such manipulation.

(B) is also Out of Scope. The assumption concerns whether the manipulation of images constitutes fraud, not why the images were submitted in the first place. The fact that the scientists were mandated to submit images is irrelevant to whether or not the submitted images were fraudulent.

(C) is Extreme. The author does not assume that fraud is *impossible* in the absence of digital images.

(E) is Extreme. The author merely discusses one area of widespread fraud; the conclusion doesn't require that it be the *only* one.

16. (D) Flaw

Step 1: Identify the Question Type
The phrase "vulnerable to criticism" indicates a Flaw question. Notice any disconnect between the evidence and conclusion, and keep in mind the common LSAT flaws.

Step 2: Untangle the Stimulus
The author concludes that a belief of others is mistaken. Thus, the author's conclusion should be paraphrased as the negation of that belief: The works of contemporary artists do not enable many people to feel more aesthetically fulfilled than they otherwise could. The author's reason is that there are already more than enough great artworks to satisfy any imaginable taste.

Step 3: Make a Prediction
The author assumes that just because there is an exhaustive cumulative body of artwork—more than anybody could hope to appreciate in a lifetime and wide-ranging enough to cover every taste—that people cannot derive additional aesthetic benefit from new works of art. This argument likely seems inherently flawed, but in a way that might not be easy to articulate. A glance at the answer choices reveals that two of the answers are phrased as Overlooked Possibilities and three are phrased as Unwarranted Assumptions. Either type is equally plausible and a prediction could be created for both. Either the author overlooks the possibility that many people *can* gain additional aesthetic fulfillment from contemporary works, or the author presumes, without providing justification, that many people cannot derive additional aesthetic benefit from new works of art. Also, keep in mind that on the LSAT, *many* means "at least some," but not necessarily a majority.

Step 4: Evaluate the Answer Choices
(D) matches the prediction. It highlights the possibility that, although the catalog of great artworks is extensive, not everyone has access to it. If that is the case, then those people might find additional aesthetic fulfillment from contemporary art.

(A) conflicts with a piece of evidence. All evidence must be accepted as true, and therefore a direct contradiction cannot describe an argument's logical flaw. If it is true that not all contemporary artists share the stated belief, then the author has lied or made a factual mistake, but has *not* necessarily made a flaw in *reasoning*.

(B) does not accurately describe an assumption of the argument. The author discusses only what people *can* and *can't* do, not what they *will* or *won't* do.

(C) is a Distortion. The argument does not assume that the value of an artwork is based on the degree to which human beings appreciate it. The author judges them to be *great* independent of humans' appreciation. The stimulus never mentions what standards artworks must meet to achieve greatness.

(E) is a Distortion. While it connects terms from the evidence and conclusion, it does not accurately describe the argument's assumption (which is what is meant by "presumes, without providing justification"). This answer sets up a proportional relationship between the amount of art and the amount of aesthetic fulfillment one can derive from any contemporary piece of art: the more art, the less fulfillment from *any* individual piece of art. The argument, however, is not that the amount of aesthetic fulfillment derivable from a *single* contemporary artwork is limited, but that new artworks do not add *more* fulfillment than could be found in the existing catalog. The argument, on the other hand, indicates that with all the great art already in existence, there's no new artwork that will cause people to have *extra* aesthetic fulfillment.

17. (B) Inference

Step 1: Identify the Question Type
A question stem that asks you to use information in the stimulus to support the truth of one of the answers (direction of support flowing downward) indicates an Inference question. Inventory the facts, looking for Formal Logic, statements that can be combined, or any emphasized facts.

Step 2: Untangle the Stimulus
The stimulus creates a chain of requirements. First, before the government health service pays for patients to take Antinfia, it requires that the manufacturer prove the drug's cost-effectiveness. However, doing so requires clinical trials, which, in turn, require widespread circulation of the drug. Nevertheless, widespread circulation isn't possible unless the government health service financially supports Antinfia.

$$\text{If } \begin{array}{c} \textit{gov't} \\ \textit{pays} \end{array} \rightarrow \begin{array}{c} \textit{Antinfia} \\ \textit{provides} \\ \textit{cost-} \\ \textit{effective} \\ \textit{ness} \\ \textit{info} \end{array} \rightarrow \begin{array}{c} \textit{massive} \\ \textit{clinical} \\ \textit{trials} \end{array} \rightarrow \begin{array}{c} \textit{widespread} \\ \textit{circulation} \end{array} \rightarrow \begin{array}{c} \textit{gov't} \\ \textit{pays} \end{array}$$

This just creates an infinite loop of A →B →C →D →A.

Step 3: Make a Prediction
This situation doesn't qualify as circular reasoning, but the Formal Logic does take one full circle. The government health service will not pay to cover Antinfia prescriptions until other conditions are met, which themselves will not happen until the government health service begins paying for Antinfia. Thus, it can be deduced that none of the actions listed in the stimulus will occur.

Step 4: Evaluate the Answer Choices
(B) is a valid inference. According to the stimulus, widespread circulation requires government aid. So if government aid is not forthcoming, then widespread circulation will never occur.

(A) is Extreme. The stimulus indicates only that the government health service will not pay for Antinfia without cost-effectiveness data. It cannot be assumed that such a requirement applies to all medicines.

(C) is Out of Scope and wholly speculative. The stimulus never discusses patients or their possible actions.

(D) is Out of Scope. The author never makes any recommendations or expresses any opinion regarding what the government health service *should* do.

(E) is a Distortion. The chain in the stimulus shows that such data will never be gathered. So it is impossible to know whether or not Antinfia is cost-effective.

18. (E) Flaw

Step 1: Identify the Question Type
The phrase "vulnerable to criticism" indicates a Flaw question. Notice any disconnect between the evidence and conclusion, and keep in mind the common LSAT flaws.

Step 2: Untangle the Stimulus
The journalist concludes that a dislike of vegetables is sometimes genetic. The reason is that, in a study, all those who disliked vegetables shared a particular gene (XRV2G).

Step 3: Make a Prediction
The journalist's conclusion asserts a claim of causation: Genetics is the cause of some people's dislike of vegetables. The evidence is merely a correlation: All the people who disliked vegetables happened to share the same gene. It's possible, however, that this was just coincidence, and the gene has nothing to do with a dislike of vegetables.

Step 4: Evaluate the Answer Choices
(E) may not have matched your prediction, but it points out a weakness in the journalist's causal argument. The journalist asserts that all the volunteers who disliked vegetables shared the gene. However, the journalist doesn't provide any information on the gene's occurrence among the volunteers who liked vegetables. If those volunteers *also* shared the XRV2G gene, then the causal link between the gene and an aversion toward vegetables is damaged.

(A) is Extreme. The journalist never indicates that *all* human traits are based on genetics.

(B) describes a representativeness flaw, which often appears in Flaw stimuli that contain a study. However, that flaw type is not in play here. The journalist specifically points out that the groups were both large and diverse. Therefore, nothing indicates that study groups were not representative of the human population. Additionally, the journalist draws a limited conclusion about "some cases," not a general conclusion about all of humanity.

(C) is a more complicated way of saying that the journalist confuses necessity and sufficiency, which does not describe the flaw here. The evidence does not present a phenomenon that *always* causes another, it merely points out a correlation.

(D) describes something the journalist overlooks, but doesn't describe a flaw. For an overlooked possibility to be the correct answer to a Flaw question, the possibility must, if true, damage the argument. Were this possibility true, it would not undermine the journalist's qualified conclusion, which tentatively suggests genetics have something to do with a dislike of vegetables. Even if genes other than XRV2G caused the dislike, the conclusion would still be true.

19. (C) Point at Issue

Step 1: Identify the Question Type
A question stem that directs you to identify what two speakers disagree about is a Point at Issue question. Summarize each speaker's statement to recognize the point of disagreement, or assess the answers utilizing the Decision Tree.

Step 2: Untangle the Stimulus
Ana, based on libertarian beliefs, opposes the smoking ban. She reasons that the government should not protect people from harming themselves.

Pankaj replies that the ban would apply only to public places and that people could still smoke in private.

Step 3: Make a Prediction
Note that Pankaj never explicitly indicates that he favors the ban. Therefore, whether or not the ban is appropriate is not at issue. Instead Pankaj addresses Ana's evidence. By starting his argument with the contrast Keyword *[b]ut* and pointing out that the ban applies only in public, not in private, he implies that the purpose of the ban is not to protect people from their own smoking habit, but rather to protect others.

Step 4: Evaluate the Answer Choices
(C) matches the prediction. Ana clearly believes that the smoking ban is intended to protect people from themselves, while Pankaj's argument suggests that cannot be the case, because people would still be allowed to smoke in private.

(A) is incorrect because Pankaj does not express or imply a position on what is or is not the government's business.

(B) is incorrect because Pankaj does not express or imply a position on whether the government should be restrained in any way.

(D) is incorrect because both speakers would agree on this. Pankaj explicitly states this fact, while Ana seems to think that the ban covers all smoking.

(E) is Out of Scope. There is no way to discern what either would believe regarding this statement. Both may agree, for example, that the government should regulate private behavior if it harms others.

20. (B) Flaw

Step 1: Identify the Question Type
The phrase "vulnerable to criticism" indicates a Flaw question. Notice any disconnect between the evidence and conclusion, and keep in mind the common LSAT flaws.

Step 2: Untangle the Stimulus
The agricultural scientist concludes that apples were probably not cultivated in a particular region 5,000 years ago. The reason is that today's cultivated apples are much larger than wild apples. However, the only remains of apples found in the region from 5,000 years ago are the same size as today's wild apples.

Step 3: Make a Prediction
The agricultural scientist makes a scope shift, assuming that the situation today is reflective of the past. The author assumes that because today's cultivated apples are larger than wild apples, that apples cultivated 5,000 years ago were also larger. This assumes there are no distinctions between the two time periods. For example, the scientist assumes that commercial fertilizers and pesticides used today are *not* responsible for the larger size of commercial apples today. The scientist also assumes that 5,000 years ago, apples had been cultivated long enough to have already developed into a larger size.

Step 4: Evaluate the Answer Choices
(B) is correct. It puts forward an overlooked possibility that, if true, would undermine the conclusion. This choice suggests that small apples from 5,000 years ago might very well have been cultivated.

(A) is Out of Scope. The scientist's conclusion is limited to the particular region and other regions are, therefore, irrelevant.

(C) is Extreme. The argument draws a conclusion about apples in one specific region based on a size comparison. It never assumes that *all* apples come in *only* two sizes.

(D) essentially says that the evidence contradicts the conclusion. However, while the evidence doesn't necessarily *lead* to the conclusion, it also doesn't prohibit it. Nothing in the stimulus indicates that apples *were* in fact cultivated in the region 5,000 years ago.

(E) describes circular reasoning, which is not present here. For circular reasoning to be the correct flaw answer, a piece of evidence must be reiterated in the conclusion, which is not the case here.

21. (B) Assumption (Necessary)

Step 1: Identify the Question Type

An assumption *required* by the argument is a necessary assumption. Build the core, basic bridge between the evidence and conclusion. You can use the Denial Test to check your answer.

Step 2: Untangle the Stimulus

The author concludes that the happy life tends to be the good life, which the author then defines as a morally virtuous life. So the conclusion is actually that the happy life is the morally virtuous life. The evidence indicates that happiness consists of a sense of approval of one's character and projects. All of the discussion of what happiness is *not* and what the good life is *not* can be disregarded in the paraphrase of the argument.

Step 3: Make a Prediction

Both the evidence and conclusion are about happiness. However, the evidence connects happiness with a "sense of approval of one's character and projects," while the conclusion connects happiness with "a morally virtuous life." Thus, the argument boils down to

Evidence:

If	*X (happiness)*	→	*Y (sense of approval of one's character and projects)*

Conclusion:

If	*X (happiness)*	→	*Z (morally virtuous life)*

That means that the Assumption is

If	*Y (sense of approval of one's character and projects)*	→	*Z (morally virtuous life)*

Step 4: Evaluate the Answer Choices

(B) matches the prediction. Negated, it makes the argument fall apart. If people who approve of their own character and projects (i.e., happy people) *don't* tend to lead morally virtuous lives, then the author has no basis in saying that happy lives mean virtuous lives.

(A) is Extreme. While the author says the good life should be defined as a morally virtuous life rather than a life of material well-being, that does not dictate that the two are mutually exclusive. The author merely asserts that those two concepts are not identical. In addition, **(A)** only links two concepts from the conclusion, but does not link the conclusion back to the evidence.

(C) suffers from the same basic defect as **(A)**, but focuses on the evidence rather than the conclusion. In defining genuine happiness as a sense of approval of one's character rather than merely pleasurable feelings, the author does not imply any particular relationship between those two things. The author says that they are not necessarily synonymous. The author might very well believe that approval of one's character and projects does tend to result in pleasurable feelings. **(C)** only links two concepts from the evidence, but does not link the evidence to the conclusion.

(D) goes Out of Scope, because the author neither asserts nor implies what anybody's *goal* is.

(E) links one concept from the evidence and one from the conclusion, but doesn't link the correct ones. Although the concept of "sense of approval" is integral to the argument, the concept of "material well-being" is not; rather, "material well-being" is merely a tangential definition that the author dismisses. Therefore, a *required* assumption will not include that concept. This is why it is so important to properly paraphrase the argument in Step 2—to home in on the concepts that are core to the evidence and conclusion and to dismiss the other filler.

22. (C) Parallel Flaw

Step 1: Identify the Question Type

A question stem that directs you to match arguments with similar *flawed* reasoning is a Parallel Flaw question. Identify the flaw type in the stimulus before seeking an answer containing the same flaw.

Step 2: Untangle the Stimulus

The author concludes that a good way for small-scale organic farms to solve their waste disposal problems is to return organic wastes to the soil. The evidence consists of a Formal Logic principle: The return of organic wastes to the soil is a good solution *only if* the wastes are nontoxic and not too much energy is expended in transporting them. In other words:

If	returning organic wastes to the soil is a good solution	→	nontoxic AND not too much energy

Additionally, the author asserts that the wastes from small-scale organic farms are indeed nontoxic and not too much energy is expended in transporting them, so the author has ultimately also asserted

If	nontoxic AND not too much energy	→	returning organic wastes to the soil is a good solution

Step 3: Make a Prediction
The principle in the first sentence of the stimulus sets out two conditions necessary for the return of organic wastes to the soil to qualify as a "good solution." The second sentence indicates that small-scale organic farming meets both of those necessary conditions. However, the conclusion acts as though those conditions are *sufficient* to guarantee that returning organic waste to the soil is a good solution for small-scale organic farms. In other words, the author confuses sufficiency with necessity, reversing the terms of the argument without negating. While it is certainly possible that returning organic wastes to the soil is a good solution for small-scale organic farms, it is not *guaranteed* to be the case. The correct answer will include evidence that a particular result requires a certain condition, and that the condition has been met. The conclusion will then state that the result is thereby guaranteed.

Step 4: Evaluate the Answer Choices
(C) is a match. The first sentence indicates that viability requires four things. The idea for a website information service fulfills these four things and so it must, therefore, be viable. This choice also reverses the terms of the Formal Logic rule without negating.

(A) is not a match. The first sentence indicates a series of *sufficient conditions* that would guarantee plant health. The next piece of evidence indicates that greenhouse plants meet all the listed sufficient conditions. The stimulus, however, lists a series of *necessary conditions* and indicates that those necessary conditions have been met. Additionally, there is a scope shift from greenhouse plants to commercially produced plants, which assumes that all commercially produced plants are grown in greenhouses.

(B)'s evidence could be translated to say:

If	equal access and globalization	→	each country can optimize its use of resources

The evidence also suggests that those sufficient conditions will occur in 20 years. However, that indicates that the *sufficient* conditions will be met, not the *necessary* condition(s)—like the stimulus did. Additionally, this conclusion also shifts scope to discuss "desired results"; it's unclear whether those "desired results" actually refer to each country being able to optimize its use of resources. That kind of ambiguity does not appear in the stimulus.

(D) presents Formal Logic that follows an "if and only if" structure, which means the sufficient condition(s) are both sufficient and necessary and the necessary condition(s) are also both sufficient and necessary—essentially, A ↔ B. Therefore, it does not match the argument in the stimulus. Further, this argument is not flawed.

(E) is not a match. The evidence presents a Formal Logic statement (if a meal is nutritious, then it includes carbohydrates and protein), but doesn't actually indicate whether or not the necessary condition was met. This answer choice doesn't delineate what the other 20 percent of the meal included, so the author makes the unwarranted assumption that it did not include at least one carbohydrate or protein. That is not the same flaw as the original stimulus.

23. (A) Strengthen
Step 1: Identify the Question Type
A question stem that asks you to support the argument or conclusion in the stimulus (the direction of support flows upward) indicates a Strengthen question. Find the answer choice that makes the conclusion more likely to be true.

Step 2: Untangle the Stimulus
The hypothesis that you are asked to strengthen is that phenazines serve as molecular pipelines to convey nutrients through the bacteria colony. The argument also points out that phenazines are antibiotic molecules that fend off other bacteria, but the scientist doesn't use this information to support the hypothesis.

Step 3: Make a Prediction
As is periodically the case for Strengthen or Weaken questions, the stimulus presents a bald claim that has no evidentiary support. Make sure you understand the conclusion and look for a reason that makes it more likely to be true.

Step 4: Evaluate the Answer Choices
(A) is correct, even though it may initially appear irrelevant. However, it presents a difference between bacteria colonies

that don't produce phenazines and those that do. Bacteria colonies that lack phenazines arrange themselves to increase the number of bacteria connected to the surrounding environment (ostensibly to access essential nutrients found there) whereas the colonies that produce phenazines do not arrange themselves in the same manner. This may be because phenazines make it unnecessary; i.e., phenazines provide access to nutrients so a wrinkled surface would be redundant. This choice provides a mere correlation (between the *absence* of phenazines in colonies that do not need nutrients transported and the *presence* of phenazines in colonies that do), which is not sufficient to *prove* the hypothesis, but it is sufficient to *support* it.

(B) is Out of Scope, as it relates to the antibiotic function of phenazines, but not the hypothesized function. This choice doesn't provide any information about access to or transport of nutrients.

(C) is an Irrelevant Comparison. This choice presents a similarity (rate of growth) between both types of bacteria communities, whereas the correct answer provided a difference (which indicates that phenazines are a significant factor). This choice addresses the *amount* of nutrients in the environment, but not their conduction. Indeed, matching growth rates suggest that phenazines may *not* be involved in nutrient transport and that both types of bacteria colonies use some other type of nutrient transport.

(D) is wrong for the same reason as **(B)**. It relates to the antibiotic function of phenazines, which is unconnected to the scientist's claim regarding the function of nutrient transport.

(E) is a 180. It weakens the argument because it suggests that in bacteria colonies with phenazines, interior bacteria are not getting the nutrients they need to survive. This makes it less likely that phenazines are providing access to those nutrients.

24. (A) Inference

Step 1: Identify the Question Type

A question stem that asks you to use information in the stimulus to determine which answer must be true indicates an Inference question. Inventory the facts, looking for any Formal Logic, statements that can be combined, or emphasized facts.

Step 2: Untangle the Stimulus

The library preservationist discusses an upcoming restoration project, presenting several conditions manuscripts must meet if they are to be restored. First, the preservationist says *most* of medieval manuscripts of acknowledged cultural significance will be restored and that therefore *some* medieval manuscripts of suspect authenticity will be restored. Additionally, the preservationist presents two

necessary conditions that must be met for a manuscript to be restored:

If	*restored*	→	*safety ensured*
If	*restored*	→	*frequently consulted*

Step 3: Make a Prediction

There is a variety of certainty levels within these statements. The two Formal Logic statements are the most certain, while the statements about *most* and *some* manuscripts are less so. It is likely that the correct answer will combine one of the definite statements with one of the less definite statements, and the resulting deduction will almost certainly be a *some* statement. Also, because this stimulus provides somewhat unfortunate information, that will almost certainly be the focus of the right answer. Because *some* medieval manuscripts of suspect authenticity *will* be restored, yet manuscripts will be restored *only if* researchers frequently consult them, it can be deduced that researchers frequently consult some medieval manuscripts of suspect authenticity.

Step 4: Evaluate the Answer Choices

(A) matches the prediction.

(B) is Extreme. Only *most* of the medieval manuscripts widely acknowledged to be of cultural significance will be restored, and thus their safety during the process can be ensured. The stimulus doesn't provide information about those manuscripts that will not be restored.

(C) mentions both conditions necessary for restoration. However, **(C)** is not a deduction that can be made. While all the manuscripts *that will be restored* are those that can be restored safely and are frequently consulted by researchers, it is not necessarily true that all those that *can* be restored safely are *also* frequently consulted. Just because it's true that if A → B and C, that doesn't mean that if B → C.

(D) is not supported by the information in the stimulus. While there is a reference to physical deterioration, there are no statements concerning which manuscripts are most susceptible to deterioration.

(E) is not a deduction that can be made from the statements. While researchers must frequently consult any manuscript that is to be restored, only *most* of the culturally significant manuscripts will be restored. Those that aren't restored may be culturally significant but not frequently consulted.

25. (B) Strengthen

Step 1: Identify the Question Type

The question stem explicitly asks you to strengthen the argument. Identify the assumption and firm up the bridge between the evidence and the conclusion.

Step 2: Untangle the Stimulus

The author concludes that direct-mail advertising is not bad for the environment. The reason is that direct-mail advertising promotes the purchase of products by phone or online, rather than in-person. This cuts down on driving, which pollutes the air.

Step 3: Make a Prediction

The judgment that something is good is similar to a recommendation, in that it presumes the pros outweigh the cons. You can strengthen these arguments by adding an additional pro or removing a possible con. Here, the author overlooks the possibility that pollution produced by shipping would outweigh that saved from customers ordering online or by phone. Or, perhaps people wouldn't buy those products at all, if they weren't advertised in the mail. A correct strengthen answer choice could indicate that either of those overlooked possibilities is not in play, or it could add some other benefit of direct-mail advertising.

Step 4: Evaluate the Answer Choices

(B) is correct. While initially it might not seem to provide much support, it addresses a possible weakener: that direct-mail advertising increases the overall number of purchases consumers make. Overall pollution increases due to making those products, shipping those products, consumers going to retail stores to acquire those products, and so on. If consumers were going to go out and acquire those products anyway, then the direct-mailing and in-home purchase may be less damaging to the environment than if the consumer had left the home to acquire the product.

(A) is a 180. It indicates an effect of direct-mail advertising that would result in more trips to the store and, thus, more pollution.

(C) makes an Irrelevant Comparison. Whether a person is more likely to purchase a product from a direct-mail advertisement or a magazine is immaterial. Although direct-mail advertisements consist of products to be purchased from the home, those advertised in magazines may cause consumers to go out and buy those items at retail stores or it may cause them to purchase those items online/via phone. Without knowing whether those purchase decisions cause a net increase/decrease in the amount of pollution or whether those products purchased by either type of advertisement increase overall sales rather than just replace in-store sales, it cannot be determined that **(C)** strengthens the argument.

(D) indicates that companies using direct-mail advertising are targeting certain customers (rather than blindly sending out paper mail to the masses), but this choice doesn't mention anything that specifically suggests direct-mail advertising isn't bad for the environment. At best, this choice suggests that direct-mail advertising isn't as bad as it could be.

(E) is too ambiguous. This answer doesn't clarify whether direct-mail advertising results in sales that *replace* in-store sales or *add* to the overall number of sales.

26. (D) Parallel Reasoning

Step 1: Identify the Question Type

The direction to identify *similar* patterns of reasoning indicates a Parallel Reasoning question. Find the answer containing an argument that uses the same type of evidence to reach the same type of conclusion as the argument in the stimulus. You can begin by characterizing and comparing conclusions.

Step 2: Untangle the Stimulus

The author concludes that new countries are likely not monarchies. The two pieces of evidence are that the older a country is, the more likely it is to be ruled by a monarch, and that most countries are not monarchies.

Step 3: Make a Prediction

As a first step, characterize the conclusion and eliminate any answers that have a conclusion of a different type or level of certainty. This conclusion is a conditional statement with a result expressed as a probability that something is *not* the case. A quick glance at the answers reveals that four of them contain conclusions that are conditional statements with an uncertain result, but only two of them indicate something is *not* likely. Still, two answers remain in contention, so the next step is to map out the evidence.

Evidence (Proportional Relationship): The older (more X), the more likely ruled by monarch (more likely Y).

Evidence (Factual Statement): Most not ruled by monarch (most not Y).

Conclusion: If new (not X), not ruled by monarch (not Y).

Remember that the order in which the pieces of the argument are presented does not matter, but the correct answer must contain the same components.

Step 4: Evaluate the Answer Choices

(D) is a match. It includes a statement about *most* novels, a proportional relationship between a novel's popularity and the likelihood it will be turned into a movie, and a conditional conclusion about what will *probably not* occur.

(A) does not match. The evidence lines up correctly, but the conclusion adds a new term, discussing the popularity of a *movie* rather than a novel, as was discussed in the evidence.

(B) is incorrect because the conclusion discusses the popularity of novels while the evidence concerns the popularity of movies. Like **(A)**, this choice introduces a new term. Additionally, the conclusion is phrased with a positive result (*will* probably be made into a movie), rather than negative (probably *not* ruled by a monarch).

(C) should be eliminated because it places the proportional relationship in the conclusion and the conditional statement of a probable result in the evidence, rather than vice versa.

(E) varies from the stimulus in a couple places. First, the proportional relationship in the stimulus is directly proportional (more old, more likely monarchy), whereas the relationship in this choice is inversely proportional (more complex, less likely to become a movie). Additionally, this conclusion is phrased as resulting in a positive result (will probably be made into a movie), rather than a negative result (probably not ruled by a monarch).

Section III: Logical Reasoning

Q#	Question Type	Correct	Difficulty
1	Paradox	C	★
2	Weaken	B	★
3	Main Point	D	★
4	Assumption (Necessary)	E	★
5	Paradox	C	★
6	Assumption (Sufficient)	C	★★
7	Flaw	A	★★★★
8	Strengthen	A	★★
9	Main Point	E	★
10	Weaken	D	★★
11	Flaw	A	★★★★
12	Strengthen	C	★★
13	Principle (Identify/Strengthen)	C	★
14	Flaw	B	★
15	Role of a Statement	B	★★
16	Inference	D	★
17	Principle (Identify/Weaken)	D	★
18	Assumption (Necessary)	C	★★★
19	Principle (Apply/Inference)	D	★
20	Inference	B	★★★
21	Principle (Identify/Strengthen)	E	★★★★
22	Flaw	E	★★
23	Parallel Reasoning	C	★★★
24	Inference	A	★★★
25	Parallel Flaw	D	★★

1. (C) Paradox

Step 1: Identify the Question Type

The phrase "reconcile the ... apparently paradoxical recommendations" identifies this as a Paradox question. Take note of the apparently contradictory statements and find the answer that allows both those statements to be true.

Step 2: Untangle the Stimulus

The dentist recommends brushing after every meal to remove sugars that promote the growth of bacteria, which produce acids that dissolve minerals in tooth enamel and lead to cavities. However, to help prevent cavities, the dentist also recommends chewing gum—even gum containing sugar—when one is not able to brush after a meal.

Step 3: Make a Prediction

The apparent discrepancy here is that sugars can ultimately *lead* to cavities, yet the dentist recommends chewing gum (even gum with sugar) to *prevent* cavities. There are a number of possible resolutions to this paradox, so remember to keep your prediction general. The correct answer choice will explain why chewing gum containing sugar can actually help to prevent cavities that are caused by sugars.

Step 4: Evaluate the Answer Choices

(C) is correct. The dentist states in his argument that cavities result from certain bacteria, which produce acid that dissolves minerals in tooth enamel. If **(C)** is true, then chewing gum helps prevent cavities because it stimulates saliva, the effects of which counteract the effects of the sugars.

(A) is an Irrelevant Comparison. Knowing the relevant amounts of sugar found in a piece of chewing gum and in an average meal does not explain why chewing gum after a meal (essentially adding more sugar) can help prevent cavities.

(B) is Out of Scope. Whether or not tooth decay can be reversed if it is caught before a cavity develops does not help to explain why chewing gum in particular can prevent cavities.

(D) is Out of Scope. Information about how long sugars can be on teeth before bacteria proliferate may be a nice thing to know, but it does not help to explain why chewing gum after a meal can prevent the formation of cavities. If anything, it deepens the paradox. If there is a 24-hour window before brushing actually needs to occur, then the recommendation to chew gum makes less sense, because one can simply wait until brushing is practical.

(E) may be tempting because it provides a direct benefit that results from chewing gum. However, knowing that chewing gum contributes to the *overall* health of the oral tract is not enough, on its own, to explain why chewing gum helps specifically to prevent the formation of cavities.

2. (B) Weaken

Step 1: Identify the Question Type

The question stem explicitly asks you to weaken the argument. Identify the argument's assumption and attack it.

Step 2: Untangle the Stimulus

The author's conclusion, signaled by the Keyword *thus*, is that the theory that New Zealand's varied bird population results from the lack of competition from mammals is false. In other words, the author believes that New Zealand's indigenous birds did experience competition from native mammals. The author supports this conclusion by citing the discovery of fossils of a primitive land mammal unearthed in New Zealand.

Step 3: Make a Prediction

The author discredits the theory in the argument simply by proving that New Zealand was home to one native land mammal. The argument provides no information, however, about whether that primitive land mammal existed at the same time as or competed with the birds in such a way as to impact their population. For the conclusion to be true, the author must assume that the land mammals and birds lived at the same time and were in direct competition with each other. Because the question asks you to weaken the argument, the correct answer will likely present information that shows one of these assumptions is not true.

Step 4: Evaluate the Answer Choices

(B) is correct. If the recently discovered land mammal became extinct *before* the native bird population was established, then there is no reason to believe that the birds and land mammals competed. Thus, the theory that the varied bird population owes its existence to the lack of competition from mammals is possible after all.

(A) is a 180. This choice strengthens the argument, because a higher number of mammal species may increase the chances that native birds faced competition.

(C) is Out of Scope. The existence of primitive *reptile* and *insect* species has no impact on the theory that New Zealand's bird population results from the lack of competition from *mammals*.

(D) is a Distortion. The contrapositive of this choice indicates that countries with rich and varied native bird populations don't have rich and varied mammal populations. However, the author doesn't make the stronger claim that New Zealand had a rich and varied *mammal* population; the author merely suggests that birds and mammals competed to some extent. That conclusion could be true, despite what **(D)** says because it does not address the issue of competition.

(E) is Out of Scope. The situation on other island countries has nothing to do with New Zealand.

3. (D) Main Point

Step 1: Identify the Question Type
The question stem explicitly asks you to identify the conclusion, or main point, in the restaurant owner's argument. Be cautious of misleading conclusion Keywords.

Step 2: Untangle the Stimulus
The contrast Keyword *but* signals the transition from background information about the newspaper reporter to the restaurant owner's belief about the newspaper reporter: The reporter is not a true restaurant critic. The last sentence provides an analogy to support the owner's belief.

Step 3: Make a Prediction
The correct answer will match the owner's conclusion that the newspaper reporter is not a true restaurant critic. Watch out for answer choices that discuss evidence, summarize the entire argument, or speculate beyond the argument.

Step 4: Evaluate the Answer Choices
(D) matches the prediction and includes a verbatim restatement of the conclusion.

(A) restates evidence that shows the newspaper reporter lacked training.

(B) also restates evidence about the reporter's background that the owner mentions to support the conclusion that the reporter is not a true restaurant critic.

(C) is a concession that the restaurant owner makes about the newspaper reporter, but this aside does not represent the owner's overall main point.

(E) is the analogy that the restaurant owner presents to support the conclusion that the newspaper reporter is not a true restaurant critic. While this sentence is opinionated, nothing else in the stimulus supports it, and so it cannot be the conclusion.

4. (E) Assumption (Necessary)

Step 1: Identify the Question Type
The question asks for "an assumption required by the argument," so this is a Necessary Assumption question. Bridge the gap between the evidence and conclusion and consider using the Denial Test to check your answer.

Step 2: Untangle the Stimulus
The author concludes that the hypothesis about the formation of the solar system is false. In other words, the solar system was not formed from a cloud of gas and dust produced by a supernova. The author's evidence is that because supernovas produce the isotope iron-60, iron-60 would have been present in the early history of the solar system, and there is no evidence of iron-60 in meteorites that formed during that time period.

Step 3: Make a Prediction
The author bases the conclusion on the simple fact that no iron-60 was found in early forming meteorites. For the conclusion to work, she must assume that those meteorites would contain iron-60 if iron-60 were present early in the history of the solar system. If it were possible that the meteorites might not contain iron-60 even if iron-60 were present, then the conclusion would be weakened.

Step 4: Evaluate the Answer Choices
(E) matches the prediction. The author must assume this is true because she claims the hypothesis is wrong simply because meteorites that formed early on did not have iron-60 in them. A denial of **(E)** is "If there had been iron-60 present in the early history of the solar system, it would *not* be found in meteorites formed early in the solar system's history." If that was true, the argument would be torn apart.

(A) is a Distortion. Although this choice discusses meteorites formed early in the solar system's history, it focuses on *extra* chemical elements that supernovas likely *don't* produce. The author focuses on *missing* chemical elements that supernovas *do* produce. Whether or not meteorites contain elements that don't come from supernovas does not impact the author's claim.

(B) is Out of Scope. How *other* solar systems are formed is unrelated to an argument about the formation of *our* solar system. While the comparison to other solar systems might *strengthen* the author's argument, this information is not *necessary*.

(C) is Out of Scope. Whether supernovas produce significant amounts of any form of iron *other* than iron-60 has no effect on the author's claim, which centers on evidence about iron-60 only.

(D) is also Out of Scope because it focuses on meteorites that formed *relatively late* in the solar system's history. The author's evidence references only meteorites that formed *early* in the solar system's history.

5. (C) Paradox

Step 1: Identify the Question Type
The phrase "resolve the apparent discrepancy" identifies this as a Paradox question. Paraphrase the apparently contradictory statements and find the answer that allows both statements to be true.

Step 2: Untangle the Stimulus
The safety expert claims that treating tuna with carbon monoxide to prevent it from turning brown is harmless. However, the expert also claims that such treatment could result in more people getting sick from eating tuna.

Step 3: Make a Prediction

Remember to keep your predictions general, as there are several ways to resolve this paradox. The correct answer will explain how it is possible that more people could get sick from eating tuna treated with carbon monoxide even though the treatment itself is harmless.

Step 4: Evaluate the Answer Choices

(C) is correct. If treated tuna doesn't show signs of spoilage, then people might eat the tuna without realizing the risk. Thus, it makes sense that more people may get sick from eating treated tuna, even though the treatment itself is not harmful.

(A) is Out of Scope. This explains how it is possible for carbon monoxide to sicken workers in fish processing plants, but does not explain how the carbon monoxide treatment could result in more people getting sick from *eating* tuna.

(B) is Out of Scope. This choice may indicate that the number of people getting sick will increase simply because the overall number of people eating tuna has increased. However, this doesn't explain why the *carbon monoxide treatment* may make tuna dangerous.

(D) is Out of Scope. Whether or not treating tuna with carbon monoxide is the *only* way to keep it from turning brown fails to explain how the treatment itself could result in more people getting sick.

(E) is Out of Scope. While this choice explains why tuna is treated with carbon monoxide in the first place, it does not explain why the treatment may cause more people to get sick.

6. (C) Assumption (Sufficient)

Step 1: Identify the Question Type

The phrase "conclusion … is most strongly supported if … assumed" identifies this as a Sufficient Assumption question. Identify the answer choice that provides an additional piece of evidence that guarantees the truth of the conclusion. Don't worry if you identified and approached this as a Strengthen question due to the phrase "strongly supported"; looking for information that makes the conclusion more likely to be true could still lead you to the correct answer. Adding the author's assumption to the argument will always strengthen it.

Step 2: Untangle the Stimulus

The Keyword *[c]learly* indicates the astrophysicist's conclusion: that describing GRBs as *short* and *long* is no longer useful. The evidence is that traditionally GRBs have been classified as either *short* or *long* based on their duration, but an unusual GRB occurred that was long in duration but had all the other properties of a *short* GRB.

Step 3: Make a Prediction

On a Sufficient Assumption question, the correct answer will provide an additional piece of evidence that, if added to the

rest of the evidence, guarantees the truth of the conclusion. Here, the astrophysicist cites one unusual GRB that didn't fall neatly into either the *short* or *long* categories, using this to claim that these labels are no longer useful. To the author, this *one* exception calls into question the usefulness of the traditional classification system. The correct answer will add a piece of evidence that supports the idea that classifying GRBs based on duration no longer makes sense.

Step 4: Evaluate the Answer Choices

(C) is correct. If it is true that duration is not as important as other properties in the classification of the unusual GRB, then the astrophysicist's claim that having duration be the defining feature is no longer useful is completely true.

(A) is Out of Scope. Whether or not other GRBs with unusual properties have been sighted does not impact the astrophysicist's claim that the *short* and *long* labels used to classify them are no longer useful. If anything, this weakens the astrophysicist's claim, because it would be rather extreme to reject a classification system because of one anomaly.

(B) is a 180. If it is possible to sometimes classify GRBs on the basis of duration alone, then there is evidence that the descriptive labels *short* and *long* are still useful.

(D) is if anything a 180. This choice eliminates one other possible classification system, thereby suggesting that the *short* and *long* descriptive labels might still be useful.

(E) is Out of Scope. The issue is whether classifying GRBs based on duration is still useful; the ease of using different wording does not guarantee that the earlier labels have "outlived their usefulness."

7. (A) Flaw

Step 1: Identify the Question Type

The phrase "vulnerable to criticism" identifies this as a Flaw question. Consider how the conclusion goes beyond the evidence and keep in mind common LSAT flaws.

Step 2: Untangle the Stimulus

The Keyword *[s]o* identifies the author's conclusion: For patients with a greater tendency to laugh, even laughing a little during their recovery from illness helps more than laughing a greater amount helps other patients. The author provides information from a study as support. First, viewing comic videos helped strengthen patients' immune systems, indicating that laughter aids in the recovery from illness. Second, patients who started out with a greater tendency to laugh experienced much greater gains.

Step 3: Make a Prediction

The author makes a subtle but important scope shift. The conclusion is a comparison between the *amount* that patients laughed, but the evidence fails to provide any information about how much patients actually laughed at the comic videos. Instead, the evidence provides a comparison between patients' initial *propensity* toward laughter. To claim that patients with a greater tendency to laugh were helped more than others merely by laughing a little, the author assumes that patients with a greater tendency to laugh did not laugh either the same amount or more than other patients at the videos. Find an answer choice that paraphrases this issue.

Step 4: Evaluate the Answer Choices

(A) is correct and matches the prediction. The author fails to consider the possibility that patients whose tendency to laugh was greater originally laughed more at the videos than the other patients laughed.

(B) is an Irrelevant Comparison. The argument is about *improvement* in patients' immune systems, not the relative strength of patients' immune systems.

(C) describes a representativeness flaw, which is not at play here. The author does not make a conclusion about the immune systems of the entire population based on a sample of hospital patients.

(D) describes a causal flaw, which in this case isn't applicable. The author does not *conclude* that patients' tendency to laugh affected the gains in their immune systems, and therefore can't be mistaking cause and effect. The problem with the conclusion is the unsupported *comparison* of the *amount* of laughter. Both the assertion that laughter strengthens immune systems and the correlation between greater gains and patients' tendency to laugh appear in the evidence and must be accepted as true.

(E) is Out of Scope. *Speed* of recovery does not factor in the argument.

8. (A) Strengthen

Step 1: Identify the Question Type

The phrase "most supports the argument" identifies this as a Strengthen question. Break down the argument into the conclusion and evidence, and find an answer choice that makes the conclusion more likely to be true.

Step 2: Untangle the Stimulus

The author concludes in the first sentence that, in response to feedback from a female guppy, a male guppy will change its courting patterns. The author supports the argument with a study involving male guppies that have more orange on one side of their body than the other. In the study, courting males were more likely to display the side with more orange, and females were drawn to those males showing more orange.

Step 3: Make a Prediction

The author claims that it is the female's feedback (the fact that they were drawn to males with more orange showing) that causes the males to show the side with more orange. The evidence provided, however, only suggests a correlation. For

the author's conclusion to work, that connection needs to be stronger. The correct answer will either somehow indicate that the males' display was indeed a result of the females' feedback or will remove some other reason why the males would tend to show the side with more orange.

Step 4: Evaluate the Answer Choices

(A) is correct. A model female guppy cannot provide feedback, and so can't indicate preference. The fact that males courting the impartial model were similarly indifferent about which side they showed makes it more likely that the different behavior seen in the original study was a result of the female guppy's feedback. This doesn't prove the argument, but it does strengthen the correlation between females' preference and males' display.

(B) is Out of Scope. The preferences of females from other species don't affect the likelihood that male guppies changed their courting behavior because of feedback from a female guppy.

(C) is Out of Scope. This choice suggests scientists aren't that interested in the relationship between color and offspring, but doesn't actually provide any information about the guppies themselves. Therefore, it has no impact on the argument.

(D) is Out of Scope. The coloring of the female guppies has no impact on the author's conclusion that male guppies change their courting patterns based on feedback from female guppies.

(E) is a bit of a 180. If the males and females could not directly interact with each other, feedback would be limited to only sight. Therefore, it is if anything less likely that feedback from females caused the male guppies to show their more orange side.

9. (E) Main Point

Step 1: Identify the Question Type

The question stem explicitly asks you to identify the conclusion, or main point, of the politician's argument. Be cautious of misleading Conclusion Keywords, but pay attention to any other Keywords that may help indicate the politician's opinion.

Step 2: Untangle the Stimulus

There is a lot going on in the politician's argument, so break it down into manageable pieces. The Keyword *because* indicates not only that the politician's evidence follows that Keyword, but that the conclusion comes before it. The politician concludes that it would be dangerous to act on the basis of "this argument." To understand the conclusion fully, paraphrase the proponents' argument, given in the first sentence: a unilateral reduction in nuclear arms would cause other countries to reduce their nuclear arms, leading to an international agreement to reduce arms. Thus, the politician believes that it would be dangerous for a country to unilaterally reduce its nuclear arms based on the thinking that an international agreement to reduce arms would be eventually reached.

Step 3: Make a Prediction
The correct answer will match the politician's conclusion that it would be dangerous for a country to unilaterally reduce its nuclear arms because of a false assumption that doing so would lead to an international agreement on nuclear arms reduction. Notice that the politician does not necessarily advocate *against* nuclear disarmament; rather, the politician argues that reducing nuclear arms *unilaterally*, as the proponents' argument suggests, would be a mistake. Watch out for answer choices that discuss evidence, summarize the entire argument, or speculate beyond the argument.

Step 4: Evaluate the Answer Choices
(E) is correct and matches the prediction.

(A) is Out of Scope. It not only restates part of the politician's evidence, but also discusses conventional weapons, which the politician never mentions.

(B) is a 180. It restates part of the argument made by proponents of unilateral nuclear arms reduction, an argument against which the politician argues.

(C) distorts a piece of evidence in the last sentence. The politician states that countries on the verge of civil wars cannot be relied upon to conform to international military policy, not that they cannot be relied upon to disclose the extent of their nuclear capability.

(D) is Extreme. The politician never suggests that an international agreement on nuclear disarmament is unlikely to *ever* be achieved. Rather, the politician merely argues that the proponents' causal argument is not sound, and therefore might not necessarily lead to an international agreement on disarmament.

10. (D) Weaken

Step 1: Identify the Question Type
The question stem reads as if it might be a Flaw question because of the language "criticize the reasoning," but read carefully. The question stem asks for an answer choice that, "*if true*, would provide the strongest basis for criticizing the reasoning of the advertisement." Thus, rather than asking you to point out what is already wrong with the argument, this Weaken question asks you to find additional information that makes the conclusion less likely to be true.

Step 2: Untangle the Stimulus
The advertisement concludes in the last sentence that one should receive a complete course of treatment for whiplash injury from the Lakeside Injury Clinic any time one has an accident involving a fall or a bump on the head. The

advertisement cites two main pieces of evidence. First, car accidents are the leading cause of whiplash, an injury caused by the sudden sharp motion of the neck. Second, a fall or a bump on one's head can also cause a sudden sharp motion of the neck.

Step 3: Make a Prediction
The basis of the advertisement's conclusion is that a fall or a bump on the head *can* cause a sudden sharp motion of the neck, which *can* cause whiplash. To then claim that people should get a complete course of whiplash treatment after any fall or bump on the head, the advertisement assumes that an accident involving a fall or a bump on the head *will* cause whiplash frequently enough to warrant the treatment. Find an answer choice that invalidates this assumption and therefore weakens the advertisement's conclusion.

Step 4: Evaluate the Answer Choices
(D) is correct. If it is very uncommon for a sudden sharp motion of the neck to result from a fall or a bump on one's head, then there is no reason to believe that one should receive a complete course of treatment for whiplash injury after *any* accident involving a fall or a bump on the head.

(A) is a Distortion. Although part of the evidence states that being shoved from behind may cause a sudden sharp motion of the neck, the advertisement's conclusion focuses only on a fall or a bump on the head.

(B) is a Distortion and has no impact on the argument. The argument states that auto accidents are the most common cause of whiplash injury and that an accident involving a fall or a bump on the head can also cause whiplash. Whether one experiences a fall or a bump on the head during a car accident or otherwise is irrelevant to whether one should receive a complete course of whiplash treatment.

(C) is Out of Scope. Non-automobile accidents that do not involve a fall or a bump on the head yet cause whiplash injury are not covered by the advertisement's conclusion and are therefore irrelevant. If anything, this choice merely increases the types of accidents that should be followed by a complete course of whiplash treatment at Lakeside Injury Clinic.

(E) is an Irrelevant Comparison. The advertisement does not compare the appropriate treatments for whiplash caused by different types of accidents. The fact that there is only one type of treatment is consistent with the advertisement's recommendation that people who have had accidents involving a fall or a bump on the head receive the same complete course of care.

11. (A) Flaw

Step 1: Identify the Question Type
The question stem explicitly asks you to identify the flaw in the argument. Consider how the conclusion goes beyond the evidence and keep in mind common LSAT flaws.

Step 2: Untangle the Stimulus

The Keyword *[c]onsequently* identifies the author's conclusion: Proceed with the development of the hiking trail. The first part of the stimulus presents an objection made by a group of citizens who oppose the development, claiming that hikers would likely litter the area if the trail were developed. The author dismisses the group's concern, however, stating that most of the trail's users will be hikers who care about the environment.

Step 3: Make a Prediction

Notice that the author never presents any independent evidence about why it is a *good* idea to develop the nearby abandoned railroad grade into a hiking trail. Instead, the author merely dismisses *one* objection. However, there may be many other reasons not to develop the hiking trail. Find an answer choice that paraphrases this flaw.

Step 4: Evaluate the Answer Choices

(A) matches the prediction. The author bases the conclusion that the hiking trail should be developed mainly on a claim that an objection based on litter is weak.

(B) is Extreme because the author never confuses *each* individual member of a set and that set itself. Rather, the author limits the evidence to "[m]ost trail users." This choice represents a parts-versus-whole flaw, a less common type of LSAT flaw.

(C) describes circular reasoning, which is not at play here. The problem is that the author doesn't provide any evidence for the trail development, not that the author uses the conclusion *as* evidence.

(D) is incorrect because the author never cites information about a *few* to draw a conclusion about *most*. Instead, the author provides evidence about *most* trail users to recommend a course of action.

(E) describes an ad hominem attack, a flaw type that shows up occasionally on the LSAT. However, the author attacks the citizens' objection, not the citizens themselves.

12. (C) Strengthen

Step 1: Identify the Question Type

The question stem explicitly asks you to strengthen the argument. Break down the argument into the conclusion and evidence, and find an answer choice that makes the conclusion more likely to be true.

Step 2: Untangle the Stimulus

The author concludes that the people and entities who have been predicting an imminent and catastrophic shortage of scientists and engineers are turning out to be wrong. In other words, the author does not believe that there will be an *imminent* shortage of people in those fields. The evidence Keyword *since* identifies why the author believes the

doomsayers are wrong. First, the salaries of scientists and engineers are not noticeably rising and, second, unemployment in these fields is as high as unemployment in other fields.

Step 3: Make a Prediction

The author supports the argument about the future based on information about the field in the present. However, for any prediction based on current trends, the author must be assuming that those trends will continue. Here, the author is assuming the science and engineering fields will remain in demand. In other words, the author must assume that there are people who are interested in those fields now and will become scientists and engineers in the future.

Step 4: Evaluate the Answer Choices

(C) matches the prediction. If it is true that there has been a significant increase in the number of students in science and engineering university programs, then the author's conclusion that there will not be an impending shortage of those professionals is more likely.

(A) doesn't necessarily strengthen or weaken the conclusion. The fact that the *proportion* of science and engineering research being done at corporations is higher now than it was five years ago does not necessarily make it more likely that there will not be an upcoming shortage. Proportion is not the same as total volume; there is no way to know if the overall amount of research being carried out has increased, decreased, or remained stable, simply shifting around among universities, corporations, and the government. Therefore, there is no way to judge the upcoming demand for scientists and engineers.

(B) is a Distortion. The author does mention that salaries have not noticeably risen, but the salary range is unspecified and success is subjective. There is no way to know if the fields of science and engineering offer the prospect of financial success or not.

(D) is a 180. If the author says there's not going to be a shortage, and **(D)** indicates that there is a shortage already within some specializations, then that would weaken, rather than strengthen, the argument. Furthermore, the argument is about the fields of engineering and science as a *whole*, not about shortages or overages within specializations, so **(D)** could also be construed as an Irrelevant Comparison about specialties.

(E) is Out of Scope. Whether or not the skills learned in science and engineering programs need to be kept current through continuing education has no impact on the conclusion. The issue is about whether there will be enough scientists and engineers in the near future, not what those who do enter the fields need to do to keep their knowledge and skills current.

13. (C) Principle (Identify/Strengthen)

Step 1: Identify the Question Type
The question explicitly asks you to find the principle in the answer choices. Furthermore, there are two arguments, and the principle must *justify* (i.e., strengthen) *both* of them. Summarize both arguments, determine the common goal of each one, and paraphrase that common goal in broad language. Expect wrong answers to focus too much on one argument to the exclusion of the other.

Step 2: Untangle the Stimulus
Rhonda starts out with a recommendation to help others when "the cost is not too great." Her reasoning is that such actions will help you lead a richer life. Brad also recommends helping people, but not just anyone—only close friends and family. Brad's reasoning is that these people will remember your good deeds, and you'll earn their help when you need it.

Step 3: Make a Prediction
Rhonda and Brad both make qualified recommendations to help others, although Rhonda is not as restrictive about whom you should help. In both cases, though, the reasoning involves some kind of personal gain. In Rhonda's case, the benefit is a richer life; in Brad's case, the gain is reciprocal help. So generally (i.e., as a principle), both speakers encourage helping others for the benefits you'd receive from doing so. The correct answer will hinge on this basic idea.

Step 4: Evaluate the Answer Choices
(C) supports both speakers. It may seem more cynical than either's argument, yet Rhonda recommends helping for the sake of a richer life, while Brad recommends helping so that others will help you in return. Both are based on benefiting oneself.

(A) is a 180 of Brad's point. Brad says to limit your help to those who would return the favor someday, so it would be extreme to do what would "*most* benefit the *most* people."

(B) is consistent with Brad's argument, which is based on reciprocity. However, Rhonda's argument does not approach the idea of how others would treat you. She doesn't mention any sort of expectations.

(D) is also consistent with Brad's argument. However, Rhonda's argument does not depend on others returning the favor.

(E) is Out of Scope. Neither argument broaches the subject of pride. Even if Rhonda's "richer lives" is construed as including the feeling of pride, Brad certainly makes no such similar declaration.

14. (B) Flaw

Step 1: Identify the Question Type
The question directly asks for a flaw in the columnist's argument. Break the argument down into the evidence and conclusion, and consider why the reasoning is not convincing.

Step 2: Untangle the Stimulus
The columnist addresses a proposal to ban the practice of stringing cable and electric lines from the same poles. Activists claim the cable lines make it easier for animals to get close to the fatal electric lines. However, the columnist refutes the activists (a classic argumentative pattern), essentially concluding that banning the practice is not worthwhile. The columnist's evidence is that some animals are still electrocuted by power lines even in areas where cable TV lines are underground and not sharing the same poles.

Step 3: Make a Prediction
Notice that the columnist doesn't actually argue against the ban, but rather attacks a specific line of reasoning: "This particular argument for banning the practice fails." The columnist's evidence indicates that the proposed ban will not *completely* eliminate harm to animals. However, the activists never claimed that separating the wires would provide full protection from danger. They only claim that shared poles make it *easier* for animals to get killed, which suggests that a ban would merely make electrocution *less likely*. It's possible that, even though some animals will inevitably continue to be electrocuted, the proposed ban could still save many from harm. The correct answer will point out this overlooked possibility.

Step 4: Evaluate the Answer Choices
(B) points out the columnist's error. The columnist rejects the activists' proposal because some animals would still be electrocuted, ignoring the fact that the proposal might effectively *reduce* such incidents.

(A) brings up the concept of necessity and sufficiency. However, the columnist doesn't confuse these ideas. According to the columnist, the fact that some animals are electrocuted in areas with underground TV wires is *enough* to show the activists' argument is inadequate; however, the columnist does not indicate that that is the *only* reason why the argument is inadequate.

(C) would be a flaw if the columnist rejected the proposal as entirely unnecessary. However, the columnist merely says that one example of the activists' reasoning is flawed. The conclusion is limited, and therefore other potential benefits are Out of Scope.

(D) describes an ad hominem attack, which is not in play here. The columnist never attacks the activists personally—only their argument.

(E) is Out of Scope. The columnist never mentions other proposals, let alone their potential effectiveness.

15. (B) Role of a Statement

Step 1: Identify the Question Type
The question presents a claim from the stimulus and asks for its "role ... in the argument," indicating a Role of a Statement question. Start by locating and underlining the claim in question, and then break the argument down into its component parts.

Step 2: Untangle the Stimulus
The second sentence is the claim in question. The Keyword *[t]herefore* in the last sentence indicates the author's conclusion: this ancient reptile was probably warm-blooded. The main piece of evidence is in the last half of that sentence, after the Keyword *for*: "such insulation" would not be useful to cold-blooded animals. "Such insulation" refers to the hair mentioned in the statement in question.

Step 3: Make a Prediction
The statement in question provides a Formal Logic statement that says if *Thrinaxodon* had whiskers, it also had hair on its body, which is the *insulation* mentioned later in the main evidence. The correct answer will indicate that the claim is used as part of the evidence.

Step 4: Evaluate the Answer Choices
(B) correctly identifies the statement as part of the evidence supporting the conclusion.

(A) starts off correct, identifying the statement as a supporting premise. However, this choice gets the conclusion wrong, describing the additional evidence (indicated by the Keyword *for*) rather than the actual conclusion that the animal was likely warm-blooded.

(C) is incorrect by suggesting that the statement in question is the conclusion.

(D) is a 180. The statement is a needed link in the evidence used to *support* the author's conclusion; it is not a hypothesis that the author tries to disprove.

(E) is a 180 because the statement *is* used to support the conclusion. Additionally, it doesn't explain *why* the animal was warm-blooded; it merely provides a reason to conclude that it was warm-blooded.

16. (D) Inference

Step 1: Identify the Question Type
The question asks for something that would logically fill in the blank at the end of the stimulus. The blank is a conclusion that will be supported by the evidence before it. In other words, the correct answer will be an inference, backed up by the other statements in the stimulus. Approach this question in the same way you would any other Inference question.

Step 2: Untangle the Stimulus
The first statement indicates that many countries tax income to fund the government. However, doing so doesn't promote savings and investment. Taxing consumption, on the other hand, *would* promote savings. Finally, countries want to improve their economies, and increasing savings rates is the *only* way to do that.

Step 3: Make a Prediction
The strong language of the last statement is important. The economist claims that increasing savings rates is the *only* way to improve these countries' economies. Because improving the economy is described as an "important challenge," then increasing savings rates would also be important. Furthermore, because taxing income does nothing for savings while taxing consumption *does*, that suggests the countries should stop their current practice of taxing income and instead focus on taxing consumption.

Step 4: Evaluate the Answer Choices
(D) correctly summarizes the economist's likely recommendation for these countries. Taxing consumption would encourage savings, the rate of which needs to increase to improve the economy.

(A) is a Distortion and Extreme. The economist states that these countries should be taxing consumption rather than taxing income. Savings and investment are mentioned as things that are not encouraged by taxing income—not as things that should or should not be taxed. Additionally, the economist cites that *many* countries need to improve their economy, but that does not mean though that *most* countries should undertake the economist's suggestion. It is unknown what proportion of countries needs to make a change to their tax policy.

(B) is Extreme and a Distortion. Increasing the savings rate is necessary (the "only way") to improve the economy, but it is not sufficient. In addition, the economist never claims that the economy would improve *rapidly*.

(C) is a Distortion. Taxing consumption would encourage savings, but there's no suggestion that this would raise adequate funds for the government. Additionally the word *most* overstates the author's limited recommendation to *many* countries.

(E) is Extreme. Taxing income may not be as beneficial as taxing consumption for the countries in question, but that doesn't make it *detrimental* to *any* country.

17. (D) Principle (Identify/Weaken)

Step 1: Identify the Question Type
The question stem asks for a principle in the answer choices, making this an Identify the Principle question. However, the correct answer will also *undermine*, or weaken, the argument. Start by breaking down the argument and identifying what would weaken the conclusion. Then, broaden the language to turn that weakener into a general principle.

Step 2: Untangle the Stimulus

Meade concludes that it's acceptable for governments to ban risky behavior. This is supported by the idea that risky behavior not only can harm the perpetrator, but can also place emotional and financial costs on others.

Step 3: Make a Prediction

Meade bases a conclusion about government intervention in individuals' lives solely on the idea of protecting others' interests. However, the evidence never mentions what constitutes grounds for legal restrictions. Meade assumes that the government has the right to restrict any behavior that can present a risk to others, even those not directly involved in such behavior. A conflicting principle that suggests governments should *not* be restricting such activities would weaken Meade's reasoning.

Step 4: Evaluate the Answer Choices

(D) is correct. If preventing harm to others were *not* a good enough reason to ban certain actions, then Meade would not be justified in suggesting that governments outlaw risky behaviors solely for that reason.

(A) has no effect on Meade's argument. Whether endangering social ties is harmful or not, there's still no indication of what governments have the right to outlaw.

(B) is Out of Scope. Personal obligation does not indicate whether governments have the right to outlaw certain actions.

(C) is a Distortion. Notice that this choice indicates that costs to others is *necessary* for governments to be justified in restricting personal freedom, not *sufficient*, which the stimulus indicates. However, this choice is still *consistent* with Meade's argument, just not logically identical. So, saying that the government should step in *only* when others are in danger would either do nothing or support Meade's assertion that government should outlaw risky behavior.

(E) is an Irrelevant Comparison. Personal obligation, whether to others or oneself, does not indicate whether *governments* have the right to outlaw certain actions.

18. (C) Assumption (Necessary)

Step 1: Identify the Question Type

The question directly asks for an assumption. Because that assumption is "required by the argument," this is a Necessary Assumption question. Look for the gap between the evidence and the conclusion, and use the Denial Test if needed.

Step 2: Untangle the Stimulus

According to the author, Sanderson was acting immorally when he failed to tell his cousin about the rumored factory closing. This is because intentionally misleading someone is morally wrong, whether one misleads by actively lying or by withholding information.

Step 3: Make a Prediction

By the author's standards, withholding information is morally wrong if one has the *intention* of misleading someone else. Therefore, for it to logically follow that Sanderson was in the wrong, the author must assume he intended to mislead his cousin. Initially, it may seem like misdirection was Sanderson's intent, because the stimulus states that, by not divulging the rumor, Sanderson knew his cousin would believe the opposite of the rumor: that the factory would stay open. However, the key to this question is that the factory's closing is just a *rumor*, not a *fact*. The logic of this argument depends on whether or not Sanderson actually believed the rumor. If he did—as the author must assume—then he acted immorally. If he didn't, then the argument falls apart.

Step 4: Evaluate the Answer Choices

(C) is correct. Sanderson *must* believe the rumors about the factory closing. You can check this answer with the Denial Test. If Sanderson did *not* believe the rumors and thought the factory was going to stay open, then he wasn't trying to mislead his cousin; he was just protecting his cousin from gossip. In that case, the author's accusation of immorality wouldn't hold.

(A) is Out of Scope. The argument of morality is not based on whether the cousin *wants* to know. Even were Sanderson fulfilling his cousin's wishes by withholding information, Sanderson would still be deceiving and thus would still be acting immorally, based on the author's evidence.

(B) is irrelevant. Even if other people *did* spread the rumor to the cousin, *Sanderson* didn't, and therefore the author might still be correct in saying he acted immorally.

(D) is an irrelevant hypothetical. The author states that lying and failing to mention something with the intent to mislead are both morally wrong. Sanderson failed to mention the rumor, which, if he did so in order to deceive, would be enough to prove he acted immorally. The argument is not dependent on whether he *also* would have lied if pressed.

(E) is Out of Scope. While this explains why Sanderson failed to mention the rumor, the concept of personal gain as a motivating factor is not brought up in the author's discussion of morality.

19. (D) Principle (Apply/Inference)

Step 1: Identify the Question Type

The question directly indicates this is a Principle question, and it also suggests that the stimulus will contain multiple principles. Because the principles are found in the stimulus and not the answer choices, this is an Apply the Principle question. The correct answer will be a specific circumstance that conforms directly to the logic of those principles.

Step 2: Untangle the Stimulus

The author provides two principles for judges' rulings, each dependent on whether or not a precedent has been set. If there is a precedent, the rule is:

> **If**   *precedent doesn't contradict society's values*   →   *judges must follow the precedent*

If there is no precedent, the rule gives an "If, but only if" type construction:

> **If**   *judges can follow their own views*   ↔   *those views don't contradict public opinion*

Step 3: Make a Prediction

It cannot be predicted which principle will be invoked, or what the specific circumstance will be. However, the correct answer will certainly need to mention whether or not a precedent has been set as that is the first condition that determines whether to invoke the first or second principle. The situation in the correct answer will follow the logic of whichever principle is relevant.

Step 4: Evaluate the Answer Choices

(D) is correct. Judge Watanabe's case has no precedent, which means the second principle applies. There is no public opinion to contradict. So, by the second principle, Judge Watanabe is free to decide based on personal views.

(A) is a 180. There is no precedent, but Judge Swoboda follows personal views that conflict with public opinion. That violates the second principle.

(B) is a 180. There is no precedent, but Judge Valenzuela goes against public opinion in favor of his own beliefs. That violates the second principle.

(C) is a 180. Judge Wilson is ruling on a case involving a precedent set by Judge Levinsky. The precedent doesn't conflict with societal values; therefore, the first principle dictates that the precedent must be followed. Judge Wilson violates that by ruling otherwise.

(E) is a 180. Judge Balila rules contrary to multiple precedents, despite their conformity with societal values. That conflicts with the first principle.

20. (B) Inference

Step 1: Identify the Question Type

For this question, the stimulus is a set of statements used to support the hypothesis in the correct answer. The hypothesis will be an inference, directly backed up by the author's information. Make an inventory of the statements, connecting any Formal Logic and noting repeated or emphasized ideas.

Step 2: Untangle the Stimulus

The author mentions a study of volunteers who have amusia—a condition in which one has trouble distinguishing different melodies or remembering simple ones. Scientists played two different tones, but the volunteers were unable to tell them apart. However, when multiple tones were played in sequence, the volunteers were able to detect changes in timing.

Step 3: Make a Prediction

Based on the study, the volunteers have trouble recognizing different pitches, but are okay with timing. So if these people are having trouble distinguishing and remembering melodies, this suggests that amusia is more likely to involve pitch problems than timing issues.

Step 4: Evaluate the Answer Choices

(B) follows directly from the study, because identifying changes in pitch, and not timing, was a problem for the volunteers with amusia.

(A) is Extreme. While the volunteers had no difficulty with timing, nothing suggests their abilities were *heightened* beyond what's normal.

(C) is a 180. The stimulus doesn't indicate that the volunteers were able to tell pitches apart when they were part of a melody. The stimulus specifically says the volunteers were unable to discern a difference between the tones. The only thing they could discern were changes in *timing*. That's different than identifying changes in tone *based* on timing.

(D) is Extreme. While timing certainly seems to be less problematic than pitch, the study does not rule out either that both play *some* part or that other factors may also be required for the ability to tell melodies apart. To say it is pitch *alone*, therefore, goes beyond any information in the stimulus.

(E) is Out of Scope. There is no information about innate versus learned abilities.

21. (E) Principle (Identify/Strengthen)

Step 1: Identify the Question Type

The question explicitly asks for a Principle. Furthermore, that principle, found in the answer choices, will be used to *justify*, or strengthen, the given argument. Start by breaking the argument down, and then broaden the assumption into more general language.

Step 2: Untangle the Stimulus

The critic complains that contemporary novels are socially insignificant. This is because readers need to experience the characters' moral perspectives in order to enter the world of the novelist's mind. However, contemporary novelists are more concerned with including spectacles intended to compel readers to keep reading rather than to highlight injustices.

Step 3: Make a Prediction

The literary critic makes two jumps in this argument: one within the evidence and one from the evidence to the conclusion. The correct answer will likely focus on the latter. The critic suggests that by worrying about driving the plot, novelists don't let readers recognize any sense of injustice. The critic assumes that this means readers aren't experiencing any sense of moral perspective. Because such experience is needed to enter the world of the novelist's mind, the critic can logically conclude that readers are unable to enter the novelist's mind. However, the conclusion jumps one step too far, suggesting that therefore these novels are socially *insignificant*. That means the critic assumes a contemporary novel cannot be socially significant if it doesn't allow readers to enter the world of the novelist's mind. The correct answer will mimic that assumption in general language.

Step 4: Evaluate the Answer Choices

(E) conforms to the critic's assumption. If having social significance requires that readers enter the novelist's mind, then contemporary novels—which fail to satisfy that requirement—would be considered insignificant.

(A) is Out of Scope. The critic never mentions anything about the continued purpose of any art form over time. Nor is the critic concerned with what the *novelist* wants.

(B) is a Distortion. While the critic may agree with this principle, it doesn't strengthen the idea that novels that *don't* let readers empathize with characters are of little social significance.

(C) is a Distortion. According to the critic, the requirement for significance is that readers experience the *characters'* moral perspectives, not engage their own moral sensibilities.

(D) is also a Distortion. The argument is that without readers experiencing the point of view of the characters, contemporary novels are *insignificant*. If contemporary novels allowed readers to see those injustices, it's possible they still might not be significant. Experiencing the novel from the moral perspective of the characters is necessary, but not sufficient. So, this choice negates the logic of the argument without reversing.

22. (E) Flaw

Step 1: Identify the Question Type

The question describes the argument as "vulnerable to criticism," which is standard language for a Flaw question. Furthermore, the question stem already identifies the flaw: the author "fails to take [something] into account." The correct answer will identify an overlooked possibility.

Step 2: Untangle the Stimulus

The author concludes that recommendations meant to reduce the chances of infection from certain pathogens are counterproductive. This is backed up by a study showing that people who follow those recommendations get infected more often than do people who deviate from those recommendations.

Step 3: Make a Prediction

Whenever a study presents two groups of people, there is always an assumption that the groups are similar in all relevant respects other than the one being tested. In this case, the groups should differ only in whether they follow the recommendations or not. The author overlooks the possibility that there is something *else* different about the first group that makes them more likely to contract diseases from those pathogens.

Step 4: Evaluate the Answer Choices

(E) mentions a key distinction that could skew the results. If the people who carefully follow the recommendations are self-selected (because they are more susceptible to infection), then the study's comparison isn't valid. The recommendations might be keeping them from contracting diseases more often than they currently are.

(A) is Out of Scope. Even if pathogens could reproduce elsewhere, the argument is only about the recommendations for pathogens found in meat-based foods.

(B) is irrelevant. The argument is not about how many people follow the recommendations precisely, but whether those recommendations help. The stimulus specifically mentions that those in the relevant group in the study *do* follow precisely all the standard recommendations.

(C) is Out of Scope. It doesn't matter if the symptoms can be easily recognized. All that matters is whether people are becoming infected or not.

(D) is irrelevant. The author doesn't overlook the possibility that following the *appropriate* set of recommendations would prevent infection. That idea is consistent with the conclusion that the *current* standard recommendations are counterproductive. The author's contention is that the current set is counterproductive, so even if true, **(D)** would not weaken the argument because the author may likely believe there is an appropriate set of recommendations.

23. (C) Parallel Reasoning

Step 1: Identify the Question Type
The question asks for an argument "most similar" to the one in the stimulus, a sure sign of Parallel Reasoning. Use logic and structure to compare each answer to the stimulus.

Step 2: Untangle the Stimulus
By the evidence, Carriage Books has never earned a profit with a nonfiction book, yet it earned a profit on every book it published in the past year. The argument logically concludes that none of the books from the past year were nonfiction.

Step 3: Make a Prediction
This argument is based on solid Formal Logic. The Formal Logic in the evidence is the statement that no nonfiction book has ever turned a profit. That translates to:

If   *profit*   →   *~ nonfiction*

Additionally, the evidence states that every book published last year made a profit, which means every published book met the sufficient condition. The argument properly concludes that since the sufficient condition was triggered, the necessary condition must have followed; in other words, none of the published books were nonfiction. The correct answer will follow the same structure: one condition (earning a profit) excludes another (books being nonfiction). Because all events within one timeframe (last year) met the sufficient condition, all events met the necessary condition as well.

Step 4: Evaluate the Answer Choices
(C) matches the construct perfectly. One condition (receiving a bonus) excludes another (being in the marketing division).

If   *receive bonus*   →   *~ marketing division*

Because all systems analysts within one timeframe (last year) met the sufficient condition, the necessary one follows as well.

(A) is flawed and doesn't follow the logic pattern. The Formal Logic in the evidence translates to:

If   *represented by Mira Roberts*   →   *~ win important role in major movie*

To be parallel, the evidence needs to say the sufficient condition was met, but the fact that all of Mira Roberts's actors simply had an important acting role doesn't match—it doesn't specify whether that important role was in a major movie or not. Additionally, the conclusion is logically flawed to indicate that none of those actors worked in a movie at all last year. Even if representation by Ms. Roberts and important

roles in major movies are mutually exclusive, that doesn't mean that the actors could not have appeared in a movie last year at all (for example, in a minor role of a major movie or a major role in a minor movie).

(B) is logically proper. However, the evidence is not about a collection of events happening within a specific timeframe. This just mentions a single member of a larger group and assigns it the proper characteristic, which is not what the original argument does.

(D) is also logically proper. However, the evidence brings in a new concept, which is not what the original argument does. This argument starts with the right kind of logic:

If   *James Benson*   →   *~ business with Waldville*

However, the evidence then introduces the maintenance of business files rather than discussing events over a specific timeframe. That's not the same as the stimulus.

(E) is flawed. Even if Conway Flooring has a lot of customers in Woodridge (and must not have installed hardwood floors for them), it could still install hardwood flooring in other cities. The original argument did not have such an overlooked possibility.

24. (A) Inference

Step 1: Identify the Question Type
The question asks for something that "must be true" based on the given claims, indicating an Inference question. Such questions often feature Formal Logic, and this is no exception. Be sure to translate carefully and look out for answers that confuse sufficient and necessary conditions.

Step 2: Untangle the Stimulus
As expected, the two claims both provide Formal Logic. The first is about unemployed artists, who are all sympathetic to social justice:

If   *unemployed artist*   →   *sympathetic to social justice*

The second is about employed artists, none of whom are interested in fame:

If   *employed artist*   →   *~ interested in fame*

Step 3: Make a Prediction
Taking the contrapositive of the first statement allows the two claims to be combined. Notice that the negation of

unemployed is employed, and vice versa. The contrapositive of the first statement is:

$$\text{If} \quad \sim \begin{array}{l} \textbf{sympathetic} \\ \textbf{to social} \\ \textbf{justice} \end{array} \quad \rightarrow \quad \begin{array}{l} \textbf{employed} \\ \textbf{artist} \end{array}$$

According to the second claim, employed artists are not interested in personal fame. Thus, it can be concluded that artists who are not sympathetic to social justice are also uninterested in personal fame:

$$\text{If} \quad \sim \begin{array}{l} \textbf{sympathetic} \\ \textbf{to social} \\ \textbf{justice} \end{array} \rightarrow \begin{array}{l} \textbf{employed} \\ \textbf{artist} \end{array} \rightarrow \sim \begin{array}{l} \textbf{interested} \\ \textbf{in fame} \end{array}$$

By the contrapositive, any artist that *is* interested in personal fame *is* sympathetic to justice:

$$\text{If} \quad \begin{array}{l} \textbf{interested} \\ \textbf{in fame} \end{array} \rightarrow \begin{array}{l} \textbf{unemployed} \\ \textbf{artist} \end{array} \rightarrow \begin{array}{l} \textbf{sympathetic} \\ \textbf{to social} \\ \textbf{justice} \end{array}$$

The correct answer will likely be one of these combined deductions. The wrong answers will distort the Formal Logic or introduce concepts not mentioned in the stimulus.

Step 4: Evaluate the Answer Choices

(A) correctly combines the logic.

(B) is a Distortion. It starts from the necessary term of the second Formal Logic statement. However, there is no deduction that follows from those that are uninterested in fame.

(C) goes backward on the logic. By the second claim, employed artists are *not* interested in personal fame, but that doesn't mean all *un*employed artists *are* interested in fame. **(C)** negates without reversing.

(D), like **(C)**, goes backward on the logic, but this time it is the logic of the first claim. All unemployed artists are sympathetic to justice, but there could be employed artists who are also sympathetic to justice.

(E) distorts the logic of the second statement. Clearly, all artists must be either employed or unemployed. That means all artists must be either sympathetic to social justice (if employed) or *not* interested in fame (if unemployed).

25. (D) Parallel Flaw

Step 1: Identify the Question Type
The phrase "most similar" indicates Parallel Reasoning, but the reasoning is described as "flawed." That makes this a Parallel Flaw question. Find the flaw in the original argument

and look for an answer that commits the exact same error in its reasoning.

Step 2: Untangle the Stimulus
The author mentions that there are two possible suspects for a burglary. One suspect is cleared with a solid alibi, so the author concludes that the second suspect *must* be the burglar.

Step 3: Make a Prediction
The word *must* in the conclusion suggests an overlooked possibility. Sure enough, the author is considering only the two *current* suspects. The actual burglar may not be under suspicion yet. The correct answer will match this flawed logic: there are two possible outcomes; one is eliminated, so the author concludes the other must be the case, ignoring unmentioned alternatives.

Step 4: Evaluate the Answer Choices
(D) matches. There are two locations under consideration. Evansville is eliminated, so the author concludes Rivertown must be the winner. This ignores the possibility that Baxim may find another location.

(A) starts off well, offering two possibilities. However, the author states that one *is* being done and concludes that the other will *not* be done. That reverses how the original argument works. While this logic is indeed flawed (the zoo could still do both), it's not the same flaw. Additionally, the evidence that there is "good reason to believe" is weaker than the "ironclad alibi" in the stimulus.

(B) contains a flaw, confusing a sufficient condition (picking Watson from a lineup) for a necessary condition. However, the original argument did not contain this errant Formal Logic structure. This argument does not provide two possible outcomes for a situation and thus is not parallel.

(C) provides—loosely—two outcomes (take on debt or be unable to compete). However, it doesn't entirely eliminate one possibility, it just says one is worse than the other, and thus makes a recommendation—which is not parallel to anything in the original argument.

(E) is close. It does offer two possible outcomes (Slater and Gonzales). However, the candidates are described as the *only* ones viable. The original argument never suggested the two suspects were the *only* possible burglars. Plus, the evidence and conclusion here are qualified enough ("little chance" and *likely*) to allow for alternative outcomes, meaning this argument is not flawed.

Section IV: Logic Games
Game 1: Radio News Updates

Q#	Question Type	Correct	Difficulty
1	Acceptability	B	★
2	"If" / Must Be True	E	★
3	"If" / How Many	B	★
4	Must Be False (CANNOT Be True)	D	★
5	Completely Determine	A	★★★
6	"If" / Could Be True	E	★

Game 2: Realtor's Houses

Q#	Question Type	Correct	Difficulty
7	"If" / Must Be True	E	★
8	Completely Determine	C	★★
9	"If" / Must Be True	D	★★
10	Could Be True	A	★
11	"If" / Must Be True	E	★
12	Rule Substitution	B	★★★

Game 3: Sunken Ship Artifacts

Q#	Question Type	Correct	Difficulty
13	Acceptability	B	★
14	"If" / Minimum	A	★★
15	Must Be False (CANNOT Be True)	E	★★
16	"If" / Must Be True	A	★
17	How Many	C	★★★
18	Must Be False (CANNOT Be True)	C	★★

Game 4: Summit Company Workpieces

Q#	Question Type	Correct	Difficulty
19	Partial Acceptability	A	★
20	Must Be True	E	★★★
21	"If" / Must Be True	C	★★★
22	"If" / Must Be True	E	★★★★
23	Could Be True	E	★★★★

Game 1: Radio News Updates

Step 1: Overview

Situation: A radio station broadcasting daily news updates

Entities: Five reports—two general (international and national) and three local (sports, traffic, weather)

Action: Distribution/Sequencing Hybrid. No definitive action is mentioned until the first two rules. By the first rule, the reports will be divided into two segments (Distribution). By the second rule, the reports will be ordered by length within each segment (Sequencing). You could also view this as a Strict Sequencing game because all five reports are placed in one continuous order. The twist there would be that the first three slots would compose the first segment and slots four and five would compose the second segment. Regardless of how you categorize the game, your sketch should reflect the sequencing element and the two segments.

Limitations: Each of the five reports will be featured exactly once, three in the first segment and two in the second segment (Rule 1). Each report is categorized as either general interest or local interest, which will likely be important later. Furthermore, Rule 2 hints that reports will have different lengths, but no lengths are provided. Those will also likely be determined later.

Step 2: Sketch

Typically, you'll get enough information from the overview to generate your initial sketch. However, in this game, it's necessary to take a quick glance down at the rules too. The first two rules provide information that helps clarify the action(s) of the game. Start by listing the five reports by initial, separating them into their two categories, ideally using uppercase and lowercase letters to differentiate them. Then, set up two rows or columns—one for each segment. The first segment will have three ordered spaces and the second segment will have two. Add a label to indicate that the sequence goes from longest to shortest.

$$\begin{array}{cc} \underline{\text{Gen}} & \underline{\text{local}} \\ \text{IN} & \text{stw} \end{array}$$

Seg 1: ___ ___ ___

Seg 2: ___ ___

Long ————————— Short

Step 3: Rules

Rules 1 and 2 provide the action(s) and limitations for the game.

Rule 3 requires that each segment gets at least one local interest story (s, t, or w). That simply means that s, t, and w cannot all be in the same segment. It also means that if

international and national are in the same segment together it must be Segment 1.

NO stw

Rule 4 sets the national report as the longest of all. That means it will take up the first spot in one of the segments. Draw N next to the first slots. You can also draw ~N next to later slots in each row if that's helpful for you to track.

Rule 5 sets the sports report as the shortest of all. That means it will take up the last spot in one of the segments. Because the last slots are not aligned, draw ~s next to the first slots in each row and the second slot in segment 1 if that's helpful for you to track.

Rule 6 sets the international report as longer than the weather report. Because the reports are only ordered within each segment, this only matters if these reports are in the same segment. If they are, I must precede w:

If I & w together → I...w

This means that international can still be the shortest report in a segment and weather can still be the longest report in a segment, as long as they're in separate segments.

Step 4: Deductions

Despite so many rules and so few entities, this game offers no concrete deductions. There are no Blocks of Entities, Established Entities or Duplicates. Numbers are important, but don't allow for any absolute deductions. There are a couple of ways Limited Options could be set (where national goes or where sports goes), but neither one allows any other entity to be established with certainty. With three New-"If" questions and an Acceptability question, there will be plenty of sketches to help out with the two remaining non-New-"If" questions.

Your Master Sketch should reflect this general setup and contain these deductions:

$$\begin{array}{cc} \underline{\text{Gen}} & \underline{\text{local}} \\ \text{IN} & \text{stw} \end{array} \quad \text{NO stw}$$

Seg 1: ___ ___ ___
    ~s ~s ~N

N   ~N

Seg 2: ___ ___ ←s
    ~s ~N

I & w together → I...w

Long ————————— Short

Step 5: Questions

1. (B) Acceptability

As with any Acceptability question, go through the rules one at a time and eliminate answers that violate those rules.

Rules 1 and 2 merely set up the structure, so no answers violate them. **(E)** violates Rule 3 because the second segment has no local interest report (sports, traffic, and weather are all in the same segment). **(A)** violates Rule 4 because it orders national shorter than international. **(C)** violates Rule 5 because it orders sports longer than traffic. **(D)** violates Rule 6 because weather is ordered longer than international in the first segment. That leaves **(B)**—the only one that doesn't violate the rules—as the correct answer.

2. (E) "If" / Must Be True

For this question, traffic will be the last (i.e., shortest) report in the first segment. By Rule 5, sports is shorter than traffic, so sports must be in the second segment. As the shortest report of all, sports will be the last report of the second segment, making **(E)** the correct answer.

```
1: ___ ___  t

2: ___  s
```

For the record, the national report could still be in either segment, eliminating **(A)** and **(D)**. And either the international or weather report could be in the second segment, eliminating **(B)** and **(C)**.

3. (B) "If" / How Many

For this question, national will be the first report of the second segment. The second report of that segment will have to be a local interest report (Rule 3). So, the international report must be in the first segment.

```
1: ___ ___ ___  l

2:  N   s/t/w
```

The question asks how many reports could be first (i.e., longest) in the first segment. It can't be national, which is in the second segment here, and it can't be sports, which is the shortest report of all. That leaves three reports: international, traffic, and weather. However, because the international report is already in the first segment, the weather report would be shorter if it were in the first segment (Rule 6). That means the international and the traffic reports are the only two that could be first in the first segment, like so:

```
1:  l   t   s        t   l   s
            or
2:  N   w            N   w
```

That makes **(B)** the correct answer.

4. (D) Must Be False (CANNOT Be True)

The correct answer to this question must be false. The remaining four answers will all be possible.

The first sketch for the previous question shows that international could be the first report of the first segment, national could be the first report of the second segment, and weather could be the last report of the second segment. That eliminates **(A)**, **(C)**, and **(E)**. National could be the first report of either segment. That eliminates **(B)**.

If weather were the first report of the first segment, it would be the longest report of the segment. However, national and international have to be longer (Rules 4 and 6), so they would both have to be in the second segment. However, that would leave the second segment without a local interest report, violating Rule 3. That cannot happen, making **(D)** the correct answer.

5. (A) Completely Determine

The correct answer to this question will be the only one that allows every report to be placed with certainty. If an answer leaves anything open-ended, it will be eliminated.

Testing **(A)**, if international is the last report of the first segment, then it is also the shortest report of that segment. Neither weather nor sports can be longer than international (Rules 5 and 6), so they must both be in the second segment, sports being shorter (i.e., later) than weather. That fills up the second segment. That leaves national and traffic to fill out the first segment, with national being first (i.e., longest) to satisfy Rule 4.

```
1:  N   t   l

2:  w   s
```

Because the order of the entire update is determined, that makes **(A)** the correct answer. For the record: Placing national in either segment does nothing to determine where sports goes for certain. Similarly, placing sports in either segment does nothing to determine where national goes for certain. That eliminates **(B)**, **(C)**, and **(D)**. If weather was the last report of the first segment, sports would have to be the last report of the second segment. However, any of the remaining reports could lead off the second segment. With so much undetermined, that eliminates **(E)**.

6. (E) "If" / Could Be True

For this question, traffic will be the first (i.e., longest) report of the first segment. National cannot be shorter than traffic (Rule 4), so national must be the first report of the second segment. The second segment still needs a local interest report (Rule 3), so the second report of that segment will be sports or weather. If it were sports, then international and weather, in that order (Rule 6), would round out the first segment. If it were weather, then sports would be the final (i.e., shortest) report of the first segment (Rule 5), with international taking up the remaining spot in the middle of the first segment.

1: _t_ _I_ _w_   _t_ _I_ _s_

or

2: _N_ _s_   _N_ _w_

That makes **(E)** the only answer possible (in the second outcome), and thus the correct answer.

Game 2: Realtor's Houses

Step 1: Overview
Situation: A realtor showing houses to a client

Entities: Five houses (designated by neighborhood—Quarry, Riverton, Shelburne, Townsend, Valencia)

Action: Strict Sequencing. Determine the order in which the houses are shown. Because the rules mention specific positions and use restrictive phrases such as "immediately before," this is Strict Sequencing.

Limitations: One house is shown from each neighborhood, each exactly once. That makes this standard one-to-one Sequencing.

Step 2: Sketch
List the houses' neighborhoods by initial and set up five numbered spaces to determine the order:

$$Q\ R\ S\ T\ V$$

$$\underline{\quad}\ \underline{\quad}\ \underline{\quad}\ \underline{\quad}\ \underline{\quad}$$
$$1\quad 2\quad 3\quad 4\quad 5$$

Step 3: Rules
Rule 1 limits the house in Riverton to two spaces: first or second. Draw R with an arrow to those two slots.

Rule 2 limits the house in Townsend to two spaces: first or fifth. Draw T with an arrow to those two slots.

Rule 3 limits the third space to two houses: the one in Quarry or the one in Valencia. Add Q/V to the third space in the sketch.

Rule 4 prevents the houses in Quarry and Shelburne from being shown consecutively. Draw No QS and No SQ to the side.

Step 4: Deductions
There are no Blocks of Entities, Duplications, or Established Entities that yield any definitive deductions. However, the first three rules each provide a potential source for Limited Options.

If you opt not to use Limited Options, your Master Sketch would look something like this:

However, if you do examine the first three rules for Limited Options possibilities, here's what you'll find:

Rule 3 is the least valuable. Placing V third would lead to no further deductions, and placing Q third would prevent S from being second or fourth, but that's hardly a lot to work with.

Either Rule 1 or Rule 2 would be valuable for Limited Options. Even better is realizing that, by combining those rules, there are only three pairs of outcomes for R and T: R first and T fifth; R second and T first; or R second and T fifth. Each of these outcomes would fill in at least 40 percent of the sketch, so it would be worth the time considering *three* options.

Option I: R first and T fifth. That leaves three consecutive spaces in between. By Rule 4, Q and S cannot be consecutive. To split them up, one must be shown second and the other one fourth—in either order. That leaves V to be third.

$$\text{I)}\quad \underline{R}\ \underline{Q/S}\ \underline{V}\ \underline{S/Q}\ \underline{T}$$
$$\quad\quad 1\quad 2\quad 3\quad 4\quad 5$$

Option II: R second and T first. That leaves the last three spaces open. Again, Q and S cannot be consecutive. To split them up, Q and S must be shown third and fifth, leaving V to be shown fourth. S cannot be third (Rule 3), so Q would be third and S fifth.

$$\text{II)}\quad \underline{T}\ \underline{R}\ \underline{Q}\ \underline{V}\ \underline{S}$$
$$\quad\quad 1\quad 2\quad 3\quad 4\quad 5$$

Option III: R second and T fifth. That leaves two consecutive spaces in between. By Rule 4, Q and S cannot be consecutive, so one of them must shown first. By Rule 3, only Q or V can be third. Any of the remaining neighborhoods could be fourth.

$$\text{III)}\quad \underline{Q/S}\ \underline{R}\ \underline{Q/V}\ \underline{\quad}\ \underline{T}$$
$$\quad\quad 1\quad 2\quad 3\quad 4\quad 5$$

With three New-"If" questions and only one standard Non-"If" question, this set could still be handled deftly without Limited Options. However, it's always worth taking a moment to consider them and see how valuable they could be.

Step 5: Questions

7. (E) "If" / Must Be True
For this question, the house in Quarry is shown fourth. In that case, the house in Valencia must be shown third (Rule 3). That makes **(E)** the correct answer.

$$\underline{\quad}\ \underline{\quad}\ \underline{V}\ \underline{Q}\ \underline{\quad}$$
$$1\quad 2\quad 3\quad 4\quad 5$$

For the record, the Limited Options show how the remaining answers could be false. In Option I, the house in Quarry could be fourth, with the house in Riverton first and the house in

Townsend fifth. That eliminates **(B)** and **(D)**. In Option III, the house in Quarry could be fourth, with the house in Riverton second and the house in Shelburne first. That eliminates **(A)** and **(C)**.

8. (C) Completely Determine

The correct answer will be the one that allows the entire order of the houses to be determined with no uncertainty. The remaining answers will each leave some part of the order open-ended.

If the house in Quarry is shown third, that means both Options II and III are still in play, thus the house in Townsend could still be shown first or fifth. There are still multiple possible outcomes, which eliminates **(A)**.

If the house in Riverton is shown first, that places you squarely in Option I. However, the houses in Quarry and Shelburne would still have to be split between second and fourth (by rule 4), so that order cannot be determined. That eliminates **(B)**.

If the house in Shelburne is shown second, that places you definitively in Option I again. It also nails down the location of Shelburne and Quarry, and thus the entire order is determined, making **(C)** the correct answer. Even if you didn't have the Limited Options, placing the house in Shelburne second would mean that the house in Riverton would have to be first (Rule 1). That would make the house in Townsend fifth (Rule 2). Finally, the house in Quarry cannot be next to one in Shelburne (Rule 4), so Quarry would be fourth, leaving Valencia third. So, either approach would completely determine the order.

For the record: If the house in Townsend is shown fifth, the house in Riverton could still be shown first or second, as in Options I and III. That eliminates **(D)**.

If the house in Valencia is shown fourth, the house in Quarry would be shown third (Rule 4). However, the house in Townsend could still be shown first or fifth, as shown in Options II and III. That eliminates **(E)**.

9. (D) "If" / Must Be True

For this question, the house in Shelburne will be shown before the one in Quarry. That means Shelburne cannot be shown fifth. It also cannot be shown fourth because that would place Quarry next to it in fifth, violating Rule 4. It cannot be shown third (Rule 3), so it must be shown first or second. If it were shown first, the houses in Riverton and Townsend would be shown second and fifth, respectively (Rules 1 and 2). That would leave the houses in Quarry and Valencia to be shown third and fourth, in either order.

$$\frac{S}{1} \quad \frac{R}{2} \quad \frac{Q/V}{3} \quad \frac{V/Q}{4} \quad \frac{T}{5}$$

If the house in Shelburne were shown second, the house in Riverton would be shown first (Rule 1), causing the house in Townsend to be shown fifth (Rule 2). The houses in Shelburne and Quarry cannot be consecutive (Rule 4), so Quarry would be fourth, leaving Valencia to be third.

$$\frac{R}{1} \quad \frac{S}{2} \quad \frac{V}{3} \quad \frac{Q}{4} \quad \frac{T}{5}$$

In either case, Townsend must be fifth, making **(D)** the correct answer. The remaining answers are all possible, but need not be true. [Note: Limited Options help greatly here. The house in Shelburne could only be shown before the house in Quarry in Options I and III. In both cases, the house in Townsend must be shown fifth.]

10. (A) Could Be True

The correct answer will be the one answer that is possible. The remaining answers will all be definitely false.

If the house in Quarry is shown first, then the houses in Riverton and Townsend would be shown second and fifth, respectively (Rules 1 and 2). The house in Valencia would be shown third (Rule 4), leaving the house in Shelburne to be shown fourth. That does not violate any of the rules, making **(A)** the correct answer.

$$\frac{Q}{1} \quad \frac{R}{2} \quad \frac{V}{3} \quad \frac{S}{4} \quad \frac{T}{5}$$

A quick consultation of the Limited Options also makes quick work of this question. Scanning the three options, you see Quarry is a possibility as the first neighborhood in Option III, so that immediately makes **(A)** the right answer.

For the record, the Limited Options also show why all of the remaining answers must be false. The fifth house shown could only be in Shelburne or Townsend. That eliminates **(B)** and **(E)**. Furthermore, the house in Valencia is neither first nor second in any of the options, which eliminates **(C)** and **(D)**.

11. (E) "If" / Must Be True

For this question, the house in Valencia is shown third. The houses in Quarry and Shelburne cannot be shown consecutively, so one must be shown before Valencia and the other one after.

$$\frac{}{1} \quad \frac{}{2} \quad \frac{V}{3} \quad \frac{}{4} \quad \frac{}{5}$$
$$\quad\; Q/S \qquad\qquad S/Q$$

That means the houses in Riverton and Townsend must also be split. Riverton cannot be fourth or fifth (Rule 1), so it will be before Valencia. That means Townsend will be after Valencia. Townsend cannot be fourth (Rule 2), so it will be fifth.

$$\frac{\quad}{1} \;\; \frac{\quad}{2} \;\; \frac{V}{3} \;\; \frac{S/Q}{4} \;\; \frac{T}{5}$$
R; Q/S

That makes **(E)** the correct answer. The fourth house could still be in either Quarry or Shelby; therefore, **(A)** and **(D)** each *could* be true, but need not be. In addition, Riverton could still be first, which means neither **(B)** nor **(C)** have to be true. Again, the Limited Options would also make short work of this question: If the house in Valencia is shown third, that means only Options I and III are in play. The only single entity definitively placed in the same slot in both of those options is that the house in Townsend is shown fifth, which is correct answer **(E)**.

12. (B) Rule Substitution

For this question, Rule 1 will be removed and replaced by one of the answer choices. The correct answer must reestablish the restriction of the original rule (the house in Riverton must be shown first or second) without adding any new restrictions that were not already in place.

Blocking Riverton from being fourth does not prevent it from being fifth, which was not allowed by the original rule. That eliminates **(A)**.

The original rules did not specifically say that Riverton had to precede Valencia. However, if that were true, then Riverton could not be fifth. It also could not be third (Rule 3). If it were fourth, this rule would make Valencia fifth. That would make Townsend first, placing Quarry and Shelburne consecutive. That's unacceptable (Rule 4). So, a rule placing Riverton before Valencia would force Riverton to be first or second—replicating the original rule. Furthermore, Riverton always had to precede Valencia. By the original rules, if Valencia were before Riverton, Riverton would have been second, making Valencia first. Townsend would have been fifth, forcing Quarry and Shelburne to be consecutive. Again, that's unacceptable. So, placing Riverton before Valencia resets the original restrictions without adding any new ones. That makes **(B)** the correct answer.

For the record: Valencia was always limited to third or fourth, but that wouldn't restrict Riverton, which the original rule did. That eliminates **(C)**.

Quarry never had to be consecutive with Riverton. That would be an unwarranted new restriction, which eliminates **(D)**.

Limiting what happens if Townsend is *not* fifth will not be enough. That still allows Riverton to be unrestricted if Townsend *is* fifth. That eliminates **(E)**.

Game 3: Sunken Ship Artifacts

Step 1: Overview

Situation: Artifacts recovered from a sunken ship

Entities: Five artifacts (V, W, X, Y, Z); three countries (Iceland, Norway, Sweden)

Action: Distribution. Determine the country from which each artifact originated. Each artifact came from one and only one of the three countries.

Limitations: By definition, an artifact can only originate from one country. However, there are no limits set on the countries. Each country can be the origin of any number of artifacts—even none.

Step 2: Sketch

Each artifact will be assigned to its country of origin. So, list the artifacts at the top and set up a table with a column (or row, if preferred) for each country. Because no information is given about the number of artifacts from each country, leave the columns empty for now.

Step 3: Rules

Rule 1 creates a Block of Entities: W and Y will be from the same country.

Rule 2 limits X to two countries: Norway or Sweden. That means it cannot come from Iceland. Add "No X" under Iceland. Alternately, you can make a shorthand note to the side (X = Nor or Swe) or draw an X beneath the sketch with arrows pointing to Norway and Sweden.

Rule 3 sets up a numeric restriction: More artifacts come from Iceland than from Norway. Make a shorthand note of this to the side or put the greater than sign right in the top of the column labels:

At the very least, one artifact must originate in Iceland. Add one slot in that column. Note: Iceland could be the origin of just that one artifact, as long as Norway is the origin of none.

Rule 4 provides some Formal Logic. If V is from Iceland, Z is from Sweden. Jot this down with its contrapositive. You can change the negatives of the contrapositive into positives

given the limited number of countries. So, for example, not being from Sweden is the same as being from Iceland or Norway:

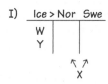

Step 4: Deductions

There's one major Block of Entities: W and Y. If they were both from Iceland, then Norway could still be the origin of an artifact, and Sweden is unlimited for any remaining artifacts. Similarly, if W and Y were both from Sweden, there would still be room for more there as long as at least one artifact comes from Iceland. However, by Rule 3, if W and Y were from Norway, then Iceland would have to be the origin of three artifacts: V, X, and Z—which would violate Rules 2 and 4. Therefore, W and Y cannot be from Norway.

This opens up the possibility of Limited Options. In the first option, W and Y would be from Iceland. In that case, X could still be from Norway or Sweden, and V and Z could each be from any of the countries.

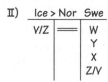

In the second option, W and Y would be from Sweden. If X were from Norway, then there would have to be two artifacts from Iceland (Rule 3). However, they would have to be V and Z, which would violate Rule 4. So, X cannot be from Norway, meaning it must be from Sweden (Rule 2). That leaves V and Z. Neither one could be from Norway because that would leave just one artifact for Iceland (the other one of V and Z), violating Rule 3. Something must come from Iceland (Rule 3), but V and Z cannot both be from Iceland (Rule 4). So, only one of them is from Iceland (either one), and the other must come from Sweden.

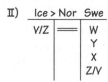

Limited Options could also be set up from the beginning depending on where X comes from. (The option with X from Norway forces W and Y to be from Iceland.) As always, Limited

Options are not necessary to complete this game. However, they can be beneficial here.

13. (B) Acceptability

The correct answer here will be acceptable—the one answer that doesn't violate any rules. Go through the rules one at a time, and eliminate the four answers that violate those rules.

(A) violates Rule 1 by having W and Y originate in different countries. **(E)** violates Rule 2 by having X originate in Iceland. **(C)** violates Rule 3 by having an equal number of artifacts from Iceland and Norway. **(D)** violates Rule 4 by having V originate in Iceland, but Z in Norway, not Sweden. That leaves **(B)** as the correct answer.

14. (A) "If" / Minimum

For this question, Y and Z originate in Iceland, so this must be Option I because Y is only from Iceland in Option I. With Y from Iceland, W must originate there, too (Rule 1). The contrapositive of Rule 4 says that if Z is from Norway or Iceland (as it is here), then V must be from Norway or Sweden. The question asks for the minimum number of artifacts that can come from Sweden, so V should be assigned to Norway to minimize Sweden's number of artifacts. Likewise, X can originate in Sweden or Norway, but to keep Sweden's number minimal, X should be assigned to Norway. That leaves Sweden empty:

Ice	Nor	Swe
W	X	
Y	V	
Z		

That means Sweden can have the absolute minimum: zero artifacts. That makes **(A)** the correct answer.

15. (E) Must Be False (CANNOT Be True)

The correct answer to this question must be false no matter what. The remaining four answers could be true. By the major deduction, W and Y cannot be from Norway. That makes **(E)** the correct answer.

For the record: In the sketch for the previous question, V can be from Norway with X, which eliminates **(A)**. Also, in that sketch, W and Z are from Iceland, which eliminates **(C)**. If you set up Limited Options based on W and Y, a little re-sketching shows that V and Y can be from Iceland in Option I:

Ice	Nor	Swe
W		Z
Y		
V	↖ ↗	
	X	

That eliminates **(B)**.

Option II shows that W and Z could both be from Sweden. That eliminates **(D)**. If you didn't set up Limited Options, you could temporarily skip this question and move to the next. The next question sets up the sketch from Option II.

16. (A) "If" / Must Be True

For this question, W and X originate in Sweden. If you set up Limited Options, this is Option II. If not, this question provides the source of that option. By the logic described for Option II in the Deductions section, Norway would be empty, making **(A)** the correct answer.

II)	Ice > Nor	Swe
V/Z	===	W
		Y
		X
		Z/V

Something always has to originate in Iceland, which eliminates **(B)**. The remaining answers are all possible, but need not be true.

17. (C) How Many

The answer to this question will be the number of entities, any of which could originate in Norway—but not necessarily all at once. By Deduction 1, W and Y cannot. The sketch from the second question of the set shows that V and X can both originate in Norway. That leaves Z. A quick test shows that this is possible. If Z is from Norway, then there must be at least two artifacts from Iceland (Rule 3). V could not be from Iceland (Rule 4), nor could X (Rule 2). That would leave W and Y. Then, V and X could both be from Sweden.

Ice	Nor	Swe
W	Z	V
Y		X

That means V, X, and Z could each originate in Norway—and only those three. That makes **(C)** the correct answer.

18. (C) Must Be False (CANNOT Be True)

The correct answer to this question must be false. That means the four wrong answers will all be possible.

If V were the only artifact from Sweden, then X would be from Norway (Rule 2). The remaining artifacts (W, Y, and Z) could all be from Iceland. This is acceptable, which eliminates **(A)**. This is a variation on Option I.

If V and Z were the only artifacts from Sweden, then X would be from Norway (Rule 2). The remaining artifacts (W and Y) would be from Iceland. This is acceptable, which eliminates **(B)**. This is a variation on Option I.

If W and Y were the only artifacts from Sweden, then X would be from Norway (Rule 2). Iceland would need two artifacts (Rule 3), but that would leave V and Z for Iceland—violating Rule 4. This is impossible, making **(C)** the correct answer. Note that neither of the two options shows W and Y as the only artifacts from Sweden. For the record:

If X and Z were the only artifacts from Sweden, then the remaining artifacts (V, W, and Y) could all be from Iceland, or W and Y could be from Iceland with V from Norway. Either way is acceptable in Option I, which eliminates **(D)**. In addition, if V, W, X, and Y were the only artifacts from Sweden, then Z would be from Iceland. This is also acceptable, as shown in Option II, which eliminates **(E)**.

Game 4: Summit Company Workpieces

Step 1: Overview

Situation: Employees of Summit Company working on a set of workpieces

Entities: Four employees (J, K, L, M); four days (Monday, Tuesday, Wednesday, Thursday); four unnamed workpieces

Action: Strict Sequencing. Determine the order in which each workpiece is transferred from employee to employee over a four-day workweek. Essentially, the employees J, K, L, and M will be ordered on each of the four days, so this is just Sequencing … quadrupled! Some may identify this as a Hybrid game with a Matching component (i.e., match the employees to the workpieces) or even a variation on a rare Process game (i.e., work out how the original assignments change over the course of the week). Ultimately, an exact label is not as important as understanding what you need to develop an effective sketch.

Limitations: On Monday, each employee will be assigned to one of the four workpieces. Each day after that, each employee will be reassigned to a workpiece other than the one that employee was assigned the previous day. In other words, no employee can be assigned to the same workpiece two days in a row. This is an important rule to save for later. Write a shorthand note to the side (e.g., "No employee consecutive") or draw the four restricted blocks ("No JJ," "No KK," "No LL," "No MM").

Step 2: Sketch

The schedule for this game is built over four days, Monday through Thursday. That should be at the top of the sketch, calendar style. For each day, there needs to be four spaces to determine the employee assigned to each workpiece. It's important to note that the workpieces are never referred to by name, so they are interchangeable. In other words, the order of employees is not unique to any particular workpiece. So, don't bother giving the workpieces names. Just have four unlabeled rows, each of which could represent any one of the workpieces.

Furthermore, you can start by assigning each employee to any one workpiece on Monday. It doesn't matter which ones. Think of them merely as "one workpiece, another one, another one, and another one."

	Mo	Tu	We	Th
	J	___	___	___
	K	___	___	___
	L	___	___	___
	M	___	___	___

Step 3: Rules

Rules 1, 2, and 3 set up three restricted blocks: No workpiece can ever transfer from J to M, from K to J, or from L to J. You can draw these rules to the side ("No JM," "No KJ," "No LJ"), or use some deductions to enter this information directly into the sketch.

It's important to note that these are one-way restrictions. In other words, a workpiece cannot transfer from J to M, but it could still transfer from M to J.

Step 4: Deductions

When a rule states that something *cannot* happen, always consider what *can* happen. In this case, by Rule 1, no workpiece can transfer from J to M, and J cannot work on the same workpiece two days in a row (Overview). That means the workpiece J works on one day can only be transferred to K or L the next day. In the sketch, add "K/L" to the space on Tuesday for the workpiece to which J was assigned on Monday.

Similarly, by Rule 2, no workpiece can transfer from K to J, and K cannot work on the same workpiece two days in a row. So, the workpiece K works on one day can only be transferred to L or M the next day. By Rule 3, no workpiece can transfer from L to J, and L cannot work on the same workpiece two days in a row. So, the workpiece L works on one day can only be transferred to K or M the next day. Add "L/M" and "K/M" to the spaces on Tuesday for the workpieces to which K and L, respectively, were assigned on Monday.

Furthermore, note that J is restricted in some way by each rule of the game. As noted previously, any piece J works on can only be transferred to K or L. However, more telling, J can never be assigned to a workpiece to which K or L was just assigned. And J can never work on the same piece two days in a row. That means the only employee that can transfer a workpiece to J is M. Because of that, and because J has to work on some workpiece every day, there is a big deduction to note:

Whatever workpiece M is assigned to one day must be transferred to J the following day.

So, add J to the space on Tuesday for the workpiece to which M is assigned on Monday. On Wednesday, that same workpiece must then transfer to either K or L, because J cannot transfer to M (Rule 1) or work on the same piece two days in a row (Overview).

	Mo	Tu	We	Th
	J	K/L	___	___
	K	L/M	___	___
	L	K/M	___	___
	M	J	K/L	___

That leaves a lot of uncertainty. However, this game will be much more about recognizing possible sequences for individual workpieces than about filling in the entire sketch.

Step 5: Questions

19. (A) Partial Acceptability

The correct answer to this question will list a possible complete set of transfers from one day to the next. As with any standard Acceptability question, use the rules to eliminate answers that are unacceptable. The one answer that does not violate any rules will be the correct answer.

By Rule 1, there can never be a transfer from J to M. That eliminates **(E)**. By Rule 2, there can never be a transfer from K to J. That eliminates **(D)**. By Rule 3, there can never be a transfer from L to J. That eliminates **(C)**. There are no more rules, but there are restrictions from the overview. According to the overview, each employee must work on one workpiece each day. That eliminates **(B)**, in which two workpieces are transferred to K (from J and L) and no workpiece is transferred to L. That leaves **(A)** as the correct answer.

20. (E) Must Be True

The correct answer to this question will list a transfer that must occur on some day after Monday. The remaining four may be possible, but need not occur. From the big deduction, M must always transfer to J, making **(E)** the correct answer. For the record:

J *can* transfer to either K or L, but neither one *must* occur. That eliminates **(A)** and **(B)**. K can transfer to L, but can also transfer to M. That eliminates **(C)**. And L can transfer to M, but can also transfer to K. That eliminates **(D)**.

21. (C) "If" / Must Be True

For this question, one workpiece will be transferred back and forth between the same two employees for the entire workweek. The correct answer will list the only two employees who could do this. The remaining four answers will list employees who would have to transfer to a third employee at some point.

J can transfer a workpiece to K or L, but neither one could transfer it back to J the next day (Rules 2 and 3). That eliminates **(A)** and **(B)**.

K can transfer a workpiece to L, and L can transfer it back to K the next day, followed by one last transfer from K to L. This is acceptable, and they are the only pair that can accomplish this. That makes **(C)** the correct answer.

For the record: either K or L could transfer a workpiece to M, but M would have to transfer that piece to J the following day based on the major deduction. That eliminates **(D)** and **(E)**.

22. (E) "If" / Must Be True

For this question, L works on a piece on Tuesday and Thursday. Either J or K could have worked on that piece on Monday and transferred it to L on Tuesday. L could then transfer the piece to either K or M on Wednesday, but only K would be able to transfer it back to L on Thursday. Therefore, that piece must go to K on Wednesday.

Mo	Tu	We	Th
J/K	L	K	L

The question asks for something that must be true of this workpiece only. Because K works on it on Wednesday, **(E)** is the correct answer. **(A)** and **(B)** could be true, but need not be, while **(C)** and **(D)** must be false.

23. (E) Could Be True

The correct answer will list a possible outcome for Tuesday. The remaining four answers will list something that cannot happen.

If J transfers to K and K transfers to M, then M still has to transfer to J (Deduction 1). That leaves L to work on the same workpiece two days in a row. That's not allowed, which eliminates **(A)**.

Mo	Tu	We	Th
J	K		
K	M		
L	L		
M	J		

If J transfers to L and L transfers to M, then M still has to transfer to J. That leaves K to work on the same workpiece two days in a row. That's not allowed, which eliminates **(B)**.

Mo	Tu	We	Th
J	L		
K	K		
L	M		
M	J		

J cannot transfer to M (Rule 1). That eliminates **(C)**.

If K transfers to L and L transfers to K, then M still has to transfer to J. That leaves J to transfer the final workpiece to M, which violates Rule 1. That eliminates **(D)**.

Mo	Tu	We	Th
J	M		
K	L		
L	K		
M	J		

If K transfers to L and L transfers to M, then M still transfers to J, leaving the last workpiece to transfer from J to K. That is acceptable, making **(E)** the correct answer.

Mo	Tu	We	Th
J	K	__	__
K	L	__	__
L	M	__	__
M	J	__	__

PrepTest 73

The Inside Story

PrepTest 73 was administered in September 2014. It challenged 30,943 test takers. What made this test so hard? Here's a breakdown of what Kaplan students who were surveyed after taking the official exam considered PrepTest 73's most difficult section.

Hardest PrepTest 73 Section as Reported by Test Takers

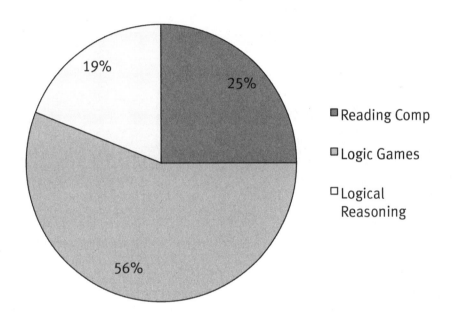

Based on these results, you might think that studying Logic Games is the key to LSAT success. Well, Logic Games is important, but test takers' perceptions don't tell the whole story. For that, you need to consider students' actual performance. The following chart shows the average number of students to miss each question in each of PrepTest 73's different sections.

Percentage Incorrect by PrepTest 73 Section Type

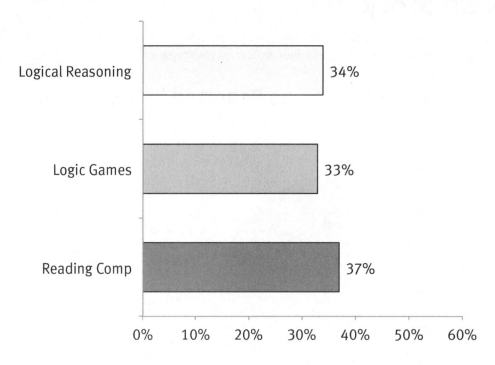

Actual student performance tells quite a different story. On average, students were almost equally likely to miss questions in all three of the different section types, and on PrepTest 73, Reading Comprehension and Logical Reasoning were somewhat higher than Logic Games in actual difficulty.

Maybe students overestimate the difficulty of the Logic Games section because it's so unusual, or maybe it's because a really hard Logic Game is so easy to remember after the test. But the truth is that the testmaker places hard questions throughout the test. Here were the locations of the 10 hardest (most missed) questions in the exam.

KAPLAN

Location of 10 Most Difficult Questions in PrepTest 73

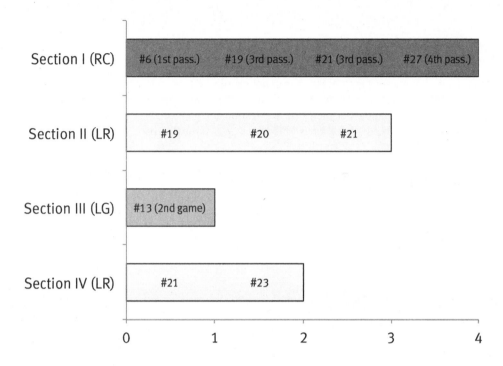

The takeaway from this data is that, to maximize your potential on the LSAT, you need to take a comprehensive approach. Test yourself rigorously, and review your performance on every section of the test. Kaplan's LSAT explanations provide the expertise and insight you need to fully understand your results. The explanations are written and edited by a team of LSAT experts, who have helped thousands of students improve their scores. Kaplan always provides data-driven analysis of the test, ranking the difficulty of every question based on actual student performance. The 10 hardest questions on every test are highlighted with a 4-star difficulty rating, the highest we give. The analysis breaks down the remaining questions into 1-, 2-, and 3-star ratings so that you can compare your performance to thousands of other test takers on all LSAC material.

Don't settle for wondering whether a question was really as hard as it seemed to you. Analyze the test with real data, and learn the secrets and strategies that help top scorers master the LSAT challenge.

7 Can't–Miss Features of PrepTest 73

- Really? No Strict Sequencing games? After a streak of 19 released tests with a Strict Sequencing game, PT 73 did not not have one. (Although, it did have a Loose Sequencing game.)
- After no Method of Argument questions on the previous test, PT 73 had three of them—the most since September 2009 (PT 58).
- PrepTest 73 did not contain a single Point at Issue question—the first time that question type was entirely missing since December 2010 (PT 62).
- The Reading Comprehension section tied for the fewest number of Inference questions ever on a single test with seven. The other time there were so few was December '01 (PT 36).
- I've Got You Babe! One section has eight consecutive answers that spell out B-A-B-E-B-A-B-E.
- Question 24 of the second Logical Reasoning section says " ... a democracy cannot thrive without an electorate that is knowledgeable about important political issues. ..." Well, although participation may not necessarily mean knowledgeable, Scotland did see 86% turnout for its independence referendum just 11 days prior to the administration of PT 73.

- Test takers preparing for this test in September 2014 got some good advice from Taylor Swift in the weeks leading up to the exam. If you encounter a tough question, passage, or game, just "Shake It Off"—which was the #1 song for the first two weeks of the month.

PrepTest 73 in Context

As much fun as it is to find out what makes a PrepTest unique or noteworthy, it's even more important to know just how representative it is of other LSAT administrations (and, thus, how likely it is to be representative of the exam you will face on Test Day). The following charts compare the numbers of each kind of question and game on PrepTest 73 to the average numbers seen on all officially released LSATs administered over the past five years (from 2012 through 2016).

Number of LR Questions by Type: PrepTest 73 vs. 2012–2016 Average

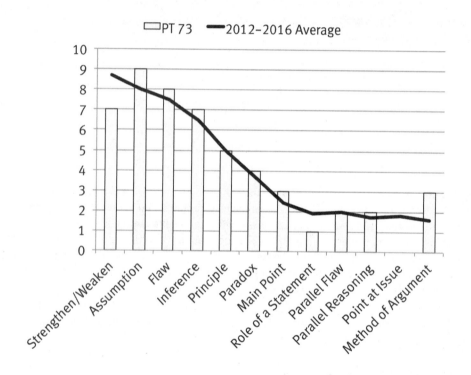

Number of LG Games by Type: PrepTest 73 vs. 2012–2016 Average

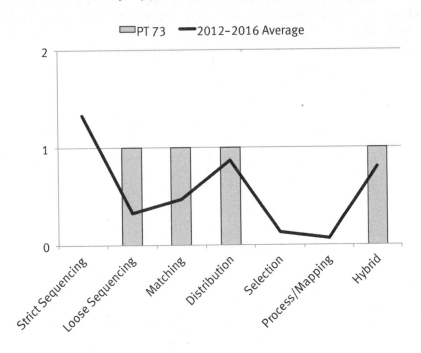

Number of RC Questions by Type: PrepTest 73 vs. 2012–2016 Average

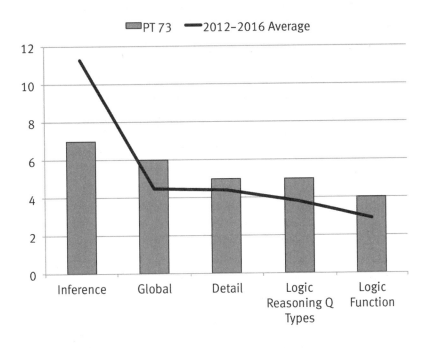

There isn't usually a huge difference in the distribution of questions from LSAT to LSAT, but if this test seems harder (or easier) to you than another you've taken, compare the number of questions of the types on which you, personally, are strongest and weakest. And then, explore within each section to see if your best or worst question types came earlier or later.

Students in Kaplan's comprehensive LSAT courses have access to every released LSAT, and to an online Qbank with thousands of officially released questions, games, and passages. If you are studying on your own, you have to do a bit more work to identify your strengths and your areas of opportunity. Quantitative analysis (like that in the previous charts) is an important tool for understanding how the test is constructed, and how you are performing on it.

KAPLAN

Section I: Reading Comprehension
Passage 1: Natural Selection

Q#	Question Type	Correct	Difficulty
1	Global	A	★
2	Detail	B	★
3	Detail	D	★
4	Inference	B	★
5	Inference	A	★
6	Logic Function	E	★★★★
7	Global	C	★

Passage 2: Cameron's "Fancy-Subject" Photos

Q#	Question Type	Correct	Difficulty
8	Global	B	★
9	Logic Function	A	★
10	Logic Reasoning (Strengthen)	D	★★
11	Logic Reasoning (Parallel Reasoning)	C	★★
12	Inference (EXCEPT)	E	★★
13	Inference	E	★★★
14	Logic Function	B	★★
15	Global	B	★★

Passage 3: Marcuse's Mistake

Q#	Question Type	Correct	Difficulty
16	Global	C	★
17	Detail	B	★
18	Logic Function	E	★★★
19	Detail	A	★★★★
20	Inference	E	★★★
21	Inference	A	★★★★

Passage 4: Justice and Property

Q#	Question Type	Correct	Difficulty
22	Global	B	★★★
23	Detail	A	★★★
24	Logic Reasoning (Method of Argument)	D	★
25	Logic Reasoning (Parallel Reasoning)	E	★
26	Inference	D	★★★
27	Logic Reasoning (Method of Argument)	A	★★★★

Passage 1: Natural Selection

Step 1: Read the Passage Strategically
Sample Roadmap

line #	Keyword/phrase	¶ Margin notes
1	objected	Darwin: nat sel main force in evolution, but not the only one
3	main; but not	
4	exclusive	
5	Nonetheless	Strict const: nat sel is ONLY force
9	all	
10	every	
16	If	Nat sel --> adaptation
17	right; every	Strict const view: all attributes due to adaptation
19	But in fact; numerous	
20	examples; not	Auth: ev says not so
22	little to do	
23	For example; while it is true	Ev from genetics
28	most; neither	Most mutations neither + nor -
29	revealed	
31	Most	
32	no effect	
34	but	
35	not explainable	
37	Additionally	More ev: paleontology
38	undermined	Dinosaur extinction
		Smaller animals survived
48	But; while	
50	does not conform	Goes against strict const. view
52	For that view assumes	
56	In a sense	
57	dumb luck	

Discussion

The passage begins with Darwin's view that natural selection was the primary—but not the only—means of evolution. A group of Darwinians have taken this view to the extreme, claiming that natural selection explains all observable biological phenomena. Lines 10–12 provide the assertion of these "strict constructionists." Reading actively, you can expect the author to weigh in on this assertion.

Paragraph 2 goes on to explain how natural selection manifests itself in adaptations. According to the strict constructionists, these adaptations give rise to every attribute present in species. The author challenges this directly, citing examples of many attributes that can't be explained as adaptations that aid in a species' reproductive success.

Paragraph 3 begins with the illustration Keywords "[f]or example," therefore you know this paragraph will provide support for the author's view. According to research in population genetics, DNA's evolution is made up in large part of neutral mutations that neither enhance nor hamper a species' reproductive success.

The continuation Keyword [a]dditionally (line 37) signals more evidence for the author's argument. Paragraph 4 provides evidence from the field of paleontology to support the argument. Dinosaurs' extinction millions of years ago wasn't due to natural selection, but to the unlucky fact of their size. Smaller animals fare better after catastrophic events (such as the impact of an extraterrestrial body), but it's not as though natural selection anticipated a comet strike and rewarded animals whose sizes were more conducive to postimpact conditions.

The passage's **Topic** is natural selection, and its **Scope** is the primacy of natural selection in evolution. The **Purpose** is to challenge the view of the strict constructionist Darwinians. The **Main Idea** is that contrary to the strict constructionists' view, natural selection is not the exclusive mechanism through which evolutionary processes occur.

1. (A) Global

Step 2: Identify the Question Type
This is a Global question because it asks for the passage's "main point."

Step 3: Research the Relevant Text
The entire text is relevant because this is a Global question; therefore, base your prediction on the Main Idea you determined during Step 1.

Step 4: Make a Prediction
The main point of the passage is that the strict constructionists are wrong to believe that natural selection is the only force behind evolution.

Step 5: Evaluate the Answer Choices
(A) is therefore correct.

(B) is a Distortion. Strict constructionist Darwinians do believe that natural selection is responsible for the failure of extinct species, but **(B)** doesn't take the author's view into account.

(C) is too narrow. It gives the main point of paragraph 3, but that paragraph only exists to support the author's rebuttal of the strict constructionists.

(D) gives the view that the author sets out to refute, but without giving the author's view; **(D)** is incomplete.

(E) is too narrow, only including the evidence from paragraph 3 and not that from paragraph 4.

2. (B) Detail

Step 2: Identify the Question Type
This is a Detail question because it asks for what is true "according to the author."

Step 3: Research the Relevant Text
The discussion of environmental changes from 65 million years ago occurs in the last paragraph.

Step 4: Make a Prediction
Lines 43–48 say that smaller mammals, which could not compete with the large dinosaurs of the Cretaceous period, were better able to survive the changes in climate that accompanied the extraterrestrial impact.

Step 5: Evaluate the Answer Choices
(B) is therefore a match.

(A) isn't mentioned. No other environmental changes are discussed in the passage.

(C) is Out of Scope. The author calls the survival of the smaller mammals "the result of dumb luck" (line 57), and no mention is made of their intelligence.

(D) is also Out of Scope. No information is given about the range of environments inhabited by the smaller mammals.

(E) is also Out of Scope. The author doesn't say how quickly the smaller mammals were able to reproduce.

3. (D) Detail

Step 2: Identify the Question Type
This is a Detail question because it asks about what the author asserts, or states directly.

Step 3: Research the Relevant Text
"Mutations of genetic material" is a Content Clue leading you to paragraph 3.

Step 4: Make a Prediction
In paragraph 3, the author says that most genetic mutations produce neither beneficial nor deleterious attributes in

species. The evolution of DNA is mostly due to "neutral, nonadapative changes" (lines 29–31).

Step 5: Evaluate the Answer Choices

(D) is therefore correct.

(A) is not supported by the passage, which refers to the "persistence" of genetic mutations "from one generation to the next" (lines 34–35).

(B) is a Distortion. Mass extinctions are discussed in paragraph 4.

(C) makes an unwarranted distinction between behavior and appearance, when the author suggests that genetic mutations alter both.

(E) is not mentioned. Smaller species are only discussed in the context of paragraph 4. Nothing in the passage indicates that larger species experience more mutations.

4. (B) Inference

Step 2: Identify the Question Type

Any question asking what "the author would be most likely to agree with" is an Inference question.

Step 3: Research the Relevant Text

The question stem has no Content Clues to focus your research, so the correct answer will be consistent with the author's larger viewpoint.

Step 4: Make a Prediction

You know the author's Main Idea—that natural selection does not account for the evolution of every single one of a species' attributes, so a valid inference must be true based on this idea.

Step 5: Evaluate the Answer Choices

(B) is supported by paragraph 4. Smaller mammals fared better than large animals after the extraterrestrial impact of 65 million years ago, but the animals were already smaller by the time of the impact, so their size couldn't have been an adaptation to the impact.

(A) is Extreme. The author says there are "numerous examples of attributes that are not adaptations for reproductive success," but this doesn't mean that natural selection plays almost no role at all.

(C) is contradicted by the last sentence of paragraph 3, which says that changes get passed down from one generation to another despite having no impact on a species' reproductive success.

(D) is a Distortion. In the specific case of the extraterrestrial impact that led to the dinosaurs' extinction, the dinosaurs' large size was a disadvantage, but to say that large species generally can't survive in "harsh environmental conditions" is too general.

(E) distinguishes between form and behavior of species, but the author doesn't say that natural selection can explain the form of "most species." In fact, that idea undercuts the passage's argument.

5. (A) Inference

Step 2: Identify the Question Type

This is an Inference question because it asks about the author's *stance*, or attitude, toward a part of the passage.

Step 3: Research the Relevant Text

The author refers directly to the arguments of the strict constructionist Darwinians in paragraphs 1 and 2.

Step 4: Make a Prediction

With questions asking about the author's attitude, predict whether that attitude is positive, negative, or neutral. In paragraph 2, the author says what would be true "if the strict constructionists are right" and then goes on to dispute it. Therefore, the author's attitude toward the strict constructionists' argument is one of clear opposition.

Step 5: Evaluate the Answer Choices

(A) is a good characterization of the author's attitude.

(B) is too soft. The author doesn't just disapprove of the strict constructionists' argument; two and a half paragraphs are spent refuting it.

(C) doesn't take the author's argument into account. The passage is very clear in its disagreement with the strict constructionists' view.

(D) is a 180. The author doesn't seem to be on the side of the strict constructionists. All the facts provided contradict the strict constructionists' argument.

(E) is also a 180. If the author endorsed the strict constructionists' view, the passage would provide facts to support it.

6. (E) Logic Function

Step 2: Identify the Question Type

Any question asking for the function of a paragraph is a Logic Function question.

Step 3: Research the Relevant Text

Use your Roadmap to determine the function of a paragraph.

Step 4: Make a Prediction

The second paragraph is intended to give the implication of the strict constructionists' theory, and then to set the scene for the author's rebuttal of this theory.

Step 5: Evaluate the Answer Choices

(E) is therefore correct.

(A) is incorrect because the author never explains exactly why the strict constructionists' views are so much more extreme than those of Darwin.

(B) is the function of paragraphs 3 and 4, not of paragraph 2.

(C) is incorrect because the evidence described in subsequent paragraphs hasn't necessarily gotten a lot of attention; the evidence is being given to correct the strict constructionists' misconceptions.

(D) is a Distortion. Paragraph 2 doesn't provide arguments in favor of the strict constructionists' ideas.

7. (C) Global

Step 2: Identify the Question Type
This is a Global question because it asks for the "primary purpose of the passage."

Step 3: Research the Relevant Text
You've already determined the passage's Purpose during Step 1. Use that to form your prediction.

Step 4: Make a Prediction
The author's argument throughout the passage has one goal—to correct the misconception of the strict constructionists regarding natural selection's role in evolution.

Step 5: Evaluate the Answer Choices
(C) is therefore correct.

(A) doesn't reflect the author's tone toward the strict constructionists' hypothesis (see lines 37–40 for an example of this tone).

(B) is too neutral. The author isn't merely outlining two sides of a debate; the author is getting involved and making arguments.

(D) has the right tone, but the theory advanced by the strict constructionists is not a *traditional* one; rather, it is a new one (see *recently* in line 6).

(E) is a Distortion. The author does say that the strict constructionists have "recently risen to prominence," but instead of exploring why, the author just goes on to undermine their argument.

Passage 2: Cameron's "Fancy-Subject" Photos

Step 1: Read the Passage Strategically
Sample Roadmap

line #	Keyword/phrase	¶ Margin notes
5	unmistakable; often comical	Fancy subject photos defined
7	more connection to	
9	than they do to	
13	of course	Comic charm not intentional
14	life and charm; If	
15	succeeded	
18	extravagantly awful	Auth approves of actual results over Cameron's aim
19	rather than	
19–20	most vital	
21	precisely	Realism of photos give truth
24	rather than	
27	:	
34	can	
36	cannot; always	Cannot avoid seeing the real sitters
38	can	
39	can	
41	can never	
44	special; treasures	Cameron's photos combine amateur w/ artistic
45	unfathomably peculiar; —	
47	for example	Example
50	But	
53	While	Passing is a delight
57	shameless delight	

Discussion

The author introduces the **Topic**—Julia Cameron's "fancy-subject" photos—right away, and mentions the comic traces they bear. The author goes on to credit those traces with the life and charm the photos still display. Apparently, this was all unintentional; Cameron's goal was to create "seamless works of illustrative art" (line 16). But from the use of emphasis/opinion Keywords such as "of course" (line 13) and "most vital" (lines 20–21), you know that the author values Cameron's work for reasons other than what would be expected of a typical masterpiece.

The author explains in paragraph 2 that the camera's realism is what lends truth to Cameron's attempt at artificiality. No matter how much she dresses up her sitters, the viewer can't ignore the fact that these are humans in costume just trying to sit still through the taking of the photos. Unlike theater or painting, which can allow the spectator to suspend disbelief, Cameron's photos never stop being pictures of actors.

The final paragraph continues the lovefest. Cameron's photos are special because they juxtapose artistry and amateurism. Then the author cites an example, *The Passing of Arthur*, in which the viewer can clearly make out the common household objects that are meant to stand in for a boat and oars. Instead of this being a drawback, however, this obviousness imbues the photo with a sense of magic, mystery, and delight. It's clear now that the **Scope** of the passage is the artistic value of Cameron's photos. The author's laudatory tone gives away the **Purpose**: to point out what makes Cameron's work so special. Thus, the **Main Idea** is that the value of the photos lies in the unintentional interplay between realism and artifice, between amateurism and artistry.

8. (B) Global

Step 2: Identify the Question Type
Any question asking for the "main point of the passage" is a Global question.

Step 3: Research the Relevant Text
Instead of rereading specific parts of the text, use the work you did in Step 1 to predict your answer.

Step 4: Make a Prediction
The main point is that viewers can appreciate Cameron's photos because they can simultaneously perceive both the loftiness of her artistic goals and the comic truthfulness of the sitters.

Step 5: Evaluate the Answer Choices
(B) is therefore correct.

(A) gets half the main point. The author also appreciates the artistry that lives alongside the circumstances of the photos' creation.

(C) is too negative. Yes, any comparison to great Western painting is belied by the photos' comic elements, but the author thinks this is what makes Cameron's work so charming.

(D) is a 180. The author says that in Cameron's photos, it's impossible to forget that you're looking at people who are posed and arranged in costume. Furthermore, according to the author, that makes the photos all the better.

(E) prizes the information about the sitters in the photos above the imaginary scenes portrayed in the photos, but the author says that the value lies in perceiving both at the same time.

9. (A) Logic Function

Step 2: Identify the Question Type
This is a Logic Function question because it's asking why the author mentions the props.

Step 3: Research the Relevant Text
The props are mentioned in lines 46–50.

Step 4: Make a Prediction
To understand why the author mentions the props in *The Passing of Arthur*, look to the previous sentence (lines 43–46). In that sentence, the author says that Cameron's photos are special because they combine amateurism and artistry. That the props are clearly identifiable as broomsticks and drapery must, therefore, be an example of Cameron's amateurism.

Step 5: Evaluate the Answer Choices
(A) is therefore correct.

(B) mentions theater, which is discussed at the end of paragraph 2. *The Passing of Arthur* is not theater, but rather a picture of actors.

(C) is a Distortion. Cameron's ingenuity comes from the pictures being artistically pleasing despite, or in many cases because of, their amateurism. The use of common household props can hardly be seen as evidence of ingenuity.

(D) is a 180. According to the author, Cameron never intended her photographs to be ironic (lines 14–16).

(E) is another 180. The author's appraisal of Cameron's work is overwhelmingly positive.

10. (D) Logic Reasoning (Strengthen)

Step 2: Identify the Question Type
This is a Strengthen question because the correct answer, if true, will bolster a claim made by the author.

Step 3: Research the Relevant Text
Review the author's contention in lines 34–36, and then determine what kind of information would explain that claim.

Step 4: Make a Prediction
In lines 34–36, the author says that narrative paintings allow us to suspend our disbelief, but narrative photographs do not. In other words, when we look at a painting, we can pretend the subject of the painting really is the persona portrayed, but such fantasy is impossible with a photo. Therefore, the right answer must be a difference between paintings and photographs that creates this contrast.

Step 5: Evaluate the Answer Choices
(D) explains the contrast perfectly. If a painter can suppress things about a sitter that are incongruous with the person he or she is portraying, then the viewer can more easily pretend that he or she is really looking at Mary Madonna or Jesus or John the Baptist.

(A) wouldn't explain why we can suspend disbelief looking at a painting. Once the painting or photograph is done, it wouldn't matter how long it took to sit for either.

(B) is a 180. If paintings can depict situations that are obviously impossible, that would make it harder, not easier, for a viewer to suspend disbelief in a narrative painting.

(C) is irrelevant. Whether the sitters have to be present at the same time should have no effect on how a viewer perceives the finished product.

(E) is a 180. Anything that calls our attention to the artist's deliberate stylistic choices would make it more difficult for us to suspend disbelief while viewing a painting.

11. (C) Logic Reasoning (Parallel Reasoning)

Step 2: Identify the Question Type
This is a Parallel Reasoning question because the correct answer will be most analogous to the relationship between Cameron and her photographs.

Step 3: Research the Relevant Text
Without a specific place to research, use your big-picture understanding of Cameron and her fancy-subject pictures to form your prediction.

Step 4: Make a Prediction
According to the author, the relationship between Cameron and her photos is *peculiar* (line 45) because she intended them to be works of high art, and they still achieve that status, even though it's impossible to ignore their more lowbrow elements. The correct answer will reflect this dichotomy.

Step 5: Evaluate the Answer Choices
(C) is directly in line with the author's assessment of Cameron's work. Paragraph 3, in particular, points out the artistry of Cameron's photos, despite the obviousness of elements like the household props in *The Passing of Arthur*.

(A) is a Distortion. Cameron's photographs did perhaps contain incongruous elements, but the effect of that was not

to increase distance between the viewer and the sitters depicted in the photos.

(B) would be parallel if Cameron meant her photographic depictions to somehow subvert imagery from the Bible, or mythology, or any of her actors' source material. However, no such intention is discussed in the passage.

(D) is Outside the Scope. Nothing in the passage indicates that Cameron intended for her photographs to serve any practical function.

(E) goes against Cameron's intention, which was not to depict an appearance of truth, but rather to create "works of illustrative art" (line 16).

12. (E) Inference (EXCEPT)

Step 2: Identify the Question Type
This is an Inference question because it asks for what "the author would agree with." Be careful, though: Here, you're to determine which answer choice either receives no support from the author or goes *against* the author's views.

Step 3: Research the Relevant Text
Because the author wrote the entire passage, no specific set of lines is more relevant than any other. Be prepared to check the answer choices against the passage—and against your understanding of the author's Main Idea.

Step 4: Make a Prediction
You know that the author values Cameron's work highly, so prepare to choose any negative answer choice as the correct "odd man out." Otherwise, proceed to the answer choices and eliminate any that are consistent with the passage.

Step 5: Evaluate the Answer Choices
(E) is directly at odds with the last sentence of paragraph 1. Cameron intended for her work to be seen as *seamless*. In other words, she didn't want us to notice or focus on the sitters themselves or on the obviousness of her props. Nevertheless, the author says that the conspicuousness of the conditions under which the photos were taken is the reason why they're successful as art.

(A) is supported by lines 21–24 and lines 34–38. A painting allows us to suspend our disbelief far more readily than does a photograph (which, the author says, is more realistic).

(B) is supported by lines 43–46.

(C) is essentially the author's point in paragraph 2. The tension between the real and the artificial is what makes these photographs *wonderful* (line 26).

(D) is supported by lines 6–13 and lines 27–31.

13. (E) Inference

Step 2: Identify the Question Type

The phrase "provides the most support for inferring" is a clear sign of an Inference question.

Step 3: Research the Relevant Text

Cameron's era is discussed throughout the passage, although the end of paragraph 1 does make a reference to other Victorian photography.

Step 4: Make a Prediction

Predicting the correct answer to an Inference question is tough without specific lines to reference. Therefore, go straight to the answer choices, selecting only the answer choice that *must* be true based on the information provided.

Step 5: Evaluate the Answer Choices

(E) is a valid inference. Lines 31–32 characterize the photography process as an *ordeal* during which the sitters try "desperately hard to sit still." It must therefore be true that photos could not be taken instantaneously in Cameron's time.

(A) is unsupported. Just because Cameron concerned herself with depicting "scenes from the Bible, mythology, Shakespeare, or Tennyson" (lines 3–4) doesn't mean that other photographers weren't interested in documenting contemporary life.

(B) is Outside the Scope. The socioeconomic background of Victorian photographers is not discussed in the passage.

(C) is Outside the Scope. Nothing in the passage says how popular publicity stills of actors were at the time.

(D) is unsupported. The passage only discusses Cameron's sitters; there's no way of knowing from the passage whether or not professional artist's models existed in Cameron's era.

14. (B) Logic Function

Step 2: Identify the Question Type

This is a Logic Function question because it asks for the purpose of a particular discussion in the passage.

Step 3: Research the Relevant Text

The discussion of suspension of disbelief occurs in lines 34–42.

Step 4: Make a Prediction

The main point of paragraph 2 is that the reality of Cameron's photos—that they are composed of real people dressed up theatrically—is unavoidable. The discussion of suspension of disbelief serves to contrast Cameron's photos with other art forms, such as theater, in which the illusion takes over. Unlike those forms, the photos don't allow us to forget that we are viewing real people in all their discomfort. That, the author claims, is why the photos are charming.

Step 5: Evaluate the Answer Choices

(B) is a paraphrase of that idea.

(A) is a Distortion. Cameron's photos aren't just an example used to prove the author's point; they are the central subject of the passage.

(C) is a 180. The author's appraisal of Cameron's work is anything but negative.

(D) is Outside the Scope. The author neither introduces nor refutes any criticisms of Cameron's photography.

(E) is a 180. The author's point in lines 34–42 is that Cameron's pictures are unlike painting and drama in that they don't allow us to suspend our disbelief as viewers. Both painting and drama can allow for that suspension of belief.

15. (B) Global

Step 2: Identify the Question Type

Any question asking for the "main purpose of the passage" is a Global question.

Step 3: Research the Relevant Text

Instead of rereading specific parts of the text, use the work you did in Step 1 to predict your answer.

Step 4: Make a Prediction

The author's Purpose is to argue for a positive interpretation of Cameron's work based on the interplay between its serious artistic merit and its comic traces.

Step 5: Evaluate the Answer Choices

(B) is therefore correct.

(A) overstates the importance of *The Passing of Arthur*, which the author just uses as an example to prove a point in paragraph 3. Also, the author never chronicles Cameron's artistic development. That would require a timeline or some other series of events from Cameron's artistic life.

(C) is too neutral. The author's main argument is that what may initially seem like weakness or amateurism in her photographs is actually the source of their charm and vitality.

(D) is too negative. The author does mention in passing that Cameron's goal was to make seamless artworks, but the main purpose of the passage isn't to point out why that goal was futile.

(E), like **(A)**, also overemphasizes an artistic work that was used only as an example. Additionally, the author never lays out any criticisms of *The Passing of Arthur* that would warrant defense.

Passage 3: Marcuse's Mistake

Step 1: Read the Passage Strategically
Sample Roadmap

line #	Keyword/phrase	¶ Margin notes
2	principal	Critics assumption: advertising creates false needs
4	manipulative; Central	
6	maintained	Marcuse: we satisfy false needs instead of out real needs
9	because	
12	not to	
13	but rather to	
14	thereby	
16	supposed	Marcuse: advertising takes real needs, puts them on items
21	thereby	
22	Since; thus	Consumers never really fulfilled
24	never	
26	Unfortunately	
28	extremely problematc; If; right	Auth: If Marcusians right, can't separate real from false needs
29	cannot	
31	For	
32	necessary	
35	But, in fact; major mistake	Auth: Marcusians' mistaken assumption
40	Moreover	
43	If	Auth: we are actively willing to get satisfaction thru products
44	and if	
49	no doubt true	
51	does not	
52–53	does not mean	
53	however	Auth: we can find own kind of fulfillment

Discussion

The author begins this passage as do many LSAT authors—by pointing out the belief of someone else. In this case, it's critics of advertising, who point to the creation of false needs as the source of advertisers' manipulative power over us. The critics base this belief on the writings of Herbert Marcuse. Marcuse believed that mass market culture creates false needs whose satisfaction only strengthens corporate power, to our collective detriment. Through satisfying these false needs, we fool ourselves into thinking we're truly satisfied.

Paragraph 2 details more of Marcuse's argument. According to him, ads create a connection between our real needs and consumer products. Chasing the product, which is a mere substitute for what we're truly seeking, rather than the true sources of fulfillment leaves us forever unsatisfied.

It shouldn't surprise you that the first word of paragraph 3 is *unfortunately*—this is the author finally weighing in on Marcuse's ideas. According to the author, the Marcusian critique depends on consumers' inability to distinguish between real and false needs. To draw a distinction, we'd have to somehow eschew "forces of persuasion" (line 32) that are inextricably bound to our "instinctive judgments" (line 34).

However, the author says the Marcusians' "major mistake" (line 35) is that they assume without warrant that our responses to ads are not rational and autonomous. The author believes we are more than capable of recognizing what the Marcusians consider insidious techniques. We can devise—and attain—our own definition of genuine fulfillment through the products hawked to us by mass market culture.

The **Topic** of the passage is consumer advertising. The **Scope** is Marcuse's critique of advertising. The author's **Purpose** is to refute Marcusian arguments concerning false versus real needs. Therefore, the **Main Idea** is that Marcusians are wrong to accuse advertisers of preying on false needs because consumers can distinguish between the two and have autonomy in determining how to use mass market culture to attain both their real and false needs.

16. (C) Global

Step 2: Identify the Question Type

Any question asking for the passage's "main point" is a Global question.

Step 3: Research the Relevant Text

The entire text is relevant to a Global question. Use your work from Step 1 to predict the answer here.

Step 4: Make a Prediction

The main point, as determined during Step 1, is that the Marcusian attack on advertisers is based on a misguided conception of false needs. Consumers can determine their

own needs and fulfill them using consumer products, if they so choose.

Step 5: Evaluate the Answer Choices

(C) is a perfect match.

(A) is Outside the Scope. The author isn't trying to argue that advertising is beneficial to society. The author's merely arguing that Marcusians can't indict advertisers using their "false needs" argument.

(B) is a 180. The author believes that consumers *are* able to distinguish between their real and false needs and that the advertisers "are unable to induce unwilling behavior in rational, informed adults."

(D) is a Distortion. It broadens the Marcusians' argument and makes it *typical* of advertising critics. Furthermore, the author goes beyond simply stating that the Marcusians "do not fully consider" something, and says that their underlying assumptions represent a "major mistake" (line 35).

(E) is Half-Right/Half-Wrong. The "false needs" distinction made by the Marcusians doesn't overlook consumers' needs; it assumes that consumers can't distinguish between their real and false needs, and thus can't autonomously govern their needs and meet them through mass market culture.

17. (B) Detail

Step 2: Identify the Question Type

The categorical language of this question stem ("the author states") indicates a Detail question.

Step 3: Research the Relevant Text

Marcuse's beliefs are discussed in paragraphs 1 and 2.

Step 4: Make a Prediction

According to the author, Marcuse believed that advertisers create psychological links between our real needs and consumer items, thus displacing our real needs onto commercialized products.

Step 5: Evaluate the Answer Choices

(B) is stated in lines 17–21.

(A) is Outside the Scope. The author doesn't mention where Marcuse thinks advertisers derive their strategies.

(C) misuses a detail from lines 39–40, which are part of the author's argument, not Marcuse's.

(D) is a Distortion. Marcuse, according to the author, doesn't discuss independent decision-making as one of consumers' needs from paragraph 2.

(E) is Outside the Scope. The author doesn't say what Marcuse believes regarding advertisers' responses to the Marcusian critique.

18. (E) Logic Function

Step 2: Identify the Question Type
This is a Logic Function question because it asks for the *function* of a part of the passage, paragraph 1 in this case.

Step 3: Research the Relevant Text
Whenever a Logic Function question asks for the purpose of an entire paragraph, consult your Roadmap to form your prediction.

Step 4: Make a Prediction
The purpose of paragraph 1 is to introduce the views of "some critics of advertising" (line 1) and to locate those views in the writings of one theorist, Herbert Marcuse.

Step 5: Evaluate the Answer Choices
(E) is therefore correct.

(A) is Outside the Scope. The author doesn't give any information about the world from which Marcuse's critiques sprang. The passage doesn't even tell you what country or time period Marcuse lived in.

(B) is a Distortion. It's Marcuse, not the author, who believes that mass-market culture contributes to the creation of false needs. Furthermore, the way in which Marcuse's false needs are created is discussed in paragraph 2.

(C) only takes into account the second half of the paragraph and doesn't mention Marcuse at all.

(D) is a Distortion. The author gives the view of "some critics of advertising" (line 1), but that isn't to say that this view is prevailing. Remember from your work in Formal Logic that *some* just means "at least one."

19. (A) Detail

Step 2: Identify the Question Type
This is a Detail question because it asks for a claim that the author attributes to Marcuse. In other words, it concerns what the author explicitly states.

Step 3: Research the Relevant Text
Marcuse's claims are discussed in paragraphs 1 and 2.

Step 4: Make a Prediction
The author attributes many claims to Marcuse between lines 6 and 25. Instead of listing them all, be prepared to check the answer choices against this part of the text.

Step 5: Evaluate the Answer Choices
(A) is a paraphrase of lines 6–9.

(B) is a Distortion. According to Marcuse, people in modern societies fool themselves into thinking they've satisfied their needs, but that doesn't mean that modern societies are somehow less able than their earlier counterparts when it comes to satisfaction. In fact, earlier societies fall Outside the Scope.

(C) is Extreme. This is not a claim the author attributes to Marcuse. The author attributes claims to Marcuse in the first two paragraphs, after that, the author addresses Marcuse's underlying assumptions and what's wrong with them. So, **(C)** is an extreme version of the author's analysis of Marcuse in paragraph 3, but not a claim the author directly attributes to Marcuse.

(D) is Outside the Scope. The political systems that may or may not benefit from advertising aren't part of Marcuse's views as discussed in the passage.

(E) goes wrong when it says that the secondary needs engendered by ads "become real needs." Marcuse never believes this. Rather, he defines those as "false needs."

20. (E) Inference

Step 2: Identify the Question Type
Any question asking you to define a word or phrase as it's used in context is an Inference question.

Step 3: Research the Relevant Text
The phrase in question is located in line 32, but for this type of question, context is key. Read around the phrase to understand how the author is using it.

Step 4: Make a Prediction
The author says that if the Marcusians are right, then "forces of persuasion" have become so ingrained in society that they make it very difficult to separate our real needs from the ones advertisers have allegedly conspired to create. These forces must be all the factors that manipulate us into thinking our conditioned judgments are instinctive.

Step 5: Evaluate the Answer Choices
(E) is therefore correct.

(A) is Outside the Scope. No one in the passage, not even Marcuse, accuses advertisers of making "intentionally dishonest claims."

(B) is a Distortion. The author says that if the Marcusians are right, then "forces of persuasion" affect our instinctive judgments, but that doesn't mean that the forces themselves are innate or instinctive.

(C) talks about emotion, which goes unmentioned in paragraph 3. Furthermore, **(C)** doesn't include the idea of these "forces of persuasion" influencing consumers' behavior in unconscious ways.

(D) gets into state manipulation, but this kind of political idea is Outside the Scope of the passage.

21. (A) Inference

Step 2: Identify the Question Type
This is an Inference question because it asks you to infer the statement that would logically complete the passage.

Step 3: Research the Relevant Text

Read the last several lines of the passage and determine where the author is headed with the argument.

Step 4: Make a Prediction

Notice that each answer choice begins with *therefore*—a Conclusion Keyword. Based on the structure of the author's argument throughout paragraph 4, the author would conclude that the reasoning behind the Marcusian critique does not form a rational basis from which to attack advertising. As you evaluate the answer choices, eliminate all the choices that venture into new territory.

Step 5: Evaluate the Answer Choices

(A) is a good match for your prediction and is consistent with the author's Main Idea.

(B) is a 180 and Outside the Scope. The author doesn't feel that Marcusian claims are rationally justified. Additionally, nowhere in the passage does the author suggest that critics of advertising are politically motivated.

(C) goes Outside the Scope with a recommendation for changes in the beliefs of corporate leaders. Furthermore, the author doesn't necessarily believe that advertising is abusive to consumers in the first place.

(D) is a Distortion. The author says that Marcusians don't currently have a solid argument against advertising, but that doesn't mean that the author believes advertising to be mostly beneficial to society.

(E) is a Distortion. According to the author, Marcusians believe that all of us are susceptible to having our real needs conflated with the false ones created by advertisers. So, Marcusians do not make a claim that advertisers exert power over just "those few people." Furthermore, the author believes that the advertisers *are* able to exert economic power over consumers, it's just that rational, informed adults are able to recognize that power and then willingly opt whether or not to participate.

Passage 4: Justice and Property

Step 1: Read the Passage Strategically
Sample Roadmap

line #	Keyword/phrase	¶ Margin notes
Passage A		
1	fundamental	2 principles for justice in property
3	(1) [before justice]	(1) acquisition
6	(2) [before justice]	(2) transfer
9	if	
10	exhaustively	Implications of principle for entitlement
21	However; not all	Real world: injustive happens
24	for example	
25	raises the issue	
27	ought	Rectification of injustice (principle)
28	?	
33	should	
34	must	
Passage B		
37	requires	I.N.A. defined
41	clear; mean to	I.N.A. purpose
48	One; obvious	
48–49	way of reasoning	Arg re: Native Am land claims
50	:	Native Am here first
54	illicitly	Land stolen
55	lack	
56	Ideally; should	
57	impractical	
58	might; But	
59	wrong can most easily be righted	Land should be restored if possible
60	feasible	

Discussion

Don't be intimidated by the theoretical nature of passage A. Focus on its structure and its big picture. The passage begins by citing two principles involved in a theory of justice regarding property. Paragraph 1 ends by naming those two principles and the purpose of each.

Next, passage A takes the logic of these principles one step further. In a perfect world, people who acquired or transferred property in accordance with the relevant principles (and only those people) would be entitled to the property. Of course, the world isn't perfect, and the author addresses that in the final paragraph of passage A.

Because there exists injustice regarding property, another principle (the principle of rectification) becomes relevant. To rectify injustice, we must gather information about previous injustices to determine the ownership situation that should have resulted. Then we must take action to align property with the appropriate ownership situation.

The **Topic** of passage A is property, its **Scope** is the theory underlying justice in property, and its **Purpose** is to outline principles that are fundamental to the theory. The **Main Idea** of passage A is that a theory of justice regarding property involves a framework for determining just acquisition and transfer of property, as well as a system for rectifying injustice.

Passage B steps out of the theoretical and into the practical. In 1790, Congress enacted a law, still in effect today, designed to protect Native Americans from fraudulent acquisition of their lands by anyone not entitled to them. The Act has provided justification for lawsuits brought by Native Americans to recover certain lands.

The second paragraph of passage B outlines an argument in favor of restoring Native Americans' land to its rightful owners. From the author's tone ("one might almost say obvious" in line 48), you might think that the author is putting forward this argument as his or her own. But this isn't necessarily the case. Your success on LSAT Reading Comprehension (and beyond) will depend on your ability to tell when an author is making an argument and when the author is describing an argument belonging to someone else.

The **Topic** of passage B is also property, its **Scope** is Native American land claims, and its **Purpose** is to discuss the moral reasoning involved in rectifying injustice with respect to those claims. Its **Main Idea** is that a moral case can be made for returning unjustly acquired lands to their rightful Native American owners.

Before going to the questions, take a few moments to determine the relationship between your Comparative Reading passages. In this case, passage A describes a theoretical moral framework, and passage B applies similar moral reasoning to a particular property issue.

22. (B) Global

Step 2: Identify the Question Type
This is a Global question because it asks for the "main purpose" of each passage.

Step 3: Research the Relevant Text
You already determined the Purpose of each passage during Step 1. Use that as the basis for your prediction.

Step 4: Make a Prediction
Passage A's Purpose is to discuss the principles involved in the theory of justice regarding property. Passage B's Purpose is to analyze the moral and legal issue involved with a particular property case, the rightful ownership of Native American lands.

Step 5: Evaluate the Answer Choices
(B) is therefore correct.

(A) is incorrect on two counts. Passage A does not provide a solution to a problem, and passage B doesn't criticize any solution. If anything, passage B is the one that provides a proposed solution to the injustice faced by Native Americans.

(C) is a Distortion. Passage A mentions the principles of justice in acquisition and justice in transfer, but doesn't provide any details on the content of those principles. Also, passage B examines a case, but a case that seems to violate morality, not exemplify a moral ideal.

(D) is a 180 because passage B doesn't deal in theory at all.

(E) is too pointed in its analysis of passage A. The author of passage A isn't making an argument for or against anything—the passage is merely outlining a set of principles. Additionally, passage B's discussion of Native American land claims, although an example, is not a counterexample to any widely held moral principles.

23. (A) Detail

Step 2: Identify the Question Type
This is a Detail question because it asks about what both passages "explicitly mention."

Step 3: Research the Relevant Text
Use your Roadmap to identify topics common to both passages.

Step 4: Make a Prediction
Passage A discusses principles of property acquisition and of property transfer, while passage B concerns a specific law governing transfer of land (i.e., property transfer) from Native Americans to others. Therefore, the correct answer should mention transfer of property in some way.

Step 5: Evaluate the Answer Choices
(A) is therefore correct.

(B) is close, but the discussion of rectification of injustice in passage A can't be said to be "a legal basis for recovery of property." Such a legal basis is mentioned only in passage B (lines 44–47).

(C) is mentioned only in the second paragraph of passage A. Passage B doesn't speak about a just world in the same abstract way.

(D) is discussed in the final paragraph of passage B (lines 57–58), but not in passage A.

(E) is mentioned only in passage B (lines 51–54), and not in passage A.

24. (D) Logic Reasoning (Method of Argument)

Step 2: Identify the Question Type

This is a Method of Argument question because it asks about the relationship between parts of the passages—in other words, what one part does in regard to the other.

Step 3: Research the Relevant Text

Go back to your Roadmap to determine what the author of passage A is doing overall and how that relates to the second paragraph of passage B.

Step 4: Make a Prediction

Passage A, particularly in its last paragraph, discusses a principle for rectifying injustice when it comes to property. That principle supports the moral reasoning in the second paragraph of passage B, which is all about rectifying the unjust theft of Native American lands.

Step 5: Evaluate the Answer Choices

(D) is therefore correct.

(A) is a 180. The second paragraph of passage B isn't theoretical at all; it presents an argument about a very tangible case, so it does not get *broader*.

(B) is also backward. The second paragraph of passage B presents an argument, not a set of facts.

(C) is incorrect because passage A and passage B have the same subject matter—property rights—but passage B examines a specific case related to the general theory presented in passage A.

(E) is a 180. The argument in the second paragraph of passage B is entirely consistent with the principle of rectification presented in passage A.

25. (E) Logic Reasoning (Parallel Reasoning)

Step 2: Identify the Question Type

This is a Parallel Reasoning question because it seeks the answer with the relationship "most analogous to" the relationship between the two passages.

Step 3: Research the Relevant Text

For this question, the entire text is relevant. Use the relationship you determined in Step 1 to guide your prediction and your evaluation of the answer choices.

Step 4: Make a Prediction

Passage A provides a general overview of legal principles when it comes to justice regarding property. Passage B examines one particular case of property transfer and outlines an argument for restoring Native American lands to their rightful owners.

Step 5: Evaluate the Answer Choices

(E) is parallel, because passage A does provide a high-level, *fundamental* view (line 1 even uses the word *fundamental*), and passage B discusses a specific case (similar to the Thales building).

(A) is a 180 in that gambling is more general than card playing, yet passage B has a more specific focus than passage A.

(B) would be correct if passage A argued specifically for denying Native Americans the right to get their lands back under the Indian Nonintercourse Act. However, passage A doesn't make an argument that directly opposes passage B.

(C) presents two documents that are not closely related enough to be parallel to passages A and B, because pruning a fruit tree does not necessarily relate to cooking in general.

(D) would suggest that the passages have opposite tones toward the same subject matter, when in reality, both passages present arguments supported by principles of justice.

26. (D) Inference

Step 2: Identify the Question Type

This is an Inference question because it asks what the author of one passage would "most likely" think about something mentioned in the other passage (a common question in Comparative Reading).

Step 3: Research the Relevant Text

Go to paragraph 1 of passage B to determine the stated purpose of the Indian Nonintercourse Act, and then cite the part of passage A that relates to it.

Step 4: Make a Prediction

The Indian Nonintercourse Act was designed to regulate "transfers of lands" from Native Americans to others (line 38) and to "guarantee security" against fraud (line 42). That certainly relates to the principle of justice in transfer discussed in paragraph A (lines 6–8). Therefore, this act, according to passage A, would be a way for the government to ensure compliance with the principle of justice in transfer.

Step 5: Evaluate the Answer Choices

(D) is a match for this prediction.

(A) is Outside the Scope. Passage B doesn't say that Indian land holdings were in any way illegitimate prior to the passage of the Indian Nonintercourse Act.

(B) is Outside the Scope. Passage B doesn't say anything about the Indian Nonintercourse Act being enacted to follow up on existing property law.

(C) doesn't apply here because the principle of justice in acquisition relates to property with no previous owner, not property that's changing hands from one owner to another.

(E) goes too far. The Indian Nonintercourse Act is a preventive measure requiring the government's pre-approval of Native American land transfers. It doesn't specify what should be done to correct unjust land transfers that have already occurred.

27. (A) Logic Reasoning (Method of Argument)

Step 2: Identify the Question Type
The phrase "difference in approach" indicates a Method of Argument question.

Step 3: Research the Relevant Text
This question is more global in scope, so use your Roadmap and understanding of the big picture to form your prediction.

Step 4: Make a Prediction
Passage A outlines principles of justice when it comes to property, and then applies those principles to the idea of rectification. Passage B is much more narrow in scope and examines one particular historical issue of property, outlining an argument that Native Americans' dealings with European settlers have not conformed to principles of justice.

Step 5: Evaluate the Answer Choices
(A) is therefore correct.

(B) is incorrect because passage A doesn't distinguish between competing views. Only one view of justice in property is discussed.

(C) is incorrect because passage B doesn't cite the views of any established authorities. Furthermore, the argument made in paragraph 2 of passage B isn't necessarily endorsed by the author. Additionally, passage A does not necessarily make a recommendation, the author merely claims what could be done to rectify injustice.

(D) is incorrect because passage B does in fact provide an argument (or a "way of reasoning," as lines 48–49 put it). Conversely, passage A raises an issue (line 25) and asks if anything should be done (lines 27–28), but does not necessarily advocate the proposed solution.

(E) is incorrect because passage A sets out neither to bolster nor undermine any one view. Furthermore, the argument in the second paragraph of passage B is presented without any authorial point of view.

Section II: Logical Reasoning

Q#	Question Type	Correct	Difficulty
1	Assumption (Necessary)	C	★
2	Paradox	E	★
3	Flaw	A	★
4	Principle (Apply/Inference)	D	★
5	Flaw	D	★
6	Principle (Identify/Strengthen)	D	★
7	Parallel Flaw	C	★★
8	Assumption (Necessary)	B	★
9	Weaken	C	★★
10	Assumption (Sufficient)	A	★★
11	Main Point	B	★★
12	Assumption (Sufficient)	A	★★★
13	Flaw	B	★★★
14	Method of Argument	E	★
15	Flaw	B	★★
16	Method of Argument	A	★
17	Parallel Reasoning	B	★
18	Flaw	E	★★★
19	Weaken	B	★★★★
20	Assumption (Necessary)	E	★★★★
21	Inference	E	★★★★
22	Strengthen	A	★★★
23	Inference	C	★★
24	Paradox	D	★★★
25	Inference	C	★

1. (C) Assumption (Necessary)

Step 1: Identify the Question Type

This question stem explicitly asks for an assumption *required* by the argument. Determine the conclusion, then the evidence, and then what would have to be true for the conclusion to follow from the evidence.

Step 2: Untangle the Stimulus

The conclusion of the argument is signaled by the Keyword *[s]o*: 60 percent of the technicians employed by the city's selected contractor are unqualified. The evidence is that the Heating Technicians Association certified only 40 percent of the contractor's technicians.

Step 3: Make a Prediction

When seeking a necessary assumption, if the argument contains Mismatched Concepts, bridge the gap between terms that differ, even subtly, between the evidence and the conclusion. "Not certified" doesn't necessarily mean "not qualified," but this author is equating the two. Therefore, to form this argument, the author must be assuming that certification is the only way to be qualified.

Step 4: Evaluate the Answer Choices

(C) is a match for this prediction. If you were unsure about **(C)**, apply the Denial Test. If technicians who lack certification *can* still be qualified technicians, then the editorial's conclusion doesn't have to follow from the evidence, and the argument falls apart.

(A) doesn't have to be true for the argument to work. The conclusion is about qualification, which isn't necessarily tied to pay.

(B) is not necessary to the logic here. Other contractors are Outside the Scope.

(D) is also Outside the Scope. It doesn't matter who installed the heating systems that are in need of upgrade. That first sentence of the argument is just background information.

(E) is also Outside the Scope. The contractor's ties to city officials have no bearing on either certification or qualification for the job.

2. (E) Paradox

Step 1: Identify the Question Type

The phrase "explain the discrepancy" is a telltale sign of a Paradox question. The stimulus will contain a contradiction that the correct answer choice will resolve.

Step 2: Untangle the Stimulus

Contrast Keywords such as *but* or *yet* often signal the paradox. In this case, the contradiction lies in the different responses to being thanked. When a customer hears a salesperson say "thank you," the response is also "thank you." However, when someone hears thanks for a favor, the response is "you're welcome."

Step 3: Make a Prediction

If a solution to the paradox doesn't spring to mind, don't waste precious test time speculating. All you need heading into the answer choices is to know what *kind* of information you're seeking: some reason why a store transaction is different enough from a favor to warrant a different response to being thanked.

Step 4: Evaluate the Answer Choices

(E) provides just such a reason. If a customer in a commercial transaction feels that the benefits are mutual, then he or she might think that thanks are warranted in both directions, as opposed to a favor, which doesn't provide such benefits.

(A) is a 180. If anything, it deepens the mystery because in that case you would expect a customer to say "you're welcome" to a salesperson instead of "thank you."

(B) explains why salespeople say "thank you," but not why customers respond differently to their thanks than to the thanks of a friend on the receiving end of a favor.

(C) doesn't solve Jeneta's paradox because it's the behavior of the customer, not the salesperson, that needs explaining.

(D) is an Irrelevant Comparison. Whether or not someone responds to being thanked by habit or by conscious decision, there's still a difference in responses that needs to be explained. More information would need to be given about the habits in responding to friends versus salespeople for this to explain the discrepancy.

3. (A) Flaw

Step 1: Identify the Question Type

Anytime you see a question stem asking why a particular argument is "vulnerable to criticism," you're looking at a Flaw question. Determine why the conclusion doesn't necessarily follow from the evidence, keeping the classic flaws in mind.

Step 2: Untangle the Stimulus

The argument concludes that it's rarely smart business for video game makers to sell the movie rights to popular games. The evidence is the experience of StarQuanta, which sold the rights to its game *Nostroma*, only to see the film version tank and subsequent versions of the game sell poorly.

Step 3: Make a Prediction

To reach such a broad conclusion, you would expect the author to cite case after case of failed game-to-movie adaptations. However, the author only cites one. An argument can't conclude that a practice isn't advisable just because it failed once. This kind of unwarranted generalization doesn't fly on the LSAT—or in front of a judge.

Step 4: Evaluate the Answer Choices

(A) accurately characterizes this argument's flaw.

(B) is a Distortion. The author never inferred that the public disliked the film adaptation *because* critics disliked it. The author merely asserted that both disliked it.

(C) describes the flaw of circular reasoning, which doesn't occur here. The author's conclusion and evidence are different.

(D) is another Distortion. The author is arguing that successful games don't usually become successful movies, so the argument wouldn't assume the opposite.

(E) describes the classic flaw of confusing necessity and sufficiency, but no such error exists here. This type of logical flaw usually only occurs in arguments that employ Formal Logic.

4. (D) Principle (Apply/Inference)

Step 1: Identify the Question Type
The wording of this question stem indicates that the stimulus will state a general principle and that the correct answer will be a specific situation that properly applies it.

Step 2: Untangle the Stimulus
The principle is a straightforward if-then statement: If a company's external consultant has business interests with that company, then that consultant's advice is likely to result in the company's executive being overpaid.

Step 3: Make a Prediction
It's impossible to know exactly what the correct answer will say, but as you evaluate the answer choices, read them carefully and eliminate any that don't conform to the principle. Note the level of certainty of the principle: It uses the phrase "likely to be overcompensated." Eliminate answer choices that use more absolute language.

Step 4: Evaluate the Answer Choices
(D) conforms perfectly to the principle. Troskco's external consultant has contracts (i.e., "business interests") with Troskco, and the consultant advised Troskco on the executive's compensation, so according to the principle from the stimulus, that executive is "probably overpaid."

(A) is Extreme ("definitely overpaid" vs. "likely to be overcompensated" in the stimulus) and says nothing about an external consultant. The discussion of the "average employee" is Outside the Scope.

(B) also says nothing about an external consultant, let alone one who has other business dealings with Troskco. Furthermore, the history of the company's profits are Outside the Scope.

(C) is a Distortion. The principle tells you one condition under which an executive is likely to be overpaid, but it doesn't tell you that that's the *only* situation resulting in overcompensation. **(C)** essentially goes from the principle of

"If X → Y " and then makes an incorrect contrapositive of "If ~X → ~Y."

(E) is a Distortion similar to **(C)**, in that it negates without reversing. Additionally, **(E)** is also Extreme ("definitely not overpaid").

5. (D) Flaw

Step 1: Identify the Question Type
The wording of this question couldn't be more direct. The argument contains a flaw, or a disconnect between evidence and conclusion, and your job is to correctly identify it.

Step 2: Untangle the Stimulus
The science writer's conclusion is at the end of the argument—Lemaître's theory is inadequate. The evidence for this is that although the theory predicts phenomena that are readily observed, another theory makes the same prediction.

Step 3: Make a Prediction
There's absolutely no reason why both theories can't be adequate, especially if they both correctly predict the same thing. The science writer, therefore, has no basis to favor one theory over another.

Step 4: Evaluate the Answer Choices
(D) is a paraphrase of this prediction. That one theory correctly predicts observations doesn't undermine another theory that predicts the same things.

(A) is Outside the Scope. The science writer's argument never appeals to expert authority.

(B) describes the classic flaw of equivocation, in which an author uses the same term in different ways within one argument. However, no terms are used inconsistently here.

(C) is Outside the Scope. The science writer does cite a causal relationship in Lemaître's theory between the "primeval atom" explosion and the beginning of the universe. However, that causal relationship is just background info on the theory; it isn't central to the argument.

(E) accuses the science writer of something that doesn't happen in the argument. No assumption is made that Lemaître's theory and the oscillating universe theory are the *only* two theories explaining the beginning of the universe.

6. (D) Principle (Identify/Strengthen)

Step 1: Identify the Question Type
In addition to the word *principle*, this question stem also asks for the answer that will "justify the reasoning" in the argument. That means the correct answer, as well as being a broadly stated rule, will confirm a central assumption in the argument. Therefore, treat this question as you would any Strengthen question.

Step 2: Untangle the Stimulus

The critic concludes that one shouldn't criticize the comedy *Quirks* just because it may not be realistic. The critic concedes that the film might not be realistic, but it is funny, which is the main criterion for success in a comedy.

Step 3: Make a Prediction

For the critic's argument to work, *Quirks* should avoid criticism purely by virtue of its success within its genre; that is, the film is a comedy that is funny. Stated more broadly, the argument assumes that a film that is successful within its genre is successful, period.

Step 4: Evaluate the Answer Choices

(D) matches this principle.

(A), if valid, actually weakens the critic's argument. If films should be judged on the accuracy of their portrayals, and *Quirks* doesn't accurately depict real people, then there are valid grounds for criticizing the film.

(B) is Out of Scope. It doesn't strengthen the critic's argument because the argument points to the film's humor—not its popularity—to defend it from criticism.

(C) is a Distortion that doesn't help the critic's argument. The critic doesn't assume that the film is funny *because* it's stylized. The critic says it's funny *despite* being stylized, and that's all that matters.

(E) is irrelevant to the critic's argument because the argument doesn't rely on *Quirks* having a single genre or multiple genres.

7. (C) Parallel Flaw

Step 1: Identify the Question Type

The phrase "flawed reasoning" signals a Flaw question. The phrase "most similar to" signals a Parallel Reasoning question. Therefore, identify the logical flaw in the stimulus and find the answer choice with the same flawed reasoning.

Step 2: Untangle the Stimulus

The argument concludes that Party Y's accusations against Party X are ill-founded simply because Party Y was recently caught doing the same thing it accuses Party X of doing.

Step 3: Make a Prediction

Party Y may have been in the wrong, but that doesn't mean Party X isn't in the wrong either. If your friend argues that you should eat better, it's not logically sound to reply, "What about you? You eat fast food three meals a day." Sure, your friend would be a hypocrite, but that has no bearing on the strength of your friend's argument. Put more formally, this argument rejects a position on the basis of the hypocrisy of the entity holding the position—a variation on the classic *ad hominem* flaw. Find the answer choice that commits the same flaw.

Step 4: Evaluate the Answer Choices

(C) does exactly that. Just because the plaintiff recently did the same thing he or she now accuses the defendant of doing doesn't mean that the plaintiff's accusations are baseless.

(A) is a flawed argument because it essentially concedes the plaintiff's point and then shifts attention toward morality. However, it does not bring up anything about the plaintiff's past behavior, so it is not parallel.

(B) comes close to the flaw in the stimulus, but notice that **(B)** concludes something different from what the stimulus concludes. The stimulus concludes that certain accusations are ill-founded, whereas **(B)** just calls them hypocritical.

(D) makes an unwarranted assumption that accusations made within a certain time frame of the election are not substantial. That's a logical flaw, but not the same as the flaw in the stimulus.

(E) would be correct if the evidence accused the plaintiff of voting only for campaign laws that benefited the plaintiff's party. However, it accuses the plaintiff of a different offense—committing an *ad hominem* flaw—which is not what the defendant stands accused of, so **(E)** is not a perfect match.

8. (B) Assumption (Necessary)

Step 1: Identify the Question Type

This question stem asks you to determine the assumption required for the argument to work. Find and bracket the conclusion, summarize the evidence, and then predict the missing link.

Step 2: Untangle the Stimulus

The biologist argues that animals' eyes are adapted only to their needs rather than to an abstract sense of good eye design. The evidence is the box jellyfish, which has well-designed lenses that can produce sharp images. However, the box jellyfish has retinas that can receive only images containing prominent features, not fine detail.

Step 3: Make a Prediction

The biologist must be assuming that the visual needs of the box jellyfish only go as far as perceiving prominent features of the object it's looking at. Think about what would happen to the argument if you applied the Denial Test to this assumption. If the box jellyfish were bumping into things left and right because it needed sharper vision that it didn't have, then its eyes wouldn't be adapted to its needs, and the biologist's argument would be seriously impaired.

Step 4: Evaluate the Answer Choices

(B) is a perfect match for this prediction.

(A) is Outside the Scope. Whether or not other types of jellyfish have retinas similar to those of box jellyfish is irrelevant to the argument.

(C) doesn't have to be true to make this argument work. The biologist is making an argument about what the box jellyfish *needs*, not what it would benefit from.

(D) is incorrect because it doesn't matter to the argument how the box jellyfish inherited its forward retinas.

(E) is also Outside the Scope. It doesn't matter to the argument what box jellyfish use their vision for. It matters whether or not they need to have sharp vision or vision that only makes out prominent features of objects. Put to the Denial Test, **(E)** would say that vision is a secondary means of detecting prey. That would not tear apart the argument about what the box jellyfish needs from its eyes.

9. (C) Weaken

Step 1: Identify the Question Type

Any question that asks for the answer choice that *undermines* an argument is a Weaken question. Find the conclusion, evidence, and assumption. Then predict the kind of information that would invalidate the assumption.

Step 2: Untangle the Stimulus

The columnist concludes that tobacco companies are wrong to claim that advertising doesn't affect people's tendency to smoke. The evidence is research showing reductions in the overall number of smokers, as well as the number of first-time smokers, in countries that have restricted tobacco advertising.

Step 3: Make a Prediction

Note the words "significant causal impact" in the conclusion. The columnist phrased it using a bit of a double negative, but the argument is essentially that advertising restrictions can cause a decline in smoking. To weaken a causal argument, look for an alternate cause or some other information that undermines the cause-effect relationship. Put another way, you can weaken a causal argument by invalidating the columnist's assumption that there's no other cause for the observed effect.

Step 4: Evaluate the Answer Choices

(C) supplies an alternate cause. If negative attitudes toward smoking are already present in countries that restrict tobacco advertising, then the citizens of those countries were likely to curb their smoking habits anyway, and the ad restrictions may not be to blame.

(A) focuses only on those that already smoke, whereas the argument indicated that the number of smokers went down, *especially* first-time smokers, when advertising is restricted. **(A)** also indicates the current smokers were *unlikely* to quit, but that still leaves open that some do quit once advertising is removed. Therefore, on its own **(A)** does not invalidate the columnist's assumptions.

(B) makes an Irrelevant Comparison between broadcast and print media. The argument makes no distinction between the two.

(D) is Outside the Scope. When people start smoking and how long they continue smoking once they start have no effect on the columnist's argument.

(E) is Outside the Scope. The columnist's argument isn't about the effects of advertising in general; it's about whether or not restricting tobacco advertising leads to a reduction in smoking.

10. (A) Assumption (Sufficient)

Step 1: Identify the Question Type

In this assumption question, the question stem seeks the answer choice that is enough, all by itself, to ensure that the conclusion follows from the evidence (note the Formal Logic word *if*). As always, find the conclusion and the evidence and bridge the gap, looking out for any Formal Logic within the argument.

Step 2: Untangle the Stimulus

The actor's conclusion is the first sentence. Brecht's plays are not successful. The evidence is twofold. First, the roles in Brecht's plays are so incongruous that audiences have a hard time figuring out the characters' personalities. Second, audiences have to care what happens to at least some of the characters in a play for that play to succeed.

Step 3: Make a Prediction

The evidence is a bit of a jumble, so rearrange it to find the gap. The conclusion is that Brecht's plays aren't successful. In the evidence, the actor says that audiences have to care about the characters for a play to be successful. This may not sound like Formal Logic, but there is a necessary condition (caring about the characters) and a sufficient one (successful play). You could put it like this:

If	*succeed as drama*	→	*care about characters*

The contrapositive would be as follows:

If	*~ care about characters*	→	*~ succeed as drama*

The other piece of evidence is that audiences can't discern the characters' personalities in Brecht's plays. When combined with the conclusion, that is:

If	*~ discern personalities*	→	*~ succeed as drama*

Therefore, the missing link is between being unable to discern characters' personalities and not caring about the characters. The argument, therefore, works if it's true that audiences have to be able to discern characters' personalities to care about them.

If	~ discern personalities	→	~ care about characters

If	care about characters	→	discern personalities

The argument in full is this chain:

If	~ discern personalities	→	~ care about characters	→	~ succeed drama

Therefore, the assumption just connects the first two terms of the chain.

Step 4: Evaluate the Answer Choices

(A) is, therefore, correct. Anyone who doesn't "take any interest" in a character certainly doesn't care about that character.

(B) explains why audiences would have a hard time discerning the personalities of Brecht's characters. However, that doesn't add to the logical chain that must lead us to Brecht's plays being unsuccessful.

(C) just restates the last sentence of the argument, but doesn't add anything new to help connect the pieces of the argument.

(D) creates a conditional relationship between the actors' failure to discern their characters' personalities and the audience's failure to do so. Nevertheless, that connection doesn't bridge the real gap in the argument.

(E) does nothing except to invert the necessary-sufficient relationship in the last sentence of the argument.

11. (B) Main Point

Step 1: Identify the Question Type

This is a Main Point question because it asks for the "main conclusion" of the argument.

Step 2: Untangle the Stimulus

The legislator says the city should accept the streetlights as a gift from the lighting company. Some would object to this, but the legislator makes it clear that the city is forbidden from showing favoritism. The lighting company won't be able to influence the city's decisions on park lighting contracts. At most, all the company will get out of their gift is visibility for their products.

Step 3: Make a Prediction

On most Main Point questions, you won't be able to identify the conclusion from noticeable Keywords such as *hence*, *so*, or *therefore*. Instead, zero in on the clearest statement of opinion. The phrase "surely there would be no problem" gives it away. The legislator wants to convince people that it's not a problem to accept the gift of streetlights from the lighting company. That's the main point. Everything else in the argument is designed to support that point.

Step 4: Evaluate the Answer Choices

(B) is a good paraphrase of the conclusion.

(A) is support for the legislator's conclusion. *Because* the fears of those objecting to the gift are unfounded, it shouldn't be a problem to accept the gift, as the mayor has proposed.

(C) is, if anything, a 180. The argument does mention that the lighting company could have an ulterior motive of wanting to display its products to visiting mayors, but that is still not enough for the legislator to recommend against the city accepting the gift of streetlights. The legislator doesn't ever weigh in on whether the lighting company is acting appropriately, just that their actions are not sufficient to preclude the city from accepting the gift.

(D) is a fact that the legislator uses to dispel any concern about unethical motives on behalf of the lighting company. **(D)** is not the idea that the whole argument is driving toward.

(E) is conceded by the legislator as a possibility, but ultimately, says the legislator, that shouldn't stop the city from accepting the lighting company's gift.

12. (A) Assumption (Sufficient)

Step 1: Identify the Question Type

Because this question says that the conclusion can be properly drawn *if* the correct answer choice is assumed, this is a Sufficient Assumption question. Look for the piece of information that guarantees the conclusion will follow from the evidence.

Step 2: Untangle the Stimulus

The conclusion is the first part of the sentence: The chairperson should not have publicly released the Election Commission's report. The Keyword *for* points to the evidence: The chairperson failed to consult with any of the members of the commission prior to releasing the report.

Step 3: Make a Prediction

The evidence says the chairperson didn't consult any of the commission's members about the report. Therefore, says the conclusion, the chairperson should not have released the report. If one assumes that consultation of at least one commission member is required to release the report, then the evidence leads straight to the conclusion. Try putting that assumption into the argument and see how it flows.

Evidence: The chairperson didn't consult anyone on the commission before releasing the report.

Assumption: At least one commission member must be consulted before releasing the report.

Conclusion: The chairperson should not have released the report.

Step 4: Evaluate the Answer Choices

(A) is a Sufficient Assumption. You may have initially thought **(A)** went too far, but **(A)** says that express consent from most of the commission's members is required to release the report (the phrase "only if" signals necessity). The evidence says that the chairperson didn't consult anyone about the report (meaning that no one could have possibly given consent). Put those two together, and it must follow that the report was released impermissibly, as the conclusion states. As long as the answer to a Sufficient Assumption question guarantees the conclusion, it doesn't matter whether it contains Extreme language.

(B) requires a lot of logical gymnastics to make the argument whole. Even if members of the commission could have signed the report without being consulted about it, you'd still have to know that consult was *required* prior to the report's release for the conclusion to follow.

(C) attempts to equate "having serious reservations about the report" with "not being consulted about the report," and that's not warranted. **(C)** on its own, in conjunction with the evidence, doesn't force the conclusion to follow.

(D) is too tentative with the language of "had they been consulted." **(D)** requires each of the commission's members to say, "Yes, hypothetically, if you would have consulted me, I would have said yes," but the argument says the chairperson was unjustified in releasing the report because he or she didn't actually consult them, not because he or she didn't ask them a hypothetical question about consulting them.

(E) doesn't make the conclusion follow from the evidence. The evidence simply says the chairperson didn't consult the commission's members. To reach the conclusion, you have to know that the commission *must* be consulted before the report is released, not just that some of them preferred not to release the report.

13. (B) Flaw

Step 1: Identify the Question Type

The question stem lets you know right away that this argument contains a flaw, or a disconnect between evidence and conclusion. As you dissect the argument, look for faulty assumptions or overlooked possibilities.

Step 2: Untangle the Stimulus

The reformer's conclusion is in the last sentence: Imprisoning more people doesn't reduce crime. The evidence comes in the form of a survey. The past 20 years have not seen a significant reduction of the national crime rate, despite the fact that the percentage of the population in prison has gone up, as has public spending on prisons.

Step 3: Make a Prediction

This is one of those arguments that seems sound, until you think about what it's leaving out. While it may be true that the national crime rate isn't decreasing, that could still be seen as a good thing if the crime rate was on its way to *increasing*. What if locking up all those additional people is the reason why the crime rate is holding steady and not going up? In that case, putting more people in prison would be helpful. However, the reformer ignores this possibility, and in so doing commits a logical flaw.

Step 4: Evaluate the Answer Choices

(B) is, therefore, correct.

(A) is invalid because the reformer doesn't infer that the national crime rate has increased. The argument only mentions that it hasn't significantly decreased.

(C) might be tempting, if you thought the issue here had to do with numbers versus percentages. However, the argument deals only in percentages: The crime rate is the number of crimes per 100,000 people, and the argument cites the percentage of the population in prison. Therefore, the absolute number of people in the country is irrelevant.

(D) is Outside the Scope. The reformer doesn't recommend or even hint at any alternative measures for reducing crime. The argument is simply that incarcerating more people isn't the way to go.

(E) is another answer choice dealing in numbers and proportions, when the reformer never tries to argue for a correlation between number of crimes and number of prisoners.

14. (E) Method of Argument

Step 1: Identify the Question Type

If a question stem asks you to determine how one person "responds to" another person in an exchange, it's a Method of Argument question. Focus on the argumentative technique Winona uses, not on what she assumes or what would strengthen her argument.

Step 2: Untangle the Stimulus

The question is about Winona, but you have to read Inez's argument for context. Inez argues that spending on space exploration is an absolute must because it yields invaluable technological advances that improve our everyday lives. Winona disagrees, saying that if the technological advances are what we're really after, we should just invest in those rather than doing it indirectly through space exploration.

Step 3: Make a Prediction
Winona responds to Inez by pointing out that the end goal that Inez prizes—the technological advances—can be met in ways other than the one Inez proposes. In other words, Winona is suggesting a more direct route to Inez's goal.

Step 4: Evaluate the Answer Choices
(E) is, therefore, correct.

(A) is Outside the Scope. Winona makes no prediction as to whether or not space exploration will continue to yield useful technology.

(B) is a Distortion. Winona isn't arguing against funding space exploration. Her argument is that if one is justifying pouring money into space exploration on the sole grounds that it yields useful technology, then one might as well just spend the money on the technology itself.

(C) is Outside the Scope. Winona doesn't point out a contradiction; she offers an alternative recommendation.

(D) is Outside the Scope of Winona's argument. Winona doesn't focus on the cost of space exploration programs, but rather that their desired outcomes, per Inez, can be met more directly.

15. (B) Flaw

Step 1: Identify the Question Type
This is a Flaw question because it asks how the argument is "vulnerable to criticism." Find the conclusion, evidence, and assumption, and then note the disconnect in the reasoning. Keep classic flaws in mind as you predict an answer.

Step 2: Untangle the Stimulus
The consultant concludes that LRG's advertising campaign was poorly conceived. The evidence is that after ignoring the consultant's advice and hiring a competitor, sales are poor, especially in the case of LRG's new products.

Step 3: Make a Prediction
Aside from a serious case of "sour grapes," this consultant is committing a big causal-argument faux pas. The consultant blames LRG's "ill conceived" ad campaign for low sales, failing to acknowledge a whole host of alternate reasons for lower sales. Perhaps there's a recession and consumers have curtailed overall spending in LRG's sector of the economy. Maybe there was a recall on one of LRG's top-selling products. These are two of countless possibilities that the consultant overlooks.

Step 4: Evaluate the Answer Choices
(B) accurately states the consultant's logical flaw.

(A) is not something the argument takes for granted. The consultant is trying to argue that LRG's poor advertising campaign led to poor sales, not that the advertising campaign led to the worst sales possible.

(C) is also not something the argument takes for granted. The consultant points out that LRG's new products are selling especially poorly, but it's not assumed that they should have outsold established products.

(D) is a Distortion. Just because the consultant blames bad advertising for low sales (especially of new products) doesn't mean that the argument is crediting good advertising with high sales (of established products).

(E) describes the flaw of confusing necessity with sufficiency. No such Formal Logic blunder exists in this argument.

16. (A) Method of Argument

Step 1: Identify the Question Type
The phrase "argument proceeds by" is a clear sign of a Method of Argument question. Keep your focus on *how* the author structures evidence and conclusion rather than on *what* the argument specifically claims.

Step 2: Untangle the Stimulus
The conclusion is signaled by *thus* in the last sentence. The Pritzker Prize should go to the best building rather than to the best architect. The evidence for this is that architects are judged by their buildings, which are the result of teamwork. Movies are also the result of teamwork, and that's why the top award in cinema doesn't go to an individual, but to the film itself.

Step 3: Make a Prediction
The author's argument can be distilled to this idea: Because we dole out awards in a certain way in one discipline, we should do the same for a comparable discipline. So the author is drawing an analogy to one field to support a recommendation for another field.

Step 4: Evaluate the Answer Choices
(A) is a match for this prediction.

(B) is a Distortion. The author points out similarities, not differences, between architecture and film. Furthermore, no value judgment on "inherent value" is made on one over the other.

(C) is backward. The author's criticism of how prizes are awarded in architecture isn't transferred to film. In fact, the author points to the awarding of prizes in film as a model for how it should be done in architecture.

(D) is a 180. The author is arguing that film *is* analogous enough to architecture that conclusions about how achievements should be recognized in architecture *can* be made based on practices in film.

(E) would be correct if the author said that the top prizes for movies are wrongly given to individuals. Instead, the author makes a recommendation for how something should be done in architecture based on how top prizes in movies are *rightly* awarded.

17. (B) Parallel Reasoning

Step 1: Identify the Question Type

This is a Parallel Reasoning question because it asks you to find the answer choice whose reasoning is "most similar to" that of the stimulus.

Step 2: Untangle the Stimulus

The argument consists of two Formal Logic statements. The evidence says that between Suarez and Anderson, if one of them isn't the most qualified candidate for sheriff, then the other one is. The conclusion says that if we elect the most qualified candidate, and it isn't Suarez, then we must elect Anderson.

Step 3: Make a Prediction

Remember that two arguments are parallel if (and only if) they use the same kind of evidence to reach the same kind of conclusion. The evidence says that if one of two people isn't most qualified, then the other one is. Therefore, says the conclusion, if we select the most qualified person, and it's not person A, then it must be person B. Put in Formal Logic notation, the argument is:

Evidence:

If	~ S most qualified	→	A most qualified

Conclusion:

If	pick most qualified AND ~ pick S	→	pick A

As you evaluate the answer choices, keep your focus on the structure of each argument and not its specific terms.

Step 4: Evaluate the Answer Choices

(B) is a parallel argument. Substitute "Suarez" for "Dillon," "Anderson" for "Ramsey," and "lowest bidder" for "most qualified candidate," and you'll have an exact replica of the stimulus.

(A) doesn't use parallel evidence; it doesn't say that if Qiu isn't the lowest bidder, then Caldwell is (which is the structure of the stimulus). Furthermore, in order to have a parallel conclusion, **(A)** would have to conclude that the contract is awarded to one of the two people named in the argument.

(C) does not give a parallel piece of evidence. The first Formal Logic statement does not indicate whether Kapshaw or Johnson is the lowest bidder. Therefore, when the argument shifts from "is not awarded the landscaping contract" in the evidence to the conditional "if the contract goes to the lowest bidder" in the conclusion, it does not match the stimulus. The

fact that the conclusion also reverses the order of Kapshaw and Johnson is immaterial because the contrapositive of "If ~J → K" would still be "If ~K → J."

(D) diverges from the stimulus in two key ways. First, in its evidence, it doesn't say (as the stimulus does) that if one of the two people isn't the lowest bidder, then the other one is. Second, **(D)** makes a prediction about what *will not* happen, while the stimulus predicts what *will* happen if a certain set of conditions is met.

(E) gives parallel evidence ("If ~P → S"), but like **(D)**, it also makes a prediction in its conclusion about what will *not* happen, thus making it different from the stimulus. The conclusion should have the part about the contract being awarded to the lowest bidder on the sufficient side rather than the necessary side, and it should state that Sullivan *does* get the contract on the necessary side to be parallel.

18. (E) Flaw

Step 1: Identify the Question Type

This is about as clearly worded a question stem as you'll see in Logical Reasoning. Find the flaw by noting the disconnect between the evidence and conclusion.

Step 2: Untangle the Stimulus

The critic's conclusion is signaled by [*h*]*owever*: it's wrong to say that 15th-century painters mastered painting better than did their 16th-century counterparts. This conclusion is in response to an art historian who argues that 15th-century painters were better because their paintings were more planimetric. However, the degree to which a painting is planimetric, according to the critic, is irrelevant, so the art historian's conclusion is wrong.

Step 3: Make a Prediction

The critic's position essentially boils down to "the art historian's conclusion is wrong because he used irrelevant evidence to support it." That's not a valid counterargument. The 15th-century painters can still show more mastery than the 16th-century painters for different reasons than the one the art historian gave. Just because the argument supporting a conclusion is weak doesn't mean the conclusion itself can't be true.

Step 4: Evaluate the Answer Choices

(E) is, therefore, correct.

(A) is Outside the Scope. The critic never cites any other views held by the art historian.

(B) describes the classic LSAT flaw of equivocation, in which a key term is used inconsistently throughout an argument. However, the critic only uses the word *mastery* in one sense here.

(C) introduces the concept of necessity versus sufficiency, which is a flaw more commonly seen in arguments involving

Formal Logic. Even if the art historian's argument is construed as "If more planimetric → more mastery," then the critic dismisses that argument by indicating the *sufficient* condition (more planimetric) is inadequate to guarantee the necessary side, and that's why the historian's conclusion is false. However, **(C)** incorrectly suggests the critic treats the *necessary* condition's (more mastery) inadequacy as sufficient to guarantee the art historian's conclusion is wrong.

(D) isn't the flaw because no contradictory claims are made in the critic's argument. The argument bases its conclusion not on a contradiction, but on a dismissal of the evidence in an opposing argument.

19. (B) Weaken

Step 1: Identify the Question Type

In this Weaken question, as in any other, identify the conclusion, evidence, and central assumption of the argument. Then predict the kind of information that would invalidate that assumption.

Step 2: Untangle the Stimulus

The argument concludes that the carved flint object found in a Stone Age Irish tomb is likely the head of a communal speaking staff and not, as some archaeologists believe, the head of a warrior's mace. The evidence, signaled by the Keyword [*b*]*ecause*, is that the flint object is too small to be a mace. Furthermore, the object depicts an open mouth, which symbolizes speaking.

Step 3: Make a Prediction

The author assumes that there's no other purpose for the object that's more reasonable than the one suggested. Therefore, any fact suggesting that small stone objects depicting open-mouthed heads could serve other purposes would weaken the argument. Additionally, any fact suggesting that the head of a communal speaking staff would not normally be present in a Stone Age Irish tomb would weaken the argument.

Step 4: Evaluate the Answer Choices

(B) is correct. If communal objects (such as speaking staffs) were passed from one generation to the next in Stone Age Ireland, then it's unlikely that one would be buried with its owner. **(B)** certainly doesn't obliterate the argument, but if **(B)** is true, then it's a little harder to believe that the object was a communal speaking staff, and that's all you need for a valid weakener.

(A), if anything, strengthens the argument ever so slightly by suggesting that this particular tomb is unlikely to house weapons, thereby challenging the view of the archaeologists.

(C) doesn't affect the argument. Just because the object possessed a rare artistry doesn't mean it couldn't have been used for the purpose the author claims.

(D) is Outside the Scope. The argument doesn't say whether politically prominent people were more or less likely to be buried with communal speaking staffs in their tombs.

(E) doesn't directly attack the argument. Even if a speaking staff with a stone head *symbolizes* a warrior's mace, it would still be a speaking staff, so the author's argument wouldn't be weakened. Just because something symbolizes something else, doesn't mean that the object (speaking staff) *is* what it symbolizes (the head of a warrior's mace).

20. (E) Assumption (Necessary)

Step 1: Identify the Question Type

The phrase "relies on" means this question is asking for the necessary assumption in the argument. Determine what must be true for the conclusion to follow from the evidence.

Step 2: Untangle the Stimulus

The conclusion is signaled by *so*: Farmers have to give up chemical fertilizers if they want to significantly improve soil structure. The evidence is that local farmers have abandoned the planting of soil-renewing "green-manure" crops in the advent of chemical fertilizers, and this abandonment has hurt soil structure.

Step 3: Make a Prediction

The argument advocates stopping the use of chemical fertilizers to improve soil structure, but the soil structure isn't poor because farmers started using fertilizers. It's poor because they stopped planting green-manure crops. Therefore, to justify its recommendation, this argument assumes that getting rid of chemical fertilizers is the only way to get farmers to bring back green-manure crops.

Step 4: Evaluate the Answer Choices

(E) is a match for this prediction.

(A) doesn't have to be true for the argument to work. Alfalfa is cited as one of potentially many green-manure crops farmers could grow, so the soil could be rejuvenated with other green-manure crops besides alfalfa. **(A)** may also be considered Extreme due to the word *most*. Put to the Denial Test, if just under half of farmers abandon fertilizers and grow alfalfa, it's still possible the general soil structure could be significantly improved, especially depending on which farmers decide to do so and what percentage of the land they control.

(B) is a Distortion. It combines green-manure crops and chemical fertilizers, when the argument gives no indication that green-manure crops need help to grow.

(C) is Extreme and therefore flunks the Denial Test. Even if soil structure is not the *most* important factor influencing the soil quality of a farm field, the argument can still hold up.

(D) isn't necessary to the argument. The argument alleges that soil structure declines in the absence of green-manure crops, not in the presence of chemical fertilizers.

21. (E) Inference

Step 1: Identify the Question Type

The phrase "can properly be inferred" is a sure sign of an Inference question. Make as many connections as possible between the statements and select only the answer choice that *must* be true.

Step 2: Untangle the Stimulus

In Spanish 101 last semester, most students had perfect attendance. However, every student who earned a grade below B minus missed at least one session.

Step 3: Make a Prediction

Some Inference questions, such as this one, are ripe for prediction if you properly combine statements. You know that most students had perfect attendance. You also know that every student who got a grade below B minus did not have perfect attendance. Put those two statements together, and it must be true that most students in Spanish 101 last semester got a grade of B minus or higher. Here's the second sentence of the stimulus in Formal Logic, along with its contrapositive:

If	grade below B minus	→	missed at least 1 session
If	didn't miss session	→	grade not below B minus

Most students, according to the first sentence, didn't miss a session. Therefore, most students didn't get grades below B minus.

Step 4: Evaluate the Answer Choices

(E) is, therefore, correct.

(A) is not a valid inference because the grade threshold between those who missed class and those who didn't was B minus. Beyond that, you don't know what grade anyone earned. For example, it's possible the highest grade in the class was a B plus. It's also possible those specific students that got an A minus or higher were not part of the majority of students that attended every class.

(B) is a Distortion. You know that each student who scored below B minus missed at least one session. Nevertheless, these "B minus or below" students could be a small portion of the overall number of students who missed class.

(C) is close, but it doesn't have to be true. Those students with perfect attendance could have all gotten a grade of B minus.

(D) doesn't have to be true. Based on the stimulus, it could be true that the group of students who missed one or more classes is the exact same group that received a grade lower than B minus.

22. (A) Strengthen

Step 1: Identify the Question Type

This is a Strengthen question because it asks for the answer choice that *supports* an argument made in the stimulus.

Step 2: Untangle the Stimulus

Faced with the threatened disappearance of native salmon in Lake Clearwater, officials introduced sockeye salmon. The initial population of salmon split in two, taking over different depths of the lake and not interbreeding. Now, there are two genetically distinct populations of sockeye salmon. Researchers explain this genetic difference by hypothesizing that each population modified its genes in response to its respective habitat.

Step 3: Make a Prediction

In any argument that attempts to explain a certain phenomenon, the assumption is that no other explanation is better. In this case, the researchers assume that there isn't a more plausible alternative explanation for the genetic difference between the two populations. Therefore, to strengthen the argument, find the answer choice that eliminates such an alternative.

Step 4: Evaluate the Answer Choices

(A) does just that. The genetic difference between the two populations could be explained by one of them interbreeding with the native salmon, but if, as (A) says, that didn't happen, then it's a little more likely that the researchers' hypothesis is the correct one. Remember that a Strengthener does not need to completely prove the argument; it just needs to make the argument more likely to be valid.

(B) doesn't help the researchers' argument, because their argument focuses not on *whether* the sockeye population split off into two genetically distinct populations, but on *why* the populations became genetically distinct. The composition of the native salmon when they were numerous doesn't impact whether the two groups of sockeye salmon adapted genetically to their new habitats.

(C), if anything, weakens the researchers' hypothesis by suggesting that most salmon populations don't spend their time exclusively in one habitat or the other. If that's the case, it's less likely that sockeye salmon would adapt genetically to one of the habitats.

(D) is a 180. The hypothesis indicates *each* group has genetically adapted to its habitat. However, if one of the populations is "virtually identical" to the original group that was introduced that would mean that only one of the two groups (deep or shallow) may have made adaptations.

(E) has no effect on the researchers' argument. The number of sockeye salmon relative to the native salmon has nothing to do with whether or not they have adapted genetically to their respective habitats.

23. (C) Inference

Step 1: Identify the Question Type
This is an Inference question because it asks for the answer choice supported by the statements in the stimulus. Accept each statement as true and determine what is most *strongly supported* based on the stimulus.

Step 2: Untangle the Stimulus
The stimulus says that if a developing country's businesspeople are willing to be first-time investors in new modern industries, that country can boost its economic growth considerably. Then the stimulus gives two big obstacles to this. First, it's inherently risky to be the first to invest in an industry. Second, any businesspeople that do successfully take the risk will see their profits decline once competitors enter their industry.

Step 3: Make a Prediction
The two obstacles cited in the second half of the stimulus make it clear that unless developing countries do something to sweeten the deal for their businesspeople, those countries are unlikely to see big economic gains from new investment in modern industries. Scan the answer choices for this or any other statement that must be true given the stimulus.

Step 4: Evaluate the Answer Choices
(C) must be true. If developing countries provide added incentive for businesspeople to take the necessary risk involved in investing in modern industries, then those countries improve their prospects for economic growth.

(A) is unsupported. The stimulus says that once a modern industry has been established in a developing country, other investors follow, and competition grows. Nevertheless, that doesn't mean that economic growth isn't promoted.

(B) makes an Irrelevant Comparison by bringing in traditional industries, which the stimulus doesn't discuss.

(D) is Extreme and a Distortion. The stimulus says that a developing country can increase economic growth if its businesspeople invest in modern industries. That's not the same as saying that economic growth is impossible without such investment. Put differently, **(D)** takes a sufficient condition from the stimulus and turns it into a necessary one.

(E) is a Distortion. The stimulus says that it's "very risky" to be the first one to invest in a given industry, but that doesn't mean that industries with at least one business carry little risk. It's possible that those industries starting up second, third, fourth, and so on also carry significant investment risk, even if it is not *as* high as it was for the first industry.

24. (D) Paradox

Step 1: Identify the Question Type
This is a Paradox question because it asks for the answer choice that "most helps to explain the ... conflict." Find the discrepancy in the stimulus and then select the answer choice that resolves it.

Step 2: Untangle the Stimulus
A majority of the concertgoers surveyed expressed dissatisfaction with their local concert hall. In particular, they said they wanted wider seats and better acoustics. However, when presented with the prospect of tearing down the concert hall and rebuilding it with those desired features, the concertgoers opposed the idea.

Step 3: Make a Prediction
Don't try to guess at why the concertgoers don't want the concert hall rebuilt to their liking; the potential reasons are too numerous. Instead, go to the answer choices and eliminate any that don't resolve the conflict in the concertgoers' stated opinions.

Step 4: Evaluate the Answer Choices
(D) resolves the paradox. If a new concert hall is already being built nearby, and the current one is being repurposed, then there's no reason for the concertgoers to support tearing down and rebuilding the current one.

(A) only resolves the paradox if you assume that the concertgoers so thoroughly dislike this particular group that they will go to any lengths to oppose whatever the group sponsors. However, the stimulus doesn't indicate this at all.

(B) is Outside the Scope. The people who live in the vicinity of the concert hall and the people who took the survey don't have to be the same group. In fact, there may not be any overlap between the two groups at all.

(C) is also Outside the Scope. The stimulus does not indicate that those surveyed are in any way financially tied to the construction industry. Per **(C)**, if those surveyed were somehow tied to the construction industry, they *would* be more likely to advocate for tearing down the old hall, but the stimulus says they are against doing that. Furthermore, the stimulus stated that renovations to the existing hall are off the table, so a comparison of the financial benefits of new construction versus renovations is irrelevant.

(E) is a 180. It deepens the paradox because if building a new concert hall would attract popular singers and musicians to the city, then that would be an incentive for the concertgoers to promote the new construction rather than oppose it.

25. (C) Inference

Step 1: Identify the Question Type
Any question asking you to fill in the blank at the end of an argument with a conclusion is an Inference question.

Determine the conclusion that can logically be drawn from the given statements.

Step 2: Untangle the Stimulus
The student wants to find a book that she quoted in her research paper. From there, the student builds a logical chain: No book means no accurate citation, and no accurate citation means no quotation, and the paper will be better with a quotation than without one.

Step 3: Make a Prediction
Don't assume that correct answers can't be predicted on Inference questions. This stimulus is straightforward, so you can find the answer by translating the student's statements into Formal Logic.

$$\text{If} \quad \sim book \rightarrow \begin{array}{c} \sim acc. \\ citation \end{array} \rightarrow \sim quot. \rightarrow \begin{array}{c} paper \\ not \\ as \\ good \end{array}$$

By stringing those statements together it becomes clear that if the student doesn't find the book, the paper's quality won't be optimal. Search for this in the answer choices.

Step 4: Evaluate the Answer Choices
(C) is a match for this prediction.

(A) doesn't properly complete the argument. Nothing in the argument suggests that the student must include a citation at all, let alone an inaccurate one.

(B) isn't a valid inference. The student's statements indicate that she will complete the paper no matter what. The only question is how good the paper will be, depending on whether the student finds the book.

(D) is a 180, it goes against the student's statement that "without an accurate citation, I will be unable to include the quotation."

(E) is unsupported because the student gives every indication that there will be a completed paper, quotation or no quotation.

Section III: Logic Games
Game 1: Instrumental CD

Q#	Question Type	Correct	Difficulty
1	Acceptability	B	★
2	"If" / Must Be True	C	★
3	"If" / Could Be True	B	★
4	"If" / Could Be True	E	★
5	Partial Acceptability	E	★★
6	"If" / Could Be True	D	★
7	"If" / Must Be False (CANNOT Be True)	A	★★

Game 2: Symposium Speakers

Q#	Question Type	Correct	Difficulty
8	Acceptability	A	★
9	Must Be False (CANNOT Be True)	B	★★
10	"If" / Must Be False (CANNOT Be True)	A	★★
11	Partial Acceptability	C	★★
12	"If" / Could Be True	C	★★
13	Rule Substitution	E	★★★★

Game 3: Historic Building Owners

Q#	Question Type	Correct	Difficulty
14	Acceptability	A	★
15	Must Be False (CANNOT Be True)	D	★★★
16	"If" / Must Be True	D	★★★
17	"If" / Could Be True	B	★★
18	"If" / Complete and Accurate List	E	★★★

Game 4: Florist's Bouquets

Q#	Question Type	Correct	Difficulty
19	Acceptability	A	★
20	"If" / Must Be True	B	★★
21	"If" / Partial Acceptability	E	★★
22	Partial Acceptability (CANNOT)	A	★★★
23	Must Be False (CANNOT Be True)	C	★★★

Game 1: Instrumental CD

Step 1: Overview
Situation: A producer organizing a CD of instrumental music

Entities: Five pieces of music (*Reciprocity, Salammbo, Trapezoid, Vancouver, Wisteria*)

Action: Loose Sequencing. Determine the order in which the pieces will appear on the CD. A glance ahead reveals that all of the rules describe relative relationships, making this Sequencing game loose instead of strict.

Limitations: The CD will simply feature all five pieces in some order, from first to fifth, no ties.

Step 2: Sketch
Because the game is Loose Sequencing, there is no need to set up a series of slots. Instead, just list the five pieces by initial and build the sketch based on the relative relationships in the rules.

Step 3: Rules
Rule 1 sets up a basic relationship: *Salammbo* before *Vancouver*.

$$S — V$$

Rule 2 provides two possible outcomes for three of the pieces. *Trapezoid* will appear either before or after both *Reciprocity* and *Salammbo*. The order of *Reciprocity* and *Salammbo* is not defined. Draw out both possibilities:

Rule 3 sets up two more possible outcomes for three pieces. *Wisteria* will appear either before or after both *Reciprocity* and *Trapezoid*. The order of *Reciprocity* and *Trapezoid* is not defined. Again, draw out both possibilities:

Step 4: Deductions
Normally, Loose Sequencing games require connecting all of the rules into one complete diagram by using the deduction of Duplication. However, there is only one concrete rule. Rules 2 and 3 each set up the possibility of Limited Options. Limited Options are more effective using Rule 2 because it duplicates *Salammbo* from Rule 1. Any combination of Rules 2 and 3 would require four separate options. They can all be drawn out, but that could be excessive for a game with mostly New-"If" questions. It will depend on your comfort with Limited Options and personal preference on whether you'd want to draw them all out.

Even if you don't draw out all four options, by Rule 1, *Salammbo* must be earlier than *Vancouver*; therefore, add V after S in both options provided by Rule 2:

These would be the two primary options. In either option, *Wisteria* can come before or after R and T to satisfy Rule 3. If you opt to draw out all four options you'll have these results:

Regardless of whether you go with two or four options, be sure to keep track of all the relationships while working on the questions.

Step 5: Questions

1. (B) Acceptability
This is a standard Acceptability question. Go through the rules one at a time and eliminate answers that violate those rules.

(D) violates Rule 1 by having *Salammbo* later than *Vancouver*. **(A)** violates Rule 2 by having *Trapezoid* later than *Reciprocity* but earlier than *Salammbo*. **(E)** violates Rule 2 by having *Trapezoid* later than *Salammbo* but earlier than *Reciprocity*. **(C)** violates Rule 3 by having *Wisteria* later than *Trapezoid* but earlier than *Reciprocity*. That leaves **(B)** as the correct answer.

2. (C) "If" / Must Be True
For this question, *Salammbo* is established as the fourth song. That means *Vancouver* must be fifth (Rule 1). The remaining pieces must all come before *Salammbo*, including *Trapezoid*. By Rule 2, that means *Trapezoid* must also be earlier than *Reciprocity*, making **(C)** the correct answer. This can also be noted by looking at the Limited Options. *Salammbo* could only be fourth in the first option, in which *Trapezoid* must be earlier than *Reciprocity*.

3. (B) "If" / Could Be True
For this question, *Reciprocity* will be the first piece. *Trapezoid* will have to come later than *Reciprocity*, which means it will also have to come later than *Salammbo* (Rule 2), which still must come earlier than *Vancouver* (Rule 1). In the Limited

KAPLAN

Options, this is the second option. Furthermore, *Wisteria* will be later than *Reciprocity*, so it will also have to come later than *Trapezoid* (Rule 3):

R   S
— — — — —
1   2   3   4   5
⎵⎵⎵
T–W; V

In that case, *Salammbo* must be second. *Vancouver* can be in any position after that, including third. That makes **(B)** the correct answer. For the record, because *Salammbo* must be second, **(A)** and **(D)** are impossible. *Wisteria* has to come later than *Reciprocity*, *Salammbo,* and *Trapezoid*, so it cannot be third and *Trapezoid* cannot be last. That eliminates **(C)** and **(E)**.

4. (E) "If" / Could Be True

For this question, *Trapezoid* will be second. With only one piece before it, it cannot come later than both *Reciprocity* and *Salammbo*. Therefore, it must come earlier than both (Rule 2). In addition, *Salammbo* must also come earlier than *Vancouver* (Rule 1). This is the first option of the Limited Options. In this scenario, there is only one piece remaining that could be first: *Wisteria*.

W   T
— — — — —
1   2   3   4   5
⎵⎵⎵
R; S–V

With *Wisteria* first, **(A)**, **(B)**, and **(D)** are all impossible. *Vancouver* must come later than *Wisteria*, *Trapezoid,* and *Salammbo*, so it cannot be third. That eliminates **(C)**, leaving **(E)** as the only answer possible, and thus the correct answer.

5. (E) Partial Acceptability

The correct answer to this question will be two pieces that could be first and second, in the order listed. The remaining four answers will list two pieces that cannot be first and second, respectively. Go through the rules one at a time, just as with a typical Acceptability question. If there are multiple answers remaining, test them individually by considering what the entities in the third, fourth, and fifth places could be.

If *Vancouver* were second, *Salammbo* would have to be first (Rule 1), not *Reciprocity*. That eliminates **(A)**.

If *Trapezoid* were to appear after *Salammbo*, it would also have to appear after *Reciprocity* (Rule 2). That eliminates **(C)**.

If *Wisteria* were to appear later than either *Reciprocity* or *Trapezoid*, it would have to appear after them *both*, not just one (Rule 3). That eliminates **(B)** and **(D)**. That leaves **(E)** as the only answer possible, as shown in the following acceptable outcome:

W   S   V   R   T
— — — — —
1   2   3   4   5

Note: This question could also be answered effectively by using sketches from other questions. The sketches for the third and fourth questions show what happens when *Reciprocity* is first and *Trapezoid* is second, respectively. That work helps eliminate **(A)**, **(B)**, and **(C)**. From there, you can test the remaining two answers as described previously or wait until the final question, in which *Wisteria* is first. That sketch verifies the possibility of *Salammbo* being second in that case, immediately verifying **(E)** as possible.

6. (D) "If" / Could Be True

For this question, *Vancouver* will be second. That means *Salammbo* must be first (Rule 1). That means *Trapezoid* will be later than *Salammbo*, which means *Trapezoid* will also be later than *Reciprocity* (Rule 2). *Reciprocity* and *Trapezoid*, in that order, will take up two of the last three spaces. *Wisteria* will take up the remaining space, either before or after both *Trapezoid* and *Reciprocity* (Rule 3). That allows for two possible outcomes:

S   V   W   R   T
— — — — —
1   2   3   4   5

or

S   V   R   T   W
— — — — —
1   2   3   4   5

In that case, **(D)** is the only answer possible (in the first outcome), making it the correct one.

7. (A) "If" / Must Be False (CANNOT Be True)

For this question, *Wisteria* will be first. That doesn't allow for any definite deduction. Either option from Rule 2 is possible, so test them both (which can be easily done from the Limited Options). If you drew out all four options, then only Options Ia and IIa are in play.

For the first option, *Trapezoid* will be earlier than both *Reciprocity* and *Salammbo*, with *Salammbo* also appearing earlier than *Vancouver*. In that case, *Trapezoid* must be second.

W   T
— — — — —
1   2   3   4   5
⎵⎵⎵
R; S–V

In the second option, *Trapezoid* will be later than both *Reciprocity* and *Salammbo*. Again, *Salammbo* will also be earlier than *Vancouver*. In that case, either *Reciprocity* or *Salammbo* could be second and either *Trapezoid* or *Vancouver* could be last:

W
— — — — —
1   2   3   4   5
⎵⎵⎵
R–T
/
S–V

The correct answer to this question will be the one that must be false in both options. The remaining answers will all be possibly or definitely true in either option, if not both. *Trapezoid* can only be second in the first option. In the second option, it must come later than *Wisteria*, *Reciprocity*, and *Salammbo*. It cannot be third there. Therefore, it can never be third, making **(A)** the correct answer. For the record:

Vancouver could be third or fourth in the second option. That eliminates **(B)** and **(D)**. *Salammbo* could be fourth in the first option. That eliminates **(C)**. *Trapezoid* could be last in the second option. That eliminates **(E)**.

Game 2: Symposium Speakers

Step 1: Overview
Situation: People speaking at a business symposium

Entities: Five speakers (Long, Molina, Xiao, Yoshida, Zimmerman); two rooms (Gold and Rose)

Action: Distribution/Sequencing Hybrid. Determine in which room each speaker speaks (Distribution), and then determine what time—1:00, 2:00, or 3:00—those speeches occur (Sequencing).

Limitations: Each speaker will speak once in one of the two rooms. Three speakers will be assigned to one room and two to the other. Both rooms will have a 1:00 and a 2:00 speech, while the room with three speakers will also have a 3:00 speech.

Step 2: Sketch
The sketch should have two columns, one for each room. Within each column, there should be two definite slots, one for the 1:00 speech and one for the 2:00 speech. A third row should be set up for the 3:00 speech, but no slot can be entered until it is determined which room will have that speech. The slots will be filled by the speakers, who should be listed by initial. If desired, a note can be added that 3:00 will feature just one speaker.

L M X Y Z

	Gold	Rose
1	___	___
2	___	___
3		___ ← 1 speaker

This sketch would be fine to set up horizontally as well with 1:00, 2:00, 3:00 as the columns and Gold and Rose as the rows. Whichever configuration you prefer is fine.

Step 3: Rules
Rule 1 provides two pieces of information about Molina and Long. First, Molina will speak earlier than Long. That means Long cannot speak at 1:00 and Molina cannot speak at 3:00. Add "~L" and "~M" next to the respective rows. Second, Molina and Long will be in the same room. Draw some note indicating this (e.g., here they're boxed to indicate they're together).

$$\boxed{\begin{array}{c} M \\ \vdots \\ L \end{array}}$$

Rule 2 prevents Xiao and Yoshida from speaking earlier than Zimmerman. This does *not* necessarily mean that they must both speak *later than* Zimmerman: One of them can speak at the same time as Zimmerman. Be careful not to translate this incorrectly. You can either translate it negatively, like this:

$$\begin{array}{cc} \cancel{X} & \cancel{Y} \\ / & / \\ /Z & /Z \end{array}$$

Or affirmatively like this:

$$XZ \quad \text{or} \quad \begin{array}{c} Z \\ \vdots \\ X \end{array}$$

$$YZ \quad \text{or} \quad \begin{array}{c} Z \\ \vdots \\ Y \end{array}$$

Because Zimmerman doesn't have to be before Xiao and Yoshida, they could still speak at 1:00, as long as Zimmerman does, too. However, Zimmerman cannot speak at 3:00, because that would be the only speech at 3:00, forcing both Xiao and Yoshida to speak earlier. Add "~Z" next to 3:00. That means Zimmerman can only speak at 1:00 or 2:00—a restriction that will later lead to a crucial deduction.

Rule 3 sets up some Formal Logic: If Long is in the Gold Room, then Xiao and Zimmerman will both be in the Rose Room. Be sure to set up the contrapositive, as well: If either Xiao or Zimmerman is *not* in the Rose Room (i.e., *is* in the Gold Room), then Long is *not* in the Gold Room (i.e., *is* in the Rose Room).

$$\frac{\text{Gold}}{L} \rightarrow \frac{\text{Rose}}{X} \text{ AND } \frac{\text{Rose}}{Z}$$

$$\frac{\text{Gold}}{X} \text{ OR } \frac{\text{Gold}}{Z} \rightarrow \frac{\text{Rose}}{L}$$

Step 4: Deductions
Every rule provides significant information that involves multiple entities, so each one should be considered carefully. The last two rules both affect three speakers, but the last rule is conditional. Rule 2 is absolute and provides the greatest substance.

Zimmerman cannot speak later than Xiao or Yoshida. As previously described, that means Zimmerman could not speak at 3:00. That leaves 1:00 or 2:00. If Zimmerman speaks at 1:00, then Xiao and Yoshida could speak at any time without violating the rules. However, if Zimmerman were to speak at 2:00, then Xiao and Yoshida would be limited to speaking at 2:00 and 3:00. That would leave Long and Molina to be the two speakers at 1:00, one in each room. That would violate Rule 1. Therefore, Zimmerman cannot speak at 2:00, which leads to the most important deduction of the game: Zimmerman must speak at 1:00.

This leads to a few potential sources for Limited Options, none of which are as fruitful as one would hope.

The first opportunity is to set up two options depending upon the room in which Zimmerman speaks. However, nothing can be deduced if Zimmerman speaks in the Rose Room. Furthermore, if Zimmerman speaks in the Gold Room, Long would have to speak in the Rose Room (Rule 3) along with Molina (Rule 1). However, their times still cannot be determined as it would still be impossible to determine which room gets the 3:00 speech.

It might also seem worthwhile to set up Limited Options based on the room to which Long and Molina are assigned, but again this doesn't amount to much. Neither option—even with the information from Rule 3—would make it possible to determine which room gets the 3:00 speech or which times Long and Molina speak for certain.

Setting up any of these sets of Limited Options wouldn't be detrimental, but none of them is beneficial enough to be considered necessary. The concrete deductions are valuable enough to tackle this game efficiently:

L M X Y Z

	Gold	Rose	
1	___	___	~L, Z
2	___	___	
3		___	← 1 speaker, ~M

$$\frac{Gold}{L} \rightarrow \frac{Rose}{X} \text{ AND } \frac{Rose}{Z}$$

$$\frac{Gold}{X} \text{ OR } \frac{Gold}{Z} \rightarrow \frac{Rose}{L}$$

$$\begin{array}{c} M \\ \vdots \\ L \end{array}$$

Step 5: Questions

8. (A) Acceptability

As with any Acceptability question, go through the rules one at a time, eliminating answers that violate those rules.

(D) violates Rule 1 by making Long's speech earlier than Molina's. **(E)** violates Rule 1 by putting Long and Molina into different rooms. **(B)** violates Rule 2 by making Xiao's speech earlier than Zimmerman's. **(C)** violates Rule 3 by putting Long in the Gold Room and not putting Xiao in the Rose Room. That leaves **(A)** as the correct answer.

9. (B) Must Be False (CANNOT Be True)

The correct answer to this question will list two speakers who cannot speak at the same time. The remaining four answers will list a pair of speakers who could speak at the same time.

Looking at the sketch, Zimmerman must speak at 1:00 (by the Deductions) and Long cannot speak at 1:00 (Rule 1). So, Zimmerman and Long cannot speak at the same time, making **(B)** the correct answer.

For the record, this question could also be skipped and dealt with efficiently after drawing sketches for the third and fifth questions of the set. The sketch for the third question shows Long and Yoshida speaking at the same time, eliminating **(A)**. The sketch for the fifth question shows Molina and Xiao speaking at the same time as well as Yoshida and Zimmerman, eliminating **(C)** and **(E)**. That leaves just two answers to test, and **(D)** can be eliminated with a quick sketch like so:

	Gold	Rose
1	Z	M
2	X	Y
3		L

10. (A) "If" / Must Be False (CANNOT Be True)

For this question, Xiao will speak at 3:00, but the room still cannot be determined. Still, everyone else will have to speak at 1:00 and 2:00. By the Deductions, Zimmerman will speak at 1:00. By Rule 1, Molina must also speak at 1:00, and Long will speak at 2:00. That leaves Yoshida to be the second speaker at 2:00.

	Gold	Rose	
1	___	___	Z, M
2	___	___	Y, L
3			X

While the times are completely determined, there's no way to figure out the room to which anyone is assigned. Still, it's impossible for Long and Yoshida to be in the same room because they're speaking at the same time. That makes **(A)** the correct answer.

11. (C) Partial Acceptability

This question asks for an acceptable assignment, in order, for just the Gold Room. Start by going through the rules one at a time, just as with a typical Acceptability question. If there are multiple answers remaining, test them individually by considering what's *not* listed (in this case, the speakers in the Rose Room).

(A) violates Rule 1 by having Long speak earlier than Molina. **(B)** violates Rule 1 by having Molina speak in a room without Long. **(D)** violates Rule 2 by having Yoshida speak earlier than Zimmerman, and **(E)** violates Rule 3 by having Zimmerman speak in the Gold Room while Long is also speaking in the Gold Room. That leaves **(C)** as the correct answer.

12. (C) "If" / Could Be True

For this question, Yoshida will speak at 1:00. By the Deductions, Zimmerman also speaks at 1:00. That means the remaining speakers must speak at 2:00 or 3:00. By Rule 1, Molina will speak at 2:00 and Long will be the one speaker at 3:00. That means Xiao must speak at 2:00.

	Gold	Rose	
1	__	__	Z, Y
2	__	__	M , X
3		L	

Again, the times are completely determined, but no speaker can be placed in either room with certainty. With that, Molina will speak at 2:00 and could speak in the Gold Room, making **(C)** the correct answer.

13. (E) Rule Substitution

For this question, Rule 2 will be removed and replaced by one of the answer choices. The correct answer must reestablish the restriction of the original rule (Xiao and Yoshida cannot speak earlier than Zimmerman) without adding any new restrictions that were not already in place.

Having Long speak at 3:00 does nothing to reestablish the relationship between Xiao, Yoshida, and Zimmerman and also adds a restriction to Long that wasn't originally in place. That eliminates **(A)**.

Blocking Molina from speaking earlier than Zimmerman would not prevent Xiao or Yoshida from speaking before Zimmerman, which the original rule *did* prevent. That eliminates **(B)**.

If one of Xiao or Yoshida were forced to speak after Zimmerman, then the other speaker could still speak *before* Zimmerman, which wasn't allowed by the original rule. That eliminates **(C)**.

Forcing Xiao or Yoshida to speak at 2:00 does not prevent Zimmerman from speaking at 3:00, which would never be allowed by the original rule. That eliminates **(D)**.

Having Zimmerman speak at 1:00 guarantees that Xiao and Yoshida cannot speak any earlier, reestablishing the original rule. Furthermore, by the original deductions, Zimmerman had to speak at 1:00, so this would not add any further unwarranted restrictions, making **(E)** the correct answer.

Game 3: Historic Building Owners

Step 1: Overview

Situation: Three families owning village buildings in the 17th century

Entities: Five buildings (forge, granary, inn, mill, stable); three families (Trents, Williamses, Yandells)

Action: Distribution. Determine which buildings were owned by each family.

Limitations: Each building was owned by just one of the families, and each family owned at least one building. With five buildings to distribute, either one family owned three buildings while the others owned one each, or two families owned two buildings while the remaining family owned just one.

Step 2: Sketch

Each building will be assigned to one family. So, list the buildings by initial and set up a table with a column (or row, if preferred) for each family. Each family owned at least one building, so start off with one slot in each column, leaving space to add more as needed. Make a note of the numeric possibilities, as numbers are often very important in Distribution games.

$$
\begin{array}{c}
\text{f g i m s} \\
\begin{array}{c|c|c}
T & W & Y \\
\hline
\underline{} & \underline{} & \underline{}
\end{array}
\quad
\begin{array}{c}
3{:}1{:}1 \\
\text{or} \\
2{:}2{:}1
\end{array}
\end{array}
$$

Step 3: Rules

Rule 1 further limits the numbers: The Williamses owned more buildings than the Yandells. That means the Williamses owned at least two buildings, so add a second slot under their column. That leaves one more slot to assign. It cannot go to the Yandells, otherwise they would have owned the same number of buildings as the Williamses. Therefore, the Yandells owned just one building. Close off their column.

Rule 2 restricts certain buildings from being owned by the same family. No family owned both the forge and the inn or both the forge and the mill. Draw these rules to the side:

$$
\frac{f}{i} \quad \frac{f}{m}
$$

Rule 3 sets up two possible outcomes, at least one of which must have happened: The Trents owned the stable or the Yandells owned the inn. It is possible that both of these happened. You can either draw this rule in shorthand to the side (as shown here), or use Rule 3 to set up Limited Options.

$$
\frac{T}{s} \quad or \quad \frac{Y}{i}
$$

Step 4: Deductions

In the first option, the Trents will get the stable. However, that means anybody can now have owned the inn. The Yandells and the Williamses may have owned any of the remaining buildings, and the Trents could still have owned a second building. This option offers very little.

However, the second option is more helpful. In that option, the Yandells will get the inn. By Rule 1, that's it for the Yandells. The remaining four buildings will be distributed among the Trents and the Williamses. However, by Rule 2, neither family can own both the forge and the mill. So, those two buildings must be split—one to the Trents and one to the Williamses. Add "f/m" to both columns. The Williamses will also receive at least one of the granary and stable.

$$
\text{II)} \quad
\begin{array}{c|c|c}
T & W & > \quad Y \\
\hline
f/m & m/f & \underline{\quad i \quad} \\
& g/s &
\end{array}
$$

In either option, the fifth slot could still be assigned to either the Trents or the Williamses. With Rules 1 and 3 built entirely into the sketches, just keep track of the restrictions from Rule 2 as you head to the questions.

Step 5: Questions

14. (A) Acceptability

The correct answer here will be acceptable—the one answer that doesn't violate any rules. Go through the rules one at a time, and eliminate the four answers that violate those rules.

(D) and **(E)** violate Rule 1 by assigning the Williamses the same number or fewer buildings than the Yandells. **(C)** violates Rule 2 by having the Trents own both the forge and the mill, and **(B)** violates Rule 3 by assigning neither the stable to the Trents nor the inn to the Yandells. That leaves **(A)** as the correct answer.

15. (D) Must Be False (CANNOT Be True)

The correct answer to this question will be a pair of buildings that couldn't have both been owned by the Trents. The remaining four answers all could have been.

By Rule 3, the Trents could have owned the stable. In that case (as seen in the first option), the Trents could still have owned any of the remaining buildings. That eliminates **(C)** and **(E)** as possible. However, if the Trents did not own the stable (only possible in the second option), then the inn would have been owned by the Yandells. In that case, the

Trents could not own the inn. Because the Trents cannot have owned the inn without the stable, **(D)** is impossible and thus the correct answer.

For the record, the Trents could own the forge and the granary in Option II, leaving the Williamses with the mill and stable—that eliminates **(A)**. Also, the Trents could own the granary and mill in Option II, leaving the Williamses with the forge and stable—that eliminates **(B)**.

16. (D) "If" / Must Be True

For this question, the Yandells owned the mill. Because they owned only one building (Rule 1), that will be it. This places you in Option I. The remaining buildings must be distributed between the Trents and the Williamses.

Per Option I, because the Yandells did not own the inn, the Trents must have owned the stable (Rule 3). By Rule 2, neither remaining family could have owned both the forge and the inn, so those must be split between the Trents and the Williamses. The Williamses still owned at least one other building (Rule 1). With only the granary remaining, that must be their second building.

T	W	Y
s	f/i	m
i/f	g	

With that, the Williamses must have owned the granary, making **(D)** the correct answer.

17. (B) "If" / Could Be True

For this question, one of the families owned the granary and the inn, but it's not stated which family. The Yandells could only own one building (Rule 1), so it wasn't them. Also, because the Yandells didn't own the inn here, you must be in Option I where the Trents must have owned the stable (Rule 3). With that, the Trents could not have owned the granary and the inn. If they did, they would have owned three buildings, and the Williamses had to have owned at least two and the Yandells one. That would be six buildings, and there are only five to assign.

That means the Williamses must have owned the granary and the inn. By Rule 2, they cannot own the forge, so that must have been owned by the Trents or the Yandells. The mill is a Floater and could still have been owned by any of the three families.

T	W	Y
s	g	
	i	

From that, given that this question is asking for what "could be true" an assignment of the mill to any family would be

correct. Sure enough, the Trents could have owned the mill, leaving the forge for the Yandells. That makes **(B)** the correct answer.

18. (E) "If" / Complete and Accurate List

For this question, the Trents owned just one building. The correct answer will list every building that one could be. The incorrect answers will either leave out a possible building or include a building that it cannot be—or both.

A quick glance at the Limited Options shows that, if the Trents owned just one building, it would have to be one of three: the stable (first option) or the forge or the mill (second option). That's the exact list in **(E)**, making that the correct answer. To verify that:

If the Trents owned just the stable, the Yandells could have owned the forge and the Williamses could have owned the granary, inn, and mill:

T	W	Y
s	g	f
	i	
	m	

This is acceptable, so the correct answer must list the stable. That eliminates **(A)**, **(B)**, and **(D)**.

If the Trents *didn't* own the stable, the Yandells would have owned the inn (Rule 3). That means the forge and the mill would be split between the Trents and the Williamses. The Williamses would then get rest: the granary and the stable.

T	W	Y
f/m	m/f	i
	g	
	s	

This is acceptable, so the correct answer must also list the forge and the mill, eliminating **(C)** and making **(E)** the correct answer.

Game 4: Florist's Bouquets

Step 1: Overview
Situation: A florist creating bouquets for a customer

Entities: Three bouquets; five flowers (lilies, peonies, roses, snapdragons, tulips)

Action: Matching. Determine which flowers will be used in each bouquet.

Limitations: Each bouquet will contain at least one type of flower, but as many as all five types. However, there are no limitations set on the flowers. They each can be used in any number of bouquets—and there's no indication that they all have to be used.

Step 2: Sketch
Because of the uncertainty with the numbers, simply list the flowers by initial and set up a column (or row) for each of the three numbered bouquets. Add one space in each column, with space to add more.

Step 3: Rules
Rule 1 prevents any flower from being in both bouquets 1 and 3. Make a note of this to the side.

1 ≠ 3

Rule 2 indicates that bouquets 2 and 3 must have *exactly* two flowers in common. Start by adding a second slot under each of those columns. Then, use a connector or an equal sign to indicate that those two flowers in each column must be the same.

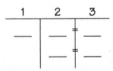

It's important to note that each bouquet can still get more flowers, none of which would be shared.

Rule 3 establishes snapdragons in bouquet 3. However, it cannot be determined whether or not this is one of the two flowers shared with bouquet 2, so do not place it in one of those slots. Instead, add an *S* under the third column that can be placed in one of the shared spots or a separate spot depending on the situation.

Rule 4 provides two pieces of information in a Formal Logic statement. If a bouquet has lilies, it will also have roses; if a bouquet has lilies it cannot have snapdragons. Set that Formal Logic statement up with its contrapositive:

L → R AND ~S
~R OR S → ~L

Rule 5 provides just one more simple piece of Formal Logic: If a bouquet has tulips, it will also have peonies. Again, draw that out with its contrapositive:

T → P
~P → ~T

Step 4: Deductions
Unfortunately, major deductions are not to be found in this game despite the wealth of rules. There are no Blocks of Entities and no obvious Limited Options to consider. Numbers will be crucial to this game, but there are still too many possibilities to determine anything with certainty.

The only source of deductions is the one Established Entity from Rule 3: Snapdragons are in bouquet 3. Because of that, there can be no snapdragons in bouquet 1 (Rule 1), and there can be no lilies in bouquet 3 (Rule 4). However, bouquet 2 can still have lilies, as long as it shares two *other* flowers with bouquet 3—and that's it. From there, work through the questions strategically, and keep referring back to the rules and previous sketchwork when you get stuck. Entering the question set, your Master Sketch should look something like this:

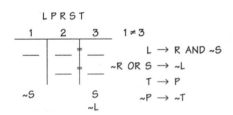

Step 5: Questions

19. (A) Acceptability
As with typical Acceptability questions, go through the rules one at a time, eliminating answers that violate those rules.

(B) violates Rule 1 because bouquets 1 and 3 both have peonies. No answers violate Rule 2. **(E)** violates Rule 3 because there are no snapdragons in bouquet 3. **(D)** violates Rule 4 because bouquet 3 has lilies and snapdragons (and it *should* have roses). **(C)** violates Rule 5 because bouquet 2 has tulips but no peonies. That leaves **(A)** as the correct answer.

20. (B) "If" / Must Be True
For this question, bouquet 1 will contain lilies. By Rule 4, it will also contain roses. That means bouquet 3 cannot contain lilies or roses (Rule 1). Bouquet 3 already has snapdragons, but needs at least one more flower (Rule 2). The only remaining flowers are peonies and tulips. The bouquet cannot have tulips without peonies (Rule 5). So, bouquet 3

will contain snapdragons and peonies alone or snapdragons with peonies *and* tulips.

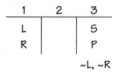

1	2	3
L		S
R		P
		~L, ~R

Either way, bouquet 3 must contain at least peonies along with the snapdragons, making **(B)** the correct answer. The remaining answers are all possible, but need not be true.

21. (E) "If" / Partial Acceptability

For this question, bouquet 1 will contain tulips. By Rule 5, it will also contain peonies. That means bouquet 3 cannot contain tulips or peonies (Rule 1). Bouquet 3 already has snapdragons, so it also cannot have lilies (Rule 4). That leaves only one other flower: roses. Because it has to have at least two flowers (Rule 2), bouquet 3 must get the roses. Furthermore, because that is all bouquet 3 can have, those must be the two flowers shared with bouquet 2.

1	2	3
T	S ≠	S
P	R ≠	R
	~T, ~P, ~L	

While bouquet 3 is restricted by bouquet 1, bouquet 2 does not have those same restrictions. An acceptable set of flowers for bouquet 2 must include roses and snapdragons, but may contain more. **(D)** is the only answer to do so, making it the correct answer.

22. (A) Partial Acceptability (CANNOT)

The correct answer will list a set of flowers that cannot be the complete set for bouquet 2. The four incorrect answers will all list acceptable flower combinations for bouquet 2.

Bouquet 2 is the most unlimited bouquet; it's the only one that can have any of the five flowers. The only restriction is that it must share two of its flowers with bouquet 3. The major restriction to bouquet 3 is that, because it has snapdragons, it cannot have lilies (Rule 4). So lilies are the only flowers that cannot be shared between bouquets 2 and 3.

If bouquet 2 only has two flowers, those are the two that must be shared with bouquet 3. Because they cannot share lilies, that makes **(A)** impossible, and thus the correct answer. For the record, bouquets 2 and 3 could share tulips and peonies. In that case, bouquet 2 could have just those two flowers, or it could have roses that it doesn't share with bouquet 3. That means **(B)** and **(D)** are possible and can be eliminated.

1	2	3
	T ≠	T
	P ≠	P
	(R)	S

Bouquets 2 and 3 could also share snapdragons and roses (as seen in the previous question), in which case bouquet 2 could also add peonies or peonies and tulips. That means **(C)** and **(E)** are also possible and can be eliminated.

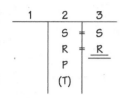

1	2	3
	S ≠	S
	R ≠	R
	P	
	(T)	

23. (C) Must Be False (CANNOT Be True)

The correct answer will definitely be false. The four incorrect answers will all be possible. With so many possible outcomes and so few deductions, it is helpful to use previous work to narrow down the answers.

A quick glance at the first question, an Acceptability question, offers immediate help. The correct answer there shows that bouquet 1 can have lilies and roses, while bouquet 3 can have peonies, snapdragons, and tulips. That immediately eliminates **(A)** and **(E)**.

With the third question of the set, bouquet 1 gets tulips and peonies. It need not have any more, so **(B)** is also possible and can be eliminated.

Finally, the four wrong answers to the previous question list acceptable arrangements for bouquet 2. One of those acceptable arrangements is peonies, roses, and snapdragons. That means **(D)** is possible and can be eliminated.

And just like that, there's only one answer left: **(C)**. That is the correct answer. To verify:

If bouquet 2 had only lilies, peonies, and roses, it would have to share two of those flowers with bouquet 3. However, because bouquet 3 has snapdragons, it cannot have lilies (Rule 4). Therefore, it must share peonies and roses with bouquet 2. By Rule 1, that means bouquet 1 couldn't have peonies, roses, or snapdragons. With no peonies, it could not have tulips (Rule 5). With no roses, it could not have lilies (Rule 4). That means there would be no flowers for bouquet 1, which is unacceptable.

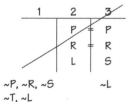

1	2	3
	P ≠	P
	R ≠	R
	L	S
~P, ~R, ~S		~L
~T, ~L		

That is why **(C)** cannot be true and is thus the correct answer.

Section IV: Logical Reasoning

Q#	Question Type	Correct	Difficulty
1	Weaken	D	★
2	Principle (Identify/Strengthen)	D	★
3	Flaw	E	★
4	Method of Argument	C	★
5	Main Point	A	★
6	Strengthen/Weaken (Evaluate the Argument)	E	★
7	Principle (Identify/Inference)	E	★
8	Inference	D	★★★
9	Role of a Statement	D	★★
10	Flaw	E	★★
11	Main Point	B	★★
12	Inference	A	★★
13	Assumption (Necessary)	B	★★
14	Inference	C	★★
15	Paradox	A	★
16	Inference	E	★
17	Weaken	C	★★
18	Parallel Flaw	C	★★
19	Assumption (Necessary)	B	★
20	Strengthen	D	★★★
21	Parallel Reasoning	E	★★★★
22	Paradox	D	★★★
23	Principle (Apply/Inference)	E	★★★★
24	Assumption (Sufficient)	E	★★
25	Flaw	E	★★
26	Assumption (Necessary)	A	★★★

1. (D) Weaken

Step 1: Identify the Question Type
The question asks you to *undermine* an argument, which is a common LSAT way of saying Weaken. Identify the author's assumption and find an answer that attacks it.

Step 2: Untangle the Stimulus
The Keyword [*c*]*learly* indicates the author's conclusion: Chocolate affects one's ability to taste coffee. The evidence is an experiment involving two groups of people. Both groups were asked to taste five coffees. The first group was also given chocolate, while the second group was not. The "chocolate" group thought all of the coffees tasted pretty much the same, while the "non-chocolate" group noted some differences among the coffees.

Step 3: Make a Prediction
There are two classic problems with this argument. First is the confusion of correlation and causation, with the author claiming chocolate caused the tasting problem just because it happened to be present. Second is unconfirmed consistency between the two groups. The only difference cited was the chocolate, but there could be other unmentioned differences. Both problems hinge on the same assumption: Chocolate was the only distinctive factor that affected the first group's tastes. To weaken this, find something that suggests another cause of the tasting discrepancy.

Step 4: Evaluate the Answer Choices
(D) cuts right into the author's assumption. If the "chocolate" group was asked to try again without the chocolate and *still* couldn't tell the difference, then that would suggest the chocolate is irrelevant to their tasting deficiency.

(A) is a 180. If the group assignments were random, that takes away any bias and reduces the chance that anything else differentiated the groups other than the chocolate.

(B) is another 180. Seeing the same result with a larger sample would only help validate the author's findings.

(C) is an Irrelevant Comparison. The physical states of chocolate and coffee have no bearing on whether consuming one affects the ability to taste the other.

(E) has no effect on the argument. Even if the people in the "non-chocolate" group differed in how much they detected, that doesn't change the fact that they all noticed *some* difference while the "chocolate" group did not.

2. (D) Principle (Identify/Strengthen)

Step 1: Identify the Question Type
The question explicitly asks for a *principle*, but one that will "justify the [residents'] reasoning" provided. That indicates an Identify the Principle question that uses the skills of a Strengthen question. The correct answer will use broader wording to validate the residents' reasoning.

Step 2: Untangle the Stimulus
The residents of a certain community are arguing against a family trying to build a house on the family's land. They argue that building a house would destroy the community's artistic heritage by changing the landscape—one that was immortalized in a painting by a beloved local artist.

Step 3: Make a Prediction
The residents' argument hinges entirely on preserving the community's artistic heritage, which the residents clearly feel is more important than some house the landowners want to build on that property. In broader terms, the residents assume that the artistic heritage of a community outweighs the personal desires of one landowner.

Step 4: Evaluate the Answer Choices
(D) matches the residents' logic perfectly, focusing directly on their concern: preservation of a community's artistic heritage over the desires of landowners.

(A) is a Distortion, if not a 180. The residents are trying to preserve an historic landscape, not a building. In fact, they're trying to *prevent* a building from being erected.

(B) is Out of Scope. Nothing is stated about purchasing the land for the public trust.

(C) is a Distortion. The residents are the ones demanding preservation, not the artist—who has no say in the matter because it's stated that he recently died.

(E) is also a Distortion. The residents do not feel the house in question would "obstruct access" to the land, only that it would alter the landscape.

3. (E) Flaw

Step 1: Identify the Question Type
Asking why an argument is "vulnerable to criticism" is standard LSAT language for saying find the flaw. Look for why the evidence doesn't logically establish the conclusion, and keep an eye out for common LSAT flaws.

Step 2: Untangle the Stimulus
Moore claims that UV-radiation-blocking sunscreens aren't really protecting users from the radiation that causes skin cancer. As evidence, Moore cites scientific studies showing how, on average, people who use such sunscreens regularly develop the same amount of skin cancer as those who don't.

Step 3: Make a Prediction
The scientific studies separate people into two groups: those who wear UV-protecting sunscreen regularly and those who don't. However, that is the only difference cited between the two groups. To declare the sunscreens ineffective, Moore must assume that both groups were equally susceptible to skin cancer in the first place. If there's something else distinctive about the sunscreen wearers that would usually make them *more* cancer prone, then the sunscreen could

have worked—reducing the likelihood of cancer to the same level of people who don't wear sunscreen. Moore overlooks this possibility, and that's a flaw.

Step 4: Evaluate the Answer Choices

(E) precisely identifies Moore's mistake. If the people who regularly wear sunscreen spend more time in the sun, they'd usually be open to *more* skin cancers due to greater exposure to UV radiation. In that case, contrary to Moore's reasoning, sunscreen *would* be seen as effective by preventing these people from getting more cancers than others.

(A) is Out of Scope. Whether sunscreens have any added benefits has no bearing on whether they work at protecting users from skin cancer.

(B) is a Distortion. Different degrees of severity are ultimately not an issue here. The only question is: Do sunscreens prevent skin cancer by blocking radiation or not? It's a "yes or no" issue, not a "how much" one.

(C) is Out of Scope. Sunscreens that are not designed to block radiation are irrelevant. The argument is about radiation-blocking sunscreen versus no radiation-blocking sunscreen.

(D) is Out of Scope. The evidence doesn't mention the probability of anybody getting skin cancer, and there's nothing presented that would be described as "impossible to challenge."

4. (C) Method of Argument

Step 1: Identify the Question Type

The phrase "reasoning technique" is another way of saying method of argument. The question stem already starts things off by stating the psychologist is "attempting to undermine an argument." From there, use Keywords and structure to determine *how* the psychologist is trying to weaken a point of view as opposed to relying too much on *what* the psychologist is saying.

Step 2: Untangle the Stimulus

The argument being attacked here is that the laborious nature of Freudian psychotherapy makes it most effective. However, the psychologist isn't convinced. As counterevidence, the psychologist makes a parallel reference to auto repair shops, suggesting that the same logic (i.e., the shops with the most laborious process are most effective) would be unacceptable.

Step 3: Make a Prediction

This is a classic case of counterargument by analogy. The psychologist tries to weaken the original argument by showing how the same argument in a similar circumstance would be improper. The correct answer will describe this common technique.

Step 4: Evaluate the Answer Choices

(C) is a perfect match. The psychologist presents an analogy (regarding auto repair shops) in which trying to reach the same conclusion (labor-intensive equals effective) is no good.

(A) is inaccurate because the psychologist introduces a specific counterexample, not a general principle.

(B) is a Distortion and, at worst, a 180. The original argument's premises are that Freudian psychotherapy is difficult and time-consuming. The psychologist does not question that—in fact, she seems to agree with that assessment. What the psychologist objects to is using that description as a sign of effectiveness.

(D) is a Distortion. The original argument does not use an analogy; the psychologist does … and she probably wouldn't consider her own analogy faulty at all.

(E) is Out of Scope. There are no causes or effects described here. Even if, stretching the logic here, the original argument is said to describe the difficulty of Freudian psychoanalysis as the cause of its effectiveness, the psychologist never suggests the argument is backward (i.e., the effectiveness is actually the cause of the difficulty).

5. (A) Main Point

Step 1: Identify the Question Type

The question asks for the argument's *conclusion* or main point. Use Keywords and look for the one statement supported by everything else.

Step 2: Untangle the Stimulus

The opening Keyword [*w*]*hile* sets up a notable contrast. The author admits that biodiversity is important to the survival of life in general, but then suggests that this doesn't require the survival of every single species. After all, life on Earth just needs certain niches to be filled, and there are multiple candidates to fill some of those niches.

Step 3: Make a Prediction

With no major logic Keywords to help out, look for the strongest opinion, then try adding your own Keywords to confirm what's evidence ("because") and what's a conclusion ("therefore"). In this case, the strongest opinion appears to be that we don't need every species to survive for biodiversity. Why does the author believe that? *Because* there are multiple species that could fill the niches needed for survival. Using *because* validates that the details about niches are evidence to back up the main point: Biodiversity does not require the survival of all species.

Step 4: Evaluate the Answer Choices

(A) is a match. Everything in the argument after this claim is just reasoning to support it.

(B) is presented as a fact, not an opinion. Facts tend to be evidence, not conclusions.

(C) paraphrases the very first statement, but that's just a statement the author concedes before moving on to the main argument. The Keyword *while* often indicates this process of logic: While [I agree about this point], [here's my alternate conclusion].

(D) is the evidence to back up the main point, not the conclusion itself.

(E) is Out of Scope. The author never mentions any species that are the "most indispensible."

6. (E) Strengthen/Weaken (Evaluate the Argument)

Step 1: Identify the Question Type
A question that asks you to evaluate an argument is a twist on a Strengthen/Weaken question. The correct answer will question the assumption in a way that will strengthen or weaken the argument depending on the answer. Start by predicting the assumption, and then find an answer that questions the validity of that assumption.

Step 2: Untangle the Stimulus
The clinician mentions that patients with immune system disorders usually take two drugs—one to treat the disorder, and one to prevent bone loss caused by the first drug. The Keyword [s]*ince* indicates evidence that will ultimately lead to the clinician's point. In this case, there's a new drug that helps grow new bone cells. Therefore, the clinician concludes that patients should take this new drug along with the other two drugs.

Step 3: Make a Prediction
The word *should* indicates a recommendation, a common argumentative technique on the LSAT. Recommendations come with a built-in assumption: The pros or benefits of the recommended course of action outweigh any potential cons. In this case, the clinician assumes the benefits of the new drug outweigh any unstated risk to adding it to the current set of drugs. The correct answer will question whether this addition is worth the recommendation.

Step 4: Evaluate the Answer Choices
(E) does the job. If the new drug is ineffective when combined with the other drugs, there's no real benefit and the recommendation is pointless. However, if the new drug *is* still effective, the recommendation is sound.

(A) is irrelevant to the argument. The size of drug classes has no bearing on whether taking the new drug is worthwhile.

(B) is a good question, but unfortunately has no bearing on the argument at hand. The correct answer needs to question the clinician's recommendation, not the unfortunate side effects of the original drug used to treat the disorder.

(C) is an Irrelevant Comparison. How the cost of the two drugs compare wouldn't matter because the clinician recommends

taking *both*. The question still stands: Is adding the new drug a good idea or not?

(D) is Out of Scope. The question is whether it's wise to take the new drug or not. It doesn't matter how long people have been using the current drug.

7. (E) Principle (Identify/Inference)

Step 1: Identify the Question Type
The question directly asks for a principle to which the given argument conforms. Because the stimulus is an argument, break it down into evidence and conclusion. Then, find an answer that makes the same logical argument, only in broader terms.

Step 2: Untangle the Stimulus
The critic is discussing the city's new concert hall, which was built on a hilltop to give it the image of "elevated purpose." However, the critic isn't buying that logic. The critic's opinion, and in this case the conclusion, is that the concert hall fails at being a civic building. This is *because* the concert hall is far from the city center. As further support, the critic cites an example of something that *does* work as a civic building: the art museum. By being located in the downtown area, the museum encourages social cohesion and gives the city life.

Step 3: Make a Prediction
By the critic's reasoning, lofty locations far from the city do not make for a successful civic building. Instead, success is based on what the art museum provides: social cohesion and a lively city. The correct answer will generalize this logic.

Step 4: Evaluate the Answer Choices
(E) matches the critic's logic exactly. Making social cohesion and a lively city the purpose of civil buildings fits the critic's praise of the art museum and argument against the concert hall.

(A) is a Distortion and, at worst, a 180. The critic doesn't value elevated sites, as evidenced by the criticism against the concert hall.

(B) is a Distortion. The critic mentions social cohesion as an attribute of a successful civic building, not something that depends on the presence of civic buildings.

(C) is a 180. The critic is against the concert hall, a building already located on a spectacular site.

(D) is Out of Scope. The critic makes no mention of city design or complementing civic buildings.

8. (D) Inference

Step 1: Identify the Question Type
The question asks for something that can "reasonably be concluded" based on the findings provided. That means the correct answer will be supported by the given information,

making this an Inference question. Be sure to combine information when possible to form logical deductions.

Step 2: Untangle the Stimulus

Before the findings are presented, the author provides a fact about fluoride: Minerals containing fluoride dissolve in the rain, releasing fluoride into a region's groundwater. The findings indicate a discrepancy: The concentration of fluoride in the groundwater is higher in areas where the only difference is a higher concentration of sodium in the soil.

Step 3: Make a Prediction

They key here is that, where the fluoride levels differ, the sodium level is the *only* other significant difference. That suggests sodium is a significant factor in determining how much fluoride is released in a region's groundwater. Furthermore, because fluoride is released when fluoride-bearing minerals dissolve, that would appear to be when sodium's role takes effect.

Step 4: Evaluate the Answer Choices

(D) is directly implied by the findings described.

(A) is Out of Scope and Extreme. Minerals are directly identified as *a* source of fluoride, but there's no suggestion whether this is or is not the *primary* source.

(B) is a 180 that contradicts the first sentence. If fluoride-bearing minerals dissolve in the rain, fluoride enters the region's groundwater, and thus it *would* affect fluoride levels in different locations.

(C) is an Irrelevant Comparison. The source of sodium is not mentioned. The findings don't indicate it comes from sodium-bearing minerals, let alone compares such minerals to fluoride-bearing ones.

(E) is Out of Scope. Again, the findings don't indicate whether the sodium in sodium-rich regions come from sodium-bearing minerals. There's no indication how high the concentration of such minerals are.

9. (D) Role of a Statement

Step 1: Identify the Question Type

This question refers to a statement in the stimulus and asks you to identify how it "figures in the argument." That's standard wording for a Role of a Statement question. Find the statement and underline or make a mark next to it. Then, after dissecting the argument, figure whether the statement is a conclusion or some part of the evidence—in which case, consider why the author included that statement.

Step 2: Untangle the Stimulus

The statement in question about the lack of evidence is the very last one in the argument. The rest of the stimulus starts off with a strong opinion: Fraenger is probably wrong about the artist Bosch being a member of the fringe group Brethren of the Free Spirit. When an author contradicts another's point of view, that contradiction is often the conclusion—and that's the case here. The author concedes that Fraenger's idea would explain some of Bosch's art, but the rest of the evidence backs up the author's dissent: Information points to Bosch being a mainstream churchgoer and, even if Bosch ever switched, there's no evidence of him going to the Brethren.

Step 3: Make a Prediction

The last two statements, including the statement in question, are part of the author's evidence in attacking Fraenger's point of view. The correct answer will point out this function.

Step 4: Evaluate the Answer Choices

(D) is perfect. As predicted, the final statement is there to call Fraenger's hypothesis into question, and, because it states that there was "no evidence" of Bosch's membership in the Brethren, that "question[s] the sufficiency" of Fraenger's information.

(A) is Extreme. The author says Fraenger's hypothesis is "unlikely to be correct," not that it's guaranteed to be false.

(B) is a Distortion. Not being a member of the Brethren is hardly enough evidence to support Bosch being in a mainstream church. The last two claims merely work in conjunction to support the author's criticism of Fraenger.

(C) starts off well by saying the statement counters Fraenger's hypothesis, but the statement is about a lack of evidence. That's not the same as attacking Fraenger's credibility. In fact, that would counter the second sentence in which the author mentions Fraenger's hypothesis *has* credibility.

(E) is a Distortion. The statement is about Bosch's religious affiliation; it has nothing to do with his art's subject matter.

10. (E) Flaw

Step 1: Identify the Question Type

If an argument is "vulnerable to criticism," there's a flaw. The correct answer will identify why the evidence does not soundly support the conclusion. Keep an eye out for common argumentative flaws.

Step 2: Untangle the Stimulus

The salesperson insists that the Super XL vacuum is superior to the old vacuum. The evidence comes from a quick demonstration. First, the salesperson ran the old vacuum once over a dirty carpet. Then, the Super XL was run over the same carpet and picked up some dirt that was left behind from the old one.

Step 3: Make a Prediction

The major problem is that the two vacuums were tested under different conditions. The old one was tested on a fully dirty carpet. The Super XL was tested on a partially cleaned carpet, which might have been much easier for any vacuum to finish. Unless the two vacuums are subjected to the same tests and conditions, the comparison is invalid. The correct answer will call the salesperson out on this.

Step 4: Evaluate the Answer Choices

(E) gets to the heart of the problem. The salesperson ignores how the vacuums would perform under the same conditions. If both vacuums were to pick up the same amount from the same starting point, the salesperson's claim would not hold.

(A) is a Distortion. Even if there was still dirt left after the Super XL trial, that dirt was also left behind by the old vacuum. Therefore, while the Super XL may not be 100 percent effective, it could still be better than the old vacuum.

(B) is Out of Scope. The salesperson's claim is about the Super XL's current performance, not its future performance.

(C) is Extreme. The salesperson merely claims Super XL is *better* than the old vacuum. The salesperson never goes so far as to say it's the best.

(D) is a Distortion. Regardless of the actual total amount of dirt removed by each, the salesperson's argument rests on the fact that the old vacuum left dirt behind that was picked up by the Super XL. The salesperson wouldn't care if the old vacuum picked up more dirt—it still left some behind that the Super XL got.

11. (B) Main Point

Step 1: Identify the Question Type

This question asks for the argument's "overall conclusion," a sure sign of a Main Point question. Use Keywords to follow the structure and look for a strong opinion supported by the content around it.

Step 2: Untangle the Stimulus

The manager starts off by introducing a needed solution to a pending problem: The company needs to change its vendor contracts to avoid weakening its supply chain. This is followed by an argument by [*s*]*ome* people: A weak supply chain is not an immediate concern, so don't worry about it. The Keyword [*b*]*ut* indicates the manager's rebuttal, saying it would be irresponsible to ignore the problem now. To support this, the manager offers an analogy to financial planning in which ignoring the concern of distant retirement would be similarly irresponsible.

Step 3: Make a Prediction

Making a point by contradicting other people's view is a common technique on Main Point questions. In this case, the manager's primary conclusion is the strong opinion that pushing off the supply chain problem is *irresponsible*. The correct answer will highlight this point of view.

Step 4: Evaluate the Answer Choices

(B) is a perfect paraphrase of the manager's point.

(A) is an accurate summary of [*s*]*ome* people's argument, but that's not the manager's conclusion. That's the point the manager disputes.

(C) rephrases the opening statement. However, the rest of the argument indicates if that condition were to go through, it would be *irresponsible*. Therefore, **(C)** is missing the author's opinion on whether or not changes should be made to the vendor contracts.

(D) is a Distortion. While the analogy suggests that both situations are subject to a similar problem with procrastination, the manager never states any recommendation for the company and the financial planner to use the "same practices."

(E) is a Distortion. Financial planning is brought up merely as an analogy to make a point about the argument's true focus: the company. Furthermore, the phrase "only if" is more restrictive than the analogy suggests.

12. (A) Inference

Step 1: Identify the Question Type

The correct answer will be "supported by" the given information. That means it can be inferred from the stimulus, making this an Inference question. Because the stimulus is said to consist of *information*, don't look for an argument. Just gather details and look for ways to combine facts by using duplicated concepts.

Step 2: Untangle the Stimulus

The stimulus presents a lot of information about book sales from last year. First, overall sales were the highest they've ever been, as were cookbook sales in particular. In addition, most (i.e., more than 50%) of those cookbooks were not for beginners—which had never been the case. Back to sales figures, professional cooks bought more cookbooks than ever before. Finally, there's information about one book: *Problem-Free Cooking*. It's for beginners and is available worldwide.

Step 3: Make a Prediction

Start by addressing the single book—*Problem-Free Cooking*. Because it's for beginners, it could only be part of the minority of cookbook sales (because most cookbooks sold last year were *not* for beginners). However, there's no indication how well it sold in comparison to other beginner cookbooks, or any individual cookbook for that matter. Therefore, that book is pretty much a nonissue. Instead, focus on the strong numbers: Total books sales have never been higher. Total books bought by professional chefs have never been higher, and total cookbook sales have never been higher. Furthermore, nonbeginner cookbooks make up the biggest-ever proportion of cookbooks sold. Taking the biggest proportion ever of the biggest overall sales figures can only mean that nonbeginner cookbooks had its highest sales of all time.

Step 4: Evaluate the Answer Choices

(A) is indisputable. If the total number of cookbooks sold was up and nonbeginner cookbooks grabbed its biggest percentage ever (i.e., the biggest portion of the biggest overall value), that can only translate to the biggest sales figure ever for that type of title.

(B) is not supported. In fact, because most cookbooks sold last year were *not* for beginners, this seems less likely to be true. It's still possible, but there's not enough information to know about the performance of any single book.

(C) is tempting, but it's a Distortion. It's true that beginner cookbooks make up a smaller *percentage* of sales for the first time. However, if total sales went up high enough, a smaller percentage could still result in higher sales overall. (For example, if beginner's cookbooks accounted for 60 percent of 10,000 overall cookbooks, that would be 6,000 beginner's cookbooks, but if beginner's cookbooks accounted for 40 percent of 20,000 overall cookbooks, that would be 8,000 beginner's cookbooks—a smaller percentage, but still increased sales.)

(D) is a Distortion. Yes, professional cooks bought more books than they ever have. However, nonprofessional cooks could still make up the vast majority of cookbook sales—nonbeginner or otherwise.

(E) is not supported. *Problem-Free Cooking* is merely described as a beginner book in a big market. There's no mention of its sales figures, let alone in comparison to any other individual cookbook—nonbeginner or otherwise.

13. (B) Assumption (Necessary)

Step 1: Identify the Question Type

This question directly asks for the argument's assumption. Because the argument *relies* on that assumption, this is a Necessary Assumption question.

Step 2: Untangle the Stimulus

The author starts off with some facts (i.e., evidence): Around Mars, scientists found methane. However, methane falls apart when exposed to the sun's UV radiation. The author concludes (as indicated by the Keyword *so*) that this means the methane must have appeared recently.

Step 3: Make a Prediction

The use of the phrase "must have" in the conclusion is a sure sign of overlooked possibilities. Surely, the methane would be destroyed by exposure to the sun's UV radiation, suggesting a relatively short life. However, what if it *doesn't* get exposed to the sun—floating around and staying on the unlit side of Mars. In that case, the methane could potentially exist undisturbed for eternity. The author doesn't consider

such a scenario and must assume that the methane cannot escape the UV radiation of the sun.

Step 4: Evaluate the Answer Choices

(B) is a match. Exposure to sunlight is what would make methane short-lasting, allowing the author to declare the methane as recent. By the Denial Test, if some methane is *not* eventually exposed to sunlight, it could conceivably survive indefinitely, destroying the author's assertion. Be careful not to eliminate **(B)** as Extreme just because of the word *all*. The argument's conclusion says *any* methane must have been released recently, so the language of the assumption can also be that comprehensive.

(A) is sufficient (i.e., would support the author's cause), but not necessary. If Mars never had methane before 2003, that would confirm the recent age of the methane. However, Mars could still have had methane for millennia before 2003, all of which was previously destroyed. Thus, any past history of methane is irrelevant to dating the current batch of methane.

(C) is Out of Scope. When the methane is able to be detected is irrelevant to whether or not it is recent. If the methane is falling apart, that would likely be due to sun exposure. However, that doesn't help determine how long the methane was around before such exposure. Maybe it's relatively new or maybe it's centuries old.

(D) is irrelevant. If it was exposed to UV radiation, then that means it was subject to destruction. However, that has no bearing on how long ago it was released in the first place.

(E) is an Irrelevant Comparison. Methane's reaction around Earth is not needed to complete the argument that the Martian methane is recent.

14. (C) Inference

Step 1: Identify the Question Type

The stimulus will contain merely *statements*, which will be used to support the correct answer. That means the correct answer will be a logical inference based on what's given.

Step 2: Untangle the Stimulus

According to the environmentalist, pollution from cars is a serious problem. However, gas prices don't reflect that problem, so they aren't high enough to discourage people from contributing to the problem. The environmentalist believes that could change by raising taxes on gasoline.

Step 3: Make a Prediction

A heavy reliance on contrast Keywords ([*b*]*ut* and *however*) is often a sign that an author is leading up to a point. In this case, everything in the first couple of sentences is just a buildup to the final claim (with the *however*): Higher taxes on gas would better reflect its involvement in pollution, resulting in a better incentive for drivers to cut back on their contribution. The correct answer will be consistent with this point, without bringing in unmentioned concepts.

Step 4: Evaluate the Answer Choices

(C) accurately expresses the environmentalist's claim in the last sentence. Make gas prices reflect its cost to the environment, and people will be more likely to cut back on gas purchases.

(A) is a Distortion. The environmentalist does say that if gas prices reflected the cost of pollution it would result in decreased pollution. However, that does not mean that even if pollution wasn't reduced that he wouldn't still recommend that gas prices reflect the cost of pollution for other reasons. For example, perhaps a price adjustment could raise revenue for alternative energy research.

(B) is another Distortion. Consumers' knowledge of pollution problems may not change regardless of gas prices. It's just that higher prices might encourage more people to *do* something about it. Even if consumers don't understand the environmental problems responsible for the price hike, they may still opt to purchase less gas based on the increased cost.

(D) is an Extreme Distortion, due to the word *only*. The environmentalist never suggests that the cost of gas is the *only* cost people consider. Consumer response to other costs is never discussed.

(E) is another Extreme Distortion due to the phrase "only if." Increasing consumer consideration due to gas prices reflecting the cost of pollution is touted as *one* way of reducing pollution (i.e., sufficient), but the environmentalist never said it is the *only* (i.e., necessary) way. It's possible there are still other ways to reduce pollution, including more efficient engines, an increase in public transportation costs, and so on.

15. (A) Paradox

Step 1: Identify the Question Type

This question asks for something that will *explain* something. That indicates a Paradox question. In this case, there will be a surprising fact that will seem to contradict another claim. Look for an answer that explains how that fact can be true without actually contradicting the other claim.

Step 2: Untangle the Stimulus

The stimulus provides information about a particular species of dragonfly whose larvae can only survive in the water, but are prey for some animals including a certain crayfish. While one would expect this predator to threaten the dragonfly population, the opposite appears to be the case—the dragonfly thrives better in the presence of the crayfish than in its absence.

Step 3: Make a Prediction

Normally, living near another animal that is prone to eating your larvae would seem dangerous. Why is that not the case here? While it's not worth predicting an exact explanation, consider that the correct answer will likely indicate another factor in crayfish-populated areas that would contribute to the dragonfly's survival. Also consider the fact that the dragonfly's larvae *need* water to survive—that's likely to play a significant role in the correct answer.

Step 4: Evaluate the Answer Choices

(A) helps clear things up a bit. If crayfish dig such water-retaining chambers, that gives the dragonfly larvae a place to survive that would be unavailable in areas without the crayfish. Dragonflies in dried-out areas without the water chambers would lose their larvae, reducing the chance of survival.

(B) is Out of Scope. Even if the crayfish don't eat the adults, they still eat the larvae—which still leaves the question of why dragonflies are doing better in environments with the crayfish.

(C) is a 180. If the crayfish don't help eliminate other predators (a potential benefit to the dragonfly larvae), then that environment would still be just as dangerous as environments without the crayfish—even more so because of the added threat of the crayfish itself. Therefore, if one potential benefit of crayfish (eliminating other predators) is removed, then the mystery is deepened—not explained.

(D) is an Irrelevant Comparison. The quantity of locales for the crayfish don't matter. The paradox revolves around dragonfly survival in areas with and without the crayfish.

(E) is irrelevant and a possible 180. If the crayfish population is not affected by the dragonfly population, then it has no incentive to leave the dragonflies alone. Thus, this would not explain why the dragonfly larvae do better with the crayfish around. The *opposite* situation would clear things up. In other words, if the crayfish population *was* negatively affected by a decrease in the dragonfly population, then the crayfish would likely encourage a healthy dragonfly population to protect themselves.

16. (E) Inference

Step 1: Identify the Question Type

This question asks for something "supported by" (i.e., inferred from) the given *information* (i.e., not an argument). That makes this an Inference question. Combine information when possible and look for an answer directly backed up by one or more claims in the stimulus.

Step 2: Untangle the Stimulus

According to the author, high blood pressure is commonly caused by stress. Some people can reduce their stress by calming their minds—which most people can do through exercise. The lower stress can result in lower blood pressure. The logical chain looks something like this:

$$\text{If} \quad \text{exercise} \rightarrow \frac{\text{calm}}{\text{mind}} \rightarrow \frac{\text{lower}}{\text{stress}} \rightarrow \frac{\text{lower}}{\text{blood}} \\ \text{pressure}$$

Note though that it's not a true Formal Logic chain because each arrow is not a true guarantee. *Most* people that exercise can calm their minds (but not necessarily all), and *some* of those that calm their mind can lower stress and blood pressure (but again, not necessarily all).

Step 3: Make a Prediction
The language is quite reserved language here with no concrete statements. Stress is one common cause, but not said to be the *most* common cause. *Some* people can lower blood pressure by calming their mind, but that's an indefinite number. Furthermore, while most people can calm their minds through exercise, there's no indication that this guarantees the lower blood pressure that some people can get. Be wary of extreme answers, and look for one that merely discusses the *possible* benefits of exercise and calming the mind.

Step 4: Evaluate the Answer Choices
(E) is just as laid-back as the author's claims. The author never guarantees anything, but the facts do support the idea that exercise *can* help calm the mind (and thus reduce stress) for *some* people.

(A) is a Distortion. It's only mentioned that reducing stress can cause lower blood pressure, not the other way around.

(B) is Extreme. The author says that *some* people can lower their blood pressure by reducing stress, not *most*. Additionally, **(B)** focuses only on those that have high blood pressure, but the stimulus doesn't indicate whether those "some people" that lower their blood pressure by reducing stress are amongst those that have high blood pressure due to their stress to begin with.

(C) is a Distortion and Extreme. While exercise is one way to calm the mind and thus reduce stress, there may be plenty of other ways to keep stress levels down for those who don't exercise. Therefore, it is unknown if *most* of those who don't exercise have high stress levels.

(D) is a 180. The connection described between exercise and lower blood pressure is far from *direct*. Exercise affects blood pressure only through the intervening effects of a calm mind and lower stress.

17. (C) Weaken

Step 1: Identify the Question Type
The question directly asks for something that *weakens* the argument, making this a Weaken question. Identify the conclusion and the evidence, and look for an answer that attacks the assumption connecting them.

Step 2: Untangle the Stimulus
The author mentions a correlation between atmospheric soot and a particular ailment. While most authors would jump to a claim of causation, the Keyword [*h*]*owever* indicates the author is taking a different approach. In fact, the author claims there is *no* causality. As evidence, the author states that many sooty cities are also exposed to other air pollutants.

Step 3: Make a Prediction
The author seems wise to avoid the common flaw of causation versus correlation. In fact, the author even weakens the prospect of causality by bringing in another possible cause of the ailment—other pollutants. However, that piece of evidence is the author's downfall. By bringing up another possible cause, the author is assuming that the true culprit is indeed those other pollutants and not the soot itself. To weaken this, the correct answer will discredit the other pollutants as the cause, making it more likely the soot is, in fact, to blame.

Step 4: Evaluate the Answer Choices
(C) hurts the author's argument. If there are just as many, if not more, cases of the ailment in sooty cities *without* the other pollutants, that suggests the other pollutants are a nonissue, returning the focus back to the soot as the probable cause—contrary to the author's point.

(A) is a 180. If, in high-pollutant areas, the number of ailments is equally high with or without soot, that bolsters the author's contention that the soot is free from blame.

(B) doesn't affect the argument because it's based on the condition of the ailment being rare in areas of low soot. However, there's no evidence that condition is in play. It's possible the ailment is prevalent all over, just more so in high-soot areas. Additionally, even if the ailment only occurs in areas with soot, it's possible those areas also have other air pollutants, so **(B)** still wouldn't determine whether it was the soot or the other pollutants that are the cause of the ailment.

(D) is also based on a condition that may or not be met. If that condition (a correlation between the other pollutants and the ailment) is not met, then the whole answer would be irrelevant. That is, the author may even agree with the statement, but believe that the *if* is never triggered and so it would be moot, making **(D)** not a valid weakener.

(E) is a 180. This increases the likelihood of other factors causing the ailment, strengthening the author's contention that the soot is free from blame.

18. (C) Parallel Flaw

Step 1: Identify the Question Type

This question asks for an argument with reasoning "similar to" that of the given argument. That indicates Parallel Reasoning. Moreover, the reasoning is described as "flawed," so this is a Parallel Flaw question. Identify the flaw in the given argument, and find an answer with an argument that commits the exact same error.

Step 2: Untangle the Stimulus

The author observes that, as summer is ending, rain hasn't fallen in a valley that usually gets some rain in the summer. Therefore, the author concludes that rain is likely to fall in the final week.

Step 3: Make a Prediction

The author is basing a conclusion on what *usually* happens in the summer. However, with just one week left to the summer, the odds of rain are dwindling fast. The author fails to consider that this summer just might be one of those exceptional rainless summers. The correct answer will include this same unwarranted last-minute prediction. In broader terms, find an answer in which something hasn't occurred that usually occurs, with the author predicting it will still *probably* occur, even though the end is so close.

Step 4: Evaluate the Answer Choices

(C) matches every step of the way. As with the original argument, something hasn't occurred that usually occurs (errors in the journal), and the author predicts it will still *probably* occur, even though the end is so close (last two pages).

(A) has no flaw. Errors are said to occur only *sometimes*, not *usually*, and saying that they *may* still occur isn't as bold as saying they'll *probably* occur. The author's language and logic here are acceptable.

(B) has different logic. In the original argument, something hasn't occurred yet, but the author predicts it likely still will occur. Here, something hasn't occurred yet, and the author predicts that it probably *won't*. Note also in **(B)** the author says there are "generally few errors in an issue." That's not the same as saying there are generally "a few errors" as it does in **(C)**. "Generally few errors" could mean that many if not most issues are error-free; however, "generally a few errors" means there's an expectation that each issue has some errors.

(D) has different logic. In the original argument, something hasn't occurred that usually *does*. Here, something hasn't occurred that usually *doesn't* anyway. The conclusions also don't match up—with the original predicting something will

probably happen, and this argument predicting something probably *won't* happen.

(E) makes an entirely different error. In the original, summer wasn't over yet. Here, the proofreading is done—no more chance to find the errors that usually appear. There is no parallelism. Furthermore, this author criticizes Aisha for not finding errors, which would be like criticizing the sky for not raining. Certainly, that's not what the original author did.

19. (B) Assumption (Necessary)

Step 1: Identify the Question Type

This question directly asks for an assumption, and one on which the argument *depends*. That makes this a Necessary Assumption question. Find the missing link between the evidence and conclusion, and be sure that the argument would be invalid without that assumption.

Step 2: Untangle the Stimulus

The author is criticizing young people for their pessimistic views on preventing bad things from happening. This negativity is going to make them less motivated. Therefore, the author makes a plea: To stop this from happening, we must encourage children to believe in a brighter future. Note the Keyword *therefore* indicating this is the conclusion.

Step 3: Make a Prediction

In a moment of bright-eyed optimism, the author makes an illicit jump from evidence about youngsters becoming unmotivated to a conclusion about helping them believe in better futures. The author must assume that instilling these beliefs in children will help with the motivation problem. Otherwise, why bother?

Step 4: Evaluate the Answer Choices

(B) is the unstated belief underlying the author's argument. If getting people to believe in better futures did *not* prevent the loss of motivation, the author's intention would go unfulfilled.

(A) is a Distortion. It reverses the argument. The author feels that believing in the future will help develop motivation, not the other way around.

(C) is a Distortion, with an Out of Scope component. While the author surely seems to favor optimism over pessimism, there's no indication that the author finds optimistic visions of the future to be *illusory* (i.e., deceptive).

(D) is Extreme. The author's intention is to restore motivation to help reduce—not necessarily *eliminate*—the world's problems. Even so, the author never goes so far as to suggest that this *will* work.

(E) is both Out of Scope and a Distortion. The original cause of the world's problems is irrelevant. Moreover, even if that cause was an inability to believe in a better future, that's not to say such a belief affects one's motivation. Also, what's true for previous generations does not necessarily apply to today's youth. For those reasons, this answer makes no true connection between the evidence (need to increase motivation) and the conclusion (must make children believe in a better future).

20. (D) Strengthen

Step 1: Identify the Question Type

This question comes right out and asks for something that strengthens the given argument. Break the argument into evidence and conclusion, and find an answer that validates the author's assumption.

Step 2: Untangle the Stimulus

The author introduces evidence of a correlation in stroke patients: Nerve cell deterioration matches up with high levels of glutamate, a protein that can kill certain nerve cells if it leaks from damaged cells. *Thus* indicates the author's conclusion: Leaked glutamate causes long-term brain damage.

Step 3: Make a Prediction

There are a couple of assumptions here, and the correct answer could play off of either of them. The word *cause* quickly signals a common assumption: A correlation between two events implies one caused the other. In this case, the author assumes that leaked glutamate—and nothing else—is the cause of brain damage. A correct answer would make that more likely. This is similar to the second assumption. The Formal Logic trigger *if* in the evidence implies that leakage from damaged cells is a merely a sufficient way (i.e., one possible way) for glutamate to kill nerve cells. However, that is not necessary (i.e., the only way) for glutamate to kill nerve cells. The correct answer could make it more likely that any harmful glutamate comes from leakage.

Step 4: Evaluate the Answer Choices

(D) backs up the author's claim. If glutamate can only come from leaky damaged cells, that eliminates other potential sources of the glutamate, making leaked glutamate more likely to be the cause of the damage. Remember that a strengthener need not prove the argument, it only needs to make it more likely.

(A) is a 180. If other neurotransmitters, besides glutamate, could damage nerve cells, that offers an alternative cause that the author overlooks.

(B) is also a 180. If there's a wide variety of abnormalities in the blood, then there are other possible candidates for the cause of brain damage.

(C) is a Distortion. Even if glutamate is the only one that leaks from damaged cells, there could be other damaging proteins that come from elsewhere that are responsible for the brain damage. The brain damage may even still occur under processes not at all discussed in the stimulus.

(E) has no effect on the argument. Whether the damaged nerve cells can stay intact has no bearing on whether the leaked glutamate is killing off *other* nerve cells.

21. (E) Parallel Reasoning

Step 1: Identify the Question Type

The question is asking for an argument with reasoning "most similar to that" of the argument in the stimulus. That indicates Parallel Reasoning. Look for easily comparable pieces. Otherwise, generalize the stimulus in broad terms and find an answer that matches the argument's structure piece by piece.

Step 2: Untangle the Stimulus

According to the original argument, Amanda has only ever written two types of songs: blues and punk rock. Most punk rock songs have just three chords, at most. Based on that, the author makes a qualified prediction about her next song: If it's not blues, it will probably have at most three chords.

Step 3: Make a Prediction

There are some easy-to-compare components here: a situation with only two options, a characteristic of *most* things that fit a category, a qualified prediction. However, a glance ahead shows that almost every answer has the same three components (except for (B), which concludes with an assertion about the past rather than a prediction). Broaden the scope and find an answer with the same logical structure: Certain items (Amanda's songs) have always been one of two types (blues or punk). Most of one type (punk) have a certain trait (three or fewer chords). Therefore, if the next item isn't the other type (blues), it will probably have the same trait. Algebraically, this would be:

$$\text{If } W \text{ (song Amanda has written)} \rightarrow X \text{ (blues) or } Y \text{ (punk)}$$

Most Y are Z (3 chords or fewer)

$$\text{If next one is } \sim X \rightarrow \text{probably Z}$$

Step 4: Evaluate the Answer Choices

(E) matches the structure every step of the way. Certain items (Gupta family pets) have always been one of two types (fish or parrot). Most of one type (parrots) have a certain trait (noisy). Therefore, if the next item isn't the other type (fish), it will probably have the same trait.

$$\text{If } W \text{ (Gupta family pet)} \rightarrow X \text{ (fish) or } Y \text{ (parrot)}$$

Most Y are Z (noisy).

If	**next one is ~X**	→	**probably Z**

(A) starts off perfectly—two types of items (fish and parrots), with one type (parrots) having a trait (noisy). However, in this argument, the conclusion is based on the condition that the next item *is* that type, rather than the condition that it *isn't* the *other* type. That doesn't line up.

(B) also falls apart at the conclusion. Instead of using the pet type to predict the next pet's trait, it uses the trait to determine the type of past pets.

(C) is Extreme in the conclusion. The original conclusion is only about the next one song. This argument's conclusion is about *any* pet that will *ever* be owned.

(D) Distorts the conclusion. Again, there are two types of items (fish and parrots), with one type (parrots) having a trait (noisy). However, this argument implies that not selecting that type would result in an animal that doesn't share that trait. That would be like the original author saying "if the next song isn't a punk rock song, it will probably have more than three chords." That, however, never happens.

22. (D) Paradox

Step 1: Identify the Question Type
The word *resolve* usually indicates a Paradox question. Sure enough, the information in question will have an "apparent discrepancy." Look for the two ideas that seem to contradict one another, and find an answer that explains how they can actually be consistent with one another.

Step 2: Untangle the Stimulus
The contrast Keyword [*y*]*et* indicates the split between one fact and its unexpected counterpart. Before the [*y*]*et*, the author explains that yogurt ads are usually more influential than milk ads. However, the example that follows involves a supermarket that advertised its store-brand products and found that sales of the advertised milk increased more than that of the advertised yogurt.

Step 3: Make a Prediction
As with most paradoxes, this all boils down to a mystery: If yogurt ads are usually more influential than milk ads, why did the store's milk sales show more improvement? There could be many reasons, so don't try to predict a specific one. Just be on the lookout for an answer that brings up an overlooked factor that would explain why the milk had a superior performance or why yogurt sales didn't get its expected dominating sales bump.

Step 4: Evaluate the Answer Choices
(D) would explain things. If yogurt sales nationwide are down dramatically, then the yogurt ads could still have been more effective, but unlike the milk ads, which merely had to drive sales up, the yogurt ads had to be extra persuasive to prevent the same sharp drop seen elsewhere and even pull off a little increase.

(A) is a 180. If there's increased demand for the store-brand yogurt, and that's the one that was advertised, it's even more unusual that its sales couldn't keep up with the milk sales.

(B) doesn't help. All this does is say that people who want milk usually don't intend to buy yogurt too. However, there's no comparison of how many people typically go to buy milk versus how many go to buy yogurt, so this still doesn't explain why milk sales improved more than yogurt sales.

(C) is an Irrelevant Comparison. The discrepancy here is about milk versus yogurt, not store-brand versus other brand.

(E) doesn't provide enough information. This might work if the store-brand milk is usually more expensive than other brands and the advertised price is now cheaper—in which case milk ads would be more likely to cause a switch in brands. However, if the store-brand milk is usually the cheapest anyway, then the discrepancy remains unresolved, perhaps even deepened. If consumers tend to purchase the store brand of yogurt and yogurt ads are usually quite effective, then it's even more peculiar that milk increases are ahead of yogurt increases.

23. (E) Principle (Apply/Inference)

Step 1: Identify the Question Type
Because the question stem asks about a principle, this is quickly identified as a Principle question. The format is fairly unique, but the same skills apply as with any Principle question. In this case, you are given a principle that, when used in context of the stated problem, will be applied to the correct answer choice in order to support it. When you use the given information to support (*justify*) the answer choices, that's an Inference question. Use those skills as well.

Step 2: Untangle the Stimulus
Shayna has a problem. Should she congratulate Daniel, thus expressing insincere praise, or should she not congratulate Daniel and hurt his feelings? To help her make a decision, a principle is given: Never be insincere unless you truly feel the other person would prefer kindness.

If	**congratulate**	→	**insincere**
If	**~ congratulate**	→	**hurt feelings**

Principle:

If	insincere	→	**truly believes the other person prefers kindness over honesty**

If	**~ truly believe the other person prefers kindness over honesty**	→	sincere

Step 3: Make a Prediction

At first, the principle seems to give Shayna a clear solution to her problem: Don't be insincere. Instead, refuse to congratulate Daniel even though his feelings will be hurt. However, the principle provides one *possible* exception depending on whether she believes Daniel would prefer kindness or not. The use of the word *possible* is important here. If she truly believes Daniel would prefer kindness, then she *may* want to congratulate him after all—but the principle doesn't say that she absolutely *should*. However, if she *doesn't* believe Daniel would prefer kindness, then the one exception doesn't apply and she's back to the original solution: Don't congratulate Daniel. The correct answer will likely specify which belief she holds and present the appropriate solution.

Step 4: Evaluate the Answer Choices

(E) applies the principle properly. If Shayna has no belief about Daniel's preference for kindness, then the exception doesn't apply and she should not be insincere. Therefore, no congratulations for Daniel.

(A) completely ignores the principle. If Shayna doesn't believe Daniel prefers kindness, then this would violate the principle's recommendation to never be insincere.

(B) is a Distortion. The principle states that Shayna's decision should be based on what *she believes* about Daniel's preference, not about what *his* actual preference is.

(C) is a Distortion. The principle states that Shayna's decision should be based on what she believes *Daniel's* preference is, not what *her* preference would be.

(D) puts Daniel in an awful spot. This basically suggests that Daniel is getting hurt either way—through being ignored or receiving insincere congratulations. However, the principle does not use hurt feelings as a deciding factor. It uses Shayna's beliefs about Daniel's feelings, which are still unknown—so the principle can't be applied here.

24. (E) Assumption (Sufficient)

Step 1: Identify the Question Type

The question is directly asking for an assumption that would allow the argument to conclude properly. It also says the argument will be valid *if* that assumption is in place, making it a Sufficient Assumption question. Look for Mismatched Concepts between the evidence and the conclusion, and find an answer that connects them.

Step 2: Untangle the Stimulus

Clearly indicates the author is starting right off with the conclusion: Democracies need effective news media to thrive. The phrase *[a]fter all* indicates the evidence to support this claim: For a democracy to thrive, the electorate needs to be informed about political issues, and that requires access to unbiased information about the government. Broken down into Formal Logic, it would look like this:

Conclusion:

If	thrive	→	**effective news media**

Evidence:

If	thrive →	**knowledgeable** →	**access to unbiased electorate gov't info**

Step 3: Make a Prediction

The argument is all about what a democracy needs to thrive. However, the evidence only goes so far as saying it needs an electorate with access to unbiased information. The author then leaps to the conclusion that it needs effective news media. Why effective news media, which the evidence doesn't address at all? The author is assuming that effective news media is needed to get the unbiased information needed by the electorate. (Feel free to add your own joke about unbiased news media here.)

Step 4: Evaluate the Answer Choices

(E) provides the right connection between the electorate's need for unbiased information and the need for effective news media.

(A) is a classic Distortion, confusing necessity and sufficiency. The author says that a democracy cannot thrive *without* effective news media—making news media necessary—but that's not the same as suggesting (or assuming) that any democracy *with* effective news *will* thrive (suggesting it's sufficient). Furthermore, **(A)** makes no connection to the mismatched concepts in the evidence; it only recycles the terms from the conclusion.

(B) is a Distortion. Like **(A)**, it also works backward on the Formal Logic, but this time it's the logic of the evidence. A knowledgeable electorate requires unbiased info, not the other way around—access to unbiased info does not necessarily guarantee a knowledgeable electorate. Like **(A)**, **(B)** still makes no connection between the evidence and the conclusion; the need for effective news media remains a mismatched concept in the conclusion.

(C), like **(B)**, is another Distortion of the evidence, turning a necessary condition (democracy needs a knowledgeable electorate) into a sufficient condition (a knowledgeable electorate *will* allow a democracy to thrive). Once again, it still doesn't tie in the author's conclusion about the need for effective news media.

(D) is a Distortion. The electorate does need access to unbiased information, but that doesn't mean exposure to biased information is going to destroy the democracy. Also, once again, this still doesn't connect the evidence to the mismatched concept in the conclusion about the need for effective news media.

25. (E) Flaw

Step 1: Identify the Question Type
As straightforward as a question gets on the LSAT. Simply put, find the flaw. Be on the lookout for commonly tested flawed techniques.

Step 2: Untangle the Stimulus
Being tired can be a problem for Roberta. That's the only time she's prone to being irritable and losing her keys. And now, she's been yawning and she's just lost her keys. Things aren't looking so good, so the author concludes that Roberta's sure to be irritable.

Step 3: Make a Prediction
It all sounds reasonable, but the Formal Logic word *only* should be a red flag that the logic may not hold up as good as it sounds. By the first two statements, Roberta is irritable and loses things *only* when she's tired—which means being tired is a necessary condition for both.

If	irritable	→	tired
If	loses things	→	tired

However, that does not mean that she's going to lose things and/or be irritable *every* time she's tired—and that's where the author gets tripped up. At this point, Roberta has lost her keys, which must mean she's tired. However, while being tired is necessary for Roberta to be irritable, it's not sufficient. So the author cannot logically conclude that she's going to be irritable. That's the flaw, and the correct answer will point out

this classic case of confusing necessary and sufficient conditions.

Step 4: Evaluate the Answer Choices
(E) pinpoints the flaw perfectly. The author takes a necessary condition for Roberta being irritable (being tired), and acts like it's sufficient to claim she's irritable.

(A) is a Distortion. The author never states or suggests any connection between tiredness and yawning. Any connection is in the mind of the reader.

(B) describes the flaw of circular reasoning, which the author does not commit here.

(C) reverses the argumentative structure. The author takes general information about Roberta to make a conclusion about a specific instance, not the other way around.

(D) correctly identifies the problem of necessity versus sufficiency. However, it's *given* that Roberta is losing things (her keys), so the author is not using the logic for that. The mistake is made in making the conclusion about her being irritable, which the correct answer properly identifies.

26. (A) Assumption (Necessary)

Step 1: Identify the Question Type
The question directly asks for an assumption, and one that the argument *requires*, making this a Necessary Assumption question. Break the argument into evidence and conclusion, and look for something that *must* be true for that conclusion to be properly drawn.

Step 2: Untangle the Stimulus
The farmer is promoting genetically engineered crops, which produce their own pest-controlling toxins so that you don't have to use insecticides, which have been known to harm wildlife. Therefore, the farmer believes that genetically engineered crops will help wildlife populations get back to normal.

Step 3: Make a Prediction
It sounds promising, but there's a major hole in this argument. The farmer mentions that insecticides are harmful to wildlife, but what about those genetically engineered crops and the toxins they release? Couldn't those toxins *also* harm wildlife? The farmer must assume otherwise. The correct answer will eliminate that, or a similar, overlooked possibility on the farmer's part.

Step 4: Evaluate the Answer Choices
(A) must be true for the farmer's argument to hold. After all, using the Denial Test, if the genetically engineered crops did *not* cause less harm to wildlife, then they would be no help to the wildlife population.

(B) is irrelevant. The argument is about whether genetically engineered crops would help wildlife populations. Whether an alternative (slightly reducing pesticide usage) could also work has no bearing on the effectiveness of the farmer's recommendation. Even if a slight reduction *didn't* work, the genetically engineered crops *could*.

(C) is Extreme. What harms wildlife according to the farmer is *excessive* spraying of insecticides. So it is not necessary that genetically engineered crops eliminate insecticide use entirely.

(D) is Out of Scope. Cost is irrelevant to the question of whether these crops would help wildlife populations.

(E) is Extreme. The prevention of excessive insecticide use does not have to be the *only* factor affecting wildlife population recovery. There could be other fringe benefits for the wildlife, and the farmer's argument would still hold.

PrepTest 74

The Inside Story

PrepTest 74 was administered in December 2014. It challenged 28,585 test takers. What made this test so hard? Here's a breakdown of what Kaplan students who were surveyed after taking the official exam considered PrepTest 74's most difficult section.

Hardest PrepTest 74 Section as Reported by Test Takers

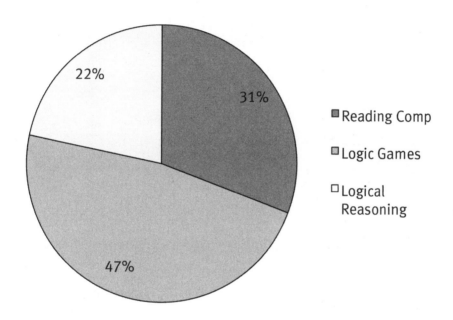

Based on these results, you might think that studying Logic Games is the key to LSAT success. Well, Logic Games is important, but test takers' perceptions don't tell the whole story. For that, you need to consider students' actual performance. The following chart shows the average number of students to miss each question in each of PrepTest 74's different sections.

Percentage Incorrect by PrepTest 74 Section Type

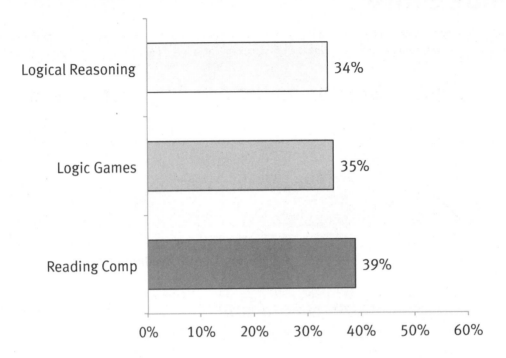

Actual student performance tells quite a different story. On average, students were almost equally likely to miss questions in all three of the different section types, and on PrepTest 74, Reading Comprehension was somewhat higher than Logic Games in actual difficulty.

Maybe students overestimate the difficulty of the Logic Games section because it's so unusual, or maybe it's because a really hard Logic Game is so easy to remember after the test. But the truth is that the testmaker places hard questions throughout the test. Here were the locations of the 10 hardest (most missed) questions in the exam.

Location of 10 Most Difficult Questions in PrepTest 74

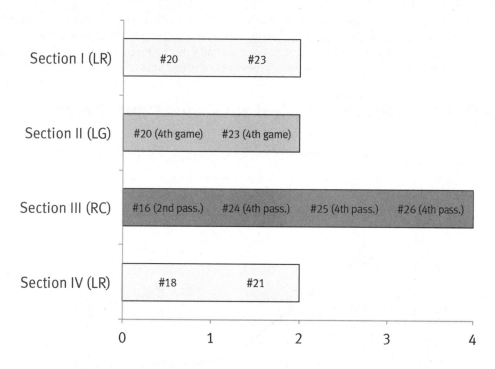

The takeaway from this data is that, to maximize your potential on the LSAT, you need to take a comprehensive approach. Test yourself rigorously, and review your performance on every section of the test. Kaplan's LSAT explanations provide the expertise and insight you need to fully understand your results. The explanations are written and edited by a team of LSAT experts, who have helped thousands of students improve their scores. Kaplan always provides data-driven analysis of the test, ranking the difficulty of every question based on actual student performance. The 10 hardest questions on every test are highlighted with a 4-star difficulty rating, the highest we give. The analysis breaks down the remaining questions into 1-, 2-, and 3-star ratings so that you can compare your performance to thousands of other test takers on all LSAC material.

Don't settle for wondering whether a question was really as hard as it seemed to you. Analyze the test with real data, and learn the secrets and strategies that help top scorers master the LSAT challenge.

7 Can't-Miss Features of PrepTest 74

- 17 combined Assumption and Strengthen/Weaken questions isn't unusual, but PT 74 was the first time since December '05 (PT 48) that there were at least five more Strengthen/Weaken questions than Assumption questions (11 vs. 6 on both tests).
- For the second straight test there were no Point at Issue questions.
- PT 76 featured two Hybrid games. It was just the second time since December '07 (PT 53) that a single test contained two Hybrid games.
- Of those two Hybrid games, neither featured a Sequencing action. That was the first time in LSAT history that a test with multiple Hybrid games had neither of them contain a Sequencing action!
- PT 74's Reading Comp section contained two 8-question passages for the first time since December '07 (PT 53).
- There were Inference questions galore in the Reading Comp section! With 14 total Inference Qs, it was the most in an RC section since June '09 (PT 57).
- For the second consecutive administration date, Taylor Swift held down the #1 song on the Billboard charts. However, this time the song was "Blank Space." Given that there's no guessing penalty on the LSAT, hopefully no test takers left any blank space on any questions when filling out their answer sheets!

PrepTest 74 in Context

As much fun as it is to find out what makes a PrepTest unique or noteworthy, it's even more important to know just how representative it is of other LSAT administrations (and, thus, how likely it is to be representative of the exam you will face on Test Day). The following charts compare the numbers of each kind of question and game on PrepTest 74 to the average numbers seen on all officially released LSATs administered over the past five years (from 2012 through 2016).

Number of LR Questions by Type: PrepTest 74 vs. 2012–2016 Average

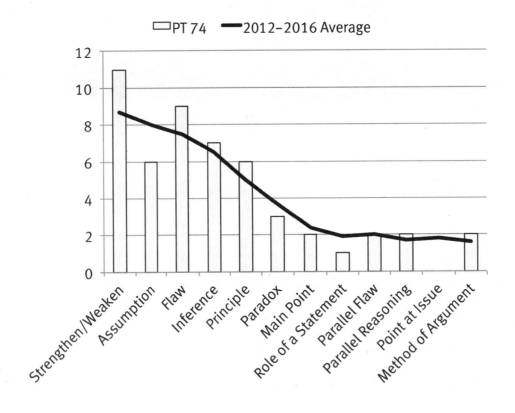

Number of LG Games by Type: PrepTest 74 vs. 2012–2016 Average

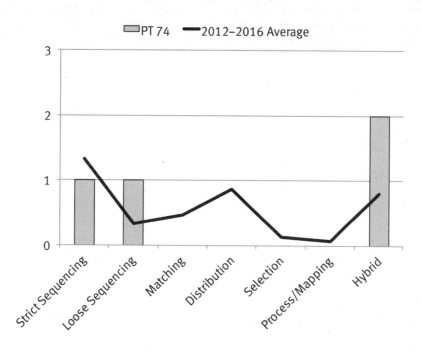

Number of RC Questions by Type: PrepTest 74 vs. 2012–2016 Average

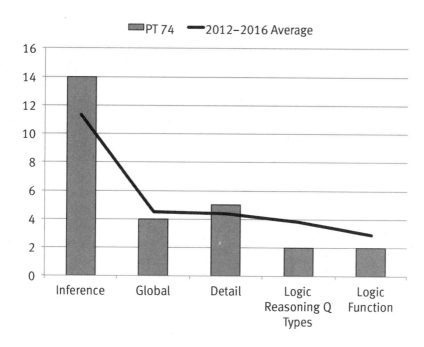

There isn't usually a huge difference in the distribution of questions from LSAT to LSAT, but if this test seems harder (or easier) to you than another you've taken, compare the number of questions of the types on which you, personally, are strongest and weakest. And then, explore within each section to see if your best or worst question types came earlier or later.

Students in Kaplan's comprehensive LSAT courses have access to every released LSAT, and to an online Qbank with thousands of officially released questions, games, and passages. If you are studying on your own, you have to do a bit more work to identify your strengths and your areas of opportunity. Quantitative analysis (like that in the previous charts) is an important tool for understanding how the test is constructed, and how you are performing on it.

Section I: Logical Reasoning

Q#	Question Type	Correct	Difficulty
1	Inference	C	★
2	Strengthen	C	★
3	Principle (Identify/Inference)	B	★
4	Strengthen	C	★
5	Flaw	C	★
6	Weaken	A	★
7	Principle (Identify/Inference)	E	★
8	Assumption (Necessary)	A	★
9	Paradox	E	★
10	Strengthen	E	★★
11	Inference	D	★
12	Assumption (Sufficient)	E	★★
13	Main Point	A	★★
14	Role of a Statement	D	★
15	Paradox	E	★
16	Flaw	D	★★
17	Strengthen	A	★★★
18	Flaw	A	★★★
19	Parallel Reasoning	A	★★
20	Assumption (Sufficient)	E	★★★★
21	Strengthen/Weaken (Evaluate the Argument)	B	★★★
22	Inference	E	★★★
23	Weaken	D	★★★★
24	Inference	B	★★★
25	Parallel Flaw	D	★★

1. (C) Inference

Step 1: Identify the Question Type

The question stem calls attention to the blank that ends the stimulus. The blank concludes a sentence that starts with "[i]n other words," so the task is to paraphrase the first part of the stimulus and apply it logically to complete the stimulus's final sentence.

Step 2: Untangle the Stimulus

The incomplete sentence is meant to state that which the author considers "the problem with letting children read Jones's books." The author of the stimulus states that problem by way of an analogy: Jones's books are like candy—tasty, but not nutritious—and reading them takes away children's appetite for better literature (just as filling up on candy kills the appetite for a healthy meal).

Step 3: Make a Prediction

To predict the correct answer, paraphrase the author's candy analogy in a way that applies to Jones's books. Something along the lines of "they discourage children from reading better books" will work nicely.

Step 4: Evaluate the Answer Choices

(C) is a match for this prediction. It sums up the reason that the author considers children reading Jones's books a problem.

(A) is too literal. It doesn't apply the author's candy analogy to books and reading.

(B) is a 180. The author considers Jones's books too easy, and says that children who read them will be disinclined to challenge themselves with anything harder.

(D) is Outside the Scope. The author says nothing about the *message* conveyed by Jones's books nor about parental instruction.

(E) is a Distortion of the author's analogy. For the author, the problem isn't that children exposed to Jones's books will spend too much time reading, but that they will be less likely to read other (and better) books than Jones's.

2. (C) Strengthen

Step 1: Identify the Question Type

The question stem defines the right answer as a fact ("if true") that will support the author's conclusion (a *hypothesis* in this case). This is a Strengthen question.

Step 2: Untangle the Stimulus

The conclusion (the archaeologist's hypothesis) is the stimulus's final sentence: The Greek stonemasons created uniformly bulging columns in the Parthenon by consulting scale drawings. The evidence is simply that such a scale drawing was found at Didyma, another ancient Greek architectural site. The author assumes that Greek stonemasons that created the Parthenon acted similarly to the stonemasons at Didyma.

Step 3: Make a Prediction

The correct answer will provide a fact that makes it more likely that the stonemasons working at the Parthenon used techniques or plans similar to those of the stonemasons working at Didyma. Be careful not to over-determine the prediction; the author does *not* imply that work at the Parthenon followed that at Didyma or that work at one site influenced work at the other.

Step 4: Evaluate the Answer Choices

(C) provides a broad fact that makes the author's assumption more likely. If Greek builders routinely used scale drawings, it makes it more likely that the stonemasons building the Parthenon did as well.

(A) is Outside the Scope. The fact that modern builders cannot recreate a feature of the Parthenon sheds no light on how the ancient Greek stonemasons worked.

(B) is a Distortion or possibly a 180. The author does not imply that stonemasons building the Parthenon learned to use scale drawings from those working at Didyma. He simply cites Didyma as an example of how construction was apparently completed at another Greek architectural site. However, if the Didyma scale drawing did not occur until after the Parthenon's construction, that adds the possibility that scale drawing was *not* known to the masons at the time of the Parthenon's construction. So, (B) may weaken the argument.

(D) is an Irrelevant Comparison. The relative size of the columns at each site has no bearing on whether scale drawings were used to plan or build them.

(E) is Outside the Scope. Knowing that the Parthenon stonemasons were an experienced group doesn't make it more or less likely that they used scale drawings to accomplish their task.

3. (B) Principle (Identify/Inference)

Step 1: Identify the Question Type

According to the question stem, the correct answer is a principle (a broad, general rule) to which the situation or recommendation described in the stimulus *conforms* or matches. To predict the correct answer, paraphrase the stimulus and determine the rule it implies.

Step 2: Untangle the Stimulus

The first sentence is a recommendation: The government should not use lottery money for health services. The second sentence gives the author's reason: Lottery revenues may drop, leaving health services—which are "essential to our community"—with an insufficient budget.

Step 3: Make a Prediction

The recommendation in the stimulus is specifically about health services and lottery money, but each is defined by a broader characteristic. Health services are *essential* and lottery revenue fluctuates and may drop. So, the stimulus implies the following rule: The government should not use revenue sources that may drop to fund essential services. Use that as a prediction and you will zero in on the correct answer.

Step 4: Evaluate the Answer Choices

(B) paraphrases the author's reasoning ("must be funded from reliable sources" rather than "should not be funded from an unreliable one"), but does so accurately, matching the prediction quite clearly.

(A) is an Irrelevant Comparison. The stimulus doesn't get into how governmental funding should be distributed overall.

(C) is a Distortion. The author says that health services shouldn't receive "any part of" its budget from lottery funds. This answer states that health services shouldn't be "entirely dependent on" lottery revenue.

(D) is another Distortion. The author stipulates that health services are "essential to the community." That's one of the author's reasons for recommending against the use of lottery funds, but it is not a principle to which the *argument* conforms.

(E) is Outside the Scope. This answer gives a new recommendation, one that might make lottery funds less susceptible to shortfall in the future, but it does not state a rule to which the argument *in the stimulus* conforms.

4. (C) Strengthen

Step 1: Identify the Question Type

The question stem defines the right answer as a fact ("if true") that will support the scientist's reasoning, making this a Strengthen question.

Step 2: Untangle the Stimulus

The scientist's conclusion—her hypothesis—is at the end of the stimulus: "the heating up of the squirrel's tail probably plays a role in repelling rattlesnakes." The author gives three pieces of evidence: (1) We already know that squirrels puff out their tails and wag them to harass rattlesnakes; (2) we now know that squirrels' tails heat up when they're trying to harass rattlesnakes; and (3) rattlesnakes sense body heat. The scientist must assume that the snakes have a negative reaction to the heat they sense in the squirrels' tails.

Step 3: Make a Prediction

The correct answer will make the scientist's assumption more likely to be true, thus strengthening her hypothesis.

Step 4: Evaluate the Answer Choices

(C), if true, definitely supports the scientist's reasoning. This answer provides confirmation that the snakes react negatively to the heated tails just as she hypothesized they would.

(A) is Outside the Scope. The scientist's hypothesis hinges on how the snakes react to the squirrels' heated tails, not on whether snakes exhibit a similar behavior.

(B) is Outside the Scope. This answer simply provides another reason why squirrels puff out and wag their tails. It must not be the only reason they do though because the stimulus explicitly states that they do so to harass rattlesnakes.

(D) is Outside the Scope. If the squirrels' ability to puff, wag, and heat helps keep other predators away, then more power to the squirrels. Finding out that these behaviors repel hawks or lynxes, however, makes it no more or less likely that the squirrels' heated tails play a role in deterring rattlesnakes.

(E) is Outside the Scope. The scientist's hypothesis is not impacted by the squirrel's ability to *sense* heat. Moreover, the evidence makes clear that the squirrel can produce heat and that the snakes can sense it.

5. (C) Flaw

Step 1: Identify the Question Type

The wording of this question stem is quite direct. The argument in the stimulus contains an error in reasoning, and your job is to correctly identify and describe it.

Step 2: Untangle the Stimulus

The critic's conclusion is that we should reject Fillmore's claim. The critic's reason (or evidence) is simply that Fillmore stands to benefit if his claim is accepted. The critic must assume that whenever someone makes an argument the acceptance of which would benefit him or her, that argument should be rejected.

Step 3: Make a Prediction

Pointing out that someone stands to benefit if his or her argument is accepted does not necessarily impugn the argument. This information might make us question the motives of the person making the argument, but without more, it provides no justification for rejecting the argument.

Step 4: Evaluate the Answer Choices

(C) hits the nail on the head, accurately describing the critic's error in reasoning. Fillmore's potential benefit was the only reason ("solely on the grounds") that the critic rejected Fillmore's argument.

(A) clearly describes the flaw of confusing necessity for sufficiency. The critic's argument contains none of the Formal Logic elements required for this flaw to appear.

(B) describes a flaw that could only occur in an argument in which the conclusion was an assertion of fact ("[i]t concludes that something is true"). In the critic's argument, the conclusion was a recommendation ("we *should* reject Fillmore's argument").

(D) is Outside the Scope. The critic's argument does not appeal to any other person's views. The critic simply urges us to reject Fillmore's argument on the grounds that accepting the argument benefits Fillmore.

(E) is a Distortion. There's nothing inconsistent or contradictory in the critic's reasoning. His evidence simply isn't strong enough to justify his conclusion. Had the critic simply said, "The fact that Fillmore stands to benefit from this argument raises some eyebrows and should make us skeptical," his position would be solid. The critic could reasonably recommend additional study or debate, but he overreaches by concluding that Fillmore's argument should be *rejected* for this reason.

6. (A) Weaken

Step 1: Identify the Question Type
This is a straightforward Weaken question stem. The correct answer will provide a fact making it less likely that the author's conclusion follows from her evidence.

Step 2: Untangle the Stimulus
The author's conclusion, a recommendation, comes right at the end of the argument: People who drink grapefruit juice should take smaller doses of certain medicines (those in which absorption is increased by a chemical found in grapefruit juice) and should drink only prescribed amounts of grapefruit juice. The author's evidence is simple: It is always best to take "the lowest effective dose" of a medication. The author must assume that her recommendation—lower doses of medicine along with prescribed amounts of grapefruit juice—will result in the lowest effective dose of the medications.

Step 3: Make a Prediction
To weaken this argument, you'll need a fact suggesting that the author's recommendation might not result in the lowest effective dose of the medications. The fact offered might suggest that the dose resulting from the author's recommendation is too low or too high, or even that the resulting dose is difficult or impossible to calculate. Regardless, the correct answer will be the only one that calls into question the assumption that following the author's recommendation will result in "the lowest effective dose."

Step 4: Evaluate the Answer Choices
(A) fits the bill. If the amount of the active chemical in grapefruit juice varies from glass to glass, then recommending a prescribed amount of grapefruit juice would result in variable doses of the medication being absorbed by the patient. Some days, the patient might get less than an effective dose, and some days, more.

(B) is an Irrelevant Comparison. The prices of grapefruit juice and those of medicines are not at issue.

(C) is Outside the Scope. The experiment described here simply proves that the chemical is, in fact, the active ingredient in grapefruit juice. The author has already stipulated this fact, so **(C)** adds nothing to the argument.

(D) is Outside the Scope. *How* the active chemical in grapefruit juice works is irrelevant to the argument about what should be prescribed.

(E) is Outside the Scope. This answer choice offers an interesting piece of trivia about the phenomenon discussed in the argument, but it has no bearing on the validity of the author's recommendation.

7. (E) Principle (Identify/Inference)

Step 1: Identify the Question Type
From the question stem, you learn that the stimulus will describe a recommendation. The correct answer will be a broad-based rule, or principle, that corresponds to that recommendation and the reasons given for it.

Step 2: Untangle the Stimulus
The salesperson recommends an identically priced but less powerful air conditioner on the grounds that the power supplied by a less powerful air conditioner is sufficient for the buyer's needs. The salesperson must assume that other things (such as price) being equal, it is preferable to purchase the air conditioner that supplies the minimum power sufficient for the buyer's needs.

Step 3: Make a Prediction
The salesperson's assumption makes an ideal prediction. Because this is a Principle question, the correct answer may refer to a broader category—e.g., appliances or household items—inclusive of air conditioners, but the rule it states will be exactly the same as that which the salesperson assumes regarding air conditioners.

Step 4: Evaluate the Answer Choices
(E) matches the prediction and is correct. Sure enough, the rule stated here applies to all "household appliances," but it matches the salesperson's reasoning point by point.

(A) is a Distortion of the stimulus. The buyer does decide between two items with identical prices, but the salesperson made a specific recommendation to consider power as the determining factor. **(A)** just indicates that both products "can satisfy the needs of the consumer," but it doesn't conform to what the salesperson advises about selecting the less powerful product.

(B) is a 180. The salesperson recommends buying a less powerful, but identically priced, air conditioner. Clearly, he does *not* recommend less powerful appliances *only if* they are less expensive.

(C) introduces the term "best value," making it difficult to assess in light of the stimulus. Does the salesperson consider the equally priced but more powerful air conditioner a better value? In that case, the rule in (C) contradicts the stimulus. Does the salesperson consider the less powerful air conditioner a better value because it will result in lower electric bills down the road? Without more information, there is no way to tell if this rule corresponds to the salesperson's recommendation.

(D) is Outside the Scope. Nothing in the stimulus suggests which of the two air conditioners would produce the higher sales commission. The stimulus tells us that the air conditioners are identically priced. If anything, that suggests that the sales commissions for the two products would be comparable as well.

8. (A) Assumption (Necessary)

Step 1: Identify the Question Type
The question stem defines the correct answer as "an assumption that the argument requires." This is a Necessary Assumption question in which the correct answer is a statement that, if false, would prevent the editorialist's conclusion from following from his evidence.

Step 2: Untangle the Stimulus
The editorialist's conclusion, found at the end of the stimulus, is signaled by [*t*]*hus*: Focusing on the flaws of our leaders is pointless. His evidence is that the relevant question is how the nation's "institutions and procedures" allow flawed politicians to obtain power.

Step 3: Make a Prediction
The editorialist must assume that focusing attention on leaders' flaws will not help to answer the relevant question about institutions and procedures.

Step 4: Evaluate the Answer Choices
(A) is the perfect match for this prediction.

(B) is Outside the Scope. A prediction that focusing on leaders' flaws will be increasingly common in the future is not necessary for the author's argument that such a focus is pointless.

(C) confirms that the nation's institutions and procedures are empowering flawed leaders, but this doesn't address whether focusing on leaders' flaws will or will not help us understand why that is.

(D) is Extreme. A quick use of the Denial Test on (D) would yield "one person in the nation" has started to work on the "real question." A single person wouldn't impact the argument. The author doesn't comment on whether or not the "real question" has yet been addressed. His point is that focusing on the leaders' flaws is pointless precisely because it is irrelevant to such a critical examination.

(E) is also Outside the Scope. This simply brings up an additional result of focusing on leaders' flaws. Such an additional impact is not necessary to the editorialist's argument.

9. (E) Paradox

Step 1: Identify the Question Type
The reference to an "apparent discrepancy" in the question stem signals a Paradox question. The correct answer will provide a fact that helps to *resolve* the seeming inconsistency in the stimulus.

Step 2: Untangle the Stimulus
The apparent discrepancy is signaled by "[d]espite this" at the beginning of the stimulus's final sentence: Doctors say that, for some people, taking calcium supplements with lead in them is preferable to taking no calcium supplements *even though* lead in the bloodstream is a public health concern and may lead to anemia and nerve damage. Note that while this analysis suggests a cost-benefit analysis, you learn here only about the risks of lead, but nothing about the benefits of calcium.

Step 3: Make a Prediction
To resolve the paradox in the stimulus, the correct answer will have to provide a reason that, despite the dangers associated with lead, doctors would be justified in recommending the use of calcium supplements which contain lead. While it is difficult to anticipate the exact wording of the correct answer, it will either suggest a benefit to taking calcium supplements or a risk to not taking them.

Step 4: Evaluate the Answer Choices
(E) helps to explain why doctors continue to recommend the supplements. Without them, lead may be drawn into the bloodstream, compounding the risks of lead outlined in the stimulus.

(A) is Outside the Scope. Other sources of lead are irrelevant to the discussion of supplements. Besides, the stimulus stated that trace amounts of lead from food sources may be safely stored in the bones.

(B) is Outside the Scope. The paradox in the stimulus is not impacted, as far as we know, by our certainty that other sources of lead have been eliminated.

(C) is Outside the Scope. Lead is associated with anemia and nerve damage. The fact that other things are also factors in these conditions is irrelevant to the paradox about calcium supplements.

(D) is a 180. If additional calcium increases the risks associated with lead, we should be even more confused about why doctors would recommend supplements.

10. (E) Strengthen

Step 1: Identify the Question Type
According to the question stem, the correct answer will help justify the application of a principle to a specific recommendation. That makes this a Strengthen question. The Application serves as the conclusion and the Principle as evidence.

Step 2: Untangle the Stimulus
The conclusion (the Application) is that Matilde should not buy the antique vase. Why not? The evidence (the Principle) provides the following rule:

If	purchase antique	→	confidence in authenticity AND aesthetic appreciation

Contraposed:

If	~ confidence in authenticity OR ~ aesthetic appreciation	→	~ purchase antique

The antique's investment potential alone is not enough to justify purchase. The author must assume that at least one of the two sufficient conditions in the contrapositive *has* been met in Matilde's case (in other words, that one of the two necessary conditions in the original rule has *not* been met).

Step 3: Make a Prediction
The correct answer will provide a fact that suggests that (1) Matilde should not be confident in the vase's authenticity, (2) Matilde does not appreciate the vase aesthetically, (3) Matilde is only interested in the vase as an investment, or (4) that two or more of these conditions apply.

Step 4: Evaluate the Answer Choices
(E) hits on the first of the predictions. In this case, the antique's authenticity cannot be verified, so a recommendation against Matilde's purchase is justified.

(A) does not provide a fact that would, based on the Principle in the stimulus, justify recommending against Matilde's purchase of the vase. If anything, it suggests that she is capable of verifying the vase's authenticity.

(B) does not provide a fact that would, based on the Principle in the stimulus, justify recommending against Matilde's purchase of the vase. We don't know if she can verify its authenticity or whether she appreciates it aesthetically.

(C) is a 180. In this case, Matilde can both verify the vase's authenticity and she appreciates it aesthetically. Both conditions necessary to justify a purchase recommendation

are met. That doesn't guarantee that she *should* buy the vase, but nothing from the given Principle indicates she shouldn't.

(D) does not provide a fact that would, based on the Principle in the stimulus, justify recommending against Matilde's purchase of the vase. Here, Matilde clearly appreciates the vase aesthetically, but we don't know if she can verify its authenticity.

11. (D) Inference

Step 1: Identify the Question Type
The question stem indicates an Inference question. The correct answer is the one supported by the critic's statements in the stimulus.

Step 2: Untangle the Stimulus
In the stimulus, the critic describes and evaluates Waverly's art history textbook. The critic quotes Waverly's stated goal: to be objective in her accounts of various works of art. The critic follows this by saying that no one is ever objective when writing about art and stating that Waverly writes much better when discussing art she likes than when discussing art she does not like.

Step 3: Make a Prediction
Leave aside your own opinions about art and art critics, and predict the answer based exclusively on the critic's statements. If the critic is correct (and remember the question stem's condition: "The critic's statements, *if true* …"), you can infer that Waverly did not achieve her stated goal of being objective about the art she discusses. This is what the correct answer will say.

Step 4: Evaluate the Answer Choices
(D) matches the prediction. It is a solid inference based on the critic's statements.

(A) is a Distortion of Waverly's goal, which is to write objectively, not to be free of preferences. Note that this choice refers to Waverly's *beliefs* while the stimulus deals only with her *claims*.

(B) is Outside the Scope. Waverly's stated goal is to avoid praising or denigrating works of art in her writing; this tells us nothing about how she *feels* about the works of art discussed in the book. Her book may well include art about which she is indifferent.

(C) is either a 180 or a deep Distortion of the stimulus. This answer directly contradicts Waverly's *stated* goal. To accept this answer, you'd have to assume something for which the stimulus gives no support: that Waverly's true intentions were different than her stated goal.

(E) is much like **(C)** in that it claims that Waverly's true intentions are at odds with her stated goal. The stimulus tells us nothing about Waverly's state of mind or hidden motive.

12. (E) Assumption (Sufficient)

Step 1: Identify the Question Type
Because this question stem defines the correct answer as one that, if true, ensures that the author's conclusion "follows logically" from her evidence, this is a Sufficient Assumption question. Look for the piece of information that guarantees the conclusion will follow from the evidence.

Step 2: Untangle the Stimulus
The stimulus opens with some background information to set up the context, but the conclusion is confined to the stimulus's final sentence: The Sals culture did not smelt iron. The evidence is that the culture had no distinct word for iron.

Step 3: Make a Prediction
The author assumes that the culture had a distinct word for any metal its people smelted.

If	smelt metal	→	word
If	~ word	→	~ smelt metal

This provides a perfect prediction for the correct answer.

Step 4: Evaluate the Answer Choices
(E) matches the prediction, phrasing it as a blanket statement about all cultures. If it is true that a culture always has a distinct word for any metal smelted by its people, then the author's conclusion must follow from her evidence.

(A) reverses the order of the terms in the author's conditional assumption without negating those terms. This statement is about how to know that a culture *did* smelt a metal while the argument in the stimulus is about how to know that the Sals did *not* smelt iron.

(B) is Outside the Scope. The argument in the stimulus is about a metal that the Sals did not *smelt*, not about one with which they were not *familiar*.

(C) is irrelevant. The author stipulated that the Sals culture smelted copper and bronze and had distinct words for copper and bronze. Knowing that all cultures that smelted these metals had distinct words for them adds nothing to the argument, which is about iron, a metal the author claims the Sals did *not* smelt.

(D) introduces a term—"familiar with"—that falls Outside the Scope of the argument, which is confined to a metal that the Sals culture did not smelt and for which it had no distinct word. **(B)** falls Outside the Scope of the stimulus for the same reason.

13. (A) Main Point

Step 1: Identify the Question Type
Because the correct answer will "accurately express the overall conclusion" of the argument in the stimulus, this is a Main Point question.

Step 2: Untangle the Stimulus
The argument's conclusion is the recommendation in the first sentence: Organizations seeking to increase support for higher education need to convince the public that such support produces a society-wide benefit. The rest of the stimulus explains why the author believes this (it will make the public more receptive) and, thus, serves as evidence for the conclusion in the first sentence.

Step 3: Make a Prediction
The correct answer will paraphrase the first sentence of the stimulus.

Step 4: Evaluate the Answer Choices
(A) is correct. This answer substitutes "seeking to encourage higher education programs" for "wanting to enhance support for higher education programs," and substitutes "must persuade the public that these programs" for "need to convince the public that such programs." Otherwise, the two sentences are identical.

(B) states, in broader terms, the example used to illustrate the author's *evidence*.

(C), like **(B)**, focuses on the example used in the author's *evidence*.

(D) paraphrases the author's *evidence*, the second sentence in the stimulus.

(E) articulates the assumption underlying the analogy the author implies between higher education programs and road building. An assumption is something implicit to an argument while the main point is always explicit.

14. (D) Role of a Statement

Step 1: Identify the Question Type
This question stem is quite direct. The correct answer "describes the role played in the argument" by the following claim: "[T]he risk of a satellite orbiting Earth colliding with other satellites or satellite fragments is likely to increase dramatically in the future."

Step 2: Untangle the Stimulus
The statement at issue is a paraphrase of the stimulus's first sentence, boiled down to just the prediction that the author makes. Predictions are routinely the conclusions of arguments, and indeed, that is the case here. This is confirmed by the opening phrase of the stimulus's second sentence—"[a]fter all"—which indicates the beginning of the author's evidence.

Step 3: Make a Prediction

The claim in the question stem, a prediction, plays the role of *conclusion* in the argument.

Step 4: Evaluate the Answer Choices

(D) is correct.

(A) is a Distortion. The claim in question *is* the argument's conclusion; it need not provide evidence for itself.

(B) is a Distortion. The claim in question *is* the argument's conclusion; the role described here is that of *subsidiary* evidence.

(C) describes a *subsidiary* conclusion, but the claim at issue here is the argument's *final* conclusion; it does not support any additional conclusion(s) drawn in the argument.

(E) is, like **(A)** and **(B)**, a Distortion of the role played by the claim. The claim—a prediction, mind you—is the main point of the argument. That prediction certainly is essential to the author's argument. The very first part of the first sentence—which indicates that currently no satellite is at significant risk—is background information, but after the contrast Keyword *but* the author's argument begins.

15. (E) Paradox

Step 1: Identify the Question Type

While this question stem doesn't contain common terms such as "apparent discrepancy" or "seeming contradiction," you know it is a Paradox question because the right answer will *explain* a phenomenon. You can safely anticipate that the stimulus will describe what appears to be a paradoxical set of facts.

Step 2: Untangle the Stimulus

The paradox is signaled by *although* in the stimulus's second sentence. Young chicks were successfully treated for *Salmonella* bacteria yet showed a higher incidence of bacteria overall.

Step 3: Make a Prediction

The correct answer will explain how the treatment could reduce *Salmonella* bacteria while, apparently, stimulating other types of bacteria. The stimulus in this Paradox question strongly suggests that *Salmonella* may act as a deterrent to other types of bacteria.

Step 4: Evaluate the Answer Choices

(E) matches the prediction. If, in fact, the other bacteria would have been hindered by the presence of *Salmonella*, the situation described in the stimulus is pretty easily explained.

(A) is a 180. The phenomenon described in the stimulus occurred only one week after the treatment, so **(A)** makes the situation even more confusing than it was originally.

(B) is Outside the Scope. The fact stated in this answer choice might help explain why the *Salmonella* treatment was successful, but it does nothing to explain why concentrations of other bacteria increased.

(C) is Outside the Scope. The situation described in the stimulus occurs over one week during the chicks' lives. What might happen later in life is irrelevant.

(D) adds an additional fact (about the *incidence of illness* from bacteria) that does nothing to explain the paradox (which is about *concentrations* of bacteria). Also, even if incidence of illness was positively correlated with higher concentrations of the bacteria, then one would expect that the treated chicks (those with the higher concentrations of other bacteria) would have the higher incidence of illness. However, **(D)** indicates the opposite, thereby potentially deepening the mystery.

16. (D) Flaw

Step 1: Identify the Question Type

The task in this Flaw question is to describe the reasoning error in the respondent's argument. Read the debater's argument, and then consider how the respondent attempts to refute it, identifying the key mistake in the respondent's logic.

Step 2: Untangle the Stimulus

The debater concludes that the hierarchical nature of lecturing is a weakness because, he says, students learn best through peer interaction, but lecturing places the lecturer as the students' superior.

The respondent considers the hierarchy in lecturing a strength. All learning, she says, is hierarchical because simpler subjects are prerequisite to more complex ones. But this response doesn't confront the debater's point head on. While the debater addresses hierarchy among the participants in the learning environment, the respondent addresses hierarchy among the subjects being taught.

Step 3: Make a Prediction

The respondent's problem is a type of equivocation. While she uses the word *hierarchy*, she is talking about a different kind of hierarchy than the debater was discussing. The correct answer will describe how the respondent uses a key term in a different way than the debater does or applies a key concept to a different aspect of the debate than the debater does. In short, the respondent misunderstands how the debater is using the word *hierarchy*.

Step 4: Evaluate the Answer Choices

(D) is a match for this prediction. The respondent applies *hierarchy* to the subject matter rather than to the teacher and students.

(A) is a Distortion. The respondent makes no concessions to the debater; she just misunderstands him.

(B) is Outside the Scope. Neither speaker claims that teaching methods are or are not fungible across disciplines, and the respondent is clear that mathematics is just an example of her point.

(C) is Outside the Scope. The two speakers limit their arguments to whether hierarchy is a strength or weakness of lecturing. Additional strengths and weaknesses aren't at issue, so the respondent's argument is not flawed by ignoring them.

(E) is a Distortion. The respondent uses mathematics as one example of her evidence. Her problem is that her evidence is on a topic different than that of the debater, not that the example in her evidence is insufficiently representative.

17. (A) Strengthen

Step 1: Identify the Question Type
This is a straightforward Strengthen question stem. The correct answer will be a fact that makes the argument's conclusion more likely to follow from its evidence.

Step 2: Untangle the Stimulus
In this argument, the author concludes that Han purple, an ancient Chinese pigment, was *probably* accidentally invented by someone trying to make common white glass. The author's evidence is that the white glass of that time and Han purple contained the same chemical ingredients, *and* both substances were made at high heat, with lead mixed into the ingredients to reduce their melting point. Notice that the author says white glass was common at the time, but does not say whether Han purple was less common. He also does not say whether Han purple is found in the same area as white glass or give any evidence suggesting that Han purple was made in the same workshops or by the same artisans who made white glass. To conclude that Han purple was accidentally invented by people trying to make white glass, however, he must be assuming those things to be true.

Step 3: Make a Prediction
The correct answer will add a fact that makes the author's scenario more likely. It might say that objects in Han purple and white glass came from the same area, that evidence suggests they were made in the same workshops or by the same artisans, or that objects of white glass were common earlier than those featuring Han purple.

Step 4: Evaluate the Answer Choices
(A) strengthens the argument by providing evidence that objects of white glass and Han purple were produced in the same small area. This clears up one of the doubts we might have had about the likelihood of the author's hypothesis.

(B) is Outside the Scope. The fact that objects made of the two materials had different uses does not explain how the materials were invented. Think of the now famous story of how the adhesive used in Post-It notes came about. It was

accidentally invented by someone trying to make a super strong adhesive. The fact that the Post-It adhesive and the super strong adhesive are used for different products says nothing about how they were invented.

(C) is Outside the Scope. It would be useful to know if those who could make Han purple also knew how to make white glass, but just knowing that few people could make Han purple neither strengthens nor weakens the argument.

(D) is, if anything, a 180. If the ingredients used in the two products were quite limited, it would be more likely that Han purple and white glass had a common source. Knowing that the ingredients could be found in many places gives the author one more question to clear up.

(E) is Outside the Scope. The fact in **(E)** might simply indicate that white glass was more popular, or was cheaper to produce, than Han purple. It doesn't indicate that white glass was first or provide any reason for thinking Han purple was a happy accident in the process of producing white glass.

18. (A) Flaw

Step 1: Identify the Question Type
This question stem indicates a Flaw question. It tells you that the medical researcher's argument is "vulnerable to criticism" and asks for a correct answer that describes the error in reasoning.

Step 2: Untangle the Stimulus
The medical researcher makes a causal claim: Mild sleep deprivation probably enhances the body's defenses against illness. His evidence is a 1-million-person study (so sample size is *not* the issue here) that showed those sleeping less than eight hours per night had a lower illness rate than those sleeping more than eight hours per night. The medical researcher assumes this correlation (less sleep = less illness) shows a causal relationship. Note that the medical researcher's language is very cautious ("probably bolsters"); he does not claim that mild sleep deprivation is the only cause or that it will prevent illness altogether.

Step 3: Make a Prediction
All arguments that use a correlation as evidence of causation are suspect in three ways: (1) Causation may be reversed (here, it could be that vulnerability to illness causes people to sleep more); (2) there could be a third factor (here, something else might cause some people to both have a higher incidence of illness and to sleep more); or (3) the correlation might be pure coincidence (here, given the size of the study, this seems the least likely problem with the argument). The correct answer will probably critique the medical researcher for failing to rule out one of the first two causality problems.

Step 4: Evaluate the Answer Choices
(A) suggests the second of the three common correlation-causation flaws and is, therefore, correct.

(B) is not a valid criticism of the medical researcher's argument. The researcher does not claim that mild sleep deprivation is the only, or even the most important, factor in combating illness.

(C) introduces a claim of sufficiency that the medical researcher simply does not make.

(D) gets the correlation-causation relationship backward. The medical researcher *has* observed a correlation and from that draws a causal conclusion. There is no reason to think that the medical researcher assumes that all causal relationships produce observable correlations.

(E) is Outside the Scope. The medical researcher does not recommend mild sleep deprivation, and neither states nor implies that it has no negative consequences.

19. (A) Parallel Reasoning

Step 1: Identify the Question Type
The length of this question alone is a clue that this is a Parallel Reasoning question. That is confirmed by the question stem, which tells you that the correct answer is the one with an argument that "most closely parallels" that in the stimulus.

Step 2: Untangle the Stimulus
The argument here contains strict, valid Formal Logic. It can be diagrammed quite cleanly:

Evidence 1 and 2:

	X (temp below freezing)	→	Y (impatiens dead)	→	~Z (not bloom)
If					

The contrapositive would be this:

	Z (bloom)	→	~Y (impatiens not dead)	→	~X (temp not below freezing)
If					

The author indicates that the trigger of the contrapositive is true: Z (bloom) and thereby concludes ~X (temp not below freezing).

Step 3: Make a Prediction
The correct answer will be the only one that has an identical diagram. It would have two connected conditional statements and a negation of the second conditional statement's necessary clause in the evidence, and then a negation of the first conditional statement's sufficient clause as the conclusion:

If	X	→	Y
If	Y	→	Z
If	~Z	→	~X

Note that it doesn't matter whether the X, Y, or Z are positive or negative terms. As long as two Formal Logic statements chain together and the conclusion goes from one end of the contrapositive of the chain to the other (~Z → ~X).

Step 4: Evaluate the Answer Choices
(A) matches perfectly and is correct.

If	X (highly adaptable)	→	Y (thrive)
If	Y (thrive)	→	Z (have adverse effect)
If	~Z (not have adverse effect)	→	~X (not highly adaptable)

(B) goes wrong by having a conditional conclusion that only negates the second statement, and thus negates the Y term as a conclusion rather than the X term. Additionally, it has slight discrepancies among the Y terms:

If	X (thrives)	→	Y (adaptable)
If	Y (adapts)	→	Z (adverse effect)

Therefore,

If	~Z (no adverse effect)	→	~Y (has not adapted)

(C) goes wrong by having a conditional conclusion that only negates the second statement, and thus negates the Y term as a conclusion rather than the X term:

If	X (introduced)	→	Y (adverse effect)
If	Y (adverse effect)	→	Z (adapts well)

Therefore,

| If | ~Z (not adapt well) | → | ~Y (no adverse effect) |

(D) goes wrong in a number of ways, but primarily by having no Z term at all; this argument simply goes from hypothetical to predictive:

| If | X (introduction would have adverse effect) | → | Y (should not be introduced) |

| If | X (introduction will have adverse effect) | → | Y (should not be introduced) |

(E) goes wrong in a number of ways. First, the evidence statements do not link up in the same way as those in the stimulus do; and second, the author continually makes slight changes in the terms in ways that alter the meaning of the argument:

| If | X (would damage) | → | Y (should not be introduced) |

| If | ~Y (is introduced) | → | Z (risk can be reduced through population control) |

| If | Y (introduction is likely) | → | Z (populations should be controlled) |

20. (E) Assumption (Sufficient)

Step 1: Identify the Question Type
This question stem indicates a Sufficient Assumption question. The correct answer, if true, guarantees that the conclusion will follow logically from the evidence.

Step 2: Untangle the Stimulus
Formal Logic is fairly common in Sufficient Assumption questions. This stimulus consists of four conditional statements, three in the evidence and one that stands as the conclusion. Diagramming the statements helps make short work of the argument analysis:

Evidence 1:

| If | city builds convention center | → | several nat'l orgs will hold conventions there |

Evidence 2:

| If | several large conventions are held there | → | # of visitors will increase |

Evidence 3:

| If | # of visitors increases | → | city tax revenues increase |

Therefore, the conclusion:

| If | city builds convention center | → | city tax revenues increase |

The argument is nearly complete, but the first and second statements have a slight distinction between two terms of the evidence. The author assumes that conventions held by national organizations will be large conventions. If that's true, the argument is sound all the way through.

Step 3: Make a Prediction
The correct answer will have to close up the one gap in the author's argument. It will state, in so many words that the conventions of national organizations are large conventions.

Step 4: Evaluate the Answer Choices
(E) paraphrases the author's assumption, matching the prediction perfectly.

(A) is Outside the Scope. The city's tax revenues could increase in ways other than through increased tourism. That has no effect on the argument. **(A)** is an incorrect contrapositive of the third piece of evidence.

(B) is Outside the Scope. The fact here, which sounds reasonable enough, is not sufficient to establish the author's conclusion from his evidence because this does not establish that the conventions at the new center will be large conventions. The third piece of evidence already indicates that more visitors means more tax revenue.

(C) is Outside the Scope. This is just like **(A)**. The city's tax revenues could increase in ways other than through increased tourism without having any effect on the argument. This choice reverses the Formal Logic without negating it.

(D) is Outside the Scope. The fact here is nice to know, and may suggest an additional benefit to building the new convention center, but it does nothing to establish that the conventions held there will be large conventions. A Sufficient Assumption question needs an answer that guarantees the truth of the conclusion, and **(D)** would merely strengthen the conclusion—not guarantee it.

21. (B) Strengthen/Weaken (Evaluate the Argument)

Step 1: Identify the Question Type
This is a variety of Strengthen/Weaken question. The correct answer is something that is relevant to the validity of the argument in the stimulus. Note that each answer choice contains a question. How the question in the correct answer choice is answered will impact the argument for better or worse. How the questions in the wrong answers are answered will have no impact on the argument in the stimulus.

Step 2: Untangle the Stimulus
The author of the stimulus concludes that dogs have an aversion to being treated unfairly. His evidence is a study. In the study, two dogs were placed side by side and given the same command, but when both obeyed, only one was given a treat. After a while, the dogs who did not receive treats stopped obeying. The author clearly assumes that because both dogs initially obeyed and only one got a treat, the dogs who did not receive treats perceived their treatment as *unfair*.

Step 3: Make a Prediction
This experiment fairly begs (excuse the dog pun) for a simpler explanation. Rather than impute a human response—"That's not fair!"—to the dogs, maybe the unrewarded dogs just stopped obeying because they didn't get treats. There's an easy way to check for this: Don't give either dog a treat. If both stop obeying, it's certainly not because one or the other thought the treatment was *unfair*, but simply because it was treats that motivated their good behavior all along.

Step 4: Evaluate the Answer Choices
(B) poses the question suggested by the prediction, and it is correct.

(A) doesn't give us information helpful to understanding why, *over time*, the dogs who did not receive rewards stopped obeying.

(C) needs more information to be of use in assessing the interpretation offered in the stimulus. We would need to know if these dogs behaved differently when they received rewards than when they did not.

(D) is Outside the Scope. The author's argument is an attempt to interpret the behavior of dogs who stopped obeying, not to explain why rewards are helpful in getting dogs to obey.

(E) offers a question that would, even if we knew the answer, lead to irrelevant information. Did some dogs perceive unfairness earlier than others? Or were some dogs just quicker to stop obeying because they didn't get treats? Knowing how long dogs took to stop obeying doesn't tell us *why* they stopped obeying.

22. (E) Inference

Step 1: Identify the Question Type
As you read this question stem, notice the "direction" of the support. Here, the statements in the stimulus offer support for the correct answer, so this is an Inference question.

Step 2: Untangle the Stimulus
This stimulus boils down to two statements, one negative and one affirmative: Income satisfaction is not strongly correlated with the amount of income, and income satisfaction depends on income relative to others in one's neighborhood. We also learn that most people live among neighbors who share their economic class status.

Step 3: Make a Prediction
Combining the two statements in the stimulus leads to a variety of inferences; for example, simply getting a raise might not be enough to make a person happy with his or her income, or a person might be content with a low salary if that salary is higher than what most of his or her neighbors make. Don't press too hard for a perfect prediction here; know what the stimulus statements say and use them to evaluate the answer choices.

Step 4: Evaluate the Answer Choices
(E) follows from the stimulus. If satisfaction with one's income comes from having a higher income than most people in one's neighborhood, then giving everyone a raise will do little or nothing to make most people more satisfied with their own salaries.

(A) is a 180. According to the stimulus, satisfaction with income is relative. Those with higher incomes tend to live among neighbors who share their high-income status. Based on the stimulus, we would expect some people in these neighborhoods (those making more than most of their neighbors) to be happy with their incomes and some to be dissatisfied. The same situation is expected in middle-class neighborhoods.

(B) is Outside the Scope. Nothing in the stimulus suggests that age is a factor, positive or negative, in income satisfaction.

(C) is a 180. According to the stimulus, satisfaction and dissatisfaction with income is determined by relative income levels *within* neighborhoods, not across them.

(D) is well Outside the Scope of the stimulus, which has nothing to say about the factors that influence people's satisfaction with their lives on the whole.

23. (D) Weaken

Step 1: Identify the Question Type
This is a clear Weaken question stem. The correct answer will make the geologist's conclusion less likely to follow from her evidence.

Step 2: Untangle the Stimulus
In this stimulus, you must keep track of various opinions. First, you get some helpful background: The dominant view holds that petroleum was formed from plant and animal remains deep in the Earth's crust. The geologist concludes that the theory of those challenging the dominant view has been refuted; i.e., she believes that the dominant view is correct. Her evidence is that biomarkers (molecules indicating living organisms) are found in petroleum. For the geologist's argument to work, she must assume that the biomarkers came from the remains of plants and animals deep in the Earth's crust.

Step 3: Make a Prediction
A fact suggesting that the biomarkers are not from the remains of plants and animals deep in the Earth's crust will weaken this argument. Remember, the correct answer will weaken the geologist's position, and thus the dominant view. The correct answer strengthens the theory of those who challenge the dominant view.

Step 4: Evaluate the Answer Choices
(D) is correct. It weakens the geologist's argument by suggesting that the biomarkers found in petroleum might come from a source other than the remains of plants and animals deep in the Earth's crust. Those who challenge the dominant view would welcome the fact in **(D)**.

(A) is Outside the Scope. The geologist is using the presence of biomarkers to argue that petroleum is formed from the fossil remains of plants and animals. Fossils without biomarkers have no impact on her argument. The fact in **(A)** suggests another avenue of investigation perhaps, but one that would, if proven, *strengthen* the geologist's argument.

(B) is Outside the Scope. The geologist does not claim that petroleum dates to the formation of the Earth, and those who challenge the dominant view don't believe that petroleum comes from fossils, so the fact in **(B)** is moot for both sides of this debate.

(C) is Outside the Scope. Much like the fact in **(B)**, the statement here is not one with which either side in the debate would take issue. It simply doesn't impact either theory.

(E) is Outside the Scope. Again, as with the facts in **(B)** and **(C)**, everyone involved in the debate could agree with this statement without altering their points of view. The geologist and those who hold the dominant view would say, "This is true, and these are the deposits from which petroleum is formed." Those who oppose the dominant view would say, "Yes, it is true, but those are not the deposits from which petroleum is formed."

24. (B) Inference

Step 1: Identify the Question Type
The identifying language in this Inference question stem is clear: The correct answer is the one that can be "properly inferred" from the statements in the stimulus.

Step 2: Untangle the Stimulus
The stimulus consists of one Formal Logic rule and an application of that rule. Here's a helpful paraphrase of the stimulus: If an accident 1) causes personal injury *or* causes over $500 in property damage, *and* 2) the driver is able to report the accident, then the driver is required to report the accident to the DMV. Ted (a driver in an accident) is not required to report his accident.

Step 3: Make a Prediction
From the fact that Ted is not required to report his accident, you can infer that *either* 1) Dan's accident did not cause personal injury *and* did not cause over $500 in property damage *or* 2) that Dan is not capable of reporting his accident. At least one of those conditions must be true.

Step 4: Evaluate the Answer Choices
(B) must be true based on the stimulus. Being a driver in an accident that caused over $500 in property damage would require a report *unless* the driver was incapable of reporting.

(A) is a Distortion. If Dan is incapable of reporting, he is released from the requirement to report. In the case of his incapacity, we can draw no valid conclusions about the type or extent of injuries and damage.

(C) is Outside the Scope. If the accident did not cause personal injury and did not cause property damage in excess of $500, then the rule does not require anyone to report. Moreover, there is no indication that this was a two-car accident or that any other person was involved. It is possible, of course, that another rule requires someone to report the accident (say a witness or an emergency worker), but any other rule is Outside the Scope of this stimulus.

(D) is a Distortion. Injury is certainly one reason a driver might be incapable of reporting an accident, but nothing in the rule or its application in the stimulus suggests that it is the only reason. What if bad weather knocked out the phones at 911 and the DMV, for example? Ted could be unhurt but still incapable of reporting the accident.

(E) cannot be guaranteed. For one, **(E)** is not strong enough to release Ted from an obligation to report. To do that, we would need to know that no one was injured *and* that the accident did not lead to more than $500 in property damage. The other possibility is of course that Ted is not required to report simply because he's unable to do so, even if there was an injury or $500 or more in property damage.

25. (D) Parallel Flaw

Step 1: Identify the Question Type
This question stem calls for an answer containing an argument that is "most similar in its flawed pattern of reasoning" to the argument in the stimulus. This is a Parallel Flaw question.

Step 2: Untangle the Stimulus
The stimulus features an argument that commits the classic Necessity versus Sufficiency flaw. From evidence that immunity to infection from a microorganism is sufficient to prevent symptoms from that microorganism, the author concludes that a lack of symptoms from the microorganism is evidence of immunity.

If	*immunity*	→	*~ harmful symptoms*
If	*~ harmful symptoms*	→	*immunity*

The problem with the argument is that someone who is not immune might not manifest symptoms for some other reason. The student *could* properly conclude that manifesting symptoms is evidence that a person is *not* immune, but not the other way around. As it stands, the student has properly reversed, but not negated, the terms in the conditional statement.

Step 3: Make a Prediction
The correct answer will feature an argument that commits the same flaw. It will say that A is sufficient for B, and then conclude that B is sufficient for A. The argument, like that in the stimulus, will reverse, but not negate, the terms in the conditional statement.

Step 4: Evaluate the Answer Choices
(D) is the perfect match. From evidence that excessive taxation is sufficient to hamper growth, the author concludes that slow growth is evidence of excessive taxation.

If	*excessive taxation*	→	*~ expansion*
If	*~ expansion*	→	*excessive taxation*

(A) introduces too many terms (morally right, just, and best serve the interests of everyone) to be parallel to the stimulus. An argument parallel to the stimulus, but using the scenario in **(A)**, would simply say: Everything morally right is just. The fact that Action X is just is evidence that it is morally right.

(B) has an argument that is flawed because it negates, but does not reverse, the terms in the conditional statement.

If	*advertiser*	→	*persuade*
If	*~ advertiser*	→	*~ persuade*

An argument parallel to the stimulus, but using the scenario in **(B)**, would say: Advertisers try to persuade people that claims are true. That fact that fiction writers try to persuade people that claims are true is evidence that they are advertisers. Additionally, the conclusion in **(B)** as written is not the right level of certainty because it says writers of fiction *probably* don't persuade, whereas no similar word of likelihood is used in the original stimulus.

(C) has an argument without a flaw. If the medicine really does cure the disease or alleviate the symptoms, the fact that Isabel still shows symptoms is, indeed, evidence that she did not take the medicine.

(E) has an argument that does not involve Formal Logic, so it cannot be parallel to the argument in the stimulus. The argument here simply makes a leap from what doctors do to what must be helpful in preventing disease.

Section II: Logic Games
Game 1: Band Solos

Q#	Question Type	Correct	Difficulty
1	Acceptability	C	★
2	"If" / Must Be True	D	★
3	Must Be False EXCEPT	E	★★
4	Must Be False (CANNOT Be True)	A	★
5	"If" / Must Be True EXCEPT	E	★

Game 2: Art Historians' Lectures

Q#	Question Type	Correct	Difficulty
6	Acceptability	E	★
7	Must Be True	B	★
8	"If" / Could Be True	E	★
9	Must Be False (CANNOT Be True)	A	★
10	"If" / Could Be True	A	★★

Game 3: Colored Rugs

Q#	Question Type	Correct	Difficulty
11	Acceptability	A	★
12	Must Be True	C	★★
13	"If" / Must Be True	E	★★★
14	"If" / Must Be False (CANNOT Be True)	D	★★
15	"If" / Could Be True	B	★★
16	"If" / Could Be True EXCEPT	A	★★★

Game 4: Graduation Photographers

Q#	Question Type	Correct	Difficulty
17	Acceptability	E	★★
18	"If" / Must Be True	D	★★
19	Partial Acceptability	B	★★★
20	Complete and Accurate List	B	★★★★
21	"If" / Must Be True	A	★★★
22	Partial Acceptability (CANNOT)	B	★★★
23	Rule Substitution	C	★★★★

Game 1: Band Solos

Step 1: Overview

Situation: Band members playing solos during a concert

Entities: Six band members (guitarist, keyboard player, percussionist, saxophonist, trumpeter, violinist)

Action: Loose Sequencing. Determine the order in which the members play their solos. A glance ahead at the rules reveals what makes this game loose instead of strict. While the first rule is definitely a Strict Sequencing type because it's about a specific slot, the relationships among entities are all defined in relative terms ("some time before" and "some time after"). These relationships are what dictate the final sketch, which is ultimately predominantly a Loose Sequencing diagram. However, if you draw out six slots and then build the loose sketch from Rules 2–4 underneath or to the side of those slots, that would also be fine.

Limitations: Each member performs one solo and, by definition, each solo will be performed by a single band member. This is a classic one-to-one sequencing.

Step 2: Sketch

Start by listing the entities by initial. Because the ultimate sketch will be a Loose Sequencing diagram, there is no need to draw a series of spaces. However, as mentioned, there would be no disadvantage if you had drawn one anyway.

Step 3: Rules

Rule 1 prevents the guitarist from performing fourth. If you drew a series of spaces, add "~G" under the fourth space. Otherwise, make a shorthand note to the side: "G ≠ 4."

Rule 2 provides a basic loose relationship, with the percussionist performing before the keyboard player:

$$P— K$$

Rule 3 creates a relationship among three band members. In order, the violinist will perform before the keyboard player, who will perform before the guitarist. This can be combined with Rule 2:

Rule 4 sets up two possible outcomes for the saxophonist, who will perform after the percussionist or the trumpeter, but not both. That's another way of saying that the saxophonist must perform after one and before the other. Draw out both possible outcomes:

$$P — S — T$$
$$or$$
$$T — S — P$$

Step 4: Deductions

The fourth rule is a definite source for setting up Limited Options. As with most Loose Sequencing games, use duplicates to expand each option and see all of the relationships.

In both options, use the percussionist to connect the combined sequence from Rules 2–3 to Rule 4. In the first option, be sure not to connect the keyboard player to either the saxophonist or the trumpeter, because they are unrelated.

In Option I, there are numerous outcomes. The first soloist can be either the percussionist or the violinist (neither of whom must be preceded by another member), and the last soloist can be either the trumpeter or the guitarist (neither of whom must precede another member).

The second option establishes more. The keyboard player and the guitarist are preceded by all of the remaining members, so they must perform fifth and sixth, respectively. The violinist can then perform any of the first four solos. The remaining members perform in order (though not necessarily consecutive): trumpeter, saxophonist, and percussionist.

If you had opted to use a Strict Sequencing sketch, you could build negative deductions underneath the slots as well. For example, for Rule 2, you would also note "~P" under slot 6 and a "~K" under slot 1. For Rule 3, "~V" under slots 5 and 6, "~G" under slots 1 and 2, and "~K" under slot 6. Also, given that the keyboard player is after both the percussionist and violinist, a "~K" under slot 2, too, and given that the guitarist is after all three of the percussionist, violinist, and keyboardist, a "~G" under slot 3. Finally, for Rule 4, "~S" under slots 1 and 6.

Lastly, be sure not to forget Rule 1. The LSAT does not provide rules that go unused, so it is sure to come into play at some point. Given the negative deductions from Rules 2–4 and Rule 1, it can be determined that the guitarist can only be the fifth or sixth solo. Additionally, because the guitarist is already established as sixth in Option II, Rule 1 will only be tested with Option I.

Step 5: Questions

1. (C) Acceptability

This is a typical Acceptability question. Go through the rules one at a time and eliminate answers that violate those rules.

(A) violates Rule 1 by having the guitarist fourth. **(D)** and **(E)** violate Rule 2 by having the percussionist perform after the keyboard player. Neither of the remaining answers violates Rule 3, but **(B)** violates Rule 4 by having the saxophonist perform after *both* the percussionist and the trumpeter. That leaves **(C)** as the correct answer.

2. (D) "If" / Must Be True

For this question, the percussionist performs before the saxophonist, which means the saxophonist must perform before the trumpeter (Rule 4). That means the percussionist performs before the trumpeter, making **(D)** the correct answer.

For the record, this is the basis for Option I. In that case, the percussionist could be first or second, but does not have to be either. That eliminates **(A)** and **(B)**. Moreover, there is no relationship between the saxophonist and either the violinist or the keyboard player. That eliminates **(C)** and **(E)**.

3. (E) Must Be False EXCEPT

Four of the answers to this question must be false (i.e., cannot happen) no matter what. The correct answer will be the one that could be true.

The keyboard player must perform after the violinist (Rule 3), so the keyboard player cannot be first. That eliminates **(A)**.

The guitarist must perform after the keyboard player (Rule 3). The keyboard player has to perform after both the percussionist (Rule 2) and the violinist (Rule 3), so the guitarist must perform after them, too. That means the guitarist cannot be second, which eliminates **(B)**, and cannot perform before the percussionist, which eliminates **(D)**.

Because the guitarist needs to perform after three other members (percussionist, violinist, and keyboard player), the guitarist appears only to be able to perform fourth, fifth, or sixth. However, here's the first non-Acceptability question to test Rule 1. The guitarist cannot perform fourth (Rule 1)—so the guitarist must be fifth or sixth. If the guitarist performed fifth, the saxophonist could not perform sixth because the saxophonist needs to perform before the percussionist or the trumpeter (Rule 4). Additionally, if the guitarist performed sixth, there would be nobody afterward. Thus, the guitarist can never precede the saxophonist, which eliminates **(C)**. That leaves **(E)** as the correct answer, which is possible under the conditions of Option I as follows:

V	P	K	S	T	G
1	2	3	4	5	6

4. (A) Must Be False (CANNOT Be True)

The correct answer to this question will be a band member that can never perform third. The remaining four answers will list members that could.

The guitarist must perform after the keyboard player (Rule 3). The keyboard player has to perform after both the percussionist (Rule 2) and the violinist (Rule 3), so the guitarist must perform after them, too. That means the guitarist must be preceded by at least three members and

thus can never perform third. That makes **(A)** the correct answer.

For the record, the following acceptable sequences show how the remaining listed entities could all be third:

Keyboard Player:	V	P	K	S	T	G
Saxophonist:	V	T	S	P	K	G
Trumpeter:	P	S	T	V	K	G
Violinist:	T	S	V	P	K	G
	1	2	3	4	5	6

5. (E) "If" / Must Be True EXCEPT

For this question, the violinist will perform fourth. That could happen in either option, so both scenarios should be accounted for. In either one, the keyboard player must perform later, followed by the guitarist (Rule 3). So, they must be the fifth and sixth performers, respectively. That leaves the percussionist, the saxophonist, and the trumpeter. The saxophonist must perform after the percussionist or the trumpeter, but before the other (Rule 4). In other words, the percussionist and the trumpeter will play in either order with the saxophonist in between:

I)	P	S	T	V	K	G
	1	2	3	4	5	6

II)	T	S	P	V	K	G
	1	2	3	4	5	6

All of the answers are true in either case except for **(E)**, because the trumpeter could perform before *or after* the saxophonist. That makes **(E)** the correct answer.

Game 2: Art Historians' Lectures

Step 1: Overview

Situation: Art historians giving a series of public lectures

Entities: Four historians (Farley, Garcia, Holden, Jiang); four topics (lithographs, oil paintings, sculptures, watercolors)

Action: Strict Sequencing. Determine the order in which the historians speak and the order of the topics. Because each set of entities will be ordered, this is merely Sequencing on two levels. Some may want to label this game a Hybrid of Sequencing (order the historians) and either Matching or Distribution (assign the topics). Ultimately, it's not significant how the game is construed. No points are awarded on Test Day for proper classification. What's more important is that any of these designations would lead to the same sketch and application of the rules.

Limitations: The four lectures are given one at a time. Each historian gives just one lecture, and each lecture is on a different topic.

Step 2: Sketch

The sketch needs spaces to determine the order of both the historians and the lecture topics. Draw a set of four spaces and use the top and bottom to order the historians and topics, respectively. If preferred, you can draw two sets of spaces, one atop the other, using one to order the historians and the second to order the topics. List the entities by initial to the side of the slots:

FGHJ ___ ___ ___ ___

l o s w ___ ___ ___ ___
         1   2   3   4

Step 3: Rules

Rule 1 provides a relative order for three of the lecture topics. The oil paintings and watercolors lectures must be before the lithographs one. Note that the oil paintings and watercolors lectures can be given in either order.

o ⋱
    l
w ⋰

Because of that, the lithographs lecture cannot be either of the first two lectures, and neither the oil paintings lecture nor the watercolors lecture can be last. If desired, draw "~l" under the first two spaces, and "~o; ~w" under the last space.

Rule 2 dictates that Farley's lecture precedes the oil paintings lecture.

F ⋱
    o

Because the top row is the historians and the bottom row is the lectures, note the rule so that the F is on a higher slot than the o so it visually corresponds to the sketch. From this

rule, it can be deduced that the first lecture cannot be on oil paintings, and Farley cannot give the last lecture. If desired, draw "~o" under the first space and "~F" above the last.

Rule 3 provides some order for three of the historians. Holden must lecture before both Garcia and Jiang. Note that Garcia and Jiang can lecture in either order.

   ⋰G
H
   ⋱J

Because of this, Holden cannot give either of the last two lectures, and neither Garcia nor Jiang can give the first lecture. If desired, draw "~H" above the last two spaces and "~G; ~J" above the first space.

Step 4: Deductions

The biggest deduction in this game comes from recognizing the Duplicated entity: oil paintings. That lecture must come before the lithographs lecture (Rule 1) and after Farley's lecture (Rule 2):

F
 ⋱
  o … l

This adds a new restriction to Farley, who now has to speak before at least *two* lectures. That means Farley cannot give either of the last two lectures—nor can Holden (Rule 3). Therefore, the last two lectures must be given by Garcia and Jiang, in either order. That means Farley and Holden will give the first two lectures, in either order.

As for the topics, the first lecture cannot be on lithographs (Rule 1) or oil paintings (Rule 2). It can only be on sculptures or watercolors. The last lecture cannot be on oil paintings or watercolors (Rule 1). It can only be on lithographs or sculptures. Note that sculptures is a Floater and has no restrictions.

F/H   H/F   G/J   J/G
___   ___   ___   ___
w/s   l/s
 1   2   3   4
~l

There are a few ways to set up Limited Options at this point. For example, two options based on whether Farley is first or second; two options based on whether oil paintings is second or third; two options based on whether lithographs is third or fourth. Each pair has at least one option that offers significant deductions. It's certainly worth taking a moment to consider them before moving to the questions, but this game can be managed effectively without them, too.

Step 5: Questions

6. (E) Acceptability

As with any Acceptability question, go through the rules one at a time, eliminating answers that violate those rules.

(A) violates Rule 1 by having lithographs earlier than oil paintings and watercolors. **(D)** violates Rule 2 by having Farley after oil paintings. And **(B)** and **(C)** violate Rule 3 by having Harley between Garcia and Jiang instead of earlier than them both. That leaves **(E)** as the correct answer.

7. (B) Must Be True

The correct answer to this question must be true no matter what. The remaining four answers could be or must be false.

Because the sculptures lecture is a Floater, it could be first, which would make it impossible for Farley's lecture to be earlier. That eliminates **(A)**.

Holden's lecture must be one of the first two lectures (Rule 3), and the lithographs lecture must be one of the last two (Rule 1). Therefore, Holden must lecture before the lithographs lecture, making **(B)** the correct answer. For the record:

Again, there is no restriction on the sculptures lecture, so it could be last, making it impossible to be earlier than any other lecture. That eliminates **(C)** and **(D)**, and it's possible for Garcia to give the watercolors lecture third (as seen in the sketch for the following question), in which case neither one would be earlier than the other. That eliminates **(E)**.

8. (E) "If" / Could Be True

For this question, the watercolors lecture will be third. That means the lithographs lecture must be last (Rule 1). That leaves the sculptures and oil paintings lectures. The oil paintings lecture must be after Farley's lecture (Rule 2), so the oil paintings lecture must be second with Farley giving the first lecture, which must be on the remaining topic: sculptures. Holden has to lecture before the remaining historians, so Holden lectures second with Garcia and Jiang giving the last two lectures in either order.

F	H	G/J	J/G
s	o	w	l
1	2	3	4

With that, only **(E)** is possible—Jiang could give the lithographs lecture as the last lecture—making **(E)** the correct answer.

9. (A) Must Be False (CANNOT Be True)

The correct answer to this question will be false no matter what. The four wrong answers will be possibly or definitely true.

Farley has to lecture before the oil paintings lecture, which must be given before the lithographs lecture. Thus, it is impossible for Farley to give the lithographs lecture, making **(A)** the correct answer. This is just a combination of Rules 1 and 2. For the record:

The sketch for the previous question shows that either Garcia or Jiang can give the watercolors lecture and that Holden can

give the oil paintings lecture. That eliminates **(C)**, **(D)**, and **(E)**. And the question stem for the very next question states that Garcia can give the sculptures lecture. That eliminates **(B)**.

10. (A) "If" / Could Be True

For this question, Garcia will give the sculptures lecture. Holden has to give one of the first two lectures (Rule 3), as does Farley, who must lecture before the oil paintings lecture (Rule 2), which must be before the lithographs lecture (Rule 1). With the first two speeches accounted for, Garcia can only lecture third or fourth, with Jiang lecturing in the other spot. Test out both possibilities.

In both possibilities, the remaining lectures have to be on lithographs, oil paintings, and watercolors, with lithographs coming after the other two (Rule 1). So oil paintings and watercolors will be the first two lectures, with lithographs taking the last open spot—which will be Jiang's lecture. The oil paintings lecture has to be given after Farley's lecture, so oil paintings will be second and Farley will be first in both options. That means Holden is left to give the second lecture and watercolors is left to be the first.

F	H	G	J
w	o	s	l
1	2	3	4

or

F	H	J	G
w	o	l	s
1	2	3	4

With that, only **(A)** is possible (in the second option), making that the correct answer.

Game 3: Colored Rugs

Step 1: Overview

Situation: Rugs being woven out of colored thread

Entities: Three rugs; six colors (forest, olive, peach, turquoise, white, yellow)

Action: Selection/Distribution Hybrid. Determine which colors will be used to make the rugs (Selection), then determine which rugs those colors will be used to make (Distribution).

Limitations: Exactly five of the six colors will be selected. Each color selected will be used in only one rug. Each rug can have one color (solid) or more (multicolored).

Step 2: Sketch

Start by listing the colors by initial. Make a note to the side that five of them will be selected. As the game proceeds, circle any color that is definitely selected and cross out any color that is not. Then, set up a table with a column (or row) for each of the three rugs. Each rug will have at least one color, so draw one slot to start each column.

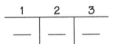

There are a few things to note immediately. Five of the six colors are selected, which means only one color will be left out. If you can determine which color is *not* selected, then you automatically know that all of the others *are* selected.

Next, the sketch has three slots to start, which means two more need to be added. Those final two slots can be split among two rugs (creating two two-colored rugs and one solid rug) or placed together on one rug (creating one three-colored rug and two solid rugs). When a game has strong numeric restrictions, Numbers will often play a key role in making deductions. In this case, Numbers can be used to set up Limited Options, as discussed later. Two sketches can be set up now or, at least, make a note to the side about the numeric outcomes (2:2:1 or 3:1:1).

Also note that the rugs are never identified by name or number—not in the overview, the rules, or the questions. There are simply three rugs. So if one rug has three colors, it doesn't matter if it's Rug 1 or Rug 2. Each rug is just one of the three rugs. They are all interchangeable. Therefore, when you do draw out options, don't worry which rug gets which color. Just be sure that the colors are assigned without violating the rules.

Step 3: Rules

Rule 1 restricts the use of white. If it's used, it must be on a rug with two other colors (i.e., a three-colored rug). This does *not* mean that any rug with three colors must include white;

it's possible that white isn't selected at all. However, white cannot be used in a solid rug or a rug with just two colors.

$$W \rightarrow \boxed{\begin{array}{c} W \\ \hline \\ \hline \end{array}}$$

Rule 2 is some typical Formal Logic with a major implication. If a rug uses olive, it must also use peach. By contrapositive, if a rug does not use peach, it cannot use olive.

$$O \rightarrow \boxed{\begin{array}{c} O \\ \hline P \end{array}}$$

$\sim P \rightarrow \sim O$

(Impossible)

However, there are two things to note about this rule. First, olive cannot be used on a solid rug. If it's used, it has to be on a multicolored rug.

Second, by the contrapositive, if peach is not selected, neither is olive. However, five of six colors must be used, so it is not possible to select neither peach nor olive. Thus, peach must be selected no matter what. If olive is used, peach must be used, and if olive is not used, then peach is one of the five remaining colors that must be used. Circle P in the list of colors.

Rules 3, 4, and 5 restrict three pairs of colors from being used in the same rug. Note these restrictions in shorthand to the side:

Step 4: Deductions

The biggest deduction to make immediately is that peach must be selected (as noted with Rule 2). That provides an instant and confident point on the second question of the game.

There are no definite Blocks of Entities in this game, but there are various opportunities for Limited Options using Numbers and/or significant entities (white and olive, notably). The most fruitful options start with Numbers.

As recognized in the overview, the colors can be assigned to the rugs numerically in one of two ways—2:2:1 or 3:1:1. In the first option (2:2:1), a lot can be determined. There is no rug with three colors, so white cannot be used (Rule 1). That means all of the other colors must be selected. Olive must be used with peach (Rule 2), so that will be one of the multicolored rugs. Forest and turquoise cannot be used together, so they will be split between the remaining two rugs. Yellow will take the final space on the remaining two-colored rug.

The second option (3:1:1) is not as valuable. A lot depends on which colors are selected. However, it's good to note that neither white (Rule 1) nor olive (Rule 2) can be used on the two solid rugs.

I)

1	2	3
O	F/T	T/F
P	Y	

II)

1	2	3
	~W	~W
	~O	~O

If Option II is too spare for your liking, it can be further split into two more options based on the selection of either white or olive. It is not necessary to create three options, especially since the majority of the questions are "If" questions. The question explanations will not refer to any further options, but here are two ways you could further split Option II:

1) Based on white: If white is selected, the sketch remains virtually unchanged. However, if white is *not* selected, every other color is. In that case, olive has to be included with peach in the multicolored rug (Rule 2). Peach cannot be used with either turquoise (Rule 4) or yellow (Rule 5), so those colors will be assigned to the solid rugs, leaving forest as the third color in the multicolored rug.

IIa)

1	2	3
W		
	~O	~O

IIb)

1	2	3
O	T	Y
P		
F		

2) Based on olive: If olive is selected, it must be used in the multicolored rug with peach (Rule 2). Peach cannot be used with either turquoise (Rule 4) or yellow (Rule 5), so the third color must be forest or white. The solid rugs can be forest, turquoise, or yellow. If olive is *not* selected, every other color is. That includes white, which must be in the three-colored rug. The last three rules provide numerous restrictions, but no definite deductions.

IIa)

1	2	3
O	F/T/Y	F/T/Y
P		
F/W		

IIb)

1	2	3
W		
	~O	~O
~O		

Step 5: Questions

11. (A) Acceptability

The correct answer here will be acceptable—the one answer that doesn't violate any rules. Go through the rules one at a time and eliminate the four answers that violate those rules.

(E) violates Rule 1 by using white in a rug with only one other color. **(C)** violates Rule 2 by using olive in a rug without peach. **(D)** violates Rule 3 by putting forest and turquoise together. Nothing violates Rule 4, but **(B)** violates Rule 5 by putting peach and yellow together. That leaves **(A)** as the correct answer.

12. (C) Must Be True

The correct answer must be true no matter what. The remaining answers could be or must be false.

From Rule 2, peach must be selected whenever olive is selected. And if olive is *not* selected, peach must *still* be selected along with everything else. Therefore, peach is always selected, making **(C)** the correct answer. For the record:

Forest and turquoise can each be used on a two-colored rug, as seen in Option I. That eliminates **(A)** and **(B)**—and neither turquoise nor yellow must be selected, as seen in this possible outcome:

1	2	3
W	F	T/Y
O		
P		

That eliminates **(D)** and **(E)**.

13. (E) "If" / Must Be True

For this question, peach will be used in a solid (i.e., one-colored) rug. With peach used up, no other rug can use olive (Rule 2), so olive is not selected at all. That means all of the remaining colors (forest, turquoise, white, and yellow) are. White must be in a three-colored rug, so there will be one three-colored rug and two solid rugs. Forest and turquoise cannot be used together (Rule 3), so they will be split: one in the three-colored rug and one by itself. Yellow will be the final color of the three-colored rug.

1	2	3
W	P	T/F
F/T		
Y		

White and yellow are definitely used together, making **(E)** the correct answer. **(C)** must be false because yellow is part of the three-colored rug, and the remaining answers—**(A)**, **(B)**, **(D)**—are all possible, but need not be true.

14. (D) "If" / Must Be False (CANNOT Be True)

For this question, there will be two solid rugs. That means the third rug must be three-colored. Unfortunately, that's Option II, which is very open-ended. However, there are still ways to manage this question effectively without drawing each answer out.

For starters, consider what the question is asking for. The correct answer will be two colors that cannot both be used for solid rugs. The wrong answers will list colors that *could be* the two solid rugs.

From there, use previous work and duplicated entities to save time. Three of the answers list peach as a solid rug, which was the basis for the sketch in the previous question. In that sketch, the second solid rug could only be forest or turquoise, which eliminates **(A)** and **(C)**. The second solid rug could *not* be yellow. That makes **(D)** the correct answer. For the record:

Option IIb based on white shows that the two solid rugs could be turquoise and yellow. That eliminates **(E)**. Incidentally, the sketch for the next question also shows that it is possible. Option IIa based on olive shows that the two solid rugs could be forest and yellow. That makes **(B)** possible, which can also be seen even more clearly in the following sketch:

	1	2	3
	O	F	Y
	P		
	W		

15. (B) "If" / Could Be True

For this question, forest and peach will be used together. However, the question doesn't indicate whether they're used alone on a two-colored rug or combined with a third color. Consider both possibilities.

If they were used as a two-colored rug, the numbers dictate that there would have to be another two-colored rug and a solid rug. That would mean no three-colored rugs and thus no white (Rule 1). However, olive could no longer be placed with peach, so olive would also be left out (Rule 2). Leaving out white and olive would not leave enough colors. (Option I also shows quickly that this is not possible.)

So, forest and peach must be used as part of a three-colored rug. Because of peach, the third color could not be turquoise (Rule 4) or yellow (Rule 5). It must be either white or olive. The remaining two rugs will be solid, neither of which could be white (Rule 1) or olive (Rule 2). So, they must be the remaining two colors: turquoise and yellow.

	1	2	3
	F	T	Y
	P		
	W/O		

With that, it's possible that white is not used, making **(B)** the only possible answer.

16. (A) "If" / Could Be True EXCEPT

For this question, one rug will be solid yellow. However, this does not immediately help determine the status of the other two rugs. They could still be two two-colored rugs or one three-colored and a second solid rug. Consider both possibilities.

If the other two rugs were both two-colored, there would be no three-colored rugs and hence no white (Rule 1). That means every other color would be used. Olive would have to be in a rug with peach (Rule 2). But the final rug would be left with forest and turquoise, which would violate Rule 3. (This could also have been seen as impossible in Option I.)

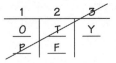

That means the other two rugs must be one three-colored rug and a second solid rug.

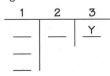

There is no way to determine for sure which colors will be used or which rugs will use them. However, the numbers indicate that there must be two solid rugs, which means **(A)** cannot be true, making that the correct answer. All of the remaining answers are possible. For the record: The sketch in the explanation of the second question of the set shows that **(B)**, **(C)**, and **(E)** are all possible. The sketch for the question before this one shows **(D)** is possible.

Game 4: Graduation Photographers

Step 1: Overview

Situation: Photographers being assigned to photograph graduation ceremonies

Entities: Six photographers (Frost, Gonzalez, Heideck, Knutson, Lai, Mays); two universities (Silva and Thorne)

Action: Selection/Distribution Hybrid. Determine which photographers are assigned (Selection), and then determine the university's ceremony to which each photographer is assigned (Distribution).

Limitations: No photographer is assigned to both ceremonies. At least two photographers are assigned to each ceremony, which means at least four of the six photographers are going to be selected.

Step 2: Sketch

List the photographers by initial and set up a table with a column (or row) for each university. Draw two spaces in each column to meet the minimum requirement, with space to add more if needed.

F G H K L M

Sil	Tho
—	—
—	—

Use the entity list for the selection part of the game, circling entities that must be selected and crossing off ones that cannot.

Step 3: Rules

Rule 1 states that Frost and Heideck are definitely selected, and that they will be assigned to the same ceremony. Circle F and H in the entity list, and draw the block off to the side.

$$\boxed{\begin{array}{c} F \\ H \end{array}}$$

Rule 2 restricts Lai and Mays from being assigned to the same ceremony. However, this does not mean that one must be assigned to Silva and the other to Thorne. One—or even both—of them may not be assigned at all. So do not draw anything into the Master Sketch. Instead, make a shorthand note to the side that L and M cannot be together.

Rule 3 is standard Formal Logic. If Gonzalez is assigned to Silva, then Lai is assigned to Thorne. Be sure to draw this out and its contrapositive (if Lai is *not* assigned to Thorne, Gonzalez *cannot* be assigned to Silva):

$$\frac{Sil}{G} \rightarrow \frac{Tho}{L}$$

$$\sim\frac{Tho}{L} \rightarrow \sim\frac{Sil}{G}$$

Be careful with this rule. This does not prevent Gonzalez and Lai from being assigned to the same ceremony. The rule does not specify what happens if Gonzalez is assigned to Thorne. In that case, it is possible for Lai to be assigned to Thorne, too.

Rule 4 is more Formal Logic, but one with an extremely helpful interpretation. The basic rule is pretty standard. If Knutson is not assigned to Thorne, then Heideck and Mays are. By contrapositive, if Heideck and Mays aren't both assigned to Thorne (i.e., at least one or the other is not), then Knutson must be.

$$\sim\frac{Tho}{K} \rightarrow \frac{Tho}{H} \text{ \& } \frac{Tho}{M}$$

$$\sim\frac{Tho}{H} \text{ OR } \sim\frac{Tho}{M} \rightarrow \frac{Tho}{K}$$

However, there's more to this rule than meets the eye. If translated properly, it allows for an exceptional chance to set up Limited Options.

Step 4: Deductions

The Formal Logic of Rule 4 is in a classic format: If one thing doesn't happen, then a second thing must. In this case, if Thorne doesn't get Knutson, it must get Heideck and Mays. In other words, at least one of those two scenarios must take place; Thorne must get either Knutson or the team of Heideck and Mays, at the very least. It's also possible that all three are assigned to Thorne!

However, the core of the rule allows for two options—one in which Thorne gets Heideck and Mays, and one in which Thorne gets Knutson.

In the first option, Heideck and Mays will be assigned to Thorne. Remember that Knutson could still be assigned there, but need not be. However, with Heideck assigned there, so must Frost (Rule 1). Furthermore, because Mays is assigned to Thorne, Lai cannot (Rule 2). With Lai not assigned to Thorne, Gonzalez cannot be assigned to Silva (Rule 3). That leaves only two people who can be assigned to Silva: Knutson and Lai. They must be assigned to Silva to meet the minimum requirement. The only person left is Gonzalez, who may be assigned to Thorne, but may also be left out.

I)
Sil	Tho
K	H
L	M
	F

~G

In the second option, Knutson is assigned to Thorne. However, there's nothing more to be deduced. Heideck and Mays are not restricted, and the block of Frost and Heideck could still be assigned to either ceremony.

II)

Sil	Tho
—	K
—	—

As is typical, one option is fairly complete while the second is still fairly open-ended. However, the block of Frost and Heideck (Rule 1) allows for the opportunity to break the second option into two more well-developed options. While not necessary, it can be useful. If attempted, here's how it would work:

In one scenario, Frost and Heideck would be assigned to Silva. That would fulfill Silva's minimum assignment. However, other photographers could still be assigned to Silva and there's no restriction as to who will be the second photographer at Thorne, and Thorne could still get more than two.

IIa)

Sil	Tho
F	K
H	—

In the other scenario, Frost and Heideck would be assigned to Thorne. That leaves three photographers (Gonzalez, Lai, and Mays), at least two of whom must be assigned to Silva. Lai and Mays cannot both be assigned to Silva (Rule 2), so Silva must get Gonzalez and one other. However, with Gonzalez assigned to Silva, Lai must be assigned to Thorne (Rule 3), leaving Mays to be the second and final photographer at Silva.

IIb)

Sil	Tho
G	K
M	F
	H
	L

Note that these last two options could not be set up by Rule 1 alone. They only come about in conjunction with Rule 4. Regardless, with only two "If" stems in the question set, success in this game depends on spending ample time with the setup and understanding the implication of the rules.

Step 5: Questions

17. (E) Acceptability

As with typical Acceptability questions, go through the rules one at a time, eliminating answers that violate those rules.

(B) violates Rule 1 because Frost and Heideck are not assigned to either ceremony. **(C)** violates Rule 2 because Lai and Mays are both assigned to Thorne. **(A)** violates Rule 3 because Gonzalez is assigned to Silva, but Lai is not assigned to Thorne. **(D)** violates Rule 4 because Knutson is not assigned to Thorne, but neither are Heidick and Mays. That leaves **(E)** as the correct answer.

18. (D) "If" / Must Be True

For this question, Heideck and Lai will be assigned to the same ceremony. That could be either ceremony, but Limited Options pays off tremendously here. Heideck and Lai are split up in Option I, so they could only be together in Option II. The only thing that's known for sure in Option II is that Knutson is assigned to Thorne, and that's what **(D)** says, making it the correct answer.

For further proof, if Heideck and Lai are together, then Mays cannot be with them (Rule 2). In that case, Heideck and Mays cannot be assigned to the same ceremony. Because of that, it's impossible for both Heideck and Mays to be assigned to Thorne. Therefore, by the contrapositive of Rule 4, Knutson must be assigned to Thorne.

For the record, the following acceptable outcome shows that all of the remaining answers could be false:

Sil	Tho
F	K
H	G
L	

19. (B) Partial Acceptability

Because the answers list only the assignments to Silva, this is a Partial Acceptability question. As with standard Acceptability questions, start by using the rules one at a time to eliminate any answers that violate those rules. If multiple answers remain, consider what's *not* listed, i.e., who would be assigned to Thorne in each case.

(D) violates Rule 1 by assigning Heideck without Frost. The remaining rules are harder to test without knowing who's assigned to Thorne. There are two ways to approach the rest here.

The first, and more effective, method is to use the Limited Options. The photographers assigned to Silva in Option I are Knutson and Lai, but that's not one of the answers. That means the correct answer must be possible in Option II. However, Knutson must be at Thorne in Option II, which means **(A)**, **(C)**, and **(E)** are impossible. That leaves **(B)** as the correct answer.

Without using Limited Options, you could start by testing Rule 4. **(A)**, **(C)**, and **(E)** list Knutson at Silva. By Rule 4, that means Heideck and Mays should be assigned to Thorne. However, **(A)** puts Heideck at Silva and **(E)** puts Mays at Silva. Those answers are unacceptable. That leaves **(B)** and **(C)**.

Both answers place Gonzalez at Silva. That brings up Rule 3, which means Lai is assigned to Thorne for those two answers. By Rule 2, that means Mays cannot be assigned to Thorne. So, by the contrapositive of Rule 4, Knutson must be assigned to Thorne.

$$
\begin{array}{c|c}
\text{Sil} & \text{Tho} \\
\hline
\underline{G} & \text{L} \\
& \text{K} \\
\underline{} & \sim\text{M}
\end{array}
$$

However, Knutson is assigned to Silva in **(C)**, so that's unacceptable. That means **(B)** must be the correct answer.

20. (B) Complete and Accurate List

The correct answer will list every photographer who must be assigned no matter what. The wrong answers will leave out someone who must be assigned or include a photographer that does not have to be assigned.

By Rule 1, Frost and Heideck must be assigned, but every answer includes them. From there, Limited Options is very useful. Knutson is assigned in both options, which means Knutson will always be assigned. So, the correct answer must include Knutson, which eliminates **(A)**, **(D)**, and **(E)**.

Without Limited Options, you would start by testing Knutson (who appears in multiple answers). If Knutson were not assigned, then Heideck and Mays would be assigned to Thorne (Rule 4), along with Frost (Rule 1). That would leave Gonzalez and Lai for Silva, but that would violate Rule 3. Therefore, it's impossible to leave out Knutson, which is why Knutson must be assigned and must be listed in the correct answer.

From there, Lai need not be included. This can be quickly tested by drawing a sketch based on Option IIa:

$$
\begin{array}{c|c}
\text{Sil} & \text{Tho} \\
\hline
\text{F} & \text{K} \\
\text{H} & \text{G}
\end{array}
$$

That eliminates **(C)**, leaving **(B)** as the correct answer.

21. (A) "If" / Must Be True

For this question, only four photographers will be assigned. That means exactly two photographers for each ceremony. With Limited Options, this can only happen in Option II, in which Knutson must be assigned to Thorne—specifically Option IIa because more than two photographers are assigned to Thorne in Option IIb.

That automatically makes **(A)** the correct answer.

$$
\begin{array}{c|c}
\text{Sil} & \text{Tho} \\
\hline
\text{F} & \text{K} \\
\text{H} & \underline{} \\
\hline
\end{array}
$$

Without Limited Options, consider which one of the ceremonies must get Frost and Heideck (Rule 1). It cannot be Thorne because that would leave Thorne without Knutson,

which would then force a third photographer, Mays, to be assigned to Thorne (Rule 4). So, Frost and Heideck must be assigned to Silva, confirming **(A)** as the correct answer.

22. (B) Partial Acceptability (CANNOT)

The correct answer will be an unacceptable assignment to Thorne. The four incorrect answers will all list acceptable assignments to Thorne.

None of the rules are directly violated by any of the answers. Therefore, it is necessary to consider who would be assigned to Silva for each answer.

If Frost, Gonzalez, Heideck, and Mays were assigned to Thorne, that would leave Knutson and Lai for Silva. That's perfectly acceptable, as seen in Option I. That eliminates **(A)**.

If Frost, Heideck, Knutson, and Mays were assigned to Thorne, that would leave Gonzalez and Lai for Silva. However, that violates Rule 3. That is unacceptable, making **(B)** the correct answer. For the record, Frost and Heideck could be assigned to Silva for all of the remaining answers without violating any rules. They would all be acceptable versions of Option IIa.

23. (C) Rule Substitution

The correct answer to this question will be a new rule that could replace Rule 4 without changing the game in any way. It must restore the restriction of Rule 4 (Knutson not assigned to Thorne means Heidick and Mays must be assigned to Thorne) without adding any new restrictions.

(A) and **(B)** present rules based on Knutson being assigned to Silva; however, the original rule was about what happened when Knutson was not at Thorne, which meant Knutson was either at Silva *or* unassigned, so neither of these give an equivalent trigger to the original rule. Furthermore, by the original rule, even if Knutson was at Silva, that would mean Heideck and Mays have to be assigned to Thorne, but neither of these rules restores that requirement. Both answers allow for Mays to simply be unassigned. That eliminates both answers.

When translated properly, **(C)** claims that Frost and Mays must be assigned to Thorne if Knutson is not:

$$
\sim\frac{\text{Tho}}{\text{K}} \rightarrow \frac{\text{Tho}}{\text{F}} \,\&\, \frac{\text{Tho}}{\text{M}}
$$

Frost has to be assigned with Heideck. So, this means if Knutson is not assigned to Thorne, Frost (and Heideck) and Mays will be assigned to Thorne, which is exactly what the original rule stated. The addition of Frost is not new because Frost's inclusion was always implied by Rule 1. This restores the original condition exactly, making **(C)** the correct answer. For the record:

According to **(D)**, if Knutson is not assigned to Thorne, Heideck and Lai must split. However, that does not necessarily assign Heideck (or Mays) to Thorne, as the original rule intended. That eliminates **(D)**.

When translated, **(E)** claims that Knutson must be assigned to Thorne unless Heideck *or* Mays is there. In other words, if Knutson is *not* assigned to Thorne, then Heideck *or* Mays must be. The original rule did not allow that choice. The original rule required Heideck *and* Mays to be assigned to Thorne. That eliminates **(E)**.

Section III: Reading Comprehension
Passage 1: Perfumes as Art

Q#	Question Type	Correct	Difficulty
1	Global	D	★★★
2	Inference	E	★★
3	Inference	A	★
4	Inference	A	★★
5	Inference	B	★
6	Logic Reasoning (Parallel Reasoning)	B	★★
7	Inference	B	★
8	Global	D	★

Passage 2: Stealing Thunder

Q#	Question Type	Correct	Difficulty
9	Global	C	★★★
10	Inference	B	★
11	Detail	D	★★
12	Logic Function	A	★
13	Inference	D	★★
14	Detail	E	★★
15	Inference	A	★★
16	Inference	D	★★★★

Passage 3: Free Will and Its Implications

Q#	Question Type	Correct	Difficulty
17	Global	B	★
18	Detail	A	★★
19	Logic Function	B	★
20	Inference	C	★★★
21	Logic Reasoning (Parallel Reasoning)	C	★★★

Passage 4: Mario Garcia and the Mexican American Generation

Q#	Question Type	Correct	Difficulty
22	Detail	E	★
23	Inference	A	★★
24	Inference	B	★★★★
25	Inference	B	★★★★
26	Detail	D	★★★★
27	Inference	E	★★★

Passage 1: Perfumes as Art

Step 1: Read the Passage Strategically
Sample Roadmap

line #	Keyword/phrase	¶ Margin notes
4	seems odd; so few	Auth: great perfume not taken seriously
6	:	
7	?	
8	While; very serious	
10	yet	Example
13	And yet; ought	
14	undeniable	painting similar to perfume making
23	Thus	Old Masters paint process
29	So, too	perfumers combine scents
37	brilliant	
38	thus; no less	
39	than	perfumers are artists
44	Perhaps one reason	why perfumes undervalued
44–45	so often undervalued	
46	not particularly watchful	
47	cynical	
48	tamper	
49	cheap	corp. substitute formulas
53	indeed	
54	Consequently	perfume not given its due
55	hopelessly entangled	
56	ill-served	

Discussion

This Humanities passage begins with something the author finds *odd*. Art appreciators spend so much time dissecting and analyzing paintings, but not perfumes. Then, in line 7, the author poses the question directly: Why aren't great perfumes taken more seriously as artworks? LSAT passages rarely, if ever, pose a question without providing at least one potential answer, so you can expect that to come in subsequent paragraphs. Nevertheless, because the question was asked so clearly in paragraph 1, you now have the **Topic** (perfumes) and the **Scope** (their value, or perceived lack thereof, as works of art).

Paragraph 2 starts to lay out the *undeniable* parallels between painting and perfume-making. The specific details of how the Old Masters layered oil paint over fabric aren't as important yet. Just note that the author is using paragraph 2 to describe how painters carefully layer oil paint to create a picture.

Paragraph 3 draws a straight line from the work of the Old Masters to the work of the finest perfumers, who also combine elements to create an aesthetic experience for the senses. The Keyword *thus* in line 38 signals the crux of the author's argument here: Perfumers' work is just as rich and artistically satisfying as that of composers or painters.

Notice that the original question from paragraph 1 still hasn't been answered, so the author does that in paragraph 4. *Perhaps* great perfumes are undervalued because their modern purveyors are large corporations who care more about turning big profits than preserving the integrity of their perfumes' ingredients. These companies alter the formulas for their scents without even telling their customers. As a result, fine perfume is not touted as art, and art lovers, therefore, don't appreciate it as such.

The author's **Purpose** here is to argue for the status of fine perfume as art and to explain why it isn't afforded such status. The **Main Idea** is that a great perfume is just as artistically valuable as any painting or piece of music.

1. (D) Global

Step 2: Identify the Question Type
This is a Global question because it asks for the "main point of the passage."

Step 3: Research the Relevant Text
The entire text is relevant here, so instead of researching a specific part, use your understanding of the big picture from Step 1 to help you form your prediction.

Step 4: Make a Prediction
The author's main point is that like literature, painting, or any of the other great arts, perfume-making is an art form worthy of respect.

Step 5: Evaluate the Answer Choices
(D) is therefore correct.

(A) is a 180 and too narrow. The author says in paragraph 4 that the large corporations in charge of manufacturing perfume value profit over artistic merit.

(B) is a point the author makes in paragraph 3, but that point is in support of a larger idea about the artistic value of perfumes.

(C) is something the author doesn't even mention until paragraph 4, and even then it's only mentioned to explain why perfumes are often undervalued.

(E) distorts the author's intent in making the analogy between oil painting and perfume-making. The author only mentions oil painting as a comparison point to perfume-making; the main idea of the passage isn't about painting.

2. (E) Inference

Step 2: Identify the Question Type
This is an Inference question because it asks you to determine what the author "would … be most likely to believe."

Step 3: Research the Relevant Text
The author discusses the process of perfume-making in paragraph 3 and mentions formulas in paragraph 4.

Step 4: Make a Prediction
The author has a strong point of view on the artistic integrity of perfume-making. Paragraph 4 criticizes big corporations for *tampering* with old formulas to cut corners, so the author would feel a perfumer was justified in changing a formula only if doing so helped to preserve the integrity of the original perfumer's work.

Step 5: Evaluate the Answer Choices
(E) is therefore correct.

(A) is a Distortion. *Joy Parfum* is just one example of a great perfume cited in the passage; the author doesn't believe that *every* perfume should aspire to mimic that perfume's formula.

(B) is a 180. This is exactly what the author criticizes big corporations for doing.

(C) is unsupported because the author seems to have no issue with perfumers combining synthetic and natural compounds (lines 14–18). No preference is indicated for one over the other.

(D) is incorrect because the author doesn't prize consumer appeal when it comes to making perfume. A perfume's artistic worth is what matters here.

3. (A) Inference

Step 2: Identify the Question Type
Any question asking you to define a term as the author uses it in context is an Inference question.

Step 3: Research the Relevant Text
Line 29 is relevant, of course, but you must also read the surrounding lines to understand how the term "noses" fits into the author's overall argument.

Step 4: Make a Prediction
In lines 29–33, the author says that "noses" with talent experiment with combinations of scents to create perfumes. Therefore, the term "noses" must refer to the creators of the perfumes.

Step 5: Evaluate the Answer Choices
(A) is therefore correct. The author even uses the word *perfumer* in line 37.

(B) is incorrect because perfume collectors are only alluded to in paragraph 1, and they aren't the ones making the perfumes.

(C) doesn't make sense because the "noses" the author refers to are the artists creating the perfumes, not the perfumes themselves.

(D) isn't touched on until paragraph 4, and has nothing to do with the process of perfume-making discussed in paragraph 3.

(E) isn't mentioned in the passage at all.

4. (A) Inference

Step 2: Identify the Question Type
This is an Inference question because it asks for the statement for which "the passage provides the most support."

Step 3: Research the Relevant Text
The author discusses works of art throughout the first three paragraphs.

Step 4: Make a Prediction
Because the author makes many statements about art, it may be too time-consuming to predict every valid inference that can be made from those statements. As you evaluate the answer choices, however, remember that the correct answer *must* be true and has explicit support in the passage.

Step 5: Evaluate the Answer Choices
(A) is directly supported by lines 37–43, where the author says that perfumers can appeal to our memories to create an artistically satisfying experience.

(B) is Extreme. While the author does say that great perfumes combine small sensations harmoniously (lines 29–33), this combination doesn't have to be detectable in *all* works of art.

(C) is also Extreme. The author isn't pleased with the big corporations for skimping on quality to save money manufacturing perfumes, but that's a far cry from saying that any artwork created with commerce in mind *inevitably* fails.

(D) is unsupported. The author does cite the Old Masters as examples of great artists, but it doesn't have to be true that the best artworks get better as they get older.

(E) goes against the author's argument that perfume-making is an art form equally as valid as literature or the visual arts.

5. (B) Inference

Step 2: Identify the Question Type
This is an Inference question because it asks you to determine the author's *likely* opinion about something discussed in the passage.

Step 3: Research the Relevant Text
Joy Parfum is mentioned at the end of paragraph 1.

Step 4: Make a Prediction
In paragraph 1, the author says that serious artistic types rarely seek out great perfumes like *Joy Parfum*, although these curators don't hesitate to extol the virtues of great works of literature, music, and architecture. In the author's mind, *Joy Parfum* is on par with any of those other great artworks.

Step 5: Evaluate the Answer Choices
(B) accurately captures the author's positive attitude toward *Joy Parfum*.

(A) is a 180. The author says that art appreciators aren't interested in *Joy Parfum* (lines 9–12).

(C) is unsupported. The author cites *Joy Parfum* as an example of a great perfume, not necessarily as an unparalleled achievement in perfume-making.

(D) is a Distortion. The author's tone throughout the passage suggests that great perfumes (of which *Joy Parfum* is one) can be appreciated by anyone with a sense of smell.

(E) is Out of Scope. The author never discusses other perfumes from the same time period.

6. (B) Logic Reasoning (Parallel Reasoning)

Step 2: Identify the Question Type
The phrase "most analogous to" signals a Parallel Reasoning question. Find the answer choice most similar to the "bean counters" from line 47.

Step 3: Research the Relevant Text
Lines 47–51 discuss the "cynical bean counters" cited in the question stem.

Step 4: Make a Prediction
In lines 47–51, the author takes corporate perfume manufacturers to task for sacrificing the artistic quality of

great perfume formulas to save a buck. Therefore, the correct answer will involve a similar kind of penny-pinching.

Step 5: Evaluate the Answer Choices

(B) is a perfect match.

(A) is a Distortion. The author isn't criticizing perfume manufacturers for appealing to popular tastes; the quality of the perfumes' ingredients is at issue here.

(C) comes close, but ultimately isn't parallel because the corporations mentioned in paragraph 4 aren't said to be facing financial difficulties.

(D) introduces tax benefits, an idea not discussed with respect to the corporate perfumers.

(E) would be parallel if the companies in Paris and Zurich pinched pennies on certain great perfumes to fund the manufacture of other perfumes, but the author says nothing of the sort.

7. (B) Inference

Step 2: Identify the Question Type

Any question stem asking for a statement that a certain part of the passage "most strongly supports" is an Inference question.

Step 3: Research the Relevant Text

As the question stem indicates, the last paragraph is relevant here.

Step 4: Make a Prediction

The author's main point in paragraph 4 is that large corporations in charge of perfume formulas substitute cheap ingredients for better ones, and the result is a decline in quality that it's assumed will go unnoticed by the consumer. The correct answer will be consistent with this idea.

Step 5: Evaluate the Answer Choices

(B) can be inferred from lines 47–51. If companies are trying to maximize profits by using cheaper ingredients, then an extremely profitable perfume isn't necessarily of highest quality.

(A) is unsupported. The author hints at the idea that customers don't know their perfumes' formulas are being tampered with, but nothing in the passage suggests that customers don't even know the names of the best perfumes.

(C) is a Distortion. Perfume companies do alter formulas without telling their customers, but that doesn't mean these perfumers neglect to pay attention to their customers' desires.

(D) is Extreme and a Distortion. Just because the author cites a current tendency to tamper with formulas doesn't mean that such tampering *never* occurred in the past.

(E) is Out of Scope. The author never mentions which perfumes generate the most profits for their sellers.

8. (D) Global

Step 2: Identify the Question Type

This is a Global question because it asks you to determine the "organization of the passage."

Step 3: Research the Relevant Text

Your biggest help here is your Roadmap, in which you laid out the structure of the passage as a whole.

Step 4: Make a Prediction

In paragraph 1, the author asks a question: Why aren't perfumes valued as much as other artworks? Then the author makes the case for why perfumes are artworks by comparing them primarily to paintings. Finally, the author gives a possible reason for why perfumes are undervalued, answering the question posed in paragraph 1.

Step 5: Evaluate the Answer Choices

(D) is the only answer choice that matches every element of the passage.

(A) is incorrect because the author provides only one explanation for why perfumes aren't as highly valued as other artworks—there's no "one possible explanation" and an "alternative explanation."

(B) is incorrect because the author doesn't present a thesis in paragraph 1, and the passage never anticipates and then rejects a potential counter to the author's main argument.

(C) goes wrong on three counts. The author doesn't challenge any received wisdom in paragraph 1. The middle paragraphs make an analogy that helps support the author's contention about perfumes; these paragraphs don't respond to any challenge. And finally, concrete examples aren't given in paragraph 4; a general explanation is given.

(E) is incorrect because even if you characterize paragraph 1 as the presentation of a problem (perfumes not being aesthetically valued as much as they should be), the middle paragraphs can't be characterized as "consequences" of that problem.

Passage 2: Stealing Thunder

Step 1: Read the Passage Strategically
Sample Roadmap

line #	Keyword/phrase	¶ Margin notes
4	While; no point	"stealing thunder" defined
7	believe	lawyers reveal bad info before opposition reveals
8	should	
9	otherwise; hostile	
10	more damaging	
11	Although	
14	in fact, effective	simulated trials show ST effective
17	not only	
18	also supported	psych research supports too
20	For one thing (1)	credibility
25	thus	
26	may also (2)	previewing makes juries more critical of opposition
27	thus	
33	Also (3)	decrease scarcity; makes bad info old news
36	thus	
41	Thus	
44	Finally (4); because	lets lawyer spin if able
48	However; therefore	
49	effective only	
52	therefore	
54	But	
55	limitations; :	
56	very damaging	warning: ST could backfire (bad impression)
57	negative impression	

Discussion

The first sentence of this Law passage introduces the **Topic** (stealing thunder) and defines it in a legal setting. The idea behind stealing thunder is that a lawyer reveals potentially negative information about his or her client before opposing counsel has the chance to reveal it. In other words, one lawyer beats another to the punch, and "many lawyers believe" (line 7) that it's generally a helpful strategy. So the **Scope** of the passage appears to be whether or not stealing thunder is an effective litigating technique.

Paragraph 2 introduces simulated research that corroborates the belief of these lawyers. Both trial simulations and psychological findings suggest that stealing thunder can be effective. Lines 21–43 detail the psychological explanations for its effectiveness—it creates a sense of credibility and, therefore, of persuasiveness; it gives juries the chance to develop resistance to opposing counsel's arguments; and it reduces the value of the damaging information by making it "old news." You don't need to memorize all these reasons; just mark them in your Roadmap for easy reference.

The word [ʃ]*inally* at the beginning of paragraph 3 signals yet another factor contributing to the value of stealing thunder: It gives lawyers the chance to "spin" the damaging testimony. Nevertheless, in line 48 ([*h*]*owever*), the author issues a caveat. This "spin" only works if there's a reasonably positive interpretation of the negative information, one that jurors can latch onto as they solidify their view of the case. If the information is too negative, stealing thunder can backfire, creating a bad early impression in jurors' minds. The **Purpose** of the passage is to present evidence suggesting that stealing thunder is effective. The **Main Idea**, therefore, is that the value of stealing thunder has been corroborated by experimental evidence and psychological findings.

9. (C) Global

Step 2: Identify the Question Type
Any question stem asking you to identify the "main point of the passage" is a Global question.

Step 3: Research the Relevant Text
The entire passage is relevant to a Global question. Instead of rereading specific parts, use the Main Idea you predicted during Step 1 to form your answer.

Step 4: Make a Prediction
The Main Idea of the passage is that experimental and psychological evidence supports lawyers' belief in the usefulness of stealing thunder.

Step 5: Evaluate the Answer Choices
(C) is therefore correct.

(A) is a 180. The author says in the beginning of paragraph 2 that no evidence supporting stealing thunder has been gathered from actual trials.

(B) is too negative, leaving out all of the evidence in support of the effectiveness of stealing thunder.

(D) is also too negative. It echoes the limitations discussed in the last few lines of the passage, but it doesn't say anything about the psychological evidence in favor of stealing thunder as a general strategy.

(E) is a Distortion. The author doesn't say that the research mentioned was designed to confirm the usefulness of stealing thunder. Furthermore, the author, not the researchers, identified a potential limitation to the strategy's effectiveness in paragraph 3.

10. (B) Inference

Step 2: Identify the Question Type
This is an Inference question because it asks you to determine what "can be most reasonably inferred" from the text.

Step 3: Research the Relevant Text
To infer the correct example of stealing thunder, it would help to go back to paragraph 1, where the author defines the strategy.

Step 4: Make a Prediction
In lines 1–4, the author says that stealing thunder is the practice of lawyers revealing potentially damaging information about their client when they sense that opposing counsel intends to reveal it too. The correct answer will be an example of such a revelation.

Step 5: Evaluate the Answer Choices
(B) fits the definition of stealing thunder perfectly. The client's past plagiarism certainly has bearing on the copyright infringement case, so the defense lawyer would be stealing thunder by revealing it first.

(A) isn't stealing thunder because it's not something a lawyer is revealing about his or her own client.

(C) isn't stealing thunder because the opposition has already revealed the damaging information.

(D) isn't stealing thunder because it's not a revelation of negative information about one's own client.

(E) goes too far. Stealing thunder isn't about admitting a client's guilt; that would essentially concede the whole case. Rather, the strategy of stealing thunder seeks to simply downplay potentially damaging testimony by revealing it first.

11. (D) Detail

Step 2: Identify the Question Type
This is a Detail question because it asks about something the author has mentioned explicitly in the passage.

Step 3: Research the Relevant Text
Factors contributing to the success of stealing thunder are discussed throughout paragraph 2 and the first several lines of paragraph 3.

Step 4: Make a Prediction
There are multiple psychological factors that make stealing thunder a useful strategy. Check your Roadmap against the answer choices for a match.

Step 5: Evaluate the Answer Choices
(D) is mentioned in lines 50–52.

(A) is Out of Scope. The author doesn't mention anything about an ideal amount of time that should elapse between a lawyer's thunder-stealing and the opposition's presentation of the same information.

(B) is also Out of Scope. The author doesn't discuss the skill level needed to assess jurors' reactions to thunder-stealing.

(C) is another Out of Scope answer. Stealing thunder is described as a technique in which lawyers present information; direct testimony from clients isn't cited as a factor in the success of the technique.

(E) is one final Out of Scope answer. The impact of screening jurors isn't discussed as a factor in regard to the effectiveness of stealing thunder.

12. (A) Logic Function

Step 2: Identify the Question Type
The phrase "author discusses ... primarily to" indicates a Logic Function. Determine why the author mentions jurors' cognitive framework.

Step 3: Research the Relevant Text
Lines 56–59 are relevant, as well as your Roadmap for paragraph 3.

Step 4: Make a Prediction
In the last few lines of the passage, the author discusses a potential limitation of the technique of stealing thunder. Priming jurors with negative information about a client can create a bad impression that forms a "cognitive framework." In other words, the author suggests that negative information could create a pattern of thinking in the jury that influences how they interpret later information.

Step 5: Evaluate the Answer Choices
(A) is therefore correct.

(B) is a 180. The cognitive framework discussed in line 58 is said to be created by the lawyers stealing thunder, not by any preconceptions jurors walked in with.

(C) is a Distortion. The discussion of a cognitive framework indicates that jurors will construe information through a lens they develop early in the trial. However, that is not to say that damaging evidence that is spun early in a trial will definitively be more impactful than damaging evidence presented later. That depends on how damaging the initial information was, and whether or not the jurors formed an early negative impression. Also, it depends on how and who presents the damaging evidence later. Without more information, the author wouldn't say for certain which would have a greater impact.

(D) is a Distortion. The author says in paragraph 3 that jurors have a tendency to solidify their opinions on a case, but the author doesn't argue that stealing thunder is most effective "as early as possible" in a trial.

(E) mashes together the discussion of very harmful information in paragraph 3 with the idea of creating credibility from paragraph 2. However, the "cognitive framework" that the author describes has more to do with conditioning a jury to interpret later information in a certain light than with how credible they find testimony.

13. (D) Inference

Step 2: Identify the Question Type
Any question stem that asks about the "author's attitude" toward something discussed in the passage is an Inference question.

Step 3: Research the Relevant Text
Stealing thunder is the Topic of the entire passage, so the entire text is relevant. Use the author's Main Idea and general point of view to form your prediction.

Step 4: Make a Prediction
The author's attitude toward stealing thunder is generally positive, mainly because its usefulness is supported by a lot of experimental and psychological research. Look for positive language in the answer choices and eliminate any that are too negative.

Step 5: Evaluate the Answer Choices
(D) captures the author's positive attitude.

(A) is Out of Scope and too negative. The frequency with which stealing thunder is employed as a strategy has no bearing on the author's argument, and generally the author's attitude is more positive than *concerned*.

(B) makes a distinction the author never makes. The passage never expressed skepticism about the value of stealing thunder outside the opening statements of a trial.

(C) is too negative. The author never shares any concern regarding the research results discussed in paragraph 2.

(E) again uses the word *skeptical*, but the author expresses no doubts about the usefulness of stealing thunder when it's done by less experienced lawyers.

14. (E) Detail

Step 2: Identify the Question Type
This is a Detail question because it focuses on the evidence marshaled by the author in his characterization of stealing thunder.

Step 3: Research the Relevant Text
The author's basis for characterizing stealing thunder as an effective technique is provided in paragraph 2.

Step 4: Make a Prediction
In lines 13–20, the author gives the sources of the evidence in favor of stealing thunder. The two sources are trial simulations and psychological research.

Step 5: Evaluate the Answer Choices
(E) is therefore correct. "Research not directly concerned with legal proceedings" is another way of describing the psychological research in paragraph 2.

(A) is Half-Right/Half-Wrong. The author never cites client surveys to argue that stealing thunder can be effective.

(B) is a 180. Statistical evidence is never brought in, and the author says explicitly at the beginning of paragraph 2 that no actual trials have been studied.

(C) is Half-Right/Half-Wrong. The author never mentions evidence of judges' decisions in court cases. In fact, the technique of stealing thunder is discussed mainly in relation to the decision of juries.

(D) also mentions studies of lawyers' behavior in courtrooms, but the author says that such studies have yet to occur in the real world. Furthermore, the observations detailed in paragraph 2 can hardly be said to be informal.

15. (A) Inference

Step 2: Identify the Question Type
This is an Inference question because it asks what the author "most likely means" when using a particular phrase.

Step 3: Research the Relevant Text
Line 14 is relevant, but context is key in determining what an author means by using a given phrase.

Step 4: Make a Prediction
According to paragraph 1, the whole reason to steal thunder in the first place is to reduce the damage done by potentially negative information about one's client. Therefore, for the technique to be *effective*, it needs to make the negative information seem less negative in a jury's eyes than it would if the opposition had revealed it first.

Step 5: Evaluate the Answer Choices
(A) is therefore correct.

(B) is a Distortion. Stealing thunder is said to provide jurors with the chance to develop their own counterarguments to the opposition's attempt at persuasion, but those counterarguments aren't necessarily provided to the jury by attorneys.

(C) is Extreme. That stealing thunder is effective doesn't mean that it *always* results in cases being decided in favor of the clients whose lawyers use the technique.

(D) is Out of Scope. The author never suggests that the goal of stealing thunder is to better hold the jury's attention.

(E) is Out of Scope. The author doesn't mention whether the timing of thunder-stealing is dramatic or not as a factor contributing to its effectiveness.

16. (D) Inference

Step 2: Identify the Question Type
This is an Inference question because it asks about what the passage "most strongly implies."

Step 3: Research the Relevant Text
Lawyers' beliefs about stealing thunder are mentioned mainly in paragraph 1.

Step 4: Make a Prediction
In lines 7–10, the author says that if a lawyer believes that the opposition will present certain damaging information, it may be best to steal thunder. Otherwise, there's no reason to present the negative testimony. The correct answer will be consistent with this belief.

Step 5: Evaluate the Answer Choices
(D) is therefore a valid inference.

(A) brings in an idea from the end of the passage, where the author says a lawyer may need to weigh how negative the information is and how easily it can be *spun*. However, this isn't presented as something that "many lawyers" believe.

(B) doesn't have to do with lawyers' beliefs and goes against lines 50–51, which say that jurors often have little information about a case in the beginning.

(C) is Out of Scope. The author doesn't say that many lawyers believe such careful deliberations need to take place. The decision to steal thunder is mainly predicated on whether the opposition will try to reveal the information too. Although the author does say that jurors may respond in differing ways, opposing lawyers' reactions to the information are irrelevant.

(E) is a Distortion. Much of the passage presents psychological findings that support the usefulness of stealing thunder, but that doesn't mean lawyers need to know these findings to decide whether to steal thunder.

Passage 3: Free Will and Its Implications

Step 1: Read the Passage Strategically
Sample Roadmap

line #	Keyword/phrase	¶ Margin notes
Passage A		
4	radically	Nuero view on behavior
5–6	all that matters	Application to law
6	but	
7	even though	
9	Indeed	
11	deluding	
15	insight suggests	implications for criminal justice
16	should abandon	
18	dominant	
19	Instead	
19–20	should focus	Auth: deter, don't punish
21	If	
23	then	
Passage B		
29–30	long been argued	Neuro findings support determinism
30	however	free will AND determinism
33	argued	Ayer: soft determinism
35	even	
36	distinguished	Free vs constrained actions
40–41	for example	
49	argued	Ayer: if not constrained --> free
50	not	
51	but	
52	Although	
53	one could	
56	therefore; even though	Free acts can be determined

Discussion

Passage A, a Natural Sciences passage, takes a basic tenet of neuroscience—that behavior arises only from the operations of the brain—and applies it to the law. The law assumes that rationality can be determined definitively, but according to passage A, a person can believe that he or she is behaving rationally despite a brain scan revealing activity only in emotional, nonrational centers of the brain.

Therefore, says passage A, we should reexamine a criminal justice system that is based mainly on punishment and retribution for crimes. A nonrational person won't be rehabilitated through punishment or deterred by the threat thereof. The **Topic** of the passage is human behavior, and its **Scope** is the implications of recent discoveries about human behavior on the law. The **Purpose** is to argue for a modification to criminal justice policy based on neurological findings. Passage A's **Main Idea** is that in light of what certain research suggests about free will and rational choice, the criminal justice system should move away from a strict focus on punishment.

Passage B starts by pointing out that neurological findings bolster the arguments of those who believe in determinism and not in free will. But, says passage B, free will and determinism are not mutually exclusive for everyone. You can expect this author to go into more detail on this idea, and in the next paragraph the author cites Alfred J. Ayer, who, in his theory of "soft determinism," made a distinction between free actions and constrained actions.

Passage B ends by discussing Ayer's view that any action that is not constrained is free, even if that free action has a cause. The author extends this by pointing out that a disease-free brain may therefore generate unconstrained (i.e., free) actions that are nonetheless in some way determined. The **Topic** of passage B is also human behavior, but here, the **Scope** is whether free will and determinism can coexist. The **Purpose** is to discuss Ayer's theory of soft determinism, and the **Main Idea** is that some philosophers, such as Ayer, have posited that freely performed actions can still have a deterministic element.

Before going to the questions, always note similarities and differences between Comparative Reading passages—you're guaranteed to see questions about them. In this case, both passages deal with neurological research and its implications for behavior. While passage A uses those implications to argue for a specific change to public policy, passage B simply explores one philosopher's theory on the extent to which determinism governs behavior.

17. (B) Global

Step 2: Identify the Question Type
This is a Global question because it asks for what both passages are concerned with.

Step 3: Research the Relevant Text
Instead of locating the answer in a specific set of lines, use your work from Step 1 to predict where the passages overlap.

Step 4: Make a Prediction
Both passages examine how much the question of free will versus determinism is affected by neurological research.

Step 5: Evaluate the Answer Choices
(B) is therefore correct.

(A) is only examined in passage A (lines 15–18).

(C) is also only examined in passage A (lines 19–24).

(D) is also only examined in passage A (lines 9–19).

(E) is only examined in passage B (lines 39–48).

18. (A) Detail

Step 2: Identify the Question Type
This is a Detail question because it requires you to scan the passages for an element of passage B that does not appear in passage A.

Step 3: Research the Relevant Text
The question stem is worded generally here, so any part of the passages is fair game.

Step 4: Make a Prediction
Don't make a list of concepts in passage B and then cross off the ones that appear in passage A—it would be too time-consuming. Instead, just check the answer choices against passage A. Anything that is mentioned in A is an incorrect answer. Likewise, anything not mentioned in B is an incorrect answer.

Step 5: Evaluate the Answer Choices
(A) is discussed in passage B's exploration of Ayer's theory (lines 39–43), but appears nowhere in passage A.

(B) is mentioned in passage A (line 10).

(C) is mentioned in passage A (lines 1–3).

(D) is mentioned in passage A (lines 9–11).

(E) isn't discussed in either passage. The word "immoral" does appear, but only in passage A (line 18).

19. (B) Logic Function

Step 2: Identify the Question Type
Any question that asks for the *purpose* of a given line, quote, or other reference is a Logic Function question.

Step 3: Research the Relevant Text

David Hume is mentioned in line 34, but you'll also need to read the surrounding lines to determine how the reference is used in context.

Step 4: Make a Prediction

David Hume is mentioned as someone who had argued the ideas behind soft determinism two hundred years before Alfred J. Ayer did. So, the reference is intended to legitimize Ayer's theory by citing an older philosopher who had the same ideas.

Step 5: Evaluate the Answer Choices

(B) is therefore correct.

(A) is too negative. Passage B is exploring Ayer's ideas in a neutral fashion, so there's no need to criticize him.

(C) is incorrect because passage B ties Ayer's ideas to contemporary brain research in the last paragraph.

(D) is an Irrelevant Comparison of two things in passage B: David Hume and mechanistic descriptions of the brain. Nothing in passage B indicates that these mechanistic descriptions are as old as Hume's ideas. In fact, passage B calls these descriptions constantly "new" (line 1).

(E) is Half-Right/Half-Wrong. It does "add intellectual respectability," but not to the notion that the brain "should *not* be described mechanistically." Hume and Ayer argue that "even in a deterministic world, a person can still act freely" (lines 35–36). So, they believe that free will *can* coexist with the mechanistic descriptions determined by neuroscientists.

20. (C) Inference

Step 2: Identify the Question Type

Any question asking about the authors' attitudes toward something in the passages is an Inference question.

Step 3: Research the Relevant Text

There isn't a specific place to research the answer. Instead, look for places in each passage where the author is making arguments or expressing opinions.

Step 4: Make a Prediction

Passage A has a clear stake in the ideas it discusses—lines 19–24 advocate for a change to criminal justice policy. However, passage B makes no such arguments. In fact, there's no indication whatsoever of the author's opinion on soft determinism. Passage B is much more neutral than passage A.

Step 5: Evaluate the Answer Choices

(C) is a good match for neutral.

(A) is a 180. Passage A is more engaged with its ideas than is passage B.

(B) is not neutral enough to characterize passage B, which doesn't say anything dismissive about Ayer's ideas.

(D) is incorrect because passage B doesn't display any irony, or expression of meaning through language that normally signifies the opposite. Passage B's discussion of determinism is much more direct.

(E) would be correct if passage B called Ayer's ideas "doubtful" or "hard to believe," but no such characterization exists.

21. (C) Logic Reasoning (Parallel Reasoning)

Step 2: Identify the Question Type

This is a Parallel Reasoning question because, just as in the Logical Reasoning section, this question asks you to find an argument "most analogous to" a given argument in the passages.

Step 3: Research the Relevant Text

Go back to passage A and review its argument. Then rephrase that argument in general terms to find a match in the answer choices.

Step 4: Make a Prediction

Passage A argues for a more lenient, less punitive social policy on the grounds that those we purport to punish don't always have the capacity we believe they do. The correct answer will advocate for a similar policy on similar grounds.

Step 5: Evaluate the Answer Choices

(C) is a parallel argument because passage A argues that the existing criminal justice policy is based on mistaken notions of how much rational control people have over their behavior.

(A) might be parallel if it said that word processor use or design is based on faulty reasoning and that word processors should, therefore, be used differently. Nevertheless, no such recommendation is made.

(B) may have been tempting because it uses the terms *rational* and *irrational*, but it misses the mark in its conclusion. **(B)** merely says the models are wrong, whereas passage A moves one step further and makes a practical recommendation.

(D), in addition to being somewhat circular in its reasoning, doesn't recommend a specific course of action the way that passage A does.

(E) doesn't advocate for a change in policy the way that passage A and correct answer choice **(C)** do.

Passage 4: Mario Garcia and the Mexican American Generation

Step 1: Read the Passage Strategically
Sample Roadmap

line #	Keyword/phrase	¶ Margin notes
1	argues	Garcia's arg
4	more	
5	than; recognized	
7	persuasive	Auth: Garcia persuasive
11	however; suffers; two flaws	Auth: study flawed
12	First	Flaw #1
14–15	not entirely consistent	
15	Indeed; undermines	
17	tends to conceal	Garcia hides differences among groups
23	diametrically opposed	Ex. two opposing groups
27	but dismisses	Garcia: differences not significant
28	insignificant	
30	But; one need only note	
30–31	fierce controversies	
33	to recognize	Auth: difference significant
35	not by; but by	
37	Second; may be exaggerating	Flaw #2 Garcia overstates representativeness of views
43	argues	
46	hence	Garcia: new generation more politically active
49	according to	
51	However; not clear	
52	Without	Auth: unclear if population shared views
57	one cannot assume	

Discussion

A quick scan of this Social Sciences passage reveals an easily digestible structure, with many helpful Keywords at the beginnings and ends of each paragraph. The passage also follows a common LSAT pattern: It begins by introducing a scholar's argument and then evaluates it. The more Reading Comprehension you do in practice, the better you'll become at anticipating this pattern and knocking out passages like this early in your 35 minutes.

Paragraph 1 gives Garcia's argument—the so-called Mexican American Generation was more radical and diverse than scholars had previously thought. And in lines 7–10, the author gives him some credit for making a persuasive case. But the contrast Keyword *however* in line 11 tells you that the author has some critiques in store—two, to be exact. The **Topic** is therefore Garcia's study, and the **Scope** appears to be its strengths and weaknesses, with a heavy lean toward the weaknesses.

Paragraph 2 outlines the author's first gripe with Garcia's study. Garcia undermines his argument about the Mexican American Generation's political diversity by downplaying the very real differences among various groups. The details about the League of United Latin American Citizens and the Congress of Spanish-Speaking People are examples that should be marked for reference later—extended examples tend to show up in questions. The Keyword *but* in line 30 signals the author's objection to Garcia's characterization of these differences as insignificant.

Paragraph 3 gives the author's second critique of Garcia's study. The passage alleges that Garcia extended the views of activists to cover the ethnic Mexican population as a whole. Garcia cites the increased political activity of the Mexican American Generation as proof of an increase in the activism of the whole ethnic population. *However*, says the author in line 51, Garcia doesn't take into account the variables that could have rendered the Mexican American Generation politically unrepresentative.

The author's overall **Purpose** is to critically evaluate Garcia's study. The **Main Idea**, therefore, is that despite some persuasive evidence, Garcia's study suffers from inconsistent historical analysis and a failure to demonstrate the representativeness of the political views he analyzes.

22. (E) Detail

Step 2: Identify the Question Type
This is a Detail question because it begins with the telltale phrase "according to the passage."

Step 3: Research the Relevant Text
The two advocacy groups mentioned in the question stem are discussed in lines 18–26.

Step 4: Make a Prediction
According to lines 18–26, the League of United Latin American Citizens differed from the Congress of Spanish-Speaking People in that the League was more assimilationist; that is, its goal was to encourage Mexican Americans to join mainstream U.S. culture. The Congress sought to retain native culture and language.

Step 5: Evaluate the Answer Choices
(E) is therefore correct.

(A) is Out of Scope. The passage doesn't say how broadly popular the League's goals were with other U.S. citizens.

(B) is a 180. It was the Congress of Spanish-Speaking People that sought equal rights for resident aliens (lines 24–26).

(C) is not really a difference between the two groups because line 29 says that the goals of these groups "centered on liberal reform."

(D) would, if anything, be a goal of the Congress of Spanish-Speaking People, a group that "advocated bilingual education" (line 25).

23. (A) Inference

Step 2: Identify the Question Type
Two phrases identify this as an Inference question: "it can be inferred" and "... would most probably agree."

Step 3: Research the Relevant Text
This question asks about Garcia's ideas, so look at the bulk of the first paragraph, lines 26–30, and lines 40–51.

Step 4: Make a Prediction
Lines 7–10 deal directly with the 1930s and 1940s. In these lines, Garcia is said to have provided evidence that activists from these decades anticipated many reforms pushed by activists in later decades. The correct answer will be a valid inference based on this statement.

Step 5: Evaluate the Answer Choices
(A) is therefore correct.

(B) is Out of Scope. Garcia never argues that the political diversity of Mexican American activists decreased over time.

(C) is a 180. Lines 9–10 characterize the activists of the 1960s and 1970s as "more militant."

(D) is a Distortion. Bilingual education and equal rights for resident aliens were goals of the Congress of Spanish-Speaking People (lines 24–26). It is unknown if that group accounted for *most* of the political activists.

(E) is a 180. Garcia claims that the goals of the activist groups were focused on liberal reform and *not* revolution (lines 28–30).

24. (B) Inference

Step 2: Identify the Question Type
This is an Inference question because it asks about what "the passage suggests."

Step 3: Research the Relevant Text
This question stem has a couple of important content clues. First, it focuses on Garcia's views, narrowing the relevant text to lines 1–5, 26–30, and 40–51. Second, note the timeframe: between 1930 and 1960. That interval is mentioned explicitly in line 44, so read around that line.

Step 4: Make a Prediction
Between 1930 and 1960, according to Garcia, a new generation of Mexican Americans arose that was more politically active than the previous generation due to its being more acculturated, or assimilated to the dominant culture. The correct answer is the one that must be true based on this assertion.

Step 5: Evaluate the Answer Choices
(B) is an almost direct paraphrase of Garcia's argument in lines 43–46.

(A) goes outside Garcia's argument to bring in ethnic consciousness, a concept that doesn't arise until the author brings it up in line 56.

(C) is a 180. Garcia argues that the acculturation of the new Mexican American generation *increased* their level of political activity.

(D) distorts Garcia's argument in lines 47–51. Garcia does argue that these Mexican American leaders wanted to achieve full civil rights for all Mexican Americans. However, the passage doesn't say that they used "political militancy" to achieve this end.

(E) also distorts lines 47–51. It's not valid to equate "moved to political protest" with "determined to achieve full civil rights for all United States residents of Mexican descent." Furthermore, the passage says that the rhetoric of World War II slogans was *inclusive,* which isn't the same as *patronizing.*

25. (B) Inference

Step 2: Identify the Question Type
The phrase "it can be inferred" is a sure sign of an Inference question.

Step 3: Research the Relevant Text
Pay careful attention to that question stem—it focuses on the author's opinion, not Garcia's. So, scan your Roadmap for places where the author's view on the Mexican American activists emerges.

Step 4: Make a Prediction
Lines 15–18 and 30–36 reveal that the author believes the political differences between certain groups of activists to be

of utmost significance. Lines 51–60 reveal that the author believes that outlook of the Mexican American activists may not have extended to the ethnic population at large. The correct answer will be consistent with these statements by the author.

Step 5: Evaluate the Answer Choices
(B) is directly supported by lines 26–36, in which the author cites the "fierce controversies" and "intense and lively debate" among these activist groups as proof that their common goal of liberal reform was secondary to their political differences.

(A) is a Distortion. The author seems persuaded by Garcia's claim that the later activists were more militant, but this wasn't necessarily because of their goal of liberal reform.

(C) is a 180. The author says that post-1930 Mexican American political history has not been characterized by consensus (lines 34–36).

(D) is unsupported. The author doesn't say what proportion of activists lined up behind groups such as the League of United Latin American Citizens versus groups such as the Congress of Spanish-Speaking People.

(E) is Out of Scope. Neither the author nor Garcia hints at whether the activists fully achieved their political goals, and if not, why they didn't.

26. (D) Detail

Step 2: Identify the Question Type
This is a Detail question because it deals with what the author *expresses* or states directly.

Step 3: Research the Relevant Text
Your Roadmap should already show you where the author's statements of opinion are. Look within these lines for Keywords expressing uncertainty: "Garcia may be exaggerating" in line 37; "it is not clear" in line 51.

Step 4: Make a Prediction
In line 37, the author is unsure whether the views of the Mexican American activists accurately represented the views of the population as a whole. In line 51, the author phrases this uncertainty in another way: The activists' political outlook may not have extended beyond them—Garcia doesn't provide enough evidence to substantiate this claim.

Step 5: Evaluate the Answer Choices
(D) is therefore correct.

(A) is incorrect because the author discusses an increase in the *proportion*, not the number, of Mexican Americans born in the United States. But even if **(A)** had used the word *proportion,* the author claims that a higher percentage of Mexican Americans *can't* be assumed to correlate with increased political activism (lines 57–60), so there is no uncertainty by the author on that point.

(B) is Out of Scope. The author mentions the earlier historians only in passing (line 5).

(C) is a 180. The author is clear in lines 34–36 that there was little or no consensus among various groups of Mexican American activists.

(E) is also a 180. The author says in line 23 that the League of United Latin American Citizens and the Congress of Spanish-Speaking People were "often diametrically opposed."

27. (E) Inference

Step 2: Identify the Question Type
The phrase "the passage supports which one of the following statements" indicates an Inference question.

Step 3: Research the Relevant Text
"Ethnic consciousness among Mexican Americans" is a helpful content clue leading you to the author's contention in lines 52–60.

Step 4: Make a Prediction
In lines 52–60, the author discusses "variations in ethnic consciousness" that are created by variations in patterns of bilingualism and rates of immigration by Mexicans. The author also says that an understanding of the diversity of ethnic consciousness is necessary to validate Garcia's assumptions. The correct answer will be consistent with these ideas.

Step 5: Evaluate the Answer Choices
(E) is directly supported by lines 52–57.

(A) is a Distortion. While the author does say that variations in rates of immigration and naturalization help to create variations in ethnic consciousness, the passage doesn't say that the correlation has to be direct. Higher immigration rates could potentially have led to a decrease in ethnic consciousness.

(B) sounds very similar to what the author says one *cannot* assume (lines 57–60).

(C) is unsupported. The author says that varying patterns of bilingualism can affect levels of ethnic consciousness, but even if you assume bilingualism to be a measure of assimilation, nothing in the passage suggests that assimilation and ethnic consciousness are inversely correlated.

(D) is Out of Scope. The author doesn't discuss the varying levels of influence that Mexican American leaders exerted over the ethnic Mexican population at large.

Section IV: Logical Reasoning

Q#	Question Type	Correct	Difficulty
1	Flaw	B	★
2	Main Point	C	★
3	Strengthen	E	★
4	Assumption (Necessary)	D	★
5	Principle (Identify/Strengthen)	D	★
6	Assumption (Necessary)	B	★
7	Inference	A	★★
8	Flaw	B	★
9	Paradox	B	★★
10	Strengthen/Weaken (Evaluate the Argument)	C	★
11	Inference	A	★★
12	Principle (Identify/Paradox)	D	★
13	Inference	D	★
14	Method of Argument	A	★★
15	Flaw	C	★★
16	Assumption (Sufficient)	E	★★
17	Method of Argument	E	★★
18	Flaw	E	★★★★
19	Parallel Reasoning	C	★★★
20	Flaw	D	★★★
21	Principle (Identify/Inference)	A	★★★★
22	Flaw	C	★★★
23	Principle (Apply/Inference)	E	★★★
24	Weaken	D	★★
25	Parallel Flaw	A	★★★
26	Strengthen	B	★

1. (B) Flaw

Step 1: Identify the Question Type
This is an unusual and uncommon question format. The first speaker, Ming, makes some comments. The question asks for Carol's interpretation of those comments. Carol's interpretation most likely isn't accurate, otherwise the question would have just asked for Ming's main point without involving Carol. Therefore, there's bound to be a flaw to Carol's interpretation.

Step 2: Untangle the Stimulus
According to Ming, trans fat is unhealthy, so consumers are fortunate that it's been removed from cookies. Carol isn't so pleased. She complains that, even though the cookies have no trans fat, they're still not healthy.

Step 3: Make a Prediction
There's just one problem with Carol's response: Ming never said cookies (or any dessert for that matter) were healthy. Ming merely said that cookies no longer had a particular unhealthy ingredient: trans fat. That just means they're less *un*healthy—still unhealthy, but not as much. Carol didn't catch that and instead reacted as if Ming was praising non–trans fat cookies as a health food. That flawed interpretation will be addressed in the correct answer.

Step 4: Evaluate the Answer Choices
(B) perfectly matches Carol's mistaken interpretation.

(A) is a 180. This is more in sync with Ming's *actual* meaning rather than Carol's erroneous translation.

(C) is a Distortion. All this does is define "not healthy" foods as "unhealthy." While logical, it ignores Carol's focus on the non–trans fat cookies.

(D) is Out of Scope. Ming and Carol are both talking about cookies with *no* trans fat.

(E) is Out of Scope. Ming brings up consumers, but Carol's comments don't address them at all. No recommendation is made about when to purchase cookies; there's just an assessment of whether or not they're healthy. So consumers are irrelevant to Carol's response.

2. (C) Main Point

Step 1: Identify the Question Type
The question asks for the historian's "overall conclusion," which makes this a Main Point question. Use Keywords to guide you, and look for the one sentence (typically a strong opinion rather than a given fact) that is supported by everything else.

Step 2: Untangle the Stimulus
The historian starts off with some historical data: The economy's productivity outpaced population growth for the first time during the Industrial Revolution, which led to better living standards. The historian then presents one economist's

theoretical interpretation of this data: Productivity grew because of the values of hard work and thrift that were spreading. The contrast Keyword *but* indicates the historian's inevitable rebuttal (LSAT authors love to dismiss others' opinions in favor of their own): Interpretations like that need to be backed up by facts. Because of that, the historian recommends ignoring the economist's view until there is evidence for the purported spread of values.

Step 3: Make a Prediction
The Conclusion Keyword *so* in the historian's rebuttal is a solid indicator of the main point here. Ultimately, the historian is calling for a dismissal of the economist's view until there's evidence to support the claims about values.

Step 4: Evaluate the Answer Choices
(C) matches the historian's main point practically word for word.

(A) is part of the basis for the argument, but it's merely a fact, not a conclusion.

(B) is also part of the opening facts. This may be tempting due to the Keyword *thus* in the stimulus, but this is not the historian's conclusion. Instead, it's the conclusion of the facts that merely serve as background for the argument.

(D) is a Distortion. The historian does question the claim about the spread of values, but is open to considering it if evidence is provided. The historian never goes so far as to say the spread of values was absolutely not a factor.

(E) is also a Distortion. The historian merely suggests that there's currently no evidence for the spread of values, not that it absolutely didn't happen.

3. (E) Strengthen

Step 1: Identify the Question Type
The question directly asks for something that strengthens the argument. Find the author's conclusion and evidence, and look for an answer that validates the assumption connecting them.

Step 2: Untangle the Stimulus
A community group is helping out with a master plan to plant trees in a new park. The plan is to use native species that are not too large. To achieve this, the community group has donated trees purchased from a local nursery (Three Rivers) known for selling native trees. The author concludes (with the Conclusion Keyword [*t*]*hus*) that these trees will mostly likely conform to the master plan's standards.

Step 3: Make a Prediction
The author's argument rests solely on the evidence of where the trees were purchased. There's no indication that these trees fit the regulations of the master plan: native trees that aren't too tall. The author merely assumes that the trees sold by the nursery are indeed native and not too tall. The

evidence already confirms that the nursery specializes in native trees, so the correct answer will likely validate that they're not too tall.

Step 4: Evaluate the Answer Choices

(E) supports the author's view that the master plan will be followed because the donated trees come from that nursery, and the master plan calls for trees that aren't very large.

(A) is a 180 because it contradicts the master plan outlined in the first sentence.

(B) is a potential weakener. The cottonwood is mentioned by the author as a very large tree that would be unacceptable. If the nursery sells those trees, then the donated trees could go against the master plan.

(C) is irrelevant. The community group donated trees, not shrubs. This does nothing to further validate whether or not the *trees* are consistent with the master plan.

(D) is Out of Scope. The master plan does not call for any non-native trees, so the difficulty of finding such trees would be irrelevant.

4. (D) Assumption (Necessary)

Step 1: Identify the Question Type

The question directly asks for the assumption, which is said to be *required*, making it a Necessary Assumption question. Start by identifying the author's conclusion and evidence and look for an answer that must be true for that conclusion to be logically drawn.

Step 2: Untangle the Stimulus

This argument is about *Diplodocus*, a dinosaur with a long neck. Paleontologists originally felt that *Diplodocus* raised its neck to reach high-growing vegetation for food, but this was recently called into question because the neck bones couldn't go up that way. However, the neck could go *down*, which would allow access to ground-level and even underwater plants. Because of this, the author concludes (using the Conclusion Keyword [*t*]*hus*) that *Diplodocus* must have eaten these low-growing plants instead.

Step 3: Make a Prediction

The author's insistence that this dinosaur *must* have eaten low-growing plants comes across as short-sighted. While the neck's ability to reach low-growing plants suggests the *possibility* of such a diet, that's a long way from suggesting that *must* be the case. The author is assuming that this possibility is a certainty, i.e., there is no other food *Diplodocus* would have eaten other than low-growing plants (or there is no other way for the *Diplodocus* to eat other, higher growing vegetation). The correct answer will state this general claim or deny a specific alternative that the author feels is not the case.

Step 4: Evaluate the Answer Choices

(D) has to be true for the author's argument to follow. If *Diplodocus could* access high-growing vegetation without raising its neck, then it wouldn't be limited to the ground and underwater plants. However, the author claims the dinosaur *is* limited to those plants, so the author must assume it *can't* reach those higher-growing plants.

(A) may strengthen the author's point of view, but it's not necessary. Even if modern ground-feeding animals *didn't* have the same neck structure, *Diplodocus* could still have the same limited diet claimed by the author.

(B) is Out of Scope. The dinosaur's field of vision is not in question here, only what the dinosaur ate.

(C) is Extreme. It might strengthen the idea that *Diplodocus* never raised its head, thereby restricting it to low-growing vegetation, but it is not necessary. Even if it *were* possible for *Diplodocus* to supply blood to an elevated brain, the neck bones still made such elevation impossible. The author's argument would go unaffected.

(E) is Out of Scope. The author already indicated that the neck of the *Diplodocus* allowed it to reach the underwater vegetation from dry land. So, whether it could also kneel or walk into the water is irrelevant. If anything, **(E)** weakens the argument by suggesting the *Diplodocus* would have been limited in reaching its food source. Using the Denial Test on this answeryields that the *Diplodocus was* able to browse for vegetation in these other ways—that certainly would not crush the argument, and thus, **(E)** cannot be correct.

5. (D) Principle (Identify/Strengthen)

Step 1: Identify the Question Type

This Principle question clearly asks for a principle that has to be identified in the correct answers. Furthermore, that principle will be used to *justify* an argument, which means this question will utilize the skills of a Strengthen question. Start by looking for a connection between the evidence and the conclusion, then find an answer that states that connection in broader terms.

Step 2: Untangle the Stimulus

The official is arguing that the government should not provide assistance for rebuilding destroyed hiking trails despite the determination and commitment of the local residents. "The reason" (a clear indication of evidence) is because future landslides in the area could lead to further serious injuries.

Step 3: Make a Prediction

The official's argument is pretty straightforward: Government assistance to this project should be withheld because of the possibility of future injury. However, this is a specific argument for this particular project. To validate such a decision, the correct answer will suggest applying the same reasoning to other such circumstances. In short, the government should not help out with any project that could lead to serious injury in the future.

Step 4: Evaluate the Answer Choices

(D) matches the logic of the official's argument perfectly.

(A) is a Distortion. The official doesn't directly state any conditions under which the residents should be denied rebuilding. The official is only concerned about government involvement.

(B) is a 180. If residents' determination were a factor in determining government support, the officer's denial of support would be contradictory.

(C) is a 180. If government assistance required a strong commitment to community, the officer's denial would be unwarranted. The residents are displaying the requisite commitment.

(E) is a Distortion. The official recommends against government assistance, but never goes so far as to discourage the residents from continuing on their own.

6. (B) Assumption (Necessary)

Step 1: Identify the Question Type

The question asks for something the scientist is *assuming,* and the argument *requires* that assumption. That makes this a Necessary Assumption question. The correct answer will identify something that must be true for the scientist's argument to work.

Step 2: Untangle the Stimulus

The scientist has an optimistic way of looking at a potential problem. While humans may be the cause of large-scale climate change, the scientist claims this could actually be a *good* thing. The scientist argues that, if climate change is indeed affected by our behavior, we could just take control and modify climate trends.

Step 3: Make a Prediction

This argument requires a major leap in logic. The scientist's claim that we could *control* climate change is based solely on the idea that we may be *responsible* for climate change. This assumes we can control things for which we are responsible. The correct answer will connect that gap between responsibility and control.

Step 4: Evaluate the Answer Choices

(B) does the job perfectly. After all, using the Denial Test, if humans *couldn't* control their relevant behaviors, then we'd have no chance to control climate change if we were responsible.

(A) is an Irrelevant Comparison. The comparison to other causes has no effect on whether we could change *our* role in climate change.

(C) is not necessary. The author claims that humans "may be responsible," and the evidence states "[*I*]*f* human behavior is

responsible." The argument is hypothetical, not reliant on humans actually being the cause.

(D) is an Irrelevant Comparison. The argument is about controlling climate change, not who it more greatly affects.

(E) is another Irrelevant Comparison. The ease in identifying our problematic behavior has no bearing on the argument. Even if such behavior was difficult to identify, the argument is about whether we could control climate change by changing those behaviors.

7. (A) Inference

Step 1: Identify the Question Type

This question asks for something that would fill in the blank at the end of the stimulus. A quick glance up shows that the blank is preceded by the Keywords "conclude that." That means the blank will be filled with a conclusion that can be drawn, or inferred, from the given information. That makes it an Inference question. Use the evidence provided and connect ideas to look for a logically deducible conclusion.

Step 2: Untangle the Stimulus

A study of a group of heart patients indicated that those who didn't know whether they needed surgery experienced less pain than those who *did* know. The conclusion will be based on this and the assumption that not knowing what's going to happen is more stressful than knowing.

Step 3: Make a Prediction

They key to drawing an inference here is to see how the two groups of patients compare. Those patients who were still waiting to find out if they need surgery were (presumably) under more stress, yet they felt less pain. On the other hand, those who knew what was going to happen were less stressed, but were in more pain. As odd as that may sound, the implication is that greater stress may have the paradoxical effect of reducing pain. The correct answer will identify this correlation.

Step 4: Evaluate the Answer Choices

(A) correctly identifies the implied connection between higher stress and lower pain.

(B) is a Distortion. The author claims that the stress is affected (presumably) by knowing or not knowing about the future. There is no implication that the pain plays any causal role in the stress they're experiencing.

(C) is at worst a 180. The patients who had information withheld from them actually experienced *less* pain, which suggests a better condition, not worse.

(D) is a Distortion. The stress is said to be caused by the knowledge (or lack thereof) of the type of treatment needed. There is no connection implied between stress and blood flow.

(E) is an Irrelevant Comparison. The author's connection is between pain and *knowing* what treatment is in store. There is no indication how many patients actually require surgery or which group would be more likely to require surgery versus a different treatment.

8. (B) Flaw

Step 1: Identify the Question Type
When an argument is described as vulnerable to criticism, that means there is a flaw in the reasoning. Dissect the argument and look for an answer that identifies why the evidence does not logically back up the conclusion.

Step 2: Untangle the Stimulus
According to the author, the shape of a Kodiak bear's bones allow the bear to walk upright naturally. The author then concludes that walking upright must be an innate ability rather than a learned one.

Step 3: Make a Prediction
The author's conclusion about instinctual versus learned behavior is based on evidence that the behavior is *natural*. That assumes *natural* behavior is *solely* instinctual and not learned. The author not only erroneously equates *natural* and *instinctive*, but also assumes there's only one possible explanation rather than some combination of instinct and learning.

Step 4: Evaluate the Answer Choices
(B) points out this classic overlooked alternative. LSAT authors frequently solve the scientific question of nurture versus nature by choosing one side exclusively over the other rather than considering a combined effect.

(A) is Out of Scope. The evidence is general information about Kodiak bears, not data taken from a small sample of bears.

(C) is invalid because the word *behavior* is consistent throughout, always referring to the act of standing upright.

(D) is Extreme. The author definitely makes the mistake of choosing one explanation to the exclusion of another, but this mistake is only applied to the behavior of standing upright. The author does not ascribe this opinion to *all* behavior.

(E) is a Distortion. The scientific evidence here (about bone shape) is verifiable, so the author is not appealing to science merely because a scientist said so.

9. (B) Paradox

Step 1: Identify the Question Type
The question asks for something that will explain a certain tendency people have. If it needs to be explained, that means it probably doesn't make sense in context of the rest of the stimulus, resulting in a paradox. Look for the potential contradiction and find an answer that provides a resolution while maintaining the validity of everything.

Step 2: Untangle the Stimulus
The author starts by noting that people are often interested in or moved by individual anecdotes, but don't really care about statistical data. Then comes the paradox (identified with the Keyword *although*): The anecdotes that capture people's attention are often unrepresentative and misleading, yet people's beliefs about society are still pretty accurate.

Step 3: Make a Prediction
This is certainly a mystery. How are people's beliefs about society so accurate when they ignore factual statistics and pay more attention to manipulative personal stories? While it's not necessary to predict an exact response, know that the correct answer will clarify how people's opinions can go unchanged despite the exposure to misleading information.

Step 4: Evaluate the Answer Choices
(B) helps clear things up. If people are aware of how anecdotes can be unrepresentative, they'll know the anecdotes are misleading and won't let those anecdotes improperly skew their beliefs.

(A) is irrelevant. People largely ignore statistics anyway, so it doesn't matter how much is revealed or covered up by statistics.

(C) is a 180. Anecdotes are said to be misleading. If they actually had an influence on people's beliefs, then one would expect people's beliefs to be misguided, not accurate.

(D) is irrelevant. Whether anecdotes can somehow make statistics clearer or not, there's still no explanation for how people exposed to misleading information can maintain an accurate view of society. Furthermore, the author states anecdotes are about unrepresentative cases, which would seem to make them less likely to be helpful in explaining statistics anyway.

(E) is a 180. If people's beliefs are affected by emotional response, then the misleading anecdotes would be more likely to make people change their minds and start believing *in*accurate ideas.

10. (C) Strengthen/Weaken (Evaluate the Argument)

Step 1: Identify the Question Type
The question asks for something that would help *evaluate* the given argument. The correct answer will pose a question that, depending on how it's answered, will strengthen or weaken the argument. The validity of an argument hinges on its assumption, so look for an answer that questions the author's assumption.

Step 2: Untangle the Stimulus
The argument presents a paleontologist who discovered some tissue preserved from a *T. rex*. She found that the tissues contained collagen proteins similar to collagen proteins found in chickens. The author concludes (indicated

by the Keyword *therefore*) that this evidence strengthens the theory that dinosaurs and birds are related.

Step 3: Make a Prediction
The author's conclusion is about whether dinosaurs and birds are related, but this is based solely on evidence that they share collagen proteins. This makes the unwarranted assumption that collagen proteins somehow indicate whether two animals are related. The correct answer will question whether having these proteins in common is really enough to claim a relationship.

Step 4: Evaluate the Answer Choices
(C) raises a perfect question. What if unrelated animals could share similar proteins? If they could, then it's just as likely that dinosaurs and birds are *unrelated*, going against the author's point. However, if unrelated animals are not likely to share those proteins, then birds and dinosaurs at more likely to be related, further validating the author's point.

(A) is Out of Scope. The difficulty in finding dinosaur tissue has no bearing on whether dinosaurs and birds are related.

(B) is Out of Scope. Even if there were evidence against the theory of a dinosaur-bird connection, that would have no bearing on whether this particular protein evidence supports that theory or not.

(D) is an Irrelevant Comparison. The argument is about whether this evidence supports *some* relation between dinosaurs and birds, not whether that relation is stronger than other relations.

(E) is Out of Scope. Whether or not researches *assumed* such a similarity before the discovery wouldn't change the debate about whether dinosaurs and birds are related. The timeline of when the theory of a *T. rex*-chicken relation was hypothesized wouldn't change whether the physical evidence supported the theory or not.

11. (A) Inference

Step 1: Identify the Question Type
The question asks for something "strongly supported by the information" in the stimulus. That means the given information will be used to draw an inference. Do not look for an argument. Instead, use Keywords to derive intention and look for ways to combine ideas to make deductions.

Step 2: Untangle the Stimulus
The stimulus describes a professor who occasionally taught class after full nights of performing research. On those occasions, she felt worn down and unfocused. However, when her students were asked to identify which lessons followed her all-night research sessions, a lot of them couldn't tell.

Step 3: Make a Prediction
The Keyword [*I*]*nterestingly* suggests the last sentence will be significant here. Why is it interesting that her students couldn't tell which classes followed her late-night research? Because the professor felt fatigued and figured it was affecting her performance. Yet the students didn't seem to notice, suggesting that the professor's performance wasn't quite as poor as she thought. The fatigue probably made her over-critical of her own performance. The correct answer will likely address this dichotomy between her fatigue-fueled perception and her actual observed performance.

Step 4: Evaluate the Answer Choices
(A) summarizes the information perfectly, albeit in fancy language. Simply put, this is saying that the effect the professor "felt" sleeplessness had on her (i.e., the subjective effect) was more serious than the effect actually observed by her students (i.e., her overt behavior).

(B) is Extreme. While the professor was certainly more aware of the effects than her students, that's not to say that *nobody* could better assess the effect.

(C) is an Irrelevant Comparison. The effect of sleep deprivation on any other job performance is never addressed.

(D) is another Irrelevant Comparison. Extended sleep deprivation is never addressed.

(E) is a 180. Very few of the students actually realized the professor was suffering from sleep deprivation—not very astute at all.

12. (D) Principle (Identify/Paradox)

Step 1: Identify the Question Type
The question asks for a principle which will be identified in the correct answer. In a never-before-seen twist, the principle will be used to *reconcile* an "apparent conflict," which means the principle is going to be used to resolve a paradox. Despite the novel mix, this question doesn't require any new skills. Start with standard paradox skills by looking for the discrepancy between the prime minister's claims. Then, look for a solution in broad, principle-like terms that would eliminate the contradiction and allow both claims to remain valid.

Step 2: Untangle the Stimulus
The prime minister's first claim is that the government should satisfy the needs of its own nation's citizens before satisfying the needs of people from other nations. However, this seems to go against the second claim, which basically states that people in all countries are equally worthy and equally deserving of having their needs satisfied.

Step 3: Make a Prediction
If citizens of all nations deserve an equal opportunity to have their needs satisfied, why should the prime minister's

government put its nation's own citizens ahead of everyone else? It's not worth predicting a specific reason, especially on a Principle question. Instead, go to the answers looking for a broadly worded policy that gives a nation the right to prioritize its own citizens even when other nations have citizens with equally deserving needs.

Step 4: Evaluate the Answer Choices
(D) helps explain the prime minister's seemingly hypocritical suggestion. Generally, when everyone has equally worthy needs (as is the case here), those needs should be met primarily by the people's own government. So, that allows the prime minister's government to focus on its own nation's people, while (optimistically) confident that other nations' people will be helped by their own government.

(A) is a 180. This states that people shouldn't get help unless their needs are more important than others' needs. If that were true, then nobody should get help because nobody's needs are more important to satisfy than anyone else's.

(B) is another 180. This states that the only time a government should give priority to its people is when its people's are *more* worthy. Nevertheless, the people of the prime minister's government are *not* more worthy, so this would make the prime minister's recommendation completely unwarranted.

(C) is a Distortion. The prime minister said that *people* are all equal, and thus objectively no one group should take priority over another. The prime minister did not weigh in on how important the *needs* of specific groups are. For example, although the people may be of equal worth, perhaps one group only needs better Internet connections, whereas another needs food. Thus, their needs could be of greater/lesser importance. That said, **(C)** still wouldn't explain why the prime minister has prioritized his own citizens because nothing has been established about what needs his citizens have versus citizens of other countries.

(E) is Out of Scope. The author doesn't mention other ways to satisfy people's needs, so there's no way to know if the prime minister's nation *has* other ways that would warrant the extra priority.

13. (D) Inference

Step 1: Identify the Question Type
The question asks for something that "must be true" based on the given statements. That means the correct answer will be a logical inference. Because the answer *must* be true, expect some Formal Logic and look out for answers that sound reasonable but are not absolutely true.

Step 2: Untangle the Stimulus
According to the mayor, every street in town will get at least one monthly sweeping. However, some neighborhoods will

qualify for additional sweepings if needed. If a qualified neighborhood requests extra sweepings, it will receive them.

If	qualified & request	→	swept more than once/ month

Step 3: Make a Prediction
The outline is pretty direct. Any neighborhood that needs extra sweeping and asks for it will get it. Sounds great! Just remember that this does *not* exclude other neighborhoods from getting extra sweepings. While neighborhoods that need the extra sweeping will definitely be qualified and have any requests approved, other neighborhoods could get an extra sweeping, too. The correct answer will follow the absolute logic of the mayor's statements.

Step 4: Evaluate the Answer Choices
(D) is logically sound. The very last sentence says that such requests "*will* be satisfied immediately," so that means the one monthly sweeping plus any requested interim sweepings.

(A) is a Distortion. The mayor cites "excessive dirt" from *major* construction jobs as a qualification, but that doesn't mean any old construction job will qualify a neighborhood.

(B) is a subtle Distortion. All requests for additional sweepings will be approved, but what if a qualified neighborhood doesn't put in a request? In that case, they could still get just their single monthly sweeping. So, **(B)** does not have to be true.

(C) is a Formal Logic Distortion. While qualified neighborhoods are guaranteed extra sweepings (upon request), that doesn't mean *only* those neighborhoods can get extra sweepings. Other neighborhoods may be eligible, too.

If	swept more than once/ month	→	qualified

(E) is another Formal Logic Distortion, which could be considered just the contrapositive of **(C)**. While other neighborhoods may not be guaranteed extra sweepings (as qualified ones are), that's not to say they'll definitely be denied.

If	~ qualified	→	~ swept more than once/ month (even if requested)

14. (A) Method of Argument

Step 1: Identify the Question Type
While this question stem isn't complete, a quick glance at the answers shows that each one describes an action the journalist may be performing (e.g., "pointing out," "defending," "defining"). That means the correct answer will describe the *way* the argument is made, which is a Method of Argument question. (The word *by* at the end of the stem is a common signal of this question type.) Use Keywords to concentrate on the journalist's technique rather than focusing on the content.

Step 2: Untangle the Stimulus
According to the journalist, it's unethical for journalists to outright lie to get a story, but they will often hide information in order to get new information. Some people find both actions unethical, but the journalist feels otherwise. According to the journalist, there's a difference between letting a lie go undenied (e.g., withholding information) and actively encouraging a lie. It's only the latter the journalist finds truly unethical.

Step 3: Make a Prediction
There are two actions being described here: withholding information (not telling somebody the truth about what you know) and lying. An argument is made by some people, but the Keyword [*h*]*owever* indicates the journalist disputes this argument. To do so, the journalist draws a *distinction* between the two actions. The correct answer will describe this method of disputing an argument about two actions by drawing a distinction between them.

Step 4: Evaluate the Answer Choices
(A) is exactly what the journalist does. The journalist points out the difference between not revealing the truth and lying to show that people shouldn't conclude that both of those otherwise similar actions are unethical.

(B) is Out of Scope. The journalist uses generic language at all times, never providing a "clear instance" (i.e., a specific example).

(C) is a 180. The journalist does define lying as "saying something untrue" in the first sentence and "actively encouraging a false belief" at the end. However, the journalist argues that this definition does *not* apply to "all of the cases" because it does *not* apply to the discussed concept of withholding information.

(D) is Out of Scope. Even if there was an "ethical principle" behind the disputed argument (e.g., actions based on untruths are all unethical), the journalist rebuts it by discussing an unrecognized distinction, not by presenting any particular counterexamples.

(E) distorts the logic. The journalist's moral principle is the distinction between the acceptability of not revealing the truth and the unacceptability of actively lying. The journalist

is *using* that principle to defend how journalists act in those cases, not the other way around (i.e., using the cases to defend the principle).

15. (C) Flaw

Step 1: Identify the Question Type
The question asks what makes the economist's reasoning *questionable*. That means it's asking for the flaw in the argument. Break the argument apart and look for an answer that expresses why the evidence does not adequately back up the conclusion.

Step 2: Untangle the Stimulus
The economist is rebutting colleagues who want to lower interest rates to stimulate the economy. The economist claims the economy is already growing just fine, thus suggesting that there is no reason to lower interest rates.

Step 3: Make a Prediction
That's a rather strong conclusion. The economist has fairly argued that lowering interest rates isn't needed to stimulate the economy. However, to claim there is "no reason" whatsoever to lower interest rates ignores any other potential benefit. This is a classic case of overlooked possibilities, and the correct answer will point out the economist's narrow-minded reaction.

Step 4: Evaluate the Answer Choices
(C) gets it exactly right. Denying the need to stimulate the economy eliminates that one reason for lowering interest rates, but there could be many other reasons that weren't addressed.

(A) is Out of Scope. The economist's evidence is the economy's currently sustainable growth rate. However, there's no indication that this evidence comes from expert testimony. It could very well be general knowledge.

(B) mentions a confusion between growth and what stimulates growth. The economist's language indicates no such confusion. The economist admittedly doesn't state what has stimulated the current economic growth, but that's irrelevant. The fact remains that the economy no longer needs lower interest rates as a stimulus.

(D) is a Distortion. The economist isn't saying that one way to stimulate growth (lowering interest rates) is the only way. The economist says there's no other *reason*, other than stimulating the economy, to lower interest rates. That's not the same as saying there's no other *way* to stimulate the economy. The economist acknowledges the economy has already been stimulated and, thus, does not further discuss other potential ways to stimulate it.

(E) is Out of Scope and Extreme. The economist never says that lowering interest rates further will suddenly make things worse (i.e., go from sustainable to unsustainable). It's just that the economy appears to be doing fine without further lowering rates and, thus, there's no need to do so.

16. (E) Assumption (Sufficient)

Step 1: Identify the Question Type
This question asks for an assumption that allows for a proper argument. The conclusion is said to follow *if* the assumption is in place, making this a Sufficient Assumption question. That means there will most likely be Mismatched Concepts that need to be connected.

Step 2: Untangle the Stimulus
The author starts off by describing a majority opinion: Caravaggio's realistic artwork with its use of light and shadow indicates that he was one of the earliest Baroque painters. However, the author feels there may be a problem. If Caravaggio is considered Baroque, that would contradict Mather's definition of Baroque paintings. So, either the commentators or Mather are mistaken.

Step 3: Make a Prediction
Mather's definition of Baroque involves grandiose features such as opulence and extravagance. However, the evidence makes no mention of whether or not these features are present in Caravaggio's work. If they *were* present, then the commentators could consider him Baroque while still upholding Mather's definition. However, the author claims somebody is mistaken, so the author is assuming that Caravaggio's works *didn't* have these features.

Step 4: Evaluate the Answer Choices
(E) gets it exactly right. If Caravaggio's paintings didn't have the described features, then Mather's definition holds and the commentators are wrong, or Caravaggio *is* Baroque and Mather's definition is contradicted—just as the author concludes.

(A) is Out of Scope. What features are shared by any paintings has no bearing on whether those features confirm or deny the views of the commentators or Mather.

(B) is a Distortion. This verifies that it's okay for Caravaggio's work to be considered realistic, but it does nothing to suggest whether the commentators or Mather prevail as to the classification of Caravaggio as Baroque.

(C) is Out of Scope. The argument is only about Caravaggio and whether he painted in the Baroque style.

(D) is thrown off by the word *usually*. If realistic artwork *usually* didn't have the features described, it's still possible that Caravaggio was an exception. In that case, both the commentators and Mather could be right, contrary to the author's point. Therefore, **(D)** does not guarantee the conclusion.

17. (E) Method of Argument

Step 1: Identify the Question Type
The question asks for the *technique* used in the argument, which means it's a Method of Argument question. However, the question stem already provides part of the technique: The author is trying to weaken the argument of people who support jury nullification. Use Keywords and structure to determine how the author argues against the proponents' viewpoint.

Step 2: Untangle the Stimulus
The argument starts with a description of jury nullification (a jury can free a lawbreaker if the jury finds the law unfair) and the proponent's argument (this protects against injustice). However, neither of these statements helps with the question at hand. The author's objection starts with the Keyword [*b*]*ut*. At that point, the author cites that jury nullification assumes juries will be objective. However, if juries aren't objective, they can make serious mistakes.

Step 3: Make a Prediction
The author mentions "serious mistakes" as a potential problem that could result from using jury nullification. That's pretty much the author's sole method for rebutting the proponents' position: showing how it could have grave results.

Step 4: Evaluate the Answer Choices
(E) is a match. The author argues that applying the doctrine of jury nullification could have undesirable consequences ("serious mistakes").

(A) is a Distortion. The proponents are motivated by preventing injustice, but the author has no problem with that motive. It's the potential result that the author objects to.

(B) is a Distortion. There is a potential inconsistency with needing objectivity and potentially not getting it, but that's all part of the author's evidence. The proponents' support doesn't have any such inconsistency.

(C) is Extreme. The proponent's sole support for jury nullification is that it would protect against injustice. However, the author doesn't say that's *false*—that it absolutely *wouldn't* protect against injustice. It just relies too much on objectivity, which can be a problem in *certain* cases (when juries use their own perceptions).

(D) is Out of Scope. The author provides no examples or counterexamples, just some reasoned general claims.

18. (E) Flaw

Step 1: Identify the Question Type
The question directly asks for the flaw in the pharmacist's argument. Look for a reason why the evidence doesn't adequately back up the conclusion.

Step 2: Untangle the Stimulus

The pharmacist's argument is based on a study of insomnia patients whose condition improves after ingesting melatonin, a hormone usually produced by the pineal gland. The pharmacist uses this study to conclude (indicated by the Keyword [*thus*]) that the pineal gland produces less melatonin as we grow older.

Step 3: Make a Prediction

The argument seems nice. After all, if melatonin helped the patients, then their bodies probably weren't producing an adequate amount of melatonin. However, the patients are all relatively older and *all* suffer from insomnia, a rather convenient demographic for the pharmacist. Unfortunately, without comparison to other people (i.e., younger people and/or those without insomnia), it's hard to tell if this is normal for people in general or just unique to these individuals. The correct answer will point out this use of an unvaried study group.

Step 4: Evaluate the Answer Choices

(E) is a match. The sample used (older people with insomnia) is not exactly representative of people in general.

(A) is a Distortion and not a flaw. In the study, an action (ingesting melatonin) does have an effect (reduces insomnia). However, it would be perfectly reasonable to say that ingesting melatonin was intended to reduce insomnia. Even so, that wasn't the author's point.

(B) is a Distortion. While the manufacturers of the melatonin supplements may have an incentive for people to use their product, their claim is not flawed just because the manufacturers have that incentive. Instead, their claim was made on factual data, but alas that data was not representative—therein lies the flaw.

(C) is wrong because every term is used consistently throughout the argument.

(D) is a Distortion. The only cause-and-effect relationship suggested here is that ingesting melatonin causes insomnia symptoms to subside. However, the author does not confuse this relationship, and it makes no sense that reduced insomnia would cause patients to start ingesting melatonin.

19. (C) Parallel Reasoning

Step 1: Identify the Question Type

The question asks for an argument "similar to that" in the stimulus. That indicates Parallel Reasoning. The components of the correct answer should logically match those of the stimulus exactly. If anything doesn't logically compare, the answer should be eliminated. Keep in mind that the *logic* has to match, even if the argumentative components are presented in a different order.

Step 2: Untangle the Stimulus

The stimulus starts with a qualified assertion that is the conclusion: The concert was *probably* not promoted properly. The evidence involves a concert expert, Wells, who had made a prediction earlier: As long as the promotion was done well, the concert would sell out.

If	~ poorly promoted	→	sell out

However, the concert did not sell out (necessary term did not occur), which is why the author concludes the concert was *probably* poorly promoted (sufficient term did not occur).

If	~ sell out	→	poorly promoted (probably)

Step 3: Make a Prediction

The expert's prediction uses Formal Logic, which forms the basis of the argument. If the promotion was not poorly promoted (~X), the concert would sell out (Y). ~X → Y. The evidence indicates the necessary term did not happen (~Y), i.e., the concert did *not* sell out. So, the author concludes that the promotion probably *was* mishandled (X) (using the qualified word *probably* because the logic is still based on one expert's opinion). The correct answer will match this structure exactly: If ~X → Y; ~Y, therefore, probably X.

Step 4: Evaluate the Answer Choices

(C) matches every step of the way. An expert (experienced home renovator) makes a prediction based on a condition (if the repair was done right, the damage would be unnoticeable); the result doesn't happen (the damage *is* noticeable), so the author concludes that the condition was probably not met (the repair was probably not done right).

If	properly repaired	→	~ noticeable

Noticeable, therefore, probably ~ properly repaired

(A) is a Distortion. The expert's prediction is not as certain as the one in the stimulus. It is based on a condition (if surgery performed by a highly skilled surgeon), but then it only predicts that the patient would *probably* survive. Also, when the results don't happen (the patient doesn't survive), the author concludes the surgery was performed poorly—a completely different condition than the one raised by the expert.

(B) is another Distortion. This choice mixes things up. It should be the expert that gives a conditional prediction with the author making a qualified assertion. However, here the author gives the conditional prediction (if it were properly labeled, it would contain organic compounds), and the expert gives a qualified assertion (the sample probably did not contain organic compounds). The author does still make a qualified assertion of his own ("the sample probably is not labeled correctly"), but the overall structure is already askew. Also, like **(A)**, the expert's statement is not fully certain ("the sample *probably* did not contain any organic compounds"), whereas in the stimulus the expert had no such qualification.

(D) is a 180. It goes wrong in several ways, but foremost is that in this case, the author concludes the expert (the builder) was wrong, which is the opposite of how the author regards the expert's claim in the stimulus.

(E) is a Distortion. The expert does have a parallel conditional prediction: If tests were properly conducted, then lead would be found in the soil.

$$\text{If} \quad \text{\emph{properly conducted}} \quad \rightarrow \quad \text{\emph{lead}}$$

However, the evidence states that the results *did* happen (lead *was* found), and the author concludes that the condition *was* probably met (tests *were* probably conducted properly). That goes backward on the Formal Logic rather correctly forming a contrapositive. To be correct, it should have said this: So, since the tests did *not* find lead in the soil, they probably were *not* properly conducted.

20. (D) Flaw

Step 1: Identify the Question Type
An argument that's described as "vulnerable to criticism" has a flaw in its reasoning. Break the argument into evidence and conclusion, and determine why those components do not logically connect.

Step 2: Untangle the Stimulus
The Keyword *for* in the opening sentence indicates a common "this is my conclusion, because of this evidence" structure. In this case, the economist concludes that global recessions can't be prevented, which is based on the logic that preventing a recession requires it to be predictable.

$$\text{If} \quad \text{\emph{global recession prevented}} \quad \rightarrow \quad \text{\emph{predictable}}$$

However, the economist adds that even the best techniques in use couldn't predict a recession.

Step 3: Make a Prediction
The economist's conclusion is very strong ("recessions can *never* be prevented"), hinging on the idea that recessions have to be predictable. However, the last sentence merely states that economists can't predict recessions with the "techniques at their disposal." What if there were better, more reliable techniques that economists haven't devised yet? In that case, recessions may be predictable at some point—just not with the current methods. The economist fails to consider that, and that's the flaw in this argument.

Step 4: Evaluate the Answer Choices
(D) correctly identifies the economist's overlooked possibility. Maybe techniques will improve and recessions will become predictable, allowing them potentially to be prevented.

(A) is a potential flaw, but not one the economist makes. The stated premises are distinct from the conclusion.

(B) is irrelevant. Even if the author *did* establish such a claim of predictive ability, economists have still always failed.

(C) is a classic flaw, but not one the economist makes. The predictability of a recession is always treated as necessary and never treated as a sufficient term that would ensure prevention.

(E) is a subtle Distortion. The economist does infer that something will not occur (recessions won't be prevented), but the evidence is not that recessions *can't* be predicted, it's that they *haven't* been.

21. (A) Principle (Identify/Inference)

Step 1: Identify the Question Type
This question directly asks for a principle that needs to be identified. However, there's a significant twist. The correct answer will be a principle that *conflicts* with the stimulus. Start by identifying the principle underlying the stimulus, then look for an answer that contradicts that principle.

Step 2: Untangle the Stimulus
A respected community member, Mr. Hanlon, recently reported an alien sighting. Unfortunately, despite the extraordinary nature of an alien sighting, the letter writer is not happy with the newspaper's article. The letter writer complains that the newspaper is unjustified in its bias, treating Mr. Hanlon with more skepticism than if he were to report something a little less fantastic (e.g., a meteor).

Step 3: Make a Prediction
The letter writer's problem is the disparity in the newspaper's tone, treating Mr. Hanlon more critically because he was talking about aliens rather than something a little less fanciful. That means the letter writer believes that all claims should be treated fairly, especially those from respected community members. The correct answer will contradict this, suggesting the newspaper was justified in treating Mr. Hanlon's extraordinary claim with skepticism.

Step 4: Evaluate the Answer Choices
(A) conflicts properly with the letter writer's point. What makes this challenging is the use of double negatives and

reliance on Formal Logic. This answer refers to extraordinary claims (such as Mr. Hanlon's alien sighting). Simply put, it says that such a claim *can* be criticized (*not* presented *un*critically) if there's no high-quality evidence to back it up. As the question asks, the letter writer's argument conflicts with this principle by calling such criticism *unjustified*.

(B) is Out of Scope. It says that any evidence from a solely intermediary source should be taken with skepticism. However, the evidence of aliens comes directly from the observer (Mr. Hanlon), so this principle doesn't apply and thus is not conflicted.

(C) is Out of Scope and perhaps a 180. This principle is based on a source who has been trusted in the past. There's no evidence that the media has ever dealt with Mr. Hanlon in the past, so the principle doesn't apply and thus can't be conflicted. However, if the newspaper has used Mr. Hanlon in the past, then this principle would conflict with the *newspaper*, but would agree with the letter writer. Thus, it *wouldn't* conflict with the entity called for by the question stem.

(D) is a Distortion. The letter writer's argument is against the newspaper for its reporting, not against the person observing a phenomena (Mr. Hanlon). He is not the one that publicized his claim.

(E) is a Distortion. The letter writer's argument is against the newspaper's treatment of Mr. Hanlon, not with its decision to publish the report.

22. (C) Flaw

Step 1: Identify the Question Type
The question directly states that there's a flaw in the argument. Find why the evidence does not directly support the conclusion, and be on the lookout for common LSAT flaws.

Step 2: Untangle the Stimulus
This argument discusses two types of fish, one found in Flower Lake and one found in Blue Lake. They have the same type of teeth for scraping algae and were thus expected to be related. If they *were* related, the algae-scraping teeth would have evolved just once. However, evidence shows the fish are actually *not* closely related. Using the Keyword [*t*]*hus*, the author concludes that the algae-scraping teeth did *not* evolve just once.

If	closely related	→	1 evolution
If	~ closely related	→	~ 1 evolution

Step 3: Make a Prediction
Those confident with Formal Logic probably pounced on the flaw before the argument even finished. The logic is based on a conditional statement: If the fish were related, the algae-scraping evolved just once. However, this says *nothing* about what would happen if the fish were *not* closely related. Their traits could also have evolved just once, contrary to the author's conclusion. The author negates the terms without reversing them. Being closely related is a sufficient condition for guaranteeing one evolution, not a necessary condition—a classic LSAT flaw committed by this author.

Step 4: Evaluate the Answer Choices
(C) describes this frequently tested logical flaw.

(A) is Out of Scope. Nothing is claimed or inferred to have caused something else to occur.

(B) is a Distortion. The author concludes that algae-scraping evolved more than once because the two fish aren't closely related, not because support for a single evolution has gone unconfirmed.

(D) is Out of Scope. There is no evidence that states the evolution was *likely* to have occurred multiple times, so the author doesn't use such evidence to conclude evolution *did* occur multiple times.

(E) is a Faulty Use of Detail. While the opinion of some biologists are presented, their statements are merely a backdrop for the author's argument. The argument itself does not incorporate their claims at all.

23. (E) Principle (Apply/Inference)

Step 1: Identify the Question Type
Be sure to take care in dissecting this question. The stimulus will describe some constitutional requirements, which will likely be general rules (or principles). The correct answer will present a specific situation that forces someone to *violate* one of those principles.

Step 2: Untangle the Stimulus
The stimulus lays out two requirements for selling a state-owned entity. First, it must accept the highest bid it can get. Second, it must ensure that the citizens of Country F maintain majority ownership for at least one year.

If	sell	→	*highest price AND citizens have majority ownership for at least one year*

Step 3: Make a Prediction

Do not spend too much time contemplating an exact scenario. Instead, as per the question, the correct answer will present a situation in which at least one of the two requirements must go unmet. That would involve the country accepting a bid that's either lower than it could get otherwise or one in which the citizens give up majority ownership within a year.

Step 4: Evaluate the Answer Choices

(E) would definitely cause a problem. This sale would force a restriction requiring that citizens get majority ownership, which would satisfy the second constitutional requirement. However, that restriction automatically lowers the selling price, which would force the government to violate the first constitutional requirement.

(A) is a 180. The citizens currently own the entire corporation. If this highest bid is accepted, then *non*citizens would get a minority share, leaving a majority share for citizens. Both requirements would be satisfied, not violated.

(B) is Out of Scope. The requirements only address the bidding price and the ownership. If the mine is sold for the highest price and the citizens maintain majority ownership, then it doesn't matter where operations and sales take place.

(C) has too many variables to ensure something will be violated. World Oil is said to make "one of the highest offers," not necessarily *the* highest. Furthermore, if their bid were accepted, it would merely be unknown if citizens would maintain majority ownership. It's certainly *possible* that a requirement will be violated, but it's also possible that everything will work out and nothing gets violated.

(D) is a 180 and Out of Scope. The highest bid would still give citizens majority ownership. As long as that bid is accepted, nothing is violated. The existence of a second bid that's close is irrelevant.

24. (D) Weaken

Step 1: Identify the Question Type

This question asks directly for something that weakens the given argument. Consider the assumption that connects the evidence to the conclusion and look for an answer that contradicts that assumption.

Step 2: Untangle the Stimulus

At the Keyword [*c*]*learly*, the author states the conclusion: The dietary supplement Activite must be effective at promoting energy and alertness. The evidence is that the manufacturers are giving away a month's supply for free, which wouldn't seem to be in their best interest.

Step 3: Make a Prediction

It's unusual that the author's conclusion is about the product's effectiveness (how it *must* be effective, no less) given that there is no evidence whatsoever about how well it

works. The only evidence is the promotional giveaway, as if that somehow speaks to the product's effectiveness. The giveaway could indicate some ulterior motive that the author certainly overlooks. The author assumes no such other motive exists, so the correct answer will contradict the author by suggesting one.

Step 4: Evaluate the Answer Choices

(D) indicates something the author didn't consider. Perhaps the product is ineffective, but the company offers it for "free" and then overcharges for shipping, making money from people who probably wouldn't buy it otherwise.

(A) is Out of Scope. Even if there are alternate sources of the same nutrients, this product could still work just fine.

(B) is an Irrelevant Comparison. The existence of other similar products does not change the idea that Activite could still work.

(C) is a Distortion. Even if the product is not *fully* effective in the first month, it could still be effective enough to encourage people to buy more and ultimately get its full effect. Besides this answer talks about *most* supplements. Activite could be a more effective exception.

(E) is Out of Scope. The potential existence of side effects does not affect whether or not the product works.

25. (A) Parallel Flaw

Step 1: Identify the Question Type

The correct answer will contain an argument "parallel to" the one in the stimulus. Furthermore, that reasoning is described as "flawed," so it's a Parallel Flaw question. The correct answer not only needs to have the same type of evidence and the same type of conclusion, but it also must commit the same error in connecting the two.

Step 2: Untangle the Stimulus

The stimulus presents information about a majority group: Most critics of the prime minister disapprove of increasing the income tax. One person, Theresa, approves of a higher income tax. *So* (an indicator of the conclusion), the author claims she probably approves of the prime minister.

Step 3: Make a Prediction

The problem here is that information is only given about people who *don't* approve of the prime minister's performance. Most of *them* disapprove of a higher income tax. But what about people who *do* approve of the prime minister's performance? They may not want a higher income tax, either. In that case, Theresa could hold a minority opinion as part of *either* group. The correct answer will commit the same error: Based on the opinion (don't raise income tax) of the majority of one group (most critics of the prime minister), the author wrongfully concludes that someone with the opposite opinion (it's okay to raise income tax) is probably not part of the original group (does not criticize the prime minister).

Step 4: Evaluate the Answer Choices

(A) matches the flawed logic piece by piece. Based on the opinion (logging will reduce the risk of fires) of the majority of one group (most supporters of logging), the author wrongfully concludes that someone with the opposite opinion (logging will *not* reduce the risk) is probably not part of the original group (does *not* support the logging).

(B) does have the majority of one group (most people who expect a population increase) expressing an opinion (a new school should be built). However, the idea that someone is not part of the original group is used as *evidence* rather than being the *conclusion*. The author does go on to commit a logical flaw, but it's not the same as the original.

(C) also has a majority of one group (most people who think the economy has improved) expressing an opinion (their own situation has improved). However, again, the idea that someone is not part of the original group is used as *evidence* rather than being the conclusion. Another flawed argument, but again not for the same reason as the stimulus.

(D) is not flawed. The person in this case (Donna) *is* part of the original group (people who oppose a study), so the author rightfully concludes that she *probably* holds the opinion of the majority of that group (build the freeway).

(E) has a different structure than the stimulus. The person in this case (Eduardo) *is* part of the original group (people who expect a blizzard). Not only is that not parallel, but there's an unwarranted shift from believing a weather report to merely seeing it.

26. (B) Strengthen

Step 1: Identify the Question Type

This question is very clear, directly asking for something to strengthen the argument. Find an answer that validates the assumption that links the author's evidence to the conclusion.

Step 2: Untangle the Stimulus

The author makes a conclusion right away: The decrease in mourning doves in an area was probably due to a loss of nesting sites. The evidence is that the doves started to disappear when sprinklers were installed in the orchards where the doves nested.

Step 3: Make a Prediction

There are two problems with this argument. The first is that the sprinklers were installed in the same orchard as the doves' nesting sites, but there's no indication that these sprinklers interfered with the nesting sites or caused them to be lost. The author assumes the sprinklers *did* interfere. The second problem is a classic case of correlation versus

causation. Doves started to decrease around the time that the sprinklers were installed around their nesting sites, but that doesn't mean the sprinklers *caused* the dove population to decrease. The author assumes they did. The correct answer will either show how the sprinklers affected the nesting sites or strengthen the connection between the sprinklers and population size.

Step 4: Evaluate the Answer Choices

(B) strengthens the assumption that the loss of nesting sites in the trees impacted the mourning dove population. If the mourning doves had plenty of other potential nesting sites, then the loss of the orchard should not have decreased their population. However, if the orchard had the *only* trees in the area that the doves were willing to nest in, then it is more likely that the installation of the sprinklers, and a potential proximate loss of nesting sites, decreased the local mourning dove population.

(A) is a 180. This weakens the argument by suggesting a different explanation for the bird's dwindling numbers—they're now being hunted.

(C) is Out of Scope. Even if another bird species ceased nesting in the orchard, that still leaves the same correlation versus causation issue unresolved. Maybe the sprinklers caused the decrease in numbers, but it may still have been an alternative cause.

(D) is Out of Scope. This suggests a reason why the mourning dove might *want* to stay in the area, but does nothing to support *why* they started to disappear.

(E) is a Distortion. Even if fruit trees (commonly found in orchards) are attractive, there's still no evidence that the sprinklers affected the nesting sites in those trees. Also, fruit trees could grow in areas other than orchards, making this answer ultimately irrelevant.

PrepTest 75

The Inside Story

PrepTest 75 was administered in June 2015. It challenged 23,238 test takers. What made this test so hard? Here's a breakdown of what Kaplan students who were surveyed after taking the official exam considered PrepTest 75's most difficult section.

Hardest PrepTest 75 Section as Reported by Test Takers

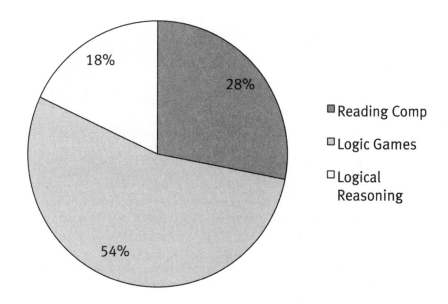

Based on these results, you might think that studying Logic Games is the key to LSAT success. Well, Logic Games is important, but test takers' perceptions don't tell the whole story. For that, you need to consider students' actual performance. The following chart shows the average number of students to miss each question in each of PrepTest 75's different sections.

Percentage Incorrect by PrepTest 75 Section Type

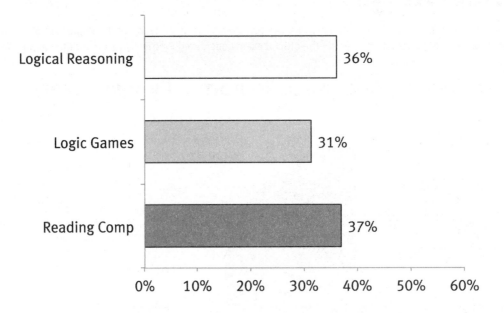

Actual student performance tells quite a different story. On average, students were almost equally likely to miss questions in all three of the different section types, and on PrepTest 75, Reading Comprehension and Logical Reasoning were somewhat higher than Logic Games in actual difficulty.

Maybe students overestimate the difficulty of the Logic Games section because it's so unusual, or maybe it's because a really hard Logic Game is so easy to remember after the test. But the truth is that the test maker places hard questions throughout the test. Here were the locations of the 10 hardest (most missed) questions in the exam.

Location of 10 Most Difficult Questions in PrepTest 75

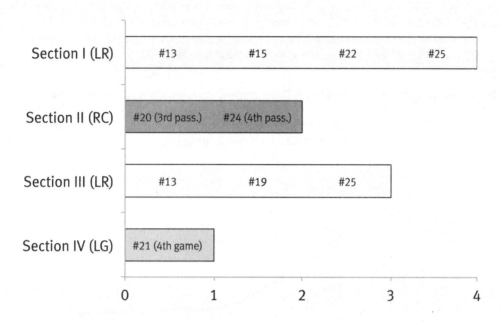

The takeaway from this data is that, to maximize your potential on the LSAT, you need to take a comprehensive approach. Test yourself rigorously, and review your performance on every section of the test. Kaplan's LSAT explanations provide the expertise and insight you need to fully understand your results. The explanations are written and edited by a team of LSAT experts, who have helped thousands of students improve their scores. Kaplan always provides data-driven analysis of the test, ranking the difficulty of every question based on actual student performance. The 10 hardest questions on every test are highlighted with a 4-star difficulty rating, the highest we give. The analysis breaks down the remaining questions into 1-, 2-, and 3-star ratings so that you can compare your performance to thousands of other test takers on all LSAC material.

Don't settle for wondering whether a question was really as hard as it seemed to you. Analyze the test with real data, and learn the secrets and strategies that help top scorers master the LSAT.

7 Can't–Miss Features of PrepTest 75

- This was the first PrepTest numbered in the "70s" with 100, rather than 101 questions.
- PrepTest 75 marked the first time since September 2007 (PT 53) that an LSAT was administered without any Strict Sequencing games, and it was only the third released LSAT ever to have two Distribution games.
- The fourth and final game on PrepTest 75—Business Newsletter—has an extremely rare feature: one entity that occupies two spaces. (Even the LSAT experts were talking about that one.)
- In Logical Reasoning, PrepTest 75 was the third consecutive LSAT with no Point at Issue questions.
- PrepTest 75 was the only test released in 2014–2015 in which no Reading Comprehension passage had eight questions.
- Test takers who made good predictions in Reading Comprehension saved a lot of time reading through answers. Only 7 of the 27 answers in RC were (D) or (E).
- The #1 song in the country when PrepTest 75 was released was Wiz Khalifa's "See You Again" from the *Furious 7* soundtrack. LSAT students know you need to be fast *and* furious on this test.

PrepTest 75 in Context

As much fun as it is to find out what makes a PrepTest unique or noteworthy, it's even more important to know just how representative it is of other LSAT administrations (and, thus, how likely it is to be representative of the exam you will face on Test Day). The following charts compare the numbers of each kind of question and game on PrepTest 75 to the average numbers seen on all officially released LSATs administered over the past five years (from 2012 through 2016).

Number of LR Questions by Type: PrepTest 75 vs. 2012–2016 Average

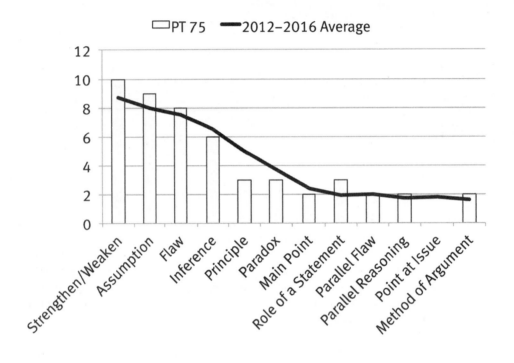

Number of LG Games by Type: PrepTest 75 vs. 2012–2016 Average

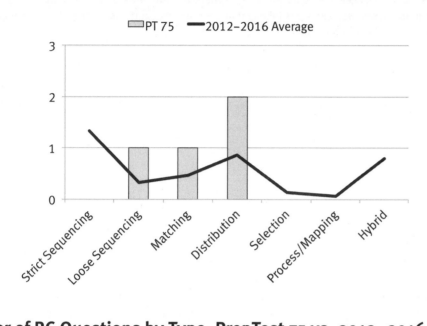

Number of RC Questions by Type: PrepTest 75 vs. 2012–2016 Average

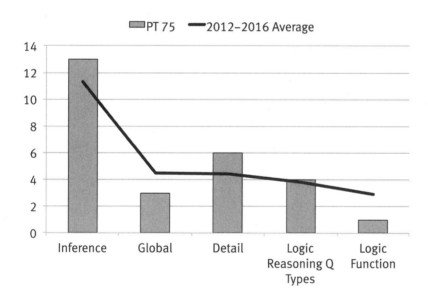

There isn't usually a huge difference in the distribution of questions from LSAT to LSAT, but if this test seems harder (or easier) to you than another you've taken, compare the number of questions of the types on which you, personally, are strongest and weakest. And then, explore within each section to see if your best or worst question types came earlier or later.

Students in Kaplan's comprehensive LSAT courses have access to every released LSAT and to an online Q-Bank with thousands of officially released questions, games, and passages. If you are studying on your own, you have to do a bit more work to identify your strengths and your areas of opportunity. Quantitative analysis (like that in the previous charts) is an important tool for understanding how the test is constructed and how you are performing on it.

Section I: Logical Reasoning

Q#	Question Type	Correct	Difficulty
1	Assumption (Necessary)	B	★
2	Principle (Identify/Strengthen)	C	★
3	Assumption (Necessary)	A	★
4	Method of Argument	E	★★
5	Weaken	C	★
6	Paradox	D	★★
7	Flaw	E	★
8	Main Point	C	★
9	Strengthen	A	★
10	Principle (Identify/Strengthen)	E	★
11	Weaken	D	★★
12	Flaw	D	★★
13	Inference	C	★★★★
14	Role of a Statement	A	★
15	Strengthen	C	★★★★
16	Role of a Statement	C	★
17	Inference	D	★★★
18	Flaw	B	★★
19	Paradox	B	★
20	Inference	E	★★
21	Strengthen	B	★★★
22	Parallel Flaw	C	★★★★
23	Assumption (Sufficient)	C	★★★
24	Flaw	E	★★★
25	Parallel Reasoning	A	★★★★

1. (B) Assumption (Necessary)

Step 1: Identify the Question Type

This is a Necessary Assumption question because it asks for the assumption that the argument *requires*.

Step 2: Untangle the Stimulus

The pundit concludes that the city erred when it sold the right to assess parking fees to a private company. The evidence is that the private company has made huge profits from raising parking fees—profits that the pundit says could have gone to the city.

Step 3: Make a Prediction

In order for the pundit's conclusion to be valid, one has to assume that the city had the same capacity as the private company to raise parking fees.

Step 4: Evaluate the Answer Choices

(B) matches this prediction perfectly. Remember that on Necessary Assumption questions, the Denial Test is a great way to double-check your answer or to evaluate an answer choice if prediction is tough. In this case, to deny (B) would be to say that the city *could not* have raised parking fees had it not sold away the rights. If that's the case, the city would never have seen that extra money, and the pundit's argument is in jeopardy.

(A) is Outside the Scope. The pundit is concerned with whether or not the city made a mistake to sell the rights at all, not with how many companies were willing to pay for those rights.

(C) is Extreme. It broadens the issue to say *all* municipal functions "should always" be handled by the municipality. However, the pundit's argument focuses specifically on one function, so (C) doesn't have to be true for the argument to work.

(D) is not necessary for the argument to be valid. Using the Denial Test, even if the revenue from parking fees *is* the only factor to consider when setting rates, the pundit can still argue that it was a mistake for the city to privatize parking fee collection. After all, in the pundit's case, the only consideration was about how much revenue the private companies have been able to raise.

(E) is Outside the Scope. The relative efficiency of private companies versus city officials when it comes to parking fees is not at issue.

2. (C) Principle (Identify/Strengthen)

Step 1: Identify the Question Type

The phrase "[w]hich one of the following principles" identifies this as an Identify the Principle question. Furthermore, "justify the reasoning" indicates that the correct answer will be a broadly stated principle that strengthens the argument.

Step 2: Untangle the Stimulus

The argument's conclusion is signaled by *therefore*: popular science publications should stop trying to reach a wide audience with their explanations of new scientific developments. The evidence describes a dilemma: when these publications try to reach wide audiences, they skimp on scientific accuracy. When they aim for more scientific rigor, they succeed but lose their broad appeal.

Step 3: Make a Prediction

In order for its recommendation to be valid, the argument assumes that getting the science right is a more important goal to achieve than appealing to a broad swath of the public. The correct answer will be a general principle supporting this.

Step 4: Evaluate the Answer Choices

(C) is worded in the negative, but says the exact same thing as the prediction.

(A) could help publications reconcile the goal of reaching a wide audience with that of staying scientifically accurate, but the author recommends disregarding wide audiences altogether.

(B) doesn't affect the argument. The author argues against trying to reach wide audiences because doing so risks getting the science wrong, not because doing so is merely difficult. How recent the science is is not mentioned.

(D) is a 180 because it weakens the author's argument in favor of abandoning the goal of reaching a wide audience.

(E) misses the point of the argument. The excessive use of metaphor in science publications often muddies the science, but the author isn't arguing for or against the abandonment of metaphors entirely, so (E) doesn't strengthen the reasoning.

3. (A) Assumption (Necessary)

Step 1: Identify the Question Type

This is a Necessary Assumption question because it seeks an assumption "on which the critic's argument relies."

Step 2: Untangle the Stimulus

The critic bleakly concludes that rock music no longer has anything going for it. The evidence is that rock music has always been bad, both musically and socially, but at least back in the LP era, album covers featured distinctive visual art. Nowadays, though, the success of digital music has all but eliminated LPs.

Step 3: Make a Prediction

The critic assumes that innovative visual art disappeared along with the old LP covers. The correct answer will paraphrase this idea.

Step 4: Evaluate the Answer Choices

(A) is therefore correct. Applying the Denial Test, if digital music *is* actually distributed with accompanying innovative visual art, then rock music does still have at least one positive feature, and the critic's argument is impaired.

(B) is a 180. It goes against the argument by suggesting that rock LPs, which feature innovative visual art, are still being mass-produced.

(C) is Extreme. It doesn't have to be true that rock LPs were the only LPs to contain innovative album cover art. Even if other genres also had innovative art, the critic could still speak highly of those rock albums that had it, too.

(D) doesn't have to be true for the critic's argument to be valid. Even if today's LPs do not have innovative album cover art, the critic can still argue that rock music has nothing to recommend it these days.

(E) is an Irrelevant Comparison. The critic says that rock music is currently "musically bankrupt and socially destructive," so it doesn't need to be true that rock music was even worse in the past for the argument to work.

4. (E) Method of Argument

Step 1: Identify the Question Type
This is a Method of Argument question because it asks you to determine "how the ... argument proceeds."

Step 2: Untangle the Stimulus
The scientist concludes that babbling is a linguistic task. The evidence is a study in which researchers set out to determine whether babbling was a linguistic task or just random sounds. Their results were the opposite of those one would expect for nonlinguistic vocalizations, so babbling must therefore be a linguistic task.

Step 3: Make a Prediction
On Method of Argument questions, focus on what the argument *does*, not on the specifics of what it says. Here, the scientist establishes the argument's conclusion by presenting a scientific observation and then ruling out one of two competing explanations for the observation, thereby settling on the other explanation.

Step 4: Evaluate the Answer Choices
(E) is therefore correct.

(A) doesn't take into account any of the experimental evidence presented, and the scientist never makes any counterarguments in order to disprove anything.

(B) would be correct if the scientist said that researchers started out assuming that babbling was a nonlinguistic task, but no such principle was held as true by the researchers prior to their experiment.

(C) is a Distortion. The scientist does describe an experiment used to answer a question, but the point of the argument is not to establish that the experiment was *necessary* to answer the question. The scientist merely uses the experiment as evidence to draw a larger conclusion.

(D) is partially correct in that the scientist does present an explanation. However, the scientist never mentions anyone's assertions that the explanation is "unlikely to be correct," let alone counters them.

5. (C) Weaken

Step 1: Identify the Question Type
The phrase "weaken the ... argument" is a clear indication of a Weaken question.

Step 2: Untangle the Stimulus
The environment minister's conclusion is that planting lots of trees will help the country fulfill its commitment to reducing carbon dioxide emissions over the next decade. The evidence is that trees absorb carbon dioxide.

Step 3: Make a Prediction
In order for the environment minister's prediction to come true, planting trees would have to absorb more carbon dioxide than it releases. Otherwise, the relative amount of carbon dioxide in the atmosphere would increase. Therefore, the argument is weakened by anything suggesting that planting trees can actually increase carbon dioxide emissions.

Step 4: Evaluate the Answer Choices
(C), if true, weakens the argument by suggesting that planting trees could increase the overall amount of carbon dioxide.

(A) doesn't weaken the argument. Nothing in the minister's reasoning indicates that the government wouldn't be able to financially incentivize landowners to give up their land for tree planting. Alternatively, they could just plant the trees on public land.

(B) would affect the argument if you knew how much deforested land would need to be replanted with trees to absorb a given amount of carbon dioxide. Without this information though, **(B)** isn't a weakener.

(D) is Outside the Scope because the minister is specifically concerned with how the country can fulfill the commitment it has made, which is to reduce carbon dioxide emissions in the 10 years allotted. Whether different commitments would be better is immaterial.

(E) is Outside the Scope. The country has committed itself to combating global warming by decreasing its carbon dioxide output. Other gases are therefore irrelevant to the fulfillment of that commitment.

6. (D) Paradox

Step 1: Identify the Question Type
If a question stem asks for the answer choice that "most helps to account for" a given phenomenon or discrepancy, it's a Paradox question.

Step 2: Untangle the Stimulus

The stimulus describes a contradiction concerning SUV safety. In an accident, SUVs, though expensive, are safer for their occupants than are smaller vehicles. However, auto safety experts still conclude that the rising popularity of SUVs is cause for concern.

Step 3: Make a Prediction

You don't have to have a hard-and-fast prediction for Paradox questions. But you do need to know how to spot the correct answer when you come to it. In this case, the correct answer will explain why auto safety experts are still alarmed despite the popularity of vehicles that are relatively safer.

Step 4: Evaluate the Answer Choices

(D) explains the discrepancy by suggesting that SUV-involved collisions produce more fatalities generally. In other words, the SUV occupants are safer, but it's now the people in the smaller vehicles that are in more danger.

(A) is a 180. It deepens the paradox because it suggests that SUV owners will drive more carefully, which should relieve auto safety experts, not unnerve them.

(B) is Outside the Scope. It introduces the idea of fuel consumption, which doesn't come up at all in the stimulus.

(C) doesn't explain the paradox because it suggests that more people will be riding in safer vehicles. If that's the case, why the alarm? Unless an increase in passenger numbers indicates an increase in danger, this choice doesn't explain the safety experts' alarm.

(E) doesn't account for the experts' concern because, on balance, SUVs are safer cars, so knowing that they are equally as likely as smaller vehicles to be involved in collisions shouldn't necessarily cause alarm.

7. (E) Flaw

Step 1: Identify the Question Type

This is a Flaw question because it asks how the argument is "vulnerable to criticism." Find the conclusion, evidence, and assumption, then note the disconnect in the reasoning.

Step 2: Untangle the Stimulus

The political advertisement is firmly against Sherwood's bid for reelection to city council. Sherwood apparently campaigns against higher taxes, but while Sherwood was on the city council, the council voted to raise taxes. Therefore, the argument says, Sherwood should be defeated at the polls.

Step 3: Make a Prediction

This argument commits the classic fallacy of division, which is just a fancy way of saying that it imputes a characteristic of a whole to each of its constituent parts. In this case, it can certainly be true that Sherwood voted against higher taxes but was just outvoted by her colleagues.

Step 4: Evaluate the Answer Choices

(E) accurately states the advertisement's logical flaw.

(A) is almost a 180. The political advertisement draws a conclusion about a specific person based on a more general assertion about a collective to which that person belongs. Conversely, **(A)** suggests that the argument makes a broader generalization on a specific instance.

(B) would be relevant if the advertisement suggested that higher taxes were somehow unavoidable. But whether or not higher taxes can be avoided doesn't figure into the argument.

(C) describes the common Formal Logic flaw of necessity versus sufficiency. However, no Formal Logic is involved in this argument.

(D) describes an ad hominem attack, but the advertisement doesn't target Sherwood's character. Rather, the advertisement assumes that Sherwood must have taken the same actions taken by the city council as a whole.

8. (C) Main Point

Step 1: Identify the Question Type

Any question stem asking you to find the "main conclusion" of an argument is a Main Point question.

Step 2: Untangle the Stimulus

On a Main Point question, the entire task is to determine an argument's conclusion. Therefore, you're unlikely to find those helpful Keywords that point directly to conclusions in the stimuli for other question types. Instead, look for a strong statement of the author's point of view and use the One-Sentence Test to find the single sentence the client would insist on in making that point.

Step 3: Make a Prediction

The client's point of view comes in the third sentence. The catering company has decided to raise its rates, arguing that their expanding client base has necessitated hiring new staff. But the client concludes that the catering company should reconsider. The last sentence is support for the conclusion: raising rates, in the client's view, would compromise the company's mission to provide low-cost catering.

Step 4: Evaluate the Answer Choices

(C) is a match for this prediction.

(A) restates the first sentence of the argument, but this is merely background information on which the client bases the argument.

(B) is a 180. The client clearly argues that the catering company should *not* raise its rates.

(D) is evidence that the client uses to support the claim that the company shouldn't increase its rates.

(E), like **(D)**, is support for the client's conclusion, and not the conclusion itself.

9. (A) Strengthen

Step 1: Identify the Question Type

The phrase "strengthens the support for the … hypothesis" indicates a Strengthen question.

Step 2: Untangle the Stimulus

The scientists hypothesize that the erratic flight style of the red admiral butterfly evolved to help them avoid predators. Their evidence is that because the red admiral is not poisonous, it needed to evolve other means of avoiding predators in order to survive.

Step 3: Make a Prediction

In order for the scientists to reach their hypothesis, they assume that the red admiral's flight style didn't evolve for any other reason than to avoid predators. They further assume that poisonous species of butterfly don't also have the same irregular flight style. The correct answer will validate either of these assumptions.

Step 4: Evaluate the Answer Choices

(A), if true, strengthens the argument by suggesting that poisonous butterflies, which predators already avoid, don't need an irregular flight style. It's therefore more likely that the flight style developed to help avoid predators. **(A)** doesn't prove the conclusion, but it does make it more likely.

(B) doesn't affect the argument because other causes of death for butterflies are Outside the Scope.

(C) doesn't strengthen the argument unless you know that those other species with the same flight pattern have developed those flight patterns to avoid predators. Simply knowing that other species have the same flight style as the red admiral doesn't explain why that style evolved.

(D) is an Irrelevant Comparison. How other varieties of insects behave doesn't matter unless it helps indicate whether the irregular flight pattern evolved as a means to avoid predators. **(D)** may even weaken the argument if it is suggesting that the red admiral's flight style evolved to conserve energy rather than to help them avoid predators.

(E) is Outside the Scope because the scientists don't assume that the red admiral's predators feed exclusively on the red admiral.

10. (E) Principle (Identify/Strengthen)

Step 1: Identify the Question Type

This is an Identify the Principle question in which the correct answer will be a broadly stated rule that "supports the reasoning," or strengthens the argument.

Step 2: Untangle the Stimulus

The author argues that copyright statutes grant copyright protections for too long a period of time. The support for this conclusion is that the cost to society of granting additional

years of copyright (the creation of protected monopolies) exceeds the benefit (the incentive to produce original works).

Step 3: Make a Prediction

To strengthen this argument, the argument assumes that society should adopt statutes that produce societal benefits larger than their societal costs. The correct answer will be a broad principle that restates this idea.

Step 4: Evaluate the Answer Choices

(E) is therefore correct.

(A) is Outside the Scope because the argument concerns the effects of copyright statutes, not their aims. Furthermore, the statutes as written do not have *inconsistent* aims. They are set up to benefit society and encourage people to create original works. The author just thinks they provide too much benefit, as written, and thus have the unintended consequence of having a societal cost.

(B) doesn't strengthen the argument because the author never points to any changing conditions that impact whether or not copyright statutes are still justified.

(C) is Outside the Scope of the argument. The author doesn't argue for expanding copyright statutes to all countries; rather, the author argues that those countries that have adopted such statutes grant protections for too long a period.

(D) is also Outside the Scope. The author relies on a societal cost-benefit analysis to support the reasoning; the argument doesn't trade on whether or not copyright laws limit or enhance individual *rights*.

11. (D) Weaken

Step 1: Identify the Question Type

The phrase "calls into question" indicates a Weaken question.

Step 2: Untangle the Stimulus

The police chief concludes that his policing strategy has decreased crime in the city by 20 percent. The strategy boasts real-time crime data and an allocation of resources to the areas with the highest crime rates.

Step 3: Make a Prediction

Causal arguments such as this one are very common in Logical Reasoning, particularly in Strengthen and Weaken questions. Here, the chief notices an effect (the decline in the city's crime rate) and argues for a cause (the chief's own policing strategy). To weaken a causal argument, find an answer choice that suggests an alternative cause.

Step 4: Evaluate the Answer Choices

(D) provides that alternative cause by associating the city's decreasing crime rate with an overall decline in crime nationwide. The police chief surely didn't implement the strategy throughout the whole country, so the strategy may not be responsible for the city's lower crime rate.

(A) is an Irrelevant Comparison. Even if the city's crime rate is still relatively high, it can still be lower than it once was thanks to the chief's strategy.

(B) is also an Irrelevant Comparison because the argument is restricted to the chief's own tenure and the rates immediately before the chief started. It doesn't incorporate any other periods—certainly not from decades earlier.

(C) is not a valid weakener because it's not relevant to the argument to know when exactly during the chief's tenure the crime rate decreased. Perhaps the strategy was implemented quickly and successfully, and that's why it has since leveled off. In that case, **(C)** could be seen as a strengthener.

(E) is an Irrelevant Comparison because the chief is making an argument about the city as a whole. The relative crime rates of different parts of that city don't figure into the argument.

12. (D) Flaw

Step 1: Identify the Question Type
Because the question stem indicates that the commentator's argument is already "vulnerable to criticism," this is a Flaw question.

Step 2: Untangle the Stimulus
The commentator concludes that the Duke of Acredia was correct in asserting that concern for the people's welfare is necessary for good governance.

If	successful governance	→	concern for the welfare of the people

The evidence is that the fall of Acredian governments *always* coincided with the rule of leaders who disregarded the people's welfare.

If	~ successful governance	→	~ concern for the welfare of the people

Step 3: Make a Prediction
The word *necessary* in the argument's conclusion may have tipped you off to the flaw that the commentator commits. In his conclusion, the commentator makes the mistake of negating without reversing. The evidence says that when governments have fallen, the rulers have *always* "viciously disregarded the people's needs." The commentator mistakes a sufficient condition with a necessary one.

Step 4: Evaluate the Answer Choices
(D) accurately describes this flaw.

(A) is a Distortion. The argument doesn't concern the conditions necessary for the welfare of the people; the argument concerns one condition the commentator claims is necessary for successful governance of the people.

(B) comes close, but goes wrong when it alleges that the commentator's inference is based on the fact that the absence of concern for the people's welfare has always *led to* failure. The evidence doesn't describe causation. Instead, the evidence says "when ... governments have fallen," their falls have always been when rulers were not concerned with the people. So, the evidence *does* set up Formal Logic, but not in the order of a causal relationship in which the lack of care *caused* the government's failure.

(C) is not the argument's flaw because the commentator gives no information about the sources used to gather the argument's evidence.

(E) is incorrect because the commentator isn't doing anything nearly as broad as assessing the character of past leaders. Moreover, even if the argument were to assess these leaders' character with words such as *concerned* or *vicious*, it doesn't pretend to do so using an objective standard.

13. (C) Inference

Step 1: Identify the Question Type
This is an Inference question because it asks for the answer choice "most supported by [the] statements."

Step 2: Untangle the Stimulus
Dr. Khan starts by sharing a discrepancy: recent observations of the solar system don't confirm earlier ones, which showed the presence of a comet reservoir. Professor Burns infers from this discrepancy that the earlier observations must therefore be incorrect. However, the recent observations happened under poor conditions.

Step 3: Make a Prediction
Determine what must be true from Dr. Khan's statements. If the recent observations occurred under poor conditions, then any conclusions based on those observations would be called into question. Therefore, Professor Burns may be rash in tossing out the earlier observations based solely on newer ones that could be untrustworthy.

Step 4: Evaluate the Answer Choices
(C) is therefore a valid inference.

(A) can't be inferred. It doesn't have to be true that the recent observations would have definitely confirmed the earlier ones had they been carried out under better conditions.

(B) is a Distortion. The recent observations don't have to confirm the earlier ones; Dr. Khan is simply implying that Professor Burns is wrong to claim that the recent observations invalidate the earlier ones.

(D) isn't a valid inference. For all we know, Dr. Khan may believe that the recent observations, if made under better conditions, *would* be enough to invalidate the earlier ones. But since the recent observations were made under poor conditions, we'll never know.

(E) is Extreme. Dr. Khan doesn't imply that the recent observations are *worthless*. The poor conditions under which the recent observations were made are not sufficient to throw out the earlier observations, but that doesn't mean the recent observations might not have some other value.

14. (A) Role of a Statement

Step 1: Identify the Question Type

This is a Role of a Statement question because it asks you to determine the "role played in the argument" by a particular claim.

Step 2: Untangle the Stimulus

The author begins by conceding a point: society would improve if people avoided impoliteness. The word [*b*]*ut* beginning the second sentence signals the author's point of view: despite the earlier point, society would not be served by laws mandating politeness. The last sentence provides support: enforcing those laws would create more problems than would impoliteness.

Step 3: Make a Prediction

The sentence in question is the author's main point, or conclusion. The first sentence provides background, and the last sentence is evidence.

Step 4: Evaluate the Answer Choices

(A) is therefore correct.

(B) is a 180. It's the last sentence that serves as evidence to support the author's conclusion.

(C) is two steps removed. The claim in question is the author's main point, one that the rest of the argument is designed to support.

(D) is incorrect because the statement in question is itself the main conclusion. It is neither a premise of the argument, nor an illustration of such. In fact, the whole argument speaks in generalizations; there are no specific illustrations.

(E) is incorrect because the author never describes a phenomenon in the argument. Rather, each sentence of the argument describes a hypothetical situation. **(E)** also indicates the claim in question is not the conclusion, when in fact it is.

15. (C) Strengthen

Step 1: Identify the Question Type

The phrase "strengthen the ... argument" is a clear indication of a Strengthen question.

Step 2: Untangle the Stimulus

Don't be thrown by the scientific subject matter. This argument, like many others, attempts to explain a phenomenon. In this case, the phenomenon is the oval orbits of most planets that revolve around distant stars. This is contrasted with planets in our solar system, several of which have circular orbits. However, the astronomer notes that comets with oval orbits in our solar system got those orbits through encounters with planets within the same solar system. Therefore, says the astronomer, those distant planets probably acquired their oval orbits in the same way.

Step 3: Make a Prediction

The astronomer assumes that just because at least some comets in our solar system with oval orbits acquired those orbits through encounters with other objects, the same must be true of planets with oval orbits around distant stars. In other words, the author assumes that the same conditions causing the oval orbits of comets are present for planets orbiting distant stars. The correct answer will validate this assumption.

Step 4: Evaluate the Answer Choices

(C) strengthens the argument by indicating that there are indeed other planets that the planets in oval orbits could have encountered. **(C)** doesn't prove that the astronomer is correct, but it makes the conclusion more likely to be true.

(A) references the relative size of planets, which doesn't figure into the argument. You don't know from the argument whether the planets thrown into oval orbits are usually the smaller ones. Knowing which object would adjust its orbit doesn't make it any more likely that the oval orbits of distant planets were actually caused by close encounters with other planets.

(B) doesn't affect the astronomer's argument, which is concerned with whether encounters with other planets render a planet's orbit oval in shape. Even if some of the planets orbiting our sun do have oval orbits, there's no information in **(B)** indicating what caused those oval orbits, so **(B)** can't be a strengthener.

(D) helps to confirm a piece of the astronomer's evidence—that comets *can* change to oval orbits based on close encounters with other objects—but it doesn't help validate the conclusion the astronomer draws about the planets orbiting distant stars.

(E) is a 180. It weakens the argument by suggesting that no other objects could have affected the orbit of planets surrounding a distant star, even though we know most of those distant planets have an oval orbit.

16. (C) Role of a Statement

Step 1: Identify the Question Type

A question stem asking you to determine the "role played in the argument" by any claim is a Role of a Statement question.

Step 2: Untangle the Stimulus

The argument's conclusion comes in the second sentence: irrigating crops with seawater would be cheaper than most other irrigated agriculture if the crops were grown near oceans. The evidence is threefold: The water used in such irrigation would not have to be pumped far. The greatest expense in irrigated agriculture comes from pumping the water, and such expenses increase with the distance the water is pumped.

Step 3: Make a Prediction

The claim in question, that the greatest expense in irrigated agriculture is in pumping the water, is given in support of the conclusion that irrigating crops with seawater is cheaper if the crops are grown near oceans. Simply put, the claim is one of the pieces of evidence.

Step 4: Evaluate the Answer Choices

(C) is therefore correct.

(A) is incorrect because there are no claims in the argument that the author disproves.

(B) is a 180. Not only is the statement question not held out as a hypothesis, but it supports the argument's conclusion rather than undermining it.

(D) is incorrect because the argument's conclusion is the conditional prediction in the second sentence. The claim in question is a fact supporting that prediction.

(E) describes a subsidiary conclusion. **(E)** is correct in that the claim in question is not the argument's conclusion. However, the argument provides no evidence to support the idea that pumping water is the greatest expense in irrigated agriculture.

17. (D) Inference

Step 1: Identify the Question Type

This is an Inference question because it asks you to accept the stimulus (the "statements above") as true, and then determine which answer choice they "most strongly support."

Step 2: Untangle the Stimulus

The stimulus outlines a worry of critics: gloomy news about the economy decreases public confidence in the economy, of which everyone has direct daily experience. Journalists can't be concerned, though, with the effects of their work if they're to do that work well. Further, people don't turn to journalists unless it's on a matter of which they have no direct experience.

Step 3: Make a Prediction

On Inference questions, try to link statements together to see if a prediction emerges naturally. People don't defer to journalists on matters they directly experience. Because everyone has direct daily experience with the economy, it must be true that people don't defer to journalists when it comes to reports on the economy.

Step 4: Evaluate the Answer Choices

(D) is a good paraphrase of this inference.

(A) is a Distortion. The critics may very well be right that people's confidence in the economy has an effect on it, but the stimulus is more concerned with the critics' worry about the effects of bleak news reports on the economy. Those news reports aren't affecting people's confidence, but their confidence may still be affecting the economy.

(B) is a Distortion. The stimulus suggests that people aren't terribly affected by bad news reports on matters of which they have direct experience, but that doesn't mean that the critics' worry carries over to matters like foreign policy, of which people don't have daily experience. In that case, the news reports *may* affect people's foreign policy views, but perhaps the impact of people's mood on foreign policy is not discernible.

(C) restates the critics' worry, but that doesn't mean that the worry must be valid. If anything, this is a 180 because the author's statements, taken together, indicate that the worry might be unfounded.

(E) paraphrases the journalists' view, but that doesn't mean that this view is valid. It could still be true that journalists *should* be concerned about the effects of their work; this stimulus is merely suggesting that those effects aren't significant when it comes to people's perceptions of the economy.

18. (B) Flaw

Step 1: Identify the Question Type

Any question stem asking you to determine why an argument is "vulnerable to criticism" is a Flaw question.

Step 2: Untangle the Stimulus

The police captain rejects recent claims that there's graft in her precinct. The evidence for this is that the chief of police has indicated that gifts over $100 in value qualify as graft, and no such gifts have exchanged hands within the precinct.

Step 3: Make a Prediction

This would be a solid argument as long as gifts over $100 in value are the *only* possible instances of graft. The police chief never indicated that, however; the captain merely assumed it. The definition of graft could be large enough to encompass many different actions, some of which may have occurred at the precinct in question.

Step 4: Evaluate the Answer Choices

(B) is a good paraphrase for this overlooked possibility.

(A) is not the flaw because there's no "limited sample." The police captain accounts for every single officer in the precinct, and the accusations of graft are focused only on that precinct.

(C) is Outside the Scope. The captain's rebuttal focuses only on certain actions that the officers in the precinct did not take. No appeal is made to their character as individuals.

(D) is also Outside the Scope because it widens the focus of the argument to corruption, but the captain's argument focuses only on graft.

(E) is incorrect because the problem with the argument is that the evidence isn't enough to establish the conclusion, not that the evidence and conclusion contradict each other.

19. (B) Paradox

Step 1: Identify the Question Type

The phrase "most helps to resolve the apparent paradox" indicates a Paradox question.

Step 2: Untangle the Stimulus

In each region of the economist's country, the average full-time hourly wage went up last year. However, for the country as a whole, the same average wage decreased over the same time period.

Step 3: Make a Prediction

Perhaps more jobs were added in lower-paying regions of the country as compared to higher-paying regions. Whatever occurred, the correct answer has to explain how the country's overall average full-time hourly wage decreased despite an increase in that average wage for each region.

Step 4: Evaluate the Answer Choices

(B) resolves the paradox. If employers moved more jobs from higher-paying regions of the country to lower-paying regions, then there were fewer jobs at the highest earning levels, thereby depressing the overall hourly wage.

(A) means that the decrease in the overall full-time hourly wage is part of a three-year trend, but that doesn't explain the contradiction with the increase in last year's regional average.

(C) doesn't explain the discrepancy because it's Outside the Scope. The unemployment rate doesn't have a strong enough relationship to the average full-time hourly wage.

(D) comes close to explaining the discrepancy, but it needs to demonstrate that the higher-paying regions saw a smaller rate of wage growth than did the lower-paying regions.

(E), in order to resolve the paradox, would require us to know the relative distribution and frequency of manufacturing jobs versus service sector jobs. The stimulus doesn't provide this information.

20. (E) Inference

Step 1: Identify the Question Type

This is an Inference question because it asks for the "conclusion … most strongly supported by the information." This means that the right answer must be true given the stimulus.

Step 2: Untangle the Stimulus

In a comparison of the brains of recently deceased people with schizophrenia to those of recently deceased people without the disorder, a significant percentage of the former showed damage to a brain structure. This damage must have occurred while these people's brains were developing in utero.

Step 3: Make a Prediction

Putting all these statements together, the stimulus suggests that prenatal damage to a structure of the brain could contribute to the development of schizophrenia later in life.

Step 4: Evaluate the Answer Choices

(E) is therefore correct. Note the qualified language of this answer choice. The stimulus doesn't prove that prenatal damage to the subplate causes schizophrenia, but it certainly *may be* a cause.

(A) is Extreme. It extrapolates the statistical results of the study to the population at large, but without a whole lot more information, you can't determine that **(A)** "will eventually" be true.

(B) moves Outside the Scope from potential causes of schizophrenia to effective treatments, a leap that doesn't sustain a valid inference. No information is given regarding whether the subplate can be repaired, and even if it can, that the outlook for that treatment is *promising*.

(C) isn't supported by the stimulus, which only discusses subplate damage that occurred before the second fetal trimester. After that point, the stimulus doesn't provide any information to infer **(C)**.

(D) is Outside the Scope. It's safe to say from the stimulus that prenatal damage to the subplate could contribute to schizophrenia, but that doesn't necessarily mean that such damage has to arise from genetic factors.

21. (B) Strengthen

Step 1: Identify the Question Type

The phrase "support the prediction" indicates a Strengthen question.

Step 2: Untangle the Stimulus

The device's maker predicts that ranchers will buy the GPS device at its current price. This prediction comes despite the fact that outfitting all the cattle in a herd with the device is far costlier than other means of restricting cattle movement. The device works by making noises in a cow's ears when it strays outside its pasture.

Step 3: Make a Prediction

In order to strengthen the argument, the correct answer must make the prediction more likely to come true. In this case, ranchers need to be incentivized to purchase a device that's more expensive. The correct answer will describe some benefit of the new GPS device that outweighs its cost.

Step 4: Evaluate the Answer Choices

(B) supports the prediction by suggesting that only a few cattle need to be outfitted with the new GPS device. If the right few cattle are outfitted, then the rest of the herd will follow them back to the home range when the device is triggered, and ranchers don't need to shell out lots of money to outfit the whole herd.

(A) doesn't affect the argument because the device's maker predicts that ranchers will buy the device "at its current price," not at the promise of some future lower price.

(C) removes one possible objection to buying the device (animal cruelty), but **(C)** still doesn't make it any more likely that ranchers will fork over the extra money for the device.

(D) equates the device's effectiveness with that of fences, but because fences remain cheaper, **(D)** doesn't support the prediction that ranchers will buy the new device at the higher price.

(E), like **(A)**, introduces a condition that could lower the price of the device, but the device's maker predicts sales "at its current price."

22. (C) Parallel Flaw

Step 1: Identify the Question Type

This is a Parallel Flaw question because the reasoning in the stimulus is flawed, and the correct answer choice will be an analogous argument with the same flawed reasoning.

Step 2: Untangle the Stimulus

The Keyword *therefore* signals the conclusion: it's more economical to shop at a food co-op than at a supermarket. The evidence is that food co-ops are a type of consumer cooperative, and consumer cooperatives usually offer the same products as other stores but at cheaper prices.

Step 3: Make a Prediction

Notice the word *usually* in the stimulus. Consumer cooperatives *usually* offer cheaper products than other stores do, but not always. So, it could just as easily be true that food co-ops are unusually expensive or that supermarkets are unusually cheap. Put simply, the correct answer choice will compare a member of category A to a member of category B on the basis of what is *usually* (but not necessarily *always*) true about the categories as a whole.

Step 4: Evaluate the Answer Choices

(C) matches the stimulus exactly. Members of category A (users of private transportation) "tend to generate more pollution per mile" than category B (users of public transportation). However, to conclude that every member of category A (e.g., bicyclists) creates more pollution per mile than every member of category B (e.g., public bus users) is flawed in the same way as the stimulus.

(A) would need to be different in two ways to be parallel. If it concluded that a specific sports car used more gasoline *per mile* than another car that wasn't a sports car, then it would be parallel. But **(A)** doesn't delineate specific members of its categories, and it draws a conclusion about total gas usage based on evidence about gas usage per mile. Thus, it doesn't match the conclusion in the stimulus.

(B) fails on several points. First, **(B)**'s evidence doesn't say that frozen vegetables are *usually* better than fresh vegetables in those respects—there needs to be a qualifier like the one in the stimulus. Additionally, to be parallel it would need to have brought up individual members of each group rather than focus on the groups themselves. Finally, **(B)** brings up an additional consideration (spoilage) to determine which type of vegetable is *better*, whereas the stimulus focuses on just cost in the conclusion and evidence. So, to fix those issues, a parallel statement would be that it was *cheaper* (not better) to buy a frozen eggplant than to buy a fresh tomato, since fresh vegetables are *usually* more expensive than frozen ones.

(D) entirely misses the stimulus's assumption that a member of a group can be definitely compared to a member of another group based on a comparison that usually holds true.

(E) states its conclusion as a superlative ("the best way to lose weight") rather than comparing two alternative ways of losing weight in the same way that the stimulus compares two food stores. Also like **(B)**, there is no qualifier similar to *usually* in **(E)**'s evidence.

23. (C) Assumption (Sufficient)

Step 1: Identify the Question Type

This is a Sufficient Assumption question because the editorial's conclusion will follow logically *if* the correct answer is assumed.

Step 2: Untangle the Stimulus

The editorial concludes that it's wrong to blame the railroad company, even in part, for accidents that occur when drivers go around the gates that bar them from crossing railroad tracks. The evidence proceeds by making a distinction between this situation, in which licensed drivers are adults capable of higher decision-making, and a situation in which one has a duty to keep a small child from endangerment.

Step 3: Make a Prediction

The evidence says drivers are adults who should know better, and the conclusion says that these drivers therefore can't blame the railroad company for accidents. This conclusion is fully established if it's true that capable adults who willfully go around protective gates are completely responsible for any ensuing accidents.

Step 4: Evaluate the Answer Choices

(C) is therefore correct.

(A) doesn't help establish the editorial's conclusion that the railroad company is not to blame in this instance. In fact, **(A)** doesn't touch on the issue of culpability at all.

(B) might be correct if the editorial were attempting to distribute responsibility between the railroad company and the automobile driver, but the editorial in fact claims that drivers who go around the company's gates and cross the tracks indemnify the railroad company against any fault.

(D) mashes together two concepts from the argument. Small children are used as part of an example of a situation in which the responsibility for accidents may fall to the party restricting access; these children have nothing to do with drivers at railroad crossings.

(E) doesn't establish the editorial's conclusion. The editorial claims that the railroad company is not even partially responsible for accidents, so it's not enough to assume simply that the company's responsibility is limited.

24. (E) Flaw

Step 1: Identify the Question Type

Because the stimulus says the "reasoning in the . . . argument is questionable," you know this is a Flaw question. Furthermore, you know to be on the lookout for an overlooked possibility.

Step 2: Untangle the Stimulus

The researcher concludes that a well-constructed survey's results will not be affected by respondents' desire to meet the surveyors' expectations. The evidence is twofold: some surveys don't accurately reflect respondents' views because people give answers they think the surveyor wants to hear, but well-constructed surveys are worded such that respondents can't determine what the surveyor expects to hear.

Step 3: Make a Prediction

The researcher makes the faulty assumption that survey respondents will refrain from entertaining beliefs about surveyors' expectations just because the respondents aren't given any indication of what those expectations are. In other words, the researcher overlooks the possibility that respondents will use their made-up beliefs about surveyors' expectations to answer the survey's questions.

Step 4: Evaluate the Answer Choices

(E) matches the prediction.

(A) is irrelevant to the researcher's argument because the researcher never claims that such well-constructed surveys are flawless. The claim is merely that these surveys' results won't be affected by respondents' ideas about what the surveyors expect them to say.

(B) isn't the overlooked possibility here because the researcher's argument is concerned primarily with people whose answers *are* likely to be influenced by the surveyors' expectations.

(C) is irrelevant to the argument because the researcher is concerned with people's beliefs about their surveyors' expectations, not whether or not those expectations actually exist.

(D) isn't a flaw in the argument because the argument is concerned with people who do want to meet their surveyors' expectations.

25. (A) Parallel Reasoning

Step 1: Identify the Question Type

The phrase "reasoning … is most similar to" indicates a Parallel Reasoning question.

Step 2: Untangle the Stimulus

The conclusion of the argument comes in the first sentence: the availability of television reduces the amount that children read. The evidence is a couple of correlations: without television available, reading increases. But once television is reintroduced, reading levels drop back to their previous amounts.

Step 3: Make a Prediction

Your first task in abstracting the argument is to characterize its conclusion. Here, the conclusion is an assertion of fact; namely, an assertion of a causal relationship. The evidence is also statements of fact that assert correlation. The correct answer will use the same type of evidence to reach the same type of conclusion.

Step 4: Evaluate the Answer Choices

(A) is a parallel argument. Its first two sentences are correlations that support the conclusion (signaled by [*thus*]) that a constant money supply leads to stable interest rates.

(B) does provide a causal conclusion, but the evidence is not parallel. It would be parallel if it provided evidence that the absence of candy is correlated with a healthy appetite and that the reintroduction of candy is correlated with a disrupted appetite. But the evidence doesn't match this.

(C) has a conclusion that states a causal relationship, but its evidence also establishes causal relationships—unlike the correlations in the stimulus—so **(C)** is not fully parallel.

(D) concludes that factors other than the one in question affect a certain outcome (not an exact match to the causal conclusion in the stimulus) and backs up this conclusion with two examples, a tactic the stimulus never employs.

(E), like the stimulus, concerns a decline in reading. But it's the two arguments' structures, not their subject matter, that make them parallel. The evidence in **(E)** would be a match if it said that the absence of activities coincided with a boost in adult reading and that the availability of activities coincided with a drop in reading. So, **(E)**'s evidence is not parallel because it only discusses when reading time is low and because it focuses on the time spent on activities rather than the availability of the activities.

Section II: Reading Comprehension
Passage 1: Video Technology and Indigenous Cultures

Q#	Question Type	Correct	Difficulty
1	Global	C	★
2	Inference	A	★
3	Logic Reasoning (Parallel Reasoning)	B	★
4	Detail	C	★
5	Detail	A	★
6	Inference	D	★
7	Inference	E	★★

Passage 2: Handling Judicial Bias

Q#	Question Type	Correct	Difficulty
8	Detail	B	★★
9	Logic Function	A	★★
10	Inference	A	★★
11	Inference	C	★★
12	Inference	B	★★
13	Inference	C	★★
14	Inference	E	★★★

Passage 3: Eye for an Eye

Q#	Question Type	Correct	Difficulty
15	Global	C	★
16	Detail	A	★★
17	Logic Reasoning (Method of Argument)	D	★★★
18	Inference	C	★★
19	Inference	E	★★
20	Logic Reasoning (Strengthen)	B	★★★★

Passage 4: Does Solid Glass Flow?

Q#	Question Type	Correct	Difficulty
21	Global	E	★
22	Detail	B	★★
23	Inference	A	★★★
24	Inference	D	★★★★
25	Detail	B	★★★
26	Logic Reasoning (Parallel Reasoning)	B	★★
27	Inference	C	★★★

Passage 1: Video Technology and Indigenous Cultures

Step 1: Read the Passage Strategically
Sample Roadmap

line #	Keyword/phrase	¶ Margin notes
5	struggling ... even more ...	indig. people filming own cultures
6	profound ... Because	
12	sharply divided	Anthropologists divided
13	One faction	1st group (Weiner)
15	final assault	
16	argues	Video – Western culture
20	believes	
21	inevitably	Weiner: video robs indig. culture
23	Thus ... concludes ... costs	
25	Moreover ... maintains	
28	naive	
29	But ... opponents contend	2nd group (Ginsburg)
31	One such	
32	concedes	
34	but	
37	Unlike ... maintains	
40	In fact	Ginsburg: video doesn't make indig. Western
41	believe ... especially	Ginsburg: video helps indig. people preserve culture
42	invaluable opportunity	
47	lends credence	Turner's work supports Ginsburg
48		Kayapo use of video
50		
52	In contrast	Kayapo contradict Weiner
60	not so at odds	

Discussion

The passage begins by describing a recent phenomenon: cheaper video equipment has become available to indigenous cultures, and now those cultures, which were previously subject to documentation by Western ethnographic filmmakers, have begun to turn the cameras on themselves. The last sentence of paragraph 1 notes that reaction to this phenomenon among Western anthropologists is "sharply divided." Reading this sentence actively, you can probably guess that the passage will go on to detail this division.

Paragraph 2 outlines the position of "one faction" in the debate and identifies its leader, James Weiner. The position of Weiner et al. is that video technology is inherently Western in its ethos and that by using such technology, indigenous peoples lose what made them culturally distinct in the first place. By now, the **Topic** (the use of video technology by native peoples) and **Scope** (the debate over the impact of this technology) should start to become apparent.

Paragraph 3 begins with the contrast Keyword [b]ut, signaling a shift to the other faction in the debate. This faction is represented by Faye Ginsburg, who argues that Weiner's position is reductive; simply picking up a video camera doesn't infuse the holder with Western cultural conventions. Ginsburg argues the opposite: video technology can help indigenous societies strengthen their native languages and traditions.

Paragraph 4 introduces evidence to support Ginsburg's position. Terence Turner's fieldwork with the Kayapo people has shown that video representations of Kayapo traditions conform to the same principles as the traditions themselves and provide an aesthetic mirror to their ceremonies. The **Purpose** of the passage is therefore to outline the debate among anthropologists concerning video's impact on native peoples and to share evidence that supports one side in the debate. The **Main Idea** is that there are two distinct schools of thought about how video technology has affected indigenous cultures, but some evidence supports the latter school.

1. (C) Global

Step 2: Identify the Question Type
This is a Global question because it asks for the answer choice that "completely summarizes the passage."

Step 3: Research the Relevant Text
The entire text is relevant because this is a Global question, so base your prediction on the Main Idea you determined during Step 1.

Step 4: Make a Prediction
The main point of the passage is that anthropologists disagree over the impact of video technology on native cultures, but fieldwork exists to support the idea that

indigenous people don't lose their culture just by using video technology.

Step 5: Evaluate the Answer Choices
(C) is therefore correct.

(A) only encapsulates the view of Weiner and those in his camp. It doesn't take into account any of paragraphs 3 and 4.

(B) distorts the first paragraph of the passage. Yes, ethnographers have attempted to eliminate the "colonial gaze," but the passage focuses on a different transformation of their discipline. Furthermore, nothing in the passage states that the "colonial gaze" has been eliminated successfully.

(D) doesn't take into account the argument presented in paragraph 2 or the evidence presented in paragraph 4.

(E) is Extreme. Turner's fieldwork doesn't conclusively *validate* the position of Ginsburg. Moreover, the Scope of the passage is the debate itself, not the evidence concerning the Kayapo people.

2. (A) Inference

Step 2: Identify the Question Type
This is an Inference question because it asks you to characterize the attitude of someone in the passage toward something mentioned in the passage.

Step 3: Research the Relevant Text
Paragraph 3 contains Faye Ginsburg's argument. Look for any language that compares or contrasts her with James Weiner.

Step 4: Make a Prediction
Line 31 characterizes Ginsburg as Weiner's *opponent*, suggesting that she fundamentally disagrees with his position.

Step 5: Evaluate the Answer Choices
(A) is therefore correct.

(B) is incorrect because nothing in the passage suggests that Ginsburg is reluctant to critique Weiner's ideas.

(C) is too timid. Line 35 says that Ginsburg calls Weiner's idea about video technology's effects "little more than boilerplate technological determinism." Hardly mild language.

(D) is incorrect because Ginsburg is not neutral when it comes to Weiner's position.

(E) is a 180. Ginsburg is not supportive of Weiner's position; in fact, she flatly disagrees with it.

3. (B) Logic Reasoning (Parallel Reasoning)

Step 2: Identify the Question Type
This is a Parallel Reasoning question because it asks for the answer choice "most analogous to" a portion of the passage.

Step 3: Research the Relevant Text

The Kayapo and their use of video technology are discussed in paragraph 4.

Step 4: Make a Prediction

Lines 47–60 describe the Kayapo's use of video to document their ceremonial performances. These representations "conform to the same principle of beauty embodied in the ceremonies themselves." The correct answer will be an example of a culture appropriating the tools of another culture while retaining the features that make their own culture unique.

Step 5: Evaluate the Answer Choices

(B) is a good match.

(A) is a 180. The Kayapo didn't move to another culture and alter that culture; the Kayapo incorporated one element of Western culture and used it to help preserve elements of their own society.

(C) is also a 180. The Internet is reshaping the way the authors write, but the Kayapo did not allow the camera to reshape their culture.

(D) is not analogous to the passage because the Kayapo were not imitating any cultural features from an earlier time. Historical homage doesn't figure into the Kayapo's use of video.

(E) is not parallel because the European artists are rejecting elements of their own culture and moving in a different direction. The Kayapo are taking devices from an outside culture in service of their own.

4. (C) Detail

Step 2: Identify the Question Type

The phrase "according to the passage" is a clear indication of a Detail question.

Step 3: Research the Relevant Text

Weiner's claims are detailed in paragraph 2. Specifically, "Western ontology" is mentioned in line 21.

Step 4: Make a Prediction

Line 22 says that according to Weiner, Western ontology is "based on realism, immediacy, and self-expression."

Step 5: Evaluate the Answer Choices

(C) is therefore correct.

(A) is mentioned as a feature of traditional Kayapo ceremonies (lines 54–59).

(B) is mentioned as something Weiner says anthropologists naively ascribe to films made by indigenous cultures (lines 25–28).

(D) is mentioned in line 2 as a characteristic of early ethnographic films.

(E) is a characteristic Weiner imputes to anthropologists who find ethnographic films culturally truthful simply because they were made by native peoples.

5. (A) Detail

Step 2: Identify the Question Type

This is a Detail question because it asks about which information is provided by the passage.

Step 3: Research the Relevant Text

Without any specific content clues, the entire passage is relevant, so save your research for Step 5.

Step 4: Make a Prediction

The passage provides enough information to answer a whole slew of questions. So, instead of predicting them all, check each answer choice against the passage.

Step 5: Evaluate the Answer Choices

(A) is answered in lines 50–52. The Kayapo use video technology to create legal records so they can hold the Brazilian government to the agreements it makes with the Kayapo.

(B) is not answered in the passage. The idea of the "noble savage" is mentioned in lines 30–31, but the passage doesn't say where the idea came from.

(C) is not answered. The only specific indigenous culture mentioned is the Kayapo, and the passage says that they have adopted video technology.

(D) is not answered. Ginsburg concedes in lines 32–34 that no Western cultural object that has entered circulation since the fifteenth century has remained neutral, but no specific technologies from that time are mentioned.

(E) is not answered. Line 7 confirms that inexpensive video equipment is now more available, but the author never says how the equipment became inexpensive.

6. (D) Inference

Step 2: Identify the Question Type

This is an Inference question because it asks what Turner "would be most likely to agree with."

Step 3: Research the Relevant Text

Terence Turner's research is discussed in paragraph 4. Within that paragraph, Weiner is mentioned in lines 52–53.

Step 4: Make a Prediction

Turner's findings contradict Weiner's position that video technology imposes Western culture on its users. Therefore, Turner would believe that Weiner's position doesn't allow for instances in which native peoples could use Western technology but still preserve their own unique cultural identity.

Step 5: Evaluate the Answer Choices

(D) is therefore correct.

(A) is Outside the Scope because Weiner makes no argument that depends on the *diversity* of traditional practices among native peoples.

(B) is not a position Turner would take regarding Weiner's argument because even if video technology is *available* worldwide, Turner is more concerned with Weiner's argument that indigenous cultures will be altered as a result.

(C) is not a position Turner would take regarding Weiner's argument because Weiner seems to demonstrate concern for preserving traditional indigenous practices. In fact, that concern underlies Weiner's suspicion of video technology.

(E) is not something Turner would likely agree with because Weiner's position has more to do with video's effect on native peoples rather than the effect of Western technologies in general.

7. (E) Inference

Step 2: Identify the Question Type

This is an Inference question because it asks what an author means by using a particular term. Therefore, the correct answer will not be directly stated, but must be inferred.

Step 3: Research the Relevant Text

Line 35 is relevant, of course, but to grasp the author's full meaning, you must read the surrounding lines for context.

Step 4: Make a Prediction

In line 35 and the surrounding lines, the author summarizes Ginsburg's position on Weiner's claims. Ginsburg considers it "technological determinism" to say that using a video camera automatically makes one Western. In other words, "technological determinism" refers to the idea that technology determines the cultural identity of indigenous peoples.

Step 5: Evaluate the Answer Choices

(E) is therefore correct.

(A) might be tempting if you use the dictionary definition of "determinism." But in the context of the passage, "determinism" has more to do with Weiner's idea that cultures are altered by their use of technology.

(B) mischaracterizes the influence of video technology. The debate is about the influence of video on native cultures, not about its influence on field anthropologists.

(C) uses a meaning of "determinism" that might be familiar to biologists, but in the context of this passage, it doesn't reflect Weiner's argument about native peoples' relationship to video technology.

(D) introduces the idea of a culture's ethical values, an idea which is Outside the Scope of both Weiner's and Ginsburg's arguments.

Passage 2: Handling Judicial Bias

Step 1: Read the Passage Strategically
Sample Roadmap

line #	Keyword/phrase	¶ Margin notes
1	current	Current approach to
2	heavily emphasizes	recusal based on
4	avoidance of both	appearances
12	vague … at best	Auth: rules vague
15	without	
16	mistake	
17	focus on	Auth: shouldn't focus on appearances
18	rather than	
24	overlooked	bias overlooked
26	only if	Justice occurs thru reasoning
29	Therefore … best way	
30	require	Auth: judges should explain reasoning
31	Accordingly … should	
32	eliminate	
33	unreliable	
34	should … replaced by … requirement	
38	should not	
40	but rather … should be required	
43	potential objection	Objection: judge's reasoning not "real"
44	however … adequate	
45	thus	
46	However	Auth: if no fault in reasoning no complaint
49	only if	
50	If	
53	then	

Discussion

This Law passage begins by summarizing the current approach to recusal and disqualification of judges, which "heavily emphasize appearance-based analysis." Judges are expected to recuse themselves in instances of impropriety or even the appearance of impropriety. Jurisdictional rules vary regarding whether or not parties to a court can themselves request recusal. You can expect this author to express a point of view about these rules, and that point of view comes in paragraph 2.

Paragraph 2 lays out the author's position: the current rules are "vague ... at best." In the author's view, it's a mistake to focus too much on appearances at the expense of discovering sources of actual bias. Such bias may not be apparent to the parties to a court proceeding or even to judges themselves, so appearance-based analysis provides a shaky foundation on which to base ethical rules.

Paragraph 3 provides the author's suggestion for a revision of the rules. Instead of focusing on the appearance of impropriety, rules governing judicial ethics should focus on the reasoning behind a judge's ruling. Judges should be required to make such reasoning transparent. If judges recuse themselves, they should explain why, and if they do not, they should explain the legal basis for the judgment they reach.

In paragraph 4, the author anticipates a potential objection to this recommendation. Some might allege that the judge's written reasoning is not the real reasoning used to reach a decision. *However*, the author contends, there are no grounds for complaint if the legal reasoning is deemed sound by a knowledgeable observer. If another objectively impartial judge could have reached the same legal conclusion as the judge in question, then no harm is done.

This is a relatively challenging Law passage, but sticking closely to the author's point of view can help you sort it out. The **Topic** is judicial bias, and the **Scope** is approaches to setting rules for handling such bias. The author's **Purpose** is to critique the current approach and propose a new approach. The Main Idea is that our legal system should replace the current appearance-based approach with an approach focused on a judge's underlying legal reasoning.

8. (B) Detail

Step 2: Identify the Question Type
The phrase "[a]ccording to the passage" indicates a Detail question.

Step 3: Research the Relevant Text
"A weakness of current rules" is a content clue leading you to paragraph 2, where the author critiques the current approach to recusal and disqualification of judges.

Step 4: Make a Prediction
Lines 12–16 say that the current rules provide "vague guidance at best" and that they fail to provide an idea of whose perspective matters or how the facts should be interpreted.

Step 5: Evaluate the Answer Choices
(B) is therefore correct.

(A) is a Distortion. Judges' reasoning isn't discussed until the author recommends a new approach in paragraph 3.

(C), like **(A)**, introduces judicial reasoning, which is part of the author's recommendation. Furthermore, paragraph 3 indicates that the author highly values transparency in judicial reasoning.

(D) is mentioned as a feature of the recusal rules in some jurisdictions (lines 10–11). But the author doesn't directly criticize this feature.

(E) is a 180. The author says in paragraph 2 that the current rules focus too much on the appearance of propriety.

9. (A) Logic Function

Step 2: Identify the Question Type
This is a Logic Function question because it asks you to determine the "primary purpose" of part of the passage.

Step 3: Research the Relevant Text
The second paragraph is relevant, but in order to form your prediction, consult your margin notes rather than rereading the entire paragraph.

Step 4: Make a Prediction
Paragraph 2 provides the author's evaluation of the current approach to recusal that was discussed in paragraph 1.

Step 5: Evaluate the Answer Choices
(A) is therefore correct.

(B) is a Distortion. The author's solution is provided in paragraph 3, and it is never rejected anywhere in the passage.

(C) is incorrect because the author doesn't discuss any problems in the first paragraph. Furthermore, no examples of such problems are given in the passage.

(D) is a 180. Far from being an objective discussion of the history leading to the current approach, the author uses paragraph 2 to take issue with the current approach.

(E) is a Distortion. The author's own thesis doesn't occur until paragraph 3.

10. (A) Inference

Step 2: Identify the Question Type
This is an Inference question because it asks how an author *regards* something mentioned in the passage. Don't worry if

you thought this might be a Detail question; you would execute Steps 3 and 4 in largely the same way.

Step 3: Research the Relevant Text

Lines 49–50 are relevant, as well as the context of the surrounding lines.

Step 4: Make a Prediction

The author says that the principle that a right of recourse arises only if harm arises is a principle "under the law." Furthermore, it's a principle on which the author bases a rebuttal to a potential objection to the recommendation made in paragraph 3. The author must therefore consider this principle fairly ironclad.

Step 5: Evaluate the Answer Choices

(A) is consistent with the way the author uses the principle to further the passage's argument.

(B) misuses a point from lines 25–26, in which the author says that the law's function is to settle "normative disputes."

(C) is a Distortion. The principle in lines 49–50 is why it's *not* a concern that judges might hide their real reasoning.

(D) is a 180. If this principle were unfair to parties to legal proceedings, then the author would not have used the principle to support the passage's Main Idea.

(E) is a Distortion. The principle in lines 49–50 has nothing to do with the *current* means of addressing judicial bias, which is discussed in paragraphs 1 and 2. The principle in lines 49–50 instead relates to the author's proposed solution.

11. (C) Inference

Step 2: Identify the Question Type

The phrase "can be inferred from the passage" is a clear indication of an Inference question.

Step 3: Research the Relevant Text

The author primarily discusses "weakness of statutes" in paragraph 2.

Step 4: Make a Prediction

In paragraph 2, the author faults the current rules for basing disqualification on a vague standard of "whether the judge's impartiality might reasonably be questioned." According to the author, no guidance is given as to whose perspective to consult or how to interpret the facts of the case.

Step 5: Evaluate the Answer Choices

(C) is consistent with lines 22–24.

(A) is a 180. The author says at the beginning of paragraph 2 that the rules concerning recusal and disqualification provide "vague guidance at best." So, they are certainly not "excessively rigid."

(B) is a Distortion. The author does suggest requiring judges to make their reasoning transparent, but there's no indication that this requirement is incompatible with current rules.

(D) is a 180. Rather than conflicting with statutes allowing people to request disqualification of judges, the professional codes of conduct mentioned in **(D)** likely form the basis for these statutes.

(E) can't be inferred because the author makes no prediction concerning the outcomes of potential requests for disqualification.

12. (B) Inference

Step 2: Identify the Question Type

Any question that asks about what the passage "suggests" is an Inference question.

Step 3: Research the Relevant Text

The author recommends that judges be required to provide their written legal reasoning at the end of paragraph 3, and further support for this recommendation comes in paragraph 4.

Step 4: Make a Prediction

In paragraph 4, the author says that the judge's reasoning is acceptable "as long as a knowledgeable observer cannot find fault" with it. This provision is intended to respond to critics who allege that judges might not be giving their real reasoning.

Step 5: Evaluate the Answer Choices

(B) is a valid inference. If faulty reasoning cannot in principle be detected, then the author would presumably have refrained from making the recommendation in lines 40–42.

(A) is Extreme. The author mentions earlier in the passage that sources of bias are not always apparent, so it's hard to conclude that bias can be *eliminated* altogether.

(C) is a 180 because it is an objection that the author anticipates and seeks to counter in lines 46–54. Additionally, even if some situations arise where judges attempt to conceal their reasoning, the passage does not suggest that that would be the *usual* practice of judges.

(D) is Outside the Scope. The author isn't concerned with public perception of judges' impartiality. The author is instead concerned with ways to ensure that bias doesn't affect the outcome of cases.

(E) is a 180 because the author argues against recusal when there is only an "appearance of bias." The author would not have proposed a solution where judges must provide written legal reasoning if the effect would be to cause recusals based merely on an appearance of impropriety.

13. (C) Inference

Step 2: Identify the Question Type

This is an Inference question because it asks you to find the answer choice that is "an example of" something mentioned in the passage. The correct answer won't be stated directly by the author, but will instead be consistent with the passage.

Step 3: Research the Relevant Text
Lines 43–46 are of importance here, but be sure to read around these lines for context.

Step 4: Make a Prediction
The "real reasoning" referred to in these lines is reasoning that might not be reflected in a judge's official written explanation of a decision. In other words, this "real reasoning" could actually reflect a judge's bias against a party to a court proceeding.

Step 5: Evaluate the Answer Choices
(C) is therefore a valid inference. The reasoning described in **(C)** is the kind of reasoning that could conceal a judge's "undetected bias" (line 46).

(A) is unsupported. The author says in lines 38–39 that judges should not be required to explain why they chose not to recuse themselves.

(B) is Outside the Scope. The "undetected bias" mentioned in line 46 has nothing to do with whether or not a judge's reasoning can be understood by laypeople.

(D) is a Distortion. The author says that a knowledgeable observer should not be able to find fault with a judge's stated reasoning in explaining a decision, not in that judge's concealed and potentially biased "real reasoning."

(E) is a Distortion. The author makes a distinction between the reasoning contained in a judge's written explanation, which should be based on legal principles, and potential "real reasoning," which can be based on bias.

14. (E) Inference

Step 2: Identify the Question Type
The looser language in this question stem ("author would be most likely to consider") indicates an Inference question.

Step 3: Research the Relevant Text
The author analyzes the effects of the current approach to recusal and disqualification in paragraph 2.

Step 4: Make a Prediction
The author says that it's a mistake to base the current approach to recusal and disqualification primarily on appearances, which can be deceiving. That focus on appearances, says the passage, could lead jurists to miss actual sources of bias. Line 33 even calls the current system an "unreliable mechanism."

Step 5: Evaluate the Answer Choices
(E) is consistent with the "unreliable mechanism" described in the passage.

(A) is Outside the Scope. The author doesn't discuss the attitudes of the general public toward the current standards.

(B) is also Outside the Scope. The author doesn't say how judges personally feel about their professional codes of conduct. The effects of the current system are of primary importance to the author.

(C) is a Distortion. The author never suggests a difference between how often unbiased judges are removed from cases and how often biased ones are allowed to sit on cases.

(D), like **(C)**, suggests that the author gives an indication of how frequently judges are removed from cases in certain instances, but no such indication exists in the passage.

Passage 3: Eye for an Eye

Step 1: Read the Passage Strategically
Sample Roadmap

line #	Keyword/phrase	¶ Margin notes
Passage A		
1–3		
4	lower standards	Augustine: 2 wrongs don't make a right
5	yet … indeed	Auth: may be just to repay lies with lies
6	some justification	
8	:	
11	Just as	Lying to liars—fairness
12	so	
14	Two	2 moral Qs involved
15	first	
17	second	
21	Surely	Exception: pathological liar
23	But … not … sufficient	tall tales don't justify lying
Passage B		
28	holds	
32	That is	Kant: rational beings authorize repayment of behavior
34	Consequently	
38	might be concluded	Kant argument could mean duty to punish
41	But	
42	seems excessive … since	Auth: duty too extreme
46	The point … rather	
49	leads to	
50	rather than	Auth: Kant argument means right, not duty

Discussion

Passage A begins by offering the view of Saint Augustine, who believed that one shouldn't respond to a liar by lying. In Augustine's view, two wrongs never make a right. In paragraph 2, the author gives the counterpoint: some see responding to lies by lying as inherently just. The author doesn't offer her own point of view on this debate, but instead outlines two questions involved in the debate. One question asks whether a liar and an honest person have the same claim to be told the truth, and the other asks whether one is more justified in lying to a liar than to others.

Passage A ends with a case study in which it may not be justified to reply to a liar with lies. If the liar in question is pathological, meaning that he compulsively tells tall tales that are harmless, lying in response to him may actually do a disproportionate amount of harm to "self, others, and general trust." The **Topic** of passage A is lying, the **Scope** is whether it's justified to repay lies with lies, the **Purpose** is to discuss the debate over whether such lying is justified, and the **Main Idea** is that while many believe it is justified to repay lies with lies, other considerations may affect that justification in certain cases.

Passage B begins by outlining Kant's view that rational beings, by virtue of their rationality, authorize others to behave toward them as they themselves behave. So, according to Kant, to respond in kind to a rational person's immoral behavior is merely part of treating that person as a rational being.

In the second paragraph, the author takes this logic one step further. If we feel we should treat rational beings as rational, then we might conclude that Kant's argument saddles us with a duty to repay bad behavior with similarly bad behavior. But, says the author, that might be going too far. Instead, Kant's argument leads to a right, not a duty. If a rational being behaves immorally, we then have a right to respond as that rational being has implicitly authorized us to do.

The **Topic** of passage B is Kant's view of reciprocal behavior. The **Scope** is the implications of that view. The **Purpose** is to discuss and evaluate those implications. The **Main Idea** is that Kant's argument leads us to conclude that we have a right, but not a duty, to behave toward rational beings as they behave toward us.

On Comparative Reading passages, always note areas of overlap between the passages; the questions are sure to ask about them. In this case, both passages explore whether it is justified to repay an improper action with a similarly improper action. Passage A, however, restricts its discussion to the practice of lying, while passage B explores immoral actions in general.

15. (C) Global

Step 2: Identify the Question Type
This is a Global question because it asks what both passages are "concerned with answering."

Step 3: Research the Relevant Text
The entire text is relevant to a Global question. Use your work from Step 1 to predict the answer here.

Step 4: Make a Prediction
The passages overlap in their discussion of whether it is proper to respond in kind to another person's wrongdoing.

Step 5: Evaluate the Answer Choices
(C) is therefore correct.

(A) is touched upon briefly in the last paragraph of passage A, but passage B doesn't discuss the idea of harm.

(B) is Outside the Scope. The idea of criminality doesn't appear in either author's analysis.

(D) is discussed in passage B, but not in passage A.

(E) is also discussed in passage B, but not in passage A.

16. (A) Detail

Step 2: Identify the Question Type
This is a Detail question because it asks about information introduced—that is, stated directly—in one or both passages.

Step 3: Research the Relevant Text
The question stem directs you to restrict your research to passage A only.

Step 4: Make a Prediction
Several considerations are introduced in passage A. Instead of predicting them all, check each answer choice against the passage.

Step 5: Evaluate the Answer Choices
(A) is discussed primarily in the last paragraph of passage A, in which the author asserts that one may do unwarranted harm by lying in response to the lies of a person whose behavior is known to be pathological.

(B) is a Distortion. Passage A discusses the consequences that can ensue when people do reciprocate another's wrongdoing, but not the ones that ensue when people do *not* reciprocate.

(C) is a 180. It is not mentioned in A, but it is mentioned in passage B where the author discusses how Kant viewed rational beings.

(D) is also discussed in passage B, but not in passage A.

(E) is a Distortion. Neither passage offers specific *instances* of harm done to people whose wrongdoing was reciprocated. The discussion of the pathological liar in lines 19–27 is merely hypothetical.

17. (D) Logic Reasoning (Method of Argument)

Step 2: Identify the Question Type

This is a Method of Argument question because it asks how each passage advances its argument.

Step 3: Research the Relevant Text

Both passages are relevant in this case, but instead of rereading them, use your Roadmap and your global understanding of the passages to predict your answer.

Step 4: Make a Prediction

Each passage explores a view concerning the reasonableness of responding to wrongdoing with wrongdoing, and then shows how unreasonable implications can result from that view.

Step 5: Evaluate the Answer Choices

(D) is therefore correct.

(A) is a Distortion. Neither author argues against any objections to a particular theory.

(B) is incorrect because neither author bases a main argument on an analogy. Saint Augustine uses an analogy in lines 1–2 of passage A, but this is not how either author structures either passage as a whole.

(C) is incorrect because even if you consider the pathological liar in passage A to be a specific case, passage B contains no such case but rather remains abstract in its discussion.

(E) is incorrect because neither passage attempts to redefine a key term.

18. (C) Inference

Step 2: Identify the Question Type

This is an Inference question because it asks what an author "would be most likely to agree with."

Step 3: Research the Relevant Text

Passage A is the only passage relevant here.

Step 4: Make a Prediction

You may not be able to predict the correct answer verbatim, but the correct answer will be compatible with passage A's Main Idea that it may not always be justified to repay a liar with lies.

Step 5: Evaluate the Answer Choices

(C) is a valid inference. Passage A says that a liar may have forfeited his or her right to be told the truth (lines 12–13, 21–22), but in certain cases, it might not be justified to lie to that person (lines 23–27).

(A) is within the scope of passage B. Passage A doesn't discuss rational beings.

(B) is Outside the Scope of passage A, which concerns only how to respond to wrongdoing—not how to respond to actions that are morally neutral.

(D) is almost a 180. Passage A suggests that it may be justified to respond to a wrong with a similar wrong (lines 11–13). The specific case of the pathological liar does indicate one case where it would be *improper* to respond in kind, but it would be extreme to say there is "no circumstance in which there is sufficient reason."

(E) is Outside the Scope. Nothing in passage A suggests that an *innocent* person forfeits the right to be dealt with honorably.

19. (E) Inference

Step 2: Identify the Question Type

This is an Inference question because it asks you to "characterize the difference" between a concept in passage A and one found in passage B.

Step 3: Research the Relevant Text

The lines cited in the question stem are relevant, but be prepared to read around those lines to get a sense of context.

Step 4: Make a Prediction

Lines 11–13 describe an inherent right to be treated well by others, a right that one forfeits by doing wrong. Line 50 describes a right to treat others poorly in response to their own wrongdoing.

Step 5: Evaluate the Answer Choices

(E) is therefore correct.

(A) is Half-Right/Half-Wrong. Both passages discuss moral rights; the law doesn't enter into the discussion.

(B) is a Distortion. Nothing in passage B suggests that the right to treat others poorly in response to their own wrongdoing is a right granted by any specific authority figure.

(C) is incorrect because in each passage, the kind of right referred to is one held by an individual, not held by a group.

(D) is a 180. Passage A discusses a kind of right that can readily be forfeited by those who do wrong.

20. (B) Logic Reasoning (Strengthen)

Step 2: Identify the Question Type

This is a Strengthen question because it asks you to find the answer choice that, if true, makes arguments from the two passages compatible.

Step 3: Research the Relevant Text

Both the last paragraph of passage A and the first paragraph of passage B are relevant in this case.

Step 4: Make a Prediction

In the last paragraph of passage A, the author argues that a pathological liar's tall tales don't on their own justify lying to him because the harm done to him by lying to him outweighs the negligible harm of his tall tales. In passage B, Kant argues that rational beings implicitly authorize reciprocal treatment when they act immorally. These arguments are compatible if it were demonstrated that a pathological liar is somehow outside the realm of rationality.

Step 5: Evaluate the Answer Choices

(B) is therefore correct.

(A) is a Distortion and Outside the Scope. Lying in response to a pathological liar is not in itself pathological, and Kant's argument concerns whether the *original* bad behavior comes from a rational being. The rationality of *our* response to that behavior doesn't figure into the argument.

(C) is a 180. If pathological liars should be treated as rational beings, then, according to Kant's argument, it would in fact be justified to respond to those liars with lies of our own, an idea that contradicts the argument at the end of passage A.

(D) supports passage B's author's view regarding the implications of Kant's argument, but doesn't reconcile that argument with the one laid out in passage A.

(E) certainly bolsters Saint Augustine's argument from the beginning of passage A, but it does nothing to reconcile passage A's author's argument with that of Kant in passage B.

Passage 4: Does Solid Glass Flow?

Step 1: Read the Passage Strategically
Sample Roadmap

line #	Keyword/phrase	¶ Margin notes
1	strange	
3–4		Wrong belief: window glass flows
8	but ... confusion ... probably	
9	misunderstanding	why people believe this
12	but	
14	rather	Glass has transition temp
18	but	
20	However ... debunks	Zanotto's study debunks belief
25	But	Zanotto's calculation
31		More of Zanotto's findings
36		
37	but	
38	since	
39	demonstrates	Zanotto's study supports scientists views
40	dramatically	
45	probably results ... instead	Auth: changes in manufacturing methods true cause
46	Until	
53	Later	Auth traces changes in glass manufacturing
55	Today	

Discussion

Don't be thrown by the arcane subject matter of this Natural Sciences passage. Like many passages of this type, this passage outlines a commonly believed explanation for a phenomenon, presents evidence undermining that explanation, and suggests an alternative explanation. In this case, the common belief has to do with the perceived viscosity of glass. The variations in thickness of old window glass have often been thought to be the result of glass flowing very slowly over time. The second half of paragraph 1 outlines the basis of this misperception. Many people misunderstand the atomic structure of glass. This structure is similar from liquid glass to solid glass, but these different phases of glass diverge when it comes to thermodynamics. Rather than a precise freezing point, glass has what's known as a transition temperature, and once molten glass is cooled below the lower end of that range, it begins to take on the physical properties of a solid. By now, it should become clear that the **Topic** is glass, and the **Scope** is explanations for why glass thickness can vary within the same antique window.

Paragraph 2 begins with the contrast Keyword [*h*]*owever*, signaling a shift. Here, the author introduces Zanotto's study, which debunks the persistent belief mentioned earlier. The author concedes that gravity can cause some solids to flow slightly. But Zanotto calculated the time it would take for us to perceive the flow of solid glass, and that time period amounts to longer than the age of the universe.

Paragraph 3 provides more information gleaned by the study. Chemical composition can alter the rate of flow of glass, but only slightly, and certainly not enough to be noticeable after only a handful of centuries (which is the age of medieval stained-glass windows). Zanotto's study lends statistical credence to the position already held by scientists.

Now that the "persistent belief" has been thoroughly called into question, the author uses paragraph 4 to provide an alternative explanation. Rather than a viscous flow, changes in manufacturing methods are the reason why antique window glass displays differences in thickness from top to bottom. The rest of the paragraph lays out a few of those changes from before the nineteenth century all the way to today. The **Purpose** of the passage is therefore to supplant a commonly held belief about why glass thickness varies in older glass. Therefore, the **Main Idea** is that differences in thickness in old window glass are explained not by the properties of glass itself, but by changes in how glass has been manufactured over the centuries.

21. (E) Global

Step 2: Identify the Question Type
This is a Global question because it asks for the "main point" of the passage.

Step 3: Research the Relevant Text
You already determined the **Main Idea** of the passage during Step 1. Use that as the basis for your prediction.

Step 4: Make a Prediction
The main point of the passage is that the difference in thickness between the top and bottom of glass windowpanes is better explained by the manufacturing process than by the flowing of glass.

Step 5: Evaluate the Answer Choices
(E) is therefore correct.

(A) just reiterates the second half of paragraph 2. But Zanotto's calculations are only provided to support the larger point that window glass has not flowed enough to cause a noticeable difference in thickness from top to bottom.

(B) is a point made in paragraph 4, but that point only serves to help explain the author's broader position concerning why glass varies in thickness.

(C) describes Zanotto's discovery, but that discovery is not the focus of the passage. Zanotto is only mentioned to help debunk the commonly held belief with which the author takes issue.

(D) misrepresents the author's point of view. According to paragraph 4, there aren't several factors explaining the difference in thickness between the top and bottom of old windows; the author points to only one factor.

22. (B) Detail

Step 2: Identify the Question Type
This is a Detail question because it deals with what the passage explicitly mentions. The correct answer choice will be a question directly answered by the information in the passage.

Step 3: Research the Relevant Text
There are no content clues here, so the entire passage is relevant text. Save your research for Step 5.

Step 4: Make a Prediction
It's nearly impossible to predict the correct answer to a question like this one, so check each answer choice against the passage, using the content clues within them to pinpoint the relevant text.

Step 5: Evaluate the Answer Choices
(B) is answered in paragraph 4. Lines 46–52 describe how glass was made before the nineteenth century. The Keyword [*l*]*ater* in line 53 signals a shift to the nineteenth century, which is contrasted in lines 55–57 with the approach to glassmaking [*t*]*oday*.

(A) is not answered by the passage. Lines 46–52 describe the glassmaking process and indicate that there was an "only way" to do it until the nineteenth century. No distinctions were made between different periods leading up to the nineteenth century.

(C) is not answered by the passage. Medieval windows are the earliest ones discussed in the passage.

(D) is not answered by the passage. Germanium oxide glass is mentioned at the beginning of paragraph 3 as a type of glass that flows relatively easy, but it's not stated that this glass was used in stained-glass windows.

(E) is not answered by the passage. Line 35 states that medieval stained glass contains impurities, but no information is given as to how those impurities came about.

23. (A) Inference

Step 2: Identify the Question Type
This is an Inference question because it asks about the author's view, or attitude, toward part of the passage.

Step 3: Research the Relevant Text
The results of Zanotto's study are discussed in the end of paragraph 2 and throughout paragraph 3.

Step 4: Make a Prediction
Because the author uses the results of Zanotto's study to discredit the belief held by laypeople that glass viscosity accounts for the difference in thickness between the top and bottom of old windows, you can properly infer that Zanotto's findings support the author's view. Furthermore, the last sentence of paragraph 3 says that Zanotto's study demonstrates what many scientists had already reasoned.

Step 5: Evaluate the Answer Choices
(A) matches the prediction.

(B) is a 180. Scientists can't have thought the issue had been settled because the author says that glass researchers find it strange that the myth about flowing glass persists (lines 1–4).

(C) is a Distortion. The author explains in paragraph 1 how the mistaken hypothesis about window glass came to be believed. Zanotto's study doesn't figure into that discussion.

(D) is incorrect because there aren't two incompatible views that the author attempts to reconcile. Rather, the author spends the passage undermining one explanation for a phenomenon and endorsing another.

(E) is another Distortion. There are two hypotheses to explain the phenomenon discussed in the passage, but according to the author, one of them is valid and supported by evidence.

24. (D) Inference

Step 2: Identify the Question Type
This is an Inference question because it asks about what "the passage suggests." That looser language means that the correct answer won't be stated directly, but rather supported by the passage.

Step 3: Research the Relevant Text
The atomic structure of glass is discussed in paragraph 1, specifically in lines 8–19.

Step 4: Make a Prediction
According to the passage, the atomic structure of glass remains constant in its amorphousness from solid to liquid states. However, solid and liquid glass differ thermodynamically. At any temperature above the lower range of the glass transition temperature, molten glass retains the properties of a liquid.

Step 5: Evaluate the Answer Choices
(D) is a valid inference.

(A) is a Distortion. The last few lines of paragraph 1 indicate that glass does not always behave as a liquid.

(B) warps a detail from paragraph 2 about the length of time needed to perceive the flow of glass. That length of time is described as "a period well beyond the age of the universe" (lines 29–30), not simply a few millennia.

(C) is a Distortion because paragraph 1 says that molten glass behaves as a solid when it is cooled below the lower range of its glass transition temperature. That suggests that at this transition temperature, it still behaves as a liquid.

(E) isn't a valid inference because the passage describes conditions under which glass will flow, despite the fact that its atoms are not arranged in a fixed crystalline structure.

25. (B) Detail

Step 2: Identify the Question Type
This is a Detail question because it asks about something explicitly attributed by the author. The correct answer will state or paraphrase information already contained.

Step 3: Research the Relevant Text
The false belief that window glass flows noticeably downward over time is discussed in paragraph 1.

Step 4: Make a Prediction
Lines 7–10 say that the myth about glass originates from a misunderstanding of the atomic structure of glass. Because that structure is amorphous, people believe that even solid glass takes on the properties of a viscous liquid.

Step 5: Evaluate the Answer Choices
(B) is therefore correct.

(A) is a Distortion. No one mistakenly believes that glass has a fixed crystalline structure. Rather, the author says that people misinterpret the implications of the amorphous atomic structure of glass.

(C) is another Distortion. The mistaken belief about glass has nothing to do with the changes in manufacturing methods; those changes are instead at the heart of the author's own attempt to counter this mistaken belief.

(D) is incorrect because paragraph 1 suggests that all glass has the same transition temperature. The author doesn't attempt to debunk any inaccurate beliefs about transition temperatures.

(E) is incorrect because liquid and solid glass are actually thermodynamically dissimilar, according to the passage (lines 12–13). So, this is not an erroneous assumption.

26. (B) Logic Reasoning (Parallel Reasoning)

Step 2: Identify the Question Type
The phrase "most analogous to" indicates a Parallel Reasoning question.

Step 3: Research the Relevant Text
"Persistent belief" is a content clue leading you to lines 1–7.

Step 4: Make a Prediction
The persistent belief discussed in the passage is the belief that the difference in thickness between the top and bottom of old windows is explained by the viscous flow of glass. The correct answer probably won't mention glass at all; instead, it will describe a similar belief, namely that a phenomenon is explained by properties of the material itself rather than manufacturing methods.

Step 5: Evaluate the Answer Choices
(B) is a perfect match. The "early pottery" mentioned in **(B)** parallels the old windows discussed in the first lines of the passage.

(A) is a Distortion. The manufacturing process has more to do with the author's explanation and less to do with the belief cited at the beginning of the passage. Furthermore, the belief in the passage seeks to provide a cause for a phenomenon, not to predict whether that phenomenon can be changed.

(C) might be parallel if it said that people blamed the materials used to make appliances—rather than the manufacturing techniques—for the shorter life spans of those appliances. However, even in that scenario, the varying level of thickness in window glass is not commensurate with a flaw causing a window to have a shorter life span.

(D) is incorrect because the persistent belief in the passage is about a certain phenomenon. **(D)** merely compares two different types of material and deems one inferior.

(E) might be parallel if the passage said that people believe that newer windows don't have differences in thickness because their glass is more durable. But the persistent belief in lines 1–7 doesn't compare older glass to newer glass.

27. (C) Inference

Step 2: Identify the Question Type
"The passage suggests" is a clear sign of an Inference question.

Step 3: Research the Relevant Text
The transition temperature of glass is mentioned primarily in lines 13–19.

Step 4: Make a Prediction
The passage defines the glass transition temperature as a range of a few hundred degrees Celsius within which glass transforms its physical properties from those of a liquid to those of a solid. However, Celsius is also mentioned in lines 41–43, which state that in order for glass to noticeably flow, it must be heated to at least 350 degrees Celsius.

Step 5: Evaluate the Answer Choices
(C) is a valid inference. The temperature of 350 degrees Celsius is mentioned in paragraph 3 as the lowest temperature to which glass would have to be heated to flow noticeably. In other words, it's the lowest end of the transition temperature, at which glass takes on the properties of a liquid. Therefore, it is strongly supported that the upper extreme of the transition temperature is well above 350 degrees.

(A) is a comparison with no basis in the passage. The author suggests that the age of glass is irrelevant to its transition temperature.

(B) is a Distortion. Zanotto has calculated the amount of time it would take for glass to flow noticeably, but nothing in the passage details when and how precisely the glass transition temperature has been calculated.

(D) is unsupported by the passage, which says that once molten glass is cooled below the lower end of the transition temperature, it stops flowing and takes on the properties of a solid. Therefore, the transition temperature *does* affect the tendency of glass to flow downward.

(E) isn't a valid inference because nothing in the passage suggests that certain types of glass have more precise transition temperatures than others. Furthermore, lines 41–43 indicate 350 degrees Celsius is the minimum for glass in general, so there wouldn't be any types below 350 degrees Celsius.

Section III: Logical Reasoning

Q#	Question Type	Correct	Difficulty
1	Inference	C	★
2	Assumption (Necessary)	B	★
3	Principle (Identify/Strengthen)	C	★
4	Inference	D	★
5	Paradox	A	★
6	Strengthen	B	★
7	Flaw	B	★
8	Main Point	C	★
9	Parallel Reasoning	E	★★
10	Flaw	C	★★
11	Method of Argument	E	★★★
12	Strengthen	B	★★
13	Weaken	C	★★★★
14	Parallel Flaw	D	★★
15	Assumption (Sufficient)	E	★★
16	Flaw	A	★
17	Assumption (Necessary)	B	★★★
18	Flaw	E	★★
19	Assumption (Necessary)	C	★★★★
20	Role of a Statement	D	★★★
21	Strengthen	E	★★★
22	Weaken (EXCEPT)	A	★★★
23	Assumption (Necessary)	A	★
24	Inference	B	★★
25	Assumption (Necessary)	A	★★★★

1. (C) Inference

Step 1: Identify the Question Type
The correct answer will fill in the blank at the end of the given argument. The Keyword [o]*bviously* indicates that the last sentence, including the blank, will logically follow from the information before it. That means the last sentence is a supported inference.

Step 2: Untangle the Stimulus
New technology is presenting a lose-lose situation here. When companies adopt new technology, people who can master it do well. The rest lose their jobs. When companies *don't* adopt new technology, they become obsolete and *all* their employees lose their jobs.

Step 3: Make a Prediction
The blank will be the *obvious* conclusion regarding companies that resist new technology. According to the evidence, those companies will lose out to other companies, and employees will all lose their jobs. The correct answer will be consistent with this rather bleak outcome.

Step 4: Evaluate the Answer Choices
(C) cuts right to the idea of inevitable job loss.

(A) is a 180. Dislocated workers are the *more* likely scenario as employees lose their jobs.

(B) is a Distortion and a 180. Those who possess technical skills only retain their jobs in businesses that *apply* new technology. In industries that *resist* technology, *everyone* is affected.

(D) is a 180. Jobs will be lost, not created.

(E) is Out of Scope and a possible 180. The author is merely talking facts, and there's no support for a recommended course of action. Even if there were, resisting technology is going to lead to job loss—hardly an action that should "take priority over" anything.

2. (B) Assumption (Necessary)

Step 1: Identify the Question Type
This question directly asks for an assumption, which is said to be *required* by the argument. That makes this a Necessary Assumption question. The correct answer must be true for the conclusion to follow from the evidence.

Step 2: Untangle the Stimulus
Sales of the Hydro, a fuel-efficient vehicle, are increasing while sales of other fuel-efficient vehicles are going down. The Hydro's manufacturer attributes this to the Hydro's great price and low fuel consumption. The Keyword [h]*owever* indicates the author's disagreement. The author claims that the Hydro and its competitors have pretty much the same price and fuel consumption. The Keyword *so* indicates the author's alternative conclusion: the great sales are due to

something else: people wanting to show off how environmentally friendly they are.

Step 3: Make a Prediction
In determining why the Hydro's sales are so different from those of other fuel-efficient vehicles, the author is justified in rejecting two factors that are *not* different among the competing vehicles. However, why choose people's desire to look good for the neighbors as the difference-maker? The author doesn't even consider other potential factors, assuming that keeping up appearances is the one likely to affect sales. Furthermore, the author rejects price and fuel consumption because of their similarity among vehicles, but never actually says there's something *different* about the Hydro that helps people appear more environmentally friendly. There *must* be a difference to claim that as a cause of higher sales.

Step 4: Evaluate the Answer Choices
(B) must be true. After all, using the Denial Test, if the Hydro is *not* seen as being different from its competitors, then the author has no reason to cite appearances as a contributing factor.

(A) is Extreme. The Hydro does not have to be the *most* popular. Its sales can increase even while far more popular vehicles have slight dips in their sales.

(C) is an Irrelevant Comparison and a 180. A better safety record is irrelevant and would, if anything, provide an alternative explanation for sales that doesn't involve mere appearances.

(D) is a Distortion. The author's point is about people wanting to appear environmentally friendly; it's not about them wanting to own the same thing as their neighbors.

(E) is a Distortion and a possible 180. There's a difference between actually *being* interested in the environment and wanting to *appear* interested. At worst, if Hydro buyers don't really care about the environment, it's harder for the author to justify attributing sales to their wanting to appear environmentally friendly.

3. (C) Principle (Identify/Strengthen)

Step 1: Identify the Question Type
The question asks for a principle that will *justify*, or strengthen, the author's judgment. So, this is an Identify the Principle question that mimics a Strengthen question. The correct answer will support the author's reasoning in broad terms.

Step 2: Untangle the Stimulus
A homeowner is trying to file a complaint with the Licensing Bureau against a nightclub. She was supposed to use a particular form, but someone at the Licensing Bureau gave her a different form, and she used that one instead. The

nightclub wants the complaint dropped because the wrong form was used. The author disagrees (indicated by the Keyword [*b*]*ut*), claiming this would not be fair.

Step 3: Make a Prediction
Specifically, the author says it would be unfair to dismiss the homeowner's complaint, even though she clearly used the wrong form. The only evidence that could back up the author's judgment is that the homeowner was *given* the wrong form by the Licensing Bureau itself. The correct answer will generalize this: if somebody uses the wrong form because it was *given* to her, then it's not fair to dismiss the complaint.

Step 4: Evaluate the Answer Choices
(C) generalizes the circumstances exactly, thus supporting the author's claim.

(A) is Out of Scope. There's no evidence whether the homeowner was informed of the regulations or not. It's possible she was informed but was still given the wrong form.

(B) is Out of Scope. The author never mentions how difficult any of the forms are to fill out.

(D) is Out of Scope. The Bureau staff gave the homeowner the wrong form, but that doesn't necessarily indicate a lack of understanding of the procedures. It could have been a simple mistake.

(E) is Out of Scope. The question asks for justification as to why it's unfair for the homeowner, not why it's unfair for the business. Furthermore, there's nothing that suggests the nightclub wasn't allowed to defend itself anyway.

4. (D) Inference
Step 1: Identify the Question Type
The correct answer will be "supported by the information above," which means this is an Inference question. Look for ways to connect statements and make logical deductions.

Step 2: Untangle the Stimulus
Two general relationships are presented. Sickly birds have smaller spleens than healthy birds, and predators tend to kill birds with smaller spleens than those killed by accident.

Step 3: Make a Prediction
If predators tend to kill birds with smaller spleens and smaller spleens usually indicate more sickly birds, it stands to reason that predators tend to kill birds that are more sickly.

Step 4: Evaluate the Answer Choices
(D) makes the logical connection between what predators kill and the birds' health.

(A) is Extreme. Predators kill birds with smaller spleens (i.e., sickly birds) "in general." That hardly means they're *unable* to kill healthy birds.

(B) is also Extreme. Predators may kill lots of birds with smaller spleens, but there could still be countless more such birds that escape. Most such birds may survive after all.

(C) is Out of Scope. There's no evidence that the predators can *sense* sickness. Perhaps sickly birds are just slower and make easier targets.

(E) is an Extreme Distortion. What's described is merely a correlation between spleen size and sickness. There's no indication of causality, let alone whether spleen size would be a *main* cause.

5. (A) Paradox
Step 1: Identify the Question Type
The stimulus will provide an "apparent conflict," which the correct answer will *resolve*. Solving the mystery behind a conflict is the hallmark of a Paradox question.

Step 2: Untangle the Stimulus
As expected with a Paradox question, there's something *surprising*. In this case, home ownership is supposed to indicate economic prosperity, but unemployment is high in various regions where home ownership is prevalent.

Step 3: Make a Prediction
So, the mystery can be summarized simply as this: why would regions with so much home ownership—that should be home to economically prosperous residents—experience such high levels of unemployment? It's not worth predicting an exact explanation, but expect the correct answer to provide a reason why people struggle to find jobs in a good economy.

Step 4: Evaluate the Answer Choices
(A) could resolve the issue. Even though the economy of the region overall is great and there are plenty of jobs, unemployment is high because homeowners don't live near those jobs and would struggle to move closer.

(B) is a 180. If the jobs were moving *closer* to homeowners, the mystery deepens. Why are so many people still unemployed?

(C) is Out of Scope. If different social systems don't affect the level of unemployment, then the question still remains: why is unemployment so high in these regions?

(D) is a 180. If homeowners are more likely to help each other find jobs, it's even *less* clear why they're still unemployed.

(E) is a Distortion. This might explain the first piece of information: why home ownership is a sign of economic prosperity. However, that doesn't address the central conflict about why unemployment is so high in these cases.

6. (B) Strengthen

Step 1: Identify the Question Type
The correct answer "adds ... support," or strengthens, the given reasoning. Find the conclusion, which is said to be a *hypothesis*, and look for an answer that validates the assumption leading to that conclusion.

Step 2: Untangle the Stimulus
The hypothesis here is meant to explain the unusual eating habits of the tobacco hatchworm. If the first thing it feeds on after hatching is a nightshade plant, then that's the only type of plant it will ever eat. Otherwise, it's not as picky. The hypothesis is that this is due to a chemical found only in nightshade plants: indioside D. Once the worm tastes it, the worm's taste buds adapt to the chemical and everything else tastes terrible.

Step 3: Make a Prediction
The hypothesis is based on the suggested effect of the chemical on the worm's taste receptors. No other explanations are even suggested. That means the scientists are rejecting other possibilities, assuming that the eating habits are solely based on the chemical and taste. The correct answer will provide further evidence that the chemical and/or taste play a role in the worm's eating habits.

Step 4: Evaluate the Answer Choices
(B) provides some helpful evidence. If nightshade-eating hornworms *with* taste receptors keep eating nightshade plants, but nightshade-eating hornworms *without* taste receptors eat other plants, then that strengthens the hypothesis that taste receptors are a factor in the eating habits.

(A) is an Irrelevant Comparison. The argument is about why such worms would prefer nightshade plants over *non-nightshade* plants, not about any preference among different varieties of nightshade plants.

(C) is Out of Scope. The frequency of eggs being laid on nightshade plants would indicate *how often* hornworms develop the eating habits described, but the hypothesis is about *why* the worms have such eating habits.

(D) is a 180. If nightshade plants contain other unique chemicals, then there's reason to believe that even if taste is still a factor, it's something *other* than indioside D that plays a role.

(E) doesn't actually help, and could even be a 180. Even if the taste receptors react to *several* chemicals, that's not enough to suggest that indioside D is one of those chemicals. Even if that were the case, this would still create doubt by suggesting that there may be explanations other than indioside D.

7. (B) Flaw

Step 1: Identify the Question Type
The question asks why the given argument is *flawed*, making this easily identified as a Flaw question. Look for an answer that describes why the evidence does not adequately back up the conclusion.

Step 2: Untangle the Stimulus
The employee was given some feedback about a presentation: it should have had more detail. The Keyword [*s*]*o* expresses the employee's conclusion: this is wrong. There was no reason for more detail. The evidence is that too much detail would cause an audience to lose interest.

Step 3: Make a Prediction
The employee is right to worry about *too much* detail, but the boss merely requested *more*. There could have been room to add more detail without going overboard, but the employee fails to consider that—and that's the flaw in the argument.

Step 4: Evaluate the Answer Choices
(B) directly points out the employee's unwarranted leap from "more detail" to "too much detail."

(A) is Out of Scope. The employee is only rejecting one assessment about detail, not necessarily making any commentary or assumptions about the boss's assessments in general.

(C) is a Distortion. Even if there were other ways to lose an audience's attention, too much detail would still cause the audience's minds to wander—and the employee would be perfectly justified in wanting to avoid that.

(D) gets the logic backward. The employee rejects the assessment in a single case (advice on the employee's presentation) based on a generalization ("people's attention tends to wander") about what affects audiences in general.

(E) suggests the flaw of equivocation. However, the word *detail* is used consistently throughout the argument. It always refers to information (e.g., stats or data).

8. (C) Main Point

Step 1: Identify the Question Type
The question asks for the "overall conclusion," so this is a Main Point question. Look for the one claim that is supported by everything else.

Step 2: Untangle the Stimulus
The author starts with information about the media being proven wrong for touting the scandal-involved politician Clemens as honest. This information is then used to *demonstrate* a point: local media is often too deferential toward public figures. As further evidence, the author cites a newspaper editor who confessed that reporters ignored leads that could have exposed Clemens earlier.

Step 3: Make a Prediction

All of the information about Clemens consists of facts and details (i.e., evidence). These merely serve as a specific example to support (or, as the Keyword indicates, *demonstrate*) the author's broader main point (i.e., conclusion): local media show too much deference toward public figures.

Step 4: Evaluate the Answer Choices

(C) is the central point of the argument.

(A) is merely an established fact from the first sentence, not a conclusion.

(B) is a fact from the second sentence. However, that fact is used to *demonstrate* the broader point about media's treatment of public figures in general.

(D) is the fact in the last sentence, but it's still part of the specific situation that demonstrates the author's broader point about the local media in general.

(E) is implied, but it doesn't express the author's stated conclusion that there's "too much" of this kind of behavior.

9. (E) Parallel Reasoning

Step 1: Identify the Question Type

The correct answer will be an argument with reasoning "similar to" that of the given argument. That indicates a Parallel Reasoning question. Compare structural components, and find the answer that reaches the same type of conclusion using the same logic as the stimulus.

Step 2: Untangle the Stimulus

The given argument is based on Formal Logic. If there were ever life on the Moon, there would be signs. However, we have never found any signs, so there must never have been life there.

Step 3: Make a Prediction

The author basically uses a contrapositive to reach the conclusion:

If	**life on Mars**	→	**signs**

If	**~ signs**	→	**~ life on Mars**

However, the reasoning is not quite that sound. The conclusion is concrete ("there has *never* been life on the Moon"), but the evidence just states we haven't *found* any signs. That doesn't mean the signs don't exist. Even though this question isn't presented as a Parallel Flaw question, the correct answer should still follow the same questionable format: if an event were to occur (life on Moon), there would be evidence (signs). We haven't *seen* that evidence, so the event doesn't happen.

Step 4: Evaluate the Answer Choices

(E) matches the logic exactly. If an event were to occur (army plans an attack), there would be evidence (troop movements or weapons transfer). We haven't *seen* that evidence, so the event doesn't happen.

If	**planning an attack**	→	**troop movements OR transfer of weapons**

If	**~ troop movements AND ~ transfer of weapons**	→	**~ planning an attack**

Again, the same unsound reasoning applies: intelligence reports don't indicate troop movements or weapon transfers, but that doesn't mean they haven't actually happened.

(A) falls apart immediately by presenting a known piece of evidence ("We know that the spy is a traitor"). Nothing was known in the original argument. Also, there's no Formal Logic here.

(B) has Formal Logic, but the conclusion is qualified ("it is unlikely") rather than unjustifiably strong. Also, the evidence is different. Instead of citing a lack of evidence (e.g., "there's no sign of mayonnaise"), it merely says the refrigerator is *almost* empty.

(C) fails on a couple of levels. For starters, "will probably go" in the conclusion doesn't denote the same unwarranted strength as the original stimulus. Also, the terms in the Formal Logic don't exactly match: *Hendricks's* view on criminal penalties is not an exact match of *voters'* concern with fighting crime.

(D) has the Formal Logic: if an event were to occur (rodents affecting harvest), there would be evidence. However, instead of citing a lack of evidence to kick off a contrapositive, the author states that they *have* found evidence and concludes that the event *did* occur.

If	**rodents responsible**	→	**signs**

If	**signs**	→	**rodents responsible**

This argument improperly confuses necessity and sufficiency (i.e., it reverses without negating—a necessary versus sufficient flaw). However, that was not a problem with the original argument.

10. (C) Flaw

Step 1: Identify the Question Type
The correct answer will describe why the given argument is *flawed*, making this easy to spot as a Flaw question.

Step 2: Untangle the Stimulus
The phrase "I still believe" is a clear indication of the host's conclusion: the defendant is still guilty, despite a strong alibi, evidence of innocence, and an acquittal. And what evidence does the host have? Merely the fact that the prosecutor brought up charges in the first place.

Step 3: Make a Prediction
So, despite all of the evidence to the contrary, the host is still siding against the defendant based on the opinion of one person: the prosecuting attorney. However, opinions are just that—opinions. Without actual evidence to contradict the acquittal, the alibi, and everything else, the host's reliance on the prosecutor's actions are dubious at best.

Step 4: Evaluate the Answer Choices
(C) correctly exposes the host's reliance on an authority figure (the prosecutor) rather than having any actual evidence.

(A) is a Distortion. The host does conclude that a view (the defendant is innocent) is false. However, there *is* plenty of evidence for the defendant's innocence.

(B) suggests circular reasoning. However, the host's argument is based on what the prosecutor did, so the host's evidence and assumptions—although still flawed—are not merely a repeat of the conclusion.

(D) is Out of Scope. The argument is solely about legal guilt. Moral standards are never addressed.

(E) is a Distortion. While it *is* said that the defendant was "quickly acquitted," that's not the host's reason for doubting the judgment. The host dismisses the judgment because of the prosecutor's actions.

11. (E) Method of Argument

Step 1: Identify the Question Type
This is certainly an unusual question stem. However, when analyzed carefully, it's merely asking for the professor's argumentative strategy, i.e., *how* the professor presents the argument. So, this is a Method of Argument question. As an added benefit, the question already provides half the answer: the professor argues that the critics haven't properly established their point. The correct answer will complete the thought by expressing the *grounds*, or evidence, for the professor's claim.

Step 2: Untangle the Stimulus
Critics argue that Sauk's works lack aesthetic merit because he uses the same style as another writer who would disagree with Sauk's political ideals. The professor concedes those points, but claims they have no effect on the craft of Sauk's writings. As indicated by the Keyword [s]o, the professor concludes that the critics are wrong.

Step 3: Make a Prediction
The last sentence is the professor's conclusion, which rejects the critics' claim (just as the question stem suggested). The *grounds* for this claim are presented immediately before it: even though the critics make valid points, those points can't be said to devalue the merit of Sauk's works. The correct answer will express that piece of evidence.

Step 4: Evaluate the Answer Choices
(E) accurately expresses the professor's reasoning. The critics may have good points, but they're not relevant. Sauk's works are still subtly and powerfully crafted.

(A) is a 180. The professor concedes the critics' points, agreeing that Sauk is an imitator with different political views.

(B) is a Faulty Use of Detail. This is what the professor is arguing, not the *grounds*, or evidence, in support of that argument.

(C) is a Distortion. While it *is* claimed that some critics would reject Sauk's political ideals, the professor never cites that as a motivation for their assessment.

(D) is another 180. The author admits that the critics' claims (Sauk's imitative style and different political views) are indeed correct. The professor just disagrees with the critics' assessment that Sauk's work lacks aesthetic merit.

12. (B) Strengthen

Step 1: Identify the Question Type
The stimulus presents a policy (usually associated with Principle questions), as well as an application of that policy. The application will be the conclusion based on the policy, which serves as the evidence. You don't need to broaden or narrow anything—just justify the application—which is why this is a Strengthen question rather than a Principle question.

Step 2: Untangle the Stimulus
The application concludes that a factory's safety inspector should reject a new welding process because there's no evidence that it will make things safer. This application is based on the Formal Logic of the policy:

$$\text{If } \begin{array}{l} \textit{new process} \\ \textit{approved} \end{array} \rightarrow \begin{array}{l} \textit{used for over a} \\ \textit{year at} \\ \textit{another} \\ \textit{factory OR} \\ \textit{shown to} \\ \textit{increase} \\ \textit{safety} \end{array}$$

Step 3: Make a Prediction

Approval requires a one-year testing cycle *or* a display of safety. Even though the new welding process failed to display safety, it could *still* meet the other requirement: the one-year test at another factory. To justify rejecting the new welding process, it should be shown that the process doesn't meet that other requirement. Essentially, the application formed the contrapositive, but didn't add the term before the *and* on the sufficient side.

$$\text{If } \begin{array}{l} \textit{~ used for over} \\ \textit{a year at} \\ \textit{another factory} \\ \textit{AND ~ shown} \\ \textit{to increase} \\ \textit{safety} \end{array} \rightarrow \begin{array}{l} \textit{~ new process} \\ \textit{approved} \end{array}$$

Step 4: Evaluate the Answer Choices

(B) fills in the missing gap. If the process wasn't used anywhere else at all, then it hasn't been used for more than a year. Add that to the evidence that it hasn't been shown to increase safety, and that's enough to say it shouldn't be approved.

(A) is Out of Scope. While problems may *sound* like a good reason to reject the process, the policy still allows acceptance under the condition that it was used somewhere else safely for more than a year. It doesn't necessarily matter what happened at the factory where it was *first* introduced. Perhaps there have been many other factories that have subsequently used it without incident for more than a year.

(C) is a Distortion and Out of Scope. This suggests that the new welding process is just as safe, if not *safer*, than some current processes. However, the policy only involves approving new processes, not about necessarily eliminating ones currently used. The processes that are currently used that are "not demonstrably safer" may be for tasks other than welding, and are thus irrelevant. The author's point goes unjustified because it's not known if the welding process was tested elsewhere.

(D) is Extreme and a Distortion. The question is only about the new welding process, not *any* new process. And besides,

there's still no evidence about how much this new process was used elsewhere.

(E) is a Distortion. It doesn't matter how *many* other factories use the process. The requirement is based on how *long* it's been used elsewhere. Unless that one factory has been using it less than a year, this is not enough to reject the new process.

13. (C) Weaken

Step 1: Identify the Question Type

This question directly asks for something that weakens the given argument.

Step 2: Untangle the Stimulus

Grad students are complaining that TAs should be treated as and receive benefits like other university employees. The Keyword [*h*]*owever* indicates the administrator's contrary point: the only reason TAs are used is to help them pay for college. The evidence is that TAs are solely students who couldn't otherwise pay for their education.

Step 3: Make a Prediction

While the TA population may consist entirely of students who need financial help, the administrator is making a rather strong claim that this is the *sole* reason for the TA program. This suggests that the university has no reason to use TAs other than generous altruism. Any answer that suggests an ulterior motive will undermine the administrator's argument.

Step 4: Evaluate the Answer Choices

(C) implies that TAs are being used to support the university's economic interest—hardly the selfless goal the administrator was boasting about.

(A) is irrelevant. The administrator's point is that the university is merely helping the TAs fund their education. Benefits are a nonissue, so it doesn't matter whether the administrator is aware of the benefits costs.

(B) is Out of Scope. The presence of adjunct faculty has no effect on why the university employs TAs.

(D) is a Distortion. The administrator states that TAs are paid to fund their *education*. Even if they're paid beyond *tuition* costs, the extra stipend may still be used for other educational purposes such as books or lab fees. In that case, the administrator's argument would still hold.

(E) is Out of Scope. The work ethic of TAs does not change the administrator's reasoning for hiring them in the first place.

14. (D) Parallel Flaw

Step 1: Identify the Question Type

The question directly asks for parallel reasoning that is described as *flawed*, so this is a Parallel Flaw question. The correct answer will not only have the same logical structure as the stimulus, but it will also contain the same logical flaw.

Step 2: Untangle the Stimulus
Branson points out that air pollution is most prevalent in large cities. So, Branson suggests moving people out of the large cities. That would reduce pollution in those cities, and thus reduce pollution in the country as a whole.

Step 3: Make a Prediction
Branson overlooks a fundamental issue: moving people out of the city doesn't eliminate pollution. The pollution will just move with people to the rural areas. So, pollution may go down in the city, but the overall level won't necessarily change. The correct answer will try to apply the same faulty logic: concluding that something will be reduced overall (pollution) by moving it from where it appears most (large cities) to someplace else (rural areas).

Step 4: Evaluate the Answer Choices
(D) makes the same mistake. It concludes that something will be reduced overall (caloric intake) by moving it from where it appears most (major meals) to someplace else (snacks). And just as Branson's country will still produce the same amount of pollution overall, Javier will still consume the same number of calories overall.

(A) doesn't match from the get-go. The conclusion is not about reducing something overall. It's a claim about "most of" something, which should be part of the evidence. **(A)** is flawed because although Monique is spending *more* on housing, it is unknown if she spends *most* of her salary on housing.

(B) talks about having *more* of something (living space), rather than reducing something. Regardless, the evidence isn't about moving that something from one place to another, so the logic doesn't line up. The logic of **(B)** is sound—not flawed—provided Karen's family has a typical apartment and would move to a typical single-family home.

(C) also stumbles immediately by not having a conclusion about reducing something overall. Again, this has a conclusion about "most of" something, which should be part of the evidence. **(C)** is flawed because it is unknown if Ward's farm is representative of the rest of the county. Although the county as a whole has switched most fields planted with other crops to corn, there's no guarantee that Ward's farm has followed suit. Furthermore, there's no information on what proportion of Ward's fields were planted with other crops to begin with. It's possible it's been untended or used as grazing land, so even a switch to corn for those fields that were planted might not mean *most* of the farm is now planted with corn.

(E) again fails to present a conclusion about reducing something overall. And again, the conclusion is about "most of" something, which should be part of the evidence. **(E)** is flawed because although pollution would be reduced if people switched to public transportation, it is unknown if

most pollution would be eliminated. Perhaps the majority of pollution was not related to transportation.

15. (E) Assumption (Sufficient)

Step 1: Identify the Question Type
The question asks for something that, *if* it were *assumed*, would complete the logic of the argument. That makes it a Sufficient Assumption question. The correct answer will logically close the gap between the evidence and the conclusion.

Step 2: Untangle the Stimulus
A lot of people claim that safety is an important factor in buying a car. However, of these people, only half researched objective safety details while the other half just looked at ads. The Keyword [*t*]*hus* indicates the author's conclusion: the latter half doesn't really consider safety all that important.

Step 3: Make a Prediction
The author makes quite a jump in logic. The evidence and conclusion are about the same group of people, but the evidence merely mentions their information source (nonobjective ads), while the conclusion judges their concerns about safety (they're not really concerned). The assumption will connect those concepts: people who don't research objective sources of safety aren't really concerned about safety. Or, to put it in contrapositive terms, people who *are* concerned about safety *do* research objective sources.

Step 4: Evaluate the Answer Choices
(E) makes the logical connection between safety concerns and the buyers' sources of information.

(A) is Out of Scope. This argument isn't concerned with what people would consider the *most* important factor in a buying decision.

(B) is a Distortion. Even if the promotional information is incomplete, the second group of people might think it's enough to make a sound judgment of safety. In that case, they *would* still be interested in safety, contrary to the author's point.

(C) is a Distortion. This suggests that some car buyers *may* not be telling the truth. However, it doesn't say which ones. It's possible that the ones who just check ads are still telling the truth, contradicting the author's point.

(D) is a Distortion. Even if people know the ads are subjective, they could still trust the ads and consider the safety information to be valid. In that case, they could still be telling the truth about their safety concerns.

16. (A) Flaw

Step 1: Identify the Question Type
The question is directly asking for the flaw in the argument. Be on the lookout for some commonly tests flaws.

Step 2: Untangle the Stimulus

The Keyword [*t*]*hus* indicates the author's conclusion: if an organism can't perform planned locomotion, it doesn't have a central nervous system. The evidence is that planned locomotion requires certain activities, which in turn require a central nervous system.

Step 3: Make a Prediction

By Formal Logic, the evidence states that organisms require a central nervous system for planned locomotion, meaning a central nervous system is *necessary*.

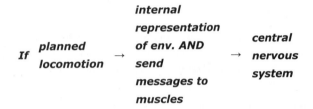

	planned	→	*internal representation of env. AND send messages to muscles*	→	*central nervous system*
If	*locomotion*				

However, the author concludes that organisms *unable* to perform planned locomotion *don't* have central nervous systems.

If	*~ planned locomotion*	→	*~ central nervous system*

That logic by the author negates without reversing. By contrapositive of the faulty conclusion, that also means if it *did* have a central nervous system, it *could* perform planned locomotion.

If	*central nervous system*	→	*planned locomotion*

The author concludes that the central nervous system is *sufficient*. That's not supported by the evidence, making this a classic case of the author confusing necessity and sufficiency.

Step 4: Evaluate the Answer Choices

(A) indicates the author's all-too-common flaw.

(B) is a Distortion. It does work backward from the intermediate requirement of sending messages to muscles to the original sufficient statement of planned locomotion. However, there are a few inconsistencies. Nothing indicates that the messages to the muscles definitely come from the nervous system. Furthermore, this answer merely discusses locomotion, not necessarily *planned* locomotion. If any animals were capable of *unplanned* locomotion, the author makes no assumptions about them.

(C) is an Extreme Distortion. The author does mention that planned locomotion requires forming a representation of the environment, but never suggests that planned locomotion is the *only useful* result of such a representation.

(D) is Out of Scope. The author merely discusses what factors are involved in planned locomotion, not the reason such factors arose in the first place.

(E) is a Distortion. The author only makes assumptions about a *central* nervous system, not a *rudimentary* nervous system. Besides, the argument is about how it relates to planned locomotion, not the internal representation.

17. (B) Assumption (Necessary)

Step 1: Identify the Question Type

The question directly asks for an assumption, and one that that argument *requires*, making it a Necessary Assumption question.

Step 2: Untangle the Stimulus

Thus indicates the author's conclusion: all rockets need both short and long nozzles on the engines to work most effectively throughout their ascent. The evidence is that the different nozzle sizes work better at different pressures—short nozzles are best for the lower atmosphere (high pressure), and long nozzles are best for the upper atmosphere (lower pressure).

Step 3: Make a Prediction

Different nozzles would certainly work best on any rocket going through the different layers of the atmosphere. However, the author's conclusion is about *all* rockets. Do all rockets go through the different layers? That would have to be true for the author's argument to work.

Step 4: Evaluate the Answer Choices

(B) must be true. Consider the Denial Test. What if there were some rockets that *didn't* pass through the upper atmosphere; they just rose through the lower atmosphere, then descended. Those rockets would only need short nozzles, not long nozzles. The author's point would be invalid—not *every* rocket would need both nozzle sizes.

(A) is Out of Scope. The difficulty of installing the different nozzles doesn't matter. Even if they were harder to install, they could still be necessary.

(C) is a Distortion. The argument is not about whether a rocket *can* reach high altitudes, it's about how it can do so *most effectively*.

(D) is a subtle Distortion. This suggests that equal pressure between the nozzles and atmosphere is needed for the rocket to work effectively at all. However, that doesn't have to be true. The argument is about what would be *most* effective. Even if rockets worked effectively with single-size nozzles, the use of long and short nozzles could still be the *most* effective solution.

(E) is yet another subtle Distortion. The author claims that short and long nozzles both need to be present, but not necessarily on the same engines. Perhaps each rocket has multiple engines, with each engine used at different altitudes. In that case, the engines used at lower altitudes would need short nozzles while the other engines would need long nozzles. There wouldn't need to be any individual engine with both nozzles.

18. (E) Flaw

Step 1: Identify the Question Type
The question directly asks for the flaw in the consumer advocate's argument. Look for a reason why the evidence doesn't adequately back up the conclusion.

Step 2: Untangle the Stimulus
The Keyword [*t*]*herefore* indicates the conclusion: toy manufacturers shouldn't overstate the danger of their products. The evidence is that manufacturers are overstating dangers merely to protect themselves from lawsuits, and dangers should be overstated only if that will reduce injuries.

Step 3: Make a Prediction
The given principle is the key here: overstating dangers should be done *only if* it reduces injuries. To conclude that labels *shouldn't* overstate dangers, the author must be assuming that the warnings don't actually reduce injuries. But what if they *do*? What if, even though manufacturers aren't *trying* to reduce injuries (just trying to protect themselves), the labels *still* help reduce injuries anyway? The author overlooks that possibility, continuing to assume that injuries will not be reduced.

Step 4: Evaluate the Answer Choices
(E) needs to be translated a little, but gets to the core problem. The author does assume that an action (overstating dangers) would only have an effect (reduce injuries) if that were the motive. But because that's *not* the manufacturers' motive, the author assumes the labels won't have that effect.

(A) is a Distortion. The author never identifies anything necessary to reducing injury. Instead, the effect of reducing injury is itself a necessary condition for using labels with overstated dangers.

(B) is Out of Scope. This argument is only concerned with labels that *do* overstate dangers. It doesn't matter what happens with labels that *don't*.

(C) is Out of Scope. There is no sample. The evidence and conclusion are both about toys in general.

(D) is a Distortion. The author doesn't assume that labels that overstate dangers won't *prevent* injuries. The author just

assumes that they won't necessarily *reduce* the number of injuries.

19. (C) Assumption (Necessary)

Step 1: Identify the Question Type
The question outright asks for an assumption, and one on which the argument *depends*, making this a Necessary Assumption question.

Step 2: Untangle the Stimulus
The author concludes, as indicated by [*t*]*hus*, that drinking tea boosted immune system defenses. The evidence is that the blood cells in people who drank only tea responded twice as fast to germs as blood cells in people who drank only coffee.

Step 3: Make a Prediction
Why did tea drinkers' blood cells act so much more quickly? The author assumes it must have had something to do with the tea. However, there could be another explanation. Alas, the author assumes otherwise—that nothing else (e.g., something about the coffee) was responsible for the discrepancy in blood cell response time.

Step 4: Evaluate the Answer Choices
(C) must be true. If everyone started out with the same response time, the author is implying response time got *faster* in tea drinkers. But what if, instead, the response time just got *slower* in coffee drinkers? Then the tea would have been ineffective, denying the author's reasoning. The author *must* assume that the coffee had no such effect. A quick check using the Denial Test rephrases **(C)** as "drinking coffee *did* cause the blood cell response time to double." If true, that would destroy the author's argument.

(A) is not necessary. The author only mentions the people who drank tea or coffee exclusively, but there could have been other people in the study who did drink both but were irrelevant to the author's argument.

(B) is Out of Scope. Other health benefits have nothing to do with whether the tea was responsible for the immune system response discrepancy.

(D) is Out of Scope. Using the Denial Test, even if coffee drinkers *did* have healthier lifestyles, the tea could still have been responsible for boosting immune defenses. This does not need to be true for the argument to work.

(E) is also Out of Scope. Even if tea has a unique chemical to boost immune defenses, that doesn't mean it can't share some other chemical with coffee that fights disease in some other way. Testing **(E)** with the Denial Test indicates that the two drinks *do* share a chemical that helps fight disease. That fact would in no way invalidate the author's conclusion about tea leading to improved immune response times.

20. (D) Role of a Statement

Step 1: Identify the Question Type

This question stem is rather long, but it's merely asking for "the role played" by a particular claim from the stimulus. That makes this a Role of a Statement question. Start by marking the claim in question in the stimulus. Then, break the argument down and consider *how* the marked claim fits within the structure.

Step 2: Untangle the Stimulus

The statement in question (about transportation being more expensive on monohulls than on regular ships) is the second sentence. As for the rest of the argument, the conclusion comes at the very end, indicated by the Keyword [*t*]*hus*: monohulls will be profitable. The evidence is that monohulls have advantages similar to jet planes, which were also able to be profitable despite how expensive it was to use them initially.

Step 3: Make a Prediction

The statement in question (travel on monohulls will be much more expensive) doesn't sound good for the author's conclusion about their potential profitability. However, the author then brings up the analogy to jet planes to show why that statement regarding cost won't necessarily affect profitability in the long run. The correct answer will express how the statement is presented as a possible problem that's explained away by the jet analogy.

Step 4: Evaluate the Answer Choices

(D) expresses the statement's role exactly.

(A) is a Distortion. The statement in question compares monohulls to other ships, not jets.

(B) is another Distortion. The author is merely comparing monohulls to other ships, not drawing an analogy between them. The analogy in the argument is between monohulls and jets.

(C) is a 180. The distinction actually goes *against* the author's claim that monohulls will be profitable until the analogy overrules it.

(E) is a Distortion. The author's main conclusion is solely about monohulls. Comparing the ships' distinction to the planes' distinction is all part of the evidence. The statement in question also only discusses the relative transportation costs of each type of ship, but does not otherwise make distinctions about their characteristics.

21. (E) Strengthen

Step 1: Identify the Question Type

The question asks for something that will strengthen the given argument. Find an answer that validates the connection between the evidence and the conclusion.

Step 2: Untangle the Stimulus

The Keyword [*t*]*herefore* indicates the conclusion: maté probably originated in Paraguay. Why? Because maté is more varied and more widely used in Paraguay than anywhere else.

Step 3: Make a Prediction

The argument is all about maté. The evidence is about its varieties and usage, while the conclusion is about its origin. The correct answer will validate the connection made by the author between those concepts—specifically that the place where maté is most varied and most widely used is most likely its place of origin.

Step 4: Evaluate the Answer Choices

(E) makes a helpful proportional connection between usage and origin. If a place uses something *more widely* as it's used for a *longer* time, then it stands to reason that the place with the *widest* usage (as is the case with maté in Paraguay) is likely to be where it's been used the *longest*, i.e., where it was first used.

(A) doesn't help in the same way as **(E)** because it doesn't give a proportional relationship. Even though variety may be an indication of how long something has been used, it still wouldn't necessarily mean Paraguay was the origin, even if it's been there a "very long time." For instance, even if there's a lack of variety in places where maté is relatively new, that doesn't mean the area with the *most* variety is the origin (where it's been around the longest). Maybe the origin country also lacks a lot of variety (e.g., uses only its purest variety).

(B) is a 180. This suggests that maté originated elsewhere and was brought to Paraguay as people migrated there.

(C) is Out of Scope. Even if Paraguayan people believe they have the *best* maté, that doesn't mean it originated there. After all, New Yorkers and Chicagoans often debate who has the best pizza, but it still originated in Italy.

(D) doesn't help. This just means maté is primarily consumed in South America, but it doesn't pinpoint Paraguay as the origin.

22. (A) Weaken (EXCEPT)

Step 1: Identify the Question Type

According to the question, a group of opponents are going to argue why family income has decreased. Four answers will counter, i.e., weaken their argument. The correct answer will be the exception—the one that strengthens or has no effect on the argument.

Step 2: Untangle the Stimulus

In a certain country, average family income decreased over an eight-year period. A political party's opponents argue that this decrease was caused by the party's economical mismanagement.

Step 3: Make a Prediction

The opponents provide no stated evidence, but they are concluding a causal relationship (economic mismanagement caused family income to drop). Such an argument would be weakened by indicating an alternate cause, e.g., another reason why average family income went down. Four answers will suggest alternate causes; the correct answer will not.

Step 4: Evaluate the Answer Choices

(A) is the exception. Even if family income went up in 1996, it still went down overall by 2004, and this answer does nothing to reject economic mismanagement as a cause for that decrease.

(B) weakens the argument directly by providing a "noneconomic" cause: fewer families with multiple incomes.

(C) weakens the argument by freeing the government of guilt and citing outside factors as the cause.

(D) weakens the argument by pointing to another noneconomic cause: the working population is getting younger, and younger people earn less money. No economic mismanagement there.

(E) directly weakens the opponents' claim by citing a *previous* party's policies as the cause for lower family incomes.

23. (A) Assumption (Necessary)

Step 1: Identify the Question Type

The question asks for what the argument "requires assuming," which means this is a Necessary Assumption question. Find the answer that must be true for the argument to work.

Step 2: Untangle the Stimulus

The author is comparing two groups of amateur gardeners. The first group chooses when to plant based on phases of the moon. The second group plants when the weather first gets warm in the spring. The author concludes (indicated by the Keyword [*s*]*o*) that the first group won't lose as many plants to frost. The evidence is that a frost can follow the first warm spell of spring.

Step 3: Make a Prediction

If the first warm spell of spring is followed by a frost, then plants from the second group of gardeners are certainly at risk. To better avoid frost damage, gardeners would have to wait a little longer before planting. The author must be assuming that gardeners using the moon phases must be doing this—waiting a little longer. That's the only way they'd be less at risk for frost damages.

Step 4: Evaluate the Answer Choices

(A) must be true. Using the Denial Test, if gardeners using moon phases planted at the *same time or earlier* than the other gardeners, they would be exposed to the exact same risk when a frost hits. The author must assume that they plant

a little later in the season when there's less likely to be an unexpected frost.

(B) would certainly help the author's point: if phases of the moon affected frosts, then gardeners watching the phases could better predict a frost and avoid it. But despite its helpfulness, this isn't *required*, as the question demands. Even if the moon phases had *no* effect on frosts, they could still indicate a later planting time, helping gardeners avoid frost by happenstance.

(C) is an Irrelevant Comparison. Even if they all planted the *same* types of plants, the author's point could still be valid. Again, this *could* be helpful if the first group used frost-resistant plants and the second group didn't. However, that distinction isn't drawn here, and it still wouldn't *need* to be true.

(D) is Out of Scope. Whether gardeners understand what they're doing has no effect on the author's argument.

(E) is Out of Scope. The argument is about amateur gardeners, not professional ones. Nothing would need to be true about the pros for this argument to work.

24. (B) Inference

Step 1: Identify the Question Type

The correct answer will be "strongly supported" by the given information. That means it will be a deducible inference. Accept the given information as true, and combine whatever statements you can to make deductions.

Step 2: Untangle the Stimulus

The columnist is talking about the tourism industry in developing countries. On average, tourism companies owned by foreigners take in about 70 percent of tourism profits—a number that generally increases as a country becomes a popular tourist destination. This can be offset if tourists use locals for some services.

Step 3: Make a Prediction

Seventy percent is the *average* percentage going to foreign owners, which means there must be countries where the percentage is even *higher*. And those countries must be among the most popular if the percentage generally increases as popularity increases. The last line about tourists needs to be treated carefully. It merely says that tourists *can* counteract this situation. It doesn't say they *will*, and it doesn't say by how much. If the correct answer uses this information, it must retain the conservative language. Otherwise, the correct answer will merely be based on the facts from the first two sentences.

Step 4: Evaluate the Answer Choices

(B) is supported by the opening statistics. If the percentage of profits that goes to foreign owners increases with a country's popularity, then there must be *some* countries among the most popular that make above-average profits. And if the average is 70 percent, that's already well above *most* of the profits.

(A) is a Distortion. The author merely mentions that tourists *can* do this, but never comes out and suggests that they *should*.

(C) is possible, but not supported. If an average of 70 percent of tourism goes to foreigners, that means an average of 30 percent goes to locals. However, the countries where locals make an above-average percentage could still provide less than half of the services.

(D) is Extreme and a Distortion. Locals may get a smaller *percentage* of tourism profits, but they can still make more money if the total profits increase substantially. (For example, 25 percent of $20 million ($5 million) is still more than 30 percent of $10 million ($3 million).) Also, the profit figures deal only in tourism income. Even if the local people lose out on some of those revenues, nothing in the stimulus prevents them from possibly offsetting that loss by making more in a different industry. So, it is not supported that the locals will get "progressively poorer."

(E) is Extreme. Tourists who use local services can counteract foreign owners' profits to *some* degree, but they may still use foreign tourism business for some aspects of their vacation. It can't be said that they won't contribute "in any way" to foreign owners' profits.

25. (A) Assumption (Necessary)

Step 1: Identify the Question Type
The argument given "depends on assuming" the correct answer, which means this is a Necessary Assumption question.

Step 2: Untangle the Stimulus
The Keyword *therefore* indicates the conclusion: it's impossible to tell if the population of certain amphibians is being affected by industrial pollution. The evidence is that the population of most amphibians is affected by weather variations.

Step 3: Make a Prediction
If weather was a potential factor, then it would certainly be challenging to blame pollution. However, the argument's conclusion is about certain amphibian species identified by scientists in the first sentence. It's only said that *most* amphibians are affected by weather, not necessarily *all* amphibians—and certainly not necessarily the ones the scientists are talking about. In order for the argument to work properly, the author *must* assume that the amphibians cited are among those affected by the weather.

Step 4: Evaluate the Answer Choices
(A) is necessary for the author's argument. Be careful interpreting all of the negatives. This basically says that the amphibians in question are not *un*affected by the weather (i.e., they *are* affected by weather).

(B) is a 180. To claim it's impossible to blame pollution, weather would have to have the *same* impact as pollution. Then it would be impossible to tell the difference. This says the exact opposite.

(C) isn't necessary. The author isn't saying it must be one or the other, exclusively. Even if the population could be affected by a combination of the two—or even an unmentioned third factor—the author can still validly claim that pollution is impossible to confirm.

(D) is a Distortion. This only relates how pollution can affect *certain* amphibians, but not necessarily the same amphibians in question in this argument.

(E) is Out of Scope. There's no distinction made as to whether the claimed pollution is severe or not, so it's impossible to apply the logic of this answer to the argument. Also, the answer can be eliminated using the Denial Test: if industrial pollution is severe, it *cannot* create more weather variations that would occur naturally. That fact wouldn't ruin the author's claim that it is impossible to determine what's causing the amphibian populations to decline.

Section IV: Logic Games

Game 1: Employee Bonuses

Q#	Question Type	Correct	Difficulty
1	Acceptability	C	★
2	"If" / Could Be True	B	★
3	"If" / Must Be True	A	★
4	Must Be True	E	★
5	"If" / Must Be True	D	★
6	Could Be True EXCEPT	B	★★

Game 2: Landscaper's Trees

Q#	Question Type	Correct	Difficulty
7	Acceptability	D	★
8	"If" / Must Be True	B	★
9	Complete and Accurate List	C	★★
10	"If" / Could Be True	A	★★★
11	Completely Determine	A	★★★

Game 3: Librarians' Desk Duty

Q#	Question Type	Correct	Difficulty
12	Acceptability	A	★
13	Must Be False (CANNOT Be True)	E	★
14	"If" / Must Be False (CANNOT Be True)	B	★
15	"If" / Must Be True	A	★★
16	"If" / Must Be True	C	★
17	"If" / Must Be True	D	★★
18	Rule Substitution	C	★★★

Game 4: Business Newsletter

Q#	Question Type	Correct	Difficulty
19	Acceptability	D	★★★
20	"If" / Must Be True	A	★★
21	Must Be False	E	★★★★
22	"If" / Must Be True	D	★★★
23	Could Be True EXCEPT	D	★★★

Game 1: Employee Bonuses

Step 1: Overview

Situation: An HR department giving out bonuses to employees

Entities: Seven employees—four in Finance (Kimura, Lopez, Meng, Peterson) and three in Graphics (Vaughan, Xavier, Zane); three bonus values ($1,000, $3,000, $5,000)

Action: Distribution. Determine the bonus for each employee. Each employee can only receive exactly one of the bonuses, which is why this is categorized as Distribution rather than Matching. However, the game could work conceptually as other actions, too. For instance, each bonus could be matched to a different employee, in which case, although each employee still receives exactly one bonus, each bonus could be repeated. Additionally, there is an argument for calling it a Sequencing game given that Rule 2 calls for some employees to be in a *larger* denomination group than some others. Remember, though, that however you classify a game is substantially less important than assuring you have a Master Sketch that allows you to build in rules and spot deductions.

Limitations: Each employee gets one bonus, but there's no limit to how many employees get each bonus.

Step 2: Sketch

List the employees by initial, using uppercase and lowercase letters to distinguish the two subgroups (Finance and Graphics). Set up a column for each bonus. The employees will be distributed once each.

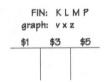

Note that the overview never states that each bonus value will be given out, so one or more columns may be blank. Therefore, don't add any slots in the columns until they've been established.

This sketch is consistent with a standard Distribution game, in which one set of entities is assigned once apiece to subgroups. However, some may find it unusual to assign people to bonuses—the real world usually works the other way around. That would suggest a sketch in which the seven people are listed on top, with one slot below each to assign the bonus. That type of setup would indicate a Matching game as noted as a possibility in Step 1.

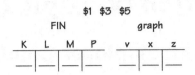

In fact, the answers to the first question (an Acceptability question) use that setup. Ultimately, either sketch would work fine for this game, with no change in how deductions are made. These explanations will use the Distribution instead of the Matching configuration because a Distribution sketch would also be parallel to a Sequencing approach. However, neither the Distribution nor the Matching approach is superior. It is simply a matter of personal preference.

Step 3: Rules

Rule 1 sets a restriction on the three Graphics employees (Vaughan, Xavier, and Zane). None of them will receive a $1,000 bonus. Add "~v," "~x," and "~z" under the $1,000 column.

Rule 2 suggests that some people in each department may be rated Highly Effective. Within each department, those rated Highly Effective will make more than those not. Because the ratings haven't been assigned yet, draw a note to the side that expresses the rule: "Each dept: Not High Eff $ < High Eff $."

Rule 3 rates all of the employees. Lopez, Meng, and Xavier are Highly Effective. The rest are not. Mark L, M, and x (e.g., star them, circle them, or underline them) to indicate this rating.

Step 4: Deductions

There's not much to work with, but there's enough to make some serious deductions. Start with the Finance Department. Two of them (Lopez and Meng) are Highly Effective; the others (Kimura and Peterson) are not. That means Lopez and Meng must get bigger bonuses than Kimura and Peterson.

$$K \& P < L \& M$$

That means Lopez and Meng cannot get $1,000 bonuses, and Kimura and Peterson cannot get $5,000 bonuses. Note that neither pair has to receive the same bonuses. In other words, Lopez and Meng can get different bonuses, as long as both of their bonuses are greater than Kimura's and Peterson's.

There are a few ways the Finance bonuses can work out. However, it's helpful to note that if one Finance person gets a $3,000 bonus, that will be significant. For example, if Kimura receives a $3,000 bonus, then Lopez and Meng must both get $5,000 bonuses. Peterson could then get either $1,000 or $3,000. Don't worry about considering every outcome, but do take note of the limited ways these bonuses can be paid out.

The Graphics department provides even bigger deductions. There, Xavier is Highly Effective, while Vaughan and Zane are not. So, Xavier gets the biggest bonus. However, none of the Graphics employees get a $1,000 bonus (Rule 1). That can only mean Vaughan and Zane get $3,000 bonuses and Xavier gets $5,000.

One final note: Even though Meng and Lopez are Highly Effective while Vaughan and Zane are not, Meng and Lopez do not necessarily have to receive bigger bonuses than Vaughan and Zane. Rule 2 only applies to employees *in the same department.*

A Master Sketch of this game—set up as a Distribution game—would look something like this:

```
FIN:  K L̇ Ṁ P
                      * = high eff
graph:  v x̊ z        not high eff < high eff

   $1    $3    $5
          v     x
          z           K & P < L & M

   ~L          ~K
   ~M          ~P
```

Step 5: Questions

1. (C) Acceptability

As with all Acceptability questions, the four wrong answers will each violate one or more rules. Use the rules to find the violators, and eliminate them. While the first rule is easily tested here, the second and third rules will need to be tested together.

(B) and **(E)** violate Rule 1 by giving $1,000 bonuses to a Graphics employee. **(A)** violates Rule 2 by giving Highly Effective employee Xavier (Rule 3) the same bonus as everyone else in the Graphics department. **(D)** violates Rule 2 by giving Highly Effective employee Meng (Rule 3) the same bonus as co-Finance employee Kimura, who is *not* Highly Effective. That leaves **(C)** as the correct answer.

2. (B) "If" / Could Be True

For this question, Lopez and Meng receive different bonuses. As Highly Effective employees, they cannot get $1,000 bonuses, so one must get $3,000 and the other $5,000. The non-Highly Effective Finance employees (Kimura and Peterson) can now only get $1,000 bonuses.

```
   $1    $3    $5
   K     v     x
   P     z     M/L
         L/M
```

Lopez could get a $3,000 bonus, making **(B)** the correct answer. All four of the other answers must be false.

3. (A) "If" / Must Be True

For this question, only one person gets a $1,000 bonus. It cannot be a Graphics employee (Rule 1), so it must be a Finance employee—and it cannot be a Highly Effective employee (Rule 2). That means either Kimura or Peterson gets the $1,000 bonus. The other must receive a $3,000 bonus so that Meng and Lopez (the Highly Effective Finance employees) can get bigger bonuses: $5,000 each.

```
   $1     $3    $5
   K/P    v     x
          z     M
          P/K   L
```

Meng has to get a $5,000 bonus, making **(A)** the correct answer. **(B)**, **(D)**, and **(E)** all could be true, but need not be, and **(C)** must be false.

4. (E) Must Be True

The correct answer to this question must be true, which means the four wrong answers could be false.

None of the Graphics employees get a $1,000 bonus, and it's possible for Kimura and Peterson to get $3,000 bonuses with Meng and Lopez getting $5,000 bonuses. Nobody needs to get a $1,000 bonus, which eliminates **(A)**.

Two employees (Vaughan and Zane) already receive $3,000 bonuses. However, nobody else needs to. It's possible for Kimura and Peterson to get $1,000 bonuses while Meng and Lopez get $5,000 bonuses. That eliminates **(B)**.

Still, it *is* possible for Kimura and Peterson to both get $3,000 bonuses, which makes it possible that *four* employees get $3,000 bonuses. So, there could be more than three such employees, eliminating **(C)**.

Xavier definitely gets a $5,000 bonus. However, nobody else needs to. It's possible that Kimura and Peterson get $1,000 bonuses while Lopez and Meng get $3,000 bonuses. That eliminates **(D)**.

Because there are Highly Effective employees in each department, only those employees can get $5,000 bonuses. There are only three such employees (Rule 3), so that confirms **(E)** as the correct answer.

5. (D) "If" / Must Be True

For this question, only two employees get a $5,000 bonus. One of them is Xavier. The other must come from the Finance department. It must be a Highly Effective Finance employee, so it must be Lopez or Meng. The other one still has to make more than Kimura and Peterson, so the other will receive a $3,000 bonus with Kimura and Peterson receiving $1,000 bonuses.

$1	$3	$5
K	v	x
P	z	M/L
	L/M	

Peterson gets a $1,000 bonus, making **(D)** the correct answer. **(A)**, **(B)**, and **(C)** could be false, and **(E)** must be false.

6. (B) Could Be True EXCEPT

The four wrong answers here all could be true. The correct answer will be the one that must be false.

Two employees (Vaughan and Zane) already receive $3,000 bonuses. There could also be exactly two employees who receive $1,000 bonuses (Kimura and Peterson).

$1	$3	$5
K	v	x
P	z	L
		M

(A) is possible, so that can be eliminated.

However, Kimura and Peterson are the only employees who even *can* receive $1,000 bonuses. Therefore, the number of employees who get $1,000 bonuses can never exceed the number who get $3,000 bonuses because there will always be at least two in the $3,000 bonus category—Vaughan and Zane. That makes **(B)** impossible, and thus the correct answer. For the record:

The mini-sketch for the previous question shows that both **(C)** and **(E)** are possible. Kimura and Peterson can get $1,000 bonuses while Xavier, along with exactly one of Meng or Lopez, can get $5,000 bonuses. **(D)** is possible if Kimura and Peterson get $1,000 bonuses, and Xavier is the only employee to get a $5,000 bonus.

$1	$3	$5
K	v	x
P	z	
	L	
	M	

Game 2: Landscaper's Trees

Step 1: Overview

Situation: A landscaper planting trees in three lots

Entities: Seven trees (hickory, larch, maple, oak, plum, sycamore, walnut); three lots (1, 2, 3)

Action: Distribution. Determine in which lot each tree is planted. Each tree must be planted somewhere, but no tree can be planted in more than one lot. That's why this is a Distribution game rather than a Matching game.

Limitations: There are exactly seven trees, and each tree must be planted. There is no limit to how many trees can be planted in each lot. At this juncture, a lot could receive anywhere from zero to seven trees.

Step 2: Sketch

A standard Distribution sketch will do. List the trees by initial, and set up columns for the three lots. Because the overview sets no numbers on the lots, do not add slots to the columns until rules or deductions dictate.

Step 3: Rules

Rule 1 sets the makeup for one of the lots: hickory, oak, and *exactly* one other. This could be any of the three lots, so draw this Block of Entities to the side, including a single blank space to be filled in later.

H
O
—

Rule 2 prevents maple and walnut from being together.

Rule 3 establishes at least one tree on lot 1: larch or walnut. However, larch and walnut cannot be planted together. So, add "L/W" under lot 1. Additionally, depending on which type of notation you find more helpful, either make a note about the restriction ("Never LW") or add W/L to your sketch with arrows pointing to lots 2 and 3.

Rule 4 establishes at least one tree on lot 2: maple or oak. And they cannot be together. So again, add "M/O" under column 2 and, depending on which type of notation you find more helpful, either note the restriction ("Never MO") or add O/M to your sketch with arrows pointing to lots 1 and 3.

Rule 5 adds a numeric restriction: lot 3 has to include more trees than lot 1.

Step 4: Deductions

Rule 1 presents a significant Block of Entities consisting of three trees. That block is restricted by the last rule. It can no longer be placed on lot 1. After all, if there were three trees on lot 1, there would have to be at least four trees on lot 3. That would be all seven trees, leaving nothing for lot 2 and thus violating Rule 4.

Therefore, the block from Rule 1 can only be placed on lot 2 or lot 3. This is a great opportunity for Limited Options.

In the first option, the block with hickory, oak, and one other will be placed on lot 2. That leaves four trees to be planted in the remaining lots. The only way to make sure lot 3 gets more trees than lot 1 is to place three trees on lot 3 and one on lot 1. The one tree on lot 1 will be larch or walnut (Rule 3).

Maple cannot be on lot 2 with oak (Rule 4). With no more room on lot 1, maple must be placed on lot 3.

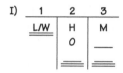

In the second option, the block with hickory, oak, and one other will be placed on lot 3. That leaves four trees to be planted in the remaining lots. Lots 1 and 2 each have at least one tree, but lot 1 cannot get three (Rule 5). So, lot 1 gets only one or two trees, with lot 2 getting three or two trees. That means lot 2 gets at least a second tree, so add a slot to that column. Furthermore, with oak on lot 3, maple must be one of the trees on lot 2 (Rule 4).

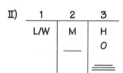

Note: These options could also be derived by using Rule 4. Maple and oak are both duplicated in the rules, making it significant which one is placed on lot 2. Each option would automatically place the block from Rule 1, leading to the exact same set of options.

Also note that plum and sycamore are never mentioned in the rules. They are Floaters and can be placed anywhere there's an empty space. Make a notation, such as starring them, in your Master Sketch. Because there are two Floaters, they are entirely interchangeable.

The final Master Sketch will look something like this:

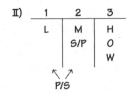

Step 5: Questions

7. (D) Acceptability

As with any Acceptability question, go through the rules one at a time, eliminating answers that violate those rules.

(A) violates Rule 1 by placing hickory and oak on lot 2 with nothing else. None of the answers violate Rule 2. **(C)** violates Rule 3 by not having larch or walnut on lot 1. **(E)** violates Rule 4 by not placing maple or oak on lot 2. **(B)** violates Rule 5 by putting the same number of trees on lots 1 and 3. That leaves **(D)** as the correct answer.

8. (B) "If" / Must Be True

For this question, hickory will be on lot 2. This is the basis for the first Limited Option. In that option, lot 3 must include maple, making **(B)** the correct answer.

9. (C) Complete and Accurate List

The correct answer to this question will list every tree that could possibly be planted on lot 1—not necessarily all at once though. The four wrong answers will list trees that *cannot* ever be on lot 1 or leave out trees that *could* be.

By Rule 5, lot 1 cannot include the three-tree block with hickory and oak. Otherwise, there would have to be four trees on lot 3, leaving nothing for lot 2, thus violating Rule 4. So, hickory cannot be on lot 1. That eliminates **(A)** and **(B)**.

By Rule 3, lot 1 must contain larch or walnut. Either one is acceptable, so that eliminates **(E)**, which does not list larch.

The only difference between **(C)** and **(D)** is that **(C)** lists sycamore. Because both plum and sycamore are Floaters, they're interchangeable. There'd be no reason one could be on lot 1 and the other could not. Therefore, if there were a second tree planted on lot 1, it could be either plum or sycamore. That eliminates **(D)**, which is missing sycamore.

That leaves **(C)** as the correct answer. To save time, it would have been very effective to skip this question temporarily and work on the next one first. In the next question, the sketch places the larch on lot 1, and the correct answer places the sycamore on lot 1. That means the correct answer to this

question would have to include those two trees, and **(C)** is the only one to do so.

10. (A) "If" / Could Be True

For this question, walnut is planted on lot 3. This could only happen in the second option because in the first option maple is established on lot 3, and maple and walnut cannot be together by Rule 2. So, using the second option, walnut would fill up lot 3. Larch would have to be planted on lot 1 (Rule 3). The remaining trees—the two Floaters (plum and sycamore)—can both go on lot 2, or they can be split so that one goes on lot 1 and the other goes on lot 2.

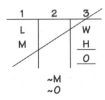

The sycamore could be planted on lot 1, making **(A)** the correct answer.

This question could still be successfully approached even without the Limited Options. Placing walnut on lot 3 would still force larch to lot 1 (Rule 3). Maple couldn't be on lot 3 with walnut (Rule 2). It also couldn't be on lot 1 with the larch because that would place at least three trees on lot 3 (Rule 5), leaving only two trees for lot 2. The block with oak from Rule 1 would have to be placed on lot 3, but then lot 2 would be without maple or oak, violating Rule 4. So, the maple must be on lot 2.

```
        1    2    3 ╱
        L         ╱ W
        M        ╱  H
              ╱     O
           ╱
          ~M
          ~O
```

At that point, the oak couldn't be on lot 2 (Rule 2). To satisfy numbers, the block with the oak can only be placed on lot 3. So, that lot will include hickory, oak, and walnut, and that's it. Plum and sycamore would be placed either one each on lots 1 and 2 or both on lot 2.

11. (A) Completely Determine

The correct answer to this question will be a tree that, when planted on lot 2, will make it possible to determine exactly where every other tree is planted with no uncertainty.

If the walnut is on lot 2, then the larch would have to be on lot 1 (Rule 3). The maple couldn't be on lot 2 (Rule 2), so the oak would have to be (Rule 4). Lot 2 would have to include hickory and one other tree (Rule 1)—in this case, the walnut. Lot 2 would then be filled. To satisfy Rule 5, the remaining four trees would have to be split one onto lot 1 and three onto lot 3. Lot 1 is already done with larch, so the remaining trees (maple, plum, and sycamore) will round out lot 3.

1	2	3
L	W	M
	O	P
	H	S

So, planting walnut on lot 2 would lead to just one possible outcome, making **(A)** the correct answer. For the record:

Plum and sycamore are Floaters. Either one could be placed on lot 2 with maple or oak. Because there would be multiple outcomes in either case, that eliminates **(B)** and **(C)**.

Placing the maple on lot 2 would force out oak. By the numbers of Rule 5, the block with oak (including hickory and one other) would be forced onto lot 3. However, lot 1 could still have either larch or walnut, and plum and sycamore could be planted anywhere.

1	2	3
L/W	M	H
		O
		___

~W

With too many possibilities, that eliminates **(D)**.

If larch is on lot 2, then walnut would be on lot 1 (Rule 3). However, lot 2 could contain either maple or oak, so there are still multiple outcomes.

1	2	3
W	L	
	M/O	

That eliminates **(E)**.

Game 3: Librarians' Desk Duty

Step 1: Overview

Situation: Librarians being scheduled for desk duty

Entities: Seven librarians (Flynn, Gomez, Hill, Kitson, Leung, Moore, Zahn)

Action: Loose Sequencing. Determine the order in which the librarians are scheduled for desk duty, from Monday to Saturday. A look ahead at the rules shows that every rule involves relative ordering (i.e., one person is on duty at some undefined point *earlier* than another). That makes it Loose Sequencing—even though there will be one "tie" in the sequence for the two librarians on Saturday.

Limitations: There are seven librarians, but only six days. One librarian will be on duty every weekday, Monday through Friday. Two will be on duty on the last day, Saturday. Every librarian will be on duty exactly once.

Step 2: Sketch

As with any Sequencing game, simply list the entities by initial. Because it's Loose Sequencing, the final diagram is likely to be a tree, so drawing a series of slots is not necessary. However, if you also drew out seven slots, that's fine given the brief nature of the task. The slots can be a helpful visual reminder for remembering the double duty of Saturday, but the rules themselves do not allow entities to be built into definite slots of a Strict Sequencing sketch.

F G H K L M Z

Mo Tu We Th Fr Sa

___ ___ ___ ___ ___ ___
___

Step 3: Rules

Rule 1 provides a simple relationship: Hill is on duty before Leung.

H — L

Rule 2 sets up a relationship among three librarians: Hill and Moore are on duty before Gomez. Note that no relationship is defined between Hill and Moore, so they could be scheduled in either order. You can add this rule directly to the sketch from Rule 1.

Rule 3 provides more connections. Flynn is on duty before Kitson and Moore, but the relationship between Kitson and Moore is undefined. That information can all be attached to the evolving sketch.

Rule 4 is a final simple relationship: Kitson is on duty before Zahn. Add that to the Loose Sequencing sketch.

Rule 5 states that Leung must be on duty before Flynn, with one exception: when Leung is scheduled for Saturday. The Formal Logic of this rule is technically set up as follows:

$$\sim(L...F) \rightarrow \frac{Sa}{L}$$

$$\sim\frac{Sa}{L} \rightarrow L...F$$

However, rather than jotting the Formal Logic down, the rule can be used to make a deduction as discussed in Step 4 next.

Step 4: Deductions

The last rule sets up two possible outcomes. The first is when Leung is scheduled for Saturday. In that case, Leung is simply one of two Saturday librarians, and the rule provides no further restrictions. Per the rule, Flynn could be earlier than Leung or could be scheduled simultaneously with Leung on Saturday (although Rule 3 already prohibits Flynn from performing on Saturday). The second is when Leung is scheduled for any other day. In that case, Leung must be on duty before Flynn. These should be drawn out as Limited Options.

The first option involves Leung being scheduled for Saturday. In that case, nothing else is deduced. Simply mark L as "Sa" (or add L under Saturday if a sketch with slots is used).

In the second option, Leung must be placed before Flynn. This leads to some bigger deductions. Flynn will be preceded by Leung, who in turn still needs to be preceded by Hill (Rule 1). Flynn must still be placed before Moore (Rule 3), who must be placed before Gomez (Rule 2). That puts five librarians in order. The last two librarians are Kitson, who is still scheduled after Flynn (Rule 3), and Zahn, who is still scheduled after Kitson (Rule 4).

With everyone in order, the first three librarians in the schedule must be Hill, Leung, and Flynn, in that order. So, they will be on Monday, Tuesday, and Wednesday. The remaining four librarians will be scheduled after Flynn on the last three days.

$$\text{II)} \quad \underline{\text{Mo}} \; \underline{\text{Tu}} \; \underline{\text{We}} \diagdown \begin{matrix} \text{M} - \text{G} \\ \\ \text{K} - \text{Z} \end{matrix}$$
$$\text{H} - \text{L} - \text{F}$$

Step 5: Questions

12. (A) Acceptability

The correct answer here will be acceptable—the one answer that doesn't violate any rules. Go through the rules one at a time and eliminate the four answers that violate those rules.

(E) violates Rule 1 by scheduling Hill *later* than Leung. No answer violates Rule 2. **(C)** violates Rule 3 by scheduling Flynn *later* than Kitson and Moore. **(D)** violates Rule 4 by scheduling Kitson *later* than Zahn. **(B)** violates Rule 5 because Leung is not on Saturday, which means Leung should be scheduled *earlier* than Flynn, not *later*. That leaves **(A)** as the correct answer, which is acceptable because Leung is scheduled for Saturday, negating the need for Leung to be scheduled before Flynn.

13. (E) Must Be False (CANNOT Be True)

The correct answer to this question will be a librarian that *cannot* be on duty on Tuesday. The remaining four will be librarians that *could* be on duty on Tuesday.

If Leung is on duty on Saturday, then Flynn doesn't have to be preceded by anyone. The same is true of Hill. So, either Flynn or Hill could be on duty on Monday, allowing the other to be on duty on Tuesday. That eliminates **(A)** and **(B)**.

Kitson merely has to be on duty after Flynn. If Flynn was on duty on Monday, then Kitson could be scheduled on Tuesday. That eliminates **(C)**. This is also the case for Moore, which eliminates **(D)**.

Zahn has to be on duty after Kitson (Rule 4), who in turn has to be on duty after Flynn (Rule 3). That means Zahn will always have at least two librarians scheduled ahead of him. So, he couldn't possibly be on duty earlier than Wednesday. With Tuesday an impossibility, **(E)** is the correct answer.

14. (B) "If" / Must Be False (CANNOT Be True)

For this question, Kitson will be on duty before Moore. This could happen in either option, so consider the general implications. Kitson still needs to be on duty after Flynn (Rule 3), and Moore still needs to be on duty before Gomez (Rule 2).

$$\begin{matrix} & & \text{L} \\ & & \diagup \\ \text{H} & & \text{G} \\ \diagup & & \diagup \\ \text{F} - \text{K} - \text{M} \\ & & \diagdown \\ & & \text{Z} \end{matrix}$$

The question is asking for something that *cannot* be true. In this case, Kitson must be on duty earlier than Gomez. It cannot be the other way around, making **(B)** the correct answer. **(A)**, **(C)**, **(D)**, and **(E)** all could be true.

15. (A) "If" / Must Be True

For this question, Zahn must be on duty on Thursday. This cannot happen in the second option because Zahn needs to be scheduled after too many people (Hill, Leung, Flynn, and Kitson). Therefore, if Zahn is on duty on Thursday, it can only occur in the first option. In that option, Leung must be on duty on Saturday. Flynn couldn't possibly be on duty on Saturday, so Flynn must be on duty earlier than Leung, making **(A)** the correct answer.

This can be seen without Limited Options as well. If Zahn is on Thursday, Kitson must be on duty earlier (Rule 4), which means Flynn must as well (Rule 3).

That leaves one more space in the schedule before Zahn. Leung couldn't be on duty before Zahn without also scheduling Hill earlier (Rule 1). Likewise, Gomez couldn't be on duty before Zahn without also scheduling Moore earlier (Rule 2). Therefore, Leung and Gomez have to be scheduled *later* than Zahn. One of Hill and Moore will be scheduled before Zahn and one after. Regardless of everyone's exact positions, Flynn is guaranteed to be before Leung. **(B)**, **(C)**, **(D)**, and **(E)** all could be false.

Mo	Tu	We	Th	Fr	Sa
__	__	__	Z	__	__

F — K   H/M   L, G, M/H

16. (C) "If" / Must Be True

For this question, Moore will be on duty on Tuesday. That can only happen in the first option (in the second option, Leung is on Tuesday). In the first option, with Moore on Tuesday, Flynn—before Moore per Rule 3—must be on duty on Monday. The only other entity that is guaranteed a specific date for desk duty in the first option is Leung on Saturday. That makes **(C)** the correct answer.

Mo	Tu	We	Th	Fr	Sa
F	M	__	__	__	L

Even without the Limited Options, it is known that Moore on Tuesday means Flynn on Monday (Rule 3). And, because Flynn is first, she'll automatically be on duty before Leung, which can only happen with Leung scheduled on Saturday (Rule 5). Answers about Thursday—**(A)** and **(B)**—or about Zahn—**(D)** and **(E)**—are all incorrect because they could be false.

17. (D) "If" / Must Be True

For this question, Flynn will be on duty earlier than Hill, which automatically points to the second option because in the first option Hill is before Flynn. In the second option, the New-"If" schedules Flynn before Hill, who must be on duty earlier than Leung (Rule 1). That means Flynn will be scheduled before Leung, which means Leung must be scheduled on Saturday (Rule 5).

$$
\begin{array}{c}
\overset{\text{Sa}}{} \\
\text{H} - \text{L} \\
{}^{\diagup} \\
\text{F} - \text{M} - \text{G} \\
{}_{\diagdown} \\
\text{K} - \text{Z}
\end{array}
$$

The only librarians who can also be scheduled on Saturday are Gomez and Kitson—the only other librarians who do not have to be scheduled earlier than someone else. So, every other librarian, including Moore, must be scheduled earlier than Leung. That means **(D)** must be true. **(A)**, **(B)**, **(C)**, and **(E)** all provide relationships that could be false.

18. (C) Rule Substitution

This question removes Rule 3 from the game and asks for a substitution that doesn't change any of the game's restrictions. In other words, the correct answer will be a rule that does exactly what the original Rule 3 did without adding any new restrictions. So, the correct answer must ensure Flynn's position before Kitson and Moore.

Restricting Flynn from Thursday does nothing to place Flynn before or after Kitson and Moore. This rule would allow Flynn to be on Friday or Saturday, which was never allowed by the original rule. That eliminates **(A)**.

By the original rules, Flynn and Hill were indeed the only librarians who could be on duty on Monday. However, this rule only works if Flynn were on duty on Monday. If Hill were on duty, this rule does nothing to connect Flynn with Kitson and Moore. That eliminates **(B)**.

If Hill and Leung are the only librarians that can be on duty before Flynn, then Flynn would have to be on duty before everyone else, including Kitson and Moore. This rule would also force Flynn to be on duty before Gomez and Zahn, but that was always true anyway because Moore is on duty before Gomez (Rule 2), and Kitson is on duty before Zahn (Rule 4). So, Rule 3 is back in effect, and there are no new restrictions. That makes **(C)** the correct answer. For the record:

Having Flynn on duty before Gomez does not necessarily place Flynn on duty before Moore. That eliminates **(D)**.

Having Flynn on duty before Zahn does not necessarily place Flynn on duty before Kitson. That eliminates **(E)**.

Game 4: Business Newsletter

Step 1: Overview

Situation: Setting up an issue of a business newsletter

Entities: Five slots (numbered 1 through 5); four feature types (finance, industry, marketing, technology) and one non-feature type (graphic)

Action: Matching. Determine in which slots the features will be assigned. What makes this game difficult to classify is that it doesn't fit the standard model of any one game type. It appears to have Strict Sequencing elements (the slots are described as "consecutive" in the first rule) and even Selection elements (some features may not be included). However, the rules and questions focus primarily on Matching concepts: assigning features—which can be repeated—to various slots. Whatever the label, the sketch shouldn't change, and the rules will be interpreted the same. Those factors are more important to managing the game than fixating on what the exact label should be.

Limitations: There are five slots and four feature types, as well as a non-feature type (graphic). Three features must be included, but there could be more. It's possible that some feature types will go unused, and there's no indication that feature types can only be used once. So, for example, it's possible that the three features are all finance. The game is very open-ended, made even more so by the first rule, which suggests that features can be spread out over multiple slots.

Step 2: Sketch

The sketch may be the most standard aspect of the game. There should be five slots numbered 1 through 5. Those slots will be filled with the entities, which should be listed by initial—including four uppercase letters for the features and one lowercase "g" for the non-feature graphic.

$$\text{F I M T } g$$

$$\overline{}\ \overline{}\ \overline{}\ \overline{}\ \overline{}$$
$$1\quad 2\quad 3\quad 4\quad 5$$

Step 3: Rules

Rule 1 introduces the idea of features taking up multiple slots. If that happens, the slots must be next to one another. Make a shorthand of this to the side (e.g., "multi-slot features consecutive"). There are two things to note: First, if one feature does take up two slots, it's still considered *one* feature. To satisfy the requirement from the overview, there would still need to be at least two more features. Second, this only applies to single multi-slot features. It does not apply if there are two separate features of the same type. So, for example, one finance feature that takes up two slots would have to be in consecutive slots (e.g., 2 and 3). However, two *separate* finance features could be split up (e.g., slots 2 and 5).

Rule 2 is conditional. If there are any finance or technology features included, one of them must be in slot 1. By contrapositive, if slot 1 has neither finance nor technology, then there can be no finance or technology features at all in the issue.

$$\text{F or T} \rightarrow \frac{\text{F/T}}{1}$$

$$\frac{\sim\text{F/T}}{1} \rightarrow \sim\text{F \& }\sim\text{T}$$

Note: If there are no finance or technology features, then there's no restriction to the first slot.

Rule 3 limits the number of industry features to one. There doesn't *have* to be one, but there can't be more.

$$1 \text{ I feature MAX}$$

Step 4: Deductions

This game is way too open-ended to allow for deductions. There are no Blocks of Entities. There are no Established Entities. No entities are Duplicated in the rules. Numbers are important, but there can be anywhere from three to five features, and those features can be placed in single slots or spread out among multiple slots. And everything (except for industry) can be repeated as needed. This game will be all about understanding the rules and their implications.

Step 5: Questions

19. (D) Acceptability

As with typical Acceptability questions, go through the rules one at a time, eliminating answers that violate those rules.

(E) violates Rule 1 by splitting up a single marketing feature into two nonconsecutive slots. **(B)** violates Rule 2 by placing a graphic in slot 1 when there are technology features listed in the issue. **(C)** also violates Rule 2 by placing an industry feature in slot 1 when there's a finance feature listed in the issue. **(A)** violates Rule 3 by listing two industry features. That leaves **(D)** as the correct answer. (Note that even though this choice lists an industry feature in two slots, it's still listed as a single feature. So, this does not violate Rule 3.)

20. (A) "If" / Must Be True

For this question, there are no technology features but at least one finance feature. By Rule 2, that means slot 1 must include a finance feature.

$$\frac{\text{F}}{1}\quad \overline{}\ \overline{}\ \boxed{\frac{\text{F}}{4\quad 5}}$$

That makes **(A)** the correct answer. This question merely tests an understanding of Rule 2.

21. (E) Must Be False

The correct answer to this question must be impossible. The four wrong answers will all be possible, if not definitely true.

There could be a single industry feature in slot 1, as long as there were no finance or technology features in the issue. That eliminates **(A)**.

With a finance feature included, slot 1 would have to be a finance or technology feature (Rule 2). If slot 2 had the *only* finance feature, then slot 1 could still have technology. This is acceptable, which eliminates **(B)**.

Similarly, with a technology feature included, slot 1 would have to be finance or technology. If slot 3 had the *only* technology feature, slot 1 could still have finance. This is acceptable, which eliminates **(C)**.

If slot 1 had a feature that wasn't finance or marketing, it would have to be technology or industry. Filling slot 1 with a technology feature would ensure Rule 2 isn't violated. This is acceptable, which eliminates **(D)**.

If slot 5 had a feature—not a graphic—that wasn't industry or marketing, it would have to be finance or technology. However, by Rule 2, that would mean there would also have to be a finance or technology feature in slot 1. That would mean another feature that's *not* industry or marketing, making **(E)** impossible and thus the correct answer.

22. (D) "If" / Must Be True

For this question, there will be one industry feature and it will be in slot 1. According to the overview, there need to be at least two more features. With slot 1 occupied by an industry feature, the issue can no longer contain any finance or technology features (Rule 2). And there cannot be any more industry features (Rule 3). So, to fulfill the feature quota, there must be at least two marketing features. However, they can occupy any of the remaining four slots.

$$\overset{\textcircled{\scriptsize 1}\,\textcircled{\scriptsize 2+}}{F\ I\ M\ \cancel{T}\ \cancel{g}}$$

$$\frac{I}{1}\ \overline{}\ \overline{}\ \overline{}\ \overline{}$$
$$\ 1\ \ \ 2\ \ \ 3\ \ \ 4\ \ \ 5$$

The industry feature may be spread over multiple slots, but it certainly doesn't have to be. That eliminates **(A)** and **(B)**.

$$\boxed{\frac{I}{1\ \ 2}}\ \overline{3}\ \overline{4}\ \overline{5}$$

M, M

$$\boxed{\frac{I}{1\ \ 2\ \ 3}}\ \frac{M}{4}\ \frac{M}{5}$$

The marketing features could be assigned to slots 4 and 5, so they don't have to be assigned to either slot 2 or 3. That eliminates **(C)**.

$$\frac{I}{1}\ \overline{}\ \overline{}\ \frac{M}{4}\ \frac{M}{5}$$

There must be at least two marketing features, and slot 1 is already taken up by an industry feature. Even if one marketing feature was assigned to slot 5, the other one would *still* have to be assigned to slot 2, 3, or 4. There's no way to avoid putting at least one marketing feature in those slots.

$$\frac{I}{1}\ \underbrace{\overline{}\ \overline{}\ \overline{}}_{M}\ \frac{M}{5}$$

(D) must happen, making it the correct answer. For the record: The marketing features could be assigned to slots 2 and 4, so they don't have to be assigned to either slot 3 or 5—those slots could be graphics.

$$\frac{I}{1}\ \frac{M}{2}\ \frac{g}{3}\ \frac{M}{4}\ \frac{g}{5}$$

Even though slots 2 and 4 are not consecutive, this does not violate Rule 1. Remember, that rule only applies to a single multi-slot feature. Two separate marketing features can still be split up.

23. (D) Could Be True EXCEPT

Four answers to this question will be possible. The correct answer will be the exception—the one that must be false no matter what. For each answer, it's important to remember that each issue must include at least three features (according to the overview).

With only one finance feature, the issue still needs at least two more features. If there are no industry or marketing features, the other features would be technology ones. That is acceptable, which eliminates **(A)**.

With only one industry feature, the issue still needs at least two more features. If there are no finance or marketing features, the other features would be technology ones. That is acceptable, which eliminates **(B)**.

With only one finance feature, the issue still needs at least two more features. If there are no marketing or technology features, the other features would be finance ones. That is acceptable, which eliminates **(C)**.

With only one marketing feature, the issue still needs at least two more features. If there are no finance or technology features, the other features would be industry ones. However, there cannot be more than one industry feature. This is not acceptable, making **(D)** the correct answer. This question merely tests knowledge of the numbers limitation from the overview along with Rule 3. For the record:

With only one marketing feature, the issue still needs at least two more features. If there are no industry or technology features, the other features would be finance ones. That is acceptable, which eliminates **(E)**.

PrepTest 76

The Inside Story

PrepTest 76 was administered in October 2015. It challenged 33,229 test takers. What made this test so hard? Here's a breakdown of what Kaplan students who were surveyed after taking the official exam considered PrepTest 76's most difficult section.

Hardest PrepTest 76 Section as Reported by Test Takers

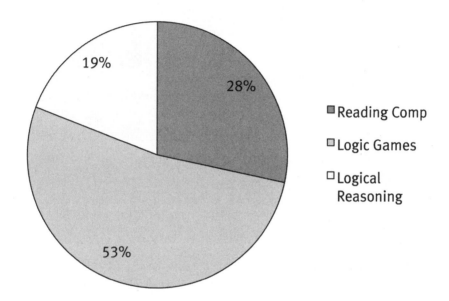

Based on these results, you might think that studying Logic Games is the key to LSAT success. Well, Logic Games is important, but test takers' perceptions don't tell the whole story. For that, you need to consider students' actual performance. The following chart shows the average number of students to miss each question in each of PrepTest 76's different sections.

Percentage Incorrect by PrepTest 76 Section Type

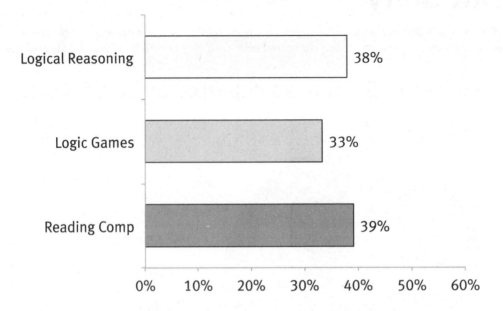

Actual student performance tells quite a different story. On average, students were almost equally likely to miss questions in all three of the different section types, and on PrepTest 76, Reading Comprehension and Logical Reasoning were somewhat higher than Logic Games in actual difficulty.

Maybe students overestimate the difficulty of the Logic Games section because it's so unusual, or maybe it's because a really hard Logic Game is so easy to remember after the test. But the truth is that the test maker places hard questions throughout the test. Here were the locations of the 10 hardest (most missed) questions in the exam.

Location of 10 Most Difficult Questions in PrepTest 76

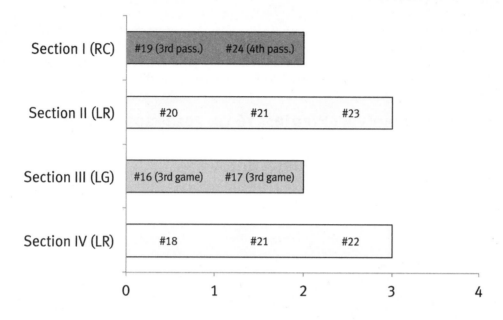

The takeaway from this data is that, to maximize your potential on the LSAT, you need to take a comprehensive approach. Test yourself rigorously, and review your performance on every section of the test. Kaplan's LSAT explanations provide the expertise and insight you need to fully understand your results. The explanations are written and edited by a team of LSAT experts, who have helped thousands of students improve their scores. Kaplan always provides data-driven analysis of the test, ranking the difficulty of every question based on actual student performance. The 10 hardest questions on every test are highlighted with a 4-star difficulty rating, the highest we give. The analysis breaks down the remaining questions into 1-, 2-, and 3-star ratings so that you can compare your performance to thousands of other test takers on all LSAC material.

Don't settle for wondering whether a question was really as hard as it seemed to you. Analyze the test with real data, and learn the secrets and strategies that help top scorers master the LSAT.

7 Can't–Miss Features of PrepTest 76

- With 12 Assumption questions, PrepTest 76 is tied for the most ever on a single LSAT. The only other time this happened was back in June of 2009 (PT 57).
- This was the first PrepTest since June '02 (PT 37) with no Main Point questions.
- PrepTest 76 featured two Strict Sequencing games—after only one on the three previous tests combined.
- In the second logic game—Newspaper Photographs—you'll want to check out a rarely used triple option setup.
- Answer choices (A) and (E) were never correct two times in a row, but choice (C) was correct three times in a row … twice!
- PrepTest 76 was only the second LSAT (and first since December '09 (PT 59)) on which a Comparative Reading passage had eight questions.
- The second Comparative Reading passage discussed scientists calculating orbits. Maybe that was on the mind of test takers who had just seen *The Martian*, which was the #1 movie in America the week this test was administered.

PrepTest 76 in Context

As much fun as it is to find out what makes a PrepTest unique or noteworthy, it's even more important to know just how representative it is of other LSAT administrations (and, thus, how likely it is to be representative of the exam you will face on Test Day). The following charts compare the numbers of each kind of question and game on PrepTest 76 to the average numbers seen on all officially released LSATs administered over the past five years (from 2012 through 2016).

Number of LR Questions by Type: PrepTest 76 vs. 2012–2016 Average

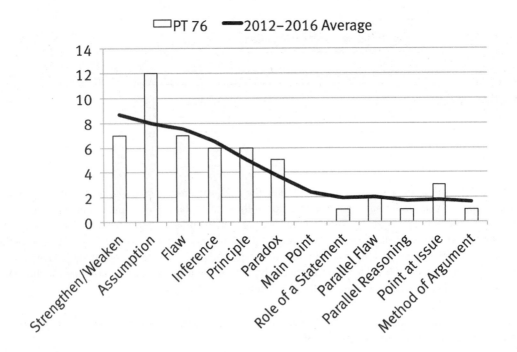

Number of LG Games by Type: PrepTest 76 vs. 2012–2016 Average

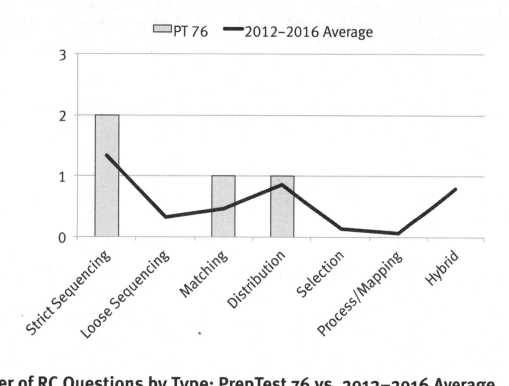

Number of RC Questions by Type: PrepTest 76 vs. 2012–2016 Average

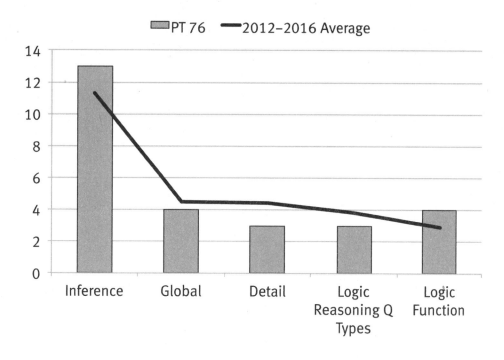

There isn't usually a huge difference in the distribution of questions from LSAT to LSAT, but if this test seems harder (or easier) to you than another you've taken, compare the number of questions of the types on which you, personally, are strongest and weakest. And then, explore within each section to see if your best or worst question types came earlier or later.

Students in Kaplan's comprehensive LSAT courses have access to every released LSAT and to an online Q-Bank with thousands of officially released questions, games, and passages. If you are studying on your own, you have to do a bit more work to identify your strengths and your areas of opportunity. Quantitative analysis (like that in the previous charts) is an important tool for understanding how the test is constructed and how you are performing on it.

Section I: Reading Comprehension
Passage 1: Arnold Schoenberg

Q#	Question Type	Correct	Difficulty
1	Global	C	★
2	Logic Reasoning (Parallel Reasoning)	B	★
3	Logic Function	D	★★
4	Detail (EXCEPT)	A	★
5	Inference	D	★
6	Inference	A	★★★

Passage 2: Biotechnology Patents

Q#	Question Type	Correct	Difficulty
7	Global	D	★
8	Inference	B	★
9	Detail	B	★
10	Inference	C	★★
11	Logic Function	B	★
12	Inference	D	★★★
13	Inference	D	★★

Passage 3: Haudenosaune Wampum

Q#	Question Type	Correct	Difficulty
14	Global	B	★★
15	Logic Function	E	★
16	Logic Function	C	★★
17	Inference	C	★★
18	Inference	B	★★
19	Inference	E	★★★★

Passage 4: Negative Evidence in Science

Q#	Question Type	Correct	Difficulty
20	Global	C	★★★
21	Detail	C	★★
22	Inference	C	★★
23	Inference	D	★★★
24	Inference	B	★★★★
25	Logic Reasoning (Parallel Reasoning)	A	★★
26	Inference	B	★★
27	Logic Reasoning (Parallel Reasoning)	E	★★★

Passage 1: Arnold Schoenberg

Step 1: Read the Passage Strategically
Sample Roadmap

line #	Keyword/phrase	¶ Margin notes
1–5		Quote—music sounds bad
8	But	NOT re: Schoenberg, but Beethoven
11	But	B & S controversy
12	controversy	B became popular
15	but	over time
17	significantly	
20	Like	B & S evolved
23	three	S—3 styles
28	ought to love	1) late-Romantic
34	Because … in his view … inevitable	2) atonal
35	he felt	
36	because	
37	compelled	
39	Finally	3) 12-tone
42	Awe-inspiring	Styles became more
44	more violent … therefore	difficult to follow
45	more difficult	
46	But	Auth:
47	but	Schoenberg's impact
51	essential	
54	disturbing … not because	
55	but because	

Discussion

The passage opens with a quote about some harsh-sounding music. Paragraph 2 suggests that this quote could easily apply to the music of Arnold Schoenberg, but it was actually about a piece by Beethoven.

Paragraph 3 describes how Schoenberg and Beethoven were both controversial, but mentions that Beethoven eventually became popular as people were able to listen to his music multiple times.

Paragraph 4 describes Schoenberg and Beethoven as innovators. At this point, the passage starts to concentrate primarily on Schoenberg's music, making him the **Topic**. This is also the start of a three-paragraph discussion of Schoenberg's three-stage stylistic evolution, which serves as the **Scope**. This paragraph mentions the first style: late-Romantic music.

Paragraph 5 introduces the second style: atonal music, which Schoenberg saw as a natural progression needed to express his ideas. Paragraph 6 brings up the third style: 12-tone music, which further refined atonal music. All three styles showed off Schoenberg's skills, but were also increasingly hard to listen to.

In paragraph 7, the author finally expresses a strong point of view: the style of music is not as important as the message the music conveys. This leads to a clearer understanding of the author's intentions. The **Purpose** is to evaluate the importance of Schoenberg's music. The author's praise of Schoenberg constitutes the **Main Idea**: Schoenberg's music was vital because it exposed listeners to emotions and truths never before heard in music.

1. (C) Global

Step 2: Identify the Question Type
This is a Global question because it asks for the "main point of the passage."

Step 3: Research the Relevant Text
Global questions are based on the entire text. Use the Main Idea as a perfect prediction here.

Step 4: Make a Prediction
Despite how some see Schoenberg's music as "shrill" and "difficult to follow," the author ultimately praises Schoenberg for his "awe-inspiring level of technical mastery" and his expression of "emotional states that music had not recorded before."

Step 5: Evaluate the Answer Choices
(C) correctly identifies the author's advocacy of Schoenberg's value in the face of critical reception.

(A) focuses too much on the negative reaction and not on the author's praise. And while the author would probably encourage a wider appreciation for Schoenberg's music, the passage never confirms this has happened.

(B) is a Distortion. While Schoenberg and Beethoven share similarities, the author never suggests that they should be regarded as equals.

(D) is a 180. Line 49 directly states that Schoenberg was important "*not* because of the 12-tone system," but because of the message his music conveyed.

(E) is Out of Scope. The author never mentions how quickly, if at all, Schoenberg's music was accepted. This answer also fails to convey the author's appreciation for Schoenberg's music.

2. (B) Logic Reasoning (Parallel Reasoning)

Step 2: Identify the Question Type
The correct answer will be "analogous to" information provided in the passage. That makes this a Parallel Reasoning question.

Step 3: Research the Relevant Text
The word *disturbing* is in line 54, but the entire last sentence (lines 53–56) provides the relevant context.

Step 4: Make a Prediction
According to the last line, it is *not* the harshness of Schoenberg's music that makes it disturbing. What's disturbing is that it "unflinchingly faces difficult truths." The correct answer will describe another work that similarly addresses harsh realities.

Step 5: Evaluate the Answer Choices
(B) is a match. Difficult truths are exactly the kinds of things that "people would prefer to ignore."

(A) is Out of Scope. Vulgar language may be offensive, but it doesn't necessarily address "difficult truths."

(C) is Out of Scope. This would imply that Schoenberg was stealing from other composers, which is never mentioned or suggested.

(D) is Out of Scope. Political philosophies are never discussed. Furthermore, philosophies deal with personal beliefs rather than truths.

(E) is a Distortion. Saying a truth is unfamiliar doesn't mean it's difficult to face. In fact, people are probably *very* familiar with difficult truths and just don't want to listen to them.

3. (D) Logic Function

Step 2: Identify the Question Type
The phrase "in order to" indicates a Logic Function question. It's asking *why* the author included the opening quote.

Step 3: Research the Relevant Text
Beyond the quote itself, the second and third paragraph provide ample context for why the quote was included.

Step 4: Make a Prediction

According to the second paragraph, the quote describes a work by Beethoven. The third paragraph mentions how Beethoven is seen as an icon now, but he didn't develop that status until over a century after Kotzebue's remarks. So, the purpose here is to show—as the author later feels should apply to Schoenberg—that music initially deemed discordant could become appreciated over time.

Step 5: Evaluate the Answer Choices

(D) matches the contrast between early reaction and later reconsideration.

(A) is a Distortion. While the quote does refer to Beethoven's music, it is still one critic's opinion and not necessarily "accurate."

(B) mistakenly attributes the quote to a work of Schoenberg. While it resembles the reaction people have to Schoenberg's works, it's actually about the overture to Beethoven's *Fidelio*.

(C) takes one person's initial reaction and stretches it to a claim about all of Beethoven's works. However, Beethoven's works are now appreciated, and Beethoven is considered a cultural icon. The author also never suggests his works are uneven in quality.

(E) is Out of Scope. While critical consensus about Beethoven may have changed over the years, it is possible that Kotzebue's reaction was entirely consistent with other critics of his time.

4. (A) Detail (EXCEPT)

Step 2: Identify the Question Type

The question asks for what the author "alludes to," which may seem to indicate an Inference question. However, the answer choices here are lifted straight from the passage, making this a Detail question. Either way, four answers will come directly from the passage. The correct answer will not.

Step 3: Research the Relevant Text

The passage discusses both composers in the second, third, and fourth paragraphs.

Step 4: Make a Prediction

While impossible to predict what the correct answer will say, it helps to locate support for the wrong answers. They will all include similarities, which can be found by the Keywords [b]oth (line 11) and [λ]ike (line 20). Expect an answer choice to point out an attribute of one composer that does not necessarily apply to the other.

Step 5: Evaluate the Answer Choices

(A) is correct because it only applies to Schoenberg (line 25). The passage never indicates the style in which Beethoven worked.

(B) is a similarity. These descriptors come directly from the quote about Beethoven's overture in the first paragraph. And

the second paragraph states that this description also "characterizes the reaction of many listeners" to Schoenberg's music.

(C) is directly stated about both composers in lines 11–12.

(D) is mentioned in lines 20–21 about how both composers were alike.

(E) is an attribute of both composers mentioned in lines 12–13.

5. (D) Inference

Step 2: Identify the Question Type

The question asks for what the author "appear[s] to value." Because it merely appears as such (and thus isn't directly stated), this is an Inference question.

Step 3: Research the Relevant Text

The author's opinion is found primarily in the last paragraph.

Step 4: Make a Prediction

In lines 50–53, the author describes what makes Schoenberg's music *essential*: the inclusion of emotional aspects "music had not recorded before."

Step 5: Evaluate the Answer Choices

(D) is a perfect paraphrase of the *essential* quality of Schoenberg's work.

(A) is a Faulty Use of Detail. The technical mastery is described as *awe-inspiring* (line 42), but that doesn't make it more valuable than something *essential*. Lines 46–47 even say, "[b]ut the real issue for any piece of music is not how it is made, but what it has to say."

(B) is a Faulty Use of Detail. Shifting harmonies were just a part of Schoenberg's late-Romantic music (line 26). Nothing indicates that this was particularly valuable.

(C) is a 180. In line 49, the author states that the 12-tone system was *not* what made Schoenberg important.

(E) is a 180. In lines 46–47, the author suggests that the message is more important than the style. So the progression of styles wasn't important. What mattered is that he was able to say something through his music.

6. (A) Inference

Step 2: Identify the Question Type

The question asks for something *inferred* that the author is "most likely to agree with." That makes this an Inference question.

Step 3: Research the Relevant Text

The question asks about the relationship between Schoenberg's three styles, which are described in paragraphs 4–6.

Step 4: Make a Prediction

According to lines 32–33, Schoenberg took the first style of music (late-Romantic) and kept pushing it further and further until it transitioned into the second style (atonal). Schoenberg felt that second style was *inevitable*. Then, by lines 39–41, the third style (12-tone) took the second style and gave it order and stabilization. The correct answer will indicate this sense of purposeful transition.

Step 5: Evaluate the Answer Choices

(A) matches Schoenberg's intention of progress and development.

(B) is a 180. Schoenberg directly stated that the shift between the first two styles was an "inevitable step in the historical development of music." That makes it seem intentional, not *inexplicable* at all.

(C) is Half-Right/Half-Wrong. The progression between the first two styles was indeed *natural*, but so was the second progression. Schoenberg's goal in the third style was to bring order to the second style (lines 40–41).

(D) is Half-Right/Half-Wrong. The progression from the second to the third style was indeed *natural*, but so was the progression from the first to the second, which Schoenberg felt was *inevitable* (line 34). There were no *inexplicable* departures.

(E) is a 180 and a Distortion. The second style was not an *inexplicable* departure from the first—it was *inevitable* (line 34). Additionally, the third style built upon the second style, not the first one.

Passage 2: Biotechnology Patents

Step 1: Read the Passage Strategically
Sample Roadmap

line #	Keyword/phrase	¶ Margin notes
1	convinced	Biotech people
2	should	want protection
5	increasingly	But are
6	because	patents bad?
8	However	
9	hindering	
12	focus of increased scrutiny	
14	threat	Some patents restrict
20	fear	access to materials
23	In other instances	1) fear legal action
27	For example	2) patent holder
31	fear	wants exchange
35	While it is true	Auth:
37	also undoubtedly true	Arguments mistaken
41	seem to be confusing	1) legal action expensive
43	mistakenly assume	2) courts allow
47	questionable ... First	noncommercial exceptions
51	Second	3) patents are good
54	Moreover	for innovation
55	spur rather than hinder ... because	
56	compelling	

Discussion

Paragraph 1 opens with two biotechnology groups, each with a vested interest in protecting its intellectual property. Industries want to protect their commercial products, and academic institutions want to retain their funding. The Keyword [*h*]*owever* in line 8 is when the focus of the passage becomes clear. The **Topic** is biotechnology patents, and the **Scope** is the concerns scientists have about the effect of patents on basic research.

Paragraph 2 outlines the concerns. Researchers feel that patents prevent access to useful research material because either A) patent holders will sue anyone who tries to access that material, or B) patent holders will demand some sort of compensation in exchange for such access.

In paragraph 3, the author disputes these concerns (**Purpose**), suggesting that researchers are *confusing* the issue and *mistakenly* assuming that patents prevent basic research (**Main Idea**). For one thing, companies don't always take issues to court because it's expensive; they'll only sue if something threatens their place in the market system. Furthermore, courts tend to side with people who want to access material for noncommercial purposes. The author wraps up by pointing out the benefit of patents: They give scientists a "compelling incentive to innovate."

7. (D) Global

Step 2: Identify the Question Type
This is a Global question because it asks for the "main point of the passage."

Step 3: Research the Relevant Text
Because this is a Global question, the entire passage is relevant.

Step 4: Make a Prediction
The Main Idea from Step 1 provides an adequate prediction: researchers are mistaken in their belief that biotechnology patents are preventing them from performing basic research.

Step 5: Evaluate the Answer Choices
(D) is correct.

(A) is a 180. This is consistent with the opinions expressed in paragraph 2, but the author directly disputes this concern in paragraph 3.

(B) is too narrow. This expresses the conflict raised at the end of paragraph 1, but completely ignores the author's response in paragraph 3.

(C) is Out of Scope. The author says nothing about academics or industries being penalized. Furthermore, if anything the author thinks the current patent system is *fair* because he calls the concerns regarding perceived threats *questionable* (line 47).

(E) is too narrow, focusing on just one detail from paragraph 3 that supports the broader argument that patents are not as restrictive as some researchers believe.

8. (B) Inference

Step 2: Identify the Question Type
The question asks for something researchers are "most likely to" accept, making this an Inference question.

Step 3: Research the Relevant Text
The question points directly to lines 30–31, but be sure to use the entire sentence and any surrounding sentences for context.

Step 4: Make a Prediction
In lines 30–34, the researchers in question are afraid that patent holders will demand high fees to use their materials for basic research. So, as a general rule, they would prefer it if patent holders were *not* allowed to charge such exorbitant fees.

Step 5: Evaluate the Answer Choices
(B) accurately addresses these researchers' concern.

(A) is a 180. Competition is what makes industries charge high fees for patented materials. These researchers oppose such a system.

(C) is a 180. These researchers *want* access to materials and are disgruntled about paying too much for them.

(D) is a Faulty Use of Detail. Fear of litigation is the first concern in paragraph 2. The researchers in lines 30–31 have a *different* concern: having to provide a lot of money in exchange for access.

(E) is a Faulty Use of Detail. Funding is mentioned in paragraph 1 as a reason why biotechnology researchers in academics support patents. The researchers in question though—from lines 30–31—are worried about what they have access to, not how much funding they receive.

9. (B) Detail

Step 2: Identify the Question Type
The phrase "[a]ccording to the passage" indicates a Detail question. The correct answer will be directly stated in the passage.

Step 3: Research the Relevant Text
The reason why university researchers support patents is described in paragraph 1.

Step 4: Make a Prediction
In lines 4–7, university researchers support patents "because of their reliance on research funding that is in part conditional on the patentability of their results."

Step 5: Evaluate the Answer Choices
(B) is a perfect match.

(A) is Out of Scope. The passage never mentions the quantity or quality of their research.

(C) may be consistent with the author's point of view, but the passage never states that university researchers share this opinion.

(D) is Out of Scope. The passage never mentions partnerships between universities and corporations. It also never mentions any groups feeling "unfairly exploited."

(E) is Extreme. While some researchers (and maybe an increasing number—lines 4–5) may believe this, the passage never states that *most* researchers hold this view.

10. (C) Inference

Step 2: Identify the Question Type
This is an Inference question because it asks for something with which the author is "most likely to agree."

Step 3: Research the Relevant Text
The question asks about the author's point of view. That is found exclusively in paragraph 3, which makes it the most likely source of the correct answer.

Step 4: Make a Prediction
The author makes many points over the 25 lines of paragraph 3. Start with the overarching point (patents are not as problematic as some believe), eliminate answers that stray too far, and use content clues in the answers to perform any necessary research.

Step 5: Evaluate the Answer Choices
(C) is correct. In lines 47–51, the author states that litigation is expensive and would only be done to protect market position. Basic, noncommercial research wouldn't be worth the expense.

(A) is not supported. Lines 35–37 do suggest that materials were more freely shared in the early days, but it's never suggested that researchers weren't *entitled* to protection.

(B) is a Distortion. Some researchers fear such excessive fees (lines 30–34), but there's no indication that patent holders *typically* charge such fees.

(D) is another Distortion. Lines 6–7 confirm that academic institutions rely on such funding, but the author never expresses whether they rely "too heavily" on it.

(E) is Out of Scope. The concerns against patenting have to do with patent holders withholding access to useful materials. The innovative quality has no bearing on the issue.

11. (B) Logic Function

Step 2: Identify the Question Type
The phrase "primarily in order to" indicates a Logic Function question. Focus on *why* the author mentions the early days in context of the passage.

Step 3: Research the Relevant Text
The early days are mentioned in line 38, but the purpose of mentioning them is only seen by looking at the entire first sentence of paragraph 3. Also, consider how that sentence is used as a transition from paragraph 2.

Step 4: Make a Prediction
Paragraph 2 describes the concerns researchers have about patents. In the first sentence of paragraph 3, the author concedes that researchers have shifted to a market model. Nonetheless, researchers have always tried to protect their materials, "even in the early days." That phrase suggests that this is nothing new. You could go back to a time when ideas were exchanged more freely, but you'd *still* find some people trying to protect themselves.

Step 5: Evaluate the Answer Choices
(B) accurately describes how the phrase indicates that nothing is new. These kinds of practices have happened before.

(A) is a Distortion. Lines 35–37 do provide the absolute briefest account of any sort of evolution, but the *also* in line 37 suggests that the author included the reference to the early days to bring up a new point—not just to provide the history.

(C) is Out of Scope. The author expresses no such longing to return to the early days.

(D) is also Out of Scope. It brings up the level of technological sophistication, which is never mentioned here.

(E) is a 180. The author's point in paragraph 3 is that patents are fine, and the fact that some researchers have always wanted protection *supports* the idea that patents are acceptable.

12. (D) Inference

Step 2: Identify the Question Type
This is an Inference question because the passage provides "support for inferring" the correct answer.

Step 3: Research the Relevant Text
There are no content clues here, so the entire passage is relevant.

Step 4: Make a Prediction
Don't bother trying to predict the correct answer here. Eliminate answers that are clearly wrong, and use content clues in the answers to do any necessary research.

Step 5: Evaluate the Answer Choices
(D) is consistent with the second concern raised in paragraph 2. In lines 23–27, patent holders that do not sue can still "refuse to make such materials available" unless they get something in exchange.

(A) is an unsupported comparison. Policy makers (mentioned in line 13) may be scrutinizing patents more carefully, but there's no suggestion of how much they favor new restrictions or how that compares to what academic researchers believe.

(B) is Extreme. Lines 47–51 suggest that patent holders would sue only if they felt their market position threatened, but there's no indication that *most* patent holders actually feel threatened.

(C) is Extreme. Lines 4–7 suggest that funding is *partially* conditional on patentability, but that doesn't mean that academic institutions would be *unable* to get funding without patents.

(E) is Out of Scope. There is no mention of how many biologists are "willing to teach."

13. (D) Inference

Step 2: Identify the Question Type
This is an Inference question because it asks for something with which the author is "most likely to agree."

Step 3: Research the Relevant Text
The question asks about the author's point of view, which is all in paragraph 3. The question also refers to a situation involving "noncommercial research," a topic mentioned in lines 47 and 53.

Step 4: Make a Prediction
In lines 44–47, the author implies it's *questionable* whether patent infringement would be an issue in noncommercial research. First, the cost may not justify legal action in noncommercial situations; further, lines 51–54 suggest that courts have a tendency to grant exceptions to noncommercial research anyway. Therefore, the author most likely believes that the research described should not pose any problem.

Step 5: Evaluate the Answer Choices
(D) is correct. Even if a patent holder *does* try to sue, judges traditionally side with noncommercial research projects.

(A) is Extreme. Patent holders *may* demand high payment (lines 23–34), but that doesn't mean it will *probably* happen.

(B) is a 180. Lines 51–54 suggest that judges allow for exceptions in noncommercial cases.

(C) is unsupported. The passage never suggests any action that universities would take on their own researchers.

(E) is part Extreme and part Out of Scope. The corporation *may* ask for something in exchange (lines 27–30), but there's nothing in the passage to suggest it *probably* will. Also, the passage does not suggest that a corporation would actively offer both funding and access to patented materials.

Passage 3: Haudenosaune Wampum

Step 1: Read the Passage Strategically
Sample Roadmap

line #	Keyword/phrase	¶ Margin notes
4	primarily	Historians:
6	insisted … primarily	wampum = $
7	While	Auth:
9	due to	misinterpretation
10	misinterpreted	Wampum actually
12	However … true significance	political message
18	two	Loose beads
22	for example	= simple ideas
28	for example	Ex. communicate
35	thought that	with spirits
36	such that	String wampum = political message
37	however	Haud. Conf. made wampum
40	major impetus	primarily political
42	primarily	Wampum belts
43	evident	= depict rules
48	Ex	Belts indicate gov't business
58	Thus	
60	although	
61	effectively	

Discussion

Paragraph 1 starts right off with the **Topic**: wampum—beads used for mostly political communication by the Haudenosaune. Historians insist that wampum was primarily a form of currency, but the author asserts that this was a misinterpretation. This indicates that the **Scope** of the passage will be what wampum represents. The author's response to historians signals the **Purpose**: to clarify what wampum actually represents. And the phrase "true significance of wampum" gives away the **Main Idea**: Wampum was *not* supposed to be currency but instead a way of conveying messages, including important political ones.

Paragraph 2 begins to describe the chronological development of wampum's usage. Wampum was first used as loose beads, some white and some purple, to convey simple ideas. An example is given of how the beads represented different spirits and were used to communicate with these spirits. The Keyword [*l*]*ater* in line 33 indicates the next phase of wampum: string wampum. By stringing beads together, the Haudenosaune could send basic political messages.

Paragraph 3 introduces the next major stage, starting with the formation of the Haudenosaune Confederacy. The confederacy drafted a constitution, and its rules were encoded in wampum belts, which consisted of multiple wampum strings. Through a series of examples, it's shown how the wampum beads are arranged to indicate sociopolitical circumstances. Ultimately, wampum belts were successfully used as a way to "frame and enforce" confederate laws.

14. (B) Global

Step 2: Identify the Question Type

This is a Global question because it asks for the "main point" of each passage.

Step 3: Research the Relevant Text

No need to research any particular text here. The Main Idea from Step 1 will serve as a sufficient prediction.

Step 4: Make a Prediction

The point of the passage is that, despite what historians claim, wampum was *not* used primarily as currency but instead developed over time as a way to convey important information.

Step 5: Evaluate the Answer Choices

(B) is correct, saying that wampum was not intended as money and discussing the evolution of wampum as a form of communication. All of the details are accurate.

(A) is too narrow and a Distortion. Wampum started as just loose beads. Strings came [*l*]*ater* (line 33).

(C) is Extreme. While Europeans may have used wampum "solely to purchase goods" (line 11), that doesn't mean the

Haudenosaune stopped using it as a form of communication. Thus, it was not *exclusively* used as a form of currency.

(D) is a Distortion. The establishment of the confederacy marked the beginning of wampum *belts*. But wampum was used before then in the form of loose beads and wampum strings.

(E) is another Distortion. It's fair to say that historians let the commercial use of wampum overshadow its communicative use in European transactions, but that doesn't mean they overlooked the communicative roles from *before* the Europeans arrived.

15. (E) Logic Function

Step 2: Identify the Question Type

The phrase "offered primarily as" indicates a Logic Function question. It's asking *why* the author mentions the fishing practice. As additional help, the question states that the fishing practice serves as an "instance of," i.e., an example.

Step 3: Research the Relevant Text

The fishing practice is described in lines 28–33. The phrase "for example" indicates that the practice illustrates the point made directly beforehand, so use the previous sentences for more context.

Step 4: Make a Prediction

Right before the claim about the fishing practice, the passage describes how the different colors represent different spirits. The phrase "for example" in lines 21–22 indicates that this is an example of the previous point: "Even in the form of loose beads, wampum could represent basic ideas." So ultimately, the fishing practice—which involves tossing loose beads into the water—is an example of how wampum in loose bead form could be used in such a way.

Step 5: Evaluate the Answer Choices

(E) is correct. Loose beads were the first stage in the evolution of wampum, and the fishing practice shows how loose beads were used.

(A) is a Faulty Use of Detail. The beads in this case were merely thrown into the water. Nothing was encoded until the development of wampum belts, as described in lines 43–45.

(B) is a Distortion. The Europeans may have changed historians' perception of how wampum was used, but there's no suggestion that the fishing practice itself was ever altered.

(C) is a Faulty Use of Detail. The Haudenosaune Confederacy didn't come about until 1451, *after* wampum was used only in loose bead form.

(D) is not supported. By line 28, the practice was described through *legend*. There's no indication that wampum was being studied when this legend was discovered.

16. (C) Logic Function

Step 2: Identify the Question Type
The phrase "serves primarily to" indicates a Logic Function question.

Step 3: Research the Relevant Text
The question asks about the last paragraph, so consider the entire paragraph. Margin notes will be useful.

Step 4: Make a Prediction
The last paragraph is all about how wampum evolved into belts, which represented the provisions of the Haudenosaune Confederacy.

Step 5: Evaluate the Answer Choices
(C) is correct. By creating belts, the wampum was used to symbolize constitutional provisions.

(A) is too narrow. While the paragraph does describe how wampum belts evolved from wampum strings (lines 45–48), that's just one sentence. This ignores the rest of the paragraph, which discusses the symbolic nature of the belts.

(B) is also too narrow. The comparison between belts and strings is found in lines 45–48, but this overlooks the rest of the paragraph, which discusses what the belts represent.

(D) is a Distortion. The author does provide several examples of wampum codes (lines 48–57), but they're just random samples. It's hardly a complete *outline* of the constitution.

(E) is a Distortion. The last sentence confirms that wampum was used *effectively*, but the paragraph only describes what wampum was *meant* to symbolize. It never actually gives *evidence* of its effectiveness. So, the paragraph's primary purpose was to tell *how* the wampum was used, not whether it ensured "compliance with the law."

17. (C) Inference

Step 2: Identify the Question Type
This question asks for what can be *inferred* and what the author is "most likely to agree with." That indicates an Inference question.

Step 3: Research the Relevant Text
There are no content clues, so the entire text is relevant.

Step 4: Make a Prediction
The correct answer here cannot be predicted. Instead, check the answers one at a time using content clues to do any necessary research.

Step 5: Evaluate the Answer Choices
(C) is supported. The association between colors and spirits is described before the Keyword [*l*]*ater* (line 33), so it's definitely a precursor. And the later uses include "truce requests" (line 36) and "political purposes" (line 42), which do not utilize the spiritual associations.

(A) is not supported. Lines 7–11 indicate that wampum only became currency because of how Europeans misinterpreted it. There's no indication that Haudenosaune would have gone that route otherwise.

(B) is a 180. The use of colors was in the "simplest and oldest form of wampum" (lines 19–20), long before the confederacy.

(D) is a Distortion. While the associations may have changed once beads were formed into strings, there's no indication that color associations further changed when belts were introduced.

(E) is an unsupported hypothetical. Even if the Europeans *were* aware of the communicative role of wampum, they still could have just ignored that and used the wampum however they wanted.

18. (B) Inference

Step 2: Identify the Question Type
This is an Inference question because it asks for something the passage "provides the most support for inferring."

Step 3: Research the Relevant Text
There is no content clue here, so the entire passage is relevant.

Step 4: Make a Prediction
The correct answer cannot be predicted, so eliminate answers that are outside the scope of the passage, and use content clues to do any necessary research.

Step 5: Evaluate the Answer Choices
(B) is correct. The formation of the confederacy led to the invention of belts (lines 43–45), which were definitely more complex than the mere strings that were used before then.

(A) is a 180. Lines 7–11 suggest that wampum only developed an economic purpose because of European misinterpretation.

(C) is Out of Scope. There's no indication that the Haudenosaune ever stopped using wampum to represent the constitution or went on to use something else.

(D) is a subtle Distortion. While wampum *belts* were used to indicate and enforce edicts and policies, wampum could still have been used more often in other forms. It's possible that wampum strings were more common and used for purposes unrelated to the confederate policies. Line 4 does indicate that wampum was used primarily for political purposes, but to say wampum "served primarily" for official edicts and policies of the confederacy is not supported in the passage.

(E) is Out of Scope. In fact, lines 56–57 suggest that, even in belts, wampum still used the same "two colors" as always. Interpretation came from the *arrangements* of the colors, not different shades.

19. (E) Inference

Step 2: Identify the Question Type

This is an Inference question because it asks for something *inferred* that the author is "most likely to agree with."

Step 3: Research the Relevant Text

There are no content clues, so the entire passage is relevant.

Step 4: Make a Prediction

The correct answer cannot be predicted. Eliminate any answers that are clearly not supported, and use content clues to do any relevant research.

Step 5: Evaluate the Answer Choices

(E) is supported multiple times throughout paragraph 3. In the examples, the author says that longhouses *usually* meant a particular nation (line 49), fires *possibly* indicated talks (line 50), and lines "seem to have indicated" relationships (line 53). Those phrases all indicate inconclusive results.

(A) is Out of Scope. The passage never discusses objects similar to wampum, nor does it discuss what groups other than the Haudenosaune used.

(B) is a 180. The author states that Europeans "misinterpreted the significance of wampum," which suggests that they were not as aware as this answer suggests.

(C) is a 180. Line 11 states that Europeans used wampum "solely to purchase goods."

(D) is a 180 on multiple fronts. First, the use of wampum in loose bead and string form predated the Haudenosaune Confederacy. Only wampum *belts* seemed to come later. Also, the confederacy formed from "warring tribes" (lines 37–38), suggesting that any peaceful association was hardly *long term* when the belts were introduced.

Passage 4: Negative Evidence in Science

Step 1: Read the Passage Strategically

Sample Roadmap

line #	Keyword/phrase	¶ Margin notes
Passage A		
1	main	negative evid. = disprove
2	power	
3	fundamental point … :	
4	for example	
5	but	
8	no value	can't prove
9	tantamount	
10	disproof … Moreover	can disprove
11	At the heart	
13	not only … but also	
15	Indeed … only if	negative evid. vital
17	However	Auth rebuts
18	does not adequately	
20	But	Which premise disproved?
28	but	Negative evid.
31	never … But	not conclusive
Passage B		
34		Predict Uranus orbit
41	incorrect	Failed
42	One possible explanation	
43	Incorrect … Another	
44	error	Changed aux. assms.
45	changed	
46	concluding	
49		Found Neptune; prediction correct
53	Once again	Didn't predict Merc. orbit
54	hypothesized	
56	However … never	No Vulcan—
58	Error … Finally	Newton wrong?
62	rejection	
63	increased confidence	Einstein theory confirms

Discussion

Passage A starts off with Karl Popper's view of scientific evidence: positive evidence (i.e., supporting evidence) can never provide proof, but negative evidence (i.e., contradicting evidence) absolutely provides disproof. Based on that, Popper argues that negative evidence (**Topic**) is vital and that theories can't be truly scientific unless they're tested against negative evidence. The conclusive value of negative evidence is the **Scope** of the passage.

In paragraph 2, the author claims that Popper is ignoring reality. So, the **Purpose** is to refute Popper's claims. According to the author, scientific theories usually have multiple *auxiliary* assumptions. A failed prediction can just mean one of the assumptions was off—but which one is unknown. So, negative evidence isn't as conclusive as Popper suggests—which is the author's **Main Idea**.

Passage B discusses two experiments by astronomers. In the first, they tried to predict the orbit of Uranus using Newton's theories and auxiliary assumptions. The prediction failed, but they had assumed that there were no planets nearby. They changed the assumption, found Neptune, and the calculations worked. In the second experiment, they tried to predict Mercury's orbit. They failed again, and again changed the assumption—but no new planet was found. So, Einstein came up with a new theory, and all the calculations worked. Newton's theory was then rejected.

The **Topic** of passage B is predicting planetary orbits. The **Scope** is testing theories based on the results of predictions. The **Purpose** is merely describing what happened. The **Main Idea** is that, while Newton's theories held up in one situation, failed predictions and assumptions in another situation led to the rejection of Newton's theories.

While passage B never uses the term "negative evidence," the failed predictions in both experiments are perfect examples. So, both passages are ultimately focused on how negative evidence can be used to test theories. However, passage A is focused on scientific theories in general, while passage B stays focused on a specific scientific field—astronomy.

20. (C) Global

Step 2: Identify the Question Type

The question asks for the "central topic" of both passages, making this a Global question.

Step 3: Research the Relevant Text

For Global questions, there's no need to go back into the passages. The information gleaned from Step 1 will be enough to predict the answer.

Step 4: Make a Prediction

Both passages focus on testing theories and whether contrary (i.e., negative) evidence is enough to disprove them.

Step 5: Evaluate the Answer Choices

(C) is correct. Even though the phrase "negative evidence" never appears in passage B, the unexpected results described directly illustrate the concept.

(A) is mentioned in passage A, but passage B never discusses the relationship between positive and negative evidence.

(B) mentions planetary orbits, which are only focused on in passage B. Passage A never specifically discusses planets.

(D) brings up techniques for confirming a theory. Passage A only concentrates on using negative evidence, a technique for *disproving* theories.

(E) is a 180. Both passages suggest that experimentation is relevant, not irrelevant.

21. (C) Detail

Step 2: Identify the Question Type

The question asks for something *mentioned* in one passage and *illustrated* in the other. The correct answer will be directly stated somewhere, making this a Detail question.

Step 3: Research the Relevant Text

There are no content clues here, so the entire text is relevant.

Step 4: Make a Prediction

The experiments in passage B illustrate a few concepts from passage A. The failed prediction results are a prime example of "negative evidence" (seen throughout passage A). The assumptions about the existence of Neptune and Vulcan illustrate "auxiliary premises" (line 23 of passage A). The Uranus experiment illustrates that negative evidence isn't always conclusive (lines 30–32). And the rejection of Newton's theory illustrates that negative evidence *can* "disprove [theories]" (line 14). Any of these can be the correct answer.

Step 5: Evaluate the Answer Choices

(C) is correct, because passage A does mention disproving a theory (line 14), and passage B has the example of Newton's theory of gravity being rejected.

(A) is a Distortion. The theories that rely on experimental results can be repudiated, but there's no mention of disputing the results themselves.

(B) is illustrated by the Uranus experiment. However, revision is never mentioned in passage A.

(D) is illustrated twice in passage B, but passage A never mentions planets or their orbits.

(E) is referred to in passage A (lines 14–15 suggest that such theories are not truly scientific). However, the theories in passage B are all testable, so there's no illustration of one that's *not* testable.

22. (C) Inference

Step 2: Identify the Question Type

This is an Inference question because it asks for something that "most clearly illustrates" a term.

Step 3: Research the Relevant Text

Start by reviewing lines 22–26 for full context of what constitutes a "disturbing force." Then, use that to research passage B appropriately.

Step 4: Make a Prediction

Lines 25–26 discuss the "absence of" a disturbing force, and this is an example of an *auxiliary* premise. In lines 37–39, the author discusses an *auxiliary* assumption about the absence of planets near Uranus. So, the disturbing force would be "planets near Uranus," which is what Neptune is (lines 48–51).

Step 5: Evaluate the Answer Choices

(C) is a match.

(A) is a Distortion. Scientists made assumptions about the absence of planets *near* Uranus, not Uranus itself.

(B) is a Faulty Use of Detail. Astronomers had an assumption about the "mass of the sun" (line 36), not the absence of the sun.

(D) is a Distortion. In the second experiment, the scientists likely assumed the absence of planets *near* Mercury, not Mercury itself. Vulcan would be the kind of planet they originally assumed was absent.

(E) is Out of Scope. Passage B never mentions the moon.

23. (D) Inference

Step 2: Identify the Question Type

This is an Inference question because it asks for something the author "means to suggest."

Step 3: Research the Relevant Text

The phrase in question appears in line 7, but be sure to use the entire sentence for context. Then, the question asks about the author's opinion, which is found only in paragraph 2. Contrast Keywords [*h*]*owever* (line 17) and [*b*]*ut* (line 31) offer good places to check.

Step 4: Make a Prediction

In lines 6–10, Popper's "hyperbolic application" asserts that "negative evidence is tantamount to disproof." The word *hyperbolic* itself suggests an extreme point of view. Sure enough, in lines 17–19, the author claims that Popper's application "does not adequately capture" what scientists actually face. And by lines 31–32, the author asserts that negative evidence is *not* conclusive, as Popper suggests. So, the author feels that the *hyperbolic* view is not as absolute as Popper suggests.

Step 5: Evaluate the Answer Choices

(D) matches the author's belief that Popper's view is "too radical" (*hyperbolic*) and not as conclusive as Popper thinks.

(A) is a Distortion. Popper applies the idea to scientific research, to which logical asymmetry *does* apply. The author just feels it's not always conclusive.

(B) is a 180. [*H*]*yperbolic* suggests *overestimation*. Popper thinks negative evidence will *always* disprove theories, but the author suggests that that's not always true.

(C) is a Distortion. The reasoning behind logical asymmetry is not in itself flawed. It's Popper's *application* of that reasoning that's extreme.

(E) is a Distortion. The idea of logical asymmetry *is* relevant, it just doesn't allow for the extreme conclusion that Popper suggests (i.e., positive evidence has no value, and negative evidence will always disprove).

24. (B) Inference

Step 2: Identify the Question Type

The question asks for what one author is "most likely to" do with information from the other passage. That makes this an Inference question.

Step 3: Research the Relevant Text

The correct answer will take something from passage B and support the last sentence of passage A. So, start with the last sentence of passage A (lines 31–32), and use that to research passage B appropriately.

Step 4: Make a Prediction

The last sentence of passage A claims that "negative evidence rarely is [conclusive]." There are three instances of negative evidence in passage B. In lines 40–41, results did not match predictions of Uranus's orbit. In lines 53–54, results did not match predictions of Mercury's orbit. In line 56, Vulcan was not found. However, the last two pieces of evidence *were* ultimately used to conclusively reject Newton's theory. Only the first results about Uranus's orbit were shown to be inconclusive, with Newton's theory holding up under new assumptions.

Step 5: Evaluate the Answer Choices

(B) is correct.

(A) is a Distortion. The discovery of Uranus (mentioned in line 33) didn't disprove or contradict any theory, as negative evidence would do.

(C) is a 180. This failure ultimately led to Newton's theory being rejected, suggesting that it *was* conclusive.

(D) is a 180. This failure *was* conclusive, destroying an assumption that led to the rejection of Newton's theory.

(E) is a Distortion. A successful prediction would be positive evidence. The last sentence of passage A is about the inconclusiveness of *negative* evidence.

25. (A) Logic Reasoning (Parallel Reasoning)

Step 2: Identify the Question Type
This is a Parallel Reasoning question because it asks for something in one passage that is "most analogous" to something in the other.

Step 3: Research the Relevant Text
The black swan is mentioned in lines 3–5. The developments leading to the rejection of Newton's theory are described in lines 52–64.

Step 4: Make a Prediction
The black swan is a piece of negative evidence that disproves the theory that "all swans are white." A parallel circumstance would involve a piece of negative evidence that disproved Newton's theory of gravity. Two pieces of negative evidence caused Newton's downfall: first, the failed prediction of Mercury's orbit (lines 52–54); second, the failure to find Vulcan (line 56). So, Mercury and Vulcan are the two bodies that played a role in disproving Newton's theory.

Step 5: Evaluate the Answer Choices
(A) is a match.

(B) is a 180. Newton's theory was upheld after new assumptions led to revised and confirmed predictions for Uranus.

(C) is a 180. The discovery of Neptune confirmed a new assumption that helped *validate* Newton's theory.

(D) is Out of Scope. Venus is never mentioned in the passage.

(E) is a Faulty Use of Detail. While there may have been assumptions about the "mass of the sun" (line 36), the sun was never mentioned in the evidence against Newton's theory.

26. (B) Inference

Step 2: Identify the Question Type
The question asks for something *inferred* that an author is "likely to be skeptical of." That makes this an Inference question.

Step 3: Research the Relevant Text
Without any content clues, all of the text is relevant.

Step 4: Make a Prediction
If the author of passage B would be skeptical about a claim, then there would be evidence to contradict that claim. The entire results of the Uranus experiment show that negative evidence is not conclusive and couldn't be used to disprove Newton. That contradicts Popper's claim in lines 9–10 that negative evidence is tantamount to disproof. The results of

the Mercury experiment were used to disprove Newton's theory, so that questions the claim in lines 31–32 that negative evidence is rarely conclusive. And the fact that confirmed calculations "increased confidence in Einstein's theory" suggests that positive evidence *can* have value, as opposed to Popper's claim in line 8.

Step 5: Evaluate the Answer Choices
(B) is a match. By showing that positive evidence "increased confidence" in a theory, passage B suggests positive evidence *does* play a role.

(A) is Out of Scope. Passage B's examples address Popper's views, but never address whether these views were Popper's "main contribution" to science or not.

(C) is a 180. Both experiments described in passage B involve auxiliary assumptions. That would suggest agreement with this claim, not skepticism.

(D) is Out of Scope. Passage B never addresses logical asymmetry.

(E) is not supported. In both experiments described, negative evidence was found. But the author of passage B never suggests whether these experiments were an "attempt to refute" theories. Even if they weren't, passage B could still agree that scientific research involves both attempts to support *and* to refute theories.

27. (E) Logic Reasoning (Parallel Reasoning)

Step 2: Identify the Question Type
The correct answer asks for a situation "analogous to" one described in passage B. That makes this a Parallel Reasoning question.

Step 3: Research the Relevant Text
The discovery of Neptune is described in lines 44–51.

Step 4: Make a Prediction
In the experiment described, scientists were testing a theory by predicting the orbit of Uranus. The prediction failed because they assumed that no other planet was nearby. They then discovered Neptune, which *was* nearby. Once they factored that in, the calculations finally matched the prediction. The correct answer will contain a similar situation in another field of science: a theory is tested, but predictions don't match; something new is discovered, and that allows the predictions to be confirmed.

Step 5: Evaluate the Answer Choices
(E) is logically the same. A theory is tested (law of conservation of energy), but predictions don't match (combined energy was less than expected); something new is discovered (an undetected particle), and that allowed the prediction to be confirmed.

(A) does not match. Here, Galileo's predictions are shown to be wrong. In the passage, the discovery of Neptune allowed for a revision that helped *confirm* the predictions.

(B) is Out of Scope. This uses evidence to "settle a debate," which is something that is never done in passage B.

(C) does not match. Here, Alvarez makes a prediction and finds evidence to support the prediction. However, there's no mention of his prediction *not* matching in the first place.

(D) does not match. Here, Brunhes simply uses evidence to reach a conclusion. There is no theory tested and no unmatched predictions that are overturned by the discovery of something new.

Section II: Logical Reasoning

Q#	Question Type	Correct	Difficulty
1	Flaw	B	★
2	Inference	B	★
3	Point at Issue	C	★
4	Flaw	C	★
5	Assumption (Necessary)	C	★
6	Principle (Identify/Strengthen)	D	★
7	Paradox	C	★★
8	Method of Argument	E	★
9	Weaken	B	★★
10	Assumption (Sufficient)	B	★
11	Paradox	A	★★
12	Weaken	B	★★
13	Inference	D	★★
14	Strengthen	E	★★
15	Inference	A	★★
16	Flaw	C	★★
17	Inference	D	★★★
18	Assumption (Necessary)	B	★★★
19	Flaw	C	★★★
20	Paradox	E	★★★★
21	Parallel Flaw	B	★★★★
22	Assumption (Sufficient)	A	★★★
23	Principle (Identify/Strengthen)	E	★★★★
24	Assumption (Necessary)	D	★★★
25	Strengthen	D	★★
26	Principle (Parallel)	E	★★★

1. (B) Flaw

Step 1: Identify the Question Type
The phrase "vulnerable to criticism" indicates that there's a flaw in the argument. Look for why the conclusion does not logically follow from the given evidence.

Step 2: Untangle the Stimulus
According to the evidence, industrial by-products can increase hormonal activity in reptiles. Some alligators were recently spotted with abnormalities that could only be caused by an increase in hormonal activity. So, the author concludes that there must have been industrial by-products in the swamp.

Step 3: Make a Prediction
The abnormalities had to be caused by increased hormonal activity, but industrial by-products are just one way of making that happen. By placing the blame solely on the by-products, the author overlooks other factors that could lead to the necessary hormonal activity.

Step 4: Evaluate the Answer Choices
(B) exactly describes what the author is overlooking.

(A) is Out of Scope. The alligators in question had the abnormalities that *are* caused by increased hormonal activity. There's no need to explain other abnormalities.

(C) is a 180. The author concludes that the by-products were in the "swamp's ecosystem," which *would* include any food eaten by the alligator. So, this is something that *is* considered—not overlooked.

(D) is an Irrelevant Comparison. Whether or not other animals had the abnormalities, the argument is about what caused these abnormalities in the first place.

(E) is Out of Scope. There's no information here about the exact number of alligators, so there's no basis to question the sample as unrepresentative. Besides, the argument is not about alligators in general, but about these specific alligators and their abnormalities.

2. (B) Inference

Step 1: Identify the Question Type
When a question asks for something that fills in a blank, look at the Keyword before that blank. In this case, the Keyword is [s]o, which means it will contain a conclusion. And a conclusion is meant to be an Inference based on the supporting evidence. (This is not a Main Point question because the conclusion is not actually stated—it needs to be inferred.)

Step 2: Untangle the Stimulus
According to the government official, it's good that foreign citizens cannot be cabinet secretaries because that position would require foreign citizens to perform duties they shouldn't be performing. As it turns out, cabinet undersecretaries would have to perform the same duties when the actual secretary is not around.

Step 3: Make a Prediction
The major point here is that foreign citizens should not be performing the duties of a cabinet secretary. If undersecretaries can be expected to perform those duties on occasion, then logic would dictate that foreign citizens should not hold the position of undersecretary either.

Step 4: Evaluate the Answer Choices
(B) is exactly what follows from the official's statements.

(A) is Out of Scope. There is no information here to support any granting of citizenship.

(C) is Extreme. While the official may conclude that *foreign* citizens should not be appointed as secretaries, there's no reason to exclude local citizens who have never served as undersecretaries.

(D) is a 180. The official directly states that it "is wise" that foreign citizens *not* serve as secretaries.

(E) is unsupported. The statements merely claim that undersecretaries *are* expected to stand in on occasion. There is no evidence given for why they *shouldn't*.

3. (C) Point at Issue

Step 1: Identify the Question Type
There are two speakers, and the question asks for a claim they "disagree over." That makes this a Point at Issue question.

Step 2: Untangle the Stimulus
Seeing that people in student government are all outspoken, Doris recommends more students to join so that they can become more outspoken. Zack points out a classic flaw in Doris's argument: student government doesn't *make* people more outspoken; those students were outspoken *before* joining.

Step 3: Make a Prediction
Zack's last sentence directly addresses the point at issue. Zack says joining student government will "do nothing" to make people more outspoken, contrary to Doris's suggestion.

Step 4: Evaluate the Answer Choices
(C) is the point at issue. Use the Decision Tree to confirm: 1) Does Doris have an opinion about this answer? Yes, she feels it *does* help. 2) Does Zack have an opinion about this? Yes, he feels it will "do nothing." 3) Are those opinions different? Absolutely.

(A) is certainly something that Doris favors. However, Zack offers no opinion on this. It's not that he feels students *shouldn't* be more outspoken, but that student government is not going to help.

(B) is exactly what Doris is encouraging. However, while Zack points out that becoming involved in student government won't help with making people outspoken, Zack could still encourage people to join for other reasons.

(D) is a 180 because this is something Doris and Zack agree on. They both state that student government people are outspoken. What they disagree on is what *made* them outspoken. Doris feels it was student government, while Zack says they were outspoken *beforehand*.

(E) is a Distortion. Zack would clearly disagree, but this logic distorts Doris's statements. **(E)** suggests that student government is the *only* way for students to become more outspoken. While Doris believes joining student government is sufficient, that doesn't mean students couldn't become more outspoken in other ways.

4. (C) Flaw

Step 1: Identify the Question Type
The given argument is said to be "vulnerable to criticism," which means this is a Flaw question. Determine why the evidence does not logically back up the conclusion.

Step 2: Untangle the Stimulus
Critics of a study of chameleons are complaining about the small sample size. The biologist concedes that point, but concludes that critics have no need to be skeptical. As evidence, the biologist refers to the reputation and status of the study's author.

Step 3: Make a Prediction
No matter how much expertise is involved, the study is still based on a mere six chameleons. Citing the author's credentials does nothing to address this concern. In short, the biologist is appealing to authority without providing any actual evidence.

Step 4: Evaluate the Answer Choices
(C) exactly expresses the appeal to authority flaw.

(A) is a possible flaw in the study, but the biologist does not make this mistake. The biologist's mistake is defending the study merely based on who conducted it.

(B) is irrelevant. The biologist has no need to explain this. The argument is merely about whether or not the results of the study are valid.

(D) mentions the critics' expertise, which is not relevant. The question is whether or not the study is valid based on its *author's* expertise, not how much expertise the critics have.

(E) is an Irrelevant Comparison. It doesn't matter how high the standards are for the critics. The biologist is only concerned about how well regarded the study's author is, and that's not relevant to whether the study is valid.

5. (C) Assumption (Necessary)

Step 1: Identify the Question Type
The question directly asks for an assumption, and one that is *required* by the argument. That makes this a Necessary Assumption question.

Step 2: Untangle the Stimulus
Despite what some analysts claim, the political scientist concludes that the government does *not* support freedom of expression. This is because the government recently accepted a protest pushing ideas the government supports, and governments that support freedom of expression would accept expressing ideas they support *and* oppose.

Step 3: Make a Prediction
The political scientist is suggesting that the government is playing favorites, only accepting protests with messages it supports. However, only the one protest is mentioned. There's no evidence of what the government would say to protests with a message it *doesn't* support. The political scientist assumes that the government would reject those protests, thus making the government not truly supportive of freedom of expression.

Step 4: Evaluate the Answer Choices
(C) must be true. After all, using the Denial Test, if the government *would* accept a protest with a message it opposed, then it would do everything a supportive government would, contradicting the political scientist's claim.

(A) is Out of Scope. The political scientist's argument does not require that the government actually help organize the rally. That may help strengthen the argument that the government plays favorites, but it's not needed. In order to confirm that the government does not truly support freedom of expression, something *is* needed to point at the government actually limiting that freedom.

(B) is Out of Scope. The argument is merely based on the government's support of the message, not the content of the message itself.

(D) is a Distortion. Groups don't have to *fear* government retaliation. Even if groups *weren't* afraid, the government could still be unsupportive of people expressing opposing ideas. **(D)** would strengthen the argument, but it's not required.

(E) is also not necessary. If the government *was* only acting out of fear of backlash, that could support the argument that the government isn't truly supportive. However, even if they *weren't* acting out of fear, the government could still be unsupportive of people expressing opposing ideas.

6. (D) Principle (Identify/Strengthen)

Step 1: Identify the Question Type

The question directly asks for a principle that will "justify the reasoning" provided. That means this is an Identify the Principle question that mimics a Strengthen question. Break the argument into evidence and conclusion, and look for a broadly worded answer that conforms to the argument's logic.

Step 2: Untangle the Stimulus

Convicted criminals are now being asked to pay a $30 "victim surcharge," which helps provide support for victims of violent crimes. Unfortunately, this fee is charged to *all* criminals. That may be fine for criminals who commit violent crimes, but the lawyer argues that this is unfair to criminals who commit less serious crimes, such as petty theft.

Step 3: Make a Prediction

As a general rule, the lawyer is arguing that criminals should not have to pay to support people affected by the more violent crimes of other criminals. The correct answer will be consistent with that principle.

Step 4: Evaluate the Answer Choices

(D) is a match.

(A) is Out of Scope. This argument is not about how severe the penalty is, but whether or not it's fair to make certain criminals pay it in the first place.

(B) is an Irrelevant Comparison. The argument is not about "overall penalties." It's only about a particular surcharge and who should have to pay it.

(C) is Out of Scope. The lawyer's claim of fairness is based on the type of crime committed, not how much of the $30 surcharge actually goes to the victims. So whether "all proceeds" are used for services is immaterial.

(E) is a Distortion. The lawyer is merely arguing that thieves should *not* pay the "victim surcharge." There's no mention of what fines they *should* pay.

7. (C) Paradox

Step 1: Identify the Question Type

The correct answer will *explain* something that occurred, making this a Paradox question.

Step 2: Untangle the Stimulus

According to the economist, the country in question is focusing more on services and less on manufacturing. With that, the country has reduced international trade.

Step 3: Make a Prediction

As with any Paradox question, ask "why." In this case, why would a greater focus on services lead to less international trade? It's not important to predict an exact answer, but know that the correct one will answer that question.

Step 4: Evaluate the Answer Choices

(C) provides an explanation. If markets for services were primarily local, then a country focusing on services would have less need to deal with outside markets.

(A) is a 180. If international trade covered manufactured goods *and* services, then the country's switch from one to the other should have made no difference.

(B) is an Irrelevant Comparison. The skills required for employment in either sector have nothing to do with international trade.

(D) is a Distortion. If a country wanted to cut back on unemployment, this may explain why it would shift focus to a more service-based economy. However, it does nothing to explain why international trade is going down.

(E) is a 180. If services were less expensive in other countries, then it would make sense to *increase* trade with those other countries. That makes the *decrease* in international trade even more inexplicable.

8. (E) Method of Argument

Step 1: Identify the Question Type

The word *by* is the key to recognizing this as a Method of Argument question. Simply put, the question asks for *how* Ortiz criticizes Merton (i.e., *by* doing what?).

Step 2: Untangle the Stimulus

Merton refers to a study that shows a greater rate of heart disease among people who live on busy streets. Merton argues that car exhaust pollution is to blame. Ortiz isn't convinced, suggesting that the people on those streets might just have unhealthy lifestyles.

Step 3: Make a Prediction

Merton is convinced that pollution is the cause, but Ortiz raises the question of an alternate cause. That questioning of possible alternatives is the Method of Argument.

Step 4: Evaluate the Answer Choices

(E) is correct. Ortiz suggests that Merton cannot be *sure* of pollution as the cause without ruling out the possibility of "other lifestyle factors."

(A) is a Distortion. Ortiz questions the conclusion Merton derives from the study, not the study itself.

(B) is a Distortion. Ortiz raises the question of other *causes* of heart problems, not other *effects* of air pollution.

(C) is not supported. There's no suggestion that Merton misunderstands the findings. What Ortiz questions is the conclusion Merton derives *from* those findings.

(D) is a Distortion. Merton does not draw a "general conclusion." Merton comes up with a specific conclusion about air pollution, and Ortiz counters with the general alternative possibility of "lifestyle factors."

9. (B) Weaken

Step 1: Identify the Question Type
The question directly asks for something that weakens the argument.

Step 2: Untangle the Stimulus
About 10 years ago, fish started to die out in two lakes: Quapaw and Highwater. At that point, fishing was banned at Quapaw but not at Highwater. Since then, the fish have returned at Quapaw, but fish numbers are still dwindling at Highwater. The author concludes that the fish population recovered at Quapaw because of the fishing ban.

Step 3: Make a Prediction
This is a classic case of Correlation versus Causation. Yes, the fish population happened to recover at the one lake with a fishing ban. But was the fishing ban really the cause? The author assumes so. To weaken that assumption, the correct answer will offer an alternative explanation or show how the fishing ban had no direct effect on the fish population.

Step 4: Evaluate the Answer Choices
(B) weakens the argument. If people weren't really fishing at Quapaw *before* the ban, then the fishing ban wouldn't have changed much. So, there must be another reason why the fish population recovered.

(A) might help explain why Highwater Lake continues to have troubles, but it doesn't offer any explanation why things improved at Quapaw Lake. The fishing ban is still a plausible explanation.

(C) is an Irrelevant Comparison. The size of the lakes has no bearing on why the fish population improved in Quapaw but not in Highwater.

(D) has no effect on the argument. Even if other lakes have seen increased fish populations, there's still the question of why. Maybe those lakes had fishing bans, too.

(E) is another Irrelevant Comparison. The argument is not about the number of *varieties* of fish but the total population overall.

10. (B) Assumption (Sufficient)

Step 1: Identify the Question Type
The question asks for something that, *if* assumed, would make the argument sound. That makes this a Sufficient Assumption question.

Step 2: Untangle the Stimulus
Because the Asian elephant always has some feet on the ground, the author concludes that it doesn't actually run.

Step 3: Make a Prediction
This is a fundamental case of Mismatched Concepts. The author's conclusion about running ability is based solely on evidence about feet being on the ground. The author assumes

that any animal that keeps its feet on the ground cannot run. Or, as a contrapositive, any animal that *can* run must get all of its feet off the ground.

Step 4: Evaluate the Answer Choices
(B) is a match. If an animal needs to have all of its feet off the ground to run, then an animal that *doesn't* get all its feet off the ground (e.g., the Asian elephant) cannot run, as the author concludes.

(A) is a Distortion. The Asian elephant *can* accelerate, so this logic does not guarantee the author's conclusion.

(C) is an Irrelevant Comparison. It doesn't matter how fast the elephant is compared to other animals. The argument is about whether or not it can technically *run*.

(D) is Out of Scope. Saying the elephant's behavior is *unusual* has no bearing on whether it can run or not.

(E) is Out of Scope. Even if elephants were not alone in keeping their feet on the ground while *walking*, this does nothing to connect to the conclusion about whether they can run.

11. (A) Paradox

Step 1: Identify the Question Type
The question asks for something that will "explain [a] surprising result," making this a Paradox question. Look for the central mystery, and consider why things happen as they do.

Step 2: Untangle the Stimulus
A hardware store has two brands of hammers: Maxlast and Styron. Normally, the store sells an equal number of each. However, when the Maxlast brand was put on sale and displayed in the front of the store, people actually bought more Styron hammers.

Step 3: Make a Prediction
How bizarre. If people normally buy both hammers equally, one would think that placing Maxlast hammers in a more prominent location at a cheaper price would increase *that* brand's sale. So, why did people walk past them and buy more hammers of the other brand, which were still selling at full price? The correct answer will provide a reason why people passed on what should have been a great deal.

Step 4: Evaluate the Answer Choices
(A) offers an explanation. When people first enter the store, they don't pay close attention to the displays. So, people looking for a hammer wouldn't notice the display of cheaper Maxlast hammers and would walk on by. They would then head to the hammer section, where only one hammer brand remains: Styron.

(B) does not help. Neither the quality nor the service was said to change, so this wouldn't explain why people suddenly shifted their preference toward the one hammer *not* discounted and *not* displayed in the front. It's also too far a stretch to infer that the temporary lower price made people associate Maxlast with inferior quality, so it's still unclear why Styron was the bigger seller.

(C) does not help. The mystery is not why some people *did* buy Maxlast. The mystery is why more people *didn't*.

(D) is a 180. If the Maxlast hammer sale was advertised, it's even *more* unusual that a greater number of people opted for the Styron hammers.

(E) does not help. Even if people didn't make a special trip just to buy the hammer on sale, this still doesn't explain why, when people *did* go shopping there, they suddenly shifted to buying more Styron hammers.

12. (B) Weaken
Step 1: Identify the Question Type
The question directly asks for something that will weaken the given argument.

Step 2: Untangle the Stimulus
Two groups of mice were taught to navigate a maze. One group was given gingko, the other was not. The mice given gingko did better at remembering the maze a day later. Still, the author is skeptical, concluding that gingko was not the *direct* cause. As evidence, the author states that gingko reduces stress, and reducing "very high stress" could improve memory.

Step 3: Make a Prediction
If reducing stress in general helped improve recall, the author would have a solid argument. Then, gingko *would* be an indirect factor, only helping the mice by reducing their stress. However, the author only notes that reducing "very high stress levels" could improve memory. Perhaps reducing normal stress levels has no effect. In that case, if the mice in question weren't overly stressed to begin with, then it *is* possible that gingko was the direct cause—contrary to the author's argument.

Step 4: Evaluate the Answer Choices
(B) weakens the argument. If none of the mice had very high stress levels, then there's no evidence that reducing their normal stress levels would have had any effect. That makes it possible that the gingko itself *was* the direct cause.

(A) is a 180. Even if the mice were given higher doses than needed, the gingko still could have reduced high stress levels, making gingko an *indirect* factor, as the author suggests.

(C) is irrelevant. Even if *some* such harmful substances exist, gingko did *not* impair the memory. So, this has no effect on whether gingko directly or indirectly aided in memory improvement.

(D) is Out of Scope. It doesn't matter what substances in ginkgo helped. If it helped reduce high levels of stress, it would still have an indirect effect, as the author claims.

(E) is also Out of Scope. The argument is not about how long it takes to *learn* the maze. The question is about what helped the one group of mice better *remember* the maze.

13. (D) Inference
Step 1: Identify the Question Type
The correct answer "must be true" based on the statements given, making this an Inference question.

Step 2: Untangle the Stimulus
There's just one claim here. Some politicians who supported free trade among Canada, the United States, and Mexico do *not* publicly support free trade with other Latin American countries.

Step 3: Make a Prediction
There's not much to deduce here. What's more important is understanding what this claim does *not* mention. The claim is about a group of people who supported the original free trade agreement. There's no information at all about politicians who *didn't* support that agreement, so the correct answer should not mention them. Also, the group in question does not publicly favor free trade with other Latin American counties. However, there's no information about anyone who *does* publicly favor such an extension of free trade. The correct answer should also exclude those people. All that's known is that a group of politicians exists who supported the initial free trade agreement but do *not* publicly support one with other Latin American countries. That also leaves the door open that they could support trade with other Latin American countries, just not *publicly*.

Step 4: Evaluate the Answer Choices
(D) must be true. If some politicians who favored the original deal do *not* publicly favor extending the deal, then it's impossible that every politician who favored the original deal publicly favors the new deal.

(A) does not have to be true. The original statement is about politicians who *did* favor the Canada-U.S.-Mexico deal but did *not* publicly favor the new Latin American deal. There's no information about politicians who *didn't* favor the original deal or ones that *do* publicly favor the new deal.

(B) does not have to be true. There's no information about politicians who *do* publicly favor extending free trade, so it's impossible to deduce whether they supported the original agreement or not.

(C) is a Distortion. Nothing suggests that these politicians changed their positions. They may have always refused to support free trade with other Latin America countries, while still supporting free trade among the original three. Another possibility is that they openly supported the first agreement, but are just silent in their support of the second agreement (i.e., they're refusing to support it *publicly*).

(E) is a Distortion. These politicians may not *publicly support* extending free trade, but that doesn't mean they actively *oppose* it. They may just keep quiet and reply "no comment" when asked.

14. (E) Strengthen

Step 1: Identify the Question Type
The correct answer will *justify* the application provided, which means it will strengthen the logic.

Step 2: Untangle the Stimulus
According to the principle, if someone commits copyright infringement, anyone who *knowingly* helps that person is also guilty. The application pronounces the Grandview Department Store guilty of copyright infringement because someone used its photo-printing kiosk to print a copyrighted photograph.

Step 3: Make a Prediction
By the principle, the department store would be guilty if it "knowingly aided" the person copying the photo. However, there's no evidence of that here. The correct answer will indicate how the store *knowingly* provided such aid.

Step 4: Evaluate the Answer Choices
(E) is correct. By this logic, because the department store provided a service that could lead to copyright infringement (the picture-printing kiosk), it "knowingly aided" the customer, justifying its guilt per the principle.

(A) is an Irrelevant Comparison. Copyright infringement likely *does* apply equally to full-service and self-service facilities. However, this still provides no evidence that the store "knowingly aided" anyone.

(B) is Out of Scope. There's no evidence that the store *witnessed* the infringement. Even if it did, there's still the question of whether it "knowingly aided" the infringer.

(C) is also Out of Scope. There's no evidence that the store *didn't* post such a note. And if it did, this would make the store seem *less* liable. And note or not, there's still nothing indicating the store "knowingly aided" the copyright violator.

(D) is Out of Scope, too. There's no evidence that the store does *not* monitor the kiosk. And even if it didn't, this does not necessarily imply "knowingly aiding" the customer.

15. (A) Inference

Step 1: Identify the Question Type
The correct answer will complete the argument and fill in the blank. The blank ends a sentence that will be [o]bviously concluded from the preceding lines, making this an Inference question.

Step 2: Untangle the Stimulus
According to the author, the purpose of journalism is to help people make informed decisions. However, sensationalistic gossip provides information that is, for the most part, irrelevant.

Step 3: Make a Prediction
The conclusion will be about sensationalistic gossip. Because it does not provide relevant information for people, it does not serve the purpose of journalism described in the first sentence. The correct answer will note this non-journalistic quality of sensationalistic gossip.

Step 4: Evaluate the Answer Choices
(A) is a match.

(B) is a Distortion. While the gossip portion itself does not achieve the purpose of journalism, that doesn't mean it stops *other* portions of that newspaper or television news program from achieving journalism's purpose.

(C) is an Irrelevant Comparison. The stimulus has no comparison between current news and past news of any kind.

(D) is not supported. While this gossip does not qualify as journalism, it may certainly be considered a form of entertainment.

(E) is Extreme. The gossip may not be considered journalism, but it may still provide *some* value—e.g., perhaps it increases sales or viewership so more people are likely to consume the portions of the paper or news program that *do* have journalistic merit.

16. (C) Flaw

Step 1: Identify the Question Type
The question directly asks for the flaw in the argument.

Step 2: Untangle the Stimulus
A survey showed that 40% of people want Conservative legislators, 20% want Moderate legislators, and 40% want Liberal legislators. The author then concludes that most people want legislature to match those percentages.

Step 3: Make a Prediction
This is a gross misapplication of statistics. There's no evidence that people want to see a mixed legislature. They would probably prefer to see a legislature that is 100% their choice (e.g., 100% Conservative). The author is mistakenly taking the survey results of the entire group and assigning those numbers to each person.

Step 4: Evaluate the Answer Choices
(C) expresses the flaw of taking the group results and applying them to the individual responders.

(A) is a Distortion. The evidence *and* conclusion are about what people would "like to see," not about what is *actually* the case or what "should be" the case.

(B) is a Distortion. The conclusion uses the same numbers as the evidence, but the numbers are applied differently. There is no restated claim.

(D) is Out of Scope. The beliefs of the researchers are irrelevant to the author's misuse of statistical results.

(E) gets the details backward. The evidence is precisely quantified figures, while the conclusion mentions what is *roughly* the case. Regardless of which was precise and which was an estimate, the flaw still lies in the misapplication of statistics from individuals to the group—not in the switch from specific to approximate numbers.

17. (D) Inference

Step 1: Identify the Question Type

The question states that the given information will *support* the correct answer. Because the answer is being supported, this is an Inference question.

Step 2: Untangle the Stimulus

The city leader discusses two proposals: a tourism plan and a new automobile manufacturing plant. They would each create an equal number of jobs, and the tourism plan would bring in $2 billion. The manufacturing plant plan would cost more money, but the leader states that it would still be a reasonable expense.

Step 3: Make a Prediction

If it would be reasonable to spend money getting a new auto manufacturing plant, then spending *less* money on a proposal that would be equally, if not more, beneficial (i.e., the tourism plan) would have to be considered reasonable, too.

Step 4: Evaluate the Answer Choices

(D) is supported. If the auto plant idea is reasonable, then so is the tourism plan that would cost less, create the same number of jobs, and bring in a lot of money.

(A) is not supported. The leader only mentions the two options, of which the tourism plan is cheaper. However, there may be other options not mentioned, and the *least* expensive one may not be worth considering.

(B) is a Distortion. The leader finds it reasonable to reach out to *automobile* manufacturers, but that doesn't mean manufacturing plants "in general" are a good idea.

(C) is not supported. The leader mentions the relative cost of both plans, but never suggests the city can only afford one.

(E) is a 180. The leader directly states that a new automobile manufacturing plant would "create as many jobs" as the tourism plan.

18. (B) Assumption (Necessary)

Step 1: Identify the Question Type

The question asks for an *assumption* that the argument *requires*, making this a Necessary Assumption question.

Step 2: Untangle the Stimulus

The author urges people to not trust an article about patients who can predict changes to their medical status. As evidence, the author cites a similar claim that was ultimately disproven about more babies being born during full moons.

Step 3: Make a Prediction

For these cases to be *analogous*, as the author claims, the logic would have to be the same. The baby claim was deemed faulty because people were shown to have selective memory: they just remembered the busy nights during a full moon, not the busy nights without a full moon. To be analogous, the predicting patient claim would have to be faulty for the same reason: people just happen to remember when the patients' predictions are accurate, and not when the patients guess wrong.

Step 4: Evaluate the Answer Choices

(B) must be true for the analogy to hold. This suggests that, like the baby incident, medical staff have selective memory. They're less likely to remember patients who make predictions that don't happen. Instead, they're just more likely to remember the accurate predictions, fueling the rumor that patients are prophets. Using the Denial Test, if the medical staff *are* just as likely to remember the patients' predictions regardless of whether the predictions are accurate, then the selective memory analogy no longer holds.

(A) is not necessary. While the baby claim was "empirically disproven," the author still doesn't trust the article in question because it is based on anecdotal evidence. Also, even if empirical evidence to disprove the article is forthcoming, it certainly doesn't need to be disproven *soon*.

(C) is Out of Scope. It doesn't matter if the patients were serious or not. The analogy hinges on what the medical staff remembers and whether those stories can be trusted.

(D) is a Distortion. The point of the baby claim analogy is to show that people *thought* babies were born more during full moons. However, the suggestion is more likely that baby births were *equally* likely to be high with or without a full moon. The argument does not need it to be true that babies were born *less* under a full moon.

(E) is Out of Scope. The author's problem with the article is the reliability of anecdotal evidence, not how "widely held" the belief is.

19. (C) Flaw

Step 1: Identify the Question Type
The question asks why the reasoning is *flawed*, making this easy to identify as a Flaw question.

Step 2: Untangle the Stimulus
According to the politician, union leaders are upset about countries working together to control manufacturing. The concern is that this leads businesses to move labor to where worker protection is weak and wages are lower. Union leaders understandably want to stop this from happening. However, the politician argues that multinational control should *not* be stopped because union leaders are trying to protect their own interests.

Step 3: Make a Prediction
The problem is that the politician has no actual evidence to reject the union leaders' claims. The politician merely points a finger at their motives without actually addressing their claims. It's possible that their points are still valid even if they are looking out for their own interests.

Step 4: Evaluate the Answer Choices
(C) correctly points out how the politician rejects an argument merely because the outcome would benefit the union leaders themselves.

(A) is Extreme. The politician is merely rejecting this one argument about multinational control, not *all* viewpoints that union leaders express. For example, they may express some viewpoints that are not related to their self-interest, and the politician would not be able to dismiss those based on the same reasoning.

(B) is Out of Scope and possibly Extreme. There's no mention of "political motivations." The union leaders are motivated by maintaining high worker wages. Furthermore, even if the union leaders' desire to keep wages high is somehow considered a political motivation, **(B)** says the politician assumes *anyone* with political motivations is unreliable, but the politician's reasoning may be just limited to union leaders.

(D) is not supported. There is no suggestion that union leaders don't have other arguments to back their claim. If anything, the politician *overlooks* any such arguments and focuses solely on union leaders protecting their interests.

(E) is Extreme. The politician is arguing against a particular group of union leaders. There's no suggestion that this argument extends to leaders of *all* unions. However, even if the politician does accurately attribute the viewpoint to *all* union leaders, the politician's argument is still flawed in that it fails to address their argument.

20. (E) Paradox

Step 1: Identify the Question Type
The correct answer here will *explain* a circumstance, making this a Paradox question.

Step 2: Untangle the Stimulus
Job prospects for chemistry majors are better than ever. Yet, over the past 10 years, while the number of students entering college as chemistry majors has stayed the same, fewer students are actually graduating with chemistry degrees.

Step 3: Make a Prediction
Paraphrase the paradox as a question of why: why are fewer students getting chemistry degrees if the number of students entering the program hasn't changed? Something must have changed in the past 10 years that is preventing an increasing number of students from graduating with the chemistry degree they went in for—and it's not dampened job prospects.

Step 4: Evaluate the Answer Choices
(E) provides an explanation. The classes have changed and become less appealing. In that case, students initially interested in chemistry may decide to bail in favor of something more exciting.

(A) doesn't help. This has probably always been true and wouldn't explain why the number of chemistry grads has *decreased* over the years. Those without the necessary background may not have been trying to major in chemistry in the first place.

(B) suggests that chemistry is not alone in its decreasing number of graduates, but still offers no explanation of *why* that's occurring. If anything, it adds more mystery. Why are those *other* departments suffering, too?

(C) could explain why some students change majors throughout college. However, it does not explain why it has happened significantly more often for chemistry majors over the 10-year period.

(D) makes an Irrelevant Comparison. It doesn't matter how chemistry job prospects compare to other sciences. Those job prospects for chemistry jobs are still the best they've ever been, so it's hard to understand why *fewer* students are graduating with chemistry degrees.

21. (B) Parallel Flaw

Step 1: Identify the Question Type
The correct answer will contain reasoning *parallel* to the reasoning in the stimulus, and that reasoning is described as *flawed*. That makes this a Parallel Flaw question. The correct answer must contain a flaw that is exactly the same as the one in the stimulus.

Step 2: Untangle the Stimulus

The author argues that human-borne diseases are probably not to blame for animal extinctions that occurred 46,000–56,000 years ago. Over 55 species disappeared, and no one disease could kill off that many species.

Step 3: Make a Prediction

The evidence adequately suggests that the extinctions were not caused by any one specific human-borne disease. However, the extinctions could have been caused by *several* human-borne diseases, each responsible for some extinctions. The correct answer will commit the same logical error: suggesting a whole group of entities cannot accomplish something because no single member could accomplish it alone, ignoring the possibility of multiple members working together.

Step 4: Evaluate the Answer Choices

(B) makes the same mistake. This argument suggests that a group of entities (the two people involved) cannot accomplish something (repair the apartment) because no one member could fix both the door and window. It ignores the possibility that the apartment can be fixed by *both* of them, each responsible for one task. Although it does not match the level of certainty by omitting a word parallel to the word *probably*, it does contain the same group vs. member flaw.

(A) rejects something as the cause of a problem, but does not generalize about a group based on what one individual member cannot do.

(C) does reject the possibility of dinner by using the fact that no single restaurant appeals to everyone. However, it makes no sense that they would go to *multiple* restaurants for dinner together, so this doesn't match the overlooked possibility of the stimulus.

(D) is, among other problems, backward. The original argument used evidence about individual diseases to make a conclusion about a group of diseases. **(D)** uses evidence about a group of art to make a conclusion about an individual piece of art.

(E) is flawed because, even though the vaccine does help some people, it still *could* be correct that some people get no benefit from it. However, this is not the same logic as the stimulus. It draws no conclusion about a group of entities based on individual members.

22. (A) Assumption (Sufficient)

Step 1: Identify the Question Type

This question asks for something *assumed*, and the argument will be logical *if* that assumption is included. That makes this a Sufficient Assumption question.

Step 2: Untangle the Stimulus

A tax preparation company puts a particular disclaimer on all of its emails. However, the author argues that the disclaimer has no purpose. After all, if an email were to encourage something illegal, the disclaimer would not provide legal protection, which would be the sole purpose of such a disclaimer.

Step 3: Make a Prediction

The author has a point, *if* the email were to encourage something illegal. In that case, it wouldn't provide any legal protection, and would thus fail to serve its only purpose. But what if an email *doesn't* encourage anything illegal? In that case, the disclaimer may provide legal protection and thus could serve some purpose. The author suggests otherwise, assuming that the disclaimer wouldn't provide legal protection in *either* case, whether the email encouraged something illegal or not.

Step 4: Evaluate the Answer Choices

(A) completes the argument. As the author states, the disclaimer provides no protection when emails *do* encourage illegal activities. If, as this suggests, there's no protection needed when emails *don't* encourage illegal activities, then the disclaimer has no effect and thus serves no purpose, as the author claims.

(B) doesn't help. Even if the company is subject to penalties when emails encourage illegal activity, that still doesn't confirm that the disclaimer serves no purpose on other emails.

(C) is Out of Scope. The argument is about the disclaimer serving its purpose of offering legal protection, which is not based on whether the client ignores the message or not.

(D) is irrelevant. Sure, emails that encourage illegal activities are still not legally protected if people actually followed the advice. But this fails to address emails that do *not* encourage illegal activities. Disclaimers in those emails could still provide protection, whether people follow the advice or not.

(E) is Out of Scope. Customer behavior doesn't matter. This still ignores what would happen if emails did *not* encourage illegal behavior. The disclaimer in those emails could still provide some protection from those people who would perform illegal tax activities if they could.

23. (E) Principle (Identify/Strengthen)

Step 1: Identify the Question Type

The correct answer will be a principle, making this an Identify the Principle question. Because the principle will "support the reasoning" provided, it also acts as a Strengthen question. Validate the argument by finding an answer that conforms to the logic in broader terms.

Step 2: Untangle the Stimulus

Some people *try* to help their friends who are having marital problems, but they usually fail. Thus, the author concludes that these people's actions are unjustified.

Step 3: Make a Prediction

That's a rather harsh judgment. The author is basically saying that, even if people mean well, their actions are unjustified if they don't succeed. In other words, actions are justified *only if* they actually help.

Step 4: Evaluate the Answer Choices

(E) broadly summarizes the author's judgment that actions are not justified unless they actually help.

(A) is irrelevant. It doesn't matter *how* good the intentions are. The author still claims that such attempts are "usually ineffectual" and unjustified if unsuccessful.

(B) is a 180. The consequences are all that matter to the author.

(C) is a Distortion. All that matters to the author is whether the problem gets solved or not—regardless of intention.

(D) is a Distortion. Per the author, intentions are certainly irrelevant to deeming an action *unjustified*. However, the author doesn't mention what kinds of actions *are* justified. So, adding **(D)** wouldn't help determine whether the specific attempts to resolve the marital problems of one's friends are justified or unjustified.

24. (D) Assumption (Necessary)

Step 1: Identify the Question Type

The question asks for an *assumption* that is *required*, making this a Necessary Assumption question.

Step 2: Untangle the Stimulus

This argument opens with someone else's claim: authors who try to please their readers cannot produce books that impart truth. The argument's evidence attempts to explore the implications of that claim. If the claim were true, then a book's truthfulness could be judged by its sales figures, because a popular book must give pleasure, and thus must be at least partially untrue. On the basis of that reasoning, the argument concludes by rejecting the claim: authors who try to please their readers *can* produce books that impart truth.

Step 3: Make a Prediction

The argument's reasoning has several holes in it. Turn the argument's "What if?" strategy against it. What if readers purchase or read books without knowing whether the book will please them, or what if they sometimes choose to read books they know will not please them? Then sales figures and popularity wouldn't indicate readers' pleasure. What if books fail to please even when authors wrote them with the intention to please? Result and intention are not the same

thing, yet the argument assumes that they are. Finally, what if a book could give pleasure even if the author had not tried to please the reader? If that were true, the argument's central premise falls apart. Here again, the argument treats an author's intentions and a book's results as equivalent.

Step 4: Evaluate the Answer Choices

(D) is one of the argument's central assumptions, saying that books that give readers pleasure *must* be written with that intention. If books can produce pleasure even if their authors did not try to please their readers, then the argument's rejection of the original claim would be invalid.

(A) is a 180. By equating sales figures with pleasure, the argument assumes that people do choose to read books that they know will give them pleasure.

(B) is a 180. The argument assumes that books that give pleasure *are* indicative of an author's intention to give pleasure.

(C) is Out of Scope. The argument is about whether or not the books *can* impart truth, regardless of readers' concerns.

(E) is a 180. The argument assumes that popularity and pleasure are equivalent.

25. (D) Strengthen

Step 1: Identify the Question Type

The question directly asks for something that will strengthen the given argument.

Step 2: Untangle the Stimulus

The author argues that most new shows by Wilke & Wilke will be canceled. As evidence, the author cites their poor record from the previous year. Also, their new shows are all police dramas, which have not done so well lately.

Step 3: Make a Prediction

The author is making a prediction based on past performance. Predictions always assume constancy. In other words, the author assumes that there's no drastic change or difference that would impact the prediction. So, to strengthen the prediction that Wilke & Wilke will fail, the correct answer will validate that Wilke & Wilke are offering nothing new that would suggest a different outcome.

Step 4: Evaluate the Answer Choices

(D) helps the author out. Not only are Wilke & Wilke trotting out a relatively unpopular genre, but they're repeating a strategy that provided no success at all for them last year. That suggests a continued struggle for Wilke & Wilke.

(A) is an Irrelevant Comparison. The author concluded that *most* of their new shows would be canceled. That's over half, regardless of the quantity produced. If Wilke & Wilke increased their production, perhaps they have a better chance this year of having *some* more shows stick around—but not a better chance of the majority doing so.

(B) doesn't help. Even if, last year, most of their shows were cancelled and most of their shows were police dramas, then it could only be inferred that *some* of their police dramas were canceled. However, their biggest success story from last year may have been a police drama. By putting all their efforts there, maybe they can repeat the magic and go against the author's claim.

(C) is Out of Scope. This indicates that last year Wilke & Wilke only succeeded with shows other than police dramas. They aren't making any shows like that this year, so this information is irrelevant to the new lineup of all police dramas.

(E) is Extreme. Even if the *most* popular shows weren't police dramas, some police dramas could have been popular enough to warrant trying out a few new ones.

26. (E) Principle (Parallel)

Step 1: Identify the Question Type
The question asks for something that *conforms* to a principle. However, the principle is not given but merely *illustrated* by the stimulus. So, this is a Parallel Principle question. Start by identifying the general rule behind the argument in the stimulus, then find an answer that is logically consistent with that principle.

Step 2: Untangle the Stimulus
The author is concerned about a company that profited from committing fraudulent acts. The author argues that the company should be penalized to compensate for those profits.

Step 3: Make a Prediction
The author's general problem is seeing profit coming from misdeeds. The correct answer will provide another specific example of someone who shouldn't be allowed to profit from wrongdoing.

Step 4: Evaluate the Answer Choices
(E) is a match. Like the corporation, the convicted criminal is able to profit from a misdeed. And like the original argument, this recommends a course of action that will prevent the criminal from profiting.

(A) suggests a penalty that will prevent a recurrence of the original misdeed. However, the original argument was not concerned with recurrence, and this argument makes no mention of profiting.

(B) also places a penalty to safeguard against recurrence, which is not the same as the original. Also, there's no indication that the money is meant to "offset any profit."

(C) is not a match. The original argument is concerned about the penalty itself, not who benefits from the penalty.

(D) does not match. The penalty here is more about taking away a future privilege than offsetting a previous benefit.

Section III: Logic Games
Game 1: Recruiting Criminal Accomplices

Q#	Question Type	Correct	Difficulty
1	Acceptability	D	★
2	Partial Acceptability	C	★
3	"If" / Could Be True	D	★
4	"If" / Must Be False (CANNOT Be True)	B	★
5	"If" / Could Be True	A	★
6	"If" / Must Be True	B	★

Game 2: Newspaper Photographs

Q#	Question Type	Correct	Difficulty
7	Acceptability	B	★
8	"If" / Must Be True	C	★
9	"If" / Must Be True	D	★
10	Could Be True	A	★★
11	"If" / Could Be True	C	★★
12	"If" / Could Be True	E	★★★
13	"If" / Could Be True	C	★★

Game 3: Campus Art Gallery

Q#	Question Type	Correct	Difficulty
14	Partial Acceptability	A	★
15	Must Be True	C	★★★
16	"If" / Must Be True	B	★★★★
17	"If" / Could Be True	E	★★★★
18	"If" / Could Be True	B	★★★

Game 4: Publishing Cookbooks

Q#	Question Type	Correct	Difficulty
19	Acceptability	E	★
20	"If" / Could Be True	C	★
21	"If" / Could Be True	B	★
22	Completely Determine	A	★★
23	Rule Substitution	B	★★★

Game 1: Recruiting Criminal Accomplices

Step 1: Overview
Situation: A detective investigating when a criminal recruited a series of accomplices

Entities: Seven accomplices (Peters, Quinn, Rovero, Stanton, Tao, Villas, White)

Action: Strict Sequencing. Determine the order in which the accomplices were recruited.

Limitations: Each accomplice was recruited "one at a time," so this is a standard one-to-one Sequencing game.

Step 2: Sketch
The words "immediately before" in the first rule and an established position in the fourth rule indicate that this is Strict Sequencing. So, list the entities by initial, and set up seven numbered slots in order.

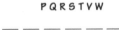

PQRSTVW

__ __ __ __ __ __ __
1   2   3   4   5   6   7

Step 3: Rules
Rule 1 prevents Stanton and Tao from being recruited consecutively, in either order.

Rule 2 provides a relative sequence: Quinn is recruited some time before Rovero.

Q...R

That means Quinn cannot be the last accomplice recruited, and Rovero cannot be the first. Add "~Q" and "~R" under the respective slots.

Rule 3 creates a Block of Entities: Villas is recruited immediately before White.

That means Villas cannot be the last accomplice recruited, and White cannot be the first. Add "~V" and "~W" under the respective slots.

Rule 4 establishes Peters as the fourth recruit. Add P to the fourth slot in the sketch.

Step 4: Deductions
Deductions are scarce in this game. There is one Block of Entities (Villas and White), but it can be placed in any pair of positions before or after Peters. There is no clear source of Limited Options. There is one Established Entity: Peters. That provides a couple of minor deductions. With Peters fourth,

Villas cannot be third (because that would not allow White to be immediately after, as Rule 3 dictates), and White cannot be fifth (because that would not allow Villas to be immediately before, as Rule 3 dictates). There are no Numbers issues here, and there are no Duplications. Every entity is mentioned in the rules, so there are no Floaters. Thankfully, the game consists of two Acceptability questions and four New-"If" questions—a good sign that few deductions were expected in the first place. Going into the questions, the Master Sketch should look something like this:

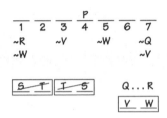

Step 5: Questions

1. (D) Acceptability
As with any Acceptability question, use the rules one at a time to eliminate answers that violate those rules.

(A) violates Rule 1 by having Stanton immediately after Tao. **(E)** violates Rule 2 by having Quinn after, not before, Rovero. **(B)** violates Rule 3 by having Villas and White separated (and in the wrong order). **(C)** violates Rule 4 by having Peters fifth instead of fourth. That leaves **(D)** as the correct answer.

2. (C) Partial Acceptability
As with standard Acceptability questions, the four wrong answers will be unacceptable because they will violate the rules. Start by using the rules one at a time to test the answers. If there are multiple answers remaining, start considering where the unlisted accomplices would be placed.

None of the answers directly violate Rules 1 or 2. **(B)** violates Rule 3 by not having Villas immediately before White. **(E)** violates Rule 4 because the answers list the accomplices recruited from second to sixth, which includes the fourth accomplice, but Peters is not listed.

From there, test the remaining answers by using the rules to determine where the unlisted entities would be placed. Remember that these answers list the accomplices from second to sixth, so the unlisted entities must be placed first and seventh.

(A) does not include Rovero or White. Rovero must be recruited after Quinn (Rule 2), and White must be recruited after Villas (Rule 3). That would leave nobody to be first, so this list is unacceptable.

(C) does not include Rovero or Tao. Rovero must be recruited after Quinn (Rule 2), so Rovero could be placed seventh. That would place Tao first, which is far enough away from Stanton.

$$\frac{T}{1} \quad \frac{V}{2} \quad \frac{W}{3} \quad \frac{P}{4} \quad \frac{Q}{5} \quad \frac{S}{6} \quad \frac{R}{7}$$

That would all be acceptable, making this the correct answer. For the record:

(D) does not include Quinn or Tao. Quinn must be recruited before Rovero (Rule 2), so Quinn would have to be first. That would place Tao seventh, but that would place Tao immediately after Stanton. That violates Rule 1, making this unacceptable.

3. (D) "If" / Could Be True

For this question, Tao is recruited second.

$$\frac{}{1} \quad \frac{T}{2} \quad \frac{}{3} \quad \frac{P}{4} \quad \frac{}{5} \quad \frac{}{6} \quad \frac{}{7}$$

By Rule 1, Stanton cannot be recruited first or third, so Stanton must be one of the last three accomplices recruited. There must be two consecutive spaces for Villas and White, so they must be recruited either fifth and sixth or sixth and seventh. Either way, they will take up the last three spaces along with Stanton. That leaves Quinn and Rovero, in that order (Rule 2), to be first and third. Because Villas and White are a block, Stanton cannot come in between them, so draw out the two possibilities:

$$\text{I)} \quad \frac{Q}{1} \quad \frac{T}{2} \quad \frac{R}{3} \quad \frac{P}{4} \quad \frac{S}{5} \quad \frac{V}{6} \quad \frac{W}{7}$$

$$\text{II)} \quad \frac{Q}{1} \quad \frac{T}{2} \quad \frac{R}{3} \quad \frac{P}{4} \quad \frac{V}{5} \quad \frac{W}{6} \quad \frac{S}{7}$$

With that, Villas could be sixth, making **(D)** the correct answer.

4. (B) "If" / Must Be False (CANNOT Be True)

For this question, Quinn and Rovero become a block. By Rule 2, Q would be before R (QR). Along with Villas and White (Rule 3), there are now two blocks that need to fit into the sketch. With Peters fourth, there are only three spaces before Peters and three spaces after. It is impossible to place both blocks before or after Peters. Therefore, one block must be placed before Peters and one block after. It doesn't matter which block goes where.

However, when one block is placed before Peters, it will go either first and second or second and third. Either way, the block must overlap the second position. Similarly, the block after Peters will go either fifth and sixth or sixth and seventh. Either way, that block must overlap the sixth position.

$$\text{I)} \quad \frac{V/W}{1} \quad \frac{}{2} \quad \frac{P}{3} \quad \frac{}{4} \quad \frac{}{5} \quad \frac{Q/R}{6} \quad \frac{}{7} \quad \boxed{VW} \quad \boxed{QR}$$

$$\text{II)} \quad \frac{Q/R}{1} \quad \frac{}{2} \quad \frac{}{3} \quad \frac{P}{4} \quad \frac{}{5} \quad \frac{V/W}{6} \quad \frac{}{7} \quad \boxed{QR} \quad \boxed{VW}$$

Stanton is not part of either block, so Stanton will never be in one of the positions taken up by either block. So, Stanton can never be second or sixth. That makes **(B)** the correct answer.

5. (A) "If" / Could Be True

For this question, White is recruited before Rovero, and Rovero is recruited before Tao. By Rule 3, Villas must be recruited immediately before White. Altogether, this creates a long string of entities:

$$\boxed{VW} \ldots R \ldots T$$

With Peters taking up the fourth spot, the block of Villas and White is restricted. It cannot be placed after Peters, because there would not be enough room after it for both Rovero and Tao. So, the block must be placed before Peters, either first and second or second and third:

$$\text{I)} \quad \frac{V}{1} \quad \frac{W}{2} \quad \frac{}{3} \quad \frac{P}{4} \quad \frac{}{5} \quad \frac{}{6} \quad \frac{}{7}$$

$$\text{II)} \quad \frac{}{1} \quad \frac{V}{2} \quad \frac{W}{3} \quad \frac{P}{4} \quad \frac{}{5} \quad \frac{}{6} \quad \frac{}{7}$$

By Rule 2, Quinn must also be recruited before Rovero, so that creates a string of Quinn, Rovero, and Tao, in that order (Q ... R ... T). That leaves Stanton, who cannot be placed next to Tao (Rule 1). Stanton cannot come last, or else he would be next to Tao. Stanton also cannot be sixth, because then Tao would be last and they would still be consecutive. So, the last two accomplices recruited must be Rovero and Tao, in that order. Then, Quinn and Stanton can take up the remaining positions, in either order.

$$\text{I)} \quad \frac{V}{1} \quad \frac{W}{2} \quad \frac{Q/S}{3} \quad \frac{P}{4} \quad \frac{S/Q}{5} \quad \frac{R}{6} \quad \frac{T}{7}$$

$$\text{II)} \quad \frac{Q/S}{1} \quad \frac{V}{2} \quad \frac{W}{3} \quad \frac{P}{4} \quad \frac{S/Q}{5} \quad \frac{R}{6} \quad \frac{T}{7}$$

With that, Quinn could be first, making **(A)** the correct answer.

6. (B) "If" / Must Be True

For this question, White is recruited immediately before Quinn. This creates a three-entity block with Villas, White, and Quinn (VWQ). With Peters fourth, there are only two places to add a three-entity block: first through third or fifth through seventh. However, the block includes Quinn, who must be recruited before Rovero (Rule 2).

$$\boxed{\text{VWQ}} \ldots \text{R}$$

So, the block cannot be at the end, which means it must be first through third.

That leaves Rovero, Stanton, and Tao to be the last three accomplices recruited. Stanton and Tao cannot be recruited consecutively (Rule 1), so Rovero has to come in between them. That would place Stanton and Tao fifth and seventh, in either order, with Rovero in the middle at sixth.

I) $\dfrac{\text{V}}{1} \quad \dfrac{\text{W}}{2} \quad \dfrac{\text{Q}}{3} \quad \dfrac{\text{P}}{4} \quad \dfrac{\text{S/T}}{5} \quad \dfrac{\text{R}}{6} \quad \dfrac{\text{T/S}}{7}$

The sixth accomplice must be Rovero, making **(B)** the correct answer.

Game 2: Newspaper Photographs

Step 1: Overview

Situation: A newspaper choosing photos for its next edition

Entities: Three sections (Lifestyle, Metro, Sports) and three photographers (Fuentes, Gagnon, Hue)

Action: Matching. Determine which photographer's photos will be assigned to each section. (While some may label this game something other than Matching, understanding the general action would ultimately lead to the same sketch. Those skills should prevail over worrying about the exact categorization.)

Limitations: Each section will have exactly two photographs, which means there will be six photographs in total. With only three photographers to assign, at least one photographer will be assigned multiple times. However, the overview never states that each photographer *will* be assigned. That's not mentioned until the first rule. Be careful about making such assumptions. This game is forgiving, but other games *can* include entities that are never used. Also note that the overview never states that the two photographs in a section are taken by different photographers. Thus, for example, it is possible that the two photographs in the Lifestyle section are both taken by Fuentes.

Step 2: Sketch

The sections are more fixed, with the photographers being more variable. Plus, in context of the situation, it makes more sense to assign photographers to the different sections. So, list the photographers by initial, and set up a chart with a column for each section. Draw two slots in each column to assign the photographers.

$$\begin{array}{ccc} & \text{FGH} & \\ \text{Lif} & \text{Met} & \text{Spo} \\ \hline \rule{0pt}{1.2em} \underline{\quad} & \underline{\quad} & \underline{\quad} \\ \underline{\quad} & \underline{\quad} & \underline{\quad} \end{array}$$

Step 3: Rules

Rule 1 sets some limitations on the photographers. Each one will be assigned at least once, but cannot be assigned more than three times. Make a note of that to the side in shorthand:

Each pho. 1–3x

Rule 2 states that at least one photographer has to be assigned to both Lifestyle and Metro. Either set one slot in Lifestyle equal to a slot in Metro (adding "=" between them across the column), or set a note to the side:

At least 1 Lif = 1 Met

Rule 3 creates a numeric restriction: the number of photos by Hue in Lifestyle must be equal to the number of photos by Fuentes in Sports. Make a note of that to the side:

$$\# \frac{\text{Lif}}{\text{H}} = \# \frac{\text{Spo}}{\text{F}}$$

Rule 4 prevents Gagnon from being assigned to Sports. Draw "~G" under the Sports column.

Step 4: Deductions

Each of the first three rules has a numeric component, which means Numbers will be important in this game. By Rule 1, each photographer will be used at least once, but no more than three times. With three photographers and six spots, there are only two ways to arrange the numbers: 1) Each photographer is assigned twice. 2) One photographer is assigned once, another twice, and the last one three times (2:2:2 or 1:2:3). While worth noting, this does not provide any concrete deductions.

By Rule 2, at least one photographer must be assigned to both the Life and the Metro section, but that could be any of the three. Rule 3 offers the best chance at some deductions.

By Rule 3, there must be an equal number of photos by Hue in the Lifestyle section as there are by Fuentes in the Sports section. There are only three possible outcomes for that number: 0, 1, or 2. Each outcome would establish substantial information, so it may be worth considering a rare foray into three Limited Options.

A quick glance ahead at the questions indicates that five out of the seven questions are New-"If" questions. So, while Limited Options can be helpful, the numerous "If" questions allow for enough sketching to make this game equally manageable without them. If you do set up Limited Options, here's what would happen:

$$\text{I)} \quad \begin{array}{ccc} \text{Lif} & \text{Met} & \text{Spo} \\ \hline \rule{0pt}{1.2em} \text{F/G} & \text{F/G} & \text{H} \\ \text{F/G} & \underline{\quad} & \text{H} \end{array}$$

In the second option, there would be one photo by Hue in Lifestyle and one photo by Fuentes in Sports. Because there are no photos by Gagnon in Sports (Rule 4), the second photo in Sports would have to be by Hue. The second photo in Lifestyle could be by Fuentes or Gagnon. Any photographer could be the one assigned to both Lifestyle and Metro. No further deductions can be made.

$$\text{II)} \quad \begin{array}{ccc} \text{Lif} & \text{Met} & \text{Spo} \\ \hline \rule{0pt}{1.2em} \text{H} & \underline{\quad} & \text{F} \\ \text{F/G} & \underline{\quad} & \text{H} \end{array}$$

In the third option, there would be two photos by Hue in Lifestyle and two photos by Fuentes in Sports. Because Hue is the only photographer assigned to Lifestyle, Hue must have at least one photo in Metro (Rule 2). That leaves one photo in Metro, which has to be assigned to Gagnon, who is the only photographer not yet assigned.

III)	Lif	Met	Spo
	H	H	F
	H	G	F

Step 5: Questions

7. (B) Acceptability

As with any Acceptability question, go through the rules one at a time, eliminating answers that violate those rules.

(E) violates Rule 1 by including *four* photographs by Hue (one in Lifestyle, two in Metro, one in Sports). **(C)** violates Rule 2 by not having a photographer in common between Lifestyle and Metro. **(D)** violates Rule 3 by having no photographs by Hue in Lifestyle, but one photograph by Fuentes in Sports. **(A)** violates Rule 4 by including a photograph by Gagnon in Sports. That leaves **(B)** as the correct answer.

8. (C) "If" / Must Be True

For this question, both photos in the Lifestyle section will be by Hue—that's Option III. If you didn't do Limited Options, you'd simply create a new sketch with the new "if." With both photos in the Lifestyle section by Hue, that means both photos in the Sports section must be by Fuentes (Rule 3). Because Hue is the only photographer in Lifestyle, there must also be at least one photo by Hue in Metro (Rule 2). There is one photo left in Metro, which must be assigned to Gagnon because per Rule 1 each photographer must be assigned at least once.

Lif	Met	Spo
H	H	F
H	G	F

With only one photo by Gagnon, **(C)** is the correct answer.

9. (D) "If" / Must Be True

For this question, Lifestyle will have one photo by Gagnon and the other by Hue—that's Option II. If you didn't set up Limited Options, just set up a new sketch incorporating the new "if." Because only one Lifestyle photo is by Hue, there must be just one photo in Sports by Fuentes (Rule 3). The second photo in Sports cannot be by Gagnon (Rule 4), so it must be by Hue. Because Gagnon and Hue are the photographers assigned to Lifestyle, at least one of them must also be assigned to Metro (Rule 2). The second photo in Metro could be by any of the photographers.

Lif	Met	Spo
H	G/H	F
G		H

There must be just one photo by Hue in Sports, making **(D)** the correct answer. **(A)**, **(B)**, and **(C)** *could* be true, but need not be. **(E)** must be false.

10. (A) Could Be True

The correct answer to this question will be an acceptable set of assignments for Fuentes. The four wrong answers will all be impossible.

If Fuentes had one photo in each section, the second photo in each section would have to be by Gagnon or Hue. With one photo by Fuentes in Sports, Hue would have to have one photo in Lifestyle (Rule 3). Gagnon cannot have a photo in Sports, so the second photo there would also have to be by Hue. Gagnon still has to be assigned at least once, so the second photo in Metro will be by Gagnon.

Lif	Met	Spo
F	F	F
H	G	H

This is acceptable, making **(A)** the correct answer. Fortunately, the correct answer was right at the top. Test takers could have saved time by temporarily skipping this question and drawing a sketch for the next question. The sketch for the next question allows for this very scenario and could have been used to verify this answer immediately.

As for the wrong answers: if there were two photos by Fuentes in the Sports section, there would also have to be two photos by Hue in the Lifestyle section (Rule 3), making **(B)** impossible because it has a photo by Fuentes in Sport.

As for **(D)**, those two photos by Fuentes in the Sports section would again force two of Hue's photos into the Lifestyle section (Rule 3), and this time there is room for them. However, because Hue is the only photographer in the Lifestyle section, there also must be a photo by Hue in the Metro section (Rule 2), and the final photo in Metro would have to be by Gagnon, who hasn't been assigned yet. **(D)**, however, also has a photo by Fuentes in the Metro section, creating three photos there, which is impossible.

If there were one photo by Fuentes in the Sports section, there would have to be a photo by Hue in the Lifestyle section (Rule 3), making **(C)** impossible because it has the Lifestyle section filled with two photos by Fuentes.

In **(E)**, Fuentes has one photo in the Sports section and can still be assigned two more times. However, in this case, Fuentes could not be assigned both photos in Metro because that would leave only Hue and Gagnon in Lifestyle, with no common photographer between Lifestyle and Metro, violating Rule 2. That means **(E)** is impossible.

11. (C) "If" / Could Be True

For this question, the two photos in Lifestyle are assigned to Fuentes and Hue—Option II. With Hue assigned to just one photo in Lifestyle, there must be just one photo in Sports by Fuentes (Rule 3). The second photo in Sports cannot be by Gagnon (Rule 4), so it must be by Hue. Gagnon still has to be assigned at least once, so one of the photos in Metro must be by Gagnon. The second Metro photo must be by one of the photographers assigned to Lifestyle (Rule 2), which means it will be by either Fuentes or Hue.

Lif	Met	Spo
F	G	F
H	F/H	H

Hue could have a photo in Metro, making **(C)** the correct answer.

12. (E) "If" / Could Be True

For this question, one of the sections will have two photos by Gagnon. Gagnon cannot be assigned to Sports, so this could only happen in Lifestyle or Metro. Draw out both possibilities.

If there were two photos by Gagnon in Lifestyle, there would have to also be a photo by Gagnon in Metro (Rule 2). That's three photos for Gagnon, and that's all (Rule 1). With no photos by Hue in Lifestyle, there would be no photos by Fuentes in Sports (Rule 3), so the Sports photos must both be by Hue. Fuentes still needs to be assigned at least once, so Fuentes will be assigned the second photo in Metro.

Lif	Met	Spo
G	G	H
G	F	H

If there were two photos by Gagnon in Metro, there would have to be a photo by Gagnon in Lifestyle (Rule 2). That's Gagnon's maximum of three photos. The second photo in Lifestyle could be by Fuentes or Hue. As for Sports, both photos can't be by Fuentes because there aren't two photos by Hue in Lifestyle (Rule 3), so at least one photo in Sports will be by Hue. The other one will be by either Fuentes or Hue. Fuentes will have to have a photo in either the Lifestyle or Sports section (Rule 1).

Lif	Met	Spo
G	G	H
F/H	G	H/F

The first option here was enough to verify that both photos in Sports could be by Hue, making **(E)** the correct answer. The

second option helps verify why the remaining answers all must be false.

13. (C) "If" / Could Be True

For this question, the two photos in Metro will be by Fuentes and Hue. Gagnon still needs to be assigned, and cannot be assigned to Sports (Rule 4). With Metro filled up, Gagnon must be assigned a photo in Lifestyle. The second photo in Lifestyle must be assigned to someone assigned to Metro (Rule 2), so it will be either Fuentes or Hue.

Lif	Met	Spo
G	F	
F/H	H	

If the second photo in Lifestyle is by Fuentes, there would be no photos by Hue in Lifestyle. That would mean no photos by Fuentes in Sports (Rule 3), so both Sports photos would be by Hue.

Lif	Met	Spo
G	F	H
F	H	H

If the second photo in Lifestyle is by Hue, there would be one photo by Hue in Lifestyle. That would mean exactly one photo by Fuentes in Sports (Rule 2). The other Sports photo would have to be by Hue.

Lif	Met	Spo
G	F	F
H	H	H

In that second option, Lifestyle could have photos by Gagnon and Hue, making **(C)** the correct answer. The remaining answers all must be false.

Game 3: Campus Art Gallery

Step 1: Overview

Situation: Students working shifts at an art gallery exhibit

Entities: Five students (Grecia, Hakeem, Joe, Katya, Louise)

Action: Strict Sequencing. Determine the schedule, in order from Monday to Friday, for the five students.

Limitations: Each day will include 2 shifts (first and second) for a total of 10 shifts. The shifts are "nonoverlapping," so they are distinct. Each student will be assigned to exactly two of those shifts. Each shift is worked by just one student, so there is no sharing of shifts.

Step 2: Sketch

The idea of multiple shifts may seem intimidating. However, there's not much going on here that's different from any standard Sequencing game. Set up the order from Monday to Friday, but just place *two* spaces under each day. Draw them one on top of the other so that there's a distinct row for each shift (rather than a consecutive line of 10 slots with the first and second shift alternating between slots). Because each student will be used twice, list two of each by initial:

```
        G G H H J J K K L L
        Mo  Tu  We  Th  Fr
1:      ___ ___ ___ ___ ___
2:      ___ ___ ___ ___ ___
```

Step 3: Rules

Rule 1 prevents any student from working two shifts on the same day. Make a shorthand note to the side ("Never 2 shifts same day"), or draw a block using the letter "X" as a variable, like so:

Rule 2 creates a Block of Entities. Louise will work on two consecutive days:

Both shifts will be the second shift, so draw this block next to the bottom row of the sketch.

Rule 3 states that both of Grecia's shifts will be the first shift. Furthermore, they *cannot* be consecutive. Next to the top row of the sketch, draw two Gs. To represent them being nonconsecutive, add a note to the side: "No GG."

Or, draw the Gs with at least one space in between, with an ellipsis to indicate the possibility of more spaces:

$$G \text{\_\_\_} \ldots G$$

Rule 4 assigns Katya to Tuesday and Friday, but with no indication of which shift on either day. So, draw a K under each day.

Rule 5 creates a Block of Entities with Hakeem and Joe. They must work together at least one day. They *could* work together twice, but do not have to. Note that when they *do* work together, this rule does not indicate who works the first shift and who works the second. When you draw the block, you can draw both possibilities, like so:

Or you can use slash notation, like so:

```
H/J   at least
J/H   once
```

Rule 6 prevents Grecia and Louise from working together on any day.

```
G̶    L̶
L̶    G̶
```

Step 4: Deductions

There's a lot going on in this game, and investing in some good deductions really pays off in the questions. There is one Block of Entities that needs to appear: Hakeem and Joe (Rule 5). With Katya already working on Tuesday and Friday, Hakeem and Joe can only work together on Monday, Wednesday, or Thursday.

By itself, that's not information for Limited Options. However, the key issue in this game involves two very important Duplications: Grecia and Louise. They never work on the same day as one another. And, because nobody can work two shifts in one day (Rule 1), Grecia and Louise will work on four completely different days. None of those days will include Hakeem *and* Joe, so those two can only be together on whatever day is left. Knowing that Louise's days must be consecutive and Grecia's days *can't* be, the placement of Hakeem and Joe will be significant. Time to consider Limited Options.

If Hakeem and Joe were together on Monday, that would leave Tuesday through Friday for Grecia and Louise. Louise couldn't work Tuesday and Wednesday, otherwise Grecia would work consecutive shifts on Thursday and Friday. Similarly, Louise couldn't work Thursday and Friday, otherwise Grecia would work consecutive shifts on Tuesday and Wednesday. So, the only way this works is if Louise works Wednesday and Thursday, with Grecia working on Tuesday and Friday. Grecia works the first shift on her days, and Louise works the second shift on her days. With Grecia working the first shift on Tuesday and Friday, Katya must work the second shifts on those days (Rule 4). The first shifts on Wednesday and Thursday would be by Hakeem and Joe, in either order.

```
I)   Mo  Tu  We  Th  Fr
1:  J/H  G  J/H  H/J  G
2:  H/J  K   L    L   K
```

If Hakeem and Joe were together on Wednesday, Louise would work Monday and Tuesday or Thursday and Friday. However, if Louise worked Monday and Tuesday, Grecia would be left with consecutive days Thursday and Friday. If Louise worked Thursday and Friday, Grecia would again be left with consecutive days Monday and Tuesday. Either way, Rule 3 would be violated, making this option impossible.

So, the only other option is to put Hakeem and Joe on Thursday. In that case, Louise's consecutive shifts would have to be on either Monday and Tuesday or Tuesday and Wednesday. Either way, Louise will be on Tuesday's second shift (Rule 2)—along with Katya (Rule 4), who will then take the first shift. One of Grecia's shifts will be the day Louise does *not* work (Monday or Wednesday). Her second shift will have to be the only day left: Friday. She'll take the first shift (Rule 3), and Katya will be on Friday with her (Rule 4) in the second shift.

```
II)  Mo  Tu  We  Th   Fr
1:  ___  K  ___  J/H   G
2:  ___  L  ___  H/J   K
```

Step 5: Questions

14. (A) Partial Acceptability

The correct answer here will be acceptable—the one answer that doesn't violate any rules. However, the answers only list the second shift. Start by testing the rules one at a time, eliminating answers that violate those rules. With any remaining answers, consider who would be assigned the first shift, then test those answers to the rules.

Without seeing the first shift, Rule 1 cannot be tested. **(C)** violates Rule 2 by having Louise work only one second shift. **(D)** also violates Rule 2 by having Louise work shifts that are not consecutive. **(B)** violates Rule 3 by having Grecia work a second shift. The remaining rules cannot be tested without knowing who works the first shift.

With **(A)**, Louise is assigned Tuesday and Wednesday. Katya would be the first shift on Tuesday (Rule 4). Grecia cannot be assigned Tuesday or Wednesday (Rule 6) and cannot be assigned to both Thursday and Friday (Rule 3). So, Grecia would have to be assigned Monday and one other day. Hakeem and Joe would have to work one day together, so that would have to happen on Thursday. Grecia's second day

would then be Friday, leaving Joe to round out the schedule on Wednesday.

```
A)   Mo  Tu  We  Th  Fr
1:   G   K   J   J   G
2:   H   L   L   H   K
```

That is acceptable, making **(A)** the correct answer. For the record:

(E) has Louise working Monday and Tuesday. Grecia could not work those days (Rule 6). Because she cannot work consecutive days, she would have to work Wednesday and Friday. However, this answer would then have Grecia on Friday with Joe, violating Rule 4 by leaving no room for Katya.

```
E)   Mo  Tu  We  Th  F̶r̶
1:  ___  K   G   ___  G
2:   L   L   H    J   J
                        K?
```

15. (C) Must Be True

The correct answer to this question must be true. The remaining answers could be true, but could also be false.

Limited Options makes short work of this question. In the first option, Grecia *could* work on Tuesday, Hakeem *could* work on Wednesday, and Joe *could* work on Thursday. That means **(A)**, **(B)**, and **(D)** all could be false. As for **(E)**, although Louise does not work on Tuesday in the first option, in the second option, she *does* work on Tuesday, which means **(E)** could be false. That leaves **(C)**, which must be true—Joe is never on Tuesday.

This could also be handled deftly without Limited Options. Temporarily skip this question, and use sketches drawn for later "If" questions. The sketches eventually lead to the same options, allowing for equally effective elimination.

As final proof, Joe cannot work on Tuesday because then Joe would work with Katya (Rule 4). With Tuesday filled up, Louise and Grecia would have to be each assigned to one of the other four days (Rule 6). But that would leave no day to have Joe and Hakeem together, violating Rule 5.

16. (B) "If" / Must Be True

For this question, Hakeem will work on Wednesday. That cannot be the same day as Joe. Otherwise, Wednesday would be filled. Then, Louise would have to be on consecutive days, Monday and Tuesday or Thursday and Friday. But that would force Grecia to be on the other two consecutive days, violating Rule 3. With Katya already working on Tuesday and Friday (Rule 4), Hakeem and Joe can only work together on Monday or Thursday, as already outlined in the Limited Options in Step 4.

For this question, Hakeem will be the first shift on Wednesday, making Joe take the first shift on Thursday in the first option.

I)

	Mo	Tu	We	Th	Fr
1:	J/H	G	H	J	G
2:	H/J	K	L	L	K

In the second option, Hakeem could be with Grecia or Louise on Wednesday. Either way, Joe's second shift would have to occur on Monday, with either Grecia or Louise.

II)

	Mo	Tu	We	Th	Fr
1:	___	K	___	J/H	G
2:	___	L	___	H/J	K
	J	H			
	L/G	G/L			

In either case, Joe always works on Monday and Thursday, making **(B)** the correct answer.

17. (E) "If" / Could Be True

For this question, Grecia and Joe have to work together one day. It couldn't be on Tuesday or Friday because Katya works those days (Rule 4). That leaves Monday, Wednesday, or Thursday. There also has to be a day with Hakeem and Joe (Rule 5). As outlined in Step 4, Hakeem and Joe could only be together on Monday or Thursday. If they were together on Monday, Louise would have to be on Wednesday and Thursday so that Grecia's shifts could be split between Tuesday and Friday. However, that would force Grecia to be with Katya both days and never with Joe. So, that option cannot apply here.

That means only the second option applies, with Hakeem and Joe on Thursday. That means Grecia could be with Joe on either Monday or Wednesday. Test them both.

If Grecia and Joe were together on Monday, Grecia would be the first shift (Rule 3), putting Joe on the second shift. Louise's consecutive days would have to be Tuesday and Wednesday. Katya would be on Tuesday and Friday. Grecia's second shift would be on Friday, leaving Hakeem to work the first shift on Wednesday.

	Mo	Tu	We	Th	Fr
1:	G	K	H	J/H	G
2:	J	L	L	H/J	K

If Grecia and Joe were together on Wednesday, Grecia would be the first shift (Rule 3), putting Joe on the second shift. Louise's consecutive days would have to be Monday and Tuesday. Katya would be on Tuesday and Friday. Grecia's second shift would be on Friday, leaving Hakeem to work the first shift on Monday.

	Mo	Tu	We	Th	Fr
1:	H	K	G	J/H	G
2:	L	L	J	H/J	K

Either way, Joe would be on Thursday and could work either shift that day. That makes **(E)** the correct answer. For the

record, **(A)** is impossible because Grecia is not on Tuesday in either case. The remaining answers list possible *days* for each student, but Hakeem can only work the *first* shift on Monday or Wednesday, and Joe can only work the *second* shift on Wednesday.

18. (B) "If" / Could Be True

For this question, Katya works the *second* shift on Tuesday—that's only possible in Option I. Using that option, only **(B)** is possible, making it the correct answer. The other answer choices all must be false. Check back in Step 4 to see the deductions that led to Option I if necessary.

Game 4: Publishing Cookbooks

Step 1: Overview
Situation: A publisher scheduling the release of six cookbooks

Entities: Six cookbooks (K, L, M, N, O, P) and two seasons (fall and spring)

Action: Distribution. Determine in which season each cookbook will be published.

Limitations: Each cookbook will be published in just one season. There's no minimum or maximum number of cookbooks for each season.

Step 2: Sketch
List the cookbooks. Then, set up a chart with two columns: one for fall and one for spring. Because there's no minimum or maximum number of cookbooks in each season, leave the columns empty for now.

```
        KLMNOP
     Fall   Spring
            |
            |
```

Step 3: Rules
Rule 1 prevents M and P from being published in the same season. That means one will be published in the fall and the other in the spring. Set up a slot in each column and enter "M/P" in each slot.

Rule 2 creates a Block of Entities with K and N. They could go in either season, so draw the block to the side.

Rule 3 introduces some Formal Logic. If K is published in the fall, then O is published in the fall. By contrapositive, if O is published in the spring (i.e., *not* in fall), then K must be published in the spring (i.e., *not* in fall):

Note that this does *not* mean that K and O have to be published in the same season. If K is published in the spring, it's not certain that O is published then, too. It's perfectly acceptable for K to be published in the spring while O is published in the fall.

Rule 4 is more Formal Logic. If M is published in the fall, then N must be published in the spring. By contrapositive, if N is

published in the fall (i.e., *not* in spring), then M must be published in the spring (i.e., *not* in fall):

$$\frac{Fall}{M} \rightarrow \frac{Spring}{N}$$

$$\frac{Fall}{N} \rightarrow \frac{Spring}{M}$$

Note that this does *not* mean that M and N are published in different seasons. They cannot be both published in the fall—publishing either one in the fall results in the other being published in the spring. However, if either one is published in the spring, then the logic dictates nothing. It's possible that both are published in the spring.

Step 4: Deductions
The block of K and N allows for Limited Options. In the first option, K and N would be published in fall. In that case, with K in the fall, O would also be in the fall (Rule 3). And with N in the fall, M would have to be in the spring (contrapositive of Rule 4). With M in the spring, P would have to be in the fall (Rule 1). That leaves L, which is unrestricted by the rules (i.e., a Floater). L could be published in either season.

In the second option, K and N would be published in the fall. In that case, neither piece of Formal Logic is triggered. So, M and P could still be published in either order. O could now be published in either season without violating the rules. And L is still a Floater, so L could also be published in either season.

```
II)  Fall   Spring
     M/P    P/M
             K
             N
       ↖↗↖↗
        LO
```

Limited Options could also be set up using the first rule. If M were published in the fall, P would be published in the spring. With M in the fall, N would be there, too. That would bring along K. With K in the fall, O would be there, too. L would be a Floater and could be published in either season. If M were published in the spring, P would be published in the fall. However, that's as far as that option would go.

Either way, Limited Options are great but hardly necessary in this game. The biggest key is to avoid mistranslating Rules 3 and 4. As long as you stay consistent to the logic, the questions can be readily handled with or without Limited Options.

Step 5: Questions

19. (E) Acceptability

As with all Acceptability questions, go through the rules one at a time, eliminating answers that violate those rules.

(B) violates Rule 1 by having M and P in the same season. **(A)** violates Rule 2 by having K and N in different seasons. **(C)** violates Rule 3 by having K in the fall, then putting O in the spring. **(D)** violates Rule 4 by having M in the fall, then putting N also in the fall. That leaves **(E)** as the correct answer.

20. (C) "If" / Could Be True

For this question, M is published in the fall. That means P is published in the spring (Rule 1). With M in the fall, N must also be published in the spring (Rule 4). N must be published with K (Rule 2), so K will be in the spring.

Fall	Spring
M	P
	N
	K

With P, N, and K in the spring, any answer containing any of those cookbooks must be false. That eliminates **(A)**, **(B)**, **(D)**, and **(E)**—leaving **(C)** as the right answer. Both L and O *could* be in the fall.

21. (B) "If" / Could Be True

For this question, N will be published in the fall. That only happens in Option I of the Limited Options set up in Step 4. The question can still be handled quickly even without the Limited Options. If N is in the fall, K will be published in the fall, too (Rule 2). Also, with N published in the fall, M couldn't be in the fall (Rule 4), so M would be published in the spring. That would mean P is published in the fall (Rule 1). Finally, with K in the fall, O must be there, too (Rule 3). That leaves L, which is entirely unrestricted and could be published in either season.

Fall	Spring
N	M
K	
P	
O	

The fastest path to the right answer for a "Could Be True" question in a game that contains a Floater may be to consider any answer about the Floater right away. L is never restricted by the rules, so it could always go in either season. That makes **(B)** the correct answer.

22. (A) Completely Determine

The correct answer to this question will make it possible to determine in which season every cookbook is published for certain. The remaining answers will all allow for some uncertainty. Given that L is a Floater, it will need to be nailed down, and four of the answer choices do just that. Also, answers that trigger a Formal Logic rule are more likely to be correct.

If K is published in the fall, then so is N (Rule 2) and so is O (Rule 3). With N published in the fall, M would have to be published in the spring (Rule 4), which would mean P is published in the fall (Rule 1). Publishing L in the spring would make every cookbook scheduled.

Fall	Spring
K	L
N	M
O	
P	

That makes **(A)** the correct answer. For the record:

No matter when O and P are published, it would not be possible to determine in which season L is published. That eliminates **(B)**.

If P is published in the fall, then M is published in the spring (Rule 1). However, N and K could still be published in either season, no matter when L is published. That eliminates **(C)**.

If K is published in the spring, then so is N (Rule 3). However, that doesn't help determine in which seasons M and P are published, no matter when L is published. That eliminates **(D)**.

If M is published in the fall, then P is published in the spring (Rule 1) and N is published in the spring (Rule 4). If N is published in the spring, so is K (Rule 2). However, even placing L in the fall does nothing to confirm in which season O is published. That eliminates **(E)**.

Fall	Spring
M	P
L	N
	K

23. (B) Rule Substitution

For this question, Rule 4 is removed from the game. The correct answer will be a rule that could replace Rule 4 without changing anything from the original setup. In other words, it will reestablish the original rule without adding any new restrictions.

L was never involved in any of the original rules, so adding a condition based on when L is published would change the game. That eliminates **(A)**.

(B) tries a different piece of Formal Logic. If N is published in the fall, then so is P. By Rule 1, that would mean M is published in the spring. So, the effect of this rule would be: If N is published in the fall, then M is published in the spring. By contrapositive, if M is published in the fall (i.e., *not* the spring), then N would have to be published in the spring (i.e., *not* the fall). That's an exact replacement for Rule 4, making this the correct answer. For the record:

(C) states that publishing M in the spring would place P in the fall, which would always happen by Rule 1. However, that makes no connection between M and N, so this would not help replace Rule 4.

(D) contradicts the original rule that was removed. By this logic, if N is published in the spring, then so is M. However, the contrapositive of this says that if M is published in the fall (i.e., *not* the spring), then N must be in the fall (i.e., *not* the spring). That's the exact opposite of the original rule.

(E) is valid by the original rules. If O is published in the spring, then so is K (Rule 3), which means so is N (Rule 2). However, this makes no connection between M and N, so it does not help replace Rule 4.

Section IV: Logical Reasoning

Q#	Question Type	Correct	Difficulty
1	Assumption (Sufficient)	C	★
2	Principle (Identify/Assumption)	B	★
3	Paradox	D	★
4	Point at Issue	B	★
5	Flaw	C	★
6	Parallel Flaw	D	★
7	Role of a Statement	C	★
8	Strengthen	E	★
9	Principle (Identify/Inference)	C	★★
10	Point at Issue	E	★★
11	Principle (Apply/Inference)	B	★
12	Assumption (Necessary)	B	★★★
13	Flaw	D	★★
14	Assumption (Sufficient)	B	★
15	Flaw	D	★
16	Assumption (Necessary)	B	★★
17	Inference	A	★★
18	Assumption (Necessary)	E	★★★★
19	Inference	A	★★★
20	Assumption (Necessary)	C	★★
21	Weaken	C	★★★★
22	Parallel Reasoning	A	★★★★
23	Weaken	D	★★★
24	Assumption (Necessary)	D	★★★
25	Paradox	C	★★★

1. (C) Assumption (Sufficient)

Step 1: Identify the Question Type
The question asks for something that makes the argument valid "if ... assumed," making this a Sufficient Assumption question.

Step 2: Untangle the Stimulus
Aisha states that Vadim will be laid off. Despite his excellent programming skills, the firm is laying off a programmer, which always involves laying off the programmer hired most recently.

Step 3: Make a Prediction
There's no evidence that Vadim is the most recently hired programmer. But if he is, then he would definitely be the first person laid off according to the company policy, ensuring Aisha's argument is correct.

Step 4: Evaluate the Answer Choices
(C) is correct, making Aisha's argument complete.

(A) is a Distortion. The layoff is based on how long programmers have worked *at the firm*. Experience can involve earlier work at other companies, which is surely not considered in this decision.

(B) is Out of Scope. The decision is made purely on what policy dictates, regardless of how clearly it was explained.

(D) is irrelevant. Vadim's work has been exemplary, but maybe he's still the worst of the bunch. However, the quality of the work doesn't matter. The decision is based on who was hired most recently.

(E) is Out of Scope. The argument is not about whether the policy is good or bad. It's about whether the policy applies to Vadim, which it only does if he's the most recently hired programmer.

2. (B) Principle (Identify/Assumption)

Step 1: Identify the Question Type
The correct answer will be a principle *underlying* the response, making this an Identify the Principle question that acts like an Assumption question.

Step 2: Untangle the Stimulus
As an artist, Wanda values visual stimuli in her work area. She likens herself to a writer who values written stimuli. Vernon accepts the analogy, but says there's a catch: writers value *good* writing as stimuli, not tabloids. He then questions Wanda's visual stimuli of laundry and garbage.

Step 3: Make a Prediction
Vernon is okay with an artist having stimuli, but doesn't feel that junk qualifies. Vernon is acting on the principle that proper artistic stimuli should at least be *good* stimuli.

Step 4: Evaluate the Answer Choices
(B) gets to Vernon's concern. If quality matters, then laundry piles and empty glass bottles are certainly as questionable as Vernon suggests.

(A) is Out of Scope. Vernon is not concerned with Wanda's *health*, but rather her ability to be inspired by the clutter around her.

(C) is too specific. Vernon definitely suggests that tabloids are inferior to "good writing." However, tabloids have nothing to do with Wanda's circumstance, so a principle about them would not pertain.

(D) is a Distortion. Vernon is not so much concerned about the messiness itself. If the mess contained something appropriately stimulating as opposed to laundry and garbage, Vernon might accept the mess.

(E) is a Distortion. Vernon's unhappiness with Wanda's choice of stimuli doesn't mean he encourages working in an empty area. He just wants Wanda's stimuli to be less junk and more *good* stuff.

3. (D) Paradox

Step 1: Identify the Question Type
The question asks for something that will "account for" the given results. That suggests that the results are not what one would expect, making this a Paradox question.

Step 2: Untangle the Stimulus
Although designating an animal as *endangered* leads to greater legal protection of that animal, many animals start to disappear even *more* quickly after they're listed as endangered.

Step 3: Make a Prediction
For Paradox questions, always ask "why." In this case, why are endangered animals dying out more quickly when being labeled as endangered gives them legal protection? Something must happen to these animals after they're placed on the endangered list. The correct answer will describe something that makes them more vulnerable.

Step 4: Evaluate the Answer Choices
(D) helps resolve the mystery. Calling animals *endangered* makes them more desirable to collectors, who will be more eager to find and collect that rare species before it disappears forever.

(A) is Out of Scope. The increased rate of disappearance only occurs *after* the animal is listed. It doesn't matter how long it takes for that official listing to take place.

(B) doesn't help. Even though some endangered animals may not get enough affection to warrant a public campaign, they would still be subject to stricter laws and restrictions. Their rapid decline is still a mystery.

(C) doesn't help. No matter how many animals are listed, laws and restrictions should still protect them, or at least not exacerbate their diminished numbers.

(E) is a 180. If endangered animals become harder to find and poach, then it's even *more* unusual that they're dying off more quickly.

4. (B) Point at Issue

Step 1: Identify the Question Type
There are two speakers, and the question asks for a point over which they *disagree*. That makes this a Point at Issue question.

Step 2: Untangle the Stimulus
Sefu wants the town council to adopt his development plan. Annette recommends Sefu take the council to other towns that have successfully adopted the same plan. Sefu is hesitant because the vote affects him directly and he wants to avoid the appearance of impropriety.

Step 3: Make a Prediction
Sefu probably agrees that taking the council to other towns would help sell the development plan. However, the question is whether he *should*. Annette says he should, but Sefu feels otherwise. That's the point at issue.

Step 4: Evaluate the Answer Choices
(B) is correct. Using the Decision Tree, Annette has an opinion about this (she says he *should*), and Sefu has an opinion (he implies he *shouldn't*). And they do disagree.

(A) is a 180. Sefu and Annette both seem to want the development plan to succeed. They disagree over the idea of aiding that success by taking the council on a trip.

(C) is not a contentious point. Only Sefu mentions his having a vested interest. Annette makes no mention of that and accordingly has no opinion about it.

(D) is a 180. Annette brings this point up directly, but Sefu doesn't dispute it. The problem Sefu has is taking the council *himself* to see those success stories.

(E) is definitely something Sefu advocates. However, Annette never addresses it. It's possible that she would agree, but wasn't aware of that issue until Sefu brought it up.

5. (C) Flaw

Step 1: Identify the Question Type
The question directly asks why the argument is flawed. However, the question provides some extra assistance, stating that the answer is something the scholar "presumes without giving sufficient justification." In other words, the answer will express an unwarranted assumption.

Step 2: Untangle the Stimulus
As some religions have adapted to modern times, worship attendance for those religions has increased. The scholar concludes that other religions will see the same results if they also keep up with the times.

Step 3: Make a Prediction
This is a classic error of Causation versus Correlation. While it's a remarkable coincidence that worship increased just after the modern updates, there's still no evidence that those updates were definitely the *cause* of the attendance increase. The scholar mistakenly assumes as much, as the correct answer should mention.

Step 4: Evaluate the Answer Choices
(C) is exactly the causal assumption made by the scholar.

(A) is not suggested. The scholar concludes that the attendance will increase for any religion that *can* modernize, but never suggests or assumes that there are religions that *can't*.

(B) is Out of Scope. The argument only connects modernization to attendance. Whether the message changes or not has no effect on the argument.

(D) is Extreme. The scholar concludes that modernization guarantees increased attendance, but never implies it is the *only* way to do so.

(E) is Extreme. The attendance increase does not have to be *irreversible*. As long as the increase occurs at all, the scholar's argument stands.

6. (D) Parallel Flaw

Step 1: Identify the Question Type
The correct answer will be an argument that "most closely resembles" the one in the stimulus. Furthermore, the reasoning in both arguments will be *flawed*, making this a Parallel Flaw question. Be sure to find the answer that commits the exact same logical flaw as the stimulus argument.

Step 2: Untangle the Stimulus
Being in the regional band requires a lot of practice or great talent. Lily is in the regional band and is talented, so the author concludes she doesn't really practice.

Step 3: Make a Prediction
Participation in the band requires *at least* one of two qualities: practice or talent. The word *or* is inclusive and allows the possibility of *both*. In other words, it's possible that participants could practice hard *and* be talented. The author makes it exclusive (i.e., you can only do one or the other, not both), and there's no logical basis for that. The correct answer will similarly provide two possible requirements and then suggest that meeting one excludes the possibility of meeting the other.

Step 4: Evaluate the Answer Choices

(D) is a match. There are two possible requirements (to stay informed, one must read the newspaper or watch the news on TV), and the author suggests that meeting one (informed Julie reads the paper) means not meeting the other (she doesn't watch TV news).

(A) only lists one requirement (good weather), so it cannot make the same inclusive/exclusive error.

(B) does provide two requirements (Chicago or Toronto) for going on vacation, but Lois doesn't actually go on vacation. Thus, the requirements are irrelevant, and the logic doesn't match.

(C) is a Distortion. "Neither ... nor" means "not one... *and* not the other." So, the requirement for Johnson is that Horan doesn't run *and* Jacobs doesn't run. That's not the same "one or the other" requirement from the stimulus. And while the logic *is* flawed (classic Necessity vs. Sufficiency), it's not the *same* flaw as the original.

(E) is a Distortion. There are two possible requirements, but this argument says that *not* meeting one requires meeting the other—the opposite of the stimulus. Moreover, there's no indication that Wayne definitely gets a ride home, so the requirements are irrelevant anyway.

7. (C) Role of a Statement

Step 1: Identify the Question Type

The question provides a claim from the stimulus and asks for its *role* in the argument, making this a Role of a Statement question. Start by locating the claim in question, which in this case is the very last sentence of the argument. Then, break the argument into evidence and conclusion, and determine why the dietitian included that final claim.

Step 2: Untangle the Stimulus

The dietitian argues that eating fish can lower one's cholesterol. The evidence involves a study of two groups, one that ate fish and one that didn't. After the study, the people who ate fish had lower cholesterol than the people who didn't. Before the study, the cholesterol level of each group was roughly the same.

Step 3: Make a Prediction

The direct evidence for the dietitian's claim is the lower cholesterol level *after* the study. So, why mention the cholesterol level *before* the study? Well, if the first group had lower levels to begin with, then nothing would have changed. The lower cholesterol would be a preexisting condition, possibly caused by other factors. By citing the initial results, the dietitian eliminates that possibility and makes it more likely for the fish to be responsible.

Step 4: Evaluate the Answer Choices

(C) is correct. It rules out the possibility that the lower cholesterol levels were caused by something else *before* the study.

(A) is a 180. If the first group had lower levels to begin with, *that* would be an objection, suggesting an alternative possibility. However, the claim in question suggests the exact opposite.

(B) is inaccurate. The conclusion here is the very first sentence, not the claim in question.

(D) is Out of Scope. There is no background info on the *purpose* of this study.

(E) is a Distortion. The starting cholesterol levels do not explain why eating fish can lower those levels.

8. (E) Strengthen

Step 1: Identify the Question Type

The question directly asks for something that would strengthen the given argument.

Step 2: Untangle the Stimulus

The author is singing the praises of satnavs, concluding that they help save gas and increase safety. They give drivers shorter routes, which can reduce fuel usage. And drivers don't get distracted looking at maps.

Step 3: Make a Prediction

Satnavs clearly have a lot of advantages, but are there any disadvantages? The author assumes otherwise, or at least that any advantages are more significant than the disadvantages. To strengthen the argument, the correct answer will either eliminate a disadvantage or add yet another reason why satnavs are awesome.

Step 4: Evaluate the Answer Choices

(E) supports the author's claim. If people take fewer risks, that bolsters the claim that satnavs "promote safety."

(A) is an Irrelevant Comparison. It doesn't matter who uses satnavs more frequently. What matters is whether or not satnavs are better for safety and fuel usage.

(B) offers no help. This explains *why* people would want to find a shorter route, but does nothing to support the idea that satnavs are a safer and more fuel-efficient solution.

(C) is irrelevant. It doesn't matter how *likely* people are to use satnavs. The argument is whether satnavs help when they *are* used.

(D) is irrelevant and a 180 at worst. The argument is about how satnavs can help when they *are* used. If anything, this just suggests people ignore satnavs anyway, so they don't even get the chance to help.

9. (C) Principle (Identify/Inference)

Step 1: Identify the Question Type

The question asks for a *proposition* illustrated by the stimulus. That makes this an Identify the Principle question, and the principle will be inferred by broadening the scope of the situation described.

Step 2: Untangle the Stimulus

Managers should encourage employees to do their best, but threats and rewards aren't good enough. Employees have to *want* to do their best. So, the author recommends that managers give away some of their responsibilities to provide employees with the most effective motivation.

Step 3: Make a Prediction

The specific solution for the managers is to give up some responsibilities to employees so that the managers can better motivate the employees. The correct answer will describe this sacrificial act in more general terms.

Step 4: Evaluate the Answer Choices

(C) matches the idea. By partially relinquishing control (i.e., passing off responsibilities), managers can enhance their effectiveness as managers (i.e., better extract the best performance from employees).

(A) is a Distortion. Giving employees more responsibility is intended to increase their performance, not give them a better sense of "how power should be used."

(B) is Out of Scope. There's no mention of "prestige" or "job security."

(D) is Extreme. Giving more decision-making authority to employees doesn't mean they should be considered the *best* people to carry out those decisions. It just needs to encourage employees to perform their personal best.

(E) is Extreme. Harnessing self-interest (i.e., getting employees to *want* to do a good job) can help benefit managers, but that doesn't necessarily apply to the "company as a whole."

10. (E) Point at Issue

Step 1: Identify the Question Type

The question asks about two speakers and what they "disagree over," making this a Point at Issue question.

Step 2: Untangle the Stimulus

Richard argues that abstract art fails to represent anything, meaning it's not actually "art." He concludes that others will eventually agree. Jung-Su refutes this by saying that abstract art *does* represent, just not in a literal sense. Abstract art defies everyday perspectives and only represents the "formal features" of objects. Thus, it *is* art.

Step 3: Make a Prediction

The debate here focuses on whether abstract art qualifies as art or not, based on the requirement of representation. Richard says abstract art does *not* represent, so does *not* qualify as art. Jung-Su says the opposite. The correct answer will focus on this question of whether abstract art represents anything, thus qualifying it as art.

Step 4: Evaluate the Answer Choices

(E) is the point at issue. Richard has an opinion about this (it *fails* to be representational), as does Jung-Su (it *does* represent, but only formal features), and they certainly disagree.

(A) is a 180. Richard agrees with this, in that abstract art rejects *any* representation. But so does Jung-Su, who says that abstract art rejects "literal representation" in favor of a "purely formal" one. So, they agree about this.

(B) is stated by Richard, but Jung-Su does not dispute this requirement. The disagreement is over whether abstract art *meets* that requirement.

(C) is Out of Scope for Richard, who is only concerned with abstract art, not music.

(D) is stated by Richard. Jung-Su may hold the personal belief that it's *not* an aberration, but could still concede the point that it "will be seen as an aberration" by others.

11. (B) Principle (Apply/Inference)

Step 1: Identify the Question Type

The stimulus will contain *principles* that will be used to *justify* the correct answer. That means the general principle will be given, and you must apply the principle to the specific situation in the correct answer, which should conform to the same logic.

Step 2: Untangle the Stimulus

There are two principles. The first is that someone who intentionally brings about misfortune should be blamed for it. However, *some* people who bring about misfortune unintentionally should be free of blame. That brings up the second principle: if someone causes misfortune that couldn't be reasonably expected, that person should *not* be blamed.

Step 3: Make a Prediction

The first claim is absolute: if one *knows* there's going to be trouble, that person should be blamed. The key here is not to be fooled by the middle sentence. Only *some* people who unintentionally cause misfortune should be cleared of blame. However, that allows for exceptions. The only situation that ensures being free from blame is if the misfortune was reasonably unforeseeable. If misfortune *is* foreseeable, the question of blame is open. Look for an answer in which someone acts *knowing* that misfortune will happen (making that person to blame) or in which someone acts with *no* reasonable expectation of misfortune (clearing the blame).

Step 4: Evaluate the Answer Choices

(B) is supported. While misfortune occurred (bankruptcy), Oblicek had no expectation and could not reasonably foresee that misfortune occurring. By the second principle, that frees Oblicek from blame.

(A) is a Distortion. Who knows why Riley was oblivious to the problem of parking in the middle of Main Street? However, an accident was entirely (and very reasonably) foreseeable, so the question of blame still looms.

(C) is a Distortion. Gougon was concerned, but he did not *know* his guests would become ill. While his decision was perhaps unwise, it's not enough to trigger the first principle and assign him blame.

(D) puts the blame on Dr. Fitzpatrick even though he did not *know* the blood pressure would go up. The fact that nobody else was involved is irrelevant to the first principle, which does not apply here.

(E) blames Kapp for the fire even though she didn't *know* it was going to happen. The first principle only states that people who *do* know are to blame.

12. (B) Assumption (Necessary)

Step 1: Identify the Question Type

The question asks for an *assumption* that the argument *requires*, making this a Necessary Assumption question.

Step 2: Untangle the Stimulus

The smell of lavender has been shown to reduce stress, and "intense stress" can make people more likely to get sick. Therefore, the researcher concludes that people who smell lavender regularly are less likely to get sick.

Step 3: Make a Prediction

Only "intense stress" is said to impair the immune system. Other stress levels, whether they be low, normal, or slightly high, may all have no effect on the immune system. So, regularly inhaling the scent of lavender would only help if it lowered stress down from *intense*. The researcher assumes that this is what happened.

Step 4: Evaluate the Answer Choices

(B) must be true. Some of these people *must* be highly stressed without the lavender. Otherwise, the lavender is not reducing *intense* stress and thus could not be said to have any effect on the immune system.

(A) is Out of Scope. This argument is only about lavender. Whether or not other scents could help in other ways has no bearing on the argument.

(C) is an Irrelevant Comparison. It doesn't matter how these people's susceptibility compares to other people's. What

matters is whether or not the lavender reduces their personal level of susceptibility.

(D) is not necessary. While the argument only mentions reducing stress, that doesn't imply that lavender can't have other, more significant effects that reduce susceptibility to illness.

(E) is a potential 180. It restricts the stress-relieving effect of lavender to just those people who experience intense stress. However, the first sentence of the stimulus says the scent of lavender can reduce stress generally. It's just those with intense stress that might get the decrease in susceptibility to disease, but anyone that smells it could get the stress-relief benefits.

13. (D) Flaw

Step 1: Identify the Question Type

The correct answer expresses why the argument is "vulnerable to criticism," which is a common LSAT phrase meaning the argument has a flaw.

Step 2: Untangle the Stimulus

Adjusting for inflation, the average family income increased over the past five years. The author concludes that the Andersen family's income increased because their income this year is average for families.

Step 3: Make a Prediction

The evidence is only about the Andersen family's income *this* year. What about their income five years ago? This argument only works if they maintained an average income. However, if their income was above average in the past, then they could have experienced a decrease. The author overlooks such a possibility.

Step 4: Evaluate the Answer Choices

(D) expresses the author's error.

(A) is not accurate. In both usages, *average* refers to the same statistical calculation.

(B) is not true. The conclusion refers to the family's "real income," which the author defines as "adjusted for inflation."

(C) is Out of Scope. The argument is only about the Andersen family. Even if most families' incomes are below average, the *average* income is still determined mathematically based on summing all the incomes and dividing them by the number of families—nothing requires an equal *number* of data points on either side of the average income value.

(E) is Extreme. While the author does assume that government statistics are reliable, that doesn't mean the government made *no* errors in gathering estimates.

14. (B) Assumption (Sufficient)

Step 1: Identify the Question Type
The correct answer will complete the argument *if* it were *assumed*, making this a Sufficient Assumption question.

Step 2: Untangle the Stimulus
Some counterfeiters carefully measure the images on real currency in order to make their counterfeit currency. Hence, the author concludes that images on banknotes *must* be difficult to measure accurately in order to stop counterfeiters.

Step 3: Make a Prediction
While creating difficult-to-measure images seems like a strong solution, it seems hasty to say this *must* be done. What if there are other actions that could just as easily prevent counterfeiting? The author is assuming that there are no viable alternatives, which is why prevention must involve difficult-to-measure images.

Step 4: Evaluate the Answer Choices
(B) is the assumption. This suggests that any other anti-counterfeiting method could be overcome by going back to accurately measured images. At that point, the counterfeiters cannot be stopped. So, no solution will work unless the images are, indeed, difficult to measure.

(A) is a 180. If copying technology is now this precise, then counterfeiters no longer need to measure anything, making the author's recommendation unnecessary.

(C) is a 180. If government has better printing technology, then an anti-counterfeiting solution need not involve hard-to-measure images. Instead, a solution can involve a complex printing pattern that only government printers can manage.

(D) suggests that there are many countries that *could* heed the author's advice. However, this still doesn't ensure that creating such images is necessary for counterfeit protection.

(E) does not guarantee the conclusion. Even if new designs can help minimize the *amount* of counterfeit currency, it still wouldn't entirely prevent it. What would entirely prevent it? There still could be several things that could be done, so **(E)** does not assure that difficult-to-measure images must be added.

15. (D) Flaw

Step 1: Identify the Question Type
The correct answer will point out why the argument is *flawed*, making this a Flaw question.

Step 2: Untangle the Stimulus
Dr. Sullivan advocates using nutritional supplements for a certain disease. However, Dr. Sullivan is getting paid to make that endorsement. Thus, Armstrong concludes that nutritional supplements should *not* be used.

Step 3: Make a Prediction
The problem is that Armstrong has no actual evidence against using nutritional supplements. By focusing exclusively on Dr. Sullivan's role as a paid spokesperson, Armstrong ignores any merit in Dr. Sullivan's claims.

Step 4: Evaluate the Answer Choices
(D) correctly expresses this ad hominem error of attacking the person making the argument rather than the argument itself.

(A) is not accurate. *Supplement* refers to the same kind of medication throughout the argument.

(B) is a 180. Armstrong is *rejecting* the voice of authority.

(C) is a Distortion. Armstrong does ignore the question of efficacy, but does not appeal to people's emotions. Instead, Armstrong appeals to questionable motives.

(E) is a Distortion. Armstrong doesn't assume that supplements *can't* be used in conjunction with other treatments (that would go against the very definition of a supplement). Armstrong merely argues that they *shouldn't* be used.

16. (B) Assumption (Necessary)

Step 1: Identify the Question Type
The question asks for an *assumption* that the argument *requires*, making this a Necessary Assumption question.

Step 2: Untangle the Stimulus
The economist is discussing the effects of a stronger economy. More parents will go back to work and need day care for their children. However, many day-care workers will quit to find better-paying jobs outside the day-care industry. According to the economist, this means finding day care will become more difficult for parents.

Step 3: Make a Prediction
There is a major overlooked possibility here. Sure, many day-care workers will look for new jobs. However, when one person quits, there may be plenty of other candidates ready to replace that person. The economist assumes otherwise, suggesting that nobody new will step in when the current day-care workers quit.

Step 4: Evaluate the Answer Choices
(B) must be true. The economist's argument hinges on day-care workers quitting and leaving an unfilled void. Using the Denial Test, if this *weren't* true, then there would be a host of new day-care workers, and the economist's argument is ruined.

(A) does not have to be true. Even if most new jobs *don't* pay well, there may still be enough well-paying jobs to lure day-care workers away.

(C) is a subtle Distortion. Even if day-care *centers* didn't lose workers, there could still be fewer independent day-care providers, fewer nannies, etc. In that case, the economist's argument still holds, so **(C)** does not have to be true.

(D) is a Distortion. While the economist implies that higher employment and departing day-care workers *will* lead to a shortage of day care, that doesn't mean day-care shortage couldn't happen under other conditions.

(E) is Out of Scope. The cost of day care is entirely unmentioned and irrelevant.

17. (A) Inference

Step 1: Identify the Question Type
The question asks for an answer "strongly supported" by the given *information*. That means the correct answer will be an inference.

Step 2: Untangle the Stimulus
According to the author, ostrich farming can be done on less land than cattle farming. Also, ostrich farming only requires two pairs of ostriches to start. Cattle farming requires a bull and an entire herd of cows. Starting an ostrich farm is more costly, but it can be more lucrative in the long run.

Step 3: Make a Prediction
It's impossible to predict exactly what the correct answer will say. However, it will be consistent with the facts about ostrich farming, including the need for less land, the smaller number of animals needed to start (even if they do cost more), and the considerably larger revenue it can produce.

Step 4: Evaluate the Answer Choices
(A) is supported. Two pairs of ostriches are needed to start up ostrich farming, and a herd of cows and a bull are needed to start up cattle farming. Land is also required, but less land is needed for ostriches than for cattle. So, because the author states that ostrich farming is more expensive to start up, it can be inferred that the four ostriches are more expensive than the herd of cows and a bull.

(B) is a Distortion. Ostrich farming may seem like a *better* source of income, but that doesn't mean cattle ranching is bad.

(C) is an Irrelevant Comparison. There's no information at all about food consumption.

(D) is a Distortion. Ostrich farming *can* bring in five times as much money, but that could be an upper limit, not the average. Even still, five times more income does not necessarily translate to five times more *profit*, which also has to factor in operational costs.

(E) is not supported. While the start-up costs may be expensive, it's possible that a bigger income is earned quickly enough to recoup those costs within a year.

18. (E) Assumption (Necessary)

Step 1: Identify the Question Type
The question asks for an *assumption* that the argument *requires*, making this a Necessary Assumption question.

Step 2: Untangle the Stimulus
This argument is about hairless dogs in Mexico and Peru. Hairlessness is too rare for these dogs to be unrelated (i.e., they didn't "emerge on two separate occasions"). However, there are no wild hairless dogs, and there's too much rough terrain between Mexico and Peru for them to have traveled over land. The author concludes that they *must* have gotten from one place to the other by boat.

Step 3: Make a Prediction
The argument focuses on how these related dogs got separated. The author rules out a couple of explanations. They don't have wild ancestors, so they didn't just migrate in different directions after evolving in the wild. And Mexico and Peru are separated by "mountainous jungle," so they probably didn't just walk themselves over from one country to the next. However, the author then decides they *must* have traveled from one place to the other by boat, overlooking any other explanation. The author assumes that no explanation other than "transported by boat" exists.

Step 4: Evaluate the Answer Choices
(E) must be true because it eliminates the likelihood of the dogs being transported a different way: over land. If this *weren't* true, and it was just as easy to travel over land, then trading expeditions could have taken dogs either way, negating the author's assertion that it *must* have been by boat.

(A) is not necessary. Even if such dogs are found elsewhere in the world, this doesn't address *how* they got from one place to the other. The author's argument still stands.

(B) is a Distortion. What's important is that any trade expeditions from *Peru* came by boat. Mexico could have done most of its trading over land with other countries, and the dogs still would have had to come from Peru by boat.

(C) is Extreme. The author merely claims that the dogs were *probably* transported during trading expeditions. That doesn't mean boats were never used for other purposes.

(D) is not necessary. The dogs didn't have to be traded themselves. They could have just hopped on the boats as stowaways or been given to people as gifts.

19. (A) Inference

Step 1: Identify the Question Type
The correct answer "must be true" based on what's given, making it an Inference question.

Step 2: Untangle the Stimulus

In Australia, researchers have found microdiamonds in the earth's crust that were formed 4.2 billion years ago, just 300 million years after the earth itself was formed.

Step 3: Make a Prediction

There are three dates to keep track of here. The earth formed 4.5 million years ago. Some microdiamonds formed in the crust 300 million years later. Present-day researchers found those microdiamonds. What happened in between those dates is unknown. Just stick to the timeline, and don't infer anything beyond what's known.

Step 4: Evaluate the Answer Choices

(A) is true. The crust *must* have started forming by that point because that's when the microdiamonds started forming there.

(B) does not have to be true. The microdiamonds are the earliest fragments "yet identified," but the crust could have started forming millions of years prior in any other part of the world.

(C) is not necessarily true. All that's known is that the crust was definitely forming, if not fully formed, by about 4.2 billion years ago. When it started to form and when it finished are unknown. It could have taken billions of years, or it could have taken just a couple of million.

(D) is not supported. They are described as the oldest fragments "yet identified," but that doesn't rule out the possibility of even older components that could be discovered in the future.

(E) is unsupported. The particular crystals discovered were formed 4.2 billion years ago, but there's nothing to suggest that there are no newer crystals that started forming eons after the crust was done forming.

20. (C) Assumption (Necessary)

Step 1: Identify the Question Type

The question asks for an *assumption* that is *required* by the argument, making this a Necessary Assumption question.

Step 2: Untangle the Stimulus

In the past, public squares provided an important forum for open discussion. Today, the Internet serves the same purpose, so the author concludes that the Internet should allow an equal amount of free expression.

Step 3: Make a Prediction

The issue here is one of Mismatched Concepts. The Internet is said to be replacing public squares as an open forum for discussion. However, the conclusion is that the Internet should have equal "freedom of expression." The author never mentions the role of free expression in public forums. For this argument to work, the author must assume that public forums depend upon that freedom of expression.

Step 4: Evaluate the Answer Choices

(C) must be assumed, claiming public forums would be less effective without free expression. Using the Denial Test, if forums could be *equally* effective without free expression, then the author's argument would be unsound.

(A) is Extreme. The author merely claims that the Internet should have "as much freedom of expression" as public squares. That doesn't have to be "complete freedom."

(B) is not necessary. The argument is not about everyone having equal access. Besides, nothing suggests that, in the past, everyone had equal access to public squares.

(D) is an Irrelevant Comparison. It doesn't matter what kind of discussion is more common. As long as the forum for important discussion exists, the author's argument stands. So, this is not necessary for the argument.

(E) is Out of Scope. Even if other types of public forums *do* exist, the author could still validly claim that the Internet should grant freedom of expression.

21. (C) Weaken

Step 1: Identify the Question Type

The correct answer will *undermine* the argument, which is a common LSAT term that means to weaken the argument.

Step 2: Untangle the Stimulus

Some children completed a program in which they learned to play chess. After the program was over, most of these children showed improvement in their schoolwork. The author concludes that their chess-playing skills contributed to their academic improvement.

Step 3: Make a Prediction

This is a classic case of Causation vs. Correlation. The students improved at school after the program, but were the chess skills (i.e., reasoning power and spatial intuition) really the *cause* of that improvement? The author assumes so, overlooking other possible causes. The correct answer will likely suggest that students improved in school for some other reason.

Step 4: Evaluate the Answer Choices

(C) offers an alternative explanation. If the chess team requires a high grade average, then students may have just wanted to join the team and were motivated to work harder. That suggests the higher performance was due to hard work, not necessarily the particular skills they learned in the chess program.

(A) is Out of Scope. Where other kids learn chess has no bearing on what made this particular group improve at school.

(B) is an Irrelevant Comparison. How these students compare to others before the program has no bearing on what caused their performance to improve. Even if they were high-performing kids to begin with, it's still possible the chess skills made them even better.

(D) is Out of Scope. The argument is not about reaching the *highest* level of achievement. Even if more effective solutions exist (e.g., study sessions), the chess skills could still provide *some* contribution to improved school performance.

(E) is an Irrelevant Comparison. The argument is about what led to improved school performance, not which students are better chess players.

22. (A) Parallel Reasoning

Step 1: Identify the Question Type

The question asks for an argument that is *similar* in its reasoning to the given argument. That makes this a Parallel Reasoning question.

Step 2: Untangle the Stimulus

On Wednesdays, Kate usually buys guava juice, which she can only get at the health food store. So, the author concludes she must go to the health food store some Wednesdays.

Evidence:

If	Wednesday	→	usually buys guava juice	→	at health food store

Conclusion: *Some Wednesdays Kate shops at the health food store.*

Step 3: Make a Prediction

This argument is logically sound. The correct answer will follow the same general format: on a particular occasion (Wednesdays), an event usually happens (Kate buys guava juice) that can only happen under certain circumstances (at the health food store). So, the author concludes that the circumstances must occur sometimes on the given occasion.

Step 4: Evaluate the Answer Choices

(A) is a match. On a particular occasion (dinner at Cafe Delice), an event usually happens (food prepared in the institute's kitchen) that can only happen under certain circumstances (by institute teachers). So, the author concludes that the circumstances must occur sometimes on the given occasion.

Evidence:

If	CD dinner	→	usually prepared in main kitchen	→	by CI teachers

Conclusion: *Some CD dinners are prepared by CI teachers.*

(B) is Extreme. The original argument is about what *usually* happens and what *sometimes* occurs. This argument is about "all dinners" and what *must* occur.

(C) does provide an event that usually happens (preparing food in the kitchen), but does not say it can *only* happen under certain circumstances. It just says that all teachers are *allowed* to use that kitchen. That allows other people to use it, too, so the conclusion is not as sound.

(D) is a Distortion. Most teachers *can* use the kitchen, but that doesn't mean they usually *do*. This also allows other people to use the kitchen, which makes the conclusion less sound.

(E) is a Distortion. Like the original, there's a particular occasion (dinner at Cafe Delice) on which an event usually happens (institute teachers prepare the meal). However, that event does not *have* to happen at the institute kitchen. The teachers are the only ones who can cook there, but they can just as likely cook elsewhere. This argument does not match.

23. (D) Weaken

Step 1: Identify the Question Type

The question is direct and asks for something that weakens the given argument.

Step 2: Untangle the Stimulus

The city is looking to switch from picking up recycling biweekly to weekly. The city claims this is more cost-effective because more recyclables collected means more revenue for the city. The editor argues otherwise, suggesting that the city won't really be collecting more recyclables.

Step 3: Make a Prediction

The argument is predicting what will happen under the new program, and predictions always hinge on the same assumption: relevant circumstances will go unchanged. In this case, the editor assumes that people will continue to put out an equal amount of recyclables under the new program. If the editor is overlooking a possible change that would cause people to put out *more* recyclables, then the argument is weakened.

Step 4: Evaluate the Answer Choices

(D) suggests a significant change. The new program will be easier to follow, and people will be more likely to put out their recyclables. That would allow for more recyclables to be collected, contrary to the editor's claims.

(A) is an Irrelevant Comparison, if not a 180. The cost of recycling compared to general trash collection has no bearing on the argument. Besides, this suggests that nothing is going to change, which is consistent with the editor's assumption.

(B) is an irrelevant hypothetical. It doesn't matter what would happen if more recyclables *were* collected. The argument is about whether the new plan would lead to such an increase or not.

(C) is irrelevant. The city's argument, as well as the editor's, is based entirely on *how much* is collected, not how long it takes to collect it.

(E) is a 180. Contractor fees do not affect how much recycling people will do. But, if contractors *did* raise fees, that would likely raise costs and give the editor another reason to dispute the city's program.

24. (D) Assumption (Necessary)

Step 1: Identify the Question Type
The question asks for an *assumption* that the argument *requires*, making this a Necessary Assumption question.

Step 2: Untangle the Stimulus
Some science courses are intended to be so difficult that only the most committed students pass them. However, the professor notes that the least enthusiastic students are passing the course. Hence, the professor concludes that these courses are not doing what they intend.

Step 3: Make a Prediction
The courses are meant to ensure that only the most committed students pass. To conclude that these courses are failing their purpose, the professor must believe some *less* committed students are passing. However, the evidence only mentions passing students that are least *enthusiastic*—a Mismatched Concept. The professor must assume that these least enthusiastic students are less committed to majoring in science.

Step 4: Evaluate the Answer Choices
(D) must be true, connecting the lack of enthusiasm with the lack of commitment. If this *weren't* true, and unenthusiastic students could nonetheless be highly committed, then the courses might be serving their purpose after all.

(A) is a Distortion. The only purpose mentioned for the courses is to pass committed students. This answer still does not make the needed connection between enthusiasm and commitment.

(B) is Out of Scope. The professor is not arguing whether science departments *should* (let alone "need to") weed out those that are not the most committed. The argument is merely about whether such programs are working.

(C) is a 180 at worst. This makes it so that the programs are weeding out the least *and* some of the most enthusiastic students. In that case, enthusiasm becomes irrelevant, and the professor has no argument as to whether the programs are properly targeting *committed* students.

(E) is Out of Scope. The professor never gives any indication whether courses *should* be designed this way. The argument is solely about whether they *work*.

25. (C) Paradox

Step 1: Identify the Question Type
The question asks for something that will *resolve* a discrepancy, making this a Paradox question.

Step 2: Untangle the Stimulus
To warn predators, birds and reptiles create hissing sounds so similar that the author suggests that the sounds first developed in a common ancestor. However, the common ancestors would have had predators that couldn't hear those sounds.

Step 3: Make a Prediction
Paradox questions come down to a question of "why." In this case, why would these warning sounds develop in a creature whose predators couldn't hear it? The ancestor must have found these sounds effective against predators somehow, and the correct answer should suggest how.

Step 4: Evaluate the Answer Choices
(C) resolves the issue. Even though the predators couldn't *hear* the sound, they could *see* the physical effect of producing the sound, which explains why the ancestor developed the sound in the first place.

(A) is a 180. If the predators *and* the ancestor itself couldn't hear the sound, then it's even more inexplicable why this sound developed in the first place.

(B) doesn't help. If the common ancestor had various techniques to threaten predators, it would make sense for modern birds and reptiles to use *those* as well. But this still doesn't explain the hissing sounds, which would have gone unheard by predators.

(D) is an Irrelevant Comparison. Even if hissing required little energy, the predators still couldn't hear it. Thus, the question remains why those sounds would be used at all if they had no effect on predators.

(E) is Out of Scope. The number of predators doesn't help explain why the ancestor would have developed a technique that couldn't be detected by whatever number of predators it had.

PrepTest 77

The Inside Story

PrepTest 77 was administered in December 2015. It challenged 29,115 test takers. What made this test so hard? Here's a breakdown of what Kaplan students who were surveyed after taking the official exam considered PrepTest 77's most difficult section.

Hardest PrepTest 77 Section as Reported by Test Takers

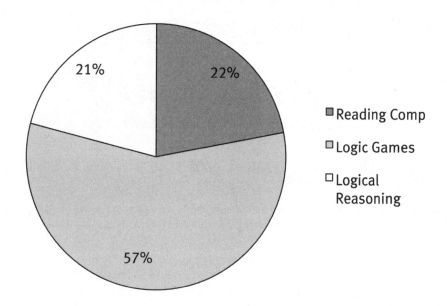

Based on these results, you might think that studying Logic Games is the key to LSAT success. Well, Logic Games is important, but test takers' perceptions don't tell the whole story. For that, you need to consider students' actual performance. The following chart shows the average number of students to miss each question in each of PrepTest 77's different sections.

Percentage Incorrect by PrepTest 77 Section Type

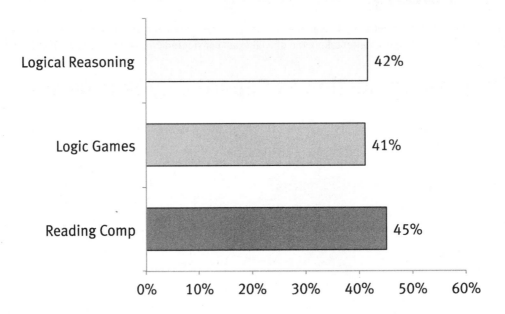

Actual student performance tells quite a different story. On average, students were almost equally likely to miss questions in all three of the different section types, and on PrepTest 77, Reading Comprehension and Logical Reasoning were somewhat higher than Logic Games in actual difficulty.

Maybe students overestimate the difficulty of the Logic Games section because it's so unusual, or maybe it's because a really hard Logic Game is so easy to remember after the test. But the truth is that the test maker places hard questions throughout the test. Here were the locations of the 10 hardest (most missed) questions in the exam.

Location of 10 Most Difficult Questions in PrepTest 77

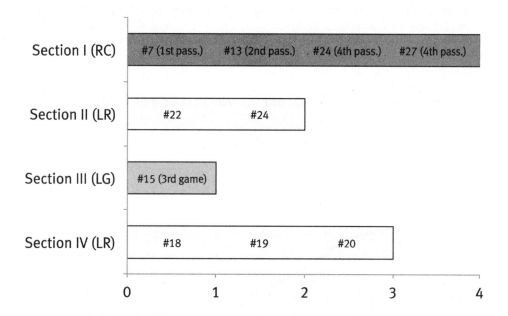

The takeaway from this data is that, to maximize your potential on the LSAT, you need to take a comprehensive approach. Test yourself rigorously, and review your performance on every section of the test. Kaplan's LSAT explanations provide the expertise and insight you need to fully understand your results. The explanations are written and edited by a team of LSAT experts, who have helped thousands of students improve their scores. Kaplan always provides data-driven analysis of the test, ranking the difficulty of every question based on actual student performance. The 10 hardest questions on every test are highlighted with a 4-star difficulty rating, the highest we give. The analysis breaks down the remaining questions into 1-, 2-, and 3-star ratings so that you can compare your performance to thousands of other test takers on all LSAC material.

Don't settle for wondering whether a question was really as hard as it seemed to you. Analyze the test with real data, and learn the secrets and strategies that help top scorers master the LSAT.

7 Can't–Miss Features of PrepTest 77

- PrepTest 77 featured two Hybrid logic games—just the sixth time that had happened in a decade!
- After the test, everyone was talking about Game 3, Office Selection. Find out how LSAT experts handled this game, one unlike any other in LSAT history.
- In Logical Reasoning, PrepTest 77 featured five Role of a Statement questions. That's tied—with PrepTest 42 from December 2003—for the most ever on a single test.
- In most Logical Reasoning sections, Questions 15 to 24 are considered the Danger Zone, with the highest concentration of difficult questions. On PrepTest 77, call it the Dangr Zon, because the correct answer was never (E) on any of those questions ... in either LR section!
- PrepTest 77's Reading Comprehension section contained seven Global questions, the most since September 2006 (PT 50), which had eight.
- Who says the LSAT isn't timely? PrepTest 77 featured a passage on the punishment of white collar crime ... the same month *The Big Short* was released...
- ... and the paired passages were about feminism and gender studies, just in time for *The Hunger Games: Mockingjay Part 2*. There are worse tests to take, right, Katniss?

PrepTest 77 in Context

As much fun as it is to find out what makes a PrepTest unique or noteworthy, it's even more important to know just how representative it is of other LSAT administrations (and, thus, how likely it is to be representative of the exam you will face on Test Day). The following charts compare the numbers of each kind of question and game on PrepTest 77 to the average numbers seen on all officially released LSATs administered over the past five years (from 2012 through 2016).

Number of LR Questions by Type: PrepTest 77 vs. 2012–2016 Average

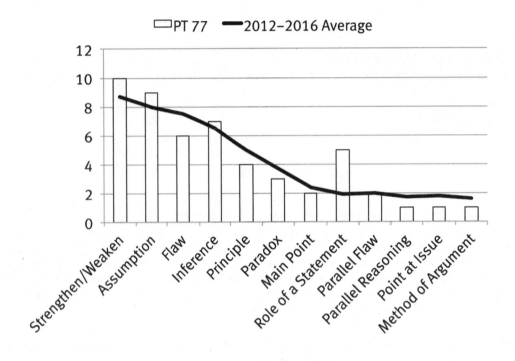

Number of LG Games by Type: PrepTest 77 vs. 2012–2016 Average

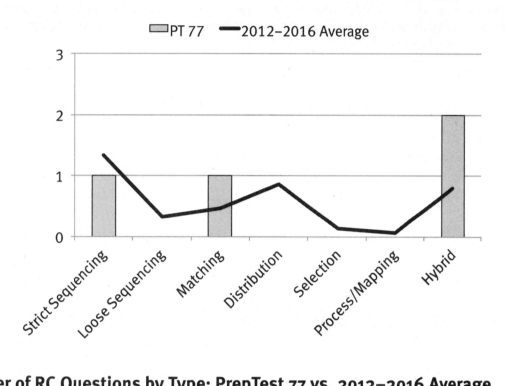

Number of RC Questions by Type: PrepTest 77 vs. 2012–2016 Average

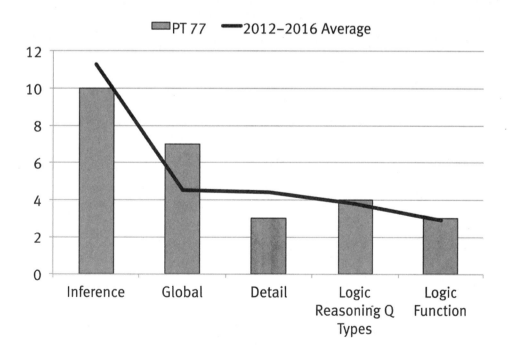

There isn't usually a huge difference in the distribution of questions from LSAT to LSAT, but if this test seems harder (or easier) to you than another you've taken, compare the number of questions of the types on which you, personally, are strongest and weakest. And then, explore within each section to see if your best or worst question types came earlier or later.

Students in Kaplan's comprehensive LSAT courses have access to every released LSAT and to an online Q-Bank with thousands of officially released questions, games, and passages. If you are studying on your own, you have to do a bit more work to identify your strengths and your areas of opportunity. Quantitative analysis (like that in the previous charts) is an important tool for understanding how the test is constructed and how you are performing on it.

Section I: Reading Comprehension
Passage 1: Federal Theater Project Negro Units

Q#	Question Type	Correct	Difficulty
1	Global	C	★
2	Detail (EXCEPT)	A	★
3	Inference	C	★
4	Logic Function	D	★
5	Inference	B	★
6	Inference	E	★
7	Logic Reasoning (Strengthen)	C	★★★★

Passage 2: Corporate Crime Punishment

Q#	Question Type	Correct	Difficulty
8	Global	E	★★
9	Global	D	★
10	Inference	C	★★
11	Detail	E	★★★
12	Global	A	★
13	Inference	A	★★★★

Passage 3: Women and Gender in History

Q#	Question Type	Correct	Difficulty
14	Global	B	★
15	Inference	C	★★
16	Detail	A	★★
17	Logic Reasoning (Method of Argument)	D	★★
18	Inference	B	★★
19	Inference	E	★★★

Passage 4: Lamarckian Hereditary Mechanism

Q#	Question Type	Correct	Difficulty
20	Global	B	★★
21	Logic Function	C	★★
22	Inference	D	★
23	Global	B	★★
24	Logic Function	E	★★★★
25	Inference	B	★★★
26	Logic Reasoning (Strengthen)	A	★★★
27	Logic Reasoning (Parallel Reasoning)	E	★★★★

Passage 1: Federal Theater Project Negro Units

Step 1: Read the Passage Strategically
Sample Roadmap

line #	Keyword/phrase	¶ Margin notes
3	Although	1930's
7	most important ... though	FTP
8	until recently ... little-studied	New studies "Negro Units"
14	Defying	Closest to nat'l black theater
16	overcoming	
17	arguably	
19	truly	
24	Thus	FTP introduced during creative period
28	gave rise to	Debates about content motivated by broader debates
29	vigorous ... heated ... :	Led to diverse productions
30	favored	Ex. Swing Mikado
31	preferred	
33	advocated	
36	motivated ... larger ... whether	
37	should	
39	whether it should	
41	whether it should	
42	disagreements ... resulted in	
45	Among them	
49	challenged	
52	Although	FTP short-lived, but valuable
53	provided a lifeline	
55	allowed	

Discussion

Paragraph 1 introduces a short-lived government program from the 1930s, the Federal Theater Project (FTP), that sponsored theater performances across the United States. The author then introduces the **Topic**, "Negro Units": a subset of the FTP that is now being recognized for its valuable focus on African American theater. This newfound recognition serves as the **Scope** of the passage. As will be noted throughout the passage, the author doesn't express many strong opinions. So, the **Purpose** of this passage is to merely describe the significance of the Negro Units.

Paragraph 2 gives some social context, indicating that the FTP appeared at a time of major developments in African American art. Negro Unit producers debated about what to perform. These debates were spurred by larger debates about the intended audience and the cultural impact. This led to a diverse selection of productions. The author provides an example of *The Swing Mikado*—a musical casting black people in white roles that challenges people's perspectives.

Paragraph 3 sees the end of the FTP. While it only lasted a few years, it helped save theater during the Great Depression, and the Negro Units helped African American artists bring their diverse productions to a nationwide audience. The author's **Main Idea** combines this result with the gist of the first paragraph: Negro Units are now being recognized for their ability to give African American artists a literal stage for voicing their diverse ideas.

1. (C) Global

Step 2: Identify the Question Type
This is a Global question because it asks for the "main point of the passage."

Step 3: Research the Relevant Text
Global questions are based on the entire text. Use the Main Idea as a perfect prediction here.

Step 4: Make a Prediction
The Negro Units have recently been recognized as important in helping African American artists bring their diverse beliefs to American audiences through the theater.

Step 5: Evaluate the Answer Choices
(C) correctly summarizes the recent recognition of the Negro Units' value.

(A) is Extreme and a Distortion. The Negro Units are being recognized for their legacy and contribution to African American theater, not their talent or stage performance. Further, the author states that they are "*[o]ne* of the most important" parts of the FTP, not necessarily *the* most influential.

(B) is Out of Scope. The author only cites the effect of the FTP and does not address its effect relative to any other government programs.

(D) is too narrow and not supported. Some producers favored folk dramas (lines 29–30), but there is no indication that this is what Negro Units are "best known" for—and this would hardly be the point of the whole passage.

(E) is too narrow, focusing only on details in the last paragraph about theater in general. It completely misses the author's focus on the Negro Units and their contribution to African American theater.

2. (A) Detail (EXCEPT)

Step 2: Identify the Question Type
Four answers will list what the FTP did, "[a]ccording to the passage." That means these will be details directly stated in the passage. The correct answer will not be mentioned or will distort what is actually said.

Step 3: Research the Relevant Text
The FTP in general is described in lines 1–7. Some answers are likely to be found there. The rest of paragraph 1 describes what the Negro Units did, and they are part of the FTP. That should aid with any remaining answers.

Step 4: Make a Prediction
There are many details in the first paragraph, so it's not worth predicting which ones will populate the wrong answers. Furthermore, there are an infinite number of facts that are *not* mentioned, so it's impossible to predict the correct answer. Just use details from the passage to knock out answers that are mentioned and/or look for something that clearly goes out of scope.

Step 5: Evaluate the Answer Choices
(A) is not mentioned, and is thus the correct answer. In fact, this would be impossible because the FTP "existed for only four years" (line 3).

(B) mentions operation in multiple cities, which is found in line 14.

(C) mentions the production of African American plays, which is found in line 10.

(D) mentions designers and technicians, who are listed among the employed in line 12.

(E) mentions weekly performances, as found in line 6.

3. (C) Inference

Step 2: Identify the Question Type
The correct answer will be something with which the author is "most likely to agree." That means it won't be stated directly, but it will be a valid Inference supported by the text.

LSAT PrepTest 77 Unlocked

Step 3: Research the Relevant Text

There are no context clues for reference, so the entire passage is relevant.

Step 4: Make a Prediction

The correct answer can be supported by anything from the text, so prediction will be impossible here. Instead, stay focused on the scope of the passage, and eliminate answers that distort or misrepresent what is said.

Step 5: Evaluate the Answer Choices

(C) is supported by lines 42–44, in which the philosophical and aesthetic debates described in paragraph 2 "resulted in a wide range of productions reflecting ... diverse views."

(A) is not supported. In fact, the FTP is said to have had weekly audiences up to "half a million people" (lines 6–7). It's implied at the end that the FTP was merely in place to support theater during the Great Depression.

(B) is an unsupported comparison. There's no mention of how polarized the views of Harlem Renaissance artists were. The only polarized views described are those of the Negro Unit producers.

(D) is Out of Scope. There is no mention of today's artists, let alone their artistic contribution.

(E) is an unsupported comparison. Urban dramas and folk dramas were among the plays debated among producers (lines 29–32), but there's no indication which one was more popular.

4. (D) Logic Function

Step 2: Identify the Question Type

The phrase "in order to" at the end of the question reveals that this is asking *why* the author references the Harlem Renaissance. That makes this a Logic Function question.

Step 3: Research the Relevant Text

While the Harlem Renaissance is mentioned only in the beginning of the second paragraph, it's important to understand how that relates to what follows. Use the roadmap and margin notes for paragraph 2 for full context.

Step 4: Make a Prediction

The author mentions that the FTP followed ("came on the heels of") the Harlem Renaissance. The Keyword *Thus* (line 24) gives away the point this leads to: the FTP came along at a time when the African American community was already teeming with diverse social ideas, and it was this diverse set of beliefs that led to the debates described throughout the rest of the paragraph. So, the author mentioned the Harlem Renaissance to provide insight into what African American society was like at the time, which impacted the FTP and its Negro Units.

Step 5: Evaluate the Answer Choices

(D) correctly addresses the author's ultimate goal of providing context: the historical background that led to the subsequent debates among Negro Unit producers.

(A) is too focused on details. Yes, it was a successful artistic movement. Yes, it preceded the Negro Units, but *why* did the author mention this? That's what the question is asking for. The author has no need to just provide examples of other artistic movements. The author's focus is on what made the Negro Units so valuable, and the Harlem Renaissance is mentioned only to further that agenda.

(B) is Out of Scope. There's no mention of "overall political advancement of the African American community."

(C) is Out of Scope. The author never discusses why Negro Units "fell into obscurity."

(E) is a Faulty Use of Detail. Any relationship between African American culture and mainstream U.S. culture is only mentioned as part of the debate within Negro Units, not as part of the Harlem Renaissance.

5. (B) Inference

Step 2: Identify the Question Type

The question asks for what the author "most likely means," which indicates an Inference question. The correct answer will be supported by the text and will indicate the intended definition of "a truly national black theater."

Step 3: Research the Relevant Text

The question stem points to lines 19–20, but the entire description of the Negro Units from lines 7–20 provide a clearer picture.

Step 4: Make a Prediction

The author claims that the concept of a "national black theater" was nearly attained by the Negro Units. What they did was produce plays with African American ideas for African American audiences throughout the United States. So, the "national black theater" would be the ideal: the ultimate concept of bringing African American ideas to a nationwide audience through performing arts.

Step 5: Evaluate the Answer Choices

(B) accurately describes a large-scale artistic endeavor to spread African American ideas.

(A) equivocates with respect to the term *theater*. This answer uses *theater* to mean a physical building (a "performing arts center"), whereas the author uses *theater* to refer to the general artistic medium.

(C) distorts the government's intentions. The government was just promoting theater in general. The Negro Units promoted African American arts. Even so, that promotion actually happened. The "truly national black theater" is more of an ideal that Negro Units "came close ... to founding."

(D) is a Distortion. "Theater" refers to the full production of such plays, not just the plays themselves. Besides, there's no indication of this having to be "endorsed by scholars."

(E) also mistranslates the word *theater*. *Theater* is meant to refer to the artistic medium, not a physical "playhouse."

6. (E) Inference

Step 2: Identify the Question Type
According to the question, there will be "support for inferring" the correct answer, making this easy to spot as an Inference question.

Step 3: Research the Relevant Text
The question asks about the producers of *The Swing Mikado*, which is brought up at the end of the second paragraph (line 45). The correct answer will be consistent with the details about that play (lines 45–51). Also, the play is provided as an example of a work that sprung from the debates described earlier (lines 29–44), so those will also provide helpful context.

Step 4: Make a Prediction
The Swing Mikado is described as a musical that casts black performers in what's traditionally a "white classic." This play "challenged" audience members and their perceptions. The producers who chose such a play fit the description of those who argued for "adapting dramas written by white playwrights" (lines 33–34).

Step 5: Evaluate the Answer Choices
(E) matches the use of African American actors performing a traditionally white drama.

(A) is a 180. The play challenged audiences, which suggests that it intentionally touched on controversial ideas.

(B) is a 180. By challenging the audience to think, the producers most likely *approved* the idea of combining instruction and entertainment.

(C) is not supported. The play is merely described as a "musical," not necessarily a folk drama. Moreover, there's no mention of exploring "rural roots."

(D) is also not supported. Again, the play is merely described as a "musical," not necessarily an urban one, and there's no mention of "contemporary dilemmas."

7. (C) Logic Reasoning (Strengthen)

Step 2: Identify the Question Type
The question directly asks for something that would "strengthen" a point, making this a Strengthen question such as those found in the Logical Reasoning section.

Step 3: Research the Relevant Text
The claim in question is the author's point at the end of paragraph 1 (lines 17–20). That claim is supported by the details of the Negro Units in lines 7–14.

Step 4: Make a Prediction
The author describes a lot of Negro Unit accomplishments: defying external forces and hiring hundreds of theater folk to bring African American ideas to stages across the United States. However, there's no evidence about what happened before that. To conclude that Negro Units "came closer than any other group … to founding a truly national black theater," the author must assume that no previous group accomplished as much toward that goal as the Negro Units. The correct answer will validate that assumption.

Step 5: Evaluate the Answer Choices
(C) helps the author's cause. If previous African American plays were exclusively produced in Eastern cities, then performing in "cities spread throughout the United States" allowed the Negro Units to be closer to "truly national" than groups that just performed on the East Coast.

(A) is a 180, suggesting that previous groups used predominantly African American ideas, just like the Negro Units.

(B) is irrelevant. Even if other projects didn't have government funding, their accomplishments could still have led to something closer to "truly national" than what the Negro Units accomplished.

(D) brings up audience size, which doesn't necessarily help the author's claim. Even if earlier groups had smaller audiences on average, those audiences could have been consistent throughout the country, allowing those groups to be more "truly national" than the Negro Units.

(E) doesn't help at all. At worst, those hard-to-find documents could potentially indicate a group that was closer than the Negro Units in establishing a "national black theater." The difficulty in finding those documents is irrelevant.

Passage 2: Corporate Crime Punishment

Step 1: Read the Passage Strategically
Sample Roadmap

line #	Keyword/phrase	¶ Margin notes
1	How severe	Punishment for corp crime?
2	e.g.	
4	? ... argue	
5	sole ... should	
6	:	Some econ. say it should just exceed profit
7	should exceed	
8	For example	
11	would feel ... justice	
12	In arguing thus ... hold	Econ: morals are irrelevant
15	such as	
17	should not	
18	argue ... should	
19	rather than	
20	But ... highly impractical ... if not	Auth: econ. proposal is impractical
21	impossible ... complicated	
22	acceptable	
23	needs to	
26	must	
27	holds ... must	
28	Otherwise	
30	even if	
32	ultimately	
34	A true reckoning ... therefore	Need to factor detection ratios
35	have to take	
36	but	
39	according to ... to be just	
40	requires	Auth: penalties too high
42	but	
44	astronomical ... necessary	
45	might arguably	
47	Thus	Need some other criterion
49	such as	
50	necessary	
51	practical ... as well as ... just	

Discussion

The passage opens with a question, which is fantastic. Opening questions usually indicate what the passage will concentrate on, and that's certainly the case here. It introduces the **Topic** (punishment for corporate crimes), and the question itself is the **Scope**: how severe should punishment for corporate crimes be? "Some economists" offer one response: the punishment should be based solely on the reckoning of cost and benefit. In other words, calculate the profit a company made through the crime, and penalize them above that value.

Paragraph 2 raises the idea that people often judge some crimes worse than others and want the more serious offenders to be more severely punished. The economists reject that, saying morals should be left out of the equation. Stick to the law and focus on offsetting profits.

In paragraph 3, the author speaks up. Starting with the Keyword *But*, the author's **Purpose** becomes clear: to refute the economists' claims. The author calls the economists' approach "impractical" and cites a complicating factor: detection ratios (i.e., the odds of getting caught). If the economists want a "true reckoning of cost and benefit" (line 34), that calculation should include the detection ratio. The example shows how this would work: if the likelihood of getting caught for a crime is 1 in 10, the penalty would be 10 times the profit (e.g., $60 million penalty for a crime that netted $6 million).

Paragraph 4 describes the potential problem. With detection ratios close to the 1-in-10 scenario as previously illustrated, penalties would be enormous. Companies would have to shut down, and people would be out of work. That leads to the author's **Main Idea**: punishment for corporate crimes should factor in criteria other than just cost and benefit reckoning to ensure penalties are both just and practical.

8. (E) Global

Step 2: Identify the Question Type
This is a Global question because it asks for the "main point of the passage."

Step 3: Research the Relevant Text
Because this is a Global question, the entire passage is relevant.

Step 4: Make a Prediction
The Main Idea from Step 1 provides an adequate prediction: corporate crime penalties should not be based solely on reckoning cost and benefit, but should consider other factors to ensure practicality.

Step 5: Evaluate the Answer Choices
(E) is correct. It addresses the impractical nature of using just cost and benefit reckoning, and suggests additional criteria as a supplement.

(A) is a Distortion. By paragraph 3, detection rates would not "supplement" the reckoning of cost and benefit; they would be included in that calculation (lines 34–35). And that approach leads to "astronomical penalties" (line 44) that are hardly practical.

(B) is a 180. When detection ratios are taken into account, that results in the "astronomical penalties" (line 44) decried by the author.

(C) is a Distortion. The author never states that economists are doing communities any "injustice," and the effect on communities is not the focus of this passage.

(D) is a Distortion. A true reckoning *would* take detection ratios into account (lines 34–35). Furthermore, the author's purpose does not involve satisfying moral standards or sending a message to corporations.

9. (D) Global

Step 2: Identify the Question Type
The question asks for the "primary purpose" of the entire passage, making this a Global question.

Step 3: Research the Relevant Text
For Global questions, the entire passage is relevant.

Step 4: Make a Prediction
The Purpose was identified as soon as the author used the Keyword *But* at the beginning of paragraph 3: to criticize the economists' approach to punishing corporate crime.

Step 5: Evaluate the Answer Choices
(D) is a perfect match.

(A) is Out of Scope. The author never addresses the courts themselves.

(B) is Out of Scope. The passage is about punishing those crimes, not describing the motives behind them.

(C) is a Faulty Use of Detail. While some communities may want to do this (as per paragraph 2), it is not the author's focus.

(E) is a Distortion. The author does advocate for a new approach, but is much more general ("some other criterion" in lines 47–48). Moral weight is offered as one example, but the author is not necessarily pushing that idea entirely.

10. (C) Inference

Step 2: Identify the Question Type
The question asks for something which the author is "most likely" to suggest, making this an Inference question.

Step 3: Research the Relevant Text
The question asks for a penalty the author might endorse for a crime with a 1-in-10 detection rate. The impact of that detection rate is described in lines 28–33. The author then

outlines a general suggestion in lines 47–51 that counteracts the potential problems described in lines 43–47.

Step 4: Make a Prediction

In lines 50–51, the author wants to ensure that penalties are "practical as well as just," as opposed to what the economists propose, which would involve "astronomical penalties" and could "put convicted corporations out of business." However, by lines 28–33, if a penalty isn't big enough, companies would just take the 1-in-10 chance repeatedly, knowing that the profit made from their multiple successes will far outweigh the handful of times they get caught. So, to be practical, the author would endorse a middle ground penalty that is large enough to deter illicit behavior without causing financial ruin.

Step 5: Evaluate the Answer Choices

(C) is just the kind of middle ground the author would support.

(A) is too small a penalty to be practical. Companies would gladly give up that profit knowing that they could just commit the crime again and keep the profit when they *don't* get caught.

(B) is also too small to be practical. Companies would still be willing to risk committing further crimes "even if the potential penalty is somewhat larger than the profit" (lines 30–31).

(D) is a 180. This would be the kind of "astronomical penalty" the author argues against.

(E) is a 180. This is exactly the kind of scenario the author wants to avoid.

11. (E) Detail

Step 2: Identify the Question Type

The question asks for a view that the author "ascribes" to the economists. That means it will be stated directly in the passage, making this a Detail question.

Step 3: Research the Relevant Text

A quick glance indicates that each answer refers to "a community's moral judgment." The economist's view of that is presented in paragraph 2.

Step 4: Make a Prediction

According to the economists, a community's moral judgment "should not be a factor in determining penalties" (line 17).

Step 5: Evaluate the Answer Choices

(E) matches the economists' view about disregarding the community's judgment when calculating penalties.

(A) is Out of Scope. The economists make no claim about the reliability of the community's judgment.

(B) is a 180. The economists outright claim that judgments *should not* be a factor, not even "occasionally."

(C) may be the case, but the economists never express that point of view.

(D) is a Distortion. The community's judgment may be irrelevant to assessing the *penalty* for the crime, but could still be relevant to determining a company's morality. However, the economists are not interested in determining a company's morality.

12. (A) Global

Step 2: Identify the Question Type

This question asks for the "organization of the passage" in its entirety. That makes this a Global question.

Step 3: Research the Relevant Text

The organization of the passage should be outlined clearly in the margin notes.

Step 4: Make a Prediction

Consider the purpose of each paragraph in order. Paragraph 1 poses a question and provides one answer (the economists' proposal). Paragraph 2 discusses one factor involved in that response (the role of morality). Paragraph 3 introduces a complication (detection ratio). Paragraph 4 describes the consequence and pushes for an alternative solution. The correct answer should hit these major points in order.

Step 5: Evaluate the Answer Choices

(A) is a perfect rundown from top to bottom.

(B) is perfect until the very end. The author does raise a criticism (the detection ratio), but the author does not reject that criticism. The criticism is accepted and spurs the author's call for an alternate solution.

(C) distorts the passage by focusing too much on the "ethics of [the economists]." The author has nothing against their ethics. The problem is in the application of the detection ratio.

(D) goes astray by mentioning two answers that are identified and compared. The author only raises one answer to the initial question and then rejects it. If there's a second answer, it's the author proposal at the very end, but the author never compares it to anything or identifies any assumption underlying it.

(E) goes Out of Scope quickly by mentioning the "consequences of failing to solve the problem."

13. (A) Inference

Step 2: Identify the Question Type

This is an Inference question because it asks for something with which the economists are "most likely to agree."

Step 3: Research the Relevant Text
Be careful. The question asks about the economists' point of view, not the author's. Be sure to use the economists' arguments as presented in paragraphs 1 and 2.

Step 4: Make a Prediction
There's a lot of text, so don't predict an exact answer. Instead, start by testing the answers against a general summary of the economists' proposal: penalize companies based on the reckoning of cost and benefit (paragraph 1), and only worry about affecting earnings rather than assessing morality (paragraph 2). If needed, go back to those paragraphs to confirm support for any answer that seems plausible.

Step 5: Evaluate the Answer Choices
(A) is correct. By lines 17–19, all that matters is that the law affects earnings. As further support, the author claims that following the economists' "reckoning of cost and benefit only" plan could put corporations out of business, suggesting that this is not a concern for the economists.

(B) is a Distortion. The community's opinion should be a factor in determining the *penalty*, but could still be a factor in assigning moral weight. However, the economists have no concern with assigning moral weight.

(C) would be correct if it stopped before the word *unless*. However, that *unless* suggests a possible exception when it would be okay to consider moral offensiveness. The economists do not allow for such exceptions.

(D) is Extreme and a Distortion. The detection ratio that should be involved is about the likelihood of being caught for a crime, not the likelihood of "recommitting" the crime. Furthermore, even if this answer did get the definition of detection ratio right, there's no indication that it's the "main factor" in calculating penalties.

(E) is Out of Scope. The economists' proposal is simply based on the reckoning of cost and benefit. There's no mention in their proposal of factoring in prior convictions.

Passage 3: Women and Gender in History

Step 1: Read the Passage Strategically
Sample Roadmap

line #	Keyword/phrase	¶ Margin notes
Passage A		
2	both ... dramatic	1990's
3	and	in history, shift from studying individual women to general gender issues
10	seemed ... retreat	
12	:	
18	but ... also reveals	Studying "women" too narrow
19	so often dismissed ... too	
24–26		Studying "gender" allows greater emphasis
27	And yet ... lost	Auth: focus on gender
28	share the suspicion	obscures individual
29	obscure ... as ...	accomplishments
30	much as ... reveals	
31	overlook	
Passage B		
35	promote	Aug.'s laws promote family
37	resting upon	
38	particular ...	Defined women as domestic
39	attention	
44	thereby	Good women = good state
45	particular ...	
46	attention	
47	:	
48	Thus	
49	more	Values of women recognized but restricted
50	but also more	
52	became clear	
53	unusual	
55	should	
58		Art reflected domestic vision of women
61		

Discussion

According to passage A, women's history (**Topic**) became more mainstream in the 1990s, but with less focus on specific women and more focus on generic studies of gender relations. Instead of revealing individual accomplishments, articles discussed the cultural role of broader ideas like masculinity and domesticity. This shift toward gender issues is the **Scope**.

In paragraph 2, the author explains how just studying women can be seen as merely "celebratory," a way to remember who those women were. Nevertheless, "gender" studies can help analyze social and political structures. By paragraph 3, the author is questioning the value of this shift (**Purpose**), claiming that this focus on gender issues can cause us to overlook the effect certain individual woman had on the world (**Main Idea**).

Passage B starts off discussing emperor Augustus's desire to bring back good old-fashioned morality to Rome after the Triumviral Wars (over 2,000 years ago). He did so by passing laws promoting family. These laws (**Topic**) encouraged women to perform domestic roles as mothers and wives.

Paragraph 2 further discusses the role women played in these laws (**Scope**). Augustus viewed women as integral to his plan. Simply put, if women just stayed home and were good mothers and wives, there would be peace and prosperity in Rome. This gave women more visibility, but restricted them to those domestic roles. Paragraph 3 describes how art of that era expressed this supposedly "idealized" world created by Augustus. The author here expresses no opinion, so the **Purpose** is merely to describe the situation. The **Main Idea** is that Augustus's laws encouraged women to take on domestic roles in order to ensure political stability in Rome.

14. (B) Global

Step 2: Identify the Question Type
The question asks for the "central topic" of each passage, making this a Global question.

Step 3: Research the Relevant Text
All of the text is relevant to this question. Instead, focus on the Main Idea of each passage, as discovered in Step 1.

Step 4: Make a Prediction
Passage A is focused on the study of gender roles and how it allows for analysis of social and political structures. Passage B is focused on a specific sociopolitical event in history, but one that focuses on the role of women in that event. So, the central idea of both passages revolves around gender issues in a social and political context.

Step 5: Evaluate the Answer Choices
(B) is correct.

(A) mentions a decline in studying individual women, which is only addressed in passage A.

(C) mentions ancient Rome, which is only discussed in passage B.

(D) mentions the role of masculinity, which is only brought up in passage A (and hardly the central topic).

(E) mentions the "celebratory" goals of women's history, a concept only broached in passage A.

15. (C) Inference

Step 2: Identify the Question Type
The question asks for something with which the author of passage A is "most likely to agree." That makes this an Inference question.

Step 3: Research the Relevant Text
The question is too vague to suggest any particular reference point in the passages. Instead, use the general ideas and the roadmap to get a sense of the correct answer.

Step 4: Make a Prediction
The author of passage A expresses the strongest opinions in paragraph 3, suspecting that analysis of gender roles "obscures" the "ways in which individual women engaged their worlds." The analysis in passage B matches that suspicion by describing the general role of women under Augustus's laws without providing any information about individual women.

Step 5: Evaluate the Answer Choices
(C) accurately matches the analysis in passage B to the description in passage A.

(A) is not supported. No comparison is made between the gender roles described in passage B and those in modern times.

(B) is a Distortion. The analysis in passage B focuses more on women's domestic role than it does on "femininity" per se. Even if it did focus on femininity, the author of passage A never suggests that studying masculinity is equally important.

(D) is not supported. There is no information in either passage about the role of domesticity in recent politics.

(E) is Out of Scope. There's no suggestion that historians were unaware of any of these laws.

16. (A) Detail

Step 2: Identify the Question Type
"According to" the passage typically indicates a Detail question, and the language is strong enough here (e.g., it's not asking for something *suggested* or *implied*) to indicate that the correct answer will be directly stated.

Step 3: Research the Relevant Text
The shift that happened in the 1990s is described at the very beginning of passage A. Note that the question asks for what

the focus shifted *to*, so don't worry about what it shifted away *from*.

Step 4: Make a Prediction

The opening sentence mentions the transition "to the issue of gender issues" (line 4). In the subsequent lines, this is said to involve "turning to an exploration of the social systems that underlay the relationships of men and women" (lines 7–9).

Step 5: Evaluate the Answer Choices

(A) matches the verbiage of lines 7–9 practically word for word.

(B) is a Distortion. There's no suggestion that gender studies are "bringing attention" to something "previously ignored." If anything, this better fits the kind of women's studies people are moving away from, as described in lines 23–24 (finding lost ancestors and restoring them in our memories).

(C) is a Distortion. The author never mentions gender bias affecting traditional scholarship.

(D) is Out of Scope. There is no criticism of earlier historians.

(E) is a Distortion. While some specific articles might focus on domesticity, that's not the general focus in studying women's history. Also, there's no mention of "documenting shifts in the conception of domesticity."

17. (D) Logic Reasoning (Method of Argument)

Step 2: Identify the Question Type

The question asks for the "relationship" between both passages. The answers will describe *how* the authors present their material and *how* they relate. Finding *how* arguments proceed is the hallmark of a Method of Argument question.

Step 3: Research the Relevant Text

The question refers to the passages as a whole, so there's no particular reference point for research.

Step 4: Make a Prediction

Passage A is a general discussion of the shift toward gender studies in history. Passage B describes the laws of Augustus, a specific event that illustrates the shift described in passage A. The correct answer should address this connection.

Step 5: Evaluate the Answer Choices

(D) is a match. The "trend in scholarship" is the shift toward gender studies. Passage A does indicate some strengths (paragraph 2) and weaknesses (paragraph 3), and the study in passage B is a perfect example of that trend.

(A) is a 180. The author of passage A is suspicious of the trend and complains that it "obscures as much as it reveals." That's hardly an endorsement.

(B) falls apart because passage A never addresses passage B directly. Besides, there's no mention of overlooked evidence.

(C) doesn't work because, while the evidence in passage B is consistent with what's described in passage A, they have

different goals in their conclusions. Passage A expresses opinions about fairly recent trends, while passage B is more of a factual account of ancient events.

(E) is off because there's no argument in passage B for passage A to advance.

18. (B) Inference

Step 2: Identify the Question Type

This question asks for something in passage A that "most closely" corresponds to something in passage B. That makes this an Inference question.

Step 3: Research the Relevant Text

Start by analyzing the provided lines for passage B. Then, use content clues in that text to search for matching ideas in passage A.

Step 4: Make a Prediction

The question provides a reference to lines 36–43, which describe laws allocating "domestic" roles to women to help preserve "peace and stability" to Rome. This lines up nicely with the articles described in lines 14–16 about how "domesticity ... shaped culture and politics."

Step 5: Evaluate the Answer Choices

(B) matches the wording from passage A that corresponds to the details referenced in passage B.

(A) is a 180. The "history of women per se" is what historians are said to "retreat from" (lines 10–11). That would be a focus on women as individuals, which is not what passage B entails.

(C) is a 180. Rediscovering and honoring lost ancestors is part of the "celebratory" study of women's history (lines 21–24), which focuses on individual women. Nothing in passage B does that.

(D) is Out of Scope. There's nothing in the lines of passage B that discusses the role of masculinity.

(E) a Distortion. There's nothing in the passage B lines referenced that suggests that anything was obscured.

19. (E) Inference

Step 2: Identify the Question Type

This is an Inference question because it asks for something with which the author of passage A is "most likely to agree."

Step 3: Research the Relevant Text

There are no content clues, so all of the text is relevant.

Step 4: Make a Prediction

Passage B describes details of the laws passed in ancient Rome by Augustus. It matches the kind of scholarship described throughout passage A in that it focuses on general gender issues instead of the role of any women in particular. However, despite concerns about aspects being overlooked (paragraph 3), the author of passage A does concede that analyses like that of passage B can "offer an analytic framework within which to analyze social and political structures."

Step 5: Evaluate the Answer Choices

(E) is supported in that the details of passage B do provide insight into Roman politics and culture, an advantage that passage A does admit exists.

(A) is Out of Scope. The author of passage A never discusses the integration of women's history as being "far from complete."

(B) is a 180. The author of passage A is suspicious of abandoning such efforts and would hardly claim such actions to be "justified."

(C) is a Distortion. Passage B does illustrate the current trend, but that trend is toward gender studies, not a specific focus on women's political influence.

(D) is a 180. Gender roles are the focus of recent studies and *are* seen as significant.

Passage 4: Lamarckian Hereditary Mechanism

Step 1: Read the Passage Strategically
Sample Roadmap

line #	Keyword/phrase	¶ Margin notes
4	basic idea	Lamarck: organisms adapt, pass to offspring
7	ridiculed	
8	for example	
11	adamant	Most bio. disagree
12	But	
13	attempting to revive	Steele: evidence in immune system
14	claim ... evidence	
18	:	How does immune system work?
23	unusual	
24	most common	DNA → RNA, mutates
27		immune system finds defense
29		
30	hypothesizes	Steele: RNA → DNA
31	Indeed	
33	But	
34	troublesome question ... :	New DNA to reprod system?
38	? ... believe this is possible	
39	elegant ... but speculative	Steele: Yes, via virus
44	But ... even if	actually happen?
45	?	
47	we must make do	
48	claim	Steele offers circumstantial evidence
51	claim	
55	not so	Some bio, still not convinced
56	easily swayed ... suggest ... less ...	
57	radical	

Discussion

Paragraph 1 opens by introducing the **Topic**: the evolutionary theory of Jean-Baptiste de Lamarck. Lamarck suggested that animals adapt to their environment and pass those adaptations on to their offspring. While most biologists dismiss Lamarck's theory, one scientist claims to have found supporting evidence involving the immune system. This attempt at confirming Lamarck's theory is the **Scope** of the passage.

Before getting to Steele's ideas, paragraph 2 provides some background on immune systems. Immune systems help defend against diseases, in part, through mutation. When DNA is copied over to RNA, some immune system cells mutate—a process described as a genetic "typo." The immune system finds out which mutation works, which then helps the body defend itself.

Paragraph 3 introduces Steele's belief that this altered RNA will turn back into DNA, a general process that has been observed previously. However, the author raises the question of whether this new DNA could replace the DNA in the reproductive system and thus be passed on to offspring. Steele believes so, suggesting that the new DNA could be brought to the reproductive system by a virus.

The author raises more questions in paragraph 4, most importantly: does this actually happen? It's never been seen, but Steele insists that he and his team have found evidence. He claims reproductive genes have a "signature" with instructions for the immune system. Mutations to those genes would indicate that information was indeed transferred from somewhere else. Despite this evidence, some biologists are not convinced.

The author raises a lot of questions, but the focus remains on Steele's theories. So, the author's **Purpose** is to merely inform the reader. The **Main Idea** is that Steele and his team claim to have evidence supporting Lamarck's theory that genetic adaptations can be passed along to offspring.

20. (B) Global

Step 2: Identify the Question Type
The question asks for the "main point" of the passage, making this a Global question.

Step 3: Research the Relevant Text
For Global questions, there's no need to go back into the passage. The Main Idea from Step 1 will be enough here.

Step 4: Make a Prediction
Stay neutral with this. Steele and his team claim to have found evidence supporting Lamarck's theory that genetic adaptations can be passed along to offspring.

Step 5: Evaluate the Answer Choices
(B) matches, citing Steele's evidence for a Lamarckian system that would pass along genetic characteristics.

(A) is Extreme. Steele claims to have found evidence, but the lackluster response of biologists shows that he hasn't quite "proven" anything yet.

(C) goes against what's said in paragraph 3, which claims that Steele "believes" changes can be passed along to offspring, but this is merely "speculative." That doesn't suggest that he succeeded.

(D) is a Distortion. The author never compares Steele's work to the standard theory of evolution, and the tone of this answer is too negative for what's really a more neutral passage.

(E) is a Distortion on many fronts. RNA reverting back to DNA had already been "observed frequently" (line 33), and there's no suggestion that this was the "main obstacle" to accepting Lamarck's theory. Furthermore, by the end, Lamarck's theory is *still* not generally accepted.

21. (C) Logic Function

Step 2: Identify the Question Type
The phrase "primarily in order to" indicates a Logic Function question. The question is asking *why* the author refers to a mutation as a "typo."

Step 3: Research the Relevant Text
The term "typo" appears in line 25, but be sure to read the entire sentence from 24–27 for context.

Step 4: Make a Prediction
"Typo" refers to a mutation that occurs when DNA is "transcribed" (i.e., copied) into RNA. In other words, when a DNA strand is copied, a change occurs that is akin to a typo—a slight error in the copy that results in something little different.

Step 5: Evaluate the Answer Choices
(C) correctly expresses the concept of a minor error copying one thing to another.

(A) is a 180 because these mutations *are* adaptive—changing to help the body defend itself.

(B) is a 180. The mutation is *very* consequential, helping the body defend itself against diseases.

(D) is Out of Scope. There's no suggestion that this change is easily overlooked.

(E) is a clever Distortion. The analogy to a text-based "typo" makes it easier to understand what's happening. However, the author's intention is to clarify what the mutation is like. The author does not compare scientific analysis and textual analysis.

22. (D) Inference

Step 2: Identify the Question Type

The question asks for the author's attitude, which the passage "strongly suggests." That's the sign of an Inference question.

Step 3: Research the Relevant Text

Steele's theory is described throughout paragraphs 3 and 4. Look for Keywords indicating the author's voice throughout those paragraphs.

Step 4: Make a Prediction

The author doesn't express any views directly about Steele's theory. The author does raise many questions, but Steele always has an answer. However, it is telling that the author keeps noting that Steele merely "hypothesizes" (line 30) about things he and his team "believe" (lines 38 and 41). The author even qualifies one claim as "speculative" (line 39). While the author doesn't outright dismiss Steele's theory, the author is much more in sync with the biologists who are "not so easily swayed" (lines 55–56).

Step 5: Evaluate the Answer Choices

(D) fits the author's constant questioning and refusal to admit Steele's theories as anything more than just beliefs.

(A) is a 180. With so many questions, the author seems hardly confident that Steele is correct.

(B) is not supported. The author doesn't express any ill feelings toward Steele and never professes any allegiance to Darwinism.

(C) is a Distortion. The author does seem to have trust issues, but they have nothing to do with the "novelty" of the theory.

(E) is not supported. Steele has answers to every question posed, which suggests plenty of rigor on his part. The author holds no grudge against Steele for being lazy.

23. (B) Global

Step 2: Identify the Question Type

The question asks what the passage is "primarily concerned with," making this a Global question.

Step 3: Research the Relevant Text

With Global questions, there's no need to go back to the text. For this question, just consider the author's Purpose as determined in Step 1.

Step 4: Make a Prediction

The author's purpose for the passage is merely to introduce Steele's theory and the evidence he supplies for that theory.

Step 5: Evaluate the Answer Choices

(B) gets it right. The author is merely describing Steele's attempt to support Lamarck's much-ridiculed theory of evolution.

(A) is a Distortion. The passage describes a modern attempt to support the theory, not the development of that theory in the first place.

(C) is too narrow. A series of questions about the immune system is raised in paragraph 2, but the rest of the passage moves past that into reproductive systems and passing genes on to offspring.

(D) is a Distortion. While Steele and his team may feel the theory has merits, the author is not concerned with evaluating those merits. The author is only concerned with Steele's findings.

(E) is Out of Scope. The author is only focused on Lamarck's theory, not on the philosophy of science in general.

24. (E) Logic Function

Step 2: Identify the Question Type

The question directly asks for the function of the last paragraph.

Step 3: Research the Relevant Text

Use the margin notes for paragraph 4, and be sure to determine how that relates to the previous paragraphs.

Step 4: Make a Prediction

The bulk of the last paragraph describes the "circumstantial evidence" that Steel provides to support the theory he argues for earlier in the passage.

Step 5: Evaluate the Answer Choices

(E) correctly identifies the discussion of evidence to support Steele's neo-Lamarckian theory (i.e., the theory meant to revive Lamarckism).

(A) is a Distortion. While the last paragraph states that some biologists are not entirely swayed, it doesn't present "various objections" to Steele's theory.

(B) is a 180. Steele *does* provide supporting evidence, even if that evidence hasn't been generally accepted.

(C) is Out of Scope. The author offers no revision to Steele's theory.

(D) is Out of Scope. The author offers no suggestions for further research.

25. (B) Inference

Step 2: Identify the Question Type

This question asks for something the passage "suggests" that the author would "agree with." That makes this an Inference question.

Step 3: Research the Relevant Text

There are no context clues here, so the entire passage is relevant.

Step 4: Make a Prediction

With no hints in the question stem, the correct answer could reference anything from anywhere in the passage. In this case, go through the answers one at a time, eliminating those that are clearly wrong. Then, use content clues in the remaining answers to do any necessary research.

Step 5: Evaluate the Answer Choices

(B) is supported by paragraph 3. While reverse transcription has been observed frequently "in other contexts," the author states that Steele merely "hypothesizes" that immune cell RNA would do it, too. That suggests he hasn't actually observed it happening yet.

(A) is not supported. The author never suggests that the doubting biologists are mistaken.

(C) takes a lot of details and mixes them up improperly. Lines 41–43 suggest that viruses carry DNA that has *already been altered*. The virus itself does not alter the DNA.

(D) is a 180. As Steele's theory is described, the passing along of characteristics takes place when DNA is transferred out of the immune system and into the reproductive system.

(E) is Extreme. While Steele's theory may still be considered "speculative," the author never suggests that direct observation is the key to moving a theory from speculation to science.

26. (A) Logic Reasoning (Strengthen)

Step 2: Identify the Question Type

The question directly asks for something that would strengthen Steele's position. Treat this question as it would be treated in Logical Reasoning.

Step 3: Research the Relevant Text

Steele's position is laid out in paragraph 4, with evidence provided in paragraph 3.

Step 4: Make a Prediction

The gist of Steele's theory is that the DNA that's altered in the immune system is transferred to the reproductive system by a virus (lines 41–43). However, Steele has never seen this happen and only has circumstantial evidence. If there were actual evidence of DNA being transported by a virus, that would help Steele out.

Step 5: Evaluate the Answer Choices

(A) helps greatly. If a virus was shown to bring new DNA into reproductive cells and make a change, then Steele would have something more than mere conjecture.

(B) is a 180. Steele says that the appearance of such patterns in reproductive genes suggests a transfer from the immune system (lines 51–55). If those patterns are also found in nervous system genes, it's possible the patterns are found everywhere and may not have been transferred from one place to another.

(C) adds nothing to Steele's argument. The way this process is described—the immune system will "test out different defenses until it finds one that does the job" (lines 27–29)—already appears to be random trial and error. This doesn't help Steele's claim that mutations are then transferred by a virus.

(D) is a Faulty Use of Detail, supporting Lamarck's supposed presumption in lines 8–10. However, this does not support *Steele's* theory about passing along immune system mutations to offspring.

(E) discusses "acquired immunities" as opposed to those that developed through genetic mutation. So, that doesn't help Steele out.

27. (E) Logic Reasoning (Parallel Reasoning)

Step 2: Identify the Question Type

The correct answer asks for evidence "analogous to" that described in the last paragraph. That makes this a Parallel Reasoning question.

Step 3: Research the Relevant Text

The evidence in the last paragraph is described in lines 48–55.

Step 4: Make a Prediction

The question stem presents a situation with a copy of an ancient text. One scholar hypothesizes that the text isn't wholly original and was changed by a copyist at some point. This would be similar to Steele finding DNA in the reproductive system and hypothesizing that it's not original DNA and it was changed at some point. Steele's evidence in the last paragraph involves a "distinct pattern of mutations" that doesn't match the standard "signature" of reproductive cells. To complete the analogy in the question stem, the scholar should have evidence of "distinct" changes that don't match the "signature" style of the original era.

Step 5: Evaluate the Answer Choices

(E) fits the analogy. This is evidence of "distinct" changes that don't match a previous style.

(A) does not match. This offers no evidence that the changes were "distinct" to a later era.

(B) does not match. Even if there was admittance of a change, that's not parallel to finding "distinct" changes.

(C) does not match. This doesn't provide evidence of changes "distinct" to a particular era.

(D) doesn't match. This definitely indicates changes, but doesn't have any "distinct" pattern to parallel the evidence in paragraph 4.

Section II: Logical Reasoning

Q#	Question Type	Correct	Difficulty
1	Strengthen	C	★
2	Strengthen	D	★
3	Assumption (Necessary)	E	★★
4	Weaken	A	★
5	Parallel Flaw	A	★
6	Assumption (Necessary)	D	★
7	Strengthen	E	★★
8	Principle (Identify/Strengthen)	A	★
9	Assumption (Sufficient)	B	★★
10	Strengthen/Weaken (Evaluate the Argument)	C	★
11	Main Point	B	★★
12	Principle (Parallel)	B	★
13	Inference	B	★
14	Flaw	A	★★
15	Assumption (Sufficient)	C	★★
16	Principle (Identify/Strengthen)	B	★★★
17	Method of Argument	B	★★★
18	Flaw	D	★★
19	Paradox	B	★★★
20	Role of a Statement	B	★★★
21	Strengthen	A	★
22	Flaw	A	★★★★
23	Inference	D	★★
24	Assumption (Necessary)	A	★★★★
25	Inference (EXCEPT)	D	★★

1. (C) Strengthen

Step 1: Identify the Question Type

The question asks for something that will "justify" or strengthen the environmentalists' point. Look for the conclusion and any evidence, and find an answer that makes the connection more logically sound.

Step 2: Untangle the Stimulus

An electric utility is weighing two options for a new power plant: natural gas–fired or waste-to-energy. The environmentalists recommend the waste-to-energy plant, despite the fact that it produces more pollution than a gas-fired plant.

Step 3: Make a Prediction

In a way, this works very much like a Paradox question. Why would the environmentalists push an option that is liable to be worse for the environment? As with any recommendation, there are always overlooked advantages or disadvantages to consider. In this case, the environmentalist must know of some benefit to waste-to-energy plants or some problem with gas-fired plants that hasn't been mentioned. The correct answer will fill in one of those missing gaps.

Step 4: Evaluate the Answer Choices

(C) provides a resolution. Even if the waste-to-energy plant isn't quite as efficient as the gas-fired plant, it's still a much better solution than keeping what's currently available. While it may not *completely* justify the choice over the gas-fired plant, it *helps* push things in the right direction—and that's all the question asks for.

(A) is a 180. This just makes gas-fired plants seem like a better option, making it less understandable why the environmentalists would choose the waste-to-energy plant.

(B) is irrelevant. This does nothing to justify the choice of one plant over another.

(D) is a 180. If air pollution is the most serious problem, then they seem *less* justified choosing the option that will produce more air pollution.

(E) is irrelevant. Even if power plants contribute relatively little to air pollution overall, that doesn't help justify choosing the higher-polluting option.

2. (D) Strengthen

Step 1: Identify the Question Type

The question directly asks for something that strengthens the given argument. Find the evidence and conclusion, and look for an answer that validates the assumption between them.

Step 2: Untangle the Stimulus

The anthropologist concludes that cooking allows us to get the calories we need to support our large brains. "After all" (which indicates evidence), we developed big brains when we started to control fire, and people don't get enough calories from eating just raw food.

Step 3: Make a Prediction

The evidence provides information about people who eat raw food and what happened when our ancestors controlled fire. However, the conclusion is about *cooking* food, which is never directly addressed in the evidence. The anthropologist assumes that there's something distinct about cooking food that helps us get the calories we need. The correct answer will provide a needed distinction.

Step 4: Evaluate the Answer Choices

(D) supports the anthropologist by providing something distinct about cooking food that allows us to get more calories.

(A) is a 180. If cooked foods and raw foods had the same number of calories, then cooking would do nothing to gain us more calories.

(B) is an Irrelevant Comparison. The argument is about raw vs. cooked food, not meat vs. vegetables.

(C) is a 180. If the body gets the same amount of calories from food no matter what, then cooked food offers no advantage and does nothing to give us the extra calories we need.

(E) is an Irrelevant Comparison. The argument is about cooking the food, regardless of whether it's domesticated or wild.

3. (E) Assumption (Necessary)

Step 1: Identify the Question Type

The question directly asks for an assumption, and one that is "required by the argument." That makes this a Necessary Assumption question.

Step 2: Untangle the Stimulus

Commercial honeybees face a lot of problems, but the author argues there's a root cause for all of these problems: inbreeding. The evidence is that inbreeding has reduced the bees' genetic diversity.

Step 3: Make a Prediction

What does genetic diversity have to do with these problems? For the author's argument to make any sense, there must be *some* connection between genetic diversity and the host of problems described.

Step 4: Evaluate the Answer Choices

(E) makes the necessary connection. After all, using the Denial Test, if a lack of diversity did *not* make honeybees more vulnerable, then the reduced diversity that stems from inbreeding would be irrelevant, making the whole argument fall apart.

(A) is an Irrelevant Comparison. The relative likelihood of inbreeding does nothing to connect it to the problems the commercial bees face.

(B) is irrelevant. Even if inbreeding practices *could* be undone, there's still no evidence that inbreeding is truly the cause of all the problems.

(C) is irrelevant. Whether the diversity is still dropping or has leveled out, there's still no evidence that limited diversity is really the cause of the problems.

(D) is a 180. This suggests that problems would occur regardless of how diverse the population is. That would make inbreeding *less* likely to be the root cause.

4. (A) Weaken

Step 1: Identify the Question Type
The question outright asks for something that will weaken the given argument. Find an answer that attacks the assumption between the evidence and conclusion.

Step 2: Untangle the Stimulus
The argument starts off with some statistical information: the northern cardinal was hardly seen in Nova Scotia in 1980. Twenty years later, they became a common sight. Because winters warmed up a little during those 20 years, the author argues that those warmer temps are responsible for the sudden increase in cardinals.

Step 3: Make a Prediction
The phrase "responsible for" indicates a causal argument. In this case, the author is taking evidence of a correlation (more cardinals appeared during the same time temperatures rose) and concluding that one thing caused the other (higher temps *caused* the increase in cardinals). The most common way to weaken such an argument is to find an alternate cause, for instance some other reason the cardinals are suddenly more prevalent.

Step 4: Evaluate the Answer Choices
(A) provides an alternative explanation. The birds aren't there more for the warmer weather. They're coming for the food!

(B) is irrelevant. What matters is why they were spotted more in 2000 than in 1980. No matter how easy the bird is to spot, the author can still say weather impacted the population increase.

(C) is irrelevant. If other songbirds are also more common, the author could claim that warm weather was responsible for their increased numbers, too.

(D) just says that populations of nonmigratory birds (such as the cardinal) fluctuated more than other birds. But what caused that fluctuation? It could have been warmer weather, thus confirming the author's view.

(E) is a 180. If there were *fewer* predators in the area, *that* would weaken the argument, suggesting that the increased cardinal population was due to a threat being removed. *More* predators suggests that the cardinals are moving to Nova

Scotia regardless for some other reason—perhaps because of the warmer weather.

5. (A) Parallel Flaw

Step 1: Identify the Question Type
The question asks for an argument "parallel in its reasoning" to the argument given. Moreover, the given argument is described as "flawed." That makes this a Parallel Flaw question. Identify the error in the stimulus, and look for an answer that commits the exact same error.

Step 2: Untangle the Stimulus
The author cites a connection between personality and genes. The author then concludes that personalities don't change because genes don't change.

Step 3: Make a Prediction
While personality is linked to genes, it may also be linked to other things. So, even if genes don't change, something else could change that would affect personality. The correct answer will commit this same flaw: concluding that one thing won't change (personality) because it's connected to something else that doesn't change (genes), overlooking other factors that could induce change (e.g., personal relationships).

Step 4: Evaluate the Answer Choices
(A) matches piece by piece. The author concludes that one thing won't change (understanding of WWI) because it's connected to something else that doesn't change (what happened in the war), overlooking other factors that could induce change (e.g., the discovery of missing documents).

(B) is the opposite logic, claiming that two things are connected but saying that changing one *could* change the other.

(C) tries to tempt people by sticking to the same topic (genes). However, the logic here is about actively stopping something rather than something changing. That's not the same.

(D) makes a shift between long-term effects and short-term effects, concepts not involved in the original argument.

(E) is a 180. This makes a connection between two things, but concludes that if one thing *does* change, then the other thing *changes* as well.

6. (D) Assumption (Necessary)

Step 1: Identify the Question Type
The question asks for the assumption on which the argument "depends," making this a Necessary Assumption question.

Step 2: Untangle the Stimulus
After some political brouhaha, former PM Brooks has been released from prison and is now willing to join the government of dictator McFarlane. The problem is that

McFarlane's supporters don't like Brooks, and McFarlane's opponents won't support anyone in his government. So, the analyst concludes that Brooks won't get a lot of supporters.

Step 3: Make a Prediction
It is clear that Brooks is not going to get support from anyone who supports or opposes McFarlane. However, those are two extremes. What about people in the middle who don't really have a strong opinion about McFarlane? Maybe Brooks could drum up lots of support from those people. The analyst is convinced otherwise, so the analyst must assume this can't happen—that there just aren't enough people who are ambivalent about McFarlane.

Step 4: Evaluate the Answer Choices
(D) must be true. If most people *didn't* have one of these opinions, then there would be plenty of potential supporters of Brooks. The analyst must assume that most people *will* have an opinion.

(A) is irrelevant. The legitimacy of McFarlane's government has no bearing on how many supporters Brooks has.

(B) is irrelevant. Even if there *was* more corruption now than during Brooks's reign, people could *still* be unhappy with Brooks.

(C) is irrelevant. The author's argument is based on people's alignment with McFarlane, regardless of how much or how little Brooks's views overlap.

(E) is irrelevant. Whether the charges are valid or not, Brooks still seems to be out of favor with a lot of folks.

7. (E) Strengthen

Step 1: Identify the Question Type
The question directly asks for something that Strengthens the given argument.

Step 2: Untangle the Stimulus
Because amber is more valuable when it contains fossilized life, forgers will add normal-looking insects to their fake amber to drive up prices. *Therefore*, the author concludes that amber pieces with normal-looking insects are likely to be fake.

Step 3: Make a Prediction
The author reversed the logic! By the evidence, if amber is faked, forgers will add normal-looking insects:

> *If   fake   →   normal insect*

The author concludes that if there's a normal-looking insect, it's likely to be fake:

> *If   normal insect   →   fake*

That's not proper logic. While forgers are likely to put normal insects in their fake amber, normal insects could appear in real amber, too. The author assumes otherwise, likely believing that real amber would contain something else (e.g., not-so-normal insects).

Step 4: Evaluate the Answer Choices
(E) validates the author's assumption. By getting trapped in awkward positions, insects in real amber are more likely to look bizarre, bolstering the author's claim that normal-looking insects are more likely the sign of a fake.

(A) suggests that there's a good chance that forgeries will get sold, but does nothing to support the idea that normal-looking insects are any indication of a fake.

(B) is an Irrelevant Comparison. Here, size doesn't matter. The argument is all about spotting fakes.

(C) is an Irrelevant Comparison. Whether insects are worth more than plants or not, the argument is about recognizing fakes. This adds nothing to that argument.

(D) is a 180. The author is suggesting otherwise, saying you can spot a fake merely by looking at how normal the insect inside the amber appears.

8. (A) Principle (Identify/Strengthen)

Step 1: Identify the Question Type
The question directly asks for a principle, and one that will "justify" the given argument. That makes this a common Identify the Principle question that acts like a Strengthen question. The correct answer will be a broader take on the specific argument provided.

Step 2: Untangle the Stimulus
The author is concerned about the surge in crimes due to the Internet. The Internet is impersonal, so people are liable to loosen their morals and decide it's okay to hurt other people. Because of this, the author concludes that people should be educated about proper Internet ethics.

Step 3: Make a Prediction
Specifically, the author is advocating for education about the Internet to curb people's immorality. As a general rule (i.e., a principle), the author assumes that education can somehow affect people's morals.

Step 4: Evaluate the Answer Choices
(A) works. If education increases one's sense of moral responsibility, then that would justify the author's proposal to solve the moral problems caused by the Internet.

(B) is Out of Scope. The author's solution is about educating people. Creating a set of guidelines is not the same thing.

(C) is a 180. If educating people *increased* the amount of harm they could cause, that would make matters worse.

(D) is irrelevant. What acts people are morally opposed to have no bearing on whether education will help restore morality.

(E) is Out of Scope. The argument is not concerned with placing blame. It's about taking action to prevent moral lapses.

9. (B) Assumption (Sufficient)

Step 1: Identify the Question Type
According to the question, the argument given is proper "if" the correct answer "is assumed." That makes this a Sufficient Assumption question. Look for an answer that logically connects the evidence to the conclusion.

Step 2: Untangle the Stimulus
The columnist starts right off with the conclusion: video games are not art. The evidence is that video games are interactive, and art requires an experience controlled by the artist.

Step 3: Make a Prediction
Art requires an experience controlled by the artist. If video games did not have that necessary control, then the author can justly conclude that they're not art. However, the author merely states that video games are interactive. So, the author assumes that interactivity somehow takes away the artist's control, which would then solidify the conclusion that video games are not art.

Step 4: Evaluate the Answer Choices
(B) is the author's assumption, suggesting that a video game's interactivity prevents its artist from having the control needed to make it art.

(A) is Out of Scope. Nothing in the argument addresses the creators' intentions.

(C) is a 180. The author implies that video games *can* produce a rich aesthetic experience, and this would allow video games to be art, contrary to the author's point.

(D) is irrelevant. Art is not said to be dependent on *who* creates it, but whether that person has *control*.

(E) is a 180 at worst. If the players' choices are irrelevant, that makes it more likely that the experience *is* ultimately controlled by the creator, thus contradicting the author's point.

10. (C) Strengthen/Weaken (Evaluate the Argument)

Step 1: Identify the Question Type
This question asks for something that will "help in evaluating" the given argument. This is a variation on Strengthen/Weaken questions called Evaluate the Argument. The correct answer will be something that questions the assumption. The answer to that question will determine whether the argument is strong or weak.

Step 2: Untangle the Stimulus
Rumors are swirling that, after detergents with phosphates were banned in a local town, some rebels went to another town to buy their precious phosphate-filled detergents. However, the author has a theory: some people *did* follow the law and went phosphate-free. The evidence is that there was less phosphate in the wastewater.

Step 3: Make a Prediction
Does the reduction in phosphate levels really indicate a switch to phosphate-free detergents, or is the author overlooking another reason why the phosphate levels dipped? The author assumes it's all about the switch, and the correct answer will question if this is the case.

Step 4: Evaluate the Answer Choices
(C) raises a perfect question. What if the wastewater treatment plant treated phosphates differently? If it did, perhaps its new policies are responsible for the lower phosphate levels, hurting the author's claim that it was about people switching detergents. However, if the plant made no changes, then maybe people *did* switch, and the author's claim is supported.

(A) offers no help. The motive for those who defied the new regulation does nothing to determine if other people were following the rules or not.

(B) is Out of Scope. The argument is entirely dependent on phosphate levels. Other pollutants add no value.

(D) doesn't help. It doesn't matter whether wastewater makes up a majority or a small portion of phosphate pollution overall. The argument is about what led to the drop in phosphates in that wastewater.

(E) doesn't help. Whether officials tried to step in or not, the question remains: were there people who switched detergents?

11. (B) Main Point

Step 1: Identify the Question Type
The question asks for the "conclusion of the argument," making this a Main Point question.

Step 2: Untangle the Stimulus
Genetically engineered plants are risky because, at any moment, concerns can be raised that would destroy people's trust in those foods. Prices for such foods aren't high enough to offset the risk, making such crops a bad idea for farmers.

Step 3: Make a Prediction
Note the complete lack of Conclusion Keywords. Each sentence leads to the next with no transition. In a case like this, the One-Sentence Test is needed. What is the one sentence supported by everything else? That's often the most opinionated claim, and that would be the second sentence here: it is unwise for farmers to grow such crops. Why is it

unwise? *Because* such crops bring along a great amount of risk (sentence 1), and *because* their prices are not high enough to make up for that risk (sentence 3). Adding *because* before those claims confirms that they work more as evidence in support of the main point: farmers should not grow genetically engineered plants.

Step 4: Evaluate the Answer Choices

(B) perfectly paraphrases the conclusion.

(A) is evidence, not the conclusion. The risk is evidence *why* it's an unwise idea. Some may note that this claim is supported by its own piece of evidence ("because at any time ..."). So, this is *a* conclusion, but it is merely a subsidiary conclusion that in turn supports the main conclusion.

(C) is evidence, not the conclusion. The lack of compensation is *why* growing such crops is unwise.

(D) is preceded by the word *because* in the stimulus, indicating that it's evidence.

(E) is a Distortion. The author states that studies *could* be published that would diminish consumer confidence, but there's no claim that this is already the case.

12. (B) Principle (Parallel)

Step 1: Identify the Question Type

The word *principle* indicates a Principle question. However, the passage "illustrates" a principle that the correct answer will also illustrate. That makes this a Parallel Principle question. Start by expressing the stimulus in broad terms, and look for an answer that applies that same broad idea to a new topic.

Step 2: Untangle the Stimulus

Vaccination involves exposing patients to a mild pathogen so that they develop a resistance to that pathogen and avoid a harsher reaction in the future.

Step 3: Make a Prediction

Start by taking out the "pathogen" context to come up with a broader idea: in order to reduce the effect of a problem in the future, people are exposed to a minor form early on to build up their resistance to the problem. The correct answer will follow this principle, but in a new context.

Step 4: Evaluate the Answer Choices

(B) matches the principle perfectly. To reduce the effect of a problem in the future (treachery and cruelty), people are exposed to a minor form early on (as allegories in fairy tales) to build up their resistance to the problem (make them less vulnerable).

(A) doesn't match. In this case, instead of exposing people to a mild form of something, directors are taking something away.

(C) is a 180. Instead of using a milder form of something to address a problem, the firefighters are creating something *more* intense.

(D) doesn't match. Instead of exposing people to a milder form of something, the business is taking something away.

(E) is a Distortion. In this case, police are using a minor form of a problem to encourage people to avoid more serious forms. This is not the same as helping people become better able to handle the problem.

13. (B) Inference

Step 1: Identify the Question Type

The correct answer fills in the blank in the stimulus, which is preceded by the phrase "it follows that." That means what fills the blank will be directly backed up by the information before it, which makes it an Inference.

Step 2: Untangle the Stimulus

When nations don't interact much, they don't really understand each other's needs and problems, and sympathy and justice depend on that understanding.

Step 3: Make a Prediction

A lack of interaction impedes understanding, which is necessary for sympathy and justice. If understanding is that important, then losing it would have a major effect on sympathy and justice. So, what follows (and should therefore fill in the blank) is that those countries that barely interact are short on the needed understanding, which is going to affect their ability to share sympathy and justice.

Step 4: Evaluate the Answer Choices

(B) adequately expresses the potential consequence of little to no interaction.

(A) distorts the Formal Logic. Sympathy and justice *depend on* understanding, which means understanding is necessary. But that doesn't make such understanding enough to guarantee that there *will* be sympathy and justice.

(C) is Extreme. Nations that don't interact may not share sympathy or justice, but there's nothing to suggest that this is the root of "almost all" of their problems.

(D) is an Extreme Distortion. The stimulus mentions nothing about eliminating conflict and never suggests that there's *no way* to do so.

(E) is Extreme. This suggests that nations *must* have interaction to know a little about each other. However, while the stimulus does mention how little knowledge countries have with little interaction, it's still possible for nations to have some trace of understanding even with no interaction at all.

14. (A) Flaw

Step 1: Identify the Question Type

The question directly asks for a flaw in the activist's argument.

Step 2: Untangle the Stimulus

The activist is concerned about pollutants in the water that contribute to incurable cancer and birth defects. The activist wants to "significantly" reduce these problems and concludes "Clearly" that shutting down polluting industries is the only solution. The evidence is that these industries wouldn't comply with regulations.

Step 3: Make a Prediction

Saying that this is the *only* solution is a sure sign that the activist is overlooking something. While there *is* a link between pollutants and health problems, pollutants may not be the *only* factor—and may not even be the most significant factor. The correct answer will address this overlooked possibility.

Step 4: Evaluate the Answer Choices

(A) addresses the issue. If there are other factors that contribute to a significant number of health problems, then the activist loses the ability to claim shutting down factories is the *only* solution.

(B) is Out of Scope. The argument is only about significantly reducing cancer and birth defects in people. The effect of pollutants on other animals is not an issue here.

(C) is a 180. If the activist assumed that there were several different causes, then shutting down industries wouldn't be the *only* solution.

(D) is a Distortion. If industries wouldn't comply with regulations, the activist wouldn't have much reason to believe they would volunteer on their own. And even if they did, this still doesn't address the problem that pollutants might not be the most significant factor in cancer and birth defects.

(E) is Out of Scope. Even if some pollutants *did* have some benefits, there's no indication that they would be beneficial enough to affect the activist's cause of preventing cancer and birth defects.

15. (C) Assumption (Sufficient)

Step 1: Identify the Question Type

The correct answer will complete the argument "if" it is "assumed," making this a Sufficient Assumption question.

Step 2: Untangle the Stimulus

The political leader is convinced that offering a compromise to her opponents will benefit her side. As evidence, the leader presents the two possible outcomes: 1) The opposition agrees, and a compromise is reached. 2) The opposition says no, and they get blamed for failing to compromise.

Step 3: Make a Prediction

The problem is that the leader only directly says that the second outcome (opposition says no) will actually benefit her side. The leader never says that the first outcome (an actual compromise) would be a benefit. The leader assumes as much because, if it *is* a benefit, then her side *does* benefit either way, validating her conclusion.

Step 4: Evaluate the Answer Choices

(C) directly matches the assumption.

(A) is not good enough. A desire to compromise does not necessarily mean a compromise would be beneficial.

(B) is just not enough. If the opposition *never* compromises, then the leader's side is guaranteed a rejection, which would be an automatic benefit. However, "rarely" compromising allows for a possible exception. In that case, there's no guarantee that the compromise would be a benefit.

(D) is Out of Scope. Any benefit to the opposition has no bearing on benefits to the leader's side.

(E) is not enough. Even if the opposition *does* compromise, there's still no evidence that a compromise will certainly benefit the leader's side.

16. (B) Principle (Identify/Strengthen)

Step 1: Identify the Question Type

The question asks for a principle that will "justify" the given argument. That makes this a common Identify the Principle question in which the principle will effectively Strengthen the argument.

Step 2: Untangle the Stimulus

Some people think it's okay to push a remedy even if doesn't work. However, the author argues otherwise, claiming there *is* a danger. Those people using the ineffective remedies could be ignoring solutions that actually help.

Step 3: Make a Prediction

In general terms, something that *seems* harmless can still be harmful if it prevents people from getting something that will actually help.

Step 4: Evaluate the Answer Choices

(B) matches. This makes the ineffective folk remedies harmful because they interfere with something that would benefit people (i.e., effective treatments).

(A) does not match. People do *not* believe that the folk remedies are harmful, so this doesn't apply.

(C) is Out of Scope. The argument is not about blaming people for being dishonest.

(D) is Out of Scope. The author is not placing responsibility on anyone.

(E) is Out of Scope for the same reason as **(D)**. The author is not placing responsibility on anyone.

17. (B) Method of Argument

Step 1: Identify the Question Type
While not a complete question, the phrase "proceeds by" indicates that the question is asking for *how* the argument is made, making this a Method of Argument of question.

Step 2: Untangle the Stimulus
The author takes issue with a radio station that's pushing how popular its new format is. The station cites how much its call-in listeners rave. The author isn't convinced, and compares the station's logic to someone saying a politician is popular based on a survey of that politician's supporters.

Step 3: Make a Prediction
The comparison between the radio station's claim and the politician example is a very common argumentative technique: analogy. The politician situation is clearly absurd: of course a candidate will appear popular if you only talk to people voting for that candidate. The analogy shows how the station's argument is equally absurd: of course the new format will appear popular if you only consider the people who call your station to make requests. The correct answer will express this use of analogy to highlight flawed reasoning.

Step 4: Evaluate the Answer Choices
(B) accurately described the method. The author refers to a clearly flawed inference (the politician's popularity) to argue against a similar inference (the radio station's claim) via analogy.

(A) is a clever Distortion. The author certainly *implies* that the radio station's results are based on biased feedback. However, the author doesn't directly make that claim. The author hides behind an analogy, and *that* is the way the argument actually proceeds.

(C) is a Distortion. The politician argument does not use the same evidence as the radio station argument, and it's certainly not "more reasonable."

(D) is a 180. The example used is not a *counterexample*. Its logic is consistent with the radio station's and is flawed in the same way to show similarity.

(E) is Out of Scope. The author does not expose any contradiction.

18. (D) Flaw

Step 1: Identify the Question Type
The phrase "vulnerable to criticism" is common LSAT language indicating that something is wrong with the argument. So, this question is asking what that flaw is.

Step 2: Untangle the Stimulus
This historian starts right off with the conclusion: those who deny Shakespeare's authorship are motivated solely by snobbery. As evidence, the historian points out that those

naysayers just happen to be descendants of the very upper-class people they claim actually wrote the plays.

Step 3: Make a Prediction
It is rather coincidental that the people making these claims just happen to be descendants. However, the author takes that one step too far by saying their motives are *purely* snobbish. While it is possible that their sense of entitlement is *partially* a factor, there's still a chance they have other motives. The correct answer will address this overlooked possibility.

It's very important to note one thing: while it may seem that the author disagrees with such outrageous claims, the author never outright *states* that these people are wrong. The argument is purely about their motives and not about the actual truth of their claims (making this a variation of the classic ad hominem attack).

Step 4: Evaluate the Answer Choices
(D) is the flaw. The author is too focused on these people's background to consider other, potentially more valid motives.

(A) is an Extreme Distortion. The author never actually addresses the truth of the claims. Even if the author isn't entirely convinced in this case, that's a far cry from assuming that claims motivated by snobbery *cannot* be true.

(B) is not a flaw. If someone *is* "purely motivated" by one thing, then it's perfectly logical to assume that no other motivation exists. The author's actual flaw is saying that these people are purely motivated by snobbery in the first place.

(C) is Out of Scope. The author's argument is solely about the people trying to discredit Shakespeare. The motives of those who *do* give Shakespeare credit are irrelevant.

(E) suggests circular reasoning. However, the author's evidence and assumption are distinct enough from the conclusion. The author's assumption does not require the conclusion to be true.

19. (B) Paradox

Step 1: Identify the Question Type
The question asks for something that "helps to explain" a situation, making this a Paradox question. Look for the central mystery (i.e., *why* does something unexpected happen?), and find an answer that provides a solution.

Step 2: Untangle the Stimulus
The stimulus describes two sets of lemurs. The first live in rain forests with year-round foliage. The second live in forests where leaves fall off the trees in winter. For some reason, the second group is much more active during the night than the first group.

Step 3: Make a Prediction
Paradox questions always boil down to a central mystery. In this case, why is the second group so much more active at night than the first group during the winter? The only known difference is that the second group lives where the leaves are gone in winter, while the first group lives where the leaves stay up year-round. Most likely, there's something about the missing foliage that makes the second group more active at night. Don't try to predict *exactly* what that would be (there are too many possibilities), but know the correct answer will probably tie the increased nighttime activity to the missing leaves.

Step 4: Evaluate the Answer Choices
(B) solves the mystery. If both groups have high-flying predators during the day, then the first group is a little safer during the winter with its canopy of leaves. They can get things done during the day and rest a little more at night. The second group is more exposed with all the leaves gone. They'd be more likely to avoid going out during the day and wait until night to do their business. That would be why they're more active at night than the first group.

(A) is a 180. This gives both groups equal competition during the day, which should result in equal activity at night. Unless there's something significantly different about one group's competition, the mystery goes unsolved.

(C) is a 180. This puts both groups at equal risk during the day, which would suggest equal activity at night. There's still no understanding why their nighttime activities are different.

(D) brings up a difference between the two groups, but there's no direct connection between size and nighttime activity. If anything, one might expect the larger animals would be more active because they need to eat more, but this would be the complete opposite of what actually happens.

(E) doesn't help. Giving the second group a more limited diet doesn't explain why they would be more active at night. Even if the limited diet makes it harder for the second group to find food, the mystery is why the second group *increases* its nighttime activity so much more—not why it spends more time overall.

20. (B) Role of a Statement

Step 1: Identify the Question Type
The question provides a claim from the stimulus and asks for its "role" in the argument. That makes this a Role of a Statement question.

Step 2: Untangle the Stimulus
The critic presents a common view: "literary" fiction is meant to be interpreted, while "genre" fiction is just for fun. However, the critic argues that these labels are meaningless. Nothing should be interpreted because that diminishes the work's emotional impact.

Step 3: Make a Prediction
The claim in question is the very last sentence. However, that's not the conclusion. By adding the word *because* before it, its role becomes clear: *because* evaluating a work takes away the emotional impact, the critic feels there should be no such interpretation, making the distinction between "literary" and "genre" fiction pointless. That identifies the claim in question as evidence, which is ultimately used to support the critic's conclusion about the labels being improper.

Step 4: Evaluate the Answer Choices
(B) correctly identifies the last sentence as evidence for the critic's conclusion.

(A) is mistaken. The conclusion is that separating "literary" and "genre" fiction is a "specious distinction."

(C) is off because the critic's conclusion is that the distinction between "literary" and "genre" fiction is false. The claim in question is not an implication of that conclusion.

(D) is a Distortion. The only distinction mentioned is that between "literary" and "genre" fiction. However, the critic *disputes* rather than considers that distinction. And the claim in question explains why that distinction is wrong.

(E) is Out of Scope. There's no clear objection that the claim in question seems to address.

21. (A) Strengthen

Step 1: Identify the Question Type
The correct answer will "justify" the application provided, making this a Strengthen question. However, this is a relatively common variation in which a principle is given along with a supposed application of that principle. The application is usually incomplete. The correct answer will fill in the missing piece so that it applies properly.

Step 2: Untangle the Stimulus
The principle is that people who neither fault themselves for a behavior nor promise to stop shouldn't criticize that behavior in others. This supposedly applies to Shimada, who has not promised to stop being late to things, and thus shouldn't criticize McFeney for the same behavior.

Step 3: Make a Prediction
By the principle, criticizing others should be avoided by people who don't promise to stop their own behavior *and don't fault themselves for that behavior*. The application leaves out the part about the lack of self-criticism. For the application to be complete, it must include a claim that Shimada does not fault himself for his tardiness.

Step 4: Evaluate the Answer Choices
(A) fills in the missing piece of the puzzle. If Shimada does not criticize his own tardiness, then that (along with his refusal to vow quitting such behavior) would set off the principle, denying him the right to criticize McFeney.

(B) is Out of Scope. The frequency of the behavior in question is not part of the principle.

(C) is Out of Scope. How McFeney acts toward Shimada has no bearing on applying the principle to Shimada.

(D) is a 180. If Shimada *does* criticize himself, then the principle doesn't apply. It only applies to people who *don't* fault themselves.

(E) is Out of Scope. The frequency of the behavior is not addressed in the principle.

22. (A) Flaw

Step 1: Identify the Question Type
The question directly asks for a flaw in the reasoning.

Step 2: Untangle the Stimulus
The author is arguing for access to multiple newspapers because no individual newspaper could fully cover every story, and every important story should be covered fully.

Step 3: Make a Prediction
The author commits a very subtle scope shift. By the evidence, no single newspaper could fully cover *every single story*. However, the author only states that all sides of *important* stories should be covered. Perhaps one newspaper can cover all sides of the *important* stories, while skimping out on some of the less significant stories. In that case, one newspaper *would* be enough. The author overlooks this possibility, and that's the flaw.

Step 4: Evaluate the Answer Choices
(A) addresses the error. Just because a single newspaper can't fully cover *every* story doesn't mean it can't fully cover every *important* story.

(B) is a Distortion. The author isn't arguing that two newspapers will definitely do the job. It's possible that it would take three, four, or even more newspapers to get the kind of coverage the author expects.

(C) is not accurate. The author's conclusion (people should have access to multiple papers) is not just supported by factual evidence, but also by evidence of what newspapers *should* do (they should cover all sides of important stories).

(D) is Extreme. The author's argument does not depend on people having access to *all* newspapers, just "more than one."

(E) is not a *logical* flaw in the argument. Some people might subjectively believe that the argument should address more than just important studies, but that's not a *reasoning* flaw, which the question asks for.

23. (D) Inference

Step 1: Identify the Question Type
The correct answer "follows logically" from what is given, which means it will be an Inference directly backed up by the stimulus.

Step 2: Untangle the Stimulus
The information discusses a company called Moradco. Most of its mines in Velyena have never violated regulations, while every one of its gold mines worldwide *has* violated regulations.

Step 3: Make a Prediction
The last claim provides a little Formal Logic. If one of Moradco's mines is a gold mine, it has violated regulations:

$$\textbf{\textit{If}} \qquad \textbf{\textit{gold mine}} \qquad \rightarrow \qquad \textbf{\textit{violate}}$$

By contrapositive, any mine that has *not* violated regulations is *not* a gold mine:

$$\textbf{\textit{If}} \qquad \textbf{\textit{\~ violate}} \qquad \rightarrow \qquad \textbf{\textit{\~ gold mine}}$$

By that logic, because most of the mines in Velyena have *not* violated regulations, most of the mines in Velyena must *not* be gold mines.

Step 4: Evaluate the Answer Choices
(D) is the right logical deduction.

(A) is not supported. There's no information on the number of mines Moradco operates anywhere.

(B) is not supported. There's no information on how many total mines Moradco operates anywhere.

(C) is a Distortion. *Most* of the mines in Velyena have never violated regulations. But there could still be plenty that *have* (say 50 of the 500 mines in Velyena). Those mines could all be gold mines and could certainly be the majority of Moradco's worldwide gold mines.

(E) is a Distortion. While most of the mines in Velyena are not gold mines, that could be an exceptional area. It's still possible that Moradco has predominantly gold mines throughout the rest of the world.

24. (A) Assumption (Necessary)

Step 1: Identify the Question Type
The question asks for an "assumption" on which the argument "relies," making this a Necessary Assumption question.

Step 2: Untangle the Stimulus
Tariffs are great for the few people who make the product being taxed. Most people, though, oppose tariffs because

they hike up costs. *So*, the author concludes that politicians who vote against tariffs are more likely to be reelected.

Step 3: Make a Prediction
The author took quite a leap. The evidence is just that people don't like tariffs. The conclusion suddenly brings up the reelection of politicians, implying that a vote for tariffs can potentially end a politician's career. The only way this is true is if the anti-tariff folks are so passionate that they insist on voting against politicians who favor tariffs.

Step 4: Evaluate the Answer Choices
(A) must be true, suggesting that opponents are as likely or more likely to base their voting decision on the tariff than anyone else. Using the Denial Test, if this *wasn't* true, opponents would be *less* likely to base their decision on tariffs. In that case, tariffs wouldn't be as big a problem as the author insists.

(B) is not necessary. The argument is not about what politicians *actually* do, but what the author recommends they *should* do.

(C) is Out of Scope. The argument is only discussing product-specific tariffs, not general tariffs.

(D) is Extreme. The author's argument is only about tariffs. There's no need to shun *all* measures that benefit few people.

(E) is not necessary. Whether people know the trouble of tariffs or not has no bearing on the potential reelection of politicians.

25. (D) Inference (EXCEPT)

Step 1: Identify the Question Type
The correct answer will be based on the information given, making this an Inference question. However, unlike most Inference questions that look for something absolutely supported, this one states that four answers *could* be true. The correct answer will be the exception: the one that *cannot* be true based on what's given.

Step 2: Untangle the Stimulus
The author provides a direct relationship between seals and dolphins: the longer one can stay underwater, the deeper one can dive. Then two pairs of animals are compared. Dolphins can dive deeper than fur seals, and elephant seals can stay underwater longer than Weddell seals.

Step 3: Make a Prediction
Start by using the relationship described, then make deductions about the four animals provided. Because dolphins can dive deeper than fur seals, dolphins must be able to stay underwater longer:

dolphins   >   fur seals

And because elephants seals can stay underwater longer than Weddell seals, elephant seals can dive deeper:

elephant seals   >   Weddell seals

There is *no* connection between the two pairs. For instance, there's no way of knowing whether dolphins can surpass elephant seals and Weddell seals, are inferior to both, or are somewhere in between. The correct answer will lead to an impossible scenario (i.e., one in which fur seals dominate dolphins or Weddell seals dominate elephant seals).

Step 4: Evaluate the Answer Choices
(D) is impossible, and thus the correct answer. If fur seals can surpass elephant seals, then they must also surpass Weddell seals (fur > elephant > Weddell). However, dolphins surpass fur seals, which means they would be able to stay submerged the longest and dive the deepest of all (dolphins > fur > elephant > Weddell). In this scenario, there's no way Weddell seals could surpass dolphins.

(A) is possible. This would rank dolphins in between elephant seals and Weddell seals (elephant > dolphin > Weddell). Then, fur seals would just have to be inferior to dolphins, too. That's fine.

(B) is possible. This would rank Weddell seals between dolphins and fur seals (dolphin > Weddell > fur). Then, elephant seals would just have to be superior to Weddell seals, too. That's fine.

(C) is possible. This would rank Weddell seals superior to dolphins and fur seals (Weddell > dolphin; Weddell > fur). Then, elephant seals would just have to be superior to Weddell seals. That's fine.

(E) is possible. This would rank fur seals between elephant seals and Weddell seals (elephant > fur > Weddell). Then, fur seals would just have to be inferior to dolphins, too. That's fine.

Section III: Logic Games
Game 1: Community Festival Performances

Q#	Question Type	Correct	Difficulty
1	Acceptability	A	★
2	"If" / Could Be True	B	★
3	Must Be False (CANNOT Be True)	D	★★
4	Earliest	C	★
5	Complete and Accurate List	C	★

Game 2: Ceramic Bowl Display

Q#	Question Type	Correct	Difficulty
6	Acceptability	E	★
7	"If" / Could Be True	D	★
8	"If" / Must Be True	C	★
9	"If" / Must Be True	A	★
10	"If" / Must Be False (CANNOT Be True)	B	★★
11	Must Be True	B	★★★
12	"If" / Must Be True	A	★

Game 3: Office Selection

Q#	Question Type	Correct	Difficulty
13	Partial Acceptability	B	★★★
14	Must Be True	C	★★★
15	Could Be True	A	★★★★
16	"If" / Could Be True	E	★★★
17	Must Be True	E	★★★

Game 4: Community Committee Volunteers

Q#	Question Type	Correct	Difficulty
18	Partial Acceptability	E	★
19	"If" / Could Be True EXCEPT	C	★★
20	Must Be True EXCEPT	B	★★★
21	"If" / Complete and Accurate List	B	★★★
22	Completely Determine	C	★★★
23	Rule Substitution	C	★★★

Game 1: Community Festival Performances

Step 1: Overview
Situation: Entertainers performing at a community festival

Entities: Six entertainers (Robinson, Shahpari, Tigay, Wu, Yeaton, Zane)

Action: Strict Sequencing. Determine the order in which the entertainers perform.

Limitations: No two entertainers perform at the same time, so this is one-to-one Sequencing. However, the schedule is split in that the first three performances are in the morning and the last three are in the afternoon.

Step 2: Sketch
List the entities by initial and set up six numbered slots in order, using the times provided. Draw a line to separate the morning and afternoon slots, labeling each side.

```
          R S T W Y Z
      morn    |    aft
    ___ ___ ___ | ___ ___ ___
     9  10  11  |  2   3   4
```

Alternatively, you could list the morning slots above the afternoon slots to indicate morning and afternoon. Choose whichever configuration is your preference.

```
              R S T W Y Z
      morn   ___ ___ ___
              9  10  11

      aft    ___ ___ ___
              2   3   4
```

Step 3: Rules
Rule 1 sets up a loose relationship: Robinson performs sometime before Zane.

$$R \ldots Z$$

That means Robinson cannot perform last (4:00 P.M.), and Zane cannot perform first (9:00 A.M.). If helpful, add "~R" and "~Z" under the respective slots.

Rule 2 creates a block: Yeaton must perform immediately after Wu:

That means Wu cannot perform last (4:00 P.M.), and Yeaton cannot perform first (9:00 A.M.). Again, if helpful, add "~W" and "~Y" under the respective slots.

Rule 3 limits Tigay to the afternoon. Draw "~T" under the first three slots, or draw T above the last three slots with arrows pointing to the slots.

Rule 4 limits Zane to the morning. Draw "~Z" under the last three slots, or draw Z above the first three slots with arrows pointing to the slots.

Step 4: Deductions
The Duplication of Zane in Rules 1 and 4 is significant. If Zane is restricted to the morning and Robinson has to perform before Zane, then Robinson is also restricted to the morning. That means Robinson and Zane will be two of the three morning performers. The third morning performer cannot be Tigay (Rule 3). That leaves Shahpari, Wu, and Yeaton. Shahpari is a Floater—which you can mark with a star or other notation in the list of entities—and could certainly be the third morning performer. Wu could be also, as long as Yeaton performs immediately afterward in the afternoon (Rule 2). Yeaton could not perform in the morning because there would not also be space for Wu immediately before Yeaton given that Robinson and Zane are already in the morning, so Yeaton cannot be the third morning performer. Thus, Yeaton must perform in the afternoon.

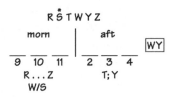

It's possible to set up Limited Options depending on who performs with Robinson and Zane in the morning (Wu or Shahpari). However, as long as the previously mentioned deductions are made, Limited Options are nice but ultimately not needed.

Step 5: Questions

1. (A) Acceptability
As with any Acceptability question, use the rules one at a time to eliminate answers that violate those rules.

(E) violates Rule 1 by having Robinson scheduled after Zane. **(D)** violates Rule 2 by scheduling Tigay in between Wu and Yeaton. **(C)** violates Rule 3 by scheduling Tigay third, which would be in the morning. **(B)** violates Rule 4 by scheduling Zane fourth, which would be in the afternoon. That leaves **(A)** as the correct answer.

2. (B) "If" / Could Be True
For this question, Wu must perform in the morning. By Rule 4, so must Zane, which means so must Robinson (Rule 1). That fills up the morning, leaving Shahpari, Tigay, and Yeaton for the afternoon. By Rule 2, Yeaton must perform *immediately* after Wu. The only way to do that is to have Wu perform at

11:00 A.M. and Yeaton at 2:00 P.M. That leaves Robinson and Zane to perform at 9:00 A.M. and 10:00 A.M., respectively. Shahpari and Tigay will perform at 3:00 P.M. and 4:00 P.M., in either order.

$$\frac{R}{9} \quad \frac{Z}{10} \quad \frac{W}{11} \quad \Big| \quad \frac{Y}{2} \quad \frac{S/T}{3} \quad \frac{T/S}{4}$$

In that case, only **(B)** is possible, making it the correct answer. The other answers all must be false.

3. (D) Must Be False (CANNOT Be True)
The correct answer will be a time at which Shahpari is unable to perform. The remaining answers will list times at which Shahpari *could* perform.

By the work in the second question, Shahpari could perform at 3:00 P.M. That eliminates **(E)**. If Shahpari performed in the morning, it could be at any time, with Robinson and Zane performing at the remaining two morning times. That eliminates **(A)**, **(B)**, and **(C)**, leaving **(D)** as the correct answer. For further proof:

If Shahpari performs in the afternoon, the only person left to perform in the morning with Robinson and Zane would be Wu. In that case (as seen in the second question), Wu would have to perform at 11:00 A.M. so that Yeaton could perform immediately afterward (Rule 2) at 2:00 P.M. That would force Shahpari elsewhere, unable to perform at 2:00 P.M.

4. (C) Earliest
The correct answer to this question will be the earliest time at which Wu could perform. As seen in the second question, Wu could perform as early as 11:00 A.M., which eliminates **(D)** and **(E)**. In fact, that's the earliest Wu could perform. If Wu performed earlier in the morning, then Yeaton would also perform in the morning (Rule 2), along with Zane (Rule 4) and thus Robinson (Rule 1). That would be too many performers in the morning. Therefore, the only time (and thus the earliest time) Wu could perform in the morning is 11:00 A.M., making **(C)** the correct answer.

5. (C) Complete and Accurate List
The correct answer to this question will list every entertainer that must perform in the afternoon. By Rule 3, that list must include Tigay. The list must also include Yeaton. After all, if Yeaton performed in the morning, so would Wu (Rule 2), as would Zane (Rule 4) and thus Robinson (Rule 1). That would be too many morning performers.

The correct answer to the Acceptability question has Shahpari perform in the morning, and the second question has Wu perform in the morning. Thus, neither Shahpari nor Wu has to perform in the afternoon. Furthermore, Robinson and Zane can never perform in the afternoon. That means Tigay and

Yeaton are the only people who must perform in the afternoon, making **(C)** the correct answer.

Game 2: Ceramic Bowl Display

Step 1: Overview

Situation: A selection of crafted ceramic bowls being put on display

Entities: Eight potters (Larsen, Mills, Neiman, Olivera, Park, Reigel, Serra, Vance)

Action: Sequencing/Selection Hybrid. Determine which of the bowls will be displayed (Selection), and place the selected bowls in order (Sequencing).

Limitations: There are eight bowls, each one crafted by one of the eight potters. For the Selection element, exactly six of the eight bowls will be chosen. For the Sequencing element, there are six consecutively numbered positions, one bowl per position.

Step 2: Sketch

For the Sequencing element, a set of six numbered slots will suffice. For the Selection element, simply list the potters by initial and note that six out of the eight will be selected. As the game proceeds, circle potters whose bowls are chosen and cross out those whose bowls are not chosen.

L M N O P R S V   –Pick 6

—— —— —— —— —— ——
 1   2   3   4   5   6

Step 3: Rules

Rule 1 affects the selection. If Larsen's bowl is selected, then Mills's bowl cannot be. By contrapositive, if Mills's bowl is selected, then Larsen's bowl cannot be. Essentially, that means the display cannot include both Larsen's and Mills's bowls.

$$L \rightarrow \sim M \quad \text{(Never LM)}$$
$$M \rightarrow \sim L$$

Note that this does not mean the display must include one of their bowls. Only six bowls are selected, so it's possible that both of their bowls are rejected.

Rule 2 places a major restriction on Park's bowl. If it's included in the display, it has to be next to both Olivera's and Serra's bowl (i.e., in between those two bowls). The order of Olivera's and Serra's bowls are not defined.

$$P \rightarrow \underline{OPS} \text{ or } \underline{SPO}$$

This means that Park's bowl cannot be placed on either end, so add "~P" under slots 1 and 6.

Rule 3 restricts Reigel's bowl to position 1 or 6. This does *not* mean that Reigel's bowl is definitely selected. So, it's still possible for two other bowls to be placed in positions 1 and 6, with Reigel's bowl not selected. However, it can be noted that

Reigel's bowl will not be placed in positions 2–5. Draw "~R" under those slots and/or make a shorthand rule to the side.

$$R \rightarrow 1 \text{ or } 6$$

Rule 4 prevents Serra's bowl from being placed in position 2 or 4. Again, Serra's bowl is not definitely selected. However, if it is, it cannot be placed in position 2 or 4. Add "~S" under those two slots.

Rule 5 restricts Neiman's bowl to one position: fifth. It's still possible that Neiman's bowl won't be selected. However, if it is, it must go in position 5.

$$N \rightarrow 5$$

Step 4: Deductions

There are a couple of opportunities for Limited Options in this game, most notably based on the last rule. If Neiman's bowl is selected, that establishes a bowl in position 5, which does place a significant restriction on Park's bowl, but leads to no further concrete deductions. If Neiman's bowl is *not* selected, that helps limit whose bowl *is* selected, but allows for no absolute placement.

While Limited Options are always worth considering, a glance ahead reveals that, of the game's seven questions, five are "If" questions and one is an Acceptability question. Those questions will provide a lot of information, so it's more important now to pay attention to significant entities and any Numbers restrictions.

The only entity Duplicated in the rules is Serra. By Rule 2, if Park's bowl was selected, Serra's bowl would have to be next to it. However, Serra's bowl cannot be in position 2 or 4 (Rule 4), which means Park's bowl cannot be in position 3. Also by Rule 2, Park's bowl cannot be on the end because it needs to be in between two other bowls. That limits Park's bowl to positions 2, 4, and 5. However, Park's bowl can also go unselected, leaving too many options to consider.

In terms of Numbers, six bowls must be selected, but the selection cannot include both Larsen's and Mills's (so you could almost treat them as one entity labeled as "L/M" in the entities list). That means at least one of their bowls will go unselected. That leaves only one more bowl that can go unselected. Once that second bowl is determined, then everyone else's bowl must be selected. This will be a significant point throughout the game. Finally, the only entity that has no rules about it is Vance's bowl, so you can mark it with a star in the list of entities to indicate that it is a Floater.

If you opted to include all the negative deductions, a final Master Sketch would look something like this:

L/M N O P R S V̇   -Pick 6

P → OPS or SPO

1	2	3	4	5	6
~P	~R	~R	~R	~R	~P
	~S	~P	~S	N̄	

Step 5: Questions

6. (E) Acceptability

As with any Acceptability question, go through the rules one at a time, eliminating answers that violate those rules.

(A) violates Rule 1 by including Larsen's bowl but also including Mills's bowl. **(D)** violates Rule 2 by not placing Park's bowl next to Olivera's bowl. **(C)** violates Rule 3 by putting Reigel's bowl in position 5—it is supposed to be limited to position 1 or 6. No remaining answers violate Rule 4, but **(B)** violates Rule 5 by putting Neiman's bowl in position 2—it is supposed to be limited to position 5. That leaves **(E)** as the correct answer.

7. (D) "If" / Could Be True

For this question, Neiman's bowl and Park's bowl are selected. By Rule 5, Neiman's bowl must go in position 5. Park's bowl has to be surrounded by Olivera's and Serra's (Rule 2), which means Park's bowl cannot go in position 1 or 6. Park's bowl cannot go into position 4 because Neiman's bowl is in the way. Park's bowl cannot go in position 3, because Serra's bowl couldn't be in either position next to it (Rule 4). Therefore, Park's bowl would have to be in position 2, placing Olivera's and Serra's bowls in positions 1 and 3, in either order.

L/M Ⓝ Ⓞ Ⓟ R Ⓢ V

O/S	P	S/O		N	
1	2	3	4	5	6

With that, the only bowls that could be in position 1 are Olivera's or Serra's, making **(D)** the correct answer.

8. (C) "If" / Must Be True

For this question, Larsen's bowl is established in position 6, and Olivera's bowl is established in position 2. With Larsen's bowl included, Mills's bowl must be out (Rule 1)—cross it off the entity list for this new sketch. Placing Olivera's bowl in position 2 limits the placement of Park's bowl. By Rule 2, Park's bowl would have to be next to Olivera's bowl in position 1 or 3. However, Park's bowl would also have to be next to Serra's bowl, which means it cannot be in position 1. In addition, putting Park's bowl in position 3 would put Serra's bowl in position 4, which violates Rule 4. Therefore, Park's bowl cannot be included—cross it off the entity list, too. With Mills's and Park's bowls eliminated, everyone else's bowl must be selected. That includes Neiman, Reigel, Serra, and Vance. Neiman's bowl would have to be in position 5

(Rule 5). With Larsen's bowl in position 6, Reigel's bowl would have to be in position 1 (Rule 3). Serra's bowl can't be in position 4 (Rule 4), so Vance's bowl must go there, placing Serra's bowl in position 3.

Ⓛ/M̶ Ⓝ Ⓞ Ⓡ Ⓢ Ⓥ

R	O	S	V	N	L
1	2	3	4	5	6

With Serra's bowl established in position 3, **(C)** is the correct answer.

9. (A) "If" / Must Be True

For this question, Park's bowl is in position 4. By Rule 2, that means Olivera's and Serra's bowls must be in positions 3 and 5, in either order. With position 5 filled, there's no place left for Neiman's bowl. So, Neiman's bowl must be eliminated—cross it off the entity list for this new sketch. That leaves the bowls of Larsen, Mills, Reigel, and Vance. Given that only one of Larsen's and Mills's bowls can be chosen, the bowls of Reigel and Vance both must be chosen.

L/M N̶ Ⓞ Ⓟ Ⓡ Ⓢ Ⓥ

_	O/S	P	S/O	_	
1	2	3	4	5	6
~R					

Reigel's bowl cannot be displayed in position 2 (Rule 3). So, the only bowls left that can fill position 2 are Larsen's, Mills's, and Vance's, making **(A)** the correct answer.

10. (B) "If" / Must Be False (CANNOT Be True)

For this question, Larsen's bowl will be in position 1 and Olivera's bowl will be in position 4. With Larsen's bowl included, Mills's bowl must be out (Rule 1). Only one more bowl needs to be eliminated.

Ⓛ/M̶ N Ⓞ P R S V

L	_	_	O	_	_
1	2	3	4	5	6

Olivera's bowl limits the placement of Park's bowl, which would have to be surrounded by both Olivera's and Serra's bowls if included (Rule 2). So, Park's bowl could only be in position 3 or 5. However, if Park's bowl was in position 3, Serra's bowl would have to be in position 2, violating Rule 4. If Park's bowl were in position 5, Serra's bowl would be in position 6. However, that would leave no place for Neiman's bowl (Rule 5) or Reigel's bowl (Rule 3). That would eliminate too many bowls. There is no position to place Park's bowl. Therefore, Park's bowl must be the second bowl eliminated, making **(B)** the correct answer.

11. (B) Must Be True

The correct answer will be a potter whose bowl *must* be selected. The remaining four answers will list potters whose bowls could be left out.

Previous work helps make short work of this question. The correct answer to the Acceptability question and the sketch for the fourth question of the set show that Neiman's bowl need not be selected. That eliminates **(A)**. For the fifth question of the set, Park's bowl was left out. That eliminates **(C)**.

A little extra work with the sketch from the second question of the set puts an end to the testing. In that case, if either Larsen's or Mills's bowl is in position 4, then either Reigel's or Vance's bowl could be in position 6.

$$\frac{O/S}{1} \quad \frac{P}{2} \quad \frac{S/O}{3} \quad \frac{L/M}{4} \quad \frac{N}{5} \quad \frac{R/V}{6}$$

In that case, either Reigel's bowl or Vance's bowl could be left out, eliminating **(D)** and **(E)**. That leaves **(B)** as the correct answer. For further proof that Olivera must be there:

If Olivera's bowl was left out, then Park's bowl couldn't be displayed (Rule 2). That would mean everyone else's bowl would have to be included: Larsen's, Mills's, Neiman's, Reigel's, Serra's, and Vance's. However, that would violate Rule 1 by including Larsen's bowl with Mills's. That's unacceptable, so Olivera's bowl cannot be left out, which means it must be included.

12. (A) "If" / Must Be True

For this question, the display will include Neiman's, Park's, and Reigel's bowls. The sketch from the second question of the set already set up what would happen if Neiman's and Park's bowls were included. Neiman's bowl would be in position 5, and Park's bowl would have to be in position 2, with Olivera's and Serra's bowls in positions 1 and 3, in either order.

This question merely adds Reigel's bowl to that display. With position 1 filled, that leaves only position 6 for Reigel's bowl (Rule 3).

$$L /M\,\cancel{N}\,\cancel{O}\,\cancel{P}\,\cancel{R}\,\cancel{S}\,V$$
$$\frac{O/S}{1} \quad \frac{P}{2} \quad \frac{S/O}{3} \quad \frac{}{4} \quad \frac{N}{5} \quad \frac{R}{6}$$

With that, Reigel's bowl is definitely next to Neiman's bowl, making **(A)** the correct answer. **(B)**, **(D)**, and **(E)** all could be true with Vance's bowl in position 5, and **(C)** must be false.

Game 3: Office Selection

Step 1: Overview

Situation: Employees putting in requests for a new office

Entities: Four employees (Jackson, Larabee, Paulson, Torillo) and four offices (W, X, Y, Z)

Action: Sequencing/Matching Hybrid. Determine the order in which the employees select offices (Sequencing), and which office each employee selects (Matching). The employee rankings add a challenging wrinkle to this game, but they are nothing more than a series of limitations used to determine the assignment of offices. Ultimately, there's no action beyond the classic order-and-assign setup. Some may feel the employee rankings add a Process element to the game. However, Process games generally involve a repeated action, which this game does not have. Additionally, because each office is used exactly once, some may feel it is a Sequencing/Distribution Hybrid instead. However, a typical Sequencing/Distribution game has a sequence within each group—not a single sequence of entities with a second type of entity assigned to the first type. In the end, it's more important to understand what needs to be accomplished than to insist on applying an absolute label to the game.

Limitations: The overview provides no clear limitations. All restrictions in this game are clarified in the rules.

Step 2: Sketch

The ultimate goal is to determine the order in which the employees select offices and determine which office each employee selects. To display that, set up two rows. The employees will be entered on top, with their office selections entered below. (Two rows of slots would also work.)

$$\begin{array}{c c c c c} & 1 & 2 & 3 & 4 \\ \text{JLPT} & \rule{1.5em}{0.4pt} & \rule{1.5em}{0.4pt} & \rule{1.5em}{0.4pt} & \rule{1.5em}{0.4pt} \\ \text{wxyz} \end{array}$$

Step 3: Rules

Rule 1 prevents two people from selecting the same office. So, each office will be selected just once.

Rule 2 limits each employee to just one office. So, no employee can get greedy and choose two offices.

Rule 3 is the most significant. When it's an employee's turn to select an office, that employee will choose the first available office listed in his or her personal ranking.

Step 4: Deductions

The key to this game is understanding how Rule 3 works and affects the selection. The first person selected will get first choice of office. That person will choose the office he or she has ranked highest.

The second employee gets to choose from whatever offices remain. If that employee's top choice is available, the

employee will select that office. Otherwise, that employee will settle for the office he or she ranked second. Either way, the second employee will get one of the top two offices on his or her list.

The third employee may still be able to get his or her first choice, if it's still available. If not, the third employee may be able to choose the second office on his or her list, If *that's* not available, the third employee will have to settle for the third office on his or her list.

The final employee is stuck with whatever office is left at the end— regardless of where that employee ranked it.

1	2	3	4
1st rank	1st or 2nd rank	1st or 2nd or 3rd rank	Any rank

So, as an example, if Jackson goes first, Jackson would choose Y—the top-ranked choice on Jackson's list. If Larabee goes second, Larabee would then choose X because it's still available and it's the highest ranked office on Larabee's list. However, if Jackson chooses Y and Paulson goes second, Paulson cannot also choose Y (Rule 1). So, Paulson would have to choose the *next* office on Paulson's list: Z. This goes on until all offices are assigned.

With four employees and no restriction to their order, there are 24 possible outcomes. It's not worth considering all 24 ahead of time, but it is interesting to note two things:

Each employee has ranked office X or Y highest. So, whoever goes first will certainly choose one of those offices. Additionally, nobody ranks W first or second, so W will never be chosen first or second. Furthermore, the only person who ranks W third is Larabee—and even if Larabee goes third, there's no way for X and Z to both be unavailable. So, as it turns out, W will always be the last office selected—which also means that the final office will always be someone's third or fourth choice.

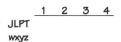

Step 5: Questions
13. (B) Partial Acceptability

The correct answer will list an acceptable selection of offices by the employees. The remaining answers will all be impossible. This would appear to be a standard Acceptability question, but the answers leave out one critical piece of information: the order in which the selection occurs.

Order or not, none of the answers violate the first two rules. Each answer lists one office per person, and no office is duplicated. That means all answers have to violate Rule 3. The only way to test that is to compare answers to the rankings provided in the overview and try to determine the order in which the selections were made.

For starters, whoever went first would have chosen his or her highest ranked office. That eliminates **(A)** and **(C)**, in which no one did that. In **(B)**, the only person who chose his or her highest ranked office is Larabee, who chose X. So, Larabee must have chosen first. After that, Jackson's and Paulson's highest preference would still be available, but not Torillo's. The next office on Torillo's list is Y, which is what Torillo chose. So, that works. With X and Y chosen, Jackson could go third, forced to choose the highest available office on Jackon's list: Z. That would leave W for Paulson.

	1	2	3	4
JLPT	L	T	J	P
wxyz	x	y	z	w

This answer works fine, making **(B)** the correct answer. For the record:

In **(D)** and **(E)**, the only person who chose his or her highest ranked office is Jackson, who chose Y. So, Jackson chose first in each answer. However, if either Larabee or Torillo went second, that person would get his or her highest preference: X. That doesn't happen in either answer, which means Paulson went second. With Y taken, Paulson would have to settle for the next office on Paulson's list: Z. However, both answers show Paulson choosing X. That can't happen, so both answers are impossible.

14. (C) Must Be True

The correct answer to this question must be true. The remaining answers may be possible, but could also be false.

Whoever goes first will certainly choose the office he or she ranked highest. So, at least that person has to get top choice, making **(C)** the correct answer. For the record:

If Jackson and Larabee go first and second, they could both choose their highest ranked offices (Y and X, respectively). Thus, more than one employee can choose the highest ranked office, which eliminates **(A)**.

In that same scenario, Torillo could go third, having to settle for the office ranked third on Torillo's list: Z. That would leave W for Paulson. Nobody would get the office ranked second on his or her list, which eliminates **(D)**.

	1	2	3	4
JLPT	J	L	T	P
wxyz	y	x	z	w
rank	1st	1st	3rd	4th

If Paulson goes first, Paulson would choose Y. After that, Jackson could go and would have to settle for the second office on Jackson's list: X. Then Larabee could go and would

also have to settle for an office ranked second: Z. Thus, more than one employee can choose an office ranked second, which eliminates **(B)**.

In that same scenario, Torillo would have to go fourth, settling for W—the last office on Torillo's list. Nobody would get the office ranked third on his or her list, which eliminates **(E)**.

	1	2	3	4
JLPT	P	J	L	T
wxyz	y	x	z	w
rank	1st	2nd	2nd	4th

15. (A) Could Be True

The correct answer for this question merely *could* be true. The wrong answers will all be impossible.

The first employee gets top choice, while the second employee gets his or her second choice, at worst. Only the last two employees might have to resort to their third choice. This could happen if Jackson goes third and chooses office Z. That would mean the first two employees chose Y and X (e.g., Paulson choosing Y first, then Torillo choosing X). If that happened, Larabee could go last. With X and Z chosen, Larabee would also settle for an office ranked third: W.

	1	2	3	4
JLPT	P	T	J	L
wxyz	y	x	z	w
rank	1st	1st	3rd	3rd

This is possible, making **(A)** the correct answer. For the record:

Only the last employee to choose is in danger of getting the office he or she ranked fourth. That's one employee and no more, which eliminates **(B)** and **(E)**. Similarly, only the last two employees could get stuck with the office they ranked third, and no more than that. That eliminates **(D)**.

There are only three offices ranked second on any employee's list: X, Y, and Z. The only way all of these employees get their second choice is for the first employee to choose the remaining office: W. However, no employee has W as a top option, so this can't happen. That eliminates **(C)**.

16. (E) "If" / Could Be True

For this question, Paulson selects office W. That's the last office on Paulson's list, which means the remaining employees must all select the other offices before Paulson goes. That means Paulson goes last.

	1	2	3	4
JLPT			P	
wxyz			w	

As usual, whoever goes first will get the office he or she ranked first. The second person will get an office he or she ranked first or second. The third person will get an office he or she ranked first, second, or third. Because of that, only one employee can get the office he or she ranked third, which eliminates **(B)**.

The three people remaining are Jackson, Larabee, and Torillo. If two of those people choose the office they ranked second, the remaining person would be first and get his or her top choice. However, this can't happen. Jackson's and Larabee's second choices would be X and Z, but Torillo would have chosen X first. Jackson's and Torillo's second choices would be X and Y, but Larabee would have chosen X first. And Larabee's and Torillo's second choices would be Y and Z, but Jackson would have chosen Y first. Therefore, **(A)** is impossible.

Three people cannot select their highest ranked office because each employee only has X or Y as a top choice—and only one person can get each office. That eliminates **(C)**.

X is Jackson's second choice, so Jackson couldn't go first and choose X. Nevertheless, if Jackson doesn't go first here, then Larabee or Torillo would, and either one of them would choose X first before Jackson gets a chance. So, Jackson won't get office X, which eliminates **(D)**.

That leaves **(E)** as the correct answer, which could happen if Torillo goes first and chooses X, leaving Larabee with the office Larabee ranked second: Z.

	1	2	3	4
JLPT	T	L	J	P
wxyz	x	z	y	w

17. (E) Must Be True

The correct answer here must be true. The remaining could all be false. Each answer lists an office that one employee *cannot* get. So, if the employee listed *could* get that office, the answer is wrong.

Jackson could choose office X if Paulson goes first and takes away Jackson's top choice of Y. That eliminates **(A)**.

Larabee could choose office W if Larabee goes last and everyone else chooses X, Y, and Z. That eliminates **(B)**.

Larabee could choose Z if Torillo goes first and takes away Larabee's top choice of X (as seen in the previous question). That eliminates **(C)**.

Torillo could certainly choose X if Torillo goes first. That eliminates **(D)**.

That leaves **(E)** as the correct answer. Sure enough, Paulson cannot select X, which is Paulson's third choice. That would require two employees to choose Y and Z before Paulson gets to choose X. However, Larabee and Torillo have X as a top choice. Even if Jackson went first and chose Y, Larabee or Torillo would go second and select X before Paulson gets the chance.

Game 4: Community Committee Volunteers

Step 1: Overview

Situation: Volunteers being assigned to a series of community committees

Entities: Five volunteers (Haddad, Joslin, Kwon, Molina, Nash), three committees (X, Y, Z), and three positions on each committee (leader, secretary, treasurer)

Action: Matching. Determine which volunteers are assigned to each committee and which position each volunteer holds on that committee.

Limitations: Each committee will consist of three volunteers, one for each of the three positions. That's a total of nine positions among three committees. With only five volunteers to choose from, some volunteers will be assigned to multiple committees. However, there is no minimum or maximum for each volunteer. Any volunteer can appear on one, two, or even all three committees.

(Note: Some may question whether every volunteer even has to be used. The overview never directly states that, although it can be argued that it's implied by the opening language: "Exactly five volunteers ... *are* being assigned." There have been games with entities that go unused, so it's wise to consider. However, Deductions in this game will make it impossible for anyone to be left out, so there is no penalty for overlooking that possibility here.)

Step 2: Sketch

Start by listing the volunteers by initial. Then, build a table with a column for each committee. In each column, there should be three slots: one for the leader, one for the secretary, and one for the treasurer. Keep all of the corresponding slots lined up and labeled for clear reference.

H J K M N

	x	y	z
lead	___	___	___
secr	___	___	___
trea	___	___	___

Step 3: Rules

Rule 1 dictates that Nash be the leader of any committee to which Nash is assigned. While it's unknown which committees Nash will join, it is certain that Nash will never be a secretary or treasurer. Add "~N" next to the secretary and treasurer rows.

Rule 2 limits Molina to one committee. That could be any of the three at this point, so add a "1" above M in the entity list to indicate this restriction.

Rule 3 establishes Kwon on Y, but not on Z. There's no indication what position Kwon will hold on Y. For now, add a "K" under column Y and "~K" under column Z.

Rule 4 establishes Joslin as the secretary for Y, but prevents Joslin from being on X or Z. Add J to the appropriate slot in column Y, and add "~J" under columns X and Z.

Step 4: Deductions

There are lots of deductions to be had in this game, so take some time to set as much up as possible. The key is to take negative information and turn it into positive information. Start with committee Z. By Rules 3 and 4, that committee cannot contain Kwon or Joslin. So, the three positions have to be filled by the remaining three volunteers: Haddad, Molina, and Nash. By Rule 1, Nash will be the leader. Haddad and Molina will be the secretary and treasurer, in either order.

With Molina on Z, Molina is done (Rule 2). That means Molina will not be on X or Y. By Rule 4, Joslin is not on X, either. Once again, that leaves three positions to be filled by the remaining volunteers: Haddad, Kwon, and Nash. Again, Nash will be the leader. Haddad and Kwon will be the secretary and treasurer, in either order.

That leaves committee Y. Joslin is the secretary (Rule 4), and Kwon will be either the leader or the treasurer (Rule 3). The remaining position belongs to either Haddad or Nash.

	x	y	z
lead	N		N
secr	H/K	J	H/M
trea	K/H		M/H
		K	
		H/N	

Step 5: Questions

18. (E) Partial Acceptability

The correct answer will be one possible assignment of volunteers to Z. The four wrong answers will be unacceptable.

Z cannot contain Kwon (Rule 3) or Joslin (Rule 4), which eliminates **(A)**, **(B)**, and **(C)**. Nash can only be a leader (Rule 1). That eliminates **(D)**, making **(E)** the correct answer. The Master Sketch confirms this possible outcome.

19. (C) "If" / Could Be True EXCEPT

For this question, the one correct answer must be false and the four incorrect answers could be true. The new "If" says Kwon will be treasurer of two committees. Kwon cannot be assigned to Z (Rule 3), so Kwon will be treasurer of X and Y. By the Master Sketch, that means Haddad will be the secretary of X and either Haddad or Nash will be the leader of Y. The assignments for Z remain uncertain.

	x	y	z
lead	N	H/N	N
secr	H	J	H/M
trea	K	K	M/H

With that, all of the answers are possible except for **(C)** because Kwon must be the treasurer for X. That makes **(C)** the correct answer.

20. (B) Must Be True EXCEPT

The four wrong answers to this question must be true no matter what. The correct answer might be possible, but could also be false.

Haddad could be assigned to Y, but Nash could be assigned to Y in lieu of Haddad. In that case, Y would consist of Nash as leader, Joslin as secretary, and Kwon as treasurer. Thus, Haddad does not have to be assigned to Y, making **(B)** the correct answer.

21. (B) "If" / Complete and Accurate List

For this question, Kwon is the leader of one committee. Nash is already the leader of X and Z, so Kwon will have to be the leader for Y. Joslin is the secretary for Y (Rule 4). That leaves Haddad or Nash to be treasurer, but Nash cannot be treasurer (Rule 1). So, Haddad is the treasurer of Y. No further deductions can be made to the other committees.

	x	y	z
lead	N	K	N
secr	H/K	J	H/M
trea	K/H	H	M/H

The question asks for a complete list of the committees that are entirely determined. That would be Y, and nothing else, making **(B)** the correct answer.

22. (C) Completely Determine

The correct answer to this question will make it possible to determine which volunteer is assigned to each position on each committee with complete certainty. The remaining answers will leave some uncertainty.

If Haddad was the leader for one committee, it would have to be Y. However, that would not help determine anything further about X or Z. That eliminates **(A)**.

If Haddad was the secretary of two committees, they would be X and Z. That would help determine the treasurer for those committees, too. However, that would leave Y open-ended, with Kwon still able to be leader or treasurer. That eliminates **(B)**.

If Haddad was the treasurer of all three committees, then Kwon would be the secretary for X and Molina would be secretary for Z. Kwon still needs a position on Y, so Kwon would be leader.

	x	y	z
lead	N	K	N
secr	K	J	M
trea	H	H	H

With everything complete, that makes **(C)** the correct answer. For the record:

If Kwon was treasurer of two committees (as seen in the second question of this game), they would be X and Y. However, the leader of Y is still uncertain, as is the secretary and treasurer of Z. That eliminates **(D)**.

If Nash is the leader of all three committees, Kwon would have to be treasurer of Y. However, the secretary and treasurer positions of X and Z would still be uncertain. That eliminates **(E)**.

23. (C) Rule Substitution

For this question, Rule 2 is removed from the game. The correct answer will be a rule that could replace Rule 2 without changing anything from the original setup. In other words, it will reestablish the original rule without adding any new restrictions.

The original rule restricted Molina to one committee. Because Kwon and Joslin cannot be on Z (Rules 3 and 4), Molina will certainly be assigned to that one committee. The correct answer will prevent Molina from being assigned to any more committees, without further restricting anyone else.

Haddad and Nash could be on all three committees. Assigning either one to more committees than Molina would allow Molina to be on two committees. That eliminates **(A)** and **(E)**.

Joslin could only be on one committee (Rule 4). If Joslin was assigned more than Molina, Molina couldn't be on any committees, which would lead to an impossible scenario. That eliminates **(B)**.

Kwon can only be on two committees. If Kwon was assigned to more than Molina, Molina would be confined to one committee, just as the original rules intended. That makes **(C)** the correct answer. For the record:

By the deductions, Haddad is at least on Z. If Molina were on *more* committees, Molina would have to be on at least two, contrary to the original rules. That eliminates **(D)**.

Section IV: Logical Reasoning

Q#	Question Type	Correct	Difficulty
1	Principle (Identify/Strengthen)	A	★
2	Point at Issue	C	★
3	Paradox	E	★
4	Strengthen	B	★
5	Assumption (Sufficient)	A	★
6	Flaw	C	★
7	Role of a Statement	D	★
8	Main Point	A	★
9	Flaw	D	★
10	Inference	D	★★
11	Weaken	D	★★
12	Flaw	A	★★
13	Inference	D	★
14	Role of a Statement	E	★★★
15	Inference	C	★★
16	Role of a Statement	B	★★
17	Strengthen	B	★★
18	Inference	D	★★★★
19	Weaken	A	★★★★
20	Assumption (Sufficient)	B	★★★★
21	Paradox (EXCEPT)	B	★★
22	Role of a Statement	C	★★★
23	Parallel Reasoning	B	★★
24	Assumption (Sufficient)	D	★
25	Parallel Flaw	B	★★
26	Assumption (Necessary)	E	★★★

1. (A) Principle (Identify/Strengthen)

Step 1: Identify the Question Type

The question directly asks for a principle, one that will "justify" the reasoning provided. That means it is an Identify the Principle question that will require the same skills as a Strengthen question.

Step 2: Untangle the Stimulus

The pundit is arguing that Grenier probably won't be elected mayor. As evidence, the pundit points out how Grenier has changed her position on wages and now voters see her as insincere.

Step 3: Make a Prediction

The pundit's prediction about Grenier's electability hinges entirely on voters' perception of insincerity. For this argument to work, Grenier must be acting on the principle that the appearance of insincerity will affect the way people vote.

Step 4: Evaluate the Answer Choices

(A) matches the principle, connecting insincerity to people's voting habits.

(B) is a 180. The fact that people view Grenier as insincere is a pretty good sign that they *did* notice her change in stance.

(C) is Out of Scope. It's not about voters *agreeing* with Grenier, it's about them viewing Grenier as insincere.

(D) is Out of Scope. The voters' financial concerns are not an issue here. It's all about Grenier's flip-flopping.

(E) is Out of Scope. The pundit never mentions what beliefs the voters have, and this does nothing to justify the conclusion about Grenier being elected.

2. (C) Point at Issue

Step 1: Identify the Question Type

The stimulus provides arguments by two speakers, and the question asks for something over which they "disagree." That makes this a Point at Issue question.

Step 2: Untangle the Stimulus

Albert condemns Swenson's book as poor scholarship, but argues that it still has some value in that it encourages further research. Yvonne uses an analogy to counter Albert: saying the book has value is the same as saying a virus has value because it encourages epidemiologists.

Step 3: Make a Prediction

Sure, viruses might give epidemiologists something to think about, but it's hard to argue that viruses are really valuable. That's the argument Yvonne is making about Swenson's book: it might encourage a few people to think about sun exposure, but that doesn't make it valuable. And that's the point at issue: Albert finds value in the book, while Yvonne finds none.

Step 4: Evaluate the Answer Choices

(C) is correct. Albert believes it *should* be considered valuable, while Yvonne feels it *shouldn't*.

(A) is only mentioned in Albert's argument. Yvonne offers no argument against that claim.

(B) is a 180. Despite the value Albert finds in the book, he does admit it's poor scholarship, and Yvonne is all too likely to agree with that claim.

(D) is a Distortion. Yvonne does not argue that the book *didn't* spur new research. She merely argues that such encouragement is not enough to consider the book valuable.

(E) is Out of Scope. All that's stated is that Swenson's book *did* stimulate new research. Neither Albert nor Yvonne addresses books that do *not* stimulate new research.

3. (E) Paradox

Step 1: Identify the Question Type

The question asks for something that will "explain" a "surprising finding." That makes this a Paradox question.

Step 2: Untangle the Stimulus

According to the researchers, people in countries with high income are more likely to become entrepreneurs than people in countries with moderate income, which makes sense because high-income countries offer more business opportunities. Somehow, though, people in *low*-income countries are even *more* likely to start new businesses.

Step 3: Make a Prediction

Using the researcher's reasoning, the high-income countries have the most business opportunities, which should make them the most likely to experience new businesses. So, why are the low-income countries, with theoretically the *fewest* business opportunities, experiencing an even higher rate of new businesses? The correct answer will provide a significant difference to low-income countries that encourages people to start new businesses despite the lack of opportunities.

Step 4: Evaluate the Answer Choices

(E) provides an explanation. It's precisely *because* of the lack of business opportunities that people in low-income countries start their own businesses; there are no other viable options. So, instead of settling for a terrible job or unemployment, they're forced to create their own business.

(A) is an Irrelevant Comparison. The number of employees in new business doesn't help explain *why* citizens of low-income countries are starting such businesses while lacking opportunities.

(B) is a 180. This gives citizens of low-income countries even *less* incentive and *less* assistance, which makes it even harder to understand why they're taking so many risks on new businesses.

(C) is a 180. If businesses in low-income countries were more likely to succeed, then *that* might explain why so many citizens there are taking the risk. However, with equal success rates, the question remains why they're starting new businesses in the face of little opportunity.

(D) just refers to the disillusion faced by entrepreneurs in high-income countries. However, there's no reason to believe that entrepreneurs in low-income countries would be any different, which means the mystery goes unresolved.

4. (B) Strengthen

Step 1: Identify the Question Type
The question asks for something that will "support," or Strengthen, the given argument.

Step 2: Untangle the Stimulus
People avoided a particular film, and its director argues that this was not because of a few negative reviews. As evidence, the director suggests that her films have small audiences to begin with, and those people had other similar films to choose from that weekend.

Step 3: Make a Prediction
The director overlooks an alternative solution for audiences: If they wanted to, they could just go out and see all the movies that interested them. If people had the option of seeing multiple movies, then perhaps they *did* avoid the director's film because of the reviews. Removing that possibility would help the director's cause.

Step 4: Evaluate the Answer Choices
(B) helps the director's defense. By limiting themselves to one movie, filmgoers were split, meaning reduced audiences for all films—regardless of what the reviews said.

(A) is a 180. If the one or two negative reviews were the *only* reviews, and *nobody* reviewed the film positively, then that is more likely to be the reason people shunned the film.

(C) is a 180. In this case, negative reviews could still explain why people shunned the movie despite more people seeing movies overall.

(D) is a 180. If other films received positive reviews while the director's film received negative reviews, this makes it *more* likely that the reviews were responsible.

(E) is irrelevant. The director admits that the number of viewers for her films is already "relatively small," so the movie choices of most people has no effect on why *her* usual audience members stayed away.

5. (A) Assumption (Sufficient)

Step 1: Identify the Question Type
The question asks for something that would help the argument reach its conclusion. The blank in the argument is preceded by the Keyword *since*. That means the blank will be

filled in with a missing piece of evidence, which is the definition of an assumption.

Step 2: Untangle the Stimulus
Despite how complex some scientific issues are, readers are often fascinated by stories about those issues. Unfortunately, the author argues that popular magazines won't cover those issues very often.

Step 3: Make a Prediction
If readers are so fascinated by these stories, why not cover them? The only evidence given is that the stories are too complex and readers of popular magazines struggle to understand them. The author must assume that such challenges override public interest when it comes to deciding what popular magazines cover.

Step 4: Evaluate the Answer Choices
(A) is a match. If editors base their decision on how likely a story is to be understood, that would make it clear why popular magazines are leaving out these complex stories despite the public interest.

(B) is a 180. If a magazine's success depends on appealing to readers, then it makes no sense for a magazine to leave out such fascinating stories.

(C) is irrelevant. How common such issues are does nothing to explain why magazines would leave them out.

(D) is irrelevant. Making readers unable to determine how much they really understand does nothing to further the magazine's decision to not cover these stories.

(E) is irrelevant. Even if people don't actively seek out such articles, that doesn't explain why popular magazines won't at least try to appeal to their readers' fascination.

6. (C) Flaw

Step 1: Identify the Question Type
The question asks why the given argument is "vulnerable to criticism," which means it is asking for the flaw in the argument.

Step 2: Untangle the Stimulus
The author is refuting the newspaper's claim that it covers the most popular high school sports. As evidence, the author cites that track is more popular in the school than basketball, yet the newspaper covers basketball and not track.

Step 3: Make a Prediction
This is a classic case of equivocation—equating two different ideas merely because they are expressed by the same word. In this case, when the author says track is more popular than basketball, *popular* refers to how many students *participate* in a sport. When the newspaper uses the term, *popular* refers to how interested people are in *reading about* the sport. Even though fewer students play basketball, basketball could still

be a more popular sport among readers. The correct answer will point out this confusion.

Step 4: Evaluate the Answer Choices

(C) is correct. The author misinterprets the meaning of *popular*, thinking it only refers to the number of students who play a given sport.

(A) is Out of Scope. The author makes no claim about one thing causing another.

(B) is a Distortion. The statistics only refer to 20 percent of the school population, but the numbers are substantial enough to confirm the author's comparison between track and basketball. There's no flaw there. The flaw comes when the author uses this comparison to argue a claim about popularity among the newspaper's readers.

(D) refers to circular reasoning (using evidence that merely restates the conclusion), but that's not the case here. The evidence and the conclusion are adequately distinct.

(E) is a 180. This not an ad hominem attack. The author uses statistical evidence to back up the conclusion, which only attacks the newspaper's claim, not the newspaper itself.

7. (D) Role of a Statement

Step 1: Identify the Question Type

The question cites a claim from the stimulus and asks for its "role in the argument." That makes this a Role of a Statement question.

Step 2: Untangle the Stimulus

Most people feel it's environmentally friendly to buy food from local farmers. The author argues otherwise. While transportation concerns are valid, some distant locations may have production practices that are more environmentally friendly and can thus be preferable overall.

Step 3: Make a Prediction

The claim in question is in the very first sentence, presented as something "widely believed." Once the author uses the Keyword *But*, it's clear the author is not convinced. By the conclusion, the author expresses the exact opposite of that opening belief: buying local food is *not* always the best choice. The correct answer will identify the opening claim as a mere belief, and one that the author refutes.

Step 4: Evaluate the Answer Choices

(D) is correct.

(A) is a Distortion. The argument is not *based* on the claim in question; it's designed to *refute* that claim.

(B) is a Distortion. While the claim does support buying local foods, this answer ignores the rest of the argument in which the author does *not* support that activity.

(C) is a Distortion. While the author ultimately suggests buying local foods is not always the best idea, the claim in question does not itself provide reason for that rejection.

(E) is a Distortion. The claim in question is "widely believed," which means it's a point *others* might argue. However, the author's conclusion argues the opposite of this claim.

8. (A) Main Point

Step 1: Identify the Question Type

The question asks for the *conclusion* of the argument, making this a Main Point question.

Step 2: Untangle the Stimulus

This author is praising technology for improving our lives, and not just for its direct effects. It has indirectly helped the growth of many businesses (design, production, testing, etc.), which helps increase economic and spiritual well-being.

Step 3: Make a Prediction

The phrase "After all" is used to indicate evidence for the sentence before it. In this case, the second sentence about the growth of various industries is evidence to support the first sentence that technology is not just helping people via direct application. The final sentence regarding the effect on jobs, taxes, and renewal is just further support for the claim in the first sentence. Thus, the main point is that first sentence: technology is improving our lives, and not just directly.

Step 4: Evaluate the Answer Choices

(A) summarizes the main point perfectly, praising technology and not just for its direct applications.

(B) is evidence, not the conclusion.

(C) is from the last sentence, but that's just further evidence for the conclusion that technology is improving our lives.

(D) is a Distortion. The author doesn't claim that it's either creation *or* direct application that's helping, and the last two sentences list more reasons than that (including testing and marketing).

(E) is Extreme. While this accurately expresses some of the ways in which technology is helping, these are not the *only* ways. The author suggests that these are ways *in addition* to direct application, as mentioned in the first sentence.

9. (D) Flaw

Step 1: Identify the Question Type

The question asks why the given argument is "vulnerable to criticism," which is a common way for asking for the flaw in the argument.

Step 2: Untangle the Stimulus

The author argues that Joshi's votes are being swayed by campaign contributions. As evidence, the author cites Joshi's sizable contributions from property developers as well as Joshi's frequent votes that benefit property developers.

Step 3: Make a Prediction

It would be easy to claim the flaw of Correlation vs. Causation here. Joshi's votes do line up conveniently with the interest of his supporters (correlation), but it's not logically proper to conclude that his votes were *influenced* by those contributions (causation). However, there's more to this story. The contributions are for Joshi's *reelection*, which means Joshi was already city councillor and probably voted before he even needed those contributions. So, even if there *is* causality, the author likely has it backwards: maybe it's his pro-developer votes that influenced the contributions and not the other way around.

Step 4: Evaluate the Answer Choices

(D) points out the author's error. The author assumes that large contributions were the cause of Joshi's actions when it really could be the other way around: large contributions are the *result* of his actions.

(A) is a clever Distortion. While this does raise the question of Correlation vs. Causation, this states the author assumes that the "earlier events" were the cause. However, the author argues that large contributions are the cause of Joshi's voting behavior, but there's no evidence that contributions were made *before* Joshi voted.

(B) raises a common flaw, but one that has no bearing here. The author makes no mention of anything that's "necessary."

(C) is Out of Scope. The author never broaches the subject of morality.

(E) suggests circular reasoning. However, the evidence describes correlated events, and the conclusion implies causality. Those are distinct ideas, and not merely a repetition of one another.

10. (D) Inference

Step 1: Identify the Question Type

For this question, the given information will "provide reason" for choosing the correct answer, which makes this an Inference question. However, unlike most Inference questions, the correct answer here will be the one that will be "reject[ed]" by the information provided. In other words, the correct answer will be the one that is false.

Step 2: Untangle the Stimulus

Some people say that government can't manage financial institutions and thus shouldn't take over failing banks. *However*, the columnist argues against that claim, saying that government wouldn't actually *run* the banks it takes over. The government would assign new managers who know what they're doing, similar to how politicians with little military

experience staff the defense department with proper officials who know what they're doing.

Step 3: Make a Prediction

The gist of the columnist's argument is that it's okay for government to take over failing banks. The day-to-day business will be handled just fine by proper managers, not the government itself. The correct answer will be contradictory to these points.

Step 4: Evaluate the Answer Choices

(D) is the correct answer. The columnist states that, even though the government would *own* the bank, it wouldn't actually *manage* the bank. That would be done by qualified managers, just like our military is managed by top appointed officials. So, such banks *can* be well managed.

(A) is Out of Scope. The columnist doesn't mention the knowledge needed for either job, so this answer couldn't be rejected.

(B) is a 180. The use of the analogy suggests that politicians certainly *are* doing a fine job in selecting military officials. That's why the columnist contradicts people who believe government couldn't manage banks as well.

(C) is Out of Scope and potentially a 180. The columnist never says anything about politicians running the bank. Besides, the columnist states that government would *not* manage day-to-day operations, supporting (and not rejecting) this idea that politicians are not right for the job.

(E) is Out of Scope. The argument is about taking over failed banks, not sound ones. It's perfectly possible that the columnist would agree with (and not reject) government leaving sound banks alone.

11. (D) Weaken

Step 1: Identify the Question Type

The question directly asks for something that weakens the given argument.

Step 2: Untangle the Stimulus

The author cites polls of university students in which graduating students are more likely to be against reducing social services than first-year students. The author uses this to conclude that university graduates would favor increased social services more than the overall population.

Step 3: Make a Prediction

This is a classic case of faulty representativeness. The poll only involves *students*, yet the author dares to apply the findings to all "people with a university education" and the "overall population." This sweeping generalization requires two assumptions: 1) The views of graduating students represent the views of anyone with a university education. 2) The views of students overall represent that of the overall population. Any answer that contradicts one of these assumptions will weaken the argument.

Step 4: Evaluate the Answer Choices

(D) weakens the argument by questioning a major assumption. The views of today's graduating students don't necessarily reflect the views of all past graduates. If so many past graduates favor *reduced* social services, that would contradict the author's belief.

(A) is a 180. This suggests that the polls were done carefully to avoid error, giving further credence to the author's argument.

(B) is a 180. This just provides reasoning *why* university graduates would favor increased services, which would only support the author's belief.

(C) is a 180. Ignoring the "retired" part, this just compares graduates to nongraduates, and graduates are less likely to favor reductions. That makes graduates more likely to favor *increases*, exactly as the author claims.

(E) is a 180. If the graduating students have stronger opinions, they'd be less likely to change their minds. The other students would be *more* likely to change their minds, eventually making pro-social service a majority opinion among graduates.

12. (A) Flaw

Step 1: Identify the Question Type

The question directly asks why the argument is flawed.

Step 2: Untangle the Stimulus

Some critics claim a particular movie will encourage bad behavior, but the author claims that view is based on a flawed survey. Thus, the author concludes that the critics are wrong.

Step 3: Make a Prediction

This is a common error on the LSAT. Yes, the survey cited was flawed. However, even if the survey was flawed, the critics' opinion could still be valid for *other* reasons. Bad evidence does not imply a bad conclusion.

Step 4: Evaluate the Answer Choices

(A) describes this classic flaw. The author infers that the critics are wrong just because their evidence is unsatisfactory (i.e., the survey was flawed).

(B) is Out of Scope. The only claim provided is one the author claims is false. There is no pejorative (i.e., disparaging) claim that's true to make such a comparison.

(C) is not a flaw here. The author doesn't rely on a sample; the author merely relies on evidence that a particular survey is flawed.

(D) is incorrect. The author *does* attack the critics' argument by attacking the study they use to support their claim. The author makes no attack on the critics themselves.

(E) gets the logic backwards. The author fails to consider that, even though their *evidence* is faulty, the critics' *conclusion* may still be true ... not the other way around.

13. (D) Inference

Step 1: Identify the Question Type

The correct answer "must ... be true" based on the information given, making this an Inference question.

Step 2: Untangle the Stimulus

The information is clear: most skilled banjo players are skilled guitar players, but not the other way around.

Step 3: Make a Prediction

Some sample numbers could help clear this up. Say there are 100 banjo players. In that case, at least 51 of them are also good guitar players. However, that overlap group of 51 people does *not* represent most guitar players. So, there must be more guitar players (say 500) than banjo players.

Step 4: Evaluate the Answer Choices

(D) must be true. After all, if there were an equal number of guitar and banjo players, then a majority overlap would be a majority overlap for *both* groups, not just one.

(A) could be true, but need not be. There could be millions of skilled guitar players who are not good at the banjo, yet only a couple of hundred skilled banjo players.

(B) is Out of Scope. There's nothing in the stimulus about success rates—only the number of people who have the skills.

(C) is Out of Scope. The stimulus only provides information about numbers, not what skills are required.

(E) is a 180. If there were more banjo players, and most of them were good guitar players, then it wouldn't be possible for most guitar players to be unable to play banjo. (To illustrate, if there were 100 banjo players, and most were good guitar players, at least 51 would be good at both. With 99 guitar players total or less, 51 players who could also play banjo would automatically be a majority, too.)

14. (E) Role of a Statement

Step 1: Identify the Question Type

This question provides a claim from the stimulus and asks for its "role" in the argument, making this a Role of a Statement question.

Step 2: Untangle the Stimulus

To start a company, one does need entrepreneurial abilities, but can also fail without proper management skills (e.g., ability to analyze trends). Hence, the author concludes that *both* entrepreneurial and management skills are important.

Step 3: Make a Prediction

The claim in question is part of the third sentence, which begins "For instance." That indicates it's part of the example used to support the claim before it: some companies fail due to a lack of managerial skills. That claim, in turn, is used to support the author's final conclusion (indicated by *Hence*) that success depends on both entrepreneurial and management skills. The correct answer will describe this two-phase function: the claim is an example to support a point that is ultimately used to support the main conclusion.

Step 4: Evaluate the Answer Choices

(E) is a match.

(A) is not accurate. The conclusion is the last sentence, not the claim in question.

(B) is a Distortion. The author's argument is not designed to explain anything.

(C) is a 180. It's a significant example that justifies the author's primary piece of evidence. While the argument could potentially function without it, it still serves as much more than a mere side note.

(D) is inaccurate. The conclusion does not mention company growth. Instead, the claim about company growth leads *indirectly* to the conclusion by supporting the claim about the need for managerial skills.

15. (C) Inference

Step 1: Identify the Question Type

The correct answer will be "supported by the information" given, making this an Inference question.

Step 2: Untangle the Stimulus

The author dismisses the efforts of outsiders bringing fresh ideas to a field. The author claims that solving problems requires understanding, which in turn requires experience.

Step 3: Make a Prediction

Notice the very strong language in the last sentence. *Only* people with understanding can solve problems, and *no one* gets that understanding without experience. So, by that logic, anyone without experience in a field will be unable to solve problems in that field. Alternatively, by contrapositive, if someone *does* come up with a solution, that person *must* have experience in that field.

Step 4: Evaluate the Answer Choices

(C) is logically deducible from the last sentence. All solutions, creative or otherwise, must come from someone with experience.

(A) is a Distortion. The author never correlates experience with creativity.

(B) is a Distortion. Experience is said to be necessary for coming up with solutions, not sufficient. It's possible that most people have the experience but are *still* unable to find solutions.

(D) is Out of Scope. The author makes no mention of variation among different levels of complexity.

(E) is Extreme. While outsiders will be incapable of devising solutions to problems, that doesn't mean they should be denied *any* responsibility without training.

16. (B) Role of a Statement

Step 1: Identify the Question Type

The question provides a claim from the stimulus and asks for its "role" in the argument. That makes this a Role of a Statement question.

Step 2: Untangle the Stimulus

According to the researcher, dinosaurs lack a feature usually found in warm-blooded creatures. Some believe that makes dinosaurs cold-blooded, but the researcher disagrees. Some dinosaurs were discovered in areas where cold-blooded animals couldn't survive.

Step 3: Make a Prediction

The claim in question is the last sentence. However, that's not the conclusion. This argument has the common structure of presenting a point of view and rejecting it. The author's conclusion is that paleobiologists are wrong, and there *were* warm-blooded dinosaurs. The claim in question, that only warm-blooded animals could survive in the area where certain dinosaurs lived, is the author's evidence in support of that conclusion.

Step 4: Evaluate the Answer Choices

(B) correctly identifies the last sentence as supporting evidence.

(A) is a 180. The last sentence *supports* the author's conclusion.

(C) is a Distortion. While it certainly contradicts the claim that all dinosaurs are cold-blooded, it doesn't negate the claim about the missing turbinates.

(D) is incorrect. The author's conclusion is that the paleobiologists are mistaken.

(E) is a Distortion. The existence of dinosaurs in Australia and Alaska is not support for *why* warm-blooded animals can't survive there.

17. (B) Strengthen

Step 1: Identify the Question Type

The question asks for something that will "justify" the given application, which makes this a Strengthen question. This is a variation that involves a principle and a specific situation that supposedly applies that principle. The application usually leaves something out from the principle, and the correct answer will add the missing piece.

Step 2: Untangle the Stimulus
The principle is that government should always allow people to express their beliefs, as long as expressing that belief isn't harmful to others. The application states that government shouldn't have repressed Calista from expressing her belief about the link between cell phones and cancer.

Step 3: Make a Prediction
The problem with the application is that the principle doesn't entirely allow *all* beliefs to be expressed. There are possible exceptions, namely beliefs that could be harmful to people. To completely match the principle, it's important to know that Calista's view isn't an exception. In other words, the correct answer needs to confirm that Calista's views aren't harmful to others.

Step 4: Evaluate the Answer Choices
(B) fills in the final piece. By confirming that Calista's beliefs are valid and can actually *help* people, her beliefs don't meet the exception of the principle and thus should not be repressed, just as the application concludes.

(A) is not enough because it doesn't reveal the results of the research. If they found no link, then Calista's beliefs *could* be harmful to people, and the principle would allow for repression.

(C) is a Distortion. It doesn't matter if she *believes* people won't be harmed. It's whether or not people are actually going to *be* unharmed that determines whether the principle applies.

(D) could be a 180. It's unknown if Calista's evidence is strong or not, and if it's not, this suggests that her beliefs could be harmful. In that case, the application could be wrong as the principle would allow for repression.

(E) depends on people being convinced. Without knowing that for sure, it's still unsure if Calista's views are harmful or not. Thus, it can't be determined if the principle properly applies or not.

18. (D) Inference

Step 1: Identify the Question Type
The question asks for something that can be "properly inferred" from the given information, which makes this an Inference question.

Step 2: Untangle the Stimulus
Reading an alphabetic language requires two things: phonemic awareness and learning how sounds are symbolized by letters. Many kids have learned to read an alphabetic language despite learning a method called "whole-language," which emphasizes the way words sound.

Step 3: Make a Prediction
The whole-language method is said to emphasize the way words sound, which fits the concept of phonemic awareness (knowing that language can be broken into sounds). However, kids learning from this method are said to be able to read alphabetic languages. By the second claim, that would require learning how sounds are represented by letters. So, it must be true that those kids were able to learn how sounds are represented by letters.

Step 4: Evaluate the Answer Choices
(D) must be true. By the second claim, because there are kids taught the whole-language method that *can* read alphabetic languages, those kids must have been able to learn how letters represent sounds.

(A) is Extreme. The stimulus only talks about what "many" children were able to do. There's no evidence that the whole-language method "invariably succeeds" at anything.

(B) is Extreme. This happened for "many" children, but it's not assured this will happen.

(C) is an Extreme Distortion. Phonemic awareness and knowledge of how sounds are represented are *necessary*, but some people can have both skills and still be unable to read alphabetic languages. And even if someone *was* unable to read such a language, they could still have one skill and not the other. They wouldn't have to be missing *both*.

(E) is a Distortion. Those students who did learn to read alphabetic languages must have learned how to represent sounds symbolically, but there's no evidence that they learned that from the whole-language method. They could have learned a second method that gave them that knowledge.

19. (A) Weaken

Step 1: Identify the Question Type
The question asks for something that "undermines" the argument, which is common LSAT language for a Weaken question.

Step 2: Untangle the Stimulus
According to studies, more pedestrians get hit by a car when using crosswalks than when not using them. The author argues this is due to a false sense of security. People think they're automatically safer in crosswalks and are less likely to look both ways before crossing.

Step 3: Make a Prediction
The author provides one reasonable explanation, but overlooks any other reason why more people are getting hit within the crosswalk. Similar arguments have appeared numerous times on the LSAT, and the author always makes the same assumption: that an equal number of people do both activities (i.e., an equal number use the crosswalk as

don't use it). However, if a lot more people use the crosswalk, there's just more opportunity there for an accident. It's pure statistics. The author would have less reason to bring up the sense of security.

Step 4: Evaluate the Answer Choices

(A) is the common weakener to this kind of argument.

(B) is irrelevant. An increase in incidents overall doesn't change the author's explanation for why more such incidents happen *in* the crosswalk rather than *out*.

(C) is a 180. This strengthens the author's contention that people have a false sense of security. They just trust the crosswalk signals and don't bother looking at the traffic themselves.

(D) is a 180. If drivers are more alert at crosswalks, then it's more likely the cause of the problem has to do with the pedestrians—exactly what the author is contending.

(E) is a 180. This says that safety measures (e.g., crosswalks) make people less cautious, which is pretty much exactly what the author is claiming.

20. (B) Assumption (Sufficient)

Step 1: Identify the Question Type

The correct answer will complete the argument "if" it is "assumed." That makes this a Sufficient Assumption question.

Step 2: Untangle the Stimulus

Selena claims to be psychic. The author concludes that determining the validity of her claim will provide proof if psychic powers really exist.

Step 3: Make a Prediction

The author argues that knowing whether Selena's claim is true or not will confirm the possibility of psychic powers. In other words, if Selena *does* have psychic powers, then they exist. If Selena does *not* have psychic powers, then they do *not* exist.

If	Selena is psychic	→	possible

If	Selena ~ psychic	→	~ possible

The first claim is logically sound. If Selena has psychic powers, then *of course* they exist. However, what if Selena is *not* psychic? The author offers no evidence that psychic powers would be impossible for anyone else. For this argument to be valid, the author is assuming that that is the case.

Step 4: Evaluate the Answer Choices

(B) is correct. This says that Selena *must* have psychic powers to prove their existence. If she doesn't, then they don't exist—and it's logical to say that if she *does* have such powers, then they *do* exist. Put those two together, and the author's conclusion is confirmed: whether Selena has such powers will determine whether they exist.

(A) is a Distortion. If Selena was found to be *not* psychic, this answer still wouldn't confirm or deny the existence of psychic powers. It would still be possible that psychic ability has just yet to be discovered.

(C) is not good enough. Even if it *were* possible to determine Selena's ability for sure, what would happen if it was determined that she was *wrong* and wasn't psychic? The argument would still be unconvincing because perhaps somebody *else* could be psychic.

(D) is a 180. This suggests that finding out Selena's claim is false would lead to uncertainty. The author argues that a conclusion would be certain either way—whether Selena's claim is true or not.

(E) is an Extreme Distortion. The author says *if* we find out about Selena's claim, then that will be good enough. This answer makes it *necessary* to find out about her claim, which is the wrong Formal Logic. There could be other ways to confirm the existence of psychic powers (e.g., proving someone *else* has them).

21. (B) Paradox (EXCEPT)

Step 1: Identify the Question Type

The question asks for something that would "explain the situation described." That makes this a Paradox question. The EXCEPT indicates that four answers will resolve the central mystery. The correct answer will be the one that does *not* explain the mystery or makes it even more mysterious.

Step 2: Untangle the Stimulus

Researchers looked at prices for 300 common drugs sold in bulk at wholesalers. While there are suggested prices for these drugs in a price guidebook, researchers found the drugs being sold for far less.

Step 3: Make a Prediction

The mystery here is: why are bulk wholesalers selling these drugs at such a big discount? There could be many reasons, so don't try to predict exactly what the answers will say. Just note a few things. First, the research only involves wholesalers that sell in bulk. So, it's likely that some answers will address something unique about wholesalers or bulk sales that make them amenable to discounts. Also, the research involves only *common* drugs, so that could also factor into the explanation. Remember that one answer will not help explain the low prices, and that will be the correct answer.

Step 4: Evaluate the Answer Choices

(B) is the correct answer. If anything, this makes the mystery even weirder. If the guide recommends prices that are *already* relatively low, why are wholesalers reducing that price even more? There's still no good explanation.

(A) helps explain. The lower prices are being caused by wholesalers trying to outprice their competitors.

(C) helps explain. If the prices fluctuate, researchers might have just stopped by when prices hit a low (perhaps a big sale). Maybe the next month would have seen prices closer to the recommendations.

(D) helps explain. If the recommended prices are already so high as to guarantee "substantial profits," then wholesalers could slash prices as noted and *still* make some profit.

(E) helps explain. Perhaps selling the drugs in bulk is significantly more cost-effective and allows for prices substantially lower than those for smaller quantities.

22. (C) Role of a Statement

Step 1: Identify the Question Type

The question presents a claim from the stimulus and asks for its "role in the ... argument." That makes this a Role of a Statement question.

Step 2: Untangle the Stimulus

The theorist lists a few pairs of emotions (e.g., hatred and anger) that share a core emotion but are impossible to tell apart without a social and behavioral context. So, the theorist concludes that music can only produce the core of an emotion because it provides no definitive social or behavioral context.

Step 3: Make a Prediction

The claim in question ("music is merely sound") is preceded by the word *for*, which indicates that it is evidence for the claim before it. The claim it's supporting ("music produces [only] the core of a given emotion") is the author's main conclusion. The claim in question is also followed by the word *and*, which indicates that it is followed by yet another piece of evidence. So, the correct answer will identify the claim in question as part of the evidence in support of the conclusion.

Step 4: Evaluate the Answer Choices

(C) is correct.

(A) commits multiple errors. First, there is no "particular instance" cited of music producing only sound. Second, the claim doesn't undermine anything. Third, the author is not "attacking" any argument.

(B) is inaccurate. The word *for* immediately before the claim identifies it as evidence, not part of the conclusion.

(D) is Extreme. The author never claims that it's *necessary* for music to be merely sound.

(E) is a 180. This is a central piece of evidence. The author wouldn't reject it at all.

23. (B) Parallel Reasoning

Step 1: Identify the Question Type

The question asks for an answer with an argument "similar in its reasoning" to the one in the stimulus. That makes this a Parallel Reasoning question.

Step 2: Untangle the Stimulus

To be intelligent, a computer needs at least one of three things. A particular computer (AR3000) is missing two of those things. So, if it's intelligent, it must have the third.

Step 3: Make a Prediction

The structure is pretty clean. An entity (computers) fits a category (intelligent) only if it has one of three qualities (creativity, self-awareness, ability to learn from mistakes). A particular entity (AR3000) is missing two of those qualities, so it must have the third quality to fit the category. The correct answer will fit this structure exactly.

Step 4: Evaluate the Answer Choices

(B) matches piece by piece. An entity (vaccines) fits a category (commonly used) only if it has one of three qualities (dead-virus, attenuated-virus, or pure DNA). A particular entity (Vaccine X) is missing two of those qualities, so it must have the third quality to fit the category.

(A) is close, but applies the logic to all members of a set of entities ("Every vaccine") rather than saying what's needed to fit a particular category (e.g., for a computer to be intelligent or for the vaccine to be commonly used—as the correct answer states).

(C) also applies the logic to all members of a set of entities ("Every vaccine") rather than saying what's needed to fit a particular category (e.g., for a computer to be intelligent or for the vaccine to be commonly used—as the correct answer states).

(D) only states that the specific virus is missing *one* of the three qualities. The conclusion is conditional, claiming the third quality exists *if* the second one is missing. The original argument had no such conditional.

(E) only states that the specific virus is missing *one* of the three qualities. The conclusion is conditional, claiming the third quality exists *if* the second one is missing. The original argument had no such conditional.

24. (D) Assumption (Sufficient)

Step 1: Identify the Question Type

The correct answer will complete the argument "if" it is "assumed." That makes this a Sufficient Assumption question.

Step 2: Untangle the Stimulus

Mallotech claims to be socially responsible, but critics raise concerns about unsanitary working conditions. If those critics are right, the author argues that Mallotech's claim is rubbish.

Step 3: Make a Prediction

If the critics are right, then Mallotech has unsanitary working conditions. However, Mallotech is merely claiming to be "socially responsible," a concept neither the critics nor the author directly addresses. How do unsanitary conditions relate to social responsibility? The author assumes that there's a connection, and the correct answer will make that connection.

Step 4: Evaluate the Answer Choices

(D) is correct. If this were true and Mallotech *did* have unsanitary working conditions, then the author is justified in saying Mallotech is not really socially responsible.

(A) is Out of Scope. There's no evidence that Mallotech is lying about anything.

(B) is Out of Scope. There's nothing in the argument about Mallotech concealing information.

(C) adds nothing to the argument. It's already acknowledged that "many" factories are unsanitary, which would imply it affects many employees. The author still makes no connection between such working conditions and the concept of social responsibility.

(E) is Out of Scope. There's no evidence that unsanitary conditions indicate poor management. Even if they did, this answer only mentions "well managed" companies. It would still be possible for poorly managed companies to be socially responsible, too.

25. (B) Parallel Flaw

Step 1: Identify the Question Type

The correct answer will be an argument "similar to" the given argument. In addition, the reasoning will be "flawed." That makes this a Parallel Flaw question. Remember that the correct answer must contain the exact same flaw as the original argument.

Step 2: Untangle the Stimulus

The author talks about dichotomous concepts—two ideas that are wholly distinct (e.g., right and wrong). However, the author then cites some pairs that are no longer considered dichotomous (e.g., plants and animals are no longer considered distinct—some things are considered *both*!). Therefore, the author recommends dropping the notion of dichotomous concepts altogether.

Step 3: Make a Prediction

That's rather drastic. A couple of examples become invalid, and the author suddenly wants to scrap *everything*. Isn't it possible that the general idea is still valid even if some

exceptions have arisen? The correct answer will contain the same flaw: dismissing an entire concept because of a handful of exceptional cases.

Step 4: Evaluate the Answer Choices

(B) commits the same flaw. In this case, the author wants to dismiss *all* anti-anxiety drugs just because a few bad ones were found.

(A) does not match. The original argument contained a conclusion about eliminating something entirely. Here, such an elimination is part of the evidence to support a conclusion about some computers.

(C) is not flawed the same way. Here, the evidence and the conclusion are both about "all intoxicated drivers." The conclusion is not based on just a handful of bad instances.

(D) does not match. The author is not using exceptional cases. This argument is based on a relationship (the longer it's kept, the more likely it's rotten). The original contained no such relationship.

(E) mentions eliminating something because it doesn't match an assumption. That's not the same as eliminating something due to the existence of a few bad examples.

26. (E) Assumption (Necessary)

Step 1: Identify the Question Type

The question asks for an "assumption" that the argument "requires." That makes this a Necessary Assumption question.

Step 2: Untangle the Stimulus

The author is discussing ballast tanks that are used to keep ships stable. As ballast tanks are filled and emptied at port, local sea creatures can get into the tanks. They can then get out when the ship reaches another port, causing major problems in their new environment. So, the author offers a solution: when the ship is midocean, take a moment to drain the tanks and refill them. Any coastal stowaways that are drained out will not be able to survive. Any midocean creatures that climb aboard will not survive when drained out at port.

Step 3: Make a Prediction

While the author's plan spells doom for any creature that finds its way into a ballast tank, it seems like it would prevent ecological disasters caused by creatures invading a new environment. The problem is that the author calls the plan "viable." Unfortunately, some plans look good in theory but don't quite work out in practice. The author is overlooking any potential glitches in the plan. For this argument to work, the author must assume that everything will work out as planned, and nothing significant will go wrong.

Step 4: Evaluate the Answer Choices

(E) must be true. The whole point of the ballast tank is to help maintain stability. If draining the tanks midocean causes a problem and the ship becomes unstable, then the author's plan would put the ship and its crew at great risk. The plan would suddenly seem less viable. So, for the plan to work, it *must* be true that ships can stay stable while going through the "drain and refill" process.

(A) is Extreme. Remember that the correct answer must be one the argument "requires." While this answer would certainly be helpful to the author's cause, it's not entirely necessary. The proposal would not have to *ensure* that *no* harmful creatures are pumped into the tank. It could merely make that scenario *less likely* and still be considered viable.

(B) is a 180. For the plan to be viable, it would be best if the "drain and refill" process could be done under *any* conditions, not just calm ones.

(C) is irrelevant. The frequency of such ecological problems has no bearing on whether the author's proposal has merit or not.

(D) does not have to be true. Even if the tanks are drained and refilled at other times, it's still possible that they're only drained in port or near the coast. The author's proposal could still work by adding midocean refills.

PrepTest 78

The Inside Story

PrepTest 78 was administered in June 2016. It challenged 23,051 test takers. What made this test so hard? Here's a breakdown of what Kaplan students who were surveyed after taking the official exam considered PrepTest 78's most difficult section.

Hardest PrepTest 78 Section as Reported by Test Takers

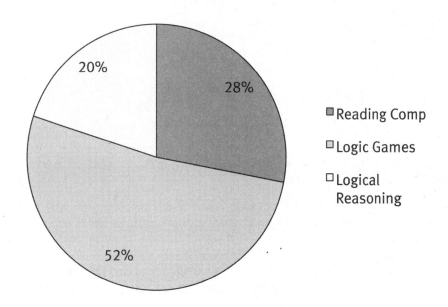

Based on these results, you might think that studying Logic Games is the key to LSAT success. Well, Logic Games is important, but test takers' perceptions don't tell the whole story. For that, you need to consider students' actual performance. The following chart shows the average number of students to miss each question in each of PrepTest 78's different sections.

Percentage Incorrect by PrepTest 78 Section Type

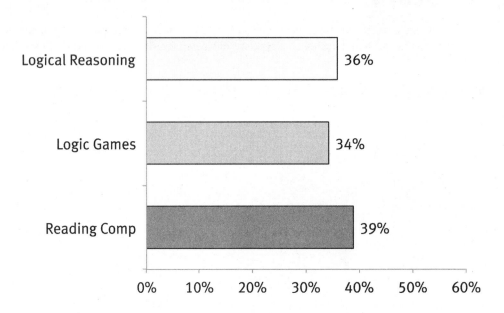

Actual student performance tells quite a different story. On average, students were almost equally likely to miss questions in all three of the different section types, and on PrepTest 78, Reading Comprehension and Logical Reasoning were somewhat higher than Logic Games in actual difficulty.

Maybe students overestimate the difficulty of the Logic Games section because it's so unusual, or maybe it's because a really hard Logic Game is so easy to remember after the test. But the truth is that the test maker places hard questions throughout the test. Here were the locations of the 10 hardest (most missed) questions in the exam.

Location of 10 Most Difficult Questions in PrepTest 78

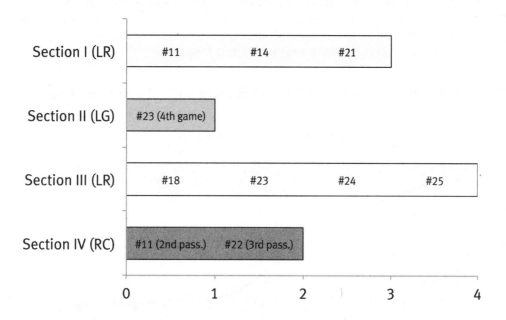

The takeaway from this data is that, to maximize your potential on the LSAT, you need to take a comprehensive approach. Test yourself rigorously, and review your performance on every section of the test. Kaplan's LSAT explanations provide the expertise and insight you need to fully understand your results. The explanations are written and edited by a team of LSAT experts, who have helped thousands of students improve their scores. Kaplan always provides data-driven analysis of the test, ranking the difficulty of every question based on actual student performance. The 10 hardest questions on every test are highlighted with a 4-star difficulty rating, the highest we give. The analysis breaks down the remaining questions into 1-, 2-, and 3-star ratings so that you can compare your performance to thousands of other test takers on all LSAC material.

Don't settle for wondering whether a question was really as hard as it seemed to you. Analyze the test with real data, and learn the secrets and strategies that help top scorers master the LSAT.

7 Can't-Miss Features of PrepTest 78

- Tough curve! PrepTest 78 was the first time since June '11 (PT 63) that 99 questions correct wasn't enough to get a 180.
- With only six Assumption questions and six Flaw questions, PrepTest 78 had the least combined Assumption and Flaw questions since October 2010 (PT 61).
- The Selection game returns! PrepTest 78 featured a Selection game for the first time since October '13 (PT 70) and for just the third time since 2010.
- The record for fewest Global questions in a Reading Comprehension section had been three, which had happened five times. However, on PrepTest 78, a new record was set with just two Global questions.
- The Comparative Reading pair of passages appeared in the Reading Comprehension section for the first time since December '09 (PT 59).
- Answer choices (A), (B), (C), (D), and (E) each appeared exactly 10 times in RC/LG. However, in Logical Reasoning, there was not the same consistency. In fact, (E) was twice as likely to occur as (D)—14 vs. 7 times.
- Section III kicks off with a question about unrepresentative polling. Then, less than 20 days after PrepTest 78 was administered, the United Kingdom voted for Brexit.

PrepTest 78 in Context

As much fun as it is to find out what makes a PrepTest unique or noteworthy, it's even more important to know just how representative it is of other LSAT administrations (and, thus, how likely it is to be representative of the exam you will face on Test Day). The following charts compare the numbers of each kind of question and game on PrepTest 78 to the average numbers seen on all officially released LSATs administered over the past five years (from 2012 through 2016).

Number of LR Questions by Type: PrepTest 78 vs. 2012–2016 Average

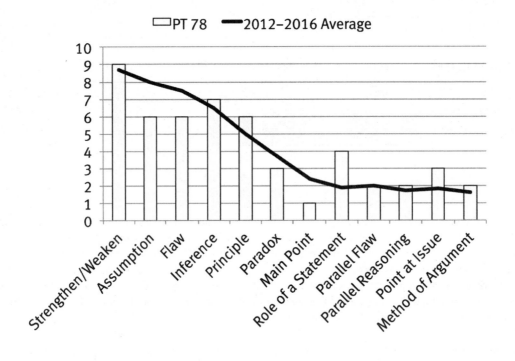

Number of LG Games by Type: PrepTest 78 vs. 2012–2016 Average

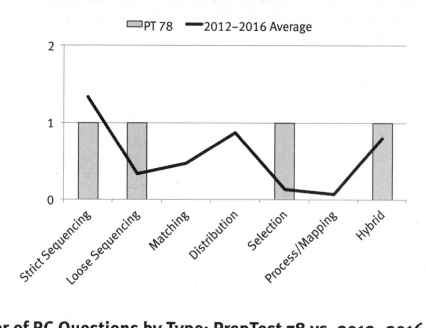

Number of RC Questions by Type: PrepTest 78 vs. 2012–2016 Average

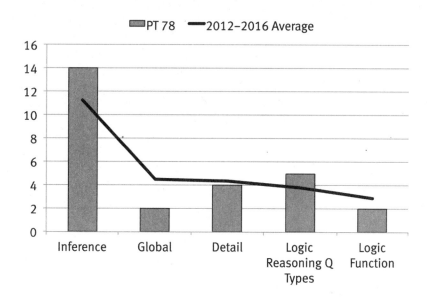

There isn't usually a huge difference in the distribution of questions from LSAT to LSAT, but if this test seems harder (or easier) to you than another you've taken, compare the number of questions of the types on which you, personally, are strongest and weakest. And then, explore within each section to see if your best or worst question types came earlier or later.

Students in Kaplan's comprehensive LSAT courses have access to every released LSAT and to an online question bank with thousands of officially released questions, games, and passages. If you are studying on your own, you have to do a bit more work to identify your strengths and your areas of opportunity. Quantitative analysis (like that in the previous charts) is an important tool for understanding how the test is constructed and how you are performing on it.

Section I: Logical Reasoning

Q#	Question Type	Correct	Difficulty
1	Principle (Identify/Strengthen)	A	★
2	Assumption (Necessary)	E	★
3	Method of Argument	A	★
4	Point at Issue	E	★
5	Method of Argument	B	★
6	Point at Issue	B	★
7	Flaw	B	★
8	Inference	C	★★
9	Flaw	A	★
10	Weaken	C	★★
11	Inference	A	★★★★
12	Strengthen	C	★★
13	Inference	D	★★
14	Assumption (Necessary)	D	★★★★
15	Principle (Identify/Inference)	E	★★★
16	Strengthen	A	★★★
17	Paradox	E	★★
18	Principle (Identify/Strengthen)	E	★★
19	Assumption (Necessary)	E	★★
20	Point at Issue	D	★★
21	Parallel Flaw	E	★★★★
22	Flaw	A	★★
23	Parallel Reasoning	B	★★
24	Principle (Identify/Assumption)	E	★★★
25	Weaken	C	★

1. (A) Principle (Identify/Strengthen)

Step 1: Identify the Question Type

The correct answer will be a broad principle that conforms to the specific content in the stimulus, making this an Identify the Principle question. Also, that principle will *justify* Hidalgo's argument, which means this Principle question will mimic a Strengthen question.

Step 2: Untangle the Stimulus

Grecia argues that people should provide their age when responding to a particular survey. Hidalgo argues that exact ages aren't needed and that respondents should just choose from a set of age ranges.

Step 3: Make a Prediction

Hidalgo's argument boils down to a simple recommendation: don't ask for specific ages because there's no need for that level of specificity. The correct answer will restate this in more general terms: there's no need to ask for specific information when that level of specificity is not needed.

Step 4: Evaluate the Answer Choices

(A) matches the logic of Hidalgo's recommendation.

(B) is Out of Scope. There's no mention of how likely people are to provide *accurate* information.

(C) is Out of Scope. There's no mention of any "secure means of storage" for information.

(D) is a Distortion. Hidalgo's intention is to *prevent* the collection of *unnecessary* information. His recommendation is more of a compromise than a suggestion to collect anything that *is* needed.

(E) is Out of Scope. Hidalgo makes no mention of revealing anything to respondents about how information is going to be used.

2. (E) Assumption (Necessary)

Step 1: Identify the Question Type

The question asks for an assumption that is *required* by the argument, making this a Necessary Assumption question.

Step 2: Untangle the Stimulus

The author is arguing that, contrary to belief, an ancient city uncovered during excavation is not actually Troy—the legendary site of the Trojan War described in the poem the *Iliad*. As evidence, the author notes that the war lasted 10 years according to the *Iliad*, and the uncovered city was too small to survive that long a war.

Step 3: Make a Prediction

The problem here is that the author's evidence does not come from historical records; it comes from a poem. The author overlooks the possibility that Homer may have taken some creative liberties with history. In order for this argument to work, the author must assume that the details described in the *Iliad* are accurate enough to make judgments about actual history.

Step 4: Evaluate the Answer Choices

(E) must be assumed. The Denial Test confirms this. If the *Iliad* were *not* accurate about the length of the war, then the basis of the author's argument falls apart. Perhaps Homer exaggerated the length, and the uncovered city could actually be Troy. That would contradict the author, so the author must assume otherwise: the poem *was* indeed accurate.

(A) is irrelevant and a 180 at worst. What scholars knew in 1893 has no effect on the author's argument about the size of the city versus the length of the war. Besides, the author's argument would be stronger if this answer *weren't* true. If scholars *did* know of other potential sites for Troy, the author would have more reason to believe this city wasn't Troy.

(B) would help the author's cause, but is not necessary. Even if the poem *did* provide clues about the specific location, there's no indication that it would match the excavation site. And the author would still have the evidence about the size of the city and the timeline of the war.

(C) would also help the author's cause, but is still not necessary. No evidence of a siege would certainly support the idea that the city was not Troy. However, even if there *were* evidence of a siege, it wouldn't have to be one from the Trojan War. It could have been a minor siege, and the author's argument still stands: it was not Troy.

(D) is a 180. This would support the theory that the city was Troy, and the author is trying to argue it was *not* Troy.

3. (A) Method of Argument

Step 1: Identify the Question Type

The word *by* indicates that the question is asking *how* Garcia responds to Flynn. That makes this a Method of Argument question. Focus on the technique Garcia uses rather than the logic behind the content.

Step 2: Untangle the Stimulus

When dangerous products cause damage, people can sue large companies and get huge payouts. Flynn argues that this is great for consumers as it encourages companies to make products safer. Garcia disagrees, arguing that this is bad for consumers. Those lawsuits can harm companies, leading to layoffs and decreased productivity and ultimately to a weaker economy.

Step 3: Make a Prediction

Flynn's argument in favor of big-payout lawsuits rests on one benefit. Garcia counters that by listing a series of overlooked downsides. The correct answer will describe this approach: arguing against a point of view by raising unconsidered negatives.

Step 4: Evaluate the Answer Choices

(A) accurately describes Garcia's technique. Garcia argues that the policy Flynn supports (getting large rewards by suing corporations) has undesirable consequences (loss of jobs, a hurt economy).

(B) is a Distortion. Garcia attacks Flynn's *conclusion*, not one of Flynn's *premises* (i.e., his evidence). Flynn's sole premise is the incentive to reduce safety risks, and Garcia does not contradict that.

(C) is Out of Scope. Garcia makes no analogy to any other argument. Garcia merely points out overlooked possibilities within Flynn's argument.

(D) is a Distortion. Garcia shows no such self-contradiction. Garcia contradicts Flynn's argument by raising new concerns that were *not* brought up by Flynn.

(E) is Out of Scope. Neither Flynn nor Garcia is trying to *explain* why any particular situation occurred.

4. (E) Point at Issue

Step 1: Identify the Question Type

The stimulus provides a dialogue, and the question asks what the two speakers "disagree over." That makes this a Point at Issue question.

Step 2: Untangle the Stimulus

Monroe argues that a project, designed to cut back as much as possible the number of homes without electricity, was a failure. As evidence, Monroe cites 2,000 homes that are still without electricity. Wilkerson counters that the project was a success because it did bring electricity to 3,000 homes that didn't have any.

Step 3: Make a Prediction

Simply put, Monroe and Wilkerson disagree over whether the project was a success or a failure. Furthermore, this disagreement is based on how each author interprets the "2,000 homes" statistic. So, Monroe and Wilkerson are arguing over whether those 2,000 homes represent a success or a failure.

Step 4: Evaluate the Answer Choices

(E) is the point at issue. Monroe argues that the 2,000 homes without electricity *does* count as a failure, while Wilkerson argues that it does *not*—it's actually a success!

(A) is a 180. Monroe and Wilkerson *agree* about the number of homes left without electricity. What they disagree about is whether that number constitutes a success or a failure for the project.

(B) is not a point at issue. Monroe doesn't address the number of homes without electricity *before* the project began. In all likelihood, Monroe would agree with Wilkerson about that figure. The real issue about the success of the project

revolves around the number of houses left without electricity *afterward*.

(C) is Extreme. Monroe's assessment of the project's failure is based on a substantial number of homes without electricity: 2,000. There's no evidence that Monroe would consider the project a failure at *any* number. It's possible that Monroe just has a threshold for homes still without electricity (say, 100 homes or less), but 2,000 homes was just too much.

(D) is not a point at issue. Monroe brings up this stated goal, but Wilkerson never disputes it. The point at issue is whether or not the project *met* that goal.

5. (B) Method of Argument

Step 1: Identify the Question Type

The word *by* indicates that the answer will describe *how* the author weakens a conclusion drawn by someone else. That makes this a Method of Argument question.

Step 2: Untangle the Stimulus

Researchers surveyed an equal number of 20-year-olds and 50-year-olds about donating blood. Because more 50-year-olds claimed to give blood, the researchers concluded that 50-year-olds are more altruistic. The author disagrees, suggesting that some people may misrepresent their behavior if they feel it doesn't live up to societal expectations.

Step 3: Make a Prediction

Basically, the author is suggesting that some of those seemingly altruistic 50-year-olds are just a bunch of liars, unwilling to admit that they're not the generous donators they're expected to be. In short, the author questions the researcher's conclusion by taking a more cynical interpretation of the survey results.

Step 4: Evaluate the Answer Choices

(B) matches the author's technique. The author uses the same data, but offers an alternative explanation (they're not more altruistic—they're just trying to make themselves look good!).

(A) is Out of Scope. The author never questions the sample group selected. The author just questions their motives in answering the survey question.

(C) is Out of Scope. The author's argument is based on people's motives when answering the survey question. The author never mentions direct observation of altruistic acts.

(D) is a Distortion. The author criticizes the motives of the people *responding* to the survey, not the researchers administering the survey.

(E) is Out of Scope. The author only makes general claims about "[m]any people." No specific examples are given.

6. (B) Point at Issue

Step 1: Identify the Question Type
This is a Dialogue/Response stimulus, and the question asks for something the speakers "disagree over." That makes this a Point at Issue question.

Step 2: Untangle the Stimulus
The only rug store in Glendale just went out of business. According to Mario, this indicates low demand for rugs in Glendale, so opening a new rug business there would be a bad idea. Renate disagrees, suggesting demand for the product is not an issue. One place closing just opens the market up for a new rug store.

Step 3: Make a Prediction
To Mario, the rug market is dead. Renate says quite the opposite: with a wide open market, now is probably a great time to open a new rug store. So, their primary disagreement is about whether opening a new rug store is a good idea or not.

Step 4: Evaluate the Answer Choices
(B) is the point at issue. Mario says it's not a good idea ("rugs would be one product to avoid"), while Renate suggest it *is* a good idea ("the market for rugs . . . is now wide open").

(A) is Out of Scope. Neither Mario nor Renate address the quality of the rugs.

(C) is either Out of Scope or potentially a 180. Neither speaker talks about whether it's possible to determine the market for rugs. However, because Mario and Renate both make judgments about the rug market, this suggests that they agree that it is possible to determine the market. They just disagree on the size of the market.

(D) is Out of Scope. Neither speaker mentions any other stores going out of business.

(E) is a Distortion. Mario clearly agrees that low demand can lead to a rug store closing. While Renate does not feel that low demand was the problem for the store in Glendale, that's not to say that low demand couldn't be the cause for other rug stores closing. Renate's opinion on this statement cannot be determined, so it cannot be the point at issue.

7. (B) Flaw

Step 1: Identify the Question Type
The question directly asks for the flaw in the argument.

Step 2: Untangle the Stimulus
The city council claims that the latest technology would prevent safety issues that could arise from expanding the airport's air traffic beyond its original capacity. The editorialist argues otherwise: the technology would *not* prevent safety issues. As evidence, the editorialist cites studies that show the latest technology does nothing to prevent safety issues.

Step 3: Make a Prediction
Unfortunately, the editorialist refers to studies from *30 years ago*. Technology could have changed drastically over that time, and it's possible that *today's* technology could prevent a decrease in safety far better than anything from 30 years ago. The editorialist completely overlooks this, and that is the flaw.

Step 4: Evaluate the Answer Choices
(B) accurately describes the flaw. The editorialist fails to consider that safety depends on what the latest technology is, assuming that what was true of the latest technology 30 years ago still holds true with today's technology.

(A) is inaccurate. The conclusion is based on "numerous studies," not a general statement. And those studies reflected what would happen at "every airport," not just a few specific instances.

(C) is Out of Scope. It doesn't matter whether or not the council was aware of the old studies. The editorialist's mistake is using those potentially outdated studies as evidence in the first place.

(D) is not accurate. There is no absence of evidence for the claim of safety. The council provides evidence: the airport would use the latest technology.

(E) is Out of Scope. This argument is entirely about whether safety would decrease or not. There's no judgment about whether this is *acceptable* or not based on other non-safety benefits.

8. (C) Inference

Step 1: Identify the Question Type
It is difficult to categorize this question by the stem alone. What fills in the blank at the end of an argument depends on what surrounds the blank. In this case, the blank completes a train of thought that is supported by everything before it. That makes it an Inference question. It could also arguably be considered a Sufficient Assumption question, but the stimulus will help you see that the argument is basically already complete; you just have to infer what completes the analogy.

Step 2: Untangle the Stimulus
Some people claim that the existence of different moral codes shows that morality is developed through culture and is not universally part of our nature. The philosopher disagrees, citing particular shared moral attitudes. The philosopher then makes an analogy to food, saying that all people share tastes but can still have different cuisines.

Step 3: Make a Prediction
The phrase "[t]his argument is flawed" is important. The philosopher argues that, despite what people say, there *could* be some universal grounds for morality even though different

cultures have different moral codes. However, the philosopher never directly states this, so it will likely fill in the blank at the end. In addition, the blank comes at the end of an analogy. So, the phrasing of the philosopher's view will conform to the logic of the analogy. For food, different cultures may have different cuisines, but those cuisines are still based on shared/universal tastes (e.g., sweetness). This compares perfectly to the philosopher's point: different cultures may have different moral codes, but those codes are still based on shared/universal moral attitudes (e.g., cruelty is wrong).

Step 4: Evaluate the Answer Choices

(C) matches the philosopher's point about shared moral attitudes despite differing moral codes.

(A) is a 180. It has been argued that moral codes are a product of culture (i.e., they're based on where they arise), but the philosopher is arguing against that, saying such reasoning is *flawed*.

(B) is a Distortion and Extreme. While there may be some resemblance among moral codes, this does not match the analogy that shared traits (tastes) can "provide the basis" for different large-scale ideas (cuisines). Nothing indicates that *most* cuisines resemble each other, so it would be too much to say the moral codes of *most* cultures resemble each other.

(D) is Out of Scope. The philosopher is not discussing whether *understanding* the basis of moral codes is possible or not.

(E) is a Distortion. The philosopher is trying to argue that universal shared moral attitudes exist, not that these moral attitudes can be changed to fit a moral code.

9. (A) Flaw

Step 1: Identify the Question Type

The question asks why the argument is "vulnerable to criticism," which means it is asking for the flaw in the argument.

Step 2: Untangle the Stimulus

The author concludes (as indicated by the word [*t*]*hus*) that more plant species make prairies better able to support plants. As evidence, the author cites a study in which prairies with more plant species had healthier plants and more nutrient-rich soil.

Step 3: Make a Prediction

This is one of the most common flaws tested on the LSAT. The evidence describes a correlation (the data lines up: more plant species correlates with plant and soil quality). The author then concludes one thing caused the other (more species was the cause of the prairie's great growing conditions). There are three flaws in this case: 1) the author overlooks alternative causes (i.e., something else could have

led to great growing conditions), 2) the causality could be reversed (i.e., the quality of the prairie is responsible for the greater number of species), and 3) it could just be a coincidence. The correct answer will identify one of these three flaws.

Step 4: Evaluate the Answer Choices

(A) describes one of the common flaws in causal arguments, just in algebraic terms. Replacing X with "more plant species" and Y with "better ability to support plants," this basically says more species caused the better plant support when the causality could be reversed (better plant support could have caused more species).

(B) is irrelevant. The author doesn't need to describe a specific mechanism to claim that one thing led to another.

(C) is a Distortion. The author never uses characteristics of one particular plot. The author uses data about prairie plots in general.

(D) is unsupported. The data is said to come from a "study of prairie plants." There's no indication that the sample size or population was unrepresentative.

(E) is Out of Scope. The author makes no claim about proportions.

10. (C) Weaken

Step 1: Identify the Question Type

This question directly asks for something that weakens the given argument.

Step 2: Untangle the Stimulus

The anthropologist describes an experiment in which two groups of students were taught how to make a Neanderthal tool. One group was taught visually and verbally, while the other group was given no oral instruction. Both groups learned equally well. So, the anthropologist concludes that Neanderthals didn't need language to make their sophisticated tools.

Step 3: Make a Prediction

The conclusion brings up *sophisticated* tools. However, the study doesn't say the students were asked to make sophisticated tools. They were just shown how to create "one of the types" of tools Neanderthals made. Maybe they learned to make a tool that was absurdly simplistic. In that case, Neanderthals may have needed language for the more sophisticated tools, raising considerable doubts about the anthropologist's claim.

Step 4: Evaluate the Answer Choices

(C) attacks the anthropologist's assumption about the tools created by the undergrads. If they made simplistic tools, then the author has no evidence to back up a claim about sophisticated tools—and the argument falls apart.

(A) has no effect on the anthropologist's argument. The argument is not about whether or not Neanderthals actually had language, but whether or not they could make their tools even "if they had no language."

(B) is a 180. If members of the second group couldn't even talk to one another and still performed equally well, the anthropologist's claim that language is unnecessary would be *strengthened*.

(D) is an Irrelevant Comparison at best and a 180 at worst. The proficiency of the instructors does not change the results. Even if it did have some effect, the silent group *still* did just as well with an inferior teacher. This could only reinforce the fact that language is really not necessary.

(E) is an Irrelevant Comparison. If the Neanderthal tools were less sophisticated, then it's still possible that language wasn't needed to create those tools (as the anthropologist claims). So, bringing up evidence about another group does not weaken the argument.

11. (A) Inference

Step 1: Identify the Question Type
The correct answer will be "supported by" the information given, which means this is an Inference question.

Step 2: Untangle the Stimulus
The author presents information about exercising to improve one's cardiovascular health. One *can* see dramatic results with moderate exercise, e.g., half an hour of walking most days of the week. Sure, one could get even *more* results from more strenuous exercise, but that's not really needed.

Step 3: Make a Prediction
It's difficult to predict exactly what the correct answer will say, but it will be consistent with the information provided: modest exercise may be good enough to help dramatically improve cardiovascular health; you could do more, but you don't need to.

Step 4: Evaluate the Answer Choices
(A) is supported. The author does claim that even modest exercise on most days can produce improvement. And if "more vigorous exercise is more effective," then strenuous exercise on most days could also certainly help—even if it's not absolutely necessary.

(B) is a Distortion. The author claims that half an hour of walking most days of the week (i.e., at least four days a week, which would be at least two hours of walking) can help. This suggests that you can take the same amount of hours and condense it into two or three days. However, the author never suggests you can do that. Instead, the author states "one should exercise most days," which means one may not get the same results by spacing things out too much. Furthermore, the first sentence says that modest exercise *can*

produce improvements in cardiovascular health. However, that is a lower level of certainty than saying it *generally* produces dramatic improvements.

(C) is a 180. Even though strenuous exercise is not necessary, the author directly says that more vigorous (i.e., strenuous) exercise would still be "more effective" than modest exercise.

(D) is Extreme. The author only discusses exercise and does not exclude other ways to improve cardiovascular health.

(E) is a 180, directly contradicting the last sentence which claims "a strenuous workout is not absolutely necessary."

12. (C) Strengthen

Step 1: Identify the Question Type
The question directly asks for something that strengthens the given argument.

Step 2: Untangle the Stimulus
The author concludes that Sartore is a better movie reviewer than Kelly. The evidence is that reviews should help people determine if they're likely to enjoy a movie or not, and when people realize they're likely to enjoy a particular movie, that is more likely to come from one of Sartore's reviews.

Step 3: Make a Prediction
The goal of a review is to help readers determine whether they're likely to enjoy a movie *or not*. The evidence only talks about Sartore's ability to help people recognize movies they *are* likely to enjoy. The author assumes that this means Sartore's reviews also help people recognize movies they are *not* likely to enjoy. The correct answer will validate this.

Step 4: Evaluate the Answer Choices
(C) strengthens the argument by looking at both goals of a movie review. Now, Sartore's reviews better help people recognize when they're likely to enjoy a movie and when they're *not* likely to.

(A) may be a tempting answer, as many people might feel technical knowledge makes one a better movie critic. However, this author's judgment is based on the reviewer's ability to help people recognize what movies they are likely to enjoy. The comparison between technical knowledge and fandom cannot be absolutely connected to that ability. At worst, some could argue that people are more likely to be persuaded by a movie fan than some stuffy technical analyst.

(B) is irrelevant. The proportion of favorable versus unfavorable reviews does nothing to indicate whether readers are influenced by these reviews or not. If Sartore is better able to help people identify if they enjoy a movie or not, then the quantity of negative and positive reviews is immaterial.

(D) is irrelevant. The argument is not based on how much readers *actually* enjoy the movie. It's based on whether the review helps them realize whether or not they're *likely* to enjoy the movie. The point of the review is not to make one enjoy the movie *more*; the point is to better ascertain which movies are worth watching and which ones are worth avoiding.

(E) is an Irrelevant Comparison. It doesn't matter how many movies they review in common. All that matters is their ability to influence readers.

13. (D) Inference

Step 1: Identify the Question Type
The correct answer will be "strongly supported by the information" provided, which means it will be a logical inference.

Step 2: Untangle the Stimulus
The author discusses specially bred fish. Their colors and unique shapes make them appealing, but there are downsides. Their shape slows them down at feeding time, so they won't eat enough when they're competing against faster ordinary fish. And when they breed, their offspring aren't as colorful or uniquely shaped.

Step 3: Make a Prediction
There are many possible inferences here, so just take time to consider the major details. The author provides various pros (colorful, interesting shapes) and cons (slow, dull offspring) of specially bred fish. They are also compared to ordinary fish. Specially bred fish are inferior, and they move more slowly due to their body shapes. Watch out for answers that are too strong or bring up concepts not addressed in the stimulus.

Step 4: Evaluate the Answer Choices
(D) is supported. Ordinary fish are said to reach food more quickly because the specially bred ones are "[h]ampered by their elaborate tails or strangely shaped fins." That directly suggests that ordinary fish lack those drawbacks.

(A) is Extreme. Special care would probably be recommended, but the stimulus merely says that specially bred fish are *often* underfed. That suggests they *could* do okay without special care. Special care is not described as a *must*.

(B) is unsupported. While specially bred fish are said to be "popular with connoisseurs," that doesn't mean other fish are not popular. Connoisseurs could very well like ordinary fish, too.

(C) is Extreme. Specially bred fish may be *popular* with connoisseurs, but that doesn't mean *most* of these fish are bought by connoisseurs.

(E) is a 180. The offspring may not be as unique, but there *are* offspring. There is no reproductive interference.

14. (D) Assumption (Necessary)

Step 1: Identify the Question Type
The question directly asks for an assumption, and one that is *required* by the argument. That makes this a Necessary Assumption question.

Step 2: Untangle the Stimulus
The ethicist concludes that the principle "if one ought to do something, then one can do it" is not always true. In other words, we can't always do what we should. As evidence, the ethicist provides an example of someone unable to fulfill a promise due to unexpected traffic.

Step 3: Make a Prediction
The ethicist argues that we can't always do what we *ought to* based on an example showing that we can't always keep our *promises*. That leads to the basic assumption that we ought to do what we promise.

If	promise something	→	ought to do it

That seems reasonable, but the ethicist makes this assumption in a situation in which the promise is *impossible* to keep. So, the ethicist must assume that an *impossible* promise is still a promise, and one still ought to do what is promised. And given that there are promises that are impossible to keep, the general principle that "if one ought to, then one can" does not always hold.

Step 4: Evaluate the Answer Choices
(D) must be assumed. This confirms that one ought to keep (i.e., is obligated to complete) any promise, even when that promise cannot be kept.

(A) reverses the logic of the necessary assumption. The Formal Logic here states that "if something ought to have been done, then it was promised."

If	ought	→	promise

However, the ethicist's assumption goes the other way: "if something is promised, then it is something that ought to be done."

If	promise	→	ought

The part about *failing* doesn't cause the terms to be negated. Failing to deliver on a promise is not the same as "not promising," and failing to do what ought to be done isn't the same as "ought not to do it."

(B) is a 180. The ethicist assumes that events like traffic jams do *not* excuse people from the obligation. It's still something they ought to do, even if they can't.

(C) is Out of Scope. This argument is about what people *should* do, not what they *shouldn't*.

(E) is Out of Scope. The ethicist does not question whether people should *make* promises, but whether people ought to *keep* those promises—even when they become impossible.

15. (E) Principle (Identify/Inference)

Step 1: Identify the Question Type
The correct answer will be a *generalization* to which the given situation conforms. That makes this an Identify the Principle question. Because the stimulus is described as a *situation*, don't look for evidence and a conclusion. Just consider what happens, and look for an answer that matches the facts, just like you would in an Inference question, but in broader terms.

Step 2: Untangle the Stimulus
As leather and fur have become less fashionable, their prices have dropped. Other materials, which are now more fashionable, have risen in price. This is despite the fact that leather and fur require more intensive labor than the new fashionable materials.

Step 3: Make a Prediction
With both sets of materials, the prices are correlated with fashion trends. It doesn't matter that leather and fur require more labor to make. So, as a general rule, it appears that the price of materials is driven by more than just labor costs.

Step 4: Evaluate the Answer Choices
(E) matches the logic. Fashion trends have moved away from leather and fur and toward other materials, and the prices of both groups have adjusted accordingly.

(A) is Out of Scope. The stimulus only provides information about the price of raw materials (e.g., leather and fur), not the final price of manufactured goods. Furthermore, even though fashion trends certainly influence the overall price of a material, it is not clear that they influence the price *more* than the cost of producing the materials. Prices have been adjusted based on fashion trends, but perhaps labor costs still play the most important role.

(B) is Out of Scope. The stimulus mentions nothing about the practicality of the materials.

(C) is a Distortion. While materials requiring little labor are becoming more fashionable *now*, labor-intensive leather and fur *were* fashionable at one point. And there's always a chance fashion can change and return to something more labor-intensive.

(D) is Out of Scope. The stimulus never mentions the appearance of the final manufactured good, and never discusses what makes something fashionable.

16. (A) Strengthen

Step 1: Identify the Question Type
Fill-in-the-blank questions cannot always be classified simply by the existence of the blank; they also depend on the Keywords in the stimulus. This question stem directly mentions that what fills in the blank will "strongly support" the argument's conclusion, which indicates a Strengthen question. The blank also concludes a sentence beginning with "[a]fter all," which indicates evidence. So, the blank could also be considered an unstated piece of evidence that completes the argument, which would make this a Sufficient Assumption question. Either way, the correct answer will create a stronger connection between the given evidence and the conclusion.

Step 2: Untangle the Stimulus
The author concludes that an outbreak of certain moths in most of the forest should not be stopped. As evidence, the author cites that the moths help in areas where the forest is crowded with immature trees.

Step 3: Make a Prediction
The author wants to keep the moths around because they are beneficial … when the forest is crowded with immature trees. However, there's no evidence that this is the case in the forest mentioned. The author just assumes it is. The correct answer will verify that *most* of the forest in discussion is crowded with immature trees.

Step 4: Evaluate the Answer Choices
(A) backs up the conclusion. If most of the forest is crowded with immature trees, then it is warranted to keep the moths around for the benefit they provide.

(B) is potentially a 180. If the forest only has a few immature trees and many mature trees, then this could pose a major problem. The moths are only said to be beneficial when a forest is overcrowded with immature trees. However, if the moths eat mature trees first, they won't impact how crowded the forest is with immature trees, and they could destroy a significant number of mature trees first.

(C) is an Irrelevant Comparison. Which trees are more often affected by forest fires has no bearing on whether the forest in question meets the conditions that would warrant keeping the moths around.

(D) does not help. This makes the outbreak more likely to happen, but still does not validate that it's a good idea for the forest in question.

(E) is irrelevant. The author doesn't want to use any countermeasures, so their effectiveness has no bearing on the argument.

17. (E) Paradox

Step 1: Identify the Question Type

The question asks for something that would *explain* the statistics provided. That makes this a Paradox question.

Step 2: Untangle the Stimulus

The city of Gastner just built a new highway to reduce traffic, but travel times in the city actually got *worse* after the new highway opened.

Step 3: Make a Prediction

Paradox questions contain a central mystery. In this case, why did commute times get *longer* when the highway was supposed to help? Something must have happened to offset the time savings granted by the new highway. There could be several options, so don't predict anything specific. Just look for an answer that mentions a side effect that would somehow create *more* traffic.

Step 4: Evaluate the Answer Choices

(E) provides an explanation. While the highway may have reduced traffic from the suburbs to the downtown area, it caused *more* traffic *in* the downtown area. Perhaps more people were willing to drive into downtown after completion of the new highway. So, people got to the city faster only to hit more traffic once they got there.

(A) is irrelevant. The new highway provided new links to the suburbs, so it should have helped by giving people additional options into the city. This doesn't explain why things got worse.

(B) is also irrelevant. Even if the new highway were only convenient for certain people, it still should have helped *them*, indirectly reducing the number of people on other roads.

(C) is a 180. This says the suburban roads were *upgraded*, which suggests improvement. That doesn't help explain why things got worse.

(D) is irrelevant. The mystery is about the increase in travel time *after* the highway opened. Roadwork that occurred during construction (i.e., *before* it opened) doesn't help explain anything.

18. (E) Principle (Identify/Strengthen)

Step 1: Identify the Question Type

The question directly asks for a principle, and one that will *justify* the given reasoning. That makes it an Identify the Principle question that mimics a Strengthen question.

Step 2: Untangle the Stimulus

The office worker has two unfinished projects and argues for working exclusively on the second project. The first one is already late, and working more on the first one would make it impossible to finish the second one on time.

Step 3: Make a Prediction

Both projects are equally important, so that has no bearing on the decision. The decision comes down to two options: 1) keep working on the already late project, and make both projects late, or 2) work on the other project, and at least have a chance of getting one project done on time. By choosing the second option, the office worker is acting on the principle that it's better to try getting *something* done on time instead of being late with everything.

Step 4: Evaluate the Answer Choices

(E) validates the office worker's logic. The office worker argues in favor of the second project (a project that could be finished on time) over the first project (a late project of equal priority).

(A) does not help. This fits the idea of devoting time exclusively to one project, but gives no justification for choosing the second project over the first.

(B) is a Distortion. The office worker is not concerned about failing to finish either project. The office worker is merely concerned about finishing the projects *on time*.

(C) is Out of Scope. Both projects are said to be "equally important." There's no suggestion that one "must be done" while the other is "merely optional."

(D) is Out of Scope. The office worker makes no mention of worries or the prospect of those worries interfering with the projects.

19. (E) Assumption (Necessary)

Step 1: Identify the Question Type

The question asks for an assumption that the argument *requires*, making this a Necessary Assumption question.

Step 2: Untangle the Stimulus

The science teacher concludes ([*t*]*herefore*) that science courses should teach evaluation of science-based arguments regarding practical issues rather than just abstract concepts. As evidence, the teacher claims that courses should teach skills useful in everyday life, and abstract concepts are rarely useful.

Step 3: Make a Prediction

The science teacher mentions that abstract concepts are not useful, but never actually states that evaluation of science-based arguments regarding practical issues *is* useful. The teacher must assume such evaluation is useful in everyday life, otherwise there'd be no reason to recommend it over abstract concepts.

Step 4: Evaluate the Answer Choices

(E) must be true. The science teacher's argument rests entirely on teaching skills that are useful. Using the Denial Test, if the ability to evaluate arguments were *not* useful in everyday life, then there would be no reason to recommend it.

The teacher's argument would fall apart. So, the teacher must assume it can be useful.

(A) is Extreme and even a 180. The science teacher does not claim that useful skills are the *only* things that should be taught. In fact, the teacher claims in the very last line that the useful skills could be taught "in addition to" abstract aspects, which the teacher already cited as "very seldom useful."

(B) is a 180. The science teacher favors argument evaluation of practical issues more than abstract aspects. In fact, the teacher argues it would be okay to teach evaluation "instead of" abstract concepts.

(C) is an Irrelevant Comparison. It doesn't matter who would be better at learning argument evaluation. The argument is only concerned with teaching it in the first place.

(D) is Out of Scope and Extreme. The argument is about what *should* be done, not what *is* or *is not* being done. Furthermore, putting **(D)** to the Denial Test would give a negated answer of "*some* secondary school science courses *do* currently teach students to evaluate arguments regarding practical issues." The existence of some schools that are already compliant with the recommendation would hardly destroy the science teacher's argument.

20. (D) Point at Issue

Step 1: Identify the Question Type
The question asks for a "point of disagreement" between two speakers, making this a Point at Issue question.

Step 2: Untangle the Stimulus
Lyle concludes that modernizing the language of old plays helps teach history. This is because modernization makes the play more accessible, even if it affects the aesthetic quality. Carl concludes ([*t*]*hus*) that modernizing language is of *no use* to teaching history. This is because it prevents full understanding, making it impossible to get a deep knowledge of the past.

Step 3: Make a Prediction
The point at issue is fairly transparent as Lyle says modernizing language is "valuable for teaching history," and Carl says it is "of no use for teaching history." Neither speaker addresses the other's evidence, so disagreement there cannot be discerned. The correct answer will stick to the core issue: whether modernizing language is valuable for teaching history.

Step 4: Evaluate the Answer Choices
(D) is the point at issue. Lyle says such modernizing *is* valuable, while Carl says it is decidedly *not*.

(A) is Out of Scope. Neither speaker assesses the pedagogical value of the original play. They only address the value of the modernization. If anything, they would probably *agree* that

the value is *different*. The real issue is whether that difference is positive or not.

(B) is a Distortion. Both speakers are concerned with the effect of modernized language, not the loss of aesthetic quality. If anything, Lyle finds the lessened aesthetic quality irrelevant while Carl offers no opinion whatsoever about the loss of aesthetic quality.

(C) is Out of Scope. Neither speaker is concerned about what would be *most* aesthetically enjoyable.

(E) is a Distortion. Lyle makes this suggestion, but Carl expresses no opinion about aesthetic qualities or loss thereof.

21. (E) Parallel Flaw

Step 1: Identify the Question Type
The correct answer will be an argument that is "parallel to" the one in the stimulus, which is described as *flawed*. That makes this a Parallel Flaw question. The correct answer must commit the exact same flaw as the argument in the stimulus.

Step 2: Untangle the Stimulus
The stimulus's author concludes that some soils contain clay and sand while other soils contain clay and organic material. This is because most soil contains clay, and almost all soil has sand or organic material.

Step 3: Make a Prediction
The problem here is that almost all soil contains sand *or* organic material. However, it's impossible to tell which one is more common. It's possible that 90% of soil has sand while only 9% has organic material (for a total of 99%—virtually all soil having one or the other), yet clay might only appear in soil with sand (90%—still most soil). Based on the two overlapping majorities, clay will certainly appear with sand *or* organic material, but there's no guarantee it will appear with sand in some soils *and* with organic materials in others, as the original argument concludes. The correct answer will make the same flawed shift from *or* to *and*. It might be helpful to set up an algebraic formula to compare the logic. The evidence is that most items (soils) have X (clay), and almost all of those items have Y *or* Z (sand or organic materials). The conclusion is that some items have X and Y *and* others have X and Z.

Step 4: Evaluate the Answer Choices
(E) matches the flawed logic. The evidence is that most items (pharmacies) have X (cosmetics), and almost all those items have Y or Z (shampoo or toothpaste). The conclusion is that some items have X and Y *and* others have X and Z. Like the original, it's possible that 90% of pharmacies have shampoo and 9% have toothpaste, and cosmetics could be sold only where shampoo is sold. There's no guarantee it would also be sold with toothpaste.

(A) has perfect evidence. However, the conclusion is conditional, based solely on *if* cosmetics are sold with toothpaste. If cosmetics are sold with shampoo, the conclusion doesn't trigger anything. So, the conclusion leaves open the door that cosmetics could be sold without toothpaste, taking away part of the original's flaw.

(B) mixes up the evidence and conclusion, concluding that most pharmacies sell cosmetics based on evidence of what *some* pharmacies sell. A conclusion about *most* pharmacies cannot be drawn from evidence about *some* pharmacies, but that's not the same flaw as the original.

(C) matches the evidence. However, the conclusion here is actually logical, not flawed. This is saying that if there's no pharmacy with cosmetics and toothpaste, then there must be some with cosmetics and shampoo. In other words, there must be pharmacies with at least cosmetics and toothpaste *or* cosmetics and shampoo, not necessarily both. This properly retains the *or* in the logic from evidence to conclusion.

(D) has the correct conclusion, but it is based on different evidence, and thus does not match. Instead of evidence that almost all pharmacies have Y or Z (shampoo or toothpaste), the evidence here is that almost all pharmacies with Y *also* have Z. That ignores all the pharmacies that *don't* have Y—a flaw not found in the original argument.

22. (A) Flaw

Step 1: Identify the Question Type
The question asks why the argument given is "vulnerable to criticism," which means it is asking for the flaw in the reasoning.

Step 2: Untangle the Stimulus
The author concludes that PCB regulation effectively reduced exposure to PCBs based on a study showing that younger test subjects had lower levels of PCBs.

Step 3: Make a Prediction
The author wisely addresses representativeness issues by admitting that "valid inferences could not be drawn from the study because of the small sample size." And yet, just two sentences later, the author claims that the study *proves* that regulations were effective. So, the flaw is the author's insistence that a conclusion is *proven* based on a study the author outright admitted could not be used to infer anything.

Step 4: Evaluate the Answer Choices
(A) identifies the flaw. This inconsistency is apparent when the author claims "inferences could not be drawn from the study" and then proceeds to draw an inference from the study.

(B) is Out of Scope. The author is only concerned about PCB levels, not other chemicals or any effects.

(C) is Out of Scope. The evidence never mentions any lack of evidence against the PCB regulations.

(D) is not applicable here. While claims of causality can sometimes confuse cause and effect, there's no reason to suggest that the author is doing that here. This answer suggests that the PCB-banning regulation could have been an *effect* (rather than the *cause*) of reduced PCB levels—but that doesn't make sense.

(E) is Out of Scope. The argument is only about exposure to PCBs, not the effects.

23. (B) Parallel Reasoning

Step 1: Identify the Question Type
The correct answer will be an argument that is "similar in its reasoning" to the given argument. That makes this a Parallel Reasoning question.

Step 2: Untangle the Stimulus
The author presents a discrepancy in learning about spies: we can learn a lot about why they fail, but much less about why they succeed. This is because spies generally don't reveal their methods unless they fail (i.e., are caught).

Step 3: Make a Prediction
The argument is based on how limited evidence can lead to lopsided information. If information is mostly limited to failures, then it makes sense that that's what we learn the most about. The correct answer will present similar results on a different topic: information will be mainly limited to one side of a situation, so that is what we mostly learn about.

Step 4: Evaluate the Answer Choices
(B) is a match. Information about motives is mainly limited to one side (motives people are aware of), so that is what we mostly learn about.

(A) draws a conclusion about a requirement and makes no mention of a situation in which we learn more about one side than another. Furthermore, the stimulus is limited to spies who were caught and those who were not, but **(A)** contains three groups of people: those who succeeded at the marathon, those who failed, and those who did not participate.

(C) concludes that something is unclear and provides a condition that would have provided more clarity. Not only does that not match the original logic, but it fails to mention how we learn more about one aspect of a situation over another.

(D) does not compare one side of a situation to another. Instead, it just describes how one category of people is already large but can be made even larger with a different label.

(E) concludes that something is *impossible*, which is far stronger than the original argument—which says "very little" can be learned about successful spies who "normally only" reveal their methods when they are caught. Furthermore, **(E)** fails to include two groups of people, one of which provides more limited information than the other. Successful spies *could* reveal information, but in **(E)** there is no way to find out what would have happened had there been no intervention in the conflict.

24. (E) Principle (Identify/Assumption)

Step 1: Identify the Question Type

The question directly asks for a principle, which makes this an Identify the Principle question. Furthermore, it is said that the argument "requires assuming" the principle. This means that this would also work like a Necessary Assumption question, only with an answer that is in broader terms than usual.

Step 2: Untangle the Stimulus

The author argues that parents should be allowed to vote on behalf of their children, *thus* giving families fair representation. As evidence, the author points out that families are often overlooked in politics because families have underage children who cannot vote.

Step 3: Make a Prediction

Allowing parents to vote on behalf of their children would certainly allow families to get more representation in elections. After all, they would be allowed to cast votes for family members who couldn't previously vote. However, is this really *fair*? The author must assume so, which means the necessary principle here is that *more* representation is *fair* representation.

Step 4: Evaluate the Answer Choices

(E) is the assumed principle, connecting the increased number of votes to the idea of fairness.

(A) is a Faulty Use of Detail. The author does bemoan the lack of attention given to families, but the conclusion (and thus the argument) is ultimately about fair representation, not how much attention people get.

(B) is Out of Scope. The author's conclusion does not rest on the condition that children lack maturity. The only reason given for children not voting is that they are *underage*. Maturity has no bearing on the argument.

(C) is Extreme. The author only recommends giving parents the right to vote on behalf of their children. There's no mention of having to serve their children's interests. Perhaps the author believes votes cast on behalf of the children should represent the children's best interests, but the votes made by the adults (for the adults) may not have to. Either way, this is not necessary to the argument.

(D) is an Irrelevant Comparison. The author is not comparing people who *can* vote to people who *cannot*. Besides, the

author is only arguing a certain action is fair, not judging any action as *not* fair.

25. (C) Weaken

Step 1: Identify the Question Type

The question directly asks for something that weakens the given argument.

Step 2: Untangle the Stimulus

The critic concludes that a newspaper's plan to avoid errors is not working. As evidence, the critic cites that the newspaper acknowledges more errors by printing corrections than a competing newspaper.

Step 3: Make a Prediction

The critic assumes that the greater number of corrections somehow indicates a failure to avoid errors. This overlooks the possibility that the newspaper *is* doing a better job at avoiding errors—it just also does a better job at admitting when it *does* make an error. Showing such an overlooked possibility would certainly weaken the critic's argument.

Step 4: Evaluate the Answer Choices

(C) weakens the argument. This suggests that the newspaper is just more diligent about acknowledging errors. Its competitor might make a *lot* more errors, but it might just not care enough to correct them.

(A) is an Irrelevant Comparison. No connection can be logically drawn between salary and avoiding errors.

(B) is an Irrelevant Comparison. How long the newspaper has been in business has no bearing on its ability to avoid errors.

(D) is a 180 at worst. If the newspaper uses more editors and *still* has to print more corrections, the critic's claim that the paper's plan isn't working is only helped.

(E) is Out of Scope. The size of the reporting staff has no bearing on whether the editorial staff is doing its job or not.

Section II: Logic Games
Game 1: Special Project Workers

Q#	Question Type	Correct	Difficulty
1	Acceptability	C	★
2	"If" / Must Be True	D	★
3	Supply the If	A	★★
4	"If" / Must Be True	E	★★
5	Completely Determine	B	★★★

Game 2: 1920s History Archives Project

Q#	Question Type	Correct	Difficulty
6	Acceptability	C	★
7	Supply the If	E	★★
8	"If" / Could Be True	A	★
9	How Many	D	★★★
10	"If" / Could Be True	E	★★
11	Must Be False (CANNOT Be True)	A	★★

Game 3: Antique Dealer Auction

Q#	Question Type	Correct	Difficulty
12	Acceptability	C	★
13	Could Be True	B	★★
14	"If" / Could Be True	D	★★
15	Must Be False (CANNOT Be True)	A	★★
16	Could Be True	E	★★★
17	Could Be True	B	★★★

Game 4: Chorus Auditions

Q#	Question Type	Correct	Difficulty
18	Acceptability	D	★
19	Must Be False (CANNOT Be True)	C	★
20	Could Be True	C	★
21	"If" / Could Be True	E	★★
22	Could Be True	B	★★
23	Rule Substitution	A	★★★★

Game 1: Special Project Workers

Step 1: Overview
Situation: Workers being considered for a special project

Entities: Seven workers (Quinn, Ruiz, Smith, Taylor, Verma, Wells, Xue)

Action: Selection. Determine which workers will be selected for the special project.

Limitations: Exactly three workers will be selected. Furthermore, exactly one of those workers will be selected as project leader, adding a second level of selection.

Step 2: Sketch
List the entities by initial. Because it is known how many people will be selected, an In/Out sketch can be used with three "In" slots and four "Out" slots. Be sure to label one "In" slot as the project leader.

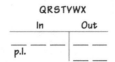

Step 3: Rules
Rule 1 provides some Formal Logic. If Quinn or Ruiz is selected, that person must be project leader. This does *not* mean Quinn or Ruiz will definitely be selected, but either one must be project leader *if* selected.

$$Q \text{ or } R \longrightarrow \text{project leader}$$

As an early deduction, it should be noted that this means Q and R cannot *both* be selected. Otherwise, they would both be project leaders, and there can only be one.

<u>Never</u>
QR

Rule 2 is more Formal Logic. If Smith is selected, then so is Taylor. Draw that out and its contrapositive:

$$S \longrightarrow T$$
$$\sim T \longrightarrow \sim S$$

Rule 3 is even more Formal Logic. If Wells is selected, then Ruiz and Verma are not. You can draw out this rule and its contrapositive:

$$W \longrightarrow \sim R \ \& \ \sim V$$
$$R \text{ or } V \longrightarrow \sim W$$

However, this rule can be interpreted more simply: it is impossible to select both Wells and Ruiz (because selecting

one requires rejecting the other), and it is similarly impossible to select Wells and Verma.

<u>Never</u>
WR
WV

Step 4: Deductions
Because every rule is conditional, it's difficult to make any substantial deductions until some condition is met. There is no specific worker who must or cannot be selected. And any worker could still be project leader. There's even one worker, Xue, who is completely unrestricted (i.e., a Floater)—which you can note with an asterisk in your entity list. There are no Blocks of Entities, no clear Limited Options, and no Established Entities. The only part of BLEND that can yield a meaningful deduction is the Numbers. Although there are too many outcomes to consider for who *is* selected, there are few deductions that can be made about who is *not* selected. First, because Quinn and Ruiz are both only able to be the project leader (Rule 1), at least one of them must not be selected. That means one of them will occupy one of the four "Out" slots. Furthermore, because Wells and Verma are mutually exclusive (Rule 3), one of the two of them also must *not* be selected.

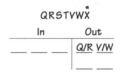

Ruiz is a Duplication in the rules (in fact the only one), but the mutual exclusivity of Wells and Ruiz cannot also be built into the Master Sketch, because it's possible one or each is already represented by the "Q/R" and "V/W" in the first two "Out" slots. So, the Ruiz Duplication does not allow the rules to be logically combined in any meaningful way at this point. With so few deductions, it's important to be confident with the rules and consider each one when new conditions are presented.

Step 5: Questions
1. (C) Acceptability
As with any Acceptability question, use the rules one at a time to eliminate answers that violate those rules.

(B) violates Rule 1 by having Quinn selected, but not as the leader. **(D)** violates Rule 2 by selecting Smith without Taylor. **(A)** violates Rule 3 by selecting Wells but also selecting Ruiz. **(E)** also violates Rule 3 by selecting Wells but also selecting Verma. That leaves **(C)** as the correct answer.

2. (D) "If" / Must Be True

For this question, Taylor and Wells are selected, and Taylor is the project leader. Because Taylor is the project leader, neither Quinn nor Ruiz can be project leader, so they cannot be selected at all (Rule 1). Because Wells is selected, Verma cannot be selected (Rule 3). That leaves Smith and Xue, either of whom could fill in the third spot on the project.

In			Out	
T	W	S/X	Q	R
pl			V	X/S

That makes **(D)** the correct answer.

3. (A) Supply the If

The correct answer will be a condition that would allow Verma to be project leader. The remaining answers would make it impossible for Verma to be project leader.

In order for Verma to be project leader, Quinn and Ruiz would have to be rejected. Otherwise, one of them would be project leader (Rule 1). Also, Wells would have to be rejected, otherwise Verma couldn't be selected for the project at all (Rule 3).

In			Out	
V	—	—	Q	R
pl			W	—

That would leave Smith, Taylor, and Xue—two of whom must be selected and one of whom must be rejected. Getting rid of Taylor would also get rid of Smith (Rule 2). That wouldn't leave enough people on the project to work with Verma. Therefore, Taylor would *have* to be selected, which eliminates **(B)**, **(C)**, and **(E)**. And the project couldn't exclude Smith and Xue because, again, that wouldn't leave enough people on the project to work with Verma. That eliminates **(D)**, leaving **(A)** as the correct answer. Sure enough, if Quinn and Smith were rejected, Verma could be project leader on a team with Taylor and Xue.

In			Out	
V	T	X	Q	R
pl			W	S

4. (E) "If" / Must Be True

For this question, Taylor is not selected. In that case, Smith is also not selected (Rule 2). That leaves Quinn, Ruiz, Verma, Wells, and Xue. As noted in Step 4, Quinn and Ruiz cannot both be selected, or else there would be two project leaders (Rule 1). Also, Verma and Wells cannot both be selected (Rule 3). This creates some major Numbers restrictions. Between Quinn and Ruiz, only one can be selected. Same with Verma and Wells. That would account for two members. The third

and final member would have to be the only remaining worker: Xue.

In			Out	
R/Q	V/W	X	T	S
pl			Q/R	W/V

That makes **(E)** the correct answer.

5. (B) Completely Determine

The correct answer to this question will create enough restrictions such that only one outcome is possible. The other four answers will still allow for multiple outcomes.

If neither Quinn nor Smith is selected, that would leave Ruiz, Taylor, Verma, Wells, and Xue. In that case, Wells could be selected along with Taylor and Xue. Or Wells could be left out, and any of the remaining three could be selected.

In			Out	
—	—	—	Q	S
			W/V	—

This leaves too many possibilities, so **(A)** can be eliminated.

If neither Quinn nor Taylor is selected, then Smith cannot be selected (Rule 2). That leaves Ruiz, Verma, Wells, and Xue. Wells cannot be selected, otherwise Ruiz and Verma would be rejected (Rule 3), leaving only two people for the project. With Wells out, that leaves three people: Ruiz, Verma, and Xue. Ruiz would be project leader (Rule 1).

In			Out	
R	V	X	Q	T
pl			S	W

That is the only possible outcome, making **(B)** the correct answer. For the record:

If neither Quinn nor Xue is selected, there are still plenty of outcomes. Wells could be selected with Smith and Taylor. Or Wells could be rejected, and either Ruiz or Verma could be selected with Smith and Taylor, among other outcomes.

In			Out	
—	—	—	Q	X
			W/V	—

There are too many possibilities, so that eliminates **(C)**.

If neither Ruiz nor Wells is selected, that leaves Quinn, Smith, Taylor, Verma, and Xue. Virtually any trio could be selected from that group, as long as Smith is not selected without Taylor.

In			Out	
___	___	___	R	W
			___	___

This results in too many outcomes, so that eliminates **(D)**.

If neither Ruiz nor Verma is selected, that leaves Quinn, Smith, Taylor, Wells, and Xue. Again, as long as Smith is not selected without Taylor, any other trio is acceptable.

In			Out	
___	___	___	R	V
			___	___

This leaves too many outcomes, so that eliminates **(E)**.

Game 2: 1920s History Archives Project

Step 1: Overview
Situation: Students being assigned to search archives for a history project

Entities: Six students (Louis, Mollie, Onyx, Ryan, Tiffany, Yoshio) and four archive years (1921, 1922, 1923, 1924)

Action: Sequencing/Selection Hybrid. Determine which students will be selected for the project (Selection), and place them in order of the years they must search (Sequencing).

Limitations: For the Selection element, exactly four of the six students will be chosen. For the Sequencing element, each individual year will be searched by exactly one student. That makes it standard 1:1 Sequencing.

Step 2: Sketch
For the Sequencing element, a set of four numbered slots will suffice. You can write out the full year or just use the last digit of each year (1, 2, 3, 4). For the Selection element, simply list the students by initial and note that four out of the six will be selected. As the game proceeds, circle students that are chosen and cross out those who aren't.

$$\text{LMORTY}$$
$$\underline{\text{Pick 4}}$$

$$\underline{\quad} \quad \underline{\quad} \quad \underline{\quad} \quad \underline{\quad}$$
$$1 \quad\quad 2 \quad\quad 3 \quad\quad 4$$

Step 3: Rules
Rule 1 assigns Louis or Tiffany in 1923. That means at least one of them will be selected. However, it could be either one, and it is still possible that both are selected. In that case, one would be assigned to 1923, and the other could be assigned to any other year. For this rule, simply establish "L/T" in the slot for 1923.

Rule 2 restricts Mollie. If she is selected, she can only be assigned to 1921 or 1922. This does not mean Mollie *must* be selected. However, it does mean that she cannot be assigned any other year. Since Louis or Tiffany is already established in 1923, simply add "~M" under the slot for 1924.

Rule 3 provides some Formal Logic for the selection. If Tiffany is selected, then so is Ryan. By contrapositive, if Ryan is not selected, then Tiffany is not.

$$T \rightarrow R$$
$$\sim R \rightarrow \sim T$$

Rule 4 provides more Formal Logic. If Ryan is selected, then Onyx must also be selected and assigned the year immediately before Ryan. By contrapositive, if Onyx is not selected, then neither is Ryan.

$$R \rightarrow \underline{O} \ \underline{R}$$
$$\sim O \rightarrow \sim R$$

Step 4: Deductions
The last rule is very significant. If Ryan is selected, that creates a block of Onyx immediately before Ryan. With Louis or Tiffany established in 1923, there is only way to assign the block of Onyx and Ryan: Onyx in 1921 and Ryan in 1922.

However, that only happens if Ryan *is* selected. If Ryan is *not* selected, that leads to even *more* deductions from Rule 3. At this point, there are major ramifications depending on whether Ryan is selected or not. That means Limited Options would be highly valuable.

In the first option, Ryan is selected. That means Onyx is selected and assigned immediately before Ryan. That could only happen by assigning Onyx to 1921 and Ryan to 1922. Louis or Tiffany will be assigned to 1923. That leaves 1924. Mollie cannot be assigned to 1924 (Rule 2), so Mollie can be crossed off. That leaves Yoshio for 1924, or either Louis or Tiffany—whoever is not assigned—to 1923.

$$\text{I)} \quad\quad \text{L} \ \cancel{M} \ \text{O} \ \text{R} \ \text{T} \ \text{Y}$$

$$\underline{O} \quad \underline{R} \quad \underline{L/T} \quad \underline{\quad}$$
$$1 \quad\quad 2 \quad\quad 3 \quad\quad 4$$

In the second option, Ryan is not selected. By Rule 3, Tiffany will also be left out. That means the remaining four students must be selected: Louis, Mollie, Onyx, and Yoshio. With Tiffany unavailable, that means Louis must be assigned to 1923. The only other restriction is that Mollie can only be assigned to 1921 or 1922. So, either Onyx or Yoshio must be assigned to 1924.

$$\text{II)} \quad\quad \cancel{L} \ \cancel{M} \ \cancel{O} \ \cancel{R} \ \cancel{T} \ \cancel{Y}$$

$$\underline{\quad} \quad \underline{\quad} \quad \underline{L} \quad \underline{O/Y}$$
$$1 \quad\quad 2 \quad\quad 3 \quad\quad 4$$

Step 5: Questions

6. (C) Acceptability
As with any Acceptability question, go through the rules one at a time, eliminating answers that violate those rules. Keep in mind that the answers are listed in chronological order: 1921, 1922, 1923, 1924.

(A) violates Rule 1 by assigning Ryan, and not Louis or Tiffany, to 1923. **(E)** violates Rule 2 by assigning Mollie to 1924. **(B)** violates Rule 3 by assigning Tiffany to the project without Ryan. **(D)** violates Rule 4 by assigning Ryan to the project without Onyx *immediately* before. That leaves **(C)** as the correct answer.

7. (E) Supply the If

The correct answer will be a condition that forces Mollie to be assigned to 1922. The wrong answers will all allow Mollie to be assigned to another year or even go unassigned.

Mollie can only be assigned to 1921 or 1922, so the correct answer is likely to establish another student to 1921. If Onyx is assigned to 1921, then 1922 would be the only year left for Mollie. However, it's also possible that Mollie is not assigned at all (as seen in Option I). That eliminates **(B)**.

If Yoshio is assigned to 1921, Louis or Tiffany is assigned to 1923. In that case, there is no longer space for Onyx and Ryan to be consecutive. That means Ryan cannot be assigned at all (Rule 4), which also means Tiffany is not assigned (Rule 3). That means everyone else must be assigned, including Mollie. (Option II makes this clear, as Yoshio could only be assigned to 1921 in Option II.) With Yoshio in 1921, Mollie would have to be assigned to 1922. That's what the question is looking for, making **(E)** the correct answer. For the record:

If Louis is assigned to 1924, Tiffany would be assigned to 1923 (Rule 1). With Tiffany assigned to 1923, Ryan would have to be assigned (Rule 3) with Onyx immediately before (Rule 4). They would be assigned to 1921 and 1922, as seen in Option I. Mollie couldn't be assigned at all, so that eliminates **(A)** and **(D)**.

If Onyx is assigned to 1924 (as could happen in Option II), Mollie could still be assigned to 1921 *or* 1922. That eliminates **(C)**.

8. (A) "If" / Could Be True

For this question, Ryan and Yoshio are both assigned—which only happens in Option I. With Ryan assigned, Onyx is also assigned and immediately before Ryan (Rule 4). With Tiffany or Louis assigned to 1923, Onyx and Ryan can only be assigned to 1921 and 1922, respectively. That leaves 1924 for Yoshio.

O	R	L/T	Y
1	2	3	4

With that, only **(A)** is possible and is thus the correct answer.

9. (D) How Many

The question asks for the number of students who could be assigned to 1921. Limited Options help a lot with this question. In Option I, only Onyx could be assigned to 1921. In Option II, Louis is assigned to 1923. Any of the remaining three students that are selected—Mollie, Onyx, or Yoshio—could be assigned to 1921. So, Mollie, Onyx, and Yoshio are the only three students who could be assigned to 1921, making **(D)** the correct answer.

As further proof, Ryan cannot be assigned to 1921 because that would leave no previous year for Onyx, violating Rule 4.

Also, neither Louis nor Tiffany could be assigned to 1921. If that happened, one would be assigned to 1921 and the other to 1923. Tiffany would definitely be assigned, but that would force Ryan to be assigned (Rule 3), which would force a block with Onyx (Rule 4) that would be impossible to place. So, Ryan, Louis, and Tiffany could *not* be assigned to 1921. That leaves the other three: Mollie, Onyx, and Yoshio.

10. (E) "If" / Could Be True

For this question, Yoshio is not assigned at all. That leaves five students. Ryan would have to be assigned, otherwise Ryan would be out, eliminating Tiffany (Rule 3) and leaving only three students.

With Ryan selected, Onyx has to be selected and assigned the year before. With Louis or Tiffany assigned to 1923, Onyx and Ryan would have to be assigned to 1921 and 1922, respectively (as seen in Option I). That leaves 1924 open. Mollie cannot be assigned to 1924 (Rule 2), so she is not assigned at all. With Mollie and Yoshio both out, that means Louis and Tiffany are both assigned. One will be assigned to 1923, the other will be assigned to 1924.

$$L \cancel{M} O R T \cancel{Y}$$

O	R	L/T	T/L
1	2	3	4

So, Louis, Ryan, and Tiffany *are* assigned for sure, and Onyx is assigned to 1921. That leaves **(E)** as the only remaining answer. Louis *could* be assigned to 1924, so **(E)** is correct.

11. (A) Must Be False (CANNOT Be True)

The correct answer will be a student who cannot be assigned to 1922. The remaining students all *could* be.

Limited Options help a lot here. In Option I, Ryan is assigned to 1922. That eliminates **(D)**. In Option II, with Louis assigned to 1923, Mollie, Onyx, or Yoshio could be assigned to 1922. That eliminates **(B)**, **(C)**, and **(E)**, leaving **(A)** as the correct answer.

For further proof, if Louis were assigned to 1922, then Tiffany would be assigned to 1923 (Rule 1). With Tiffany assigned, Ryan would have to be assigned (Rule 3), with Onyx assigned the previous year (Rule 4). With 1922 and 1923 filled, the Onyx and Ryan block could not be placed. This is impossible, so Louis cannot be assigned to 1922.

	L	T	
1	2	3	4

O	R

Game 3: Antique Dealer Auction

Step 1: Overview

Situation: An antique dealer auctioning off antiques at a shop's grand opening

Entities: Six antiques (harmonica, lamp, mirror, sundial, table, vase)

Action: Loose Sequencing. Determine the order in which the antiques are auctioned, from June 1 to June 6. The only indication that this is Loose Sequencing is the rules, which all establish relative ordering with no defined spacing. The first rule is admittedly strict, but the ultimate sketch and treatment of the entities work much more like a Loose Sequencing game than a Strict one.

Limitations: The dealer will auction each antique, exactly one per day. There are no ties in the sequence.

Step 2: Sketch

As with any Sequencing game, list the entities by initial. Because this is Loose Sequencing, no sketch is needed up front. It would be understandable to want a series of numbered slots, but they would likely go unused for the rest of the game.

Step 3: Rules

Rule 1 prevents the sundial from being auctioned first. If you've drawn slots, "~S" could be added under the first slot. Otherwise, draw a note to the side: "S ≠ 1."

Rule 2 provides Formal Logic. If the harmonica is auctioned earlier than the lamp, then so is the mirror. By contrapositive, if the mirror is *not* auctioned earlier than the lamp (i.e., the mirror *is* auctioned later), then the harmonica is not auctioned earlier (i.e., is later) than the lamp.

$$H–L \rightarrow M–L$$
$$L–M \rightarrow L–H$$

This rule allows for three possibilities:

H \
    L   or
M /

     / M
L   or
     \ H

M — L — H

Rule 3 dictates that the sundial be auctioned before the mirror and the vase, but does not indicate whether the mirror should be auctioned before the vase or vice versa.

Rule 4

Rule 4 requires the table to be auctioned earlier than the harmonica or the vase, *but not both*. So, if the table is auctioned earlier than the harmonica, the table must be auctioned *later* than the vase. Similarly, if the table is auctioned earlier than the vase, then it must be auctioned later than the harmonica. In short, the table will be auctioned before one and after the other:

$$V – T – H$$
or
$$H – T – V$$

Step 4: Deductions

Rule 4 presents two possible orders for half of the antiques (whereas Rule 2 allows for three possible orders). Further, each order includes the vase, which is also mentioned in Rule 3 along with two other antiques. That means each option would create connections among five of the six antiques. That warrants setting up Limited Options based on Rule 4.

In the first option, the table will be auctioned before the harmonica, which means the table will be auctioned after the vase. The vase will be auctioned later than the sundial (Rule 3). The sundial is also auctioned before the mirror, but that is not connected to any of the other antiques so far.

I)   S < M
      \ V – T – H

In that case, the sundial is auctioned before every other listed antique. However, by Rule 1, it cannot be auctioned first. That leaves one antique, the lamp, to be first. With the lamp first, the sundial will be auctioned second. The remaining antiques will be the vase, table, and harmonica, in that order, with the mirror being auctioned at any point in between.

I)   L – S < M
         \ V – T – H

In the second option, the table will be auctioned before the vase, which means the table will be auctioned after the harmonica. The sundial will also be auctioned before the vase (Rule 3), but there is no connection between the sundial and the table. Further, the sundial will be auctioned before the mirror, which is not connected to anything else. That leaves the lamp, which is only limited by Rule 2. However, Rule 2 is conditional, so the lamp cannot be placed with certainty.

II)   S < M   L?
      H – T – V

Step 5: Questions

12. (C) Acceptability

As with any Acceptability question, use the rules one at a time to eliminate answers until there is one answer left that does not violate any rule.

(D) violates Rule 1 by placing the sundial first. **(A)** violates Rule 2 by having the harmonica before the lamp, but then having the mirror *after* the lamp. **(E)** violates Rule 3 by having the sundial before the mirror but not the vase. **(B)** violates Rule 4 by having the table at the end, earlier than neither the harmonica nor the vase. That leaves **(C)** as the correct answer.

13. (B) Could Be True

The correct answer will be the only one that is possible. The other four must be false.

The table has to be auctioned between the harmonica and the vase (Rule 4). If the table is auctioned on the 2nd, the harmonica would have to be auctioned on the 1st because the vase still needs to be auctioned after the sundial (Rule 3). With the harmonica on the 1st, it will certainly be auctioned earlier than the lamp. That means the mirror must also be auctioned earlier than the lamp (Rule 2). But then the lamp could not be auctioned on the 3rd because there would be no room for the mirror before it.

(A) is thus impossible and can be eliminated.

The sundial could be auctioned on the 2nd, and it must precede the vase, which could certainly be on the 3rd. Then the lamp could be on the 1st, with the remaining antiques taking up the remaining spots.

This is all seen as possible in Option I. That makes **(B)** the correct answer. For the record:

The sundial must be auctioned before the mirror and the vase (Rule 3), so that eliminates **(C)** and **(D)**. Likewise, if the sundial was auctioned on the 4th and the table on the 5th, that would leave no room for both the mirror and the vase, which both have to be after the sundial (Rule 3).

That eliminates **(E)**.

14. (D) "If" / Could Be True

For this question, the table will be auctioned later than the mirror and the vase (which can only happen in Option I). If the table is auctioned later than the vase, then it must be auctioned earlier than the harmonica (Rule 4). The mirror and the vase, in either order, must both be auctioned after the sundial (Rule 3). At that point, everything would be auctioned after the sundial, but the sundial cannot be auctioned first (Rule 1). That means the remaining antique, the lamp, would be first. The sundial would be second. The table and harmonica would be fifth and sixth, respectively. The only thing that cannot be determined is the order of the vase and the mirror.

With that, only **(D)** is possible and is thus the correct answer.

15. (A) Must Be False (CANNOT Be True)

The correct answer for this question will be the antique that cannot be auctioned immediately before the vase. The remaining four antiques *could* be auctioned immediately before the vase.

By Rule 4, if the table is auctioned earlier than the vase, then the harmonica would be auctioned earlier than the table. And if the table is auctioned earlier than the harmonica, then the vase would be auctioned earlier than the table.

That means the table must be auctioned in between the harmonica and the vase. Therefore, the harmonica could never be immediately before the vase, making **(A)** the correct answer.

16. (E) Could Be True

The correct answer will be the only one that is possible. The remaining four answers all must be false.

The mirror must be auctioned after the sundial. If the mirror was auctioned on the 2nd, the sundial would be auctioned on the 1st, violating Rule 1. That eliminates **(A)**.

If the lamp is auctioned on the 2nd, the harmonica could not be auctioned on the 1st because that would require the mirror to be auctioned before the lamp (Rule 2), and there would be no room for that to happen. The sundial could not be on the 1st (Rule 1), nor could the mirror or vase (Rule 3). And the table has to be auctioned between the harmonica and the vase (Rule 4), so the table couldn't be on the 1st. That would leave nothing to be on the 1st.

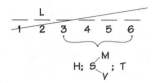

That's not possible, which eliminates **(B)**.

The vase must be auctioned after the sundial. If the vase was auctioned on the 2nd, the sundial would be auctioned on the 1st, violating Rule 1. That eliminates **(C)**.

If the lamp is auctioned on the 3rd, the sundial could not be auctioned on the 1st (Rule 1), nor could the mirror or the vase (Rule 3) or the table (Rule 4). That leaves the harmonica. If the harmonica were on the 1st, the mirror would have to be before the lamp (Rule 2), so the mirror would be on the 2nd. But that would not leave room for the sundial before the mirror, violating Rule 3.

$$\begin{array}{ccccccc} & \overset{S}{\diagup} \\ H & M & L \\ \hline 1 & 2 & 3 & 4 & 5 & 6 \end{array}$$

This is impossible, which eliminates **(D)**.

That leaves **(E)** as the correct answer, which is possible in either of the two options. Here is an example of each:

$$\begin{array}{llllllll} \text{I)} & L & S & V & T & M & H \\ & 1 & 2 & 3 & 4 & 5 & 6 \end{array}$$

or

$$\begin{array}{llllllll} \text{II)} & H & T & S & V & M & L \\ & 1 & 2 & 3 & 4 & 5 & 6 \end{array}$$

17. (B) Could Be True

The correct answer here could be true, which means the remaining answers all must be false.

The sundial cannot be auctioned on the 5th because there would be no room for both the vase and the mirror afterward, violating Rule 3. That eliminates **(A)**.

The sundial could be auctioned on the 4th, though. Then the mirror and vase would be on the 5th and 6th, in either order. The remaining antiques would be the harmonica, lamp, and table. With the mirror on the 5th or 6th, the lamp is sure to be auctioned earlier, triggering Rule 2's contrapositive. Thus, the lamp must be earlier than the harmonica. Also, given that the vase is sure to be auctioned after the table, the table must be auctioned after the harmonica (Rule 4).

$$\begin{array}{cccccc} H/V & T & V/H & S & M/V & V/M \\ \hline 1 & 2 & 3 & 4 & 5 & 6 \end{array}$$

This is possible, making **(B)** the correct answer. For the record:

If the lamp were on the 5th and the mirror were on the 6th, the contrapositive of Rule 2 would be triggered, which would require the lamp to also precede the harmonica. However, with the 5th and 6th slots filled, there is no more room after the lamp, so this is impossible. That eliminates **(C)**.

If the table were on the 3rd and the lamp on the 4th, the sundial could not be on the 1st (Rule 1), nor could the mirror or vase (Rule 3). That would leave the harmonica on the 1st. By Rule 2, the mirror would have to be before the lamp, thus on the 2nd. But that would violate Rule 3 because there would be no room for the sundial before the mirror.

$$\begin{array}{cccccc} & \overset{S}{\diagup} \\ H & M & T & L \\ \hline 1 & 2 & 3 & 4 & 5 & 6 \end{array}$$

That eliminates **(D)**.

The table has to be auctioned between the harmonica and the vase (Rule 4), so the harmonica and vase cannot be consecutive. That eliminates **(E)**.

Game 4: Chorus Auditions

Step 1: Overview
Situation: Singers auditioning for a chorus director

Entities: Six singers (Kammer, Lugo, Trillo, Waite, Yoshida, Zinn)

Action: Strict Sequencing. Determine the order in which the singers audition. Even though each singer's audition is recorded or not recorded, there is no Matching component, because it's already announced which singers are recorded and which aren't. If that information were not already concrete, then this would be a Sequencing/Matching Hybrid.

Limitations: The six singers will all be auditioned, and auditions take place one after the other, so this is standard 1:1 Sequencing. It's also noted that two of the singers, Kammer and Lugo, will be recorded while the others will not.

Step 2: Sketch
List the singers by initial, and set up a series of six numbered slots. Be sure to distinguish the two singers that are recorded; there are many ways to do so. You can just label the entity list with those that are recorded and those that aren't, you can put the recorded ones in uppercase and the non-recorded ones in lowercase, you can put an "r" under each recorded singer and an "n" under each non-recorded one, etc. It doesn't matter which you choose, just make sure they're at least distinguished in the entity list.

rec	non-rec
KL	TWYZ

$$\underline{}\ \underline{}\ \underline{}\ \underline{}\ \underline{}\ \underline{}$$
$$\ \ 1\quad 2\quad 3\quad 4\quad 5\quad 6$$

Step 3: Rules
Rule 1 establishes the fourth audition as non-recorded. Depending on your notation, you may consider adding "n" under the fourth slot. You may alternatively or additionally want to put "~K" and "~L" underneath the slot, which would also capture the rule.

Rule 2 establishes the fifth audition as recorded. Depending on your notation, you may consider adding "r" under the fifth slot. You may alternatively or additionally want to put "K/L" in the slot itself, which would also capture the rule.

Rule 3 requires Waite to audition before both recorded singers (Kammer and Lugo). Kammer and Lugo could still audition in either order. There's no need to necessarily indicate recorded/non-recorded because the sequence already completely represents the rule.

$$W\begin{matrix}\nearrow K\\ \searrow L\end{matrix}$$

Rule 4 requires Kammer to audition before Trillo. That can be immediately combined with Rule 3.

Rule 5 requires Zinn to audition before Yoshida.

$$Z-Y$$

Step 4: Deductions
Most of the deductions come from the orders established in the last three rules. That alone leads to a lot of restrictions about which entities *can't* be in certain slots (e.g., per Rule 4, Zinn can't be last and Yoshida can't be first). However, there's one more deduction to consider first. One of the recorded sessions (Kammer or Lugo) will be fifth (Rule 2). The other recorded session cannot be fourth (Rule 1), nor can it be first because Waite must audition beforehand (Rule 3). That means the other recorded session must be second, third, or sixth. However, if it were sixth, that would mean the last two sessions would both be recorded. In that case, it would be impossible for Kammer to audition before Trillo (a non-recorded audition). Therefore, the other recorded session cannot be sixth, so it has to be either second or third. That allows for Limited Options.

If the other recorded session is second, then Waite would have to audition first. Kammer and Lugo would be second and fifth, in either order. Trillo, Yoshida, and Zinn would fill in the remaining spots. Because Zinn has to precede Yoshida (Rule 5), Zinn could not be last and Yoshida could not be third.

$$I)\ \underline{W}\ \ \underline{L/K}\ \ \underline{T/Z}\ \ \underline{}\ \ \underline{K/L}\ \ \underline{T/Y}$$
$$\quad\ \ 1\qquad 2\qquad 3\qquad 4\qquad 5\qquad 6$$

If the other recorded session is third, Waite would audition first or second. Kammer and Lugo would be third and fifth, in either order. Trillo would have to audition after Kammer, so Trillo could not be first or second, and thus must be fourth or sixth.

$$II)\ \underline{}\ \ \underline{}\ \ \underline{L/K}\ \ \underline{}\ \ \underline{K/L}\ \ \underline{}$$
$$\quad\ \ 1\quad\ \ 2\quad\ \ 3\quad\ \ 4\quad\ \ 5\quad\ \ 6$$

Yoshida has to audition after Zinn, so Yoshida also cannot be first or second—otherwise, it would be in the first two auditions with Waite, leaving no room for Zinn. That would leave Zinn as the only other singer who could audition first or second along with Waite, in either order. That means Trillo and Yoshida would be fourth or sixth, in either order.

$$\begin{array}{c} \text{II)} \quad \underset{1}{\text{W/Z}} \quad \underset{2}{\text{Z/W}} \quad \underset{3}{\text{L/K}} \quad \underset{4}{\text{T/Y}} \quad \underset{5}{\text{K/L}} \quad \underset{6}{\text{Y/T}} \end{array}$$

Step 5: Questions

18. (D) Acceptability

Use the rules one at a time to eliminate answers that violate the rules. The one answer that doesn't violate the rules is acceptable and thus correct. Be sure to refer to the entity list to remember who is recorded and who is not.

(E) violates Rule 1 by placing Lugo (a recorded singer) fourth. **(C)** violates Rule 2 by placing Zinn (a non-recorded singer) fifth. **(A)** violates Rule 3 by placing Waite after Kammer (a recorded singer). Neither of the remaining answers violates Rule 4. **(B)** violates Rule 5 by placing Yoshida before Zinn. That leaves **(D)** as the correct answer.

19. (C) Must Be False (CANNOT Be True)

The correct answer to this question will be someone who cannot be second. The remaining four answers list singers who *could*.

The second singer could be either recorded singer (Kammer or Lugo), as long as Waite auditions first (as seen in Option I). That eliminates **(A)** and **(B)**.

If Trillo auditioned second, Kammer would have to audition first (Rule 4). However, that would violate Rule 3 by leaving no space for Waite before Kammer. This is impossible, making **(C)** the correct answer. For the record:

If the third singer were a recorded singer (Kammer or Lugo), then the first and second singer would be Waite and Zinn, in either order (as seen in Option II). That means either of those singers could be second, which eliminates **(D)** and **(E)**.

20. (C) Could Be True

The correct answer will be a singer who could audition sixth. The other answers will list singers who absolutely cannot audition sixth.

By Rules 3, 4, and 5, Kammer, Waite, and Zinn all must audition earlier than at least one other singer. None of them could be sixth. That eliminates **(A)**, **(D)**, and **(E)**.

If Lugo auditioned sixth, then Kammer would audition fifth (Rule 2). That would leave no room for Trillo after Kammer, violating Rule 4. So, Lugo could not be sixth, eliminating **(B)**. That leaves **(C)** as the correct answer, which can be verified in the sketch for the next question of the set.

21. (E) "If" / Could Be True

For this question, Kammer will audition immediately before Yoshida. Kammer must also audition before Trillo (Rule 4) and after Waite (Rule 3). Yoshida must audition after Zinn (Rule 5).

$$\begin{array}{c} Z \\ \boxed{KY}\!-\!T \\ W \\ \qquad \searrow \\ \qquad L \end{array}$$

The fifth audition must be Kammer or Lugo, but Kammer must now audition before Yoshida and Trillo. That means Lugo auditions fifth. The rest of the order has already been determined: Waite and Zinn will audition (in either order) before the block of Kammer and Yoshida, which must occur before Trillo auditions:

$$\begin{array}{c} \underset{1}{\text{W/Z}} \quad \underset{2}{\text{Z/W}} \quad \underset{3}{\text{K}} \quad \underset{4}{\text{Y}} \quad \underset{5}{\text{L}} \quad \underset{6}{\text{T}} \end{array}$$

With that, only **(E)** is possible, making that the correct answer.

22. (B) Could Be True

The correct answer will be a time Yoshida *could* audition. The others will list times Yoshida *could not* audition.

The quickest way to answer this question is to look at the sketch for the previous question. In that sketch, Yoshida auditioned fourth, making **(B)** the correct answer.

Limited Options also help. In both options, Yoshida is limited to the fourth and sixth auditions. Sixth is not an answer choice, so the correct answer is that Yoshida could be fourth.

23. (A) Rule Substitution

For this question, Rule 3 is removed from the game. The correct answer will be a rule that could replace Rule 3 without changing anything from the original setup. In other words, it will reestablish the original rule without adding any new restrictions.

The original rule required Waite to audition before both recorded auditions (Kammer and Lugo). By Rule 4, Kammer has to audition before Trillo, which means Waite would have been before Trillo, too. One recorded session is fifth. The other cannot be sixth without violating Rule 4, and it cannot be fourth without violating Rule 1. A recorded session also can't be first per Rule 3. So, the other recorded audition must be second or third. To restore Rule 3, the correct answer would have to force Waite before the other recorded audition (i.e., Waite must be first or second, and no recorded audition could be first) without adding any new restrictions.

If Zinn's is the only audition that could be earlier than Waite's, then Waite could only be first or second. That's a great start. If Waite goes first, it's automatically before everything. If Waite goes second, this rule makes Zinn first, so Waite would again audition before both recorded sessions. Further, neither of the remaining non-recorded auditions could have been first (not Trillo by Rule 4 nor Yoshida by Rule 6). Therefore, the original rule is restored without adding any new restrictions. That makes **(A)** the correct answer. For the record:

Requiring Waite to audition consecutively with Zinn does not force Waite to audition before a recorded session, and it adds a restriction that was not originally in place. (Waite and Zinn could be separated in Option I.) That eliminates **(B)**.

Requiring Waite to audition before Lugo forces Waite to audition before *one* of the recorded sessions, but still does not force Waite to audition before *both* recorded sessions (including Kammer's). That eliminates **(C)**.

Waite was always restricted to the first or second audition. However, adding that rule doesn't force Waite to audition before Kammer and Lugo. Kammer or Lugo could still audition first, which was not allowed by the initial rule. That eliminates **(D)**.

Adding **(E)** does restore the deduction that the first audition could never be recorded. However, adding just that restriction does not force Waite to audition before Kammer and Lugo. This places no restriction on Waite and would even allow Waite to go last.

$$\frac{Z}{1} \quad \frac{Y}{2} \quad \frac{K}{3} \quad \frac{T}{4} \quad \frac{L}{5} \quad \frac{W}{6}$$

This does not restore the original rule, which eliminates **(E)**.

Section III: Logical Reasoning

Q#	Question Type	Correct	Difficulty
1	Flaw	A	★
2	Strengthen	D	★
3	Inference	B	★
4	Role of a Statement	C	★
5	Flaw	E	★
6	Principle (Identify/Strengthen)	B	★
7	Inference	E	★
8	Strengthen/Weaken (Evaluate the Argument)	A	★
9	Paradox	E	★
10	Assumption (Sufficient)	D	★
11	Principle (Identify/Inference)	E	★★
12	Assumption (Necessary)	B	★
13	Parallel Reasoning	A	★★★
14	Role of a Statement	C	★
15	Flaw	C	★★
16	Paradox	B	★★
17	Role of a Statement	A	★★
18	Main Point	C	★★★★
19	Role of a Statement	B	★★★
20	Assumption (Sufficient)	C	★★★
21	Strengthen	A	★★★
22	Inference (EXCEPT)	E	★
23	Strengthen/Weaken (Evaluate the Argument)	C	★★★★
24	Inference	E	★★★★
25	Parallel Flaw	D	★★★★
26	Weaken	D	★

1. (A) Flaw

Step 1: Identify the Question Type
The question asks why the argument is "vulnerable to criticism," which means the correct answer will describe the argument's flaw.

Step 2: Untangle the Stimulus
A nonprofit organization sent a fund-raising letter to 5,000 people and included a survey about a social issue. The author concludes that most of those people agree with the organization's position on that issue because 283 out of the 300 people who responded agree with the organization's position.

Step 3: Make a Prediction
The author seems to ignore the fact that the survey accompanied a fund-raising letter. People who disagree with the organization are more likely to throw the survey out when they see the fund-raising letter. The people who respond are far more likely to be the people who side with the organization in the first place. And given how relatively few people responded (a mere 6%), the author makes the classic mistake of faulty representation: judging the opinions of a larger population based on a sample group that is likely to be biased.

Step 4: Evaluate the Answer Choices
(A) describes the flaw: drawing a conclusion about a population (all 5,000 people) based on the opinions of a potentially unrepresentative subgroup (the 300 people who responded to the fund-raising letter).

(B) is Out of Scope. This was a one-time survey. No assumption is made about whether opinions would change "on different occasions."

(C) is Out of Scope. There's no reason to question the accuracy of the responses.

(D) gets the logic backward. The evidence is about a small group (the respondents), and the conclusion is about a larger population (all 5,000 people), not the other way around.

(E) is a 180. The author does not assume, but completely *overlooks*, this potential influence.

2. (D) Strengthen

Step 1: Identify the Question Type
The question directly asks for something that strengthens the given argument.

Step 2: Untangle the Stimulus
The author concludes that the Roman empire's fall was caused by an unstable climate. The evidence is that the Roman empire fell during a time of climate fluctuation, a condition that makes various aspects of life difficult.

Step 3: Make a Prediction
This is a terrific example of correlation versus causation. The author assumes that two things coinciding (climate fluctuation and the fall of the Roman empire) indicate that one thing *caused* the other (climate fluctuation caused the fall). However, the correlation only involves one set of data: what the climate was like when the empire fell. What about when the empire was doing well? What was the climate like then? The author assumes it was stable, which the correct answer should validate.

Step 4: Evaluate the Answer Choices
(D) helps the author out. If this were true, the correlation would be more consistent. Climate stable? Empire good. Climate unstable? Empire falls. That makes it more likely that the climate was responsible.

(A) is a 180. This suggests that political failures, and *not* the climate, were at fault.

(B) is a 180, suggesting that climate is not as much a factor as the author claims.

(C) is a 180, placing fault on poor farming practices rather than the climate.

(E) is an Irrelevant Comparison. It indicates that food production was higher around the time of the fall than at the start of the decline, but there's no information about what production was like prior to that time period. More importantly, it does nothing to confirm that the *climate* was responsible for any change in food production.

3. (B) Inference

Step 1: Identify the Question Type
The question asks for something that would fill in the blank at the end of the argument. That blank is preceded by [*t*]*herefore*, which means the blank will be filled by something that logically follows the previous information. That makes this an Inference question.

Step 2: Untangle the Stimulus
The manager states that naturally gifted salespeople are rare, but suggests that many salespeople can *appear* naturally gifted if they have a good manager.

Step 3: Make a Prediction
The blank is preceded by *should*, which makes it a recommendation. If good managers can really turn a bunch of average salespeople into superstar performers, that would seem better than waiting around hoping to find that rare natural superstar. The correct answer will be a recommendation that favors using good managers.

Step 4: Evaluate the Answer Choices
(B) is supported.

(A) is a Distortion. Training would be better than hoping to hire a natural superstar, but evaluation may still be equally important to make sure the training is working right. Furthermore, it's not clear that managers are responsible for training and evaluation, so **(A)** is not a logical conclusion.

(C) is not supported. There's nothing to suggest that reducing responsibility will make a manager any better.

(D) is not supported. If natural superstars are so rare, it would actually seem counterproductive to move them away from sales. And there's no indication that a gifted salesperson would be a good manager.

(E) is Out of Scope. The manager makes no mention of rewarding anyone, let alone favoring the naturally talented employees.

4. (C) Role of a Statement

Step 1: Identify the Question Type
The question presents a claim from the stimulus and asks for the role it plays in the argument, making this a Role of a Statement question. Start by finding the claim and underlining or putting a mark next to it. Then break the argument into evidence and conclusion, and determine how that claim fits in.

Step 2: Untangle the Stimulus
Economists have a rule: demand and price are inversely proportional. In other words, the lower the price, the higher the demand, and vice versa. The author provides an example: as steel prices dropped, more steel was purchased. *Nevertheless*, the author sees a problem. *Obviously*, the author concludes there are exceptions to the rule, as evidenced by lace. When lace prices dropped, so did demand.

Step 3: Make a Prediction
The author is not disputing the economists entirely, but is saying their rule has exceptions, i.e., it doesn't always work. So, how does the claim in question (regarding steel) fit in to this argument? Well, steel is an example in which the economist's rule *does* work (prices down, demand up). So, the role of that claim is to illustrate how the economist's rule *can* work, even if the author later argues it doesn't *always* apply.

Step 4: Evaluate the Answer Choices
(C) is a match. It illustrates the economist's generalization, which the author concludes does not always hold.

(A) is Out of Scope. The author merely presents the claim as an example. It is never "described as inadequate evidence" for anything.

(B) is a 180. The steel is consistent with the generalization. *Lace* was brought up as an exception.

(D) is a Distortion. It definitely fits the economists' view, but it is just an example. It was never said to "lead economists to embrace" that view.

(E) is a Distortion. The author never suggests modifying the assumption, just that there are exceptions. Also, steel is consistent with the economists' view. There is only one counterexample: lace.

5. (E) Flaw

Step 1: Identify the Question Type
The question directly asks for the flaw in the argument. Furthermore, it indicates that the flaw will be an overlooked possibility.

Step 2: Untangle the Stimulus
The resident concludes ([*h*]*ence*) that at least 60 percent of local homes have integrity problems because 30 percent have inadequate drainage and 30 percent have structural defects.

Step 3: Make a Prediction
The numbers certainly add up—as long as each group in the evidence is entirely independent. In other words, the author assumes that the houses with inadequate drainage and the ones with structural defects are two completely separate groups. If there is any overlap (i.e., houses with *both* problems), then the math doesn't hold up. The author overlooks the possibility of overlap.

Step 4: Evaluate the Answer Choices
(E) is correct.

(A) is a Distortion. The argument is about percentages. It doesn't matter if there are 10 houses or 10,000 houses.

(B) is a 180 and a Distortion. The author *assumes* inadequate drainage is a problem, so that isn't overlooked. And, even though the author may not say that all *problems* with integrity are *unsafe*, overlooking that possibility is not a flaw of the argument.

(C) is Out of Scope. The author is only concerned with the percentage of problems, not how easily fixed they are.

(D) is not overlooked. The author's argument is only about houses that *do* have problems. The author only claims that at least 60 percent have problems. The author could very well feel the other 40 percent are problem-free.

6. (B) Principle (Identify/Strengthen)

Step 1: Identify the Question Type
The question directly asks for a principle that will "justify the reasoning" given. That makes this an Identify the Principle question that acts like a Strengthen question.

Step 2: Untangle the Stimulus
The author concludes ([*s*]*o*) that people shouldn't regret the missed opportunities of youth. As evidence, the author mentions how decisions impact our lives. The choices we made led to cherished relationships. If we had chosen differently and seized those opportunities, we may never have developed those relationships.

Step 3: Make a Prediction

The author reaches a conclusion about what we shouldn't regret based on evidence of the cherished relationships we have. The assumption is that we shouldn't regret any decision that led us to those cherished relationships. The correct answer will express that idea, just in broader terms.

Step 4: Evaluate the Answer Choices

(B) validates the author's assumption.

(A) is a Distortion. The author is only worried about the quality of the relationships, not whether a different decision would have gotten us *more*.

(C) is a 180. The author argues that we shouldn't regret the decisions that *did* have a big effect; they gave us the close relationships we cherish.

(D) is Out of Scope. The author is not concerned about how deeply we cherish the relationships we have. Also, the author claims we *shouldn't* regret our decisions. There's no information about people who *do* regret them.

(E) is Out of Scope. The author doesn't discuss the number of relationships one has, whether it be *few* or many. And this ignores the author's conclusion about not regretting decisions.

7. (E) Inference

Step 1: Identify the Question Type

The correct answer will be "strongly supported" by the information given, making this an Inference question.

Step 2: Untangle the Stimulus

The stimulus discusses two groups of Panamanian natives called the Kuna. One group lives on the islands and one group lives on the mainland. Unlike the mainland Kuna, the island Kuna drink a lot of flavonoid-rich cocoa and happen to suffer less from high blood pressure.

Step 3: Make a Prediction

While it may be extreme to claim an absolute cause-and-effect relationship, the correlation is hard to deny. The author is suggesting that the cocoa, while perhaps not entirely responsible, at least *partly* explains why the island Kuna have less blood pressure problems.

Step 4: Evaluate the Answer Choices

(E) is correct, drawing a loose link ("tends to prevent") between the cocoa and the blood pressure.

(A) is not supported. While the mainland Kuna do not drink the same amount of cocoa, there is no indication that this is because it (or any other flavonoid-rich food) is unavailable.

(B) is not supported. The island Kuna might just drink the cocoa because it's delicious. The benefits could just be a welcome side effect.

(C) is a 180. If low blood pressure were genetic, that wouldn't explain why the mainland Kuna experience more high blood pressure issues.

(D) is Out of Scope. The information only compares the mainland Kuna to the island Kuna. There is no information, and thus nothing to infer, about other mainland citizens.

8. (A) Strengthen/Weaken (Evaluate the Argument)

Step 1: Identify the Question Type

The question asks for something that would help *evaluate* the stated hypothesis. This is an Evaluate the Argument question, a common variation of Strengthen/Weaken questions. The correct answer will raise a question that, depending on how it's answered, can affect the validity of the argument. In short, it will question the author's assumption.

Step 2: Untangle the Stimulus

For some reason, jurors are more likely to believe scientific evidence if they hear it in court than if they hear the *very same* evidence outside of court. Legal theorists argue that this is primarily because judges sift through evidence before trial and only allow credible evidence to be presented.

Step 3: Make a Prediction

The assumption here is that jurors take the judge's decision into account when assessing credibility. The correct answer will question whether the judge has any role in their assessment.

Step 4: Evaluate the Answer Choices

(A) correctly questions the assumption. If jurors know about the judge's role, then that adds evidence to connect the jurors and the judge. If jurors *don't* know about the judge's role, then the hypothesis falls apart. The jurors couldn't possibly be influenced by something they don't even know about.

(B) doesn't help. The hypothesis is that jurors are *primarily* influenced by the judge's choices. That could be valid whether other jurors were partially influential or not at all.

(C) is a Distortion. The hypothesis is about judging the credibility of the evidence itself, not the person presenting the evidence.

(D) doesn't help. The hypothesis is that jurors are *primarily* influenced by the judge's choices. That could still hold whether jurors use any personal scientific knowledge or not.

(E) is an irrelevant hypothetical. The argument is only about why jurors are more persuaded *in* court than *out* of court, regardless of situations involving conflicting information.

9. (E) Paradox

Step 1: Identify the Question Type

The correct answer will *explain* something *surprising*, making this a Paradox question.

Step 2: Untangle the Stimulus

A study shows that word-of-mouth marketing is more effective when the person promoting a product admits they're part of a marketing campaign. This is surprising because the supposed benefit of word-of-mouth marketing is that it avoids the kind of skepticism raised by mass advertising.

Step 3: Make a Prediction

It makes sense that people would trust a friend's recommendation over a random mass-marketing ad. Friends want to help us. Companies want to make money. However, once a friend or acquaintance says, "Oh by the way, I'm being paid to promote this product," you would expect skepticism to creep back in. But the study says otherwise. Why would people be *more* successful when admitting affiliation? There must be something about the openness and honesty that removes doubt and alleviates lingering concerns that the friend is hiding something. The correct answer will align with this concept of beneficial honesty.

Step 4: Evaluate the Answer Choices

(E) helps. This suggests that honesty relaxes the customer, allowing the customer to be more open and less skeptical.

(A) is Out of Scope. The mystery is not about word-of-mouth versus mass-media ads. The mystery is about word-of-mouth with affiliations revealed versus word-of-mouth *without* affiliations revealed.

(B) is Out of Scope. The mystery revolves around why openly admitting affiliation is more effective than not admitting it. How the people "most receptive to mass-media marketing campaigns" act is irrelevant.

(C) doesn't help. It doesn't matter how the word-of-mouth campaigners got their jobs. It matters how well they *do* their job and whether admitting their affiliation helps.

(D) is Out of Scope. The cost of the campaigns is irrelevant to the effectiveness of openly admitting one's affiliation.

10. (D) Assumption (Sufficient)

Step 1: Identify the Question Type

The question asks for something *assumed* by the argument, and the conclusion is said to be logically drawn *if* that assumption is made. That makes this a Sufficient Assumption question.

Step 2: Untangle the Stimulus

The consultant concludes ([*t*]*herefore*) that Whalley will win the election by sticking with her current platform. According to the evidence, with her current platform, she'll lose with younger voters, but win by a bigger margin with older voters.

Step 3: Make a Prediction

The issue here is one of numbers versus percentages. A greater percentage of votes from the 50-and-over crowd would be great, as long as there aren't substantially more under-50

voters. If there were 100,000 younger voters but only 1,000 older voters, the percentages would be misleading. In that case, losing the younger vote 51%–49% would put her down 2,000 votes. Thus, no margin of victory with older voters could help her win the election. For this argument to work, the consultant assumes that the total number of 50-and-over voters is large enough to compensate for the loss in the under-50 crowd.

Step 4: Evaluate the Answer Choices

(D) is correct. If there are more older voters overall, then a larger margin of victory with that group ensures her victory in the election.

(A) is irrelevant. The argument is not about getting the most votes possible. It's just about winning. And the lack of an alternative platform does not guarantee that her current platform will win.

(B) is Out of Scope. The argument is based on numbers and whether the current poll numbers are indicative of a win for Whalley. The actual issues have no bearing on the argument.

(C) is irrelevant. The argument is based on Whalley sticking with her platform. What would happen if she changes does nothing to validate the conclusion.

(E) is irrelevant. The argument is about whether she could win with her current platform. It doesn't matter what would happen if she changed the platform. The consultant is not arguing about what would give Whalley the best chance of winning.

11. (E) Principle (Identify/Inference)

Step 1: Identify the Question Type

The correct answer will be a generalization, making this an Identify the Principle question. In an unusual twist, the correct answer will be a principle that is *incompatible* with the given claims. That means it is similar to an Inference question that asks for a "must be false" answer.

Step 2: Untangle the Stimulus

The stimulus compares Britain in 2000 to Britain in 1880. In 2000, the economy was much larger, while carbon dioxide emissions, per capita, were the same.

Step 3: Make a Prediction

The correct answer will be incompatible with this data. The figures show that economic growth essentially has no effect on per capita carbon dioxide emissions. The correct answer will likely express the opposite: that economic growth *does* affect carbon dioxide.

Step 4: Evaluate the Answer Choices

(E) is the correct answer. The stagnant carbon dioxide emission levels clearly show that economic growth does not *always* and *inevitably* increase emissions per person.

(A) is Extreme. The figures only show data from 1880 and 2000—nothing in between. It's possible that emissions decreased at *some* point in that 120-year span (while the economy grew), and then came back up by 2000.

(B) is Out of Scope. There is nothing in the stimulus about laws or the ability to afford such laws. And Britain's economy quintupled—which can hardly be described as "growing slowly or not at all."

(C) is a 180. This suggests that, as the economy grew, emissions could have increased at first then come back down. That's consistent with the emissions being the same in 1880 as they are in 2000.

(D) is Out of Scope. The stimulus doesn't mention population, so there's no incompatibility. Even if one assumes the real-life increase in population, this refers to *total* emissions *worldwide*. The consistency of *per capita* emissions in *Britain* would not necessarily conflict with that.

12. (B) Assumption (Necessary)

Step 1: Identify the Question Type
The question directly asks for an assumption, and one "required by the argument." That makes this a Necessary Assumption question.

Step 2: Untangle the Stimulus
The advertisement concludes ([*c*]*learly*) that it is always worth asking a lawyer for advice when writing a will. The reason is that, despite being more expensive than a do-it-yourself will-writing program, lawyers can tailor a will to fit your personal needs.

Step 3: Make a Prediction
It would certainly be worthwhile if the lawyer provides something that do-it-yourself software doesn't. The advertisement mentions that lawyers provide customization, but never actually says that do-it-yourself software *doesn't*. In order for this argument to work, it must be true that do-it-yourself software doesn't offer the same level of customization that a lawyer does.

Step 4: Evaluate the Answer Choices
(B) is correct. Using the Denial Test, if the software *can* tailor a will as well as a lawyer can, then the author has no argument why a lawyer is *always* worth the extra expense. The author must assume that the software cannot tailor a will as well as a lawyer.

(A) is an Irrelevant Comparison. The author refers to doctors as an analogy. There is no need to make any comparison between lawyers and doctors. Even if a lawyer's knowledge were *less* complex than a doctor's, it could still be complex enough to warrant giving advice for drafting a will.

(C) is not necessary. Even if a lot of people are unsatisfied with do-it-yourself software, there could still be plenty of

people who *are* satisfied. That wouldn't warrant the conclusion that lawyers are *always* worth the expense.

(D) is not necessary. How often wills adequately serve their purpose has no bearing on the issue of lawyer versus do-it-yourself program. It's also unclear from **(D)** whether those inadequate wills were prepared by an attorney or by do-it-yourself software. So, it's not even something that necessarily strengthens the advertisement either.

(E) is a Faulty Use of Detail. Doctors were only brought up as an analogy. The argument is ultimately about wills and lawyers. Whether people can or can't get a prescription without a consultation has no effect on the author's argument.

13. (A) Parallel Reasoning

Step 1: Identify the Question Type
The correct answer will be an argument that is "most similar" in reasoning to the argument in the stimulus. That makes this a Parallel Reasoning question.

Step 2: Untangle the Stimulus
The author concludes ([*s*]*o*) that indifference results in harm to nature's balance. That's because indifference leads to pollution, which in turn results in harm to nature's balance.

Step 3: Make a Prediction
This argument is a straightforward connection of Formal Logic.

Evidence:

| If | X (indifference) | $\rightarrow$ | Y (pollution) |

| If | Y (pollution) | $\rightarrow$ | Z (harm balance) |

Conclusion:

| If | X (indifference) | $\rightarrow$ | Z (harm balance) |

The correct answer will follow the same basic format.

Step 4: Evaluate the Answer Choices
(A) matches.

If	X (chocolate)	→	Y (high in calories)
If	Y (high in calories)	→	Z (fattening)
If	X	→	Z

(B) does not match. It starts with:

If	X (chocolate)	→	Y (high in calories)

But then the second sentence goes backwards:

If	Z (fattening)	→	Y (high in calories)

Those claims cannot be combined the same way as the original because the Y term is necessary in both pieces of evidence. Also, in this argument, the conclusion is flawed due to improperly chaining the statements.

(C) does not match. It starts with:

If	X (high in calories)	→	Y (chocolate)

But the second claim again starts with X:

If	X (high in calories)	→	Z (fattening)

Those claims cannot be combined the same way as the original because the X term is sufficient in both pieces of evidence. Also, in this argument, the conclusion is flawed due to improperly chaining the statements.

(D) does not match even though the evidence is perfect.

If	X (chocolate)	→	Y (high in calories)
If	Y (high in calories)	→	Z (fattening)

But then the conclusion illogically reverses the logic...

If	Z	→	X

... which is not what the original argument did.

(E) does not match. The evidence and the conclusion discuss "many desserts," which is not the same absolute logic as the original.

14. (C) Role of a Statement

Step 1: Identify the Question Type
The question provides a claim from the stimulus and asks for its "role in the argument," making this a Role of a Statement question. Start by marking the claim in the stimulus. Then look for the evidence and conclusion, and determine how the claim in question fits within that argument.

Step 2: Untangle the Stimulus
The argument concerns a school of thought called mechanism. In the 17th century, proponents produced a lot of arguments promoting mechanism. Some have theorized that so many arguments indicated a clash with democracy. *But* the author disagrees, concluding that that mechanism *supported* democracy. There were just so many arguments because they didn't work.

Step 3: Make a Prediction
The claim in question is what has been *construed* by others. The [*b*]*ut* in the following sentence indicates that the author argues *against* that claim. It's easy to get lost in all the philosophical jargon. However, the content is not all that important. What matters here is the structure. The claim in question is what some people believe, and the author goes on to refute that claim. That's its role within the argument.

Step 4: Evaluate the Answer Choices
(C) is correct. The contrast Keyword [*b*]*ut* is indicative of something the author *challenges*.

(A) is a 180. The author seeks to *contradict* the claim in question, not *establish* it.

(B) is a Distortion. The author seems to *contradict* the claim in question, not *explain* it.

(D) is a 180. The conclusion goes *against* the claim in question. The claim certainly does not support the conclusion.

(E) is not correct because the conclusion is the last sentence of the stimulus.

15. (C) Flaw

Step 1: Identify the Question Type
The question asks why the argument is *flawed*, making this a Flaw question.

Step 2: Untangle the Stimulus
The author concludes that Ishiko must be a good manager. The evidence is that Ishiko can defuse tension, and defusing

tension (along with understanding people) is needed to be a good manager.

Step 3: Make a Prediction

This is a classic case of confusing necessity with sufficiency. Look at the stimulus in Formal Logic terms. According to the first sentence, if one is a good manager, then that person must understand people and be able to defuse tension:

If   good manager   →   understand people AND defuse tension

The next piece of logic says that anyone who can defuse tension must understand people. So, if one can defuse tension, then that person can also understand people:

If   defuse tension   →   understand people

It is given that Ishiko can defuse tension. By the second piece of evidence, she must also be able to understand people. She now meets the requirements for a good manager, as presented in the opening sentence. However, those skills are merely *necessary*. They do not guarantee (i.e., they are not *sufficient* to know) that she is a good manager. The author makes that mistake, treating the necessary skills as if they were sufficient.

Step 4: Evaluate the Answer Choices

(C) accurately describes this commonly tested LSAT flaw.

(A) is a Distortion. By the second piece of logic, defusing tension is a quality that is sufficient to show an understanding of people. However, the author never treats defusing tension as necessary for understanding people. It's said to be necessary for being a good manager, but the author doesn't even get *that* right, treating it as sufficient.

(B) is a Distortion. Defusing tension is not a quality that *correlates* with being a good manager. It's a quality that is necessary (i.e., *must* be present) to be a good manager. And the author doesn't say it "results from" being a good manager. The author suggests that it *causes* Ishiko to be a good manager, or at the very least is sufficient to indicate that she's a good manager.

(D) is irrelevant. *How* managers defuse tension has no bearing on the argument. The only issue is if they can or not.

(E) is a Distortion. The author does make an assumption about a quality (defusing tension) that all good managers have. However, the author is not *assuming* Ishiko must have that quality. That's already known. The assumption is that having that quality *makes* her a good manager.

16. (B) Paradox

Step 1: Identify the Question Type

The question asks for something that would help *explain* some "strange behavior." That makes this a Paradox question.

Step 2: Untangle the Stimulus

The stimulus describes a species of bird call a babbler. They live in large groups and make barking calls to each other when predators are nearby. However, they usually blend in very well and go unnoticed. The predators only see them when they start barking, and the barking continues long after they've found a good hiding spot.

Step 3: Make a Prediction

The stimulus of a paradox usually boils down to a central mystery. In this case, if they're usually not seen by predators when they stay quiet, why do the babblers draw attention to themselves with so much barking? The correct answer will solve this mystery, likely offering a benefit of the barking that outweighs the attention it brings from predators.

Step 4: Evaluate the Answer Choices

(B) explains the barking. Instead of taking the risk that their camouflage will get detected, they gather up an army of their friends, which will help intimidate and drive away the predator.

(A) does not help. If they could just fly away fast enough, it makes no sense to suddenly start barking and give away their location.

(C) does not help. They have camouflage, so it doesn't matter how many types of predators they have. The camouflage should be enough to keep them quiet.

(D) may be tempting, but the stimulus already states that the babblers are "extremely well camouflaged" and can usually go "unnoticed by predators." And predators realize the babblers are present "only because of their shrill barks." That suggests that, even with good eyesight and relatively weak hearing, the predators' eyesight still isn't good enough to recognize babblers through their camouflage, and their hearing isn't too weak to hear babblers' barks.

(E) is Out of Scope. The presence of other prey in the area does nothing to explain the babblers' behavior.

17. (A) Role of a Statement

Step 1: Identify the Question Type

The question provides a claim from the stimulus and asks how it "figures in the argument." That makes this a Role of a Statement question. Mark the claim first. Then break the argument into evidence and conclusion, and consider how the marked claim fits within the context of the argument.

Step 2: Untangle the Stimulus
According to the author, photographs of Europa suggest that there is a warm sea beneath the ice. As a second piece of evidence, the author says seas are important for life to develop. *So*, the author concludes that there may very well be life on Europa.

Step 3: Make a Prediction
The claim in question is that there is a warm sea beneath Europa's icy surface. That is a conclusion based on the photographic evidence. However, it is not the ultimate conclusion. The author goes further and uses this claim as evidence, along with a second piece of evidence (seas are a factor in the development of life) for the main conclusion: there may be life on Europa. So, the claim in question is merely a subsidiary conclusion, one that ultimately backs up the main conclusion.

Step 4: Evaluate the Answer Choices
(A) is correct.

(B) is incorrect because the main conclusion is the last sentence: there may be life on Europa.

(C) is Out of Scope. There is no theory being discredited or disputed.

(D) is Extreme. The author also raises the consideration that seas are "a primary factor in the early development in life." That other consideration, along with the claim in question, is presented in support of the conclusion.

(E) is incorrect. The claim itself is the subsidiary conclusion. The only thing the claim supports is the main conclusion.

18. (C) Main Point

Step 1: Identify the Question Type
The question asks for the "overall conclusion," which makes this a Main Point question.

Step 2: Untangle the Stimulus
Retailers like to take advantage of the fact that consumers enjoy feeling lucky. [*B*]*ut* the author argues that retailers use price-cutting tactics a bit too much. As evidence, the author claims that such promotions ultimately affect profits and hurt customer loyalty.

Step 3: Make a Prediction
Most of the argument consists of facts, and indisputable facts serve as evidence. Conclusions are opinions, and the author's opinion is only seen once in this argument: "too often." That makes that claim the main point: retailers too often use price cuts to promote their wares. Everything after that is evidence to support this opinion.

Step 4: Evaluate the Answer Choices
(C) correctly identifies the conclusion.

(A) is how consumers feel, not the author.

(B) is a given fact, not the conclusion. The conclusion comes right after this claim, where the author uses *but* to address a perceived problem.

(D) is the evidence in the last sentence that supports the author's conclusion. It helps prove *why* using those cuts too frequently is a bad idea.

(E) is a Distortion. The author is not disputing the idea of making customers feel lucky. The author is just disputing the overuse of price cuts as a way to do so.

19. (B) Role of a Statement

Step 1: Identify the Question Type
The question provides a claim from the stimulus and asks how it "functions in the argument." That makes this a Role of a Statement question. Start by marking the claim in question. Then, after breaking the argument into evidence and conclusion, consider how that claim fits within the argument.

Step 2: Untangle the Stimulus
The jurist claims it is important for legal systems to avoid giving unfair advantages to lawbreakers. *Thus*, the jurist concludes that the legal system should make sure criminals can't profit from their crimes.

Step 3: Make a Prediction
There are only two sentences in this argument. The second sentence is the conclusion. The first sentence (which contains the claim in question) is the supporting evidence. The correct answer will identify the first sentence as supporting evidence for the conclusion.

Step 4: Evaluate the Answer Choices
(B) is correct. The first claim is a principle (i.e., a general rule), and it does support the conclusion.

(A) is a Distortion. The condition raised in the claim is said to be important for the system to remain just. That suggests that it is *necessary*, but not a guarantee that ensures justice (i.e., it is *not sufficient* for justice).

(C) is incorrect. The second sentence is the conclusion. The claim in question is merely evidence.

(D) is Extreme. The author merely concludes what the legal system "should certainly attempt." The author never claims that this is the "most important goal."

(E) is Out of Scope. The author is not refuting anything.

20. (C) Assumption (Sufficient)

Step 1: Identify the Question Type
The question directly asks for what is *assumed* by the author, and the argument will be valid *if* that assumption is made. That makes this a Sufficient Assumption question.

Step 2: Untangle the Stimulus

The author concludes that a particular contract was violated. The contract in question requires that the company president or a lawyer in the legal department be notified of any changes. However, changes were made *without* notifying the president or Yeung.

Step 3: Make a Prediction

According to the evidence, changes need to be run by the president *or any lawyer in the legal department*. It is only mentioned that the president and Yeung (whoever that is) were unaware of the changes. If any one of the legal department's lawyers were told of the changes, then the rules were followed. To claim a violation, the author assumes that the legal department lawyers were *all* uninformed.

But what about Yeung? Yeung is a distraction here. Some might wonder: doesn't the author assume Yeung is one of the lawyers? In that case, the contract is violated, right? Not necessarily. Keep in mind that the contract requires notifying the president or *any* lawyer in the legal department. So, even if Yeung *was* one of those lawyers, that doesn't confirm that the contract was violated. There could still be other lawyers who *were* notified. This only works as an assumption if the author further assumes that Yeung is the *only* lawyer in the entire legal department.

Step 4: Evaluate the Answer Choices

(C) is correct. If none of the lawyers were told about the changes, and the president wasn't told, then the contract was definitely violated.

(A) is not enough to guarantee the conclusion, as described in Step 3.

(B) is not enough. There is no information about who Grimes is, let alone Yeung. Even if they were both lawyers, there could still be other lawyers in the legal department. In that case, it's still possible that the contract was not violated.

(D) is a Distortion. What ensures that the contract is *not* being violated does nothing to confirm whether the contract *is* being violated. Adding **(D)** to the argument does not guarantee that the contract was violated; it's immaterial because the president was *not* told about the changes.

(E) is not enough. This is a valid inference based on the given evidence (because it's already known that the president was not informed). However, just setting up another conditional statement provides no evidence that the lawyers *were* uninformed. Without that information, there's still no guarantee that the contract was, indeed, violated.

21. (A) Strengthen

Step 1: Identify the Question Type

The question directly asks for something that strengthens the given argument.

Step 2: Untangle the Stimulus

The journalist concludes (*thus*) that eating less iron-rich food should reduce one's risk of Parkinson's disease. The evidence is that people with Parkinson's tend to have more iron in their diets.

Step 3: Make a Prediction

This argument is based on implied causality. The author assumes that because people with Parkinson's happen to eat more iron-rich food, the iron-rich food is a *causal* factor. Thus, eating less iron-heavy food will reduce the chances of it causing Parkinson's. However, causal arguments make three assumptions: 1) there's no alternative cause (i.e., the Parkinson's couldn't be spurred on by other foods), 2) the causality is not reversed (i.e., having Parkinson's does not cause people to eat more iron than usual), and 3) it's not a coincidence. The correct answer will validate one of these assumptions. In short, it will either eliminate an alternative cause, show how the causality is not reversed, or make a stronger connection between iron and Parkinson's.

Step 4: Evaluate the Answer Choices

(A) strengthens the argument by implying that the causality is not reversed. If a genetic predisposition causes people to eat more iron, then the presence of iron is due to the disease itself. Reducing one's intake would not take away the disease. This suggests the opposite, that the genetic predisposition is irrelevant. That makes it more likely that iron is a catalyst for the disease (as the author suggests), and not the other way around.

(B) is a 180. This destroys the link between iron and Parkinson's, showing that some people with a lot of iron *don't* get the disease.

(C) is an Irrelevant Comparison. No distinction is made between younger and older people in the argument, and this comparison does nothing to connect iron to Parkinson's.

(D) is another Irrelevant Comparison. The author's conclusion is about a wholesale reduction of iron-rich foods, regardless of how easily the body absorbs the iron. This does nothing to confirm if that would help reduce the risk of Parkinson's.

(E) is Out of Scope. The author does not put an age limit on the recommendation, and this does nothing to confirm the link between iron and Parkinson's.

22. (E) Inference (EXCEPT)

Step 1: Identify the Question Type

The correct answer will be logically determined based on a set of *statements*. That makes this an Inference question. However, this question contains an EXCEPT. Four of the answers (the wrong ones) all "could be true." The correct answer will be the exception—the one that must be false (i.e., the one that is impossible).

Step 2: Untangle the Stimulus

The chairperson starts by comparing two candidates: Modernist Maples is a better candidate than Traditionalist Tannet. The chairperson then makes an even bolder claim: *every* Modern Party member would be better than *any* Traditionalist Party member.

Step 3: Make a Prediction

In all, the comparison is merely between two parties. Anyone who is a member of the Modern Party is more qualified than anyone who is a member of the Traditionalist Party. The different members within each party may vary in quality, but even the worst member of the Modern Party will be more qualified than the best member of the Traditionalist Party. The correct answer will contradict that claim.

Step 4: Evaluate the Answer Choices

(E) must be false and is thus correct. Tannet is a Traditionalist, and the chairperson is a Modernist. By the bold claim of the stimulus, the chairperson must be more qualified than Tannet, not the other way around.

(A) could be true because it is Out of Scope. The information only discusses qualifications, not *seniority*. Furthermore, even if Maples was in the Traditionalist Party before, he's not now, and the chairperson's claim did not extend to previous members of the parties—only current members. So, **(A)** is possible.

(B) could be true. Tannet is less qualified than any Modern Party member, but there is no way to know how Tannet compares to other members of the Traditionalist Party.

(C) could be true because it is Out of Scope. The question is only based on the chairperson's bold claims. There is no way to determine what other residents believe.

(D) could be true. There is no way to determine how Maples compares to other Modern Party members. All that matters is that, even if Maples *is* the worst Modern Party candidate, he is still better than any of those Traditionalist members.

23. (C) Strengthen/Weaken (Evaluate the Argument)

Step 1: Identify the Question Type

The question asks for a question that would help "evaluate the reasoning" given. That makes this an Evaluate the Argument question. The correct answer should question the assumption in a way that would strengthen or weaken the argument depending on the response.

Step 2: Untangle the Stimulus

The businessperson was late to a meeting today and blames parking lot maintenance. The evidence is that it took the businessperson 15 minutes to find a parking space, resulting in late attendance to the meeting.

Step 3: Make a Prediction

The timing cannot be denied. The businessperson was late because it took 15 minutes to find a parking space, and then whatever time to get from that spot to the building. However, was parking lot maintenance really to blame? The businessperson believes so, which assumes that those 15 minutes finding a space and getting from that space to the building made all the difference. The correct answer will question whether 15 minutes is abnormally long or not.

Step 4: Evaluate the Answer Choices

(C) would help. If parking patterns usually allow for quick parking (say, 5–10 minutes), then the businessperson has a point—the maintenance created a delay. However, if parking patterns are usually terrible (i.e., it usually takes 15 minutes to find a spot), then the argument crumbles—the maintenance was irrelevant and thus *not* responsible.

(A) is Out of Scope. The reason for the maintenance has no bearing on whether it was responsible for the long search for a parking space.

(B) is irrelevant. If other people were late, it's still not certain whether the maintenance is to blame or if the company is just filled with people who normally arrive late. Maybe others were late because of a subway delay or because they slept in. If other people weren't late, it's still not certain if they commuted by another means of transportation or arrived at a time of day when more parking was available. Or maybe the maintenance issue was a factor, but they took more time to account for it, etc. **(B)** is not helpful in determining whether the businessperson's excuse is valid.

(D) is also irrelevant. Although it may be tempting to know the person's history, it really doesn't have bearing on this one occurrence. If the businessperson is usually on time, perhaps this was an exception. But is the maintenance to blame? This still doesn't help determine that.

(E) is irrelevant, too. The importance of the meeting has no bearing on why the businessperson was late.

24. (E) Inference

Step 1: Identify the Question Type

The correct answer will be a claim that the given statements "most strongly support," making this an Inference question. Even though the word *support* is in the question stem, this is not a Strengthen question. In a Strengthen question, the correct answer is used to support the argument in the stimulus. Here, as is typical in Inference questions, the order is reversed: the stimulus is used to support the correct answer.

Step 2: Untangle the Stimulus

The opening claim sets out what is required for a work to be called "world literature." It has to be interpreted within at least two traditions: that of the author's home country and that of an external nation. The author then presents three possible uses for a work that would allow it to be interpreted within a tradition: 1) to positively develop a tradition, 2) to negatively highlight something that should be avoided, and 3) to show something radical that inspires change.

Step 3: Make a Prediction

There are a lot of abstract ideas here. Focus on the strongest points. The opening claim provides some Formal Logic. If a work is considered world literature, it must be interpreted within at least two traditions (the author's national tradition and an external national one):

If	world literature	→	received/ interpreted within writer's own national tradition AND received/ interpreted within external national tradition

By contrapositive, if it cannot be interpreted within those two traditions, then it's not really world literature. By the last sentences, there are numerous ways to achieve such an interpretation. While an exact answer will be difficult to predict, keep in mind two things. First, the two traditions are necessary, but not sufficient. Do not mix up the Formal Logic. Second, stick to the scope: what allows for traditional interpretation and what classifies a work as world literature.

Step 4: Evaluate the Answer Choices

(E) is supported. If a work affects the development of only *one* tradition, then that allows only one interpretation. By the Formal Logic provided, that means it doesn't meet the requirement and thus cannot be considered world literature.

(A) is Out of Scope. The author never mentions anything about what makes a work "well received."

(B) is an Irrelevant Comparison. There's nothing to suggest which group of readers a work "offers more" to.

(C) is another Irrelevant Comparison. The requirement is just that the story be interpreted within both traditions. It does not matter whether one interpretation is "more meaningful" than the other.

(D) is Out of Scope. The author makes no mention of being "influenced by" other works.

25. (D) Parallel Flaw

Step 1: Identify the Question Type

The question asks for an argument with reasoning "most similar" to that in the stimulus. Furthermore, that reasoning is described as *flawed*, making this a Parallel Flaw question. Find the flaw in the stimulus, and look for the answer that contains the exact same flaw.

Step 2: Untangle the Stimulus

The author concludes ([*h*]ence) that there are more sociology majors than psychology majors in a particular class. The evidence is that most sociology majors are in the class and most psychology majors are not.

Step 3: Make a Prediction

The problem here is a shift from percentages to numbers. More than 50% of sociology majors are in the class, and fewer than 50% of the psychology majors are. However, the *number* of students from each major depends on how many students there are in the first place. If there are 10 sociology majors but 100 psychology majors, then just 20% of psychology majors could be in the class (20), and that would automatically be more than all of the sociology majors. The correct answer will make the same mistake: it will provide evidence about two percentages and conclude that the group with the greater percentage has the greater *number*.

Step 4: Evaluate the Answer Choices

(D) is a match. This provides evidence about two percentages (more than 50% of veggies at Valley Food and less than 50% of veggies at Jumbo Supermarket) and concludes that the group with the greater percentage has the greater number. Perhaps Valley Food only offers 3 different vegetables, 2 of which are organic, but the Jumbo Supermarket offers dozens of vegetables, 10 of which are organic.

(A) does not match. The two percentages are not used to make a faulty conclusion about one group having a greater number than the other.

(B) has a couple of flaws, but not the same flaw found in the stimulus. This provides evidence of a numeric comparison (one is more than another) and uses that to conclude what a percentage believes ("most Silver Falls residents must be in favor… "). It's possible that only a small number of residents were in favor of increased spending on either issue, which means although more prefer road spending than park spending, those that prefer road spending may not be a majority. Also, the conclusion indicates that most people are *against* spending on parks. Of those surveyed, it may not be their first choice for increased spending, but they may support increased spending for parks nonetheless. Flaws for sure, but not the same as in the stimulus.

(C) is flawed, but not because of its use of percentages. There's only one percentage. And if most trees fit a particular category (e.g., local), then that means more trees fit that category than any other. However, that's only true of the arboretum itself. It's flawed to extrapolate that information from the arboretum to the "San Felipe area" in general.

(E) is surely flawed, but for reasons that are very different from the original. This does shift from percentages in the evidence to numbers in the conclusion. However, the argument shifts scope from the percentages that have photos to the number of houses *on sale*. The original argument does not make that kind of improper shift in scope, so this is not a match.

26. (D) Weaken

Step 1: Identify the Question Type
The question directly asks for something that weakens the given argument.

Step 2: Untangle the Stimulus
The film director argues that the film studio is sure to recover the high production costs of the movie. Even if the movie itself doesn't earn enough money to cover the costs, the special effects technology being developed for the movie can be used on later films.

Step 3: Make a Prediction
The film director is taking a long-term perspective on the high production costs. If the film does well, the studio gets its money back. If the film fails, the studio can still make its money back by reusing the new technology to make other films. Unfortunately, the director only says that the technology *could* be used in later films. If for some reason the technology *doesn't* get used again, then the costs are sunk ... and so is the author's argument.

Step 4: Evaluate the Answer Choices
(D) weakens the argument. If technology used on unpopular films tends to be abandoned, then there *is* a risk of the studio losing money. The film could do poorly, and the technology budget would go to waste. The author's argument is shot.

(A) is a 180. If studios get to control the new technology, then they can use it as often as they need until they get their money back. That supports the director's assertion that the risk is minimal.

(B) is also a 180. If innovative special effects bring in huge crowds in general, then it's unlikely that this movie will be unpopular. That supports the idea that the risk of losing money is low.

(C) is irrelevant. The director already accounts for inadequate ticket sales. Even if this movie's ticket sales (no matter how good they are) don't offset the costs, the director maintains that the new technology could be reused on other films. The studio can still get its money back that way.

(E) is another 180. This is exactly what the director is banking on. If the current film doesn't do well, then the technology can be used to cut expenses on later films, allowing the technology costs to be recovered in the future.

Section IV: Reading Comprehension
Passage 1: Jury Nullification

Q#	Question Type	Correct	Difficulty
1	Inference	E	★
2	Inference	D	★
3	Logic Reasoning (Parallel Reasoning)	C	★
4	Inference	D	★
5	Inference	E	★★★
6	Logic Reasoning (Method of Argument)	A	★

Passage 2: Sociohistorical Interpretations of Art

Q#	Question Type	Correct	Difficulty
7	Global	B	★★★
8	Inference	C	★
9	Inference	E	★
10	Detail (EXCEPT)	D	★
11	Inference	C	★★★★
12	Logic Function	B	★★★
13	Logic Function	A	★★
14	Inference	E	★

Passage 3: Clay Tokens and the Evolution of Written Language

Q#	Question Type	Correct	Difficulty
15	Global	A	★★
16	Inference	D	★★★
17	Detail	B	★
18	Detail	B	★★
19	Inference	C	★★
20	Inference	C	★★★
21	Inference	A	★★★
22	Logic Reasoning (Weaken)	B	★★★★

Passage 4: CFCs and the Ozone Layer

Q#	Question Type	Correct	Difficulty
23	Detail	E	★★
24	Logic Reasoning (Strengthen)	A	★★
25	Inference	D	★★★
26	Logic Reasoning (Evaluate the Argument)	D	★★★
27	Inference	B	★★★

Passage 1: Jury Nullification

Step 1: Read the Passage Strategically
Sample Roadmap

line #	Keyword/phrase	¶ Margin notes
Passage A		
2	disregard	Jury null.—override judge/facts
3	contrary	motives for null.
9	few; problems	causes problems
10	great	
11	First	
12	Because	1) Juries don't explain reason
13	impossible	
15	evil	
16	rather than; good	
17	Second; insufficient	2) Juries lack override
21	because; irrelevant	
23	Third; not	3) Not the jury's job
30	Nevertheless	Auth: should disagree in public instead
Passage B		
35	however	Police/prosec. can be overzealous
36	overzealous	
38	for example	juries can compensate
43	assisting	
44	both	Jury null. assists legislature when laws are broad
47	must	
48	settle	
50	unjust; useful	jury null. can indicate problems with laws
52	problem	
55	should ignore; but	Jury null. due to external factors rare
56	uncommon	
60	nevertheless	Need unanimous decision to nullify
61	appropriate	

Discussion

Passage A immediately introduces the **Topic**: jury nullification. This is when juries take matters into their own hands, regardless of the judge's instructions or the facts of the case. The author provides several reasons why juries do this (mercy for the defendant, dislike of the victim, civil disobedience), but complains that there are major problems with jury nullification. These problems are the **Scope** of the passage.

The next three paragraphs outline three such problems: 1) Juries don't have to explain their decisions, so there's no way to determine their motives. 2) Juries don't always have enough evidence to make such a decision. 3) It's not the jury's job to interpret or evaluate the laws; that's what legislators and judges are for.

In the final paragraph, the author of passage A argues that it's okay for jurors to disagree with the law, but such debates should be left out of the courtroom. The **Purpose** of passage A is to describe why jury nullification is bad. The **Main Idea** is that there are various problems with jury nullification.

Passage B has a different perspective. This author claims that police and lawyers can be overzealous in prosecuting criminals, and juries can offset such behavior. In the second and third paragraphs, the author discusses the **Topic** of jury nullification, with the **Scope** of discussing its advantages.

Paragraph 2 discusses how jury nullification can *help* legislatures by deciding what laws apply and what laws don't in certain cases. They do this because laws are often broadly worded to accommodate unexpected variations and competing views. Paragraph 3 mentions how jury nullification can send a signal that a particular law is problematic and unfair.

The author of passage B concedes that decisions could be based on factors that should be ignored, but argues this is rare. After all, nullification requires unanimous agreement among 12 people with diverse perspectives. The **Purpose** of passage B is to discuss the advantages of jury nullification. The **Main Idea** is that jury nullification can actually help legislatures and promote fairness.

The main relationship between these passages is that they take polar opposite views on the value of jury nullification. Passage A is all about the problems, while passage B sees a lot value in it.

1. (E) Inference

Step 2: Identify the Question Type

The question asks for something the author of passage B *suggests*, making this an Inference question.

Step 3: Research the Relevant Text

The question asks for a description of "some laws" that would justify jury nullification. Paragraph 2 of passage B discusses the nature of the laws themselves.

Step 4: Make a Prediction

In lines 44–48, the laws that justify jury nullification are described as "general laws," created from the need "for broad language." The correct answer will describe this broad, general characterization.

Step 5: Evaluate the Answer Choices

(E) is an exact match.

(A) is Out of Scope. While the laws may be fairly complicated, the author never states or directly suggests this.

(B) is Out of Scope. The author never describes the laws as out-of-date.

(C) is a Distortion. While some may consider general laws to be permissive, the author never directly addresses this quality as a reason for jury nullification.

(D) is Out of Scope. The author never describes laws as intruding on anything.

2. (D) Inference

Step 2: Identify the Question Type

The question asks about the "attitude" of the author of passage B. Attitudes are not directly stated but are directly inferred from the author's language, making this an Inference question.

Step 3: Research the Relevant Text

The attitudes of both authors are prevalent through the passages, so the entire text is relevant.

Step 4: Make a Prediction

The difference in the authors' attitudes is stark. The author of passage A is highly critical of juries, suggesting that they could sometimes be using their power for "evil ends" (lines 14–16), and they could be acting on "insufficient evidence" (line 17). The author of passage B is more supportive, suggesting that juries are "assisting the legislature" (line 43) and performing "a useful function" (lines 50–51). The question asks about passage B's author, so the correct answer will describe that author's more accepting stance on what juries are doing.

Step 5: Evaluate the Answer Choices

(D) matches the attitude of passage B's author.

(A) is a 180. The author of passage B approves of what juries are doing, which suggests a *more* trusting attitude.

(B) is Out of Scope. Neither author addresses the ability of jurors to "understand the laws."

(C) is Out of Scope and a 180 at worst. Only the author of passage A raises this concern. The author of passage B never addresses it and, if anything, would be *less* concerned given the author's more supportive stance.

(E) is Out of Scope. Passage B never addresses the concept of effecting social change.

3. (C) Logic Reasoning (Parallel Reasoning)

Step 2: Identify the Question Type
The correct answer will be titles to two documents that indicate a relationship "most analogous" to that of passage A and passage B. That makes this akin to a Parallel Reasoning question from LR. Consider the relationship between passages A and B, and look for two titles that describe a similar relationship on a different topic.

Step 3: Research the Relevant Text
Titles would reflect the main point of an entire passage, so all of the text is relevant. Instead, use the Purpose and Main Idea from Step 1.

Step 4: Make a Prediction
The relationship between passages A and B is that passage A talks about the negatives of jury nullification, while passage B touts jury nullification as helpful. The correct answer will provide two titles that offer the same relationship on a different topic: the first indicating a discussion of problems, and the second indicating a discussion of how something is helpful.

Step 5: Evaluate the Answer Choices
(C) matches the relationship. The first title refers to "inherent dangers," just as passage A talks about the problems of jury nullification. And the second title refers to how something can "assist the law," exactly as passage B does with jury nullification.

(A) is Half-Right/Half-Wrong. It brings up "pros and cons" in the second title, suggesting that passage B does the same. However, passage B only pushes the pros. The one con raised in passage B is immediately dismissed.

(B) may be tempting because the first title indicates "three central issues," which perfectly mimics the three problems brought up in passage A. However, the second title discusses "unexpected benefits," and passage B makes no suggestion that the benefits mentioned are *unexpected*.

(D) is Half-Right/Half-Wrong. While the second title fits, the first title mentions "troublesome history," which does not match passage A. Passage A never talks about the history of jury nullification.

(E) is Extreme. Even if it's implied, the author of passage A never directly argues for banning jury nullification. The bigger issue though is the second title, which mentions *inevitability*. That does not match passage B, which only mentions that juries *can* use jury nullification in certain cases (lines 36–38).

4. (D) Inference

Step 2: Identify the Question Type
The question asks for what the authors are "most likely to disagree over." That means it will not be directly stated, but will be directly supported by the information in the passages, making this an Inference question.

Step 3: Research the Relevant Text
There are no content clues or line references, so the entire text of both passages is relevant.

Step 4: Make a Prediction
To make a prediction here, it helps to consider the primary point at issue between both passages. The author of passage A argues that it's bad when juries take the law into their own hands. Passage B says that this is fine, and they actually *help* legislatures when they do that. The correct answer is likely to be consistent with this core disagreement.

Step 5: Evaluate the Answer Choices
(D) is correct. The author of passage A says there are legislators and judges whose job is to interpret the law. It's *not* the jury's job (lines 23–28). The author of passage B suggests otherwise, saying that juries can use their "own discretion" (lines 37–38) to determine whether a law "should be applied to a particular defendant" (lines 41–43).

(A) is too one-sided. Only the author of passage A decries the fact that juries don't have to reveal their reasoning. Passage B offers no opinion on this subject, so disagreement cannot be logically inferred.

(B) is a 180. The author of passage A agrees that such scrutiny and debate is acceptable…. as long as it's done in public (lines 29–32). And the author of passage B also seems to favor scrutiny, suggesting it could be helpful.

(C) is Out of Scope. Passage A brings up elected officials, but never discusses any *bias* in their decisions. Passage B similarly does not discuss the issue of bias.

(E) is Out of Scope for passage A. Only passage B raises the issue of overzealousness on the part of police and prosecutors.

5. (E) Inference

Step 2: Identify the Question Type
The question asks for what the author of passage A would be "likely to" say in response to a claim in passage B. There will be no directly stated response, but it will be backed up by what the author of passage A says, making this an Inference question.

Step 3: Research the Relevant Text
The claim passage B makes about jury nullification being justified occurs in lines 36–40. However, the support for a response by passage A's author would come from the problems raised in paragraphs 2–4.

Step 4: Make a Prediction

The author of passage A has three problems with jury nullification. The question is: which one would dispute the claim that juries are justified in deeming a case too trivial? The first problem (paragraph 2) involves juries not revealing their motives. That doesn't really apply here. The second problem (paragraph 3) raises concerns about insufficient evidence. That could certainly apply here. The author of passage A could argue that juries are not justified because they don't have all the facts.

The third problem (paragraph 4) is also a potential reason—the author of passage A could argue that juries are not justified because it's not their job to make that decision. The correct answer will address one of the two plausible arguments.

Step 5: Evaluate the Answer Choices

(E) is correct. Passage A directly discusses how "juries often have insufficient evidence to make a reasoned nullification decision" (lines 17–18).

(A) is irrelevant. While the author of passage A does admit that "instances of jury nullification are probably few" (lines 8–9), the rarity of such cases has no bearing on whether juries are *justified* in making such a decision.

(B) is Out of Scope. The author of passage A makes no mention of prosecutors presenting cases, nor what appearance such presentations would give.

(C) is Out of Scope. The author of passage A does not address the likelihood of agreement among jurors. Besides, if juries are not in accord, then jury nullification wouldn't happen, as it requires unanimous consensus (lines 57–61). The question is about whether juries are justified when they *do* make that decision.

(D) is a Distortion. The author of passage A could argue that this is not the jury's responsibility (as discussed in lines 23–28), but that doesn't mean jurors lack the *expertise*.

6. (A) Logic Reasoning (Method of Argument)

Step 2: Identify the Question Type

The question asks for the *relationship* between both passages. The answers describe *how* the authors present their material and *how* they relate. Finding *how* arguments proceed is the hallmark of a Method of Argument question.

Step 3: Research the Relevant Text

The relationship is defined by the passages as a whole, so all of the text is relevant.

Step 4: Make a Prediction

The relationship between the passages boils down to their opposing Main Ideas on jury nullification. Passage A describes the problems with jury nullification, while passage

B supports it by pointing out its usefulness. The correct answer will focus on this discrepancy.

Step 5: Evaluate the Answer Choices

(A) is a match.

(B) is Out of Scope for passage B, which never discusses *improvements* to jury nullification.

(C) is Out of Scope. Neither passage focuses on "jury behavior."

(D) is part Distortion, part Out of Scope. Passage A does describe problems with jury nullification, but never suggests that they are *intractable* (i.e., hard to control). Further, passage B offers no solutions. Passage B just focuses on a more positive assessment of the same action.

(E) is Out of Scope. Passage A does not raise any questions.

Passage 2: Sociohistorical Interpretations of Art

Step 1: Read the Passage Strategically
Sample Roadmap

line #	Keyword/phrase	¶ Margin notes
3–4	for example	Sociohistorical interp. art imposes class ideals
8–9	fail to clarify; however; two different ways	Auth: ignores that there are 2 different motives
11	first	1. Art for display
13	For instance	2. Art to mirror ideals
16	second	
18	like	
20	prefer	Auth: critics focus on 2nd motive
21	because	Make 2 assumptions
25	however; must	
28	must also	
31	Historically	Two classes commission art
35	not always	Tastes not prone to great art
39	interested largely	
40	obsessed	
41	As a result	
44	for example	
45	Moreover; against	Much art anti-elite ideals
47	unwillingly; misgivings; Because	Critics must assume ideals there, but hidden
49	must	
50	claim	
52	disapproved	

Discussion

The passage opens up with the **Topic**: sociohistorical interpretations of art. Critics who take this view (including Richard Taruskin, who is mentioned frequently throughout the passage) suggest that art merely reflects the ideals of the dominant or governing class. With the contrast Keyword *however*, the **Scope** becomes clear: there are problems with such an interpretation. It also sets up the **Purpose**: to criticize sociohistorical interpretations.

In paragraph 2, the author discusses two reasons art was produced for the elite. The first was for display—a chance for the elitist to say, "Hey, look at my house! I paid a really famous architect to make it for me. See how great my tastes are?" The second was to promote the elitist's personal ideals.

In paragraph 3, the author mentions that sociohistorical critics focus only on the second motive, as it conveniently fits their idea of art reflecting the ideals of the elite. Once again, the author interrupts with *however*, exposing two assumptions these critics make. First, they assume that the elite even *had* agreed-upon ideals they wanted to convey. Second, they assume that artists would never pervert the system for their own reasons.

The last two paragraphs present evidence that directly questions those two assumptions. By questioning those assumptions, the author's **Main Idea** is confirmed: art is not just about reflecting the ideals of the elite, as sociohistorical critics would suggest.

Paragraph 4 attacks the first assumption by showing how art was usually commissioned by two classes: aristocrats and the wealthy middle class. Neither of these groups exhibited high-minded ideals that enduring art would embody. Paragraph 5 attacks the second assumption, suggesting that the elite were unwillingly supporting art that actually went *against* their ideals. To maintain their view, sociohistorical critics would have to use some elaborate analysis to show that art actually *does* support elite ideals, just in hidden ways.

7. (B) Global

Step 2: Identify the Question Type

This is a Global question because it asks for the "main point of the passage."

Step 3: Research the Relevant Text

Because this is a Global question, the entire passage is relevant.

Step 4: Make a Prediction

The Main Idea from Step 1 provides an adequate prediction: art is not just about reflecting the ideals of the elite, as sociohistorical critics would suggest.

Step 5: Evaluate the Answer Choices

(B) is correct. It calls the sociohistorical interpretation "overly simplistic," suggesting that there's more to art than what they claim.

(A) is too narrow. It is a Faulty Use of Detail, focusing only on details from paragraph 4. This ignores the sociohistorical view and the author's criticism of that view.

(C) might be implied by some of the details in paragraph 2, but completely misses the point of the entire passage regarding the sociohistorical interpretation of art.

(D) is too narrow. It is a Faulty Use of Detail, focusing only on the one problem raised in the last paragraph. This ignores the other assumptions raised and questioned in preceding paragraphs.

(E) is also too narrow and a Faulty Use of Detail. It mentions a detail raised at the end of the first paragraph and explained in the second paragraph. However, that's just one step on the author's path to the bigger picture: a wholesale criticism of sociohistorical interpretation.

8. (C) Inference

Step 2: Identify the Question Type

The question asks what the author "most probably means" by a certain phrase. That meaning will not be stated directly but will be directly implied, making this an Inference question.

Step 3: Research the Relevant Text

The question points to lines 12–13. The example that follows in lines 13–16 helps provide a better understanding of the author's meaning.

Step 4: Make a Prediction

The author is discussing how some members of the elite commissioned art "for display." As an example, the author mentions hiring a famous architect to build a house, even one that is impossible to live in, all for the purpose of reflecting "great credit on one's taste." In other words, it's all about showing off and making a good impression.

Step 5: Evaluate the Answer Choices

(C) matches the implied self-centered meaning.

(A) is a Faulty Use of Detail. The idea of *display* is part of the *first* motive presented in the paragraph. Making political statements (or expressing ideals) is part of the *second* motive.

(B) is Out of Scope. There's no mention of or suggestion of attracting customers to a business. In fact, the example provided is about a home, not a business.

(D) is Out of Scope. The creation of "something for display" reflects the member of the elite who commissioned the art, not the artist who created it.

(E) is a 180. As the example shows, it's all about reflecting credit on one's taste, even if one is *not* satisfied with the final product. ("What do you mean I can't live there?!?")

9. (E) Inference

Step 2: Identify the Question Type
The question asks for an *attitude* that can be *inferred* from the passage, making this an Inference question.

Step 3: Research the Relevant Text
Matthew Arnold's views are presented in lines 36–41.

Step 4: Make a Prediction
Arnold uses some harsh words to describe the two classes. He calls aristocrats *Barbarians* and mocks the middle class as "obsessed with respectability." The correct answer will be a word that describes this derisive attitude.

Step 5: Evaluate the Answer Choices
(E) works perfectly.

(A) is a 180. Name-calling is hardly a sign of respect.

(B) is Out of Scope. There's no indication that Arnold shares their feelings.

(C) is a 180. If Arnold didn't care, he likely wouldn't resort to cheap attacks.

(D) is a Distortion. Arnold certainly has a negative attitude, but "disappointment" suggests that he expected better. ("Oh, aristocrats—you could have been so much more!")

10. (D) Detail (EXCEPT)

Step 2: Identify the Question Type
The question asks for issues directly raised in the passage, making this a Detail question. Furthermore, this is an EXCEPT question, which means the correct answer will be the one detail that is *not* found in the passage.

Step 3: Research the Relevant Text
Complications primarily begin in paragraph 3, but are found throughout all of the last three paragraphs.

Step 4: Make a Prediction
It's impossible to predict something that is *not* in the passage, but a quick reminder of the major complications can help efficiently eliminate the wrong answers, which all *are* in the passage. Paragraph 4 raises the question of patrons who lacked the kind of ideals that would inspire great art. And paragraph 5 raises the issue of artists who might actually create anti-establishment art unbeknownst to those paying for it. Start by eliminating answers that match these broader issues.

Step 5: Evaluate the Answer Choices
(D) is correct, as the passage never brings up the concept of "reselling…. artwork for a profit."

(A) is raised in lines 45–46, which mentions art that "went against the grain of elite values." This shows that artists *did* subvert the ideals of the patrons, contrary to the assumption raised in lines 28–30.

(B) is raised in lines 41–44. These eccentric patrons are "in the margins," not exactly aligned with the ideals suggested by the sociohistorical critics.

(C) is raised in lines 34–36 as a direct questioning of sociohistorical critics' assumptions.

(E) is raised in lines 45–47 as art that directly goes against the sociohistorical critics' view.

11. (C) Inference

Step 2: Identify the Question Type
The question asks for something the passage *suggests*, making this an Inference question.

Step 3: Research the Relevant Text
Taruskin is mentioned many times in the passage. However, it's only in the last paragraph (lines 47–52) that the author describes a view Taruskin is forced to accept ("must engage" in line 49).

Step 4: Make a Prediction
According to the last line, some anti-establishment art endured. Because of that, Taruskin has to believe that this art actually *supported* elite ideals, but did so in "hidden ways."

Step 5: Evaluate the Answer Choices
(C) matches the view expressed in the final sentence.

(A) is Extreme. Taruskin must believe there are works that embodied elite ideology in hidden ways, but it never says the artists who made such works were "the *most* talented artists throughout history."

(B) is Out of Scope. The passage is about historical art, not "artists working today." Besides, there's no discussion of the "most successful artists," a decisively Extreme concept.

(D) is unsupported. There's no suggestion as to which class the artists themselves belong.

(E) is an Extreme 180. It not only refers to the "most talented artists throughout history" (which is unwarranted by the language of the passage), but also talks only about subverting elite ideology. Taruskin's view is the *opposite*, suggesting that those works only *appear* to subvert the ideology, but actually support the ideology in hidden ways.

12. (B) Logic Function

Step 2: Identify the Question Type
The question directly asks for the function of the third paragraph.

Step 3: Research the Relevant Text
The purpose of paragraph 3 can best be identified by referring to the margin notes for that paragraph.

Step 4: Make a Prediction
In paragraph 3, the author identifies the kind of art that fits the sociohistorical view. The author then describes what "must be the case" in order for "this kind of analysis to work." In other words, the author presents assumptions required by that view, which was introduced in the first paragraph.

Step 5: Evaluate the Answer Choices
(B) is a match.

(A) is Out of Scope. The author does not reject anything in the third paragraph. The author only raises assumptions that are rejected in the *following* paragraphs.

(C) is inaccurate. The information in the second paragraph is never contradicted. The author merely mentions how critics look at only one side of the situation and ignore the other. Plus, this ignores the assumptions raised.

(D) is inaccurate. There is no conclusion in the second paragraph. It just outlines two ways art was commissioned.

(E) is Extreme. The author raises assumptions, but never reaches a "definitive conclusion."

13. (A) Logic Function

Step 2: Identify the Question Type
The question asks for the *reason* a particular claim was made. That means asking *why* it was included, making this a Logic Function question.

Step 3: Research the Relevant Text
The question points to lines 18–19, but consider the purpose of the entire paragraph and how it relates to the rest of the passage.

Step 4: Make a Prediction
The second paragraph describes two ways art was produced for the elite. The Raphael frescoes are mentioned as an example of the second way (lines 16–19), which involves producing art that "expressed and mirrored one's ideals." The correct answer will certainly express this illustrative function, but consider how this relates to the rest of the passage, which concerns the sociohistorical critics. In the very next paragraph (lines 20–21), the author mentions how those critics prefer the method described in lines 16–19. So, the frescoes are not just an example of any old method, but of the very one preferred by the critics.

Step 5: Evaluate the Answer Choices
(A) is correct, citing the frescoes as an example that is consistent with the sociohistorical view.

(B) is a Distortion. While the Vatican is certainly a religious locale (and the art is said to be commissioned by a pope—a religious figure), it's just a setting for the example. The author does not express any ideas about religious influence.

(C) is Extreme. The author never claims either method discussed in the second paragraph is the *most* common.

(D) is a Faulty Use of Detail. The idea of subverting ideals is not mentioned until the end of the third paragraph and has no direct connection to Raphael's frescoes.

(E) is a 180. The frescoes are an example of the method that *does* fit the pattern preferred by the critics.

14. (E) Inference

Step 2: Identify the Question Type
The question asks for something the passage *suggests* and that Matthew Arnold is "most likely to" claim. That indicates an Inference question.

Step 3: Research the Relevant Text
The question asks about Matthew Arnold, whose views are raised at the end of the fourth paragraph. Further, it asks about people in the middle class, whom Arnold addresses in lines 40–41.

Step 4: Make a Prediction
Arnold calls the middle class "Philistines, obsessed with respectability." So, if the middle class were patrons of the arts, Arnold would likely claim they were doing so to feed their obsession with gaining respect.

Step 5: Evaluate the Answer Choices
(E) is a match.

(A) is not supported. Arnold says the middle class is "obsessed with respectability," not actually concerned with art or society as a whole.

(B) is Out of Scope. There's no mention of what kind of art the middle class liked or disliked. There's also nothing mentioned about the middle class's opinion of the aristocracy's artistic tastes.

(C) is Out of Scope. The author never discusses profit as a motive.

(D) is a 180 at worst. The middle class is said to have tastes that do *not* lend themselves to enduring art. Further, Arnold makes no mention of patronage ensuring "the production of high-quality art."

Passage 3: Clay Tokens and the Evolution of Written Language

Step 1: Read the Passage Strategically
Sample Roadmap

line #	Keyword/phrase	¶ Margin notes
3	Though	Clay tablets:
5	instead	abstract symbols, not pictographs
6	for example	Older tokens
7	but	S-B says precursor to writing
9	Because of; seemingly sudden	
10	long puzzled	
15	Often ignored	
16	concluded; without evidence	
19	overlooked	
30	theorizes	Early tokens simple
		clay envelopes had impressions of tokens
		S-B: envelope held records
		more industry → more tokens
39	replaced	Tokens replaced by marks on tablets
41	first	led to mature writing
43	eventual evolution	example
45	suggests; :	
46	At first	
47	a little later	
51	Eventually	

Discussion

The passage opens with the discovery of ancient clay tablets in which the writing consisted of abstract symbols instead of pictographs (i.e., pictures representing words). Researchers were surprised by such an early appearance of abstract writing. However, excavations have also uncovered a bunch of even older tokens, which one researcher (Denise Schmandt-Besserat) claims are precursors to the written word. It's this last sentence that sets up the **Topic** (clay tokens) and **Scope** (their role as precursors to writing) of the passage.

The second paragraph describes the tokens. The earliest ones were basic shapes, and lots of them were found along with clay envelopes. The tokens were used to indicate the contents, which Schmandt-Besserat claims were records of temple contributions made by villagers. Later tokens took more advanced shapes as villagers started creating a greater variety of more sophisticated crafts.

The third paragraph charts the evolution from tokens to actual writing. Over time, the tokens were replaced with marks on the envelopes, and these marks eventually added numerals to indicate amounts. And this is how writing developed, according to Schmandt-Besserat. The final half of the paragraph is just an extended example that illustrates this evolution. With no clear author's point of view, the **Purpose** of this passage was merely to describe the role of tokens and Schmandt-Besserat's theory. The **Main Idea** is that, according to Schmandt-Besserat, these tokens were used to indicate the content of clay envelopes and served as a precursor to the written word.

15. (A) Global

Step 2: Identify the Question Type

The question asks for the "main point" of the passage, making this a Global question.

Step 3: Research the Relevant Text

All of the text is relevant to this question. Instead, focus on the Main Idea of the passage, as discovered in Step 1.

Step 4: Make a Prediction

The main point is devoid of any strong opinion. It all boils down to Schmandt-Besserat's theory that the tokens found within the clay tablets were a predecessor to the written word.

Step 5: Evaluate the Answer Choices

(A) is correct.

(B) is Extreme. The author merely presents Schmandt-Besserat's views. Her views are never said to be *confirmed*.

(C) is Extreme and a Faulty Use of Detail. Nothing suggests that the envelopes and tokens were *required* to solve anything. And the archaeologists were puzzled about the

appearance of abstract writing (lines 9–11), *not* the appearance of "sophisticated crafts" (which were only brought up in lines 36–37).

(D) is a Distortion. The evidence indicated the tokens and inscriptions formed the basis for *writing*, not for "modern language"—which may imply both a written and oral component. Furthermore, the passage describes the evolution of the tokens into *one* ancient written language—not multiple modern *languages*. Finally, although the transition from clay tokens to markings on clay tablets may have shown the dawn of the written word, the passage does not indicate that Schmandt-Besserat had a "detailed picture of the way in which" this lead to *modern* languages.

(E) is Extreme and a Distortion. Again, Schmandt-Besserat's views are merely presented, never *confirmed*. Moreover, only the symbols on the tablets are said to be abstract, not the people's *language* or their *crafts*.

16. (D) Inference

Step 2: Identify the Question Type

The question asks for something with which Schmandt-Besserat is "most likely to agree," which makes this an Inference question.

Step 3: Research the Relevant Text

The question asks about Schmandt-Besserat's view on the society where tokens were used. These views are presented throughout the second and third paragraph.

Step 4: Make a Prediction

The question is very vague, but stick to the basic concepts behind Schmandt-Besserat's views. In the second paragraph, she discusses how villagers made contributions to the temple, and tokens were used to indicate what they contributed. In the third paragraph, the society stopped using tokens, as they were easily replaced by marks on the tablets. The correct answer is hard to predict, but will be consistent with these ideas.

Step 5: Evaluate the Answer Choices

(D) fits the scenario as described. Once the society realized you could just make a mark on an envelope to indicate its contents, the token was "replaced" by such marks (lines 38–40). There was no need for both the marks *and* the tokens.

(A) is not supported. Even if Schmandt-Besserat is right and the envelopes contained records of temple contributions, that's not necessarily an indication of a "strong centralized government authority."

(B) is an Irrelevant Comparison. The passage never brings up the importance of, or even the presence of, religious rituals.

(C) is Extreme. While Schmandt-Besserat's theory involves villagers contributing to a communal pool of grain and livestock, that is not to say that *anything* they made became the property of *everyone*.

(E) is a Distortion. The token just happened to be made of clay, but there's no reason to suggest they couldn't have been made of other materials in the absence of clay.

17. (B) Detail

Step 2: Identify the Question Type
The question asks for something the passage *states*, making this a Detail question.

Step 3: Research the Relevant Text
The writing on the tablets found in Uruk is described in lines 3–6.

Step 4: Make a Prediction
According to lines 3–6, the writing on the tablets from Uruk used "numerous abstract symbols" and "relatively few pictographs."

Step 5: Evaluate the Answer Choices
(B) is directly stated in line 5.

(A) is a Faulty Use of Detail. 1992 is when Schmandt-Besserat published her book on the tokens. There is no date given for when the Uruk tablets were deciphered.

(C) is a Distortion. It's the *tokens* described later in the passage that evolved into writing, not the Uruk tablets. Also, "linguistic system" is too general because it was just a written language—not oral—that the tokens gave rise to.

(D) it Out of Scope. There is no mention of languages "commonly spoken along the Jordan and nearby rivers."

(E) is a Distortion. The archaeologists were not surprised at the age of the language, they were surprised by how early such *writing* appeared.

18. (B) Detail

Step 2: Identify the Question Type
This question asks for something known about the token system "[a]ccording to the passage." That means it will be directly stated in the passage, making this a Detail question.

Step 3: Research the Relevant Text
The token system is described throughout the second paragraph.

Step 4: Make a Prediction
There are a lot of details about the token system throughout the second paragraph. It's not necessary to predict the exact detail the LSAT will select, but take quick stock of the basics: The tokens were used to indicate the contents of the envelopes. The original shapes were basic, but later shapes got more elaborate as the crafts became more sophisticated. Look for anything consistent with these facts, and confirm that it is mentioned in the passage.

Step 5: Evaluate the Answer Choices
(B) is mentioned in lines 33–37.

(A) is a 180. The example provided in the last paragraph shows that tokens *could* represent quantity (lines 46–47). The tokens were replaced because it was just as easy to represent quantity through marks on the envelope.

(C) is Extreme. Schmandt-Besserat's theory in lines 28–33 was based on recognizing known symbols, but that doesn't mean it was *only* for that reason that the token system could be understood.

(D) is Out of Scope. There's no mention of anyone claiming the tokens had a religious function.

(E) is a Distortion. The tokens took new forms (lines 34–37), but were never said to become "unwieldy and cumbersome."

19. (C) Inference

Step 2: Identify the Question Type
The question asks what the author "most likely means" by using a particular term. This intended definition will be suggested by the context around the term, making this an Inference question.

Step 3: Research the Relevant Text
The question points directly to line 10, but the word *abstract* is used in a phrase that begins "this seemingly sudden appearance....," which refers to the example right before. That example describes the symbols for *sheep* (a circled cross) and *metal* (a crescent with five lines).

Step 4: Make a Prediction
Picture a circled cross. Then picture a crescent with five lines. Do those images look like sheep or metal? Not even close. These symbols look nothing like the words they represent. So, in calling the writing *abstract*, it means just that: it represents items but looks nothing like those items.

Step 5: Evaluate the Answer Choices
(C) fits the description of the *sheep* and *metal* symbols.

(A) is a Distortion. While the symbols don't *look* like sheep or metal, that doesn't necessarily mean they were "hard to decipher."

(B) is a 180. They represent *sheep* and *metal*, objects which are certainly tangible (i.e., can be physically touched).

(D) is a 180. While *metal* can be considered a general category, *sheep* is a fairly specific animal.

(E) is unsupported. Nothing suggests that these symbols were *ceremonial*, and there's no comparison made between these symbols and "most daily speech."

20. (C) Inference

Step 2: Identify the Question Type

The question asks for something that can be *inferred*, making this an Inference question.

Step 3: Research the Relevant Text

The question directly points to the second paragraph.

Step 4: Make a Prediction

The second paragraph has a lot of information, so a lot can be inferred about the tokens. Just focus on some of the most prominent information: The tokens were used to indicate the contents of the envelopes. The original shapes were basic, but later shapes got more elaborate as the crafts became more sophisticated. Look for an answer that is consistent with these details and has direct support in the passage.

Step 5: Evaluate the Answer Choices

(C) is supported. The early forms are described as just shapes, e.g., spheres and pyramids (lines 20–21), while later forms actually looked like something, e.g., bowls or jars with handles (lines 35–36).

(A) is not supported. There were many different tokens, so it's certainly possible that each token represented a different unique item. It's never suggested that any particular token represented more than one item.

(B) is not supported. While later tokens started to represent nonagricultural products, there is no suggestion that such products were "preferred as contributions."

(D) is Extreme and Out of Scope. There is no mention of what tasks were "most important." Besides, the second paragraph never even mentions liquids, let alone storage and transportation of them.

(E) is a Distortion and a Faulty Use of Detail. The evolution to written language is not brought up until the third paragraph. Further, the author never compares them and suggests equal abstractness or flexibility.

21. (A) Inference

Step 2: Identify the Question Type

The question asks what the author is "most likely to agree" about, making this an Inference question.

Step 3: Research the Relevant Text

The question refers to the *sheep* symbol mentioned in paragraph 1.

Step 4: Make a Prediction

As described in lines 6–7, the symbol for *sheep* was just a circled cross. It didn't actually look like a sheep at all. That suggests a random choice. Anything would have been just fine; the Sumerians just settled on a circled cross.

Step 5: Evaluate the Answer Choices

(A) is supported. Because the symbol didn't actually look like a sheep, it could just have easily been two dots and a triangle. The important thing was that everyone knew that it was supposed to mean sheep.

(B) is not supported. While the symbols look different (a circled cross vs. a crescent with five lines), the meaning appears to be derived the same way: just pick some random shapes and assign them meaning.

(C) is not supported. There's no evidence why a circled cross was used or how a circled cross would have any stronger connection to agriculture than to human industry.

(D) is not supported and is a Distortion. Schmandt-Besserat studied the tokens, not necessarily the Sumerian symbols. Plus, there's no evidence of when those symbols were initially studied, whether it was before or after Schmandt-Besserat's studies.

(E) is Out of Scope. There is no mention of "political life," and it's difficult to imagine how much a circled cross could actually reveal about such political life.

22. (B) Logic Reasoning (Weaken)

Step 2: Identify the Question Type

The question asks for something that would "call into question" Schmandt-Besserat's reasoning. That makes this a Weaken question, like the ones found in the Logical Reasoning section.

Step 3: Research the Relevant Text

The question directly points to the theory in lines 28–33. Be sure to also consider the evidence for that theory in the previous lines.

Step 4: Make a Prediction

Schmandt-Besserat's theory is that the envelopes contained records of "villager's contributions to temple-based grain and livestock pools." The evidence is that the token impressions revealed inscriptions that matched known inscriptions of farm products. While grain and livestock are certainly farm products, there's nothing that suggests that these were being donated to temple-based community pools.

Schmandt-Besserat overlooks any other type of transaction that might have involved those products. To weaken her theory, the correct answer will suggest that there may have been a *different* reason for recording quantities of farm products.

Step 5: Evaluate the Answer Choices

(B) weakens Schmandt-Besserat's theory. If records were used to indicate an exchange of agricultural products for services (e.g., "Build me a fence and I'll give you two chickens"), then it's possible that the records discovered had nothing to do with contributions to a communal pool of agricultural goods.

(A) is irrelevant. Different sizes of the envelopes could just have indicated different quantities of contributions, different preferences of construction by the envelope-makers, or it could have just been coincidence that the envelopes varied. Schmandt-Besserat's theory holds just fine.

(C) is irrelevant. The tokens were used up until 3100 B.C. (lines 38–40). It's certainly possible that the older tablets were used to record temple-based contributions, while later tablets (after 3000 B.C.) were used for different purposes.

(D) is irrelevant. The evidence states that the envelopes were "inscribed with impressions of tokens," which suggests that it's perfectly plausible that the tokens were never actually placed inside the envelope. Furthermore, a lack of (archaeological) evidence is not evidence of absence. Remember your flaws from Logical Reasoning! So, this would not affect Schmandt-Besserat's theory at all.

(E) does not weaken her theory. While there may be *other* records that indicated labor, the envelopes discovered still showed symbols of agricultural products and so could still have been records of *those* contributions.

Passage 4: CFCs and the Ozone Layer

Step 1: Read the Passage Strategically
Sample Roadmap

line #	Keyword/phrase	¶ Margin notes
1	well established	UV → skin cancer
3	Fortunately; most damaging	ozone protects
7	however	CFCs attack ozone
8	alerted to	chlorine devastating
9	pioneering	
12	should	
19	attack; deplete	
20	diminishing	
22	observed	
28	devastating	
30	both	
31	As a result	
39	even if	Lots of CFCs in atmosphere
41	pressing	M&R: need to take action
42	threat	
44	As a result	
50	attacks; especially	Critics at first
51	However	Evidence confirmed problem
52	especially	Anti-CFC policies adopted
54	led to	
55	ban	
57	banned; leading to	

Discussion

The passage opens with some science. Ultraviolet (UV) light from the sun contributes to skin cancer. *Fortunately*, the Earth has a layer of ozone that protects us.

Unfortunately, that layer is under attack. According to scientists Molina and Rowland, the ozone layer is fragile and can be destroyed by chemicals known as CFCs. That would take away some of our protection from skin cancer.

In paragraph 3, Molina and Rowland discover that the atmosphere is filled with ozone-destroying CFCs, and the situation is only getting worse. This compels them to educate the public and advocate change.

Initially, there are skeptics—chiefly scientists making money in the CFC business, of course. However, Molina and Rowland get some powerful backup in the form of a *giant hole in the ozone layer*. That catches people's attention, leading to new laws and regulations banning and replacing CFCs.

There's a lot of potential here for getting buried under the weight of scientific jargon—chlorofluorocarbons, freon, troposphere, diffusion. However, when simplified, this passage boils down to a very basic structure. It's merely about the ozone layer (**Topic**) and its susceptibility to CFCs (**Scope**), and it was written to inform the reader (**Purpose**) that CFCs can destroy the helpful ozone layer. The efforts of scientists Molina and Rowland brought about changes to prevent that problem from getting worse (**Main Idea**).

23. (E) Detail

Step 2: Identify the Question Type
The correct answer will be a question that is directly answered somewhere in the passage. Because the answer to that question will be directly stated, this is a form of Detail question.

Step 3: Research the Relevant Text
The question provides no content clues, so all the text is relevant.

Step 4: Make a Prediction
Because the question can bring up anything from anywhere in the passage, there's no need to attempt to predict the correct answer. Instead, consider each answer one at a time, eliminating ones that ask about concepts outside the scope of the passage. Use the answer choices to do any necessary research, and make sure the question in the correct answer is directly answered in the passage.

Step 5: Evaluate the Answer Choices
(E) is answered in lines 24–31, which mentions chlorine as the element of CFCs that reacts with ozone "in a way that…. destroys the ozone" (lines 29–30).

(A) is never mentioned. While it is mentioned that Molina and Rowland did research, their actual experiments were never described.

(B) is never mentioned. The passage never brings up actual numbers. The closest figure is in lines 34–36, which mentions that the atmosphere had about five years' worth of CFCs. But that's not a concentration, and that was in 1974, not 1987.

(C) is never mentioned. Testifying before Congress was mentioned at the end of the third paragraph. That paragraph starts in 1974, but the testifying occurred "as a result" of the scientists' advocacy. That could have been any number of years later.

(D) is Out of Scope. The passage only discusses CFCs. While other such chemicals may very well exist, none of them are mentioned here.

24. (A) Logic Reasoning (Strengthen)

Step 2: Identify the Question Type
The question asks for something that would *strengthen* the scientists' argument, making this a Strengthen question like the ones found in Logical Reasoning.

Step 3: Research the Relevant Text
The long-term effects of CFCs, according to Molina and Rowland, are described in paragraph 3.

Step 4: Make a Prediction
In lines 36–41, Molina and Rowland conclude that the ozone layer would continue to be destroyed even if we stopped producing CFCs. This is based on evidence of the rate at which CFCs break down and the fact that there is five years' worth of CFCs in the atmosphere. The author assumes that nothing would change and CFCs would, indeed, continue to destroy the ozone layer after we stop production. The correct answer will be something that validates a continued loss of ozone under such circumstances.

Step 5: Evaluate the Answer Choices
(A) would directly back up the scientists' claim, showing a continued depletion of the ozone after we stop production of CFCs.

(B) would not help. If these other chemicals were less harmful to the ozone, then there's no support for the idea that the ozone would continue being depleted if CFC production halted.

(C) is irrelevant. This is already supported by the passage, but does not strengthen the idea that the ozone layer would still be in trouble if CFC production stopped.

(D) is irrelevant. The approval of the scientists' *methods* does nothing to support the *results* they predict.

(E) is irrelevant. This suggests that the problem will continue because some countries won't stop producing CFCs. However, it does not support whether the problem would continue if those countries *did* stop.

25. (D) Inference

Step 2: Identify the Question Type
The question asks for something "strongly supported" by the passage, making this an Inference question.

Step 3: Research the Relevant Text
There are no context clues here, so the entire passage is relevant.

Step 4: Make a Prediction
With no hints in the question stem, the correct answer could reference anything from anywhere in the passage. In this case, go through the answers one at a time, eliminating those that are clearly wrong. Then, use content clues in the remaining answers to do any necessary research.

Step 5: Evaluate the Answer Choices
(D) is supported. The regulations are designed to reduce CFC production, thus preserving the ozone layer. This *indirectly* helps with skin cancer rates, as the ozone layer protects us from skin-cancer-producing UV light (lines 1–6).

(A) is a Distortion. According to lines 11–13, the ozone layer should be fine in "the absence of pollutants." That would certainly include chlorine, but there could still be plenty of other damaging pollutants if chlorine was not around. Furthermore, lines 13–14 indicate that there is "natural production and destruction of the gas [ozone] over time." So, ozone destruction does naturally occur, but it also naturally regenerates.

(B) is Extreme. The first sentence merely says that UV light *contributes* to skin cancer, not that it is the *primary* cause.

(C) is Out of Scope. While other chemicals are not mentioned specifically in the passage, there most certainly could be plenty of other such damaging chemicals.

(E) is a Distortion. The upward flow of CFCs does not have to be *mainly* over Antarctica. There could be other reasons for the hole appearing there (e.g., the ozone layer is just thinner there).

26. (D) Logic Reasoning (Evaluate the Argument)

Step 2: Identify the Question Type
The question asks for something that would be "useful in determining" whether something is valid. That makes this an Evaluate the Argument question, similar to those found in Logical Reasoning.

Step 3: Research the Relevant Text
The effect of CFCs on the ozone layer is described in detail in paragraph 2.

Step 4: Make a Prediction
The question wants an experiment that will test whether a CFC substitute would be safer for the ozone. According to lines 23–25, CFCs themselves are not directly the problem. The problem occurs when they break down into their constituent elements, particularly chlorine. It's the chlorine that reacts with the ozone and destroys it (lines 29–33). So, a good experiment for a CFC substitute would be to make sure that the chemical (or its components) doesn't have the same damaging effect that chlorine has.

Step 5: Evaluate the Answer Choices
(D) would properly test the replacement. If the chemical or its components were similar to chlorine, they would likely be equally damaging to the ozone. However, if the chemical were completely *unlike* chlorine, there would be one less reason to worry about the ozone.

(A) is irrelevant. The whole question is about whether it would affect the ozone layer. Effects on *other* forms of oxygen would not matter at all.

(B) would not help. The question is whether it would react with *ozone*, not just any chemicals found in the atmosphere.

(C) is a Distortion. The chemical is meant to replace one with chlorine, so the effects on chlorine would have no bearing on how the replacement chemical would affect *ozone*. There's no concern about it *reacting with* chlorine, but there is a concern about the replacement becoming chlorine or chlorine-like and reacting with *ozone*.

(E) is a Distortion. The problem is not that CFCs break down into components. The problem is that they break down into *chlorine*. So, if the chemical did not contain chlorine, then it wouldn't matter at all whether the chemical breaks down or not.

27. (B) Inference

Step 2: Identify the Question Type
The correct answer will be "strongly supported" by the passage, making this an Inference question.

Step 3: Research the Relevant Text
With no line references or content clues, the entire text is relevant.

Step 4: Make a Prediction
Because of the open-ended nature of the question, it is not worth trying to make an exact prediction. However, a quick glance does show that four answers mention "refrigerant chemicals," which are brought up only in the very last sentence of the passage (line 60). The new ones are called "more environmentally friendly," which at least suggests that newer refrigerant chemicals don't have the same damaging effect on the ozone layer as CFCs do.

Step 5: Evaluate the Answer Choices

(B) is supported by the last sentence, which calls refrigerant chemicals "more environmentally friendly" than CFCs. The whole problem with CFCs is the release of chlorine, so new refrigerant chemicals must not release as much.

(A) is Extreme. Just because CFCs were used doesn't mean there was *no* other known refrigerant chemical at the time.

(C) is Out of Scope. No information is given for why CFCs were used, let alone whether they were "energy efficient" (or even the *most* energy efficient).

(D) is not supported. The Montreal Protocol was an international agreement that came out in 1987 (lines 54–55). CFCs were already banned in North America by the late 1970s (lines 56–57).

(E) is also not supported. Refrigerant chemicals are described as "more environmentally friendly" (line 60). While this does not prove that they are entirely free of harmful chemicals, it certainly does not suggest that they are damaging either.

PrepTest 79

The Inside Story

PrepTest 79 was administered in September 2016. It challenged 33,563 test takers. What made this test so hard? Here's a breakdown of what Kaplan students who were surveyed after taking the official exam considered PrepTest 79's most difficult section.

Hardest PrepTest 79 Section as Reported by Test Takers

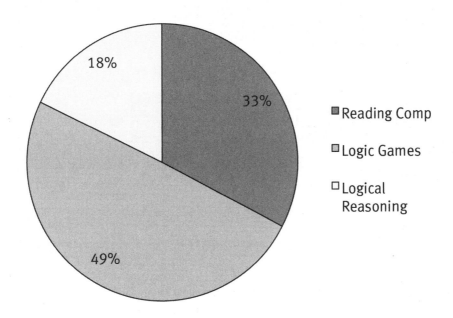

Based on these results, you might think that studying Logic Games is the key to LSAT success. Well, Logic Games is important, but test takers' perceptions don't tell the whole story. For that, you need to consider students' actual performance. The following chart shows the average number of students to miss each question in each of PrepTest 79's different sections.

Percentage Incorrect by PrepTest 79 Section Type

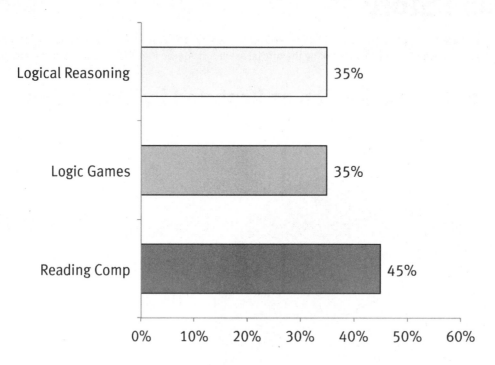

Actual student performance tells quite a different story. On average, students that took PrepTest 79 were about as likely to miss questions in Logical Reasoning as they were in Logic Games, and Reading Comprehension was much higher than Logic Games in actual difficulty.

Maybe students overestimate the difficulty of the Logic Games section because it's so unusual, or maybe it's because a really hard Logic Game is so easy to remember after the test. But the truth is that the test maker places hard questions throughout the test. Here were the locations of the 10 hardest (most missed) questions in the exam.

Location of 10 Most Difficult Questions in PrepTest 79

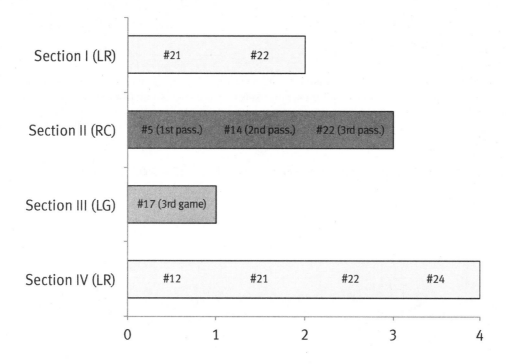

The takeaway from this data is that, to maximize your potential on the LSAT, you need to take a comprehensive approach. Test yourself rigorously, and review your performance on every section of the test. Kaplan's LSAT explanations provide the expertise and insight you need to fully understand your results. The explanations are written and edited by a team of LSAT experts, who have helped thousands of students improve their scores. Kaplan always provides data-driven analysis of the test, ranking the difficulty of every question based on actual student performance. The 10 hardest questions on every test are highlighted with a 4-star difficulty rating, the highest we give. The analysis breaks down the remaining questions into 1-, 2-, and 3-star ratings so that you can compare your performance to thousands of other test takers on all LSAC material.

Don't settle for wondering whether a question was really as hard as it seemed to you. Analyze the test with real data, and learn the secrets and strategies that help top scorers master the LSAT.

7 Can't–Miss Features of PrepTest 79

- With 10 Assumption questions, PrepTest 79 was only the second test since September '09 (PT 58) with 10 or more.
- Although there were two Parallel Flaw questions, PrepTest 79 was only the second test *ever* with no Parallel Reasoning questions. The other time was in September '09 (PT 58).
- PrepTest 79 featured two Distribution games—which was only the fourth time that had ever happened on a released test, as of the time of PT 79's release.
- Although Loose Sequencing game sketches feature branches to indicate relative relationships, Game 4 on PrepTest 79 was a *Strict* Sequencing game that featured a first-of-its-kind twist where the strict sequence branched. Check out the explanations for this game that was the talk of the test.
- Many students have reservations about the Natural Science passage. Complex language in biology, chemistry, and physics passages may be difficult for some test takers. However, the topic of the Natural Science passage on PrepTest 79 is: bodybuilding! Hanz and Franz approve!
- (C)eize the day! If you had to guess on the last question of each section, but you always selected answer choice (C), you got three of the four right!

- LSAC never reveals when its questions were written, but Question 20 of the first Logical Reasoning section showed up at a time when public debate included its subject matter on an almost daily basis leading up to the 2016 U.S. presidential election.

PrepTest 79 in Context

As much fun as it is to find out what makes a PrepTest unique or noteworthy, it's even more important to know just how representative it is of other LSAT administrations (and, thus, how likely it is to be representative of the exam you will face on Test Day). The following charts compare the numbers of each kind of question and game on PrepTest 79 to the average numbers seen on all officially released LSATs administered over the past five years (from 2012 through 2016).

Number of LR Questions by Type: PrepTest 79 vs. 2012–2016 Average

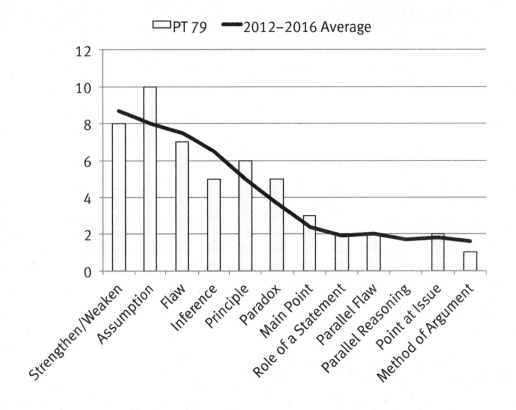

Number of LG Games by Type: PrepTest 79 vs. 2012–2016 Average

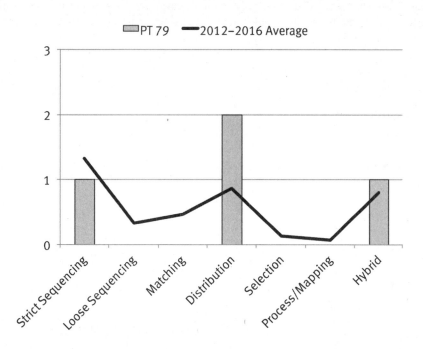

Number of RC Questions by Type: PrepTest 79 vs. 2012–2016 Average

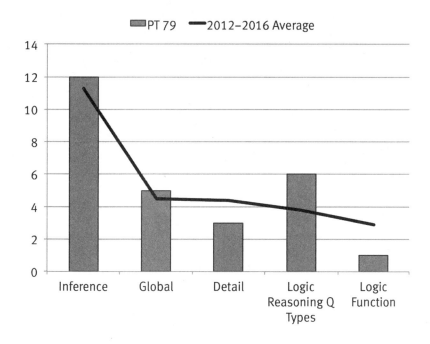

There isn't usually a huge difference in the distribution of questions from LSAT to LSAT, but if this test seems harder (or easier) to you than another you've taken, compare the number of questions of the types on which you, personally, are strongest and weakest. And then, explore within each section to see if your best or worst question types came earlier or later.

Students in Kaplan's comprehensive LSAT courses have access to every released LSAT and to an online question bank with thousand of officially released questions, games, and passages. If you are studying on your own, you have to do a bit more work to identify you strengths and your areas of opportunity. Quantitative analysis (like that in the previous charts) is an important tool for understandin how the test is constructed and how you are performing on it.

Section I: Logical Reasoning

Q#	Question Type	Correct	Difficulty
1	Paradox	C	★
2	Flaw	E	★
3	Paradox	D	★
4	Assumption (Necessary)	D	★
5	Paradox	B	★
6	Flaw	B	★
7	Assumption (Necessary)	A	★
8	Inference	E	★
9	Main Point	B	★
10	Strengthen	C	★★
11	Point at Issue	C	★
12	Strengthen	A	★
13	Flaw	E	★★
14	Principle (Identify/Strengthen)	E	★
15	Flaw	A	★
16	Principle (Parallel)	B	★
17	Strengthen/Weaken (Evaluate the Argument)	C	★★
18	Assumption (Necessary)	A	★★★
19	Principle (Identify/Strengthen)	D	★★★
20	Inference (EXCEPT)	D	★★★
21	Weaken	E	★★★★
22	Role of a Statement	E	★★★★
23	Strengthen	D	★★★
24	Assumption (Necessary)	B	★★
25	Inference	A	★★
26	Parallel Flaw	E	★★★

1. (C) Paradox

Step 1: Identify the Question Type

The question asks for something that "helps to resolve the apparent discrepancy," making this a Paradox question.

Step 2: Untangle the Stimulus

The installation of a new electronic toll system led to fewer delays, shorter travel times, and less pollution per trip. Nonetheless, overall pollution from cars stayed the same.

Step 3: Make a Prediction

The correct answer will answer the central mystery: why is pollution not going down overall? The key here is to notice the discrepancy between the two facts. The benefits described (shorter travel time, tailpipe pollution) are said to be "per car trip." That would be great if the number of car trips stayed constant. However, if more trips were taken, that would solve the mystery. More trips could increase pollution enough to balance out the per-trip reduction.

Step 4: Evaluate the Answer Choices

(C) matches the prediction. If more vehicles use the highway, then reducing pollution per trip might not be enough to make up for the additional cars on the road.

(A) is irrelevant. The price of tolls has no bearing on pollution levels.

(B) is irrelevant. It was never said that the system *eliminated* delays, just that they declined significantly. Even with some delays, there was still a reduction in per-trip pollution, so this doesn't explain why there's still more pollution overall.

(D) does not help. It was never said that *all* trips were shorter, just that they were 10% shorter *on average*. Even if the shortest trips were relatively unchanged, there's still no explanation why pollution didn't drop.

(E) is irrelevant. Even if some people didn't take advantage of the new system, enough must have to result in fewer delays and shorter trips. In that case, pollution still should have dropped, so there's no resolution.

2. (E) Flaw

Step 1: Identify the Question Type

The question asks why the argument presented is *flawed*, clearly indicating a Flaw question.

Step 2: Untangle the Stimulus

The author concludes that not trusting one's neighbors makes one disrespect the law. The evidence is a study that claims neighborhoods where people lock their doors experience more burglaries than other neighborhoods.

Step 3: Make a Prediction

The phrase "leads to" in the conclusion indicates a causal argument. The author is assuming that people locking their doors (implying they don't trust their neighbors) is the reason why there are more burglaries (implying disrespect for the law). Consider the three classic flaws in a causal argument: 1) The author overlooks an alternative cause, i.e., another reason for the higher rate of burglaries. 2) The author might have the causality backward, i.e., maybe people are locking their doors *because* of the burglary rate, not the other way around. 3) It might just be a coincidence. The correct answer will address one of these three common flaws.

Step 4: Evaluate the Answer Choices

(E) is correct, indicating that the author may have the causality backward. Locked doors could be an effect of high burglary rates, not the cause.

(A) is a commonly tested flaw, but not one that's present here. The evidence does not cite anything as sufficient for a particular result. It only cites statistics indicating a correlation.

(B) mentions a "moral conclusion," but the author does not mention morality.

(C) claims the evidence is contradictory, but that's not true. There are different results in different areas, but there's no contradiction.

(D) implies circular reasoning, but the evidence and the conclusion are distinct. The conclusion is about trust and respect for the law, and the evidence is about locking doors and burglaries.

3. (D) Paradox

Step 1: Identify the Question Type

The correct answer will "resolve the apparent discrepancy," making this a Paradox question.

Step 2: Untangle the Stimulus

According to the author, the government is getting more successful at eliminating counterfeit bills. *Yet* counterfeiters are still easily passing off fake bills to merchants and banks.

Step 3: Make a Prediction

The correct answer will address the central mystery: How are counterfeiters getting away with fake bills so easily if the government is cracking down? It helps to notice a key scope shift between the two claims. The *government* is getting better at removing the fake bills from circulation, but counterfeiters are more easily fooling *merchants and banks*. This could be resolved by showing a clear difference between the government and merchants/banks that makes the latter group more susceptible to counterfeiting.

Step 4: Evaluate the Answer Choices

(D) resolves the situation. If merchants and bank tellers are getting lax, they're less likely to spot counterfeit bills. Thus, counterfeiters can get away with more before the government finds the fake bills and takes them away.

(A) is a 180. If such campaigns are more effective than ever, then it's even more of a mystery why the counterfeiters are having an easier time passing along fake bills.

(B) is a 180. If the bills are getting harder to copy, then it's even more of a mystery why counterfeiters are not having difficulty.

(C) is irrelevant. Even if the counterfeiters are unaware of the government's success, that doesn't explain why merchants and banks are being easily fooled while the government is succeeding.

(E) is irrelevant. Even if the government keeps putting more money and effort into removing counterfeit bills from circulation, that still wouldn't affect whether counterfeiters are able to more easily put the fake bills into circulation via merchants and banks. The government is only spending money on pulling the counterfeit bills out, not keeping it from getting put into circulation to begin with.

4. (D) Assumption (Necessary)

Step 1: Identify the Question Type
The question directly asks for an assumption, and one that is "required by the argument," making this a Necessary Assumption question.

Step 2: Untangle the Stimulus
The author concludes (*thus*) that we won't find advanced civilizations within 50 light-years of earth. The evidence is that such a civilization would have discovered us by now and could easily have made contact.

Step 3: Make a Prediction
Sure, if extraterrestrial beings were that close and as technically advanced as us, they *could* have easily contacted us. That doesn't mean they *would* have. Perhaps the evidence they've found suggests that contacting us would be a bad idea. The author just assumes anyone who *could* contact us easily *would*.

Step 4: Evaluate the Answer Choices
(D) must be assumed. After all, using the Denial Test, if other civilizations *didn't* want to contact us, then the author's point is invalid. Life could be out there, they're just ignoring our calls. The author must assume they *would* want to contact us.

(A) is not necessary. It doesn't matter whether scientists are looking specifically for advanced life forms or just for any life forms at all. The argument is about whether scientists will *find* advanced life forms.

(B) is irrelevant. The author's argument is about finding advanced civilizations *within* 50 miles. Whether or not such civilizations exist farther away has no bearing on that argument.

(C) is irrelevant. The argument is not about communicating with and understanding other civilizations. It's only about

whether we'll find them or not. Fully deciphering the messages is optional, at best.

(E) is Extreme. It's not important that intelligent life recognize *all* signs of intelligent life on Earth, just that they find anything at all and try to make contact.

5. (B) Paradox

Step 1: Identify the Question Type
The correct answer will "resolve the apparent conflict," making this a Paradox question.

Step 2: Untangle the Stimulus
It was expected that removing traffic lights and street markings on a busy street would lead to more accidents. On the contrary, the number of accidents *decreased*.

Step 3: Make a Prediction
The central mystery is this: why were there fewer accidents when the traffic lights and street markings were taken away? This could be solved by showing some other significant difference that would have resulted in safer driving.

Step 4: Evaluate the Answer Choices
(B) offers a resolution. People started driving more carefully. That's why there were fewer accidents.

(A) is a 180. If people ignored traffic lights and street markings in the first place, then taking those signals away should have done nothing—yet the number of accidents still went down.

(C) is a 180. If people didn't notice, that suggests they were just driving as usual. With no other change in circumstance, it's even harder to understand why the number of accidents went down.

(D) is irrelevant. The mystery revolves around the number of accidents, so safety is the only issue at hand. Besides, this just further suggests that the situation should have been far worse.

(E) does not help. Even if people knew the change was coming, this offers no understanding of what changed to reduce the number of accidents. The mystery remains.

6. (B) Flaw

Step 1: Identify the Question Type
The correct answer will describe why the argument is "vulnerable to criticism," a common phrase that indicates a Flaw question.

Step 2: Untangle the Stimulus
The argument being made is that body size universally influences mating decisions. The evidence comes from studies of college students and personal ads.

Step 3: Make a Prediction

The author is drawing a conclusion about "all societies" in general based on a very particular subset of people: college students and people using personal ads. This is a classic case of representativeness: basing a very broad conclusion on a potentially unrepresentative sample. The correct answer will identify this illogical argumentative technique.

Step 4: Evaluate the Answer Choices

(B) accurately identifies the likelihood of an unrepresentative sample in the evidence.

(A) is a Distortion. The author is not claiming one thing causes another. If it's interpreted that way, it could be suggested that body size is the cause of mating decisions. However, in that case, it makes no sense to raise the possibility of a third event that could cause both body size and mating decisions.

(C) is a Distortion. The author is not making any claim about cause and effect. And even if one interprets the conclusion to suggest that body size causes mating decisions, there's no stated evidence about mating decisions having multiple causes.

(D) reverses and distorts the logic of the argument. The author uses a claim about certain people to draw a conclusion about entire societies, not the other way around. Further, the author does not apply anything to anyone individually.

(E) is a Distortion. This suggests a different representative issue: small sample size. However, there's no evidence of the sample size. The author could have looked over a very large number of reports and analyses. The representative flaw here is based on the *type* of people involved in the evidence, not the *number*.

7. (A) Assumption (Necessary)

Step 1: Identify the Question Type

The question directly asks for an assumption, and one that is *required*, making this a Necessary Assumption question.

Step 2: Untangle the Stimulus

The journalist concludes that the new mayor is not introspective. The evidence is that the mayor is bold and makes confident, certain assertions.

Step 3: Make a Prediction

The evidence is solely about the mayor's boldness and assertiveness, but the conclusion is about being introspective. These are completely different concepts. The journalist assumes they are connected. Specifically, the journalist assumes that being bold and assertive prevents one from being introspective.

Step 4: Evaluate the Answer Choices

(A) connects the mismatched concepts and is correct.

(B) confirms that assertiveness makes the mayor popular, but it does nothing to justify a conclusion about being introspective.

(C) connects boldness and assertiveness, but the conclusion about being introspective remains disconnected and unsupported.

(D) is a Distortion. Even if people who lack confidence are introspective, that doesn't mean bold and assertive people can't be.

(E) is irrelevant. The new mayor *is* bold, so it doesn't matter what people who *aren't* bold are like. Besides, this still fails to connect the conclusion's mismatched concept of being introspective.

8. (E) Inference

Step 1: Identify the Question Type

The question stem indicates that the stimulus will be a series of statements (instead of a full argument), and they will provide support for the correct answer. That means the correct answer will be an inference backed up by the stimulus.

Step 2: Untangle the Stimulus

In a study, macaque monkeys less than a week old imitated some, but not all, gestures made by scientists. The ones they *did* imitate (lip smacking and sticking out the tongue) are ones adult macaques use with babies. The other gestures are not used this way.

Step 3: Make a Prediction

Based on the results, this suggests that baby macaques must innately know which gestures would be used by adult macaques and will only imitate those particular gestures.

Step 4: Evaluate the Answer Choices

(E) is supported, as gestures used by adult macaques are the only gestures the babies imitated.

(A) is a 180. If they naturally mimicked "whatever they see," then they would have also imitated the open/closed mouth and hand gestures. So, this statement must be false based on the stimulus.

(B) is not supported. It is only stated that they *don't* imitate hand gestures, not that they *can't*.

(C) is not supported. While these gestures are used "when interacting with babies," there's no suggestion that they are for entertainment purposes. The gestures might be used as a form of communication.

(D) is not supported. The babies might be mimicking the gestures, but that does not suggest that they think the human scientists are actually monkeys. The babies might simply recognize the gestures regardless of who or what species uses them.

9. (B) Main Point

Step 1: Identify the Question Type
The correct answer will express the "conclusion drawn in the argument" making this a Main Point question.

Step 2: Untangle the Stimulus
The author presents the view of "some scientists": the skeletons are of people with a growth disorder. As usually happens when an argument opens with *some people's* view, the author disagrees: the skeletons were of a unique species of people who just got smaller over time. The author then presents evidence that contradicts the "growth disorder" view and supports the "smaller people" view.

Step 3: Make a Prediction
The main point is the author's rejection of the scientists' view: the skeletons were of particular people who became smaller over time, not people with a growth disorder.

Step 4: Evaluate the Answer Choices
(B) is correct, accurately expressing the author's point of view.

(A) presents the scientists' view, but completely misses the author's rejection of that view in favor of an alternate one.

(C) is merely evidence that contradicts the scientists' view. It is not the author's conclusion.

(D) is merely evidence in support of the conclusion drawn by the author.

(E) may be assumed by the author, but it is not the conclusion stated regarding the skeletons found in Indonesia.

10. (C) Strengthen

Step 1: Identify the Question Type
The question directly asks for something that will strengthen the argument.

Step 2: Untangle the Stimulus
The author concludes ([*therefore*) that the atmosphere would get cooler when there's more snow and ice on Earth's surface. The evidence is that snow and ice reflect more sunlight to space than water and land, and the atmosphere gets cooler as more sunlight is reflected.

Step 3: Make a Prediction
The evidence is only half helpful. It adequately shows the cooling effect that snow- and ice-covered land has on the atmosphere. However, the evidence does not describe the effect of water and land on the atmosphere. While they may not reflect as much sunlight, they could possibly have a *greater* cooling effect in other ways. The author assumes otherwise: that snow and ice will have a greater cooling effect than land and water. The correct answer will verify this.

Step 4: Evaluate the Answer Choices
(C) is correct. If water and land have the effect of warming the atmosphere and snow and ice have a cooling effect, that strengthens the suggestion that covering more land with snow and ice will lead to more cooling.

(A) is irrelevant. It doesn't matter how cold it has to be to snow in the first place. The argument is about whether having snow on the ground will make the atmosphere even colder.

(B) is a 180. If there are other factors to consider, then it's possible that the reflection of sunlight by snow and ice will not be enough to cool the atmosphere.

(D) is a 180. If heat comes from sunlight passing through the atmosphere, and ice and snow reflect *more* sunlight through the atmosphere, that would contradict the idea that more sunlight would make the atmosphere cooler.

(E) is an Irrelevant Comparison. The argument is about ice and snow versus water and land, not different colors of land/soil.

11. (C) Point at Issue

Step 1: Identify the Question Type
The correct answer will identify a claim that two speakers "disagree over," making this a Point at Issue question.

Step 2: Untangle the Stimulus
Nick is arguing that the university should not hire the Pincus family's competitor to build the library because the Pincus family has donated to the university, and universities should be loyal to donors. Pedro argues that there should be no preferential treatment to donors and that the decision should be based solely on which bid is most competitive.

Step 3: Make a Prediction
Pedro and Nick disagree about the criteria for choosing a bid. Pedro only considers the competitiveness, while Nick says to consider donor loyalty. This stems from a more basic issue: Nick feels donor loyalty should influence the decision, while Pedro says donors shouldn't receive any special privileges. The correct answer will address the issue of whether donor loyalty should have any influence.

Step 4: Evaluate the Answer Choices
(C) is correct. Nick feels that donations do confer privileges, as he argues that the Pincus family should get preferential treatment because of their donations. Pedro directly argues otherwise: donors should not get any special privileges.

(A) is a Distortion. Nick definitely agrees with **(A)**. Pedro might also agree that loyalty can be considered for *some* business decisions. It just doesn't apply here because there *is* no loyalty. Donations (according to Pedro) don't confer such standing.

(B) is not supported. Neither Nick nor Pedro make any suggestion about the Pincus family's motivation. It's actually possible that Nick and Pedro agree that the Pincus family had self-serving motivations, but Pedro simply argues that they don't deserve any special privileges.

(D) is not supported. Neither Nick nor Pedro make any distinction between new and long-term donors.

(E) is not supported. Neither Nick nor Pedro indicate which bid is more competitive. That cannot be determined with certainty from either speaker.

12. (A) Strengthen

Step 1: Identify the Question Type

The correct answer will "strongly support" the conclusion, making this a Strengthen question. While most fill-in-the-blank questions are Inference questions, this one is different because the blank is preceded by the Keyword *since*. That indicates that the blank will be an additional piece of evidence in support of the author's conclusion. The question could also conceivably be categorized as an Assumption question because whatever fills in the blank will need to tie together the evidence and conclusion.

Step 2: Untangle the Stimulus

Because new antibiotics such as ampicillin are more profitable than older ones like penicillin, drug companies want to stop producing old antibiotics and start pushing the new ones. However, the author concludes ([*t*]*hus*) that these new antibiotics are likely to lead to an outbreak of diseases caused by drug-resistant bacteria. The stated evidence is that these new antibiotics kill a wider variety of bacteria than do older ones.

Step 3: Make a Prediction

The evidence is solely about how many bacteria are killed. From that, the author makes a drastic jump to the conclusion, warning about a potential outbreak. The author must assume that killing off a wide variety of bacteria will somehow lead to an outbreak of drug-resistant-bacteria-borne diseases. The correct answer will verify this assumption.

Step 4: Evaluate the Answer Choices

(A) is correct, connecting the killing of many bacteria to the flourishing of drug-resistant bacteria—the supposed cause of the predicted outbreak.

(B) is irrelevant. The prior use of older antibiotics has no effect on determining whether the new ones will lead to an outbreak.

(C) is irrelevant and a 180 at worst. The price and profit margin of penicillin has no bearing on whether the new antibiotics would lead to an outbreak. At worst, if the profit margin of penicillin *does* increase, drug companies may not stop making it. So, the new antibiotics might not be pushed as much, and the predicted outbreak could potentially be avoided.

(D) is irrelevant and a 180 at worst. The cost of treatment has no bearing on whether an outbreak will occur. If anything, a higher cost might lead fewer people to use the new antibiotics, thus *reducing* the possibility of an outbreak.

(E) is a 180. This suggests that ampicillin (one of the new antibiotics) can kill off a lot of bacteria that are currently drug-resistant, making it *less* likely that such drug-resistant bacteria will cause an outbreak.

13. (E) Flaw

Step 1: Identify the Question Type

The correct answer will describe why the reasoning is *flawed*, making this a Flaw question.

Step 2: Untangle the Stimulus

Weingarten argues that zoos place animals in unnatural environments in order to amuse humans, thus making zoos unethical. *However*, the author concludes that Weingarten's claim should be rejected, i.e., zoos are not unethical. The evidence is that Weingarten is okay with people having pets, which also involves placing animals in unnatural environments to amuse humans.

Step 3: Make a Prediction

There is some logic in calling out Weingarten's hypocrisy. He has two conflicting views: zoos are unethical, but pets are okay. One of them must be mistaken, but which one? The author just decides the claim about zoos is mistaken. However, it's possible that Weingarten is *correct* about that claim, but is mistaken in his approval of owning pets. So, the author's flaw is rejecting a claim solely because of a contradiction, when that claim could just as likely be accepted in favor of the competing claim.

Step 4: Evaluate the Answer Choices

(E) is correct. The author rejects Weingarten's claim merely because of Weingarten's inconsistent view regarding pets.

(A) is a Distortion. The author's argument is based on Weingarten's view that owning pets is okay. There's no implication or assumption that Weingarten himself actually owns any.

(B) is inaccurate. The author is comparing the general idea of zoos to the general idea of owning pets. No particular cases are mentioned.

(C) is inaccurate. Weingarten's conclusion is clear: zoos are unethical. There's no misrepresentation.

(D) invokes the flaw of necessity vs. sufficiency. However, there are no conditional statements, and nothing is deemed necessary to claiming a practice is unethical.

14. (E) Principle (Identify/Strengthen)

Step 1: Identify the Question Type

The correct answer will be a principle that will *justify* an argument. That makes this an Identify the Principle question that acts like a Strengthen question. Take note that there are two speakers, and the question asks for the principle that justifies the *first* speaker's claims.

Step 2: Untangle the Stimulus

The activist argues that President Zagel should resign because people feel she rigged the election, making her ineffective. President Zagel argues that she can't resign. Her evidence is that two other presidents resigned in the past 10 years, and her resigning would cause the world to view her country as politically unstable.

Step 3: Make a Prediction

With any recommendation, the assumption is that the support provided is enough to outweigh any considerations against that recommendation. In this case, the activist's support for recommending the president's resignation is her inability to govern effectively. The president provides another consideration: the world may perceive her country as politically unstable. So, the activist is assuming that the president's ineffectiveness outweighs the potential of a bad reputation for the country. The correct answer will be a general rule that validates that assumption.

Step 4: Evaluate the Answer Choices

(E) matches the prediction. If effective leadership is more important than a good reputation, then the activist has a stronger case than the president.

(A) is a Distortion. The activist's argument is not about making the country politically stable or fixing the election system. The activist is only concerned about removing the president for the sake of effective governing.

(B) is a Faulty Use of Detail. Only the president seems to be concerned about the country's reputation. That activist is only concerned about effective governing.

(C) is an Irrelevant Comparison. There's no indication whether previous scandals were any more or less serious than the president's rigging scandal, so this offers no basis for making a judgment call about the president.

(D) is Out of Scope. There is no conclusive evidence, so, while the activist may agree with this claim, it offers no justification for ousting a president based merely on a "widespread belief."

15. (A) Flaw

Step 1: Identify the Question Type

The correct answer will describe an "error of reasoning," making this a Flaw question.

Step 2: Untangle the Stimulus

A book claims that successful people always benefited from luck.

> **If**   **successful**   →   **luck**

But the author claims this is ridiculous; i.e., luck is not a factor. The evidence is that success requires hard work.

> **If**   **successful**   →   **hard work**

Step 3: Make a Prediction

The first issue that may stand out is the author's implication that hard work and luck are mutually exclusive. In other words, the author is erroneously assuming you can't be lucky *and* work hard at the same time. Unfortunately, none of the answers address that scope shift, so there must be another flaw. In this case, the phrases "without exception" and "requires" indicate some Formal Logic. In essence, the book claims success requires luck (as all successful people benefited from luck). The author argues that success requires hard work, implying that luck is not *good enough*, i.e., not sufficient. However, the book never claimed luck was sufficient, just that it was necessary. The correct answer will point out the author's mistake in suggesting otherwise.

Step 4: Evaluate the Answer Choices

(A) accurately describes the flaw of necessity vs. sufficiency. The author mistakenly takes the book's claim that luck is required and assumes the book is suggesting that luck is sufficient.

(B) is a Distortion. The view presented by the author (success requires hard work) is not attributed to a particular source. It's said to be known by "anyone who has studied successful people," so there is no need to establish any authority.

(C) suggests circular reasoning, but the evidence and the conclusion are distinct. The premise regarding hard work is not based on any assumptions regarding the conclusion about luck.

(D) is a Distortion. The relationship between causes (luck, hard work) and effects (success) is consistent. The author never gets it backwards (e.g., suggesting that success is the cause of luck).

(E) is a 180. The author *does* attack the substance, questioning the involvement of luck. The author makes no attack on the book itself.

16. (B) Principle (Parallel)

Step 1: Identify the Question Type

The correct answer will be a specific circumstance that "conforms most closely to [a] principle," making this a

Principle question. The principle will be applied to the answer choices, but the principle is not given. It is *illustrated* by the specific argument provided. Thus, the principle must be identified first, and then reapplied to the answers. This is a rare Parallel Principle question.

Step 2: Untangle the Stimulus
The president concludes that it's a good thing the media raised a discussion of the university's standards. Even though the media was mistaken, the president states that it's important to stay vigilant regarding academic standards.

Step 3: Make a Prediction
To formulate the principle, take the president's specific argument and broaden the scope. In this case, the principle is that it's good to discuss a certain topic because, even if there was a mistaken accusation regarding that topic, it's important to pay attention to that topic. The correct answer will apply the exact logic of that principle to another specific situation.

Step 4: Evaluate the Answer Choices
(B) applies the principle perfectly. It's good to discuss a certain topic (oversight) because, even though there was a mistaken accusation regarding that topic (the scandal was mistakenly attributed to oversight, but was really a single case of corruption), it's important to pay attention to that first topic (oversight).

(A) does not match. There is no mistaken accusation. Plus, it's indicating a causal nature between the two topics, and praising the discussion of both of them, which doesn't align with the original argument.

(C) does not match. In the original argument, there was concern that it was one thing (low academic standards), when it was really another thing (one case of dishonesty). In **(C)**, it is *both* things (lack of oversight and corruption). Furthermore, it is not clear that the *harm* mentioned is parallel to the results of the case of dishonesty in the original argument.

(D) does not match. This condemns the mistaken accusation, which completely contradicts the more positive "it's okay because at least we're talking about something important" tone of the original argument.

(E) does not match. This argument praises the discussion of corruption not because of the importance of staying vigilant, but because corruption played "the largest role in the scandal." The original argument did not weigh the role of standards against anything else.

17. (C) Strengthen/Weaken (Evaluate the Argument)

Step 1: Identify the Question Type
The question asks for something "useful to know in evaluating" the argument. That makes this a variation of a Strengthen/Weaken question known as Evaluate the Argument. The correct answer will raise a question that,

depending on how it's answered, would affect the validity of the argument. In essence, it will pose a question about the argument's assumption.

Step 2: Untangle the Stimulus
The politician is arguing that replacing the city's street signs with new, more readable signs is waste of time and money. The evidence is that nobody's complaining about the current signs.

Step 3: Make a Prediction
The politician makes two assumptions. First, the politician assumes that public opinion is the primary deciding factor. Even though the public hasn't complained, there could still be good reason to replace the signs. Second, the politician claims that the project would be a waste of time and money. That is only true if the time and money would be otherwise spent on something better or more useful. The correct answer will question either one of those assumptions.

Step 4: Evaluate the Answer Choices
(C) is correct, questioning the assumption about what the time and money would be otherwise spent on. The plan is to replace the signs "over the next decade." If the city already replaces at least 10% of its signs every year, then the plan is not a waste of time—all signs would have been replaced anyway. However, if the city only replaced a very small percentage of its signs annually (e.g., 1%), then the politician's point is valid: why spend all that money replacing signs that people are okay with?

(A) is irrelevant. Regardless of what specific features are used, there's no way of evaluating whether installing the new signs would be worthwhile or not.

(B) is an Irrelevant Comparison. Regardless of which signs are more expensive, the politician's argument is unaffected. Replacing the current signs could waste money no matter how much the new signs cost, whether they're cheaper or more expensive.

(D) is also an Irrelevant Comparison. Other cities may have different reasons to either replace (e.g., people there *do* complain) or not replace (e.g., not enough money). Their decisions offer no legitimate basis for judging the politician's decision.

(E) is irrelevant. It doesn't matter how the new signs were designed or who was consulted. It's still uncertain if installing those signs would be worthwhile or not.

18. (A) Assumption (Necessary)

Step 1: Identify the Question Type
The question asks for something the argument "requires assuming," making this a Necessary Assumption question.

Step 2: Untangle the Stimulus

The author concludes ([t]*herefore*) that most of the surveyed scientists reject the Minsk Hypothesis. The evidence is that the Minsk Hypothesis is contradicted by combining Wang's Law with the results of the Brown-Eisler Experiment, two things accepted or recognized by almost all scientists surveyed.

Step 3: Make a Prediction

The author claims that the scientists know about and accept two separate pieces of evidence (Wang's Law, Brown-Eisler Experiment). However, the Minsk Hypothesis is contradicted by *combining* those two pieces of evidence. The author has spotted that issue, but there's no evidence that the scientists have made the connection yet. It's only stated that they know about the two pieces separately. The author must assume that the scientists have already made the connection tying Wang's Law and the Brown-Eisler Experiment to the Minsk Hypothesis.

Step 4: Evaluate the Answer Choices

(A) is correct, as it must be assumed. Using the Denial Test, if the scientists were *not* aware of the connection to the Minsk Hypothesis, they would have no basis for rejecting it. The author must assume they are aware of the connection.

(B) is Extreme. These do not have to be the *exact* same group of scientists. It's possible there are one or two scientists who accept Wang's Law but haven't heard about the Brown-Eisler Experiment yet (or vice versa). Such anomalies would not affect the author's conclusion.

(C) is irrelevant. All that matters is that the scientists know the results. It makes no difference whether or not they know *how* those results were obtained.

(D) is irrelevant. The conclusion is about the "scientists surveyed," not about scientists in general.

(E) is irrelevant. Even if Wang's Law has not been entirely confirmed, the scientists still accept it. Proving Wang's Law true is not necessary.

19. (D) Principle (Identify/Strengthen)

Step 1: Identify the Question Type

The correct answer will be a principle that "helps to justify" the argument, making this an Identify the Principle question that acts like a Strengthen question.

Step 2: Untangle the Stimulus

The author concludes ([t]*hus*) that even the most skillful translation of a book will be flawed. The evidence is that a translation cannot stay entirely faithful to both the meaning of the original text and the original author's style. Some compromise must be made.

Step 3: Make a Prediction

The author assumes that the compromise made automatically results in a "flawed approximation." The correct answer will be a general rule that validates that assumption.

Step 4: Evaluate the Answer Choices

(D) is correct, confirming the author's assumption that the compromise between meaning and style automatically results in a flawed approximation.

(A) is a Distortion. The author never argues that the meaning or the style *should* be compromised, just that something inevitably *is*. Besides, this offers no justification for the characterization of translations as "flawed approximations."

(B) raises the question of whether a compromise is successful, a concept about which the author makes no claim.

(C) is irrelevant. The balance between faithfulness to meaning and faithfulness to style does nothing to justify calling any translations a "flawed approximation."

(E) is a Faulty Use of Detail. It is consistent with the opening claim that any translation (even the most skillful) cannot be faithful to both meaning and style. However, it does nothing to justify the conclusion that such translations are "flawed approximations."

20. (D) Inference (EXCEPT)

Step 1: Identify the Question Type

The correct answer will be based on accepting all the given statements as true. That makes this an Inference question. However, while most Inference questions ask for something supported or true, this question does not. Here, four answers "could be true," while the correct answer will be the exception: the one that cannot be true (i.e., it must be false).

Step 2: Untangle the Stimulus

According to the sociologists, certain technologies (TV, phones, electronic media) lead to uncritical thinking. Unfortunately, critical thinking is the *only* way to protect against demagogues that exploit people's emotions to distort reality.

If	*adequately protected against demagogues*	→	*critical thinking*
If	*~ critical thinking*	→	*~ adequately protected against demagogues*

Step 3: Make a Prediction

With an Inference question asking for such an absolute answer (the one that *must* be false), look for the strongest claims that can be more directly contradicted. In this case, the sociologist claims that critical thinking is the *only* adequate protection against demagogues. Any answer that suggests something else is adequate or critical reasoning is not enough will absolutely contradict the sociologist, and thus could not be true.

Step 4: Evaluate the Answer Choices

(D) is correct. According to the sociologist, critical thinking is the *only* adequate protection. In that case, it *cannot* be true that an orderly system of government by itself would be adequate.

(A) could be true. Technology does encourage uncritical thinking, which would make people susceptible to demagogues. However, there's no way to know for sure whether demagogues are present or not in any given society. It's possible (even if unlikely) that demagogues only appear in non-technological societies, making the technological ones fortunate in that there are no demagogues to exploit their uncritical thinking.

(B) could be true. Demagogues exploit people's emotions, but it's never said that they're the only type of people to do so. There certainly could be other people who exploit emotions.

(C) is an Irrelevant Comparison that could be true. The sociologist makes no comparison between highly emotional people and less emotional people, so it's very possible highly emotional people are more easily exploited.

(E) could be true. The sociologist offers no information about the erosion of media freedoms, so this claim could be true or false. There's no support either way.

21. (E) Weaken

Step 1: Identify the Question Type

The question directly asks for something that weakens the given argument.

Step 2: Untangle the Stimulus

The author concludes ([*t*]*hus*) that taking lots of B vitamins and folic acid can reduce the risk of getting Alzheimer's disease. The evidence is that B vitamins and folic acid convert homocysteine, a substance found in high levels in people with Alzheimer's, into other substances that are not connected to Alzheimer's.

Step 3: Make a Prediction

Most directly, the author is assuming that removing homocysteine will certainly reduce people's risk of Alzheimer's, as if there were no other way the risk could stay constant. This could be weakened by showing that the risk

doesn't change or that removing homocysteine would have no effect.

However, there's also an implication of causality. Homocysteine levels are higher in people with Alzheimer's, but the author is implying that homocysteine is the *cause* of Alzheimer's, so reducing homocysteine would remove a potential cause. There are three ways to weaken this causal argument: 1) Show an alternative cause of Alzheimer's. 2) Show the author mistakenly reversed causality; i.e., having Alzheimer's is the cause of high homocysteine levels, not the other way around. 3) Indicate that it's just a coincidence and that the two factors are in fact unconnected.

Step 4: Evaluate the Answer Choices

(E) weakens the argument by indicating that the author may have the causality reversed. If the high levels of homocysteine are caused *by* Alzheimer's, then replacing homocysteine would have no effect. Something else is causing Alzheimer's, and the B vitamins and folic acid wouldn't stop that from happening.

(A) has no effect on the argument. Even if lots of Alzheimer's patients have normal homocysteine levels, high levels could still create a greater risk of developing the disease. In that case, taking B vitamins and folic acid won't guarantee anything, but it could still reduce the risk.

(B) is Out of Scope. The author's argument is about reducing the risk of Alzheimer's. Even if there are other harmful effects, the risk of Alzheimer's would still be reduced.

(C) is also Out of Scope. This would be a problem if the author only recommended supplements. However, even if supplements are inefficient, there could be other ways to increase B vitamins and folic acid without compromising efficiency. Thus, the author's argument goes unaffected.

(D) is also Out of Scope. Even if there are other factors that affect the risk of Alzheimer's, it's still possible that replacing homocysteine could have *some* effect of its own and reduce the risk.

22. (E) Role of a Statement

Step 1: Identify the Question Type

The question presents a claim from the stimulus and asks for "the role played" by that claim in the argument. That makes this a Role of a Statement question.

Step 2: Untangle the Stimulus

The advocate concludes ("[a]s a result") that increasing a good's price will benefit people with the most money, not the people who actually need that good. This contradicts the economists, who argue that price gouging (increasing price in absence of competition) favors those who need that good because they're the ones willing to pay for it. *But* the advocate claims that "willingness to pay" and *need* do not correlate with one another.

Step 3: Make a Prediction

The claim in question (which follows the Keyword [*b*]*ut*) is the advocate's rebuttal of the economist's view. That rebuttal is then used to support the advocate's conclusion in the final sentence. The correct answer will address the claim's role as a rebuttal or as support for the advocate's conclusion, or both.

Step 4: Evaluate the Answer Choices

(E) matches the claim's purpose, albeit in a convoluted way. The "reasoning that [the argument] rejects" is the economist's view. That view (price gouging reduces buyers to those who need the good) assumes that the more someone is willing to pay for a good, the more that person *needs* that good. The claim in question denies that assumption, just as this answer indicates.

(A) is a Distortion. The advocate is disputing a purported *effect* of an action (price gouging benefiting those who need a certain good) and claiming a different *effect* will occur (price gouging will benefit those with the most money). The advocate neither disputes nor advocates for any *explanations*.

(B) is incorrect. The conclusion is the last sentence, not the claim in question.

(C) is a 180. The claim is not part of the reasoning being disputed; it's the evidence *against* the reasoning being disputed.

(D) is a 180. The advocate does not question the validity of the claim in question. The advocate accepts that claim and uses it to reject the economist's view.

23. (D) Strengthen

Step 1: Identify the Question Type

The question directly asks for an answer that will strengthen the argument.

Step 2: Untangle the Stimulus

The zoologist concludes ([*t*]*hus*) that prehistoric cave bears were not exclusively herbivores (plant-eaters). The evidence is that blood samples from modern meat-eating bears had the same level of heavy nitrogen as bone samples from prehistoric cave bears, and meat-eaters usually have more heavy nitrogen in their tissues than herbivores.

Step 3: Make a Prediction

If both prehistoric cave bears and modern bears had the same concentration of heavy nitrogen, it would certainly suggest a similar diet. So, if the modern bear eats meat, it stands to reason that the prehistoric bears did, too. The problem is that the zoologist compared blood samples to bone samples. That assumes that heavy nitrogen levels are

consistent from blood to bone. If bone samples usually have a higher concentration of heavy nitrogen than blood, then the prehistoric bears would have had lower levels in their blood, which would suggest a different (perhaps all-plant) diet. To strengthen the zoologist's claim, it should be shown that heavy nitrogen levels do not vary between bone and blood.

Step 4: Evaluate the Answer Choices

(D) strengthens the argument. This confirms that heavy nitrogen levels stay constant between bone and blood, making the comparison between prehistoric bones and modern blood more valid.

(A) is Out of Scope. It doesn't matter where the heavy nitrogen comes from. The argument only depends on the amount of heavy nitrogen found in the bears.

(B) is Out of Scope. What's important is that the ultimate level of heavy nitrogen in blood can be inferred from bone samples. The *rate* of accumulation is irrelevant.

(C) is also Out of Scope. The number of samples doesn't matter. All that matters are the results.

(E) is an Irrelevant Comparison. What matters is that the levels of the prehistoric bears match *any* bear that eats any amount of meat from any source. Differing heavy nitrogen levels among differing types of bears or bears with meat from different sources, does nothing to support the zoologist's conclusion about prehistoric bears.

24. (B) Assumption (Necessary)

Step 1: Identify the Question Type

The correct answer will be an "assumption required" by the argument, making this a Necessary Assumption question.

Step 2: Untangle the Stimulus

The phrase "[t]hey are mistaken" indicates the biologist's conclusion, a rejection of the computer scientists' view. They claim a computer program encapsulating the information in a human genome is all you need to create artificial intelligence. The biologist rejects this claim, thus concluding that human genome information is not enough. The evidence is that the brains are controlled by the "interactions of proteins" within the genome.

Step 3: Make a Prediction

The biologist is implying that the interactions of proteins are what really govern the human brain (and would thus lead to intelligence). If the biologist claims that encapsulating the information in a genome is not enough, the biologist must be assuming that the genome does not provide information on the interactions of proteins.

Step 4: Evaluate the Answer Choices

(B) is correct, making the necessary connection between genome information and the inability to get protein interaction.

(A) is a Distortion. It is not *necessary* that computers are incapable of simulating the protein interactions. It's merely necessary that encapsulating genome information is not enough to provide those interactions. Even if those interactions *could* be simulated by a computer, the biologist could still argue that genome information would not be enough to create those simulations. More would be needed.

(C) is Extreme. Modeling the human brain does not have to be the *only* way. Even if there were other ways, the biologist could still claim that encapsulating genome information would not be enough.

(D) is not necessary. It doesn't have to be difficult to get that information. Even if it were really easy for a computer, the biologist could still have a point that such information would not be enough.

(E) is an Irrelevant Comparison. It doesn't matter which program would be harder to write. The question is whether encapsulating genome information would be enough by itself for making artificial intelligence, regardless of the difficulty of programming protein interactions.

25. (A) Inference

Step 1: Identify the Question Type
The correct answer will be "strongly supported" by the information provided. That makes this an Inference question.

Step 2: Untangle the Stimulus
The stimulus describes an advertising ploy that involves giving away free computers that constantly play ads. The ads adapt to people's Internet usage so that the ads reflect the users' interests. Advertisers can afford this because the ads lead to increased sales.

Step 3: Make a Prediction
It's hard to predict exactly what the correct answer will say, but keep the general tone and message in mind. In this case, advertisers are giving away free computers that play targeted ads, and the plan is working. Watch out for answers that distort the facts, introduce unsupported elements, or are too strong in language.

Step 4: Evaluate the Answer Choices
(A) is supported. If advertisers "can afford to offer the computers for free," the plan must be working to some degree. Thus, it's logical that at least *some* people are buying the advertisers' products who otherwise wouldn't.

(B) is Extreme. This denies any other way to get effective use out of giving away free computers. While the Internet-based system seems to work, there could still be *some* way to use free computers as an advertising ploy without the Internet.

(C) is unsupported. There's no suggestion that people who get these computers spend very little online to begin with.

The suggestion is that some people who *do* get these computers just start buying *more*.

(D) is not supported. In order to afford to give away the computers, the advertisers *have* to get increased sales, but they don't necessarily *have* to play adds continuously. They might be just as able to offer such computers even if the ads only popped up every 15–30 minutes.

(E) is not supported. There is no indication that consumers have any ability to prevent information from being sent at any time.

26. (E) Parallel Flaw

Step 1: Identify the Question Type
The correct answer will be reasoning "similar to" that in the stimulus. Furthermore, that reasoning will be *flawed*, making this a Parallel Flaw question.

Step 2: Untangle the Stimulus
According to the author, some eloquent speakers can impress audiences with clear, vivid messages. Because of this, the author concludes that speakers who use obscenity, who are not eloquent, are incapable of impressing audiences.

Step 3: Make a Prediction
The flaw is that the evidence is only about some people who *are* eloquent. The evidence provides no information about ineloquent speakers, and therefore offers no justification that they can't also impress audiences. The correct answer will be flawed in the exact same way. The argument will claim that some people of a certain type (eloquent speakers) can perform a particular action (impress audiences), and then conclude that people who are *not* that type *cannot* perform that action.

Step 4: Evaluate the Answer Choices
(E) matches the flawed logic. It claims that some people of a certain type (sculptors) can perform a particular action (produce significant art), and then concludes that people who are *not* that type *cannot* perform that action. Like the original, there's no justification that musicians cannot produce significant art just like sculptors do.

(A) does not match. The logic here is not flawed. If *any* culture with no myths has no moral certainties, then the culture cited without myths cannot have certainties.

(B) does not match. The reasoning here is certainly illogical, but for various reasons that do not compare to the original. Here, some people of a certain type (authors who write one page a day) can perform a particular action (produce one book a year). However, this argument doesn't claim that serious authors (who don't write one page a day) cannot produce one book a year. And, unlike the original, the conclusion is about people who *can* write a book a year. This argument is just not parallel to the original.

(C) does not match. This compares centers of industry to centers of commerce, and centers of commerce are always centers of industry. They're part of the same group. The original argument compares people in one group (eloquent speakers) to people who are *not* in that group (those who use obscenity). This argument is certainly illogical, but not in the same way.

(D) does not match. The concept of [*m*]*ost* does not align with the original. Further, the conclusion does not outright reject the possibility of certain people being able to perform a certain act. This just claims one person *probably* wouldn't like something. It's not entirely logical, but it's not flawed in the same way as the original.

Section II: Reading Comprehension
Passage 1: Muscle Memory

Q#	Question Type	Correct	Difficulty
1	Global	C	★
2	Logic Reasoning (Method of Argument)	B	★
3	Inference	A	★
4	Inference	C	★★
5	Global	D	★★★★
6	Inference	D	★★
7	Detail	E	★★★

Passage 2: Eileen Gray

Q#	Question Type	Correct	Difficulty
8	Global	B	★
9	Inference	E	★★★
10	Inference	E	★★
11	Detail	C	★★★
12	Inference	A	★★★
13	Logic Reasoning (Principle)	B	★★★
14	Inference	C	★★★★

Passage 3: Mesolithic Woodland Clearings

Q#	Question Type	Correct	Difficulty
15	Global	B	★★
16	Detail	B	★★
17	Logic Reasoning (Strengthen)	E	★★★
18	Inference	D	★★
19	Logic Function	D	★
20	Inference	A	★★
21	Inference	A	★★★
22	Logic Reasoning (Parallel Reasoning)	E	★★★★

Passage 4: Specific Performance

Q#	Question Type	Correct	Difficulty
23	Logic Reasoning (Principle)	B	★★
24	Inference	C	★★★
25	Global	E	★★
26	Inference	A	★★
27	Logic Reasoning (Strengthen)	C	★★★

Passage 1: Muscle Memory

Step 1: Read the Passage Strategically
Sample Roadmap

line #	Keyword/phrase	¶ Margin notes
Passage A		
1	puzzling	Muscle memory common
3	yet	
6	seems easier	
7	even if	but unexplained
9	must	
10	One potential explanation	Auth theory:
17	But	more exercise → more neurons → more muscle fibers
26	Although	
29	also possible	Theory 2: It's mental
30	nothing; :	
Passage B		
39–40	think they know why	Scientists: muscles retain something
42	Because	Muscles need nuclei for protein
44	Previous	More exercise → more nuclei
49	had thought	Prev idea: extra nuclei die
52	recent	New study w/ mice: muscles got more nuclei
57	but	
58	Since	Nuclei don't die = cellular muscle memory

Discussion

Passage A gets right to the **Topic**: Muscle memory—a phenomenon in which bodybuilders who stop training are able to gain muscles more easily when they start working out again. The author expresses surprise that no explanation exists for this. Finding an explanation is the **Scope** of the passage.

The author then presents two theories. First, in the second paragraph, the author suggests neurons play a role. When weightlifting, neurons stimulate muscle fibers. More weightlifting leads to more neurons, which leads to more muscle fibers being stimulated. The body then adapts so it can continue stimulating that increased number of muscle fibers. When one quits and comes back to weightlifting, the body adapts to start where the weightlifter left off.

In the third paragraph, the author offers a different theory: it could just be in your head. When you stop training and then come back, you simply remember what your body could handle in the past. So, you don't start off slowly any more, and you get back to building muscles more quickly. The author never provides any support for the theories, so the **Purpose** is merely to present the two theories. The **Main Idea** is that muscle memory may involve neurons and muscle fibers, or it may be mental, but there's no definitive explanation.

Muscle memory is also the **Topic** of passage B. However, unlike the previous author, the author of passage B claims in the first paragraph that scientists *have* come up with an explanation. This explanation serves as the **Scope** of passage B, and the **Purpose** is to inform the reader of that explanation.

Paragraph 2 starts off with the science of muscle-building. Muscle-building requires proteins, and muscle cells have multiple nuclei to make those proteins. When exercising, muscle cells grow and merge with other cells to absorb even more nuclei. However, when exercising stops, researchers assume that the extra nuclei just die off.

Paragraph 3 introduces a study of mice that suggests otherwise. In that study, the muscle cells in mice grew and, as expected, gained new nuclei. However, when they stopped exercising, the nuclei did *not* die. They stuck around so that, should the mice start exercising again, the muscle cells still have the extra nuclei to start making the extra proteins. That leads to the **Main Idea**: new studies suggest that it's easier for people who had exercised before to build muscles because muscle cells retain the protein-producing nuclei they gained before.

Both passages are concerned with explaining muscle memory. However, while the author of passage A merely theorizes about neurons, muscle fibers, and mental explanations, the author of passage B presents scientific evidence regarding muscle cells, nuclei, and proteins.

1. (C) Global

Step 2: Identify the Question Type
The question asks for something both passages seek to answer. The correct answer will be based on the Scope and Purpose of both passages overall, making this a Global question.

Step 3: Research the Relevant Text
Because the correct answer will be based on the Scope and Purpose of the passages, there is no need to go back into the text itself.

Step 4: Make a Prediction
Both passages are focused on explanations for muscle memory, i.e., why people who have exercised before find it easier to build muscles the second time around.

Step 5: Evaluate the Answer Choices
(C) matches the main focus of both passages.

(A) brings up inconclusive explanations, which are not mentioned in passage B. Moreover, the author of passage A never actually explains *why* explanations are inconclusive.

(B) is a Distortion. Both passages focus on the effects of training, not on actual training methods or regimens.

(D) questions whether muscle memory is *psychological*, a concept only brought up in the last paragraph of passage A. Passage B does not address psychological explanations at all.

(E) also brings up *psychological* explanations, which is only addressed partially in passage A and never in passage B.

2. (B) Logic Reasoning (Method of Argument)

Step 2: Identify the Question Type
The word *by* indicates that the question is asking for *how* the author of passage B argues, making this a Method of Argument question similar to those found in Logical Reasoning.

Step 3: Research the Relevant Text
The question asks about the method used throughout passage B, so there's no specific text to research. Instead, because the question asks about how passage B differs from passage A, consider the relationship between the two passages.

Step 4: Make a Prediction
The difference between the passages is that passage B actually presents scientific evidence, while passage A merely presents unsupported theories. The correct answer will focus on passage B's use of scientific evidence.

Step 5: Evaluate the Answer Choices
(B) matches passage B's use of a scientific experiment (the one with mice), which contrasts the lack of scientific evidence in passage A.

(A) is a Distortion. The author of passage B provides evidence to explain the phenomenon of muscle memory. There is no questioning whether it's real or not.

(C) is a 180. Passage A addresses the reader personally (using the words *you* and *your*). Passage B refers to scientific evidence.

(D) is a 180. Passage A addresses psychological factors in the last paragraph. Passage B sticks to biological factors, including cells, nuclei, and proteins.

(E) is a 180. Passage A provides mere speculation. Passage B actually presents scientific evidence.

3. (A) Inference

Step 2: Identify the Question Type
The question asks for something passage B *suggests*, making this an Inference question.

Step 3: Research the Relevant Text
Because the entire passage revolves around muscle memory, everything is potentially relevant. However, the direct cause according to passage B is brought up at the very end. Start there and work backward.

Step 4: Make a Prediction
According to passage B, muscle memory is due to "extra nuclei" sticking around to make proteins (lines 58–61). This refers to the science in paragraph 2, in which muscle cells gain extra nuclei by merging with stem cells (lines 44–48). None of this is discussed in passage A, so the correct answer will revolve around this explanation.

Step 5: Evaluate the Answer Choices
(A) is correct, addressing the initial concept of muscle cells merging with stem cells.

(B) is a 180. Passage A does bring up the body's ability to adapt in lines 19–22.

(C) is a 180. Passage A brings up psychological factors in the third paragraph.

(D) is a Faulty Use of Detail. Passage B does bring up apoptosis (line 51), but that's part of the rejected assumption that extra nuclei die off. Muscle memory is based on the idea that those nuclei did *not* die off.

(E) is a 180. Passage A discusses neurons stimulating muscles in the second paragraph.

4. (C) Inference

Step 2: Identify the Question Type
The question directly asks for something that "can be inferred," making this an Inference question.

Step 3: Research the Relevant Text
There are no research clues, so the entire text is relevant. The question does ask about the author of passage A, but it

mentions making an inference from the *passages*. So, both passages will be relevant.

Step 4: Make a Prediction
The question is far too open-ended to make a specific prediction. Just stick to the global ideas (passage A deals with unsupported theories while B offers a scientific explanation), and test the answers one at a time.

Step 5: Evaluate the Answer Choices
(C) is correct. The author of passage A claims that "virtually no discussions of [muscle memory] have appeared in scientific publications." Given that the two theories in passage A make no mention of the details from the research in passage B, the author of passage A is surely working without knowledge of that research.

(A) is a 180. Neither author questions the existence of muscle memory. They both equally admit it's real.

(B) is not supported, as the author of passage A makes no mention of any of the details raised by passage B. In fact, passage A raises the possibility of entirely different theories.

(D) is not supported. The author of passage A presents two theories as merely *potential* or *possible* explanations. There is no reason to believe that the author would be against a new theory if it's plausible.

(E) is not supported. The author of passage A never mentions other species at all, so there's no way to determine how that author would feel about using the study of mice to draw inferences about human muscles.

5. (D) Global

Step 2: Identify the Question Type
The question asks for the expected target audience of each passage. The correct answer will be based on each passage in its entirety, making this an unusual twist on a Global question.

Step 3: Research the Relevant Text
The answer will be based on the entire content of each passage, so there is no specific text to research.

Step 4: Make a Prediction
Both passages discuss explanations for muscle memory, but passage A makes consistent references to lifting weights (lines 13, 15, 22, 32–33) while passage B merely refers to exercise and muscle development in general. Thus, passage A definitely has a more specific target audience than passage B.

Step 5: Evaluate the Answer Choices
(D) matches passage A's more specific target audience: bodybuilders who lift weights.

(A) is flawed on both counts. Neither passage addresses any skepticism about muscle memory. Additionally, passage A, not passage B, addresses people with personal experience (using words such as *you* and *your*).

(B) is a Distortion on both counts. Passage A's puzzlement over the lack of scientific information might be motive to address researchers, but passage A never directly calls for action. Moreover, there's no reason to believe that passage B's scientific discussion is directed at coaches or trainers.

(C) is not supported. Neither passage draws a distinction between those working out alone and those working with a trainer, so neither group could be considered a target audience.

(E) is perhaps Half-Right/Half-Wrong because the science of passage B would probably be of interest to physiologists. However, passage A only brings up psychological ideas in the last paragraph. The entire second paragraph about neurons and muscle fibers would be irrelevant to psychologists.

6. (D) Inference

Step 2: Identify the Question Type
The question asks for a view the author of passage B would be "most likely to hold," making this an Inference question.

Step 3: Research the Relevant Text
The question directly refers to the first sentence of passage A. Start with that, and consider what content in passage B would address that claim.

Step 4: Make a Prediction
The first sentence of passage A characterizes muscle memory as a "puzzling phenomenon." This refers to that author's surprise about the lack of a scientific explanation. However, passage B actually brings up scientific research that could explain muscle memory. Thus, the author of passage B would suggest that muscle memory may not be as *puzzling* as passage A suggests.

Step 5: Evaluate the Answer Choices
(D) matches the idea that the scientific evidence makes muscle memory a less puzzling phenomenon.

(A) is a 180. The author of passage B does not deny the experiences of bodybuilders. In fact, passage B provides evidence that helps explain their experiences.

(B) is a 180. There is no dichotomy. What athletes experience is consistent with what passage B suggests happens at the cellular level.

(C) is unsupported. There's no information about what "most athletes" would believe. If they were unaware of the scientific evidence raised in passage B, they might be just as puzzled as the author of passage A.

(E) is a Distortion. Passage B never suggests that the author of passage A has any misunderstanding about anything, let alone "exercise psychology," a concept that passage B never mentions.

7. (E) Detail

Step 2: Identify the Question Type
The question asks for something "explicitly mentioned," making this a Detail question.

Step 3: Research the Relevant Text
The question provides no research clues, so the entire text is relevant.

Step 4: Make a Prediction
Passage B mentions many things that are never found in passage A, including muscle cell nuclei, proteins, stem cells, apoptosis, mice, and so on. If something doesn't jump out immediately in the answers, look for answers that can be eliminated because they *are* mentioned in passage A (e.g., neurons, muscle fibers).

Step 5: Evaluate the Answer Choices
(E) is correct. The need for protein is mentioned in lines 43–44, but never in passage A.

(A) is a 180. Passage A mentions such conditions in lines 23–26.

(B) is a 180. Passage A mentions muscles adapting in lines 19–22.

(C) is a 180. Passage A mentions muscle fiber percentage in line 21.

(D) is a 180. Passage A mentions discussion in scientific publications in lines 3–4.

Passage 2: Eileen Gray

Step 1: Read the Passage Strategically
Sample Roadmap

line #	Keyword/phrase	¶ Margin notes
1	Best known	E.G. career
2	fascinating	Studied lacquer:
3	:	layering
5	Though; shifted	simple aesthetics
6	always; even	
7	forever	
13	fit well	
14	eschewed	
16	preferring	
20	This tension	Tension b/w aesthetics and structure
23	critical; but; :	Led to interior design:
26	early; later	objects artistic and functional
30	:	
34	subsequently	
35	heavily invested	
39	though	
41	prefigures; did not believe	Led to architecture
46	:	structured house as whole
47	But	inside out
52	One such	no "exterior" or "interior"
55–56	no important distinction	

Discussion

The passage opens by introducing Eileen Gray, noting the years of her life span, and mentioning her "fascinating and multifaceted career." This makes Eileen Gray the **Topic** of this typical biography passage on the LSAT. Most biography passages are organized as a progression from one stage of the person's life or career to the next. The description of her artistic career (the **Scope** of the passage) in lines 3–4 foreshadows the structure of this passage: designing ornaments, then furniture, then interiors, and then homes. This common technique is great to notice as it offers an easy way to break down the remaining content.

Sure enough, the rest of the first paragraph discusses her work with lacquer, which applies to ornaments (bowls, screens) and furniture. The first sentence claimed she is best known for such work, and the author provides ample detail on this subject. Lacquering involves a series of layers, and the aesthetic result is austere ("straight lines and simple forms"), which veered from the showier style of the Art Nouveau movement of the time.

The second paragraph reveals more about her lacquer work, noting it's not just about aesthetics. There are also structural elements (e.g., lacquering properly to prevent the wood from warping), and both are critical to her work. The passage describes her applying this technique to various objects, creating pieces that were both artistic and functional. This *subsequently* (line 34) led to the next phase in her career: interior design. As with the lacquer objects, she created areas that were aesthetically stark, yet functional.

In the third paragraph, the author moves on to the final stage in Gray's career: architecture. Again, her principles from lacquering and interior design carry forward. Individual components were layered so as to allow for multiple functions. Nothing was "exterior" or "interior." Every part of the house was designed to function as a whole.

The author offers very little in the way of opinion, so the **Purpose** of this passage is merely to inform the reader about Gray's career. The **Main Idea** is that she had a varied career that carried forward her artistic principles of combining aesthetics and function and seeing everything as part of a whole.

8. (B) Global

Step 2: Identify the Question Type
The question asks for the "main point of the passage," making this a Global question.

Step 3: Research the Relevant Text
As with most Global questions, the entire text here is relevant. Instead of going back into the text, just consider the Main Point as predicted after reading the passage.

Step 4: Make a Prediction
The main point is very objective: Eileen Gray had a varied artistic career, taking the artistic principles from her work with lacquer and carrying them through to her work in architecture.

Step 5: Evaluate the Answer Choices
(B) is correct, identifying her varied career and how the aesthetic style she developed from her work with lacquer carried forward to her "everything works as a whole" style of architecture.

(A) starts off perfectly, but veers off at the end, suggesting she never received critical acclaim. The author never mentioned any critical reception, so this could not be part of the main point.

(C) contradicts the first sentence, which suggests she is best known for her work in lacquer, not her use of modern materials (a concept only presented tangentially in lines 37–39).

(D) is a Distortion. The author does mention *hidden* elements in some of Gray's work, but never claims this makes her work "readily identifiable."

(E) is a 180. Gray *embraced* the concept of integral wholeness, which she carried forward from her work in the Japanese tradition of lacquering. There is no dissatisfaction at all.

9. (E) Inference

Step 2: Identify the Question Type
The question asks for something that would exemplify the characteristics of Gray's work. Such an example will not be stated, but can be inferred based on the descriptions in the passage. This is a common Inference variation.

Step 3: Research the Relevant Text
The passage lists several characteristics of Gray's work. Some of the most prominent appear at the end of the first and second paragraphs.

Step 4: Make a Prediction
In describing Gray's work, the author notes Gray's preference for "straight lines and simple forms" (line 17). This austere quality is raised again in line 39, which also notes another frequently discussed characteristic: functionality. The correct answer should be an aesthetically simple creation that serves a functional purpose.

Step 5: Evaluate the Answer Choices
(E) matches Gray's style. The shape is described as simple, which matches Gray's aesthetic sensibility. It's made to fit the human form, which ensures it would be functional.

(A) is a 180. Tasseled fringes and curved arms go against Gray's preference for "straight lines and simple forms."

(B) is a 180. Gray prefers "straight lines and simple forms," not "intricate carvings" of wildlife.

(C) is a 180. While the functional aspect matches, the aesthetic style of mimicking "ornate flowers" does not.

(D) is not supported. The use of many different components (beads, pearls, and shells) does not fit Gray's simpler style.

10. (E) Inference

Step 2: Identify the Question Type

The correct answer will be supported by information in the passage, making this an Inference question.

Step 3: Research the Relevant Text

There are no research clues, so the entire text is relevant.

Step 4: Make a Prediction

It's difficult to predict an answer here; there are too many possible inferences. Instead, eliminate answers that are clearly beyond the Scope of the passage, and use content clues in the answer choices to do any necessary research.

Step 5: Evaluate the Answer Choices

(E) matches Gray's progression toward functionality, as noted in lines 37–39 and 49–52.

(A) is a 180. Any hint to Gray's reputation comes from the first sentence, which suggests that she *is* best known for a particular medium: her work with lacquer.

(B) is Extreme. The author mentions that she *often* created her own furniture (lines 36–38), but does not say she constructed *most* of the furnishings she designed.

(C) is a Distortion. The technique of lacquering was not common in Paris (lines 10–11), but there's no suggestion that artists didn't use wood or even found it *inappropriate*.

(D) is not supported. There's no suggestion that she withheld anything from public viewing.

11. (C) Detail

Step 2: Identify the Question Type

The correct answer will be a question that is directly answered in the passage. That means there will be a detail in the passage that corresponds to the correct answer.

Step 3: Research the Relevant Text

With no research clues, the entire text is relevant.

Step 4: Make a Prediction

The correct answer could refer to any detail from anywhere in the passage. The only approach is to test the answers one at a time, doing research when necessary to ensure there's a direct answer to the question provided.

Step 5: Evaluate the Answer Choices

(C) is directly answered in lines 13–17, which claim that the "straight lines and simple forms" of lacquering were *not* similar to the showier style of Art Nouveau.

(A) is not answered. It is only known that lacquer was "little known in Europe" during the early days of Gray's career, but there's no indication of when it was first introduced.

(B) is not answered. The passage mentions different types of wood surfaces (bowls, screens, furniture), but never mentions any specific types of wood.

(D) is not answered. In all the discussion of her architectural design, there is no mention of using the surrounding landscape.

(E) is not answered. The only materials mentioned are the wood used in lacquering and the steel used in some of her furniture. However, neither of those were said to be used for their structurally superior strength.

12. (A) Inference

Step 2: Identify the Question Type

The question asks for the "author's attitude" toward Gray's work, which is a common variation of an Inference question.

Step 3: Research the Relevant Text

The author's voice is noticeably lacking in this passage. Instead, the attitude will be gleaned from the overall tone of the passage.

Step 4: Make a Prediction

The sole indication of the author's attitude is the use of the word *fascinating* (line 2) to describe Gray's career. The rest of the passage describes her aesthetic style that carried forward through various stages in her career. The correct answer will be positive overall and will likely stay focused on her style.

Step 5: Evaluate the Answer Choices

(A) is consistent with the author's tone. The author spends the entire passage describing her aesthetic philosophy. The opening line indicates appreciation of Gray's *fascinating* career, and lines 13–17 indicate how her philosophy helped her eschew the flourishing style adapted by her contemporaries.

(B) is a Distortion. While Gray did eschew the flourishing Art Nouveau movement, the author never suggests she was pushed to the periphery for her independent ways.

(C) is not supported. While lacquering was a traditional Japanese technique, there's no mention of any Japanese "architectural traditions."

(D) is a Distortion. There's no indication that her career developed rapidly, and there's no indication she was recognized as an "avant-garde artist."

(E) is Extreme. She may have had her own style of architectural design, but it's never suggested that she *revolutionized* the field of structural design.

13. (B) Logic Reasoning (Principle)

Step 2: Identify the Question Type
The question asks for a principle used by Gray in her work, which means this works like a Principle question in Logical Reasoning.

Step 3: Research the Relevant Text
The principles invoked in Gray's work are described throughout the second and third paragraphs.

Step 4: Make a Prediction
Gray's work is frequently described as serving multiple functions (lines 32–34, 38–39, 49–52), which emphasizes the idea that things work together "as an integrated whole" (line 45). The correct answer will express this idea of individual items being part of a whole.

Step 5: Evaluate the Answer Choices
(B) matches Gray's style of using individual objects (interior features) to create an integrated whole (overall structural design).

(A) is not supported. The author only mentions the use of wood in lacquering. There's no indication of Gray's application of that technique to other materials.

(C) is a Distortion. Gray carried forward the aesthetic and structural principles behind lacquer, but there's no indication that the actual technique of lacquering would be suitable for large structural elements.

(D) is a 180. Gray preferred "straight lines and simple forms." She never expressed interested in mixing this with "ornate elements."

(E) is not supported. Gray's work is said to have involved "hidden layers" (line 48), which suggests that visual aspects would not necessarily give evidence of those unseen components.

14. (C) Inference

Step 2: Identify the Question Type
The question asks for something the passage *suggests* and that the author "would agree with," making this an Inference question.

Step 3: Research the Relevant Text
The question asks about Gray's architectural work, which is described in the third paragraph.

Step 4: Make a Prediction
The third paragraph mentions Gray's architectural style, which involves seeing interior and exterior elements as part of a unified whole, rather than as independent components. It talks about hidden layers and how Gray felt her architecture was similar to her work with lacquer.

Unfortunately, the correct answer to this question is not based on anything in the third paragraph. The correct answer

is based on the very first sentence, a sentence that is worthy to note upon first reading the passage, but you wouldn't necessarily expect it to play a role in this question. On Test Day, it is vital that questions like these do not monopolize your time. Give them ample effort. Eliminate answers that are clearly wrong. However, know when it's time to move on. You never want to sacrifice an entire passage from later in the section, just for the sake of completing a single question.

Step 5: Evaluate the Answer Choices
(C) is the correct answer. The support from this comes from the very first line, which indicates that Gray is "best known for her work with lacquer." If that's what she's *best* known for, then she must be somewhat less known for everything else, including her work in architecture.

(A) is not supported. There is no mention of the views of any other architects.

(B) is a 180. There was no "radical shift" in her attitude. On the contrary, her architecture was based on the same attitudes she brought to her earlier work.

(D) is not supported. There is no mention of any of her work being controversial, so there is no basis for comparing her work on this quality.

(E) is a 180. Gray felt her architectural work was "like her work in lacquer" (line 46), which means they were similarly inspired by the Japanese tradition of layering.

Passage 3: Mesolithic Woodland Clearings

Step 1: Read the Passage Strategically
Sample Roadmap

line #	Keyword/phrase	¶ Margin notes
1	generally accepted	General view:
4	Whether	Mesolithic clearings used to get food
6	or whether	Auth: evidence not conclusive
7	common view	
9	however; at best; circumstantial	
13	but	
14	Furthermore	
17	generally lacking	
20	rather than	Some evidence supports
22	But	other evidence contradicts
23	while	
24	bolster	
25	may suggest a different vision	
28	argues	Tuan: humans fear wilderness
30	driven by; While	may apply to Mesolithic era
31	tempted	
32	clear	
33	If	
35	may change	
39	However	Auth: Mesolithic paths created due to fear
41	only recently; I propose	
46	alternative hypothesis	Alt view:
47	First	clearings developed where paths meet
48	Then	
51	legitimately consider	
54	finally	

Discussion

The passage opens with the **Topic**: woodland clearings. The prevailing view is that these clearings had an economic purpose: they provided a place to procure food. *However*, the author is not entirely convinced. The evidence provided is not conclusive, and there's no real evidence of animal preparation near the clearings.

The author's doubts continue in the second paragraph, in which the author bemoans the lack of archeological evidence and claims there's merely some ethnographic evidence. *But* the author is quick to point out that there is also ethnographic evidence that contradicts the prevailing view and points to *noneconomic* uses. At this point, it becomes clear that the **Scope** of the passage is determining the real purpose of the clearings.

In the third paragraph, the author suddenly digresses to introduce Yi-Fu Tuan, a geographer who talks about humans and their fear of wilderness. This seems off topic, but nothing is off topic in an LSAT passage. Sure enough, by the end of the paragraph, the author suggests this could shed light on the woodland clearings.

The author then discusses paths created by Mesolithic humans, who had a tendency to move around. The author hypothesizes that the paths were created due to the fear of wilderness, tying things back to Tuan's ideas. This leads to the final paragraph, in which the author's **Purpose** is clear: to present an alternative hypothesis about the clearings. As the paths became permanent and more frequently used, clearings emerged where the paths met, basically providing shortcuts and giving people a place to rest. So, the **Main Idea** is that, contrary to the view that clearings were used to procure food, the author believes they served a noneconomic purpose: they were just a place where people literally crossed paths.

15. (B) Global

Step 2: Identify the Question Type
The question asks for the "main idea" of the passage, making this a Global question.

Step 3: Research the Relevant Text
All of the text is relevant to this question. Instead, focus on the Main Idea of the passage, as discovered in Step 1.

Step 4: Make a Prediction
The main idea is that Mesolithic clearings may have had a noneconomic purpose, contrary to the prevailing view that they were used to procure food.

Step 5: Evaluate the Answer Choices
(B) correctly addresses the noneconomic theory as an alternative to the prevailing resource-procurement model.

(A) provides distorted information based on the wilderness discussion from the third and fourth paragraphs, but completely misses the author's focus on the Mesolithic woodland clearings.

(C) is Half-Right/Half-Wrong. It correctly notes the existence of ethnographic evidence in favor of the resource-procurement model. However, the author's point is not that there were "multiple purposes." The author's view is that there was a different noneconomic purpose, for which there is no archaeological evidence given.

(D) focuses on the wrong details (movement along paths instead of the woodland clearings). Besides, the idea of moving along paths is said to be a *fact* (line 39), not a hypothesis.

(E) is a 180 of information in the second paragraph. Instead of providing a clear explanation, some evidence supports one view while other evidence supports a conflicting view.

16. (B) Detail

Step 2: Identify the Question Type
"According to" suggests that the correct answer will be directly found in the text, making this a Detail question.

Step 3: Research the Relevant Text
The resource-procurement model is described primarily in the first paragraph.

Step 4: Make a Prediction
It's frequently called the "resource-procurement model," but the first sentence is more direct about the "resource" being procured: food. And the food in question is animals, which are either attracted to open areas or just easier to hunt when out in the open. Either way, the view is that animals entered the clearing to graze, and humans hunted them there for food.

Step 5: Evaluate the Answer Choices
(B) matches the stated view.

(A) is a Faulty Use of Detail. Pathways are part of the author's theory, not the resource-procurement model.

(C) is a Distortion. The potential use of the clearings was to attract presumably *wild* animals to be hunted, not to provide *domesticated* animals with a place to graze.

(D) is a Faulty Use of Detail. This is part of the author's theory in the final paragraph, not the resource-procurement model.

(E) mentions crops, which were never mentioned in the passage, let alone as part of the resource-procurement model.

17. (E) Logic Reasoning (Strengthen)

Step 2: Identify the Question Type
The question asks for information that "would lend support to the author's proposal," making this a Strengthen question like the ones found in Logical Reasoning.

Step 3: Research the Relevant Text
The question directly refers to the author's proposal in the next-to-last paragraph, which can be readily spotted by the phrase "I propose" (line 41).

Step 4: Make a Prediction
The author's proposal in the second-to-last paragraph is that the paths were created due to fear of the surrounding woodland. This is all based on Tuan's theory that humans fear wilderness. The author assumes that human actions (e.g., creating paths) can be motivated by the fears they have. The correct answer will strengthen that assumption by showing how people's actions can be based on their fears.

Step 5: Evaluate the Answer Choices
(E) strengthens the argument by showing how some premodern populations perform other actions (rituals) as protection from the wilderness they fear. If their fear motivates the performance of such rituals, then it's more likely that Mesolithic populations also had similar fears that motivated their creation of the paths.

(A) would not strengthen the author's proposal. It may help confirm that Mesolithic people used those paths and clearings, but offers no support that fear of wilderness was a motivator.

(B) would not strengthen the proposal. This would merely suggest that the paths were created in response to population density, not to any fear of wilderness.

(C) is irrelevant. Whether modern people use the paths offers no evidence why they were created in the first place or whether fear played any role in their creation.

(D) offers no help. This merely confirms Tuan's theory that people fear wilderness, but does not confirm that such fear was the motivator for building the paths.

18. (D) Inference

Step 2: Identify the Question Type
The question asks for something the author *suggests*, making this an Inference question.

Step 3: Research the Relevant Text
The author discusses the Mesolithic humans throughout the passage. However, the question asks what the *author* suggests and for something that *may* have been true. That suggests that the question refers to the author's theories in the last two paragraphs.

Step 4: Make a Prediction
At the end of the fourth paragraph and into the fifth passage, the author suggests that Mesolithic humans may have created paths out of fear of the wilderness (lines 41–45, 51–52) and that they created clearings for social purposes (lines 54–58).

Step 5: Evaluate the Answer Choices
(D) is supported, especially considering the author's theory that "wilderness [was] a motivating concept in the Mesolithic" (line 52).

(A) is Extreme. The author mentions this use of fire in line 22, but never suggests that Mesolithic humans were "the first" to do so.

(B) is Extreme. They used paths, but the author never claims or suggests that they were the *first* people to do so.

(C) is not supported. In fact, it is suggested that they feared nature (lines 42–45).

(E) is not supported. The only economic idea presented is the resource-procurement theory of using open clearings for hunting—hardly a "complex system."

19. (D) Logic Function

Step 2: Identify the Question Type
The phrase "in order to" indicates that the question is asking *why* the author mentions Tuan's argument, making this a Logic Function question.

Step 3: Research the Relevant Text
Tuan's argument, as the question indicates, is in the third paragraph. Be sure to consider how Tuan's argument fits within the context of the paragraph as well as the passage as a whole.

Step 4: Make a Prediction
Tuan's argument is about human fear of wilderness, an odd concept in a passage about wilderness clearings. However, the last sentence of the third paragraph indicates how this fits into the author's discussion. The author claims that applying Tuan's argument to the Mesolithic era can provide a new perspective on the woodland clearings (lines 33–35). The author then goes on to use Tuan's ideas as a basis for a new hypothesis about those clearings. And that's the true function of Tuan's argument in this passage.

Step 5: Evaluate the Answer Choices
(D) matches the prediction of Tuan's theory as a basis (groundwork) for the author's new hypothesis.

(A) is a Distortion. Tuan's theory merely supports the author's hypothesis. It is irrelevant to the generally accepted view, and thus has no effect (i.e., casts no doubt) on that theory.

(B) is a 180. Tuan's argument is the basis for the author's argument, not the hypothesis the author is challenging.

(C) is a Distortion. Tuan's argument is used as the basis for the *author's* hypothesis about clearings. Tuan himself offered no hypothesis on the clearings.

(E) is unsupported. Tuan's view is solely about human fear of wilderness. He is not said to hold any view about the Mesolithic clearings.

20. (A) Inference

Step 2: Identify the Question Type
The question asks for something that can be *inferred*, making this an Inference question.

Step 3: Research the Relevant Text
The question refers to the author's reluctance to accept the resource-procurement model. The author's misgivings are primarily laid out in the first paragraph.

Step 4: Make a Prediction
The author currently does not accept the resource-procurement model for two reasons. First, the author cites any existing evidence as "at best circumstantial" (line 9), suggesting there's no strong link between human artifacts and the clearings. Second, the author cites a lack of evidence "that preparation of animals for human consumption took place within or near such clearings" (lines 14–17). So, the author would be more likely to accept the theory if there was a stronger link between human artifacts and the clearings or if there was evidence of animal preparation near the clearings.

Step 5: Evaluate the Answer Choices
(A) is correct, as it would directly address the author's concern in lines 14–17.

(B) would be irrelevant. The author already admits that there is such evidence (lines 18–20), so such evidence has already done nothing to sway the author.

(C) would not help. The author never questions whether clearings would attract animals. Such experimental evidence would not do anything to address the author's stated concerns: the weak link between artifacts and clearings and the lack of evidence of animal preparation near the clearing.

(D) is a 180. This would suggest that the clearings were natural and not man-made, making the resource-procurement model look even *less* likely.

(E) is irrelevant. The number of clearings would offer no evidence on *why* they were created in the first place.

21. (A) Inference

Step 2: Identify the Question Type
The question asks for the closest meaning of a phrase the author uses. The meaning will not be stated directly, but will be an inference based on the context.

Step 3: Research the Relevant Text
The question directly refers to line 55, but be sure to read around that line and consider how that line fits within the context of the author's purpose.

Step 4: Make a Prediction
In line 55, the phrase "purely social phenomena" refers to the clearings described throughout the passage. This phrase is applied in the last paragraph, which describes the author's "alternative hypothesis," the one that contradicts the economic resource-procurement model. So, the phrase "purely social" indicates an entirely social basis for the clearings as opposed to an economic, food-based motivation.

Step 5: Evaluate the Answer Choices
(A) matches the author's idea that clearings arose because of noneconomic practices (the creation of paths due to the fear of wilderness).

(B) is not supported. There's no suggestion that clearings are universal (i.e., all societies create them), nor that they are unique to humans.

(C) is not supported. The idea of cutting corners and creating resting spots could very well be self-serving and have no intention of strengthening societal ties.

(D) is a Distortion. There may have been some social benefit (the clearings offered a place to rest and protection from the scary wilderness), but the author suggests that clearings merely *emerged* where paths crossed. There's no suggestion that the clearings were "intentionally created" to produce those benefits.

(E) is, at least in part, a 180. It may reveal cultural information, but the view being presented is a purely *noneconomic* one.

22. (E) Logic Reasoning (Parallel Reasoning)

Step 2: Identify the Question Type
The question asks for an argument "analogous to" another argument, making this a Parallel Reasoning question like those found in Logical Reasoning.

Step 3: Research the Relevant Text
The question directly points to the author's argument in the second paragraph.

Step 4: Make a Prediction
The author's argument in the second paragraph is that, while there may be ethnographic evidence that supports the resource-procurement model, there is other ethnographic evidence that "may suggest a different vision" (line 25). The correct answer will provide the same logic about a completely different topic: there is some type of evidence that supports one point of view, but there is other evidence of the same type that supports a different view.

Step 5: Evaluate the Answer Choices

(E) matches the logic. As with the author's argument, this presents a particular type of evidence (circumstantial evidence), of which there is some that supports one view (the defendant is guilty) and some that supports a different view (the defendant is innocent).

(A) is Half-Right/Half-Wrong. This correctly suggests that one type of evidence (circumstantial) supports one view, but there's another type (direct) that *establishes* another view. Not only are there not two different types of evidence in the passage, but the author's second set of evidence never *established* anything. Both sets of evidence in the original merely supported or suggested a point of view.

(B) does not match. Unlike the original argument, this uses the exact same evidence to arrive at two different conclusions, suggesting a difference in interpretation. The original argument presented evidence of the same *type*, but entirely different (*other*) evidence to support a different view.

(C) is Extreme and a Distortion. It may be tempting for those who concentrated on the author's claim that *most* evidence was from "ethnography rather than archaeology." However, the original argument never suggests that the evidence is *entirely* ethnographic, with *no* archaeological evidence. This answer is far too strong, and it also ignores the counterevidence raised in the second half of the paragraph.

(D) does not match. This brings up the concepts of trustworthiness and reliability, which do not logically compare to the original argument.

Passage 4: Specific Performance

Step 1: Read the Passage Strategically
Sample Roadmap

line #	Keyword/phrase	¶ Margin notes
9	But; while	Specific performance
10	better	Auth: sometimes good, sometimes not
11	alternative	
12	clearly not; suitable	
14	depends on	SP good when $ not enough
15	only	Ex.
16	reasonable	
18	For example	
24	best	
27	Nevertheless	When $ not enough
29	thus	SP can be bad
30	In fact	Ex. employment
32	detrimental	can cause friction
33	thus; should be avoided	$ would be better
37	especially if	
39	most compelling	
43	especially	
45	heighten dissatisfaction; intensify	
46	friction; Even if	
49	do better to avoid; uncomfortable	
51	permits; steer clear	
52	troublesome	
53	while	

Discussion

In the first paragraph, the author introduces "specific performance" (**Topic**), a court ruling applied in some breach of contract disputes. With specific performance, the person who violated the contract is simply ordered to do what was promised in the first place. No monetary damages are awarded. *But* the author argues that specific performance is only better than paying monetary damages in some cases. In other cases, specific performance would not be better. This is effectively the **Main Idea** of the passage. The rest of the passage merely goes into details and examples supporting this point. That makes the relative appropriateness of specific performance the **Scope**, with the **Purpose** being to describe instances when specific performance is more appropriate than monetary damages and when it's not.

The second paragraph describes when specific performance would be better. In general, it's when money wouldn't be adequate. As an example, the author cites a situation in which a seller backs out of a deal and won't sell a subjectively important object (i.e., something of personal value). In that case, the court would simply order the seller to sell the item as promised for the agreed-upon price.

The third paragraph focuses on cases when money *would* be adequate. In those cases, the author argues that specific performance would be a bad idea. As an example, the author mentions contracts involving a service to be performed (e.g., construction work). In such cases, it would be harder for courts to enforce specific performance, and it could lead to unsatisfactory service and psychological friction between parties. Monetary compensation would be a better solution.

23. (B) Logic Reasoning (Principle)

Step 2: Identify the Question Type
The correct answer will be a specific example that conforms to the general description of specific performance, as described in the passage. Finding a specific situation that conforms to a general rule is the hallmark of Principle questions, like those found in Logical Reasoning.

Step 3: Research the Relevant Text
The general description of specific performance is provided in the first paragraph.

Step 4: Make a Prediction
Specific performance is defined clearly in the first sentence (lines 1–4): compelling participants to do precisely what they agreed to do. The correct answer will provide a specific example in which there was an agreement, and all parties involved are ordered to honor the agreement.

Step 5: Evaluate the Answer Choices
(B) matches the concept perfectly. Both the analyst and the company are ordered to do what they agreed upon in the first place: the analyst is ordered to do her promised work, and the company is ordered to pay the salary it promised.

(A) does not match. In this case, the contract is simply thrown out. Nobody is made to follow through on the original agreement.

(C) does not match. Instead of ordering the contractor to fulfill the agreement, this orders the contractor to pass the burden on to somebody else.

(D) does not match. There was no breach of contract. The buyer paid for the item, and the seller provided the item. The contract was fulfilled. The question of the item's authenticity is another matter altogether.

(E) does not match. This involves awarding monetary damages, which is what specific performance is meant to avoid. Also, the engineer is not ordered to fulfill the contract, which is what specific performance is all about.

24. (C) Inference

Step 2: Identify the Question Type
The question asks for something the author would "most likely agree with," "[b]ased on the passage." That makes this an Inference question.

Step 3: Research the Relevant Text
The question asks about a situation in which someone failed to undertake employment as contracted, a concept raised in lines 38–39.

Step 4: Make a Prediction
Within the context of lines 30–39, someone refusing to undertake employment is an example of when specific performance "would actually be detrimental to those involved in the dispute and thus should be avoided."

Step 5: Evaluate the Answer Choices
(C) is supported, as the situation in the question stem fits exactly the kind of circumstance described throughout the third paragraph, which identifies when monetary damages can be superior to specific performance.

(A) is a 180. The author claims specific performance can be *detrimental*, not helpful, in such a case.

(B) is a Distortion. While the author might agree with weighing monetary factors against psychological concerns, the author already categorizes breach of employment contracts as unsuited to specific performance. Moreover, there is no indication that specific performance costs the courts less. In fact, lines 46–48 suggest otherwise.

(D) is not supported. Even under such dire circumstances, the author claims that specific performance can be *detrimental* in such cases. There is no suggestion that the author would support it as a plan B. Perhaps there are other solutions not raised in the passage.

(E) is an Irrelevant Comparison. It is only claimed in the first sentence that courts "sometimes use" specific performance. The author argues when it *should* be used, but there's no indication of the situations in which it actually *is* used more often.

25. (E) Global

Step 2: Identify the Question Type
The question asks for the "main purpose" of the entire passage, making this a Global question.

Step 3: Research the Relevant Text
Because the question asks about the passage as a whole, the entire text is relevant. Instead, use the Purpose as predicted in Step 1.

Step 4: Make a Prediction
The author claims that specific performance can be better than monetary damages in some cases, but not in others (lines 9–12). The rest of the passage merely provides examples of when one solution is better and when the other is better. That's the author's purpose.

Step 5: Evaluate the Answer Choices
(E) is correct. The author identifies situations for assessing the relative applicability of two remedies: specific performance vs. monetary damages.

(A) is a Distortion. The author never suggests that specific performance will become a "standard approach." It is merely used *sometimes*.

(B) is a Distortion. The author provides a few examples, but never offers a full "set of standards" and never argues for implementation of those standards. Also, there's no indication that specific performance is a "new legal measure."

(C) is a Distortion. The author does describe some differences between specific performance and monetary damages, but this completely ignores the author's focus on determining which solution is more applicable in certain situations.

(D) brings up evidence in contract disputes, which the author never addresses, let alone provides any guidelines for evaluating.

26. (A) Inference

Step 2: Identify the Question Type
The question asks for something the passage "strongly suggests" that the "author would agree with," making this an Inference question.

Step 3: Research the Relevant Text
With no research clues, the entire text is relevant.

Step 4: Make a Prediction
With no clues for reference, stay focused on the big picture: the author never conclusively supports monetary damages or specific performance. It all depends on whether monetary factors are adequate or not. Start with this global theme, eliminate answers that are clearly wrong, and use content clues in the answer choices to do any necessary research.

Step 5: Evaluate the Answer Choices
(A) is correct, fitting the consistent theme of the passage. The author states that specific performance would be acceptable when "monetary damages could not adequately compensate" (lines 15–18). When monetary damages *could* compensate, the court "need not consider ordering specific performance" (lines 27–30). That suggests that assessing monetary damages is a key consideration.

(B) is not supported. The author claims specific performance is reasonable for contracts selling personal property "that is unique or of such subjective importance to the buyer." However, those could be rare instances and not *usually* be the case with sales of personal property in general.

(C) is Extreme. This basically dismisses specific performance entirely, but the author admits that there are cases in which specific performance is an acceptable alternative (lines 9–12, 15–18).

(D) is an Extreme Distortion. The author cites specific performance as useful in circumstances when items have "subjective importance." However, that does not mean the objective value is low. Items can be both subjectively and objectively valuable. Besides, the author does not suggest that these are the *only* disputes in which specific performance would be successful.

(E) is not supported. The author cites examples in which one method would be more suitable than another. However, the author never suggests *offering* disputing parties the option to choose which one they'd prefer.

27. (C) Logic Reasoning (Strengthen)

Step 2: Identify the Question Type
The question asks for something that would "strengthen the author's position," which makes this a Strengthen question like those in Logical Reasoning.

Step 3: Research the Relevant Text
The question refers to "employment contract cases," which are brought up in lines 37–39.

Step 4: Make a Prediction
In the third paragraph, the author cites employment contract cases as an example of ones in which monetary damages would be more effective than specific performance. In other words, it would be better to order violating parties to just pay companies money rather than complete the work they

promised. The correct answer will validate that awarding monetary damages will be a more effective solution.

Step 5: Evaluate the Answer Choices

(C) strengthens the author's recommendation. If the people violating these contracts couldn't afford the monetary damages, then companies would get no service *and* no money. It's important that people have enough money to pay the damages.

(A) is a 180. If such compensation is hard to enforce, then it looks *less* warranted to make that recommendation.

(B) is a 180, at worst. If all remedies, including monetary compensation, involved coercion, then dissatisfaction and friction could be involved in any case. That does not make monetary compensation look any better.

(D) is a possible 180. The author claims monetary damages are better, in general, for breaches of service contracts (lines 30–36). If employment cases are very different, that may suggest monetary damages are *not* better in those cases.

(E) is a 180. This suggests that employee rights are more important than monetary considerations, contradicting the author's recommendation to award monetary damages.

Section III: Logic Games
Game 1: Bookmobile

Q#	Question Type	Correct	Difficulty
1	Acceptability	B	★
2	Must Be False (CANNOT Be True)	C	★
3	"If" / Must Be True	A	★
4	"If" / Must Be True	B	★
5	"If" / Must Be True	D	★

Game 2: National Park Rangers

Q#	Question Type	Correct	Difficulty
6	Acceptability	E	★
7	"If" / Could Be True	C	★
8	"If" / Must Be True	D	★★
9	Must Be False (CANNOT Be True)	D	★
10	"If" / Could Be True	E	★★
11	"If" / Could Be True	B	★★
12	"If" / Must Be True	A	★★

Game 3: Economics TAs

Q#	Question Type	Correct	Difficulty
13	Partial Acceptability	A	★
14	Partial Acceptability (CANNOT)	B	★★
15	Could Be True	A	★
16	"If" / Must Be False (CANNOT Be True)	C	★★
17	"If" / Must Be True	D	★★★★

Game 4: Computer Virus

Q#	Question Type	Correct	Difficulty
18	Partial Acceptability	D	★★
19	Could Be True	E	★★
20	"If" / Must Be True	A	★★★
21	Could Be True EXCEPT	C	★★★
22	Completely Determine	C	★★★
23	"If" / Must Be True	C	★★★

Game 1: Bookmobile

Step 1: Overview
Situation: A bookmobile visiting various neighborhoods

Entities: Six neighborhoods (Hidden Hills, Lakeville, Nottingham, Oldtown, Park Plaza, Sunnyside)

Action: Selection/Sequencing Hybrid. Determine which five neighborhoods will be visited (Selection) and the order in which they will be visited (Sequencing).

Limitations: Exactly five neighborhoods will be visited, one per day, with no neighborhood being visited more than once.

Step 2: Sketch
List the neighborhoods by initial. (For simplicity, use a single initial for the two-word neighborhoods, e.g., H for Hidden Hills). For the selection, write "5/6" next to the entities. As the game proceeds, circle neighborhoods that are selected and cross out the one that isn't. For the sequencing, draw five slots labeled with each day of the week, Monday through Friday.

H L N O P S – Pick 5 of 6

$\overline{\text{Mo}}$ $\overline{\text{Tu}}$ $\overline{\text{We}}$ $\overline{\text{Th}}$ $\overline{\text{Fr}}$

Step 3: Rules
Rule 1 provides two pieces of information. Hidden Hills is visited, so circle H in the entity list. However, it's not visited on Friday, so draw "~H" under Friday.

Rule 2 presents some Formal Logic. If Oldtown is visited, then it must be visited immediately before Hidden Hills.

$O \rightarrow \underline{O} \ \underline{H}$

The contrapositive for a rule like this is awkward, so this is a rare case in which a contrapositive is not needed (or, in this particular case, not really helpful).

Rule 3 is more Formal Logic. If Lakeville is visited, it must be visited on Wednesday. So, by contrapositive, if Lakeville is not visited on Wednesday, it's not visited at all:

$L \ \rightarrow \dfrac{L}{We}$

$\sim \dfrac{L}{We} \rightarrow \sim L$

Rule 4 provides two pieces of information. First, Nottingham and Sunnyside are both visited, so circle N and S in the entity list. However, they cannot be visited consecutively, so make a shorthand note of this.

$\dfrac{N \ \ S}{S \ \ N}$

Step 4: Deductions
The only potential Block of Entities is Oldtown and Hidden Hills (Rule 2), but that only exists *if* Oldtown is even visited. Moreover, even if it is, there are multiple possible outcomes. However, it is useful to note that, if Oldtown is visited, it could not be visited on Friday. It also could not be visited on

Thursday because Hidden Hills cannot be visited on Friday (Rule 1).

Rule 3 offers an opportunity for Limited Options. If Lakeville is visited, Rule 3 establishes it on Wednesday. If Lakeville is not visited, it will be the one neighborhood that is not visited. That means every other neighborhood would be. It's worth taking a moment to draw out both options.

In the first option, Lakeville is visited, and it is visited on Wednesday. Hidden Hills is also visited (Rule 1), as are Nottingham and Sunnyside (Rule 4). That leaves room for one more neighborhood. If it were Oldtown, that would create a block of Oldtown immediately before Hidden Hills (Rule 2). That block could not be placed on Thursday and Friday (Rule 1), and placing it on Monday and Tuesday would force Nottingham and Sunnyside to be consecutive, violating Rule 4. Therefore, Oldtown is not visited, making Park Plaza the fifth neighborhood. The selection is complete, but the order is still uncertain.

I) $\text{ⒽⓁⓃⓄ\!\!\!/Ⓟ\!\!\!Ⓢ}$

$\overline{\text{Mo}} \ \overline{\text{Tu}} \ \underset{L}{\overline{\text{We}}} \ \overline{\text{Th}} \ \underset{\sim H}{\overline{\text{Fr}}}$

In the second option, Lakeville is not visited. That means all of the other neighborhoods are. With Oldtown visited, it must be visited immediately before Hidden Hills (Rule 2). That means Oldtown could not be visited on Friday, and Hidden Hills could not be visited on Monday. Further, Oldtown cannot be Thursday, as Hidden Hills cannot be visited on Friday (Rule 1). Again, the selection is complete, although the sequencing is still very open-ended.

II) $\text{Ⓗ\!\!\!/Ⓛ\!\!\!ⓃⓄⓅⓈ}$

Mo	Tu	We	Th	Fr
~H			~O	~H
				~O

The one other thing to potentially note is that Park Plaza is not mentioned in the rules, so it is the game's sole Floater.

Step 5: Questions

1. (B) Acceptability
As with any Acceptability question, use the rules one at a time to eliminate answers that violate those rules.

(E) violates Rule 1 by having Hidden Hills visited on Friday. **(D)** violates Rule 2 by having Oldtown visited, but not immediately before Hidden Hills. **(A)** violates Rule 3 by having Lakeville visited on Tuesday. **(C)** violates Rule 4 by having Nottingham and Sunnyside visited consecutively. That leaves **(B)** as the correct answer.

2. (C) Must Be False (CANNOT Be True)

The correct answer will be the neighborhood that cannot be visited on Thursday. The remaining answers will list neighborhoods that *could* be visited on Thursday.

Lakeville can only be visited on Wednesday, but is not listed in the answers. By Rule 2, if Oldtown is visited, it must be on the day before Hidden Hills is visited. Because Hidden Hills cannot be visited on Friday (Rule 1), Oldtown cannot be visited on Thursday. That makes **(C)** the correct answer.

3. (A) "If" / Must Be True

For this question, Hidden Hills is visited on Monday.

H				
Mo	Tu	We	Th	Fr

That means Oldtown cannot be visited (Rule 2), so all other neighborhoods will be visited—as seen in Option I. That means Lakeville must be visited on Wednesday (Rule 3), which makes **(A)** the correct answer. The remaining answers are all possible, but need not be true.

4. (B) "If" / Must Be True

For this question, Hidden Hills is visited on Wednesday. That means Lakeville cannot be visited (Rule 3), which means all of the other neighborhoods are visited—as seen in Option II. Because Oldtown is visited, it must be visited the day before Hidden Hills, i.e., on Tuesday.

	O	H		
Mo	Tu	We	Th	Fr

That makes **(B)** the correct answer. The remaining answers are all possible, but need not be true.

5. (D) "If" / Must Be True

For this question, Nottingham is visited on Thursday. That could happen in either of the two Limited Options, so test them both.

If Lakeville is visited (Option I), it will be visited on Wednesday. Friday cannot be the day the bookmobile visits Hidden Hills (Rule 1) or Sunnyside (Rule 4), so it must visit Park Plaza on Friday (Oldtown is not visited in Option I). Hidden Hills must be visited (Rule 1), as must Sunnyside (Rule 4). So, they will be visited on Monday and Tuesday in this option, in either order.

I) Ⓗ Ⓛ Ⓝ O̶ Ⓟ Ⓢ

H/S	S/H	L	N	P
Mo	Tu	We	Th	Fr

If Lakeville is not visited, every other neighborhood is. Friday cannot be the day the bookmobile visits Hidden Hills (Rule 1), Oldtown (Rule 2), or Sunnyside (Rule 4), so it must visit Park Plaza on Friday. Oldtown must be visited the day before Hidden Hills (Rule 2). The New-"If" already placed Nottingham on Thursday, so Sunnyside cannot be visited on Wednesday (Rule 4). Thus, Sunnyside must be on Monday,

with Oldtown and Hidden Hills on Tuesday and Wednesday, respectively.

II) Ⓗ L̶ Ⓝ Ⓞ Ⓟ Ⓢ

S	O	H	N	P
Mo	Tu	We	Th	Fr

In either case, Park Plaza is visited on Friday, making **(D)** the correct answer. The remaining answers are merely possible in just one option, or not possible at all.

Game 2: National Park Rangers

Step 1: Overview

Situation: Park rangers monitoring areas in a national park

Entities: Six rangers (Jefferson, Koguchi, Larson, Mendez, Olsen, Pruitt) and three areas (1, 2, 3)

Action: Distribution. Determine the area to which each ranger is assigned.

Limitations: Each ranger will be assigned to exactly one area. Each area will receive at least one but no more than three rangers.

Step 2: Sketch

List the rangers by initial and set up a chart with three columns, one for each area. Because each area gets at least one ranger, add one space to each area. The remaining spaces will be filled in as the game proceeds.

```
J K L M O P

 1   2   3   (1-3 each)
___|___|___
   |   |
```

Step 3: Rules

Rule 1 assigns Mendez to area 3. Add "M" to column 3, but leave the column open. Other rangers could still be assigned to that area.

Rule 2 prevents Olsen and Pruitt from being assigned to area 1. Draw "~O" and "~P" under column 1.

Rule 3 provides two possible blocks: Larson with Koguchi or Larson with Mendez. However, the rule also prevents those blocks from being together. So, draw the two options off to the side, but also note that they cannot all be together.

Rule 4 provides two pieces of Formal Logic. If Olsen is assigned to area 2, Jefferson and Koguchi will be assigned to the same area. Otherwise (i.e., if Olsen is *not* assigned to area 2), Jefferson and Koguchi are *not* together. You can draw these notes to the side in shorthand. However, this rule presents Limited Options, and it's more valuable to draw two sketches and build this rule directly into those options.

Step 4: Deductions

Using the fourth rule, draw two sketches, making sure they both include Mendez in area 3 (Rule 1). In the first option, Olsen will be assigned to area 2. In the second option, Olsen will *not* be assigned to area 2.

In the first option, with Olsen in area 2, Jefferson and Koguchi will be together. They cannot be assigned to area 3 because that would put Koguchi with Mendez. Larson then couldn't be paired with Koguchi or Mendez without being assigned with

both of them, violating Rule 3. The Jefferson-Koguchi block also cannot be assigned to area 2. That would leave only Larson and Pruitt available for area 1. However, Pruitt cannot be in area 1 (Rule 2), and Larson cannot be alone (Rule 3). So, Jefferson and Koguchi must be assigned to area 1. That leaves Larson and Pruitt. Larson has to be with Koguchi or Mendez, so Larson will be in area 1 or 3 (but not 2). And Pruitt cannot be in area 1, so Pruitt will be in area 2 or 3.

In the second option, with Olsen *not* in area 2, Jefferson and Koguchi will be split, but could still go anywhere. Olsen, however, cannot be in area 1 (Rule 2), so Olsen would have to be in area 3. With Mendez already there, that leaves room for just one more ranger (there doesn't *have* to be a third ranger in area 3, but there cannot be any more). If there were a third ranger, it could be anybody except for Koguchi. Placing Koguchi in area 3 would prevent Larson from being paired with Koguchi or Mendez, thus violating Rule 3. Therefore, Koguchi must be assigned to area 1 or 2.

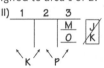

Step 5: Questions

6. (E) Acceptability

As with any Acceptability question, go through the rules one at a time, eliminating answers that violate those rules.

(D) violates Rule 1 by assigning Mendez to area 2. **(C)** violates Rule 2 by assigning Pruitt to area 1. **(A)** violates Rule 3 by assigning Larson to an area without Mendez or Koguchi. **(B)** violates Rule 4 by assigning Olsen to area 2, but not having Jefferson and Koguchi together. That leaves **(E)** as the correct answer.

7. (C) "If" / Could Be True

For this question, Olsen will be the only ranger assigned to area 2—that can only happen in Option I. As detailed in the deductions for Option I, by Rule 4, Jefferson and Koguchi will be together. They cannot be assigned with Mendez in area 3 without violating Rule 3, so they must be assigned to area 1. Pruitt cannot be assigned to area 1 (Rule 2). If Olsen is alone in area 2, Pruitt would have to be assigned to area 3. That leaves Larson, who can be assigned along with Koguchi in area 1 or Mendez in area 3.

The question asks for a possible complete assignment to area 3. Area 3 must include Mendez and Pruitt. That eliminates **(A)**, **(B)**, and **(D)**. There is room for one more, but only Larson is available. That eliminates **(E)**. If Larson is assigned to area 1, then area 3 could just be Mendez and Pruitt, making **(C)** the correct answer.

8. (D) "If" / Must Be True

For this question, exactly one ranger will be assigned to area 1. It cannot be Larson (Rule 3), Mendez (Rule 1), Olsen (Rule 2), or Pruitt (Rule 2). That leaves Jefferson or Koguchi. That means they will be split up, so Olsen cannot be assigned to area 2 (Rule 4). That means Olsen must be assigned to area 3 with Mendez, making **(D)** the correct answer. The remaining answers are all possible, but need not be true.

This question can be answered quickly with the Limited Options as well. If exactly one ranger will be assigned to area 1, you must use Option II (because Jefferson and Koguchi are both in area 1 in Option I). The only ranger that was established by the deductions for Option II is Olsen in area 3, and sure enough, that matches **(D)**.

9. (D) Must Be False (CANNOT Be True)

The correct answer will be a ranger who cannot be assigned to area 3. The remaining four answers will list rangers who could be assigned to area 3.

Area 3 must include Mendez (Rule 1). Placing Koguchi in area 3 would prevent Larson from being assigned with only Mendez or Koguchi (not both), violating Rule 3. So, Koguchi cannot be assigned to area 3, making **(D)** the correct answer. The remaining rangers all *could* be assigned to area 3, even if they don't *need* to be.

10. (E) "If" / Could Be True

For this question, Koguchi is assigned to area 2. In that case, Olsen cannot also be assigned to area 2. Otherwise, Jefferson would be with Koguchi, too (Rule 4). However, that would leave nobody for area 1 because Pruitt cannot be in area 1 (Rule 1), and Larson cannot be alone (Rule 3). This was seen as impossible in Option I, so Olsen must be in area 3, as Option II shows. That leaves Jefferson, Larson, and Pruitt. Larson must be with Koguchi or Mendez, so Larson can only be in area 2 or 3. Pruitt cannot be in area 1, so Pruitt must be in area 2 or 3. That leaves Jefferson as the only ranger who can be in area 1.

Jefferson must be in area 1, eliminating **(A)** and **(B)**. Larson must be in area 2 or 3, eliminating **(C)**. Olsen is in area 3, eliminating **(D)**. That leaves **(E)** as the correct answer. Pruitt can certainly be assigned to area 3.

11. (B) "If" / Could Be True

For this question, Larson and Olsen are assigned to the same area. Larson also has to be assigned to an area with Koguchi or Mendez. That would put three rangers in one area, which is the maximum. If they were assigned to area 3, the third ranger would be Mendez (Rule 1). If they were assigned to area 1 or 2, the third ranger would have to be Koguchi. However, Olsen cannot be assigned to area 1 (Rule 2), and if Olsen were in area 2, Jefferson would have to be added to the group with Koguchi (Rule 4), which would put four rangers in one area. Thus, it would have to be Larson, Mendez, and Olsen together in area 3, with nobody else.

Pruitt cannot be assigned to area 1, so Pruitt will go in area 2. With Olsen in area 3, Jefferson and Koguchi would have to be split between areas 1 and 2 (Rule 4).

1	2	3
J/K	P	M
	K/J	L
		O

Larson and Olsen are in area 3, so that eliminates **(C)** and **(D)**. With Mendez in area 3, there's no room for Jefferson or Pruitt in area 3, which eliminates **(A)** and **(E)**. However, Koguchi could still be assigned to area 2, making **(B)** the correct answer.

This question can also be answered quickly with the Limited Options. If Larson and Olsen are together, that can only happen in Option II (because Olsen is established in area 2, and Larson can only go to areas 1 or 3 in the Option I sketch). So, using the Option II sketch, Larson gets added to area 3 as the third and final ranger. That forces Pruitt to area 2 and leaves Jefferson and Koguchi. One will have to go to area 1 and the other to area 2 so that they stay separated (Rule 4). That also leads to **(B)**.

12. (A) "If" / Must Be True

For this question, Jefferson is assigned to area 2. In that case, Olsen cannot also be assigned to area 2. Otherwise, Jefferson would be with Koguchi, too (Rule 4). However, that would leave nobody for area 1 because Pruitt cannot be in area 1 (Rule 1), and Larson cannot be alone (Rule 3). This was seen as impossible in Option I, so this question must be asking about Option II in which Olsen must be in area 3.

```
  1    2    3
       J    M
            O
```

That leaves Koguchi, Larson, and Pruitt. With Olsen in area 3, Jefferson and Koguchi must be split up (Rule 4). Koguchi could not be with Mendez in area 3 without violating Rule 3. Therefore, Koguchi must be assigned to area 1.

```
  1    2    3
  K    J    M
            O
```

That makes **(A)** the correct answer. The remaining answers are all possible, but need not be true, except for **(C)**, which must be false.

Game 3: Economics TAs

Step 1: Overview
Situation: Teaching assistants being assigned to courses in an economics department

Entities: Six assistants (Ramos, Smith, Taj, Vogel, Yi, Zane) and three courses (Labor, Markets, Pricing)

Action: Distribution. Determine the course to which each assistant is assigned.

Limitations: Each assistant will be assigned to exactly one course, and each course will have at least one assistant.

Step 2: Sketch
List the assistants by initial and set up a chart with three columns, one for each course. Because each course gets at least one assistant, add one space to each area. The remaining spaces will be filled in as the game proceeds.

R S T V Y Z

Lab	Mar	Pri
__	__	__

Step 3: Rules
Rule 1 sets a numeric limitation to Markets. There will be exactly two assistants assigned to that course. Add a second slot to the Markets column, and close the column off.

Rule 2 creates a block, with Smith and Taj together. They could be assigned to any of the courses so far, and other assistants can be assigned with them. Draw this block off to the side.

Rule 3 dictates that Vogel and Yi be assigned to different courses. Draw a note of this to the side.

Rule 4 provides some Formal Logic. If either Yi or Zane is assigned to Pricing, they both are. By contrapositive, if they're not both in Pricing, then neither of them is. Essentially, this sets up two possible outcomes: either Yi and Zane are both in Pricing, or neither of them are. You can draw this rule off to the side or set up Limited Options.

Step 4: Deductions
By Rule 4, there are two options. In the first option, Yi and Zane are both assigned to Pricing. In the second option, neither of them is assigned to Pricing.

The first option would establish five spaces: one in Labor, two in Markets, and two in Pricing. That leaves one more space, which could go in Labor or Pricing. With Yi in Pricing, Vogel cannot be assigned to Pricing (Rule 3). Also, there's only room for one more assistant in Pricing, at most, so Smith and Taj cannot be assigned to Pricing. That means only Ramos could,

but need not be. Ramos could still be in either of the remaining courses.

In the second option, Yi and Zane will not be assigned to Pricing, but they could be assigned to either of the other courses. Note that they could be assigned together, but need not be. It is possible that one is assigned to Labor while the other is assigned to Markets. Unfortunately, that's as much as can be deduced, as the one block of entities (Smith and Taj) could still be assigned to any of the three courses.

II)
Lab	Mar	Pri

~Y,~Z

Step 5: Questions

13. (A) Partial Acceptability
The correct answer to this question will be a possible assignment for the Pricing course. As with regular Acceptability questions, start by testing the rules one at a time to see which answers violate those rules. If any answers remain, test them by considering the unlisted entities to find the one answer that is possible.

Rule 1 cannot be directly tested because the answers only list the Pricing assignments. **(D)** violates Rule 2 by assigning Taj to the course without Smith. **(E)** violates Rule 3 by assigning Vogel and Yi together. **(B)** violates Rule 4 by assigning Yi to Pricing without Zane. That leaves **(A)** and **(C)**.

As determined in setting up the first option, Smith and Taj could not be assigned with Yi and Zane. That would leave just two assistants for the remaining courses. However, Labor needs at least one and Marketing needs two (Rule 1). There wouldn't be enough assistants. That eliminates **(C)**, leaving **(A)** as the correct answer.

14. (B) Partial Acceptability (CANNOT)
The correct answer will be an assignment for Labor that cannot happen. That means the remaining four answers will list assignments that *are* possible for Labor.

Note that each answer choice lists exactly two assistants, meaning that for each answer, there will be two assistants in Labor. There must be two assistants in Markets (Rule 1). That leaves Pricing for the final two assistants.

One department must get Smith and Taj together. Of the remaining four assistants, Vogel and Yi cannot be together. So, they will be split between the remaining courses, resulting in the remaining assistants—Ramos and Zane—being split to pair up with Vogel and Yi.

Lab	Mar	Pri
—	—	—
S	V	Y
T	R/Z	Z/R

With Ramos and Zane split up, it is impossible for them to be the sole assistants in Labor. That makes **(B)** the correct answer. Any of the remaining pairs are possible assignments to Labor.

15. (A) Could Be True

The correct answer for this question will be the only one that presents a possible outcome. The remaining answers will all be false, i.e., impossible.

If Ramos and Vogel are assigned to Markets, Smith and Taj could be assigned to Labor, and Yi and Zane could be assigned to Pricing (or vice versa).

Lab	Mar	Pri		Lab	Mar	Pri
S	R	Y	or	Y	R	S
T	V	Z		Z	V	T

This is certainly possible, making **(A)** the correct answer. For the record:

If Ramos was in Markets with Taj, Smith would have to be with them (Rule 2). Similarly, if Smith was in Markets with Vogel, Taj would have to be with them. However, only two assistants can be assigned to Markets (Rule 1). That eliminates **(B)** and **(C)**.

If Smith and Zane were assigned to Pricing, then Taj (Rule 2) and Yi (Rule 4) would be also. However, that would not leave enough assistants to fill the space in Labor and the two spaces in Markets. Therefore, that eliminates **(D)**.

Additionally, if Zane is assigned to Pricing, so is Yi, which means Vogel couldn't be there (Rule 3). That eliminates **(E)**.

16. (C) "If" / Must Be False (CANNOT Be True)

For this question, Vogel is assigned to the same course as Zane. By Rule 3, Vogel and Yi cannot be together, so Yi and Zane will not be together. If Yi and Zane cannot be together, neither of them will be in Pricing (Rule 4). Thus, one must be assigned to Labor and the other to Markets. It helps to draw both possibilities.

In the first outcome, Yi is assigned to Labor, and Zane (with Vogel) is assigned to Markets. In that case, Markets is filled up. Smith and Taj could be assigned to Labor or Pricing, as could Ramos.

In the second outcome, Yi is assigned to Markets, and Zane (with Vogel) is assigned to Labor. With only one position left in Markets, there's not enough room for Smith and Taj. So, that position will be filled by Ramos, leaving Smith and Taj to be assigned to Pricing.

Lab	Mar	Pri
Z	Y	S
V	R	T

Neither outcome allows for Taj to be assigned to Markets. That makes **(C)** the correct answer. All of the remaining answers are possible in at least one option.

17. (D) "If" / Must Be True

For this question, Ramos will be assigned to one course with no other assistant. Markets requires two assistants, so Ramos could only do Labor or Pricing alone. Test both outcomes.

In the first outcome, Ramos is the only assistant assigned to Labor. Vogel and Yi must be split between Markets and Pricing (Rule 3). That leaves only one space in Markets. That's not enough for both Smith and Taj, so they must be assigned to Pricing, meaning Zane must take up the last space in Markets.

Lab	Mar	Pri
R	V/Y	Y/V
	Z	S
		T

Yi cannot be in Pricing without Zane (Rule 4), so Yi will be assigned to Markets, leaving Vogel to be assigned to Pricing.

Lab	Mar	Pri
R	Y	V
	Z	S
		T

In the second outcome, Ramos is the only assistant assigned to Pricing. Again, Vogel and Yi must be split, this time between Labor and Markets. With only one space remaining in Markets, Smith and Taj must be assigned to Labor. That leaves Zane for the final space in Markets. In this case, Vogel and Yi cannot be assigned with certainty. One will be assigned to Labor. The other will be assigned to Markets.

Lab	Mar	Pri
V/Y	Y/V	R
S	Z	
T		

In both cases, Zane is assigned to Markets, making **(D)** the correct answer. The remaining answers are all possible, but need not be true.

Game 4: Computer Virus

Step 1: Overview

Situation: A computer virus infecting computers on a network

Entities: Six computers (P, Q, R, S, T, U)

Action: Strict Sequencing. Determine the order in which the computers were infected.

Limitations: Exactly one computer was infected from outside the network. Each computer received the virus exactly once and (except for the first computer) from one of the other computers in the network.

Step 2: Sketch

At first glance, this appears to be a standard Sequencing game. However, there's an unusual twist that may not be apparent until the first rule. When a computer is infected, it can pass the virus to more than one computer, essentially creating separate sequences. In that case, a series of slots will not be useful. Instead, it will ultimately be more important to see how the virus branches out from each computer and continues infecting computers in order. For instance, if P transmitted the virus to Q and R, that would create two separate branches. In that case, it would be most helpful to use arrows to indicate transmission from one computer to the next, like so:

$$P \overset{Q}{\underset{R}{\diagup\diagdown}}$$

Note that these arrows do not work like Loose Sequencing branches. Instead of indicating relative relationships, they show direct transmission from one computer to the next.

Unfortunately, there's no way of determining when in the sequence the branches will occur. So, just list the entities and head to the rules.

Step 3: Rules

Rule 1 creates a numeric restriction. Any computer that transmitted the virus could only do so to a maximum of two other computers. Make a note of this to the side (e.g., "Max. 2 comp. get virus from 1 comp.").

Rule 2 establishes that S transmitted the virus to just one other computer. Draw S with one arrow to a blank space, and make a note of the numeric restriction:

$$S \rightarrow \underline{\quad} \quad \text{(exactly 1)}$$

Note that the computer that received the virus from S could have passed it along to another computer. So, multiple computers could have received the virus after S, but only one got it *directly* from S.

Rule 3 indicates that there will be at least one computer that passes the virus to two other computers, and that computer will infect R and S. Draw one space with two arrows leading to R and S.

Rule 4 states that computer R or T transmitted the virus to Q:

$$R/T \rightarrow Q$$

Rule 5 states that computer T or U transmitted the virus to P:

$$T/U \rightarrow P$$

Step 4: Deductions

Rules 2 and 3 can be combined because of the Duplicated entity S. By Rule 3, there is a computer that transmitted the virus to S (as well as R), and then S passed the virus along to yet another computer (Rule 2). That creates a string of four computers:

$$\underline{\quad} \overset{R}{\underset{S \rightarrow \underline{\quad}}{\diagup\diagdown}}$$

The computer that passed the virus to both R and S could be any of the remaining computers. However, S did not transmit the virus to Q (Rule 4) or P (Rule 5). That means it must have transmitted the virus to either T or U (but not both because Rule 2 says "exactly one").

The final point to consider is which computer could have been infected first (i.e., from outside the network). By the last three rules, P, Q, R, and S were all infected by another computer within the network. That means only T or U could have been the first computer infected. Note that these are the same two computers that could have received the virus from S. Therefore, between T and U, one of them will be the first computer infected, and one of them will get the virus from S.

Step 5: Questions

18. (D) Partial Acceptability

The correct answer will list a possible order of infection from the first computer infected to Q. The answers are only partial because they only list the direct route to Q, leaving out any separate branches to other computers. As with any other Acceptability question, start by going through the rules one at a time, eliminating answers that violate those rules. Then, if needed, fill in information for any remaining answers to find the only one that is possible.

Because each answer shows transmission from one computer to just one other computer, none of them will violate Rule 1. Similarly, the two answers that list S show transmission to just one other computer, so no answer violates Rule 2. By Rule 3, there must have been a computer that transmitted the virus to R, so R could not be the first computer infected. That eliminates **(A)**. Also by Rule 3, the same computer transmitted the virus to R and S. That eliminates **(B)**, which has T transmit the virus to S, but S transmits the virus to R. **(C)** violates Rule 4 because Q could not get the virus from U. Neither remaining answer violates Rule 5, as they both have T or U transmit the virus to P.

(D) lists transmission from U to P to R to Q. By Rule 3, P would also have transmitted the virus to S. By Rule 2, S would transmit the virus to one other computer. T is left, so that is acceptable.

$$U \to P \underset{S \to T}{\overset{R \to Q}{<}}$$

(E) lists transmission from U to T to P to R to Q. Again, by Rule 3, P would have also transmitted the virus to S. However, by Rule 2, S had to transmit the virus to another computer, but there are no computers left.

$$U \to T \to P \underset{S \to ?}{\overset{R \to Q}{<}}$$

Therefore, **(E)** is impossible, leaving **(D)** as the correct answer.

19. (E) Could Be True

The correct answer to this question will be a computer that could have been infected from outside the network. The remaining answers will list computers that could not, i.e., they must have been infected from *inside* the network.

R and S were infected from another computer inside the network (Rule 3), as were Q (Rule 4) and P (Rule 5). That leaves only T and U, either of which could have been infected from outside the network. That makes **(E)** the correct answer.

20. (A) "If" / Must Be True

For this question, T did not transmit the virus to any other computer. By Rule 4, that means R transmitted the virus to Q. And by Rule 5, U must have transmitted the virus to P.

One computer transmitted the virus to both R and S (Rule 3). It cannot be Q, which received the virus *from* R in this case. It cannot be T, which did not transmit the virus at all in this case. And it cannot be U, which already transmitted the virus to P in this case and cannot transmit it to another two computers (Rule 1). That means P must have transmitted the virus to R and S. So, the virus went from U to P, from P to R and S, and from R to Q. It still needs to be transmitted from S to one other computer (Rule 2), and only T is left.

$$U \to P \underset{S \to T}{\overset{R \to Q}{<}}$$

With that, **(A)** must be true and is the correct answer.

21. (C) Could Be True EXCEPT

Four answers will list computers that could have transmitted the virus to two other computers. The correct answer will be a computer that could not, i.e., a computer that could have only transmitted the virus to one other computer at most.

By Rule 2, S can only transmit the virus to one other computer, but S is not listed in the answers. P is said to transmit the virus to two computers in the last question of the game (and it also did so in the previous question). That eliminates **(A)**.

There must be a computer that transmits the virus to both R and S. That could be any of the remaining computers (P, Q, T, and U), which leaves R as the only possible answer of which computer *cannot* transfer the virus to two computers. Thus, **(C)** is the correct answer.

To confirm that R can't transmit the virus to two computers, consider which computers R *could* transmit the virus to. R can certainly transmit the virus to Q (Rule 4). However, R cannot transmit the virus to P (Rule 5) or S (Rule 3). Because of the last three rules, T or U has to be infected from outside the network (i.e., T or U must be the first computer in the sequence), and S has to transmit the virus to a computer, which cannot be P (Rule 5), Q (Rule 4), or R (Rule 3). So, S has to transmit the virus to T or U, whichever one was not infected first. That means Q is the *only* computer R can infect, confirming **(C)** as the correct answer.

22. (C) Completely Determine

The correct answer will be a piece of information that, if true, would allow the entire order of virus transmission to be determined with no uncertainty. The correct answer would have to help determine which computer was infected first, the one computer that transmitted the virus to both R and S, and the one computer infected by computer S.

If R transmitted the virus to Q, either T or U could still be the first computer infected with S infecting the other. With more than one possible outcome, **(A)** is eliminated.

If T transmitted the virus to Q, T could still be the first computer infected, but so could U. There's more than one outcome possible, so **(B)** is eliminated.

If T transmitted the virus to S, then it also transmitted the virus to R (Rule 3). Having transmitted the virus to two other computers, it could not transmit the virus to any others. That means R transmitted the virus to Q (Rule 4) and U transmitted the virus to P (Rule 5). S had to transmit to one other computer (Rule 2), and only computer U is left.

$$T \underset{S \to U \to P}{\overset{R \to Q}{<}}$$

That indicates every transmission, making **(C)** the correct answer. For the record:

If U transmitted the virus to P, then U could still be the first computer infected, but so could T. There's more than one outcome possible, so **(D)** is eliminated.

If U transmitted the virus to R, then U also transmitted the virus to S (Rule 3). Having transmitted the virus to two other computers, it could not transmit the virus to any other. That means T transmitted the virus to P (Rule 5). S must transmit the virus to exactly one computer (Rule 2), but it can't be Q (Rule 4), so the only computer left that's possible for S to transmit the virus to is T. However, it is still unknown which of T or R transmitted the virus to Q (Rule 4).

$$U \bigg\langle \begin{array}{l} R \quad Q? \\ S \to T \to P \end{array}$$

With more than one possible outcome, **(E)** is eliminated.

23. (C) "If" / Must Be True

For this question, P transmits the virus to two other computers, and it is the only computer to do so. One computer has to transmit a virus to both R and S, so it must be P in this case. Either T or U will transmit the virus to P (Rule 5). S cannot transmit the virus to Q (Rule 4), but it must transmit the virus to one other computer. Only T or U are left.

$$T/U \to P \bigg\langle \begin{array}{l} R \quad Q? \\ S \to U/T \end{array}$$

That leaves Q, which received the virus from R or T (Rule 4). Either way, all of the other computers are accounted for, so Q would not have transmitted the virus to any other computer. That makes **(C)** the correct answer. All of the remaining answers are possible, but need not be true. They could all be false, depending on whether T or U was infected first and whether R or T transmitted the virus to Q.

Section IV: Logical Reasoning

Q#	Question Type	Correct	Difficulty
1	Paradox	D	★
2	Assumption (Necessary)	A	★
3	Paradox	D	★
4	Assumption (Sufficient)	A	★★
5	Flaw	D	★★
6	Assumption (Necessary)	B	★★
7	Principle (Identify/Strengthen)	D	★
8	Assumption (Necessary)	B	★
9	Flaw	A	★★
10	Assumption (Sufficient)	A	★
11	Main Point	E	★★
12	Method of Argument	E	★★★★
13	Principle (Parallel)	C	★
14	Strengthen	D	★
15	Principle (Identify/Strengthen)	A	★
16	Parallel Flaw	D	★
17	Main Point	A	★
18	Flaw	B	★
19	Weaken	B	★★★
20	Point at Issue	B	★★
21	Assumption (Necessary)	C	★★★★
22	Strengthen	C	★★★★
23	Inference	B	★★
24	Role of a Statement	B	★★★★
25	Inference	C	★★★

1. (D) Paradox

Step 1: Identify the Question Type
The question asks for something that "helps to resolve the apparent discrepancy," making this a Paradox question.

Step 2: Untangle the Stimulus
In cold-blooded animals, cool weather weakens muscle power. The veiled chameleon is a cold-blooded animal, so its tongue naturally takes longer to retract when it gets cooler. However, it doesn't take much longer for the tongue to extend.

Step 3: Make a Prediction
The correct answer will answer the central mystery: why does it take longer for the tongue to retract, but not to extend? The solution is hinted at in the first sentence; cooler weather affects "muscle power." So, if retraction requires muscle power but extension does not, then that would resolve the issue.

Step 4: Evaluate the Answer Choices
(D) resolves the issue. Cool weather weakens muscle power. So, if retraction is powered by muscles, retraction would be slower in cool weather. Additionally, with extension driven by energy, not muscle power, there's no reason to expect a slowdown.

(A) is an Irrelevant Comparison. What is true for most cold-blooded animals has no bearing on why the chameleon's tongue only slows down during retraction.

(B) is Out of Scope. The distance the tongue can extend does nothing to explain why it doesn't slow down in cool weather.

(C) is also Out of Scope. Where the chameleon lives does nothing to explain why tongue extension does not slow down much in cool weather.

(E) is an Irrelevant Comparison. The mystery is not about chameleons versus other animals. The mystery is about why retraction slows down but extension does not. This offers no information about extension, so the mystery goes unsolved.

2. (A) Assumption (Necessary)

Step 1: Identify the Question Type
The question asks for an assumption that the argument *requires*, making this a Necessary Assumption question.

Step 2: Untangle the Stimulus
The author concludes (*so*) that Acme will have to declare bankruptcy. This is based on some Formal Logic rules. If Acme's annual earnings fall below $1 million, it must repay its bank loan in full, in which case it will go bankrupt.

	earnings below $1M	→	repay bank loan in full	→	bankruptcy
If					

Unfortunately, Acme overstated its earnings in the previous year.

Step 3: Make a Prediction
By the Formal Logic, Acme would have to declare bankruptcy if it's earnings one year dipped below $1 million. The evidence only claims that Acme overstated its earnings for one year. However, it's possible that it originally reported $2 million dollars but only earned $1.5 million. In that case, it overstated its earnings but still didn't have to declare bankruptcy. The only way the author can logically conclude Acme has to declare bankruptcy is if the earnings were actually below $1 million. That's what the author is assuming happened.

Step 4: Evaluate the Answer Choices
(A) is correct. If Acme earned *more* than $1 million last year, then the author's evidence about overstatement is irrelevant and the argument is invalid. The author must assume that the actual earnings were *less* than $1 million.

(B) is Out of Scope. The bank loan by itself is enough to cause the threat of bankruptcy. The author need not assume anything about other debts.

(C) is irrelevant. It doesn't matter how many years involved overstatement. Bankruptcy would be required even if just one year's earnings fall below $1 million.

(D) is irrelevant. The author's conclusion is based on last year's earnings, not this year's earnings. While dropping below $1 million this year would certainly confirm the author's conclusion, it's not necessary. As long as *last* year's earnings were below $1 million, the author still has a valid argument, regardless of what happens this year.

(E) is irrelevant. It's a pleasant thought, but there's no need for hypothetical situations here. The fact is that Acme *does* have to repay the loan if earnings drop below $1 million. No amount of "what ifs" are going to change that.

3. (D) Paradox

Step 1: Identify the Question Type
The correct answer will "resolve the apparent conflict," making this a Paradox question.

Step 2: Untangle the Stimulus
Hospital patients in private rooms tend to get fewer infections and are released sooner than those in semiprivate rooms. However, patients at Woodville's hospital are all placed in

semiprivate rooms, but they're not any worse off than similar patients in private rooms in nearby hospitals.

Step 3: Make a Prediction

The correct answer will address the central mystery: why are patients in semiprivate rooms at Woodville's hospital having the same experience as patients in private rooms at other hospitals? The patients are said to be similar, so it's not as if Woodville's hospital just happens to get easier patients. There must be something else about Woodville's hospital that benefits its patients. It's not worth predicting an exact solution. Just know that the correct answer will indicate something distinct about Woodville's hospital that helps make its semiprivate rooms equivalent to other hospitals' private rooms.

Step 4: Evaluate the Answer Choices

(D) resolves the issue. The rooms may technically be semiprivate, but placing only one person per room effectively creates a private environment. So, patients would still get the benefit of a private room, even though the room could, in theory, house multiple patients.

(A) does not help. Even if the doctors are all the same, the rooms at Woodville are still only semiprivate, which should still result in more problems.

(B) is Out of Scope. The age of the building has nothing to do with a patient's infection rate or length of stay. At worst, one could argue (perhaps unfairly) that Woodville's hospital being 40 years older might make it out-of-date. Nevertheless, that would just make it *more* unusual that patients are doing just as well.

(C) is a 180. This is exactly what should make semiprivate rooms more problematic—and yet patients in semiprivate rooms at Woodville's hospital are *still* doing just as well as patients in private rooms.

(E) is Out of Scope. The location of the hospital should have no effect on how people recover once they're in the hospital.

4. (A) Assumption (Sufficient)

Step 1: Identify the Question Type

The correct answer will be something that, *if* assumed, would make the argument valid. That makes this a Sufficient Assumption question.

Step 2: Untangle the Stimulus

The economist predicts that unemployment will soon decrease. The evidence is based on two possible scenarios: 1) If government spending significantly increases, the economy is stimulated and unemployment will decrease. 2) If government spending significantly decreases, businesses keep more earnings and hire more workers, so unemployment will decrease.

Step 3: Make a Prediction

Accepting the economist's logic, either of the two scenarios presented would indeed reduce unemployment. However, what if spending stays constant? What if the change in spending is not significant? Those scenarios are not accounted for. The economist's entire argument rests on the assumption that spending will indeed increase or decrease significantly.

Step 4: Evaluate the Answer Choices

(A) is correct. If government spending significantly increases or decreases next year, then either case would set off the economist's logic and confirm the prediction that unemployment will decrease.

(B) is irrelevant. Policies that are *intended* to reduce unemployment won't necessarily work. Besides, the economist's argument is based on government spending, not new policies.

(C) is not good enough. This ensures a decrease in unemployment under one condition: demand for workers increases. However, there's no way to know if that condition will be met, so this cannot confirm the economist's prediction.

(D) is Out of Scope. What will happen to the economy in the long run does nothing to confirm the economist's prediction about unemployment in the near future.

(E) is a 180. This offers a situation in which unemployment will *not* decrease, which would go against the economist's prediction. **(E)** creates two improper contrapositives of the Formal Logic chains in the evidence, negating but not reversing the terms. Those improper contrapositives would not guarantee the economist's conclusion.

5. (D) Flaw

Step 1: Identify the Question Type

Tyne is said to have *misinterpreted* something, which means she has committed a logical flaw. The correct answer will identify a word in Marisa's argument that Tyne's argument uses or addresses improperly.

Step 2: Untangle the Stimulus

Marisa argues for the need to loosen zoning regulations. The current regulations are restricting development, which leads to reduced property values. Tyne disagrees, arguing that regulations are indeed restricting development but that they're actually preserving the value of natural, undisturbed lands.

Step 3: Make a Prediction

Marisa and Tyne agree that regulations restrict development. However, Marisa is complaining about the effect on property values. Tyne brings up the "value of natural, undisturbed lands." They both use the word *value*, but Tyne completely addresses the wrong type of value. Marisa doesn't care about environmental value; she cares about money. It's that word *value* that Tyne misinterprets.

Step 4: Evaluate the Answer Choices

(D) is correct. Marisa is talking about the financial value of property, while Tyne addresses the environmental value of undisturbed land.

(A) is a 180. Marisa and Tyne are both talking about the same regulations, so there's no misinterpretation there.

(B) is a 180. Both speakers use development in the same sense: the construction of buildings on unused land.

(C) is a 180. Marisa uses *prohibitive* to mean "restrictive." Tyne's argument is consistent with that definition.

(E) is a Distortion. It's not the significance of the value that Tyne misinterprets. It's the type of value itself.

6. (B) Assumption (Necessary)

Step 1: Identify the Question Type

The question asks for something the argument "requires assuming," making this a Necessary Assumption question.

Step 2: Untangle the Stimulus

The scientist is arguing that results of animal research can be skewed. The evidence is that research animals get plenty of food but exercise very little, and studies depend on the assumption that animals are healthy (as illustrated by a pointless example).

Step 3: Make a Prediction

The results would be skewed if the assumption is wrong, i.e., the research animals are not actually healthy. However, the scientist only cites the existence of "ample food" and "little exercise." The scientist must be assuming that ample food and little exercise are actually unhealthy for the animals.

Step 4: Evaluate the Answer Choices

(B) is correct, making the necessary link between the ample food/little exercise environment and the animals' health.

(A) is a Distortion. Even if animals are healthy in a better environment, that doesn't mean the current environment is *unhealthy*, as the scientist assumes.

(C) is a 180. If access to ample food and little exercise is normal, then there's no reason to believe laboratories are artificially creating an unhealthy environment for the animals.

(D) is irrelevant. Even if some studies do take living conditions into account, that still has no effect on the scientist's argument, which is about studies that *don't*. It's *those* studies that the scientist is criticizing.

(E) is a 180. This suggests that the ample food does not necessarily lead to overeating. Animals will continue to eat the same amount. That contradicts the scientist's assumption that ample food would lead to an unhealthy environment.

7. (D) Principle (Identify/Strengthen)

Step 1: Identify the Question Type

The correct answer will be a principle that will be used to *justify* the argument given, making this an Identify the Principle question that mimics a Strengthen question.

Step 2: Untangle the Stimulus

The negotiator concludes ([*t*]*herefore*) that countries should not adopt trade policies that hinder other countries' prosperity. The evidence is that prosperity brings about political freedom.

Step 3: Make a Prediction

The conclusion is about prosperity, but the evidence suggests that the negotiator's ultimate concern is political freedom. So, the negotiator is suggesting that trade policies should not prevent political freedom in other countries. The correct answer will be a general rule that validates the negotiator's desire to protect political freedom.

Step 4: Evaluate the Answer Choices

(D) validates the negotiator's recommendation to avoid hindering prosperity, as that in turn would hinder political freedom.

(A) is a Distortion. The negotiator is not recommending policies that *encourage* freedom. The negotiator is recommending *against* policies that *hinder* freedom.

(B) brings up overall well-being, which has no bearing on the negotiator's argument.

(C) is Extreme and a Distortion. Political freedom does not have to be the *primary* motivator for seeking prosperity. Besides, this provides no justification for the negotiator's recommendation to avoid certain policies.

(E) is a Distortion. The negotiator's argument is about preventing issues in any *other* country, not necessarily problems within the negotiator's country itself.

8. (B) Assumption (Necessary)

Step 1: Identify the Question Type

The correct answer will be an "assumption required by the argument," making this a Necessary Assumption question.

Step 2: Untangle the Stimulus

The author concludes ([*t*]*hus*) that great works of art are rare. The evidence is that a combination of tremendous skill and extraordinary creativity is both necessary and sufficient for great art.

Step 3: Make a Prediction

If it takes high levels of skill and creativity to create great art, but that great art is rare, the author must assume that that combination of high skill and creativity is also rare.

Step 4: Evaluate the Answer Choices

(B) is correct. The combination of creativity and skill must be rare to claim that great art is rare. If that combination were common, then great art would also be common (as the author states that "the resulting product [of combining skill and creativity] is a great work of art").

(A) is irrelevant. Even if some artists have less-than-stellar skills, there could still be plenty of other artists who are highly skilled and capable of creating lots of great art.

(C) is a Faulty Use of Detail. This essentially repeats the first sentence of the stimulus. However, if there are enough such artists, then the author has no reason to claim that great art would be rare. So, **(C)** does nothing to fill in the gap between the evidence and conclusion.

(D) is irrelevant. The argument is not about the rarity of great *artists*, but the rarity of great *art*. Even if highly skilled and creative artists are rare, they could be prolific enough to create tons of great art.

(E) is not necessary. Even if the most skilled and creative artists create just a few great artworks, there could still be lots of such artists, which would mean plenty of great art.

9. (A) Flaw

Step 1: Identify the Question Type

The correct answer will describe why the argument is *flawed*, making this a Flaw question.

Step 2: Untangle the Stimulus

The advertisement concludes ([*s*]*o*) that eating Fantastic Flakes every morning will help you become physically fit. The evidence is that people who eat cereal tend to exercise more than people who don't eat cereal, and exercise helps you become fit.

Step 3: Make a Prediction

The evidence never directly indicates that cereal itself makes you fit. Exercise does that. People who exercise just *tend* to eat more cereal. The advertisement is thus implying that the cereal *makes* people exercise, which in turn leads to being physically fit. This is a classic case of correlation versus causation. People who exercise tend to eat cereal, but that doesn't mean cereal is the *cause* of them exercising. The correct answer will address this commonly tested flaw.

Step 4: Evaluate the Answer Choices

(A) is correct, describing the implication of causality (cereal makes you exercise more) based on a mere correlation (people who exercise happen to eat more cereal).

(B) is an Irrelevant Comparison. The advertisement is not pushing nutrition. It's only pushing the cereal's influence on exercise and thus its influence on becoming physically fit.

(C) is Extreme. Nothing is stated or implied to be the *sole* predictor of anything. The advertisement argues that the

cereal will make you fit, but it never suggests it's the only way to become fit.

(D) brings up the flaw of representativeness. However, there's no sample group in the evidence. All of the evidence is about what's true for people in general.

(E) brings up the flaw of applying a group trait to individual members. However, there is no characteristic applied to any group, and the conclusion does not apply a characteristic to individual members of any group.

10. (A) Assumption (Sufficient)

Step 1: Identify the Question Type

The question asks for something that, *if* assumed, allows the conclusion to be drawn. That makes this a Sufficient Assumption question.

Step 2: Untangle the Stimulus

The journalist concludes ([*s*]*o*) that the critics are mistaken. They claim entertainment decreases the caliber of news reporting, which means the journalist is arguing that entertainment does *not* decrease the caliber. The evidence is that the greatest journalists have been the most entertaining.

Step 3: Make a Prediction

The evidence is about the "greatest journalists," but the conclusion is about the "caliber of the reporting" itself. The journalist simply assumes that the greatest journalists provided high-caliber reporting.

Step 4: Evaluate the Answer Choices

(A) is correct, making the connection between the greatest journalists and the caliber of their reporting.

(B) is not good enough. Even if the greatest journalists have been entertainers, that still does not speak to the caliber of the reporting itself.

(C) is not good enough. This just connects greatness to value "in some sense." If that sense does not involve the caliber of the reporting, then it's irrelevant to the argument at hand.

(D) is something the journalist might agree with, but it offers no support for the conclusion about the caliber of the reporting.

(E) is a 180 at worst. This suggests that entertainment *can* be bad for news reporting, which contradicts the journalist's reasoning.

11. (E) Main Point

Step 1: Identify the Question Type

The correct answer will be the "overall conclusion," or main point, of the argument.

Step 2: Untangle the Stimulus

The linguist starts out with a fact: three out of four subfamilies of Austronesian languages are spoken only in

Taiwan, while the fourth is spoken elsewhere. *Since* indicates a piece of evidence: all four subfamilies are based on the same language, which must have originated in one area. That leads the linguist to claim that Taiwan is that source country. *Hence*, the linguist reaches the final conclusion: Austronesian-speaking people originated in Taiwan and later migrated.

Step 3: Make a Prediction

The linguist starts off with a fact. After that, the rest of the argument starts with a single piece of evidence that leads to one conclusion after the other. However, each conclusion is just a subsidiary conclusion that acts as evidence for the next one until the linguist reaches the final point (*hence*). That final conclusion, that Austronesian-speaking people originated in Taiwan and then migrated, is the overall conclusion, ultimately supported by everything else before it.

Step 4: Evaluate the Answer Choices

(E) correctly states, practically word for word from the stimulus, the overall conclusion.

(A) is merely a fact presented at the beginning. It is background information and nothing more.

(B) is too vague. This is more a principle or an assumption behind the linguist's argument. However, it does not adequately express the more specific conclusion drawn that Taiwan is the likely origin of the Austronesian-speaking peoples.

(C) is certainly *a* conclusion backed up by the facts in the argument. However, it is merely a subsidiary conclusion, one that is ultimately used as evidence to support the overall conclusion about where the *people* originated.

(D) is more a principle or assumption behind the linguist's argument. The overall conclusion actually specifies the location (Taiwan), rather than presents an open-ended concept.

12. (E) Method of Argument

Step 1: Identify the Question Type

The word *by* indicates a Method of Argument question. In essence, the question is asking, "By what method does Young respond to West?" The correct answer will describe *how* Young responds rather than *what* Young says.

Step 2: Untangle the Stimulus

West argues that Haynes is the worst of the company's three quality control inspectors. The evidence is that half of the defective appliances returned last year were inspected by Haynes. Young counters that Haynes is responsible for inspecting the vast majority of appliances.

Step 3: Make a Prediction

West's argument would be valid if every inspector inspected roughly the same number of appliances. In that case, one

would expect each inspector to be responsible for an average of one-third of the defective returns. Haynes being responsible for *half* would surely look bad. However, Young's statement counters the assumption that all inspectors are performing the same amount of work. If Haynes is responsible for most appliances to begin with, then Haynes is not as bad as West suggests. The correct answer will point out Young's countering of West's assumption.

Step 4: Evaluate the Answer Choices

(E) correctly describes Young's denial of West's presupposition (i.e., assumption) that all inspectors are inspecting roughly an equal number of appliances.

(A) is inaccurate. West's negative conclusion about Haynes is based on statistics, not on some predetermined agenda against Haynes, and Young makes no suggestion otherwise.

(B) is a Distortion. Young merely questions the validity of West's conclusion, not its relevance.

(C) is a Distortion. West's premise that half of the returned appliances with defects were inspected by Haynes is *not* disputed by Young. Instead, Young disputes an *unstated* assumption. West never states how many appliances Haynes inspects, and so Young disputes West's interpretation of the data, not the data itself.

(D) is a Distortion. This suggests that Young is saying, "Haynes is pretty bad, but he's not the *worst*." That's not Young's point at all.

13. (C) Principle (Parallel)

Step 1: Identify the Question Type

The correct answer will be a specific situation that "conforms most closely" to a principle. However, that principle is not directly provided. It is *illustrated* by the specific situation in the stimulus. Therefore, this is a relatively rare instance of a Parallel Principle question, which involves first identifying the principle, then applying it to the correct answer.

Step 2: Untangle the Stimulus

The author concludes that John, and not Emma, should be punished for breaking the window. The evidence is that, even though they both were playing with no regard to potential danger, it was ultimately John's action that broke the window.

Step 3: Make a Prediction

The author's judgment is based on who caused the accident directly, despite the fact that both players were acting improperly. The correct answer will apply the very same principle to an entirely different scenario: even if two people are doing something dangerous, only the one who directly causes an accident should be punished for it.

Step 4: Evaluate the Answer Choices

(C) applies the same principle. Even though two people (Terry and Chris) were acting dangerously, only the one who directly caused the accident (Chris) should be punished for it.

(A) does not match because only one person is involved, and nothing bad actually happened.

(B) does not match. The furniture didn't fit, so neither Linda nor Seung was directly responsible. Moreover, this does not apply punishment to one person over the other.

(D) does not match. In this case, neither Alexis nor Juan was responsible for the problem. Furthermore, this suggests that the owner should pay even though somebody *else* (the previous renter) caused the problem.

(E) does not match. This does fit the idea that two people are breaking a rule, but there is no situation where one of the two people caused damage to someone else's property. So, there is no way of applying the principle of punishing the person who caused the problem. For one, it never directly suggests Susan is responsible for her ankle injury, and not allowing her to hold the pond owner responsible is not parallel to making her compensate the owner for the damage.

14. (D) Strengthen

Step 1: Identify the Question Type

The question directly asks for something that will strengthen the researchers' argument.

Step 2: Untangle the Stimulus

The researchers present a hypothesis that the sound of a parent singing to an infant is affected by that parent's emotions. The researchers conclude in the last sentence that this hypothesis is correct. The evidence is an experiment in which psychologists were asked to listen to recordings of parents singing. For the most part, the psychologists were able to correctly identify which ones involved parents singing to an infant, and which ones involved no infant.

Step 3: Make a Prediction

The experiment adequately shows that the voices are noticeably different depending on whether a baby was present or not. However, there's still no evidence that this change in voices was due to the parents' *emotions*. To strengthen this argument, there needs to be some evidence connecting the vocal change to emotions.

Step 4: Evaluate the Answer Choices

(D) strengthens the argument, making it more likely that the emotions were somewhat responsible for the vocal differences.

(A) is an Irrelevant Comparison. The hypothesis is not about whose children produce the strongest emotions. It's about whether those emotions affect the singing voice, regardless

of whose children are involved or the intensity of the emotions.

(B) is a 180 at worst. This suggests that there were other factors involved, and perhaps the knowledge of being recorded played a role in vocal quality. In any case, it does nothing to connect vocal quality to one's emotions.

(C) confirms that emotions vary depending on whether or not an infant is present. However, it still does not strengthen the concept that those emotions are responsible for the change in vocal quality.

(E) is irrelevant. What people believe is not adequate evidence to support what actually happens.

15. (A) Principle (Identify/Strengthen)

Step 1: Identify the Question Type

The correct answer will be a principle that "helps to justify" the reasoning provided, making this an Identify the Principle question that mimics a Strengthen question.

Step 2: Untangle the Stimulus

There are claims that Shakespeare's portrayal of Richard III is inaccurate, but the author concludes that this is irrelevant. The author counters that the character is still aesthetically and morally fascinating.

Step 3: Make a Prediction

Note that the author does not dispute the claim of inaccuracy. Instead, the author merely argues that, inaccurate or not, the portrayal is still "fascinating and illuminating both aesthetically and morally." Thus, the author is acting on the principle that aesthetic and/or moral qualities are more important than accuracy.

Step 4: Evaluate the Answer Choices

(A) is correct, matching the author's preference for aesthetics over accuracy.

(B) is a 180. The author argues that accuracy is irrelevant.

(C) is Out of Scope. While it's okay for a principle to be extreme, as this answer is, this principle mistakenly defends Shakespeare based on his "historical importance." The author's defense is based on aesthetic qualities.

(D) is also Out of Scope. Again, although a principle can be extreme, as this answer is, who is responsible for creating history has no effect on the argument of whether accuracy is relevant or not in a historical drama.

(E) is a 180. The author claims inaccuracies are irrelevant, so any reason to correct them would be equally irrelevant.

16. (D) Parallel Flaw

Step 1: Identify the Question Type

The correct answer will be an argument with reasoning "most similar" to that of the original argument. Because that reasoning is described as *flawed*, this is a Parallel Flaw question.

Step 2: Untangle the Stimulus
The voter concludes that the prime minister is seeking a job at an international organization. The evidence is that anyone seeking such a job would spend a lot of time abroad, and the prime minister has been spending a lot of time abroad.

Step 3: Make a Prediction
This is a classic case of confusing necessity and sufficiency. The first claim of evidence is pure Formal Logic. Anyone seeking a job in an international organization spends a lot of time abroad:

If	seeking int'l org job	→	spend time abroad

However, other people could spend time abroad, too. Spending time abroad is not a guarantee, as the voter suggests, that one is seeking a job at an international organization. There could be plenty of other reasons for such travel. The correct answer will commit the same logical error. It will claim that anyone trying to accomplish a particular goal will perform a certain action. It will then conclude that someone performing that action must be trying to accomplish that goal, when there could be plenty of reasons for performing that action.

Step 4: Evaluate the Answer Choices
(D) matches and is correct. It claims that anyone trying to accomplish a particular goal (negotiate a loan) will perform a certain action (go to the bank).

If	negotiate loan	→	go to bank

It then concludes that Thompson, who is performing that action, must be trying to accomplish the goal. There are plenty of other reasons why someone would go to the bank.

(A) is flawed, but not for the same reason. This illogically claims Kao *must* be a golfer because *most* people in Kao's position play golf. This overlooks the possibility that Kao is not part of the majority, but that's not the same flaw as the original.

(B) does not match. It does not provide any reason to suggest that the logic is flawed. It may overlook some positive attributes that Franklin may possess, but it does not misinterpret a general claim as the original argument does.

(C) does not match. This makes an unwarranted conclusion about Ramirez having mind control based on what could have been a mere coincidence. This is illogical for sure, but not for the same reason as the original.

(E) does not match. This is flawed in that a lack of evidence against McKinsey does not necessarily indicate guilt. That's like saying the lack of evidence against unicorns suggests that they must be real. Flawed for sure, but not for the same Formal Logic–based reasoning as the original argument.

17. (A) Main Point

Step 1: Identify the Question Type
The correct answer will express the "overall conclusion," or main point, of the argument.

Step 2: Untangle the Stimulus
The first sentence is a strong opinion, suggesting the author's conclusion: debating the truth of the law of noncontradiction is pointless. That law of noncontradiction states that if two statements contradict one another, at least one of those statements must be false. So, why does the author feel debating this law is pointless? The evidence is that … well … who cares? The evidence is a bunch of talking points, and the question is only asking for the conclusion.

Step 3: Make a Prediction
The conclusion is the very first sentence: debating the law of noncontradiction is pointless.

Step 4: Evaluate the Answer Choices
(A) is correct, adequately summarizing the author's main point.

(B) expresses the principle behind the law of noncontradiction. However, that's not the *author's* conclusion. The author's conclusion is that debating that principle is pointless.

(C) is part of the evidence for what makes a debate productive. However, the ensuing evidence describes why that's irrelevant when debating the law of noncontradiction, thus leading to the actual conclusion: such a debate is pointless.

(D) is a Distortion. This takes the requirement for a productive debate and attributes it to the law of noncontradiction. It just mixes and matches random phrases from the argument without any respect for the author's meaning.

(E) is part of the last sentence. However, this lack of certainty is merely part of the evidence why the author concludes that debating the law of noncontradiction is pointless.

18. (B) Flaw

Step 1: Identify the Question Type
The phrase "vulnerable to criticism" is a common indicator of a Flaw question. The correct answer will describe why the argument is flawed.

Step 2: Untangle the Stimulus
The pundit concludes that attending a university would be useless for getting a corporate job. The evidence is that

corporations value a certain set of skills that many high school graduates already have without going to college.

Step 3: Make a Prediction
The key to recognizing the flaw here is to notice the overly strong language in the conclusion: attending a university would be "of no help" in finding a corporate job. This ignores the possibility that there is *some* benefit. Even if high students already possess some of the most sought-after skills, there could still be *something* that universities provide that high school wouldn't. The correct answer will point out this overlooked possibility.

Step 4: Evaluate the Answer Choices
(B) is correct, pointing out an overlooked benefit to college. Even if high school graduates possess the most sought-after skills, there could still be *some* skill required that only attending a university could provide.

(A) is a 180. University graduates *would* have those skills, but they already would have had them after high school. The pundit's argument still stands that college would be unnecessary.

(C) is Extreme. The pundit never claims or assumes that corporations hire *only* people with those skills. It's merely said that corporations value those skills the most.

(D) is irrelevant. The pundit's argument is merely that universities are of no help "in getting a corporate job." The pundit is not dismissing universities for other purposes, and thus does not assume that there's no other reason to attend a university.

(E) is irrelevant. It doesn't matter how students acquire those skills, whether through study or firsthand experience. All that matters is that they acquire those skills by the time they've graduated high school.

19. (B) Weaken

Step 1: Identify the Question Type
The question directly asks for something that will weaken the argument.

Step 2: Untangle the Stimulus
The archaeologist concludes that Neanderthals probably preserved meat by smoking it. The evidence is the presence of burnt lichen and grass, which produce a lot of smoke but not as much heat or light as wood.

Step 3: Make a Prediction
The archaeologist is making two assumptions. First, the archaeologist assumes that the smoke created by the lichen and grass was used for smoking meat, and for no other reason. Second, the archaeologist assumes that the light and heat produced by lichen and grass was not good enough for Neanderthals, i.e., they would have used wood (or something similar) if they really wanted light and heat. The correct

answer will contradict one, if not both, of these assumptions by suggesting that the lichen and grass was used for another reason or that it provided enough heat and light.

Step 4: Evaluate the Answer Choices
(B) is correct. Wood might make for a warmer, brighter fire if it was available. But if it wasn't, and nothing in the area was better than lichen and grass, then it's possible the lichen and grass were used for heat and light and not for smoking meats.

(A) is a 180. If there were other fireplaces that were used to produce more heat, then the fireplaces with the lichen and grass were probably used to produce smoke, which would only strengthen the archaeologist's view.

(C) is a 180, indicating that Neanderthals went to great lengths to procure lichens. This suggests that it was important to have a smoke-producing substance, thus strengthening the archaeologist's view.

(D) is Out of Scope. The archaeologist is not claiming that *all* Neanderthals preserved all of their meat by smoking it. Even if there were some later Neanderthals that developed an alternative method for some of their meat, the archaeologist's argument still stands.

(E) is a 180. This offers a reason why smoking meat would be beneficial, thus adding support to the archaeologist's claim.

20. (B) Point at Issue

Step 1: Identify the Question Type
The correct answer will be what two speakers, Edgar and Rafaela, "disagree over," making this a Point at Issue question.

Step 2: Untangle the Stimulus
Edgar argues that it's absurd to shut down some of the regional pumps. He claims the shutdown is all about saving one species of fish, but that's not worth inconveniencing thousands of people. Rafaela, however, argues there's another purpose to shutting down the pumps. If the fish are threatened, then so is the water supply. The fish are merely an indicator of a larger problem.

Step 3: Make a Prediction
Edgar and Rafaela surely disagree about shutting down the pumps. Edgar argues that they should not be shut down, but Rafaela is suggesting that they should be shut down. However, this disagreement stems from a bigger issue. Edgar believes the shutdown is all about saving the fish. Rafaela believes there's more to the shutdown than just one fish species. The correct answer will address the conflicting view on shutting down the pumps or the conflicting view on the motive for shutting down the pumps.

Step 4: Evaluate the Answer Choices
(B) is correct. Edgar would agree with this, saying the pumps are being shut down solely to save the fish. Rafaela would

disagree, arguing that there's a greater purpose that involves protecting the water supply.

(A) is not supported. Edgar agrees that people will be inconvenienced, but Rafaela does not dispute that claim. Rafaela only weighs in on the reason why such drastic measures are being taken.

(C) is not supported. Edgar agrees that these specific small fish are inconsequential, but Rafaela does not dispute that. Instead, Rafaela merely emphasizes a greater motive behind the shutdown.

(D) is not supported. Neither speaker addresses the legality of shutting down the pipes.

(E) is not supported. Neither Edgar nor Rafaela address whether the fish will actually be saved or not. The debate is over whether or not the fish are the primary motivation for shutting down the pumps.

21. (C) Assumption (Necessary)

Step 1: Identify the Question Type
The question asks for an "assumption required," making this a Necessary Assumption question. However, unlike most assumptions that are used to plug up holes in an argument, this assumption will plug up a hole in an analogy.

Step 2: Untangle the Stimulus
The author starts by drawing a distinction between engineering and two other sciences, physics and chemistry. Engineering can see how a machine works and analyze the nature of that machine. Physics and chemistry can only describe the physical conditions behind the machine's success, but cannot describe the machine's purpose. The author then makes an analogy to a distinction between physiology and the same two sciences. Physiology can see how an organism functions and analyze the nature of that organism. Physics and chemistry cannot determine those functions.

Step 3: Make a Prediction
Both parts of the analogy raise the inability of physics and chemistry to determine the function or purpose of something. However, both parts of the analogy compare physics and chemistry to two totally different fields: engineering and physiology. For this analogy to work, engineering and physiology must be comparable in some relevant sense.

Step 4: Evaluate the Answer Choices
(C) must be assumed. Using the Denial Test, if there were no connection between engineers' notions about machinery and physiologists' notions about organisms, the entire analogy would fall apart.

(A) is a Distortion. It's only important that the way physiologists *analyze* organisms is comparable to how

engineers *analyze* machinery. The organisms and machines themselves do not need to be similar.

(B) is not necessary. This just takes the wording used for physics and chemistry in the engineering analogy and repeats it with physiological terms. However, the physics and chemistry part of the analogy was never an issue. The problem is the disconnect between engineering and physiology, and this answer makes no connection.

(D) is a Distortion. The analogy emphasizes how physics and chemistry differ from other fields, but never claims these fields are "largely independent" of one another. Engineering was never said to be "largely independent" of physics and chemistry, so physiology need not be either.

(E) is Extreme. In the engineering analogy, the author never claims that machines *cannot* be reduced to mechanical or chemical processes. On the contrary, they *can*. It's just that physics and chemistry cannot express *purpose*. Therefore, the author need not assume biological process cannot be reduced to mechanical or chemical processes. They *can*, but physics and chemistry cannot express the operational principles.

22. (C) Strengthen

Step 1: Identify the Question Type
The question directly asks for something that strengthens the argument.

Step 2: Untangle the Stimulus
The author concludes (*therefore*) that the hepadnavirus is at least 25 million years old. The evidence is that the hepadnavirus inserts itself into an animal's chromosome and then gets passed down from generation to generation. One hepadnavirus fragment is found in chromosomes of both zebra finches and juncos, bird species that diverged from each other 25 million years ago. In addition, the virus fragment is found in the exact same location in corresponding chromosomes.

Step 3: Make a Prediction
The author is suggesting that the virus inserted itself into a bird at least 25 million years ago. It was genetically passed down until 25 million years ago, when that bird species diverged into two separate birds: zebra finches and juncos. The strongest evidence is the placement of the virus. Both birds have the virus in the exact same location in a similar chromosome. It can't be a coincidence ... or could it? Maybe the virus always inserts itself in the same location of a chromosome. If that were true, the virus could have inserted itself at two different times, perhaps just 1,000 years ago. The author assumes otherwise: the virus inserted itself once at least 25 million years ago, and the identical placement is not a coincidence. The correct answer will verify this assumption.

Step 4: Evaluate the Answer Choices

(C) is correct, validating the assumption that the virus inserted itself just once. If the placement of the virus is always random, it would be too coincidental that the virus was found in the *exact same spot* in both birds' chromosomes. It makes it much more likely that it was inserted once over 25 million years ago and got passed along during the split.

(A) is a Distortion. Even if viruses did have this ability, there's no evidence that the split wasn't caused by a different virus and the hepadnavirus inserted itself at different, much more recent times.

(B) is irrelevant. Even if no other viruses are present, there's still no evidence that the hepadnavirus fragments are genetically linked to the same virus from before the species diverged.

(D) is Out of Scope. There would still be the question of whether those fragments appear in the very same spot in those birds' chromosomes. If they did, then the author's argument seems less valid because if unrelated bird species all have the virus show up in the same spot of the chromosome, then the placement of the virus is not random, and thus, the zebra finch and dark-eyed junco need not have both had the virus at the time of their split. They could have each contracted the virus at different times much more recently than 25 million years ago.

(E) is also Out of Scope. Even if the hepadnavirus doesn't affect a species' survival, there's still no evidence that the same virus inserted itself into a bird 25 million years ago.

23. (B) Inference

Step 1: Identify the Question Type

The correct answer will be "properly inferred from the statements" given, making this an Inference question.

Step 2: Untangle the Stimulus

The *H. subflexa* caterpillar eats only one thing: a particular fruit that lacks linolenic acid. Many other insects require linolenic acid to grow and mature. Linolenic acid also needs to be consumed to produce a chemical called volicitin. Most caterpillars produce volicitin, but *H. subflexa* does not.

Step 3: Make a Prediction

There's a lot of information provided. However, when asked for something *properly* inferred, look for the most absolute statements with the most Formal Logic. Then find ways of combining that information.

There's not much to be said about the *H.subflexa* caterpillar. Unlike many other insects, it does not ingest linolenic acid, and unlike other caterpillars, it doesn't produce volicitin. However, there's not much to deduce from those statements. On the other hand, linolenic acid is said to be *necessary* for

two things. In many insects, it's necessary for growth. It also needs to be consumed to produce volicitin. Further, volicitin is produced in *most* caterpillars. If most caterpillars produce volicitin, and producing volicitin requires consuming linolenic acid, then most caterpillars must consume linolenic acid. Test the answers, making sure that the correct one is absolutely true based on the logic.

Step 4: Evaluate the Answer Choices

(B) must be true, and is thus correct. Most caterpillars produce volicitin, and that requires a diet that includes linolenic acid. Thus, most caterpillars must consume linolenic acid.

(A) is not supported. *H. subflexa* does not consume linolenic acid, but it doesn't need to. *Other* insects are said to need linolenic acid to grow. And *H. subflexa* does not produce volicitin. Therefore, *H. subflexa* has no stated need for linolenic acid, and there's no guarantee that it creates its own linolenic acid.

(C) is a Distortion of the Formal Logic. Linolenic acid is *necessary* to produce volicitin, but it's not *sufficient*. The caterpillars that produce volicitin must consume linolenic acid, but there may be other caterpillars that consume linolenic acid *without* producing volicitin.

(D) is unsupported. While *H. subflexa* caterpillars eat only one thing that doesn't have linolenic acid, that doesn't mean linolenic acid would be *poisonous*.

(E) is not supported. While most caterpillars need the linolenic acid absent from *Physalis* fruit, there could be plenty of other caterpillars that eat that fruit along with *H. subflexa*. Even the ones that do need linolenic acid could eat that fruit, too. They would just need to eat other foods as well.

24. (B) Role of a Statement

Step 1: Identify the Question Type

The question provides a claim from the stimulus and asks for the "role played in the argument" by that claim. That makes this a Role of a Statement question.

Step 2: Untangle the Stimulus

The politician starts with a requirement for democracy: people must be able to share ideas freely. That leads to the conclusion ([*t*]*herefore*) that the right to have unmonitored private conversations is essential to democracy. That, in turn, leads to the final conclusion (*thus*) that monitoring Internet conversations would be bad for democracy. Said differently, the politician concludes government monitoring of Internet conversations would be bad. Why? Because unmonitored conversations are essential to democracy. Why? Because democracy requires no restrictions on free sharing of ideas.

Step 3: Make a Prediction
The argument has a very basic structure. There's an opening claim, followed by a conclusion. That conclusion is then used as evidence to back up the final conclusion. So, in order, there's a claim, a subsidiary conclusion, and the main conclusion. The question asks for the role of the first statement. That's the claim that backs up the subsidiary conclusion.

Step 4: Evaluate the Answer Choices
(B) correctly identifies the first statement as a claim that supports another claim, which further supports the main conclusion. In other words, it's a claim that supports a subsidiary conclusion.

(A) is a Distortion. The first statement does support *a* conclusion, but not directly the *main* conclusion. If the first statement is said to support the main conclusion, then it only does so indirectly by supporting another conclusion first. It does not support *only* the main conclusion.

(C) is a 180. There is no support for the opening sentence. It is just an accepted claim that is used as evidence.

(D) is mistaken. The main conclusion is the last sentence, not the first. The first statement is not inferred from anything.

(E) is mistaken. The main conclusion is the last sentence, not the first. The first statement is not inferred from anything. Furthermore, the two other statements *are* used—one in support of the other. The second sentence supports the third sentence.

25. (C) Inference

Step 1: Identify the Question Type
The correct answer will be "strongly supported" by the information provided. That makes this an Inference question.

Step 2: Untangle the Stimulus
The author starts out by claiming that you can compare two chess-playing programs by seeing how each one performs under time restraints. How do you compare these programs? The author never says, so that's unknown. Instead, the author suddenly shifts scope and starts talking about comparing *computers*. If you test the same program on two different computers, the faster computer will more likely win because it can examine more moves within the time limit.

Step 3: Make a Prediction
The key to answering this question is to not be thrown by the first sentence. The first sentence suggests that there's a way to compare chess-playing programs, but it never actually says how. It just says that you *can*. All that's really mentioned is how to compare two computers. The faster computer can examine more moves in a given time limit, so the author claims the faster computer is more likely to win. That implies that the number of moves one can examine within a given time limit somehow affects one's ability to win.

Step 4: Evaluate the Answer Choices
(C) is directly supported. Faster computers are said to have a better chance of winning *because* they can examine more moves in any given time frame. Thus, under a given time constraint, more examining means a better chance of winning.

(A) is not supported. The author never discusses the criteria for comparing two programs. The only criterion provided is for how to compare two computers: whichever one works faster is better. It's possible that a program that tests fewer moves is still better because it's been better programmed to test more effective moves first.

(B) is not supported. Speed can be a factor in determining which computer is more likely to win, but there's no information about compatibility or the ability to run a particular program.

(D) is not supported. If the *same* program were running on two different computers, the faster computer would be able to test more moves. However, if it's two *different* programs, the results are unknown. Maybe the coding of the program on the faster computer is far more complex. In that case, the faster computer may still not be able to examine as many moves due to the nature of the program.

(E) is not supported. Raising the time limit on the slower computer would certainly allow it to examine more moves than it could previously. However, it depends entirely on how much you raise the time limit. If you only raise it a little, the faster computer might still be able to examine more moves and still have a better chance of winning. If you raise it a lot, you may allow the slower computer to examine many more moves and gain the upper hand. There's no guarantee of perfectly hitting the time limit that allows for an "equal chance of winning."

PrepTest 80

The Inside Story

PrepTest 80 was administered in December 2016. It challenged 31,340 test takers. What made this test so hard? Here's a breakdown of what Kaplan students who were surveyed after taking the official exam considered PrepTest 80's most difficult section.

Hardest PrepTest 80 Section as Reported by Test Takers

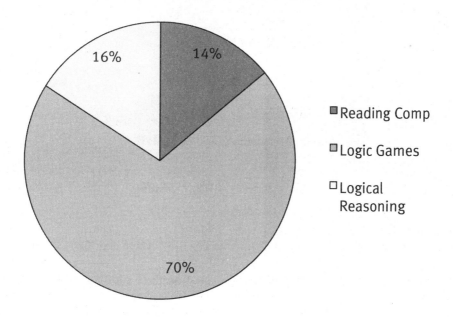

Based on these results, you might think that studying Logic Games is the key to LSAT success. Well, Logic Games is important, but test takers' perceptions don't tell the whole story. For that, you need to consider students' actual performance. The following chart shows the average number of students to miss each question in each of PrepTest 80's different sections.

Percentage Incorrect by PrepTest 80 Section Type

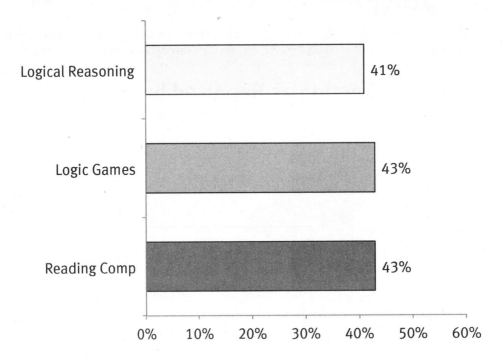

Actual student performance tells quite a different story. On average, students were almost equally likely to miss questions in all th of the different section types, and on PrepTest 80, Reading Comprehension was equal to Logic Games in actual difficulty.

Maybe students overestimate the difficulty of the Logic Games section because it's so unusual, or maybe it's because a really har Logic Game is so easy to remember after the test. That may have been the case on PrepTest 80, which featured a Process game for first time in over 20 years! But the truth is that the test maker places hard questions throughout the test. Here were the locations o the 10 hardest (most missed) questions in the exam.

Location of 10 Most Difficult Questions in PrepTest 80

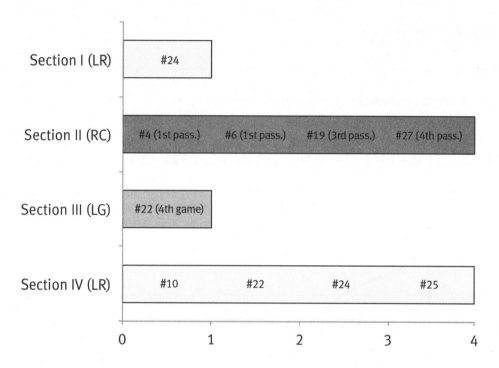

The takeaway from this data is that, to maximize your potential on the LSAT, you need to take a comprehensive approach. Test yourself rigorously, and review your performance on every section of the test. Kaplan's LSAT explanations provide the expertise and insight you need to fully understand your results. The explanations are written and edited by a team of LSAT experts, who have helped thousands of students improve their scores. Kaplan always provides data-driven analysis of the test, ranking the difficulty of every question based on actual student performance. The 10 hardest questions on every test are highlighted with a 4-star difficulty rating, the highest we give. The analysis breaks down the remaining questions into 1-, 2-, and 3-star ratings so that you can compare your performance to thousands of other test takers on all LSAC material.

Don't settle for wondering whether a question was really as hard as it seemed to you. Analyze the test with real data, and learn the secrets and strategies that help top scorers master the LSAT.

7 Can't–Miss Features of PrepTest 80

- PrepTest 80 contained the first Process logic game since September 1995 (PT 16). To put how long ago that was in perspective, just a few days after PT 16 was administered OJ Simpson was acquitted of murder.
- Although the star ratings may indicate the fourth game of the section (the Process game) gave some students trouble, that may be simply because they were afraid of the unknown. Check out the explanations to see how easily the game could be handled for those that were willing to do just a little bit of math.
- This was the first PrepTest since June '12 (PT 66) with no Role of a Statement questions. That's a pretty big omission considering there were five Role of a Statement questions on the previous year's December test (PT 77).
- PrepTest 80 featured two Distribution games—which was only the fifth time that had ever happened on a released test. Did you get déjà vu reading that comment? PrepTest 79 *also* had two Distribution games!
- Six Logic Function questions marked the most in a Reading Comprehension section since there were seven in June '04 (PT 43).
- This was not the test to guess (C). Although each answer choice would be expected to show up about 20 percent of the time, (C) was correct less than 14 percent of the time on PrepTest 80, and less than 9 percent of the time in the Logic Games section.

- The second to last question of the test was about rafting across the Pacific Ocean. Coincidentally, the #1 movie at the box office the weekend PrepTest 80 was administered was *Moana*!

PrepTest 80 in Context

As much fun as it is to find out what makes a PrepTest unique or noteworthy, it's even more important to know just how representative it is of other LSAT administrations (and, thus, how likely it is to be representative of the exam you will face on Test Day). The following charts compare the numbers of each kind of question and game on PrepTest 80 to the average numbers seen on all officially released LSATs administered over the past five years (from 2012 through 2016).

Number of LR Questions by Type: PrepTest 80 vs. 2012–2016 Average

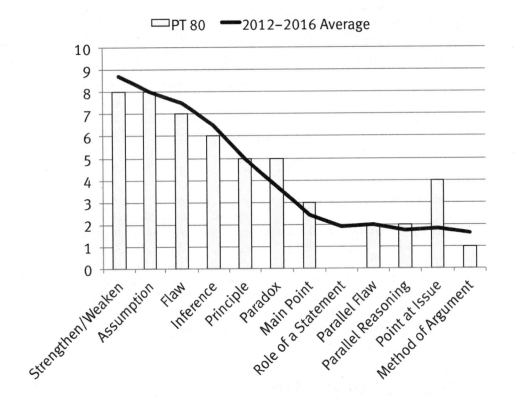

Number of LG Games by Type: PrepTest 80 vs. 2012–2016 Average

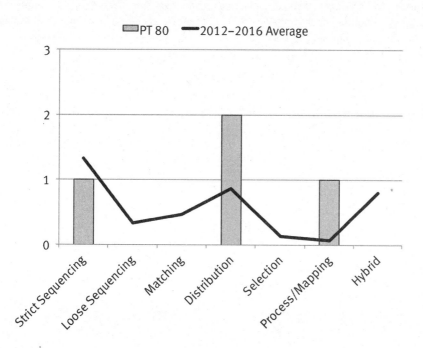

Number of RC Questions by Type: PrepTest 80 vs. 2012–2016 Average

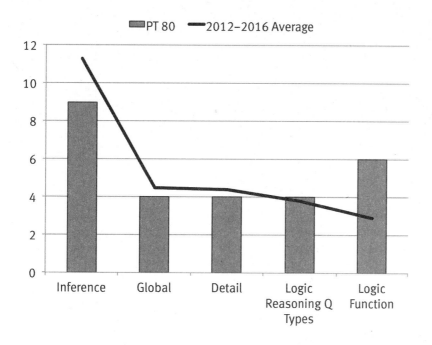

There isn't usually a huge difference in the distribution of questions from LSAT to LSAT, but if this test seems harder (or easier) to you than another you've taken, compare the number of questions of the types on which you, personally, are strongest and weakest. And then explore within each section to see if your best or worst question types came earlier or later.

Students in Kaplan's comprehensive LSAT courses have access to every released LSAT and to an online question bank with thousan_
of officially released questions, games, and passages. If you are studying on your own, you have to do a bit more work to identify yo_
strengths and your areas of opportunity. Quantitative analysis (like that in the previous charts) is an important tool for understandir_
how the test is constructed and how you are performing on it.

Section I: Logical Reasoning

Q#	Question Type	Correct	Difficulty
1	Paradox	D	★
2	Flaw	A	★★
3	Main Point	A	★
4	Principle (Identify/Strengthen)	E	★
5	Assumption (Necessary)	A	★
6	Main Point	B	★
7	Point at Issue	D	★
8	Paradox	C	★
9	Assumption (Sufficient)	D	★
10	Inference	D	★★
11	Strengthen	D	★
12	Paradox	C	★★
13	Flaw	A	★★
14	Parallel Reasoning	C	★★
15	Point at Issue	C	★
16	Flaw	B	★★★
17	Assumption (Necessary)	E	★★★
18	Point at Issue (Agree)	D	★★★
19	Weaken	A	★★★
20	Method of Argument	A	★★★
21	Principle (Apply/Inference)	B	★★★
22	Inference	D	★★★
23	Strengthen	E	★★★
24	Parallel Flaw	E	★★★★
25	Assumption (Necessary)	C	★★

1. (D) Paradox

Step 1: Identify the Question Type

The question asks for something that will "resolve the apparent conflict." That means there will be a mystery to be solved, making this a Paradox question.

Step 2: Untangle the Stimulus

A study consisted of two groups of dust-mite allergy sufferers. The first group slept on a bed with mite-proof bedding, while the other group slept on a bed without such bedding. Bedding is said to be the primary source of dust mites. Still, the special bedding provided no relief to its users, even though it reduced dust-mite allergens by 69%.

Step 3: Make a Prediction

If bedding is such a major source of dust mites, why are people with dust-mite protection still suffering? The correct answer will solve this mystery. Most likely, those people are suddenly getting exposed to a lot more dust mites elsewhere, or a 69% reduction—no matter how great that sounds—is still just not enough to reduce symptoms.

Step 4: Evaluate the Answer Choices

(D) resolves the issue. If sufferers need a 90–95% reduction to get relief, then a 69% reduction is nice but just not good enough to provide relief.

(A) is a 180. This just confirms that dust-mite allergens in bedding are particularly irritating. That makes it even more unusual that the special bedding didn't help.

(B) is Out of Scope. Exaggerated or not, people's reports were no different with or without the bedding. This doesn't explain why people didn't experience *any* relief, even with the special bedding.

(C) is also Out of Scope. It doesn't matter that the cause of the allergy isn't *fully* understood. It's still caused by dust-mite allergens in some way, and reducing those allergens should have reduced some symptoms—but that didn't happen.

(E) is Out of Scope, too. What the study participants knew about the study does not explain why the bedding was ineffective.

2. (A) Flaw

Step 1: Identify the Question Type

The question directly asks why the argument is *flawed*, making this a Flaw question.

Step 2: Untangle the Stimulus

The author provides a lot of statistics about the hair dryers sold by Wilson. Five years ago, half the hair dryers sold in the country were Wilsons. Now, only 25% of the hair dryers sold are Wilsons. Wilson still makes the same amount of money per hair dryer sold, so the author concludes that Wilson's total hair dryer income has decreased.

Step 3: Make a Prediction

The conclusion is about total income. For total income to decrease, Wilson must take in less money overall. They are making the same amount of income on each hair dryer, so that means they would have to be selling fewer hair dryers overall. However, the evidence merely indicates that Wilson's hair dryers make up a smaller *percentage* of total hair dryers sold. If people started buying a lot more hair dryers overall, Wilson could still sell just as many or even more hair dryers despite making up a smaller percentage (i.e., share) of the market. (For example, 50% of 10,000 hair dryers is still as much as 25% of 20,000 hair dryers.) The author confuses numbers and percentages. The correct answer will point out this overlooked distinction.

Step 4: Evaluate the Answer Choices

(A) matches the prediction, pointing out the confusion between percentages (market share) and numbers (total sales). If total sales nationwide increase enough, a loss of market share does not have to indicate a loss in total sales.

(B) is Out of Scope. The argument is about income and market share. Information about how profits are generated is unnecessary.

(C) is Out of Scope. The conclusion and the entire argument is solely about hair dryer sales. Sales for other products have no bearing on that.

(D) is also Out of Scope. Even if the retail price increased (i.e., the amount you'd pay in the store), Wilson is still said to receive the same *net* income per hair dryer. Given that *net* income hasn't changed, an increase in retail price just means that extra money is going somewhere else. Perhaps the cost of making each hair dryer has also gone up, or perhaps the stores are making more money per hair dryer, not Wilson.

(E) is Extreme and Out of Scope. It doesn't matter how Wilson's hair dryers compare to its other products. Besides, the author isn't trying to argue that the hair dryers are the *least* profitable.

3. (A) Main Point

Step 1: Identify the Question Type

The question asks for the "overall conclusion" of the argument, making this a Main Point question.

Step 2: Untangle the Stimulus

The argument is riddled with a bunch of philosophical buzzwords. To cut through the muck, it helps to paraphrase it in a more conversational tone: "Is being faithful a virtue? It depends on what you're faithful to. You see, virtues are supposed to be good. But resentment is a type of faithfulness, and resentment is no virtue because it means being faithful to bad things."

Step 3: Make a Prediction

So what's the point of all this? The author is ultimately trying to answer the question of whether faithfulness can be considered a virtue. The answer? That's the conclusion: it depends on what you're faithful to. Everything else is just evidence to support that point.

Step 4: Evaluate the Answer Choices

(A) is a clean paraphrase of the opening sentence, which sums up the author's conclusion.

(B) is a given fact, and facts are evidence. The fact that virtues are, by definition, praiseworthy is evidence why the author argues that faithfulness is not always a virtue.

(C) can be inferred, but is not the main point. The author does suggest that hate-based behavior (resentment) is not virtuous, but that's just evidence why faithfulness is not always virtuous.

(D) is a 180. The author claims that resentment is *in fact* a kind of faithfulness. There is no suggestion that they are "obviously different."

(E) is a Distortion. The author claims that nobody considers resentment virtuous, but never actually claims that this *should* be the case. Besides, the status of resentment is merely evidence for why faithfulness as a virtue depends on other factors.

4. (E) Principle (Identify/Strengthen)

Step 1: Identify the Question Type

The question directly asks for a principle. Because the principle will be listed in the answer choices, this is an Identify the Principle question. Further, because the correct answer will help "justify the columnist's judgment," it will also act like a Strengthen question.

Step 2: Untangle the Stimulus

The columnist's judgment comes in the last sentence: "That proposal is unacceptable." The disputed proposal involves taking additional water utility revenue and using it to build new roads instead of a new dam, as was originally the plan.

Step 3: Make a Prediction

Specifically, the columnist is rejecting a proposal, claiming it's unacceptable to take money collected by a water utility and use it to build something entirely unrelated: roads. The correct answer will justify this reasoning using the same logic, only in broader terms. In other words, something along the lines of: don't take money from one business and use it to build something unrelated to that business.

Step 4: Evaluate the Answer Choices

(E) matches the columnist's logic. If the water utility's additional charges need to be used for water-related expenses, then that justifies the columnist's argument against using those charges to build new roads.

(A) doesn't help. By this principle, as long as people know the money is going to be used for new roads, then there's no justification for calling the proposal unacceptable.

(B) is Out of Scope. There's no suggestion that a dam would benefit the entire community and/or that the new roads would only benefit some members.

(C) is Out of Scope. There's no information whether or not the customers approve of the proposal, so this offers no justification for the columnist's claim.

(D) is a Distortion. The argument is about how to use the revenue earned from the additional charges. It's never said who approved the additional charges in the first place, and the columnist is not arguing about who should or shouldn't approve those decisions.

5. (A) Assumption (Necessary)

Step 1: Identify the Question Type

The question directly asks for the assumption in the argument. The assumption is *required*, making this a Necessary Assumption question.

Step 2: Untangle the Stimulus

The final sentence offers a common "[s]ince [evidence], [conclusion]" format. The author concludes that the leopard magpie moth may become extinct. The evidence is that a plant called the Natal grass cycad is also going extinct. The moth eats this plant, which provides the moth with a predator-avoiding chemical.

Step 3: Make a Prediction

The loss of the cycad would certainly take away a source of protection for the moth. However, the author fails to consider that there just might be other sources of the helpful toxin the cycad produces. Moreover, even if other sources don't exist, the moth could still adapt and find a new way to avoid predators. The author assumes none of this will happen—that the cycad is the moth's *only* source of protection against predators.

Step 4: Evaluate the Answer Choices

(A) matches the prediction and must be assumed. After all, if there *were* other ways to become unpalatable to predators, then the extinction of the cycad would not necessarily spell doom for the moth.

(B) could help the author out, but is ultimately not necessary. Even if the moth *was* fast enough to escape predators, it could still face extinction by losing a crucial food source. This fails to make a needed connection between the cycad and the moth.

(C) is not necessary. It doesn't matter *how* predators sense the macrozamin. Whether they do sense it from appearance alone or by other means, the author still has a point.

(D) is not necessary. The moths don't need the plant to be abundant to be affected by the plant's impending extinction. Even if the moths could locate the plant at its rarest, that will be of no help should the plant disappear entirely.

(E) is Out of Scope and a 180 at worst. It may weaken the argument, because if the predators are not becoming immune that actually *helps* the magpie's chances. However, if the cycad disappears and macrozamin goes away, then it makes no difference whether the predators grow tolerant of it or not.

6. (B) Main Point

Step 1: Identify the Question Type
The question asks for the "conclusion drawn," making this a Main Point question.

Step 2: Untangle the Stimulus
The citizen uses a very common argumentative technique here: present someone else's point of view and refute it. In this case, the citizen's leaders believe that the government should use the budget surplus to pay down the national debt. The line "[t]his makes no sense" indicates the citizen's rebuttal, and thus the conclusion: the government should *not* use the surplus to pay down the debt. Everything else, including the list of other potential uses (the military, infrastructure, roads) and the analogy of homeowners paying off a mortgage, is merely evidence to back up the citizen's rebuttal.

Step 3: Make a Prediction
As often happens when an author rebuts a point of view, the rebuttal serves as the main point. Here, the citizen's conclusion is that, contrary to what the leaders suggest, the government should not use the budget surplus to pay down the national debt.

Step 4: Evaluate the Answer Choices
(B) accurately expresses the citizen's rebuttal and thus the main conclusion.

(A) takes the citizen's analogy and turns it into a recommendation. The citizen never directly states that homeowners shouldn't do this—and that's not the point. The analogy is there to argue why the government should not use the surplus to pay off the national debt.

(C) accurately expresses the citizen's belief that a homeowner's situation parallels the government's situation. However, that's merely evidence to support the citizen's rebuttal of the leaders' view of what should be done with the budget surplus.

(D) brings up a detail that implies where the budget surplus could be better spent, but misses the bigger picture that the surplus *shouldn't* be used to pay down the national debt.

(E) accurately sums up the leaders' position, but completely misses the citizen's point that this plan "makes no sense."

7. (D) Point at Issue

Step 1: Identify the Question Type
There are two speakers, and the question asks for something about which the two speakers *disagree*. That indicates a Point at Issue question.

Step 2: Untangle the Stimulus
Peraski argues that people with small cars cannot complain about people with larger gas-guzzling cars causing pollution. After all, people with small cars could produce less pollution by riding a bike, so complaining about others would be hypocritical.

Jackson concedes that people could always be better about reducing pollution. However, Jackson is okay with being hypocritical if it means speaking out against people who are even worse.

Step 3: Make a Prediction
Both speakers acknowledge that people who pollute less can be hypocritical because they're still polluting. However, they differ in their feeling toward that hypocrisy. Peraski sees hypocrisy as a reason to stay quiet. Jackson, on the other hand, does not. To Jackson, hypocrisy is no excuse for staying quiet. The correct answer will address this argument about the role of hypocrisy.

Step 4: Evaluate the Answer Choices
(D) expresses the Point at Issue. Peraski would disagree with this statement; people should *not* speak out if it reveals hypocrisy. Jackson says the opposite: people *should* speak out, despite the hypocrisy.

(A) is a 180. Peraski directly states this, but Jackson would agree. They're not arguing about the level of pollution. They're arguing over whether people should speak out about it.

(B) is a 180. Both Peraski and Jackson agree that it would reveal hypocrisy. Their disagreement is about whether or not people should speak out in light of this hypocrisy.

(C) is also a 180. Peraski implies this directly, and Jackson would not disagree. The question is this: should these drivers of small cars speak out against pollution or not?

(E) is Out of Scope. Neither speaker addresses the concept of morality, so there's no way to know whether they would agree on this or not.

8. (C) Paradox

Step 1: Identify the Question Type
The question asks for something that would "resolve the apparent discrepancy," making this a Paradox question.

Step 2: Untangle the Stimulus
For a Paradox question, look for the central mystery. In this case, abalones become large only when they can spend more energy on mating and less energy finding food and avoiding

predators. However, there's one species that became large after predators (otters) moved into their waters.

Step 3: Make a Prediction

If abalones need to spend less energy avoiding predators, how did this one species get bigger after *more* predators showed up? Perhaps something made it easy to avoid the otters, and thus their appearance was uneventful. There's another key to the mystery: abalones also need to spend less energy finding food. Perhaps the otters made it easier for the abalones to find food. The correct answer will likely draw on one or both of these potential solutions that helped the abalones out.

Step 4: Evaluate the Answer Choices

(C) is helpful on two accounts. First, it suggests that otters were eating something other than just abalones. Thus, the abalones didn't necessarily have to spend as much or more energy avoiding the otters because the otters were eating other creatures. Second, the otters were eating the abalones' competition for food, so the abalones didn't need as much energy to find food. Those are the exact conditions needed to help explain the presence of large abalones.

(A) is a 180. If the abalones and the otters compete for the same food, then the appearance of otters would have made it *harder* for the abalones to find food. That would make it *less* likely that they grew so large.

(B) is Out of Scope. It doesn't matter how many species exist. This still doesn't explain how they got large in the presence of predators.

(D) is Out of Scope. Reproductive ability is not presented as a factor in determining the size of the abalones.

(E) is also Out of Scope. The abalones developed to be larger *after* the otters showed up.

9. (D) Assumption (Sufficient)

Step 1: Identify the Question Type

This is an Assumption question, as it asks for something that is assumed. Further, the argument's conclusion can be properly drawn *if* that assumption is in place, making this a Sufficient Assumption question.

Step 2: Untangle the Stimulus

Managers encourage stiff competition among employees in the hopes that it will make employees perform their best. However, the author concludes ([t]*hus*) that stiff competition will actually make things worse. The evidence is that some people may become anxious and doubt their own abilities when faced with competition.

Step 3: Make a Prediction

The author makes a subtle shift in scope. Both the evidence and conclusion refer to the effect of stiff competition. However, the evidence merely claims it makes people anxious

and doubtful of their abilities, while the conclusion shifts to claim it affects people's actual performance. The author is assuming there's a connection between anxiety/doubt and how people actually perform.

Step 4: Evaluate the Answer Choices

(D) makes the logical connection between doubt and one's actual performance. If this were true, then the author's argument is complete: stiff competition leads to doubt, and thus impacts performance.

(A) might explain why people doubt their abilities in the face of superior competition, but that still doesn't provide a logical connection to the conclusion, which is about actual performance.

(B) is Out of Scope. The goal is not about getting everyone to perform at the same level. The goal is to maximize performance for each employee individually. Even if the winner of a competition gives the most effort, the other employees could still be giving their own individual best effort, contrary to the author's conclusion.

(C) is a Distortion. This states that, when people feel they can win a competition, they will perform better. That doesn't mean, as the author suggests, that they *won't* perform better when they *don't* think they can win. Perhaps the competition itself is enough to motivate performance.

(E) is Out of Scope. It indicates why some people might be anxious or doubtful, but it still does not make a logical connection to the conclusion, which is about actual performance.

10. (D) Inference

Step 1: Identify the Question Type

Grounds for choosing the correct answer will be made "on the basis of the statements above." That makes this an Inference question. However, unlike most Inference questions, the correct answer will not be true or supported as valid. The correct answer will be *rejected*, which means the stimulus will be used to contradict the correct answer—it must be false. Answer choices that could be true or must be true can be rejected.

Step 2: Untangle the Stimulus

The stimulus merely provides details explaining the difficulty of creating a database of every known plant species. Not only do botanists sometimes give the same plant different names (because they didn't know someone else already named it), but also DNA shows how they sometimes use the same name for plants that are actually different.

Step 3: Make a Prediction

Those wacky botanists, with such convoluted records—different plants with the same name, the same plant with different names—it's no wonder that creating a database is so complicated. However, what does this imply? What does it counter? It's almost impossible to predict. With so little to work with, there's no choice but to test each answer individually with the information given. Remember that the correct answer will be directly contradicted by what's provided.

Step 4: Evaluate the Answer Choices

(D) can be rejected. The last sentence directly states how DNA analysis can be used to identify different species. That technique could be used to identify different species, whether those species were given the same name or distinct ones. So, contrary to this claim, the botanists *do* have a viable technique.

(A) is not supported, but it can't be rejected either. There's no indication of how many problems have been identified or how many of those problems have yet to be resolved. It's still possible that *most* inconsistencies are still being worked out.

(B) certainly cannot be rejected. While it hasn't been easy to create, there must be a reason they're trying. Therefore, it's actually very likely that the database would be helpful.

(C) cannot be rejected. While the stimulus only refers to these issues in botany, there's no reason to believe similar issues aren't happening elsewhere.

(E) cannot be rejected. If a plant has multiple names, that could mean multiple botanists discovered information about it. Only searching for information under one name could easily leave out information collected by a botanist who gave it a different name.

11. (D) Strengthen

Step 1: Identify the Question Type
The question directly asks for something that strengthens the given argument.

Step 2: Untangle the Stimulus
The author concludes ([*c*]*learly*) that the knowledge of being monitored causes hospital staff to perform their work more carefully. The evidence is that there were fewer injuries caused by staff error after a program was implemented to record such errors.

Step 3: Make a Prediction
There are two problems with the argument. The first is one of the most common flaws tested on the LSAT: causation versus correlation. The evidence merely describes a correlation (errors decreased at the same time the program was implemented). The conclusion claims one thing caused the other (the monitoring program *caused* people to make fewer errors). The second problem involves a scope shift. The evidence claims that the program involved *recording* errors, but the conclusion only discusses the knowledge of being monitored. The author fails to consider that it wasn't the

monitoring but rather the actual recording of errors that made people more careful. To combat these weaknesses and make the argument stronger, the correct answer will strengthen the connection between the program and the decreased number of errors and/or make it more likely that it was the monitoring and not necessarily the recordkeeping itself.

Step 4: Evaluate the Answer Choices

(D) strengthens the argument by addressing both weaknesses. This strengthens the connection between the plan and the decreased errors by showing how errors weren't decreasing earlier. That rules out earlier causes and makes the monitoring program a more likely cause. It also makes it clearer that it's the analysis (i.e., monitoring) of the records that people noticed.

(A) is a 180. This suggests that monitoring was nothing new, making it more likely that people were concerned about some other aspect of the program. Perhaps they were always monitored, but nothing was ever recorded before and people are now nervous about having a physical record of their mistakes.

(B) is a 180. This suggests that patient errors decreased elsewhere *without* the plan. That implies there was another cause entirely.

(C) is Out of Scope. What the plan does *not* involve provides no support for whether or not the plan was responsible for changing people's behavior.

(E) is Out of Scope. It doesn't matter what the punishment is when people *did* make an error. The argument is about what caused people to make *fewer* errors. If anything, a discussion of penalties (reprimands or otherwise) could provide an alternative cause for better behavior.

12. (C) Paradox

Step 1: Identify the Question Type
The question asks for something that "helps to explain" a situation. If a situation needs explaining, that indicates a Paradox question.

Step 2: Untangle the Stimulus
In a certain area, wolves were introduced to reduce the growing moose population. Contrary to expectations, despite a healthy wolf population, the moose population actually kept growing.

Step 3: Make a Prediction
If the wolf population is doing well, why didn't they stop the moose population from growing? While it may be difficult to predict an exact solution, expect that the correct answer will show how the wolves created an unexpected benefit.

Step 4: Evaluate the Answer Choices
(C) provides an explanation. Without the wolves, the moose were susceptible to diseases that could have killed them off.

With the wolves, the disease-weakened moose are picked off, preventing the disease from spreading and thus giving the moose a better chance of staying healthy and surviving.

(A) may be tempting in that it suggests that moose predators were kept away by the wolves, helping the moose to survive. However, the other predators were still replaced by wolves, who also prey on moose. This only works if wolves are a lesser threat. However, that information is not provided, and the correct answer cannot depend on an unsubstantiated condition.

(B) tries to suggest that the mystery is not all that unusual. Other parks have the same problem. However, this still fails to explain *why* that problem exists in the first place. So essentially, this only makes matters worse by expanding the mystery to other areas.

(D) is an Irrelevant Comparison. The eating habits of a healthy moose versus unhealthy moose does nothing to explain why wolves had no effect on the moose population.

(E) is an Irrelevant Comparison. It doesn't help because it's restricted to old moose. This might explain why wolves don't affect the population of *old* moose—they'd be just as likely to die without the wolves around—but it doesn't explain why wolves had no effect on the *overall* moose population.

13. (A) Flaw

Step 1: Identify the Question Type
The question asks why the argument is *flawed*, making this easily identified as a Flaw question.

Step 2: Untangle the Stimulus
The conclusion ([*h*]*ence*) is that, if laws are not meant to make people happy, then existing laws cannot be evaluated and are thus considered legitimate just for being laws. The evidence is that, if laws *are* meant to make people happy, then existing laws *could* be criticized (i.e., evaluated).

Conclusion:

If	purpose is ~ happiness	→	~ basis for evaluation/criticism

Evidence:

If	purpose is happiness	→	basis for evaluation/criticism

Step 3: Make a Prediction
Few things are greater on the LSAT than finding an argument in which the evidence and conclusion both consist of Formal Logic. That's often a sign of a commonly tested flaw:

necessity versus sufficiency. Sure enough, the evidence claims that *if* the purpose of laws was to make people happy, that would be good enough (i.e., sufficient) to allow for critique of existing laws. However, the author suggests that we can't critique existing laws if that's *not* the purpose—as if making people happy had to be the purpose (i.e., was necessary). That's not necessarily true. It's possible that critiques are valid whatever the purpose is. The correct answer will point out this common flaw of treating a sufficient condition as if it were necessary.

Step 4: Evaluate the Answer Choices
(A) points out the common flaw being tested here. The author takes a sufficient condition (i.e., *if* the purpose of laws is to make people happy) and treats it as necessary (i.e., we can't evaluate laws without that purpose).

(B) brings up another commonly tested flaw: causation versus correlation. However, the author is not suggesting that anything caused anything else, so this flaw does not apply here.

(C) describes the flaw of equivocation (treating two different concepts as equal just because the same word is used to describe them). However, all terms are used consistently in the argument, so equivocation is not a problem here.

(D) suggests that the evidence is about how the world *should* be, but the author never makes such a claim.

(E) describes a flaw in which the evidence is about a group as a whole and the conclusion is about individual members within that group. However, there is no group here from which individual members are identified.

14. (C) Parallel Reasoning

Step 1: Identify the Question Type
The question asks for an argument "most similar to" the argument in the stimulus. That makes this a Parallel Reasoning question.

Step 2: Untangle the Stimulus
The author concludes there is no life on planet P23. The evidence is that water on the surface is required for life, and planet P23 has no water on the surface.

Step 3: Make a Prediction
The structure here uses some very fundamental Formal Logic. In order for an event to occur (life), there's a requirement (water). That requirement isn't met, so the event won't happen. Essentially, it's an argument based on employing the contrapositive:

If	life	→	water

If	~ water	→	~ life

The correct answer will use the exact same logical structure.

Step 4: Evaluate the Answer Choices

(C) is a match, employing the contrapositive exactly like the original argument. For an event to occur (increase drilling), there's a requirement (new equipment). That requirement is not met, so the author concludes the event won't happen.

If	*increasing drilling*	→	*new equipment*

If	*~ new equipment*	→	*~ increasing drilling*

(A) presents too many variables. It starts with a requirement for success (efficiency). However, the author suggests that certain employees *probably* have that requirement and then illogically concludes that such employees are needed. In addition to being illogical, this does not match the original structure of *not* meeting a requirement.

(B) is too wishy-washy with what "might be" true or is "not necessarily" true. The original argument was far more absolute. Furthermore, there is no requirement that goes unmet here.

(D) uses Formal Logic, but makes a crucial error. In this case, there is a requirement (real estate prices increase) for an event to occur (improve economy). However, this argument says the requirement *is* met, and concludes the event *is* happening. Not only is that improper Formal Logic (treating a necessary condition as if it were sufficient), but it doesn't match the original logic, which involves the requirement *not* being met.

(E) properly uses Formal Logic, but not in the same way as the original argument. Here, when one event happens (exports decrease), a result occurs (trade deficit increases). The event *does* happen, so the author concludes the result *does* occur. The logic works, but it does not employ the contrapositive based on a requirement *not* being met.

15. (C) Point at Issue

Step 1: Identify the Question Type

There are two speakers, and the question asks for something about which the speakers *disagree*. That makes this a Point at Issue question.

Step 2: Untangle the Stimulus

Sanchez argues that the school did not spend too much money on new computers because the computers were actually cheaper than assumed. Merriweather isn't concerned that the school got a good deal. The problem is that the computers were too elaborate.

Step 3: Make a Prediction

Merriweather is not disputing the fact that the computers were fairly priced. Merriweather is disputing the claim about overspending, suggesting the school *did* pay too much—not because the computers were overly expensive, but because they were unnecessarily elaborate. The correct answer will address the debate over whether the school spent more than it needed.

Step 4: Evaluate the Answer Choices

(C) describes the Point at Issue. Sanchez claims the school did *not* spend more than it should. Merriweather implies that it *did*.

(A) is a Distortion. Merriweather does not dispute the need for new computers. Merriweather merely has an issue with the particular computers purchased.

(B) is a Distortion. Merriweather is not disputing the *number* of computers purchased. Merriweather is disputing the *type* of computers purchased.

(D) is a 180. Sanchez implies that the price for that particular computer was not too high, and Merriweather *agrees*, suggesting that's not the issue. It's not about whether the school got a good deal on that particular computer model, it's about the computers purchased being unnecessarily elaborate.

(E) is Extreme and Out of Scope, as Sanchez never suggests the school was *harshly* criticized. Also, Merriweather does not address how other people reacted to the purchase.

16. (B) Flaw

Step 1: Identify the Question Type

The question directly asks for the flaw in the argument.

Step 2: Untangle the Stimulus

The argument starts with two sets of statistics. The administrator claims that only 1 in 2,000,000 flights veer off course when landing. Opponents suggest the situation is worse, claiming 1 in 20,000 flights veer off course. The administrator concludes (*so*) that the opponents' statistics are less reliable. The evidence is that the opponents' statistics are based on a partial review of air traffic control tapes while the administrator's statistics are based on a complete review of pilot reports.

Step 3: Make a Prediction

The administrator has a point about the opponents using partial data. However, the administrator overlooks a potentially more significant difference: the source of the statistics. The opponents reviewed air traffic control tapes. The administrator reviewed reports from pilots. The administrator assumes that pilot reports are just as reliable, if not more reliable, than air traffic control tapes. The correct answer will describe why this might not be valid.

Step 4: Evaluate the Answer Choices

(B) describes the flaw. The administrator assumes the pilot reports are more reliable. However, when a plane veers off course, that's often a pilot error. If pilots are reluctant to report those mistakes, that brings the administrator's entire argument into question.

(A) is Out of Scope. The argument is about the reliability of the statistics, not what would happen if the runways are built closer together.

(C) is not supported. The administrator makes no attack on the opponents' motives or integrity.

(D) is a Distortion. The administrator does not suggest the air traffic control tapes are inaccurate. The administrator merely suggests that the opponents did not see everything. Perhaps the opponents only saw an unrepresentative sample of tapes.

(E) is Extreme. The airport administrator never suggests the opponents' statistics *must* be inaccurate. Besides, the administrator doesn't question the accuracy. The administrator merely implies that the statistics are based on an incomplete review. The results are accurate, but don't represent the whole picture.

17. (E) Assumption (Necessary)

Step 1: Identify the Question Type

The question directly asks for an assumption, and one on which the argument *depends*. That makes this a Necessary Assumption question.

Step 2: Untangle the Stimulus

The author concludes ([*s*]*o*) that, when lakes are partially iced over, anglers are better off looking for trout in shallower water. The evidence is that trout generally swim in colder water. In the summer, water is colder at the bottom, and in the winter, water is colder at the top. "Turnover" occurs in the fall, bringing colder water to the surface. Then, "turnover" occurs again in late winter, bringing colder water back to the bottom.

Step 3: Make a Prediction

The colder water (which trout prefer) is near the surface during the winter, after the water turns in the fall and before it turns back in the late winter. The author's argument, however, is based on when the lake is "partially iced over." The author must assume that the ice indicates that the water is still colder near the surface, and thus the water hasn't had its end-of-winter "turnover" yet.

Step 4: Evaluate the Answer Choices

(E) must be assumed. After all, if the late-winter "turnover" *had* occurred, then the water would be colder on the bottom despite the appearance of ice on the surface. In that case, the

author has no reason to recommend shallow waters. The author must assume the "turnover" has not occurred yet.

(A) is Out of Scope. The author is never suggesting or assuming that catching trout is any *easier* at any given time of the year. The only difference is where they're likely to be found.

(B) is Out of Scope. The argument is about finding trout, and there's no indication that density plays any role in determining where the trout are.

(C) is Extreme. The author's argument is about where to find trout in deep temperate lakes, but there's no suggestion that lake trout couldn't be found in other lakes.

(D) is Out of Scope. The argument is based solely on *where* the trout are found, not *how* they feed.

18. (D) Point at Issue (Agree)

Step 1: Identify the Question Type

This is a Point at Issue question, as it asks for something supported by the argument between two speakers. However, unlike most Point at Issue questions, this asks for something with which the authors *agree*, as opposed to the usual point of disagreement.

Step 2: Untangle the Stimulus

Liang argues that children should not watch violent movies because such movies make viewers more aggressive. Sarah counters that violent movies are okay for mature audiences because such movies help people purge their aggressive emotions.

Step 3: Make a Prediction

If this were a standard Point at Issue question, the disagreement would be clear: Liang wants to restrict access to violent movies while Sarah is okay with them (even if they are referring to different audiences). Their arguments are so contrasting that it's hard to find a point of agreement. If there's anything to predict here, it's that they both agree that violent movies can have *some* effect on people, even if they don't quite agree on what that effect is. Just anticipate that the correct answer will likely be vague, as Liang and Sarah tend to disagree on a lot of the specific details.

Step 4: Evaluate the Answer Choices

(D) is a point of agreement. Liang believes violent movies have some effect (they make people more aggressive), and so does Sarah (they help people purge emotions). They may disagree on the actual effect, but they do agree there is *some* understanding of how viewers are affected.

(A) is a 180. Sarah directly claims that movies allow viewers to purge their aggression, while Liang argues that movies make people *more* aggressive. This would be a great answer to a more standard Point at Issue question, which is why it's important to read question stems carefully.

(B) is Out of Scope. Liang doesn't address mature audiences, and Sarah never discusses what mature audiences believe is acceptable.

(C) is unsupported. Liang clearly agrees with this. However, Sarah doesn't believe that violent movies cause violence in viewers. Because of that, there's no way to know how Sarah would react if she *did* believe that were true.

(E) is an Irrelevant Comparison. Neither author makes a direct comparison between children and adults, let alone who is more attracted to violent movies.

19. (A) Weaken

Step 1: Identify the Question Type
The question asks for something that "casts the most doubt" on the given argument. That makes this a Weaken question.

Step 2: Untangle the Stimulus
The politician leads right off with the conclusion: Thompson is the best candidate to lead the nation. The evidence is that Thompson is the only candidate who opposes higher taxes, a sign that most people would agree points to good leadership.

Step 3: Make a Prediction
The entire argument rests on Thompson's opposition to higher taxes—as if opposing higher taxes was the *only* significant factor in determining who's the best leader. Quite simply, this argument could be weakened by showing that opposition to higher taxes is insignificant.

Step 4: Evaluate the Answer Choices
(A) makes a direct attack. If opposing higher taxes is not a factor, then the politician's entire argument in favor of Thompson is shot.

(B) may be quite tempting, as it seems to sever the link between opposing higher taxes and being a good leader. However, this merely claims that opposing higher taxes is not *sufficient*, i.e., it's not enough by itself to guarantee good leadership. However, the politician isn't suggesting that it's enough by itself. The politician is implying that it's important or even necessary. Even if it's not sufficient, the politician could still have a point by saying it's necessary, and Thompson is the only candidate to meet that requirement.

(C) is Out of Scope. It's possible that the other candidates have equally questionable opinions on other issues. In addition, the politician could still claim that taxes are more significant than those issues. Without more information, this does not affect the politician's argument.

(D) is Out of Scope. Even if people who supported higher taxes were adequate leaders (not exactly a ringing endorsement), Thompson could still be better.

(E) is also Out of Scope. The politician is not making any claims or suggestions about people's work ethic. The argument is solely about what makes a good leader.

20. (A) Method of Argument

Step 1: Identify the Question Type
The phrase "by doing which of the following" indicates that the question is asking for *how* Garza responds as opposed to *what* Garza says. That makes this a Method of Argument question.

Step 2: Untangle the Stimulus
Patterson argues that music most likely arose during the Upper Paleolithic period because that's the source of the earliest known evidence of music: bone flutes. Garza points out that bone just happens to survive better in archaeological environments than other materials.

Step 3: Make a Prediction
Garza never comes out and claims Patterson is wrong. However, Garza implies that the evidence of bone flutes is perhaps not as conclusive as Patterson believes. There may have been earlier instruments that just didn't survive. The correct answer will describe Garza's questioning of Patterson's argument by suggesting that the evidence is inconclusive.

Step 4: Evaluate the Answer Choices
(A) describes Garza's method. Garza argues that Patterson's evidence about bone flutes may not be enough to fully support Patterson's claim about when music arose.

(B) is inaccurate. Garza does not attack the premise (i.e., evidence) behind Patterson's argument. The bone flutes *are* the earliest evidence we have of music. Garza merely raises the point that there may be other evidence we don't know about because it didn't survive.

(C) is a Distortion. Garza does not present any evidence that directly counters Patterson's claim. Garza merely suggests that Patterson's claim *may* not be fully supported.

(D) is not accurate. Garza does not draw any analogy. If anything, the comparison Garza draws between bone and other materials suggests they are *not* analogous.

(E) is not accurate. Garza provides distinct evidence and never actually draws a conclusion in contrast to Patterson. Everything in Garza's argument merely *implies* that Patterson may have overlooked something.

21. (B) Principle (Apply/Inference)

Step 1: Identify the Question Type
The correct answer will be a specific argument that is justified by a principle given in the stimulus. That makes this an Apply the Principle question.

Step 2: Untangle the Stimulus
The principle given consists of a single piece of Formal Logic: No job should require a license unless people are at risk if the job goes wrong.

Step 3: Make a Prediction

The key to this question is to translate the Formal Logic properly. In order to require a license, there must be a risk to others. By contrapositive, if there is no risk, then there's no need to require a license.

If	**require license**	→	**risk**

If	**~ risk**	→	**~ license required**

Note that the risk to others is a *necessary* condition. There *needs* to be a risk to require a license. That does not mean that a risk to others is *sufficient*. In other words, even if people are at risk, the principle does not state that a license must be required. Expect this to be a trap in at least one answer. The correct answer must conform to the proper Formal Logic. Also note that the risk must come from tasks *normally* carried out in the job.

Step 4: Evaluate the Answer Choices

(B) conforms to the logic. In this case, there is no realistic risk if an interior designer makes a mistake, so no license need be required.

(A) is a Distortion. It only claims that *some* duties carry no risk. However, those might be uncommon duties. It's still possible (and probable) that most other duties *do* carry risks if done improperly, and thus a license *could* be required.

(C) gets the logic backward. To require a license, there *must* be risk to others. However, that doesn't mean any job that carries a risk *must* require a license.

(D) also gets the logic backward. To require a license, there *must* be risk to others. However, that doesn't mean any job that carries a risk *must* require a license.

(E), just like **(C)** and **(D)**, gets the logic backward. To require a license, there *must* be risk to others. However, that doesn't mean any job that carries a risk *must* require a license.

22. (D) Inference

Step 1: Identify the Question Type

The question asks for something that "must be true" based on the given information. That makes this an Inference question.

Step 2: Untangle the Stimulus

The author presents three statistics: 1) most cars sold last year by Regis Motors were sold to Blomenville residents, 2) Regis Motors sold more cars last year than in any year before that, and 3) most cars sold last year to Blomenville residents were not from Regis Motors.

Step 3: Make a Prediction

Start with that middle statistic: last year, Regis Motors had a record-setting year. How many more cars did Regis Motors sell than in previous years? Where were those cars sold in previous years? Nobody knows the answer to these questions. There are no deductions to glean from this statistic, so it's unlikely to have anything to do with the correct answer.

The surrounding sentences, on the other hand, both refer to sales in Blomenville. Last year, cars from Regis made up less than half the sales to Blomenville residents. That means the total number of cars sold in Blomenville was more than twice as much as cars sold there by Regis alone. In addition, the number of cars Regis sold in Blomenville comprises most (more than 50%) of Regis's total sales. Putting those figures together, the total number of cars sold in Blomenville was over twice as much as most of Regis's overall sales. In other words, the total number of cars sold in Blomenville was more than 100% of Regis's overall sale. More cars were sold overall in Blomenville than Regis's entire output for the year.

If the math is too complex, picking some simple numbers can help clear it up. For example, say Regis sold 1,000 cars overall. Then at least 501 of them were sold in Blomenville. However, that's less than half the sales in Blomenville. So at least 1,003 cars were sold in Blomenville—more than all the cars sold by Regis. This is a question worth skipping if the numbers are too much to manage. Otherwise, test the answers one at a time, and eliminate ones that are clearly unsupported.

Step 4: Evaluate the Answer Choices

(D) must be true. The total sales in Blomenville were at least double the sales by Regis in Blomenville, and sales in Blomenville made up most (>50%) of Regis's overall sales. That means total sales in Blomenville were more than 100% of Regis's overall sales.

(A) is not supported. The only comparison from last year to previous years is the total number of cars sold by Regis overall. There's no way to know where those cars were sold in the past. It's possible that Regis expanded into other areas last year and increased its total sales by selling to other regions, while not making any change to its sales in Blomenville.

(B) is not supported. There is no information provided to compare sales in Blomenville from one year to the next. The only information provided about multiple years refers solely to Regis's overall sales.

(C) may be tempting, but is not supported. While most cars in Blomenville were sold to other companies, there does not have to be one particular retailer that surpassed Regis. It's possible that Regis sold just 100 cars there and 500 cars were sold by 10 other retailers who sold just 50 cars each. In that case, Regis is still the winner by a long shot.

(E) is not supported. The only mention of previous years refers exclusively to Regis's overall sales. It's possible that Regis was the only retailer in Blomenville until last year when new companies came in and cut into Regis's share.

23. (E) Strengthen

Step 1: Identify the Question Type

The question asks for something that "provides the most support" for the given argument. That means it will strengthen that argument.

Step 2: Untangle the Stimulus

The editorial's author concludes that starting school after 8:00 A.M. can reduce the number of accidents involving teenagers driving to school. There are two pieces of evidence for this. The first is scientific: Students are sleepy if they wake up before 8:00 A.M. because their body is still producing melatonin. The second is anecdotal: The number of accidents in Granville decreased after the school changed its start time to 8:30 A.M.

Step 3: Make a Prediction

The scientific evidence is pretty strong. The anecdotal evidence, on the other hand, contains a commonly tested flaw on the LSAT: causation versus correlation. The accident rate decreased during the same period that the school time was changed. However, the author implies that the later starting time of school was the *cause* of fewer accidents. This ignores other possible causes for the decrease in accidents. To combat this and thus strengthen the argument, the correct answer should reject alternate causes and/or provide more support for the link between later school starts and fewer accidents.

Step 4: Evaluate the Answer Choices

(E) strengthens the author's argument. If car accidents increased outside of Granville, that eliminates the possibility that Granville's rate was part of some regional trend. That doesn't *prove* that later start times were the cause, but it does eliminate other possible causes, thus making it more likely that the later start time was a factor.

(A) is an Irrelevant Comparison. The argument is only about teenagers, so it doesn't matter when younger children produce melatonin ... unless *they* start driving to school—but that's another issue altogether.

(B) is Out of Scope. This may provide another reason why moving up the start time is a good idea, but tardiness has nothing to do with preventing car accidents.

(C) is an Irrelevant Comparison. The argument is only about preventing accidents as teenagers drive to school. Teenagers who work during the day have no bearing on the argument.

Further, this talks about the amount of time one drives, which does not necessarily impact accident rates.

(D) is an Irrelevant Comparison. It doesn't matter what time of the day is more prone to accidents. The argument is merely focused on reducing accidents in the morning, and this offers no support that that will happen.

24. (E) Parallel Flaw

Step 1: Identify the Question Type

The correct answer will be an argument "most similar to" the one in the stimulus, and that reasoning is described as *flawed*. That makes this a Parallel Flaw question.

Step 2: Untangle the Stimulus

The author concludes that Lucinda will probably live in Western Hall. The evidence is that she's an engineering major, and most residents of Western Hall are engineering majors.

Step 3: Make a Prediction

The author misuses the logic of the term *most*. Just because most students in Western Hall are engineering majors doesn't mean most engineering majors are in Western Hall. It's possible that there are very few students in Western Hall to begin with and there a lot more engineering majors in other buildings, too. The correct answer will make the same misuse of the word *most*. The author will claim that most members of a group (Western Hall residents) possess a certain quality (engineering major) and then try to suggest that someone or something with that quality is likely to be part of that group.

Step 4: Evaluate the Answer Choices

(E) matches the logic and commits the same flaw. The author claims that most members of a group (hubs) possess a certain quality (mall) and then tries to suggest that a city with that quality is likely to become part of that group. Like the original author, this author fails to consider that there are very few hubs and there are probably a lot more malls in cities that aren't hubs.

(A) does not match and is actually more logical. Here, the author does claim that most members of a group (cities with a mall) possess a certain quality (hub). However, the author's city is now becoming part of that group, and the author reasonably suggests that it may possess the quality that most cities with a mall have.

(B) is an entirely different argument and is also more logical than the stimulus. If cities that are hubs *generally* experience something, and the city in question hasn't yet experienced it, then it is likely it *probably* will experience it in the future. Perhaps there are factors why it won't, but provided it is comparable to other hubs, the prediction that it *likely* will holds.

(C) does not match. For starters, it claims that members of a group (hubs) *always* possess a quality (excellent transportation)—which is already stronger language than that used by the original argument. Furthermore, the evidence is about what people *believe*, and they believe the city does *not* possess the quality mentioned. This is just not the same as the original.

(D) mixes up the evidence and the conclusion. The original used evidence of what was true for most students to draw a conclusion about one in particular. This argument uses evidence of one city to draw a conclusion about most cities. The logic is certainly flawed, but not in the same manner as the original.

25. (C) Assumption (Necessary)

Step 1: Identify the Question Type
The question directly asks for an assumption, and one that the argument *requires*. That makes this a Necessary Assumption question.

Step 2: Untangle the Stimulus
The oceanographer wants to reduce the amount of carbon dioxide in the atmosphere. So, the oceanographer makes a recommendation, which serves as the conclusion of the argument: pump the carbon dioxide deep into the ocean where it will dissolve in the water. The premise of this plan is that it takes hundreds of years for deeper, cooler water to mix with the warmer water. So long, carbon dioxide!

Step 3: Make a Prediction
It sounds like a great plan, but there's one little problem. The evidence claims that the *water* will take centuries to mix. However, it's possible that the carbon dioxide is less sluggish and can make its way up from the depths long before the cooler water decides to mix things up. The oceanographer must assume that once the carbon dioxide dissolves in the deep water, it will *stay* in the cool water until that water mixes upwards in a few centuries.

Step 4: Evaluate the Answer Choices
(C) must be assumed, claiming that carbon dioxide will not escape and will stay down in the depths until the cooler water mixes upwards. After all, if it *could* escape before that time, then the plan wouldn't quite work as intended.

(A) is not necessary. Even if it didn't dissolve very thoroughly, it could still dissolve enough to be trapped in the depths for centuries. The argument works with or without this claim.

(B) is Out of Scope. This is about carbon dioxide coming from evaporating water near the surface. However, it doesn't matter if this evaporating water releases a lot of carbon dioxide or not. Either way, the oceanographer's plan could still get rid of enough carbon dioxide in the atmosphere to make up for any additional carbon dioxide created by evaporation of the warmer water near the surface.

(D) is Extreme. The water may be denser, but it doesn't have to be the *main* reason carbon dioxide gets trapped. The argument would work equally well if temperature was the main factor.

(E) is Extreme. The oceanographer is not saying carbon dioxide *must* be trapped for hundreds of years to reduce its levels in the atmosphere. It's a plan, but it's not necessarily the only plan.

Section II: Reading Comprehension

Passage 1: John Rawls's Theory of Justice

Q#	Question Type	Correct	Difficulty
1	Detail	A	★
2	Logic Function	D	★
3	Global	B	★★
4	Inference	A	★★★★
5	Inference	E	★★★
6	Logic Reasoning (Weaken)	C	★★★★

Passage 2: The Great Migration

Q#	Question Type	Correct	Difficulty
7	Global	E	★
8	Detail	A	★
9	Logic Function	D	★
10	Inference	A	★★
11	Logic Function	D	★
12	Inference	C	★
13	Logic Reasoning (Strengthen)	B	★★

Passage 3: Insider Trading

Q#	Question Type	Correct	Difficulty
14	Global	D	★
15	Inference	B	★
16	Inference	C	★★★
17	Inference	E	★★
18	Logic Reasoning (Method of Argument)	B	★★
19	Logic Function	D	★★★★

Passage 4: Brain Scans

Q#	Question Type	Correct	Difficulty
20	Global	B	★★
21	Detail	A	★
22	Inference	D	★★
23	Logic Function	E	★★★
24	Logic Function	A	★★★
25	Detail	E	★
26	Inference	C	★★★
27	Logic Reasoning (Parallel Reasoning)	B	★★★★

Passage 1: John Rawls's Theory of Justice

Step 1: Read the Passage Strategically
Sample Roadmap

line #	Keyword/phrase	¶ Margin notes
2	first needs; against	Utilitarian view:
3	dominant	maximize satisfaction
4	emphasized	Rawls: no reason to violate rights of few
6	At first; seems plausible	
8	but	
9	odd consequences; Suppose	
11	Incredibly	
13	accordingly; complains	
17	If; reject	Rawls: justice based on fairness
19	ingenious; asserts	
22	key	
23	:	
25	But	What's fair?
26	clever	Example: dividing cake
27	Suppose	
35	generalizes	General idea: ignorance → ensure nobody loses → just
44	thinks	Rawls: people want primary goods
49	Hence	Auth: some people still lose out
50	should	
51	Unfortunately	

Discussion

The passage seems to open mid-conversation, wasting no time with background information or filler. The author jumps right into the **Topic** (John Rawls's theory of justice), explaining how one needs context to understand it. The rest of the first paragraph provides that context: a description of utilitarianism, the dominant approach to justice that Rawls was reacting against. Utilitarianism is about doing what satisfies the greatest number of people, a concept that Rawls complains unfairly violates certain people's rights.

The second paragraph introduces Rawls's theory, presenting it as an alternative to utilitarianism. That makes it clearer that the **Scope** of the passage is how Rawls's theory counteracts utilitarianism and the **Purpose** is to describe how Rawls's theory works as an alternative. Instead of trying to satisfy as many people as possible, Rawls's idea (which the author refers to as *ingenious*) is that justice should be based on procedures agreed upon as fair.

In the third paragraph, the author raises a valid question: what constitutes fair? Rawls has an approach called the "veil of ignorance," which the author calls *clever*. The author presents an example involving a child dividing a cake, which merely serves to illustrate the general idea described in the fourth paragraph: people are self-serving, but they don't always know what they're going to get. Therefore, instead of risking a loss for the sake of getting the best outcome, they come up with a solution that ensures no complete loss because everybody gets something.

Rawls argues, in the last paragraph, that people will apply this theory to ensure they get "primary goods," such as rights, power, and money. Give everyone something, and nobody loses. Unfortunately, despite previous praise for Rawls's ideas, the author ultimately argues that Rawls's theory is flawed and will still lead to some people gaining at the expense of others. Thus, the **Main Idea** of the passage is that Rawls's veil of ignorance theory of justice offers a clever alternative to utilitarianism, but would still have a negative impact on some people.

1. (A) Detail

Step 2: Identify the Question Type
The question asks for something directly used and mentioned in the passage, making this a Detail question.

Step 3: Research the Relevant Text
Rawls's theory is explained generally in the fourth paragraph and illustrated with the cake scenario in the third paragraph.

Step 4: Make a Prediction
The theory is most clearly explained by the cake scenario described in the third paragraph. This scenario is referred to as a "thought experiment" in the fourth paragraph (line 36).

Step 5: Evaluate the Answer Choices
(A) is a direct match to the language of the passage.

(B) is a Distortion. Rawls rejects the theory of utilitarianism, but never uses any process of elimination to explain his own theory.

(C) mentions empirical studies, of which none are mentioned anywhere in the passage.

(D) is a Distortion. Rawls asserts that fairness can help people settle on a "principle of justice" (lines 21–22), but does not derive any deductions from such principles.

(E) mentions the meaning of words, which could only logically apply to Rawls's definition of "primary goods" in the last paragraph. However, that definition does not explain the theory itself.

2. (D) Logic Function

Step 2: Identify the Question Type
The question asks for the *purpose* of something mentioned in the passage, making this a Logic Function question.

Step 3: Research the Relevant Text
The question directly points to lines 6–8, but be sure to consider that line's context within the paragraph as a whole.

Step 4: Make a Prediction
The first paragraph focuses mostly on the theory of utilitarianism. While the author (and Rawls) ultimately complain about utilitarianism, the question being asked about (essentially, why not try to maximize satisfaction?) shows how, "[a]t first sight, utilitarianism seems plausible." In other words, it points to a reason why people would have accepted utilitarianism in the first place.

Step 5: Evaluate the Answer Choices
(D) matches the idea of showing something plausible about utilitarianism.

(A) is a 180. The question illustrates why utilitarianism *does* seem plausible at first. Problems with utilitarianism are not brought up until later in the paragraph.

(B) is a Distortion. Utilitarianism is never described as "internally contradictory." In addition, the question shows off why utilitarianism is *plausible*, not problematic.

(C) is Extreme. The question merely illustrates why utilitarianism is *plausible*, not why it "must be true."

(E) is a Distortion. The question being posed describes the basic tenet of utilitarianism. It does not offer any way of *supplementing* that theory.

3. (B) Global

Step 2: Identify the Question Type

The question asks for the primary purpose of the whole passage. Any question that asks about the passage in its entirety is a Global question.

Step 3: Research the Relevant Text

As with any Global question, the entire text is relevant. Instead of going back to the text, just consider the overall Purpose as predicted when reading the passage.

Step 4: Make a Prediction

While the author offers the occasional opinion, the bulk of the passage is focused on merely describing Rawls's theory as an alternative to the flawed theory of utilitarianism.

Step 5: Evaluate the Answer Choices

(B) is correct, focusing on Rawls's theory as a reaction toward the problematic theory of utilitarianism.

(A) is too narrow. Reasons for abandoning utilitarianism are raised in the first paragraph, but this ignores the focus of the rest of the passage, which is all about Rawls's theory.

(C) is problematic for a couple of reasons. First, no information is given about the "historical development" of Rawls's theory. Further, that theory is never described as *celebrated*.

(D) is a Distortion. While the author offers the occasional opinion on Rawls's theory, the bulk of the passage is not concerned with *debating* the pros and cons. Further, it's never suggested that the theory is *complex*.

(E) is a 180, at worst. The theory is never said to be *controversial*. Further, the author brings up reservations at the end of the passage, which hardly suggests that there's concrete truth to the theory.

4. (A) Inference

Step 2: Identify the Question Type

The question asks for something with which Rawls and the author are "mostly likely to agree," making this an Inference question.

Step 3: Research the Relevant Text

Both Rawls and the author provide opinions throughout the passage, so the entire text is relevant.

Step 4: Make a Prediction

The question is too open-ended to make a specific prediction. Stick to the big picture (the veil of ignorance theory is clever, albeit flawed), and test the answers one at a time.

Step 5: Evaluate the Answer Choices

(A) is supported. Both the author and Rawls reject utilitarianism, which is about fulfilling the majority's preferences (lines 4–5). The author-approved part of Rawls's theory allows for solutions made by "individuals motivated by self-interest" (lines 40–42).

(B) is a 180. Rawls's theory is based on people motivated by self-interest, not people who set aside that self-interest.

(C) is a 180. This is the redistributionist idea raised at the very end of the passage (lines 53–55). The author's use of the word [*u*]*nfortunately* (line 51) indicates disapproval of the concept, rather than agreement.

(D) is a Distortion. In the discussion of primary goods in the last paragraph, there is no mention of what "most people" believe or what anyone would consider to be "most valuable."

(E) is a 180. Maximizing the satisfaction of the majority is a tenet of utilitarianism, the theory that both Rawls and the author reject.

5. (E) Inference

Step 2: Identify the Question Type

The question asks for the author's stance toward Rawls's theory. The author never directly asserts a stance, but the stance can be deduced by analyzing the author's language, making this an Inference question.

Step 3: Research the Relevant Text

The author's reaction to Rawls is scattered throughout the passage, notably via the Keywords *ingenious* (line 19), *clever* (line 26), and [*u*]*nfortunately* (line 51).

Step 4: Make a Prediction

The words *ingenious* and *clever* indicate that the author appreciates Rawls's theory to some extent. However, the word [*u*]*nfortunately* suggests that the author is ultimately not convinced. The original problem (some people will lose out) still exists.

Step 5: Evaluate the Answer Choices

(E) matches the author's tone, both in the clear admiration for some ideas and in the ultimate disappointment in the theory's shortcoming.

(A) is a 180. The author clearly has opinions that belie any "scholarly neutrality."

(B) is Extreme. The author may see the ultimate result as unfortunate, but that hardly qualifies as *disdain*. Furthermore, if there's any disappointment, it has nothing to do with any pretensions.

(C) is a Distortion. The author never exactly questions the theory's cogency (i.e., its effectiveness). The author merely questions whether the theory is really the right solution to the problem of utilitarianism.

(D) is Extreme. The author is impressed with the ideas, but the unfortunate end effect suggests that the author isn't entirely enthusiastic.

6. (C) Logic Reasoning (Weaken)

Step 2: Identify the Question Type

The question asks for something that would "call into question" a claim in the passage. This is the same kind of language used for Weaken questions in the Logical Reasoning section.

Step 3: Research the Relevant Text

The question is directed at the claim in lines 49–51, but use the surrounding lines for context.

Step 4: Make a Prediction

This claim in question is all part of Rawls's theory. An "individual in the original position" refers back to the fourth paragraph, which describes people motivated by self-interest but ignorant of their standing. Self-interest will lead to solutions in which individuals "will not lose, because nobody loses" (line 42). That supports the claim in question, which suggests that individuals will act so that "everyone should get at least a minimum." To weaken that idea, the correct answer will show this won't always happen—sometimes people will act in a way that leads to somebody getting nothing.

Step 5: Evaluate the Answer Choices

(C) weakens the claim. If some people are willing to risk "a complete loss," then that means they're taking a chance that somebody will get nothing, as opposed to ensuring everyone gets a minimum.

(A) does not weaken the claim. Under Rawls's theory, people can still be motivated by self-interest and put their preferences over those of others—as long as everybody gets at least *something*.

(B) is irrelevant. While this may deny the potential for Rawls's theory to work in practice (as nobody could be in the "original position"), it does not affect the *theoretical* idea that such people would agree on giving everyone a bare minimum.

(D) is irrelevant. Rawls's theory is not about guaranteeing satisfaction. It's about doing what's fair and just.

(E) is irrelevant. The availability of resources has no effect on whether people would believe in the concept of giving everyone a minimum of primary goods.

Passage 2: The Great Migration

Step 1: Read the Passage Strategically
Sample Roadmap

line #	Keyword/phrase	¶ Margin notes
4	While	Great migration
8	three catalysts; First	3 catalysts
10	Second	
13	Finally	
16	because; only then	Cause: income gap
19	Less clear; however	Why continued?
23	propose	Auth: momentum made it easier
26	typically assumed	Migrate if earnings > difficulties
30	suggests	
31	First	3 difficulties
34	Second	
36	Third	
41	show	Studies:
45	Thus	How migrating made easier
51	Additionally	

Discussion

The opening note indicates this passage was written by three people. Thankfully, there is no need to juggle multiple points of view. The passage is written in one voice, and the note is merely for grammatical purposes (e.g., to explain the use of *we* in line 23 and to accurately refer to plural *authors* in the question stems).

The first paragraph introduces the **Topic**: The Great Migration of African Americans in the United States from the South to the North. The authors provide three causes of this event: 1) Employers in the North needed more workers. 2) With fewer immigrants coming in, those employers turned to the South more for laborers. 3) Work in the South was dwindling as crop problems arose.

The second paragraph neatly sums it up: the migration was caused by a significant income gap. People in the South needed jobs, and the North needed workers. *However*, the authors then raise a significant question: why did migration continue for decades even after the income gap decreased? This question serves as the **Scope** of the passage.

The authors provide an answer in the third paragraph. Once the migration started, it created momentum that made it easier for others to migrate. The rest of the passage simply presents detailed support for this idea. First, the third paragraph outlines three difficulties that would have hindered migration: 1) a lack of information about housing and employment opportunities available; 2) the cost, in terms of time and money, of moving; and 3) the need to adapt to a new environment.

The last paragraph provides data showing how the Great Migration overcame each of those difficulties: 1) People in the South learned about opportunities through letters and conversations with original migrants who came back to visit. 2) Later migrants saved on costs by basically hitching a ride with earlier migrants returning North after a visit to the South. 3) Early migrants helped newer migrants adjust to the new environment.

The **Purpose** of the passage was to describe factors involved in the Great Migration. The **Main Idea** is that the Great Migration was initially caused by an income gap, while other factors gave the migration momentum to continue for decades afterward.

7. (E) Global

Step 2: Identify the Question Type
The question asks for the "main point of the passage." As it asks about the passage in its entirety, this is a Global question.

Step 3: Research the Relevant Text
As with any Global question, the entire text is relevant. Instead of going back into the text, use the Main Idea predicted after reading the passage.

Step 4: Make a Prediction
The passage is focused entirely on what caused the Great Migration to start and what helped it continue. While income gap was the initial cause, the authors claim that other factors reduced the difficulty of migration, helping the Great Migration continue for decades afterward.

Step 5: Evaluate the Answer Choices
(E) is correct, providing a vague (although accurate) summary of the Great Migration's initial cause and why it continued for so long.

(A) is merely a detail from the first paragraph. This misses the passage's focus on *why* this event occurred.

(B) accurately cites some of the initial causes outlined in the first paragraph, but completely omits the last three paragraphs that focus on why the migration persisted after the initial trigger.

(C) is too narrow. This highlights one of the reasons listed in the last paragraph for the extended duration of the Great Migration. However, that's just one point among many. The main point of the passage and the main reason for the continued migration involves much more than just financial costs.

(D) is a Distortion. This takes details that apply to the Great Migration and applies them to migrations in general. The authors never suggest this is true of migrations in general, and that certainly wasn't the point of the passage.

8. (A) Detail

Step 2: Identify the Question Type
The phrase "[a]ccording to the passage" suggests the answer to the question will be mentioned directly in the text. That makes this a Detail question.

Step 3: Research the Relevant Text
The authors explain why the Great Migration did not start earlier than 1915 in lines 16–19 ("began in 1915 and not earlier").

Step 4: Make a Prediction
In lines 16–19, the authors directly explain why the Great Migration did not start before 1915: "it was only then that the North-South income gap became large enough to start such a large-scale migration."

Step 5: Evaluate the Answer Choices
(A) is an exact paraphrase of the authors' claim.

(B) is Extreme. There may have been a gap in income, but that's not to say the cost of living in the North was "prohibitively high." The authors never state or suggest that this was an issue.

(C) brings up the need for specialized training, a concept that is never mentioned in the passage.

(D) is a Distortion. While momentum made it easier for later migrants to move, the authors never claim that a *lack* of momentum was what prevented migration to start in the first place.

(E) is not mentioned in the passage. The boll weevil infestation led to reduced labor demand (lines 13–15), but there's no suggestion that agricultural jobs paid "very well" before that happened.

9. (D) Logic Function

Step 2: Identify the Question Type
The question asks how two paragraphs *function*, making this easy to identify as a Logic Function question.

Step 3: Research the Relevant Text
Instead of going back into the specific text, use margin notes and focus on how the third and fourth paragraphs relate to the earlier paragraphs and the passage as a whole.

Step 4: Make a Prediction
The third and fourth paragraph outline difficulties that hinder migration and how the Great Migration overcame those difficulties. This is all part of what the authors *propose* (line 23) as a response to the question of "why migration continued"—a concept raised in the second paragraph (lines 19–21).

Step 5: Evaluate the Answer Choices
(D) correctly describes how the last two paragraphs help answer the question posed in the second paragraph.

(A) is a Distortion. The explanation in the first paragraph outlines why the Great Migration started in the first place. The third and fourth paragraphs do nothing to change that. Instead, they provide an explanation why the Great Migration *continued* afterward.

(B) mentions repercussions of the Great Migration, which are never addressed. The passage is focused merely on why it happened, not what resulted from it.

(C) is a Distortion. The last two paragraphs do not present a historical model, nor do they utilize any evidence from the first two paragraphs.

(E) is a Distortion. The claims in the first paragraph are about the initial cause of the Great Migration. The claims in the third and fourth paragraphs are completely separate and explain why the migration continued afterward. There is no additional support for the initial cause.

10. (A) Inference

Step 2: Identify the Question Type
The correct answer will be something with which the authors are "most likely to agree." It will not be directly stated but will be fully supported by information in the passage, making this an Inference question.

Step 3: Research the Relevant Text
There are no line references or content clues, so the entire text is relevant.

Step 4: Make a Prediction
It's difficult to predict an answer here; there are too many possible inferences. Instead, eliminate answers that are clearly beyond the Scope of the passage, and use content clues in the answer choices to do any necessary research.

Step 5: Evaluate the Answer Choices
(A) is supported starting in lines 25–29 and continuing throughout the rest of the passage. The likelihood of migration is not determined by expected financial gains alone. One also needs to consider potential difficulties such as uncertain prospects, travel costs, the need for cultural adjustment, and more.

(B) is Extreme. The authors never mention what triggered "nineteenth-century migrations" (i.e., ones from the 1800s), so there is no suggestion that explaining the Great Migration *must* begin with such accounts.

(C) is not supported. The authors only focus on the Great Migration and never compare it to other migrations.

(D) is Extreme. The authors only focus on the Great Migration. There is no indication of what's true for *most* large-scale migrations, let alone any migration other than the one described.

(E) is not supported. In fact, the authors suggest there were migrations as early as the nineteenth century (lines 4–6). There's no indication whether these were or not, but there's also no suggestion that there weren't large-scale migrations elsewhere in the world at any other time before the twentieth century.

11. (D) Logic Function

Step 2: Identify the Question Type
The question asks for the *purpose* of one sentence, making this a Logic Function question.

Step 3: Research the Relevant Text
The question directly asks about the last sentence of the second paragraph (lines 19–22), but be sure to consider its context within the whole paragraph as well as within the passage as a whole.

Step 4: Make a Prediction

The sentence in question mentions how the Great Migration continued for decades after it started, even though the income gap got smaller. This raises the very question that is answered by what the authors *propose* in the third and fourth paragraphs. It is essentially the setup for everything the authors discuss in the rest of the passage.

Step 5: Evaluate the Answer Choices

(D) correctly identifies the sentence as what the authors explain throughout the remainder of the passage.

(A) is a Distortion. While earlier research may have left the claim in question unexplained, there is no suggestion that earlier research was *misguided*.

(B) is a Distortion. The initial causes of the Great Migration are not extended to any other event. Further, the continued migration is based on entirely new explanations described later in the passage.

(C) is a 180. The claim in question states the income differences were narrowing after 1915, which actually suggests that the income in the North *was* indeed higher beforehand.

(E) is Extreme and a 180. It is "[l]ess clear," but that doesn't mean it *cannot* be explained. In fact, the entire second half of the passage provides an explanation.

12. (C) Inference

Step 2: Identify the Question Type

The correct answer will be a statement supported by passage, making this an Inference question.

Step 3: Research the Relevant Text

There are no line references or content clues, so the entire text is relevant.

Step 4: Make a Prediction

The correct answer could be based on anything from the passage, so it's not possible to make a solid prediction. Eliminate answers that are clearly beyond the Scope of the passage, and use content clues in the answers to do any necessary research.

Step 5: Evaluate the Answer Choices

(C) is supported. The increased labor demand in the North and the decreased labor demand in the South are mentioned in lines 8–15 as catalysts for the Great Migration. The phrase "[i]n short" in the following paragraph suggests that all of the details from lines 8–15 led to a simplistic causal factor: the income gap.

(A) is a Distortion. There may have been an overall gap in income, but there's no way of comparing individual jobs within distinct industries.

(B) is not supported. There is no indication that earlier migrants had more jobs to choose from.

(D) is not supported. The 1910s and the 1920s were when labor demand decreased in the South (lines 13–15), but there's no suggestion that wages remained constant for all workers during that time. In fact, wages are never mentioned.

(E) is Extreme. The studies in the last paragraph definitely indicate migrants returning to the South and bringing back information, but there's no indication that *most* migrants did so.

13. (B) Logic Reasoning (Strengthen)

Step 2: Identify the Question Type

The question asks for something that "would provide the most support" for the authors' analysis, making this a Strengthen question like those found in Logical Reasoning.

Step 3: Research the Relevant Text

The authors' primary conclusion starts off the third paragraph and is supported by all of the subsequent details.

Step 4: Make a Prediction

The authors are primarily focused on why the migration persisted for so long. Their proposal is that momentum made it easier for people to migrate (lines 23–25). The evidence is that many of the difficulties described in paragraph 3 were addressed by the solutions listed in paragraph 4. To further support the authors' proposal, the correct answer will merely provide further evidence that migration was made easier and that difficulties were overcome.

Step 5: Evaluate the Answer Choices

(B) supports the authors' proposal. One of the difficulties migrants faced was having to "adapt to a new culture or language" (lines 39–40). This was addressed in the last line, as early migrants provided a "cultural cushion for later migrants, so that they did not have to struggle as hard." If these migrants moved into communities with people of common origins, that would certainly help provide a "cultural cushion" to reduce the shock of entering a whole new area.

(A) is a 180. This suggests it took longer to find jobs as time went on, which would make things harder, not easier.

(C) is a 180. Fluctuations would cause uncertainty, which would be harder to deal with than constant prices.

(D) is irrelevant. This puts more pressure on Northern employers, but does nothing to explain why people from the South were more likely to migrate. Even if there were more people recruiting in the South, that doesn't mean migrating was any easier.

(E) is irrelevant. What happened after the Great Migration does nothing to support why people moved up North in the first place.

Passage 3: Insider Trading

Step 1: Read the Passage Strategically
Sample Roadmap

line #	Keyword/phrase	¶ Margin notes
Passage A		
–	–	Insider trading law
6	However	Auth: shouldn't be a crime
8	?	
16	best	Market works best when all info available
21	helps	stock prices reflect info
26	helps	Selling stock provides more accurate info
27	help ensure	
29	good	
31–32	helps to consider	Nontrading also happens
34	but	not a problem
35	rightfully	
36	No one	
Passage B		
37	basic principles	Stock market transparent
41	only	success by analysis of info
50	unfairly compromises	insider trading based on unshared info
51	:	Auth: unfair
53	difficult or impossible	
55	causes	Consequences: investors lose confidence
56	could ultimately destroy	leads to widespread problems
58	whole point	
62	thus	
63–64	could ultimately lead to	

Discussion

Passage A immediately introduces the **Topic**: insider trading, which involves making stock transactions based on information that hasn't been made public. The first paragraph states that this a crime; *however*, the author suggests in the second paragraph that it shouldn't be. The author instead raises the idea that insider trading actually aligns perfectly with the model of a properly functioning stock market. This question of whether insider trading is criminal serves as the **Scope** of the passage.

The author then describes how the stock market functions in general, in a way that parallels insider trading. Stock brokers analyze data and gain information that others don't have. They then use this knowledge to buy and sell. Nothing criminal. It's just the way the system works. The next couple of paragraphs continue this theme by further describing an effective stock market, again as a thinly veiled comparison to insider trading. Stock markets work best when everyone has access to all relevant information, and that information is reflected in the stock prices. So, if someone knows the value of a stock will drop and acts on that information, that sends a signal to others who can then better assess the stock's value. Everyone wins!

In the final paragraph, the author provides one final point in favor of insider trading. There's a similar, more common practice called "insider nontrading." This also involves making decisions based on inside information, but it results in people *not* buying or selling—and yet nobody seems to have a problem with that. In the end, the **Purpose** of the passage is to argue in favor of insider trading. The **Main Idea** is that insider trading should not be a crime because it is beneficial and works exactly the way the stock market is supposed to.

Passage B also talks about the stock market (**Topic**). The first paragraph describes the significance of transparency: making sure everyone has access to the same information to make good investing decisions. This leads to the second paragraph, which begins a discussion of insider trading and why it's bad for the stock market (**Scope**). When people act on information that others don't have, they are getting an unfair advantage that makes it difficult for others to make money.

This leads to severe consequences described in the third paragraph. When it's difficult to make money, investors lose confidence in the market. They then stop investing, which means companies lose funding, which ultimately can lead to "widespread financial repercussions." By the end, it's clear the **Purpose** of passage B is to argue against insider trading, with the **Main Idea** that insider trading gives some people an unfair advantage that, over time, can lead to financial disaster.

Both passages focus on how insider trading affects the stock market. The author of passage A sees insider trading as a benefit, while the author of passage B sees it as a problem. Despite the clear discrepancy, a lot of their arguments are based on shared common principles (e.g., open access to information and analyzing that information is crucial to success in the stock market). However, there are a few notable differences. Only passage A brings up the legality of insider trading, and only passage B goes beyond insider trading to discuss investor confidence and financial impact on companies.

14. (D) Global

Step 2: Identify the Question Type
The question asks for the "primary concern" of both passages as a whole, making this a Global question.

Step 3: Research the Relevant Text
As with all Global questions, the entire text is relevant. Use the Purpose and Main Idea of each passage, as predicted while reading the passages.

Step 4: Make a Prediction
Both passages are focused on whether insider trading is good for the stock market or not. The correct answer will raise the question of its impact on the stock market.

Step 5: Evaluate the Answer Choices
(D) correctly raises a question about each passage's central purpose. Passage A argues that insider trading is not harmful, while passage B argues that it is.

(A) is too narrow. Both passages do define insider trading, but only at one point for the sake of clarity. Both passages spend far more time discussing the benefits and problems with insider trading.

(B) brings up penalties for insider trading, a concept not addressed by either author.

(C) is a Distortion. Both authors focus on the *effect* of insider trading, not on the motive for doing so in the first place.

(E) mentions regulating insider training, a concept that neither author addresses.

15. (B) Inference

Step 2: Identify the Question Type
The question asks about the authors' attitudes. Attitudes are not stated directly but can be deduced based on the tone of each passage. This is a common variant of an Inference question.

Step 3: Research the Relevant Text
Insider trading is discussed throughout both passages, so there is a lot of relevant text. Use the big picture and Keywords to get a sense of the attitudes.

Step 4: Make a Prediction

The Main Idea of passage A is that insider trading is actually beneficial, as evidenced by the line "good for everyone" (line 29). The Main Idea of passage B is that insider trading is a problem, as evidenced by the line "unfairly compromises the market" (lines 50–51). The correct answer will express, in order, passage A's positive stance and B's negative stance.

Step 5: Evaluate the Answer Choices

(B) correctly identifies passage A's author as positive and passage B's author as negative.

(A) correctly identifies the author of passage A as positive. However, the author of passage B claims insider trading is unfair, which is hardly a neutral assessment.

(C) suggests that the author of passage A is neutral, but that author ultimately suggests that the concept of insider training is "good for everyone"—a decisively non-neutral claim.

(D) suggests that both authors are neutral. However, the author of passage A suggests that insider trading is good, and the author of passage B says it's unfair. These are not neutral claims.

(E) suggests the author of passage A is negative, which is a 180 from that author's suggestion that insider trading is "good for everyone."

16. (C) Inference

Step 2: Identify the Question Type

The question asks for something with which both authors are "most likely to agree." The correct answer will not be stated, but will be directly supported by information in the passages, making this an Inference question.

Step 3: Research the Relevant Text

There are no line references or content clues, so all of the text is relevant.

Step 4: Make a Prediction

While vague Inference questions are often difficult, if not impossible, to predict, the relationship between these passages provides some helpful information. The authors are mostly in disagreement, making it a little easier to spot points of *agreement*. Sure enough, both authors base their arguments on two general principles. First, it's important that relevant information be openly available (lines 16–18 and lines 37–40). Second, success in the market depends on analyzing the information effectively (lines 8–15 and lines 40–42). The correct answer will likely match up with at least one of these principles.

Step 5: Evaluate the Answer Choices

(C) is consistent with both authors' arguments. The author of passage A claims that analyzing stock to take advantage is part of the job (lines 8–15), and the author of passage B

claims that success depends on using analysis to get an advantage (lines 40–42).

(A) is a major point of the last paragraph of passage B, but the author of passage A presents no opinion on how insider trading impacts investor confidence.

(B) is Extreme. The author of passage A says all *relevant* information (lines 16–17) should be available, and the author of passage B only mentions information "that influences trading decisions." Neither of those phrases are enough to suggest that *all* information should be available—only information relevant to the stock market.

(D) brings up insider nontrading, which only passage A mentions. The author of passage B presents no opinion on that concept.

(E) is Extreme and likely a 180. While the author of passage A is in favor of insider trading, there is no suggestion that it offers the *best* means for spreading information. Besides, the author of passage B finds insider trading to be unfair and would certainly disagree with this claim.

17. (E) Inference

Step 2: Identify the Question Type

The question asks for a law that would conform to an author's position. That can sound very much like a Principle question in Logical Reasoning. However, passage A brings up insider trading laws, so the correct answer will not be any more general than the information provided. It will merely be supported by the information provided in the passage, making this an Inference question. Regardless of what you call it, there will be direct logical support for the correct answer.

Step 3: Research the Relevant Text

The question asks about something that conforms to a general position, which is part of the big picture. There is no specific line or paragraph to research. The entire text is relevant.

Step 4: Make a Prediction

The author of passage A is firmly in favor of insider trading, while the author of passage B is firmly against it. The correct answer will be a law that makes it acceptable to make transactions based on inside information, thus conforming to passage A and *not* passage B.

Step 5: Evaluate the Answer Choices

(E) is consistent with the position stated in passage A. As long as the information is legitimately acquired, the author of passage A finds insider trading perfectly acceptable.

(A) is a 180. The author of passage A approves of insider trading as it would "help ensure that stock prices do reflect a more accurate assessment of all the relevant facts" (lines 27–29).

(B) is a 180. The author of passage A accepts trading based on all relevant information, regardless of whether it's publicly known or learned from the inside.

(C) is a 180. The author of passage A has no opinion on the effect on investor confidence. Furthermore, this is the kind of law the author of passage B would endorse, which is the opposite of what's being asked.

(D) is not supported. The author of passage A is fine with insider trading regardless of the transaction type. There is no suggestion that selling is okay but not buying.

18. (B) Logic Reasoning (Method of Argument)

Step 2: Identify the Question Type
The word *by* indicates that the question is asking *how* the author of passage A argues, as opposed to *what* the argument says. That's the sign of a Method of Argument question like the ones found in Logical Reasoning.

Step 3: Research the Relevant Text
Methods are not derived from any one line or paragraph in particular, so the entire text is relevant here. Focus on the big picture and the overall structure of the passage.

Step 4: Make a Prediction
The correct answer has to include something the author of passage A does but not something the author of passage B does. While passage B discusses insider trading and its potential effects, passage A makes comparisons of insider trading to permissible activities. The bulk of the passage describes the stock market in general and why it's important to have information spread widely and quickly. The passage concludes with a discussion of a "widespread practice." Because insider nontrading is permissible, the author of passage A feels insider trading should be as well. The correct answer will point out this analogical approach.

Step 5: Evaluate the Answer Choices
(B) is correct, as it describes the method used by passage A, comparing a controversial activity (insider trading) with more acceptable ones (general stock market activities and insider nontrading). In lines 14–15, the author of passage A says that researching and taking advantage of knowledge that others might not means "you've done your homework." In line 36, the author of passage A emphasizes that "[n]o one" would think to criminalize insider nontrading.

(A) mentions application of principles to "particular examples." Neither author offers any specific examples of insider trading.

(C) is a 180. Passage B describes consequences in the final paragraph, so this is *not* a method that is unlike the one used in passage B.

(D) is a 180. This is not unlike passage B. Passage B directly relates the effect of insider trading to a large context in the last paragraph.

(E) brings up the motivation behind insider trading, a concept that is never addressed in either passage.

19. (D) Logic Function

Step 2: Identify the Question Type
The question asks how two references relate to one another. It's difficult to characterize this question by the stem alone. However, a glance at the answers reveals that each answer lists the purpose each reference serves within the passages, making this a Logic Function question.

Step 3: Research the Relevant Text
The question stem provides line references, but be sure to consider how those lines fit within the context of the paragraphs in which they appear as well as the passages as a whole.

Step 4: Make a Prediction
The author of passage A discusses analysis of stock information in the second paragraph, which is meant to show how insider trading is actually consistent with such analysis, and is thus not really a criminal act. The author of passage B discusses analysis as part of a transparent market, which is undermined by insider trading as described in the second paragraph. In essence, both authors bring up analysis to support conflicting opinions about insider trading. The correct answer will be consistent with that dichotomy.

Step 5: Evaluate the Answer Choices
(D) matches the opposing purposes of each reference.

(A) accurately fits the tone of passage B. However, passage A points to analysis as part of how a stock market is supposed to work. It's definitely not *unnecessary*.

(B) is a Distortion. The author of passage A never suggests that there's a "lack of transparency" in the stock market.

(C) is a Distortion on both parts. The author of passage A never suggests that anything is unfair—only the author of passage B does that. And passage B suggests that transparency makes analysis possible, not the other way around.

(E) is Extreme. The author of passage A never suggests that stock analysis is limited solely to brokers and stock-market professionals.

Passage 4: Brain Scans

Step 1: Read the Passage Strategically
Sample Roadmap

line #	Keyword/phrase	¶ Margin notes
1	problems	Brain scans: OK for medical
4	for example	problem w/ psych
6	value	Assumption: brain is modular
7	indubitable; However	
8	fundamentally	
9	different	
10	depends on a premise	
15	may in fact	Uttal: brain activity general, not modular
18	contends; rather than	
19	likely	
21	cannot be said	
22	for instance	
28	But; if; critique	Why do brain scans "light up"?
29	valid	fMRI -- measures oxygen levels
30	in fact	subtractive method
31	?	
37	But; actually	
38	:	
43	seemingly plausible	
47	immediately obvious	Problem w/ subtractive method --
48	problem; obscures	whole brain active
50	false impression	
53	striking	
54	But; ultimately	
55	attractive; because	
56	?	

Discussion

The opening sentence introduces the **Topic** (brain scans) and the **Scope** (problems with their use for measuring mental activity). The author accepts brain scans for medical uses (e.g., discovering a brain tumor). *However*, the author is less convinced about psychological applications. The author claims that psychological use of brain scans rests on the assumption that the brain is made up of independent modules.

This modular theory is disputed in the second paragraph by psychologist William Uttal. According to Uttal, mental processes are not entirely independent and are part of general brain activity. This is illustrated by the example of emotion and reasoning. The author argues that these mental processes can't necessarily be separated, as some would suggest otherwise.

In the third paragraph, the author brings up a paradox. If mental activities are not modular, why do certain areas of the brain "light up" when people perform certain tasks? As an example, the author describes an fMRI. An fMRI is meant to show how much oxygen is used in different areas of the brain at any given time. *But* the author suggests that that's not quite accurate. It actually shows a *difference*. It starts with an initial measurement of oxygen usage. When a task is being performed, the fMRI subtracts that initial value. Anything above normal is said to apply solely to the given task.

In the last paragraph, the author cites the problem with this method: it gives a false impression. Some parts of the brain might be working more, but the whole brain is still working. The subtractive method (as the author calls it) only shows what's working in excess. It fails to show the rest of the brain that may also be working on the task. So, the **Purpose** of the passage is to provide evidence against using brain scans for psychological purposes. The **Main Idea** is that brain scans are not good for psychological purposes because the brain is not necessarily modular, as assumed, and the results don't necessarily provide an accurate picture of what's really happening throughout the entire brain.

20. (B) Global

Step 2: Identify the Question Type
The question asks for the "main point of the passage" as a whole, making this a Global question.

Step 3: Research the Relevant Text
As with all Global questions, the entire text is relevant. Focus on the big picture and use the Main Idea as predicted when reading the passage.

Step 4: Make a Prediction
Ultimately, the author is arguing that brain scans are not good for psychological purposes. Using them relies on a bad

assumption (the brain is modular) and the results don't show everything that's happening in the brain.

Step 5: Evaluate the Answer Choices
(B) matches the author's concerns about using brain scans for psychological purposes (to depict mental activity).

(A) is a Distortion. The author mentions "widespread use of brain scans" (line 2), but never says anything about their usage growing *rapidly*. Besides, this puts too much emphasis on their increased usage and makes the true focus of the passage (the problems) a mere side note.

(C) is a Distortion and far too specific. This merely takes one detail from the second paragraph (lines 21–24) and twists the meaning. Even if this were accurate, it hardly expresses the point of the passage as a whole. It completely ignores everything else in the surrounding paragraphs.

(D) is Extreme and too narrow. This focuses too much on the fMRI problem and ignores the entire first two paragraphs about the modular theory. Besides, the author says the results of fMRI provide a "false impression." That doesn't mean the results are *false*. The results are accurate; they just don't provide a complete picture.

(E) is too narrow, concentrating on the rhetorical question at the end. Sure, the author suggests that the subtractive method makes the modular theory look attractive. However, the author never suggests that's the *precise* reason for its widespread currency. Besides, this completely ignores the rest of the passage that focuses on the problem with the modular theory and the subtractive method.

21. (A) Detail

Step 2: Identify the Question Type
The question asks for a fact about mental activity as it was "described in the passage." That makes this a Detail question.

Step 3: Research the Relevant Text
The correct answer will be based directly on what was stated about the modular theory, which is described in the first paragraph.

Step 4: Make a Prediction
The term "modular theory" is mentioned in line 14 and refers to the premise outlined in lines 10–13. It states that "the mind [and thus mental activity] can be analyzed into separate and distinct modules" that are "instantiated in localized regions of the brain."

Step 5: Evaluate the Answer Choices
(A) matches the text precisely.

(B) is a Distortion, if not a 180. Metabolic activity is mentioned in the third paragraph, separate from any discussion of the modular theory. Further, the modular theory suggests that any given mental activity is limited to a single distinct region of the brain. It would not suggest activity is required "in *all* parts of the brain."

(C) is unsupported. It is said that mental activity consists of physical processes (lines 15–16), but there is no indication that people have "limited control" over them.

(D) is a Faulty Use of Detail. There are certain mental activities (emotion and reasoning) that are said to be localized to these areas (lines 22–23), but that doesn't mean all mental activity in general is localized in those areas.

(E) is a 180. Reason-giving is just one mental process that is said to be localized in the prefrontal cortex (line 23). However, the modular theory considers that separate from other mental processes. So other mental activity would be *distinct* from reason-giving.

22. (D) Inference

Step 2: Identify the Question Type
The question asks for something with which the author is "most likely to agree." Therefore, the correct answer won't be stated directly, but it will be a valid inference based on the passage.

Step 3: Research the Relevant Text
The question asks about the subtractive method, which the author describes in the third paragraph and evaluates in the fourth paragraph.

Step 4: Make a Prediction
Because the question is asking about the author's opinion, the correct answer is more likely to come from the opinions presented in the fourth paragraph rather than the factual description in the third. The author argues that the subtractive method *obscures* (line 48) certain facts and provides a "false impression" (line 50). The author clearly has a problem with the method, but does suggest that the "striking images" created by it are what make it seem attractive (lines 52–56). The correct answer will be consistent with these opinions.

Step 5: Evaluate the Answer Choices
(D) is supported. While the author clearly sees the problem with the subtractive method, it does provide images that make the modular theory *attractive* (line 55).

(A) is perfect…until the last two words. The author's argument is that the results are problematic for *psychological* applications, not medical applications. The author fully accepts using brain scans for medical purposes (lines 3–7).

(B) is a 180. The subtractive method actually "obscures the fact that the entire brain is active" (lines 48–49).

(C) is not supported and likely a 180. It's actually likely that the images *do* show a lot of activity in the amygdala when someone experiences anger. However, the author's point is

that the *rest* of the brain is *also* active, even if that doesn't show up when the subtractive method is used.

(E) is a 180. The subtractive method *does* depict differential rates of oxygen use (lines 37–38). Any misconception is based on how people *interpret* that data, not on recognizing how that information is measured.

23. (E) Logic Function

Step 2: Identify the Question Type
The question asks for the "central function" of a paragraph, making this a Logic Function question.

Step 3: Research the Relevant Text
Be sure to consult the margin notes for the final paragraph, and consider how it relates to all of the preceding paragraphs.

Step 4: Make a Prediction
Start by considering the author's main purpose: the author is rejecting the modular theory. That rejection happens in the second paragraph. The modular theory is supposedly backed up by the subtractive method, as described in the third paragraph. However, the purpose of the final paragraph (which this question is asking about) is to dispute the method described in the third paragraph, thus reinforcing the author's argument in the second paragraph.

Step 5: Evaluate the Answer Choices
(E) accurately matches the author's intention. The final paragraph disputes the evidence in the third paragraph (about the subtractive method) to further the author's case that the modular theory is flawed—the point raised in the second paragraph.

(A) begins well, stating that the last paragraph criticizes the results described in the third paragraph. However, those results are *not* incompatible with the premise from the first paragraph (the modular theory). In fact, the author admits in the last sentence that the results *do* illustrate the modular theory well.

(B) is a 180. The author disputes the modular theory (the position from the first paragraph). The author never calls for that theory to be modified. Besides, the author admits in the last sentence that the results from the third paragraph actually work well with the modular theory. They would support the theory, not be a basis for modifying the theory.

(C) is a Distortion. The author never suggests any model (let alone the basis for the research in the third paragraph) is *outdated*.

(D) is a Distortion. The author does argue that the method described in the third paragraph is deceptive and thus inadequate for supporting the view in the first paragraph. However, the author never disputes the argument in the second paragraph or calls it inadequate. After all, the second paragraph contains the author's own argument.

24. (A) Logic Function

Step 2: Identify the Question Type
The phrase "in order to" indicates that the question is asking *why* the author draws an analogy, which makes this a Logic Function question.

Step 3: Research the Relevant Text
The analogy between brain scans and X-rays is made in line 5. Be sure to consider the surrounding lines for context.

Step 4: Make a Prediction
In comparing brain scans to X-rays, the author is showing how, "As applied to medical diagnosis," the value of brain scans is "straightforward and indubitable" (lines 3–7). That analogy is followed swiftly by a [*h*]*owever*, which sets up the contrasting view that brain scans are not as clearly applicable to psychology. So, the purpose of the analogy is to show how brain scans can be useful in one area, despite being inapplicable in another.

Step 5: Evaluate the Answer Choices
(A) accurately expresses the author's intention. The analogy describes a valid use for brain scans, which contrasts the rest of the passage that shows their use in psychology is not necessarily as valuable.

(B) is not supported. The author is not concerned with "new technology."

(C) is a 180 at worst. The author claims a brain scan and an X-ray are *similar*. There is no suggestion that one is any less precise than the other.

(D) is a Distortion. X-rays are not used by the author to undermine any theory. The modular theory is disputed later based on entirely different evidence.

(E) is a Distortion. Brain scans and X-rays are said to be similar, but it's never suggested that one *evolved* from the other.

25. (E) Detail

Step 2: Identify the Question Type
The phrase "[a]ccording to the passage" indicates that the correct answer will be directly stated in the passage, making this a Detail question.

Step 3: Research the Relevant Text
The question asks about William Uttal, whose ideas are presented in the second paragraph.

Step 4: Make a Prediction
The question refers directly to lines 18–21, which state that Uttal contends that mental processes are "properties of a

more general mental activity that is distributed throughout the brain."

Step 5: Evaluate the Answer Choices
(E) matches the text of the passage nearly word for word.

(A) is a 180. Uttal argues that mental processes are *not* distinct and cannot be decomposed into individual modules.

(B) is a Distortion. The author suggests that it's absurd to "cleanly separate emotion from reason-giving" (lines 25–27), but that does not mean mental processes are essentially a combination of those two activities.

(C) is a Distortion. Oxygen usage is mentioned in the third paragraph as part of the fMRI. Uttal makes no claim about oxygen, let alone that its usage is uniform throughout the brain.

(D) is a Faulty Use of Detail. The subtractive method is not mentioned until the third paragraph, and Uttal makes no claim about the method or what it can do.

26. (C) Inference

Step 2: Identify the Question Type
The correct answer will be "supported by the passage," making this an Inference question.

Step 3: Research the Relevant Text
With no line reference or content clues, the entire text is relevant.

Step 4: Make a Prediction
With no clues for reference, a specific prediction will be impossible. Stay focused on the big picture, and use content clues in the answer choices to do any necessary research.

Step 5: Evaluate the Answer Choices
(C) is supported by details in the third paragraph. Lines 34–37 directly state that the rate of oxygen use "stands as a measure of metabolic activity." Thus, the more activity there is, the more oxygen usage there is.

(A) is a 180. The author's point in the second paragraph is that mental activities in general do *not* depend on independent modules.

(B) is a Distortion. The results mentioned in the third paragraph merely suggest that the rate of oxygen usage in other areas is no higher than usual. That doesn't mean the rate is "close to zero."

(D) is Extreme. The baseline measurement is taken in a "control condition," one particular condition that occurs before completing a certain task. There is no suggestion what would be true in any region of the brain "at all times."

(E) is not supported. While the author would argue that several regions of the brain are functioning when one is angry, it's possible that only one region is functioning more than usual and thus would be the only one to "light up."

27. (B) Logic Reasoning (Parallel Reasoning)

Step 2: Identify the Question Type

The question asks for a situation that is "most analogous" to the interpretation described in the passage. That makes this a Parallel Reasoning question, such as those that are found in Logical Reasoning.

Step 3: Research the Relevant Text

The way fMRI scans are interpreted is described in the third paragraph.

Step 4: Make a Prediction

The fMRI scans are interpreted using the subtractive method. That involves starting with a control condition in which oxygen usage is measured throughout the brain. When a task is being performed, the original values are subtracted from the new values. Any region that is working more than normal is interpreted to be "associated solely with the cognitive task in question." The correct answer will describe another situation in which an area with greater-than-normal activity at one time is said to be the sole area associated with that activity.

Step 5: Evaluate the Answer Choices

(B) is correct. In this case, similar to how the brain is always active, shoppersare always coming to the store. However, the time when shopping increases is said to be the sole time people are affected by ads (just like when one area of the brain lights up due to greater-than-normal usage, it's assumed that that's the only part of the brain performing the task at hand).

(A) does not match, suggesting that one area was needed because it provided the most support. That's not the same as saying that area was *solely* responsible.

(C) does not match, suggesting that one area is affected the *most* because it uses more water than another area. However, that's not the same as saying that area is the *sole* area associated with an activity.

(D) does not match, comparing usage in two areas (home versus office) rather than making one area the sole one involved in a situation.

(E) does not match, comparing short-term to long-term effects. That has nothing to do with identifying an area solely responsible for a certain activity.

Section III: Logic Games
Game 1: Student Research Teams

Q#	Question Type	Correct	Difficulty
1	Acceptability	C	★
2	Must Be True	D	★★
3	Must Be False	D	★★
4	"If" / Could Be True	E	★
5	"If" / Must Be True	B	★★

Game 2: Mystery Novel Clues

Q#	Question Type	Correct	Difficulty
6	Acceptability	D	★
7	"If" / Could Be True	E	★
8	"If" / Could Be True	B	★★
9	"If" / Could Be True	D	★★
10	Could Be True	A	★★
11	Rule Substitution	B	★★

Game 3: Art Exhibition Paintings

Q#	Question Type	Correct	Difficulty
12	Partial Acceptability	A	★★
13	"If" / Must Be True	A	★★
14	"If" / Could Be True	E	★★
15	"If" / Must Be True	D	★★
16	"If" / Could Be True	B	★★
17	Could Be True	E	★★★
18	Must Be False (CANNOT Be True)	D	★★★

Game 4: Trading Buildings

Q#	Question Type	Correct	Difficulty
19	Acceptability	C	★★
20	Must Be False (CANNOT Be True)	A	★★★
21	"If" / Must Be True	A	★★★
22	"If" / Must Be True	E	★★★★
23	Must Be False (CANNOT Be True)	D	★★★

Game 1: Student Research Teams

Step 1: Overview
Situation: A teacher assigning students to two research teams

Entities: Five students (Juana, Kelly, Lateefah, Mei, Olga) and two teams (green and red)

Action: Distribution. Determine the team to which each student is assigned. There is also the added twist of determining who is the facilitator of each team. Some may classify this as a full-fledged Selection element, which would make the game a Hybrid. Either classification will result in a similar sketch.

Limitations: One team will have two members while the other team has three. Exactly one member on each team will be a facilitator.

Step 2: Sketch
List the students by initial and set up a table with two columns, one labeled "green" and the other "red." Each team will get at least two members, so add two slots to each column. One team will get the fifth slot. This is a rare instance in which it is possible to set up Limited Options without seeing a single rule. Number restrictions often provide important deductions, so set up two sketches. In the first sketch, the green team will get a third member. In the second sketch, the red team will get a third member.

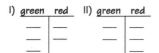

Both sketches now contain all five slots to be filled. As for the facilitator, there are a couple of ways that could be indicated in the sketch. Either set aside the top slot in each column as the facilitator, and mark it with a "fac") or leave the slots alone and star or circle the student who gets selected as facilitator once it's determined.

Step 3: Rules
Rule 1 splits up Juana and Olga. One of them will be on the green team, and one of them will be on the red team. While the order is unknown, it's important to indicate that one slot will be taken up on each team. So, draw "J/O" in one slot on each team.

Rule 2 establishes Lateefah on the green team. Add an "L" to a slot on the green team.

Rule 3 establishes that Kelly is not a facilitator. Make a note of this to the side (e.g., K not fac).

Rule 4 establishes that Olga *is* a facilitator. Star O and/or make a note to the side (e.g., O = fac).

Step 4: Deductions
If they weren't set up ahead of time, Limited Options are worthwhile to consider based on the two numeric outcomes. Have two sketches. In one, Green gets three students and red gets two. In the other, green gets two students and red gets three.

In the first option, there are two spaces established on the green team: J/O in one and L in the other. On the red team, one space is established: O/J (whoever is not on the green team). That means M and K will be split up, one on the green team and one on the red team. Add "M/K" to the remaining slots on each team.

I)
green	red
J/O	O/J
L	M/K
K/M	

In the second option, the green team is filled up. The two spaces contain J/O and L. That means everyone else will fill up the red team: O/J (whoever is not on the green team), M, and K.

II)
green	red
J/O	O/J
L	K
	M

It is unknown who the facilitator is on either team in either option. Olga is definitely one of the two facilitators, but the Limited Options setup does not definitively place Olga. Expect questions to provide more information on that twist.

Step 5: Questions

1. (C) Acceptability
As with any Acceptability question, go through the rules one at a time, eliminating answers that violate those rules.

(A) violates Rule 1 by putting Juana and Olga on the same team. **(D)** violates Rule 2 by putting Lateefah on the red team. **(E)** violates Rule 3 by making Kelly a facilitator. **(B)** violates Rule 4 by not having Olga as a facilitator. That leaves **(C)** as the correct answer.

2. (D) Must Be True
The correct answer for this question must be true no matter what. Any answer that could be false will be eliminated.

Neither Juana nor Olga are assigned to either team with certainty. So, Juana could be on the green team, and Olga could be on the red team. That eliminates **(A)** and **(C)**. Lateefah could be a facilitator, but need not be. That eliminates **(B)**. Olga must be a facilitator (Rule 4), so only one other student could be a facilitator. Thus, it must be true that Juana and Mei are not *both* facilitators. Either one of them could be, but not both—otherwise, there would be three facilitators. Therefore, **(D)** must be true, and is thus the correct answer.

For the record, Kelly cannot be a facilitator (Rule 3), but Juana could be. That eliminates **(E)**.

3. (D) Must Be False

The correct answer to this question must be false no matter what. Any answer that could be (or even must be) true should be eliminated.

If the green team has three members, as it does in Option I, then Kelly could be assigned there along with Lateefah, and it's possible for Lateefah to be the facilitator. That eliminates **(A)**.

If the red team has three members, as it does in Option II, then Kelly and Mei could be assigned together. In that case, Mei could be the facilitator. That eliminates **(B)**.

Olga is a facilitator no matter what (Rule 4), and she could be on either team with Mei. That eliminates **(C)**.

Lateefah is on the green team (Rule 2) and could be a facilitator. In that case, Olga, who also has to be a facilitator (Rule 4) would have to be facilitator for the red team. With Olga on the red team, Juana would have to be on the green team (Rule 1). That means Juana and Lateefah would be on the same team. It's impossible for them to be on different teams if Lateefah is a facilitator. That makes **(D)** the correct answer.

For the record, Olga must be a facilitator (Rule 4). If Mei is also a facilitator, she would be the facilitator for a different team, as each team only has one facilitator. Thus, **(E)** is possible and can be eliminated.

4. (E) "If" / Could Be True

For this question, Lateefah is a facilitator, which could happen in either option. However, she must be the facilitator for the green team (Rule 2). That means Olga, who is also a facilitator (Rule 4), must be the one for the red team. That means everyone else (Juana, Kelly, and Mei) are not facilitators. With Olga on the red team, Juana will be on the green team. That leaves Kelly and Mei. At least one of them must occupy a space on the red team. It could be either one. The remaining student could take up a third spot on either team.

green red
(L) (O)
J M/K
K/M

With that, only **(E)** is possible, making it the correct answer. The other answers all must be false because they place either Juana or Olga on the incorrect team.

5. (B) "If" / Must Be True

For this question, Mei is assigned to the green team, which can only happen in Option I (because in Option II, Mei is on the red team). The green team will also include Lateefah (Rule 2) and either Juana or Olga (Rule 1). That's three students on the green team. The red team will thus have the remaining two: Juana or Olga (whoever is not on the green team) and Kelly.

I) green red
J/O O/J
L K
M

With Kelly on the red team, **(B)** is the correct answer. The remaining answers are all possible but need not be true.

Game 2: Mystery Novel Clues

Step 1: Overview

Situation: An author writing a mystery novel that has seven clues contained in seven chapters

Entities: Seven clues (R, S, T, U, W, X, Z)

Action: Strict Sequencing. Determine the order, by chapter, in which the clues appear.

Limitations: All clues are mentioned exactly once, with exactly one clue in each of the seven chapters. This is standard one-to-one sequencing.

Step 2: Sketch

Simply list the clues at the top, and set up a series of seven numbered slots to which the clues will be assigned.

R S T U W X Z

___ ___ ___ ___ ___ ___ ___
1   2   3   4   5   6   7

Step 3: Rules

Rule 1 prevents T from being placed in chapter 1. Draw "~T" under the first slot.

Rule 2 creates a concrete Block of Entities. T is placed before W with exactly two spaces in between.

T ___ ___ W

Rule 3 dictates that S and Z cannot be placed consecutively, in either order.

~~S Z~~
~~Z S~~

Rule 4 dictates that W and X cannot be placed consecutively, in either order.

~~W X~~
~~X W~~

Rule 5 creates a block of U and X, which must be consecutive, in either order.

| U X | or | X U |

Step 4: Deductions

The Block of Entities with T and W is the most significant component of the game. There must be at least three spaces after T (two clues followed by W). That means T cannot be placed in chapters 5, 6, or 7. Moreover, T cannot be placed in chapter 1 (Rule 1). Thus, T can only be placed in chapters 2, 3, or 4. That means W can only be placed in 5, 6, or 7. These restrictions can be noted in several ways: Add "~T" under spaces 1, 5, 6, and 7, and add "~W" under spaces 1, 2, 3, and

4. Or, turn negatives into positives and draw "T" with three arrows pointing to spaces 2, 3, and 4 and "W" with three arrows pointing to 5, 6, and 7. Alternatively, you could draw out Limited Options, with T and W in 2, 5; or 3, 6; or 4, 7, respectively.

I)   ___ T   ___ ___ W   ___ ___
     1   2   3   4   5   6   7

II) ___ ___ T   ___ ___ W   ___
     1   2   3   4   5   6   7

III) ___ ___ ___ T   ___ ___ W
     1   2   3   4   5   6   7

It's also helpful to note that W and X are duplicated in the rules. W is now limited to three spaces (5, 6, or 7). X cannot be next to W (Rule 4). While it may not be immediately apparent, some quick testing will show that X cannot be placed into chapter 6. If it were, then W would be in either 5 or 7, violating Rule 4. Thus, X cannot be placed into chapter 6. Furthermore, because X cannot be in chapter 6, U cannot be in chapter 7 because then it couldn't be placed next to X, violating Rule 5.

The deductions about X and U can be difficult to spot. Most of the game could be managed without those deductions (especially with a good number of "If" questions), but they are very useful for one question in particular. Also, be careful not to make improper deductions. For example, even though W is in one of the last three chapters, X could be there, too—as long as they're separated. So, X could be in chapter 7 as long as W is in chapter 5 (and vice versa). Similarly, even though X cannot be in chapter 6, U could still be in chapter 5—as long as X was in chapter 4. Remember that deductions should indicate what absolutely must or cannot happen, not what merely seems unlikely. Finally, R is never mentioned in any of the rules and is thus a Floater, which can be noted with an asterisk. It can potentially be in any chapter of the book. If done with Limited Options, the final Master Sketch may look like this, with a couple other minor deductions about where U can't be based on knowing X can't be in certain chapters:

		•	R S T U W X Z				
I)	___	T	___	___	W	___	___
	1	2	3	4	5	6	7
			~U	~X		~X	~U
II)	___	___	T	___	___	W	___
	1	2	3	4	5	6	7
				~U	~X		~X
							~U
III)	___	___	___	T	___	___	W
	1	2	3	4	5	6	7
					~U	~X	

~~S Z~~
~~Z S~~
~~W X~~
~~X W~~
| U X | or | X U |

Step 5: Questions

6. (D) Acceptability

As with any Acceptability question, go through the rules one at a time, and eliminate answers that violate those rules.

(B) violates Rule 1 by putting T in the first chapter. **(A)** violates Rule 2 by having *three* chapters separate T and W. No choice violates Rule 3. **(E)** violates Rule 4 by placing X and W in adjacent chapters. **(C)** violates Rule 5 by separating U and X. That leaves **(D)** as the correct answer.

7. (E) "If" / Could Be True

For this question, X is in chapter 1. That means U must be in chapter 2 (Rule 5). That leaves only two ways to separate T and W to satisfy Rule 2. T could be in chapter 3 with W in chapter 6, or T could be in chapter 4 with W in chapter 7. Use Options II and III from the Limited Options as a starting point, and then add in the additional information to test them more thoroughly.

In Option II, with T in 3 and W in 6, that leaves chapters 4, 5, and 7 for the remaining clues: R, S, and Z. S and Z cannot be consecutive (Rule 3), so one of them must be in chapter 7. The other one will be next to R in chapters 4 and 5.

```
II)   X    U    T    _    _    W   S/Z
      1    2    3    4    5    6    7
                      \  R  /
                       Z/S
```

In Option III, with T in 4 and W in 7, that leaves chapters 3, 5, and 6 for the remaining clues: R, S, and Z. S and Z cannot be consecutive, so one of them must be in chapter 3. The other one will be next to R in chapters 5 and 6.

```
III)  X    U   S/Z   T    _    _    W
      1    2    3    4    5    6    7
                           \  R  /
                            Z/S
```

With that, only **(E)** is possible and is thus the correct answer. Z could be the clue mentioned in chapter of 3 of Option III.

8. (B) "If" / Could Be True

For this question, U is in chapter 3. That means T must be in chapter 2 or 4—so, either Option I or Option III. X also must be next to U (Rule 5), so it also must be in chapter 2 or 4. The placement of T and U will also determine where W can go, so redraw both options. In Option I, T is in chapter 2, which places W in chapter 5. Because the question stem says U is in chapter 3, that means X must be in chapter 4 (Rule 5). However, that violates Rule 4 because W and X are

consecutive. Thus, this option is impossible and can be eliminated.

```
I)   _    T    U    X    W    _    _
     1    2    3    4    5    6    7
```

In Option III, T is in chapter 4, which places W in chapter 7. X will be in chapter 2 in order to be next to U (Rule 4). That leaves chapters 1, 5, and 6 for the remaining clues (R, S, and Z). S and Z cannot be consecutive (Rule 3), so one of them must be in chapter 1. The other one will be next to R in chapters 5 and 6.

```
III)  S/Z   X    U    T    _    _    W
       1    2    3    4    5    6    7
                            \  R  /
                             Z/S
```

Only **(B)** is possible, making it the correct answer.

9. (D) "If" / Could Be True

For this question, Z is in chapter 7. This means that Option III is out because W is in chapter 7 in that option. Only Options I and II are possible. Redraw out both options.

In Option I, T is in chapter 2 and W is in chapter 5. In that option, chapters 3 and 4 are the only consecutive chapters available for U and X to be adjacent (Rule 5). However, X cannot be next to W (Rule 4), so X will be in chapter 3 and U will be in chapter 4. That leaves S and R, but S cannot be next to Z (Rule 3). So, S is in chapter 1 and R is in chapter 6.

```
I)   S    T    X    U    W    R    Z
     1    2    3    4    5    6    7
```

In Option II, T is in chapter 3 and W is in chapter 6. The block of U and X could go into either chapters 1 and 2 or chapters 4 and 5. Whichever chapters they occupy, R and S will fill in the remaining chapters. Any order and combination is possible with one exception: X cannot be in chapter 5 because it cannot be next to W (Rule 4).

```
II)  _    _    T    _    _    W    Z
     1    2    3    4    5    6    7
                     ~X
              [UX/XU] [RS/SR]
```

With that, only **(D)** is possible, making it the correct answer.

10. (A) Could Be True

The correct answer will be the only one that could be true. That means the remaining four answers are impossible.

R is a Floater and not directly restricted by any rules of the game. Thus, it seems perfectly likely that **(A)** could be true—that R could be in chapter 7. If this is correct, the remaining answers should be clearly false.

T cannot be in chapter 5 because there would not be enough room for two clues *and* W after it, violating Rule 2. That eliminates **(B)**. Similarly, W cannot be in chapter 3 because there would not be enough room for two clues *and* T before it, also violating Rule 2. That eliminates **(D)**.

If it were determined at the onset that X cannot be in chapter 6 and U cannot be in chapter 7, that would make it easy to eliminate **(C)** and **(E)**. Otherwise, some quick testing proves why those answers are impossible. If X were in chapter 6, then W could not be in chapters 5 or 7 (Rule 4). That would put W in chapter 4 at the latest. However, that would put T in chapter 1, which violates Rule 1—and W could not be earlier. So, X cannot be in chapter 6. That eliminates **(E)**. Consequently, U cannot be in chapter 7 because that would put X in chapter 6, which has already been determined as impossible. That eliminates **(C)**, confirming that **(A)** is the only answer possible and thus the correct answer.

11. (B) Rule Substitution

This question asks for a rule that could replace Rule 1 in the game and have the exact same effect. In other words, it must guarantee that T is not in chapter 1, but it also cannot add any new restrictions that weren't already in place.

A rule that eliminates U from chapter 2 is no help at all. Not only does it not prevent T from being in chapter 1, but it also restricts U in a way that wasn't originally true. U was allowed in chapter 2 from the beginning. That eliminates **(A)**.

If W is kept out of chapter 4, that would keep T out of chapter 1 based on Rule 2. This would reestablish the restriction of the original rule. And W couldn't be in chapter 4 from the original rules, so this adds no unwarranted restrictions. The effect is identical to the original Rule 1, making **(B)** the correct answer. For the record:

X being left out of chapter 6 was a deduction from the original rules. However, directly stating X is out of chapter 6 does not necessarily prevent T from being in chapter 1. The original rule is not established. That eliminates **(C)**.

If U is mentioned earlier than T, then T couldn't be first. That definitely reestablishes the original rule. However, U did not always have to be earlier than T, as seen in a sketch for the fourth question of the game. This adds an unwarranted restriction, eliminating **(D)**.

Having X before W was never required by the original rules, and this would not ensure that T is left out of the first chapter. Thus, this does not help reestablish the original rule. That eliminates **(E)**.

Game 3: Art Exhibition Paintings

Step 1: Overview
Situation: Student paintings being displayed at an art exhibition

Entities: Eight paintings, two for each student (Franz, Greene, Hidalgo, Isaacs) in one of two mediums (oil and watercolor), and four walls (1, 2, 3, 4) with two positions on each wall (upper and lower)

Action: Distribution. There are a lot of variables in this game, but the ultimate goal is to take the the eight paintings and determine the wall on which they hang and the position on that wall.

Limitations: Each student has two paintings for a total of eight paintings. Each wall has two positions for a total of eight positions. So essentially, there are eight paintings and eight spaces. For each student, one painting is an oil and one painting is a watercolor. So, there are four oils and four watercolors. Similarly, each wall has one upper and one lower position, so there are four upper positions and four lower positions. At this point, there is no limit to how many oils or watercolors appear on any given wall nor to how many oils or watercolors appear in any given position (upper or lower).

Step 2: Sketch
The fundamental basis here is to take eight paintings and assign them to the eight positions on the walls. So, start by listing the eight paintings. The eight paintings consist of two from each person, with each person having one oil and one watercolor. Each painting can be identified by an uppercase initial for the student paired with a lowercase letter to designate oil or watercolor: Fo, Fw, Go, Gw, Ho, Hw, Io, Iw.

Then, set up a table with four columns labeled 1–4. In each column, add two slots, one on top of the other. To the side, label the top slots "upper" and the bottom slots "lower."

$$F_o \; F_w \; G_o \; G_w \; H_o \; H_w \; I_o \; I_w$$

	1	2	3	4
upper	—	—	—	—
lower	—	—	—	—

Step 3: Rules
Rule 1 states that no wall can have two watercolors. That means each of the four watercolors must be on a different wall. Because there are only four walls, each wall will get one watercolor. The second painting on each wall would then have to be an oil. Essentially, this rule indicates that each wall will have one oil and one watercolor. However, it does not specify a position (upper or lower) for any wall. So, make a note to the side (e.g., each wall = 1 o and 1 w) or draw "o, w" under each column.

Rule 2 prevents any student from having both paintings on the same wall. This can be notated in several ways. You can draw each restriction individually (e.g., No FF) or you can use a variable to indicate the restriction algebraically (e.g., No XX). Or, you can simply make a shorthand note (Each wall = 2 diff. students).

Rule 3 prevents any wall from having paintings by both Franz and Isaacs.

Rule 4 establishes that one wall will have Greene's watercolor in the upper position and Franz's oil in the lower position. However, it could be any wall, so draw this to the side as a block.

Rule 5 establishes Isaacs's oil in the lower position of wall 4. Add "Io" to that slot, and cross it off the entity list.

Step 4: Deductions
There is a lot of information to work with here, so take some time to go through it thoroughly. It will save a ton of time with the questions.

Each wall has two paintings, one watercolor and one oil. One wall is already set: Gw in the upper position and Fo in the lower position. Another wall, wall 4, has Io in the lower position. The upper position has to be a watercolor. It cannot be Franz's (Rule 3), Greene's (Rule 4), or Isaacs's (Rule 2). Therefore, it must be Hidalgo's watercolor (Hw) in the upper position of wall 4.

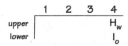

That leaves two more walls to be completed. There are four paintings left: Franz's and Isaacs's watercolors and Greene's and Hidalgo's oils. Franz's and Isaacs's watercolors cannot be together (Rule 3), so one wall will get Franz's watercolor and the final wall will get Isaacs's. Greene's and Hidalgo's oils will be split between those two walls, in either order. There is no way to determine which position any painting is in on either of these two walls.

In the end, all four walls are determined to some degree. One wall will have Gw on top and Fo on bottom. One will have Fw and either Go or Ho, in either order. One will have Iw and either Go or Ho (whichever one is not with Fw), in either order. The final wall is wall 4 with Hw on top and Io on bottom.

Step 5: Questions

12. (A) Partial Acceptability

In a Partial Acceptability question, start by going through the rules one at a time. Eliminate any answers that are clearly violated. If any answers remain, use any major deductions and consider the entities that are not listed.

Each answer only lists the paintings in the lower position of each wall. Without knowing what's in the upper position, it is impossible to test Rules 1–3 directly. However, **(D)** violates Rule 4 by having Greene's watercolor assigned to a lower position, and **(C)** violates Rule 5 by putting Isaacs's oil on wall 3, not wall 4.

The most efficient way to test the remaining answer choices is to consider any deduction that prevents a particular painting from being in a lower position. Wall 4 has Isaacs's oil in the lower position. So, the upper position has to be a watercolor. It cannot be Franz's (Rule 3), Greene's (Rule 4), or Isaacs's (Rule 2). Therefore, it must be Hidalgo's watercolor (Hw). Because Hidalgo's watercolor always has to be in an upper position, that eliminates **(B)** and **(E)**. That leaves **(A)** as the only acceptable answer.

13. (A) "If" / Must Be True

For this question, Isaacs's watercolor is displayed on wall 2 and Franz's oil is on wall 3. Franz's oil has to be in the lower position on wall 3 with Greene's watercolor in the upper position (Rule 4). Wall 4 is already complete with Isaacs's oil in the lower position and Hidalgo's watercolor in the top position. That leaves three paintings to be assigned: Franz's watercolor, Greene's oil, and Hidalgo's oil. Isaacs and Franz cannot have paintings on the same wall (Rule 3). So, with Isaac's watercolor on wall 2, Franz's watercolor must be on wall 1.

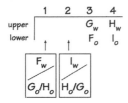

That makes **(A)** the correct answer. Greene's or Hidalgo's oil *could* be on wall 1, but only Franz's watercolor *must* be.

14. (E) "If" / Could Be True

For this question, Hidalgo's oil will be on wall 2. That means the other painting on wall 2 must be a watercolor (Rule 1 deduction). It cannot be Greene's watercolor (Rule 4), and it cannot be Hidalgo's watercolor (Rule 2). Thus, the other painting could only be either Franz's or Isaacs's watercolor, making **(E)** the correct answer. Likewise, looking back at the Deductions step, it was already determined that Hidalgo's oil was in a Block of Entities with either Franz's watercolor or Isaacs's watercolor.

15. (D) "If" / Must Be True

For this question, Greene's oil is on the same wall as Franz's watercolor. It's already been established that one wall will have Greene's watercolor and Franz's oil (Rule 4), and wall 4 has Hidalgo's watercolor and Isaacs's oil. That means the remaining wall must have the two remaining paintings: Hidalgo's oil and Isaacs's watercolor.

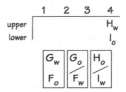

That makes **(D)** the correct answer. **(A)**, **(C)**, and **(E)** all make an upper/lower determination that could be, but does not have to be, true. **(B)** is a violation of Rule 1.

16. (B) "If" / Could Be True

For this question, Franz's oil is displayed on wall 1. It must be in the lower position with Greene's watercolor in the upper position (Rule 4). Wall 4 is also established with Hidalgo's watercolor in the upper position and Isaacs's oil in the lower position. That leaves the remaining paintings, Franz's and Isaacs's watercolors and Greene's and Hidalgo's oils, for walls 2 and 3.

	1	2	3	4
upper	Gw			Hw
lower	Fo			Io

With that, only **(B)** is possible, making it the correct answer.

For the record, **(A)** is a violation of Rule 3 given that Isaacs's oil is already established on wall 4 (Rule 5). **(C)** can be eliminated because Greene's watercolor must be on wall 1 along with Franz's oil (Rule 4). **(D)** can be eliminated because, as previously deduced in Step 4, Hidalgo's watercolor must be in the upper position on wall 4. Finally, **(E)** is a violation of Rule 5.

17. (E) Could Be True

The correct answer to this question will be the only one that could be true. The remaining answers must all be false.

Greene's watercolor must be in an upper position (Rule 4), so it's impossible for both of Greene's paintings to be in lower positions. That eliminates **(A)** and **(D)**.

Franz's oil must be in a lower position (Rule 4), so it's impossible for both of Franz's paintings to be in upper positions. That eliminates **(B)** and **(C)**. That leaves **(E)** as the correct answer.

One way this could look is this:

	1	2	3	4
upper	G_o	H_o	G_w	H_w
lower	F_w	I_w	F_o	I_o

18. (D) Must Be False (CANNOT Be True)

The correct answer to this question cannot be true, which means it will be false no matter what. That means the four wrong answers are all possible, if not definitely true.

The correct answer must be something definite. The definites given in the rules are Greene's watercolor in an upper position on the same wall as Franz's oil in a lower position (Rule 4), and Isaacs's oil in the lower position on wall 4 (Rule 5). With Isaacs's oil in the lower position, the upper position has to be a watercolor. It cannot be Franz's (Rule 3), Greene's (Rule 4), or Isaacs's (Rule 2). Therefore, it must be Hidalgo's watercolor (Hw). Because Hidalgo's watercolor always has to be in an upper position, **(D)** must be false and is thus the correct answer. All of the remaining answers are indeed possible.

Game 4: Trading Buildings

Step 1: Overview

Situation: Real estate companies looking to trade buildings

Entities: Three companies (RealProp, Southco, Trustcorp), eight buildings (Garza Tower, Yates House, Zimmer House, Flores Tower, Lynch Building, King Building, Meyer Building, Ortiz Building), and three building classes (1, 2, 3)

Action: Process. The buildings are already assigned classes, and they are already distributed among the three companies. The initial setup is provided in its entirety. The task is to take that initial setup and determine how things can be rearranged via a rule-driven process (in this case, the rules of trading). Process games are very rare on the LSAT and may be worth saving for last because they are often very unfamiliar.

Limitations: Because the initial setup is already complete, there are no limitations to find. The rules will provide all the limitations needed to answer the questions.

Step 2: Sketch

The sketch should illustrate the initial conditions of the game. In this case, there are three companies, each with a set of buildings. Set up three columns, one for each company. In each column, list the buildings each company owns by initial, along with a number to indicate its class (e.g., G1 for the class 1 Garza Tower in the RealProp column).

Real	South	Trust
G_1	F_1	K_2
Y_3	L_2	M_2
Z_3		O_2

Step 3: Rules

Rule 1 allows any company to transfer one building to another company in exchange for any one building of the same class (i.e., an even exchange).

Rule 2 allows any company to transfer one class 1 building to another company in exchange for two class 2 buildings.

Rule 3 allows any company to transfer one class 2 building to another company in exchange for two class 3 buildings.

Step 4: Deductions

The rules only provide information about what *could* happen. However, there is no indication of any trades that *must* happen. By the overview, the companies are merely *considering* trades. Thus, it is possible that one company decided not to trade anything at all. Of course, some trades are bound to happen—otherwise, this would be a very boring game.

The key here is to consider the implication of each rule to determine what could happen and what cannot happen. The first rule is the most useful. Companies are allowed to swap any two buildings of the same class at any time. That means that buildings of the same class are infinitely interchangeable. In other words, if a company has a class 2 building (e.g., Lynch Building), then that building can be exchanged for any other class 2 building at any time. This means it's ultimately more important to pay attention to the building classes than the building names. If you know a company has a class 2 building, it could effectively be any one of them. The same goes for class 1 and class 3 buildings.

The last two rules basically assign value to the building classes. Class 1 buildings are the most valuable and can only be obtained by trading two class 2 buildings. (This is like exchanging one $1 bill for two $0.50 coins.) Similarly, class 2 buildings are more valuable than class 3 buildings, again requiring two class 3 buildings to get a class 2 (i.e., like exchanging two $0.25 coins for a $0.50 coin).

$$\text{Class } 1 = \$1$$
$$2 = \$0.50$$
$$3 = \$0.25$$

There are only two class 1 buildings (Garza Tower and Flores Tower), but they require a lot to acquire. RealProp already has one, but only has two class 3 buildings in addition. Those class 3 buildings could be exchanged for a class 2 building, but that would not be enough to get the other class 1 building. Similarly, Southco has a class 1 building, but only has a single class 2 building in addition. Essentially, Southco has the same trading power as RealProp and thus cannot get both class 1 buildings, and Trustcorp starts with three class 2 buildings. Trustcorp can trade two of those buildings to get a class 1 building, but then it would have one class 1 building and just one class 2 building left. That's the same trading power as the other companies. Per the money exchanging analogy, each company has $1.50 worth of buildings. So, all companies have the same trading potential, with none of them able to get both class 1 buildings.

Finally, it helps to note that there are only two class 3 buildings, and they are both initially owned by RealProp. Because nobody else has a class 3 building, the only way to trade them is to exchange them *both* for a class 2 building. That would give another company both class 3 buildings. Once again, they could not be traded separately, so the two class 3 buildings will always be together—no matter who owns them.

Step 5: Questions

19. (C) Acceptability

The correct answer to this question will list a possible scenario after *only one* trade is made. That means only one rule will apply to the correct answer, but it's impossible to know which one. Unlike standard Acceptability questions, wrong answers here may not violate any rule—they may just apply too many. In this case, the answers have to be tested one at a time to make sure only one rule was applied.

In **(A)**, RealProp still has Garza Tower, but now has Flores Tower. However, that would require at least two trades because RealProp started with two class 3 buildings and those cannot be traded directly for a class 1 building. That eliminates **(A)**. Furthermore, as already deduced, no company can have both class 1 buildings ($2 of value).

In **(B)**, RealProp still has Garza Tower, but has traded its two class 3 buildings and somehow received two class 2 buildings. That violates the rules of trade and eliminates **(B)**.

In **(C)**, RealProp still has Garza Tower, but now has a class 2 building: Lynch Building. That could have happened by trading the two class 3 buildings (Yates House and Zimmer House) to the original owner of the Lynch Building: Southco. That is what's listed, and all of the buildings are where they started. That means only one acceptable trade was made, making **(C)** the correct answer. For the record:

In **(D)**, RealProp still has Garza Tower and the Yates House. However, RealProp now has Meyer Building (a class 2 building) in exchange for Zimmer House (a class 3 building). That's not an even exchange and is thus unacceptable. That eliminates **(D)**.

In **(E)**, RealProp has the same set of buildings it started with. Southco still has the Lynch Building, but now has the Ortiz Building (a class 2 building) in exchange for the Flores Tower (a class 1 building). That's not an even exchange and is thus unacceptable. That eliminates **(E)**.

20. (A) Must Be False (CANNOT Be True)
The correct answer to this question will be impossible, no matter how many trades are made. The four wrong answers will all be possible results.

RealProp starts with Garza Tower but only has two class 3 buildings to trade. Those could be traded for a single class 2 building, but that will still not be enough to ever trade for the Flores Tower, the remaining class 1 building. That means **(A)** can never happen and is thus the correct answer. For the record:

Southco starts with the Flores Tower. The other building it starts with is the Lynch Building, a class 2 building. That could be traded at any time for the Meyer Building, another class 2 building. That means **(B)** is possible.

Southco starts with the Lynch Building. The other building it starts with is the Flores Tower, a class 1 building. That could be traded at any time for the Garza Tower, another class 1 building. That means **(C)** is possible.

Trustcorp starts with the Ortiz Building. The other buildings it starts with are the King Building and the Meyer Building, both of which are class 2 buildings. Those could be traded together at any time for the Flores Tower, a class 1 building. That means **(D)** is possible.

Trustcorp starts with the Meyer building. The other buildings it starts with are the King Building and the Ortiz Building, both of which are class 2 buildings. Those two could be traded together at any time for the Garza Tower, a class 1 building. That means **(E)** is possible.

21. (A) "If" / Must Be True
For this question, RealProp will end up with only class 2 buildings. That means it must trade away its class 3 buildings and its class 1 building. Either remaining company can trade a class 2 building in exchange for the two class 3 buildings. However, neither remaining company could trade enough to get both class 1 buildings. Southco already has one but only has a class 2 building left to trade. TrustCorp has enough to trade for one class 1 building, but would be left with another class 2 building—not enough to get both. So, if RealProp has only class 2 buildings, then the two class 1 buildings must be split—one to Southco and one to Trustcorp.

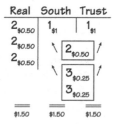

That means **(A)** must be true, making that the correct answer. For the record:

RealProp will have class 2 buildings, and all class 2 buildings are interchangeable. Thus, RealProp could end up with the Meyer Building, and not Trustcorp. That eliminates **(B)**.

Southco could trade its class 2 building for RealProp's class 3 buildings. That would leave Southcorp with a class 1 building and two class 3 buildings—no class 2 buildings. That eliminates **(C)**.

Alternatively, Southco could do nothing, and Trustcorp could trade for the class 3 buildings. That eliminates **(D)**.

Finally, Southco will end up with a class 1 building, as will Trustcorp. However, they could trade with each other, so either one could end up with the Flores Tower. That eliminates **(E)**.

22. (E) "If" / Must Be True
For this question, Trustcorp will end up with no class 2 buildings. Thus, it must trade all three class 2 buildings it

starts with. It could trade two of those class 2 buildings for one of the class 1 buildings. That would leave it with one class 1 building and just one class 2 building. It wouldn't have enough to trade for *both* class 1 buildings, so it would have to trade the remaining class 2 building in exchange for the two class 3 buildings. That's the only way Trustcorp could end up without a single class 2 building.

Real	South	Trust
		1 $1
		3 $0.25
		3 $0.25

So, Trustcorp would have a class 1 building and two class 3 buildings. The class 1 building could be either one (Flores Tower or Garza Tower), but there are only two class 3 buildings available. So, Trustcorp would have to end up with them both: Yates House and Zimmer House. Therefore, it must have the Zimmer House, making **(E)** the correct answer. For the record:

It's possible this happens with Trustcorp trading with RealProp the whole time, getting the Garza Tower for two class 2 buildings, and getting Yates House and Zimmer House for the remaining class 2 buildings. That would leave RealProp with no class 1 building, Southco with a class 1 building, and no trading done for Southco. That eliminates **(A)**, **(B)**, and **(C)**.

Real	South	Trust
2 $0.50	1 $1	1 $1
2 $0.50	2 $0.50	3 $0.25
2 $0.50		3 $0.25
$1.50	$1.50	$1.50

Alternatively, that could all happen and Trustcorp could finally swap with Southco and take the Flores Tower in exchange for the Garza Tower. That eliminates **(D)**.

23. (D) Must Be False (CANNOT Be True)

The correct answer to this question cannot be true, which means it is impossible. The remaining answers will all be possible in some way.

RealProp could own three Class 2 buildings ($1.50 of value). Specifically, RealProp could trade its Garza Tower (class 1) with Trustcorp in exchange for the Meyer Building and the Ortiz Building (both class 2). Then, RealProp could trade its two class 3 buildings with Southco to get the Lynch building (class 2). That means **(A)** is possible and can be eliminated.

The Garza Tower is a class 1 building and the Meyer Building is a class 2 building—together a $1.50 value. Those are the same classes that Southco owns at the start, so Southco can certainly make even trades for those buildings. That eliminates **(B)**.

The King Building, the Meyer Building, and the Ortiz Building are all class 2 buildings owned by Trustcorp at the beginning ($1.50 of value). Southco could swap its class 2 building for any one of Trustcorp's and then trade its class 1 building for the other two. That means **(C)** is possible and can be eliminated.

The Yates House is a class 3 building. The only way for Trustcorp to get the Yates House is to trade a class 2 building for both Yates House *and* Zimmer House (the only other class 3 building). There's no way to have Yates House without Zimmer House, making **(D)** the correct answer.

For the record, Trustcorp could end up with the Garza Tower (class 1) and the Lynch Building (class 2)—together a $1.50 value. Specifically, Trustcorp could trade any of its class 2 buildings evenly with Southco to get the Lynch Building. Trustcorp could then trade its remaining class 2 buildings with RealProp to get the Garza Tower. That means **(E)** is possible and can be eliminated.

Section IV: Logical Reasoning

Q#	Question Type	Correct	Difficulty
1	Flaw	A	★
2	Point at Issue	C	★
3	Paradox	D	★
4	Strengthen	D	★
5	Assumption (Sufficient)	C	★
6	Principle (Identify/Inference)	A	★
7	Strengthen	B	★
8	Principle (Identify/Strengthen)	A	★★
9	Main Point	E	★
10	Strengthen	C	★★★★
11	Flaw	A	★
12	Inference	E	★
13	Paradox	A	★
14	Assumption (Sufficient)	E	★
15	Inference	E	★
16	Flaw	B	★
17	Inference	B	★
18	Assumption (Necessary)	E	★★★
19	Parallel Reasoning	B	★★
20	Assumption (Sufficient)	E	★★
21	Inference	B	★★
22	Strengthen/Weaken (Evaluate the Argument)	B	★★★★
23	Parallel Flaw	A	★★★
24	Principle (Apply/Inference)	E	★★★★
25	Weaken	D	★★★★
26	Flaw	B	★

1. (A) Flaw

Step 1: Identify the Question Type

The correct answer will describe why the given argument is "vulnerable to criticism," which is common wording for a Flaw question.

Step 2: Untangle the Stimulus

The organizer concludes that the community cleanup will be successful by having at least 100 participants. The evidence is that 85 residents have signed up and last year's cleanup had over 100 participants despite only 77 residents signing up.

Step 3: Make a Prediction

Based on last year's outcome, it's reasonable for the organizer to be optimistic. Unfortunately, one exceptional outcome is not enough to guarantee a similar outcome the next time. The correct answer will describe this use of one past experience to predict a future outcome.

Step 4: Evaluate the Answer Choices

(A) correctly describes the flaw. The community organizer certainly takes a single observation (what happened last year) and implies that it's a sign of a general trend that will repeat this year.

(B) is a Distortion. The organizer assumes that a similar *number* of people will participate, but not necessarily the same actual people.

(C) is not accurate. Nothing is ever described as required. The organizer merely claims the cleanup will be successful *if* there are 100 or more participants. That indicates sufficiency, not necessity.

(D) is not necessarily true. Only 77 residents signed up last year, but over 100 participated. Who are those extra people? They may very well be nonresidents, and the organizer does not ignore that possibility.

(E) is not accurate. No such term is defined, and the organizer merely predicts a positive outcome. The organizer never suggests that any outcome would be positive.

2. (C) Point at Issue

Step 1: Identify the Question Type

The stimulus consists of two speakers and the question asks for something about which those speakers disagree, making this a Point at Issue question.

Step 2: Untangle the Stimulus

Bell is defending Klein against critics, claiming that Klein is the kind of person we want making policy decisions. Klein's policies may have been unpopular, but they were effective. Soltan agrees that the policies worked, but suggests that the lack of support for Klein will prevent her from making important decisions in the future. Soltan thus suggests that Klein should step down.

Step 3: Make a Prediction

Bell and Soltan agree that Klein's policies have been effective. Unfortunately, they disagree about what that means going forward. Bell suggests that Klein should stick around, while Soltan argues she should leave office because of lack of support. The correct answer will bring up the dispute about Klein's future tenure in office.

Step 4: Evaluate the Answer Choices

(C) gets to the heart of the debate. Soltan makes this point directly, while Bell disagrees, suggesting we need Klein to stay.

(A) is a 180. Bell claims the policies were effective (they "avoided an impending catastrophe"), and Soltan *agrees* ("Klein's policies have been effective").

(B) is a 180. Bell likes the policies but admits that Klein has critics. Soltan agrees, claiming she doesn't have political support.

(D) is also a 180. Both Bell and Soltan directly state this very point.

(E) is not supported. Bell directly makes this claim. Soltan never suggests anything about an "impending catastrophe," but Soltan never disputes that claim, either.

3. (D) Paradox

Step 1: Identify the Question Type

The question asks for something that will "resolve the apparent discrepancy," making this a Paradox question.

Step 2: Untangle the Stimulus

The psychologist held a study that produced some mysterious results. Participants were asked how much they would pay for a particular mug. They said up to $5 and no more. They were then given a similar mug and asked how much they would sell it for; most of them wanted more than $5.

Step 3: Make a Prediction

Why would people put such a different price on a similar mug? It would appear they're following the philosophy of "a bird in the hand is worth two in the bush." In other words, they believe that something you have is worth more than something you don't.

Step 4: Evaluate the Answer Choices

(D) explains the difference in price. If people put a greater value on something they own, that explains why they would put a higher price on selling their own mug than on buying a similar mug they *don't* own.

(A) is a 180. The two mugs are similar. If people's assessment is based on the inherent properties of the mug, then the values should have been the same, not different.

(B) is Out of Scope. According to the psychologist, people who were given the mug were asked to value it "immediately afterwards." It doesn't matter how people act after possessing something for a long period of time.

(C) does not help. This might provide some insight into the price they devised in the first half of the experiment. However, it offers no explanation why they came up with a higher price when asked to sell their mug.

(E) is an Irrelevant Comparison, and likely a 180. They were only given mugs, so there's no need to draw a comparison between objects people were given and objects they bought. Besides, this suggests that people *undervalue* objects they were given. That just makes it more unusual that they gave a *higher* value to the mugs they were given.

4. (D) Strengthen

Step 1: Identify the Question Type
The question directly asks for something that will strengthen the given argument.

Step 2: Untangle the Stimulus
The ecologist starts by describing the nest-building behavior of male starlings. They decorate nests with plants that help kill parasites harmful to nestlings. Researchers thus argue that the decoration is used for that very reason: to protect nestlings. *However*, the ecologist argues otherwise, concluding that the decorations are actually meant to attract females. The evidence is that starlings stop adding such decoration once eggs are being laid.

Step 3: Make a Prediction.
The fact that decoration stops after eggs are being laid does seem to weaken the theory that the decorations are for nestling protection. However, the ecologist actually provides no evidence whatsoever that the decorations are used to attract females. The correct answer should make that much-needed connection.

Step 4: Evaluate the Answer Choices
(D) is correct, as it is the only answer that suggests a connection between the decorations and female starlings.

(A) is Out of Scope. This makes it clear that they don't need the greenery for their own protection, but it offers no support that the decorations are meant to attract females.

(B) is potentially a 180. This claims that starlings don't decorate their nests if they're in an area with few parasitic insects. That may be because the males have decided the aromatic plants are not necessary for protecting nestlings given that there's significantly fewer parasites around. This strengthens the idea that the decoration is for protection against parasites, not for mating.

(C) is an Irrelevant Comparison. The speed at which nestlings grow offers no help to the ecologist's argument that the decorations are used to attract females.

(E) is Out of Scope. If this were true, it might explain why decoration would be used as protection for nestlings (which would actually strengthen the researchers' argument, not the ecologist's). However, it offers no support for the decoration being used to attract females.

5. (C) Assumption (Sufficient)

Step 1: Identify the Question Type
The question asks for something that, *if* assumed, would logically complete the argument. That makes this a Sufficient Assumption question.

Step 2: Untangle the Stimulus
The author concludes that the commission's report on disaster preparedness will not be effective. The evidence is that individual commission members have openly voiced their opinions, and effectiveness requires the commission to speak "with a unified voice."

Step 3: Make a Prediction
The key to this question is to pick up on the Formal Logic rule for effectiveness. The author claims that, for the report to be effective, the commission must speak in a unified voice.

If	effective	→	speak in unified voice

If the author believed the commission could *not* speak in a unified voice, that would be grounds to conclude the report will be ineffective.

If	~ speak in unified voice	→	~ effective

However, the author only claims that individual members have voiced their opinions ahead of time. So, the author is assuming that the voicing of opinions ahead of time will prevent the commission from speaking in a unified voice, thus making the report ineffective.

If	voicing opinions early	→	~ speak in unified voice	→	~ effective

Step 4: Evaluate the Answer Choices
(C) is correct. This makes it necessary for individual members to not speak out early. If they *did* speak out, this logic suggests that the commission couldn't speak in a uniform voice, as the author suggests. That would lead to the conclusion that the report will be ineffective.

$$\text{If } \quad \begin{array}{c} \textbf{\textit{speak in}} \\ \textbf{\textit{unified voice}} \end{array} \quad \rightarrow \quad \begin{array}{c} \textbf{\textit{~ voicing}} \\ \textbf{\textit{opinions early}} \end{array}$$

(A) is Out of Scope. By the author's argument, the effectiveness of the report depends on the commission speaking in a unified voice, not the members' commitment to effectiveness.

(B) is Out of Scope. The author is not concerned about what should or should not happen, let alone making any judgment about the press. The author is merely trying to evaluate the effectiveness of the report.

(D) is also Out of Scope. This describes how the public might have reacted had the members *not* spoken out. However, the fact remains that the members *did* speak out, so this has no bearing on the author's argument about whether or not the report will be effective.

(E) is a Distortion. The conclusion's claim of ineffectiveness is based on commission members presenting opinions publicly before the report is complete. Whether or not they had opinions (which they may not have shared) before the commission was even *formed* plays no role in this argument.

6. (A) Principle (Identify/Inference)

Step 1: Identify the Question Type
The question asks directly for a principle that is used by the engineer. The correct answer will be a general rule that matches logically to the specific argument made by the engineer. That makes this an Identify the Principle question.

Step 2: Untangle the Stimulus
The engineer is arguing that blocking out some sun rays to cut back on global warming would actually have the opposite effect. People would just emit *more* carbon dioxide and make global warming worse. The evidence comes in the form of an analogy to driving. Making roads wider and obstacle-free actually makes things worse, as drivers are willing to take more risks.

Step 3: Make a Prediction
In both the engineer's argument about global warming and the supporting analogy about roads, the attempt to make things safer actually makes things worse because people then act more recklessly. The correct answer will express this general philosophy.

Step 4: Evaluate the Answer Choices
(A) matches the logic of both situations in the argument. In both cases, conditions are intended to appear safer (wider, obstacle-free roads and fewer sun rays causing global warming), but then people take more risks (driving more recklessly and emitting more carbon dioxide).

(B) is Extreme. This suggests that the "technical fix" for global warming is no good, so we have to bring in humans. However, the engineer never suggests that human-created solutions are *required*.

(C) is Extreme and a Distortion. The engineer just discusses how the solutions can make things worse. There is no mention of the solutions being "inevitably temporary."

(D) is Extreme. The solutions described *don't* discourage risk-taking behavior, but that doesn't mean other solutions *can't*. The engineer is just dismissing these solutions that try to provide a sense of security. There may be other, better solutions that do discourage risk-taking.

(E) is Out of Scope. The engineer makes no mention of how long global warming or narrow roads have been a problem. Likewise, nothing was mentioned about letting problems go unresolved.

7. (B) Strengthen

Step 1: Identify the Question Type
The question asks for something that "adds the most support" for the argument. That makes this a Strengthen question.

Step 2: Untangle the Stimulus
The author concludes ([*t*]*herefore*) that the oil urushiol did not evolve in plants for defense. The evidence is that urushiol, found in poison oak and poison ivy, causes a lot of pain for humans but hardly affects other animals, such as the wood rat.

Step 3: Make a Prediction
The author is suggesting that the painful rashes we experience are an anomaly. Urushiol is not supposed to be about protection, it just happens to be painful to us. To strengthen this, the correct answer will provide further evidence that our reaction is unique and/or urushiol normally does not provide much in the way of defense.

Step 4: Evaluate the Answer Choices
(B) strengthens the argument, providing further evidence that urushiol hardly offers plants a defense. Animals are *eating* the plant, despite the presence of urushiol.

(A) is Out of Scope, if not a 180. If wood rats wait until the plant is dead before using it, that could suggest that they avoid the plant while it's alive. In that case, it's possible the urushiol *does* provide defense.

(C) is a 180. This suggests that chemicals often *are* used as a defense, which does nothing to help the author's argument that urushiol is not.

(D) is Out of Scope. This just confirms how harmful urushiol could be to humans, but does nothing to support the author's argument about urushiol being non-defensive. If anything, it just makes urushiol sound worse and *more* likely to be a defense.

(E) is also Out of Scope. Where these plants grow does nothing to indicate the purpose of urushiol.

8. (A) Principle (Identify/Strengthen)

Step 1: Identify the Question Type
The correct answer will be a principle that will be used to *justify* a specific argument in the stimulus. That makes this an Identify the Principle question that acts like a Strengthen question.

Step 2: Untangle the Stimulus
The politician argues that we should not praise legislation that encourages renovation and revitalization in urban areas. The evidence is that such legislation only benefits wealthy professionals and winds up hurting the people it was supposed to help.

Step 3: Make a Prediction
The idea of renovation and revitalization sounds terrific, but the politician is disappointed in the ultimate effect: the people who were supposed to be helped are being displaced. In condemning the legislation, the politician is acting on the principle that legislation should not be praised if it doesn't help in the way it was intended.

Step 4: Evaluate the Answer Choices
(A) matches the politician's reasoning. The politician's evaluation of the legislation (it should not be commended) is based on the actual results (it displaced people who were supposed to be helped), despite the good intentions.

(B) is a Distortion. The politician is more concerned that wealthy people were benefiting from the legislation, not about any "undue influence" on their part to pass that legislation.

(C) is Extreme and a Distortion. The politician is concerned about the disparity in who's benefiting from legislation, not in how the legislation is being applied. Besides, the politician never goes so far as to say the legislation should apply *equally* to everyone.

(D) is Extreme. The legislation doesn't benefit *nobody*, it just didn't benefit who it was supposed to. The wealthy professionals still benefited.

(E) is a 180. The legislation in question did give well-to-do professionals an advantage, but it seems *not* to have benefited society as a whole because long-term residents were displaced. If there were unmentioned benefits to society as a whole, those would weaken the politician's argument that the legislation should not be commended.

9. (E) Main Point

Step 1: Identify the Question Type
The question asks for the "main conclusion" of the argument, making this a Main Point question.

Step 2: Untangle the Stimulus
The pundit starts off with a strong value judgment: it's good to vote leaders out of office after a few years. What follows is "[t]he reason," which indicates that the pundit is now providing evidence to support that first sentence. Reforms usually occur when new leaders first take over, and waiting too long to make reforms can lead to more problems.

Step 3: Make a Prediction
When there's a strong opinion followed by "[t]he reason" behind it, that's as good a sign as any that that opinion is the main point: it's good to have national leaders voted out after a few years.

Step 4: Evaluate the Answer Choices
(E) neatly sums up the first sentence, which is indeed the main point supported by everything else that follows.

(A) is not the conclusion. The pundit does imply this by stating that reforms are generally undertaken early in a new government. However, this is just evidence why the pundit concludes that national leaders *should* be voted out after a few years.

(B) is Extreme. Leaders can deny responsibility, but the last sentence suggests they can also admit responsibility. There is no indication of what tends to happen more often. Besides, this is all merely evidence anyway for why some leaders should be voted out.

(C) is not the conclusion. This is just evidence why it would be a good idea to vote out older leaders after a few years.

(D) is, if anything, a 180. The pundit never argues about letting leaders stay in office. The argument is about voting leaders *out* of office.

10. (C) Strengthen

Step 1: Identify the Question Type
The question directly asks for something that will strengthen the farmer's argument.

Step 2: Untangle the Stimulus
The farmer concludes ([*t*]*hus*) that agricultural techniques that don't use commercial products are generally only investigated by government-sponsored research. The evidence is that private companies won't sponsor such research without the potential for marketable (i.e., commercial) products.

Step 3: Make a Prediction
This is a common argumentative structure in which the author denies one option and concludes there is only one other

solution. Such arguments ignore other solutions. In this case, when commercial products aren't involved, private corporations won't fund the research. So, the farmer concludes that only the government will. That assumes there are no other sources of funding for researching these agricultural techniques. The correct answer will strengthen this by denying any other options and/or making it more likely that only the government will get involved.

Step 4: Evaluate the Answer Choices

(C) strengthens the farmer's argument. This suggests, as the farmer assumes, that funding primarily comes from just two sources: private corporations and the government. So, if the private corporations are out, that just leaves the government.

(A) does not help. This suggests that the government will sponsor *some* research, but does not support the idea that it is the *only* source of sponsorship for such research.

(B) is Out of Scope. This suggests that noncommercial solutions are often viable, but does nothing to indicate who would sponsor research into those techniques.

(D) is Out of Scope. The argument is about who would sponsor noncommercial techniques. It doesn't matter who sponsors techniques that *do* use commercial products.

(E) is also Out of Scope. Even if the government focused primarily on sponsoring noncommercial techniques, it could still only be responsible for sponsoring research into just a small portion of those techniques. In that case, there would be plenty of other research that would have to be sponsored by someone else.

11. (A) Flaw

Step 1: Identify the Question Type

The correct answer will describe why the argument is "vulnerable to criticism." That's classic language indicating a Flaw question.

Step 2: Untangle the Stimulus

The spokesperson's conclusion comes at the very end: the university should rehire Hall Dining next year. The evidence is that the decision should reflect what most students want, and most students want a new food vendor. Hall Dining, for mysteriously unmentioned reasons, is the only viable option, despite the fact that Hall Dining was replaced last year by the current vendor.

Step 3: Make a Prediction

The ultimate goal of the spokesperson is to give the students what they want. However, the solution provided is to go back to the previous vendor. Perhaps there was a really good reason Hall Dining was dropped in the first place. Maybe students wanted them replaced last year and are just not happy with the current replacement. The spokesperson

overlooks the possibility that going back to Hall Dining may not be the difference students were clamoring for.

Step 4: Evaluate the Answer Choices

(A) accurately describes a flaw in the reasoning. If the student didn't know that Hall Dining was the only other option, then there's a chance they won't be happy with the switch back. The spokesperson completely overlooks this possibility.

(B) mentions an unrepresentative sample, but there's no sample group to dispute.

(C) is Extreme. The spokesperson doesn't suggest that student preference is the *only* factor. It's just that it's important. Besides, the spokesperson *does* consider other factors—the mysterious "variety of reasons" that are referenced.

(D) is Out of Scope. The spokesperson does not discount some disagreement. The argument is merely based on satisfying the preference of "the majority of students."

(E) is a Distortion. Student preference is said to be important but not necessarily the *only* grounds on which this solution is based. Besides, there's no evidence that Hall Dining will be popular. In fact, the flaw is that the spokesperson overlooks the possibility it *won't* be popular.

12. (E) Inference

Step 1: Identify the Question Type

The correct answer will be "strongly supported by the information" given, making this an Inference question.

Step 2: Untangle the Stimulus

The author provides three comparisons between canned cat food and dry cat food: 1) cats fed canned cat food eat fewer ounces per day, 2) canned cat food has more calories per ounce, and 3) feeding a cat canned food costs more per day.

Step 3: Make a Prediction

There are a lot of possible inferences, so don't try to predict just one. Look for ways to combine the information provided to make deductions. It's important to note that none of the comparisons provide actual numbers. For example, cats that eat canned food eat fewer ounces, but how much is that? Does it eat a lot less or just a little? There's no way to tell.

That makes it difficult to make deductions with the second claim about calories. If cats that eat canned food tend to eat less, they could still take in fewer calories overall if the canned food was only slightly more caloric. However, if the canned food has many more calories, then cats could still take in more calories overall even with less food.

The last sentence, on the other hand, offers a deduction along with the first sentence. For cats that eat canned food, the daily cost is higher even though they're eating fewer ounces. That must mean their food must cost more per ounce.

Step 4: Evaluate the Answer Choices

(E) is supported. If it costs more per day to feed a cat canned food and cats eat fewer ounces per day, then canned cat food must be more expensive per ounce.

(A) is not supported. It's not known how big the difference in calories is. Cats that eat canned food eat fewer ounces per day. If the canned cat food has only a few calories more, then cats could still take in fewer calories overall by eating a lot fewer ounces than would a cat eating dry cat food.

(B) is not supported. The author only presents information about canned and dry food, but there could be other options that are just not mentioned and may be more common.

(C) is Extreme. While canned food is more expensive and has more calories, that doesn't mean calories are the *only* factor involved in the extra cost.

(D) is a Distortion. This only works if one assumes that "a cat that eats fewer ounces" refers to a cat that eats canned food, and "a cat that eats more ounces" refers to a cat that eats dry food. However, there may be a third food option that the author doesn't mention. It's possible that such an option *could* cost less with cats eating even fewer ounces per day than one eating canned or dry food.

13. (A) Paradox

Step 1: Identify the Question Type

The question asks for something that will "resolve the puzzle described," making this a Paradox question.

Step 2: Untangle the Stimulus

A foundation has reconstructed an historic church in Dresden so that it can be used for church services and other events. The foundation was determined to return the church to its original form. However, that leads to a puzzling exception: the organ. Instead of restoring the original baroque organ, the foundation built a new modern one.

Step 3: Make a Prediction

If returning the church to its original form is so important, why make an exception for the organ? Don't try to predict an exact solution. Just expect that the correct answer will describe why restoring the original organ was either infeasible or unacceptable.

Step 4: Evaluate the Answer Choices

(A) provides a solution. Restoring the original baroque organ would have to be inadequate for the church's current purposes.

(B) is Out of Scope. Even if modern organs have new features, this doesn't explain why those features would warrant the foundation going against its purpose to maintain the church's original form.

(C) is a 180. If the donation was intended solely for the purpose of restoring the original organ, it's even more

unusual that the foundation ignored that request and went against the goal of bringing the church back to its original form.

(D) is Out of Scope. Even if the organ had been modified in the past, that doesn't mean it couldn't be restored to its original form. This offers no explanation why the foundation went in the other direction and made it more modern.

(E) is a 180. If the original organ was used for church services, then it's more unusual that the foundation didn't return it to its original form. It would have served the same purpose as it originally did.

14. (E) Assumption (Sufficient)

Step 1: Identify the Question Type

This is an unusual question stem, which can make it harder to identify. However, the stimulus contains a conclusion, and the correct answer will provide an unstated piece of information that, when added to the given evidence, will allow the conclusion to be properly drawn. That's the very essence of a Sufficient Assumption question.

Step 2: Untangle the Stimulus

The conclusion is that the government should not reduce import taxes on textiles. The evidence consists of two pieces of Formal Logic: 1) If reducing import taxes would benefit consumers, then it should be done. However, that could be superseded by 2) if reducing import taxes would significantly harm domestic industries, then it shouldn't be done.

Step 3: Make a Prediction

The first piece of Formal Logic provides a condition when the government *should* reduce taxes. However, the conclusion states that the government *shouldn't*, so that means the second overriding principle must be in effect. That states that taxes shouldn't be reduced if that would significantly hurt domestic industries. So, to reach the conclusion, the author is assuming that reducing taxes on textile imports would indeed cause significant harm to the industry. That would provide the grounds for rejecting the reduced taxes.

Step 4: Evaluate the Answer Choices

(E) provides the grounds for the conclusion. This suggests that reduced taxes would create significant harm, which is the very condition that would warrant saying *not* to reduce taxes.

(A) is a Distortion. While benefiting consumers would be grounds for reducing taxes, that doesn't necessarily mean that taxes should *not* be reduced without such a benefit. The only condition mentioned for not reducing taxes is if there's a significant harm.

(B) is a Distortion. The principle states that taxes should not be reduced if the industry will be "significantly harmed." Saying the textile industry won't benefit is not the same as saying it will be significantly harmed.

(C) is Out of Scope. Facing significant competition doesn't mean the industry is going to be harmed. It could thrive in the face of competition. This provides no grounds for stopping the reduction of taxes.

(D) is Out of Scope. Other measures don't affect the decision here. The only condition provided for denying the reduction of taxes is if the industry would be significantly harmed. Even if other measures provide a bigger benefit, it's still OK to lower taxes provided the industry is not harmed significantly. Thus, there would be no grounds for the conclusion to not reduce taxes on textile imports.

15. (E) Inference

Step 1: Identify the Question Type
The question asks for something that can "reasonably be concluded" from the information given. That conclusion will not be directly stated, but it will be an inference based on what's provided.

Step 2: Untangle the Stimulus
The author presents two ways in which global warming has led to rising sea levels: it causes glaciers and ice sheets to melt, and warmer water has more volume. *But* the author suggests the sea levels could have been even higher. That was prevented by artificial reservoirs, which hold water that would otherwise be in the sea.

Step 3: Make a Prediction
The author is essentially suggesting that there's more going on than people may realize. Sea levels may be rising, but that doesn't tell the whole story. Without the reservoirs, the levels would be even higher. There are a lot of potential conclusions to this situation. Don't predict one. Instead, test the answers and find one consistent with the facts without going too far or bringing in outside information.

Step 4: Evaluate the Answer Choices
(E) is supported. The rising sea level does give a glimpse into the effect of melting glaciers and ice sheets. However, some of that water may have also made its way into reservoirs, so the sea levels alone don't provide the complete picture.

(A) is not supported. The author does not suggest any dispute about how much the sea level has risen. The author merely suggests that there's more to consider than just the sea level.

(B) is not supported. The author provides no information about what occurred before reservoirs. If anything, it's likely that rising sea levels were caused by the same factors as now: melting ice and warmer water.

(C) is a 180. The author actually presents information about how global warming contributes to rising sea levels.

(D) is a Distortion. The author claims that global sea levels would have been higher without the reservoirs, but never says by how much. There is no foundation for this comparison.

16. (B) Flaw

Step 1: Identify the Question Type
The question directly asks for why the argument is *flawed*, making this a Flaw question.

Step 2: Untangle the Stimulus
The author concludes that Juan must have entered the software company's contest. The evidence is that Juan has a T-shirt with the company's new logo, and everyone who entered the contest got a T-shirt with that logo.

Evidence:

If	**contest**	$\rightarrow$	**T-shirt**

Conclusion:

If	**T-shirt**	$\rightarrow$	**contest**

Step 3: Make a Prediction
There could have been plenty of other ways for Juan to get a hold of that T-shirt. Maybe he works for the company. Maybe he bought one on the company's website. Maybe his friend entered the contest and gave him the shirt. Essentially, it boils down to a Formal Logic error. Entering the contest guaranteed people a shirt, but there's no indication that that was the only way to get a shirt (i.e., it wasn't necessary). The author reversed without negating.

Step 4: Evaluate the Answer Choices
(B) accurately describes this commonly tested flaw. Entering the contest was sufficient (i.e., it guaranteed getting a shirt), but the author acts as if it were necessary (i.e., Juan *must* have entered the contest to get that shirt).

(A) describes the commonly tested flaw of causation versus correlation, but the author is not concluding that one thing caused another to happen.

(C) is a Distortion. This describes another commonly tested flaw on the LSAT. However, the only group mentioned is people who entered the contest. The author does not draw an inference about *every* member of that group. The author only refers to Juan, who is not necessarily part of that group.

(D) describes circular reasoning, which means the evidence is based solely on the conclusion being true. However, the evidence is based on fact: Juan has the shirt. The conclusion need not be true for that evidence to be true.

(E) gets the logic backward. The author draws a conclusion about a single person (Juan) on the basis of a generalization (the general rule of contest entrants).

17. (B) Inference

Step 1: Identify the Question Type
For this question, the stimulus will "strongly support" the correct answer, meaning the correct answer will be a logical inference.

Step 2: Untangle the Stimulus
The author describes some problems with expert witnesses. Jurors often can't understand them and thus cannot evaluate their testimony. Even though expert witnesses can actually contradict one another, they can both appear competent. In that case, it's up to the jury to determine the reliability.

Step 3: Make a Prediction
This all leads to an unusual resolution. The final claim states that, when expert witnesses contradict one another, it's up to the jury to decide who is more reliable. However, the first sentence claims that juries often *can't*. In that case, juries are inevitably going to have to use a different basis for their decision.

Step 4: Evaluate the Answer Choices
(B) is exactly what the author is suggesting. If juries cannot understand and thus cannot evaluate expert testimony, they must base their decision on some other factor.

(A) is not supported. The author is not making any recommendations about what should or should not happen.

(C) is not supported. The information provided offers no suggestion about people who *can* understand the technical information, let alone their assessment of legal implications.

(D) is not supported. The author makes no recommendation about who should be selected for juries.

(E) is a 180. The author directly states that expert witnesses on opposite sides can make conflicting claims. There's no indication that they are likely to *agree* about anything.

18. (E) Assumption (Necessary)

Step 1: Identify the Question Type
The question directly asks for an assumption, and one on which the argument *depends*, making this a Necessary Assumption question.

Step 2: Untangle the Stimulus
The tax reformer concludes that the proposed tax legislation is perfectly framed. This is despite the fact that some people criticize the legislation for being too vague and some criticize it for being too specific. The reformer's evidence is that no one statement can be both too specific and too vague.

Step 3: Make a Prediction
The reformer makes one major slip. The evidence is that one *statement* cannot be too specific and too vague. However, the reformer's conclusion is about the entire legislation. The reformer overlooks the possibility that the complaints are about different statements. The reformer must assume everyone is complaining about the same statements, and thus they're just being whiny—the legislation is perfect as is.

Step 4: Evaluate the Answer Choices
(E) must be assumed. If the legislation *is* made up of a combination of vague and overly specific statements, then the criticisms may be valid. The reformer must assume otherwise to suggest the legislation is just right.

(A) is Out of Scope. Even if criticism on both sides is rare (which is hard to believe), that offers no connection to why the reformer believes the legislation is good as is.

(B) is Out of Scope. The reformer is not concerned about results. The entire argument is solely about the quality of the legislation itself.

(C) is also Out of Scope. It makes no difference to the reformer's argument whether these are the only two groups making criticisms or whether there are countless others.

(D) is Out of Scope, too. Who the legislation was meant to satisfy is immaterial. Using the Denial Test, even if the legislation *was* meant to satisfy one specific political group, and now the right and left have opposite complaints, that does not necessarily upend the tax reformer's conclusion that the legislation was framed "as it should be."

19. (B) Parallel Reasoning

Step 1: Identify the Question Type
The correct answer will be an argument "most similar" to the one presented in the stimulus. That makes this a Parallel Reasoning question.

Step 2: Untangle the Stimulus
The employee's company has blocked access to certain websites claiming they can be distracting. The employee counters that windows and decorations can also be a distraction, but those are not considered unacceptable.

Step 3: Make a Prediction
The employee is pointing out an inconsistency in the company's reasoning. The correct answer will do the same thing using similar logic: someone provides a reason why an action is unacceptable, but the author argues that the same reason does not make other actions unacceptable.

Step 4: Evaluate the Answer Choices
(B) matches the employee's call about inconsistency. Here, activists want to ban a device for the reason that extended exposure causes cancer in lab animals. However, the same reasoning does not make chemicals unacceptable.

(A) does not match. This just suggests everybody is different, and people fail to consider that sometimes. That's not the same as pointing out an inconsistency in applying the same reasoning.

(C) makes a prediction about a company needing to replace its retiring employees with new hires. This has nothing to do with suggesting that someone is applying reasoning in an inconsistent manner.

(D) does not provide inconsistent application of a reason. It merely claims that one thing (engaging characters) is not enough to guarantee a result (sales). That's not the same logic as the original.

(E) does not match. It rejects a standard of judgment because it's counterintuitive. Unlike the stimulus though, **(E)** does not indicate a discrepancy on how that standard is applied. The movie industry seems to always use that same standard.

20. (E) Assumption (Sufficient)

Step 1: Identify the Question Type
The question asks for something that, *if* assumed, would allow the conclusion to be drawn. That makes this a Sufficient Assumption question.

Step 2: Untangle the Stimulus
The author concludes ([*t*]*herefore*) that some students in French Lit 205 are not French-literature majors. The evidence is that some students in French Lit 205 are in Bio 218, and everyone in Bio 218 is a biology major.

Step 3: Make a Prediction
The evidence shows how some people in French Lit 205 are biology majors, but the author concludes that some people in that class are not French-literature majors. The author is simply assuming biology majors can't also be French-literature majors. If that were true, then the author's conclusion is confirmed. There are people in French Lit 205 who are not French-literature majors: the biology majors.

Step 4: Evaluate the Answer Choices
(E) is the assumption. If one cannot be both a biology major and a French-literature major, then those biology majors in French Lit 205 cannot be French-literature majors, confirming the author's conclusion.

(A) offers no support for the author's conclusion. If French Lit 205 is a requirement for French-literature majors, then there's no reason to suggest that anyone in that class is *not* a French-literature major.

(B) is Out of Scope. The author's argument is not about students in Bio 218. The argument is about students in French Lit 205.

(C) is an Irrelevant Comparison. It doesn't matter which major is more common at the university in general. The argument is only about who's taking the one class in question.

(D) is the same Irrelevant Comparison as **(C)** but reversed. It doesn't matter which major is more common at the university in general. The argument is only about who's taking the one class in question.

21. (B) Inference

Step 1: Identify the Question Type
The correct answer "must be true" based on the information given, making this an Inference question.

Step 2: Untangle the Stimulus
The stimulus consists of two pieces of Formal Logic: 1) in order for a book to be a literary classic, it must reveal something significant about people, and 2) if something is not worthy of serious study, then it doesn't reveal anything significant about people.

Step 3: Make a Prediction
As long as the Formal Logic is translated properly, the two statements can be combined. By the first statement, if a book is a classic, it must reveal something. Thus, by contrapositive, if it doesn't reveal anything, it can't be a classic:

If	*classic*	$\rightarrow$	*reveal*

If	*~ reveal*	$\rightarrow$	*~ classic*

By the second statement, if a book is not worthy of being studied seriously, it reveals nothing. By contrapositive, if it *did* reveal something, it *would* be worthy of serious study:

If	*~ worthy of serious study*	$\rightarrow$	*~ reveal*

If	*reveal*	$\rightarrow$	*worthy of serious study*

Putting these statements together, if a book is a literary classic, it must reveal something, which means it must be worthy of serious study. By contrapositive, if a book is not worthy of serious study, it reveals nothing, and thus cannot be a literary classic.

If	*literary classic*	$\rightarrow$	*reveal*	$\rightarrow$	*worthy of serious study*

If	*~ worthy of serious study*	$\rightarrow$	*~ reveal*	$\rightarrow$	*~ literary classic*

Anticipate that some, if not all, of the wrong answers will confuse sufficient and necessary conditions. Apply the logic properly, following the arrows in the right direction.

Step 4: Evaluate the Answer Choices

(B) directly follows the logic. In order for a book to be a classic, it must reveal something, which means it has to be worthy of serious study.

(A) is a classic trap, confusing necessary and sufficient conditions. Being worthy of serious study is necessary, but it does not guarantee that a book will be a classic.

(C) is a 180. Literary classics must reveal something about the human condition, which means they must be worthy of serious study.

(D) is possible, but does not have to be true. The logic only mentions what's true of books that are *not* worthy of serious study (they fail to reveal anything). There is no additional information guaranteed about books that *are* worthy of serious study.

(E) is possible, but does not have to be true. The logic only claims that literary classics reveal something about the human condition. There is no information guaranteed about books that are *not* literary classics. They might all reveal something as well. Don't dispute this as unlikely (which it very well may be). Instead, stay focused on the logic provided. The correct answer must be based on that and nothing else.

22. (B) Strengthen/Weaken (Evaluate the Argument)

Step 1: Identify the Question Type

The question asks for something that would "help in evaluating the argument." That makes this an Evaluate the Argument variant of Strengthen/Weaken questions. The correct answer will pose a question that, depending on how it's answered, would validate or invalidate the argument.

Step 2: Untangle the Stimulus

The author here is refuting an opinion. Scientists believed that the features of the *T. Rex* (large head, long legs, tiny arms) developed to accommodate the dinosaur's massive size. *However*, the author suggests abandoning this belief based on evidence of an earlier, much smaller dinosaur that had the same features.

Step 3: Make a Prediction

Paraphrased, the author's conclusion is that the *T. Rex*'s features did *not* develop to accommodate for the dinosaur's size. The evidence comes from another dinosaur skeleton with the same features at a fraction of the size of a *T. Rex*. This would definitely question the belief about accommodating a larger animal . . . unless the skeleton found was of a baby dinosaur. It's highly unlikely that a *T. Rex* is *born* at full height. Perhaps the dinosaur in question was still quite young and would eventually grow to the same size as a *T. Rex*. In that case, the original hypothesis could still hold. For the author's argument to stand, it must be determined whether this new

dinosaur skeleton was of a fully grown dinosaur or if it was just in its youth and yet to reach its full height.

Step 4: Evaluate the Answer Choices

(B) would help evaluate the author's argument. If the dinosaur was at the peak of its life, then the author has a point. If the dinosaur was still very young, it may have grown a lot more, and the feature could still serve to accommodate a larger animal.

(A) does not help. If the exact ratio was the same, that supports the author's claim for sure. However, even if the ratios were a little off, the general features were still the same and the author still has a point.

(C) is Out of Scope. The only comparison that's important here is between the *T. Rex* and the new dinosaur. How *T. Rex* compares to other dinosaurs has no effect on this argument.

(D) is Out of Scope. It doesn't matter if the dinosaurs were necessarily related. It's all about the size of the dinosaurs and the shared features.

(E) is also Out of Scope. It doesn't matter what size animals the dinosaurs preyed upon. All that matters are the features and why they developed.

23. (A) Parallel Flaw

Step 1: Identify the Question Type

The correct answer will be an argument with reasoning "most similar to" that in the given argument. That reasoning is said to be flawed, so this is a Parallel Flaw question.

Step 2: Untangle the Stimulus

The author concludes ([s]o) that the show *Bliss* must be the most watched show on television. The evidence is that *Bliss* is the most popular show on channel YXK, and YXK has more viewers than any other network.

Step 3: Make a Prediction

The problem is that what's true of a group comparison does not necessarily indicate what's true of individual members. In other words, just because the total viewers for YXK is the highest, that doesn't mean the same goes for each of its individual shows. It's possible that one other network has fewer viewers overall but has one outstanding show that is more popular than *Bliss*. The correct answer will commit the same error. It will claim that a group (YXK) has the highest number of something overall (most viewers), and then suggest that one member of that group (*Bliss*) has more than any other individual.

Step 4: Evaluate the Answer Choices

(A) matches the flawed logic. As with the original, this argument claims that a group (soccer players) has more of something (leg injuries) than any other group. The author then illogically claims that one member of that group (Linda) has more than any other individual. There may be one sport with fewer leg injuries overall, but which just happens to have one particular accident-prone player who got hurt more than Linda.

(B) is flawed, but not for the same reason. The evidence is about the number of awards received, while the conclusion makes a claim about being the *best* teacher. That's an unwarranted scope shift, but that's not what the original argument did wrong.

(C) is not flawed. This does not claim that the entire group (Olson Motor Company) sells the most cars. It states that the best-selling *individual* cars come from that company. So, it's logical to say its best-selling individual car is the best-selling individual car overall.

(D) is flawed, but not for the same reason. This uses extremes (highest- and lowest-paid individuals) to draw a conclusion about averages. This is not logical, but it's not the same flaw as the original, which had nothing to do with averages.

(E) does not match. This only focuses on what's true for an individual film. It does not try to apply what's true of an entire group to that individual. Furthermore, the level of certainty in **(E)**'s conclusion is *probably*. However the stimulus gave a more definitive conclusion.

24. (E) Principle (Apply/Inference)

Step 1: Identify the Question Type
The stimulus will contain a general principle that will be used to support the specific reasoning in the correct answer. That makes this an Apply the Principle question.

Step 2: Untangle the Stimulus
The stimulus provides two pieces of Formal Logic. First, for a contract to be valid, someone has to accept a legitimate offer. Second, if the person offered something reasonably believes the offer is in jest, then that offer is not legitimate.

Step 3: Make a Prediction
Once translated, the two statements can be combined. The first statement is that, if a contract is valid, there must be a legitimate offer. By contrapositive, if the offer is not legitimate, the contract is invalid.

If	valid	→	offer legitimate

If	offer ~ legitimate	→	~ valid

The second statement is that, if someone feels they are being offered something in jest, the offer is not legitimate. By contrapositive, for the offer to be legitimate, the person receiving the offer has to feel the offer is not in jest.

If	offer believed to be in jest	→	offer ~ legitimate

If	offer legitimate	→	offer ~ believed to be in jest

Combining these statements, for a contract to be valid, the offer must be legitimate, which means the person accepting the offer has to believe it was a serious offer. By contrapositive, it the person receiving the offer believes it's a joke, then the offer is not legitimate, and the whole contract is invalid. The correct answer will apply the Formal Logic properly without confusing necessary and sufficient conditions. Note that the correct answer doesn't have to use everything, it just has to be consistent.

Step 4: Evaluate the Answer Choices
(E) matches the logic of the principle. By the first statement, once the offer is illegitimate, the contract is invalid. This may have been difficult to choose as it doesn't apply the second half of the principle (regarding the offer being made in jest). However, it doesn't have to. As long as it doesn't contradict the second half (which it doesn't), it correctly applies the logic given, and is the only answer to do so.

(A) is a classic trap, as it gets the logic backward. To be valid, the offer *must* be legitimate. That means it's necessary. However, that does not mean it is sufficient, i.e., that every legitimate offer results in a valid contract. Furthermore, the fact that Sandy has not rejected the offer is not equivalent to accepting the offer.

(B) is a Distortion. If Kenta *believed* the offer was in jest, the contract would be invalid. However, Kenta didn't know that, and thus the principle provides no grounds to consider the contract invalid.

(C) is a Distortion. There is no condition that guarantees anyone accepting an offer. The *reasonable* standard of the stimulus was about whether or not an offer was legitimate, not whether or not it should be accepted.

(D) is a classic trap, as it gets the logic backward. Accepting a legitimate offer is necessary for a contract to be valid, but it is not sufficient, i.e., it does not guarantee the contract is certainly valid. Besides, the fact that nobody would believe the offer was in jest is also not sufficient to consider the offer legitimate. So this gets the logic of *both* statements backward.

25. (D) Weaken

Step 1: Identify the Question Type

The question directly asks for something that weakens the scientist's argument.

Step 2: Untangle the Stimulus

The scientist presents a timeline of events. Ages ago, there was a continent called Gondwana. That split up into the Americas and Australia. Long after that, a group of islands arose. On that island, there are certain species of iguana. Where did they come from? The scientist concludes they came from the Americas—all the way across the Pacific. They floated over on debris. The scientist doesn't think they came from Australia—even though the islands are surely closer to Australia—because the only existing species in the entire world related to the island iguanas are the ones in the Americas.

Step 3: Make a Prediction

The scientist makes a pretty good case, but makes one fatal error. The Americas is the only place in the world where a related species *currently* exists. The scientist overlooks the possibility that another related species once lived in Australia. Then, either they all migrated to the islands, or some of them migrated before the rest all died off in Australia. Either way, if related iguanas ever did live in Australia, the scientist's theory of iguanas travelling across an entire ocean on debris is suddenly called into question.

Step 4: Evaluate the Answer Choices

(D) weakens the scientist's argument. If there are fossils of related iguanas in Australia, then it's possible that the island iguanas migrated from there before the Australian population died off. There was no need for iguanas to travel across the ocean from the Americas.

(A) is Out of Scope. The argument is only about the iguanas, not any other animals on the islands.

(B) is Out of Scope. Even if there are *some* genetic differences, the two groups are still related, and the iguanas in the Americas are still the *only* related species in the world. So, **(B)** does not weaken the argument.

(C) does not weaken the argument either. Even if it's uncommon, that still means it could happen. In addition, the scientist has plenty of other evidence to make a case.

(E) is Out of Scope. The argument is only about the iguanas, and only about the ones that live on the islands. This answer talks about other immaterial plants and animals that live elsewhere.

26. (B) Flaw

Step 1: Identify the Question Type

The correct answer will describe why the argument is "vulnerable to criticism," which is wording that indicates a Flaw question.

Step 2: Untangle the Stimulus

Archaeologists recently found the largest tomb ever found in Macedonia. The author concludes that it must be the tomb of Alexander the Great. The evidence is that he was the greatest Macedonian in history and thus would have had the largest tomb.

Step 3: Make a Prediction

Sounds plausible, but what about the largest tomb that had been found before that? Did the author think *that* was Alexander the Great's? What if an even bigger tomb is found in the future? Maybe *that* will be the one that belonged to Alexander the Great—unless they find yet another one that's *even bigger*. All of this means the author is only basing a conclusion on what's been found so far without considering that other, bigger tombs have yet to be found.

Step 4: Evaluate the Answer Choices

(B) describes the author's mistake perfectly.

(A) is Extreme. The author suggests that Alexander's military success contributed to his greatness, but that doesn't mean that's the *only* way to attain greatness.

(C) is Out of Scope. The argument is only about Macedonia and Alexander as the greatest person in that area's history. It doesn't matter how the tomb compares to those in other regions.

(D) is Out of Scope. What happened after his death does nothing to change the status of all he accomplished when he was alive. The evidence still claims he was the greatest Macedonian in history. It was people *after* him that messed it all up.

(E) may be true, but it's not a logical flaw. It's perfectly reasonable to assume that the remains of a tomb can indicate the tomb's size. The flawed logic is assuming that archaeologists will never find anything bigger.

PrepTest 81

The Inside Story

PrepTest 81 was administered in June 2017. It challenged 27,606 test takers. What made this test so hard? Here's a breakdown of what Kaplan students who were surveyed after taking the official exam considered PrepTest 81's most difficult section.

Hardest PrepTest 81 Section as Reported by Test Takers

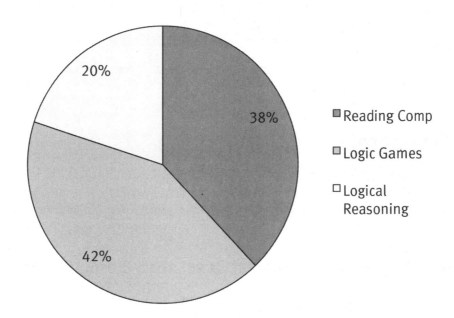

Based on these results, you might think that studying Logic Games is the key to LSAT success. Well, Logic Games is important, but test takers' perceptions don't tell the whole story. For that, you need to consider students' actual performance. Alas, PrepTest 81 is so recent that as of the time of publication we don't yet have sufficient data about student performance on this test. ***Your online materials will be updated to reflect performance data later in the fall of 2017.***

Actual student performance typically tells quite a different story. Usually students are fairly equally likely to miss questions in all three of the different section types.

Maybe students overestimate the difficulty of the Logic Games section because it's so unusual, or maybe it's because a really hard logic game is so easy to remember after the test. But the truth is that the testmaker places hard questions throughout the test. When we update the information in fall of 2017, we'll include the locations of the 10 hardest (most missed) questions in the exam.

To maximize your potential on the LSAT, you need to take a comprehensive approach. Test yourself rigorously, and review your performance on every section of the test. Kaplan's LSAT explanations provide the expertise and insight you need to fully understand your results. The explanations are written and edited by a team of LSAT experts, who have helped thousands of students improve their scores. Kaplan always provides data-driven analysis of the test, ranking the difficulty of every question based on actual student performance. The ten hardest questions on every test are highlighted with a 4-star difficulty rating, the highest we give. The analysis breaks down the remaining questions into 1-, 2-, and 3-star ratings so that you can compare your performance to thousands of other test takers on all LSAC material. ***As soon as we get sufficient data, we'll update the star ratings for PrepTest 81 in fall of 2017.***

7 Can't Miss Features of PrepTest 81

- With 10 Inference questions in LR, PT 81 had the most Inference questions since December '94 (PT 13).
- The Logic Games section has only started with a Hybrid game nine times ever. That said, PT 81 was the third test in three years to do so.
- PT 81's Reading Comprehension section contained only two Global questions. That ties June '16 (PT 78) as the fewest ever.
- What replaced those Global questions? There were four LR - Parallel Reasoning questions in the RC section. That's a new record, and equals the same number there were on PT 77–80 combined!
- (D)-lightful! There were at least two more (D)'s than (C)'s or (E)'s in all three sections!
- A/B Testing? The second LR section had some pretty unusual letter answer streaks. #7 to #15 were all either (A) or (B)—including four straight (B)'s in one stretch.
- Dangerous Curve Ahead! PT 81 was the first test since October '08 (PT 58) to require at least 83 questions correct to get a 164 (90th percentile score). Similarly, PT 81 was the first test since June '07 (PT June '07) to require at least 94 questions correct to get a 172 (99th percentile score).

PrepTest 81 in Context

As much fun as it is to find out what makes a PrepTest unique or noteworthy, it's even more important to know just how representative it is of other LSAT administrations (and, thus, how likely it is to be representative of the exam you will face on Test Day). The following charts compare the numbers of each kind of question and game on PrepTest 81 to the average numbers seen on all officially released LSATs administered over the past five years (from 2012 through 2016).

Number of LR Questions by Type: PrepTest 81 vs. 2012–2016 Average

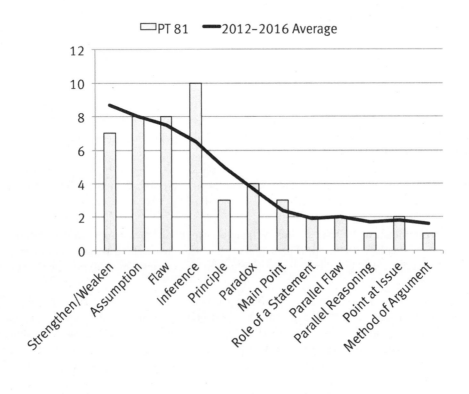

Number of LG Games by Type: PrepTest 81 vs. 2012–2016 Average

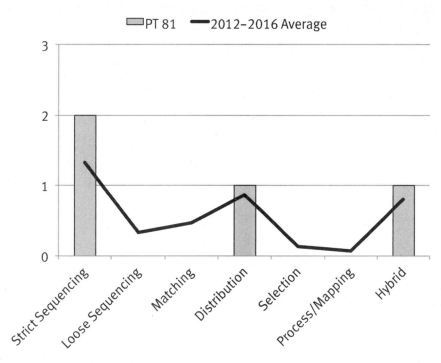

Number of RC Questions by Type: PrepTest 81 vs. 2012–2016 Average

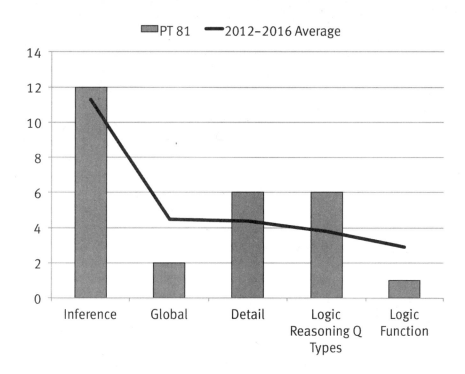

There isn't usually a huge difference in the distribution of questions from LSAT to LSAT, but if this test seems harder (or easier) to you than another you've taken, compare the number of questions of the types on which you, personally, are strongest and weakest. And then, explore within each section to see if your best or worst question types came earlier or later.

Students in Kaplan's comprehensive LSAT courses have access to every released LSAT, and to an online Qbank with thousands of officially released questions, games, and passages. If you are studying on your own, you have to do a bit more work to identify your strengths and your areas of opportunity. Quantitative analysis (like that in the previous charts) is an important tool for understanding how the test is constructed, and how you are performing on it.

Section I: Reading Comprehension
Passage 1: Wynton Marsalis and the State of Jazz

Q#	Question Type	Correct	Difficulty
1	Global	D	Check your online resources.
2	Inference	C	Check your online resources.
3	Inference	D	Check your online resources.
4	Logic Reasoning (Parallel Reasoning)	B	Check your online resources.
5	Detail	E	Check your online resources.
6	Inference	A	Check your online resources.
7	Detail	E	Check your online resources.

Passage 2: Inferential vs. Noninferential Thoughts

Q#	Question Type	Correct	Difficulty
8	Global	B	Check your online resources.
9	Logic Reasoning (Weaken)	C	Check your online resources.
10	Inference	E	Check your online resources.
11	Logic Reasoning (Parallel Reasoning)	A	Check your online resources.
12	Detail	D	Check your online resources.
13	Detail	C	Check your online resources.
14	Inference	D	Check your online resources.

Passage 3: Dowsing

Q#	Question Type	Correct	Difficulty
15	Logic Function	C	Check your online resources.
16	Detail	A	Check your online resources.
17	Logic Reasoning (Parallel Reasoning)	D	Check your online resources.
18	Inference	B	Check your online resources.
19	Detail	D	Check your online resources.
20	Inference	E	Check your online resources.

Passage 4: The Use of Independent Research by Judges

Q#	Question Type	Correct	Difficulty
21	Logic Reasoning (Principle)	C	Check your online resources.
22	Inference	A	Check your online resources.
23	Inference	D	Check your online resources.
24	Inference	B	Check your online resources.
25	Inference	C	Check your online resources.
26	Logic Reasoning (Parallel Reasoning)	B	Check your online resources.
27	Inference	D	Check your online resources.

Passage 1: Wynton Marsalis and the State of Jazz

Step 1: Read the Passage Strategically
Sample Roadmap

line #	Keyword/phrase	¶ Margin notes
3	persuasive advocacy	
4	ruled	
5	unqualified admiration	
6	unsurpassed influence	Marsalis praised
7	But	
8	increasing fire	
10	uncertain; as does	Future of Marsalis & jazz uncertain
14	In fact	After 1999, Marsalis stopped
19	drastically reduced	
20	shifting its emphasis	Columbia shift from new jazz to old
23	essentially gave up	
24	grim	
26	accused of; partly	Critics blame Marsalis
27	culpable; charge	
28	unbending; sanctifying	
30	stifling	Marsalis too traditional
31	inhibited	
33	noted	
37	Indeed	
39	great	
40	emphasis; Still; never advocated	Auth: Marsalis traditional yet innovative
41	mere	
45	However	
46	different; :	But, record execs say don't need new jazz
48	?; So	
49	shifted	
55	irresistible; :	Record companies make $ selling old jazz
56	far more profitable	
57	than	

Discussion

In the first paragraph, the author introduces a startling contrast: Jazz musician Wynton Marsalis (**Topic**) was widely praised for decades, gaining "unqualified admiration" and having "unsurpassed influence." *But* that changed, as criticism toward Marsalis led to an uncertain fate for both him and jazz music, in general.

The second paragraph goes into detail about the deterioration of both Marsalis's career and jazz. After a massive output (15 CDs in one year), Marsalis went years without releasing new music. He no longer had a record contract, and record companies stopped developing new jazz artists. It makes the reader wonder, what happened to Marsalis's sterling reputation, and how did this affect jazz as a whole? These questions serve as the **Scope** of the passage. And the **Purpose** is to answer those questions and explain what happened.

The third paragraph starts to offer some explanation, presenting the point of view of Marsalis's critics. They partially blame Marsalis for his *unbending* and *stifling* reliance on classicism, which impeded innovation.

The author defends Marsalis some in the fourth paragraph, admitting to Marsalis's emphasis on tradition, but arguing that Marsalis was using that tradition as inspiration for reinvention and expression. *However*, record companies took a different view: If traditional music is so great, then who needs new music?

And that leads to the ultimate effect described in the last paragraph: Record companies stopped pushing new artists and instead focused on making lots of money selling archived recordings of older artists. This wraps up the **Main Idea** of the passage: Despite his initial success, Marsalis's emphasis on traditional jazz styles ultimately hurt his career and led the music industry to stop supporting new jazz musicians.

1. (D) Global

Step 2: Identify the Question Type
The question asks for the "main point" of the entire passage, making this a Global question.

Step 3: Research the Relevant Text
Don't go back into the passage. Just consider the Main Idea as predicted after reading the passage.

Step 4: Make a Prediction
The Main Idea was that, despite his initial success, Marsalis's emphasis on traditional jazz hurt his career and ultimately led record companies to abandon their support for new jazz musicians.

Step 5: Evaluate the Answer Choices

(D) offers an accurate summary, bringing up Marsalis's emphasis on tradition and how that led to decreased support for new jazz artists.

(A) focuses too much on Marsalis, completely ignoring the effect on jazz music in general.

(B) addresses the author's defense of Marsalis in the fourth paragraph. However, this not only misses the point of the passage as a whole, but it also suggests that jazz now has a wider audience—a claim not supported anywhere in the passage.

(C) is a Distortion. It is never suggested that Marsalis ever moved away from traditionalism. And, if anything, the passage suggests that Marsalis's style caused the record companies to shift their focus, not the other way around.

(E) is far too narrow, focusing merely on what is mentioned in the first paragraph. However, this completely leaves out the effects described throughout the rest of the passage.

2. (C) Inference

Step 2: Identify the Question Type
The question asks what someone "most likely means" when making a claim, making this an Inference question.

Step 3: Research the Relevant Text
The quote in question is presented at the end of the third paragraph. Don't just focus on the quote itself. Consider how it relates to the point of the paragraph as a whole.

Step 4: Make a Prediction
In saying Marsalis has a "retro ideology," the executive also claims that Marsalis's ideas were more "museumlike in nature, a look back." This fits the criticism throughout the paragraph that Marsalis was *unbending* in his focus on classicism and was *stifling* in its orthodoxy. In short, the executive is suggesting that Marsalis was too caught up in the past.

Step 5: Evaluate the Answer Choices

(C) correctly identifies the idea that Marsalis was too focused on tradition.

(A) is a Distortion. Marsalis is reviving traditional ideas, but there is no suggestion that these ideas were ever *discredited*.

(B) is a Faulty Use of Detail. The author references Marsalis recombining ideas in the fourth paragraph (line 43), but this is not related to the executive's claim, which is more about Marsalis's ideas being outdated (*museumlike*).

(D) is also a Faulty Use of Detail, and a 180. It's the author who praises Marsalis for reinvention and reinterpretation (lines 41–44), not the executive. The executive is more critical and sees Marsalis as stuck in the past, rather than being inventive.

(E) is a Distortion. There is no suggestion that the ideas Marsalis used were in any way *inauthentic*.

3. (D) Inference

Step 2: Identify the Question Type
The question asks about what the author would "most likely" believe, which means the correct answer won't be directly stated, but it will be directly supported. That makes this an Inference question.

Step 3: Research the Relevant Text
The question stem refers to the "state of affairs in jazz," a phrase that (not coincidentally) appears word for word in line 24. The phrase "this grim state of affairs" indicates the author is referring to the scenario described immediately beforehand, in the second paragraph.

Step 4: Make a Prediction
The *grim* situation is that record companies have "reduced [their] roster of active jazz musicians," emphasized "reissues of old recordings," and "essentially gave up on developing new artists." That suggests the author would be much happier if record companies starting focusing on new jazz musicians again.

Step 5: Evaluate the Answer Choices

(D) is supported, as it would perfectly address the de-emphasis on new artists.

(A) is a Distortion. The author would certainly appreciate this, especially given the defense of Marsalis presented in the fourth paragraph. However, the question asks about what would make the author less negative about the state of affairs in jazz music in general, not in the treatment of Marsalis personally.

(B) is too focused on reviving Marsalis's career rather than improving the "state of affairs in jazz," as the question asks.

(C) is also too focused on defending Marsalis personally, rather than addressing the state of affairs in jazz overall.

(E) is a Distortion. The author does not have a problem with young jazz musicians. The problem is with the record companies, who are basically abandoning new jazz musicians.

4. (B) Logic Reasoning (Parallel Reasoning)

Step 2: Identify the Question Type
The question asks for a situation that is "most analogous" to one described in the passage. That makes this a Logic Reasoning question, specifically one that mimics a Parallel Reasoning question.

Step 3: Research the Relevant Text
The situation facing Marsalis is described throughout the entire passage. Use the margin notes to stay focused on the major themes, rather than getting caught up in the details.

Step 4: Make a Prediction
As described throughout the passage, Marsalis is criticized for focusing too much on traditional ideas, and this has led music companies to abandon new musicians in favor of selling older recordings. The correct answer will mimic this idea of how one's focus on tradition can lead others to abandon new ideas in favor of selling old ones.

Step 5: Evaluate the Answer Choices

(B) is a perfect match. Like Marsalis, the research firm is trying to create new products that are similar to traditional products. However, that has just led to people abandoning the new products in favor of seeking out the traditional products.

(A) does not match. Here, the unintended consequence is comparatively higher price increases. There's no focus on traditional styles or abandonment of new ideas.

(C) does not match. Here, the focus is on people finding synthetic products less attractive. There's nothing about Marsalis's situation that suggests people are less *attracted* to new music than to old music—the record companies are just focusing on marketing old music.

(D) does not match, and is a 180 at worst. If anything, Marsalis is facing competition from established companies focused on profiting from archived recordings, not some upstarts with their newfangled ideas.

(E) does not match. In this scenario, somebody tries to save one thing (endangered fish), and a new thing comes along to destroy it. Marsalis, on the other hand, is trying to use old ideas to create something new, but it's the old ideas that thrive and diminish the presence of new stuff.

5. (E) Detail

Step 2: Identify the Question Type
"According to the passage" indicates that the correct answer will be directly stated, making this a Detail question.

Step 3: Research the Relevant Text
The question asks what Marsalis encouraged young jazz musicians to do. This is not a major part of the global theme, so do a quick scan for Content Clues, e.g., *encouraged* or "young musicians." Those words should direct your attention to lines 37–39.

Step 4: Make a Prediction
In lines 37–39, it is directly stated that Marsalis encouraged young musicians to "pay attention to [jazz] music's traditions." The correct answer should say exactly that, if a bit paraphrased.

Step 5: Evaluate the Answer Choices

(E) is a perfect match.

(A) is a 180, at worst. Even though Marsalis encouraged paying attention to tradition, the author claims Marsalis himself reinvented traditional elements for innovative purposes (lines 41–44), so it would seem unlikely that Marsalis would encourage musicians to restrain that kind of impulse.

(B) is Out of Scope. While Marsalis himself composed music, there is no mention of him encouraging others to do so.

(C) is Out of Scope. There is no mention anywhere of playing with older musicians.

(D) is a Distortion. In the same sentence that indicates Marsalis's encouragement to young musicians, it is said he also seeks to *elevate* the public perception, not ignore it.

6. (A) Inference
Step 2: Identify the Question Type
The question asks for something with which the author is "most likely to agree," making this an Inference question.

Step 3: Research the Relevant Text
There are no Content Clues or line references, so the entire text is relevant.

Step 4: Make a Prediction
With no reference point to start, there are too many possible inferences to make a solid prediction. Stick to the major themes and go through the answers one at a time. Eliminate anything that goes against the main theme and use Content Clues in the choices to test what's necessary.

Step 5: Evaluate the Answer Choices
(A) is supported, even if weakly. The support for this claim comes from lines 51–53. There, the author raised contrasting opinions regarding Marsalis's traditional views. To critics, Marsalis's classicism was idolatry, i.e., seeing past musicians as idols to be worshiped and emulated. However, at least Marsalis was creating new music. For record companies, classicism was just "play the old stuff again." They rejected new music entirely, making them a little more rigid.

(B) is a Distortion. Marsalis encouraged new musicians to respect traditional views, but it's never suggested that Marsalis directly promoted those new musicians personally.

(C) is not supported. The author does mention that both critics and fellow musicians were displeased (lines 7–9), but never suggests one group was more vocal. In fact, the author only presents the views of critics (lines 27–36).

(D) is Out of Scope. The views of younger musicians are never addressed in the passage.

(E) is a Distortion. The release of fifteen CDs is mentioned in line 12, but there's no indication that this had any impact on critical perception.

7. (E) Detail
Step 2: Identify the Question Type
The correct answer will be a question that is directly answered by a detail in the passage.

Step 3: Research the Relevant Text
With no Content Clues or line references, the entire text is relevant.

Step 4: Make a Prediction
With no research clues, a prediction is not possible. Instead, go through the choices one at a time, only doing research when necessary to ensure the question in the correct choice is answered.

Step 5: Evaluate the Answer Choices
(E) is answered in lines 53–58. It's money, of course. What else would encourage record companies to do this?

(A) is not answered. Marsalis didn't *release* any music in that time, but it's not known whether or not he was *composing* any music.

(B) is Out of Scope. No description of Marsalis's fan base is given.

(C) is not answered in the passage. This may be tempting for anyone familiar with Marsalis, who did indeed release such CDs. However, the content of Marsalis's CDs are not described in this passage, and this is thus not correct.

(D) is not answered. It is only mentioned that Marsalis did not have a contract. It is never actually said why.

Passage 2: Inferential vs. Noninferential Thoughts

Step 1: Read the Passage Strategically
Sample Roadmap

line #	Keyword/phrase	¶ Margin notes
2	but	Common belief: know own thoughts; infer others'
4	while	
5	But	
6	challenged	Studies with children dispute
9	while nonetheless	
12	but	
13	argue	Psych: people infer own thoughts
15	every bit	
16	According to	
19	It follows	
20	wrong	
23	so tenaciously; illusory belief	Knowing thoughts is an illusion
25	suggest; analogous to	
28	not only; but	similar to expertise
31	whereas	
32	For instance	
35	so	
36	expert	Infer quickly; don't notice
37	fail	
38	failure; leads naturally to	
39	supposition	
42	claiming	
43	perilously close	Auth: potential dangerous claim
46	But; in fact	But, psych. avoid problem
47	do not	
48	suggest	
51	e.g.	
53	explains why	Inferences made internally
57	Thus; crucial	

KAPLAN

Discussion

The passage opens up with what common sense *suggests*: Presumably, we just know our own thoughts with complete accuracy, and we merely guess other people's thoughts. However, as could be expected in an LSAT passage, this assumption is rejected. The author presents a study in which children can accurately describe certain events, but have trouble describing their own thoughts about those events. From this, "psychologists argue" (line 13) that our thoughts are not directly observable; we're merely inferring our own thoughts, too, and we can be wrong about them.

The second paragraph presents an explanation why we insist that we know our own thoughts infallibly. Psychologists explain it through an analogy involving expertise. When we gain expertise in a field, it *appears* to change our knowledge and perception. We thought we were making inferences before and now just see the truth. However, psychologists suggest we're still making inferences; we're just getting so fast at making them that we don't even realize it. It's important to note the persistent use of phrases such as "it appears" and "the supposition." It's constantly suggested that people just *believe* they're observing things directly and infallibly, but they're not—they're just making inferences. That's a major theme of this passage.

In the third paragraph, the author brings up a potentially dangerous implication: Psychologists are almost saying our inferences are solely based on our external behaviors. *But*, the author qualifies that they're not saying that. Instead, psychologists say our inferences are based on internal activity in the brain. This activity is what makes our inferences so reliable and seemingly infallible.

There's a lot of psychological jargon here, but stay focused on the overriding theme. The **Topic** is our thoughts, and the **Scope** is whether we directly observe our thoughts infallibly or not. The **Purpose** is to present the views of psychologists (note how almost all opinions in the passage are attributed to them). The **Main Idea** is that, contrary to what people assume, psychologists argue that we do not know our own thoughts directly; we simply infer them, and those inferences are not based solely on observations of our external behavior.

8. (B) Global

Step 2: Identify the Question Type

The question asks for the "main point of the passage," making this a Global question.

Step 3: Research the Relevant Text

No need to go back into the passage. Just consider the Main Idea as predicted after reading the passage.

Step 4: Make a Prediction

The main idea is that, according to psychologists, we do not directly observe our thoughts infallibly, as is commonly

assumed. Instead, we're actually just making inferences about our own thoughts.

Step 5: Evaluate the Answer Choices

(B) is a perfect match.

(A) is a Distortion and a 180. This misinterprets the information about expertise in the second paragraph. Expertise makes it *appear* that we are observing our thoughts directly and infallibly. However, the psychologists argue that this is still just an illusion. Nobody is said to directly observe their own thoughts—not even experts.

(C) is also a Distortion and a 180. First, the psychologists' claims are not said to be "in response" to the common belief. Moreover, this contradicts lines 52–54, which state that we *can* make quick and reliable inferences.

(D) is a Distortion. The experiment with children is just a starting point for the argument made in the passage, not a primary focus. And the psychologists never blame anything on the lack of expertise.

(E) is a 180. This is the claim that the author says psychologists are "perilously close" to making (lines 43–46). However, the author immediately rejects that and suggests psychologists are *not* making that claim.

9. (C) Logic Reasoning (Weaken)

Step 2: Identify the Question Type

The question asks for something that would "call into question" an argument, making this a Weaken question like those found in Logical Reasoning.

Step 3: Research the Relevant Text

The question provides the line references for the primary argument, but it helps to consider the full details of the experiment, as described in lines 6–10.

Step 4: Make a Prediction

The psychologists conclude that people infer their own thoughts based on evidence of a study involving children. In the study, the children have trouble describing their thoughts about certain events. The psychologists assume this trouble is due to the children inferring their thoughts, and nothing else. To weaken the argument, the correct answer should provide an alternate explanation for why children have trouble describing their thoughts.

Step 5: Evaluate the Answer Choices

(C) is correct. If the children are stumbling due to limited language skills, then their inability to describe their thoughts may have nothing to do with making inferences. They may be seeing their thoughts directly, but just having a hard time expressing themselves.

(A) is a 180. This suggests kids are just as capable as adults at identifying their thoughts. That would mean kids are just as valid a source of testing as adults would be, making the experiment and the psychologists' deductions seem appropriate.

(B) is a 180. This suggests children and adults can be equally accurate (or equally inaccurate), which means children could be just as valid a sample group as anyone.

(D) is Out of Scope. The children don't have to know the difference. What matters is what the psychologists observe during the experiment.

(E) is also Out of Scope. Even if the study was intended for other reasons, it's still acceptable for psychologists to draw conclusions about other concepts from that study.

10. (E) Inference

Step 2: Identify the Question Type

The question asks what the author is "most likely to believe" regarding a claim from the passage. That makes this an Inference question.

Step 3: Research the Relevant Text

The claim in question is at the beginning of the third paragraph, but be sure to consider the context of the paragraph as a whole.

Step 4: Make a Prediction

The claim in question is one the author says psychologists are "perilously close" to making. *But* (line 46), the author immediately states that psychologists are *not* actually making that claim. The correct answer will indicate the author's belief that the claim in question is, ultimately, not supported.

Step 5: Evaluate the Answer Choices

(E) is correct. The author does not believe there is support for that claim—even if psychologists are perilously close to making it.

(A) is Out of Scope. The author never suggests that it's impossible to study thinking processes.

(B) is a Distortion. The claim in question is one that psychologists come close to making, but don't actually make. If they don't actually make that claim, then they can't possible misunderstand it.

(C) is a Distortion. The prevailing view that experiments undermine is the common belief presented in lines 1–5. The claim in question is not a prevailing view. In fact, the author says psychologists don't even really believe it.

(D) is a 180. The author claims that psychologists don't actually believe this view. And by saying that psychologists come "perilously close" to claiming it, the author suggests it's a dangerous idea and not likely to be "basically sound."

11. (A) Logic Reasoning (Parallel Reasoning)

Step 2: Identify the Question Type

The question asks for a situation "most closely analogous" to one presented in the passage. That makes this a Logic Reasoning question, specifically one that mimics Parallel Reasoning.

Step 3: Research the Relevant Text

The explanation for people's failure to notice they're making inferences is described throughout the second paragraph, primarily in lines 27–41.

Step 4: Make a Prediction

The failure is directly described in lines 35–38: We make inferences so fast that we fail to notice we're making them. Based on the surrounding lines, this is because we appear to grasp relations through expertise and just assume we're seeing things directly instead. So, the correct answer will describe someone who has developed expertise and assumes (incorrectly) that everything is now being observed directly.

Step 5: Evaluate the Answer Choices

(A) provides a good example. In this case, the anthropologist has become so familiar with his culture that he takes it for granted and just assumes he sees the truth—and he's wrong!

(B) does not match. This places a limit on studying something due to a requirement, which has nothing to do with the illusion of direct observation.

(C) does not match. The failure people have in the passage has nothing to do with an inability to go from abstract ideas to concrete experiences.

(D) does not match. Conflict of interest does not match the idea of making bad assumptions based on experience.

(E) does not match. We fail to notice our inferences because we assume we're seeing things directly, not because we're "too busy" doing something else and have to pass along the work.

12. (D) Detail

Step 2: Identify the Question Type

"According to the passage" indicates that the correct answer will be directly stated, making this a Detail question.

Step 3: Research the Relevant Text

The question asks about the result of gaining greater expertise, which is described in lines 27–32.

Step 4: Make a Prediction

According to the passage, greater expertise appears to change "our knowledge of [an] area" and our "perception of entities in that area," and it appears we are able to "grasp these entities and their relations directly."

Step 5: Evaluate the Answer Choices

(D) matches the described change in our perception and the way we understand (i.e., grasp) the relations in a particular area.

(A) is Out of Scope. Nothing is mentioned about *expressing* judgment about issues.

(B) is Out of Scope. Nothing is mentioned about taking a detail-oriented approach.

(C) is a Distortion. We may fail to notice we're making inferences, but that doesn't mean we ignore errors. You can't ignore something if you don't even realize it's there.

(E) is a Faulty Use of Detail. This refers to the sensations and emotions brought up in line 51–52. However, it is not suggested that we *reduce* our reliance on these sensations and emotions. On the contrary, they make it possible to make inferences in the first place.

13. (C) Detail

Step 2: Identify the Question Type
The question asks for something directly mentioned according to views "cited in the passage," making this a Detail question.

Step 3: Research the Relevant Text
The "illusion of direct knowledge" refers back to lines 38–41 ("the supposition that . . . we are perceiving [things] directly").

Step 4: Make a Prediction
The last sentence of the second paragraph states that "[t]his failure leads naturally" to the illusion in question. That phrase refers back to the previous sentence (lines 35–38), where psychologists claim that we make inferences so fast that we fail to notice we're making then. So, the illusion of direct knowledge comes from that failure to notice we're making inferences.

Step 5: Evaluate the Answer Choices
(C) matches the stated source according to the psychologists.

(A) is Out of Scope. There is no discussion of getting feedback on the accuracy of our inferences.

(B) is a 180. It is frequently suggested that we do *not* have unmediated (i.e., direct) knowledge of our thoughts.

(D) is a 180. It is often suggested that we *believe* our inferences are infallible (i.e., absolutely accurate), but that's not actually the case.

(E) is a Distortion. We make incredibly fast inferences which may not be infallible, but there's no suggestion that those inferences are in any way clouded or uncertain. We're certain we're right, even if that's not actually the case.

14. (D) Inference

Step 2: Identify the Question Type
The question asks for something that can "most reasonably be inferred," making this an Inference question.

Step 3: Research the Relevant Text
The use of children for the experiments is discussed in the first paragraph.

Step 4: Make a Prediction
According to lines 10–13, children have the same thoughts as adults, which makes them equally valid subjects. The difference, though, is that children are "much less capable of identifying these thoughts." That must have been the reason the study used children instead of adults, suggesting there's a benefit to using subjects that have greater trouble recognizing their thoughts.

Step 5: Evaluate the Answer Choices
(D) matches the prediction that the advantage comes from the likelihood of making mistakes (i.e., being less capable of identifying their own thoughts).

(A) is Out of Scope. The study is not about creativity, it's about whether thoughts are recognized directly or by inference.

(B) is a 180. It's the children that are more likely to be inaccurate, not the adults.

(C) is a 180. It is frequently suggested in the passage that nobody is actually infallible. Everyone makes inferences about their own thoughts.

(E) is a Distortion. The study is not about the ability to infer the thoughts of *others*. It's about inferring one's *own* thoughts.

Passage 3: Dowsing

Step 1: Read the Passage Strategically
Sample Roadmap

line #	Keyword/phrase	¶ Margin notes
2		Dowsing defined
4	For example	Ex. finding water
7	claiming	
16	skeptical	Skeptics:
17	crudeness	
18	assert	1) Crude tools = actually use subsconsious
23	Further	
24	skeptics say; while a few	
25	considerable	
26	success	2) Inconsistent results
27	generally is notably inconsistent; Finally; skeptics	
28	note	
30	unlikely	3) Hand-picked locations
32	Proponents	
33	contend	Proponents:
34	should be	1) Many techniques
35	also note	2) Studies skewed
39	Proponents	
40	claim	3) Sense electromag.
43	also claim	4) More successful than others
47	corroborated	Study supports proponents
57	significantly more accurate	
58	even	

Discussion

The first paragraph is very introductory, starting off with a definition of the **Topic**: dowsing. This involves finding things underground using basic tools. The definition is followed by a detailed example that involves finding water with a tree branch.

The second paragraph offers some opinions, which help identify the **Scope** of the passage: How effective is dowsing? According to the skeptics in the second paragraph, not very much at all. Their criticisms boil down to: 1) The methods are crude, and the tools do nothing—it's all in the dowser's subconscious; 2) studies show inconsistent results; and 3) dowsers just happen to go where success is statistically more likely in the first place.

The third paragraph offers a defense from proponents of dowsing. In short: 1) There are various distinct techniques, so you can't just lump them all together and judge; 2) studies tend to use inappropriate subjects who merely claim to be experts but have no certification; 3) successful dowsers are sensitive to underground conditions; 4) dowsers are more successful than scientists who use fancy schmancy tools.

The last paragraph presents a study that supports the last two claims of the proponents. In the study, dowsers competed against geologists and hydrologists to find water in a particular area, and the dowsers were more successful—even finding an area with *no* water when asked to do so.

The **Purpose** of this Debate passage is mostly to present the views of both parties about the efficacy of dowsing. The author does offer support for the proponents in the last paragraph, which may suggest some tacit endorsement of dowsing. But the overall **Main Idea** is pretty neutral: Some people are skeptical, but there is support that dowsers can find things underground effectively.

15. (C) Logic Function

Step 2: Identify the Question Type
The question asks for the "primary purpose of the second paragraph." In other words, it's asking for the function of the paragraph within the context around it.

Step 3: Research the Relevant Text
There's no need to reread the actual text. Just use the Margin Notes to see how the second paragraph fits within the overall structure.

Step 4: Make a Prediction
The second paragraph consists of the skeptics' criticisms of dowsing, the concept described in the first paragraph. Those criticisms are countered by proponents in the third paragraph.

Step 5: Evaluate the Answer Choices

(C) is correct. The second paragraph contains the arguments against dowsing, and the third paragraph counters those complaints.

(A) is not accurate. The second paragraph is entirely about opinions, not just supplementary details.

(B) is not accurate. There is one consistent point of view in the second paragraph, and there's no synthesis of points of view in the last paragraph.

(D) is a Distortion. The paragraph offers opinions about the details in the first paragraph. However, the opinions presented in the second paragraph are very broad and hardly "explore[d] in detail." And there are no ramifications to speak of. It's just a discussion of how one group of people finds something to be ineffective.

(E) is a Distortion and Out of Scope. The second paragraph only discusses one side of the dispute (the skeptics), and the third paragraph discusses the other side. No resolution is to be found.

16. (A) Detail

Step 2: Identify the Question Type
"According to the passage" indicates that the correct answer will be a detail that is directly stated in the passage.

Step 3: Research the Relevant Text
The skeptics' point of view is outlined throughout the second paragraph.

Step 4: Make a Prediction
The skeptics have a lot of complaints. However, the contrast Keyword *while* in line 24 indicates a brief concession: "a few dowsers have demonstrated considerable and consistent success."

Step 5: Evaluate the Answer Choices

(A) matches the skeptics' acknowledgment word for word.

(B) is a Distortion. Some scientists are mentioned in the passage (e.g., geologists and hydrologists), but any criticism toward dowsing in the passage is made solely by the skeptics, not any scientists.

(C) is a Faulty Use of Detail. This is the complaint *proponents* make in the third paragraph (lines 34–39), but there is no acknowledgment of this by the skeptics.

(D) is also a Faulty Use of Detail. Skeptics do claim that dowsers may be working subconsciously (lines 18–22), but the specific concept of being sensitive to Earth's electromagnetic field is raised by the *proponents* (lines 39–42), not the skeptics.

(E) is also a Faulty Use of Detail. Separate evaluation is encouraged by the *proponents* (lines 32–34), not the skeptics.

17. (D) Logic Reasoning (Parallel Reasoning)

Step 2: Identify the Question Type

The correct answer will have reasoning "most analogous to" that of an argument in the passage. That makes this a Logic Reasoning question along the lines of Parallel Reasoning.

Step 3: Research the Relevant Text

The skeptics' arguments are presented in the second paragraph.

Step 4: Make a Prediction

Unfortunately, the question asks for something parallel to *an* argument made by the skeptics, and they make a few. It's impossible to know which one to choose. Have a quick idea of the three arguments: 1) Dowsers' tools are crude; they're just using their subconscious; 2) studies show inconsistency; 3) dowsers just go where they're more likely to succeed in the first place. The correct answer will show someone consistent with one of these arguments.

Step 5: Evaluate the Answer Choices

(D) is perfectly parallel to the last argument. As dowsers just happen to go where water is everywhere and say "look, I found water!," the people in this answer just happen to go where fish are everywhere and say "look, I found fish!"

(A) does not match. The skeptics never claim there are tools that are more accurate than what dowsers suggest.

(B) does not match. The skeptics never accuse dowsers of having little evidence to support their claims.

(C) does not match. The skeptics never suggest that dowsers claim their abilities are innate, nor do skeptics suggest that any success of dowsing is due to intense practice.

(E) does not match. This may seem somewhat similar to the first argument, in which dowsers claim their tools work but it's all in the subconscious. However, the skeptics argue that dowsers' subconscious determination is based on "clues derived from surface conditions," not just thoughts of things that didn't actually happen.

18. (B) Inference

Step 2: Identify the Question Type

The question asks for something with which the author is "most likely to agree," making this an Inference question.

Step 3: Research the Relevant Text

The question asks about the study in the final paragraph.

Step 4: Make a Prediction

At the beginning of the paragraph, the author claims that the study corroborates the "last two claims" of the proponents. Going back to the previous paragraph, those claims were that 1) dowsers can detect changes in the electromagnetic field; and 2) dowsers can be more successful than other scientists. The facts of the study are consistent with both points.

Step 5: Evaluate the Answer Choices

(B) is correct. The study doesn't prove that dowsers can detect such changes, but the possibility is certainly there.

(A) is Extreme. While the dowsers may have had more success, that doesn't mean the other scientists would be "of little service to *any* groundwater-locating effort."

(C) is Extreme. The study may corroborate some ideas, but that's hardly the same as *proving* dowsing is the "most dependable."

(D) is Extreme and a Distortion. The study does nothing to show what makes dowsers *most* successful. Further, it makes no sense to suggest that dowsers used any tools other than their own.

(E) is a 180. While focusing on one type of terrain might indicate the study isn't a conclusive rebuttal, it definitely does *help* to refute some of the skeptics' arguments.

19. (D) Detail

Step 2: Identify the Question Type

The correct answer will be a question that is answered directly by a Detail in the passage.

Step 3: Research the Relevant Text

With no Research Clues, the entire passage is relevant.

Step 4: Make a Prediction

A prediction cannot be made here. Instead, go through the answers one at a time and research when necessary to make sure there is a directly stated answer to the question provided.

Step 5: Evaluate the Answer Choices

(D) is answered in the first sentence. Dowsing is used to detect resources (e.g., water) *or objects*—which suggests physical items other than water.

(A) is not answered. No timeline is given in the passage.

(B) is not answered. The effect of rain is not brought up.

(C) is not answered. Forked sticks are brought up as one method for finding water, but there's no mention of whether this is the most common or how it compares statistically to other methods.

(E) is not answered. Skeptics only broadly refer to using surface clues (lines 21–22), but never mention any specific clues.

20. (E) Inference

Step 2: Identify the Question Type

The correct answer is something for which there is "support for inferring," making this an Inference question.

Step 3: Research the Relevant Text

There are no Research Clues, so the entire text is relevant.

Step 4: Make a Prediction

With no clues, there's no choice but to go through the answers, eliminate those that are clearly wrong, and test the remaining answers as necessary.

Step 5: Evaluate the Answer Choices

(E) is supported. According to proponents of dowsing, successful dowsers "are not well represented in the typical study" (lines 38–39). However, the study in the last paragraph was extensive and used teams of "the most successful dowsers." Combined, that suggests the last study is not your typical study involving a poor representative sample.

(A) is a Distortion. The study in the last paragraph was conducted around narrow, tilted fracture zones. And while dowsers did find a dry zone on request, that is not to say the entire region was arid. Nor does that suggest that such fracture zones are more common in arid regions than in other regions. The comparison is unsubstantiated.

(B) is Extreme and Out of Scope. The passage only discusses studies related to finding groundwater, not other resources. Further, there's nothing to suggest that *no* reliable studies have been performed.

(C) is not supported. There's no mention in the final study what tools were used or whether they would be any different from tools used in different zones.

(D) is a Distortion. It is merely said that dowsers *were* able to locate a dry zone. That doesn't mean that other scientists *couldn't*. Perhaps they also did, or perhaps they just weren't asked.

Passage 4: The Use of Independent Research by Judges

Step 1: Read the Passage Strategically
Sample Roadmap

line #	Keyword/phrase	¶ Margin notes
Passage A		
2	?	Why oppose ind. research?
3	One; objections; distorts	1) Distorts system
5	undermining	
6	Another fear	2) Judges may research poorly
10	While; some merit; do	Auth: ind. research can be good
11	not justify	
12	First	
14	ill-suited	1) Good for specialized knowledge
19	Because	
20	considerable influence	
21	erroneous; detract	
22	could help	helps avoid errors
24	Second	2) Trial structure prevents bad results
25	reducing	
26	outlandish	
27	rather than	Supplements; doesn't replace
28	so	
Passage B		
30	Regardless	
31	should resist	Auth: Appellate should not use ind. research
33	As a general rule	
34	Thus; lack	Appellate courts lack live testimony and cross-exam
35	critical	
36	:	
39	And	Benefit of cross-exam
45	However	
50	Thus	No live comment
53	in particular	Usurps trial court's function
54	come under criticism; potential unreliability	
56	ignores	Ignores function of appellate court
57	questionable	
59	criticism	
60	full force	
61	regardless	

Discussion

The author of passage A starts with a question: Why are some trial judges against conducting independent research? As with most questions in an LSAT passage, this one is answered and serves as a focal point for the whole passage. The rest of the paragraph describes some objections: 1) Independent research can skew results and undermine other important evidence; and 2) judges may not have the best research techniques.

The author recognizes the concerns, but offers two reasons over the next two paragraphs why independent research can be good. First, in cases requiring specialized knowledge, the evidence raised by both parties can lead to conflicts and future problems that independent research can help avoid. Second, trials have a structure that reduces the chances of judges' research producing crazy results and ensures such research is a supplement to other evidence, not a replacement.

The **Topic** of passage A is independent research, with the author focused on the **Scope** of its benefits. The author's **Purpose** is to support the use of independent research. The **Main Idea** is that there are circumstances in which judges doing independent research is acceptable.

The author of passage B sticks to the **Topic** of independent research, but shifts the **Scope** to its use specifically in appellate courts. The author immediately suggests that appellate courts should *not* conduct independent research. That suggests the **Purpose** of this passage will be to explain why it shouldn't be used.

The second and third paragraph offer evidence against using independent research in appellate courts. Appellate courts lack the *critical* components of live presentation and cross-examination found in trial courts. The second paragraph focuses on the value of cross-examination, while the third paragraph explains why live presentation is valuable and how raising new information in appellate courts would steal that function from a trial courts.

The last paragraph wraps up the **Main Idea** that independent research is inappropriate in appellate courts and goes against the function of an appellate court as a court of review.

The passages are definitely of different minds about independent research. However, it should be noted that the author of passage A sticks mainly to its benefits in *trial* courts, while the author of passage B is more concerned with its use specifically in *appellate* courts.

21. (C) Logic Reasoning (Principle)

Step 2: Identify the Question Type

The question directly asks for a principle underlying both passages, making it a Logic Reasoning question of the Principle variety.

Step 3: Research the Relevant Text

The question asks about the overall arguments in both passages, so the entire text is relevant.

Step 4: Make a Prediction

The author of passage A argues that independent research is beneficial because it helps avoid conflict and supplements what is provided by the structure of the trial court. The author of passage B argues against independent research because it takes away the function of trial courts and goes against the function of the appellate court. Both authors are intent on making sure that independent research helps supplement a court's structure and function, not go against that.

Step 5: Evaluate the Answer Choices

(C) is correct. As the first author claims, independent research "supplements, rather than replaces" (lines 27–28) evidence from opposing parties. And the second author claims using independent research is bad because appellate courts would "substitute its own questionable research results for evidence that should have been tested in the trial court" (lines 57–59). So, both authors want to ensure independent research does not supersede the elements of a trial.

(A) might fit well with the author of passage B, but the author of passage A never makes a comparison between trial courts and appellate courts, so such a principle would be irrelevant.

(B) is irrelevant to passage B, which involves doing research in appellate court, which would take place *after* a trial.

(D) is Out of Scope. While the concept of questioning witnesses is raised as a side note in passage B (line 43–45), it's not a main part of the argument and has no bearing on the argument in passage A.

(E) is a 180 for passage B. The author of passage B weighs in on the reliability of some outside resources in lines 53–54, and cites the lack of their reliability as a reason *against* appellate judges using outside research at all. Furthermore, passage A makes no mention of what "[b]oth trial and appellate judges" should do and also does not discuss where outside research should have to come from.

22. (A) Inference

Step 2: Identify the Question Type

The question asks for something that "can be inferred," making this an Inference question.

Step 3: Research the Relevant Text

The question asks about both passages, and what should be done if judges *do* conduct independent research. That's raised in passage A in the third paragraph (lines 24–29), and in passage B in the third paragraph (lines 47–54).

Step 4: Make a Prediction

According to the author of passage A, independent research is guided by the structure of a trial and should be supplementary, not a substitution. And the author of passage B says that the appellate courts bringing up new information would "usurp the trial court's fact-finding function," which suggests that passage B agrees that independent research should be restricted to where it belongs: the trial courts, if anywhere.

Step 5: Evaluate the Answer Choices

(A) fits both authors' belief that independent research should conform to the function of a trial court.

(B) is not supported. Both passages raise the possibility of unreliable sources, but passage A does not lay out limits on the sources of outside research. Passage B warns of the unreliability of internet sources, but does condone the use of "reliable sources" as an alternative either.

(C) is a 180. Both authors argue that it should *not* replace such evidence.

(D) mixes the two opinions. However, passage A does not address whether it should be used in appellate courts, and passage B never directly argues that it *should* be used in trial courts.

(E) is a Faulty Use of Detail. Only passage B mentions this, and only in context of using independent research in an appellate court.

23. (D) Inference

Step 2: Identify the Question Type

The question asks for a phrase that conveys a particular meaning. These kind of definition questions are a variation on Inference questions. The definition won't be directly stated, but it will be inferred from the context. In this case, the correct answer will be "most closely related" to another phrase, which means this question also shares some qualities with Parallel Reasoning questions from the Logical Reasoning section.

Step 3: Research the Relevant Text

Start by looking at the context of the quote from passage A. That refers to judges who are concerned with their ability to "conduct first-rate research." This potential for bad research is addressed in the last paragraph of passage B.

Step 4: Make a Prediction

In the last paragraph of passage B, the author refers to the potential for an appellate court substituting "its own questionable research results" (lines 56–59), a sentiment echoing the concern raised in passage A.

Step 5: Evaluate the Answer Choices

(D) matches the prediction.

(A) refers to experts and their knowledge beyond what is printed. This has nothing to do with judges and their concern about their poor research techniques.

(B) is about judges participating in questioning witnesses, which does not reflect the author of passage B's concern about judges doing research.

(C) makes reference to live responses to information, which is not the same as being worried about researching that information in the first place.

(E) refers to using outside material, but does not mimic the concern about researching such material in a less-than-stellar way.

24. (B) Inference

Step 2: Identify the Question Type

The question asks what the author of passage B would be "mostly likely to take issue with," making this an Inference question.

Step 3: Research the Relevant Text

The question starts with a reference to lines 39–43, in which the author of passage B claims that parties in a trial can perform cross-examination on new information to ensure it is credible and reliable. This goes contrary to ideas presented in passage A about how scientific evidence "ensures conflicting and partisan testimony."

Step 4: Make a Prediction

The author of passage B does not share the concerns that scientific information will be definitively problematic. The correct answer will address this disputed concept.

Step 5: Evaluate the Answer Choices

(B) is correct. According to the author of passage B, cross-examination helps make sure specialized knowledge can be handled and introduced without a problem.

(A) is not disputed by the author of passage B. The first line of passage B is "*Regardless* of what trial courts may do . . . ." The author of passage B merely wants independent research to be removed from appellate courts, not trial courts.

(C) is Out of Scope for passage B. The discussion of cross-examination only applies to the trials at hand, not to future trials.

(D) is a 180. The author of passage B would not dispute this. If anything, cross-examination would confirm that erroneous decisions can be exposed.

(E) is a 180. The author of passage B does not dispute the structure of a trial court and its ability to involve independent research. Passage B merely argues that it goes against the function of an appellate court.

25. (C) Inference

Step 2: Identify the Question Type

This is a variation of Inference question that asks for defining a term within the context of the passage. In this case, the correct answer won't provide the actual definition, but will be another word that has the same definition in context, which also makes this similar to Parallel Reasoning questions from Logical Reasoning.

Step 3: Research the Relevant Text
Start by looking at the word *crucible* in context. The entire sentence says that new literature introduced at the appellate level "cannot be tested in the crucible of the adversarial system." This refers back to the previous paragraph, in which the author discusses the testing of new information through the critical process of cross-examination.

Step 4: Make a Prediction
The correct answer will likely be a word taken from the second paragraph of passage B that directly relates to the process of cross-examination.

Step 5: Evaluate the Answer Choices

(C) is a match. The *engine* in line 42 directly refers to the process of cross-examination.

(A) does not match. This refers to a desire to conduct research, not the process of cross-examination.

(B) does not match. Cross-examination is used to test credibility, but it's the practice of cross-examination that is important (i.e., the crucible), not the credibility of the evidence.

(D) does not match. The function in line 53 refers to the purpose of conducting the trial (fact-finding), not a specific process (cross-examination) that is used in that function.

(E) does not match. This refers to the source of information (e.g., magazine, journal), which has nothing to do with the process of cross-examination.

26. (B) Logic Reasoning (Parallel Reasoning)

Step 2: Identify the Question Type
The correct answer will be a pair of titles that indicate a relationship "most analogous" to that between the two passages. That makes this a Logic Reasoning question, similar to Parallel Reasoning.

Step 3: Research the Relevant Text
Because it refers to the relationship between both passages as a whole, the entire text is relevant.

Step 4: Make a Prediction
The major relationship between these two passages is that they take different perspectives on the use of independent research. One supports it, and one rejects it. However, they both make their judgments in different contexts. The first just says it can be beneficial, while the second merely rejects its usage in appellate courts. The correct answer should have a similar relationship: The first supporting something in some

contexts, and the second rejecting that idea in a particular context.

Step 5: Evaluate the Answer Choices

(B) is a match, with the first showing support for something (salt) in some cases, and the second saying don't do it in a particular context (people with high blood pressure).

(A) puts a negative spin on salt in both cases, which goes contrary to the positive take by the author of passage A.

(C) is Half-Right/Half-Wrong. The first title nicely mimics how the author of passage A defends independent research against the concern of judges. However, the second title talks about inconclusive research, which is not comparable to the discussion in passage B.

(D) is Out of Scope. Neither passage advocates independent research as a substitute for anything, and the author of passage B does not talk about anything coming under fire (i.e., being criticized by others).

(E) is Half-Right/Half-Wrong. The first title definitely matches the supportive stance of passage A. However, the lack of something in a sample population does not match concepts in passage B.

27. (D) Inference

Step 2: Identify the Question Type
The question asks about the "stances of" both authors, which refers to their attitudes on a topic. And the question asks how those stances can be "most accurately described." So, the stances aren't directly stated, but they are directly deduced from the language of the passages, making this an Inference question.

Step 3: Research the Relevant Text
Both passages are entirely about independent research, so all of the text is relevant. However, the question does ask directly about its use by trial judges, so stick to that context.

Step 4: Make a Prediction
Overall, the author of passage A is supportive of trial judges using independent research as a supplement, even though judges' "concerns have some merit." While there's some suggestion that the author of passage B is okay with independent research in trial courts, the primary focus of passage B is still on the use of such research in the appellate court, not the trial court. In fact, in the very first sentence, the author claims that the argument about appellate courts stands "[r]egardless of what trial courts may do," indicating that the author of passage B ultimately isn't concerned about its use in trial courts. The correct answer should indicate attitudes of support for the first author and relative ambivalence for the second.

Step 5: Evaluate the Answer Choices
(D) matches the attitudes perfectly.

(A) is a Distortion in that the author of passage A never comes across as resigned, and a 180, if anything, as passage B never seems to disapprove of independent research by trial judges.

(B) is inaccurate in suggesting that the author of passage A is ambivalent.

(C) is a 180 for the author of passage A, who is not skeptical. And the author of passage B does not seem to be harboring hostility toward independent research by trial judges.

(E) is Extreme for the author of passage A, who is certainly supportive but not quite forceful. And the author of passage B is opposed to independent research at the appellate level, but not necessarily at the trial level.

Section II: Logical Reasoning

Q#	Question Type	Correct	Difficulty
1	Paradox	D	Check your online resources.
2	Inference	B	Check your online resources.
3	Assumption (Sufficient)	D	Check your online resources.
4	Weaken	B	Check your online resources.
5	Assumption (Necessary)	E	Check your online resources.
6	Principle (Identify/Strengthen)	B	Check your online resources.
7	Inference	C	Check your online resources.
8	Flaw	D	Check your online resources.
9	Assumption (Sufficient)	C	Check your online resources.
10	Principle (Apply/Inference)	E	Check your online resources.
11	Assumption (Necessary)	B	Check your online resources.
12	Paradox	A	Check your online resources.
13	Strengthen	A	Check your online resources.
14	Main Point	C	Check your online resources.
15	Inference	D	Check your online resources.
16	Strengthen/Weaken (Evaluate the Argument)	A	Check your online resources.
17	Inference	D	Check your online resources.
18	Role of a Statement	A	Check your online resources.
19	Inference	C	Check your online resources.
20	Flaw	A	Check your online resources.
21	Principle (Parallel)	B	Check your online resources.
22	Weaken	D	Check your online resources.
23	Assumption (Necessary)	A	Check your online resources.
24	Parallel Flaw	C	Check your online resources.
25	Flaw	D	Check your online resources.
26	Point at Issue	E	Check your online resources.

1. (D) Paradox

Step 1: Identify the Question Type

The question asks for something that "most helps explain" a situation. That makes this a Paradox question.

Step 2: Untangle the Stimulus

With Paradox questions, look for a surprising contrast. In this case, a small animal called the dunnart is born with thin skin, which is unusual because most animals of its kind need thick skin for body warmth and water retention.

Step 3: Make a Prediction

The mystery is this: How does the dunnart survive with thin skin if animals of its kind normally need thick skin? The author gives a hint by stating that the skin does get thicker as the dunnart matures in its mother's pouch. So, there may be something about that pouch that helps provide the necessary benefits of thick skin (maintaining body temperature and reducing water loss) until the dunnart matures.

Step 4: Evaluate the Answer Choices

(D) is correct.

(A) is irrelevant. Even with a respiratory system, the dunnart still has thin skin that won't help maintain body temperature or reduce water loss.

(B) is an Irrelevant Comparison. Even if this is true, the thin skin won't help maintain that body temperature, nor does this address the retention of water.

(C) is an Irrelevant Comparison. The paradox is about newborns, not adults.

(E) does not help. This does not address what happens at night, when temperatures may cool drastically. Nor does it address other dunnarts that may not live in such a fortunate environment.

2. (B) Inference

Step 1: Identify the Question Type

The correct answer will fill in the blank at the end of the stimulus. That blank is preceded by the Keyword [*t*]*hus,* which indicates that the blank will be a conclusion supported by the previous text. Something supported by the information given is an inference.

Step 2: Untangle the Stimulus

The author discusses stand-up comedians who can hold an audience's attention for hours and make interesting points. This is accomplished by using humor. University professors want to achieve the same results.

Step 3: Make a Prediction

If professors want to achieve the same results, then it makes sense to conclude that they should use the same technique: humor.

Step 4: Evaluate the Answer Choices

(B) matches the prediction.

(A) is not supported. It is stated that professors *hope* to achieve the same results as stand-up comedians, which suggests they may not necessarily have the same skills.

(C) is Extreme. The author is suggesting that humor might be a valid technique, but there's no suggestion it's the *only* solution.

(D) is Extreme. Humor may make some long lectures interesting, but that doesn't mean there's *no* way it will avoid losing the audience's attention. Even with humor, there could be something else that makes the lecture unengaging.

(E) is Extreme. Some comedians might be able to address certain serious topics using humor, but the author doesn't necessarily suggest humor would be acceptable for *every* topic, including the most serious.

3. (D) Assumption (Sufficient)

Step 1: Identify the Question Type

The argument presented will be logically sound *if* the correct answer is assumed. So, the correct answer will be a sufficient assumption, i.e., an assumption that is good enough, when added to the evidence provided, to guarantee the conclusion.

Step 2: Untangle the Stimulus

The reviewer concludes ([*s*]*o*) that the advice in management books won't be very useful for most managers. The evidence is that most managers are not CEOs, and management books are written from a CEO perspective.

Step 3: Make a Prediction

This argument, like almost all Sufficient Assumption arguments, is hindered by Mismatched Concepts. The conclusion is about the usefulness of the books, while the evidence merely talks about perspective. The reviewer assumes those concepts are somehow connected. More specifically, the reviewer assumes that readers won't find books useful if those books are written from a different perspective than their own.

Step 4: Evaluate the Answer Choices

(D) is correct. This is saying a book needs to be written from the reader's perspective to be useful, i.e., if it's not written from that perspective, it won't be useful.

(A) is not good enough. Even if this were true, there's still no evidence to support whether or not such books are *useful.*

(B) is Out of Scope. It doesn't matter what readers *want* to be. The argument is based on their current perspectives, and this offers no support for whether or not the books will be useful.

(C) is irrelevant. Even if CEOs were once lower managers, their perspectives could have changed when they became CEO.

Regardless, this is still not enough to reach the conclusion about whether or not the books are *useful*.

(E) is irrelevant. It doesn't matter what managers *prefer* to read. This still offers no evidence to guarantee the conclusion about management books and whether or not they are, indeed, useful.

4. (B) Weaken

Step 1: Identify the Question Type
The question asks for something that "undermines the mayor's defense," which means it will weaken that argument.

Step 2: Untangle the Stimulus
The mayor is being accused of taking a bribe in the form of home improvements to his vacation home. The mayor argues it wasn't a bribe. His evidence is that he paid every bill for that project that was presented to him.

Step 3: Make a Prediction
The mayor is trying to suggest he paid for the project. However, he doesn't say he paid *all* the bills for that project. He just claims he paid all the bills *presented to him*. What about all of the bills that were *not* presented to the mayor? If the mayor let somebody else pay for those (say, for example, a city consultant who wants to finance a nice project for the mayor in return for continued support), then his defense falls apart.

Step 4: Evaluate the Answer Choices

(B) is correct, attacking the mayor's presumptive suggestion that he was actually paying for the whole project.

(A) is Out of Scope. The mayor is merely defending himself. Whether the consultant took bribes or not is irrelevant. Even so, this choice only states that authorities are investigating the situation, which means it's still possible there was no bribery on anyone's account.

(C) is irrelevant. It doesn't matter who did the work. For the question of bribery, all that matters is who *paid* for it.

(D) is irrelevant. The actual cost doesn't matter. If the mayor paid for it, it's not a bribe.

(E) is an Irrelevant Comparison. The consultant's salary from the city could just be a legitimately sizable amount, and it doesn't matter how that salary compares to the cost of the mayor's vacation home improvements. All that matters is who paid for the mayor's improvements, and this offers no reason to question the mayor's claims.

5. (E) Assumption (Necessary)

Step 1: Identify the Question Type
The question directly asks for an assumption, and one that is "required by the argument," making this a Necessary Assumption question.

Step 2: Untangle the Stimulus
The archaeologist is rejecting a common belief, essentially arguing that humans did not need fire to migrate to the cold climate of Europe. The evidence is that the earliest controlled fires date back just 400,000 years.

Step 3: Make a Prediction
To argue that fire wasn't necessary, the archaeologist must believe that humans were able to survive in cold Europe before they could control fire. If controlled fire goes back 400,000 years, then the archaeologist must assume that people were in Europe before that time, and hence were able to survive without fire.

Step 4: Evaluate the Answer Choices

(E) must be assumed. Using the Denial Test, if *nobody* was in Europe earlier than 400,000 years ago, then the migration to Europe happened *after* fire was controlled. In that case, the archaeologist has no reason to suggest fire wasn't needed. So, the archaeologist must believe there *were* people in Europe earlier, before fire was controlled.

(A) is not necessary. The archaeologist's argument could be valid whether early humans used fire for cooking or not.

(B) is an Irrelevant Comparison. It doesn't matter whether it's colder now or it was colder back then. Was fire needed or not? That's the focus of the argument.

(C) is Out of Scope. Whether humans utilized natural fires or not, the argument is about the need for mastery of fire. This suggests people did use fire before it was controlled, but the archaeologist does not need that to be true to claim that *mastery* of fire was necessary for migration.

(D) is Extreme. This suggests that the need for heat was the *only* reason humans mastered fire. Even if that weren't true (i.e., even if humans would have mastered fire for other reasons), the archaeologist's argument is not affected.

6. (B) Principle (Identify/Strengthen)

Step 1: Identify the Question Type
The question directly asks for a principle, which will be found in the correct answer, making this an Identify the Principle question. Further, the correct answer will "help to justify" the argument, which means this question will also utilize the skills of a Strengthen question.

Step 2: Untangle the Stimulus
The astronomer uses a common argumentative technique: negating the views of an opponent. Some people argue that a space telescope project should be cancelled for being over budget. The astronomer says otherwise, i.e., don't cancel the project. The evidence is that cancelling the project would be a waste of the money already spent, which is greater than the amount needed to finish the project.

LSAT PrepTest 81 Unlocked

Step 3: Make a Prediction

The astronomer's argument is based on a principle of money. The argument would be justified if the astronomer held the same financial principle for any project: don't cancel it if the money already spent is greater than the remaining cost.

Step 4: Evaluate the Answer Choices

(B) is correct. If the space agency has already spent more than the remaining costs and is already over budget, then it has already spent most (i.e., more than half) of the total cost. By this principle, the project should be completed, i.e., not cancelled, as the astronomer argues.

(A) is Out of Scope. The astronomer does not refer to the agency's overall budget, nor how small or large the telescope project is with respect to the overall budget.

(C) is Out of Scope, and a potential 180. The project is said to be "way over budget," but there's no indication whether this means more than twice the original budget. In any event, this principle offers a reason to cancel the project, which the astronomer is trying to avoid.

(D) is a 180. This is suggesting that the agency shouldn't spend any more money on the project, which sounds a lot like saying the project should be cancelled—contrary to the astronomer's plea.

(E) is Out of Scope. The argument is not based on the likelihood of important new discoveries. Also, it's about whether a project should be canceled or not, not what should get funding in the first place.

7. (C) Inference

Step 1: Identify the Question Type

The correct answer will be "strongly supported by" the information provided, making this an Inference question.

Step 2: Untangle the Stimulus

The naturalist claims that different primates can behave in different ways. This is illustrated by two examples describing how two different primates (a chimpanzee and an orangutan) would behave if a zookeeper dropped a screwdriver nearby. The chimp would play around with it a little, then move on to something else. The orangutan would pretend to ignore it, then use it to tear apart the cage when the zookeeper leaves.

Step 3: Make a Prediction

Two very different behaviors, indeed. The chimp would act curious, but quickly get bored. The orangutan, on the other hand, would be quite cunning—playing it cool and waiting for the zookeeper to leave before carrying out the devious plan. The correct answer will be based directly on these observations. Don't make any assumptions about what this behavior *might* indicate. The correct answer must be directly supported. It's also important to note that these are just two

examples. Be wary of answers that make overly broad claims from these examples.

Step 4: Evaluate the Answer Choices

(C) is supported, as the orangutan is said to "pretend to ignore" the screwdriver, just to deceive the zookeeper into thinking nothing is going to happen—until the zookeeper leaves. Then, we've all seen Planet of the Apes, so we know what happens next.

(A) is Extreme and Out of Scope. Some might consider the orangutan's plan a sign of high intelligence, but that's not directly supported. In any event, the stimulus only mentions two primates. Without knowing how other primates would behave, there's no support that orangutans would be the *most* intelligent.

(B) is not supported. Walking away from the screwdriver doesn't mean the chimp has an inferior memory.

(D) is not supported. While the orangutan's plan might certainly indicate a dislike for being caged, there's no evidence that the chimp is any less displeased. Perhaps the chimp just didn't take the time to concoct as destructive and devious a scheme as the orangutan.

(E) is not supported. Walking away from the screwdriver does not necessarily indicate that the chimp didn't understand its use. Perhaps the chimp understood but just wasn't interested.

8. (D) Flaw

Step 1: Identify the Question Type

The question directly asks why "the manager's argument is flawed," making this a Flaw question.

Step 2: Untangle the Stimulus

The manager concludes ([*t*]*hus*) that Liang should not receive a bonus. The evidence is that bonuses only go to exceptionally productive employees, and Liang works in a division that is not exceptionally productive.

Step 3: Make a Prediction

Poor Liang; the manager is denying her a bonus because of the performance of her division. However, the rule for bonuses is based on the productivity of the employee individually, not the division that employee belongs to. The manager's reasoning is thus unsound, judging Liang on her group's performance rather than her own individual performance.

Step 4: Evaluate the Answer Choices

(D) points out the manager's error, judging an individual member (Liang) based on the performance of her group (the whole division).

(A) is an Irrelevant Comparison. It doesn't matter how the standards compare from one division to the next. If the group

KAPLAN

didn't reach its own unique productivity goals, then the manager has a right to say it's not exceptionally productive.

(B) is Out of Scope. The profitability of the company has nothing to do with the argument at hand, which focuses on bonuses and productivity.

(C) is a Distortion. The manager uses a group's performance as a basis for judging one individual within that group, not for judging a different group.

(E) is Out of Scope. The manager is not assuming Liang won't be exceptionally productive in the future. She just wasn't productive this year (allegedly), and that's all that matters for the assignment of bonuses.

9. (C) Assumption (Sufficient)

Step 1: Identify the Question Type
The question directly asks for something assumed, and the argument will be logical *if* that assumption is in place, making this a Sufficient Assumption question.

Step 2: Untangle the Stimulus
The author concludes ([*t*]*hus*) that the journalist in question is definitely going to reveal her informant's identity. The evidence includes some Formal Logic: If the journalist's editor or a judge orders her to reveal the identity, she will.

Step 3: Make a Prediction
By the Formal Logic, there are two things that would ensure the source being revealed: the judge ordering it or the editor ordering it. The correct answer should confirm one of those two things will happen. There are two other ideas to consider: 1) The author states that the information concerns safety violations. It's unclear how this factors in to the argument, so it appears to be a glaring Mismatched Concept. There's a good chance the correct answer will show how concerns over safety violations will lead to a definite reveal of the source; 2) At the beginning, the journalist promised her source that she wouldn't reveal the source's identify—as long as the information is not false.

If	~ false	→	~ reveal
If	reveal	→	false

However, that doesn't mean the journalist will definitely reveal the source if the information *is* false, so that could be a trap answer. And even if the information is accurate, the Formal Logic suggests that a court order or an editor's order would supersede that and require her to break that promise. In short, the promise is ultimately a non-issue and should not be factored into the assumption.

Step 4: Evaluate the Answer Choices

(C) is correct. The information does concern safety. So, according to this logic, a judge will order the identity to be revealed. Thus, by the Formal Logic in the evidence, the conclusion is confirmed: the source's identity will be revealed.

(A) is not good enough. The journalist promised to keep the identity secret if the information was not false. However, that doesn't mean she would definitely reveal the identify if the information *was* false. That's an improper use of Formal Logic.

(B) is a Distortion. By this logic, it would be *necessary* that the information be safety-related for the editor to demand a name. However, it's not sufficient. Even though the the information is, in fact, safety-related, this logic does not guarantee that the editor will demand the identity be revealed.

(D) is a Distortion. Even if revealing the source is the only way to verify the information, that doesn't guarantee the journalist will break her promise and reveal the identity.

(E) is Out of Scope. What the informant understands is irrelevant. This shows that the informant wasn't ignorant. The informant knew that a judge's order would override any promise made by the journalist. However, it's still not said whether such an order was made, so there's no reason to believe the journalist would break her promise just yet.

10. (E) Principle (Apply/Inference)

Step 1: Identify the Question Type
The stimulus will contain a principle that will be used to support the correct answer. Because the principle is provided in a stimulus, this is an Apply the Principle question. And the correct answer will be directly supported by that principle, making this similar to an Inference question.

Step 2: Untangle the Stimulus
The principle is just one big piece of Formal Logic: If it's not difficult to return a borrowed item on time and the item's owner didn't say you could return it late, then you should return the item when you promised.

If	~ difficult AND ~ permission	→	return it on time
If	~ return it on time	→	difficult OR permission

Step 3: Make a Prediction
The rule is pretty straightforward. There are two things to note: 1) This rule only applies to people who promised to return it by a certain time, thus if no promise is made, then the principle doesn't apply; and 2) do not simply negate the

logic. If it's *not* difficult to return it and you *don't* have permission to keep the item late, then return the item on time. That's the rule. If it *is* difficult or you *do* have permission, the principle doesn't apply. It might be okay to return the item late, but you can't logically conclude that it absolutely is. Perhaps it's still the right thing to stick to your promise and get it back on time.

Step 4: Evaluate the Answer Choices

(E) fits the principle. A promise was made, returning the item on time is not difficult, and there's no permission to keep it late. Thus, as the Formal Logic dictates, the item should be returned on time.

(A) does not match. Even though Christopher gave permission to return the book late, that doesn't mean there's anything wrong with returning it early. The principle doesn't deny that.

(B) does not match. The Formal Logic contains the word *and*: If you don't have permission *and* it isn't difficult to return the item, then return it on time. Only one condition is met here (Wanda didn't give permission). If it is difficult to return the bicycle on time, then it may still be okay for Nick to return it late.

(C) does not match. Only one condition is met here: It's not difficult to return the car. However, Ted gave permission to return the car late, so the principle no longer applies.

(D) does not match. Yesenia did not promise to return the computer by a certain date, and the principle only applies to people who *do* make such a promise. While it seems reasonable to suggest Yesenia should return the computer on time, it does not conform to the confines of the principle in question.

11. (B) Assumption (Necessary)

Step 1: Identify the Question Type
The question directly asks for an assumption, and one that the argument *requires*, making this a Necessary Assumption question.

Step 2: Untangle the Stimulus
The author presents evidence of two gaseous substances. They both attract mosquitoes, but a bare arm attracts mosquitoes more than either one. The author concludes ([*t*]*herefore*) that the human arm must give off a different gaseous substance.

Step 3: Make a Prediction
This is a classic case of Overlooked Possibilities. The author has ruled out two possible gaseous substances and then concludes that it must be another gaseous substance. Why does it have to be a gaseous substance at all? Why can't there be some other aspect of the human arm that is attracting mosquitoes? The author does not consider that and assumes there are no other factors. The correct answer will state that

generally or introduce a specific alternative that the author assumes is non-existent.

Step 4: Evaluate the Answer Choices

(B) must be assumed. The author assumes the mosquitoes are attracted by a gaseous substance and nothing else—not even body heat. Using the Denial Test, if mosquitoes *were* attracted by body heat, then the author's persistence with gaseous substances would be seriously questioned.

(A) is not necessary. It doesn't matter whether mosquitoes communicate with each other or not. The argument is about what attracts them to the human arm in the first place.

(C) is an Irrelevant Comparison. The author does claim that mosquitoes are attracted to a bare arm "even in complete darkness," but that still could mean they're equally attracted in broad daylight. When the arm gives off more substances has no effect on the author's claims.

(D) is an Irrelevant Comparison. The argument is about what attracts the mosquitoes, not when they're most successful.

(E) is Extreme and Out of Scope. The argument is about what attracts mosquitoes. Whether or not our skin could ever repel mosquitoes has nothing to do with what happens when mosquitoes are attracted.

12. (A) Paradox

Step 1: Identify the Question Type
The question asks for something that would "resolve the apparent discrepancy" described, making this a Paradox question.

Step 2: Untangle the Stimulus
Two analyses were done on an Italian painting, one in 1955 and another in 2009. Both analyses found cobalt in the paint, a pigment not used until 1804. Based on that, the 1955 analysis logically concluded the painting was produced after 1804, *but* the 2009 analysis said otherwise—it was produced *before* 1804.

Step 3: Make a Prediction
If cobalt wasn't used until 1804, why would the 2009 analysis suggest the painting was *older* than that? The author must have omitted something critical about that 2009 analysis. It may be difficult to predict an exact explanation, but know that the correct answer will provide a reason why the 2009 analysis dated the painting to some time earlier than cobalt was first used.

Step 4: Evaluate the Answer Choices

(A) offers an explanation. The 2009 analysis showed cobalt was only found in upper layers that were added to older, damaged layers. If that's true, then the top layer with cobalt would be from after 1804, but the original, older layers could be from any time before that.

(B) does not help. Even if the new technology is more sophisticated, it still found traces of cobalt, so there's no explanation why analysts though the painting was produced before the use of cobalt.

(C) is irrelevant. It doesn't matter how many samples were taken. Cobalt was found in both cases, so there's no explanation why analysts would suggest the painting was older than the first use of cobalt.

(D) is irrelevant. Regardless of what the experts think, the painting still had cobalt, which wasn't used until 1804. There's nothing about the paint analysis that suggests it should be any earlier than that. So, if there's artistic evidence that the painting is older than 1804, then the mystery about the cobalt still remains.

(E) is a 180. This says that the use of cobalt in Italy, the source of the painting, was rare in the first few years after 1804. That would make it more likely the painting was produced even *later* than is suggested, when cobalt use was perhaps more common.

13. (A) Strengthen

Step 1: Identify the Question Type
The question directly asks for information that "strengthens the argument," making this a Strengthen question.

Step 2: Untangle the Stimulus
To reduce the spread of influenza, a campaign was run for six months to encourage frequent hand-washing and avoiding public places when sick. In that six months, there were fewer incidences of influenza, leading the author to conclude the campaign was a success.

Step 3: Make a Prediction
This is a prime example of Correlation vs. Causation. Fewer people got the flu during the campaign, so the author argues the campaign *caused* the flu rate to drop. However, the author may have identified the wrong cause. Perhaps there was some other reason people weren't getting the flu. The author suggests otherwise, assuming that people were, indeed, just encouraged by the campaign to wash their hands more and stay away from the public when sick. The correct answer will confirm this, making it more likely that the campaign was responsible.

Step 4: Evaluate the Answer Choices

(A) is correct. This offers more reason to believe people were washing their hands more often and thus listening to the campaign messages.

(B) is a 180 at worst. It's not mentioned what could help prevent the common cold. If washing hands and staying home when sick could reduce the risk of getting a cold, then this

suggests people weren't doing that. In that case, flu rates were down for another reason, not because of the campaign.

(C) is a 180. This suggests the campaign may have been irrelevant. There just might have been fewer opportunities for people to be at large gatherings where the influenza virus could be easily shared.

(D) is another 180. This directly offers an alternative explanation for the reduction in flu incidences. The campaign may have been irrelevant if people were just watching the news.

(E) does not help. This suggests that people recognized the importance of reducing the incidence of the flu, but it still doesn't show that the campaign was the factor that finally made people take action.

14. (C) Main Point

Step 1: Identify the Question Type
The question asks for the "conclusion drawn in the argument," making this a Main Point question.

Step 2: Untangle the Stimulus
The first two sentences provide factual results from a study. From these results, the author concludes that meetings need to have a clear, less-than-30-minute time frame to be truly productive.

Step 3: Make a Prediction
The correct answer will be a paraphrase of the conclusion in the last sentence, defining the circumstances needed to achieve maximum productivity.

Step 4: Evaluate the Answer Choices

(C) matches the author's claim that a clear, below-30-minute time frame is needed for maximum productivity.

(A) is a Distortion. This confuses the logic of the conclusion, which claims that a meeting "needs to have" a clear, less-than-30-minute time frame. That makes it necessary, but not sufficient. In other words, having that time frame doesn't necessarily guarantee that any such meeting *will* be maximally productive.

(B) is a fact from the study, and the facts are merely evidence to support the conclusion, not the conclusion itself.

(D) is also a fact from the study, and facts are evidence to support the conclusion, not the conclusion itself.

(E) is part of the facts, i.e., the evidence. Those facts are used to support the conclusion.

15. (D) Inference

Step 1: Identify the Question Type
The stimulus contains a set of statements, and the correct answer will be "strongly supported by" those statements. That makes this an Inference question.

Step 2: Untangle the Stimulus

The nutritionist provides an interesting contrast. Most fad diets prescribe the same nutrients to everyone, but not everyone has the same dietary needs. The nutritionist then tosses out a random recommendation to eat your fruits and vegetables.

Step 3: Make a Prediction

The opening contrast suggests that fad diets won't be appropriate for everyone. As for the fruits and vegetables comment, don't read too much into it. It's just a recommendation, but there could still be plenty of other foods that are equally helpful. The correct answer will conform to this limited information. Just be wary of answers that go beyond what's mentioned or exaggerate the nutritionist's claims.

Step 4: Evaluate the Answer Choices

(D) is supported. If different people have very different dietary needs, then those fad diets that tell everyone to eat the same few nutrients are not going to satisfy everyone's needs; hence, *some* people will not get what they need.

(A) is a Distortion. The recommendation to eat fruits and vegetables has no logical connection to the fad diets, so there's no way to conclude whether those diets include fruits and vegetables or not.

(B) is Extreme. The nutritionist recommends fruits and vegetables, but never goes so far as to say they are the *only* foods to provide widespread health benefits. There could be other such foods.

(C) is also Extreme. Not everybody has the same dietary needs, but that doesn't mean *every* single person is entirely different. There could be a group of people who all have one set of needs, but those needs are completely different from those of another group of people, whose needs are different from another group's, etc.

(E) is Out of Scope. There is no information about what foods contain what kinds of nutrients, nor is there information about which nutrients can be found in any given food.

16. (A) Strengthen/Weaken (Evaluate the Argument)

Step 1: Identify the Question Type

The correct answer here will help in "evaluating the argument," which makes this an Evaluate the Argument variation of a Strengthen/Weaken question. The correct answer will test the validity of the argument by questioning the author's assumption.

Step 2: Untangle the Stimulus

The caffeine in coffee can produce irritating stomach acid, but darker roasts (i.e., coffee produced by roasting the beans longer) have more NMP than lighter roasts, and NMP is something that helps reduce stomach acid production. (Don't

worry about what NMP actually is—all that matters for this argument is what it *does*.) *Therefore*, the author concludes that darker roasts are less irritating.

Step 3: Make a Prediction

It's good to know that darker roasts contain something that helps reduce acid production. However, the author assumes there's nothing else different about darker roasts that could counteract that benefit. Perhaps there is something else about darker roasts that could actually stimulate *more* acid production, despite the added NMP. The correct answer will question whether the NMP is enough to reduce acid levels overall or whether there's some overlooked factor.

Step 4: Evaluate the Answer Choices

(A) is correct. If the longer brewing time does increase the caffeine, then that could easily balance out the NMP, making darker roasts equally irritable. However, if the caffeine level is the same, then it is likely that darker roasts are better for your stomach.

(B) is a great question to ponder, but not relevant to the argument. The author merely claims the darker roasts will be less irritating by reducing acid production. Whether or not this causes other stomach function problems is an entirely different concern and does nothing to question the author's claims.

(C) is Out of Scope. There is no mention of coffees that contain less caffeine, and the author's argument is about reducing acid production, not reducing caffeine intake.

(D) is clever, but does not affect the author's argument. The author may well agree that more coffee (and thereby caffeine) could be consumed if the switch to dark roast was made, and if it was *too* much if might offset the benefits of dark roast. However, the conclusion was merely about the effect of darker roasts versus lighter roasts. Any change in habits beyond that are irrelevant.

(E) is Out of Scope. The argument is entirely focused on acid production. Other health benefits are interesting, but not relevant to this argument.

17. (D) Inference

Step 1: Identify the Question Type

The correct answer will be "strongly supported by the statements" provided, making this an Inference question.

Step 2: Untangle the Stimulus

The author mentions how difficult it is for film historians to determine how typical audience members respond to certain films. Two possible sources of information are presented as unhelpful: box office figures—which can't provide details about what people actually liked about a film—and movie reviews.

Step 3: Make a Prediction

In saying that box office figures "help little" and newspaper and magazine reviews "fail to provide much insight," the author is referring to how unhelpful they are in trying to determine the typical response from audience members. There's no indication what *would* be helpful, or if it's even possible. The correct answer should merely be consistent in describing the difficulty historians face, without bringing in outside information or exaggerating the claims.

Step 4: Evaluate the Answer Choices

(D) is supported. The last sentence says such reviews "fail to provide much insight," and that insight refers to historian's attempt to determine the typical audience member's view.

(A) is Out of Scope. The author makes no mention why historians don't find such reviews insightful, and there's no suggestion whether the reviews were generally written before or after a film's release.

(B) is a Distortion. The author mentions that it's especially difficult to determine audience views for early 20th-century films, but that doesn't make it *easy* to determine audience views of late 20th-century films. They may still be difficult to determine, just a little less so.

(C) is a Distortion. This confuses the detail that box office figures do not indicate what people find funny, frightening, or moving. However, that just means the figures won't reveal the specific components that people enjoyed. It's still possible those components are critical to a movie's success, even if they can't be identified directly.

(E) is not supported. The historians don't happen to find such reviews insightful, but that doesn't mean they weren't commonly written.

18. (A) Role of a Statement

Step 1: Identify the Question Type

The question stem provides a claim from the stimulus and asks for its "role in the argument," making this a Role of a Statement question.

Step 2: Untangle the Stimulus

The claim in question (the core would have a positive charge) is in the first half of the last sentence. Before dealing with that, consider the author's overall argument. In general, astronomers believe pulsars are giant balls of neutrons. (Don't get too caught up in the science. Simplifying the details into "giant balls of neutrons" is enough to stay focused on the structure of the argument.) At the contrast Keyword [*h*]*owever*, the author argues that this description also works for pulsars that are giant balls of quarks. As evidence, the author notes how a quark-filled pulsar would have a positive charge, which would attract particles that could "support a crust of neutrons"—thus

creating something that might be mistaken for the aforementioned "giant ball of neutrons."

Step 3: Make a Prediction

It's easy to get distracted by all of the science. However, boil the argument down to a simple structure. Scientists have a definition of something called a pulsar (it's a ball of neutrons). The author argues that definition applies even when it appears otherwise (when it's a ball of quarks instead). The author provides evidence that explains why the oddball pulsars still fit the original definition (a ball of quarks would have a neutron shell). The claim in question is in the last part, so its role is to provide evidence to show why quark-filled pulsars still can still have an outer coating of neutrons.

Step 4: Evaluate the Answer Choices

(A) is correct, identifying the claim as evidence to explain how non-neutron-filled pulsars (i.e., those filled with quarks) could still attract neutrons.

(B) is a Distortion and a 180. The author never challenges the idea that pulsars can be made of quarks. They absolutely can. And the claim in question explains how they work.

(C) is Out of Scope. The author says nothing about such pulsars going unrecognized by astronomers.

(D) is a 180. The claim actually shows how quark-filled pulsars *conform* to the consensus view, not challenge it.

(E) is a Distortion. The author never questions the mass of pulsars.

19. (C) Inference

Step 1: Identify the Question Type

The stimulus will contain a set of statements, and those statements will be used to "strongly support" the correct answer, making this an Inference question.

Step 2: Untangle the Stimulus

The analyst provides four requirements for the location of a particular generation station: 1) It needs to be near a natural-gas pipeline; 2) it needs to be near a large body of water; 3) it needs to be near transmission lines; and 4) residents won't oppose it. As of now, the analyst's country has extensive transmission lines, so the third requirement should be fine. The problem is there are only three large bodies of water near gas pipelines, but residents would oppose all three locations.

Step 3: Make a Prediction

With the residents being so stubborn (the author says they would oppose *any* construction project near the three bodies of water), the country is at an impasse. The only choice left is to find another body of water, but none of them are currently near natural-gas pipelines. That leaves one viable alternative if the country wants to build one of these stations: build new pipelines near another large body of water.

Step 4: Evaluate the Answer Choices

(C) is the supported inference from the analyst's information. The current sites don't meet the requirements, and building new pipelines is the only logical course of action if they want to build this type of station.

(A) is not supported. New pipelines can still be built, so there's no need to give up on natural-gas-powered generation just yet. Furthermore, perhaps existing natural-gas-powered generation stations would be sufficient to meet future electrical needs—it's only the construction of new ones that are cited as a potential problem.

(B) is not supported. The residents do oppose the currently available sites. If the station is built anyway, the residents might protest, but there's no indication they'd just pack up and move.

(D) is not supported. It's possible that such stations were already built in the past. The residents just won't approve of any *new* projects. The old stations could have been built before the public stated its views.

(E) is a 180. The analyst claims residents would oppose *any* significant construction project in those areas, not just electrical stations.

20. (A) Flaw

Step 1: Identify the Question Type
The question asks why the "reasoning is questionable" in the argument given, making this a Flaw question.

Step 2: Untangle the Stimulus
The author concludes that each generation of citizens is becoming more disinterested in politics than the next generation. The evidence is that people over 65 vote a lot while young adults don't.

Step 3: Make a Prediction
There are some representativeness issues with the author's argument; this is not an apples to apples comparison. What is true of a generation in the later stages of their lives may not have been true about them in their earlier years. Perhaps the younger generation will behave more like the older generation when they reach that point of their lives. Likewise, the older generation's current voting record may not be representative of their voting record when they were young adults.

Step 4: Evaluate the Answer Choices

(A) is correct. One generation is at an early stage of their lives and the other at a later stage. It is unknown how the older generation behaved when they were younger, and it is unknown how the younger generation will behave when they are older. So, the author makes a faulty prediction that the

young adults current behavior is indicative of what their future behavior will be.

(B) is not an issue. The argument is about percentages and rates, so actual numbers are not relevant.

(C) is accurate in that the author does not explain why people are becoming disconnected from politics. However, that's not the purpose of the argument, so there's nothing flawed (i.e., questionable) about omitting that.

(D) is Out of Scope. The author never addresses the cause of the problem, so there's nothing to confuse.

(E) is a 180. The point of the author's argument is that voting patterns *are* changing, and that future patterns are likely to show even more of a disconnect. However, the author fails to consider whether the older generation has always had a high percentage of voters, or whether they've matured into that behavior. If they've matured, then the current younger generation may do the same. Thus, the author overlooks the possibility that the voting patterns among age groups are *not* changing—it's just that older people may always be more likely to vote.

21. (B) Principle (Parallel)

Step 1: Identify the Question Type
According to the question, there is a principle to be identified from the argument given. However, the correct answer will not describe that principle. Instead, it will re-apply that principle to a new situation. That makes this a relatively uncommon Parallel Principle question.

Step 2: Untangle the Stimulus
The author concludes (*therefore*) that the city should not allow the office complex to be built just yet. The evidence is that building it would require draining a local marsh, and that raises potential problems that have yet to be assessed.

Step 3: Make a Prediction
In principle, the author is advocating not to take any rash actions when there are potential problems that should be studied first. The correct answer will apply this principle to another situation.

Step 4: Evaluate the Answer Choices

(B) matches the principle. Like the original argument, there are potential problems (recalls and lawsuits due to defects) that have not been studied yet. Based on that, it's recommended not to take action and sell the new product just yet.

(A) does not match. This outright rejects taking action because of the high cost of performing the needed assessment. That's not the same as temporarily holding back until the assessment is done.

(C) does not match. In this situation, the suggestion is to not reveal the results of the assessment just yet. That's not the same as asking the company to wait before selling the grills. In fact, it's possible the company has already started selling grills and sent some in for testing after the fact, which would go contrary to the original author's principle.

(D) is a Distortion. This tries to mimic the original argument's concern for the environment. However, the guiding principle of the original argument was not "do what's less damaging." It was all about assessing the problem before acting, and this argument leaves that out entirely.

(E) does not match. This simply makes a judgment that solving future problems overrides the costs involved. This does not compare to the original argument, which was based on assessing problems first. Further, this argument recommends taking a course of action while the original recommended temporarily holding off.

22. (D) Weaken

Step 1: Identify the Question Type
The question directly asks for something that "most weakens" the given argument, making this a Weaken question.

Step 2: Untangle the Stimulus
The author describes a study with two groups of people. The first group watched recordings of themselves on a treadmill. (That must have been exciting.) The second group watched recordings of *other* people on a treadmill. (Even more exciting.) When later asked how much they exercise, people in the first group reported an average of one hour longer. Based on that, the author concludes that watching yourself exercising can motivate you to exercise more.

Step 3: Make a Prediction
There is a lot wrong with this entire situation, but let's stick to the poor logic of the argument. First off, this is a classic case of Correlation vs. Causation. The author merely assumes that the videos motivated people, and nothing else. What's more, there's always a fundamental error when the author says something happened more often because people in a study *said* they did it more often. In this case, the people in the first group *said* they did more exercise. But did they really? Who knows? Maybe they just watched the video and thought, "Wow—I bet I exercise more than I thought. I'll just tell these research folks that I exercise a *lot*." If the correct answer doesn't show an alternative reason why people exercise more, it will likely show that people *aren't* actually exercising more; they're just making up numbers.

Step 4: Evaluate the Answer Choices

(D) weakens the argument, albeit in a very offbeat way. In the study described in this choice, people watched videos of their *identical* twin reading. In other words, they were watching people who looked *just like them*. After doing so, they overreported how much time they spent reading. So, they didn't actually read more, they just *said* they did. That

suggests the same might be happening with the treadmill study, and thus it is less likely that people are actually motivated to exercise more. Is that the best way to weaken this argument? Not by a long shot. However, it's the only choice that addresses either the assumption that there were no alternative causes of the increased exercise or the assumption that the people's self-assessments of more exercise were accurate.

(A) is an Irrelevant Comparison. The author is not concerned with finding the most effective motivator. If people exercised more after watching themselves on a treadmill, the author's argument is still valid, even if watching themselves lift weights would have been more effective.

(B) is Out of Scope. This involves hearing second-hand stories about other people. Even if that effectively motivates people, it doesn't weaken the idea that watching yourself exercise on video could also be motivating.

(C) is irrelevant. How many such participants were there? Did they make up a large portion of the study? And what group were they in? Without more details, a few stray health nuts are not going to have any effect on the author's claim.

(E) is a 180 at worst. This suggests that people *are* actually influenced by watching themselves on video. Watch yourself on a treadmill? You exercise more! Watch yourself sitting on a couch? (The most exciting video yet!) You sit around more!

23. (A) Assumption (Necessary)

Step 1: Identify the Question Type
The question asks for something the argument "requires assuming," making this a Necessary Assumption question.

Step 2: Untangle the Stimulus
The environmentalist is arguing that convincing people to reduce their personal use of fossil fuels is not going to reduce carbon usage overall. The evidence is that reducing carbon usage requires large-scale government policies.

Step 3: Make a Prediction
There's a major Overlooked Possibility here. The environmentalist is only looking at direct effects. Individual changes won't *directly* reduce carbon usage enough. However, it's possible that individual changes could *indirectly* lead to bigger changes, which may ultimately lead to the central requirement: government policies. The environmentalist assumes this wouldn't happen and that we need to start directly at government policies.

Step 4: Evaluate the Answer Choices

(A) must be assumed. After all, using the Denial Test, if personal changes *did* persuade people to get the government involved, then the environmentalist's argument is unsound. Focusing on individual efforts could pay off in the long run. The environmentalist must be assuming that won't happen.

(B) is Out of Scope. The difficulty in performing such calculations is irrelevant to the argument. The environmentalists's point is that people's efforts wouldn't be enough, even if they *did* go through the effort of determining the best course of action.

(C) is Extreme. The people encouraging personal reduction in fossil fuel usage don't *have* to be currently uninvolved in framing government policies. They could all be involved in government, but still fail, as the environmentalist suggests, by focusing on individuals instead of getting the government involved.

(D) is an Irrelevant Comparison. The argument does not depend on one course of action being easier. It depends on one being more effective.

(E) is Out of Scope. It doesn't matter which candidates people support. All that matters is whether or not the needed governmental policies can be enacted.

24. (C) Parallel Flaw

Step 1: Identify the Question Type
The correct answer will have an argument that is "similar to that" in the stimulus. Moreover, that reasoning is described as *questionable*, making this a Parallel Flaw question.

Step 2: Untangle the Stimulus
The author presents two possible sources of a painting's aesthetic value: the painting's formal qualities or its meaning. The author then argues that there's no valid support for saying it's in the formal qualities, so it must be in the painting's meaning.

Step 3: Make a Prediction
There may not be support for formal qualities, but who said there's any support for the painting's meaning? The author merely rejects one option without providing convincing evidence in favor of the second. The correct answer will follow the same flawed format: present two options, reject one for not having supportive evidence, and illogically claim the second option is correct.

Step 4: Evaluate the Answer Choices

(C) is a match. The author presents two options (economic or political forces), rejects one for not having supportive evidence (economic forces), and illogically claims the second option is correct.

(A) does not match. The author does reject one of two options. However, the original author claimed there were *only* two viable options. This author claims that there are multiple "other methods." So, this argument is flawed in that it fails to consider the other options, but that's not the same as the original argument. Furthermore, this author *does* give a viable reason to reject one of the two options specifically mentioned.

(B) does not match. The two options presented are requirements if an outcome occurs (the company being outbid). The author claims one option won't happen, so the outcome won't occur. However, this completely ignores the second requirement. And the original argument was not based on any necessary conditions. The Formal Logic is flawed, for sure. However, it's not the same flaw as the original.

(D) does not match. The author presents two outcomes if a situation occurs. The author then concludes that one outcome won't happen because the other won't happen. This displays some poor Formal Logic, for sure, but it's not the same as rejecting one option and saying the other option must be correct.

(E) does not match. If there are two options to consider here, it's whether the party changes its policies or not. However, the conclusion doesn't reject one and favor the other. It just says something bad will inevitably happen.

25. (D) Flaw

Step 1: Identify the Question Type
The question directly asks for a description of the argument's flaw.

Step 2: Untangle the Stimulus
The phrase "must be" indicates some Formal Logic. If there is to be economic growth, then there must be technological innovations. The author then claims that a ban on fossil fuels will spur technological innovations, and uses that to conclude that economic growth is imminent.

Step 3: Make a Prediction
When Formal Logic appears in a Flaw question, there's a good chance the author is going to commit the commonly tested flaw of Necessity vs. Sufficiency. Sure enough, the Formal Logic dictates that technological innovations *must* be in place first (i.e., they're necessary).

If	substantial economic growth	→	tech innovations

However, that doesn't mean tech innovations will guarantee (i.e., are sufficient for) economic growth, as the author asserts.

If	tech innovations	→	substantial economic growth

The author reversed, but failed to negate. The correct answer will describe this mistaken treatment of a necessary condition as if it were sufficient.

Step 4: Evaluate the Answer Choices

(D) is correct.

(A) describes the flaw of Circular Reasoning, but that doesn't happen here. The author misinterprets the evidence. It's not just about a mere restatement of the evidence.

(B) describes the flaw of *ad hominem*, which involves attacking people personally rather than addressing their claims. However, the author does not personally attack the critics of the ban. The author tries to addresses their claim, but fails to follow the rules of Formal Logic.

(C) is not even a flaw. This is suggesting that the author's evidence is *too* good. When's the last time you told someone, "I don't believe you—your evidence is just too convincing"?

(E) is a Distortion. This suggests the author concludes that innovation *always* brings about economic growth just because innovation *sometimes* happens before economic growth. That would be flawed logic, but it's not what the author does here. The author says substantial economic growth *must* be preceded by innovation, so, there's no *sometimes* about the author's evidence.

26. (E) Point at Issue

Step 1: Identify the Question Type

As with most Point at Issue questions, there are two speakers, and the correct answer will address something about which they both have an opinion. However, read the question carefully. Unlike most Point at Issue questions, the correct answer will be something the speakers *agree* with each other about.

Step 2: Untangle the Stimulus

Winston is unhappy with the rules for awarding Nobel Prizes. Each award can go to only three people, but many winning science results are the work of four or more people. Sanjay is also unhappy, but with another restriction: Winners have to be living. That ignores influential scientists who died before their results were recognized.

Step 3: Make a Prediction

Winston and Sanjay are both unhappy with the rules for awarding Nobel Prizes, particularly in science. In both arguments, the rules have the effect of denying credit to certain scientists (those who were left out after the first three people on a project were selected, and those who died before the project won the award). The correct answer will address this agreed-upon displeasure with people getting ignored.

Step 4: Evaluate the Answer Choices

(E) is correct. To Winston, the prizes are inaccurate because they only list three people and leave out other potential contributors. To Sanjay, the prizes are inaccurate because they don't recognize contributors who may have died.

(A) only addresses Sanjay's concerns. It's possible that Winston would agree, but there's nothing in his statements to directly suggest that.

(B) is a Distortion. It's likely that both authors want to see some changes to the science rules, but that doesn't mean science has to have its own unique rules. While both authors only talk about science here, they may have similar complaints about other disciplines as well. Perhaps they would both like to see universal changes so that the rules are consistent, but more inclusive, for all disciplines.

(C) is a Distortion. Neither author argues against the awarding of prizes to particular results. Their concerns are about the people being recognized.

(D) is Out of Scope. Neither author addresses whether the awards are based on subjective or objective criteria.

Section III: Logical Reasoning

Q#	Question Type	Correct	Difficulty
1	Point at Issue	E	Check your online resources.
2	Paradox	C	Check your online resources.
3	Main Point	A	Check your online resources.
4	Assumption (Necessary)	E	Check your online resources.
5	Inference	D	Check your online resources.
6	Paradox	E	Check your online resources.
7	Flaw	B	Check your online resources.
8	Main Point	B	Check your online resources.
9	Flaw	B	Check your online resources.
10	Inference	B	Check your online resources.
11	Parallel Flaw	A	Check your online resources.
12	Strengthen	A	Check your online resources.
13	Flaw	B	Check your online resources.
14	Inference	A	Check your online resources.
15	Flaw	A	Check your online resources.
16	Weaken	C	Check your online resources.
17	Role of a Statement	D	Check your online resources.
18	Assumption (Necessary)	D	Check your online resources.
19	Inference	C	Check your online resources.
20	Assumption (Sufficient)	E	Check your online resources.
21	Method of Argument	C	Check your online resources.
22	Weaken	D	Check your online resources.
23	Flaw	B	Check your online resources.
24	Inference	B	Check your online resources.
25	Parallel Reasoning	E	Check your online resources.

1. (E) Point at Issue

Step 1: Identify the Question Type
The question asks for something that two speakers "disagree over," making this a Point at Issue question.

Step 2: Untangle the Stimulus
Joe finds vampire stories absurd, arguing that these immortal creatures should have almost no prey remaining as they've been around for ages and all of their victims turn into vampires, too. Maria points out a flaw in Joe's analysis. In stories she's read, vampires only turn *some* other people into vampires, not *all* of their victims.

Step 3: Make a Prediction
The point at issue here is whether, in vampire stories, vampires turn everyone into vampires or just a select few.

Step 4: Evaluate the Answer Choices

(E) is correct. Joe claims this is correct, while Maria argues otherwise—in some stories, most victims are merely killed, not turned into more vampires.

(A) is Out of Scope for Maria. Joe mentions vampires' immortality, but Maria makes no mention of it, nor does she seem to dispute that claim.

(B) is Out of Scope for Maria. Joe mentions vampires existing since ancient times, but Maria neither addresses nor disputes that claim.

(C) is a Distortion of Joe's claims. Joe finds the stories absurd in that they have ridiculous consequences. However, that doesn't mean they're incoherent (i.e., confusing or unclear).

(D) is Out of Scope for both speakers. Joe argues that the premises of such stories imply that almost everyone should be a vampire by now. However, he never claims the stories actually depict this large-scale vampire population. And Maria never addresses how large the vampire population is said to be.

2. (C) Paradox

Step 1: Identify the Question Type
The correct answer will help "account for" the situation presented, making this a Paradox question.

Step 2: Untangle the Stimulus
A company wanted to help its salespeople by scanning all of their paperwork and storing it in a database that can be easily accessed by computer. They expected the salespeople would be thrilled. No more carrying around piles of papers! However, the result was not as expected. Salespeople resisted the database and refused to get their paperwork scanned.

Step 3: Make a Prediction
It definitely seems strange that the salespeople were not interested in something that seems so helpful. Why did they resist this change? The most likely explanations are that there

was something remarkably inconvenient about the database, or there is something highly beneficial about keeping work in paper form. The correct answer will address one, if not both, of these possible explanations.

Step 4: Evaluate the Answer Choices

(C) is correct. This points to a benefit of paper forms—client confidentiality. That explains why salespeople resisted the database and didn't want to submit their paperwork for scanning.

(A) does not help. This confirms that some salespeople didn't submit a lot of paperwork. However, it doesn't offer a reason why, so there's still no accounting for their resistance.

(B) is a 180. If the salespeople *didn't* have portable computers, that might explain why they resisted the database. However, if they already had portable computers, it's even more unusual that they wouldn't take advantage of the database.

(D) is a 180, at worst. If the training was inconvenient and the database was overly complicated, that might explain the resistance. However, if the salespeople found the database software so easy to use, it's even harder to understand why they wouldn't use it.

(E) is Out of Scope. The paradox has nothing to do with the building of the database. The paradox is all about why employees didn't *use* the database, no matter how much time or money it cost to build.

3. (A) Main Point

Step 1: Identify the Question Type
The question asks you what "the politician argues," which means the correct answer should express the point the politician is advocating, i.e., the main point.

Step 2: Untangle the Stimulus
The politician is making a common claim that "free speech" doesn't imply everything you say is protected. What follows are some common examples of unacceptable forms of speech, which all lead to the ultimate conclusion: Some forms of speech can lead directly to harm and are thus okay to make illegal.

Step 3: Make a Prediction
The correct answer will express the politician's claim at the end that criminalization of some speech is okay because that speech can cause harm.

Step 4: Evaluate the Answer Choices

(A) is correct.

(B) is Extreme. The politician uses examples of speech that can cause harm and concludes that such speech can be restricted. However, the author doesn't claim this is the *only* kind of speech that can be restricted. There may be other reasons to restrict other kinds of speech.

(C) is a Distortion. The only harm mentioned by the politician is that caused by certain forms of speech. The author never says anything about harm being caused by restricting speech.

(D) is Extreme. The politician argues that certain forms of speech can lead directly to harm, but never says that *any* form of speech can do so.

(E) is Out of Scope. The author never mentions any situation in which restricting freedom is *un*justified.

4. (E) Assumption (Necessary)

Step 1: Identify the Question Type
The question directly asks for an assumption on which the argument *depends*, making this a Necessary Assumption question.

Step 2: Untangle the Stimulus
According to the art critic, people who go to museums look at an artwork for under a minute, take a photo, and move on. That leads the critic to conclude that people are less willing to engage with artwork.

Step 3: Make a Prediction
This is a perfect example of Mismatched Concepts. The evidence is all about the brief time spent looking at artwork, but the conclusion raises the concept of being engaged. The art critic is assuming there's a connection between those two concepts, i.e., that time spent looking at an artwork somehow indicates how engaged one is with that artwork.

Step 4: Evaluate the Answer Choices
(E) is correct. By the Denial Test, if time spent was *not* a reliable measure of engagement, then the critic's conclusion is completely unsupported. The art critic must assume that time spent has some connection to engagement.

(A) is Out of Scope. It doesn't matter whether people see one piece of art or 100. The argument is about whether people are engaged with that art, and this makes no connection to that.

(B) is irrelevant. Why people move so quickly doesn't matter. What matters is whether or not people are losing their willingness to engage in the art.

(C) is Out of Scope. The argument is not about enjoying the museum-going experience. It's about engaging with the artwork, which is not necessarily the same concept.

(D) is Out of Scope. This may strengthen the art critic's evidence that people don't spend much time with a single piece of art—they don't even look at the photo of the art! However, regardless of the time spent with the artwork or its photo, this offers no connection to whether or not people feel engaged with the artwork.

5. (D) Inference

Step 1: Identify the Question Type
The correct answer will be "supported by the information" given, making this an Inference question.

Step 2: Untangle the Stimulus
According to the author, heavy tapestry fabrics shouldn't be used to create items that need to be frequently laundered, such as clothing. Instead, it should be used for items such as window treatments.

Step 3: Make a Prediction
The word *only* indicates Formal Logic: If it's appropriate to use heavy fabric, then the item should not be frequently laundered. By contrapositive, if an item is going to be frequently laundered, then it's not appropriate to use heavy tapestry fabrics.

If	heavy fabric appropriate	→	~ laundered frequently
If	laundered frequently	→	~ heavy fabric appropriate

The correct answer will follow this logic without improperly negating or reversing the logic.

Step 4: Evaluate the Answer Choices
(D) is correct, essentially using the contrapositive. Because skirts and jackets are said to be frequently laundered clothing, then heavy fabric would not be appropriate.

(A) is a Distortion. Heavy fabrics are appropriate for swags, but there could be other fabrics not mentioned that are also appropriate.

(B) is Extreme. The author says that appropriate applications *include* swags and balloon valances. However, there are likely plenty of other acceptable applications for heavy fabrics.

(C) is also Extreme. Appropriate applications *include* the window treatments listed, but that doesn't mean all appropriate applications *must* be window treatments.

(E) is a 180. The author specifically makes note of skirts and jackets, but the general claim is that heavy tapestry fabrics are not appropriate for "any types of clothing."

6. (E) Paradox

Step 1: Identify the Question Type
The question asks for something that "helps to explain" a discrepancy, making this a Paradox question.

Step 2: Untangle the Stimulus
New apartments in Brewsterville logically increased the supply of available housing. However, while that usually

leads to lower rents for existing apartments, the opposite happened: those rents went up.

Step 3: Make a Prediction

Why did rents for existing apartments go up when they usually go down? The correct answer will answer that question. The correct answer will likely show why even the existing apartments (instead of just the new ones) are suddenly more desirable.

Step 4: Evaluate the Answer Choices

(E) solves the mystery. If the population stayed the same, then the general trend would be expected: high prices for the new apartments and lower prices for the old ones. However, if lots of people are looking to move in to the area, then there would be increased demand for both the new *and* the existing apartments, which would logically lead to the higher prices.

(A) does not help. Even if there were supposed to be more new apartments, there's no indication why the older apartments are more desirable and worth more rent.

(B) is a 180. If the new apartments are more desirable, then they should have higher rents. It wouldn't make sense to raise the rent for the old apartments, which are less desirable.

(C) is Out of Scope. The effect in other areas has no impact on explaining the rent increase on apartments in Brewsterville.

(D) does not help. This just suggests that there were more older apartments available as people moved out. However, with more apartments available, that doesn't explain why the rent would increase.

7. (B) Flaw

Step 1: Identify the Question Type

The correct answer will describe why the argument is "vulnerable to criticism," a frequently used phrase that indicates a Flaw question.

Step 2: Untangle the Stimulus

The author argues that politicians push for more economic productivity but ignore the negative consequences. The author then provides an example of how a company could attempt to increase productivity by increasing profits, but that often leads to reducing employment. *Thus*, the author concludes that trying to increase economic productivity would lead to unemployment.

Step 3: Make a Prediction

The author provides a great example of how focusing on productivity can have undesirable consequences. However, the author then uses the details of that one example (about a corporation losing employees) and suggests the exact same consequences will happen if politicians focus on increasing economic productivity as a whole. While it's possible that focusing too much on productivity could be problematic,

there's no reason to suggest that the result would *definitely* be unemployment based on one hypothetical example. This is a common flaw of basing a broad conclusion on an unrepresentative sample.

Step 4: Evaluate the Answer Choices

(B) correctly describes the commonly tested flaw. The author assumes that what happens in one single case is going to happen when addressing the economy overall.

(A) is Out of Scope. The author is certainly concerned about potential drawbacks, particularly unemployment. However, the author never argues that the goal of increasing productivity should be *abandoned*. Perhaps the author just feels that politicians should exercise more caution.

(C) is a Distortion. The author does criticize politicians in general, but the evidence is that they do, in general, fail to consider the drawbacks. It's not said to be just a few politicians that make this mistake.

(D) is a Distortion. The author makes no comparison as to whose interests are more important. Besides, the author claims that increasing productivity would be beneficial to business owners, so there's no assumption that productivity is more important than the owners' interests.

(E) is a Distortion. The author's argument is just that there can be drawbacks, not that the drawbacks outweigh the benefits. To claim that there are drawbacks, the author merely needs to show they exist. There's no need to mention *all* drawbacks or any benefits.

8. (B) Main Point

Step 1: Identify the Question Type

The question asks for the "overall conclusion," i.e., the main point of the argument.

Step 2: Untangle the Stimulus

The author starts with the opinion that good movie reviewers should be able to give positive reviews to movies they don't personally like. This opinion is supported by two facts: 1) Movie reviewers' tastes are often very different from those of most moviegoers; and 2) the role of a movie reviewer is to help people decide which movies they might enjoy.

Step 3: Make a Prediction

In an argument, the conclusion is an opinion that is supported by evidence, which usually consists of facts. In this argument, the only true opinion is the first sentence, and that claim is supported by the facts provided. So, the conclusion is that good movie reviewers should be able to give positive reviews to movies they don't personally like.

Step 4: Evaluate the Answer Choices

(B) is correct, providing an accurate paraphrase of the conclusion in the first sentence.

(A) is a subsidiary conclusion presented in the argument as evidence to support the main conclusion; its not the main conclusion itself.

(C) is a fact presented in the argument, and facts are part of the evidence, not the conclusion.

(D) is a fact, that is used to support the subsidiary conclusion that movie reviewers have tastes that are typically different and better informed than most moviegoers.

(E) is a fact presented as evidence to support the conclusion, not the conclusion itself.

9. (B) Flaw

Step 1: Identify the Question Type
The question directly asks for the flaw in the argument.

Step 2: Untangle the Stimulus
The author presents a correlation: a certain part of the brain tends to be larger in skilled musicians than in people who don't really play music. This leads the author to conclude that playing an instrument changes the brain's structure.

Step 3: Make a Prediction
This is a prime example of the flaw of correlation vs. causation. The brain area happens to be larger in musicians (a correlation), so the author assumes that playing music is the *cause* of that area being larger. There are three problems with such causal arguments: 1) The author overlooks other causes, i.e., other factors that contribute to the size of the brain area; 2) the author may have reversed the causality, i.e., already having a larger brain area may be responsible for people choosing to play music, not the other way around; and 3) it's just a coincidence, i.e., the results are correlated but neither one directly affects the other. The correct answer will express one of these three problems.

Step 4: Evaluate the Answer Choices

(B) is correct, identifying the overlooked possibility that the author has the causality reversed, i.e., that having a larger brain area causes people to play music, not the other way around.

(A) is an Irrelevant Comparison. The author mentions piano sounds, but attributes the ability to all musicians equally. There is no comparison made or assumed about pianists versus other musicians.

(C) is a Out of Scope. The author indicates highly skilled musicians have a specific area of their brain that is larger. The author claims this is caused by playing an instrument. The author does not then take this supposed phenomenon and apply it broadly to other activities that could also (allegedly) change brain structure.

(D) is Out of Scope. The author is merely suggesting that playing an instrument can affect one particular area of the brain. That doesn't mean listening to music can't affect

another area. That has no bearing on the author's argument, so the author has no need to address it.

(E) is also Out of Scope. The argument is about how playing music affects a particular part of the brain. What makes someone a highly skilled musician or how much practice is involved is entirely irrelevant.

10. (B) Inference

Step 1: Identify the Question Type
The stimulus will provide a set of statements that will "strongly support" the correct answer, making this an Inference question.

Step 2: Untangle the Stimulus
According to the researcher, hearing just one side of a cell-phone conversation can be distracting for two reasons: 1) The listener starts to guess what the other side is saying; and 2) the cell-phone user speaks very loudly.

Step 3: Make a Prediction
There is very little to work with here, and thus very little to predict. The correct answer will be consistent with the distracting quality of hearing one side of a cell-phone conversation. Watch out for answers that exaggerate or distort these claims.

Step 4: Evaluate the Answer Choices

(B) is correct. According to the first claim, overhearing a cell-phone conversation can divert attention from *whatever* someone is doing. That would include an activity such as driving.

(A) is a Distortion. People are said to be distracted if they hear one side of a conversation, i.e., they hear somebody *else* on a cell-phone. If a driver is talking on the phone, the driver is hearing both sides, not just one. While, in real life, this statement is probably very true, it is not supported by the information provided.

(C) is a 180, at worst. The statements only support what happens when people hear one side of a call on a cell-phone, not a traditional phone. Besides, the first distraction (listeners guessing what the other side is saying) could still apply to traditional phones, which would likely make hearing one side of a traditional phone conversation similarly distracting.

(D) is Extreme. Overhearing one side of a cell-phone call might divert one's attention, but perhaps just temporarily. That doesn't necessarily mean people will completely lose track of their thoughts.

(E) is Out of Scope. The situation described is guessing what people are saying when you can't hear them, not guessing what people mean when you *do* hear them. This also makes an unsupported comparison between cell-phone conversations and other forms of conversations, which are never addressed.

11. (A) Parallel Flaw

Step 1: Identify the Question Type

The correct answer will use "parallel reasoning" to indicate the "flawed nature" of the argument provided, making this a Parallel Flaw question.

Step 2: Untangle the Stimulus

The author mentions that studies showed positive results for a promising new pain treatment. However, there was something wrong with the method for each study, so the author concludes the pain treatment is probably no good.

Step 3: Make a Prediction

The study methods may have been flawed in some way, but the results could still have been accurate. The author doesn't consider that, and the correct answer will describe a situation that commits the same flaw: Concluding that something assessed as good is likely bad because of some problem with how that item was assessed.

Step 4: Evaluate the Answer Choices

(A) is a match. The cake was assessed as good (it won the contest), but the author argues that it's probably bad because of some problem with how the cake was assessed (the criteria was not consistent). Even with inconsistent criteria, the cake could still be good, just as the pain treatment in the original argument could still be effective, despite the flawed methods in the studies.

(B) does not match. There is no judging the quality of anything or questioning the method of assessment.

(C) does not match. No method of assessment is addressed, and this author shifts from a discussion of nutritional value to a conclusion of being malnourished, a shift in scope that was never found in the original argument.

(D) does not match. No method of assessment is addressed, and the author does not claim that a positive judgment is likely wrong.

(E) does not match. This does not address any method of assessment, and the author does not say something claimed to be good is likely bad.

12. (A) Strengthen

Step 1: Identify the Question Type

The question asks for something that "strongly supports the argument" given, making this a Strengthen question.

Step 2: Untangle the Stimulus

The conclusion is a conditional prediction: If computer simulations can test safety features as effectively as test

crashes, then companies will use fewer test crashes. The evidence is that computer simulations would cost a lot less.

Step 3: Make a Prediction

This is a case of Overlooked Possibilities. If test crashes are more expensive, that could certainly provide an incentive to cut back on using them. However, the author's prediction is based on computers being equally effective in providing information about safety features. What if test crashes are used to produce more than just safety information? The author doesn't consider that and assumes there are no other benefits to test crashes that would warrant keeping them around, even if computer simulations were to provide equally reliable safety information. The correct answer will validate this assumption.

Step 4: Evaluate the Answer Choices

(A) is correct, confirming that most of the important information gleaned from test crashes is, indeed, safety-related.

(B) is a Distortion. The author's prediction is based on the condition that computer simulations become more informative. However, even if that were likely, as this choice suggests, that doesn't help verify that the prediction is any more valid. The same assumptions and overlooked possibilities persist.

(C) is Out of Scope. The author's argument is not about creating safer cars. The author just seems more intent on finding a cheaper way to test them.

(D) is a 180. The cost of designing the features has no impact on the argument, as the argument is solely about testing the features. Nonetheless, if the cost of testing is decreasing and is predicted to decrease further, then it may eventually be just as cheap as computer simulations. In that case, there'd be no need to cut back on test crashes.

(E) is an Irrelevant Comparison. What the aviation industry needs is not necessarily comparable to what the automobile industry needs. For the auto industry, there could still be particular needs served by test crashes that would not be served by computer simulations.

13. (B) Flaw

Step 1: Identify the Question Type

The correct answer will describe how the argument is "vulnerable to criticism," common wording used to indicate a Flaw question.

Step 2: Untangle the Stimulus

The legislator concludes ([s]o) that a certain act should be approved. The evidence is that a colleague recommends rejecting the act because it would deter investment. However, the legislator questions that reasoning because the colleague favored other acts in the past that deterred investment.

Step 3: Make a Prediction

The legislator is making an *ad hominem* attack. The legislator is questioning the colleague merely on her previous actions. It's possible that the colleague *is* against deterring investment, but there was an overriding concern to the earlier legislation. Instead of attacking the colleague personally for her previous voting record, the legislator should have focused on her reasoning for rejecting this act. The correct answer will describe this flaw.

Step 4: Evaluate the Answer Choices

(B) is correct, describing the legislator's failure to address the colleague's reasoning, instead concentrating on her previous voting record.

(A) is a Distortion. Attacking one's character traits is a form of *ad hominem* attack, but the legislator is not doing that. The legislator is attacking the colleague's prior actions, not her character traits.

(C) is Out of Scope. The legislator does not address which position is more popular, and does not assume either way.

(D) is Out of Scope. The legislator does not assume anything about voters. This argument is solely about the colleague's opinion and the reason to be skeptical of that.

(E) is also Out of Scope. If anything, the legislator would welcome this information as it would show a reason why the colleague's reasoning is not persuasive. The colleague doesn't really care about investment; she's just trying to placate her constituents.

14. (A) Inference

Step 1: Identify the Question Type

The correct answer would logically fill in the blank at the end of the argument given. The blank is preceded by the conclusion Keyword *so*, indicating that the blank will contain a conclusion directly supported by the given evidence. That makes this an Inference question.

Step 2: Untangle the Stimulus

The first claim is Formal Logic: To increase efficiency significantly, a computer system needs to make employees adopt a new way of working.

	efficiency significantly up	→	adapt new productive ways
If			

Then, the author claims that the new computer system for the Ministry of Transportation will fit the way employees currently work.

Step 3: Make a Prediction

The new system for the Ministry of Transportation fails to meet the necessary condition for increasing efficiency. If it merely fits with existing ways of working, then employees don't need to adopt a new way of working. The sufficient term of the contrapositive is triggered.

	~ adapt new productive ways	→	efficiency ~ significantly up
If			

Thus, by the Formal Logic in the first statement, the logical conclusion is that the new system will not increase efficiency.

Step 4: Evaluate the Answer Choices

(A) is correct, presenting the logical result of the Formal Logic based on the information given about the new system.

(B) is Out of Scope. There is nothing in the argument to support why the system wouldn't function properly.

(C) is a Distortion. Perhaps the ministry is absolutely concerned with productivity, but are misguided or unaware that their decision to maintain existing ways of working won't increase productivity, despite the new computer system. Alternatively, perhaps the ministry feels that employees are already working at peak productivity and there's just no reason to change that.

(D) is Out of Scope. The author makes no argument about whether the system would be worthwhile or not, and there's no information to support switching processes from manual to automated.

(E) is Out of Scope. The author's argument revolves on what's necessary for the system to increase efficiency. The ease of using the system is of no concern to the author.

15. (A) Flaw

Step 1: Identify the Question Type

The correct answer will described how the argument is "vulnerable to criticism," a common indication of a Flaw question.

Step 2: Untangle the Stimulus

The columnist concludes ([*s*]*o*) that car manufacturers are probably exaggerating their cars' normal fuel economy. This is based on the relatively weak fuel performance of the three cars owned by the columnist.

Step 3: Make a Prediction

There are two potential problems. The first is that the advertised fuel economy is said to occur "under normal driving conditions." Perhaps the columnist drives in abnormal conditions. However, even assuming the columnist does drive under normal conditions, the conclusion about cars in general is based on what happened with just three cars. That is far too small a sample size, making this a direct test of the flaw of representativeness.

Step 4: Evaluate the Answer Choices

(A) is correct, identifying the commonly tested flaw of using a potentially unrepresentative sample.

(B) is Extreme. The columnist doesn't have to assume *every* region has the same driving conditions. Some regions can have unusual conditions, and that would have no effect on the columnist's argument.

(C) is a 180. The columnist is accusing the manufacturers of being unreliable, not overlooking that possibility.

(D) is a Distortion. The author might be accusing manufacturers of knowingly inflating the fuel economy numbers, but that doesn't mean the cars fail to meet efficiency standards. They could be well above standards, but the manufacturers just market them as even *better*.

(E) is not accurate. The meaning of fuel economy does not change in the argument. It refers to the distance a car will travel given a certain amount of fuel (e.g., the commonly advertised "miles per gallon").

16. (C) Weaken

Step 1: Identify the Question Type

The question directly asks for something that "weakens the argument," making this a Weaken question.

Step 2: Untangle the Stimulus

According to the author, tenants don't have an incentive to conserve electricity when they don't pay the electric bill. *Thus*, the author concludes that installing meters and making the tenants pay the electric bill will lead to energy conservation.

Step 3: Make a Prediction

The author's conclusion is a prediction. Predictions generally have the same assumption: nothing relevant is going to change that might affect the expected results. In this case, the author assumes that making tenants pay for the electricity is not going to lead to some overlooked situation that would actually make energy conversation *less* likely. The correct answer will point out a potential change that *could* prevent the predicted outcome.

Step 4: Evaluate the Answer Choices

(C) is correct. This suggests that making the tenants pay would take away a strong incentive from landlords. If they stop supplying tenants with energy efficient appliances, that could make the energy conservation situation worse, not better.

(A) is irrelevant, as it does not address what would happen if tenants *do* pay the electric bills and what effect any of this has on energy conservation.

(B) is potentially a 180. If people are educated about energy conservation, then it's even more likely they'd start

conserving energy more if they suddenly became responsible for paying the electric bill.

(D) is Out of Scope. The argument is not about the likelihood or feasibility of installing electric meters. The argument is about what would happen *if* they were installed, regardless of the cost.

(E) is also Out of Scope. Even if there are other ways to get people to conserve energy, that does not mean the author's plan won't work.

17. (D) Role of a Statement

Step 1: Identify the Question Type

The question stem presents a claim from the stimulus and asks for the role it plays in the argument, making this a Role of a Statement question.

Step 2: Untangle the Stimulus

Start by identifying the claim in question, which appears in the second sentence. Then, break down the argument. The author starts by negating a position, which is often the sign of a conclusion. Sure enough, the author's conclusion is that you can't have punishments be proportional to a crime's seriousness *and* give harsher punishments to repeat offenders. As evidence, the author indicates an implication of this ineffective plan: It suggests years-old actions are relevant to new offenses. In that, all actions would be considered relevant, and that would make the proportional punishment concept impossible to apply.

Step 3: Make a Prediction

The phrase "[i]t implies" indicates that the claim in question is an implication of a position. That position is the one the author calls *unsustainable*. The correct answer will identify the claim in question as an implication of a plan the author argues won't work.

Step 4: Evaluate the Answer Choices

(D) is correct. It is an implication (i.e., consequence) of the view the author rejects.

(A) is a Distortion. The claim in question is used to support the conclusion, but the author provides no "grounds to accept" that claim. The author just presents it as fact and expects the reader to accept it without evidence.

(B) is a 180. The position that implies the claim in question is being *rejected* by the author, not defended.

(C) is a Distortion. The conclusion is in the first sentence ("[t]he position . . . is unsustainable), and the author offers no evidence to support the claim in question.

(E) is a Distortion. The claim in question is merely part of a string of evidence, but there is no intermediate conclusion for which this claim provides support.

18. (D) Assumption (Necessary)

Step 1: Identify the Question Type
The question directly asks for an assumption, and one that is "required by" the argument. That makes this a Necessary Assumption question.

Step 2: Untangle the Stimulus
The blogger describes how the media has changed from focusing on objectivity to embracing partisan reporting. The blogger argues that this change is based on changing business strategies. In the past, newspapers had no serious rivals, so their biggest goal was to avoid being offensive.

Step 3: Make a Prediction
This is a case of Mismatched Concepts. If the goal of newspapers was to avoid being offensive, what does that have to do with being objective? The blogger must assume that objective reporting was considered inoffensive—at the very least, it's not as offensive as the partisan reporting that is more prominent in today's media with its newer business strategies.

Step 4: Evaluate the Answer Choices

(D) is correct, making the requisite connection between objective reporting and the likelihood of being offensive.

(A) is a Distortion. The argument is about the partisanship of the journalism and the reporting, not of the journalists themselves.

(B) is Out of Scope. The argument is about the standards used by journalists and what may or may not offend readers. That's not necessarily the same as the preferences of readers. Objectivity may be less preferred, but also less offensive.

(C) is Out of Scope. The argument is not about how popular the media is. It's about the change in style from objective to partisan, and whether that's based on a change in views regarding offending readers.

(E) is Extreme and a 180. The blogger does not argue that there is *no* basis for being objective. If anything, the author presents a basis used in the past: trying to avoid offending the reader.

19. (C) Inference

Step 1: Identify the Question Type
The question asks for something that can be "properly inferred" from the statements provided, making this an Inference question.

Step 2: Untangle the Stimulus
The author begins with a piece of Formal Logic: A government practice that could lead to abuse of power should not be performed unless there's a compelling reason to do so. The author provides an example of keeping secrets, which can be justified. However, when the reasons are not compelling or

when even the existence of the secret is not revealed, that can lead to an abuse of power.

Step 3: Make a Prediction
It helps to translate the opening Formal Logic and its contrapositive.

$$\text{If } \begin{array}{l}\textit{undertake practice}\\ \textit{that could lead to abuse}\end{array} \rightarrow \textit{compelling reason}$$

$$\text{If } \sim \textit{compelling reason} \rightarrow \begin{array}{l}\sim \textit{undertake practice}\\ \textit{that could lead to abuse}\end{array}$$

The author claims that keeping secrets can be justified, in which case there *must* be a compelling reason for doing so. However, the author then says secrets are often kept for insubstantial reasons, in which cases it is *not* justified to keep those secrets. The author also says that concealing the existence of a secret could also lead to abuse of power. Again, by the logic, there would need to be a compelling reason for concealing that fact. Otherwise, there's no justification.

Step 4: Evaluate the Answer Choices

(C) is supported. By the statements, concealing a secret could lead to abuse of power, and the logic dictates such action should not be undertaken unless there's a compelling reason.

(A) is Extreme. If the act is not justified, it's probably because there's no compelling reason to do it. However, there's no indication that this happens in *most* cases. At worst, the author says that insubstantial reasoning happens "too often," but that doesn't necessarily mean most of the time.

(B) is a Distortion. If there's a compelling reason to keep a secret, that just means the keeping of that secret may be justified. That doesn't mean it won't facilitate abuse of power.

(D) is Extreme. If they don't have a compelling reason to conceal information, then they should not conceal that information . . . *if* it would lead to abuse of power. However, there's no certainty that all such information absolutely *will* lead to an abuse of power.

(E) is a Distortion. The requirement for keeping a secret is that there's a compelling reason to do so. Even if keeping a secret does make it easier to abuse power, a compelling reason can override that concern.

20. (E) Assumption (Sufficient)

Step 1: Identify the Question Type
The phrase "if assumed" indicates the correct answer will be an assumption that guarantees the conclusion, making this a Sufficient Assumption question.

Step 2: Untangle the Stimulus

According to the author, some musicians embrace the theory that music is just sounds with no meaning. The author concludes ([*t*]*hus*) that their music does not conform to this theory, i.e., there is some meaning—it's not just a bunch of sounds. The evidence for this is that these musicians explain their intentions before performing.

Step 3: Make a Prediction

As with almost all arguments in Sufficient Assumption questions, this one rests on Mismatched Concepts. The conclusion implies that the songs have meaning, while the evidence merely talks about how the musicians explain their intentions. The assumption connects those concepts: Explaining the intentions indicates that the music has some meaning.

Step 4: Evaluate the Answer Choices

(E) is correct. If music with no meaning is not explained, then by contrapositive, if music *is* explained, it must have meaning, confirming the author's argument.

(A) is Out of Scope. The ability to think symbolically has nothing to do with the author's argument. Also, the argument is focused on whether or not the music has meaning at all, not how *difficult* it is to create music with meaning.

(B) is a Distortion. The author claims that musicians "encourage audience acceptance," but that doesn't mean acceptance is necessary for music to have no meaning. In fact, the musicians probably believe their music has no meaning with or without audience acceptance.

(C) is a Distortion. This combines a lot of ideas from the argument (e.g., random series of sounds, meaning, audience acceptance). However, this only indicates what would make some music appealing. This does not verify the author's conclusion about whether or not music does have meaning.

(D) is a Distortion. The argument is not about whether or not people will enjoy the music. The argument is focused on whether or not the music has meaning.

21. (C) Method of Argument

Step 1: Identify the Question Type

The question asks for the author's "technique of reasoning," making this a Method of Argument question.

Step 2: Untangle the Stimulus

The author starts off by arguing that evolution does not always maximize the potential for survival. The rest of the argument is an extended example of moose, which evolved larger antlers to better fight off competition, but also makes them more visible and vulnerable to predators.

Step 3: Make a Prediction

The bulk of the argument is an example used to show how evolution does not always improve the survival rate of an organism. The correct answer will describe this technique of countering an idea via example.

Step 4: Evaluate the Answer Choices

(C) is correct. The author challenges the idea that evolution is all about survival by presenting the counterexample of moose and their antlers.

(A) is Out of Scope. The author is countering a general idea about evolution, but there is no specific competing argument that the author is attacking.

(B) is a Distortion. An analogy is used when an author compares one specific circumstance to a different but similar specific circumstance. However, the author only raises one specific circumstance to address a general claim. That's an example or counterexample, not an analogy.

(D) is a Distortion. The example raised is about moose, and it's entirely relevant to the discussion of evolution. The author would not dispute her own example.

(E) is a Distortion. The author uses an example to undermine a claim, but the claim is not shown to be self-contradictory. In fact, the claim (evolution supports survival) may be just fine in some circumstances, just not in the moose example.

22. (D) Weaken

Step 1: Identify the Question Type

The question directly asks for something that "weakens the biologist's argument," making this a Weaken question.

Step 2: Untangle the Stimulus

The biologist describes how, when exposed to various colors of light, a particular species of bacteria gravitates toward a shade of red, a light color that aids its chlorophyll in producing energy. The biologist concludes that the bacteria detect the red color by monitoring its energy levels.

Step 3: Make a Prediction

The biologist is committing a correlation vs. causation flaw. There is a correlation between energy levels and the red color, but the biologist assumes the increased energy potential is what's causing the bacteria to move toward the red light. This could be weakened by showing an alternative explanation (i.e., they are moving toward the red light for a different reason) or by showing that it's just a coincidence (i.e., the energy level has no effect on which color is chosen).

Step 4: Evaluate the Answer Choices

(D) is correct. If blue would spur an equal level of energy creation, that suggests there's another reason the bacteria are gravitating toward red only.

(A) is a 180. If the bacteria stop gravitating toward red when they don't have chlorophyll, that suggests the energy produced by chlorophyll does indeed influence the bacteria's behavior, confirming rather than weakening the biologist's assertion.

(B) is also a 180. This suggests the bacteria are seeking out maximum energy production, which only confirms the biologist's argument.

(C) is yet another strengthener. If the red area *was* warmer, that might be an alternative explanation for the bacteria's behavior. However, if the temperature is the same, as this choice suggests, then warmth is not a factor, making it more likely the biologist's claim is correct.

(E) is an Irrelevant Comparison. There's no indication here why other bacteria gravitate toward other colors. Perhaps they contain some other substance that produces energy better under other colors. In that case, that would confirm, not weaken, the biologist's claim that energy production is a major factor.

23. (B) Flaw

Step 1: Identify the Question Type

The question directly asks for an answer that describes the flaw of the argument.

Step 2: Untangle the Stimulus

The argument begins with Formal Logic: If legislation is the product of groups negotiating and compromising, then none of those groups will be satisfied. The author then concludes that, because all of the groups involved in the new trade agreement are unsatisfied, compromises must have been made.

Step 3: Make a Prediction

Formal Logic in a Flaw question? The flaw of necessity vs. sufficiency is highly probable. Sure enough, in this argument, the Formal Logic dictates that compromise is sufficient to guarantee unhappy participants.

$$\text{If} \quad compromise \quad \rightarrow \quad unhappy\ participants$$

The author then concludes that the presence of unhappy groups indicates there must have been compromises, suggesting that compromise is a necessary condition for producing unhappy parties.

$$\text{If} \quad unhappy\ participants \quad \rightarrow \quad compromise$$

That is not logically sound, and the correct answer will describe this commonly tested flaw.

Step 4: Evaluate the Answer Choices

(B) is correct. The author concludes that comprise was necessary (i.e., it must have happened) for a result (i.e.,

unhappy groups) merely from the claim that compromise leads to unhappy groups. The groups could have been unhappy for many other reasons.

(A) is a Distortion. The conclusion doesn't merely restate the evidence. It gets the logic of the evidence backward.

(C) is not accurate. This suggests the flaw of equivocation, but all terms in the argument are used consistently and never change meaning.

(D) is Extreme. The author only argues that legislation involving compromises will ensure unhappy parties. However, if there's no need for compromise, then it's possible for all parties to be satisfied. The author never assumes otherwise.

(E) is a Distortion. A trade agreement would be a piece of legislation, and there's nothing about the trade agreement that would suggest it doesn't apply to the principle at hand.

24. (B) Inference

Step 1: Identify the Question Type

The correct answer will be "strongly supported by the information" given, making this an Inference question.

Step 2: Untangle the Stimulus

Following an accident at a power plant, researchers found three radioactive isotopes (call them I, Te, and Cs), but no heavy isotopes. There are only two possible sources: spent fuel rods or the plant's core. However, isotope Te is never found in spent fuel rods (in significant quantities), and radioactive material released directly from the core would have contained heavy isotopes. So where are isotopes I, Te, and Cs coming from? The author provides one more clue: Steam was released that may have contacted the core, even though it can easily dissolve those three radioactive isotopes.

Step 3: Make a Prediction

The key here is not to get too caught up in the scientific terms. In simple terms, researchers found three chemical items in the air. One possible source? Fuel rods. But fuel rods don't contain one of the chemicals in significant quantities. That leaves the other possible source: the core. However, if they came from the core directly, there would also have been heavy isotopes. So, they must have been released *indirectly*. And that's where the steam comes in. The chemicals must have escaped from the core indirectly through the steam.

Step 4: Evaluate the Answer Choices

(B) is supported. With only two possible sources (spent fuel rods or the core) and one source eliminated (spent fuel rods don't contain enough Te), the chemicals must have come from the second source: the core. And they wouldn't be ejected directly, so they must have taken an indirect route: the steam.

(A) is a Distortion. Because direct ejection would have included heavy isotopes, it's suggested that Te (and the other non-heavy isotopes) was ejected indirectly. However, if direct ejection *had* occurred, there's no reason to believe Te wouldn't have appeared then, too.

(C) is not supported. The spent fuel rods couldn't be the source of the Te, but they still could have been broken.

(D) is Out of Scope. The author implies that the material found did *not* come from spent fuel rods or directly from the core. While it's possible that other items were found that came from these sources, there's nothing in the statements that suggest as such.

(E) is not supported. It's only stated that the spent fuel rods do not contain Te, but there's no indication what they do contain, whether it be a lot of other heavy isotopes or not.

25. (E) Parallel Reasoning

Step 1: Identify the Question Type

The correct answer will be a complete argument with reasoning "most similar" to that in the argument given. That makes this a Parallel Reasoning question.

Step 2: Untangle the Stimulus

The argument given is based on some basic Formal Logic. If two sciences (ecology and physics) were evaluated equally, ecology would not be a successful science.

If	**evaluated by** **same criteria**	→	**ecology fails**

However, it *is* successful. Therefore, the author concludes that the two sciences are *not* evaluated equally.

If	**ecology ~ fail**	→	**~ evaluated by** **same criteria**

Step 3: Make a Prediction

The argument presents a piece of Formal Logic and then reaches its conclusion by using the contrapositive. In generic terms, the argument is structured as so: If X were true, then Y would be true. However Y is *not* true, so X is not true. The correct answer will conform to this exact same structure.

Step 4: Evaluate the Answer Choices

(E) is correct, using the same argument-by-contrapositive structure. If any economic theory were adequate, accurate forecasts could be made. Accurate forecasts *can't* be made, so economic theories are *not* adequate.

If	**adequate** **description**	→	**accurate** **economic** **forecasts**
If	**~ accurate** **economic** **forecasts**	→	**~ adequate** **description**

(A) does not match. Here, there are two consequences (connected by *or*) if taxes increase. One of those consequences can't happen, so the author concludes the other one must. However, there's no indication that the condition of a sales tax increase will happen. There's also no use of the contrapositive. And, the conclusion is a prediction, which is something the original author never makes.

(B) does not match. The Formal Logic here is: If the gallery borrows some works, then its exhibit would be the largest ever. However, unlike the original argument, this argument shifts to new topics such as the demand for larger exhibits and the willingness of galleries to lend out their works. Plus, the conclusion is a prediction, which does not match the conclusion of the original argument.

(C) does not match. This simply applies the Formal Logic as it is written without using the contrapositive. In generic terms, it says: If X were true, Y would be true. X will be true, so Y will be true, too. While the logic is sound, it does not match the original. Further, it makes a prediction, which is not logically equivalent to the original argument.

(D) does not match, and it commits a logical flaw. It simply negates the Formal Logic without reversing it. In generic terms, this is saying: If X were true, Y would be true. However, X is not usually true, so Y is not usually true. That's not logically sound, and it does not match the structure of the original argument.

Section IV: Logic Games
Game 1: Rural and Urban Photo Essays

Q#	Question Type	Correct	Difficulty
1	Partial Acceptability	E	Check your online resources.
2	Could Be True	B	Check your online resources.
3	"If" / Could Be True EXCEPT	C	Check your online resources.
4	Must Be True	D	Check your online resources.
5	Could Be True EXCEPT	A	Check your online resources.
6	Rule Substitution	B	Check your online resources.

Game 2: Concert Musicians

Q#	Question Type	Correct	Difficulty
7	Could Be True	D	Check your online resources.
8	"If" / Could Be True EXCEPT	A	Check your online resources.
9	Must Be False (CANNOT Be True)	E	Check your online resources.
10	"If" / Must Be False (CANNOT Be True)	D	Check your online resources.
11	Completely Determine	E	Check your online resources.

Game 3: Amusement Center Obstacle Course

Q#	Question Type	Correct	Difficulty
12	Acceptability	D	Check your online resources.
13	"If" / Must Be True	C	Check your online resources.
14	Complete and Accurate List	B	Check your online resources.
15	"If" / Must Be True	B	Check your online resources.
16	"If" / Must Be True	A	Check your online resources.

Game 4: Managers in Manila, Sydney, and Tokyo

Q#	Question Type	Correct	Difficulty
17	Acceptability	C	Check your online resources.
18	Completely Determine	B	Check your online resources.
19	Must Be True	D	Check your online resources.
20	Could Be True	A	Check your online resources.
21	"If" / Must Be True	D	Check your online resources.
22	"If" / Could Be True	A	Check your online resources.
23	Rule Substitution	E	Check your online resources.

Game 1: Rural and Urban Photo Essays

Step 1: Overview

Situation: A magazine assigning photo essays for upcoming issues

Entities: Five photographers (Fetter, Gonzalez, Howland, Jordt, Kim) and two themes (rural and urban)

Action: Sequencing/Matching Hybrid. Determine the order in which each photographer's essay will appear (Sequencing), and determine the theme of each photographer's essay (Matching).

Limitations: Each essay is assigned to a different photographer, making the sequencing standard one-to-one sequencing. For the matching, three essays will be rural and two will be urban.

Step 2: Sketch

Draw two rows of five slots labeled 1 through 5. The top row will be used to determine the order of the photographers, so list them by initial next to that row. The bottom row will be used to determine the theme, so draw three r's and two u's next to that row.

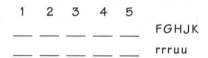

You could also draw a single row of slots and use the top of each slot for the photographer and the bottom of each slot for the theme.

Step 3: Rules

Rule 1 establishes the first essay as rural. Draw "r" in slot 1 of the bottom row, and cross one "r" off the list next to that row.

Rule 2 creates a Block of Entities. Kim and Fetter, in that order, will be consecutive.

Rule 3 dictates that Fetter and Kim have different themes. Either make a note to the side for now, or somehow notate it under the block from the previous rule. Perhaps "x" under one and "y" under the other, or "r/u" under one and "u/r" under the other, with a note that they are different.

Rule 4 assigns Gonzalez to the third essay. Draw "G" in slot 3 of the top row, and cross "G" off the list next to that row.

Rule 5 establishes that the theme for Jordt's essay is urban.

Step 4: Deductions

Numbers are important in this game. Three photographers will have rural themes, while only two have urban themes. By Rule 3, Fetter and Kim have different themes, so one of them must have a rural theme and the other will have an urban theme. So, either Fetter or Kim gets one of the two urban themes and, by Rule 5, Jordt gets the other. The remaining photographers, Gonzalez and Howland, must then have rural themes, along with either Fetter or Kim (whoever doesn't get the urban theme).

At this point, an "r" can be placed under the "G" in essay 3. Then there's the Block of Kim and Fetter. With the Established Entity of Gonzalez taking up the third essay, Kim and Fetter could only be assigned essays 1 and 2, respectively, or essays 4 and 5, respectively. These two outcomes would each establish three of the five photographers, suggesting Limited Options are worthwhile.

In the first option, Kim and Fetter are assigned to essays 1 and 2, respectively. Essay 1 is already established as rural, so essay 2 for Fetter will be urban. Howland and Jordt will be assigned to essays 4 and 5, in either order. Note that Howland's essay will be rural and Jordt's essay will be urban.

I)
1	2	3	4	5
K	F	G	H/J	J/H
r	u	r	_	_

H	J
r	u

In the second option, Kim and Fetter are assigned to essays 4 and 5, respectively. It cannot be determined which one will be rural and which one will be urban. However, that leaves Howland and Jordt for essays 1 and 2. Essay 1 is rural and Jordt has to have an urban theme. So, Howland must be assigned to essay 1, and Jordt to essay 2.

II)
1	2	3	4	5
H	J	G	K	F
r	u	r	r/u ≠ u/r	

Step 5: Questions

1. (E) Partial Acceptability

Start by using standard Acceptability tactics. Go through the rules one at a time and eliminate choices that violate those rules. Because the choices don't list the essay themes, some rules may have to be tested indirectly or in combination with other rules.

With no themes listed, Rules 1, 3, and 5 cannot be tested directly. **(A)** and **(C)** violate Rule 2 by not having Kim and Fetter consecutive. **(B)** violates Rule 4 by putting Gonzalez first, not third.

Combining Rules 1 and 5, the first essay must be rural, so it cannot be Jordt's, which must be urban. **(D)** violates that, leaving **(E)** as the correct answer.

Note that Limited Options could have been used to save even more time. By the two options, the first essay has to be assigned to Howland or Kim. That immediately narrows the choices down to **(C)** and **(E)**, and **(C)** does not match the option with Howland first because it splits up Kim and Fetter.

2. (B) Could Be True

The correct answer will be the one that is possible. The four wrong choices will be impossible, i.e., must be false.

If Fetter's essay were immediately before Jordt's, that would create a three-person block of KFJ. With Gonzalez assigned the third essay, there would be no room for such a block. That eliminates **(A)**.

Gonzalez's essay is third. If Gonzalez's essay were immediately before Howland's, then Howland's essay would be fourth. That violates no rules and is even seen as possible in Option I. Thus, this could be true, making **(B)** correct. For the record:

If Howland's or Jordt's essay were immediately before Kim's, that would create a three-person block of either HKF or JKF. With Gonzalez assigned the third essay, there would be no room for either block. That eliminates **(C)** and **(D)**.

(E) directly contradicts Rule 2, which states that Kim's essay must be immediately before Fetter's, not Gonzalez's.

3. (C) "If" / Could Be True EXCEPT

For this question, the fourth issue will have an urban theme. This could happen in either option, so draw both out. In Option I, Kim, Fetter, and Gonzalez, in that order, are assigned to the first three essays with rural, urban, and rural themes, respectively. If the fourth essay is urban, then the fifth essay must be the final rural one. Jordt must have an urban theme, so Jordt is assigned to essay 4, leaving Howland for essay 5.

In Option II, the photographers are all determined. For this question, it's now established that essay 4 (Kim's) is urban, making essay 5 (Fetter's) rural.

$$
\begin{array}{cccccc}
 & 1 & 2 & 3 & 4 & 5 \\
\text{I)} & \underset{r}{K} & \underset{u}{F} & \underset{r}{G} & \underset{u}{J} & \underset{r}{H} \\
\text{II)} & \underset{r}{H} & \underset{u}{J} & \underset{r}{G} & \underset{u}{K} & \underset{r}{F}
\end{array}
$$

With that, these options show Howland's essay as first or fifth, never fourth. That makes **(C)** impossible and thus the correct answer. Each of the remaining choices are possible in one of the two options.

4. (D) Must Be True

The correct answer for this question must be true, which means the four wrong choices may not be, i.e., could be false.

Consider the major deductions. There are two urban themes. Jordt has one. And, because Kim and Fetter must have different themes, one of them has the other. That means the remaining photographers, Gonzalez and Howland, must have rural themes. That makes **(D)** definitively true, and thus the correct answer. For the record:

(A) is certainly false, as Gonzalez is assigned the third essay and Gonzalez gets a rural theme. The fifth essay could be rural, but it could also be urban. So, **(B)** could be false. And Fetter and Kim have different themes, but it's possible that Fetter has a rural theme and Kim has an urban theme. Thus, **(C)** and **(E)** could be false.

5. (A) Could Be True EXCEPT

Four choices here could be the fourth essay. That means the correct answer will be the exception: the one that cannot be, i.e., must be false.

Limited Options help out a lot here. In Option I, the fourth essay could be either Jordt's urban essay or Howland's rural essay. In Option II, the fourth essay will be Kim's, and could be either rural or urban. That sums up choices **(B)**, **(C)**, **(D)**, and **(E)**, which means those are the incorrect "could be true" choices. Further, it's impossible for the fourth essay to be Fetter's because Gonzalez's is third and Fetter has to come immediately after Kim, not Gonzalez. That makes **(A)** impossible and thus the correct answer.

6. (B) Rule Substitution

The correct answer here will be a new rule that could replace Rule 3, regarding Fetter and Kim having different themes, without affecting the game in any way. In other words, Rule 3 will be eliminated, and the correct answer has to re-establish that exact same restriction without adding any new restrictions.

Simply establishing Howland with a rural theme is not enough. With Rule 5, Jordt has an urban theme, but that still leaves two rural themes and one urban theme. That would allow Fetter and Kim to both have rural themes. Thus, **(A)** is not good enough.

However, if both Gonzalez *and* Howland are assigned rural themes, that would help. Then, Jordt gets an urban theme by Rule 5. That leaves one urban theme and one rural theme for Fetter and Kim. That would force them to have different themes, as the original rule did. And Gonzalez and Howard were always assigned rural themes originally, so there are no new restrictions. That makes **(B)** the correct answer. For the record:

(C) does not prevent Fetter and Kim from having the same theme, and it forces Fetter to have a rural theme, which was not always the case. **(D)** adds a restriction to Jordt's essay which happens to be true based on the deductions. However, it does nothing to prevent Kim and Fetter from having the same theme. **(E)** would actually have the complete opposite effect. If Kim's essay had the same theme as Gonzalez's or Howland's, but not both, then Gonzalez and Howland would have to have different themes. So, one of them would get an urban theme along with Jordt. That would leave only rural themes for Kim and Fetter, giving them both the *same* theme, not different.

Game 2: Concert Musicians

Step 1: Overview
Situation: Musicians performing at a concert

Entities: Seven musicians (Lowe, Miller, Nadel, Otero, Parker, Sen, Thomas)

Action: Strict Sequencing. Determine the order in which the musicians will perform. Although the first two rules are loose sequencing style rules, Rules 3, 4, and 5 make this a Strict Sequencing game.

Limitations: Each musician performs, one at a time. This is standard one-to-one sequencing.

Step 2: Sketch
List the musicians by initial and draw a series of seven consecutively numbered slots.

```
        L M N O P S T

   ___ ___ ___ ___ ___ ___ ___
    1   2   3   4   5   6   7
```

Step 3: Rules
Rules 1 and 2 set up two separate loose relationships: Lowe at some point before Nadel, and Miller at some point before Thomas.

```
        L . . . N
        M . . . T
```

Rules 3 and 4 set up two similar strict relationships. There is exactly one space between Lowe and Otero, and one space between Miller and Parker, though each pair can appear in either order.

```
        L/O ___ O/L
        M/P ___ P/M
```

Rule 5 presents two options. Parker will be first or seventh (i.e., last). You can draw "P" over the sketch with arrows pointing to the first and last spots. However, Parker's placement directly affects Miller's placement, and that will have other effects. So, drawing Limited Options might be a better course of action.

Step 4: Deductions
Based on the last rule, draw two sketches. In the first, Parker will be first. By Rule 4, Miller will be third. By Rule 2, Thomas must perform after Miller, so Thomas can be anywhere but second. Nadel also cannot be second, as Nadel must perform after Lowe (Rule 1). That means the second performer could be Lowe or Otero, which would mean Lowe and Otero take up positions two and four, with Miller in between. Or, the second performer could be Sen, the Floater of the game. Also,

because Lowe has to perform before Nadel, Lowe cannot perform last.

```
   I)  P ___ M ___ ___ ___ ___
       1   2   3   4   5   6   7
          ~T                  ~L
          ~N
```

In the second option, Parker will be seventh. By Rule 4, Miller will be fifth. That means Thomas must be sixth (Rule 2). That leaves the first four slots open. The only definite order is that Lowe must perform before Nadel, so Lowe cannot be fourth and Nadel cannot be first. There's also the restriction about Lowe and Otero, but they could be in positions 1 and 3, or in positions 2 and 4 (as long as Otero is fourth).

```
   II) ___ ___ ___ ___ M   T   P
       1   2   3   4   5   6   7
       ~N          ~L
```

Step 5: Questions

7. (D) Could Be True
The correct answer will be the one that could be true. The remaining choices cannot be true, i.e., they must be false.

With Parker either first or seventh, Miller could only be third or fifth (Rule 4), never fourth. That eliminates **(A)**.

Nadel has to perform after Lowe, so can never be first. That eliminates **(B)**.

If Otero is fifth, then Miller can't be fifth, so Parker can't be seventh. Thus, Parker would be first and Miller third. This is Option I. If Otero is fifth, then Rule 3 requires Lowe to be third or seventh. However, in this option, Miller is third, and Lowe cannot be last without violating Rule 1. This is impossible, which eliminates **(C)**.

There is no rule directly restricting Sen—a Floater—so it would seem possible for Sen to perform seventh. In that case, Parker would have to perform first with Miller third, as seen in Option I. That leaves enough options for placing Lowe and Otero, as well as Nadel and Thomas. This is possible, making **(D)** correct. For the record:

If Thomas performed second, Miller would have to perform first (Rule 2). That would force Parker to perform third (Rule 4), violating Rule 5. That eliminates **(E)**.

8. (A) "If" / Could Be True EXCEPT
For this question, Otero performs earlier than Miller. This could happen in either option, so test them both. The correct answer will be the one person who cannot perform fifth. So,

eliminate any musician who could perform fifth in either scenario.

In Option I, for Otero to be before Miller, Otero would have to perform second. In that case, Lowe would have to perform fourth (Rule 3). The remaining musicians, Nadel, Sen, and Thomas, could fill in the remaining positions in any order. So any of those three could be fifth, which eliminates **(C)**, **(D)**, and **(E)**.

$$\text{I)} \quad \underset{1}{P} \quad \underset{2}{O} \quad \underset{3}{M} \quad \underset{4}{L} \quad \underset{5}{\_} \quad \underset{6}{\_} \quad \underset{7}{\_}$$

$$\underbrace{\qquad\qquad\qquad}_{N,\ S,\ T}$$

In Option II, Otero is definitely before Miller and Miller is the fifth performer there. That eliminates **(B)**.

$$\text{II)} \quad \underset{1}{\_} \quad \underset{2}{\_} \quad \underset{3}{\_} \quad \underset{4}{\_} \quad \underset{5}{M} \quad \underset{6}{T} \quad \underset{7}{P}$$

That leaves **(A)** as the correct answer, as Lowe cannot be fifth in either outcome when Otero is before Miller.

9. (E) Must Be False (CANNOT Be True)

The correct answer will be a musician who cannot perform third, i.e., it must be false that musician is third. The remaining choices will list musicians who *could* perform third.

In Option I, Miller is third, so that eliminates **(B)**.

In Option II, Lowe, Nadel, Otero, and Sen occupy the first four slots, including the third performance. Lowe and Otero must be separated by one space. So, it's possible for Lowe and Otero to perform first and third, in either order, as long as Nadel performs after Lowe (e.g., fourth). So, Lowe and Otero could each perform third, eliminating **(A)** and **(D)**.

$$\text{II)} \quad \underset{1}{L/O} \quad \underset{2}{N/S} \quad \underset{3}{O/L} \quad \underset{4}{S/N} \quad \underset{5}{M} \quad \underset{6}{T} \quad \underset{7}{P}$$

$$L \ldots N$$

The only other possibility in Option II is to have Lowe and Otero perform second and fourth. For Lowe to perform before Nadel, Lowe would have to be second with Nadel third. Nadel could be third, which eliminates **(C)**.

$$\text{II)} \quad \underset{1}{S} \quad \underset{2}{L} \quad \underset{3}{N} \quad \underset{4}{O} \quad \underset{5}{M} \quad \underset{6}{T} \quad \underset{7}{P}$$

Sen is the only musician who cannot perform third. Although Sen is not directly affected by the rules, placing Sen third would force the remaining musicians into positions that wind up violating the rules. Thus **(E)** is impossible, making it the correct answer.

10. (D) "If" / Must Be False (CANNOT Be True)

For this question, Sen and Thomas, in that order, are consecutive. If Parker were seventh, Miller would be fifth (Rule 4), forcing Thomas to be sixth (Rule 2), making it impossible for Sen and Thomas to be consecutive. So, this could only work in Option I, when Parker is first. In that case, Miller is third. The block of Sen and Thomas cannot fill the one space between Parker and Miller, and Nadel cannot perform second because Nadel has to perform after Lowe. That leaves two performers for the second slot: Lowe and Otero. If Lowe performs second, Otero would perform fourth, and vice versa. So, Lowe and Otero must be second and fourth, in either order.

$$\text{I)} \quad \underset{1}{P} \quad \underset{2}{L/O} \quad \underset{3}{M} \quad \underset{4}{O/L} \quad \underset{5}{\_} \quad \underset{6}{\_} \quad \underset{7}{\_}$$

That leaves the block of Sen and Thomas, in that order, to perform fifth and sixth, or sixth and seventh. Nadel will fill in the remaining spot.

$$\text{I)} \quad \underset{1}{P} \quad \underset{2}{L/O} \quad \underset{3}{M} \quad \underset{4}{O/L} \quad \underset{5}{S} \quad \underset{6}{T} \quad \underset{7}{N}$$

or

$$\text{I)} \quad \underset{1}{P} \quad \underset{2}{L/O} \quad \underset{3}{M} \quad \underset{4}{O/L} \quad \underset{5}{N} \quad \underset{6}{S} \quad \underset{7}{T}$$

With that, Thomas can only perform sixth or seventh, not fifth. That makes **(D)** impossible, and thus the correct answer.

11. (E) Completely Determine

The correct answer will place someone in such a way that all seven musicians can be placed with absolute certainty.

If Lowe performs fourth, Otero could still perform second or sixth, so there's still some uncertainty. That eliminates **(A)**.

If Miller performs fifth, Parker is seventh and Thomas is sixth. However, that's the setup for Option II, which still leaves a lot of uncertainty about the first four performances. That eliminates **(B)**.

If Nadel is fourth, Lowe must perform earlier. That could happen in Option II. However, in that case, Lowe could be first with Otero third, or Lowe could be third with Otero first. It's not completely determined, so that eliminates **(C)**.

If Otero is third, that could only happen in Option II with Miller fifth, Thomas sixth, and Parker seventh. Lowe would have to be first, but Nadel and Sen could then perform second and fourth in either order. That's two possible outcomes, not one. That eliminates **(D)**.

If Sen performs first, Parker must perform seventh. That means Miller performs fifth and Thomas sixth. That leaves Lowe, Nadel, and Otero for the second, third, and fourth performances. Lowe and Otero need to be separated, so Nadel must perform third, in between them. Lowe has to perform before Nadel, so Lowe must be second and Otero fourth. All seven musicians are assigned with certainty, making **(E)** the correct answer.

II) $\dfrac{S}{1} \quad \dfrac{L}{2} \quad \dfrac{N}{3} \quad \dfrac{O}{4} \quad \dfrac{M}{5} \quad \dfrac{T}{6} \quad \dfrac{P}{7}$

In a pinch, this seemed the most likely answer as it places Sen—the Floater—who was otherwise not directly restricted.

Game 3: Amusement Center Obstacle Course

Step 1: Overview

Situation: Amusement center operators designing an obstacle course

Entities: Six obstacles (rope bridge, spinning platform, tunnel, vaulting apparatus, wall, zipline)

Action: Strict Sequencing. Determine the order in which the obstacles will be placed. A quick glance at the rules reveals that they are all strict sequencing style rules.

Limitations: Each obstacle is included and separate, so this is standard one-to-one sequencing.

Step 2: Sketch

List the obstacles by initial and draw six consecutively numbered slots. (Note: You can use dual initials for the obstacles, e.g., "RB" for the rope bridge. However, just using the first initial of each obstacle is sufficient as they are distinct and presented alphabetically. Also, it can be less confusing to see six individual letters rather than a mixture of single- and double-letter items).

R S T V W Z

_____ _____ _____ _____ _____ _____
  1   2   3   4   5   6

Step 3: Rules

Rule 1 limits the spinning platform to one of two positions: third or fourth. Draw "S" above/below the sketch with arrows pointing to the third and fourth slot.

Rule 2 creates a Block of Entities with the wall and the zipline consecutive, in that order.

| W Z |

Rule 3 prevents the rope bridge and the vaulting apparatus from being consecutive, in either order.

Never | R V | or | V R |

Step 4: Deductions

By Rule 2, the wall must be before the zipline, so the wall cannot be last and the zipline cannot be first. It's also impossible to place the wall and zipline third and fourth, respectively, as that would leave no place for the spinning platform.

However, that leaves four possible placements for the wall/zipline block. With only five questions, it's not worth drawing out all four options.

It might seem tempting to set up Limited Options based on where the spinning platform goes. However, in either

position, there are still multiple places for the wall/zipline block that would also allow the rope bridge and vaulting apparatus to be separated. So, neither option would produce any fruitful deductions.

There are no Numbers deductions and no Duplication deductions. Deductions are rather sparse here. However, it's helpful to note that the tunnel is a Floater. Also, the game thankfully comes with a bunch of New-"If" questions, and that can often indicate a lack of major deductions. The final Master Sketch should reflect what's known so far:

$$S$$
$$\swarrow \searrow$$

_____ _____ _____ _____ _____ _____
  1   2   3   4   5   6
 ~Z   ~W   ~Z   ~W

Step 5: Questions

12. (D) Acceptability

As with any Acceptability question, go through the rules one at a time and eliminate answers that violate them.

(C) violates Rule 1 by putting the spinning platform fifth. **(A)** violates Rule 2 by separating the wall and the zipline. **(B)** and **(E)** violate Rule 3 by having the rope bridge and vaulting apparatus consecutive. That leaves **(D)** as the correct answer.

13. (C) "If" / Must Be True

For this question, the tunnel will be first. The spinning platform could still go third or fourth, so test them both.

If the spinning platform is third, the wall/zipline block would have to go after, either in 4/5 or 5/6—so no matter what one of the wall/zipline block will occupy slot 5. That leaves either the rope bridge or the vaulting apparatus for the second obstacle.

 T   R/V   S   _____ W/Z _____
 1   2   3   4   5   6

If the spinning platform is fourth, that leaves two sets of spaces for the wall/zipline block: second and third, or fifth and sixth. However, in either case, that would leave consecutive spaces for the rope bridge and the vaulting apparatus, violating Rule 3. This option is unacceptable.

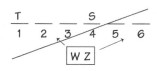

So, if the tunnel is first, the spinning platform can only be third, making **(C)** the correct answer. The remaining answers are all possible, but need not be true.

14. (B) Complete and Accurate List

The correct answer will list every possible position for the tunnel. The wrong choices will leave something out or include a position where the tunnel cannot go.

Answering this question efficiently would require finding a very challenging deduction at the beginning. Without that, this question is worth skipping and saving for last. Using sketches and outcomes from other questions can save a lot of testing. The answer to the Acceptability question shows that the tunnel can be second, and the second question of the set is based on the possibility that the tunnel can be first. Unfortunately, every answer lists those positions, so that doesn't help. However, the sketch for the last question places the tunnel sixth, so that eliminates **(A)**, which fails to list sixth.

From there, without an incredible deduction, it's all about testing. Start by testing whether the tunnel could be third. If it were, then the spinning platform would be fourth. That leaves two sets of open spaces: first and second, and fifth and sixth.

However, this cannot happen. The wall/zipline block would have to take up one set of spaces, leaving the rope bridge and the vaulting apparatus to be consecutive in the other set of spaces. This violates Rule 3 and is thus unacceptable. So, **(C)**, **(D)**, and **(E)** can all be eliminated for including the impossible position of third.

At this point, **(B)** is the only answer left and is thus correct. For the record, the tunnel cannot be fourth because that would make the spinning platform third, leading to the same problem as placing the tunnel third. You could draw one more sketch to prove that the tunnel could be fifth, but that's not necessary as all of the remaining choices have been eliminated.

15. (B) "If" / Must Be True

For this question, the rope bridge is second. That means the vaulting apparatus cannot be first or third. The first obstacle also cannot be the spinning platform, nor can it include the wall/zipline block. That leaves the tunnel as the first obstacle. That makes **(B)** the correct answer.

The remaining answers are either completely false or are possible, but not definitively true.

16. (A) "If" / Must Be True

For this question, the rope bridge and the vaulting apparatus are both earlier than the tunnel. The rope bridge and the vaulting apparatus cannot be next to one another, so there must be at least one other obstacle before the tunnel. Thus, the tunnel cannot be first, second, or third. It must be fourth, fifth, or sixth, leaving no room after it for the spinning platform. Thus, the spinning platform must also be before the tunnel.

That leaves the wall/zipline block. If that came after the tunnel, the tunnel would be fourth, making the spinning platform third, which would force the rope bridge and the vaulting apparatus to be consecutive, violating Rule 3.

So, the wall/zipline block must also be before the tunnel. That's everything, which means the tunnel must be last. Next, consider the spinning platform. If the spinning platform were third, that would create two sets of spaces: first and second, and fourth and fifth. The wall/zipline block would take one set, but that would again force the rope bridge and the vaulting apparatus to be consecutive. That can't happen, so the spinning platform must be fourth. That makes **(A)** the correct answer. The wall/zipline block will either go first/second or second/third. One of the rope bridge or vaulting apparatus will be fifth with the other one either first or third.

(B), **(C)**, **(D)**, and **(E)**, are either completely false or are possible, but not definitively true.

Game 4: Managers in Manila, Sydney, and Tokyo

Step 1: Overview

Situation: A company sending product managers to visit some cities

Entities: Four managers (Fan, Gleeson, Haley, Ibañez) and three cities (Manila, Sydney, Tokyo)

Action: Matching. Determine which managers are assigned to each city.

Limitations: Each manager is assigned at least once, and two managers are assigned to each city. That's a total of six assignments for four managers, so either one manager goes to all three cities or two managers go to two cities each.

Step 2: Sketch

List the managers by initial and set up a table with the three cities as column headings. Draw two slots under each column.

F G H I

Man	Syd	Tok
___	___	___
___	___	___

Step 3: Rules

Rule 1 sets up a Numeric Restriction. Ibañez goes to exactly two cities. Draw a second "I" in the entity list. You could also make a note to the side (e.g., "Exactly 2 I's").

Rule 2 prevents Fan and Haley from visiting the same city.

Never | F |
      | H |

Rule 3 provides some Formal Logic. If Gleeson goes to Manila, Haley goes to Tokyo. By contrapositive, if Haley does not go to Tokyo, then Gleeson cannot go to Manila.

$$\frac{Man}{G} \rightarrow \frac{Tok}{H}$$

$$\sim\frac{Tok}{H} \rightarrow \sim\frac{Man}{G}$$

Rule 4 prevents Gleeson from going to Sydney. Draw "~G" under the Sydney column.

Step 4: Deductions

Gleeson is duplicated in the last two rules. Gleeson cannot visit Sydney, which leaves Manila and Tokyo. The key question is if Gleeson visits Manila. If Gleeson does visit Manila, that triggers the Formal Logic of Rule 3. If Gleeson does *not* visit Manila, then she must visit Tokyo. Either way, some valuable deductions can be made. It is worth setting up Limited Options.

In the first option, Gleeson visits Manila. In that case, Haley vists Tokyo. That means Fan cannot visit Tokyo (Rule 2). That leaves one of Gleeson and Ibañez to be the second manager in Tokyo. Note that in Option I, Gleeson can still visit Tokyo, as managers can be sent to multiple cities.

I) | Man | Syd | Tok |
|-----|-----|-----|
| G | ___ | H |
| ___ | ___ | G/I |
| | ~G | ~F |

In the second option, Gleeson does not visit Manila. In that case, she must visit Tokyo.

II) | Man | Syd | Tok |
|-----|-----|-----|
| ___ | ___ | G |
| ___ | ___ | ___ |
| ~G | ~G | |

At this point, Numbers become important. Each city will be visited by two managers. In both options, there's at least one city that cannot be visited by Gleeson (Sydney in Option I, Manila and Sydney in Option II). In each case, that leaves Fan, Haley and Ibañez. However, Fan and Haley cannot be together (Rule 2). So, each of those cities can only get one of Fan or Haley, and the second manager must be Ibañez.

There's one final Numbers deduction to note. Ibañez must visit exactly two cities. This affects Option II, as Ibañez is already assigned twice and can no longer be assigned to Tokyo. So, the last spot in Tokyo must go to Fan or Haley.

I) | Man | Syd | Tok |
|-----|-----|-----|
| G | I | H |
| ___ | F/H | G/I |

II) | Man | Syd | Tok |
|-----|-----|-----|
| I | I | G |
| F/H | F/H | F/H |

Further, if Ibañez goes to two cities and each other employee goes to one, that would be a total of five assignments. However, there are six slots, so exactly one other employee must be assigned to a second city.

Step 5: Questions

17. (C) Acceptability

This is a typical Acceptability question. Test each rule, one at a time, and eliminate answers that violate those rules.

(A) violates Rule 1 by assigning Ibañez to just one city.
(E) violates Rule 2 by assigning Fan and Haley together to Tokyo. **(D)** violates Rule 3 by assigning Gleeson to Manila

without assigning Haley to Tokyo. **(B)** violates Rule 4 by assigning Gleeson to Sydney. That leaves **(C)** as the correct answer.

18. (B) Completely Determine

The correct answer will establish a condition that will allow all six assignments to be determined with no uncertainty. Eliminate any choice that allows for more than one outcome.

Fan can visit any pair of cities, as long as Haley visits the third. Similarly, Haley can visit any pair of cities, as long as Fan visits the third. However, in either case, it's not certain which cities are visited by whom. That eliminates **(A)** and **(C)**.

If Gleeson visits two cities, they could only be Manila and Tokyo (Rule 4). With Gleeson in Manila, Haley must visit Tokyo (Rule 3). With Tokyo filled, Ibañez still needs to visit two cities. They must be Manila and Sydney. That leaves one slot in Sydney, which must be taken up by Fan, who has nowhere else left to go. The entire outcome is determined, making **(B)** the correct answer.

	Man	Syd	Tok
I)	G	I	H
	I	F	G

For the record: If Fan and Gleeson visit Tokyo, Ibañez would be left with Manila and Sydney. Haley could visit Manila or Sydney, or both. With multiple possibilities, that eliminates **(D)**.

If Gleeson and Haley visit Tokyo, Ibañez would be left with Manila and Sydney. Fan could visit Manila or Sydney, or both. With multiple possibilities, that eliminates **(E)**.

19. (D) Must Be True

The correct answer has to be true no matter what. The wrong choices could be false or are definitely false.

In both options, Gleeson cannot visit Sydney. Fan and Haley cannot both visit Sydney, so only one of them can. The second manager visiting Sydney must be Ibañez, making **(D)** the correct answer.

20. (A) Could Be True

The correct answer to this question is the only one that could be true. The remaining choices will all be impossible, i.e., must be false.

In Option II, it is possible for Fan and Ibañez to visit Manila together. That makes **(A)** the correct answer. For the record:

Gleeson cannot visit Sydney, so Ibañez must visit Sydney to prevent Fan and Haley from being together. If Gleeson and Ibañez visit Tokyo, that would be Ibañez's second city. That would leave Fan, Gleeson, and Haley to visit Manila. However, without Haley in Tokyo, Gleeson cannot visit Manila.

And without Gleeson, that would leave Fan and Haley together, violating Rule 2. This ultimately is impossible, which eliminates **(B)**.

Ibañez has to visit Sydney, but can only visit two cities. Thus, Ibañez cannot visit Manila and Tokyo, too. That eliminates **(C)**.

Neither Fan nor Haley can visit three cities. With Ibañez visiting two cities, that would mean Fan or Haley visits three cities, Ibañez visits two, and one other manager visits one city. Somebody would be left out. That eliminates **(D)** and **(E)**.

21. (D) "If" / Must Be True

For this question, Gleeson and Haley visit a city together. Gleeson cannot visit Sydney, so it must be Manila or Tokyo.

If Gleeson and Haley visit Manila together, Haley must also visit Tokyo (Rule 3). Ibañez would then be left to visit Sydney and Tokyo. That would leave only Sydney for Fan.

Man	Syd	Tok
G	I	H
H	F	I

If Gleeson and Haley visit Tokyo together, Ibañez would be left to visit Manila and Sydney. Fan could visit Manila, Sydney, or both.

Man	Syd	Tok
I	I	G
		H

In either case, Haley visits Tokyo, making **(D)** the correct answer. The remaining choices are all possible, but need not be true.

22. (A) "If" / Could Be True

For this question, Ibañez visits Tokyo (which can only happen in Option I). If you haven't made Limited Options though and need to start from scratch, Ibañez also must visit Sydney because Gleeson cannot visit Sydney and Fan and Haley cannot visit a city together.

With Ibañez done, that leaves Manila open to Fan, Gleeson, and Haley. Again, Fan and Haley cannot visit there together. So, only one of them can visit Manila, and Gleeson must be the second manager. With Gleeson visiting Manila, Haley must visit Tokyo.

Man	Syd	Tok
G	I	H
F/H	F/H	I

With that, only **(A)** is possible, and is thus the correct answer. Ibañez cannot visit Manila in this case, and must visit Sydney and Tokyo, eliminating **(B)** and **(C)**. With both Haley and Ibañez in Tokyo, there's no room for Fan, which eliminates **(D)**. As for **(E)**, Haley could go to Manila or Sydney, but if she went to both, there'd be no city left for Fan to visit, so **(E)** is eliminated.

23. (E) Rule Substitution
For this question, Rule 2 is removed from the setup. The correct answer will provide a new condition that replicates all of the effects of Rule 2 (i.e., splitting up Fan and Haley) without adding any new restrictions.

The original restrictions did not require Gleeson and Ibañez to be split up. Also, that would not keep Fan and Haley apart. Thus, **(A)** is eliminated.

Haley was never required to visit Tokyo if Fan visits Sydney. And if Haley did have to visit Tokyo in that case, it wouldn't stop Haley from also visiting Sydney with Fan. **(B)** does not work and can be eliminated.

Restricting Fan and Haley from being together in Tokyo would not prevent them from being together in other cities. That eliminates **(C)**.

(D) sets up some clever Formal Logic. If Fan does not go to a particular city, then Haley must. However, that was not always the case. It was possible in the original for a city to not have Fan, but also not have Haley. In that case, the city could have Gleeson and Ibañez. This Formal Logic would be restrictive in a way the original rules were not, which makes **(D)** incorrect.

(E) also has some clever Formal Logic, but it works. By this rule, a city without Ibañez would have to be visited by Gleeson. By contrapositive, if a city did not have Gleeson, it must have Ibañez. In short, if one of them isn't there, the other one is, i.e., each city has to be visited by at least one of them. It's possible to have both, but you can't get rid of both Gleeson and Ibañez. By doing that, it prevents Fan and Haley from being together, establishing the original rule. And this was always true with the original rule, because splitting up Fan and Haley made it necessary to include Gleeson or Ibañez (or both) in each city. The original conditions are restored, and no new restrictions are added. That makes **(E)** the correct answer.

Glossary

Logical Reasoning

Logical Reasoning Question Types

Argument-Based Questions

Main Point Question

A question that asks for an argument's conclusion or an author's main point. Typical question stems:

> Which one the following most accurately expresses the conclusion of the argument as a whole?

> Which one of the following sentences best expresses the main point of the scientist's argument?

Role of a Statement Question

A question that asks how a specific sentence, statement, or idea functions within an argument. Typical question stems:

> Which one of the following most accurately describes the role played in the argument by the statement that automation within the steel industry allowed steel mills to produce more steel with fewer workers?

> The claim that governmental transparency is a nation's primary defense against public-sector corruption figures in the argument in which one of the following ways?

Point at Issue Question

A question that asks you to identify the specific claim, statement, or recommendation about which two speakers/authors disagree (or, rarely, about which they agree). Typical question stems:

> A point at issue between Tom and Jerry is

> The dialogue most strongly supports the claim that Marilyn and Billy disagree with each other about which one of the following?

Method of Argument Question

A question that asks you to describe an author's argumentative strategy. In other words, the correct answer describes *how* the author argues (not necessarily what the author says). Typical question stems:

> Which one of the following most accurately describes the technique of reasoning employed by the argument?

> Julian's argument proceeds by

> In the dialogue, Alexander responds to Abigail in which one of the following ways?

Parallel Reasoning Question

A question that asks you to identify the answer choice containing an argument that has the same logical structure and reaches the same type of conclusion as the argument in the stimulus does. Typical question stems:

> The pattern of reasoning in which one of the following arguments is most parallel to that in the argument above?

> The pattern of reasoning in which one of the following arguments is most similar to the pattern of reasoning in the argument above?

Assumption-Family Questions

Assumption Question

A question that asks you to identify one of the unstated premises in an author's argument. Assumption questions come in two varieties.

Necessary Assumption questions ask you to identify an unstated premise required for an argument's conclusion to follow logically from its evidence. Typical question stems:

> Which one of the following is an assumption on which the argument depends?

> Which one of the following is an assumption that the argument requires in order for its conclusion to be properly drawn?

Sufficient Assumption questions ask you to identify an unstated premise sufficient to establish the argument's conclusion on the basis of its evidence. Typical question stems:

> The conclusion follows logically if which one of the following is assumed?

> Which one of the following, if assumed, enables the conclusion above to be properly inferred?

Strengthen/Weaken Question

A question that asks you to identify a fact that, if true, would make the argument's conclusion more likely (Strengthen) or less likely (Weaken) to follow from its evidence. Typical question stems:

Strengthen

> Which one of the following, if true, most strengthens the argument above?

> Which one the following, if true, most strongly supports the claim above?

Weaken

Which one of the following, if true, would most weaken the argument above?

Which one of the following, if true, most calls into question the claim above?

Flaw Question

A question that asks you to describe the reasoning error that the author has made in an argument. Typical question stems:

The argument's reasoning is most vulnerable to criticism on the grounds that the argument

Which of the following identifies a reasoning error in the argument?

The reasoning in the correspondent's argument is questionable because the argument

Parallel Flaw Question

A question that asks you to identify the argument that contains the same error(s) in reasoning that the argument in the stimulus contains. Typical question stems:

The pattern of flawed reasoning exhibited by the argument above is most similar to that exhibited in which one of the following?

Which one of the following most closely parallels the questionable reasoning cited above?

Evaluate the Argument Question

A question that asks you to identify an issue or consideration relevant to the validity of an argument. Think of Evaluate questions as "Strengthen or Weaken" questions. The correct answer, if true, will strengthen the argument, and if false, will weaken the argument, or vice versa. Evaluate questions are very rare. Typical question stems:

Which one of the following would be most useful to know in order to evaluate the legitimacy of the professor's argument?

It would be most important to determine which one of the following in evaluating the argument?

Non-Argument Questions

Inference Question

A question that asks you to identify a statement that follows from the statements in the stimulus. It is very important to note the characteristics of the one correct and the four incorrect answers before evaluating the choices in Inference questions. Depending on the wording of the question stem,

the correct answer to an Inference question may be the one that

- *must be true* if the statements in the stimulus are true

- is *most strongly supported* by the statements in the stimulus

- *must be false* if the statements in the stimulus are true

Typical question stems:

If all of the statements above are true, then which one of the following must also be true?

Which one of the following can be properly inferred from the information above?

If the statements above are true, then each of the following could be true EXCEPT:

Which one of the following is most strongly supported by the information above?

The statements above, if true, most support which one of the following?

The facts described above provide the strongest evidence against which one of the following?

Paradox Question

A question that asks you to identify a fact that, if true, most helps to explain, resolve, or reconcile an apparent contradiction. Typical question stems:

Which one of the following, if true, most helps to explain how both studies' findings could be accurate?

Which one the following, if true, most helps to resolve the apparent conflict in the spokesperson's statements?

Each one of the following, if true, would contribute to an explanation of the apparent discrepancy in the information above EXCEPT:

Principle Questions

Principle Question

A question that asks you to identify corresponding cases and principles. Some Principle questions provide a principle in the stimulus and call for the answer choice describing a case that corresponds to the principle. Others provide a specific case in the stimulus and call for the answer containing a principle to which that case corresponds.

On the LSAT, Principle questions almost always mirror the skills rewarded by other Logical Reasoning question types. After each of the following Principle question stems, we note the question type it resembles. Typical question stems:

Which one of the following principles, if valid, most helps to justify the reasoning above? (**Strengthen**)

Which one of the following most accurately expresses the principle underlying the reasoning above? (**Assumption**)

The situation described above most closely conforms to which of the following generalizations? (**Inference**)

Which one of the following situations conforms most closely to the principle described above? (**Inference**)

Which one of the following principles, if valid, most helps to reconcile the apparent conflict among the prosecutor's claims? (**Paradox**)

Parallel Principle Question

A question that asks you to identify a specific case that illustrates the same principle that is illustrated by the case described in the stimulus. Typical question stem:

Of the following, which one illustrates a principle that is most similar to the principle illustrated by the passage?

Untangling the Stimulus

Conclusion Types

The conclusions in arguments found in the Logical Reasoning section of the LSAT tend to fall into one of six categories:

1) Value Judgment (an evaluative statement; e.g., Action X is unethical, or Y's recital was poorly sung)

2) "If"/Then (a conditional prediction, recommendation, or assertion; e.g., If X is true, then so is Y, or If you an M, then you should do N)

3) Prediction (X *will* or *will not* happen in the future)

4) Comparison (X is taller/shorter/more common/less common, etc. than Y)

5) Assertion of Fact (X is true or X is false)

6) Recommendation (we *should* or *should not* do X)

One-Sentence Test

A tactic used to identify the author's conclusion in an argument. Consider which sentence in the argument is the one the author would keep if asked to get rid of everything except her main point.

Subsidiary Conclusion

A conclusion following from one piece of evidence and then used by the author to support his overall conclusion or main point. Consider the following argument:

The pharmaceutical company's new experimental treatment did not succeed in clinical trials. As a result, the new treatment will not reach the market this year. Thus, the company will fall short of its revenue forecasts for the year.

Here, the sentence "As a result, the new treatment will not reach the market this year" is a subsidiary conclusion. It follows from the evidence that the new treatment failed in clinical trials, and it provides evidence for the overall conclusion that the company will not meet its revenue projections.

Keyword(s) in Logical Reasoning

A word or phrase that helps you untangle a question's stimulus by indicating the logical structure of the argument or the author's point. Here are three categories of Keywords to which LSAT experts pay special attention in Logical Reasoning:

Conclusion words; e.g., *therefore, thus, so, as a result, it follows that, consequently,* [evidence] *is evidence that* [conclusion]

Evidence word; e.g, *because, since, after all, for,* [evidence] *is evidence that* [conclusion]

Contrast words; e.g., *but, however, while, despite, in spite of, on the other hand* (These are especially useful in Paradox and Inference questions.)

Experts use Keywords even more extensively in Reading Comprehension. Learn the Keywords associated with the Reading Comprehension section, and apply them to Logical Reasoning when they are helpful.

Mismatched Concepts

One of two patterns to which authors' assumptions conform in LSAT arguments. Mismatched Concepts describes the assumption in arguments in which terms or concepts in the conclusion are different *in kind* from those in the evidence. The author assumes that there is a logical relationship between the different terms. For example:

Bobby is a **championship swimmer**. Therefore, he **trains every day**.

Here, the words "trains every day" appear only in the conclusion, and the words "championship swimmer" appear only in the evidence. For the author to reach this conclusion from this evidence, he assumes that championship swimmers train every day.

Another example:

Susan does **not eat her vegetables**. Thus, she will **not grow big and strong**.

In this argument, not growing big and strong is found only in the conclusion while not eating vegetables is found only in the evidence. For the author to reach this conclusion from this evidence, she must assume that eating one's vegetables is necessary for one to grow big and strong.

See also Overlooked Possibilities.

Overlooked Possibilities

One of two patterns to which authors' assumptions conform in LSAT arguments. Mismatched Concepts describes the assumption in arguments in which terms or concepts in the conclusion are different *in degree, scale, or level of certainty* from those in the evidence. The author assumes that there is no factor or explanation for the conclusion other than the one(s) offered in the evidence. For example:

> Samson does not have a ticket stub for this movie showing. Thus, Samson must have sneaked into the movie without paying.

The author assumes that there is no other explanation for Samson's lack of a ticket stub. The author overlooks several possibilities: e.g., Samson had a special pass for this showing of the movie; Samson dropped his ticket stub by accident or threw it away after entering the theater; someone else in Samson's party has all of the party members' ticket stubs in her pocket or handbag.

Another example:

> Jonah's marketing plan will save the company money. Therefore, the company should adopt Jonah's plan.

Here, the author makes a recommendation based on one advantage. The author assumes that the advantage is the company's only concern or that there are no disadvantages that could outweigh it, e.g., Jonah's plan might save money on marketing but not generate any new leads or customers; Jonah's plan might damage the company's image or reputation; Jonah's plan might include illegal false advertising. Whenever the author of an LSAT argument concludes with a recommendation or a prediction based on just a single fact in the evidence, that author is always overlooking many other possibilities.

See also Mismatched Concepts.

Causal Argument

An argument in which the author concludes or assumes that one thing causes another. The most common pattern on the LSAT is for the author to conclude that A causes B from evidence that A and B are correlated. For example:

> I notice that whenever the store has a poor sales month, employee tardiness is also higher that month. Therefore, it must be that employee tardiness causes the store to lose sales.

The author assumes that the correlation in the evidence indicates a causal relationship. These arguments are vulnerable to three types of overlooked possibilities:

1) There could be **another causal factor**. In the previous example, maybe the months in question are those in which the manager takes vacation, causing the store to lose sales and permitting employees to arrive late without fear of the boss's reprimands.

2) Causation could be **reversed**. Maybe in months when sales are down, employee morale suffers and tardiness increases as a result.

3) The correlation could be **coincidental**. Maybe the correlation between tardiness and the dip in sales is pure coincidence.

See also Flaw Types: Correlation versus Causation.

Another pattern in causal arguments (less frequent on the LSAT) involves the assumption that a particular causal mechanism is or is not involved in a causal relationship. For example:

> The airport has rerouted takeoffs and landings so that they will not create noise over the Sunnyside neighborhood. Thus, the recent drop in Sunnyside's property values cannot be explained by the neighborhood's proximity to the airport.

Here, the author assumes that the only way that the airport could be the cause of dropping property values is through noise pollution. The author overlooks any other possible mechanism (e.g., frequent traffic jams and congestion) through which proximity to the airport could be cause of Sunnyside's woes.

Principle

A broad, law-like rule, definition, or generalization that covers a variety of specific cases with defined attributes. To see how principles are treated on the LSAT, consider the following principle:

> It is immoral for a person for his own gain to mislead another person.

That principle would cover a specific case, such as a seller who lies about the quality of construction to get a higher price for his house. It would also correspond to the case of a teenager who, wishing to spend a night out on the town, tells his mom "I'm going over to Randy's house." He knows that his mom believes that he will be staying at Randy's house, when in fact, he and Randy will go out together.

That principle does not, however, cover cases in which someone lies solely for the purpose of making the other person feel better or in which one person inadvertently misleads the other through a mistake of fact.

Be careful not to apply your personal ethics or morals when analyzing the principles articulated on the test.

Flaw Types

Necessary versus Sufficient

This flaw occurs when a speaker or author concludes that one event is necessary for a second event from evidence that the first event is sufficient to bring about the second event, or vice versa. Example:

> If more than 25,000 users attempt to access the new app at the same time, the server will crash. Last night, at 11:15 PM, the server crashed, so it must be case that more than 25,000 users were attempting to use the new app at that time.

In making this argument, the author assumes that the only thing that will cause the server to crash is the usage level (i.e., high usage is *necessary* for the server to crash). The evidence, however, says that high usage is one thing that will cause the server to crash (i.e., that high usage is *sufficient* to crash the server).

Correlation versus Causation

This flaw occurs when a speaker or author draws a conclusion that one thing causes another from evidence that the two things are correlated. Example:

> Over the past half century, global sugar consumption has tripled. That same time period has seen a surge in the rate of technological advancement worldwide. It follows that the increase in sugar consumption has caused the acceleration in technological advancement.

In any argument with this structure, the author is making three unwarranted assumptions. First, he assumes that there is no alternate cause, i.e., there is nothing else that has contributed to rapid technological advancement. Second, he assumes that the causation is not reversed, i.e., technological advancement has not contributed to the increase in sugar consumption, perhaps by making it easier to grow, refine, or transport sugar. And, third, he assumes that the two phenomena are not merely coincidental, i.e., that it is not just happenstance that global sugar consumption is up at the same time that the pace of technological advancement has accelerated.

Unrepresentative Sample

This flaw occurs when a speaker or author draws a conclusion about a group from evidence in which the sample cannot represent that group because the sample is too small or too selective, or is biased in some way. Example:

> Moviegoers in our town prefer action films and romantic comedies over other film genres. Last Friday, we sent reporters to survey moviegoers at several theaters in town, and nearly 90 percent of those surveyed were going to watch either an action film or a romantic comedy.

The author assumes that the survey was representative of the town's moviegoers, but there are several reasons to question that assumption. First, we don't know how many people were actually surveyed. Even if the number of people surveyed was adequate, we don't know how many other types of movies were playing. Finally, the author doesn't limit her conclusion to moviegoers on Friday nights. If the survey had been conducted at Sunday matinees, maybe most moviegoers would have been heading out to see an animated family film or a historical drama. Who knows?

Scope Shift/Unwarranted Assumption

This flaw occurs when a speaker's or author's evidence has a scope or has terms different enough from the scope or terms in his conclusion that it is doubtful that the evidence can support the conclusion. Example:

> A very small percentage of working adults in this country can correctly define collateralized debt obligation securities. Thus, sad to say, the majority of the nation's working adults cannot make prudent choices about how to invest their savings.

This speaker assumes that prudent investing requires the ability to accurately define a somewhat obscure financial term. But prudence is not the same thing as expertise, and the speaker does not offer any evidence that this knowledge of this particular term is related to wise investing.

Percent versus Number/Rate versus Number

This flaw occurs when a speaker or author draws a conclusion about real quantities from evidence about rates or percentages, or vice versa. Example:

> At the end of last season, Camp SunnyDay laid off half of their senior counselors and a quarter of their junior counselors. Thus, Camp SunnyDay must have more senior counselors than junior counselors.

The problem, of course, is that we don't know how many senior and junior counselors were on staff before the layoffs. If there were a total of 4 senior counselors and 20 junior counselors, then the camp would have laid off only 2 senior counselors while dismissing 5 junior counselors.

Equivocation

This flaw occurs when a speaker or author uses the same word in two different and incompatible ways. Example:

> Our opponent in the race has accused our candidate's staff members of behaving unprofessionally. But that's not

fair. Our staff is made up entirely of volunteers, not paid campaign workers.

The speaker interprets the opponent's use of the word *professional* to mean "paid," but the opponent likely meant something more along the lines of "mature, competent, and businesslike."

Ad Hominem

This flaw occurs when a speaker or author concludes that another person's claim or argument is invalid because that other person has a personal flaw or shortcoming. One common pattern is for the speaker or author to claim the other person acts hypocritically or that the other person's claim is made from self-interest. Example:

> Mrs. Smithers testified before the city council, stating that the speed limits on the residential streets near her home are dangerously high. But why should we give her claim any credence? The way she eats and exercises, she's not even looking out for her own health.

The author attempts to undermine Mrs. Smithers's testimony by attacking her character and habits. He doesn't offer any evidence that is relevant to her claim about speed limits.

Part versus Whole

This flaw occurs when a speaker or author concludes that a part or individual has a certain characteristic because the whole or the larger group has that characteristic, or vice versa. Example:

> Patient: I should have no problems taking the three drugs prescribed to me by my doctors. I looked them up, and none of the three is listed as having any major side effects.

Here, the patient is assuming that what is true of each of the drugs individually will be true of them when taken together. The patient's flaw is overlooking possible interactions that could cause problems not present when the drugs are taken separately.

Circular Reasoning

This flaw occurs when a speaker or author tries to prove a conclusion with evidence that is logically equivalent to the conclusion. Example:

> All those who run for office are prevaricators. To see this, just consider politicians: they all prevaricate.

Perhaps the author has tried to disguise the circular reasoning in this argument by exchanging the words "those who run for office" in the conclusion for "politicians" in the evidence, but all this argument amounts to is "Politicians prevaricate; therefore, politicians prevaricate." On the LSAT, circular

reasoning is very rarely the correct answer to a Flaw question, although it is regularly described in one of the wrong answers

Question Strategies

Denial Test

A tactic for identifying the assumption *necessary* to an argument. When you negate an assumption necessary to an argument, the argument will fall apart. Negating an assumption that is not necessary to the argument will not invalidate the argument. Consider the following argument:

> Only high schools which produced a state champion athlete during the school year will be represented at the Governor's awards banquet. Therefore, McMurtry High School will be represented at the Governor's awards banquet.

Which one of the following is an assumption necessary to the argument?

> (1) McMurtry High School produced more state champion athletes than any other high school during the school year.

> (2) McMurtry High School produced at least one state champion athlete during the school year.

If you are at all confused about which of those two statements reflects the *necessary* assumption, negate them both.

> (1) McMurtry High School **did not produce more** state champion athletes than any other high school during the school year.

That does not invalidate the argument. McMurtry could still represented at the Governor's banquet.

> (2) McMurtry High School **did not produce any** state champion athletes during the school year.

Here, negating the statement causes the argument to fall apart. Statement (2) is an assumption *necessary* to the argument.

Point at Issue "Decision Tree"

A tactic for evaluating the answer choices in Point at Issue questions. The correct answer is the only answer choice to which you can answer "Yes" to all three questions in the following diagram.

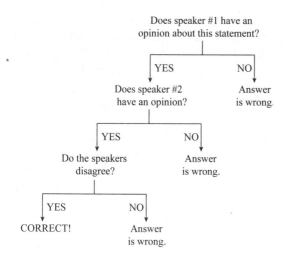

Common Methods of Argument

These methods of argument or argumentative strategies are common on the LSAT:

- Analogy, in which an author draws parallels between two unrelated (but purportedly similar) situations
- Example, in which an author cites a specific case or cases to justify a generalization
- Counterexample, in which an author seeks to discredit an opponent's argument by citing a specific case or cases that appear to invalidate the opponent's generalization
- Appeal to authority, in which an author cites an expert's claim or opinion as support for her conclusion
- Ad hominem attack, in which an author attacks her opponent's personal credibility rather than attacking the substance of her opponent's argument
- Elimination of alternatives, in which an author lists possibilities and discredits or rules out all but one
- Means/requirements, in which the author argues that something is needed to achieve a desired result

Wrong Answer Types in LR

Outside the Scope (Out of Scope; Beyond the Scope)

An answer choice containing a statement that is too broad, too narrow, or beyond the purview of the stimulus, making the statement in the choice irrelevant

180

An answer choice that directly contradicts what the correct answer must say (for example, a choice that strengthens the argument in a Weaken question)

Extreme

An answer choice containing language too emphatic to be supported by the stimulus; often (although not always) characterized by words such as *all*, *never*, *every*, *only*, or *most*

Distortion

An answer choice that mentions details from the stimulus but mangles or misstates what the author said about those details

Irrelevant Comparison

An answer choice that compares two items or attributes in a way not germane to the author's argument or statements

Half-Right/Half-Wrong

An answer choice that begins correctly, but then contradicts or distorts the passage in its second part; this wrong answer type is more common in Reading Comprehension than it is in Logical Reasoning

Faulty Use of Detail

An answer choice that accurately states something from the stimulus, but does so in a manner that answers the question incorrectly; this wrong answer type is more common in Reading Comprehension than it is in Logical Reasoning

Logic Games

Game Types

Strict Sequencing Game

A game that asks you to arrange entities into numbered positions or into a set schedule (usually hours or days). Strict Sequencing is, by far, the most common game type on the LSAT. In the typical Strict Sequencing game, there is a one-to-one matchup of entities and positions, e.g., seven entities to be placed in seven positions, one per position, or six entities to be placed over six consecutive days, one entity per day.

From time to time, the LSAT will offer Strict Sequencing with more entities than positions (e.g., seven entities to be arranged over five days, with some days to receive more than one entity) or more positions than entities (e.g., six entities to be scheduled over seven days, with at least one day to receive no entities).

Other, less common variations on Strict Sequencing include:

Double Sequencing, in which each entity is placed or scheduled two times (there have been rare occurrences of Triple or Quadruple Sequencing). Alternatively, a Double Sequencing game may involve two different sets of entities each sequenced once.

Circular Sequencing, in which entities are arranged around a table or in a circular arrangement (NOTE: When the positions in a Circular Sequencing game are numbered, the first and last positions are adjacent.)

Vertical Sequencing, in which the positions are numbered from top to bottom or from bottom to top (as in the floors of a building)

Loose Sequencing Game

A game that asks you to arrange or schedule entities in order but provides no numbering or naming of the positions. The rules in Loose Sequencing give only the relative positions (earlier or later, higher or lower) between two entities or among three entities. Loose Sequencing games almost always provide that there will be no ties between entities in the rank, order, or position they take.

Circular Sequencing Game

See Strict Sequencing Game.

Selection Game

A game that asks you to choose or include some entities from the initial list of entities and to reject or exclude others. Some Selection games provide overall limitations on the number of entities to be selected (e.g., "choose exactly four of seven students" or "choose at least two of six entrees") while others provide little or no restriction on the number selected ("choose at least one type of flower" or "select from among seven board members").

Distribution Game

A game that asks you to break up the initial list of entities into two, three, or (very rarely) four groups or teams. In the vast majority of Distribution games, each entity is assigned to one and only one group or team. A relatively common variation on Distribution games will provide a subdivided list of entities (e.g., eight students—four men and four women—will form three study groups) and will then require representatives from those subdivisions on each team (e.g., each study group will have at least one of the men on it).

Matching Game

A game that asks you to match one or more members of one set of entities to specific members of another set of entities,

or that asks you to match attributes or objects to a set of entities. Unlike Distribution games, in which each entity is placed in exactly one group or team, Matching games usually permit you to assign the same attribute or object to more than one entity.

In some cases, there are overall limitations on the number of entities that can be matched (e.g., "In a school's wood shop, there are four workstations—numbered 1 through 4—and each workstation has at least one and at most three of the following tools—band saw, dremmel tool, electric sander, and power drill"). In almost all Matching games, further restrictions on the number of entities that can be matched to a particular person or place will be found in the rules (e.g., Workstation 4 will have more tools than Workstation 2 has).

Hybrid Game

A game that asks you to do two (or rarely, three) of the standard actions (Sequencing, Selection, Distribution, and Matching) to a set of entities.

The most common Hybrid is Sequencing-Matching. A typical Sequencing-Matching Hybrid game might ask you to schedule six speakers at a conference to six one-hour speaking slots (from 9 AM to 2 PM), and then assign each speaker one of two subjects (economic development or trade policy).

Nearly as common as Sequencing-Matching is Distribution-Sequencing. A typical game of this type might ask you to divide six people in a talent competition into either a Dance category or a Singing category, and then rank the competitors in each category.

It is most common to see one Hybrid game in each Logic Games section, although there have been tests with two Hybrid games and tests with none. To determine the type of Hybrid you are faced with, identify the game's action in Step of the Logic Games Method. For example, a game asking you to choose four of six runners, and then assign the four chosen runners to lanes numbered 1 through 4 on a track, would be Selection-Sequencing Hybrid game.

Mapping Game

A game that provides you with a description of geographical locations and, typically, of the connections among them. Mapping games often ask you to determine the shortest possible routes between two locations or to account for the number of connections required to travel from one location to another. This game type is extremely rare, and as of February 2017, a Mapping game was last seen on PrepTest 40 administered in June 2003.

Process Game

A game that opens with an initial arrangement of entities (e.g., a starting sequence or grouping) and provides rules that describe the processes through which that arrangement can be altered. The questions typically ask you for acceptable arrangements or placements of particular entities after one, two, or three stages in the process. Occasionally, a Process game question might provide information about the arrangement after one, two, or three stages in the process and ask you what must have happened in the earlier stages. This game type is extremely rare, and as of November 2016, a Process game was last seen on PrepTest 16 administered in September 1995. However, there was a Process game on PrepTest 80, administered in December 2016, thus ending a 20-year hiatus.

Game Setups and Deductions

Floater

An entity that is not restricted by any rule or limitation in the game

Blocks of Entities

Two or more entities that are required by rule to be adjacent or separated by a set number of spaces (Sequencing games), to be placed together in the same group (Distribution games), to be matched to the same entity (Matching games), or to be selected or rejected together (Selection games)

Limited Options

Rules or restrictions that force all of a game's acceptable arrangements into two (or occasionally three) patterns

Established Entities

An entity required by rule to be placed in one space or assigned to one particular group throughout the entire game

Number Restrictions

Rules or limitations affecting the number of entities that may be placed into a group or space throughout the game

Duplications

Two or more rules that restrict a common entity. Usually, these rules can be combined to reach additional deductions. For example, if you know that B is placed earlier than A in a sequence and that C is placed earlier than B in that sequence, you can deduce that C is placed earlier than A in the sequence

and that there is at least one space (the space occupied by B) between C and A.

Master Sketch

The final sketch derived from the game's setup, rules, and deductions. LSAT experts preserve the Master Sketch for reference as they work through the questions. The Master Sketch does not include any conditions from New-"If" question stems.

Logic Games Question Types

Acceptability Question

A question in which the correct answer is an acceptable arrangement of all the entities relative to the spaces, groups, or selection criteria in the game. Answer these by using the rules to eliminate answer choices that violate the rules.

Partial Acceptability Question

A question in which the correct answer is an acceptable arrangement of some of the entities relative to some of the spaces, groups, or selection criteria in the game, and in which the arrangement of entities not included in the answer choices could be acceptable to the spaces, groups, or selection criteria not explicitly shown in the answer choices. Answer these the same way you would answer Acceptability questions, by using the rules to eliminate answer choices that explicitly or implicitly violate the rules.

Must Be True/False; Could Be True/False Question

A question in which the correct answer must be true, could be true, could be false, or must be false (depending on the question stem), and in which no additional rules or conditions are provided by the question stem

New-"If" Question

A question in which the stem provides an additional rule, condition, or restriction (applicable only to that question), and then asks what must/could be true/false as a result. LSAT experts typically handle New-"If" questions by copying the Master Sketch, adding the new restriction to the copy, and working out any additional deductions available as a result of the new restriction before evaluating the answer choices.

Rule Substitution Question

A question in which the correct answer is a rule that would have an impact identical to one of the game's original rules on the entities in the game

Rule Change Question

A question in which the stem alters one of the original rules in the game, and then asks what must/could be true/false as a result. LSAT experts typically handle Rule Change questions by reconstructing the game's sketch, but now accounting for the changed rule in place of the original. These questions are rare on recent tests.

Rule Suspension Question

A question in which the stem indicates that you should ignore one of the original rules in the game, and then asks what must/could be true/false as a result. LSAT experts typically handle Rule Suspension questions by reconstructing the game's sketch, but now accounting for the absent rule. These questions are very rare.

Complete and Accurate List Question

A question in which the correct answer is a list of any and all entities that could acceptably appear in a particular space or group, or a list of any and all spaces or groups in which a particular entity could appear

Completely Determine Question

A question in which the correct answer is a condition that would result in exactly one acceptable arrangement for all of the entities in the game

Supply the "If" Question

A question in which the correct answer is a condition that would guarantee a particular result stipulated in the question stem

Minimum/Maximum Question

A question in which the correct answer is the number corresponding to the fewest or greatest number of entities that could be selected (Selection), placed into a particular group (Distribution), or matched to a particular entity (Matching). Often, Minimum/Maximum questions begin with New-"If" conditions.

Earliest/Latest Question

A question in which the correct answer is the earliest or latest position in which an entity may acceptably be placed. Often, Earliest/Latest questions begin with New-"If" conditions.

"How Many" Question

A question in which the correct answer is the exact number of entities that may acceptably be placed into a particular group

or space. Often, "How Many" questions begin with New-"If" conditions.

Reading Comprehension

Strategic Reading

Roadmap

The test taker's markup of the passage text in Step 1 (Read the Passage Strategically) of the Reading Comprehension Method. To create helpful Roadmaps, LSAT experts circle or underline Keywords in the passage text and jot down brief, helpful notes or paragraph summaries in the margin of their test booklets.

Keyword(s) in Reading Comprehension

Words in the passage text that reveal the passage structure or the author's point of view and thus help test takers anticipate and research the questions that accompany the passage. LSAT experts pay attention to six categories of Keywords in Reading Comprehension:

Emphasis/Opinion—words that signal that the author finds a detail noteworthy or that the author has positive or negative opinion about a detail; any subjective or evaluative language on the author's part (e.g., *especially, crucial, unfortunately, disappointing, I suggest, it seems likely*)

Contrast—words indicating that the author finds two details or ideas incompatible or that the two details illustrate conflicting points (e.g., *but, yet, despite, on the other hand*)

Logic—words that indicate an argument, either the author's or someone else's (e.g., *thus, therefore, because, it follows that*)

Illustration—words indicating an example offered to clarify or support another point (e.g., *for example, this shows, to illustrate*)

Sequence/Chronology—words showing steps in a process or developments over time (e.g., *traditionally, in the past, today, first, second, finally, earlier, subsequent*)

Continuation—words indicating that a subsequent example or detail supports the same point or illustrates the same idea as the previous example (e.g., *moreover, in addition, also, further, along the same lines*)

Margin Notes

The brief notes or paragraph summaries that the test taker jots down next to the passage in the margin of the test booklet

Big Picture Summaries: Topic/Scope/Purpose/Main Idea

A test taker's mental summary of the passage as a whole made during Step 1 (Read the Passage Strategically) of the

Reading Comprehension Method. LSAT experts account for four aspects of the passage in their big picture summaries:

Topic—the overall subject of the passage

Scope—the particular aspect of the Topic that the author focuses on

Purpose—the author's reason or motive for writing the passage (express this as a verb; e.g., *to refute, to outline, to evaluate, to critique*)

Main Idea—the author's conclusion or overall takeaway; if the passage does not contain an explicit conclusion or thesis, you can combine the author's Scope and Purpose to get a good sense of the Main Idea.

Passage Types

Kaplan categorizes Reading Comprehension passages in two ways, by subject matter and by passage structure.

Subject matter categories

In the majority of LSAT Reading Comprehension sections, there is one passage from each of the following subject matter categories:

Humanities—topics from art, music, literature, philosophy, etc.

Natural Science—topics from biology, astronomy, paleontology, physics, etc.

Social Science—topics from anthropology, history, sociology, psychology, etc.

Law—topics from constitutional law, international law, legal education, jurisprudence, etc.

Passage structure categories

The majority of LSAT Reading Comprehension passages correspond to one of the following descriptions. The first categories—Theory/Perspective and Event/Phenomenon—have been the most common on recent LSATs.

Theory/Perspective—The passage focuses on a thinker's theory or perspective on some aspect of the Topic; typically (though not always), the author disagrees and critiques the thinker's perspective and/or defends his own perspective.

Event/Phenomenon—The passage focuses on an event, a breakthrough development, or a problem that has recently arisen; when a solution to the problem is proposed, the author most often agrees with the solution (and that represents the passage's Main Idea).

Biography—The passage discusses something about a notable person; the aspect of the person's life emphasized by the author reflects the Scope of the passage.

Debate—The passage outlines two opposing positions (neither of which is the author's) on some aspect of the Topic; the author may side with one of the positions, may remain neutral, or may critique both. (This structure has been relatively rare on recent LSATs.)

Comparative Reading

A pair of passages (labeled Passage A and Passage B) that stand in place of the typical single passage exactly one time in each Reading Comprehension section administered since June 2007. The paired Comparative Reading passages share the same Topic, but may have different Scopes and Purposes. On most LSAT tests, a majority of the questions accompanying Comparative Reading passages require the test taker to compare or contrast ideas or details from both passages.

Question Strategies

Research Clues

A reference in a Reading Comprehension question stem to a word, phrase, or detail in the passage text, or to a particular line number or paragraph in the passage. LSAT experts recognize five kinds of research clues:

Line Reference—An LSAT expert researches around the referenced lines, looking for Keywords that indicate why the referenced details were included or how they were used by the author.

Paragraph Reference—An LSAT expert consults her passage Roadmap to see the paragraph's Scope and Purpose.

Quoted Text (often accompanied by a line reference)—An LSAT expert checks the context of the quoted term or phrase, asking what the author meant by it in the passage.

Proper Nouns—An LSAT expert checks the context of the person, place, or thing in the passage, asking whether the author made a positive, negative, or neutral evaluation of it and why the author included it in the passage.

Content Clues—These are terms, concepts, or ideas from the passage mentioned in the question stem but not as direct quotes and not accompanied by line references. An LSAT expert knows that content clues almost always refer to something that the author emphasized or about which the author expressed an opinion.

Reading Comp Question Types

Global Question

A question that asks for the Main Idea of the passage or for the author's primary Purpose in writing the passage. Typical question stems:

> Which one of the following most accurately expresses the main point of the passage?

The primary purpose of the passage is to

Detail Question

A question that asks what the passage explicitly states about a detail. Typical question stems:

> According to the passage, some critics have criticized Gilliam's films on the grounds that

> The passage states that one role of a municipality's comptroller in budget decisions by the city council is to

> The author identifies which one of the following as a commonly held but false preconception?

> The passage contains sufficient information to answer which of the following questions?

Occasionally, the test will ask for a correct answer that contains a detail *not* stated in the passage:

> The author attributes each of the following positions to the Federalists EXCEPT:

Inference Question

A question that asks for a statement that follows from or is based on the passage but that is not necessarily stated explicitly in the passage. Some Inference questions contain research clues. The following are typical Inference question stems containing research clues:

> Based on the passage, the author would be most likely to agree with which one of the following statements about unified field theory?

> The passage suggests which one of the following about the behavior of migratory water fowl?

> Given the information in the passage, to which one of the following would radiocarbon dating techniques likely be applicable?

Other Inference questions lack research clues in the question stem. They may be evaluated using the test taker's Big Picture Summaries, or the answer choices may make it clear that the test taker should research a particular part of the passage text. The following are typical Inference question stems containing research clues:

> It can be inferred from the passage that the author would be most likely to agree that

> Which one of the following statements is most strongly supported by the passage?

Other Reading Comprehension question types categorized as Inference questions are Author's Attitude questions and Vocabulary-in-Context questions.

Logic Function Question

A question that asks why the author included a particular detail or reference in the passage or how the author used a particular detail or reference. Typical question stems:

> The author of the passage mentions declining inner-city populations in the paragraph most likely in order to

> The author's discussion of Rimbaud's travels in the Mediterranean (lines 23–28) functions primarily to

> Which one of the following best expresses the function of the third paragraph in the passage?

Logic Reasoning Question

A question that asks the test taker to apply Logical Reasoning skills in relation to a Reading Comprehension passage. Logic Reasoning questions often mirror Strengthen or Parallel Reasoning questions, and occasionally mirror Method of Argument or Principle questions. Typical question stems:

> Which one of the following, if true, would most strengthen the claim made by the author in the last sentence of the passage (lines 51–55)?

> Which one of the following pairs of proposals is most closely analogous to the pair of studies discussed in the passage?

Author's Attitude Question

A question that asks for the author's opinion or point of view on the subject discussed in the passage or on a detail mentioned in the passage. Since the correct answer may follow from the passage without being explicitly stated in it, some Author's Attitude questions are characterized as a subset of Inference questions. Typical question stems:

> The author's attitude toward the use of DNA evidence in the appeals by convicted felons is most accurately described as

> The author's stance regarding monetarist economic theories can most accurately be described as one of

Vocabulary-in-Context Question

A question that asks how the author uses a word or phrase within the context of the passage. The word or phrase in question is always one with multiple meanings. Since the correct answer follows from its use in the passage, Vocabulary-in-Context questions are characterized as a subset of Inference questions. Typical question stems:

> Which one of the following is closest in meaning to the word "citation" as it used in the second paragraph of the passage (line 18)?

> In context, the word "enlightenment" (line 24) refers to

Wrong Answer Types in RC

Outside the Scope (Out of Scope; Beyond the Scope)

An answer choice containing a statement that is too broad, too narrow, or beyond the purview of the passage

180

An answer choice that directly contradicts what the correct answer must say

Extreme

An answer choice containing language too emphatic (e.g., *all*, *never*, *every*, *none*) to be supported by the passage

Distortion

An answer choice that mentions details or ideas from the passage but mangles or misstates what the author said about those details or ideas

Faulty Use of Detail

An answer choice that accurately states something from the passage but in a manner that incorrectly answers the question

Half-Right/Half-Wrong

An answer choice in which one clause follows from the passage while another clause contradicts or deviates from the passage

Formal Logic Terms

Conditional Statement ("If"-Then Statement)

A statement containing a sufficient clause and a necessary clause. Conditional statements can be described in Formal Logic shorthand as:

If [sufficient clause] → [necessary clause]

In some explanations, the LSAT expert may refer to the sufficient clause as the statement's "trigger" and to the necessary clause as the statement's result.

For more on how to interpret, describe, and use conditional statements on the LSAT, please refer to "A Note About Formal Logic on the LSAT" in this book's introduction.

Contrapositive

The conditional statement logically equivalent to another conditional statement formed by reversing the order of and

negating the terms in the original conditional statement. For example, reversing and negating the terms in this statement:

| If | A | → | B |

results in its contrapositive:

| If | ~B | → | ~A |

To form the contrapositive of conditional statements in which either the sufficient clause or the necessary clause has more than one term, you must also change the conjunction *and* to *or*, or vice versa. For example, reversing and negating the terms and changing *and* to *or* in this statement:

| If | M | → | O AND P |

results in its contrapositive:

| If | ~O OR ~P | → | ~M |